READINGS IN
ARTIFICIAL INTELLIGENCE
AND
SOFTWARE ENGINEERING

D1558015

edited by

Charles Rich
and
Richard C. Waters
Massachusetts Institute of Technology
Artificial Intelligence Laboratory

MORGAN KAUFMANN PUBLISHERS, INC.
95 First Street, Los Altos, California 94022

Acquisitions Editor and President   *Michael B. Morgan*
Permissions and Coordinating Editor   *Jennifer Ballentine*
Production Manager   *Mary Borchers*
Copy Editor   *Maggie Duncan*
Cover Designer   *Beverly Kennon-Kelley*
Typesetting   *Shirley Tucker and Valerie Brewster*
Production Assistants   *Debra Kern and Lisa de Beauclair*

Library of Congress Cataloging-in-Publication Data
Readings in artificial intelligence and software engineering.

Bibliography: p.
Includes index.
1. Artificial intelligence—Data processing.
2. Electronic digital computers—Programming.
3. Programming languages (Electronic computers)
I. Rich, Charles, 1951–   . II. Waters, Richard C.
Q336.R43   1986   006.3   86-18627
ISBN 0-934613-12-5

Morgan Kaufmann Publishers, Inc.
95 First Street, Los Altos, California 94022
© 1986 by Morgan Kaufmann Publishers, Inc.
All rights reserved.
Printed in the United States of America

90 89 88 87   5 4 3 2

CONTENTS

ACKNOWLEDGMENTS

The editors would like to thank Cristina Ciro for her help in preparing the bibliography and index, and Robert Balzer, David R. Barstow, Daniel Bobrow, Martin Feather, Susan Gerhart, Cordell Green, Sol Greenspan, Elaine Kant, Jack Mostow, Beau Sheil, Elliot Soloway, and Richard Waldinger for their comments on chapter selections.

The editors would also like to thank the publishers and authors for permission to reprint copyrighted material in this volume:

INTRODUCTION

The overlap between artificial intelligence and software engineering has been an active area of research for many years. (For other overviews of this area see [Barr and Feigenbaum 82], [Biermann, Guiho, and Kodratoff 84], [Green 85], and [Mostow 85].)

The application of artificial intelligence to software engineering is of interest from at least two perspectives. On the one hand, it is of pragmatic importance to the software engineer. Artificial intelligence techniques hold the promise of achieving order of magnitude improvements in programmer productivity and program reliability.

On the other hand, software engineering has proven to be a stimulating domain for artificial intelligence research. Attempts to apply artificial intelligence techniques to the programming task have motivated further developments in knowledge representation and automated reasoning.

This volume is a collection of thirty-four archival papers covering the spectrum of work in this area. The papers are grouped into eleven sections according to the main technique (e.g., deductive synthesis, program transformations) or application focus (e.g., program verification, programming tutors) of each paper. Since many papers are relevant to more than one section, each section is introduced by a short discussion which ties together the papers in the section and points out other related papers in the volume. An extensive bibliography can be found at the back of the volume.

Automatic Programming

The ultimate goal of artificial intelligence applied to software engineering is *automatic programming*. In the limit, automatic programming would allow a user to simply say what is wanted and have a program produced completely automatically. However, it is unlikely that this kind of performance will be achieved soon. As a result, fully automatic programming has sometimes been derisively referred to as auto*magic* programming.

A much more modest level of automatic programming has, in a sense, existed for a long time. Figure 1 reproduces a chart from the April 1958 issue of the *Communications of the ACM*. The chart lists the availability of "automatic programming systems" for various computers of the time. Most of the systems listed are what are now called assemblers, a few

AUTOMATIC PROGRAMMING SYSTEMS

Computer	In library	Do not have	Computer	In library	Do not have
704	AFAC CAGE FORTRAN NYAP PACT IA REG-SYMBOLIC SAP	ADES FORC KOMPILER 3	650	ADES II BELL BELL L2, L3 DRUCO I EASE II ELI FOR TRANSIT IT RELATIVE SIR SOAP I SOAP II	BACAIC BALITAC ESCAPE FLAIR MITILAC OMNICODE SPEEDCODING SPUR
701	DUAL-607 FLOP JCS-13 KOMPILER 2 QUICK SHACO SPEEDCODING 3	BACAIC DOUGLAS GEPURS LT-2 PACT I QUEASY SEESAW SO 2 SPEEDEX	UNIVAC I, II	A2 ARITHMATIC (A3) GP MATHMATIC (AT3) NYU, OMNIFAX	A0, A1 FLOWMATIC (B–0) BIOR MJS RELCODE SHORTCODE X-1
705	ACOM AUTOCODER ELI PRINT I SOHIO SYMB. ASSEMBLY	FAIR	D'TRON 201 204 205	UGLIAC	APS DATACODE I DUMBO IT SAC STAR
702	AUTOCODER ASSEMBLY SCRIPT		UDEC III		UDECIN-1 UDECOM-3 INTERCOM
1103- 1103A	CHIP FAP FLIP-SPUR MISHAP RAWOOP-SNAP UNICODE USE	COMPILER I TRANS-USE	G-15		ALGEBRAIC
			WHIRL- WIND	COMPREHENSIVE SUMMER SESSION	
MIDAC	EASIAC MAGIC		FERUT	TRANSCODE	
			JOHNNIAC	EASY FOX	

Fig. 1. *Communications of the ACM* Volume 1 #4, April 1958, p. 8.

(notably FORTRAN for the IBM 704) are compilers. The use of the term automatic programming in Figure 1 may seem inappropriate. However, it is actually quite reasonable. In comparison with programming in absolute hexadecimal, compilers are magic.

To obtain a clearer understanding of what automatic programming is, consider more carefully the phrase "a user simply says what is wanted." In particular, ask the following questions: Who is the user? What does the user say? How is what the user says different from writing a program? Depending on how these questions are answered, several different kinds of automatic programming systems can be envisioned. (For an influential early overview of these issues see [Balzer 73].)

Suppose that the accounting department of a large company has perceived the need for a program. Figure 2 shows the agents that are involved in the creation of the needed program. At the current time, all of these agents are people. Eventually, one or more of these agents may be replaced by an automatic programming system.

Note that Figure 2 is not intended to imply a commitment to any particular view of the programming process. The main goal of the figure is to highlight the different kinds of knowledge that are involved in different parts of the process.

At the top of the hierarchy is a manager who quite likely has only a rudimentary knowledge of accounting. The manager's job is to perceive the need and initiate the process by creating a brief, vague requirement. The term "vague" is used here to highlight the fact that the only way this requirement can succeed in being brief is for it to also be incomplete, ambiguous, and/or inconsistent.

The next agent in the hierarchy is an accounting expert. The accounting expert's job is to take the manager's vague requirement and create a detailed requirement that is more or less complete, unambiguous, and consistent. A key feature of this requirement is that it is couched in terms of the basic vocabulary of accounting and is intended to be evaluated by other accountants. Thus near the top of the hierarchy, accounting knowledge plays a crucial role.

The third agent in the hierarchy is a system analyst/designer. The analyst/designer's job is to design the basic architecture of the program and to translate the requirement into a detailed specification. A key feature of this specification is that it is couched in terms of the vocabulary of programming rather than accounting. The system analyst/designer must have both extensive knowledge of programming and at least a basic understanding of accounting in order to interface between the upper

and lower parts of the hierarchy.

The agent at the bottom of the hierarchy is a programmer. The programmer's job is to create code in a high level language based on the detailed specification. The programmer is not expected to know anything about accounting. The bottom of the hierarchy is primarily concerned with programming knowledge.

Figure 2 also implicitly defines four different levels at which automatic programming might be applied. At the lowest level, the programmer is the user of an automatic programming system (a compiler), which automatically converts high-level code into machine executable code. In this case, what the user says is obviously a program.

At the next level up, the analyst/designer could use an automatic programming system that takes specifications as input. Using this system, the analyst/designer would express himself in some kind of formal specification language. This language would probably be similar to a programming language except that it would directly support abstract concepts such as quantifiers and sets without forcing the analyst/designer to specify how they should be implemented.

Going one level higher, the accounting expert could use an automatic programming system that produced programs directly from requirements. The accounting expert might express himself either in English or in some more formal requirements language. In either case, this is the first level at which the input to the automatic programming system would be something significantly different from a program. The automatic programming system would be replacing the analyst/designer as well as the programmer. As such it would need to have extensive knowledge of program design, as well as considerable knowledge of accounting.

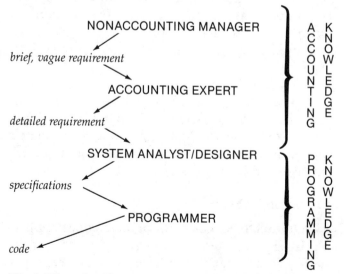

Fig. 2. Hierarchy of Agents Producing an Accounting System.

At the highest level, the manager could converse directly with an automatic programming system in free-form English. As mentioned above, this is the ultimate goal of automatic programming. Notice that at this level most of the hard problems have nothing to do with programming. The system would be replacing the accounting expert and would itself have to be an accounting expert. The primary activity of the system would be helping the manager figure out exactly what was wanted in the context of accounting.

Cutting the Problem Down

Fully automatic programming is too big a problem to be solved in a single step. In order to provide avenues of attack, researchers have cut the problem down in a number of different ways. The various approaches lead to different kinds of intermediate products and results.

One avenue of attack is to work up from the bottom of Figure 2. For example, a great deal of work has been directed toward automatically going from specifications to code. One important research approach in this area has been to develop so-called *very high level languages* (see [Schonberg, Schwartz, and Sharir, Chapter 14], [Green and Westfold, Chapter 16], and [Feather and London, Chapter 17] and systems to support them (see [Barstow, Chapter 7], [Kant, Chapter 8], and [Rowe and Tonge, Chapter 15]).

The complementary avenue of attack is to work down from the top of Figure 2. Work in this area has focused on converting free-form English into formal requirements (see [Balzer, Goldman, and Wile, Chapter 13] and on the representation of the knowledge in a requirement (see [Borgida, Greenspan, and Mylopoulos, Chapter 32] and [Greenspan, Borgida, and Mylopoulos 86]). Although not very much effort has been expended in this direction to date, this approach may turn out to be particularly important. Errors made early in the program development process are the most costly. In addition, while there are many specialized editors and other tools for program implementation, there are currently very few tools that help with requirements acquisition. As a result, an automatic system whose output was a reliable requirements document would be of great value, even if the remainder of the software process was manual.

Another way to cut down the automatic programming problem is to take a "vertical slice" through Figure 2. Given a narrow enough domain, one can construct a completely automatic programming system. This is done by designing a special-purpose problem-oriented language and implementing a special-purpose *program generator,* which compiles this language. The user creates and modifies programs in the special-purpose language without ever having to look at the programs produced. Numerous examples of program generators exist for various business and scientific applications (see [Horowitz, Kemper, and Narasimhan 85] for a survey). This is a second sense in which automatic programming exists today.

The main drawback of current program generators is their inflexibility. They work beautifully within their domain of expertise and not at all even a fraction outside of it. The only way to stretch a program generator beyond its intended domain is to manually modify the code produced by the generator. However, this is undesirable for two reasons. First, with most generators, the code created is intended only for compilation and is nearly unreadable. Modification of this kind of code is extremely error-prone. Second, a key benefit of program generators is that the output program can be modified to keep up with changing requirements by simply modifying the high-level input and rerunning the generator. Unfortunately, once the output of the generator has been manually modified, it has to be remodified each time the generator is rerun.

The main goal of research within the program generator approach has been to cover ever-broader domains with more flexibility at the boundaries. The Draco system [Neighbors, Chapter 30] and the ΦNIX system [Barstow, Chapter 31] illustrate progress in this direction.

A second kind of vertical slice through the automatic programming problem is to provide partial automation at many levels. At a minimum, such a system would perform bookkeeping and other mundane tasks. Going beyond this, it could supply varying degrees of automation for different programming tasks, such as implementation, testing, or requirements analysis. The Designer/Verifier's Assistant [Moriconi, Chapter 21], the Programmer's Apprentice [Rich and Shrobe 78] [Waters, Chapter 22], and the Knowledge-Based Software Assistant [Green, Luckham, Balzer, Cheatham, and Rich, Chapter 23]) are examples of this approach. An attractive feature of the assistant approach is that it makes it possible to take immediate advantage of incremental improvements in automation of different kinds.

Theorem-Proving Techniques

Techniques for automatically finding (or helping to find) proofs of theorems has been an early and active area of artificial intelligence research. (For a survey of this research, see [Siekmann and

Wrightson 83], [Bledsoe and Loveland 84], or [Wos *et al.*, 84]). As soon as programming languages were given a firm mathematical basis by Floyd [1967] and others, attempts began to apply automatic theorem-proving techniques to the programming task. This has been done primarily in two forms: deductive program synthesis and program verification.

Deductive Synthesis

Deductive program synthesis is based on the observation that constructive proofs are equivalent to programs because each step of a constructive proof can be interpreted as a step of computation. For example, in a constructive proof, whenever case analysis is used, an explicit method for computing which case holds in any particular situation must be supplied. In contrast, a nonconstructive proof need show only that, taken together, the cases cover all possible situations. (For a more technical discussion of the relation between constructive proofs and programs, see [Constable 71].)

A constructive theorem prover can be used to derive a program from its specification as follows. Suppose that the program to be derived takes an input x and produces an output y. Further, suppose that the specifications of the program state that a precondition $P(x)$ should be true of the input and that a postcondition $Q(x,y)$ will be true of the output. This specification is converted into the following theorem, which is given to the theorem prover.

$$\forall x \exists y [P(x) \Rightarrow Q(x,y)]$$

The process of constructive proof, in effect, discovers a method for finding y for any given x. A program that implements this method can either be constructed incrementally during the proof process or extracted from the proof as a separate post-phase. One might observe that this approach has translated one hard problem, namely automatic programming, into another hard problem, namely automatic theorem proving.

Deductive synthesis has been shown to work on a number of examples (see [Manna and Waldinger, Chapter 1] or [Dershowitz 85]). However, at the current state of the art, it is limited to the production of small programs with specifications that can be easily formalized in a logical language. Synthesis is limited to small programs, because large programs correspond to large proofs. Current theorem provers cannot discover large proofs, because they are unable to effectively control the process of searching for a proof in the space of possible deductions.

An area of work closely related to deductive synthesis is automated algorithm design. The distinction between "ordinary" program synthesis and algorithm design is mostly one of degree. Ordinary program synthesis, in effect, typically combines more or less standard algorithms. In contrast, algorithm design seeks to discover totally new algorithms.

Most of the work on algorithm design is set within the general framework of deductive synthesis (see [Bibel 80], [Barstow 82], and [Smith, Chapter 2]). It differs from ordinary deductive synthesis primarily in the system's depth of understanding. In order to support real discovery, an automatic algorithm design system needs to have a very detailed representation of the mathematical properties of the data objects involved.

An alternate approach to algorithm design has been to try to duplicate the methods used by human designers. This has lead to work on modeling human designers [Kant 85] and to investigations of the role of analysis and symbolic execution in the design process [Steier and Kant 85].

Program Verification

Given a program and its formal specification, an automatic theorem prover (either constructive or nonconstructive) can be used to verify that the program satisfies the specification. This is typically done using one of two symmetrical methods. In the first method, the precondition is passed forward over the program, yielding a logical formula describing the net effect of the program. This is done a statement at a time by combining the precondition with the axioms describing the behavior of the statement. Each step yields a new logical formula that embodies the sum total that is known to be true after the statement. Once a logical formula describing the interaction of the program as a whole with the precondition has been obtained, an automatic theorem prover is used to verify that the postcondition follows from this logical formula. The second method operates in a reverse way by passing the postcondition backward over the program and then proving that the resulting logical formula is implied by the precondition.

Like deductive synthesis, automatic program verification is limited by the fact that current automatic theorem provers cannot prove theorems that require large proofs. Two approaches have been taken to increase the size of program that can be automatically verified. First, the theorem prover can be given special-purpose knowledge (i.e., lemmas) about particular areas of programming to help it verify programs in that area. Second, human interaction can be used to guide the theorem prover. In the limit, this approach reduces the theorem prover to the role of a mechanical proof checker. (For an overview of program verification see [Boyer and Moore 85]. For a collection of current research papers see [*Verkshop* 85]. For examples of using an automated verification system, see [Boyer and Moore 79] and [Polak 79].)

Because of the great cost and effort currently required to verify a program, the main applications to date have been small, highly critical programs, such as communication protocols (see [Sunshine *et al.*, 82] and [Good, Chapter 3]) and security algorithms (see [Boyer and Moore, Chapter 4]). Another important application area has been the verification of reusable datatype implementations (see [Gerhart *et al.*, 80]).

In the discussion above, both deductive synthesis and automatic program verification are described in an all or nothing way. Given a complete specification, a complete program is derived. Given a complete program and a complete specification, a proof is derived. It is not clear whether automatic theorem provers will ever advance to the point where either of these monolithic approaches will succeed when applied to programs of commercial size. In light of this, these approaches are gradually being replaced by the view that verification and synthesis should be applied to various subproblems throughout the program development process. For example, from the viewpoint of programmer productivity, it makes good sense to verify individual properties of a program design as early as possible. As another example, the PRL system [Bates and Constable 85] combines aspects of deductive synthesis and program verification to support individual steps of program construction.

Transformational Approaches

The most active area in automatic programming research currently is the use of transformations to support program construction. A program transformation takes a part of a program and replaces it with a new (transformed) part. Typically, a program transformation is *correctness preserving*, in that the new part of the program computes the same thing as the old part. The purpose of a transformation is to make the part *better* on some scale (e.g., more efficient or more concrete). For example, a transformation might be used to replace "X**2" with "X*X." (For surveys of transformational research see [Partsch and Steinbruggen 83] and [Feather 86].)

As usually implemented, a program transformation has three parts. It has a pattern that matches against parts of a program to determine where to apply the transformation. (The program being transformed is often written in a *wide-spectrum* language [Bauer *et al.*, 78], which contains a mixture of conventional and specification-like constructs.) It has a set of applicability conditions, which further restrict the places where the transformation can be applied. (In many transformational systems, the applicability conditions are expressed in a logical language and theorem proving is used to determine whether or not they are satisfied in a given situation.) Finally, a transformation has a (usually procedural) action that creates a new program part to replace whatever the pattern matched.

There are two principal kinds of transformations: *vertical* and *lateral*. Vertical transformations define an expression at one level of abstraction in terms of an expression at a lower level of abstraction—for example, defining how to enumerate the elements of a vector using a loop. Lateral transformations specify an equivalence between two expressions at a similar level of abstraction—for example, specifying the commutativity of addition. Lateral transformations are used principally to promote efficiency and to set things up properly so that vertical transformations can be applied.

The first use of transformations was based on the notion that, in most programs, there is natural trade-off between efficiency and clarity. It is often possible to write a program in such a way that it directly mirrors its intent and is therefore self-evidently correct. Unfortunately, such a program is usually very inefficient. Lateral transformations can then be used to convert a clear but inefficient program into an efficient one.

The transformational system of Burstall and Darlington [Burstall and Darlington 77] [Darlington, Chapter 5] uses a small fixed set of powerful general-purpose lateral transformations in order to improve the efficiency of programs. Their system has demonstrated the feasibility of allowing a programmer to gain the benefit of clarity without paying the price of inefficiency.

The most common use of transformations is as the basis for *transformational implementation* [Balzer 81]. These systems approach the notion of self-evidently correct programs from a different direction by converting programs in an easily readable, very high level, wide-spectrum language into an efficient, directly executable form. This is done by iteratively applying a set of vertical and lateral transformation rules until all of the specification-like constructs in the initial program have been replaced (implemented) by conventional constructs. In contrast to the system of Burstall and Darlington, these systems use large libraries of special-purpose transformations.

In many ways, a transformational implementation system can be viewed as a special kind of program generator. The principal difference between transformational implementation systems and program generators is that the knowledge of how to implement programs is represented in a library of transformations rather than in a procedure. This makes it easier to extend and modify a transformational implementation system; however, it brings up a new problem: controlling the application of transformations.

The main difficulty in controlling the application of transformations is that, in a typical situation, many different transformations are applicable, and different results will be obtained depending on which transformation is chosen. For example, if two transformations are both applicable to the same part of a program, applying either one may modify the program in such a way that the other is no longer applicable. Choosing to apply one transformation rather than the other amounts to making an implementation decision.

With regard to vertical transformations, the control problem is typically not too severe because in most situations only one or two transformations will be applicable to a given abstract expression. However, the selection of lateral transformations is typically quite difficult and has to rely on manual control.

Existing transformational implementation systems can be divided into two classes: those that are relatively limited in power but require no user guidance and those that are capable of very complex implementations but only under user guidance. TAMPR [Boyle and Muralidharan 84] and PDS [Cheatham, Chapter 9] use simple control strategies and restrictions on the kinds of transformations that can be defined in order to obviate the need for user guidance. PDS is particularly interesting because of its emphasis on having the user define new abstract terms and transformations as part of the programming process.

The PSI system [Green 77] was one of the first systems to use a transformational implementation module for complex implementation. PSI's transformational module [Barstow, Chapter 7] operated without guidance, generating all possible low-level programs. It was assumed that another component [Kant, Chapter 8] would provide guidance as to which transformations to use. Work on complex transformational implementation systems is active both at the Information Sciences Institute, University of Southern California, (see [Balzer 85]) and the Kestrel Institute (see [Smith, Kotik, and Westfold 85]). A key focus of both these efforts has been to reduce the need for user guidance of the transfor-

mation selection process (see [Feather 82], [Fickas 85], and [Wile, Chapter 10]).

Another important classification dimension in program transformation research is between efforts that focus on the correctness-preserving nature of transformations (e.g., [Broy and Pepper, Chapter 6]) and efforts that focus on the knowledge representation aspect of transformations (e.g., [Barstow, Chapter 7]). This is not to say that Barstow does not care if his transformations produce incorrect programs, or that there is no knowledge represented by Broy and Pepper's transformations. Rather, there is a significant difference of emphasis. The correctness-preserving approach emphasizes the formal logical basis of transformations, which makes verification possible. The knowledge representation approach emphasizes the use of transformations as a vehicle for codifying programming knowledge.

Specification Techniques

As mentioned above, a principal issue in automatic programming is what language the user employs to describe the desired program. Much research has focused on three kinds of user interfaces: natural language, very high level programming languages, and examples of behavior.

Natural Language Specifications

The ultimate in automatic programming would be to support user input in unrestricted natural language. Protosystem-I [Ruth, Chapter 12] was a notable early attempt in this direction. Several other early systems for automatic programming using natural language input are surveyed in [Heidorn, Chapter 11].

The main lesson of this early work is that the essential difficulty with natural language specifications is not the syntax or semantics of natural language *per se*, but rather the informality people use when communicating about a task. The essential problem is not understanding, for example, that *the inputs to the program are* means the same as *the program's inputs are*, but rather understanding that when the user says something like

The RATS transmission times are entered into the schedule.

the user really means something like

Each RATS clock transmission time and transmission length is made a component of a new transmission entry which is entered into the transmission schedule.

(This example is taken from [Balzer, Goldman, and Wile, Chapter 13] See also [Ginsparg 78], [McCune 79], and [McCune 80].)

In response to this lesson, most automatic programming researchers now try to separate natural language processing issues (see [Grosz, Webber, and Sparck Jones 86] for a survey) from informality issues (see [Balzer, Goldman, and Wile, Chapter 13]). The current focus of automatic programming research has shifted toward designing new kinds of formal languages in which the syntactic processing is straightforward but semantic informality is allowed. Many of these new formalisms are being developed under the rubric of very high level languages.

Very High Level Languages

The archetype of a very high level language is SETL (see [Dewar, Grand, Liu, and Schwartz 79], [Freudenberger, Schwartz and Sharir 83], and [Schonberg, Schwartz and Sharir, Chapter 14]). SETL supports most of the standard constructs of any Algol-like programming language. In addition, it supports two convenient universal data structures—tuples and sets. For example, a mapping is treated as a set of 2-tuples. SETL also supports the use of universal and existential quantifiers in a program. For example, the following is the form for a SETL statement for performing some computation on every element of the set S.

$$(\forall\ x \in S)\ \ldots\ \textbf{end}\ \ \forall\ ;$$

The goal of providing such expressive facilities is to free the programmer from having to think about the detailed design of data structures. The SETL compiler will decide how data structures should be implemented. This decrease in what the programmer has to worry about is a key to the productivity gains that should be obtained by the use of very high level languages.

As it is currently evolving, the V language [Green and Westfold, Chapter 16] is in many ways similar to SETL. The GIST language [Feather and London, Chapter 17] is representative of a more ambitious direction in research on very high level languages. The goal of GIST is to provide the expressiveness of natural language while imposing formal syntax and semantics. Two examples of capabilities provided in GIST that distinguish it from SETL-like languages are: historical reference (the ability to refer to past process states) and constraints (restrictions on acceptable system behavior in the form of global declarations). (For a general discussion of other desirable features of a specification language, see [Balzer and Goldman 79].)

Not surprisingly, the more advanced features that you put into a very high level language, the harder it is to compile (and to some extent, understand, see [Swartout 83]). Compilers for SETL and V are both at least partially implemented. In contrast, although it is an active area of research (see [Fickas 85]), a GIST compiler has not yet been constructed.

When compiling languages such as SETL and V, the paramount problem is deciding how to implement the abstract data structures in the program. These decisions are needed not only to represent the data, but also to decide how to use loops to implement quantifiers in the program. Several researchers (e.g., [Low 78] and [Rowe and Tonge, Chapter 15]) have focused on the problem of data structure implementation separate from the details of any specific very high level language.

The SETL compiler operates in a procedural fashion somewhat similar to a conventional optimizing compiler. At the current time it is only moderately successful at producing efficient code. In order to make implementation choices that lead to more efficient run-time performance, the SETL compiler will have to perform a deeper analysis of the input program. Perfecting this analysis is the current focus of SETL research. Meanwhile, a declaration language is provided that the programmer can use to tell the SETL compiler how to implement particular sets. Although this is an appealing compromise in the spirit of incremental automation, it is less than satisfactory in practice. The problem is that if the full expressive power of SETL is used in writing a program, it can be very difficult for a programmer to figure out what to recommend.

The currently favored technique for compiling very high level languages is to use a program transformation system to remove the very high level constructs. For example, this approach is used for the V language [Green and Westfold, Chapter 16]. As discussed above, such transformational systems require advice on what transformations should be applied where. Unfortunately, as in the case of explicit declarations, it can be very difficult for a programmer to come up with the needed advice.

Another important trend in very high level languages is toward specialized languages for particular application areas. For applications like business data processing [Cheng, Lock, and Prywes 84], quite high level languages have been developed that can be successfully compiled using reasonably straightforward techniques.

Programming by Example

An appealing specification idea, rather different from those discussed above, is to describe a program via examples of its behavior. The appeal of this approach is that, like natural language, even people who have no knowledge of programming are familiar with examples as an descriptive technique.

Further, individual examples are easy to understand and modify.

The difficulty with programming by example is that, although examples are easy to understand by themselves, the program produced has to be more general than strictly implied by the examples given. It would be trivial to construct a program that duplicated the examples given and did nothing else. What is wanted is a program which operates on whole classes of input data in a manner analogous to, but more general than, the examples. The difficulty with generalization is that there are always many ways to generalize any set of examples.

The main effort in any programming by example system is therefore directed toward finding an appropriate level of generalization. For example, consider the program specified by the following input-output pair.

$$(A\ B\ C\ D) \Rightarrow (D\ D\ C\ C\ B\ B\ A\ A)$$

It is pretty clear from this example that the input is a list and the items in this list are doubled and reversed in the output. However, it would probably be an over-generalization to assume that doubling and reversing should be applied to elements of the input list that are themselves lists. On the other hand, it would probably be an under-generalization to assume that the input must be of length four. (See [Smith 82] and [Michalski, Carbonell, and Mitchell 83] for a discussion of generalization in the general context of machine learning.)

Early work on programming by example (see [Hardy 75], [Shaw, Swartout, and Green 75], and [Siklossy and Sykes 75]) was *ad hoc* in nature. This changed with the work of Summers [Chapter 18] who established theoretical foundations for the field. Most subsequent work (for example see [Biermann 78] and [Kodratoff and Jouannaud 84]) is based on Summers's approach.

Most of the work on programming by example uses Lisp as the target language (for a survey see [Smith 84]). The reason for this is not intrinsic to any of the techniques, but rather because of the fact that the Lisp programming environment facilitates writing programs that operate on programs.

Although it initially created a good deal of excitement, programming by example now appears to be of only theoretical interest. The problem is that the techniques do not scale up to programs of realistic complexity. Unfortunately, as input-output pairs become more complex, the problem of generalizing them appropriately becomes astronomically more complex.

There are basically only two ways to cut the generalization problem down to a manageable size. First,

more examples can be provided in order to reduce ambiguity, including examples of intermediate computation steps (see [Biermann 72], [Biermann and Krishnaswamy 76], and [Bauer, Chapter 19]). Unfortunately, when the number of examples becomes too large, this becomes an inefficient means of specification as compared with other formal techniques. Alternatively, assumptions can be built into the programming-by-example system about about the class of programs that can be produced. For example, [Andreae 85] synthesizes robot programs from examples. The system described in [Hedrick 76] assumes that the synthesized program must be a rule-based production system. Unfortunately, when the structural assumptions begin to get this strong, the programming-by-example system ends up being essentially a special kind of program generator.

A different approach to using examples is illustrated by the Tinker system [Lieberman and Hewitt 80]. Tinker does not attempt to generalize the examples automatically but rather provides a program development environment, which helps the user perform the generalization. In this context, the input-output examples are perhaps better thought of as test cases.

Intelligent Assistants

Most of the systems described above attempt to completely automate parts of the programming task. Another approach is to assist programmers rather than replace them. An advantage of this approach is that it makes it possible to construct useful systems even while the ultimate goal of automatic programming remains out of reach.

An intelligent assistant is an active agent in the programming process. In the near term, the machine will act as a programmer's junior partner and critic, keeping track of details and assisting with the routine aspects of the programming process, allowing the programmer to concentrate on the more difficult parts. As research in artificial intelligence progresses, however, it will be possible to shift more and more tasks from the programmer to the machine.

Research on intelligent assistants has uncovered two key issues. The first issue is the division of labor between the programmer and the assistant: How are the programmer and the machine going to succeed in cooperating and communicating? This brings up a second key issue: It would be impossibly tedious for the programmer to explain each instruction or decision to the assistant from first principles. Rather, the programmer needs to rely on a body of shared knowledge in order to communicate concisely.

At minimum, an intelligent assistant must understand the technical vocabulary of programming, including such terms as search, stack, side-effect, and so on. As will be discussed further below, an important part of research on automatic programming generally is concerned with identifying and codifying the specific knowledge that is required for the machine to participate in particular programming tasks.

The evolution of research on intelligent assistants has been marked by a series of influential "thought" papers, which proposed architectures for programming assistants of various kinds. This series of proposals started with [Floyd, Chapter 20], continued through the A system [Winograd 73], the Programming Apprentice [Hewitt and Smith 75], and the Lisp Programmer's Apprentice [Rich and Shrobe 78], and ends most recently with the Knowledge-Based Software Assistant [Green, Luckham, Balzer, Cheatham, and Rich, Chapter 23].

Prototype implementations of intelligent programming assistants include the Designer/Verifier's Assistant [Moriconi, Chapter 21], which emphasizes the theorem-proving capabilities of the machine, and KBEmacs (the Knowledge-Based Editor in Emacs) [Waters, Chapter 22], which emphasizes the use of a knowledge base of standard programming forms in program construction. Prototype assistants have also been constructed in the areas of program testing [Chapman 82] and project management [Kedzierski 82].

Programming Tutors

A specialized kind of intelligent programming assistant is a programming tutor. In this application, the assistant helps a novice programmer to learn programming rather than helping a expert programmer to construct programs. An interesting aspect of this application is that, in contrast with those above, the assistant is expected to know much more about programming than the user. (For a collection of papers on intelligent tutoring systems in general, see [Sleeman and Brown 82].)

A key function of a programming tutor is to examine a program written by a student programmer, find any errors in it, and then explain the errors to the student in a way that will help the student learn. In order to identify errors in a program, some theory of what errors can occur is required. The various programming tutors that have been constructed (and proposed) differ primarily in the way in which knowledge about errors is represented and in the way errors are identified.

The first system capable of finding a wide range of errors in student programs was the analyzer of

[Ruth Chapter 24]. This system relies on a grammar to specify what algorithms are expected in student programs. The grammar is used to parse student programs. Any deviation between a program and what is specified by the grammar is reported as an error. A key problem with this approach is that it is easy for a program to fail to match the grammar even though it is, in fact, correct.

Recently, [Zelinka 86] has proposed using a somewhat similar approach except that the grammar and parsing are applied to a more abstract, graphlike program representation rather than to the program text. This significantly increases the ability of the system to recognize when two programs are equivalent.

An alternate approach to finding errors is to explicitly represent what is wrong instead of what is right. For example, the MENO-II system [Soloway *et al.*, 83] contains a precompiled library of specific bug patterns. The Sniffer system [Shapiro 81] used a library of bug recognition procedures. In the system described in [Adam and Laurent 80] knowledge about errors is encoded in the form of graph transformations. A problem with the "bug library" approach is that if a program contains errors, but these errors are not in the library, then the program will appear correct to the system.

A third approach to detecting errors is to compare what a program does with its specification. This can be done either via symbolic evaluation (see [Laubsch and Eisenstadt 81]) or by comparing logical descriptions of the behavior (see [Lukey 80]). The Proust system [Johnson and Soloway, Chapter 25] combines recognition, reasoning about specifications, and knowledge about specific bugs.

A final area of investigation stimulated by the desire for intelligent tutors has been basic artificial intelligence research on the role of goals and plans in problem solving (see [Goldstein 75] and [Miller 82]).

Knowledge Representation

A recurring theme in the whole area of artificial intelligence and software engineering is: What is the knowledge that programmers know, and how can it be effectively represented in an automatic system? What programmers know can be naturally divided into two parts: programming knowledge and domain knowledge.

Programming Knowledge

The following facts illustrate the range of programming knowledge from the very basic and simple to the more specialized and complex.

(1) A stack can be implemented using an array and a pointer by . . . .

(2) Tail recursion can be converted to iteration by . . . .
(3) The convex hull of a set of points can be efficiently determined by . . .

This kind of knowledge has to do with the conventional objects of computer science (such as control constructs, arrays, and graphs) and their associated algorithms and implementation relationships. It is the knowledge found in computer science text books such as [Knuth 73] and [Aho, Hopcroft, and Ullman 74].

Knowledge representation has always been a central concern of artificial intelligence research (for an overview see [Brachman and Levesque 85]). Work on representing programming knowledge has been able to take considerable advantage of knowledge representation techniques developed in the context of other tasks. Programming has also served as a driving force for new work on representation. In particular, the following desiderata have been identified for the representation of programming knowledge (see [Rich and Waters 83]).

- *Expressiveness.* The representation must be capable of capturing a wide variety of programming knowledge, including both data abstractions and procedural abstractions.

- *Convenient Combination.* The methods for combining units of knowledge should be easy to implement and the properties of combinations should be evident from the properties of the parts.

- *Semantic Soundness.* The representation must be based on a mathematical foundation that allows correctness conditions to be stated.

- *Machine Manipulability.* It must be possible to manipulate the representation effectively and efficiently using computer tools.

- *Programming Language Independence.* The formalism should not be dependent on the syntax of any particular programming language.

Many different representations have been used for programming knowledge. One common approach is to use programming language schemas (see [Wirth 73], [Gerhart 75], [Basu and Misra 76], and [Misra 78]). Unfortunately, this approach has severe drawbacks with regard to expressiveness, convenient combination, and language independence.

Other researchers have used flowchart schemas (see [Ianov 60] and [Manna 74]), which have greater language independence but are still quite limited in expressiveness and have only somewhat improved combination properties.

The dominant current approach to representing programming knowledge is to use program transformations (see [Green and Barstow, Chapter 26] and [Barstow, Chapter 7]). Since transformations are usually stated in terms of the syntax of a particular programming language, they are not language independent. Also, because they typically have a procedural component, transformations have problems with regard to semantic soundness. However, transformations are much more expressive and more easily combined than schemas.

The work described in [Rich, Chapter 28], [Rich 82], and [Rich 85] uses a hybrid representation that combines features of program transformations and flowchart schemas with predicate calculus. This approach has advantages with regard to all of the desiderata stated above.

Two further issues in representing programming knowledge are how various items of programming knowledge are be identified in the first place and how they should be related to each other in a library. The work described in [Dershowitz, Chapter 27] explores the role of analogy in answering to these questions. [Rich, Chapter 28] defines some useful taxonomic structures for a library of programming knowledge.

Most of the research on programming knowledge described above is driven primarily by introspection and does not attempt any empirical investigation of what the average programmer actually knows. The experiments described in [Soloway and Ehrlich, Chapter 29] probe the empirical issues further. Among other things, these experiments show that the intuitions of programming knowledge researchers have been basically sound.

Domain Knowledge

A second type of knowledge required by automatic programming systems is *domain knowledge*—knowledge about the world in which the target software is to operate. The following facts illustrate domain knowledge in the area of accounting.

(1) Net salary is equal to gross salary minus deductions.
(2) If total yearly income is expected to be less than $500, then no withholding is required.
(3) There are twelve months in a year.

Since domain knowledge is an intrinsic part of stating and understanding requirements, it is an essential component of any automatic programming system that wants to go beyond automatic implementation. As a result, domain knowledge has recently begun to receive more attention in automatic programming research. One important issue is how domain knowledge and programming knowledge should interact during program synthesis (see [Manna and Waldinger 75], [Barstow 82], and [Barstow, Chapter 31]).

At the current time, there are no general-purpose automatic programming systems that take requirements as input. There are however, two very interesting special-purpose systems that do operate at least near the level of requirements. Each of these systems contains extensive domain knowledge.

The Draco system [Neighbors, Chapter 30] is a program-generator generator. Draco uses a transformational framework in which it is easy to define special-purpose program generators. When using Draco to define a program generator for a domain, a "domain designer" follows the classic program generator approach of first designing a problem-oriented language that can be used to conveniently describe programs in the domain and then specifying how to generate programs written in the problem-oriented language. The contribution of Draco is to provide a set of facilities that make it possible to specify the program generation process in a primarily declarative form. BNF is used to define the syntax of the problem-oriented language. Lateral and vertical transformations are used to define its semantics and therefore the domain knowledge. Procedures are used only as a last resort. When a program is being implemented by a Draco-based program generator, the user is expected to provide guidance as to which transformations to use. Thus the final program generator is not fully automatic.

The ΦNIX system [Barstow, Chapter 31] has extensive knowledge of the computations involved in oil well logging (determining how much oil is accessible from a given well). It probably contains more (and more detailed) domain knowledge than any other current automatic programming system. Some of this knowledge is represented in the form of program transformations, and some is procedurally embedded.

[Borgida, Greenspan, and Mylopoulos, Chapter 32] explore opportunities for applying existing knowledge representation technology, such as taxonomic hierarchies, to domain knowledge generally.

Artificial Intelligence Programming

The discussion above focuses on making programming tools more powerful by imbuing them with artificial intelligence. However, there is a completely different way in which artificial intelligence research has helped, and will likely continue to help, programmers. Artificial intelligence researchers are themselves programmers. Since the earliest days of computer science, artificial intelligence researchers have developed programming tools for their own use that have turned out to be very useful for programmers in general.

For example, in 1958, John McCarthy (who was then working at MIT) got interested in the possibility of building a program that could become intelligent by learning from experience and taking advice. To pursue this research, he first had to devise a way for his program to run interactively on a single computer while other users were doing other things. To satisfy this need he devised timesharing.[1]

In more recent history, it is significant to note that many now familiar interface features (such as windows, mice, and menus) reached their maturity in artificial intelligence programming environments before moving out into more general use. The same is true for object-oriented programming (see [Stefik and Bobrow 86]), logic programming (see [Kowalski 79] and [Cohen 85]), and constraint-oriented programming (see [Steele 80] and [Borning 81]). (For a short overview of artificial intelligence programming, see [Bobrow and Stefik, Chapter 34]. For a collection of papers on interactive programming environments in general see [Barstow, Sandewall, and Shrobe 83].)

The rate of spinoff of programming ideas from artificial intelligence has accelerated in recent years. An important reason for this is that in the programming world in general there has been an increased emphasis on rapid prototyping and the construction of large, complex, first-of-a-kind programs. Creating such programs is more a problem of exploration than implementation and does not conform to conventional software lifecycle models. (For a collection of papers on rapid prototyping as an alternative to the conventional software lifecycle, see [Squires 82].) One reason for this is that in exploratory programming, specification and implementation are inevitably intertwined (see [Swartout and Balzer 82].) The artificial intelligence programming community has always been faced with exploratory programming and has therefore had a head start on developing appropriate language, environment, and hardware features (see [Sheil, Chapter 33]).

---

[1]This anecdote is based on a memo dated January 1, 1959, from John McCarthy to Prof. P. M. Morse, regarding "A Time Sharing Operator Program for our Projected IBM 709."

I / Deductive Synthesis

The deductive approach to program synthesis transforms program synthesis into a theorem-proving task. [Manna and Waldinger, Chapter 1] provides an introduction to the key ideas of this approach, namely the correspondence between theorems and specifications and between constructive proofs and programs. Manna and Waldinger have developed a logical framework specially suited to program synthesis and illustrate its use in a number of examples. Although this logic is ultimately intended for use in automatic synthesis systems, no implementation currently exists.

[Smith, Chapter 2] describes an implemented deductive synthesis system, called CYPRESS, based on a related, but slightly different, logical framework. The major focus of the CYPRESS system is discovering divide-and-conquer algorithms. A divide-and-conquer algorithm has two parts: a method for dividing up the problem and a method for combining the solutions of subproblems. If the user chooses either a dividing method or a combining method, CYPRESS can automatically derive the other method. Given its semiautomated nature, CYPRESS is also an example of the intelligent assistant approach, along with the other examples in Section VII.

By itself, deductive synthesis is not likely to be a solution to the automatic programming problem. However, deductive methods similar to those used in these two chapters will very likely be an important component of all future automatic programming systems. Most of the systems and approaches described in this volume either explicitly or implicitly require the use of deductive techniques as part of their application.

A Deductive Approach to Program Synthesis

ZOHAR MANNA
Stanford University and Weizmann Institute
and
RICHARD WALDINGER
SRI International

Program synthesis is the systematic derivation of a program from a given specification. A deductive approach to program synthesis is presented for the construction of recursive programs. This approach regards program synthesis as a theorem-proving task and relies on a theorem-proving method that combines the features of transformation rules, unification, and mathematical induction within a single framework.

Key Words and Phrases: mathematical induction, program synthesis, program transformation, resolution, theorem proving
CR Categories: 3.64, 4.20, 5.21, 5.24

MOTIVATION

The early work in program synthesis relied strongly on mechanical theorem-proving techniques. The work of Green [5] and Waldinger and Lee [13], for example, depended on resolution-based theorem proving; however, the difficulty of representing the principle of mathematical induction in a resolution framework hampered these systems in the formation of programs with iterative or recursive loops. More recently, program synthesis and theorem proving have tended to go their separate ways. Newer theorem-proving systems are able to perform proofs by mathematical induction (e.g., Boyer and Moore [2]) but are useless for program synthesis because they have sacrificed the ability to prove theorems involving existential quantifiers. Recent work in program synthesis (e.g., Burstall and Darlington [3] and Manna and Waldinger [7]), on the other hand, has abandoned

This research was supported in part by the National Science Foundation under Grants MCS 76-83655 and MCS 78-02591, in part by the Office of Naval Research under Contracts N00014-76-C-0687 and N00014-75-C-0816, in part by the Defense Advanced Research Projects Agency of the Department of Defense under Contract MDA903-76-C-0206, and in part by the United States–Israel Binational Science Foundation.
Authors' addresses: Z. Manna, Department of Computer Science, Stanford University, Stanford, CA 94305; R. Waldinger, Artificial Intelligence Center, SRI International, 333 Ravenswood Ave., Menlo Park, CA 94025.

the theorem-proving approach and has relied instead on the direct application of transformation or rewriting rules to the program's specification; in choosing this path, these systems have renounced the use of such theorem-proving techniques as unification or induction.

In this paper we describe a framework for program synthesis that again relies on a theorem-proving approach. This approach combines techniques of unification, mathematical induction, and transformation rules within a single deductive system. We outline the logical structure of this system without considering the strategic aspects of how deductions are directed. Although no implementation exists, the approach is machine oriented and ultimately intended for implementation in automatic synthesis systems.

In the next section we give examples of specifications accepted by the system. In the succeeding sections we explain the relation between theorem proving and our approach to program synthesis.

SPECIFICATION

The specification of a program allows us to express the purpose of the desired program, without indicating an algorithm by which that purpose is to be achieved. Specifications may contain high-level constructs that are not computable, but are close to our way of thinking. Typically, specifications involve such constructs as the quantifiers *for all* ... and *for some* ..., the set constructor $\{x: \ldots\}$, and the descriptor *find z such that* ....

For example, to specify a program to compute the integer square root of a nonnegative integer n, we would write

$$sqrt(n) \Leftarrow find\ z\ such\ that$$
$$integer(z)\ and\ z^2 \leq n < (z+1)^2$$
$$where\ integer(n)\ and\ 0 \leq n.$$

Here, the *input condition*

$$integer(n)\ and\ 0 \leq n$$

expresses the class of legal inputs to which the program is expected to apply. The *output condition*

$$integer(z)\ and\ z^2 \leq n < (z+1)^2$$

describes the relation the output z is intended to satisfy.

To describe a program to sort a list l, we might write

$$sort(l) \Leftarrow find\ z\ such\ that$$
$$ordered(z)\ and\ perm(l, z)$$
$$where\ islist(l).$$

Here, *ordered(z)* expresses that the elements of the output list z should be in nondecreasing order; *perm(l, z)* expresses that z should be a permutation of the input l; and *islist(l)* expresses that l can be assumed to be a list.

To describe a program to find the last element of a nonempty list l, we might write

$$last(l) \Leftarrow find\ z\ such\ that$$
$$for\ some\ y,\ l = y <>[z]$$
$$where\ islist(l)\ and\ l \neq [].$$

Here, $u < > v$ denotes the result of appending the two lists u and v; $[u]$ denotes the list whose sole element is u; and $[]$ denotes the empty list. (Thus, $[A\ B\ C] < > [D]$ yields $[A\ B\ C\ D]$; therefore, by the above specification, $last([A\ B\ C\ D]) = D$.)

In general, we are considering the synthesis of programs whose specifications have the form

$$f(a) \Leftarrow \text{find } z \text{ such that } R(a, z)$$
$$\text{where } P(a).$$

Here, a denotes the input of the desired program and z denotes its output; the input condition $P(a)$ and the output condition $R(a, z)$ may themselves contain quantifiers and set constructors (but not the *find* descriptor).

The above specification describes an applicative program, one which yields an output but produces no side effects. To derive a program from such a specification, we attempt to prove a theorem of the form

$$\text{for all } a,$$
$$\text{if } P(a)$$
$$\text{then for some } z, R(a, z).$$

The proof of this theorem must be constructive, in the sense that it must tell us how to find an output z satisfying the desired output condition. From such a proof, a program to compute z can be extracted.

The above notation can be extended to describe several related programs at once. For example, to specify the programs $div(i, j)$ and $rem(i, j)$ for finding the integer quotient and remainder, respectively, of dividing a nonnegative integer i by a positive integer j, we write

$$(div(i, j), rem(i, j)) \Leftarrow \text{find } (y, z) \text{ such that } integer(y) \text{ and}$$
$$integer(z) \text{ and } i = y \cdot j + z \text{ and } 0 \le z \text{ and } z < j$$
$$\text{where } integer(i) \text{ and } integer(j) \text{ and } 0 \le i \text{ and } 0 < j.$$

BASIC STRUCTURE

The basic structure employed in our approach is the *sequent*, which consists of two lists of sentences, the *assertions* $A_1, A_2, \ldots, A_m$, and the *goals* $G_1, G_2, \ldots, G_n$. With each assertion or goal there may be associated an entry called the *output expression*. This output entry has no bearing on the proof itself, but records the program segment that has been constructed at each stage of the derivation (cf. the "answer literal" in Green [5]). We denote a sequent by a table with three columns: assertions, goals, and outputs. Each row in the sequent has the form

assertions	goals	outputs
$A_i(a, x)$		$t_i(a, x)$

or

	goals	outputs
	$G_j(a, x)$	$t_j(a, x)$

The meaning of a sequent is that if all instances of each of the assertions are true, then some instances of at least one of the goals is true; more precisely, the sequent has the same meaning as its *associated sentence*

$$if \ for \ all \ x, \ A_1(a, x) \ and$$
$$for \ all \ x, \ A_2(a, x) \ and$$

$$\cdot$$
$$\cdot$$
$$\cdot$$

$$for \ all \ x, \ A_m(a, x)$$
$$then \ for \ some \ x, \ G_1(a, x) \ or$$
$$for \ some \ x, \ G_2(a, x) \ or$$

$$\cdot$$
$$\cdot$$
$$\cdot$$

$$for \ some \ x, \ G_n(a, x)$$

where a denotes all the constants of the sequent and x denotes all the free variables. (In general, we denote constants or tuples of constants by a, b, c, $\ldots$, n and variables or tuples of variables by u, v, w, $\ldots$, z.) If some instance of a goal is true (or some instance of an assertion is false), the corresponding instance of its output expression satisfies the given specification. In other words, if some instance $G_j(a, e)$ is true (or some instance $A_i(a, e)$ is false), then the corresponding instance $t_j(a, e)$ (or $t_i(a, e)$) is an acceptable output.

Note that (1) an assertion or goal is not required to have an output entry; (2) an assertion and a goal never occupy the same row of the sequent; (3) the variables in each row are "dummies" that we can systematically rename without changing the meaning of the sequent.

The distinction between assertions and goals is artificial and does not increase the logical power of the deductive system. In fact, if we delete a goal from a sequent and add its negation as a new assertion, we obtain an equivalent sequent; similarly, we can delete an assertion from a sequent and add its negation as a new goal without changing the meaning of the sequent. This property is known as *duality*. Nevertheless, the distinction between assertions and goals makes our deductions easier to understand.

If initially we are given the specification

$$f(a) \Leftarrow find \ z \ such \ that \ R(a, z)$$
$$where \ P(a),$$

we construct the initial sequent

assertions	goals	outputs $f(a)$
$P(a)$		
	$R(a, z)$	z

In other words, we assume that the input condition $P(a)$ is true, and we want to prove that for some z, the goal $R(a, z)$ is true; if so, z represents the desired output of the program $f(a)$. The output z is a variable, for which we can make substitutions; the input a is a constant. If we prefer, we may remove quantifiers in $P(a)$ and $R(a, z)$ by the usual skolemization procedure (see, e.g., Nilsson [11]).

The input condition $P(a)$ is not the only assertion in the sequent; typically, simple, basic axioms, such as $u = u$, are represented as assertions that are tacitly present in all sequents. Many properties of the subject domain, however, are represented by other means, as we shall see.

The deductive system we describe operates by causing new assertions and goals, and corresponding new output expressions, to be added to the sequent without changing its meaning. The process terminates if the goal *true* (or the assertion *false*) is produced, whose corresponding output expression consists entirely of primitives from the target programming language; this expression is the desired program. In other words, if we develop a row of form

	true	*t*

or

false		*t*

where *t* is a primitive expression, the desired program is of form

$$f(a) \Longleftarrow t.$$

Note that this deductive procedure never requires us to establish new sequents or (except for strategic purposes) to delete an existing assertion or goal. In this sense, the approach more resembles resolution than "natural deduction."

Suppose we are required to construct two related programs $f(a)$ and $g(a)$; i.e., we are given the specification

$$(f(a), g(a)) \Longleftarrow find \ (y, z) \ such \ that \ R(a, y, z)$$
$$where \ P(a).$$

Then we construct an initial sequent with two output columns

assertions	goals	outputs $f(a)$	$g(a)$
$P(a)$			
	$R(a, y, z)$	y	z

If we subsequently succeed in developing a terminal row, say of form

	true	*s*	*t*

where both *s* and *t* are primitive expressions, then the desired programs are

$$f(a) \Longleftarrow s$$

and

$$g(a) \Longleftarrow t.$$

In the remainder of this paper we outline the deductive rules of our system and their application to program synthesis.

SPLITTING RULES

The splitting rules allow us to decompose an assertion or goal into its logical components. For example, if our sequent contains an assertion of form *F and G*, we can introduce the two assertions *F* and *G* into the sequent without changing its meaning. We will call this the *andsplit rule* and express it in the following notation:

assertions	goals	outputs
F and G		t
F		t
G		t

This means that if rows matching those above the double line are present in the sequent, then the corresponding rows below the double line may be added.

Similarly, we have the *orsplit rule*

assertions	goals	outputs
	F or G	t
	F	t
	G	t

and the *ifsplit rule*

assertions	goals	outputs
	if F then G	t
F		t
	G	t

There is no *orsplit rule* or *ifsplit rule* for assertions and no *andsplit rule* for goals. Note that the output entries for the consequents of the splitting rules are exactly the same as the entries for their antecedents.

Although initially only the goal has an output entry, the *ifsplit rule* can introduce an assertion with an output entry. Such assertions are rare in practice, but can arise by the action of such rules.

TRANSFORMATION RULES

Transformation rules allow one assertion or goal to be derived from another. Typically, transformations are expressed as conditional rewriting rules

$$r \Rightarrow s \quad if\ P$$

meaning that in any assertion, goal, or output expression, a subexpression of form r can be replaced by the corresponding expression of form s, provided that the condition P holds. We never write such a rule unless r and s are equal terms or equivalent sentences, whenever condition P holds. For example, the transformation rule

$$u \in v \Rightarrow u = head(v)\ or\ u \in tail(v) \quad if\ islist(v)\ and\ v \neq [\ ]$$

expresses that an element belongs to a nonempty list if it equals the head of the list or belongs to its tail. (Here, $head(v)$ denotes the first element of the list v, and $tail(v)$ denotes the list of all but the first element.) The rule

$$u \mid 0 \Rightarrow true \quad if\ integer(u)\ and\ u \neq 0$$

expresses that every nonzero integer divides zero.

If a rule has the vacuous condition *true*, we write it with no condition; for example, the logical rule

$$Q \text{ and } true \Rightarrow Q$$

may be applied to any subexpression that matches its left-hand side.

A transformation rule

$$r \Rightarrow s \quad if \, P$$

is not permitted to replace an expression of form s by the corresponding expression of form r when the condition P holds, even though these two expressions have the same values. For that purpose, we would require a second rule

$$s \Rightarrow r \quad if \, P.$$

For example, we might include the rule

$$x + 0 \Rightarrow x \quad if \, number(x)$$

but not the rule

$$x \Rightarrow x + 0 \quad if \, number(x).$$

Assertions and goals are affected differently by transformation rules. Suppose

$$r \Rightarrow s \quad if \, P$$

is a transformation rule and F is an assertion containing a subexpression r' which is not within the scope of any quantifier. Suppose also that there exists a *unifier* for r and r', i.e., a substitution θ such that $r\theta$ and $r'\theta$ are identical. Here, $r\theta$ denotes the result of applying the substitution θ to the expression r. We can assume that θ is a "most general" unifier (in the sense of Robinson [12]) of r and r'. We rename the variables of F, if necessary, to ensure that it has no variables in common with the transformation rule. By the rule, we can conclude that if $P\theta$ holds, then $r\theta$ and $s\theta$ are equal terms or equivalent sentences. Therefore, we can add the assertion

$$if \, P\theta \text{ then } F\theta[r\theta \leftarrow s\theta]$$

to our sequent. Here, the notation $F\theta[r\theta \leftarrow s\theta]$ indicates that every occurrence of $r\theta$ in $F\theta$ is to be replaced by $s\theta$.

For example, suppose we have the assertion

$$a \in l \text{ and } a \neq 0$$

and we apply the transformation rule

$$u \in v \Rightarrow u = head(v) \text{ or } u \in tail(v) \quad if \, islist(v) \text{ and } v \neq [],$$

taking r' to be $a \in l$ and θ to be the substitution $[u \leftarrow a; v \leftarrow l]$; then we obtain the new assertion

$$if \, islist(l) \text{ and } l \neq []$$
$$then \, (a = head(l) \text{ or } a \in tail(l)) \text{ and } a \neq 0.$$

Note that a and l are constants, while u and v are variables, and indeed, the substitution was made for the variables of the rule but not for the constants of the assertion.

In general, if the given assertion F has an associated output entry t, the new output entry is formed by applying the substitution θ to t. For, suppose some instance of the new assertion "*if $P\theta$ then $F\theta[r\theta \leftarrow s\theta]$*" is false; then the corresponding instance of $P\theta$ is true, and the corresponding instance of $F\theta[r\theta \leftarrow s\theta]$ is false. Then, by the transformation rule, the instances of $r\theta$ and $s\theta$ are equal; hence the corresponding instance of $F\theta$ is false. We know that if any instance of F is false, the corresponding instance of t satisfies the given specification. Hence, because some instance of $F\theta$ is false, the corresponding instance of $t\theta$ is the desired output.

In our deduction rule notation, we write

assertions	goals	outputs
F		t
if $P\theta$ then $F\theta[r\theta \leftarrow s\theta]$		$t\theta$

The corresponding dual deduction rule for goals is

assertions	goals	outputs
	F	t
	$P\theta$ and $F\theta[r\theta \leftarrow s\theta]$	$t\theta$

For example, suppose we have the goal

	$a \mid z$ and $b \mid z$	$z + 1$

and we apply the transformation rule

$$u \mid 0 \Rightarrow true \quad if \, integer(u) \, and \, u \neq 0,$$

taking r' to be $a \mid z$ and θ to be the substitution $[z \leftarrow 0; u \leftarrow a]$. Then we obtain the goal

	(integer(a) and $a \neq 0$) and (true and $b \mid 0$)	$0 + 1$

which can be further transformed to

	integer(a) and $a \neq 0$ and $b \mid 0$	1

Note that applying the transformation rule caused a substitution to be made for the occurrences of the variable z in the goal and the output entry.

Transformation rules can also be applied to output entries in an analogous manner.

Transformation rules need not be simple rewriting rules; they may represent arbitrary procedures. For example, r could be an equation $f(x) = a$, s could be its solution $x = e$, and P could be the condition under which that solution applies. Another example: the skolemization procedure for removing quantifiers can be represented as a transformation rule. In fact, decision methods for particular subtheories may also be represented as transformation rules (see, e.g., Bledsoe [1] or Nelson and Oppen [9]).

Transformation rules play the role of the "antecedent theorems" and "consequent theorems" of PLANNER (Hewitt [6]). For example, a consequent theorem that we might write as

$$to\ prove\ f(u) = f(v)$$
$$prove\ u = v$$

can be represented by the transformation rule

$$f(u) = f(v) \Rightarrow true \quad if\ u = v.$$

This rule will have the desired effect of reducing the goal $f(a) = f(b)$ to the simpler subgoal $a = b$, and (like the consequent theorem) will not have the pernicious side effect of deriving from the simple assertion $a = b$ the more complex assertion $f(a) = f(b)$. The axiomatic representation of the same fact would have both results. (Incidentally, the transformation rule has the beneficial effect, not shared by the consequent theorem, of deriving from the complex assertion $not(f(a) = f(b))$ the simpler assertion $not(a = b)$.)

RESOLUTION

The original resolution principle (Robinson [12]) required that sentences be put into conjunctive normal form. As a result, the set of clauses sometimes exploded to an unmanageable size and the proofs lost their intuitive content. The version of resolution we employ does not require the sentences to be in conjunctive normal form.

Assume our sequent contains two assertions F and G, containing subsentences P_1 and P_2, respectively, that are not within the scope of any quantifier. For the time being, let us ignore the output expressions corresponding to these assertions. Suppose there exists a unifier for P_1 and P_2, i.e., a substitution θ such that $P_1\theta$ and $P_2\theta$ are identical. We can take θ to be the most general unifier. The *AA-resolution rule* allows us to deduce the new assertion

$$F\theta[P_1\theta \leftarrow true]\ or\ G\theta[P_2\theta \leftarrow false]$$

and add it to the sequent. Recall that the notation $F\theta[P_1\theta \leftarrow true]$ indicates that every instance of the subsentence $P_1\theta$ in $F\theta$ is to be replaced by *true*. (Of course, we may need to do the usual renaming to ensure that F and G have no variables in common.) We will call θ the *unifying substitution* and $P_1\theta(=P_2\theta)$ the *eliminated subexpression*; the deduced assertion is called the *resolvent*. Note that the rule is symmetric, so the roles of F and G may be reversed.

For example, suppose our sequent contains the assertions

$$if\ (P(x)\ and\ Q(b))\ then\ R(x)$$

and

$$P(a)\ and\ Q(y).$$

The two subsentences "$P(x)$ *and* $Q(b)$" and "$P(a)$ *and* $Q(y)$" can be unified by the substitution

$$\theta = [x \leftarrow a;\ y \leftarrow b].$$

Therefore, the AA-resolution rule allows us to eliminate the subexpression "*P(a) and Q(b)*" and derive the conclusion

$$(\textit{if true then } R(a)) \textit{ or false},$$

which reduces to

$$R(a)$$

by application of the appropriate transformation rules.

The conventional resolution rule may be regarded as a special case of the above AA-resolution rule. The conventional rule allows us to derive from the two assertions

$$(\textit{not } P_1) \textit{ or } Q$$

and

$$P_2 \textit{ or } R$$

the new assertion

$$Q\theta \textit{ or } R\theta,$$

where θ is a most general unifier of P_1 and P_2. From the same two assertions we can use our AA-resolution rule to derive

$$(((\textit{not } P_1 \textit{ or } Q)\theta)[P_1\theta \leftarrow \textit{true}] \textit{ or } (((P_2 \textit{ or } R)\theta)[P_2\theta \leftarrow \textit{false}]$$

i.e.,

$$((\textit{not true}) \textit{ or } Q\theta) \textit{ or } (\textit{false or } R\theta),$$

which reduces to the same conclusion

$$Q\theta \textit{ or } R\theta$$

as the original resolution rule.

The justification for the AA-resolution rule is straightforward: Because F holds, if $P_1\theta$ is true, then $F\theta[P_1\theta \leftarrow \textit{true}]$ holds; on the other hand, because G holds, if $P_1\theta(=P_2\theta)$ is false, $G\theta[P_2\theta \leftarrow \textit{false}]$ holds. In either case, the disjunction

$$F\theta[P_1\theta \leftarrow \textit{true}] \textit{ or } G\theta[P_2\theta \leftarrow \textit{false}]$$

holds.

A "nonclausal" resolution rule similar to ours has been developed by Murray [8]. Other such rules have been proposed by Wilkins [14] and Nilsson [10].

THE RESOLUTION RULES

We have defined the AA-resolution rule to derive conclusions from assertions.
The *AA-resolution rule*

assertions	goals
F	
G	
$F\theta[P_1\theta \leftarrow \textit{true}]$ or $G\theta[P_2\theta \leftarrow \textit{false}]$	

where $P_1\theta = P_2\theta$, and θ is most general.

By duality, we can regard goals as negated assertions; consequently, the following three rules are corollaries of the AA-resolution rule.

The *GG-resolution rule*

assertions	goals
	F G
	$F\theta[P_1\theta \leftarrow true]$ and $G\theta[P_2\theta \leftarrow false]$

The *GA-resolution rule*

assertions	goals
G	F
	$F\theta[P_1\theta \leftarrow true]$ and not $(G\theta[P_2\theta \leftarrow false])$

The *AG-resolution rule*

assertions	goals
F	
	G
	$not(F\theta[P_1\theta \leftarrow true])$ and $G\theta[P_2\theta \leftarrow false]$

where P_1, P_2, and θ satisfy the same condition as for the AA-resolution rule.

Up to now, we have ignored the output expressions of the assertions and goals. However, if at least one of the sentences to which a resolution rule is applied has a corresponding output expression, the resolvent will also have an output expression. If only one of the sentences has an output expression, say t, then the resolvent will have the output expression $t\theta$. On the other hand, if the two sentences F and G have output expressions t_1 and t_2, respectively, the resolvent will have the output expression

$$\textit{if } P_1\theta \textit{ then } t_1\theta \textit{ else } t_2\theta.$$

(Of course, if $t_1\theta$ and $t_2\theta$ are identical, no conditional expression need be formed; the output expression is simply $t_1\theta$.)

The justification for constructing this conditional as an output expression is as follows. We consider only the GG case: Suppose that the goal

$$F\theta[P_1\theta \leftarrow true] \textit{ and } G\theta[P_2\theta \leftarrow false]$$

has been obtained by GG-resolution from two goals F and G. We would like to show that if the goal is true, the conditional output expression satisfies the desired specification. We assume that the resolvent is true; therefore both $F\theta[P_1\theta \leftarrow true]$ and $G\theta[P_2\theta \leftarrow false]$ are true. In the case that $P_1\theta$ is true, we have that $F\theta$ is also true. Consequently, the corresponding instance $t_1\theta$ of the output expression t_1 satisfies the specification of the desired program. In the other case, in which $P_1\theta$ is false, $P_2\theta$ is false, and the same reasoning allows us to conclude that $t_2\theta$ satisfies the specification of the desired program. In either case we can conclude that the conditional

$$if\ P_1\theta\ then\ t_1\theta\ else\ t_2\theta$$

satisfies the desired specification. By duality, the same output expression can be derived for the AA-resolution, GA-resolution, and AG-resolution.

For example, let $u \cdot v$ denote the operation of inserting u before the first element of the list v, and suppose we have the goal

assertions	goals	outputs $f(a, b)$
	$head(z) = a$ and $tail(z) = b$	z

and we have the assertion

$head(u \cdot v) = u$		

with no output expression; then by GA-resolution, applying the substitution

$$\theta = [u \leftarrow a;\ z \leftarrow a \cdot v]$$

and eliminating the subsentence

$$head(a \cdot v) = a,$$

we obtain the new goal

	$(true\ and\ tail(a \cdot v) = b)\ and$ $(not\ false)$	$a \cdot v$

which can be reduced to

	$tail(a \cdot v) = b$	$a \cdot v$

by application of the appropriate transformation rules. Note that we have applied the substitution $[u \leftarrow a;\ z \leftarrow a \cdot v]$ to the original output expression z, obtaining the new output expression $a \cdot v$. Therefore, if we can find v such that $tail(a \cdot v) = b$, the corresponding instance of $a \cdot v$ will satisfy the desired specification.

Another example: Suppose we have derived the two goals

assertions	goals	outputs $max(l)$
	$max(tail(l)) \geq head(l)$ and $tail(l) \neq []$	$max(tail(l))$
	$not(max(tail(l)) \geq head(l))$ and $tail(l) \neq []$	$head(l)$

Then by GG-resolution, eliminating the subsentence $max(tail(l)) \geq head(l)$, we can derive the new goal

	$(true\ and\ tail(l) \neq [])\ and$ $(not\ false)\ and\ tail(l) \neq [])$	$if\ max(tail(l)) \geq head(l)$ $then\ max(tail(l))$ $else\ head(l)$

which can be reduced to

	$tail(l) \neq []$	$if\ max(tail(l)) \geq head(l)$ $then\ max(tail(l))$ $else\ head(l)$

THE POLARITY STRATEGY

Not all applications of the resolution rules will produce valuable conclusions. For example, suppose we are given the goal

assertions	goals	outputs
	$P(c, x)\ and\ Q(x, a)$	

and the assertion

$if\ P(y, d)\ then\ Q(b, y)$		

Then if we apply GA-resolution, eliminating $Q(b, a)$, we can obtain the resolvent

$(P(c, b)\ and\ true)\ and\ not(if\ P(a, d)\ then\ false),$

which reduces to the goal

	$P(c, b)\ and\ P(a, d)$	

However, we can also apply GA-resolution and eliminate $P(c, d)$, yielding the resolvent

$(true\ and\ Q(d, a))\ and\ not(if\ false\ then\ Q(b, c)),$

which reduces to the trivial goal

	$false$	

Finally, we can also apply AG-resolution to the same assertion and goal in two different ways, eliminating $P(c, d)$ and eliminating $Q(b, a)$; both of these applications lead to the same trivial goal $false$.

A *polarity strategy* adapted from Murray [8] restricts the resolution rules to prevent many such fruitless applications. We first assign a *polarity* (either positive or negative) to every subsentence of a given sequent as follows:

(1) each goal is positive;
(2) each assertion is negative;
(3) if a subsentence S has form "*not* α," then its component α has polarity opposite to S;
(4) if a subsentence S has form "α *and* β," "α *or* β," "*for all* x, α," or "*for some* x, β," then its components α and β have the same polarity as S;
(5) if a subsentence S has form "*if* α *then* β," then β has the same polarity as S, but α has the opposite polarity.

For example, the above goal and assertion are annotated with the polarity of each subsentence, as follows:

assertions	goals	outputs
$(if\ P(y,\ d)^+\ then\ Q(b,\ y)^-)^-$		
	$(P(c,\ x)^+\ and\ Q(x,\ a)^+)^+$	

The four resolution rules we have presented replace certain subsentences by *true*, and others by *false*. The polarity strategy, then, permits a subsentence to be replaced by *true* only if it has at least one positive occurrence, and by *false* only if it has at least one negative occurrence. For example, we are permitted to apply GA-resolution to the above goal and assertion, eliminating $Q(b,\ a)$ because $Q(x,\ a)$, which is replaced by *true*, occurs positively in the goal, and $Q(b,\ y)$, which is replaced by *false*, occurs negatively in the assertion. On the other hand, we are not permitted to apply GA-resolution to eliminate $P(c,\ d)$, because $P(y,\ d)$, which is replaced by *false*, only occurs positively in the assertion. Similarly, we are not permitted to apply AG-resolution between this assertion and goal, whether we eliminate $P(c,\ d)$ or $Q(b,\ a)$. Indeed, the only application of resolution permitted by the polarity strategy is the one that led to a nontrivial conclusion.

The deductive system we have presented so far, including the splitting rules, the resolution rules, and an appropriate set of logical transformation rules, has been proved by Murray to constitute a complete system for first-order logic, in the sense that a derivation exists for every valid sentence. (Actually, only the resolution rules and some of the logical transformation rules are strictly necessary.) The above polarity strategy does not interfere with the completeness of the system.

MATHEMATICAL INDUCTION AND THE FORMATION OF RECURSIVE CALLS

Mathematical induction is of special importance for deductive systems intended for program synthesis because it is only by the application of some form of the induction principle that recursive calls or iterative loops are introduced into the program being constructed. The induction rule we employ is a version of the principle of mathematical induction over a well-founded set, known in the computer science literature as "structural induction."

We may describe this principle as follows: In attempting to prove that a sentence of form $F(a)$ holds for an arbitrary element a of some well-founded set, we may assume inductively that the sentence holds for all u that are strictly less than a in the well-founded ordering $<_u$. Thus, in trying to prove $F(a)$, the well-founded induction principle allows us to assume the induction hypothesis

for all u, if $u <_w a$ then $F(u)$.

In the case that the well-founded set is the nonnegative integers under the usual $<$ ordering, well-founded induction reduces to the familiar complete induction principle: To prove that $F(n)$ holds for an arbitrary nonnegative integer n, we may assume inductively that the sentence $F(u)$ holds for all nonnegative integers u such that $u < n$.

In our inference system, the principle of well-founded induction is represented as a deduction rule (rather than, say, an axiom schema). We present only a special case of this rule here.

Suppose we are constructing a program whose specification is of form

$$f(a) \Leftarrow \textit{find } z \textit{ such that } R(a, z)$$

$$\textit{where } P(a).$$

Our initial sequent is thus

assertions	goals	outputs $f(a)$
$P(a)$		
	$R(a, z)$	z

Then we can always add to our sequent a new assertion, the induction hypothesis

if $u \prec_w a$ *then if* $P(u)$ *then* $R(u, f(u))$		

Here, f denotes the program we are trying to construct. The well-founded set and the particular well-founded $\prec_w$ to be employed in the proof have not yet been determined. If the induction hypothesis is used more than once in the proof, it always refers to the same well-founded ordering $\prec_w$.

Let us paraphrase: We are attempting to construct a program f such that for an arbitrary input a satisfying the input condition $P(a)$, the output $f(a)$ will satisfy the output condition $R(a, f(a))$. By the well-founded induction principle, we can assume inductively that for every u less than a (in some well-founded ordering) such that the input condition $P(u)$ holds, the output $f(u)$ will satisfy the same output condition $R(u, f(u))$. By employing the induction hypothesis in the proof, recursive calls to f can be introduced into the output expression for $f(a)$.

As we shall see in a later section, we can introduce an induction hypothesis corresponding to any subset of the assertions or goals in our sequent, not just the initial assertion and goal; most of these induction hypotheses are not relevant to the final proof, and the proliferation of new assertions obstructs our efforts to find a proof. Therefore, we employ the following *recurrence strategy* for determining when to introduce an induction hypothesis.

Let us restrict our attention to the case where the induction hypothesis is formed from the initial sequent. Suppose that at some point in the derivation a goal is developed of form

	$R(s, z')$	$t(z')$

where s is an arbitrary term. In other words, the new goal is a precise instance of the initial goal $R(a, z)$ obtained by replacing a by s. This recurrence motivates us to add the induction hypothesis

if $u \prec_w a$ *then if* $P(u)$ *then* $R(u, f(u))$		

The rationale for introducing the induction hypothesis at this point is that now we can perform GA-resolution between the newly developed goal $R(s, z')$ and the induction hypothesis. The resulting goal is then

	true and
	not if $s <_u a$
	   then if $P(s)$
	      then false
		$t(f(s))$

This simplifies (by the application of logical transformation rules) to

	$s <_w a$ *and* $P(s)$	$t(f(s))$

Note that a recursive call $f(s)$ has been introduced into the output expression for $f(a)$. By proving the expression $s <_w a$, we ensure that this recursive call will terminate; by proving the expression $P(s)$, we guarantee that the argument s of the recursive call will satisfy the input condition of the program f.

The particular well-founded ordering $<_w$ to be employed by the proof has not yet been determined. We assume the existence of transformation rules of form

$$u <_{w_1} v \Rightarrow true \quad if \ Q(u, v)$$

capable of choosing or combining well-founded orderings applicable to the particular theories under consideration (e.g., numbers, lists, and sets).

Let us look at an example. Suppose we are constructing two programs $div(i, j)$ and $rem(i, j)$ to compute the quotient and remainder, respectively, of dividing a nonnegative integer i by a positive integer j; the specification may be expressed as

$$(div(i, j), rem(i, j)) \Leftarrow find \ (y, z) \ such \ that$$
$$i = y \cdot j + z \ and \ 0 \leq z \ and \ z < j$$
$$where \ 0 \leq i \ and \ 0 < j.$$

(Note that, for simplicity, we have omitted type requirements such as $integer(i)$.) Our initial sequent is then

assertions	goals	outputs $div(i, j)$	$rem(i, j)$
$0 \leq i$ *and* $0 < j$			
	$i = y \cdot j + z$ *and* $0 \leq z$ *and* $z < j$	y	z

Here, the inputs i and j are constants, for which we can make no substitution; y and the output z are variables.

Assume that during the course of the derivation we develop the goal

	$i - j = y_1 \cdot j + z$ *and* $0 \leq z$ *and* $z < j$	$y_1 + 1$	z

This goal is a precise instance of the initial goal

$$i = y \cdot j + z \ and \ 0 \leq z \ and \ z < j$$

obtained by replacing i by $i-j$. Therefore, we add as a new assertion the induction hypothesis.

$\begin{aligned}&\textit{if } (u_1, u_2) <_w (i, j)\\&\textit{then if } 0 \leq u_1 \textit{ and } 0 < u_2\\&\qquad\textit{then } u_1 = div(u_1, u_2) \cdot u_2 + rem(u_1, u_2)\\&\qquad\textit{and } 0 \leq rem(u_1, u_2) \textit{ and } rem(u_1, u_2) < u_2\end{aligned}$			

Here, $<_w$ is an arbitrary well-founded ordering, defined on pairs because the desired program f has a pair of inputs.

We can now apply GA-resolution between the goal

	$i-j = y_1 \cdot j + z$ and $0 \leq z$ and $z < j$	y_1+1	z

and the induction hypothesis; the unifying substitution θ is

$$[u_1 \leftarrow i-j;\ u_2 \leftarrow j;\ y_1 \leftarrow div(i-j, j);\ z \leftarrow rem(i-j, j)].$$

The new goal is

	$\begin{aligned}&\textit{true and}\\&\textit{not } (\textit{if } (i-j, j) <_w (i, j)\\&\qquad\textit{then if } 0 \leq i-j \textit{ and } 0 < j\\&\qquad\qquad\textit{then false})\end{aligned}$	$div(i-j, j)+1$	$rem(i-j, j)$

which reduces to

	$\begin{aligned}&(i-j, j) <_w (i, j) \textit{ and}\\&0 \leq i - j \textit{ and } 0 < j\end{aligned}$	$div(i-j, j)+1$	$rem(i-j, j)$

Note that the recursive calls $div(i-j, j)$ and $rem(i-j, j)$ have been introduced into the output entry.

The particular well-founded ordering $<_w$ to be employed in the proof has not yet been determined. It can be chosen to be the $<$ ordering on the first component of the pairs, by application of the transformation rule

$$(u_1, u_2) <_{N1} (v_1, v_2) \Rightarrow \textit{true} \quad \textit{if } u_1 < v_1 \textit{ and } 0 \leq u_1 \textit{ and } 0 \leq v_1.$$

A new goal

	$\begin{aligned}&i-j < i \textit{ and } 0 \leq i-j \textit{ and } 0 \leq i\\&\textit{and true}\\&\textit{and } 0 \leq i-j \textit{ and } 0 < j\end{aligned}$	$div(i-j, j)+1$	$rem(i-j, j)$

is produced; this goal ultimately reduces to

	$j \leq i$	$div(i-j, j)+1$	$rem(i-j, j)$

In other words, in the case that $j \leq i$, the outputs $div(i-j, j)+1$ and $rem(i-j, j)$ satisfy the desired program's specification. In the next section, we give the full derivation of these programs.

In our presentation of the induction rule, several limitations were imposed for simplicity but are not actually essential:

(1) In the example we considered, the only skolem functions in the initial

sequent are the constants corresponding to the program's inputs, and the only variables are those corresponding to the program's outputs; the sequent was of form

assertions	goals	outputs $f(a)$
$P(a)$		
	$R(a, z)$	z

In forming the induction hypothesis, the skolem constant a is replaced by a variable u and the variable z is replaced by the term $f(u)$; the induction hypothesis was of form

if $u <_u a$ *then if* $P(u)$ *then* $R(u, f(u))$		

However, if there are other skolem functions in the initial sequent, they too must be replaced by variables in the induction hypothesis; if there are other variables in the initial sequent, they must be replaced by new skolem functions. For example, suppose the initial sequent is of form

$$f(a) \Leftarrow find\ z\ such\ that$$

$$for\ all\ x_1,$$

$$for\ some\ x_2,$$

$$R(a, z, x_1, x_2)$$

$$where\ P(a).$$

Then the initial sequent is of form

assertions	goals	outputs $f(a)$
$P(a)$		
	$R(a, z, g_1(z), x_2)$	z

where $g_1(z)$ is the skolem function corresponding to x_1. The induction hypothesis is then of form

if $u <_w a$ *then if* $P(u)$ *then* $R(u, f(u), v, g_2(u, v))$		

Here, the skolem function $g_1(z)$ has been replaced by the variable v, and the variable x_2 has been replaced by a new skolem function $g_2(u, v)$.

(2) One limitation to the recurrence strategy was that the induction hypothesis was introduced only when an entire goal is an instance of the initial goal. In fact, the strategy can be extended so that the hypothesis is introduced when some subsentence of a goal is an instance of some subsentence of the initial goal, because the resolution rule can then be applied between the goal and the induction hypothesis. This extension is straightforward.

(3) A final observation: The induction hypothesis was always formed directly from the initial sequent; thus, the theorem itself was proved by induction. In later sections we extend the rule so that induction can be applied to lemmas that are stronger or more general than the theorem itself. This extension also accounts for the formation of auxiliary procedures in the program being constructed.

Some early efforts toward incorporating mathematical induction in a resolution framework were made by Darlington [4]. His system treated the induction principle as a second-order axiom schema rather than as a deduction rule; it had a limited ability to perform second-order unifications.

A COMPLETE EXAMPLE: FINDING THE QUOTIENT OF TWO INTEGERS

In this section, we present a complete example that exploits most of the features of the deductive synthesis approach. Our task is to construct programs $div(i, j)$ and $rem(i, j)$ for finding the integer quotient of dividing a nonnegative integer i by a positive integer j. Portions of this synthesis have been used to illustrate the induction principle in the previous section.

Our specification is expressed as

$$(div(i, j), rem(i, j)) \Leftarrow \quad find \ (y, z) \ such \ that$$
$$i = y \cdot j + z \ and \ 0 \le z \ and \ z < j$$
$$where \ 0 \le i \ and \ 0 < j.$$

(For simplicity, we again omit type conditions, such as $integer(i)$, from this discussion.) Our initial sequent is therefore

assertions	goals	outputs div(i, j)	rem(i, j)
1. $0 \le i$ and $0 < j$			
	2. $i = y \cdot j + z$ and $0 \le z$ and $z < j$	y	z

(Note that we are enumerating the assertions and goals.)

In presenting the derivation we sometimes apply simple logical and algebraic transformation rules without mentioning them explicitly. We assume that our background knowledge includes the two assertions

3. $u = u$			
4. $u \le v$ or $v < u$			

Applying the *andsplit rule* to assertion 1 yields the new assertions

5. $0 < i$			
6. $0 < j$			

Assume we have the following transformation rules that define integer multiplication:

$$0 \cdot v \Rightarrow 0$$

$$(u + 1) \cdot v \Rightarrow u \cdot v + v.$$

Applying the first of these rules to the subexpression $y \cdot j$ in goal 2 yields

	7. $i = 0 + z$ *and* $0 \le z$ *and* $z < j$	0	z

The unifying substitution in deriving goal 7 is

$$\theta = [\, y \leftarrow 0; \; v \leftarrow j\,];$$

applying this substitution to the output entry y produced the new output 0.
Applying the numerical transformation rule

$$0 + v \Rightarrow v$$

yields

	8. $i = z$ *and* $0 \le z$ *and* $z < j$	0	z

The GA-resolution rule can now be applied between goal 8 and the equality assertion 3, $u = u$. The unifying substitution is

$$\theta = [\, u \leftarrow i; \; z \leftarrow i\,]$$

and the eliminated subexpression is $i = i$; we obtain

	9. $0 \le i$ *and* $i < j$	0	i

By applying GA-resolution again, against assertion 5, $0 \le i$, we obtain

	10. $i < j$	0	i

In other words, we have found that in the case that $i < j$, the output 0 will satisfy the specification for the quotient program and the output i will satisfy the specification for the remainder program.

Let us return our attention to the initial goal 2,

$$i = y \cdot j + z \; and \; 0 \le z \; and \; z < j.$$

Recall that we have a second transformation rule

$$(u + 1) \cdot v \Rightarrow u \cdot v + v$$

for the multiplication function. Applying this rule to goal 2 yields

	11. $i = y_1 \cdot j + j + z$ *and* $0 \le z$ *and* $z < j$	$y_1 + 1$	z

where y_1 is a new variable. Here, the unifying substitution is

$$\theta = [\, y \leftarrow y_1 + 1; \; u \leftarrow y_1; \; v \leftarrow j\,];$$

applying this substitution to the output entry y produced the new output $y_1 + 1$ in the *div* program.

The transformation rule

$$u = v + w \Rightarrow u - v = w$$

applied to goal 11 yields

	12. $i-j = y_1 \cdot j + z$ $and\ 0 \leq z\ and\ z < j$	$y_1 + 1$	z

Goal 12 is a precise instance of the initial goal 2,

$$i = y \cdot j + z\ and\ 0 \leq z\ and\ z < j,$$

obtained by replacing the input i by $i-j$. (Again, the replacement of the dummy variable y by y_1 is not significant.) Therefore, the following induction hypothesis is formed:

13. $if\ (u_1, u_2) <_w (i, j)$ $then\ if\ 0 \leq u_1\ and\ 0 < u_2$ $then\ u_1 = div(u_1, u_2) \cdot u_2 + rem(u_1, u_2)\ and$ $0 \leq rem(u_1, u_2)\ and\ rem(u_1, u_2) < u_2$			

Here, $<_w$ is an arbitrary well-founded ordering.

By applying GA-resolution between goal 12 and the induction hypothesis, we obtain the goal

	14. $true\ and$ $not\ (if\ (i-j, j) <_w (i, j)$ $then\ if\ 0 \leq i-j\ and\ 0 < j$ $then\ false)$	$div(i-j, j) + 1$	$rem(i-j, j)$

Here, the unifying substitution is

$$\theta = [u_1 \leftarrow i-j;\ u_2 \leftarrow j;\ y_1 \leftarrow div(i-j, j);\ z \leftarrow rem(i-j, j)]$$

and the eliminated subexpression is

$$i-j = div(i-j, j) \cdot j + rem(i-j, j)\ and\ 0 \leq rem(i-j, j)\ and\ rem(i-j, j) < j.$$

Note that the substitution to the variable y_1 has caused the output entry $y_1 + 1$ to be changed to $div(i-j, j) + 1$ and the output entry z to be replaced by $rem(i-j, j)$. The use of the induction hypothesis has introduced the recursive calls $div(i-j, j)$ and $rem(i-j, j)$ into the output.

Goal 14 reduces to

	15. $(i-j, j) <_w (i, j)$ $and\ 0 \leq i-j\ and\ 0 < j$	$div(i-j, j) + 1$	$rem(i-j, j)$

The particular ordering $<_w$ has not yet been determined; however, it is chosen to be the $<$ ordering on the first component of the pairs, by application of the transformation rule

$$(u_1, u_2) <_{N_1} (v_1, v_2) \Rightarrow true \quad if\ u_1 < v_1\ and\ 0 \leq u_1\ and\ 0 \leq v_1.$$

A new goal is produced:

	16. $i-j < i\ and\ 0 \leq i-j\ and\ 0 \leq i$ $and\ 0 \leq i-j\ and\ 0 < j$	$div(i-j, j) + 1$	$rem(i-j, j)$

Note that the conditions of the transformation rule caused new conjuncts to be added to the goal.

By application of algebraic and logical transformation rules, and GA-resolution with the assertion 5, $0 \le i$, and assertion 6, $0 < j$, goal 16 is reduced to

	17. $j \le i$	$div(i-j, j) + 1$	$rem(i-j, j)$

In other words, we have learned that in the case that $j \le i$, the outputs $div(i-j, j) + 1$ and $rem(i-j, j)$ satisfy the specification of the div program. On the other hand, in deriving goal 10 we learned that in the case that $i < j$, 0 and i are satisfactory outputs. Assuming we have the assertion 4

$$u \le v \ or \ v < u,$$

we can obtain the goal

	18. $not(i < j)$	$div(i-j, j) + 1$	$rem(i-j, j)$

by GA-resolution.

The final goal

	19. $true$	$if\ i < j$ $then\ 0$ $else\ div(i-j, j) + 1$	$if\ i < j$ $then\ i$ $else\ rem(i-j, j)$

can then be obtained by GG-resolution between goals 10 and 18. The conditional expressions have been formed because both goals have a corresponding output entry. Because we have developed the goal $true$ and a corresponding primitive output entry, the derivation is complete. The final programs

$$div(i, j) \Leftarrow if\ i < j$$
$$then\ 0$$
$$else\ div(i-j, j) + 1$$

and

$$rem(i, j) \Leftarrow if\ i < j$$
$$then\ i$$
$$else\ rem(i-j, j)$$

are obtained directly from the final output entries.

THE FORMATION OF AUXILIARY PROCEDURES

We have remarked that mathematical induction need not be restricted to apply only to the initial assertion and goal but may legitimately be applied to any subset of the assertions and goals in the sequent. In fact, when induction is applied in this more general setting, *auxiliary procedures* may be introduced into the program being constructed. For example, in constructing a program *sort* to order a list, we might introduce an auxiliary procedure *merge* to insert a number in its place in an ordered list of numbers. In this section we develop the extended form of the induction principle that accounts for the formation of auxiliary procedures. We begin with a description of the recurrence strategy that applies to this extended induction.

Assume that we are in the process of constructing a program $f(a)$ whose specification is of form

$$f(a) \Longleftarrow find \; z \; such \; that \; R(a, z)$$

$$where \; P(a).$$

Then our initial sequent is of form

assertions	goals	outputs $f(a)$
$P(a)$		
	$R(a, z)$	z

Let goal A be any goal obtained during the derivation of $f(a)$, and assume that goal A is of form

A:		$R'(a, z')$	$t'(z')$

Suppose that by applying deduction rules successively to goal A and to the assertions $P'_1(a)$, $P'_2(a)$, ..., $P'_k(a)$ of the sequent, we obtain a goal B of form

B:		$R'(s, z'')$	$t''(z'')$

where s is an arbitrary term. (For simplicity, we assume that no goals are required other than those derived from goal A, and that none of the k required assertions have associated output entries.)

In summation, we have developed a new goal (goal B) that is a precise instance of the earlier (goal A), obtained by replacing the input a by the term s. This recurrence motivates us to define an auxiliary procedure $fnew(a)$ whose output condition is goal A; we then hope to achieve goal B by a recursive call to the new procedure.

Let us be more precise. The specification for $fnew(a')$ is

$$fnew(a') \Longleftarrow find \; z' \; such \; that \; R'(a', z')$$
$$where \; P'(a').$$

Here, the input condition $P'(a')$ is $P'_1(a')$ and $P'_2(a')$ and $\cdots$ and $P'_k(a')$. If we succeed in constructing a program that meets this specification, we can employ it as an auxiliary procedure of the main program $f(a)$.

Consequently, at this point we add a new output column for $fnew(a')$ to the sequent, and we introduce the new rows

	assertions	goals	outputs $f(a)$	$fnew(a')$
	$P'(a')$			
A':		$R'(a', z')$	$t'(fnew(a))$	z'

Note that in these rows we have replaced the input constant a by a new constant a'. This step is logically necessary; adding the induction hypothesis without renaming the constant can lead to false results. The second row (goal A') indicates that if we succeed in constructing $fnew(a')$ to satisfy the above specification, then $f(a)$ may be computed by a call $t'(fnew(a))$ to the new procedure.

By introducing the procedure $fnew(a')$ we are able to call it recursively. In other words, we are now able to form an induction hypothesis from the assertion $P'(a')$ and the goal $R'(a', z')$, namely,

if $u' \prec_{u'} a'$ *then if* $P'(u')$ *then* $R'(u', fnew(u'))$			

If this assertion is employed during a proof, a recursive call to *fnew* can be introduced into the output column for $fnew(a')$. The well-founded ordering $\prec_{u'}$ corresponding to $fnew(a')$ may be distinct from the ordering $\prec_u$ corresponding to $f(a)$.

Note that we do not begin a new sequent for the derivation of the auxiliary procedure *fnew*; the synthesis of the main program $f(a)$ and the auxiliary procedure $fnew(a')$ are both conducted by applying derivation rules to the same sequent. Those rows with output entries for $fnew(a')$ always have the expression $t'(fnew(a))$ as the output entry for $f(a)$.

Suppose we ultimately succeed in obtaining the goal *true* with primitive output entries t and t':

assertions	goals	outputs $f(a)$	$fnew(a')$
	true	t	t'

Then the final program is

$$f(a) \Longleftarrow t$$

and

$$fnew(a') \Longleftarrow t'.$$

Note that although the portion of the derivation leading from goal A to goal B serves to motivate the formation of the auxiliary procedure, it may actually have no part in the derivation of the final program; its role has been taken over by the derivation of goal B′ from goal A′.

It is possible to introduce many auxiliary procedures for the same main program, each adding a new output column to the sequent. An auxiliary procedure may have its own set of auxiliary procedures. An auxiliary procedure may call the main program or any of the other procedures; in other words, the system of procedures can be "mutually recursive."

If we fail to complete the derivation of an auxiliary procedure $fnew(a')$, we may still succeed in finding some other way of completing the derivation of $f(a)$ without using *fnew*, by applying deduction rules to rows that have no output entry for $fnew(a')$.

To illustrate the formation of auxiliary procedures, we consider the synthesis of a program $cart(s, t)$ to compute the cartesian product of two (finite) sets s and t, i.e., the set of all pairs whose first component belongs to s and whose second component belongs to t. The specification for this program is

$$cart(s, t) \Leftarrow find\ z\ such\ that$$

$$z = \{(a, b): a \in s\ and\ b \in t\}.$$

The initial sequent is then

	assertions	goals	outputs $cart(s, t)$
		$z = \{(a, b): a \in s\ and\ b \in t\}$	z

(Note that this specification has no input condition, except for the type condition $isset(s)$ and $isset(t)$, which we omit for simplicity.)

We denote the empty set by $\{\}$. If u is a nonempty set, then $choice(u)$ denotes some particular element of u, and $rest(u)$ denotes the set of all other elements. We assume that the transformation rules concerning finite sets include:

$$u \in v \Rightarrow false \quad if\ v = \{\}$$

$$u \in v \Rightarrow u = choice(v)\ or\ u \in rest(v) \quad if\ v \neq \{\}$$

$$\{u: false\} \Rightarrow \{\}$$

$$\{u: P\ or\ Q\} \Rightarrow \{u: P\} \cup \{u: Q\}$$

$$rest(u) <_{s_1} u \Rightarrow true \quad if\ u \neq \{\}$$

$$\{u: u = v\} \Rightarrow \{v\} \quad (where\ u\ does\ not\ occur\ in\ v)$$

We will not reproduce the complete derivation, but only those portions that concern the formation of auxiliary procedures.

By application of deduction rules to the initial sequent, we obtain the goal

A:

	$z' = \{(a, b): a = choice(s)\ and\ b \in t\}$	if $s = \{\}$ then $\{\}$ else $z' \cup cart(rest(s), t)$

By applying several deductive rules to this goal alone, we obtain the new goal

B:

	$z'' = \{(a, b): a = choice(s)\ and\ b \in rest(t)\}$	if $t = \{\}$
		 then $\{\}$
		 else if $s = \{\}$
		     then $\{\}$
		     else $(choice(s), choice(t)) \cup$
		         $cart(rest(s), t) \cup z''$

This goal is a precise instance of the earlier goal; consequently, our recurrence strategy motivates us to form an auxiliary procedure $cartnew(s, t)$ having the earlier goal as its output specification, i.e.,

$$cartnew(s', t') \Leftarrow \{(a, b): a = choice(s')\ and\ b \in t'\}.$$

We therefore introduce an additional output column corresponding to the new procedure, and we add to the sequent the row

	assertions	goals	outputs $cart(s, t)$	$cartnew(s', t')$
A':		$z' = \{(a, b): a = choice(s')$ $and\ b \in t')$	$if\ s = \{\}$ $then\ \{\}$ $else\ cartnew(s, t) \cup$ $cart(rest(s), t)$	z'

The induction hypothesis corresponding to this goal is then

	$if\ (u', v') <_{w'} (s', t')$ $then\ cartnew(u', v') = \{(a, b): a = choice(u')\ and\ b \in v'\}$			

By applying deduction rules to the new goal, we obtain the goal

B':	$z'' = \{(a, b): a = choice(s')$ $and\ b \in rest(t')\}$	$if\ s = \{\}$ $then\ \{\}$ $else\ cartnew(s, t) \cup$ $cart(rest(s), t)$	$if\ t' = \{\}$ $then\ \{\}$ $else\ (choice(s'), choice(t'))$ $\cup\ z''$

Applying GA-resolution between this goal and the induction hypothesis, and simplying by transformation rules, we obtain the goal

	$(s', rest(t')) <_{w'} (s', t')$	$if\ s = \{\}$ $then\ \{\}$ $else\ cartnew(s, t) \cup$ $cart(rest(s), t)$	$if\ t' = \{\}$ $then\ \{\}$ $else\ (choice(s'), choice(t'))$ $\cup\ cartnew(s', rest(t'))$

Note that a recursive call has now appeared in the output entry for the auxiliary procedure *cartnew*. By further transformation, the well-founded ordering $<_{w'}$ is chosen to be $<_{s_2}$, defined by

$$(u_1, u_2) <_{s_2} (v_1, v_2) \quad \text{if } u_2 \text{ is a proper subset of } v_2.$$

The final program obtained from this derivation is

$cart(s, t) \Leftarrow if\ s = \{\}$
$\qquad\qquad then\ \{\}$
$\qquad\qquad else\ cartnew(s, t) \cup$
$\qquad\qquad\qquad cart(rest(s), t)$

$cartnew(s', t') \Leftarrow if\ t' = \{\}$
$\qquad\qquad\qquad then\ \{\}$
$\qquad\qquad\qquad else\ (choice(s'), choice(t')) \cup$
$\qquad\qquad\qquad\qquad cartnew(s', rest(t')).$

There are a few extensions to the method for forming auxiliary procedures that we will not describe in detail:

(1) We have been led to introduce an auxiliary procedure when an entire goal was found to be an instance of a previous goal. As we remarked in the section on

mathematical induction, we can actually introduce an auxiliary procedure when some subsentence of a goal is an instance of some subsentence of a previous goal.

(2) Special treatment is required if the assertions and goal incorporated into the induction hypothesis contain more than one occurrence of the same skolem function. We do not describe the formation of such an induction hypothesis here.

(3) To complete the derivation of the auxiliary procedure, we may be forced to weaken or strengthen its specification by adding input or output conditions incrementally. We do not present here the extension of the procedure-formation principle that permits this flexibility.

GENERALIZATION

In performing a proof by mathematical induction, it is often necessary to generalize the theorem to be proved, so as to have the advantage of a stronger induction hypothesis in proving the inductive step. Paradoxically, the more general statement may be easier to prove. If the proof is part of the synthesis of a program, generalizing the theorem can result in the construction of a more general procedure, so that recursive calls to the procedure will be able to achieve the desired subgoals. The recurrence strategy we have outlined earlier provides a strong clue as to how the theorem is to be generalized.

We have formed an auxiliary procedure when a goal is found to be a precise instance of a previous goal. However, in some derivations it is found that the new goal is not a precise instance of the earlier goal, but that both are instances of some more general expression. This situation suggests introducing a new auxiliary procedure whose output condition is the more general expression, in the hope that both goals may be achieved by calls to this procedure.

Let us be more precise. Suppose we are in the midst of a derivation and that we have already developed a goal A, of form

	assertions	goals	outputs $f(a)$
A:		$R'(a, s_1, z_1)$	$t_1(z_1)$

where s_1 is an arbitrary term. Assume that by applying deduction rules only to goal A and some assertions $P'_1(a), P'_2(a), \ldots, P'_k(a)$, we obtain a goal B, of form

B:		$R'(a, s_2, z_2)$	$t_2(z_2)$

where s_2 is a term that does not match s_1. Thus, the new goal (goal B) is not a precise instance of the earlier goal (goal A). Hence, if an induction hypothesis is formed for goal A itself, the resolution rule cannot be applied between goal B and the induction hypothesis.

However, both goals A and B may be regarded as instances of the more general expression $R'(a, b', z')$, where b' is a new constant: goal A is obtained by replacing b' by s_1, and goal B is obtained by replacing b' by s_2. This suggests that we attempt to establish a more general expression (goal A') hoping that the proof of goal A' will contain a subgoal (goal B') corresponding to the original goal B, so that the induction hypothesis resulting from goal A' will be strong enough to establish goal B'.

The new goal A′ constitutes the output condition for an auxiliary procedure, whose specification is

$$fnew(a', b') \Leftarrow find \ z' \ such \ that \ R'(a', b', z')$$
$$where \ P'(a').$$

(Here, $P'(a')$ is the conjunction $P'_1(a') \ and \ P'_2(a') \cdots and \ P'_k(a')$.) Consequently, we introduce a new output column to the sequent, and we add the new assertion

assertions	goals	outputs $f(a)$ $fnew(a', b')$	
$P'(a')$			

and the new goal

A′:		$R'(a', b', z')t_1(fnew(a, s_1))$	z'

(Note again that it is logically necessary to replace the input constant a by a new constant a'.) Corresponding to this assertion and goal we have the induction hypothesis

$if (u', v') \prec_{w'} (a', b')$ $then \ if \ P'(u')$ $\quad then \ R(u', v', fnew(u', v'))$			

There is no guarantee that we will be able to develop from goal A′ a goal B′ such that the resolution rule can be applied between goal B′ and the induction hypothesis. Nor can we be sure that we will conclude the derivation of *fnew* successfully. If we fail to derive *fnew*, we may still complete the derivation of *f* in some other way.

We illustrate the generalization process with an example that also serves to show how program-synthesis techniques can be applied as well to *program transformation* (see, e.g., Burstall and Darlington [3]). In this application we are given a clear and concise program, which may be inefficient; we attempt to derive an equivalent program that is more efficient, even though it may be neither clear nor concise.

We are given the program

$$reverse(l) \Leftarrow if \ l = [\,]$$
$$then \ [\,]$$
$$else \ reverse(tail(l)) <> [head(l)]$$

for reversing the order of the elements of a list l. Here, $head(l)$ is the first element of a nonempty list l and $tail(l)$ is the list of all but the first element of l. Recall that $u <> v$ is the result of appending two lists u and v, $[\,]$ denotes the empty list, and $[w]$ is the list whose sole element is w. As usual, we omit type conditions, such as $islist(l)$, from our discussion.

This *reverse* program is inefficient, for it requires many recursive calls to *reverse* and to the append procedure $<>$. We attempt to transform it to a more efficient version. The specification for the transformed program $rev(l)$ is

$$rev(l) \Leftarrow find \ z_1 \ such \ that \ z_1 = reverse(l).$$

The initial sequent is thus

	assertions	goals	outputs $rev(l)$
A:		$z_1 = reverse(l)$	z_1

The given *reverse* program is not considered to be a primitive. However, we admit the transformation rules

$$reverse(u) \Rightarrow [] \quad if\ u = []$$

and

$$reverse(u) \Rightarrow reverse(tail(u)) <> [head(u)] \quad if\ u \neq [];$$

obtained directly from the *reverse* program.

We assume that the transformation rules we have concerning lists include:

$$head(u \cdot v) \Rightarrow u$$
$$tail(u \cdot v) \Rightarrow v$$
$$[u] \Rightarrow u \cdot []$$
$$(u \cdot v = []) \Rightarrow false$$

(where $u \cdot v$ is the result of inserting u before the first element of the list v; it is the Lisp *cons* function)

$$u <> v \Rightarrow v \quad if\ u = []$$
$$u <> v \Rightarrow u \quad if\ v = []$$
$$u <> v \Rightarrow head(u) \cdot (tail(u) <> v) \quad if\ u \neq []$$
$$(u <> v) <> w \Rightarrow u <> (v <> w)$$
$$tail(l) <_L l \Rightarrow true \quad if\ l \neq []$$

Applying transformation rules to the initial goal, we obtain a subgoal

		goals	
B:		$z_2 = reverse(tail(l)) <> [head(l)]$	*if* $l = []$ *then* [] *else* z_2

This goal is not a precise instance of goal A. However, both goals may be regarded as instances of the more general expression

$$z' = reverse(l') <> m'.$$

Goal A is obtained by replacing l' by $tail(l)$ and m' by [] (because $u <> [] = u$), and goal B is obtained by replacing l' by $tail(l)$ and m' by $[head(l)]$. This suggests that we attempt to construct an auxiliary procedure having the more general expression as an output condition; the specification for this procedure is

$$revnew(l', m') \Leftarrow find\ z'\ such\ that\ z' = reverse(l') <> m'.$$

Consequently, we introduce a new output column to the sequent, and we add the new goal

assertions	goals	outputs $rev(l)$	$revnew(l', m')$
	$z' = reverse(l') <> m'$	$revnew(l, [])$	z'

A':

The induction hypothesis corresponding to this goal is then

if $(u', v') <_w (l', m')$ then $revnew(u', v') = reverse(u') <> v'$			

By applying deduction rules to the goal A', we eventually obtain

assertions	goals	outputs $rev(l)$	$revnew(l', m')$
	$z'' = reverse(tail(l')) <> (head(l') \cdot m')$	$revnew(l, [])$	if $l' = []$ then m' else z''

B':

We succeed in applying the resolution rule between this goal and the induction hypothesis.

Ultimately, we obtain the final program

$$rev(l) \Leftarrow revnew(l, [])$$

$$revnew(l', m') \Leftarrow \quad if \ l' = []$$

$$then \ m'$$

$$else \ revnew(tail(l'), head(l') \cdot m').$$

This program turns out to be more efficient than the given program $reverse(l)$; it is essentially iterative and employs the insertion operation $\cdot$ instead of the expensive append operation $<>$. In general, however, we have no guarantee that the program produced by this approach will be more efficient than the given program. A possible remedy is to include efficiency criteria explicitly in the specification of the program. For example, we might require that the rev program should run in time linear to the length of l. In proving the theorem obtained from such a specification, we would be ensuring that the program constructed would operate within the specified limitations. Of course, the difficulty of the theorem-proving task would be compounded by such measures.

Some generalizations are quite straightforward to discover. For example, if goal A is of form $R'(a, 0, z_1)$ and goal B is of form $R'(a, 1, z_2)$, this immediately suggests that we employ the general expression $R'(a, b', z')$. Other generalizations may require more ingenuity to discover. In the *reverse* example, for instance, it is not immediately obvious that $z_1 = reverse(l)$ and $z_2 = reverse(tail(l)) <> [head(l)]$ should both be regarded as instances of the more general expression $z' = reverse(l') <> m'$.

Our strategy for determining how to generalize an induction hypothesis is distinct from that of Boyer and Moore [2]. Their system predicts how to generalize a goal before developing any subgoals in our approach, recurrences between a goal and its subgoals suggest how the goal is to be generalized.

COMPARISON WITH THE PURE TRANSFORMATION-RULE APPROACH

Recent work (e.g., Manna and Waldinger [7], as well as Burstall and Darlington [3]) does not regard program synthesis as a theorem-proving task, but instead adopts the basic approach of applying transformation rules directly to the given specification. What advantage do we obtain by shifting to a theorem-proving approach, when that approach has already been attempted and abandoned?

The structure we outline here is considerably simpler than, say, our implemented synthesis system DEDALUS, but retains the full power of that system. DEDALUS required special mechanisms for the formation of conditional expressions and recursive calls, and for the satisfaction of "conjunctive goals" (of form "*find z such that $R_1(z)$ and $R_2(z)$*"). It could not treat specifications involving quantifiers. It relied on a backtracking control structure, which required it to explore one goal completely before attention could be passed to another goal. In the present system, these constructs are handled as a natural outgrowth of the theorem-proving process. In addition, the foundation is laid for the application of more sophisticated search strategies, in which attention is passed back and forth freely between several competing assertions and goals. The present framework can take advantage of parallel hardware.

Furthermore, the task of program synthesis always involves a theorem-proving component, which is needed, say, to prove the termination of the program being constructed, or to establish the input condition for recursive calls. (The Burstall–Darlington system is interactive and relies on the user to prove these theorems; DEDALUS incorporates a separate theorem prover.) If we retain the artificial distinction between program synthesis and theorem proving, each component must duplicate the efforts of the other. The mechanism for forming recursive calls will be separate from the induction principle; the facility for handling specifications of the form

$$\text{find } z \text{ such that } R_1(z) \text{ and } R_2(z)$$

will be distinct from the facility for proving theorems of form

$$\text{for some } z, R_1(z) \text{ and } R_2(z);$$

and so forth. By adopting a theorem-proving approach, we can unify these two components.

Theorem proving was abandoned as an approach to program synthesis when the development of sufficiently powerful automatic theorem provers appeared to flounder. However, theorem provers have been exhibiting a steady increase in their effectiveness, and program synthesis is one of the most natural applications of these systems.

ACKNOWLEDGMENTS

We would like to thank John Darlington, Chris Goad, Jim King, Neil Murray, Nils Nilsson, and Earl Sacerdoti for valuable discussions and comments. Thanks are due also to Patte Wood for aid in the preparation of this manuscript.

REFERENCES

1. BLEDSOE, W.W. Non-resolution theorem proving. *Artif. Intell. J. 9*, (1977), 1–35.
2. BOYER, R.S., AND MOORE, JS. Proving theorems about LISP functions *J. ACM 22*, 1 (Jan. 1975), 129–144.
3. BURSTALL, R.M., AND DARLINGTON, J. A transformation system for developing recursive programs. *J. ACM 24*, 1 (Jan. 1977), 44–67.
4. DARLINGTON, J.L. Automatic theorem proving with equality substitutions and mathematical induction. *Machine Intell. 3* (Edinburgh, Scotland) (1968), 113–127.
5. GREEN, C.C. Application of theorem proving to problem solving. In *Proc. Int. Joint Conf. on Artificial Intelligence* (Washington D.C., May 1969), 219–239.
6. HEWITT, C. Description and theoretical analysis (using schemata) of PLANNER: A language for proving theorems and manipulating models in a robot. Ph.D. Diss., M.I.T., Cambridge, Mass., 1971.
7. MANNA, Z., AND WALDINGER, R. Synthesis: dreams ⇒ programs. *IEEE Trans. Softw. Eng. SE-5*, 4 (July 1979), 294–328.
8. MURRAY, N. A proof procedure for non-clausal first-order logic. Tech. Rep. Syracuse Univ., Syracuse, N.Y., 1978.
9. NELSON, G., AND OPPEN, D.C. A simplifier based on efficient decision algorithms. In *Proc. 5th ACM Symp. Principles of Programming Languages* (Tucson, Ariz., Jan. 1978), pp. 141–150.
10. NILSSON, N.J. A production system for automatic deduction. *Machine Intell. 9*, Ellis Horwood, Chichester, England, 1979.
11. NILSSON, N.J. *Problem-solving methods in artificial intelligence.* McGraw-Hill, New York, 1971, pp. 165–168.
12. ROBINSON, J.A. A machine-oriented logic based on the resolution principle. *J.ACM 12*, 1 (Jan. 1965), 23–41.
13. WALDINGER, R.J., AND LEE, R.C.T. PROW: A step toward automatic program writing. In *Proc. Int. Joint Conf. on Artificial Intelligence* (Washington D.C., May 1969), pp. 241–252.
14. WILKINS, D. QUEST—A non-clausal theorem proving system. M.Sc. Th., Univ. of Essex, England, 1973.

Top-Down Synthesis of Divide-and-Conquer Algorithms

Douglas R. Smith
*Kestrel Institute, 1801 Page Mill Road,
Palo Alto, CA 94304, U.S.A.*

ABSTRACT

A top-down method is presented for the derivation of algorithms from a formal specification of a problem. This method has been implemented in a system called CYPRESS. The synthesis process involves the top-down decomposition of the initial specification into a hierarchy of specifications for subproblems. Synthesizing programs for each of these subproblems results in the composition of a hierarchically structured program. The initial specification is allowed to be partial in that some or all of the input conditions may be missing. CYPRESS completes the specification and produces a totally correct applicative program. Much of CYPRESS' knowledge comes in the form of 'design strategies' for various classes of algorithms. The structure of a class of divide-and-conquer algorithms is explored and provides the basis for several design strategies. Detailed derivations of mergesort and quicksort algorithms are presented.

1. Introduction

Program synthesis is the systematic derivation of a computer program from a specification of the problem it is intended to solve. Our approach to program synthesis is a form of top-down design, called *problem reduction*, that may be described as a process with two phases—the top-down decomposition of problem specifications and the bottom-up composition of programs. In practice these phases are interleaved but it helps to understand them separately. Given a specification, the first phase involves selecting and adapting a program scheme, thereby deciding on an overall structure for the target program. A procedure associated with each scheme, called a *design strategy*, is used to derive subproblem specifications for the scheme operators. Next we apply problem reduction to each of the subproblem specifications, and so on. This process of deciding program structure and deriving subproblem specifications terminates in primitive problem specifications that can be solved directly,

without reduction to subproblems. The result is a tree of specifications with the initial specification at the root and primitive problem specifications at the leaves. The children of a node represent the subproblem specifications derived as we create program structure. The second phase involves the bottom-up composition of programs. Initially each primitive problem specification is treated by a design strategy that directly produces a target language expression. Subsequently whenever programs have been obtained for all children of a node representing specification Π they are assembled into a program for Π by instantiating the associated scheme.

One of the principal difficulties in top-down design is knowing how to decompose a problem specification into subproblem specifications. At present general knowledge of this kind (see for example [23]) is not in a form suitable for automation. Rather than attempt to formalize this general knowledge we focus on special techniques for decomposing a problem. In particular, we explore the structure common to a class of algorithms and develop methods for decomposing a problem with respect to that structure. In this paper the structure of a class of divide-and-conquer algorithms is formalized and then used as the basis for several design strategies.

The principle underlying divide-and-conquer algorithms can be simply stated: if the problem posed by a given input is sufficiently simple we solve it directly, otherwise we decompose it into subproblems, solve the subproblems, then compose the resulting solutions. The process of decomposing the input problem and solving the subproblems gives rise to the term 'divide-and-conquer' although 'decompose, solve, and compose' would be more accurate. Typically, some of the subproblems are of the same type as the input problem thus divide-and-conquer algorithms are naturally expressed by recursive programs.

We chose to explore the synthesis of divide-and-conquer algorithms for several reasons:

(1) *Structural simplicity.* Divide-and-conquer is perhaps the simplest program-structuring technique which does not appear as an explicit control structure in current programming languages.

(2) *Computational efficiency.* Divide-and-conquer algorithms naturally suggest implementation on parallel machines due to the independence of subproblems. Even on sequential machines algorithms of asymptotically optimal complexity often arise from application of the divide-and-conquer principle to a problem. In addition, fast approximate algorithms for NP-hard problems frequently are based on the divide-and-conquer principle.

(3) *Ubiquity in programming practice.* Divide-and-conquer algorithms are common in programming, especially when processing structured data objects such as arrays, lists, and trees. Current textbooks on the design of algorithms standardly present divide-and-conquer as a fundamental programming technique [1].

Artificial Intelligence **27** (1985) 43–96

0004-3702/85/$3.00 © 1985, Elsevier Science Publishers B.V. (North-Holland)

In Section 2 we illustrate the synthesis method by deriving an algorithm for finding the minimum element in a list. Sections 3 and 4 introduce basic concepts of deduction and specification respectively. Section 5 contains several basic design strategies. Special knowledge about the structure and design of divide-and-conquer algorithms is presented in Sections 6 and 7. Detailed derivations of mergesort and quicksort algorithms also appear in Section 7. Discussion of related research, a semi-automatic implementation of the synthesis method called CYPRESS, and other topics appear in Section 8.

2. A Simple Example

An informal derivation of an algorithm for finding the minimum in a list of natural numbers is given in this section in order to develop some intuition about the problem-reduction method. A formal specification for this minimization problem is[1]

$$\text{MIN}: x = z \text{ such that } x \neq nil \Rightarrow z \in \text{Bag}: x \land z \leq \text{Bag}: x$$
$$\text{where } \text{MIN}: \text{LIST}(\mathbf{N}) \to \mathbf{N}.$$

Here the problem is named MIN and it is defined to be a mapping from lists of natural numbers (denoted $\text{LIST}(\mathbf{N})$) to natural numbers ($\mathbf{N}$). Naming the input variable x and the output variable z, the formula $x \neq nil$, called the *input condition*, expresses any properties which inputs are expected to satisfy. The formula $z \in \text{Bag}: x \land z \leq \text{Bag}: x$, called the *output condition*, expresses the conditions under which z is an acceptable output with respect to input x. Here $z \in \text{Bag}: x$ asserts that z is an element of the bag (multiset) of elements in x and $z \leq \text{Bag}: x$ asserts that z is less than or equal to each element in x.

Suppose that we decide to derive a divide-and-conquer algorithm for this problem by instantiating the following functional program scheme

$$F: x \equiv \textbf{if}$$
$$\qquad Primitive: x \to Directly\_Solve: x \quad \square$$
$$\qquad \neg\, Primitive: x \to Compose \circ (\text{Id} \times F) \circ Decompose: x$$
$$\textbf{fi}$$

yielding the Min algorithm in Fig. 1[2]. Here $G \circ H$, called the composition of G

and H, denotes the function resulting from applying G to the result of applying H to its argument. $G \times H$, called the product of G and H, is defined by $G \times H: \langle x, y \rangle = \langle G: x, H: y \rangle$ where $\langle x_1, \ldots, x_n \rangle$ is an n-tuple.

Min exemplifies the structure of divide-and-conquer algorithms. When $\text{Rest}: x = nil$ then the problem is solved directly, otherwise the input is decomposed via the operator FirstRest, recursively solved via the product $(\text{Id} \times \text{Min})$, and the results composed via Min2 (Min2 returns the minimum of its two inputs). So for example:

$$\text{Min}: (2,5,1,4) = \text{Min2} \circ (\text{Id} \times \text{Min}) \circ \text{FirstRest}: (2,5,1,4)$$
$$= \text{Min2} \circ (\text{Id} \times \text{Min}): \langle 2,(5,1,4) \rangle$$
$$= \text{Min2}: \langle 2,1 \rangle$$
$$= 1$$

where $\text{Min}: (5,1,4)$ evaluates to 1 in a similar manner.

Our strategy for synthesizing Min is based on choosing a simple operator for decomposing the input list. An obvious way to decompose an input list is into its first element and the rest of the list using the operator FirstRest. Instantiating this choice into the scheme we have

$$\text{Min}: x \equiv \textbf{if}$$
$$\qquad Primitive: x \to Directly\_Solve: x \quad \square$$
$$\qquad \neg\, Primitive: x \to Compose \circ (\text{Id} \times \text{Min}) \circ \text{FirstRest}: x.$$
$$\textbf{fi}$$

We can determine the control predicate *Primitive* as follows. In order to guarantee that this recursive program terminates, the decomposition operator FirstRest must pass to the recursive call to Min a value that satisfies Min's input condition. Thus we must have $\text{Rest}: x \neq nil$ in order to meaningfully execute the **else** branch of the program. Consequently, we let the control predicate be $\text{Rest}: x = nil$.

The challenging part of the synthesis is constructing an operator that can be instantiated for *Compose*. Observe that the composite function

$$Compose \circ (\text{Id} \times \text{Min}) \circ \text{FirstRest}: x_0 \qquad (2.1)$$

must satisfy the MIN specification. Introducing names for the intermediate

$$\text{Min}: x \equiv \textbf{if}$$
$$\qquad \text{Rest}: x = nil \to \text{First}: x \quad \square$$
$$\qquad \text{Rest}: x \neq nil \to \text{Min2} \circ (\text{Id} \times \text{Min}) \circ \text{FirstRest}: x$$
$$\textbf{fi}$$

FIG. 1. Algorithm for finding the minimum element in a list.

[1] In this paper f: x denotes the application of function f to x. As usual the colon is also used in defining the domain and range of a mapping. It should be clear from context which use is intended.

[2] In this paper we use the following notational conventions: specification names are fully capitalized and set in Roman, operators are indicated by capitalizing their first letter, and scheme operators are further indicated by italics. Also, we use the list processing operators First, Rest, Cons, FirstRest, Append, and Listsplit where First: (2,5,1,4) = 2; Rest: (2,5,1,4) = (5,1,4); FirstRest: (2,5,1,4) = (2,(5,1,4)); Append: (2,5)(1,4) = (2,5,1,4); Cons: (2,(5,1,4)) = (2,5,1,4); Listsplit: (2,5,1,4,3) = ((2,5), (1,4,3)). Id denotes the identity function on any data type.

input and output values, let

FirstRest: $x_0 = \langle x_1, x_2 \rangle$,
Id: $x_1 = z_1$,
Min: $x_2 = z_2$,
Compose: $\langle z_1, z_2 \rangle = z_0$.

A specification for *Compose* is derived below. We attempt to verify that (2.1) does satisfy MIN, but since *Compose* is unknown the attempt fails. That is, no particular relation is assumed to exist between the variables z_0, z_1, and z_2 (the input/output values of *Compose*) sc the structure of (2.1) is too weak to allow the verification to go through. Although the verification fails, the way in which it fails can provide output conditions for *Compose*. In order to obtain such output conditions we attempt to recue the goal of satisfying MIN to a relation over the variables z_0, z_1 and z_2. In particular, we attempt to show that the output condition of MIN

$$z_0 \in \text{Bag}: x_0 \wedge z_0 \leq \text{Bag}: x_c \qquad (2.2)$$

holds assuming

FirstRest: $x_0 = \langle x_1, x_2 \rangle$ (**i.e.** $x_1 = \text{First}: x_0 \wedge x_2 = \text{Rest}: x_0$),
Id: $x_1 = z_1$ (i.e. $x_1 = z_1$),
Min: $x_2 = z_2$ (i.e. $z_2 \in \text{Bag}: x_2 \wedge z_2 \leq \text{Bag}: x_2$).

We reason backwards from (2.2) to sufficient output conditions for *Compose* as follows.

$z_0 \in \text{Bag}: x_0$
if $z_0 = \text{First}: x_0 \vee z_0 \in \text{Rest}: x_0$ (since $x_0 \neq \text{nil}$),
if $z_0 = x_1 \vee z_0 \in x_2$ (since $x_1 = \text{First}: x_0$ and $x_2 = \text{Rest}: x_0$),
if $z_0 = z_1 \vee z_0 = z_2$ (since $x_1 = z_1$ and $z_2 \in \text{Bag}: x_2$).

I.e., if the expression $z_0 = z_1 \vee z_0 = z_2$ were to hold then we could show that $z_0 \in \text{Bag}: x_0$. Consider now the other conjunct in (2.2):

$z_0 \leq \text{Bag}: x_0$
if $z_0 \leq \text{First}: x_0 \wedge z_0 \leq \text{Bag} \circ \text{Rest}: x_0$ (since $x_0 \neq \text{nil}$),
if $z_0 \leq x_1 \wedge z_0 \leq \text{Bag}: x_2$ (since $x_1 = \text{First}: x_0$ and $x_2 = \text{Rest}: x_0$),
if $z_0 \leq z_1 \wedge z_0 \leq z_2$ (since $x_1 = z_1$ and $z_2 \leq \text{Bag}: x_2$).

I.e., if the expression $z_0 \leq z_1 \wedge z_0 \leq z_2$ were to hold then we could show that $z_0 \leq \text{Bag}: x_0$.

We take the two derived relations

$$z_0 = z_1 \vee z_0 = z_2 \quad \text{and} \quad z_0 \leq z_1 \wedge z_0 \leq z_2$$

as the output conditions of *Compose* exactly because establishing these relations enables us to verify the **else** branch of the scheme. Thus we create the specification

COMPOSE: $\langle z_1, z_2 \rangle = z_0$
such that $(z_0 = z_1 \vee z_0 = z_2) \wedge z_0 \leq z_1 \wedge z_0 \leq z_2$
where COMPOSE: $N \times N \to N$.

The derivation of a simple conditional program

Min2: $\langle x, y \rangle = $ **if** $x \leq y \to x$ □ $y \leq x \to y$ **fi**

satisfying COMPOSE is relatively straightforward. A derivation of Min2 may be found in [27] as part of a study of design strategies for conditional programs. Strategies for synthesizing certain classes of conditional programs are presented in later sections.
The Min algorithm now has the form

Min: $x \equiv$ **if**
    Rest: $x = \text{nil} \to Directly\_Solve: x$ □
    Rest: $x \neq \text{nil} \to \text{Min2} \circ (\text{Id} \times \text{Min}) \circ \text{FirstRest}: x$.
fi

The scheme operator *Directly_Solve* must satisfy the input and output conditions of MIN but it need only do so when the input also satisfies Rest: $x = \text{nil}$, so we set up the specification

DIRECTLY_SOLVE: $x = z$
such that Rest: $x = \text{nil} \wedge x \neq \text{nil}$
    $\to z \in \text{Bag}: x \wedge z \leq \text{Bag}: x$
where DIRECTLY_SOLVE: LIST(N) $\to$ N.

The operator First can be shown to satisfy this specification. To do so we first assume $z = \text{First}: x$, Rest: $x = \text{nil}$, and $x \neq \text{nil}$, then verify that $z \in \text{Bag}: x$ and $z \leq \text{Bag}: x$ hold. Informally, $z \in \text{Bag}: x$ holds since $z = \text{First}: x$ and certainly the first element of x is one of the elements in x. $z \leq \text{Bag}: x$ holds since x has only one element, in particular First: x.
After instantiating the operator First into the scheme we finally obtain the algorithm shown in Fig. 1. Termination of Min on all non-nil inputs follows from the fact that FirstRest decomposes lists into strictly smaller lists. Note also

that we have in effect produced a proof of correctness since in the construction of Min we used correctness considerations as constraints on the way that specifications for subalgorithms were created.

To recapitulate, we started with a formal specification for a problem (MIN) and hypothesized that a divide-and-conquer algorithm could be constructed for it. We began the process of instantiating a divide-and-conquer program scheme by choosing a simple decomposition operator (FirstRest). From this choice we were able to derive the control predicate (Rest : x = nil) and a specification for the composition operator. The synthesis process was then applied (recursively) to this derived specification resulting in the synthesis of the composition operator (Min2). Finally we set up a specification for the primitive operator and applied the synthesis process to it. Synthesis consisted of verifying that a known operator satisfied the specification. In the remainder of this paper we formalize those aspects of the above derivation that have been presented informally and illustrate the formalism with more complex examples.

3. Derived Antecedents

The informal derivation presented in the previous section involved a verification attempt that failed. However, we were able to use the subgoals generated during the deduction in a useful way. In this section we generalize and formally state the deductive problem exemplified in this derivation. A formal system introduced in Section 3.2 will be used for several different purposes in the synthesis method described later.

3.1. The antecedent-derivation problem

The traditional problem of deduction has been to establish the validity of a given formula in some theory. A more general problem involves deriving a formula, called a *derived antecedent*, that satisfies a certain constraint and logically entails a given goal formula G. The constraint we are concerned with simply checks whether the free variables of a formula are a subset of some fixed set that depends on G. If G happens to be a valid formula in the current theory then the antecedent *true* should be derived—thus ordinary theorem proving is a special case of deriving antecedents.

For example, consider the following formulas.

$$\forall i \in \mathbf{N} \forall j \in \mathbf{N}[i^2 \leq j^2]$$ (3.1)

$$\forall i \in \mathbf{N}[i = 0 \Rightarrow \forall j \in \mathbf{N}[i^2 \leq j^2]]$$ (3.2)

The first is invalid, the second valid. The only difference between them is that (3.2) has a sufficient condition, $i = 0$, on the matrix $i^2 \leq j^2$ in (3.1). We call $i = 0$ an $\{i\}$-antecedent of (3.1) because i is the only variable which is free in it and if we were to include it as an additional hypothesis in (3.1) we would obtain a valid statement.

Let

$$\forall x_1 \cdots \forall x_i \forall x_{i+1} \cdots \forall x_n G$$ (3.3)

be a closed formula.[3] A $\{x_1, \ldots, x_i\}$-*antecedent* of (3.3) is a formula P whose free variables are a subset of $\{x_1, \ldots, x_i\}$ such that

$$\forall x_1 \cdots \forall x_i[P \Rightarrow \forall x_{i+1} \cdots \forall x_n G]$$

is valid. P is a *weakest* $\{x_1, \ldots, x_i\}$-*antecedent* if

$$\forall x_1 \cdots \forall x_i[P \Leftrightarrow \forall x_{i+1} \cdots \forall x_n G].$$

is valid. For example, consider formula (3.1) again:
(a) *false* is a { }-antecedent of (3.1) since

$$false \Rightarrow \forall i \in \mathbf{N} \forall j \in \mathbf{N}[i^2 \leq j^2]$$

holds;
(b) $i = 0$ is a $\{i\}$-antecedent of (3.1) since

$$\forall i \in \mathbf{N}[i = 0 \Rightarrow \forall j \in \mathbf{N}[i^2 \leq j^2]]$$

holds;
(c) $i \leq j$ is a $\{i, j\}$-antecedent of (3.1) since

$$\forall i \in \mathbf{N} \forall j \in \mathbf{N}[i \leq j \Rightarrow i^2 \leq j^2]$$

holds.

Furthermore, note that each of the above antecedents are in fact weakest antecedents since the implication signs can each be replaced by equivalence signs without affecting validity.

In general a formula may have many antecedents. Characteristics of a useful antecedent seem to depend on the application domain. For program synthetic purposes, desirable antecedents are (a) in as simple a form as possible, and (b) as weak as possible. (Criterion (b) prevents the Boolean constant *false* from being an acceptable antecedent for all formulas.) Clearly there is a tradeoff between these criteria. Our implemented system for deriving antecedents, called RAINBOW, measures each criterion by a separate heuristic function, then combines the results to form a net measure of the simplicity and weakness of an antecedent. RAINBOW seeks to maximize this measure over all antecedents.

[3]In this paper our attention is restricted to formulas involving only universally quantified variables. Hence quantifiers will be omitted whenever possible.

cedents. For example, suppose that we want a useful $\{i, j\}$-antecedent of (3.1). Three candidates come to mind: $false$, $i^2 \leqslant j^2$, and $i \leqslant j$. $false$ is certainly simple in form but it is not very weak. Both $i^2 \leqslant j^2$ and $i \leqslant j$ are weakest antecedents, however $i \leqslant j$ is the simpler of the two. Thus $i \leqslant j$ is the most desirable $\{i, j\}$-antecedent.

The generality of the antecedent-derivation problem allows us to define several well-known problems as special cases. *Formula simplification* involves transforming a given formula into an equivalent but simpler form. Formula simplification can be viewed as the problem of finding a weakest $\{x_1, \ldots, x_n\}$-antecedent of a given formula $\forall x_1 \cdots \forall x_n G$. For example, we found $i \leqslant j$ to be a result of simplifying $i^2 \leqslant j^2$. *Theorem proving* involves showing that a given formula is valid in a theory by finding a proof of the formula. In terms of antecedents, theorem proving is reducible to the task of finding a weakest $\{\ \}$-antecedent of a given formula. An antecedent in no variables is one of the two propositional constants *true* or *false*. Formula simplification and theorem proving are opposite extremes in the spectrum of uses of derived antecedents since one involves deriving a weakest antecedent in *all* variables, and the other extremes lies a use of antecedents which is crucial to the synthesis method described later.

Consider again the derivation of Min in the previous section. We reasoned backwards from the output condition of MIN (formula (2.2)) to an output condition for the unknown composition operator. Technically, we derived a $\{z_0, z_1, z_2\}$-antecedent of

$$x_1 = \text{First}: x_0 \wedge x_2 = \text{Rest}: x_0 \wedge x_1 = z_1 \wedge z_2 \in \text{Bag}: x_2 \leqslant \text{Bag}: x_2$$
$$\Rightarrow z_0 \in \text{Bag}: x_0 \wedge z_0 \leqslant \text{Bag}: x_0$$

where the goal is just (2.2) and the hypotheses are the output conditions of the operators in (2.1). This formula is an instance of a formula scheme, called SPRP, that is generic to divide-and-conquer algorithms (see Section 6). It will be seen in Sections 5 and 7 that a key step in all of the design strategies presented in this paper involves deriving an antecedent over some but not all variables of an instance of SPRP.

While the antecedent problem is in a sense more general than that of theorem proving, we will see in the next section that actually deriving antecedents is much like theorem proving.

3.2. A formal system for deriving antecedents

RAINBOW uses a problem-reduction approach to deriving antecedents that may be described by a two-phase process. In the first phase, reduction rules are repeatedly applied to goals reducing them to subgoals. A primitive rule is applied whenever possible. The result of this reduction process can be

envisioned as a goal tree in which (1) nodes represent goals/subgoals, (2) arcs represent reduction-rule applications, and (3) leaf nodes represent goals to which a primitive rule has been applied. The second phase involves the bottom-up composition of antecedents. Initially each application of a primitive rule to a subgoal yields an antecedent. Subsequently whenever an antecedent has been found for each subgoal of a goal G then an antecedent is composed for G according to the reduction rule employed.

A portion of a formal system for deriving antecedents is presented here. As mentioned above, all formulas in this paper are assumed to be universally quantified. Consequently, formulas are prepared by dropping quantifiers and treating all variables as constants. In presenting a set of rules which allow us to derive antecedents we use the notation $\overset{A}{_H}$ as an abbreviation of the formula $h_1 \wedge h_2 \wedge \cdots \wedge h_k \overset{}{\Rightarrow} A$ where $H = \{h_1, h_2, \ldots, h_k\}$. Substitutions do not play an important role in the examples of this paper so for simplicity we omit them (see however [24, 27]). Only those rules required by our examples are presented. A more complete presentation may be found in [24].

The first reduction rule, R1, applies a transformation rule to a goal. Transformation rules are expressed as conditional rewriting rules

$$r \to s \quad \text{if} \quad C$$

or simply $r \to s$ when C is *true*. By convention we treat an axiom A as a transformation rule $A \to true$. This allows rule R1 to apply axioms at any time to subformulas of the current goal. Also any hypothesis of the form $r = s$ is interpreted by R1 as a transformation $r \to s$. All transformation rules are equivalence-preserving.

R1. *Reduction by a transformation rule.* If the goal has the form $\overset{G(r)}{_H}$ and there is a transformation rule $\overset{G(r)}{_H} \to s$ if C and C can be verified without much effort then generate subgoal $\overset{G(s)}{_H}$. If A is a derived antecedent of the subgoal then return A as a derived antecedent of $\overset{G(r)}{_H}$.

R2. *Reduction of conjunctive goals.* If the goal formula has the form $\overset{B \wedge C}{_H}$ then generate subgoals $\overset{B}{_H}$ and $\overset{C}{_H}$. If P and Q are derived antecedents of $\overset{B}{_H}$ and $\overset{C}{_H}$ respectively, then return $P \wedge Q$ as a derived antecedent of $\overset{B \wedge C}{_H}$.

P1. *Primitive rule.* If the goal is $\overset{A}{_H}$ and we seek an $\{x_1, \ldots, x_n\}$-antecedent and A and H' depend only on the variables $x_1, \ldots, x_n$ where H' has the form $\wedge_{j=1}^{m} h_{i_j}$ and $\{h_{i_j}\}_{j=1, \ldots, m} \subseteq H$, then generate the antecedent $H' \Rightarrow A$.

The above rules have been presented in terms of ground instances of the relevant term and formulas. RAINBOW uses a unification algorithm to match a subterm or subformula of the goal with an expression. The rules presented above are representative of the rules actually used in RAINBOW.

Suppose that we wish to derive a $\{z_0, z_1, z_2\}$-antecedent of

$$\text{Length}:x_1 = \text{Length}:x_0 \text{ div } 2 \wedge \text{Length}:x_2 = (1 + \text{Length}:x_0) \text{ div } 2 \wedge$$
$$\text{Append}:x_0 = \langle x_1, x_2 \rangle \wedge \text{Bag}:x_1 = \text{Bag}:z_1 \wedge \text{Ordered}:z_1$$
$$\wedge \text{Bag}:x_2 = \text{Bag}:z_2 \wedge \text{Ordered}:z_2$$
$$\Rightarrow \text{Bag}:x_0 = \text{Bag}:z_0 \wedge \text{Ordered}:z_0 .$$

This antecedent problem is taken from the synthesis of a mergesort algorithm in Section 7.1. A goal tree representing a formal derivation of the antecedent

$$\text{Ordered}:z_1 \wedge \text{Ordered}:z_2$$
$$\Rightarrow \text{Union}:\langle \text{Bag}:z_1, \text{Bag}:z_2 \rangle = \text{Bag}:z_0 \wedge \text{Ordered}:z_0 \qquad (3.4)$$

is given in Fig. 2. In this example and all that follow we apply rule R2 immediately and treat each conjunct in the goal separately. The arcs of a goal tree are annotated with the name of the rule and known theorem or hypothesis used. The leaves of a goal tree are annotated with the primitive rule used. The axioms and transformation rules needed for the examples are listed in Ap-pendix A. To the left of each goal in the tree will be its derived antecedent in angle brackets.

In this example the given goal

$$\text{Bag}:x_0 = \text{Bag}:z_0 \wedge \text{Ordered}:z_0$$

is reduced by application of the rule R2 (reduction of a conjunctive goal) to Goal 1 and Goal 2. Goal 1, Bag:x_0 = Bag:z_0, is reduced to Bag:Append:$\langle x_1, x_2 \rangle$ = Bag:z_0 by replacing x_0 by Append:$\langle x_1, x_2 \rangle$. This is done by applying rule R1 and hypothesis h1. The resulting subgoal is further reduced by rule R1 together with the transformation rule

$$\text{Bag} \circ \text{Append}:\langle x_1, x_2 \rangle \to \text{Union}:\langle \text{Bag}:x_1, \text{Bag}:x_2 \rangle$$

(called L5 in Appendix A) to the subgoal

$$\text{Union}:\langle \text{Bag}:x_1, \text{Bag}:x_2 \rangle = \text{Bag}:z_0 .$$

Hypotheses h4 and h6 can now be applied (by rule R1) to generate the subgoal

$$\text{Union}:\langle \text{Bag}:z_1, \text{Bag}:z_2 \rangle = \text{Bag}:z_0 .$$

At this point no obvious progress can be made in reducing this goal. Note however that it is expressed in terms of the variables z_0, z_1, and z_2. Primitive rule P1 is applied and we obtain the derived antecedent

$$\text{Ordered}:z_1 \wedge \text{Ordered}:z_2 \Rightarrow \text{Union}:\langle \text{Bag}:z_1, \text{Bag}:z_2 \rangle = \text{Bag}:z_0 .$$

This antecedent is then returned upwards as the derived antecedent of the successive subgoals of Goal 1.

Goal 2 has no obvious reductions that can be applied to it but since it depends on one of the antecedent variables we can apply primitive rule P1 yielding the derived antecedent

$$\text{Ordered}:z_1 \wedge \text{Ordered}:z_2 \Rightarrow \text{Ordered}:z_0 .$$

In the composition phase of the derivation the antecedents generated by the primitive rules are passed up the goal tree and composed. The antecedent of the initial goal (3.4) is the simplified conjunction of the antecedents derived for its two subgoals:

$$\text{Ordered}:z_1 \wedge \text{Ordered}:z_2$$
$$\Rightarrow \text{Union}:\langle \text{Bag}:z_1, \text{Bag}:z_2 \rangle = \text{Bag}:z_0 \wedge \text{Ordered}:z_0 .$$

Hypotheses:
  h1. $x_0 = \text{Append}:\langle x_1, x_2 \rangle$
  h2. $\text{Length}:x_1 = \text{Length}:x_0 \text{ div } 2$
  h3. $\text{Length}:x_2 = (1 + \text{Length}:x_0) \text{ div } 2$
  h4. $\text{Bag}:x_1 = \text{Bag}:z_1$
  h5. $\text{Ordered}:z_1$
  h6. $\text{Bag}:x_2 = \text{Bag}:z_2$
  h7. $\text{Ordered}:z_2$

Variables: $\{z_0, z_1, z_2\}$

Goal 1: $\langle Q \rangle$ Bag:x_0 = Bag:z_0
  |R1 + h1
  $\langle Q \rangle$ Bag:Append:$\langle x_1, x_2 \rangle$ = Bag:z_0
  |R1 + L5
  $\langle Q \rangle$ Union:$\langle$Bag x_1, Bag:$x_2 \rangle$ = Bag:z_0
  |R1 + h4, R1 + h6
  $\langle Q \rangle$ Union:$\langle$Bag:z_1, Bag:$z_2 \rangle$ = Bag:z_0
  P1

where Q is
Ordered:$z_1 \wedge$ Ordered:$z_2 \Rightarrow$ Union:$\langle$Bag:z_1, Bag:$z_2 \rangle$ = Bag:z_0

Goal 2: $\langle$Ordered:$z_1 \wedge$ Ordered:$z_2 \Rightarrow$ Ordered:$z_0 \rangle$ Ordered:z_0
  P1

FIG. 2. Derivation of output conditions for Merge.

In Fig. 2 and all subsequent figures we record only the simplified form of a composed antecedent.

RAINBOW derives an antecedent by means of a depth-first search with a few pruning and ordering heuristics. The object of the search is to find an antecedent that maximizes a heuristic measure of syntactic simplicity and semantic weakness. Some of the pruning and ordering heuristics motivate the search towards subgoals that are expressed entirely in terms of the antecedent variables. For example, if there is a transformation rule that replaces non-antecedent variables in the goal with some antecedent variables then all other applicable reductions of the current goal are ignored. Other heuristics serve to avoid unnecessary search. RAINBOW spends a considerable amount of time minimizing the number of reductions applicable to a goal, thus keeping the search tree relatively small. A common difficulty arises when several potential transformations of the goal are independent in the sense that the application of one does not affect the applicability of the others. When this situation occurs the order of applying the transformations is irrelevant and a naive system can end up doing much redundant search. RAINBOW attempts to detect such sets of independent transformations and discard all but one representative member of each set. A backup approach (only partially implemented in RAINBOW) invokes checking whether the current goal has been generated and/or solved already. The pruning heuristics employed by RAINBOW are such that the derivation presented in Fig. 2 represents all but one node of the entire search tree (Goal 2 has one subgoal that proves fruitless).

4. Specifications

Specifications are a precise notation for describing a problem without necessarily indicating how to solve it. Generally, a *problem specification* (or simply a *specification*) Π has the form

$$\Pi : x = z \text{ such that } I : x \Rightarrow O : \langle x, z \rangle$$
$$\text{where } \Pi : D \rightarrow R.$$

Here the input and output domains are D and R respectively. The *input condition* I expresses any properties we can expect of inputs to the desired program. Inputs satisfying the input condition will be called *legal* inputs. For inputs that do not satisfy the input condition any program behavior is acceptable. If the input condition is *true* then it will usually be omitted. The output condition O expresses the properties that an output should satisfy. Any output value z such that O:$\langle x, z \rangle$ holds will be called a *feasible* output with respect to input x. More formally, a specification Π is a 4-tuple $\langle D, R, I, O \rangle$ where:
   D is a set called the input domain,
   R is a set called the output domain,

I is a relation on D called the input condition, and
O is a relation on D×R called the output condition.

Program F *satisfies* problem specification $\Pi = \langle D, R, I, O \rangle$ if for any legal input x F terminates with a feasible output.[4] A specification is *total* if for all legal inputs there is at least one feasible output. Otherwise, a specification is *partial*. That is, a specification is partial if for some legal inputs there does not exist a feasible output. A specification $\Pi = \langle D, R, I, O \rangle$ is *unsatisfiable* if for each legal input there is no feasible output.

The definition of 'satisfies' can be weakened slightly with the following ideas in mind. For several reasons we may not know what the input condition for a problem should be. Most importantly, the class of inputs for which there exist feasible outputs may not be known or easily described. Also, within the computational or competence limits of a synthesis system it may not be possible to find a program which works on all legal inputs. In both cases we would like the synthesis system to do the best it can and construct a program F together with an input condition under which F is guaranteed to terminate with a feasible output. These considerations lead to the following definition: Program F *satisfies* specification $\Pi = \langle D, R, I, O \rangle$ *with derived input condition* I' if for all inputs satisfying both I and I', F terminates with a feasible output.

In these terms the program synthesis problem addressed in this paper (and used in the CYPRESS system) is stated as follows: Given a specification Π find a program F and predicate I' such that F satisfies Π with derived input condition I'. A byproduct of the synthesis process is a way to convert the partial specification to a total specification. The reader may notice a parallel between the notions of derived input conditions and derived antecedents. We digress briefly in order to make the parallel explicit. A specification $\Pi = \langle D, R, I, O \rangle$ may be viewed a posing a theorem to be proved; in particular

$$\forall x \in D \exists z \in R[I : x \Rightarrow O : \langle x, z \rangle] \tag{4.1}$$

which states that Π is a total specification. Deriving a program F that satisfies Π corresponds to finding a constructive proof of (4.1). Our definition of the program synthesis problem is slightly more general. Deriving a program F that satisfies Π with derived input condition I' corresponds to constructively deriving a {x}-antecedent of (4.1). The resulting antecedent is the derived input condition. So there is a good analogy between the way that antecedent derivation generalizes theorem proving and the way that we generalize the usual notion of program synthesis.

Note that a synthesis system employing this weaker concept of satisfaction can always generate a correct output; if the given problem is too hard it can always return a do-nothing program with the Boolean constant *false* as derived

---

[4] It is assumed in this paper that all predicates involved in a specification are total.

input condition. However, as we shall see, this concept of a derived input condition plays a more serious and integral role in our method. In particular, they are used to characterize the conditions under which a synthesized sub-program can be used. Of course the synthesis of a program involves trying to make the derived input condition as weak as possible. We also note that a system based on this definition of satisfaction allows the user to ignore input conditions when formulating a specification. However, deriving an input condition requires additional computation which could be saved if the user supplies a correct or nearly correct input condition.

For example, consider the specification

$$\text{PARTITION}: x_0 = \langle x_1, x_2 \rangle$$
$$\text{such that } \text{Length}: x_0 > \text{Length}: x_1 \ \wedge$$
$$\text{Length}: x_0 > \text{Length}: x_2 \ \wedge$$
$$\text{Bag}: x_1 \leqslant \text{Bag}: x_2 \ \wedge$$
$$\text{Bag}: x_0 = \text{Union}: \langle \text{Bag}: x_1, \text{Bag}: x_2 \rangle$$
$$\text{where } \text{PARTITION}: \text{LIST(N)} \rightarrow \text{LIST(N)} \times \text{LIST(N)}.$$

This specifies the problem of partitioning a list of numbers into two shorter sublists such that each element of the first sublist is less than or equal than each element of the second sublist. This specification is partial in that for inputs of length zero or one the problem has no feasible output. CYPRESS can construct a program called Partition that satisfies PARTITION with derived input condition $x \neq nil \wedge \text{Rest}: x \neq nil$ (see Section 7.3). This predicate is used as a guard on the invocation of Partition.

5. Design Strategies for Simple Algorithms

A basic operation of the problem-reduction approach to synthesis involves treating specifications that can be satisfied by simple expressions. Two cases arise regarding such specifications. First, a specification Π may have the same domain and range as a known operator. In this case we derive the conditions under which the known operator satisfies the given specification. Alternatively, Π may have a more complex domain and/or range than any known operators. In this case we form a structure of known operators such that the structure (viewed as a function) has the correct domain and range, and derive conditions under which the structure satisfies the same known specification. If there are alternative ways to structure the same known operators then a conditional program may arise. The strategies used by a CYPRESS system for handling these cases are described below in Sections 5.1 and 5.2 respectively.

5.1. Matching an operator against a specification

In this section we present a strategy (and its formal basis) for handling

specifications that can be satisfied by a single known operator. As an example, the specification

$$\text{MSORT\_DECOMPOSE}: y_0 = \langle y_1, y_2 \rangle$$
$$\text{such that } \text{Length}: y_0 > \text{Length}: y_1 \ \wedge$$
$$\text{Length}: y_0 > \text{Length}: y_2$$
$$\text{where } \text{MSORT\_DECOMPOSE}: \text{LIST(N)} \rightarrow \text{LIST(N)} \times \text{LIST(N)}.$$

arises during the synthesis of a mergesort algorithm (see Section 7.2). The MSORT_DECOMPOSE problem involves mapping a list into a 2-tuple of shorter lists. Suppose that we have an operator, called Listsplit, that splits a list roughly in half. It is specified as follows:

$$\text{LISTSPLIT}: x_0 = \langle x_1, x_2 \rangle$$
$$\text{such that } x_0 = \text{Append}: \langle x_1, x_2 \rangle \ \wedge$$
$$\text{Length}: x_1 = \text{Length}: x_0 \text{ div } 2 \ \wedge$$
$$\text{Length}: x_2 = (1 + \text{Length}: x_0) \text{ div } 2$$
$$\text{where } \text{LISTSPLIT}: \text{LIST(N)} \rightarrow \text{LIST(N)} \times \text{LIST(N)}.$$

By x div k we mean integer division of x by k (e.g. 5 div 2 = 2). Listsplit might satisfy MSORT_DECOMPOSE since their input and output types match and neither has an input condition. To be sure though, we need to verify that if Listsplit is used to split some list y_0 into $\langle y_1, y_2 \rangle$ then y_0, y_1, and y_2 satisfy the output condition of MSORT_DECOMPOSE. Technically, this involves showing that the output condition of LISTSPLIT implies the output condition of MSORT_DECOMPOSE.

The following theorem provides the basis for deriving the conditions under which an operator satisfies a specification. It is helpful in this theorem to think of Π_k as a specification for a known operator (such as Listsplit) and Π_s as a given specification (such as MSORT_DECOMPOSE).

Theorem 5.1. *Let* $\Pi_k = \langle D_k, R_k, I_k, O_k \rangle$ *and* $\Pi_s = \langle D_s, R_s, I_s, O_s \rangle$ *be specifications. If*

(a) $D_s = D_k$,

(b) $R_k = R_s$,

(c) *J is an {x}-antecedent of*
$$\forall x \in D_s [I_s : x \Rightarrow I_k : x],$$

(d) *K is an {x}-antecedent of*
$$\forall x \in D_s \ni \forall z \in R_s [I_s : x \wedge O_k : \langle x, z \rangle \Rightarrow O_s : \langle x, z \rangle],$$

then any operator satisfying Π_k *also satisfies* Π_s *with derived input condition* J ∧ K.

Proof. Let F be any operator that satisfies Π_k, thus

$$\forall x \in D_k[I_k : x \Rightarrow O_k : \langle x, F : x \rangle]$$

holds. We must show

$$\forall x \in D_s[I_s : x \wedge J : x \wedge K : x \Rightarrow O_s : \langle x, F : x \rangle]$$

where J and K are antecedents satisfying conditions (c) and (d) respectively. Let $x \in D_s$ and assume $I_s : x \wedge J : x \wedge K : x$. By conditions (a) and (c) we can infer $I_k : x$. Since F satisfies Π_k we obtain $O_k : \langle x, F : x \rangle$. We have $F : x \in R_k$, and by condition (b) we get $F : x \in R_s$. From an instance of condition (d)

$$K : x \wedge I_s : x \wedge O_k : \langle x, F : x \rangle \Rightarrow O_s : \langle x, F : x \rangle,$$

we infer $O_s : \langle x, F : x \rangle$. Since x was taken as an arbitrary element of D_s it follows that

$$\forall x \in D_s[J : x \wedge K : x \wedge I_s : x \Rightarrow O_s : \langle x, F : x \rangle]$$

i.e., F satisfies Π_s with derived input condition $J \wedge K$. □

CYPRESS employs a strategy called OPERATOR_MATCH based on Theorem 5.1. Given a specification, OPERATOR_MATCH finds all known operators with the same input/output types. For each such operator, it then sets up and solves the antecedent-derivation problems from conditions (c) and (d). Finally that operator with the weakest derived input condition is returned as the synthesized algorithm.

Given the specification MSORT_DECOMPOSE, OPERATOR_MATCH would find the operator Listsplit and match them as follows. The antecedent-derivation problems in conditions (c) and (d) in Theorem 5.1 are set up using the following substitutions:

LIST(N) replaces D_k, R_k, D_s and R_s,
true replaces I_k and I_s,
the output condition of LISTSPLIT replaces O_k, and
the output condition of MSORT_DECOMPOSE replaces O_s.

Condition (c) becomes

$$true \Rightarrow true$$

and we trivially obtain the derived antecedent *true*. Condition (d) becomes the problem of deriving a $\{y_0\}$-antecedent of

$$y_0 = Append : \langle y_1, y_2 \rangle \wedge$$
$$Length : y_1 = Length : y_0 \, div \, 2 \wedge Length : y_2 = (1 + Length : y_0) \, div \, 2$$
$$\Rightarrow Length : y_0 > Length : y_1 \wedge Length : y_1 > Length : y_2.$$

The derivation presented in Fig. 3 yields the antecedent $Length : y_0 > 0 \wedge Length : y_0 > 1$ which simplifies to $Length : y_0 > 1$. Thus according to Theorem 5.1 Listsplit satisfies the specification MSORT_DECOMPOSE with derived input condition $Length : y_0 > 1$. Consequently we can use the operator Listsplit for the problem MSORT_DECOMPOSE provided that it is never passed an argument of length zero or one.

In applying Theorem 5.1 we assume that a specification exists for all known operators. This may seem problematic due to the need to specify the primitives in the target programming language. However, we let a primitive operator specify itself. For example, the list operator Cons is specified in CYPRESS' knowledge base by

$$CONS : \langle a, y \rangle = x$$
$$such \, that \, x = Cons : \langle a, y \rangle$$
$$where \, CONS : N \times LIST(N) \rightarrow LIST(N).$$

When this specification is used, transformations are called into play that explicate the meaning of Cons in interaction with other operators and relations.

Hypotheses: h1. $y_0 = Append : \langle y_1, y_2 \rangle$
 h2. $Length : y_1 = Length : y_0 \, div \, 2$
 h3. $Length : y_2 = (1 + Length : y_0) \, div \, 2$

Variables: $\{y_0\}$

Goal 1: $\langle Q \rangle$ $Length : y_0 > Length : y_1$
|R1 + h2
$\langle Q \rangle$ $Length : y_0 > Length : y_0 \, div \, 2$
|R1 + N2
$\langle Q \rangle$ $Length : y_0 + Length : y_0 > Length : y_0$
|R1 + N1
$\langle Q \rangle$ $Length : y_0 > 0$
P1

where Q is $Length : y_0 > 0$

Goal 2: $\langle Length : y_0 > 1 \rangle$ $Length : y_0 > Length : y_2$
derivation analogous to that for Goal 1

Fig. 3. Matching the specification of MSORT_DECOMPOSE with the specification of Listsplit.

See, for example, L1, L2, and L3 in Appendix A. The knowledge base provides a context that extends the meaning of CONS and other specifications.

5.2. Strategies for simple algorithms on composite data types

If specification Π has a complex domain and/or range, then it may be that Π can be satisfied by some simple structure of known operators. For example, consider the specification

PARTITION_COMPOSE: $(b, \langle z_1, z'_1 \rangle) = \langle z_0, z'_0 \rangle$
such that Bag: $z_1 \leq$ Bag: z'_1
$\Rightarrow$ Add: $\langle b, \text{Union}: \langle \text{Bag}: z_1, \text{Bag}: z'_1 \rangle \rangle = \text{Union}: \langle \text{Bag}: z_0, \text{Bag}: z'_0 \rangle \wedge$
Bag: $z_0 \leq$ Bag: z'_0
where PARTITION_COMPOSE: $N \times (\text{LIST}(N) \times \text{LIST}(N))$
$\to \text{LIST}(N) \times \text{LIST}(N)$

$\langle \text{Cons}: \langle b, z_1 \rangle, z'_1 \rangle$

which (in slightly stronger form) arises during the synthesis of a partition operator for a quicksort (see Section 7.3). Intuitively, this specifies the problem of adding a number b to one of two lists while preserving the property that each element in the first list is less than or equal to each element in the second list. CYPRESS has a design strategy, called STRUCTURE, that creates a list of structures of known operators that satisfy the domain and range of the given specification. For example, this strategy would suggest the structure

$\langle \text{Cons}: \langle b, z_1 \rangle, z'_1 \rangle$

and many others that are not as reasonable. Each structure in turn is matched against the given specification and the one with the weakest derived input condition is returned.

More intelligent strategies emerge from concentrating on special classes of problems. For example, the divide-and-conquer design strategies described in Section 7 require the construction of simple decomposition and composition operators. Intuitively, a decomposition operator on some data type maps a larger element of the type into smaller elements of the type (with respect to a suitable well-founded ordering). Correspondingly, a composition operator is used to construct larger elements of a type out of smaller ones. Each known data type (such as N and $\text{LIST}(N)$) has associated with it a collection of standard decomposition and composition operators which are used by the divide-and-conquer design strategies. For example, for $\text{LIST}(N)$ CYPRESS has the standard composition operators Cons and Append, and the standard decomposition operators FirstRest and Listsplit. However, on composite data types there may be no such operators known. CYPRESS has a design strategy, called COND, for constructing composite decomposition/composition operators out of known decomposition/composition operators.

COND handles PARTITION_COMPOSE as follows. A composition operator is required on the data type $\text{LIST}(N) \times \text{LIST}(N)$. This type may occur often enough that it is worth having prestored composition operators available for it, but let us assume that none are available so that we must construct one out of known composition operators on $\text{LIST}(N)$. On the data type $\text{LIST}(N)$ CYPRESS has the two known composition operators Cons and Append. COND first attempts to create structures in which a known composition operator is applied once and the identity operator is applied to the remaining input variables. The operator Append is discarded because Append and Id cannot be structured to have the same input/output type as PARTITION_COMPOSE. However, using Cons, COND generates the structures:

$$\langle \text{Cons}: \langle b, z_0 \rangle, \text{Id}: z'_0 \rangle \qquad (5.1)$$

and

$$\langle \text{Id}: z_0, \text{Cons}: \langle b, z'_0 \rangle \rangle \qquad (5.2)$$

and matches these structures against PARTITION_COMPOSE. If one structure happens to satisfy PARTITION_COMPOSE (that is, if its derived input condition is *true*) then it is returned as the composition operator. If neither structure satisfies PARTITION_COMPOSE then COND forms a conditional using the derived input conditions as the guards.

A specification for a structure is easily created from the specifications of its component operators. For example, structure (5.1) is specified by

STRUCTURE5.1: $(b, \langle z_1, z'_1 \rangle) = \langle z_0, z'_0 \rangle$
such that $z_0 = \text{Cons}: \langle b, z_1 \rangle \wedge z'_0 = z'_1$
where STRUCTURE5.1: $N \times (\text{LIST}(N) \times \text{LIST}(N))$
$\to \text{LIST}(N) \times \text{LIST}(N)$.

Theorem 5.1 is used to match STRUCTURE5.1 against PARTITION_COMPOSE as follows. Conditions (a) and (b) were satisfied by the way that COND constructed (5.1). Satisfying condition (c) yields derived antecedent *true* since the input condition of (5.1) is *true*. Satisfying condition (d) involves deriving a $\{b, z_1, z'_1\}$-antecedent of

Bag: $z_1 \leq$ Bag: $z'_1 \wedge z_0 = \text{Cons}: \langle b, z_1 \rangle \wedge z'_0 = z'_1$
$\Rightarrow$ Add: $\langle b, \text{Union}: \langle \text{Bag}: z_1, \text{Bag}: z'_1 \rangle \rangle = \text{Union}: \langle \text{Bag}: z_0, \text{Bag}: z'_0 \rangle \wedge$
Bag: $z_0 \leq$ Bag: z'_0.

In Fig. 4 the antecedent $b \leq$ Bag: z'_1 is derived. Thus (5.1) above can be used to satisfy PARTITION_COMPOSE with derived input condition $b \leq$ Bag: z'_1. An

```
Hypotheses:  h1. Bag:z1 ≤ Bag:z1'
             h2. z0 = Cons:⟨b, z1⟩
             h3. z0' = z'

Variables:   {b, z1, z1'}

Goal 1:  ⟨true⟩ Union:⟨Bag:z0, Bag:z0'⟩
                 = Add:⟨b, Union:⟨Bag:z1, Bag:z1'⟩⟩
                 |R1 + h2, R1 + h3
         ⟨true⟩ Union:⟨Bag:Cons:⟨b, z1⟩, Bag:z1'⟩
                 = Add:⟨b, Union:⟨Bag:z1, Bag:z1'⟩⟩
                 |R1 + L1
         ⟨true⟩ Union:⟨Add:⟨b, Bag:z1⟩, Bag:z1'⟩
                 = Add:⟨b, Union:⟨Bag:z1, Bag:z1'⟩⟩
                 |R1 + B4
         ⟨true⟩ Add:⟨b, Union:⟨Bag:z1, Bag:z1'⟩⟩
                 = Add:⟨b, Union:⟨Bag:z1, Bag:z1'⟩⟩
                 |R1 + B1
         ⟨true⟩ true
                 P1

Goal 2:  ⟨Q⟩ Bag:z0 ≤ Bag:z0'
             |R1 + h2, R1 + h3
         ⟨Q⟩ Bag:Cons:⟨b, z1⟩ ≤ Bag:z1'
             |R1 + L1
         ⟨Q⟩ Add:⟨b, Bag:z1⟩ ≤ Bag:z1'
                     R1 + B5, R2
         ⟨Q⟩ b ≤ Bag:z1'        ⟨true⟩ Bag:z1 ≤ Bag:z1'
             P1                        |R1 + h1
                                ⟨true⟩ true
         where Q is b ≤ Bag:z1'
```

FIG. 4. Matching STRUCTURE5.1 against PARTITION_COMPOSE.

analogous derivation for the structure (5.2) results in the derived input condition $b \geqslant \text{Bag}:z_1$. Since neither structure satisfies PARTITION_COMPOSE by itself COND combines these two results into the conditional

$$\begin{aligned}&\text{Partition_Compose}:\langle b, z, z'\rangle\rangle \equiv\\ &\quad \textbf{if}\\ &\qquad b \leqslant \text{Bag}:z' \rightarrow \langle \text{Cons}:\langle b, z\rangle, z'\rangle \quad \square\\ &\qquad b \geqslant \text{Bag}:z \rightarrow \langle z, \text{Cons}:\langle b, z'\rangle\rangle\\ &\quad \textbf{fi}\end{aligned}$$

which satisfies PARTITION_COMPOSE.

6. The Form and Function of Divide-and-Conquer Algorithms

For simplicity of exposition we will restrict our attention to the class of divide-and-conquer algorithms which have the form

$$\begin{aligned}&F:x \equiv \textbf{if}\\ &\qquad \mathit{Primitive}:x \rightarrow \mathit{Directly_Solve}:x \quad \square\\ &\qquad \neg\, \mathit{Primitive}:x \rightarrow \mathit{Compose} \circ (G \times F) \circ \mathit{Decompose}:x\,.\\ &\quad \textbf{fi}\end{aligned}$$

where G may be an arbitrary function but typically is either F or the identity function Id. A more general scheme is presented in [26]. *Decompose*, G, *Compose*, and *Directly_Solve* are referred to as the decomposition, auxiliary, composition, and primitive operators respectively. *Primitive* is referred to as the control predicate.

Our design strategies for this scheme are based on Theorem 6.1 below. The theorem is useful because it states how the functionality of the whole (instantiated scheme) follows from the functionalities of its parts and how these parts are constrained to work together. We use the theorem to reason backwards from the intended functionality of the whole scheme to the functionalities of the parts. Conditions (1), (2), (3), and (4) provide generic specifications for the decomposition, auxiliary, composition, and primitive operators respectively. Condition (1) states that the decomposition operator must not only satisfy its main output condition $\mathrm{O}_{Decompose}$, but must also preserve a well-founded ordering and satisfy the input conditions to $(G \times F)$. The derived input condition obtained in achieving condition (1) will be used to form the control predicate in the target algorithm. Since the primitive operator is only invoked when the control predicate holds, its generic specification in condition (4) is the same as the specification for the whole algorithm with the additional input condition Primitive:x. Condition (5), the Strong Problem Reduction Principle, provides the key constraint that relates the functionality of the whole divide-and-conquer algorithm to the functionalities of its subalgorithms. In words it states that if input x_0 decomposes into subinputs x_1 and x_2, and z_1 and z_2 are feasible outputs with respect to these subinputs respectively, and z_1 and z_2 compose to form z_0, then z_0 is a feasible solution to input x_0. Loosely put, feasible outputs compose to form feasible outputs.

Theorem 6.1. *Let* $\Pi_F = \langle \mathrm{D}_F, \mathrm{R}_F, \mathrm{I}_F, \mathrm{O}_F\rangle$ *and* $\Pi_G = \langle \mathrm{D}_G, \mathrm{R}_G, \mathrm{I}_G, \mathrm{O}_G\rangle$ *denote specifications, let* $\mathrm{O}_{Compose}$ *and* $\mathrm{O}_{Decompose}$ *denote relations on* $\mathrm{R}_F \times \mathrm{R}_G \times \mathrm{R}_F$ *and* $\mathrm{D}_F \times \mathrm{D}_G \times \mathrm{D}_F$ *respectively, and let* $\succ$ *be a well-founded ordering on* D_F. *If*

(1) Decompose satisfies the specification

$$\text{DECOMPOSE} : x_0 = \langle x_1, x_2 \rangle$$
$$\text{such that } I_F : x_0 \Rightarrow I_G : x_1 \wedge I_F : x_2$$
$$\wedge \; x_0 > x_2 \wedge O_D : \langle x_0, x_1, x_2 \rangle$$
$$\text{where } \text{DECOMPOSE} : D_F \rightarrow D_G \times D_F$$

with derived input condition $\neg$ Primitive : x_0;

(2) G satisfies the specification $\Pi_G = \langle D_G, R_G, I_G, O_G \rangle$;

(3) Compose satisfies the specification

$$\text{COMPOSE} : \langle z_1, z_2 \rangle = z_0$$
$$\text{such that } O_{Compose} : \langle z_0, z_1, z_2 \rangle$$
$$\text{where } \text{COMPOSE} : R_G \times R_F \rightarrow R_F ;$$

(4) Directly_Solve satisfies the specification

$$\text{DIRECTLY\_SOLVE} : x = z$$
$$\text{such that } \text{Primitive} : x \wedge I_F : x \Rightarrow O_F : \langle x, z \rangle$$
$$\text{where } \text{DIRECTLY\_SOLVE} : D_F \rightarrow R_F ;$$

(5) the following Strong Problem Reduction Principle (SPRP) holds

$$\forall \langle x_0, x_1, x_2 \rangle \in D_F \times D_G \times D_F \; \forall \langle z_0, z_1, z_2 \rangle \in R_F \times R_G \times R_F$$
$$[O_{Decompose} : \langle x_0, x_1, x_2 \rangle \wedge O_G : \langle x_1, z_1 \rangle \wedge$$
$$O_F : \langle x_2, z_2 \rangle \wedge O_{Compose} : \langle z_0, z_1, z_2 \rangle$$
$$\Rightarrow O_F : \langle x_0, z_0 \rangle] ;$$

then the divide-and-conquer program

$$F : x \equiv \textbf{if}$$
$$\text{Primitive} : x \rightarrow \text{Directly\_Solve} : x \quad \square$$
$$\neg \, \text{Primitive} : x \rightarrow \text{Compose} \circ (G \times F) \circ \text{Decompose} : x$$
$$\textbf{fi}$$

satisfies specification $\Pi_F = \langle D_F, R_F, I_F, O_F \rangle$.

Proof. To show that F satisfies the specification $\Pi_F = \langle D_F, R_F, I_F, O_F \rangle$ we show by structural induction[5] on D_F that for all $x \in D_F$, $I_F : x \Rightarrow O_F : \langle x, F : x \rangle$ holds.

Let x_0 be an object in D_F such that $I_F : x_0$ holds and assume (inductively) that $I_F : y \Rightarrow O_F : \langle y, F : y \rangle$ holds for any $y \in D_F$ such that $x_0 > y$. There are two cases to consider:

$$\text{Primitive} : x_0 = true \quad \text{and} \quad \neg \, \text{Primitive} : x_0 = true .$$

If Primitive : $x_0 = true$ then F : $x_0 = $ Directly_Solve : x_0 by construction of F. Furthermore according to condition (4) we have

$$I_F : x_0 \wedge \text{Primitive} : x_0 \Rightarrow O_F : \langle x_0, \text{Directly\_Solve} : x_0 \rangle$$

from which we infer

$$O_F : \langle x_0, \text{Directly\_Solve} : x_0 \rangle$$

or equivalently $O_F : \langle x_0, F : x_0 \rangle$.

If $\neg$ Primitive : $x_0 = true$ then

$$F : x_0 = \text{Compose} \circ (F \times F) \circ \text{Decompose} : x_0 \qquad (6.1)$$

by construction of F. We will show that $O_F : \langle x_0, F : x_0 \rangle$ holds by using the inductive assumption and modus ponens on the Strong Problem Reduction Principle. This amounts to showing that (6.1) computes a feasible output with respect to input x_0. Since $I_F : x_0$ holds and $\neg$ Primitive : x_0 holds then Decompose : x_0 is defined so let Decompose : $x_0 = \langle x_1, x_2 \rangle$. By condition (1) Decompose satisfies its specification, so we have

$$O_{Decompose} : \langle x_0, x_1, x_2 \rangle \qquad (6.2)$$

and $I_F : x_1$ and $I_F : x_2$. Consider x_1. By condition (2) we have $I_G : x_1 \Rightarrow O_G : \langle x_1, G : x_1 \rangle$ so we can infer

$$O_G : \langle x_1, G : x_1 \rangle \qquad (6.3)$$

[5] Structural induction on a well-founded set $\langle W, > \rangle$ is a form of mathematical induction described by

$$\forall x \in W[\forall y \in W[x > y \Rightarrow Q : y] \Rightarrow Q : x] \Rightarrow \forall x \in W \, Q : x$$

i.e., if $Q : x$ can be shown to follow from the assumption that $Q : y$ holds for each y such that $x > y$, then we can conclude that $Q : x$ holds for all x.

by modus ponens. Consider x_2. By condition (1) we have $x_0 > x_2$, thus the inductive assumption

$$I_F : x_2 \Rightarrow O_F : \langle x_2, F : x_2 \rangle$$

holds. From this we infer

$$O_F : \langle x_2, F : x_2 \rangle.$$ (6.4)

Next, by condition (3) we have

$$O_{Compose} : \langle Compose : \langle G : x_1, F : x_2 \rangle, G : x_1, F : x_2 \rangle,$$

or simply,

$$O_{Compose} : \langle F : x_0, G : x_1, F : x_2 \rangle.$$ (6.5)

By condition (5) we have the instance

$$O_{Decompose} : \langle x_0, x_1, x_2 \rangle \wedge O_G : \langle x_1, G : x_1 \rangle \wedge$$
$$O_F : \langle x_2, F : x_2 \rangle \wedge O_{Compose} : \langle F : x_0, G : x_1, F : x_2 \rangle$$
$$\Rightarrow O_F : \langle x_0, F : x_0 \rangle.$$ (6.6)

From (6.2), (6.3), (6.4), (6.5), and (6.6) we infer $O_F : \langle x_0, F : x_0 \rangle.$ $\square$

Notice that in Theorem 6.1 the forms of the subalgorithms Decompose, Compose, and F are not relevant. All that matters is that they satisfy their respective specifications. In other words, their function and not their form matters with respect to the correctness of the whole divide-and-conquer algorithm.

Theorem 6.1 actually treats the special case in which the auxiliary operator G is distinct from F. A more general version of this theorem appears in [26]. The principal difference is that when the auxiliary operator is F then we must include the expression $x_0 > x_1$ in the output condition of DECOMPOSE in condition (1).

7. Design Strategies for Divide-and-Conquer Algorithms

Given a problem specification Π a design strategy derives specifications for subproblems in such a way that solutions for the subproblems can be assembled (via a program scheme) into a solution for Π. Note that a strategy does not solve the derived specifications, it merely creates them.

Three design strategies emerge naturally from the structure of divide-and-conquer algorithms. Each attempts to derive specifications for subalgorithms that satisfy the conditions of Theorem 6.1. If successful then any operators which satisfy these derived specifications can be assembled into a divide-and-conquer algorithm satisfying the given specification. The design strategies differ mainly in their approach to satisfying the key constraint of Theorem 6.1—the Strong Problem Reduction Principle (SPRP).

The first design strategy, called DS1, can be summarized as follows.

DS1. First construct a simple decomposition operator on the input domain and construct the auxiliary operator, then use the Strong Problem Reduction Principle to set up a specification for the composition operator on the output domain. Finally derive a specification for the primitive operator.

The derivation of the Min program in Section 2 was controlled by this strategy. We chose a simple decomposition operator on the input domain (FirstRest) then derived output conditions for the composition operator (Min2). The assumptions used during this derivation are just those given us by the Strong Problem Reduction Principle. Also from the choice of decomposition operator we derived the control predicate (Rest : $x = $ nil) and used it to set up a specification for the primitive operator.

To see how we derive a specification for the composition operator, suppose that the given problem is $\Pi = \langle D, R, I, O \rangle$, we have selected a decomposition operator Decompose, and we have chosen an auxiliary operator G. The output conditions for Compose can be derived as follows. First, the formula

$$O_{Decompose} : \langle x_0, x_1, x_2 \rangle \wedge O_G : \langle x_1, z_1 \rangle \wedge$$
$$O_F : \langle x_2, z_2 \rangle \Rightarrow O_F : \langle x_0, z_0 \rangle$$ (7.1)

is set up. (7.1) is the same as the Strong Problem Reduction Principle of Theorem 6.1 except that the hypothesis $O_{Compose} : \langle z_0, z_1, z_2 \rangle$ is missing. We know that $O_{Compose}$ is a relation on the variables z_0, z_1, and z_2 so we derive a $\{z_0, z_1, z_2\}$-antecedent of (7.1). If $Q : \langle z_0, z_1, z_2 \rangle$ is such an antecedent then

$$O_{Decompose} : \langle x_0, x_1, x_2 \rangle \wedge O_G : \langle x_1, z_1 \rangle \wedge$$
$$O_F : \langle x_2, z_2 \rangle \wedge Q : \langle z_0, z_1, z_2 \rangle \Rightarrow O_F : \langle x_0, z_0 \rangle$$

is valid and we can take Q as the output condition $O_{Compose}$ since the Strong Problem Reduction Principle is satisfied by this choice of $O_{Compose}$. Once we have the output condition it is a simple matter to create a specification for the composition operator.

To put it another way, the SPRP can be likened to an equation in four unknowns—$O_{Decompose}$, O_G, O_F, and $O_{Compose}$. The 'locus' of the 'equation' is the set of correct instances of the divide-and-conquer scheme. In design strategy DS1 we are given O_F, we construct $O_{Decompose}$ and O_G fairly directly, leaving us with 'values' for three of the 'unknowns'. Antecedent derivation in effect allows us to 'solve for' the remaining unknown—$O_{Compose}$. The other design strategies simply attempt to satisfy the SPRP by 'plugging in values' for a different subset of the unknowns then solving for the remaining one.

The other two design strategies are variations on DS1.

DS2. First construct a simple composition operator on the output domain and construct an auxiliary operator, then use the Strong Problem Reduction Principle to derive a specification for the decomposition operator on the input domain. Finally, set up a specification for the primitive operator.

DS3. Construct a simple decomposition operator on the input domain and construct a simple composition operator on the output domain, then use the Strong Problem Reduction Principle to derive a specification for the auxiliary operator. Finally, set up a specification for the primitive operator.

In each of these design strategies we must find a suitable well-founded ordering on the input domain in order to ensure program termination. We now describe design strategies DS1 and DS2 more formally. Design strategy DS3 is discussed more fully in [26]. Section 7.1 presents DS1 and illustrates it with the derivation of a mergesort algorithm. Design strategy DS2 is presented in Section 7.2 and is illustrated by the derivation of an algorithm for merging two sorted lists. In Section 7.3 we derive a quicksort algorithm which illustrates how the design strategies handle partial specifications.

7.1. Design strategy DS1 and the synthesis of a mergesort algorithm

Each of the steps in design strategy DS1 are described below in terms of a given specification $\Pi_F = \langle D_F, R_F, I_F, O_F \rangle$. The generic description of a step is presented first, followed by its application to the problem of sorting a list of numbers.

The problem of sorting a list of natural numbers may be specified as follows

$$\text{SORT}:x = z \text{ such that } \text{Bag}:x = \text{Bag}:z \wedge \text{Ordered}:z$$
$$\text{where SORT}:\text{LIST(N)} \to \text{LIST(N)}.$$

Here $\text{Bag}:x = \text{Bag}:y$ asserts that the multiset (bag) of elements in the list y is the same as the multiset of elements in x. $\text{Ordered}:y$ holds exactly when the elements of list y are in nondecreasing order.

Design strategy DS1 stems from the construction of a simple decomposition operator.

(DS1)(1) *Construct a simple decomposition operator* Decompose *and a well-founded ordering $>$ on the input domain* D. Intuitively a decomposition operator decomposes an object x into smaller objects out of which x can be composed. It is assumed that standard decomposition operators are available on various data types. If no standard decomposition operator is available for Π_F then a structure or simple conditional is constructed, as described in Section 5.2.

Example. The input domain of the SORT problem is LIST(N). One way of decomposing a list is to split it into roughly equal length halves via the operator Listsplit. Another way is to decompose it into its first element and the remainder via FirstRest. The choice of Listsplit here leads to a mergesort algorithm, and the latter choice leads to an insertion sort [25]. An appropriate well-founded ordering on the domain LIST(N) is

$$x > y \quad \text{iff} \quad \text{Length}:x > \text{Length}:y.$$

A method for constructing well-founded orderings on a given domain may be found in [26].

(DS1)(2) *Construct the auxiliary operator* G. The choice of decomposition operator determines the input domain D_G of G. It is sufficient to let G be F if D_G is D_F and let G be the identity function Id otherwise, although other alternatives are possible. Let Π_G denote the specification of G.

Example. Since our target algorithm is to decompose its input list into two sublists it is appropriate to let the auxiliary operator be a recursive call to the sort algorithm, which we will call Msort. At this point Msort has the (partially instantiated) form

$$\text{Msort}:x \equiv \textbf{if}$$
$$\text{Primitive}:x \to \text{Directly\_Solve}:x \quad \square$$
$$\neg\, \text{Primitive}:x \to \text{Compose} \circ (\text{Msort} \times \text{Msort}) \circ \text{Listsplit}:x$$
$$\textbf{fi}$$

where Directly_Solve and Compose remain to be specified.

(DS1)(3) *Verify the decomposition operator.* The decomposition operator assumes the burden of preserving the well-founded ordering on the input domain and ensuring that its outputs satisfy the input conditions of $(G \times F)$. Consequently it is necessary to verify that our choice of decomposition operator Decompose satisfies the specification

$$DECOMPOSE : x_0 = \langle x_1, x_2 \rangle$$
such that $I_F : x_0 \Rightarrow I_G : x_1 \wedge I_F : x_2 \wedge x_0 > x_2$
where $DECOMPOSE : D_F \rightarrow D_G \times D_F$.

The derived input condition is taken to be $\neg Primitive : x_0$. If the auxiliary operator G is F then the formula $x_0 > x_1$ must be added to the output condition. Note that this step ensures that Decompose satisfies condition (1) of Theorem 6.1.

Example. Since the input condition of SORT is $true$ and the auxiliary operator is Msort we can instantiate the generic verification specification as follows

$$DECOMPOSE : x_0 = \langle x_1, x_2 \rangle$$
such that $true \Rightarrow true \wedge$
$Length : x_0 > Length : x_1 \wedge Length : x_0 > Length : x_2$
where $DECOMPOSE : LIST(N) \rightarrow LIST(N) \times LIST(N)$

or simply

$$DECOMPOSE : x_0 = \langle x_1, x_2 \rangle$$
such that $Length : x_0 > Length : x_1$
$\wedge Length : x_0 > Length : x_2$
where $DECOMPOSE : LIST(N) \rightarrow LIST(N) \times LIST(N)$.

In Section 3 we showed that Listsplit satisfies this specification with derived input condition $Length : x_0 > 1$. Again this means that we should only apply Listsplit to lists of length 2 or greater. Consequently we use $Length : x_0 \leq 1$ as the control predicate (Primitive) in Msort which now has the form

$Msort : x \equiv$ **if**
  $Length : : x \leq 1 \rightarrow Directly\_Solve : x$ ☐
  $Length : x > 1 \rightarrow Compose \circ (Msort \times Msort) \circ Listsplit : x$
fi .

(DS1)(4) *Construct the composition operator.* Our choice of decomposition and auxiliary operators in previous steps places strong constraints on the functionality of the composition operator. In particular, the output condition of the composition operator $O_{Compose}$ must satisfy the Strong Problem Reduction Principle. In this step an expression for $O_{Compose}$ is derived by finding a

$\{z_0, z_1, z_2\}$-antecedent of

$$O_{Decompose} : \langle x_0, x_1, x_2 \rangle \wedge O_G : \langle x_1, z_1 \rangle \wedge$$
$$O_F : \langle x_2, z_2 \rangle \Rightarrow O_F : \langle x_0, z_0 \rangle .$$

Next the specification

$$COMPOSE : \langle z_1, z_2 \rangle = z_0$$
such that $O_{Compose} : \langle z_0, z_1, z_2 \rangle$
where $COMPOSE : R_G \times R_F \rightarrow R_F$

is set up. Recall that the task of a design strategy is to reduce a given specification to specifications for subproblems, not to actually solve the subproblems. The synthesis process will be recursively applied to the specifications generated by the design strategy.

Example. Instantiating the formula scheme above with the output conditions, input domains, and output domains of Listsplit and Msort yields

$$Length : x_1 = Length : x_0 \text{ div } 2 \wedge$$
$$Length : x_2 = (1 + Length : x_0) \text{ div } 2 \wedge Append : x_0 = \langle x_1, x_2 \rangle \wedge$$
$$Bag : x_1 = Bag : z_1 \wedge Ordered : z_1 \wedge Bag : x_2 = Bag : z_2 \wedge Ordered : z_2$$
$$\Rightarrow Bag : x_0 = Bag : z_0 \wedge Ordered : z_0 .$$

The $\{z_0, z_1, z_2\}$-antecedent

$$Ordered : z_1 \wedge Ordered : z_2$$
$$\Rightarrow Union : \langle Bag : z_1, Bag : z_2 \rangle = Bag : z_0 \wedge Ordered : z_0$$

was derived earlier in Fig. 2. Using this antecedent we create the following specification which describes the well-known problem of merging two sorted lists.

$$COMPOSE : \langle z_1, z_2 \rangle = z_0$$
such that $Ordered : z_1 \wedge Ordered : z_2$
$\Rightarrow Union : \langle Bag : z_1, Bag : z_2 \rangle = Bag : z_0 \wedge Ordered : z_0$
where $COMPOSE : LIST(N) \times LIST(N) \rightarrow LIST(N)$.

In Section 7.2 we derive a program called Merge that satisfies this specification.

(DS1)(5) *Construct the primitive operator.* From condition (4) of Theorem 6.1 the primitive operator has the generic specification

DIRECTLY_SOLVE : $x = z$
such that $I_F : x \land \text{Primitive} : x \Rightarrow O_F : \langle x, z \rangle$
where DIRECTLY_SOLVE : $D_F \to R_F$.

Example. Instantiating the generic specification with the parts of the SORT specification and the control predicate from step (3) we obtain

DIRECTLY_SOLVE : $x = z$
such that Length : $x \leq 1$
$\Rightarrow$ Bag : $x =$ Bag : $x \land$ Ordered : z
where DIRECTLY_SOLVE : LIST(N) $\to$ LIST(N) .

The identity operator Id is easily shown to satisfy this specification using the strategy OPERATOR_MATCH described in Section 5.1.

(DS1)(6) *Construct a new input condition.* If the synthesis process cannot construct an algorithm that satisfies the specification DIRECTLY_SOLVE then we need to revise the input condition I_F and redo some earlier steps. We postpone discussion of this possibility until it arises in Section 7.3.

(DS1)(7) *Assemble the divide-and-conquer algorithm.* The operators derived in previous steps are instantiated in the divide-and-conquer scheme and then the algorithm and the current input condition I_F are returned as the results of applying the design strategy.

Example. The final form of the mergesort algorithm is

Msort : $x \equiv$ **if**
   Length : $x \leq 1 \to$ Id : x $\square$
   Length : $x > 1 \to$ Merge $\circ$ (Msort) $\circ$ Listsplit : x
fi .

The derived input condition on Msort is *true*. At this point we would apply various program transformations to obtain simpler and more efficient code.

7.2. Design strategy DS2 and the synthesis of a merge operator

In this section we describe design strategy DS2 in terms of a generic specification $\Pi_F = \langle D_F, R_F, I_F, O_F \rangle$ and apply it to the COMPOSE problem (here renamed MERGE) derived in the previous section:

MERGE : $\langle x_0, x_0' \rangle = z_0$
such that Ordered : $x_0 \land$ Ordered x_0'
$\Rightarrow$ Union : $\langle$Bag : x_0, Bag : $x_0' \rangle =$ Bag : $z_0 \land$ Ordered : z_0
where MERGE : LIST(N) $\times$ LIST(N) $\to$ LIST(N) .

Design strategy DS2 stems from the construction of a simple composition operator on the output domain.
(DS2)(1) *Construct a simple composition operator.* Intuitively, a composition operator is capable of generating the whole of its output domain by repeated application to some primitive objects, previously generated objects, and perhaps objects from an auxiliary set. It is assumed that standard composition operators are known for various common data types. If no standard composition operator is available for Π_F then a structure of simple conditional is constructed, as described in Section 5.2.

Example. The output domain of MERGE, LIST(N), has several standard composition operators: Cons and Append. If we choose Cons then the form of our target algorithm becomes

Merge : $\langle x_0, x_0' \rangle \equiv$
if
   Primitive : $\langle x_0, x_0' \rangle \to Directly\_Solve : \langle x_0, x_0' \rangle$ $\square$
   $\neg$ Primitive : $\langle x_0, x_0' \rangle \to$ Cons $\circ (G \times$ Merge$) \circ Decompose : \langle x_0, x_0' \rangle$
fi

where it remains to determine specifications for G, *Decompose*, and *Directly_Solve*.

(DS2)(2) *Construct the auxiliary function.* The choice of composition operator determines the output domain R_G of G. Again it is sufficient to let G be F if R_G is R_F and let G be the identity function Id otherwise, although other alternatives are possible. Let Π_G denote the specification of G.

Example. Since the output domain of the auxiliary operator G is **N** which differs from the output domain of F (LIST(N)) we simply choose the identity function Id for G.

(DS2)(3) *Construct a well-founded ordering on the input domain.*

Example. Our input domain is LIST(N) $\times$ LIST(N) on which we can construct the well-founded ordering defined by

$$\langle x_0, x_0' \rangle > \langle x_1, x_1' \rangle$$
iff Length × Length : $\langle x_0, x_0' \rangle >_2$ Length × Length : $\langle x_1, x_1' \rangle$
where $\langle a, b \rangle >_2 \langle c, d \rangle$ iff $a > c$ or $(a = c \wedge b > d)$.

(DS2)(4) *Construct the decomposition operator.* First, an output condition for the decomposition operator is found by deriving a $\{x_0, x_1, x_2\}$-antecedent of

$$O_G : \langle x_1, z_1 \rangle \wedge O_F : \langle x_2, z_2 \rangle \wedge$$
$$O_{Compose} : \langle z_0, z_1, z_2 \rangle \Rightarrow O_F : \langle x_0, z_0 \rangle.$$

Again, this formula is just the Strong Problem Reduction Principle with the antecedent $O_{Decompose} : \langle x_0, x_1, x_2 \rangle$ missing. The derived antecedent is used in forming the specification

$$\text{DECOMPOSE} : x_0 = \langle x_1, x_2 \rangle$$
such that $I_F : x_0 \Rightarrow I_G : x_1 \wedge I_F : x_2 \wedge x_0 > x_2 \wedge O_{Decompose} : \langle x_0, x_1, x_2 \rangle$
where DECOMPOSE : $D_F \rightarrow D_G \times D_F.$

If the auxiliary operator G is F then the formula $x_0 > x_1$ must be added to the output condition. Let Decompose be a program satisfying DECOMPOSE with derived input condition — *Primitive*.

Example. Before proceeding we name the intermediate data values in the Merge algorithm as in the following diagram:

```
                        Merge
        ⟨x₀, x₀'⟩ ─────────────────→ z₀
             │                        ↑
   Decompose │                        │ Cons
             ↓      Id × Merge        │
    ⟨a, ⟨x₁, x₁'⟩⟩ ───────────→ ⟨b, z₁⟩
```

To obtain output conditions for the decomposition operator we derive a $\{x_0, x_0', a, x_1, x_1'\}$-antecedent of

$$a = b \wedge$$
Union : $\langle$Bag : x_1, Bag : $x_1' \rangle$ = Bag : $z_1 \wedge$ Ordered : $z_1 \wedge$
Cons : $\langle b, z_1 \rangle = z_0$
$\Rightarrow$ Union : $\langle$Bag : x_0, Bag $x_0' \rangle$ = Bag : $z_0 \wedge$ Ordered : z_0.

The derivation in Fig. 5 yields the antecedent

Hypotheses h1. $b = a$
h2. Bag : z_1 = Union : $\langle$Bag : x_1, Bag : $x_1' \rangle$
h3. Ordered : z_1
h4. z_0 = Cons : $\langle b, z_1 \rangle$

Variables: $\{x_0, x_0', a, x_1, x_1'\}$

Goal 1: $\langle Q \rangle$ Union : $\langle$Bag : x_0, Bag : $x_0' \rangle$ = Bag : z_0
|R1 + h4
$\langle Q \rangle$ Union : $\langle$Bag : x_0, Bag : $x_0' \rangle$ = Bag : Cons : $\langle b, z_1 \rangle$
|R1 + L1
$\langle Q \rangle$ Union : $\langle$Bag : x_0, Bag : $x_0' \rangle$ = Add : $\langle b$, Bag : $z_1 \rangle$
|R1 + h1, R1 + h2
$\langle Q \rangle$ Union : $\langle$Bag : x_0, Bag : $x_0' \rangle$ = Add : $\langle a$, Union : $\langle$Bag : x_1, Bag : $x_1' \rangle \rangle$
P1
where Q is
Union : $\langle$Bag : x_0, Bag : $x_0' \rangle$ = Add : $\langle a$, Union : $\langle$Bag : x_1, Bag : $x_1' \rangle \rangle$

Goal 2: $\langle Q \rangle$ Ordered : z_0
|R1 + h4
$\langle Q \rangle$ Ordered : Cons : $\langle a, z_1 \rangle$
|R1 + L2, R2

$\langle Q \rangle$ $a \le$ Bag : z_1 $\langle true \rangle$ Ordered : z_1
|R1 + h2 |R1 + h3
$\langle Q \rangle$ $a \le$ Union : $\langle$Bag : $x_1' \rangle$ $\langle true \rangle$ *true*
R1 + B2, R2   P1

$\langle a \le$ Bag : $x_1 \rangle$ $a \le$ Bag : x_1 $(a \le$ Bag : $x_1' \rangle$ $a \le$ Bag : x_1'
P1   P1
where Q is $a \le$ Bag : $x_1 \wedge a \le$ Bag : x_1'

FIG. 5. Deriving an output condition for the decomposition operator in Merge.

Union : $\langle$Bag : x_0, Bag : $x_0' \rangle$ = Add : $\langle a$, Union : $\langle$Bag : x_1, Bag : $x_1' \rangle \rangle \wedge$
$a \le$ Bag : $x_1 \wedge a \le$ Bag : x_1'.

Instantiating the generic specification for DECOMPOSE above with the input domains, output domains, and output conditions of Cons, Id, and MERGE yields

MERGE_DECOMPOSE : $\langle x_0, x_0' \rangle = \langle a, \langle x_1, x_1' \rangle \rangle$
such that Ordered : $x_0 \wedge$ Ordered : x_0'
$\Rightarrow$ Ordered : $x_1 \wedge$ Ordered : $x_1' \wedge$
Length × Length : $\langle x_0, x_0' \rangle >_2$ Length × Length : $\langle x_1, x_1' \rangle \wedge$
Union : $\langle$Bag : x_0, Bag : $x_0' \rangle$ = Add : $\langle a$, Union : $\langle$Bag : x_1, Bag : $x_1' \rangle \rangle \wedge$
$a \le$ Bag : $x_1 \wedge a \le$ Bag : x_1'
where MERGE_DECOMPOSE : LIST(N) × LIST(N)
$\rightarrow$ N × (LIST(N) × LIST(N)) .

This specifies the problem of extracting the smallest element from two ordered lists and returning it with the remainder of the lists. The following simple conditional program can be derived using the COND strategy described in Section 5.2.

$$\text{Merge\_Decompose}: \langle x, x' \rangle \equiv$$
$$\textbf{if}$$
$$\quad \text{First}: x \leqslant \text{First}: x' \to \langle \text{First}: x, \langle \text{Rest}: x, x' \rangle \rangle \quad \square$$
$$\quad \text{First}: x' \leqslant \text{First}: x \to \langle \text{First}: x', \langle x, \text{Rest}: x' \rangle \rangle$$
$$\textbf{fi}$$

The derived input condition is $x_0 \neq$ nil $\land x_0' \neq$ nil. The control predicate in Merge can now be taken to be $x_0 =$ nil $\lor x_0' =$ nil.

(DS2)(5) Construct the primitive operator. As in design strategy DS1, the primitive operator has generic specification

$$\text{DIRECTLY\_SOLVE}: x = z$$
$$\text{such that } I_F : x \land \text{Primitive}: x$$
$$\to O_F : \langle x, z \rangle$$
$$\text{where DIRECTLY\_SOLVE}: D_F \to R_F.$$

Example. Instantiating the generic specification we obtain

$$\text{DIRECTLY\_SOLVE}: \langle x_0, x_0' \rangle = z_0$$
$$\text{such that Ordered}: x_0 \land \text{Ordered}: x_0' \land (x_0 = \text{nil} \lor x_0' = \text{nil})$$
$$\text{where DIRECTLY\_SOLVE}: \text{LIST(N)} \times \text{LIST(N)} \to \text{LIST(N)}.$$

The conditional function

$$\textbf{if } x_0 = \text{nil} \to x_0' \quad \square \quad x_0' = \text{nil} \to x_0 \textbf{ fi}$$

satisfies DIRECTLY_SOLVE and is easily synthesized. The strategy used by CYPRESS is described in [27] and is applicable when the input condition of a specification II involves a disjunction. II is split into several subspecifications, each the same as II except that one of the disjuncts replaces the disjunction in the input condition. The algorithms and derived input conditions synthesized for these subspecifications are used to create the branches of a conditional program.

(DS2)(6) *Create new input conditions.* This step is unnecessary in the current derivation. Discussion is postponed until Section 7.3.
(DS2)(7) *Assemble the divide-and-conquer algorithm.*

Example. The operators derived above are instantiated into the divide-and-conquer scheme yielding the algorithm

$$\text{Merge}: \langle x, x' \rangle \equiv$$
$$\textbf{if}$$
$$\quad x = \text{nil} \lor x' = \text{nil} \to \textbf{if } x = \text{nil} \to x' \quad \square \quad x' = \text{nil} \to x \textbf{ fi} \quad \square$$
$$\quad x \neq \text{nil} \land x' \neq \text{nil} \to \text{Cons} \circ (\text{Id} \times \text{Merge}) \circ \text{Merge\_Decompose}: \langle x, x' \rangle$$
$$\textbf{fi}$$

with derived input condition *true*. This version of Merge can be transformed into the simpler form

$$\text{Merge}: \langle x, x' \rangle \equiv$$
$$\textbf{if}$$
$$\quad x = \text{nil} \to x' \quad \square$$
$$\quad x' = \text{nil} \to x \quad \square$$
$$\quad x \neq \text{nil} \land x' \neq \text{nil} \to \text{Cons} \circ (\text{Id} \times \text{Merge}) \circ \text{Merge\_Decompose}: \langle x, x' \rangle$$
$$\textbf{fi} .$$

The complete mergesort program is given in Fig. 6.

7.3. Synthesis from incomplete specifications

For various reasons a specification may be partial in the sense that the input condition does not completely characterize the conditions under which the

$$\text{Msort}: x \equiv$$
$$\textbf{if}$$
$$\quad \text{Length}: x \leqslant 1 \to \text{Id}: x | \quad \square$$
$$\quad \text{Length}: x > 1 \to \text{Merge} \circ (\text{Msort} \times \text{Msort}) \circ \text{Listsplit}: x$$
$$\textbf{fi} .$$

$$\text{Merge}: \langle x, x' \rangle \equiv$$
$$\textbf{if}$$
$$\quad x = \text{nil} \to x' \quad \square$$
$$\quad x' = \text{nil} \to x \quad \square$$
$$\quad x \neq \text{nil} \land x' \neq \text{nil} \to \text{Cons} \circ (\text{Id} \times \text{Merge}) \circ \text{Merge\_Decompose}: \langle x, x' \rangle$$
$$\textbf{fi}$$

$$\text{Merge\_Decompose}: \langle x, x' \rangle \equiv$$
$$\textbf{if}$$
$$\quad \text{First}: x \leqslant \text{First}: x' \to \langle \text{First}: x, \langle \text{Rest}: x, x' \rangle \rangle \quad \square$$
$$\quad \text{First}: x' \leqslant \text{First}: x \to \langle \text{First}: x', \langle x, \text{Rest}: x' \rangle \rangle$$
$$\textbf{fi}$$

FIG. 6. Complete mergesort algorithm.

output condition can be achieved. In this section we show how this possibility can arise during the synthesis process and how a completed specification plus algorithm can be derived from a partial specification. Another purpose of this section is to show how a different factorization of the SORT problem into subproblems can be achieved.

7.3.1. Synthesis of a quicksort algorithm

Consider again the specification for the SORT problem

$$\text{SORT}: x = z \text{ such that Bag}: x = \text{Bag}: z \land \text{Ordered}: z$$
$$\text{where SORT}: \text{LIST(N)} \rightarrow \text{LIST(N)}.$$

Suppose that we apply design strategy DS2 to SORT. If Cons is chosen as a simple composition operator a selection sort algorithm will result [25, 27]. The choice of Append results in a quicksort algorithm, called Qsort, as follows. The auxiliary operator is Qsort because both inputs to Append are lists. In order to obtain an output condition for the decomposition operator we seek a $\{x_0, a, x_1\}$-antecedent of

$$\text{Bag}: x_1 = \text{Bag}: z_1 \land \text{Ordered}: z_1 \land$$
$$\text{Bag}: x_2 = \text{Bag}: x_2 \land \text{Ordered}: z_2 \land$$
$$\text{Append}: \langle z_1, z_2 \rangle = z_0$$
$$\Rightarrow \text{Bag}: x_0 = \text{Bag}: z_0 \land \text{Ordered}: z_0.$$

In Fig. 7 the antecedent

$$\text{Bag}: x_1 \leq \text{Bag}: x_2 \land \text{Bag}: x_0 = \text{Union}: \langle \text{Bag}: x_1, \text{Bag}: x_2 \rangle$$

is derived. Using this antecedent a specification for the decomposition operator is set up:

$$\text{DECOMPOSE}: x_0 = \langle x_1, x_2 \rangle$$
$$\text{such that Length}: x_0 > \text{Length}: x_1 \land$$
$$\text{Length}: x_0 > \text{Length}: x_2 \land$$
$$\text{Bag}: x_1 \leq \text{Bag}: x_2 \land \text{Bag}: x_0 = \text{Union}: \langle \text{Bag}: x_1, \text{Bag}: x_2 \rangle$$
$$\text{where DECOMPOSE}: \text{LIST(N)} \rightarrow \text{LIST(N)} \times \text{LIST(N)}.$$

In Section 7.3.2 we derive a program, called Partition, which satisfies this specification with derived input condition $x_0 \neq \text{nil} \land \text{Rest}: x_0 \neq \text{nil}$. Setting up a specification for the primitive operator we obtain

$$\text{DIRECTLY\_SOLVE}: x_0 = z_0$$
$$\text{such that Length}: x_0 \leq 1$$
$$\Rightarrow \text{Bag}: x_0 = \text{Bag}: z_0 \land \text{Ordered}: z_0$$
$$\text{where DIRECTLY\_SOLVE}: \text{LIST(N)} \rightarrow \text{LIST(N)}.$$

which is satisfied by the identity operator. Finally, putting together all of the operators derived above, we obtain the following quicksort program:

$$\text{Qsort}: x \equiv$$
$$\textbf{if}$$
$$x_0 = \text{nil} \lor \text{Rest}: x_0 = \text{nil} \rightarrow \text{Id}: x \quad \square$$
$$x_0 \neq \text{nil} \land \text{Rest}: x_0 \neq \text{nil} \rightarrow \text{Append} \circ (\text{Qsort} \times \text{Qsort}) \circ \text{Partition}: x.$$
$$\textbf{fi}.$$

The derived input condition on Qsort is *true*.

7.3.2. Synthesis of Partition

In the previous section we set up the specification

$$\begin{aligned}
\text{Hypotheses}: \quad & \text{h1. Bag}: z_1 = \text{Bag}: x_1 \\
& \text{h2. Ordered}: z_1 \\
& \text{h3. Bag}: x_2 = \text{Bag}: x_2 \\
& \text{h4. Ordered}: z_2 \\
& \text{h5. } z_0 = \text{Append}: \langle z_1, z_2 \rangle
\end{aligned}$$

$$\text{Variables}: \quad \langle x_2, x_1, x_2 \rangle$$

$$\begin{aligned}
\text{Goal 1}: \quad & \langle Q1 \rangle \text{ Bag}: x_0 = \text{Bag}: z_0 \\
& \qquad |\text{R1} + \text{h5} \\
& \langle Q1 \rangle \text{ Bag}: x_0 = \text{Bag}: \text{Append}: \langle z_1, z_2 \rangle \\
& \qquad |\text{R1} + \text{L5} \\
& \langle Q1 \rangle \text{ Bag}: x_0 = \text{Union}: \langle \text{Bag}: z_1, \text{Bag}: z_2 \rangle \\
& \qquad |\text{R1} + \text{h1, R1} + \text{h3} \\
& \langle Q1 \rangle \text{ Bag}: x_0 = \text{Union}: \langle \text{Bag}: x_1, \text{Bag}: x_2 \rangle \\
& \qquad \text{P1} \\
& \text{where } Q1 \text{ is Bag}: x_0 = \text{Union}: \langle \text{Bag}: x_1, \text{Bag}: x_2 \rangle
\end{aligned}$$

$$\begin{aligned}
\text{Goal 2}: \quad & \langle Q2 \rangle \text{ Ordered}: z_0 \\
& \qquad |\text{R1} + \text{h5} \\
& \langle Q2 \rangle \text{ Ordered}: \text{Append}: \langle z_1, z_2 \rangle \\
& \qquad \text{R1} + \text{L6, R2}
\end{aligned}$$

$$\begin{array}{lll}
\langle \textit{true} \rangle \text{ Ordered}: z_1 & \langle Q2 \rangle \text{ Bag}: z_1 \leq \text{Bag}: z_2 & \langle \textit{true} \rangle \text{ Ordered}: z_2 \\
\qquad |\text{R1} + \text{h2} & \qquad |\text{R1} + \text{h1, R1} + \text{h3} & \qquad |\text{R1} + \text{h4} \\
\langle \textit{true} \rangle \text{ } \textit{true} & \langle Q2 \rangle \text{ Bag}: x_1 \leq \text{Bag}: x_2 & \langle \textit{true} \rangle \text{ } \textit{true} \\
\qquad \text{P1} & \qquad \text{P1} & \qquad \text{P1}
\end{array}$$

$$\text{where } Q2 \text{ is Bag}: x_1 \leq \text{Bag}: x_2$$

FIG. 7. Derivation of an output condition for the decomposition operator of Qsort.

PARTITION: $x_0 = \langle x_1, x_2 \rangle$
such that Length: $x_0 >$ Length: $x_1 \wedge$
Length: $x_0 >$ Length: $x_2 \wedge$
Bag: $x_1 \leq$ Bag: $x_2 \wedge$ Bag: $x_0 =$ Union: $\langle$Bag: x_1, Bag: $x_2\rangle$
where PARTITION: LIST(N) → LIST(N) × LIST(N)

which has been renamed PARTITION. This specifies the problem of partitioning a list of numbers into two shorter sublists such that each element of the first sublist is less than or equal to each element of the second sublist. Note that for inputs of length zero or one the problem has no feasible output. The synthesis process will in effect analyze the problem and construct an algorithm, called Partition, that satisfies PARTITION with derived input condition $x_0 \neq$ nil $\wedge$ Rest: $x_0 \neq$ nil. We will derive a divide-and-conquer algorithm that is different from the usual partition algorithm. Intuitively, it works on input list x by recursively partitioning the Rest of x, then adding the First of x to the appropriate sublist. It is an unusual partitioning algorithm in that it does not make use of a partitioning element. A partitioning element can however be discovered as an optimizing refinement after the algorithm has been synthesized. The synthesis of Partition is based on design strategy DS1 and proceeds as follows.

(DS1)(1–2). *Construct a simple decomposition operator, well-founded ordering, and auxiliary operator.* The input type is LIST(N) and we choose the decomposition operator FirstRest. Again we choose the well-founded ordering used in Qsort. Let the auxiliary operator be Id since the input domain of G(N) differs from the input domain of Partition. The choice of FirstRest as decomposition operator means that we intend to construct a divide-and-conquer algorithm of the form

Partition: $x \equiv$
if
    Primitive: $x \to$ *Directly_Solve*: x ☐
    — *Primitive*: $x \to$ *Compose* ∘ (Id × Partition) ∘ FirstRest: x
fi.

(DS1)(3) *Verify the decomposition operator.* Using Theorem 5.1 it can be shown that FirstRest satisfies the specification

DECOMPOSE: $x_0 = \langle a, x_1 \rangle$
such that Length: $x_0 >$ Length: x_1
where DECOMPOSE: LIST(N) → N × LIST(N)

with derived input condition $x_0 \neq$ nil.

(DS1)(4) *Construct the composition operator.* Before proceeding we name the intermediate data values in the Partition algorithm as in the following diagram:

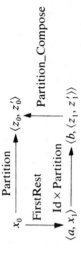

An output condition for the composition operator is obtained by deriving an $\{b, z_1, z_1', z_0, z_0'\}$-antecedent of

FirstRest: $x_0 = \langle a, x_1 \rangle \wedge$
$a = b \wedge$
Bag: $z_1 \leq$ Bag: $z_1' \wedge$ Bag: $x_1 =$ Union: $\langle$Bag: z_1, Bag: $z_1'\rangle \wedge$
Length: $x_1 >$ Length: $z_1 \wedge x_1 >$ Length: z_1'
$\Rightarrow$ Bag: $z_0 \leq$ Bag: $z_0' \wedge$ Bag: $x_0 =$ Union: $\langle$Bag: z_0, Bag: $z_0'\rangle \wedge$
Length: $x_0 >$ Length: $z_0 \wedge$ Length: $x_0 >$ Length: z_0'

The following antecedent is derived in Figs. 8(a) and 8(b):

Hypotheses: h1. FirstRest: $x_0 = \langle a, x_1 \rangle$
h2. $a = b$
h3. Bag: $z_1 \leq$ Bag: z_1'
h4. Bag: $x_1 =$ Union: $\langle$Bag: z_1, Bag: $z_1'\rangle$
h5. Length: $x_1 >$ Length: z_1
h6. Length: $x_1 >$ Length: z_1'

Variables: $\{b, z_1, z_1', z_0, z_0'\}$

Goal 1: $\langle Q1 \rangle$ Bag: $z_0 \leq$ Bag: z_0'
    P1
where $Q1$ is Bag: $z_1 \leq$ Bag: $z_1' \Rightarrow$ Bag: $z_0 \leq$ Bag: z_0'

Goal 2: $\langle Q2 \rangle$ Bag: $x_0 =$ Union: $\langle$Bag: z_0, Bag: $z_0'\rangle$
    |R1 + L4 + h1
$\langle Q2 \rangle$ Bag: Cons: $\langle a, x_1 \rangle =$ Union: $\langle$Bag: z_0, Bag: $z_0'\rangle$
    |R1 + L1
$\langle Q2 \rangle$ Add: $\langle a,$ Bag: $x_1 \rangle =$ Union: $\langle$Bag: z_0, Bag: $z_0'\rangle$
    |R1 + h4
$\langle Q2 \rangle$ Add: $\langle b,$ Union: $\langle$Bag: z_1, Bag: $z_1'\rangle\rangle =$ Union: $\langle$Bag: z_0, Bag: $z_0'\rangle$
    P1
where $Q2$ is
Bag: $z_1 \leq$ Bag: z_1'
$\Rightarrow$ Add: $\langle b,$ Union: $\langle$Bag: z_1, Bag: $z_1'\rangle\rangle =$ Union: $\langle$Bag: z_0, Bag: $z_0'\rangle$

FIG. 8(a). Deriving an output condition for the composition operator in Partition.

Goal 3: $\langle Q3 \rangle$ Length : x_0 > Length : z_0

$\qquad$ |R1 + L4 + h1

$\qquad \langle Q3 \rangle$ Length : Cons : $\langle a\ x_1 \rangle$ > Length : z_0

$\qquad$ |R1 + L3

$\qquad \langle Q3 \rangle$ 1 + Length : x_1 > Length : z_0

$\qquad$ |R1 + L8 + h4

$\qquad \langle Q3 \rangle$ 1 + Card ∘ Union : $\langle \text{Bag} : z_1, \text{Bag} : z'_1 \rangle$ > Length : z_0

$\qquad$ |R1 + B3

$\qquad \langle Q3 \rangle$ 1 + Card ∘ Bag : z_1 + Card ∘ Bag : z'_1 > Length : z_0

$\qquad$ |R1 + L7

$\qquad \langle Q3 \rangle$ 1 + Length : z_1 + Length : z'_1 > Length : z_0

$\qquad$ P1

where $Q3$ is

Bag : $z_1 \leq$ Bag : $z'_1 \Rightarrow$ 1 + Length : z_1 + Length : z'_1 > Length : z_0

Goal 4: $\langle Q4 \rangle$ Length : x_0 > Length : z'_0

$\qquad$ (Derivation similar to that for Goal 3)

where $Q4$ is

Bag : $z_1 \leq$ Bag : $z'_1 \Rightarrow$ 1 + Length : z_1 + Length : z'_1 > Length : z'_0

FIG. 8(b). Deriving an output condition for the composition operator in Partition.

Bag : $z_0 \leq$ Bag : $z'_0 \wedge$

Add : $\langle b,$ Union : $\langle \text{Bag} : z_1, \text{Bag} : z'_1 \rangle \rangle =$ Union : $\langle \text{Bag} : z_0, \text{Bag} : z'_0 \rangle \wedge$

1 + Length : z_1 + Length : z'_1 > Length : $z_0 \wedge$

1 + Length : z_1 + Length : z'_1 > Length : z'_0.

It is then used in setting up the specification

PARTITION_COMPOSE : $\langle b, \langle z_1, z'_1 \rangle \rangle = \langle z_0, z'_0 \rangle$

such that Bag : $z_1 \leq$ Bag : z'_1

$\Rightarrow$ Bag : $z_0 \leq$ Bag : $z'_0 \wedge$

Add : $\langle b,$ Union : $\langle \text{Bag} : z, \text{Bag} : z_2 \rangle \rangle =$ Union : $\langle \text{Bag} : z_0, \text{Bag} : z'_0 \rangle \wedge$

1 + Length : z_1 + Length : z'_1 > Length : $z_0 \wedge$

1 + Length : z_1 + Length : z'_1 > Length : z'_0

where PARTITION_COMPOSE : $N \times (\text{LIST}(N) \times \text{LIST}(N)) \to \text{LIST}(N) \times \text{LIST}(N)$.

In Section 5.2 we showed how design strategy COND constructs a conditional program called Partition_Compose that satisfies this specification:

Partition_Compose : $\langle b, \langle z, z' \rangle \rangle \equiv$

if $b \leq$ Bag : $z' \to \langle \text{Cons} : \langle b, z \rangle, z' \rangle$ $\square$

$\quad b \geq$ Bag : $z \to \langle z,$ Cons : $b, z' \rangle \rangle$

fi .

(DS1)(5) *Construct the primitive operator.* The specification of the primitive operator is

DIRECTLY_SOLVE : $x = \langle z, z' \rangle$

such that $x = $ nil $\not\to$ Bag : $z_1 \leq$ Bag : $z'_1 \wedge$

Bag : $x = $ Union : $\langle \text{Bag} : z, \text{Bag} : z' \rangle \wedge$

Length : $x > $ Length : $z \wedge$ Length : $x > $ Length : z'

where DIRECTLY_SOLVE : LIST(N) → LIST(N) × LIST(N)

which is unsatisfiable. The derived input condition is set to *false.*

(DS1)(6) *Construction of a new input condition.* We may need to revise the input condition for either or both of the following reasons:

(1) if Primitive : x is undefined for some legal input x then the program we are constructing will also be undefined on x;

(2) if the derived input condition I'_{DS} on Directly_Solve is not *true* then there are legal inputs x satisfying

$$I_F : x \wedge \text{Primitive} : x \wedge \neg I'_{DS} : x$$

for which we are unable to compute a feasible output. It is necessary then to revise the input condition I_F and go back and rederive the operators Decompose, Compose, and Directly_Solve. The new input condition is obtained by noting that the synthesis process to this point suggests that feasible solutions exist for inputs satisfying

$$I_F : x \wedge \neg\, \text{Primitive} : x$$

using the **else** branch of the divide-and-conquer algorithm. Furthermore, the previous step assures us that feasible solutions exist for inputs satisfying

$$I_F : x \wedge \text{Primitive} : x \wedge I'_{DS} : x.$$

Consequently, the formula

$$(I_F : x \wedge \neg\text{Primitive} : x) \vee (I_F : x \wedge \text{Primitive} : x \wedge I'_{DS} : x) \qquad (7.1)$$

approximately describes the set of inputs which we know to have feasible outputs in problem Π. We simplify (7.1) and if it differs from I_F then we take it as the new input condition and return to step 4.

Example. In the previous step the specification DIRECTLY_SOLVE proved unsatisfiable. In other words an operator could only satisfy DIRECTLY_

SOLVE with derived input condition *false*. We revise the input condition I_F by letting I'_{DS} be *false* and instantiate (7.1) yielding

$$(true \wedge \neg(x_0 = \text{nil})) \vee (true \wedge x_0 = \text{nil} \wedge false)$$

which simplifies to $x_0 \neq \text{nil}$. In effect we exclude nil as a legal input to Partition and return to an earlier stage in the synthesis and rederive Decompose, Compose, and Directly_Solve. In the following we retrace some of the previous steps.

(DS1)(3') *Verify the decomposition operator.* The input condition $I_F : x_0$ is redefined to be $x_0 \neq \text{nil}$. Thus we need to verify that FirstRest satisfies the specification

$$\text{DECOMPOSE} : x_0 = \langle a, x_1 \rangle$$
such that $x_0 \neq \text{nil} \Rightarrow \text{Length} : x_0 > \text{Length} : x_1 \wedge x_1 \neq \text{nil}$
where $\text{DECOMPOSE} : \text{LIST}(\mathbf{N}) \rightarrow \mathbf{N} \times \text{LIST}(\mathbf{N})$.

which it does with derived input condition $\text{Rest} : x_0 \neq \text{nil}$.

(DS1)(4') *Construct the composition operator.* This step does not involve the input condition so the composition operator need not be rederived.

(DS1)(5') *Construct the primitive operator.* The new specification for the primitive operator is

$$\text{DIRECTLY\_SOLVE} : x_0 = \langle z, z' \rangle$$
such that $\text{Rest} : x = \text{nil} \Rightarrow \text{Bag} : z_1 \leq \text{Bag} : z'_1 \wedge$
$\text{Bag} : x = \text{Union} : \langle \text{Bag} : z, \text{Bag} : z' \rangle \wedge$
$\text{Length} : x > \text{Length} : z \wedge \text{Length} : x > \text{Length} : z'$
where $\text{DIRECTLY\_SOLVE} : \text{LIST}(\mathbf{N}) \rightarrow \text{LIST}(\mathbf{N}) \times \text{LIST}(\mathbf{N})$

and again this is unsatisfiable. Thus we will need to find a new input condition and return to Step 4.

(DS1)(6') *Derive a new input condition.* The new input condition is found by simplifying

$$(x \neq \text{nil} \wedge \text{Rest} : x \neq \text{nil}) \vee (x \neq \text{nil} \wedge \text{Rest} : x = \text{nil} \wedge false)$$

to $x \neq \text{nil} \wedge \text{Rest} : x \neq \text{nil}$. We return again to Step 4, letting the current input condition be $x \neq \text{nil} \wedge \text{Rest} : x \neq \text{nil}$.

(DS1)(3'') *Verify the decomposition operator.* The new specification for DECOMPOSE is

$$\text{DECOMPOSE} : x_0 = \langle a, x_1 \rangle$$
such that $x_0 \neq \text{nil} \wedge \text{Rest} : x_0 \neq \text{nil}$
$\Rightarrow x_1 \neq \text{nil} \wedge \text{Rest} : x_1 \neq \text{nil} \wedge \text{Length} : x_0 > \text{Length} : x_1$
where $\text{DECOMPOSE} : \text{LIST}(\mathbf{N}) \rightarrow \text{LIST}(\mathbf{N}) \times \text{LIST}(\mathbf{N})$.

FirstRest satisfies this specification with derived input condition $\text{Rest} \circ \text{Rest} : x_0 \neq \text{nil}$.

(DS1)(4'') *Construct the composition operator.* Again the previously derived composition operator is still valid, so this step is skipped.

(DS1)(5'') *Construct the primitive operator.* The primitive operator has specification

$$\text{DIRECTLY\_SOLVE} : x = \langle z, z' \rangle$$
such that $\text{Rest} \circ \text{Rest} : x = \text{nil} \Rightarrow \text{Bag} : z \leq \text{Bag} : z' \wedge$
$\text{Bag} : x = \text{Union} : \langle \text{Bag} : z, \text{Bag} : z' \rangle \wedge$
$\text{Length} : x > \text{Length} : z \wedge \text{Length} : x > \text{Length} : z'$
where $\text{DIRECTLY\_SOLVE} : \text{LIST}(\mathbf{N}) \rightarrow \text{LIST}(\mathbf{N}) \times \text{LIST}(\mathbf{N})$. $\square$

A simple conditional program can be constructed to satisfy this specification:

$$\text{Partition\_Directly\_Solve} : x \equiv$$
if
$\qquad \text{First} : x \leq \text{First} \circ \text{Rest} : x$
$\qquad \rightarrow \langle \text{List} \circ \text{First} : x, \text{List} \circ \text{First} \circ \text{Rest} : x \rangle$
$\qquad \text{First} : x \geq \text{First} \circ \text{Rest} : x$
$\qquad \rightarrow \langle \text{List} \circ \text{First} \circ \text{Rest} : x, \text{List} \circ \text{First} : x \rangle$
fi .

CYPRESS has a design strategy for forming conditional algorithms when the inputs can be characterized as small explicit structures. For example, here the strategy would rewrite the input condition as

$$x = \text{List} : \langle \text{First} : x, \text{First} \circ \text{Rest} : x \rangle .$$

Then the constraint $\text{Bag} : x = \text{Union} : \langle \text{Bag} : z, \text{Bag} : z' \rangle$ is used to form several alternate expressions for the output variables z and z'. Each such expression is matched against the given specification and the derived input condition is used to guard the execution of the expression in a conditional (unless the derived input condition is *false*). If the derived input conditions on all expressions are *false* then the problem is unsatisfiable. This strategy was used to determine that DIRECTLY_SOLVE was unsatisfiable in earlier Steps (5 and 5').

(DS1)(6'') *Construct a new input condition.* Since an operator was constructed that satisfies DIRECTLY_SOLVE we can bypass this step.

(DS1)(7'') *Assembly of the divide-and-conquer program.* Putting together all of the operators derived above we obtain

$$\text{Partition} : x \equiv$$
if
$\qquad \text{Rest} \circ \text{Rest} : x = \text{nil} \rightarrow \text{Partition\_Directly\_Solve} : x \ \square$
$\qquad \text{Rest} \circ \text{Rest} : x \neq \text{nil}$
$\qquad \rightarrow \text{Partition\_Compose} \circ (\text{Id} \times \text{Partition}) \circ \text{FirstRest} : x .$
fi .

a scheme. In particular, the complexity of the divide-and-conquer program scheme can be expressed by a schematic recurrence relation. If design strategy DS1 is followed then the construction of a simple decomposition operator typically results in an operator requiring O(1) time. Also the primitive operator often requires only constant time. If furthermore the result of decomposition is two subproblems half the size of the input then the recurrence scheme simplifies to

$$T_{DC}(|x|) = O(1) \quad \text{if } Primitive : x$$
$$T_{DC}(|x|) = T_{Compose}(m, m) + 2T_{DS}(|x|/2) \text{ if } - Primitive : x,$$

where $|x|$ is the size of the input x, m is the size of the largest output possible from an input of size $|x|/2$, and T_H denotes the worst-case time complexity of algorithm H as a function of input size. For the SORT problem we use $|x| = Length : x$ and m is just $Length : x/2$. For Msort, the complexity of Merge is just the sum of the lengths of its inputs so the recurrence relation becomes

$$T_{Msort}(n) = O(1) \quad \text{if } n \leq 1$$
$$T_{Msort}(n) = n/2 + n/2 + 2T_{Msort}(n/2) \text{ if } n > 1$$

where $n = Length : x$. This has solution $T_{Msort}(n) = O(n \ln n)$.

CYPRESS could be extended to include complexity analysis as an integral part of its method. This would require extending each design strategy with a schematic complexity formula for its associated program scheme plus whatever operations are required to instantiate, simplify, and solve the resulting formulas. Each strategy would then return not only an algorithm plus derived input condition, but also a derived complexity analysis. One difficulty that arises is determining a suitable measurement of inputs. Some measurements will be standard, such as measuring lists by their length. Other measurements, such as m above, may require deep reasoning about a particular problem.

8.3. CYPRESS

CYPRESS is a semi-automatic implementation of the formalisms presented in this paper. It is semi-automatic in that the user supplies the key high-level decisions regarding the overall form of the target algorithm and CYPRESS carries out the formal manipulations. CYPRESS includes design strategies DS1 and DS2, several strategies for constructing conditional programs, and strategy OPERATOR_MATCH. DS1 and DS2 allow further user interaction in the choice of decomposition (resp. composition) operator and well-founded ordering. At each choice point CYPRESS first generates and presents a list of alternatives. The user is then allowed to choose from this list or to enter a new choice.

Qsort : x ≡
if
  x_0 = nil ∨ Rest : x_0 = nil → Id : x □
  x_0 ≠ nil ∧ Rest : x_0 ≠ nil → Append ∘ (Qsort × Qsort) ∘ Partition : x
fi

Partition : x ≡
if
  Rest ∘ Rest : x = nil → Partition_Directly_Solve : x □
  Rest ∘ Rest : x ≠ nil → Partition_Compose ∘ (Id × Partition) ∘ FirstRest : x .
fi

Partition_Compose : ⟨b, ⟨z, z'⟩⟩ ≡
if
  b ⩽ Bag : z' → ⟨Cons : ⟨b, z⟩, z'⟩ □
  b ⩾ Bag : z → ⟨z, Cons : ⟨b, z'⟩⟩
fi

Partition_Directly_Solve : x ≡
if
  First : x ⩽ First ∘ Rest : x → ⟨List ∘ First : x, List ∘ First ∘ Rest : x⟩ □
  First : x ⩾ First ∘ Rest : x → ⟨List ∘ First ∘ Rest : x, List ∘ First : x⟩
fi

FIG. 9. Complete quicksort algorithm.

The derived input condition on Partition is x ≠ nil ∧ Rest : x ≠ nil. The complete quicksort program synthesized in this section is listed in Fig. 9.

8. Concluding remarks

8.1. Correctness of the design strategies

The correctness of design strategies DS1 and DS2 follow from Theorem 6.1. For DS1, Steps 1 and 3 establish condition (1), Step 2 establishes condition (2), Step 4 establishes conditions (3) and (5), and Step 5 establishes condition (4) if the derived input condition on *Directly_Solve* is *true*. Once all five conditions of Theorem 6.1 are established it follows that the divide-and-conquer algorithm assembled in Step 7 satisfies the current specification. If the derived input condition on the primitive operator in Step 5 is not *true* then the design strategy enters a loop attempting to find an appropriate input condition for the given problem. As we have not investigated conditions under which the loop terminates, the design strategy DS1 can only be said to be partially correct. Analogous remarks hold for DS2.

8.2. Complexity analysis

An algorithm synthesized by means of a scheme can also be analyzed by means of

Running interpreted FRANZLISP on a VAX 11/750, synthesis times range from a few minutes for Min2 to ninety minutes for the complete quicksort algorithm. Almost all of this time is spent deriving antecedents so great payoff would result from speeding up the inference mechanism. RAINBOW was built more for conceptual clarity than efficiency. Consequently, it operates at the slow rate of about one inference per 5-10 seconds.

CYPRESS has been used to synthesize dozens of algorithms including the four sorting algorithms mentioned earlier and the top level of two convex hull algorithms (that is, a divide-and-conquer algorithm was created with specifications derived for the subalgorithms). Each of the sorting algorithms required the decomposition of the initial specification into a hierarchy of specifications that was four levels deep. While the user decided on which design strategies to apply, the derivation of each specification except the initial one was completely automatic. The main difficulty experienced in synthesizing these algorithms lay in formulating the abstract data types needed to state and reason about the problem and in formulating how various operators and relations interact. For example, just to state the problem of finding the convex hull of a finite set of planar points requires formulating abstract data types representing points, line segments, and convex polygons, and axiomatizing the relations convex_polygon_contains_point and convex_polygon_contains_point_set. For the problems we dealt with there was significant overlap between the data types and axiomatic knowledge built up for one problem and that required for related problems. For example, once we had built up CYPRESS' knowledge about lists and bags so that a sorting algorithm could be constructed it was easy to state and synthesize related problems such as MIN and (binary) search of an ordered list.

In order to gain more experience with the CYPRESS approach to program synthesis it will be necessary to develop and experiment with design strategies for many more classes of algorithms. Based on our current work the following methodology seems to be emerging regarding how to construct design strategies. First, a class of algorithms is defined and its common features abstracted into a program scheme. Second, a theorem relating the functionality of the whole to its form and the functionalities of its parts is developed. Finally, heuristic methods for proceduralizing the theorem are coded into a design strategy for the class.

8.4. Software development systems

CYPRESS has been used to explore a powerful class of tools useful in the design phase of the software lifecycle. As such CYPRESS forms just one component of a more comprehensive software engineering environment such as the proposed knowledge-based software assistant [18]. Below we critically examine the CYPRESS system with respect to how it might be integrated with and provide support to other aspects of the software development process.

It is clear that in practice there is not a clear separation between formulating specifications and designing algorithms [28]. These two activities are subsumed under the more general activity of problem understanding. Design strategies can be used to gain insight into the nature of the specified problem in several ways. We first discuss the insight gained when a design strategy succeeds and returns an algorithm plus derived input condition. We then discuss the insight gained when a design strategy fails for various reasons.

A problem specification is partial if there are legal inputs which have no feasible output. In other words, a specification is partial if the output condition is overconstrained. A derived input condition characterizes a class of inputs that either have no feasible outputs or for which the system cannot construct code to compute a feasible output. Consequently, when CYPRESS derives an input condition the user (or software development system) may wish to reexamine the specification to see if it really corresponds to his/her intentions. CYPRESS' ability to detect partial specifications depends however on clean termination of its design strategies.

A design strategy may fail on a particular problem for any of several reasons.

(1) Inapplicability of the program scheme. It may be that there is no natural way to instantiate a scheme for a particular problem. For example, during the synthesis of a mergesort-like convex-hull algorithm we were unable to develop (either with CYPRESS or by hand) a divide-and-conquer algorithm for the merge step. In a strict sense it can probably be shown that any arbitrary scheme S can be instantiated to obtain an algorithm satisfying an arbitrary solvable problem P. For example, any problem can be satisfied by an instance of the divide-and-conquer scheme by letting Primitive be true and letting Directly_Solve do all the work. However there is a more intuitive and natural sense of the notion of an instance of a scheme in which the problems corresponding to the scheme operators are of lesser complexity than that solved by the whole algorithm. In this sense it may be that no natural instance of the chosen program scheme solves a given problem.

For example, we will argue that there is probably no natural divide-and-conquer algorithm for the traveling salesman problem (TSP). All known algorithms for finding optimal solutions to the TSP run in $O(c^n)$ time for some constant c where n is the number of cities (TSP is NP-hard). One divide-and-conquer approach to TSP would seek to divide the n cities into two groups of $n/2$ cities, find optimal routes for each group, then compose the resulting routes. The recurrence relation for such an algorithm would be

$$T_{TSP}(n) = 2T_{TSP}(n/2) + T_{D+C}(n)$$

where $T_{D+C}(n)$ denotes the combined complexity of the decomposition and composition operators. If $T_{TSP}(n)$ is c^n then $T_{D+C}(n)$ is $c^n - 2c^{n/2}$. But this means that the subproblems of the algorithm have substantially the same complexity as TSP itself. Thus according to our informal definition, this would not be a natural divide-and-conquer algorithm. Other approaches have the same difficulty.

(2) *Incompleteness of the design strategy.* A design strategy will not in general be able to construct all instances of a scheme. So a given problem may be solvable by an instance of the scheme yet not by instances which a given design strategy can construct. If it is known that the scheme is applicable then failure of this kind suggests trying an alternate design strategy for the same scheme (e.g. DS2 vice DS1 for the divide-and-conquer scheme). If no other alternative design strategies are available then the specified problem may be of use to the system designer in devising a new design strategy or extending an old design strategy.

(3) *Poor choices.* Although a design strategy may be able to produce a solution to a given problem some choices in its application (e.g. the choice of decomposition operator in DS1) may lead to deadends. Failures of this kind suggest backing up and trying alternative choices.

(4) *Incomplete knowledge.* A design strategy can fail if there is not enough knowledge available concerning the problem domain. Ideally in such a case the system would be able to characterize the kind of knowledge which seems to be missing. Consider an example from this paper. Much of the data-structure knowledge used in our examples (see Appendix A) is either definitional or expresses how various operators and relations interact. If the transformation L5

$$\text{Bag} \circ \text{Append}: \langle y_1, y_2 \rangle \rightarrow \text{Bag}: y_1 \cup \text{Bag}: y_2$$

were not available then the derivation in Fig. 2 would fail at the subgoal

$$\text{Bag} \circ \text{Append}: \langle x_1, x_2 \rangle = \text{Bag}: z_0 .$$

An appropriate characterization of the difficulty would be that not enough is known about the interaction of the Bag and Append operators. Given such a characterization the user (or automated mathematical discovery system) might attempt to discover properties that fill the gap and then add them to the knowledge base.

(5) *Computational resource limitations.* If all the above difficulties are not present then failure can still occur because of limits on the amount of computational resource (e.g. time or space) that can be expended on the problem. For example, RAINBOW was occasionally unable to derive a good antecedent because of the default depth bound placed on its depth-first search. At the depth bound, RAINBOW returns the antecedent *false* if P1 is not applicable.

It is the difficulty in distinguishing these and knowing how to deal with them that suggests leaving the user in overall control of the synthesis process. The shape and direction of the synthesis process depends on the user's choices and the user's judgement of what a given failure signifies and what action to take in response.

CYPRESS was intended as an experiment in the use of schemes and design strategies to produce high-level well-structured algorithms. Our view is that the resulting algorithms will be subjected to transformation that refine their high-level constructs and introduce optimizations. For example, the sorting algorithms are expressed in terms of the abstract data type LIST(N). It would be consistent and useful to refine LISTs into arrays so that the Listsplit and Append operations can be executed in constant time. As an example of an optimizing transformation, the control predicate $\text{Length}: x \leq 1$ in Msort can be usefully specialized to $x = \text{nil} \vee \text{Rest}: x = \text{nil}$. As another example, the Partition algorithm derived in Section 7.3.2 is unnecessarily slow because the guards in Partition_Compose are computationally expensive. A way proceed is to maintain the assertion

$$\exists c \, [\text{Bag } z \leq c \wedge c \leq \text{Bag}: z']$$

throughout Partition. Either of the two numbers in the input to Partition_Directly_Solve can be used as a value for c. If the assertion can be maintained then Partition_Compose can be refined into the constant time algorithm

$$\text{Partition\_Compose}: \langle b, \langle z, z' \rangle \rangle \equiv$$
$$\textbf{if}$$
$$b \leq c \rightarrow \langle \text{Cons}: b, z \rangle, z' \rangle \quad \square$$
$$b \geq c \rightarrow \langle z, \text{Cons}: \langle b, z' \rangle \rangle$$
$$\textbf{fi} .$$

The variable c is just the usual partitioning element.

An issue we have only begun to look at is how CYPRESS could be extended to help with the problem of modifying and enhancing software. One major advantage of automated program synthesis is that any bugs in the synthesized program are traceable to either the system's knowledge or, more likely, to the initial specification. The software maintenance problem then involves modifying an old specification followed by resynthesizing code for it. Many of the synthesis decisions made for the modified specification will be the same or similar to decisions made for the old specification. The resynthesis process can be considerably shortened by using a summary of the old synthesis decisions for guidance. Such an approach could have a significant impact on the problem of modifying and enhancing software by allowing the user/programmer to maintain specifications (problem descriptions) rather than code.

8.5. Related work

A number of efforts have been made to systematize the derivation of algorithms from specifications. Perhaps the most basic is the theorem-proving approach [16, 21, 22]. Given a specification $\Pi = \langle D, R, I, O \rangle$, the theorem-proving approach seeks to extract a program F from a constructive proof of the theorem

$$\forall x \in D \; \exists z \in R[I : x \Rightarrow O : \langle x, z \rangle]. \qquad (8.1)$$

Theorem-proving techniques, more or less adapted to the special demands of program synthesis, are used to prove the theorem constructively. As explained earlier, CYPRESS is based on the slightly more general problem of extracting a program F from a constructive derivation of an $\{x\}$-antecedent of (8.1). The resulting antecedent is the derived input condition on F. The design strategies in CYPRESS can be viewed as complex special-purpose inference rules which actively seek out special structure in the specified problem in order to construct an instance of an algorithm scheme. By using larger 'chunks' of knowledge about programming and by using problem decomposition we hope to reduce the complexity of the theorem proving/program synthesis process, and enable the construction of larger well-structured programs.

Dershowitz and Manna [11] have also explored the formalization of top-down programming. They present several strategies for designing program sequences, if-then-else statements, and loops. In addition they exploit rules for transforming specifications into a stronger or equivalent form. Laaser [19] describes a system called RECBUILD that incorporates a strategy like DS1. RECBUILD was able to construct two sorting algorithms, a convex-hull algorithm, and several others. RECBUILD works by constructing various code fragments then deriving conditions under which they achieve the given output condition. Complementary code fragments are then composed to form a conditional. Follett [13] describes a system called PROSYN that produces nonapplicative algorithms, including an insertion-sort and a quicksort. PROSYN incorporates a strategy for inserting primitive operators into partially constructed programs and strategies for forming conditionals and recursive programs. Particular emphasis is placed on the analysis of constructed code in order to obtain a description of its side-effects. This analysis aids in the formulation of subprograms.

A style of programming based on instantiating program schemes is reported in [12, 14, 15]. The concern in these papers however is with instantiating the scheme operators with code rather than deriving specifications for them.

Transformation rules provide a complementary paradigm for mapping specifications to programs. Transformation rules are used in [5, 7, 20] to rewrite a specification into a target language program. CYPRESS' design strategies can be viewed as complex rules that transform a specification into a mixture of program structure and specifications for subprograms. Transformation rules can also be used to transform high-level algorithms into more efficient code [2, 3, 8]. Barstow [4] discusses the need to incorporate theorem-proving mechanisms into the transformational approach. Manna and Waldinger [21] incorporate both transformation rules and a generalized form of resolution theorem proving into a single framework.

The sorting problem has been a popular target for program synthesis methods partly due to its usefulness, simplicity of problem statement, and diversity of solutions. Some of the knowledge needed to synthesize a variety of sorting algorithms is surveyed in [17]. Darlington [10] transforms a high-level generate-and-test sort algorithm into six common sorting programs. Clark and Darlington [9] use transformation rules to derive sorting algorithms from a common specification in a top-down manner.

8.6. Summary

In this paper we have presented a problem-reduction approach to program synthesis and its implementation in the CYPRESS system. The main distinguishing feature of our approach is the use of design strategies for various classes of algorithms. Each design strategy encodes knowledge about a class of algorithms in terms of a generic form (represented by a program scheme), and a generic method for instantiating the scheme for a particular problem. In effect each design strategy provides a specialized technique for decomposing a complex problem into simpler subproblems, each described by an automatically derived specification. Another distinguishing feature of this approach is its ability to handle partial specifications. The input conditions derived by CYPRESS have many uses including the formation of guards in conditionals and providing feedback on the nature of the specified problem.

Appendix A

Listed below are all of the axioms and transformations used in the examples of this paper. Let i and j vary over N, let x and y vary over LIST(N), and let w vary over BAGS(N).

N1. $i + j > j \rightarrow i > 0$.
N2. $i > (j \operatorname{div} 2) \rightarrow i + i > j$.

L1. $\mathrm{Bag} \circ \mathrm{Cons} : \langle i, x \rangle \rightarrow \mathrm{Add} : \langle i, \mathrm{Bag} : x \rangle$.
L2. $\mathrm{Ordered} \circ \mathrm{Cons} : \langle i, x \rangle \rightarrow i \le \mathrm{Bag} : x \wedge \mathrm{Ordered} : x$.
L3. $\mathrm{Length} \circ \mathrm{Cons} : \langle i, x \rangle \rightarrow 1 + \mathrm{Length} : x$.
L4. $x \rightarrow \mathrm{Cons} : \langle i, y \rangle$ if $\mathrm{FirstRest} : x = \langle i, y \rangle$.
L5. $\mathrm{Bag} \circ \mathrm{Append} : \langle x_1, x_2 \rangle \rightarrow \mathrm{Union} : \langle \mathrm{Bag} : x_1, \mathrm{Bag} : x_2 \rangle$.

L6. $\text{Ordered} \circ \text{Append}: \langle y_0, y_1 \rangle$
$\to \text{Ordered}: y_0 \wedge \text{Bag}: y_0 \le \text{Bag}: y_1.$

L7. $\text{Card} \circ \text{Bag}: x \to \text{Length}: x.$

L8. $\text{Length}: x \to \text{Card}: w \quad \text{if } \text{Bag}: x = w.$

B1. $w = w.$

B2. $i \in \text{Union}: \langle w_1, w_2 \rangle \to i \le w_1 \wedge i \le w_2.$

B3. $\text{Card} \circ \text{Union}: \langle w_1, w_2 \rangle \to \text{Card}: w_1 + \text{Card}: w_2.$

B4. $\text{Union}: \langle \text{Add}: \langle i, w_1 \rangle, w_2 \rangle$
$\to \text{Add}: \langle i, \text{Union}: \langle w_1, w_2 \rangle \rangle.$

B5. $\text{Add}: \langle i, w_1 \rangle \le w_2 \to i \le w_2 \wedge w_1 \le w_2.$

ACKNOWLEDGMENT

I would like to thank an anonymous referee for numerous constructive comments. This research was supported in part by the Foundation Research Program of the Naval Postgraduate School with funds provided by the Chief of Naval Research and in part by the Office of Naval Research under Contract N00014-84-C-0473.

REFERENCES

1. Aho, A.V., Hopcroft, J.E. and Ullman, J.D., *Data Structures and Algorithms* (Addison-Wesley, Reading, MA, 1983).
2. Balzer, R., Transformational implementation: An example, *IEEE Trans. Software Engrg.* 7(1) (1981) 3–14.
3. Barstow, D.R., *Knowledge-Based Program Construction* (Elsevier North-Holland, New York, 1979).
4. Barstow, D.R., The roles of knowledge and deduction in program synthesis in: *Proceedings Sixth International Joint Conference on Artificial Intelligence*, Tokyo, Japan (1979) 37–43.
5. Bibel, W., Syntax-directed, semantics-supported program synthesis, *Artificial Intelligence* 14 (1980) 243–261.
6. Bledsoe, W.W., Non-resolution theorem proving, *Artificial Intelligence* 9 (1977) 1–35.
7. Broy, M. and Pepper, P., Program development as a formal activity, *IEEE Trans. Software Engrg.* 7 (1981) 14–22.
8. Burstall, R. and Darlington, J., A transformation system for developing recursive programs, *J. ACM* 24 (1977) 44–67.
9. Clark, K.L. and Darlington, J., Algorithm classification through synthesis, *Computer J.* 23(1) (1980) 61–65.
10. Darlington, J., A synthesis of several sort programs, *Acta Inform.* 11(1) (1978) 1–30.
11. Dershowitz, N. and Manna, Z., On automating structured programming, in: *Proceedings Colloques IRIA on Proving and Improving Programs*, Arc-et-Senans, France, July 1975.
12. Dershowitz, N., *The Evolution of Programs*, (Birkhäuser, Boston, MA, 1983).
13. Follett, R., Combining program synthesis with program analysis, in: *Proceedings International Workshop on Program Construction*, Bonas, France, September 1980.
14. Gerhart, S., Knowledge about programs: A model and case study, in: *Proceedings International Conference on Reliable Software*, Los Angeles CA (April 1975) 88–94.
15. Gerhart, S. and Yelowitz, L., Control structure abstractions of the backtrack programming technique, *IEEE Trans. Software Engrg.* 2(4) (1976) 285–292.
16. Green, C.C., Application of theorem proving to problem solving, in: *Proceedings First International Joint Conference on Artificial Intelligence*, Washington, DC (1969).
17. Green, C.C. and Barstow, D.R., On program synthesis knowledge, *Artificial Intelligence* 10 (1978) 241–279.
18. Green, C.C., Luckham, D., Balzer, R., Cheatham, T. and Rich, C., Report on a knowledge-based software assistant, Tech. Rept. RADC-TR-83-195, Rome Air Development Center, Griffiss Air Force Base, New York, 1983.
19. Laaser, W.T., Synthesis of recursive programs, Ph.D. Dissertation, Stanford University, Stanford, CA, 1979.
20. Manna, Z. and Waldinger, R.J., Synthesis: dreams ⇒ programs, *IEEE Trans. Software Engrg.* 5(4) (1979) 294–328.
21. Manna, Z. and Waldinger, R.J., A deductive approach to program synthesis, *ACM TOPLAS* 2(1) (1980) 90–121.
22. Minty, G. and Tyugu, E., Justification of the structural synthesis of programs, *Sci. Comput. Programming* 2(3) (1982) 215–240.
23. Parnas, D.L., On the criteria to be used in decomposing systems into modules, *Comm. ACM* 15(12) (1972) 220–225.
24. Smith, D.R., Derived preconditions and their use in program synthesis, in: D.W. Loveland (Ed.), *Sixth Conference on Automated Deduction*, Lecture Notes in Computer Science 138 (Springer-Verlag, New York, 1982) 172–193.
25. Smith, D.R., Top-down synthesis of simple divide and conquer algorithms, Tech. Rept. NPS 52-82-11, Dept. of Computer Science, Naval Postgraduate School, Monterey, CA, 1982.
26. Smith, D.R., The structure of divide and conquer algorithms, Tech. Rept. NPS52-83-002, Naval Postgraduate School, Monterey, CA, 1983.
27. Smith, D.R., Reasoning by cases and the formation of conditional programs, Tech. Rept. KES.U.85.4, Kestrel Institute, Palo Alto, CA, 1985.
28. Swartout, W. and Balzer, R., On the inevitable intertwining of specification and implementation, *Comm. ACM* 25 (1982) 438–440.

Received January 1984; revised version received February 1985

II / Program Verification

The goal of program verification is to prove that a program satisfies its specifications, ideally through the use of an automated theorem prover. Although this is an appealing prospect, automatically verifying complete software systems of commercial size and complexity is not currently feasible. Instead, current research has taken an incremental approach, e.g., proving individual properties of programs and proving the correctness of small pieces of a program. Also, current program verification systems are really intelligent assistants (see Section VII), which help a person develop proofs.

The papers in this section describe two state-of-the-art automatic theorem provers whose development has been tailored for the programming domain.

A key feature of the Gypsy system described in [Good, Chapter 3] is that it is viewed as a complete programming environment rather than just a program verifier. Gypsy contains a verification condition generator and a theorem prover that takes human advice on how to prove complex theorems. Much of the focus of the Gypsy work is on how verification can be best used as a part of the overall program development process.

[Boyer and Moore, Chapter 4] illustrates the use of the Boyer and Moore theorem prover as an interactive proof checker. Used in this way, the input to the system is the outline of a formal proof—in this case an informal published proof of the invertability of the RSA public key encryption algorithm. The theorem prover then automatically proves the lemmas corresponding to the gaps in the outline.

[Moriconi, Chapter 21] describes another program verification system, which emphasizes the intelligent assistant approach and support for incremental changes in programs and associated proofs.

Mechanical proofs about computer programs

By D. I. Good

2100 *Main Building, Institute for Computing Science, The University of Texas at Austin,
Austin, Texas* 78712, *U.S.A.*

The Gypsy verification environment is a large computer program that supports the development of software systems and formal, mathematical proofs about their behaviour. The environment provides conventional development tools, such as a parser for the Gypsy language, an editor and a compiler. These are used to evolve a library of components that define both the software and precise specifications about its desired behaviour. The environment also has a verification condition generator that automatically transforms a software component and its specification into logical formulas that are sufficient to prove that the component always runs according to specification. Facilities for constructing formal, mechanical proofs of these formulas also are provided. Many of these proofs are completed automatically without human intervention. The capabilities of the Gypsy system and the results of its application are discussed.

1. Introduction

One of the major problems with the current practice of software engineering is an absence of predictability. There is no sound, scientific way of predicting accurately how a software system will behave when it runs. There are many compelling examples of important software systems that have behaved in unpredictable ways: a Space Shuttle fails to launch; an entire line of automobiles is recalled because of problems with the software that controls the braking system; unauthorized users get access to computer systems; sensitive information passes into the wrong hands, etc. (Neumann 1983 a, b). Considering the wide variety of tasks that now are entrusted to computer systems, it is truly remarkable that it is not possible to predict accurately what they are going to do!

Within current software engineering practice, the only sound way to make a precise, accurate prediction about how a software system will behave is to build it and run it. There is no way to predict accurately how a system will behave before it can be run. So design flaws often are detected only after a large investment has been made to develop the system to a point where it can be run. The rebuilding that is caused by the late detection of these flaws contributes significantly to the high cost of software construction and maintenance. Even after the system can be run, the situation is only slightly better. A system that can be run can be tested on a set of trial cases. If the system is deterministic, a trial run on a specific test case provides a precise, accurate prediction about how the system will behave in *that one case*. If the system is re-run on exactly the same case, it will behave in exactly the same way. However, there is no way to predict, from the observed behaviour of a finite number of test cases, how the system will behave in any other case. If the system is non-deterministic (as many systems are), the system will not even necessarily repeat its observed behaviour on a test case. So in current software engineering practice, predicting that a software system will run according to specification is based almost entirely on subjective, human judgment rather than on objective, scientific fact.

In contrast to software engineering, mathematical logic provides a sound, objective way to

Phil. Trans. R. Soc. Lond. A **312**, 389–409 (1984)

make accurate, precise predictions about the behaviour of mathematical operations. For example, if x and y are natural numbers, who among us would doubt the prediction that $x+y$ always gives exactly the same result as $y+x$? This prediction is accurate not just for *some* cases or even just for *most* cases; it is accurate for *every* pair of natural numbers, no matter what they are. The prediction is accurate because there is a *proof* that $x+y = y+x$ logically follows from accepted definitions of 'natural number', ' $=$ ' and ' $+$ '.

The Gypsy verification environment is a large, interactive computer program that supports the construction of formal, mathematical proofs about the behaviour of software systems. These proofs make it possible to predict the behaviour of a software system with the same degree of precision and accuracy that is possible for mathematical operations. These proofs can be constructed *before* a software system can be run and, therefore, they can provide an objective, scientific basis for making predictions about system behaviour throughout the software life cycle. This makes it possible for the proofs actually to guide the construction of the system. In theory these proof methods make possible a new approach to software engineering that can produce systems whose predictability far exceeds that which can be attained with conventional methods.

In practice the use of this mathematical approach to software engineering requires very careful management of large amounts of detailed information. The Gypsy environment is an experimental system that has been developed to explore the viability of applying these methods in actual practice. The purposes of the environment are to amplify the ability of the human software engineer to manage these details and to reduce the probability of human error. The environment, therefore, contains tools for supporting the normal software development process as well as tools for constructing formal proofs.

2. A MATHEMATICAL APPROACH

The Gypsy verification environment is based on the Gypsy language (Good *et al.* 1978). Rather than being based on an extension of the hardware architecture of some particular computer, the Gypsy language is based on rigorous, mathematical foundations for specifying and implementing computer programs. The specification describes *what* effect is desired when the program runs, and the implementation defines *how* the effect is caused. The mathematical foundation provided by the Gypsy language makes it possible to construct rigorous proofs about both the specifications and the implementations of software systems. The language, which is modelled on Pascal (Jensen & Wirth 1974), also is designed so that the implementations of programs can be compiled and executed on a computer with a conventional von Neumann architecture.

The basic structure of a Gypsy software system is shown in figure 1. The purpose of a software system is to cause some effect on its external environment. The external environment of a Gypsy software system consists of data objects (and exception conditions). Every Gypsy data object has a name and a value. The implementation of a program causes an effect by changing the values of the data objects in its external environment (or by signalling a condition). To accomplish its effect, an implementation may create and use internal (local) data objects (and conditions). In figure 1, X and Y represent external objects, and U represents an internal object.

The specifications of a program define constraints on its implementation. In parallel with the structure of implementations, Gypsy provides a means of stating both internal and external specifications. The external specifications constrain the externally visible effects of an implementation. Internal specifications constrain its internal behaviour.

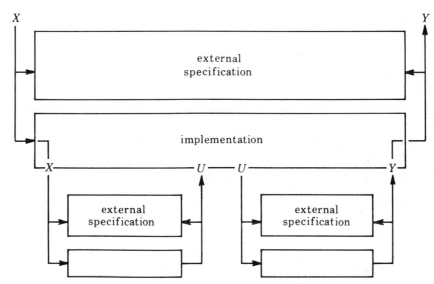

Figure 1. Gypsy software system structure.

The external specifications of a program consist of two parts: a (mandatory) environment specification and an (optional) operational specification. The environment specification describes *all* of the external data objects that are accessible to the procedure. The specification also states the type of each of these objects and whether it is a variable or a constant object. A program may change the value of a data object *only* if it is a variable object.

The type of an object specifies the kind of values it may have. The mathematical foundations of Gypsy begin with its types. The Gypsy types are all well known mathematical objects (integers, rational numbers, the Boolean values *true* and *false*, sets, sequences, mappings) or they can be easily derived from such objects (types character, record, array, buffer). For example, in Gypsy, type *integer* represents the full, unbounded set of mathematical objects. It is not restricted only to the integers that can be represented on a particular machine. For each of these pre-defined types, the Gypsy language also provides a set of primitive, pre-defined functions with known mathematical properties.

The operational specification for an implementation is a relation (a Boolean-valued function) that describes what effect is to be caused on the objects of the external environment. These relations are defined by ordinary functional composition from the Gypsy pre-defined functions.

The implementation of a Gypsy program is defined by a procedure. Running a Gypsy procedure is what actually causes an effect to be produced in its external environment. For implementation, the Gypsy language provides a set of pre-defined procedures (assign a value to an object, send a value to a buffer, remove an object from a sequence, etc.) that have precisely defined effects. It also provides a set of composition rules (*if...then...else...end, loop...end, cobegin...end*, etc.) for composing these pre-defined procedures into more complex ones. So the implementation of every Gypsy software system is some composition of the pre-defined procedures.

These composition rules are designed so that the effect that is caused by the composition can be deduced from the effects caused by its components. In particular, it is always possible to construct a set of formulas in the first-order predicate calculus that are sufficient (but not always necessary) to show that the effect caused by a procedure satisfies its specifications. These formulas are called *verification conditions*. They are the logical conditions that are sufficient to verify that the implementation meets its specifications. By constructing them, the task of proving that an implementation always causes an effect that satisfies its specifications is reduced to a task of proving a set of formulas in the first-order predicate calculus. The methods for constructing the verification conditions are based on the pioneering work of Naur (1966), Floyd (1967), Dijkstra (1968), Hoare (1969), King (1969), Good (1970). Dijkstra (1976), Jones (1980), Gries (1981), Hoare (1982) provide more recent discussions of these basic ideas and their relation to software development.

One of the most important aspects of the Gypsy composition rules is illustrated in figure 1. Only the external specifications of the components are required to construct the verification conditions for the composition. Neither the internal specifications nor the implementation of the components are required. The proof of the composition is completely independent of the internal operation of the components. Therefore, the proof of the composition can be done *before* the components are proved or even implemented; all that is required is that the components have external specifications. Because of this characteristic of the proof methods, a software system can be specified, implemented and proved by starting at the top and working downward rather than by building upward from the Gypsy pre-defined functions and procedures. Thus, when working from the top down, the proofs provide a sound, scientific basis for predicting how the system will behave long before it can be run. It is in these high levels of system design that proofs often can be most effective.

3. The Gypsy environment

The Gypsy verification environment is an interactive program that supports a software engineer in specifying, implementing and proving Gypsy software systems. The specific goals of the environment are to increase the productivity of the software engineer and to reduce the probability of human error. To meet these goals, the Gypsy environment provides an integrated collection of conventional software development tools along with special tools for constructing formal, mathematical proofs. Figure 2 shows the logical structure of the environment.

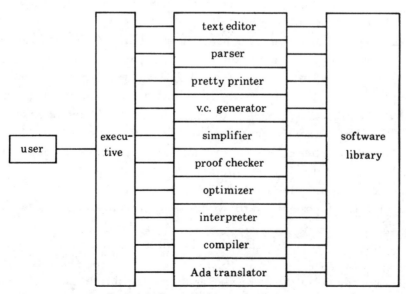

Figure 2. Gypsy environment components.

A single user interacts with the executive component of the environment to use a number of different software tools to build and evolve a software library. This library contains the various Gypsy components of the specification and implementation of a software system, as well as other supporting information such as verification conditions and proofs. The executive notes the changes that are made as the library evolves and marks components that need to be reconsidered to preserve the validity of the proofs (Moriconi 1977).

The Emacs text editor (Stallman 1980), parser and pretty printer are conventional tools for creating and modifying Gypsy text. The parser transforms Gypsy text into an internal form for storage in the library. The pretty printer transforms the internal form back into parsable Gypsy text. The interpreter, compiler (Smith 1980) and Ada translator (Akers 1983) also are fairly conventional tools for running Gypsy programs. Although the interpreter would be a very useful debugging tool, it is not well developed and it is not presently available.

The tools that are involved in constructing proofs are the verification condition generator, the algebraic simplifier, the interactive proof checker and the optimizer. The verification condition generator automatically constructs verification conditions from the Gypsy text of a program. The algebraic simplifier automatically applies an *ad hoc* set of rewrite rules that reduce the complexity of the verification conditions and other logical formulas produced within the Gypsy environment. These rewrite rules are based on equality (and other) relations that are applied by the definitions of the Gypsy pre-defined functions. The interactive proof checker has evolved from one described by Bledsoe & Bruell (1974). It provides a set of truth preserving transformations that can be performed on first-order predicate calculus formulas. These transformations are selected interactively.

The optimizer (McHugh 1983) is unique to the Gypsy environment. It produces logical formulas whose truth is sufficient to show that certain program optimizations are valid. The optimizer works in a manner similar to the verification condition generator. From the implementation of a program *and* its specifications, logical formulas called *optimization conditions* are constructed automatically. These conditions are proved, and then the compiler uses this knowledge to make various optimizations.

4. AN EXAMPLE

To illustrate the capabilities of the Gypsy language and environment, consider the design of a simple software system that filters a stream of messages. Two computers, A and B, are to be coupled by a transmission line so that A can send messages to B. These messages are strings of ASCII characters arranged in a certain format. However, certain kinds of these messages, even when properly formatted, cause machine B to crash. To solve this problem a separate microcomputer is to be installed between A and B as shown in figure 3. The microcomputer is to monitor the flow of messages from A to B, remove the undesirable messages and log them on an audit trail.

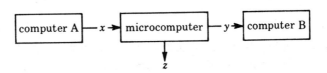

FIGURE 3. Microcomputer filter.

(a) Top level specification

The microcomputer filter will be developed from the top downwards. The process begins by defining an abstract specification of its desired behaviour. The Gypsy text for this top level specification is shown in figure 4. When using the Gypsy environment, the first step would be to create this text and store it in the software library.

```
scope message_stream_separator =
begin

    procedure separator(x:a_char_seq; var y, z:a_char_seq) =
    begin
    exit separated(msg_stream(x), y, z);
      pending;
    end;

    function msg_stream(x:a_char_seq):a_msg_seq = pending;

    function separated(s:a_msg_seq; y, z:a_char_seq):boolean =
    pending;

    type a_char_seq = sequence of character;
    type a_msg = a_char_seq;
    type a_msg_seq = sequence of a_msg;

end;
```

FIGURE 4. Microcomputer filter top level specification.

The Gypsy text defines a scope called *message_stream_separator* that contains six Gypsy units, procedure *separator*, functions *msg_stream* and *separated* and types *a_char_seq*, *a_msg* and *a_msg_seq*. (A Gypsy scope is just a name that identifies a particular collection of Gypsy units. The Gypsy units are procedures, functions, constants, lemmas and types. All Gypsy programs are implemented and specified in terms of these five kinds of units.)

Procedure *separator* is the program that will filter the messages going from computer A to B. The external environment specification of *separator* is $(x:a\_char\_seq; var\ y, z:a\_char\_seq)$. It states that *separator* has access to exactly three external data objects, x, y and z, as illustrated in figure 3. The object x is a constant, and y and z are variables. Each of the objects has a value that is a sequence of ASCII characters.

The operational specification is *exit separated*$(msg\_stream(x), y, z)$. This defines a relation among x, y and z that must be satisfied whenever *separator* halts (exits). The messages that arrive from computer A are supposed to be in a given format. However, there is no way to force A to deliver them properly, and even if it does there is the possibility of noise on the transmission line. Therefore, *separator* must be designed to extract properly formatted messages from an arbitrary sequence of characters. *Msg_stream*(x) is the function that applies the formatting rules and determines the sequence of properly formatted messages that are contained in an arbitrary sequence of characters. *Separated*(s, y, z) defines what it means for a sequence of messages s to be separated into two character strings y and z.

This top level specification does not give precise definitions for *msg_stream* and *separated*; only environment specifications for them are given. (The environment specifications for functions are interpreted in the same way as for procedures, except that the additional type name immediately preceding the ' = ' identifies the type of value produced by the function.) The precise definitions of *msg_stream* and *separated*, as well as the implementation of *separator*, are left *pending* at this stage of development. At this stage, the interface between *separator* and its external environment has been defined, and it has been acknowledged that *separator* must be prepared to deal with an input sequence that may contain improperly formed messages. Formulation of precise definitions for the pending items will be deferred to a later stage.

(b) Specification refinement

The next stage is to refine the operational specifications of *separator*. Figure 5 shows the actual Gypsy text that would be entered into the software library. This text extends scope *message_stream_separator* by replacing the old version of *separated* by the new one and by defining some new functions, types and lemmas.

In this refinement, the *separated* specification is given a precise definition in terms of two new functions *passed* and *rejected*. The definition is given by the operational specification of *separated*.

```
$extending
scope message_stream_separator =
begin

  function separated(s:a_msg_seq; y, z:a_char_seq):boolean =
  begin
  exit [assume result iff y = passed(s) & z = rejected(s)];
  end;

  function passed(s:a_msg_seq):a_char_seq =
  begin
  exit [assume result =
        if s = null(a_msg_seq) then null(a_char_seq)
        else passed(nonlast(s)) @ image(last(s)).pass fi];
  end;

  function rejected(s:a_msg_seq):a_char_seq =
  begin
  exit [assume result =
        if s = null(a_msg_seq) then null(a_char_seq)
        else rejected(nonlast(s)) @ image(last(s)).reject fi];
  end;

  function image(m:a_msg):an_image = pending;

  type an_image = record(pass, reject:a_char_seq);

  lemma null_separation =
  separated(null(a_msg_seq), null(a_char_seq),
                            null(a_char_seq));

  lemma extend_separation(s:a_msg_seq; m:a_msg;
                          y, z:a_char_seq) =
  separated(s, y, z)
  -> separated(s @ [seq: m], y @ image(m).pass,
                            z @ image(m).reject);

  lemma null_stream =
  msg_stream(null(a_char_seq)) = null(a_msg_seq);

end;
```

FIGURE 5. Microcomputer filter specification refinement.

Result is the Gypsy convention for the name of the value returned by a function, and the specification states that *result* is to be true iff $y = passed(s)$ and $z = rejected(s)$. The keyword *assume* indicates that this specification is to be assumed without proof. This is the normal Gypsy style for defining a function that is to be used just for specification.

Functions *passed* and *rejected* are defined in terms of pre-defined Gypsy functions and the function *image*. *Last* is a pre-defined function that gives the last element of a non-empty sequence, and *nonlast* gives all the other elements. The operator '@' denotes a pre-defined function that appends two sequences.

Image is a function that takes a message and produces a record of two parts, *pass* and *reject*. At a subsequent development stage, the definition of *image* will be refined to include the criterion for identifying a message that causes computer B to crash. *Image* also will define the actual output that is sent to computer B *and* to the audit trail for *each* message. If the message is of the form that will cause B to crash, the *pass* part of the record will contain a null sequence of characters and the *reject* part will contain the offending message and any other appropriate information. This record form for the result of *image* was chosen so that messages that are forwarded to B also can be audited if desired. This can be done by sending characters to both the *pass* and *reject* parts of the record. This design choice retains a large amount of flexibility for the subsequent design of the audit trail. The function *passed* applies the *image* function to each successive message m and appends the *pass* part of $image(m)$ to y. Similarly, *rejected* applies *image* to each m and appends the *reject* part to z.

(c) Specification proof

The Gypsy text for the specification refinement also contains three lemmas. These are properties that can be proved to follow from the preceding definitions. These lemmas are the beginning of a simple problem domain theory of separating messages. The lemmas (theorems) of this theory serve several important purposes. First, to the extent that they are properties that the software designer intuitively believes *should* follow from the assumed definitions, proving that they *do* follow provides confidence in these assumptions. Secondly, these properties are the basis for the implementation in the next stage. They are used in the proof of the implementation to decompose the proof into manageable parts. Thirdly, to the extent that the lemmas in this theory are reusable, they can significantly reduce the cost of other proofs that are based on the same theory (Good 1982*a*).

The *null_separation* lemma is a rather trivial one that states that if a sequence of messages s is empty, then *separated*(s, y, z) is satisfied if y and z also are empty. Lemma *extend_separation* describes how to extend the *separated* relation to cover one more message m. If *separated*(s, y, z) is satisfied, then so is *separated*$(s@[seq:m], y@image(m).pass, z@image(m).reject)$.

A formal proof of both of these lemmas can be constructed with the assistance of the interactive proof checker in the Gypsy verification environment. The proof checker provides a fixed set of truth-preserving transformations that can be performed on a logical formula. Although the proof checker has some very limited capability to make transformations without user direction, the primary means of constructing a proof is for the user to select each transformation. Expansion of the definition of a function is one kind of transformation that can be made. The user directs the proof checker to expand the definition of a particular function, and then the expansion is done automatically. Other examples of transformations provided by the proof checker are instantiation of a quantified variable, substitution of equals for equals, and use of a particular lemma. A formula is proved to be a theorem by finding a sequence of transformations that transform the formula into *true*. This sequence constitutes a formal, mathematical proof.

A complete transcript of the interactive proof of *extend_separation* is given in Appendix A. The key steps in the proof are to expand the definition of the *separated* relation and the *passed* and *rejected* functions with the <u>expand</u> command. The <u>theorem</u> command shows the state of the formula at various intermediate stages of transformation. The *null_separation* lemma is proved in a similar way.

Notice that both of these lemmas about message separation can be proved at this rather high level of abstraction without detailed knowledge of the specific format for incoming messages and without knowing the specific formatting details for the outputs *y* and *z*. These details are encapsulated in the functions *msg_stream* and *image* respectively. These definitions (which would need to be provided in subsequent refinement stages) might be quite simple or very complex. In either case, however, detailed definitions of these functions are *not* required at this stage. The use of abstraction in this way is what makes it possible to construct concise, intellectually manageable, formal proofs about large complex specifications. The next §4 (*d*) illustrates how similar techniques can be used in proofs about an implementation.

Finally, it is noted that the *null_stream* lemma cannot be proved at this stage of refinement. However, it is required in the subsequent implementation proof, and therefore, it serves as a constraint on the refinement of the definition of *msg_stream*.

(d) Implementation refinement

An implementation of procedure *separator* that satisfies the preceding specifications is shown in figure 6. The implementation contains two internal variable objects *m* and *p* of types *a_msg* and *integer* respectively. *Separator* causes its effect on its external variable objects, *y* and *z*, first by assigning each of them the value of the empty sequence of characters; then it enters a loop that separates the messages in *x* one by one, and for each message the appropriate output is appended to *y* and *z*.

The desired effect of the loop is described by the *assert* statement. It states that on each iteration of the loop, messages in the subsequence $x[1..p]$ have been separated. (The Gypsy notation for element *i* of sequence *x* is $x[i]$, and $x[1..p]$ is the notation for the subsequence $x[1],...,x[p]$.) This assertion is an *internal* specification about the operation of the procedure.

The loop operates by successively calling the procedures *get_msg* and *put_msg*. *Get_msg* assigns to *m* the next properly formatted message in *x* and increases *p* to be the number of the last character in *x* that has been examined. *Put_msg* appends to *y* and *z* the appropriate output for the new message *m*. The properties of *get_msg* and *put_msg* are stated precisely in the specifications that are given for them in figure 6. (For the variable *p*, *p'* refers to its value at the time *get_msg* is started running, and *p* refers to its value when the procedure halts. The operator <: appends a single element to the end of a sequence.)

(e) Implementation proof

The remaining task for this level of the design of the microcomputer filter is to prove that this abstract implementation of *separator* satisfies its specifications (both internal and external). This proof is possible without any further refinement of the specifications or the implementation. The current form is an instance of the one shown in figure 1. Specifications and an

```
$extending
scope message_stream_separator =
begin

procedure separator(x:a_char_seq; var y, z:a_char_seq) =
begin
exit separated(msg_stream(x), y, z);
  var m:a_msg;
  var p:integer := 0;
  y := null(a_char_seq);
  z := null(a_char_seq);
  loop assert separated(msg_stream(x[1..p]), y, z)
       & p le size(x);
    if p = size(x) then leave;
    else get_msg(x, m, p);
         put_msg(m, y, z);
    end;
  end;
end;

procedure get_msg(x:a_char_seq; var m:a_msg; var p:integer) =
begin
exit msg_stream(x[1..p]) = msg_stream(x[1..p']) <: m
    & p > p' & p le size(x);
  pending
end;

procedure put_msg(m:a_msg; var y, z:a_char_seq) =
begin
exit y = y' @ image(m).pass & z = z' @ image(m).reject;
  pending
  end;

end;
```

FIGURE 6. Microcomputer filter implementation refinement.

implementation for *separator* have been constructed, but there is no implementation of either *get_msg* or *put_msg*. This level of proof simply assumes that these procedures eventually will be implemented and proved to satisfy their specifications. However, at this level, only their external specifications are required.

It is easy to see that the *exit* specification of *separator* logically follows from the assert statement in the loop whenever the procedure leaves the loop. This follows simply from the facts that, when the loop halts, $p = size(x)$ and that for every Gypsy sequence $x[1..size(x)] = x$. It is also easy to see that the assert statement is true the first time the loop is entered. This is because the local variable p is zero, and y and z are both equal to the empty sequence. The assertion then follows from the *null_stream* and *null_separation* lemmas because in Gypsy, $x[1..0]$ is the empty sequence and the size of a sequence is always non-negative. Finally, the *extend_separation* lemma can be used to prove that if the loop assertion is true on one iteration of the loop, then it also is true on the next. These steps form an inductive proof that the loop assertion is true on every iteration of the loop (even if it never halts). The loop, however, does halt because, according to the specifications of *get_msg*, p is an integer that increases on each iteration and yet never increases beyond the number of characters in the constant x. Therefore, the loop must halt; and when it does, the *exit* specification follows from the loop assertion.

The Gypsy verification environment automates all of this argument (except the argument about the loop halting). From the Gypsy text shown in figure 6, the verification conditions generator automatically constructs the formulas shown in figure 7.

```
Verification condition separator#2
separated (msg_stream (null (#seqtype#)),
           null (a_char_seq), null (a_char_seq))

Verification condition separator#3
  H1: msg_stream (x[1..p]) @ [seq: m#1] = msg_stream (x[1..p#1])
  H2: y @ image (m#1).pass = y#1
  H3: z @ image (m#1).reject = z#1
  H4: separated (msg_stream (x[1..p]), y, z)
  H5: p le size (x)
  H6: p + 1 le p#1
  H7: p#1 le size (x)
  H8: size (x) ne p
 -->
  C1: separated (msg_stream (x[1..p#1]), y#1, z#1)
```

FIGURE 7. Separator verification conditions.

Verification condition *separator#2* is the formula that states that the loop assertion is true the first time the loop is entered. *Separator#3* is the one that states that if the assertion is true on one iteration of the loop, it also is true on the next. Lines labelled *Hi* are the hypotheses of an implication, and lines labelled *Ci* are conclusions. Both the hypotheses and the conclusions are connected implicitly by logical conjunction. The notation *m#1* denotes a value of *m* upon completing the next cycle of the loop, and similarly for *p*, *y* and *z*. The notation [*seq: m#1*] means the sequence consisting of the single element *m#1*. The verification condition generator also has constructed a *separator#4* for the case when the loop terminates. The generator, however, does not present this one because the formula has been proved automatically by the algebraic simplifier. The best way to see the effect of the simplifier is to see what the verification conditions look like without it. The unsimplified formulas are shown in figure 8. (There also is a *separator#1*, which is so trivial that the generator does not even bother to use the algebraic simplifier.)

A complete transcript of the interactive proof of *separator#3* is given in Appendix B. The key steps are to do equality substitutions based on hypotheses H1, H2 and H3 with the eqsub command and then use the *extend_separation* lemma. *Separator#2* is proved by use of the lemmas *null_stream* and *null_separation*.

Once *separator* has been proved, the process of refinement can be resumed. In general, the refinement of both specifications and implementations is repeated until all specifications and procedures are implemented in terms of Gypsy primitives.

It is important to observe that the proof of *separator* has identified formal specifications for *get_msg* and *put_msg* that are adequate for the subsequent refinements of these procedures. It has been proved that *separator* will run according to its specification if *get_msg* and *put_msg* run according to theirs. Therefore, these specifications are completely adequate constraints for the subsequent refinements. Some of the specifications may not be necessary, But they are sufficient to ensure that *separator* will satisfy its specification.

```
Verification condition separator#2
  H1: true
  -->
  C1: separated (msg_stream (x[1..0]), null (a_char_seq),
                 null (a_char_seq))
  C2: 0 le size (x)

Verification condition separator#3
  H1: separated (msg_stream (x[1..p]), y, z)
      & p le size (x)
  H2: not p = size (x)
  H3: msg_stream (x[1..p#1]) = msg_stream (x[1..p]) <: m#1
      & p#1 > p
      & p#1 le size (x)
  H4: y#1 = y @ image (m#1).pass
      & z#1 = z @ image (m#1).reject
  -->
  C1: separated (msg_stream (x[1..p#1]), y#1, z#1)
  C2: p#1 le size (x)

Verification condition separator#4
  H1: separated (msg_stream (x[1..p]), y, z)
      & p le size (x)
  H2: p = size (x)
  -->
  C1: true
  C2: separated (msg_stream (x), y, z)
```

FIGURE 8. Unsimplified verification conditions.

5. TRIAL APPLICATIONS

The Gypsy environment has been developed to explore the practicality of constructing formal proofs about software systems that are intended to be used in actual operation. Throughout its development, the environment has been tested on a number of trial applications. The two major ones are summarized in §5 (a), (b).

(a) Message flow modulator

The most recent application of Gypsy is the message flow modulator (Good *et al.* 1982 *b*). The microcomputer filter that has been specified, designed and proved in §4 is a good approximation of the modulator. The microcomputer filter example was chosen deliberately to show how it is possible to construct concise, formal proofs about much larger software systems. The modulator consists of 556 lines of implementation, and the proofs in the preceding sections apply, with only very minor alteration, to the design of the modulator. The lower level details that are unique to the modulator are encapsulated in the *msg_stream* and *image* functions.

The message flow modulator is a filter that is applied continuously to a stream of messages flowing from one computer system to another. As in the microcomputer filter, messages that pass the filter are passed on to their destination with a very minor modification. Messages that do not are rejected and logged on an audit trail. A properly formatted message consists of a sequence of at most 7200 ASCII characters that are opened and closed by a specific sequence.

The filter consists of a list of patterns. Each pattern defines a sequence of letters and digits that may be interspersed with various arrangements of delimiters (a delimiter is any character other than a letter or digit). If a message contains any phrase that matches any pattern, it is rejected to the audit trail along with a description of the offending pattern. Messages that do not contain any occurrence of any pattern are forwarded on to their destination.

In essence, the formal specifications of the modulator have the form $y = f(x, r)$ & $z = g(x, r)$, where r is the list of rejection patterns. The specification describes the exact sequences of characters that must flow out of the modulator for every possible input sequence. This includes handling both properly and improperly formatted messages in the input stream, detecting phrases that match the rejection patterns, and formatting both output sequences. The Gypsy formulation of these specifications is described in further detail in Good *et al.* (1982*b*).

The modulator was developed within the Gypsy environment as a converging sequence of prototypes. First, Gypsy specifications and proofs were constructed for the top levels of the modulator design. This design covered the basic separation of messages into the two output streams. Then, a sequence of running prototypes was implemented. The purpose of these prototypes was to help decide what some of the detailed behaviour of the modulator *should* be. These prototypes were used to investigate various approaches to handling improperly formed messages and to formatting the audit trail. Specifications for these aspects of the modulator were decided upon only after considerable experimentation with the prototypes. Next, another sequence of performance prototypes was built to evaluate the performance of various pattern matching implementations. Once adequate performance was attained, the Gypsy specifications and proofs were completed for the entire modulator.

As the final step, the proved modulator was tested in a live, operational environment on test scenarios developed by an independent, external group. Without any modification, the proved modulator passed all of these tests on the first attempt.

(b) Network interface

The first major application of Gypsy, and the most complex one to date, was a special interface for the ARPANET. Each ARPANET host has message traffic that needs to be transported over the network according to the standard Transmission Control Protocol (Version 4.0). The ARPANET, however, is assumed to be an untrustworthy courier. The special interfaces are to ensure proper message delivery across this potentially unreliable network.

Normally, each host is connected directly to the network by a bi-directional cable. Each cable is cut and an interface unit is installed at the cut (figure 9). This turns the 'dumb' cable into

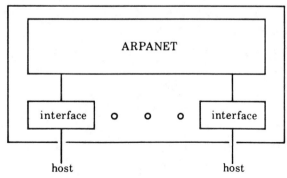

FIGURE 9. ARPANET interface.

a 'smart' one. When the smart cable receives a message from the host, the message is checked to see that it is return-addressed to the sending host. If it is not, the message is dropped. If it is properly return-addressed, then, in effect, the smart cable seals the message in a plain brown envelope that cannot be opened by the network, addresses and return-addresses the envelope and sends it to the ARPANET for delivery. In the other direction, when the cable receives an envelope from the network, it is opened and its message is examined. If the message shows no sign of damage and it is addressed to the receiving host, the message is forwarded on to the host; otherwise it is dropped. So if the network behaves in some unpredictable way and delivers an envelope to the wrong smart cable, the smart cable detects this and refuses to deliver the message to its host.

The specification for the interface unit is relatively straightforward. It states that all messages that are sent into the network must be properly return addressed and packaged and that all messages that are sent out to the host must be properly unpackaged and addressed. The implementation of the interface, however, is rather involved because of a variety of fixed, external constraints. One of the major constraints was that the interface was required to use standard ARPANET link and transport protocols; another was the hardware that was to run the interface. The interface hardware consisted of two PDP-11 minicomputers packaged into a single box. One PDP-11 was connected to the host, and the other was connected to the network. The two PDP-11s could communicate only in an extremely restricted way, and no other communication between the host and the network was allowed.

The proved network interface also was developed as a converging sequence of prototypes. First, the formal specification and proof methods were applied at the highest levels of system design. This involved a specification and proof about the concurrent host-to-host communication across the entire set of interfaces (including the ARPANET). Then, the formal specification and proof methods were applied to obtain the distribution of the interface software onto the two PDP-11 processors of the actual hardware. At this point, a sequence of running prototypes was implemented to evaluate the performance that could be attained with this design. The resources required by the initial design were much greater than those that were available, so a new design was developed and proved, and new performance prototypes were built. When adequate performance was attained, the formal specification and proof methods were applied through all the remaining levels of the interface design and implementation. The general approach that was used on the network interface is illustrated in Good (1982c).

The final result was a formally specified and proved interface, implemented in Gypsy, that operated successfully across the ARPANET with a companion interface that was implemented independently, in conventional assembly code, by Bolt, Beranek and Newman, Inc. As in the flow modulator, without any modification, the proved interface worked properly in every trial run. (A small number of inadequacies in the statement of the constraints for the message formats and protocols were detected and fixed during the prototype stage.)

(c) Economics

These trial applications indicate the kinds of specifications and proofs that are within the capability of the Gypsy environment. However, if formal specifications and proof are to be used as the basis for a new approach to software engineering, there also is the matter of economics. Table 1 shows various measures of the scale of the trial applications and estimates of the amounts of resources used.

TABLE 1. RESOURCES USED

	flow modulator	network interface
lines of Gypsy specifications	1283	3135
lines of executable Gypsy	556	4211
words of compiled PDP-11 code	3849	42271
verification conditions	304	2600
lemmas used	44	90
automatic proofs	146	2287
interactive proofs mechanically checked	198	313
lemmas assumed without proof	4	2
work-months	13	52
DEC 2060 c.p.u.-hours	220	444
page-months of file storage	45000	84465
proved, total Gypsy lines per work-day	6.43	6.42
proved, total Gypsy lines per c.p.u.-hour	8.36	16.54
proved executable Gypsy lines per work-day	1.94	3.68
proved, executable Gypsy lines per c.p.u.-hour	2.53	9.48

The 'lines of Gypsy specifications' and 'lines of executable Gypsy' must be interpreted with caution. These count actual lines of Gypsy text (excluding comments). A line count, however, obviously depends on the style in which the Gypsy text is written, and therefore these counts are quite subjective. Also, a line count is not necessarily a good measure of complexity. In spite of these obvious weaknesses, line counts are one of the most frequently quoted measures of program size.

'Lines of Gypsy specifications' refers to those lines that are used to express formal specifications. One of the important differences between the flow modulator and the network interface was the strength of their specifications. The specifications for the flow modulator were very strong; they completely defined the two output sequences as functions of the input sequence. The specifications for the network interface, however, were much weaker; they were stated as relations rather than as functions, and there are some important aspects of the behaviour of the interface that are not covered by these relations. The difference between these two specification forms is like the difference between $y = f(x)$ and $y < x$. The first defines exactly what y must be for every x and the second states only a relatively weak relation between x and y. This is an important difference to consider in interpreting the numbers in table 1.

'Lines of executable Gypsy' refers to lines of Gypsy that actually cause run-time code to be compiled. These line counts do not, for example, include type declarations. 'Words of compiled PDP-11 code' refer to the number of (16 bit) words of PDP-11 machine code that were produced by the Gypsy compiler. In both applications, the target machine was a PDP-11/03 with no operating system other than the Gypsy run-time support package. This package is not included in the word count. The two applications were compiled with different Gypsy compilers. The flow modulator was compiled through the Gypsy-to-Bliss translator (Smith 1980). The network interface was compiled with the original Gypsy compiler (Hunter 1981).

'Verification conditions' refers to the number of verification conditions constructed by the Gypsy environment. 'Lemmas used' refers to the number of these stated in the Gypsy text. 'Automatic proofs' refers to the number of verification conditions proved fully automatically by the algebraic simplifier. 'Interactive proofs mechanically checked' refers to the number of verification conditions and lemmas that required the use of the proof checker. In both applications, a small number of lemmas were assumed without proof. The four lemmas that were not proved at the time the flow modulator was completed have since been proved. The two lemmas that were not proved for the network interface were key assumptions about the problem domain.

'Work-months' refers to the total number of (22 day) working months required to complete the application. These months include the full development of the application, from initial conception through the final testing of the proved software. This includes all iterations of all levels of specifications, prototypes and proofs. Similarly, 'c.p.u.-hours' and 'page-months' also cover the full development cycle. 'Proved, total Gypsy lines' is computed from 'lines of Gypsy specifications' plus 'lines of executable Gypsy'. This gives a measure of the total number of Gypsy lines produced per working day. 'Proved, executable Gypsy lines' considers just 'lines of executable Gypsy'.

6. CONCLUSION

The Gypsy verification environment is an experimental system that has been developed to explore the practicality of a new approach to software engineering that is based on rigorous, mathematical foundations. These foundations, together with the tools provided in the Gypsy environment, make it possible for a software engineer to construct formal, mathematical proofs about a software system. By appropriate use of abstraction, the formal proofs can be kept concise and intellectually manageable even though they cover large, complex systems. These proofs provide an objective, scientific basis for predicting, accurately and precisely, how a software system will behave when it runs. These proofs can be constructed at all stages of the software life cycle, from the earliest design stages through to system maintenance. Therefore, they also provide the software engineer a basis for evaluating the effects of early design decisions at the time they are made rather than having first to build a system that runs. The proofs also provide a basis for predicting the effects of maintenace modifications.

The results of the first trial applications of the Gypsy environment have been very encouraging. The flow modulator and the network interface are non-trivial software systems. They are intended to be used in actual operation, and their predictability is a genuine, major concern. Although these applications do not approach the scale and complexity of what normally are regarded as 'large' systems, they do support the claim that a formal, mathematical approach to software engineering is technically viable. The next major research goal seems to be making this approach economically viable. Although the cost of applying this new technology in the two applications was much less than what might have been expected (and one always must weigh the cost of applying this mathematical approach against the cost of an unpredictable software system), there seem to be many ways in which the amount of resources used to apply the technology can be reduced. If this can be done, this new technology can become the basis for a new practice of software engineering that can provide dramatic improvements in the predictability and quality of software systems.

On this euphoric note, it is all too easy to be lulled into a false sense of security because it is tempting to believe that a formally specified and proved program should be absolutely correct. It should always behave perfectly and never malfunction. However, there are several reasons why a program that has been proved within the Gypsy environment may not behave exactly as expected. First, the formal specifications may not describe exactly the expected behaviour of the program. Secondly, the formal specifications may not describe all of the aspects of program behaviour. Thirdly, invalid lemmas may have been assumed without proof. Finally, either the verification environment, the compiler, the Gypsy run-time support or the hardware might malfunction.

The last of these potential sources of error, in principle, can be minimized by specifying and proving the verification environment, the compiler, the run-time support and to some degree, the hardware. These would be large complex proofs that are well beyond present capabilities; but, given sufficient cost reductions, these proofs eventually may well be possible. The first three, however, are subjective and involve some element of human judgment. Therefore, these potential sources of error cannot be eliminated. These sources of error are cited not to belittle the potential of a scientific basis for software engineering but to make clear that the formal, mathematical approach offers no absolutes. As with any other science, it must be applied in the context of human judgment.

The development and initial experimental applications of Gypsy have been sponsored in part by the U.S. Department of Defense Computer Security Center (contracts MDA904-80-C-0481, MDA904-82-C-0445), by the U.S. Naval Electronic Systems Command (contract N00039-81-C-0074), by Digital Equipment Corporation, by Digicomp Research Corporation and by the National Science Foundation (grant MCS-8122039).

APPENDIX A. FORMAL PROOF OF LEMMA *extend_separation*

The following is the complete transcript of the interactive proof of the lemma *extend_separation*. The input supplied by the human user is underlined.

```
Entering Prover with lemma extend_separation

    H1: separated (s, y, z)
->
    C1: separated (s @ [seq: m],
                   y @ image (m).pass,
                   z @ image (m).reject)


Prvr -> expand
        Unit name -> separated
Which ones?
    1. in H1: separated (s, y, z)
    2. in C1: separated (s @ [seq: m],
                         y @ image (m).pass,
                         z @ image (m).reject)

    <number-list>, ALL, NONE, PRINT, ^E: all
```

```
Prvr -> theorem
   H1: passed (s) = y
   H2: rejected (s) = z
->
   C1: y @ image (m).pass = passed (s @ [seq: m])
   C2: z @ image (m).reject = rejected (s @ [seq: m])

Prvr -> expand
      Unit name -> passed
Which ones?
   1. in H1:  passed (s)
   2. in C1:  passed (s @ [seq: m])

        <number-list>, ALL, NONE, PRINT, ^E: 2

Prvr -> expand
      Unit name -> rejected
Which ones?
   1. in H2:  rejected (s)
   2. in C2:  rejected (s @ [seq: m])

        <number-list>, ALL, NONE, PRINT, ^E: 2

Prvr -> theorem
   H1: passed (s) = y
   H2: rejected (s) = z
->
   C1: y @ image (m).pass = passed (s) @ image (m).pass
   C2: z @ image (m).reject = rejected (s) @ image (m).reject

Prvr -> qed

9.  ANDSPLIT
   11.  SIMPLIFYC
      14.  UNIFY
   12.  SIMPLIFYC
      18.  UNIFY
Theorem proved!
```

APPENDIX B. FORMAL PROOF OF VERIFICATION CONDITION *separator#3*

The following is the complete transcript of the interactive proof of the verification condition *separator #3*. The input supplied by the human user is underlined.

```
Entering Prover with verification condition separator#3

    H1: msg_stream (x[1..p]) @ [seq: m#1] = msg_stream (x[1..p#1])
    H2: y @ image (m#1).pass = y#1
    H3: z @ image (m#1).reject = z#1
    H4: separated (msg_stream (x[1..p]), y, z)
    H5: p le size (x)
    H6: p + 1 le p#1
    H7: p#1 le size (x)
    H8: size (x) ne p
->
    C1: separated (msg_stream (x[1..p#1]), y#1, z#1)

Prvr -> retain
      hypothesis labels, ALL, NONE -> h1 h2 h3 h4

Prvr -> theorem
    H1: msg_stream (x[1..p]) @ [seq: m#1] = msg_stream (x[1..p#1])
    H2: y @ image (m#1).pass = y#1
    H3: z @ image (m#1).reject = z#1
    H4: separated (msg_stream (x[1..p]), y, z)
->
    C1: separated (msg_stream (x[1..p#1]), y#1, z#1)

Prvr -> eqsub
      Hypothesis label -> h1
  msg_stream (x[1..p#1]) := msg_stream (x[1..p]) @ [seq: m#1]

Prvr -> theorem
    H1: y @ image (m#1).pass = y#1
    H2: z @ image (m#1).reject = z#1
    H3: separated (msg_stream (x[1..p]), y, z)
->
    C1: separated (msg_stream (x[1..p]) @ [seq: m#1], y#1, z#1)

Prvr -> eqsub
      Hypothesis label -> h1
  y#1 := y @ image (m#1).pass

Prvr -> theorem
    H1: z @ image (m#1).reject = z#1
    H2: separated (msg_stream (x[1..p]), y, z)
->
    C1: separated (msg_stream (x[1..p]) @ [seq: m#1],
                   y @ image (m#1).pass, z#1)
```

```
Prvr -> eqsub
          Hypothesis label -> h1
   z#1 := z @ image (m#1).reject


Prvr -> theorem
   H1: separated (msg_stream (x[1..p]), y, z)
->
   C1: separated (msg_stream (x[1..p]) @ [seq: m#1],
                  y @ image (m#1).pass,
                  z @ image (m#1).reject)


Prvr -> use
          Unit name -> extend separation


Prvr -> theorem
   H1:    separated (s$#2, y$#2, z$#2)
       -> separated (s$#2 @ [seq: m$#2],
                     y$#2 @ image (m$#2).pass,
                     z$#2 @ image (m$#2).reject)
   H2: separated (msg_stream (x[1..p]), y, z)
->
   C1: separated (msg_stream (x[1..p]) @ [seq: m#1],
                  y @ image (m#1).pass,
                  z @ image (m#1).reject)


Prvr -> proceed


11.  BACKCHAIN
   12.  UNIFY
        13.  ANDSPLIT
   13.  UNIFY
Theorem proved!.
```

REFERENCES

Akers, R. L. 1983 A Gypsy-to-Ada program compiler. Master's thesis, University of Texas at Austin. Also *Tech. Rep.* no. 39, Institute for Computing Science, The University of Texas at Austin.

Bledsoe, W. W. & Bruell, P. 1974 A man–machine theorem-proving system. In *Advance Papers of Third International Joint Conference on Artificial Intelligence* (ed. W. W. Bledsoe), **5–1** (Spring), pp. 51–72.

Dijkstra, E. W. 1968 A constructive approach to the problem of program correctness. *BIT* **8**, 174–186.

Dijkstra, E. W. 1976 *A discipline of programming.* Englewood Cliffs, N.J.: Prentice-Hall.

Floyd, R. W. 1967 Assigning meanings to programs. In *Proceedings of a Symposium in Applied Mathematics* (ed. J. T. Schwartz), vol. 19, pp. 19–32. Providence, Rhode Island: American Mathematical Society.

Good, D. I. 1970 Toward a man–machine system for proving program correctness. Ph.D. thesis, University of Wisconsin.

Good, D. I., Cohen, R. M., Hoch, C. G., Hunter, L. W. & Hare, D. F. 1978 Report on the language Gypsy, Version 2.0. *Tech. Rep.* ICSCA-CMP-10, Certifiable Minicomputer, Project, ICSCA, The University of Texas at Austin.

Good, D. I. 1982a Reusable problem domain theories. In *Formal Specification – Proceedings of the Joint IBM / University of Newcastle-upon-Tyne Seminar* (ed. M. J. Elphick), pp. 92–115. Also *Tech. Rep.* no. 31, Institute for Computing Science, The University of Texas at Austin.

Good, D. I., Siebert, Ann E. & Smith, L. M. 1982b Message Flow Modulator – Final Report. *Tech. Rep.* no. 34, Institute for Computing Science, The University of Texas at Austin.

Good, D. I. 1982c The proof of a distributed system in Gypsy. In *Formal Specification – Proceedings of the Joint IBM/University of Newcastle-upon-Tyne Seminar* (ed. M. J. Elphick), pp. 443–489. Also *Tech. Rep.* no. 30, Institute for Computing Science, The University of Texas at Austin.

Gries, D. 1981 *The science of computer programming*. New York: Springer-Verlag.

Hoare, C. A. R. 1969 An axiomatic basis for computer programming. *Commun. Ass. comput. Mach.* **12–10**, 576–580.

Hoare, C. A. R. 1982 Programming is an engineering profession. *Tech. Rep.* no. PRG-27, Programming Research Group, Oxford University Computing Laboratory.

Hunter, L. W. 1981 *The first generation Gypsy compiler. Tech. Rep.* no. 23, Institute for Computing Science, The University of Texas at Austin.

Jensen, K. & Wirth, N. 1974 *Pascal user manual and report*. New York: Springer-Verlag.

Jones, C. B. 1980 *Software development: a rigorous approach*. Englewood Cliffs, N.J.: Prentice-Hall.

King, J. C. 1969 A program verifier. Ph.D. thesis. Carnegie–Mellon University.

McHugh, J. 1983 Toward the generation of efficient code from verified programs. Ph.D. thesis, University of Texas at Austin.

Moriconi, M. S. 1977 A system for incrementally designing and verifying programs. Also Ph.D. thesis, *Tech. Rep.* ICSCA-CMP-9. The University of Texas at Austin.

Naur, P. 1966 Proof of algorithms by general snapshots. *BIT* **6**, 310–316.

Neumann, P. G. 1983a Letters from the Editor. *Software engineering Notes* **8** (3), 2–6.

Neumann, P. G. 1983b Letters from the Editor. *Software engineering Notes* **8** (5), 1–9.

Smith, L. M. 1980 Compiling from the Gypsy verification environment. Master's thesis, The University of Texas at Austin. Also *Tech. Rep.* no. 20. Institute for Computing Science, The University of Texas at Austin.

Stallman, R. M. 1980 *EMACS Manual for Twenex Users*, M.I.T. Artificial Intelligence Laboratory.

Discussion

B. A. WICHMANN (*National Physical Laboratory, Teddington, Middlesex, U.K.*). Could Dr Good comment upon the dependence of his work on the correctness of the compilers and hardware?

D. I. GOOD. Certainly, the claim that a proved program actually will run correctly is based on the assumption that it is compiled correctly and that the hardware runs correctly and on a number of other things. These are discussed briefly in the conclusion of the paper. This question, however, also raises two other important issues.

The first is program 'correctness'. This term is widely used, but I believe it is highly ill-chosen because it conveys a misleading connotation of absolute perfection. For example, when someone says they have proved that a program is 'totally correct', who would believe that it would ever do anything but always run absolutely perfectly? Yet, it is quite possible for such a program to malfunction. This is because when a program is proved, it is proved against a particular specification. The proof provides assurance that the program will run according to its specification; but, the proved program very well might do other things that are not covered by the specification, and it might do them wrong! Whenever someone claims to have proved a program, the first question should be 'what did you prove?'

The second question should be 'what did you assume?'. Every proof, whether it is about a program or anything else, is based upon certain assumptions. These may be very simple, or they may be arbitrarily complex. All that is produced in any proof is a chain of deductive steps that imply that a conclusion follows from a set of assumptions. If the assumptions are not true, then the conclusion need not be either. Thus, in the end, all that *any* proof does is to make explicit the assumptions upon which the conclusion is based. A proof provides us confidence in its conclusion to the extent that the conclusion is deduced from believable assumptions. For software systems, the simple accomplishment of identifying a precise set of assumptions that imply that a software system runs according to a particular specification is a dramatic improvement over conventional methods. There always remains, however, the question of the validity of the assumptions. For a proof to provide confidence that a system runs according to specification, its assumptions must be simple, concise, and believable.

PROOF CHECKING THE RSA PUBLIC KEY ENCRYPTION ALGORITHM[1]

ROBERT S. BOYER AND J STROTHER MOORE

Department of Computer Sciences, University of Texas, Austin, TX 78712

> The development of mathematics toward greater precision has led, as is well known, to the formalization of large tracts of it, so that one can prove any theorem using nothing but a few mechanical rules.—Gödel [11]
> But formalized mathematics cannot in practice be written down in full, and therefore we must have confidence in what might be called the common sense of the mathematician... We shall therefore very quickly abandon formalized mathematics... —Bourbaki [1].

1. Introduction. A formal mathematical proof is a finite sequence of formulas, each element of which is either an axiom or the result of applying one of a fixed set of mechanical rules to previous formulas in the sequence. It is thus possible to write a computer program to check mechanically whether a given sequence is a formal proof. However, formal proofs are rarely used. Instead, typical proofs in journal articles, textbooks, and day-to-day mathematical communication use informal notation and leave many of the steps to the reader's imagination. Nevertheless, by transcribing the sentences of the proof into a formal notation, it is sometimes possible to use today's automatic theorem-provers to fill in the gaps between published steps and thus mechanically check some published, informal proofs.

In this paper we illustrate this idea by mechanically checking the recently published proof of the invertibility of the public key encryption algorithm described by Rivest, Shamir, and Adleman [17]. We will briefly explain the idea of public key encryption to motivate the theorem proved.

In [17] a mathematical function, here called CRYPT, is defined. CRYPT(M, e, n) is the encryption of message M with key (e, n). The function has the following important properties:

1. It is easy to compute CRYPT(M, e, n).

2. CRYPT is "invertible," i.e., if M is encrypted with key (e, n) and then decrypted with key (d, n), the result is M. That is, CRYPT(CRYPT(M, e, n), d, n) = M, under suitable conditions on M, n, e and d.

3. Publicly revealing CRYPT and (e, n) does not reveal an easy way to compute (d, n). Public key encryption thus avoids the problem of distributing keys via secure means. Each user (e.g., a computer on a network) generates an encryption key and a corresponding decryption key, publicizes the encryption key to enable others to send private messages, and never distributes the decryption key.

The function defined in [17] is CRYPT(M, e, n) = M^e mod n; in addition, algorithms are given for constructing e, d, and n so that CRYPT has the three properties above. The first two properties are proved in [17]. The third property is not proved; instead the authors of [17] argue that "all the obvious approaches to breaking our system are at least as difficult as factoring n."

Robert S. Boyer received his Ph.D. in mathematics under W. W. Bledsoe at the University of Texas at Austin in 1971. J Strother Moore received his Ph.D. in computational logic under B. Meltzer at the University of Edinburgh in 1973. The automatic theorem-prover described in this paper spent its formative years proving such theorems as the commutativity of Peano multiplication in the Metamathematics Unit of the University of Edinburgh, where Boyer and Moore began collaborating in 1971. After four years of development at Stanford Research Institute, the theorem-prover could prove the uniqueness of prime factorizations and the many other theorems described in *A Computational Logic*. In 1981 Boyer and Moore joined the Computer Sciences faculty of the University of Texas at Austin as associate professors. They also hold research positions in the Institute for Computing Science and Computer Applications, The University of Texas at Austin, Austin, Texas 78712. For the past two years the theorem-prover's talents have been applied to the theorems arising in Boyer and Moore's graduate courses in programming languages and theory of computation, where it maintains a solid A average.

[1] The research reported here was supported by National Science Foundation Grant MCS-8202943 and Office of Naval Research Contract N00014-81-K-0634.

Since there is no known algorithm for efficiently factoring large composites, the security property of CRYPT is obtained by constructing n as the product of two very large (200 digit) primes.

In this paper we focus on mechanically checking the proofs of the first two properties. A precise statement of the "invertibility" property is: CRYPT(CRYPT(M, e, n), d, n) = M, if n is the product of two distinct primes p and q, $M < n$, and e and d are multiplicative inverses in the ring of integers modulo $(p - 1)^*(q - 1)$. Our mechanical proof of this theorem requires that we first prove many familiar theorems of number theory, including Fermat's theorem: M^{p-1} mod p = 1, when p is a prime and $p \nmid M$.

2. A Sketch of the Theorem-Prover. The theorem-prover we use is the current version of the system described in [2]. The theorem-prover deals with a quantifier free first order logic providing equality, recursively defined functions, mathematical induction, and inductively constructed objects such as the natural numbers and finite sequences.

The theorem-prover is a large interactive computer program. The main inputs provided by the user are new recursive definitions and conjectures to prove.

Before a proposed definition is admitted as a new axiom, certain conditions are mechanically checked to assure that there exists one and only one function satisfying the definition. The most important condition is that there exist a measure of the arguments of the function that is decreasing in a well-founded sense in each recursive call in the definition. The mechanized definitional principle can guess simple measures and well-founded relations; more complicated ones can be supplied by the user. Once a candidate measure and relation are found, the mechanical theorem-prover is invoked to prove theorems sufficient to admit the proposed definition.

Given a conjecture to prove, the theorem-prover orchestrates the application of many proof techniques under heuristic control. The main proof techniques used are:

> *Simplification*-The system applies axioms, definitions, and previously proved theorems as rewrite rules to simplify expressions. For example, if f is a defined function, it is sometimes useful to replace an instance of $f(x)$ by the corresponding instance of the definition of f. To avoid looping the simplifier contains elaborate heuristics to control the use of recursive definitions. One of the main heuristics is to expand $f(x)$ to introduce a recursive call provided the arguments to the call already occur in the conjecture. Axioms and previously proved theorems are also used as rewrite rules. For example, the theorem
>
> $$\text{prime}(p) \rightarrow [\, p|a^*b \leftrightarrow (p|a \vee p|b)\,]$$
>
> is used to replace instances of $p|a^*b$ by $(p|a \vee p|b)$ whenever the hypothesis prime(p) can be established by simplification. The simplifier also contains decision procedures for propositional calculus, equality, and those formulas of rational arithmetic that can be built up from variables, integers, $+$, $-$, $=$, $<$, and $\sim$.

> *Elimination of Undesirable Function Symbols*-The system uses axioms and previously proved lemmas to eliminate certain function symbols from the conjecture being proved. For example, it is a theorem that for each natural number i and each positive integer j there exist natural numbers $r < j$ and q such that $i = r + qj$. By replacing i with $r + qj$, the system can transform the expression i mod j to simply r and i/j to simply q.

> *Strengthening the Conjecture to be Proved*-It is frequently the case that to prove some theorem by induction, it is necessary to prove a stronger theorem than that initially posed. Our system contains several heuristics for guessing stronger

conjectures to try to prove. One heuristic involves "using" equality hypotheses by substituting one side for the other elsewhere in the conjecture and then strengthening the conjecture by throwing away the equality hypothesis. Another heuristic replaces certain nonvariable expressions in the conjecture by new variables.

For example, consider proving $(n^i)^j = n^{i*j}$, by induction on j. The induction step is

$$(n^i)^j = n^{i*j} \rightarrow (n^i)^{j+1} = n^{i*(j+1)}.$$

The conclusion simplifies to $n^{i*}(n^i)^j = n^{i+i*j}$. The system then applies the first heuristic above, using and throwing away the equality hypothesis, to obtain the goal

$$n^{i*}n^{i*j} = n^{i+i*j}.$$

The second heuristic then produces the goal $n^{i*}n^k = n^{i+k}$ by replacing $i*j$ with the new variable k. This final goal, a natural lemma about exponentiation, is then proved by a second appeal to induction.

Induction–When all else fails, it is useful to try mathematical induction. The selection of an "appropriate" induction is based on an analysis of the recursive functions mentioned in the conjecture. For example, since $n!$ is recursively defined in terms of $(n-1)!$, when n is not 0, the presence of $n!$ in a conjecture, $p(n)$, suggests a simple induction on n. The base case is $p(0)$. In the induction step, n is non-0, the inductive hypothesis is $p(n-1)$, and the induction conclusion is $p(n)$. Observe that the $n!$ in the conclusion can now be expanded by the simplifier and will produce a term involving $(n-1)!$, about which we have a hypothesis. Similarly, since we define $i \bmod j$ recursively in terms of $(i-j) \bmod j$, when $0 < j \le i$, the occurrence of $i \bmod j$ in a conjecture suggests an inductive argument in which we suppose $0 < j \le i$ and take as an inductive hypothesis the conjecture with i replaced by $i-j$.

Typically, a conjecture to be proved contains many different recursive functions and they each suggest different induction schemas. Our induction mechanism contains many heuristics for combining and choosing between the suggested inductions. That the inductions invented by the system are valid may be proved by considering the well-foundedness theorems proved when recursive functions are admitted.

Readers interested in more details of the theorem-prover should see [2] in which the system, as of May, 1978, is described at a level of detail sufficient to permit reproduction of our results. Several chapters of [2] are devoted to detailed annotated proofs by the system, including its proof of the uniqueness of prime factorizations. Improvements made to the system since the publication of [2] include the addition of the above mentioned decision procedures for equalities and simple arithmetic inequalities, the extension of the definitional principle to include reflexive functions as described in [16], and a metafunction facility permitting the incorporation of new simplifiers after they have been mechanically proved correct [3].

Finally, we have added a primitive "hint" facility so that the user can tell the theorem-prover how to prove a theorem when its heuristics lead it down blind alleys. There are two types of hints used in this paper. The first permits the user to say "use Lemma x with instantiation y." The interpretation of this hint is to obtain the lemma named, instantiate its variables as directed by y, and add the resulting formula as a hypothesis to the conjecture being proved. The system then applies its usual heuristics. The second type of hint is "induct as suggested by the recursion in f" where f is a previously admitted recursive function.

The theorem-prover is automatic in the sense that once it begins a proof attempt, no user guidance is permitted. However, every time it accepts a definition or proves a theorem, it stores the definition or theorem for future use. By presenting the theorem-prover with an appropriate sequence of lemmas to prove, the user can "lead" it to proofs it would not otherwise discover. Thus the distinction between a proof checker and an automatic theorem-prover blurs once the system remembers and uses previously proved facts. An automatic theorem-prover merely enables the user to leave out some of the routine proof steps. A sufficiently good automatic theorem-prover might enable the user to check an "informal" proof by presenting to the machine no more material than one would present to a human colleague.

When we began the encryption proofs, we initialized the theorem-prover to the current version of the lemma library listed in Appendix A of [2]. The library contains several hundred previously proved theorems. Most of the theorems in this library were irrelevant to the encryption proofs (e.g., there are many theorems about list processing functions such as REVERSE, FLATTEN, and SORT). However, among the theorems in the library are many elementary facts about addition, multiplication, and integer division with remainder. The deepest number theory result in the library is the uniqueness of prime factorizations.

3. Correctness of CRYPT. To show that $M^e \bmod n$ is easy to compute—even when the numbers involved contain hundreds of digits—Rivest, Shamir and Adleman exhibit an algorithm for computing it in order $\log_2(e)$ steps. Below we define CRYPT as a recursive version of their algorithm and prove that it computes the desired function. The notation $e/2$ below denotes integer division, i.e., the floor of the rational quotient.

The material contained in boxes in this paper represents material typed by the user and checked by the theorem-prover. The boxed material very closely resembles traditional "informal" proofs. To make this more obvious to readers unfamiliar with our formal notation, we have taken the liberty of transcribing the user type-in into conventional mathematical English. Use of the phrase "Hint:" in boxed material notes those occasions on which we gave the system explicit hints.

It may not be immediately obvious to the casual reader that each line follows from the previous ones. We have been careful to give the reader no more or less information than was given the machine and challenge the reader to do the machine's job: verify each line of the boxed material.

Box 1

We define the encryption algorithm as the recursive function CRYPT:

DEFINITION.
CRYPT(M, e, n)
$=$

if e is not a natural number or is 0,
then 1;

else if e is even,
then
   $(\text{CRYPT}(M, e/2, n))^2 \bmod n;$
else
   $(M*(\text{CRYPT}(M, e/2, n)^2 \bmod n)) \bmod n.$

LEMMA. $(x*(y \bmod n)) \bmod n = (x*y) \bmod n.$

COROLLARY. $(a*(b*(y \bmod n))) \bmod n = (a*(b*y)) \bmod n.$
(Hint: let x be $a*b$ in the preceding lemma.)

THEOREM. CRYPT(M, e, n) *is equal to* $M^e \bmod n$, *provided n is not* 1.

In Section 6 we give the actual user type-in for the material in Box 1. In order to reinforce in the reader's mind the fact that the theorem-prover assents to these claims only after proving them, we offer the following comments.

Before accepting the definition of CRYPT the theorem-prover guesses that e decreases in each recursive call and then proves it by showing that when e is a non-0 natural number, $e/2$ is strictly smaller than e.

CRYPT uses the "binary method" of computing M^e (see [15]), which is based on the observation:

$$M^e = \begin{cases} (M^{e/2})^2, & \text{if } e \text{ is even,} \\ M^*(M^{e/2})^2, & \text{if } e \text{ is odd.} \end{cases}$$

However, by doing multiplications modulo n, CRYPT keeps the intermediate results manageably small and computes $M^e \bmod n$.

The first lemma above—i.e., that $(x^*(y \bmod n)) \bmod n$ is $(x^*y) \bmod n$—establishes that the intermediate mods can be dropped. This lemma is obviously important in establishing that CRYPT computes $M^e \bmod n$. We brought this fact to the system's attention before even attempting to have the system prove properties of CRYPT.

How did the theorem-prover prove $(x^*(y \bmod n)) \bmod n = (x^*y) \bmod n$? It first tried simplification, but no known rewrites could be applied under our heuristics. The system then decided to eliminate $(y \bmod n)$ by replacing y with $r + nq$, where $r < n$. To permit this, the system case split on whether y is a natural number and n is a positive integer. The "pathological" cases, where y was not numeric or n was nonpositive, yielded immediately to simplification. In the case where y was a natural number and n was positive, the system replaced y with $r + nq$, where $r < n$. Thus $(y \bmod n)$ became r and the left hand side of the conjecture became $x^*r \bmod n$. On the right, x^*y became $x^*(r + nq)$. The simplifier then distributed the multiplication over the addition (using a previously proved lemma in the library) and obtained $(x^*r + n^*q^*x) \bmod n$, which was further rewritten to $x^*r \bmod n$ by the lemma that $i + nj \bmod n$ is $i \bmod n$. The left and right hand sides were then identical. The machine spent about 23 seconds of cpu time on the proof in Interlisp-10 on a DEC 2060.

The corollary above, that $(a^*(b^*(y \bmod n))) \bmod n$ is $(a^*(b^*y)) \bmod n$, follows trivially from the previous line, by letting x be (a^*b) and applying the associativity of multiplication. Since this observation is uninteresting to a human proof checker, the need for it in our mechanical proof exposes a deficiency in our mechanical theorem-prover. Why is this line needed by the machine? The reason has to do with the order in which rewrite rules are applied. Consider the term $((a^*b)^*(y \bmod n)) \bmod n$. The lemma just proved can be applied as a rewrite rule from left to right, to eliminate the intermediate mod and produce $(a^*b)^*y \bmod n$, to which we can then apply associativity to get $a^*(b^*y) \bmod n$. However, if we apply associativity first, we obtain $a^*(b^*(y \bmod n)) \bmod n$ and we can no longer use the first lemma from left to right.[2] The second observation solves this problem.

We did not anticipate the machine's need for the corollary. Instead, immediately after proving the lemma, we thought the machine could prove that CRYPT computes $M^e \bmod n$. We commanded it to do so and watched its proof attempt on the screen. (Imagine watching a colleague proving the theorem on the blackboard.) We saw the term $(a^*(b^*(y \bmod n))) \bmod n$ arise and remain "unsimplified" even though we knew it was $(a^*(b^*y)) \bmod n$. At that point we interjected with the corollary.

We now consider the machine's acceptance of the final theorem in Box 1, the claim that CRYPT computes the desired function. The first time we submitted the claim we did not include the hypothesis that $n \neq 1$, because the hypothesis is not noted by Rivest, Shamir and Adleman,

---

[2] This is the Knuth-Bendix problem in rewrite driven simplification. See [13] for an elegant solution to the problem in certain cases.

who imply that the algorithm always computes $M^e \bmod n$. However, the theorem-prover failed to prove the simpler conjecture and exhibited a formula showing that the encryption algorithm does not compute $M^e \bmod n$ when e is 0 and n is 1. In practice, n is always larger than 1, so the additional hypothesis is no burden.

The theorem-prover proved the final claim by induction on e. The base case is that e is not a natural number or is 0. In the induction step, it supposes e is positive and assumes the conjecture for $e/2$. Observe that this induction is precisely the one suggested by the recursion in CRYPT. The proof required about 6 minutes of cpu time.

4. Fermat's Theorem. The proof of the invertibility of CRYPT in [17] assumes the reader is familiar with elementary number theory up through Fermat's theorem. While a production model proof checker for informal proofs would come factory equipped with a good number theory library, we had no such library when we began the encryption proofs. We therefore had the system prove the following theorems:

–Many elementary facts about remainder and exponentiation.

–Suppose p and q are distinct primes, $a \bmod p = b \bmod p$, and $a \bmod q = b \bmod q$. Then $a \bmod p*q = b \bmod p*q$.[3] Hence, under the additional hypothesis $b < p*q$, $a \bmod p*q = b$.

–Suppose p is a prime and p does not divide M. Then $M*x \bmod p = M*y \bmod p$ iff $x \bmod p = y \bmod p$.[4] Hence, by letting y be 1, if p is a prime, $M*x \bmod p = M \bmod p$ iff either $p|M$ or $x \bmod p = 1$.

–The Pigeon Hole Principle: If L is a sequence of length n, every element of L is a positive integer, no element occurs twice in L, and every element of L is less than or equal to n, then L is a permutation of the sequence $[n\ n-1 \ldots 2\ 1]$.

–The following straightforward observations about permutations and the concept of the product of the elements in a sequence:

*If $L1$ is a permutation of $L2$, then the product of the elements in $L1$ is equal to that of the elements in $L2$.
*The product of the elements in $[n\ n-1 \ldots 2\ 1]$ is $n!$.
*Hence, if L is a permutation of $[n\ n-1 \ldots 2\ 1]$, then the product of the elements in L is $n!$.
*If p is a prime and $n < p$, then p does not divide $n!$.

We then had the theorem-prover check the proof of Fermat's theorem in [14]. (See Box 2.)

To prove Lemma 1 the system inducts on n and uses the previously proved lemma that intermediate mods can be dropped.

To get the system to prove the next lemma, that $j*M \bmod p$ is not a member $S(i, M, p)$, we had to instruct it to induct on i. (If left to its own devices, it chooses here to induct on i and j simultaneously.) The proof is as follows. The base case, when $i = 0$, is easy because $S(0, M, p)$ is empty. In the induction step we assume that $j*M \bmod p$ is not a member of $S(i-1, M, p)$ and must prove that it is not a member of $S(i, M, p)$. But by definition $S(i, M, p)$ is the sequence consisting of $i*M \bmod p$ followed by the sequence $S(i-1, M, p)$. The induction hypothesis establishes that $j*M \bmod p$ is not an element of the latter. It suffices to prove that $j*M \bmod p \neq i*M \bmod p$. Suppose the contrary. Then $j \bmod p = i \bmod p$, since $p \nmid M$. Thus $j = i$, contradicting $i < j$.

---

[3] Cf. Theorem 53 of Hardy and Wright's *An Introduction to the Theory of Numbers*.
[4] Cf. Theorem 55 of Hardy and Wright.

Box 2

DEFINITION. We define $S(n, M, p)$ to be the sequence:

$$[n*M \bmod p, (n-1)*M \bmod p, \ldots, 1*M \bmod p].$$

LEMMA 1. *The product of the elements in $S(n, M, p) \bmod p$ is equal to $n!*M^n \bmod p$.*

LEMMA. *If p is a prime that does not divide M and $i < j < p$, then $j*M \bmod p$ is not a member of $S(i, M, p)$.* (Hint: induct on i.)

LEMMA. *If p is a prime that does not divide M and $n < p$, then no element of $S(n, M, p)$ occurs twice.*

LEMMA. *If p is a prime that does not divide M and $n < p$, then each element of $S(n, M, p)$ is a positive integer.*

LEMMA. *If $p > 0$, then each element of $S(n, M, p)$ is less than or equal to $p - 1$.*

LEMMA. *$S(n, M, p)$ has n elements.*

FERMAT'S THEOREM. *If p is a prime that does not divide M, then $M^{p-1} \bmod p = 1$.*

(Hint: From Lemma 1 we have that the product of the elements in $S(p - 1, M, p) \bmod p$ is $(p - 1)!*M^{p-1} \bmod p$. But from the Pigeon Hole Principle we have that $S(p - 1, M, p)$ is a permutation of $[p - 1, \ldots 2, 1]$.)

The remaining lemmas above are proved by similar inductions of the system's own invention. The system's proof of the main theorem is then as follows. The hints lead it to conclude that $(p - 1)!*M^{p-1} \bmod p = (p - 1)! \bmod p$. Since p does not divide $(p - 1)!$, we can cancel $(p - 1)!$ from both sides and get $M^{p-1} \bmod p = 1$.

5. Invertibility of CRYPT. We now prove that $\text{CRYPT}(\text{CRYPT}(M, e, n), d, n) = M$, if n is the product of two distinct primes p and q, $M < n$, and e and d are multiplicative inverses in the ring of integers modulo $(p - 1)*(q - 1)$.

Box 3

LEMMA 2. *For all primes p, $(M*M^{k*(p-1)}) \bmod p = M \bmod p$.*

COROLLARY. *If p and q are prime, then*

$$(M*M^{k*(p-1)*(q-1)}) \bmod p = M \bmod p$$

and

$$(M*M^{k*(p-1)*(q-1)}) \bmod q = M \bmod q.$$

(Hint: take two instantiations of (2).)

LEMMA 3. *If p and q are distinct primes, M is a natural number less than $p*q$, and $x \bmod (p - 1)*(q - 1)$ is 1, then $M^x \bmod p*q = M$.*

RSA THEOREM. *If p and q are distinct primes, n is $p*q$, M is a natural number less than n and $e*d \bmod (p - 1)*(q - 1)$ is 1, $\text{CRYPT}(\text{CRYPT}(M, e, n), d, n) = M$.*

The proof of Lemma 2 can be seen by rearranging the exponents and mods so that $(M*M^{k*(p-1)}) \bmod p$ becomes $(M*(M^{p-1} \bmod p)^k \bmod p) \bmod p$. Fermat's Theorem can then be used to replace $M^{p-1} \bmod p$ by 1. The corollary is obvious.

To prove Lemma 3 the system first observes that, for some k, x is $k*(p - 1)*(q - 1) + 1$.

Thus, M^x mod $p*q$ is $(M*M^{k*(p-1)*(q-1)})$ mod $p*q$. Now recall the previously mentioned result that if p and q are distinct primes and a mod $p = b$ mod p and a mod $q = b$ mod q, then a mod $p*q = b$ mod $p*q$. Letting a be $M*M^{k*(p-1)*(q-1)}$ and b be M and appealing to the corollary above, the system concludes that M^x mod $p*q$ is M mod $p*q$, which, in turn, is M since $M < p*q$.

Finally, to prove the RSA Theorem itself, the system appeals to the correctness of CRYPT and the hypothesis that $n = p*q$ to reduce the conclusion to $(M^e$ mod $p*q)^d$ mod $p*q = M$. It then eliminates the intermediate mod, collects the exponents e and d and appeals to Lemma 3.

6. Sample Input to the Theorem-Prover. To illustrate the sense in which the boxed material is an English transcription of the user supplied type-in to our theorem-prover, we give below the type-in for the material in Box 1. We use the prefix syntax of Church's lambda calculus and McCarthy's LISP. It would be straightforward to arrange for the system to read and print according to a more elaborate grammar, but we prefer the simplicity of prefix notation.

DEFINITION.
(CRYPT M E N)
=
(IF (ZEROP E)
    1
    (IF (EVEN E)
      (REMAINDER (SQUARE (CRYPT M (QUOTIENT E 2) N))
                 N)
      (REMAINDER
        (TIMES M
          (REMAINDER (SQUARE (CRYPT M (QUOTIENT E 2) N))
                     N))
        N)))

THEOREM. TIMES.MOD.1 (rewrite):
(EQUAL (REMAINDER (TIMES X (REMAINDER Y N)) N)
       (REMAINDER (TIMES X Y) N))
THEOREM. TIMES.MOD.2 (rewrite):
(EQUAL (REMAINDER (TIMES A (TIMES B (REMAINDER Y N)))
                  N)
       (REMAINDER (TIMES A B Y) N))
Hint: Use TIMES.MOD.1 with X replaced by (TIMES A B).
THEOREM. CRYPT.CORRECT (rewrite):
(IMPLIES (NOT (EQUAL N 1))
         (EQUAL (CRYPT M E N) (REMAINDER (EXP M E) N)))

Readers interested in the complete list of definitions and theorems typed by the user should see section 8 of [5].

7. Conclusion. We have shown how an existing mechanical theorem-prover was used to check a recently published proof. Among the other mathematically interesting proofs performed by our theorem-prover are:

   –WILSON'S THEOREM. *If p is a prime, then* $(p - 1)!$ mod $p = p - 1$ [18];
   –the law of quadratic reciprocity [19];
   –the termination over the integers of the Takeuchi function [16]:

$$tak(x, y, z) = \text{if } x \leq y$$
$$\text{then } y$$
$$\text{else } tak(tak(x - 1, y, z),$$
$$tak(y - 1, z, x),$$
$$tak(z - 1, x, y));$$

–the soundness and completeness of a decision procedure for propositional
calculus [2];

–the existence of nonprimitive recursive functions;

–the Turing completeness of the Pure LISP programming language [8]; and

–the recursive unsolvability of the halting problem for Pure LISP [6].

We take these examples as evidence that proof checking mathematics is not only a theoretical but also a practical possibility. We doubt that the mechanical theorem-provers of today could be easily used to check theorems at the frontiers of mathematics. The less ambitious motivation behind much automatic theorem-proving research—certainly ours—is to mechanize the often mundane and tedious proofs arising in connection with computer programs. For example, our theorem-prover has been used to prove thousands of theorems related to the correctness of various programs [4], [7], communications protocols [9], and computer security [10]. Because of the high cost of bugs in software, the increasing impact of software due to cheap microprocessors, and the relatively shallow nature of most program correctness proofs, we expect to see, within the decade, commercial use of mechanical theorem-provers and formal logic in software development. The construction of an automatic theorem-prover that can advance the frontiers of mathematics, however, must still await another Gödel or Herbrand.

References

1. N. Bourbaki, Elements of Mathematics, Addison-Wesley, Reading, MA, 1968.

2. R. S. Boyer and J S. Moore, A Computational Logic, Academic Press, New York, 1979.

3. _____, Metafunctions: Proving them correct and using them efficiently as new proof procedures, in The Correctness Problem in Computer Science, R. S. Boyer and J S. Moore, Editors, Academic Press, London, 1981.

4. _____, A verification condition generator for FORTRAN, in The Correctness Problem in Computer Science, R. S. Boyer and J S. Moore, Editors, Academic Press, London, 1981.

5. _____, Proof Checking the RSA Public Key Encryption Algorithm, Technical Report ICSCA-CMP-33, Institute for Computing Science and Computer Applications, University of Texas at Austin, 1982.

6. _____, A Mechanical Proof of the Unsolvability of the Halting Problem, Technical Report ICSCA-CMP-28, University of Texas at Austin, 1982, to appear in J. Assoc. Comput. Mach.

7. _____, MJRTY–A Fast Majority Vote Algorithm, Technical Report ICSCA-CMP-32, Institute for Computing Science and Computer Applications, University of Texas at Austin, 1982.

8. _____, A Mechanical Proof of the Turing Completeness of Pure Lisp, Technical Report 37, Institute for Computing Science and Computer Applications, University of Texas at Austin, 1983.

9. Benedetto Lorenzo Di Vito, Verification of Communications Protcols and Abstract Process Models, PhD thesis ICSCA-CMP-25, Institute for Computing Science and Computer Applications, University of Texas at Austin, 1982.

10. Richard J. Feiertag, A Technique for Proving Specifications are Multilevel Secure, Technical Report CSL-109, SRI International, 1981.

11. K. Gödel, On formally undecidable propositions of Principia Mathematica and related systems, in From Frege to Gödel, J. van Heijenoort, Editor, Harvard University Press, Cambridge, MA, 1967.

12. G. H. Hardy and E. M. Wright, An Introduction to the Theory of Numbers, Oxford University Press, 1979.

13. D. E. Knuth and P. Bendix, Simple Word Problems in Universal Algebras, In Computational Problems in Abstract Algebras, J. Leech, Editor, Pergamon Press, Oxford, 1970, pp. 263–297.

14. D. E. Knuth, The Art of Computer Programming, Volume 1/Fundamental Algorithms. Addison-Wesley, Reading, MA, 1973.

15. _____, The Art of Computer Programming, Volume 2/Seminumerical Algorithms, Addison-Wesley, Reading, MA, 1981.

16. J S. Moore, A mechanical proof of the termination of Takeuchi's function, Information Processing Letters 9, 4 (1979) 176–181.

17. R. Rivest, A. Shamir, and L. Adleman, A Method for Obtaining Digital Signatures and Public-Key Cryptosystems, Communications of the ACM 21, 2 (1978) 120–126.

18. David M. Russinoff, A Mechanical Proof of Wilson's Theorem, forthcoming Masters thesis, Department of Computer Sciences, University of Texas at Austin.

19. David M. Russinoff, Proof-checking the law of quadratic reciprocity, in preparation, 1983.

III / Transformational Approaches

A wide variety of programming systems make use of program transformations as part of their knowledge representation and automation apparatus. Several of these systems are described in this section. Two others are described in [London and Feather, Chapter 17] and [Neighbors, Chapter 30]. In general, libraries of transformations play two roles. First, they are a representation of knowledge. (See Sections IX and X for further discussion of how to represent programming and domain knowledge.) Second, they are a prescription for how this knowledge should be used, namely to progressively transform one program into another.

[Darlington, Chapter 5] uses transformations to automatically improve the efficiency of a program. The input to the system is a clear ("self-evidently correct") but inefficient program; the ouput is a program that is much more efficient but usually much less clear. The system operates by applying a small number of powerful transformations to merge information from different parts of the input program and then redistribute it into a more efficient modularization. Burstall and Darlington have also developed a specialized programming language to facilitate these transformations.

Another use of transformations is to define higher-level programming constructs in terms of lower-level ones. In this use, sometimes called transformational implementation, the input to the transformation system is typically a program written in a so-called very high level language. The output is typically a program in which all the very high level constructs have been replaced by equivalent combinations of conventional constructs. Such systems typically require a large library of transformations in order to define the various very high level constructs and the ways they can be implemented.

In both of the above-mentioned uses of transformations, it is important to be able to verify that the transformations are correctness-preserving, i.e., that the transformation process does not alter the intended behavior of a program. [Broy and Pepper, Chapter 6] discusses the semantic foundations necessary to support this kind of verification.

An early landmark in research on automatic programming was the PSI system developed at Stanford. At the heart of PSI was a transformational implementation component (PECOS) that converted a very high level language program into an executable form. (Another component of PSI converted natural language input into the very high level program.) PECOS is described in detail in [Barstow, Chapter 7]. One of the most important contributions of PECOS is as a first attempt to codify a significant domain of programming knowledge in machine-usable form. The knowledge content of PECOS is discussed further in [Green and Barstow, Chapter 26].

A paramount problem in using program transformations is choosing which transformation to apply in situations where several are applicable. PECOS, for example, has a simple control structure that allows it to search all possible transformational paths, creating a variety of output programs. Another component of the PSI system, called LIBRA (see [Kant, Chapter 8]), analyzes the performance implications of alternative implementation choices and advises PECOS on which transformations to apply. Key issues in LIBRA's analysis include estimating run time behavior and identifying the most important decisions.

The PDS system described in [Cheatham, Chapter 9] is notable because it is a production quality system in regular use, in contrast with the experimental prototypes mostly described in this volume. PDS is based on an Algol-like programming language called EL1. For each new application, however, the PDS user is encouraged to define syntactic and semantic extensions of EL1 that capture the natural control structures and data abstractions of the application area and thus allow the user to write clearer and more succint programs. The user also defines transformations, to be applied in a predefined order, which map the extensions back down to basic EL1. The PDS environment provides facilities for controlling the application of alternate sets of transformations so that a single abstract program can be transformed in different ways in different situations (for example, for different target machines).

[Wile, Chapter 10] describes a generalized transformational system (POPART), which can support interactive transformational implementation in any BNF-definable programming language. A key idea in the POPART work is that the sequence of transformations chosen to implement a program is a valuable record of the development process. In particular, it should be possible to at least partially reuse ("replay") these transformations if the original very high level program is slightly modified.

An Experimental Program Transformation and Synthesis System

John Darlington
Imperial College of Science and Technology, South Kensington, Great Britain

Recommended by Erik Sandewall

ABSTRACT

This paper concentrates on the practical aspects of a program transformation system being developed. It describes the present performance of the system and outlines the techniques and heuristics used.

1. Introduction

Program transformation is a way of aiding the production of reliable, efficient programs. Programmers are encouraged to postpone questions of efficiency and first write their programs as clearly as possible. These programs are then transformed (either manually or automatically) into efficient versions by applying transformations that preserve correctness. We have developed a program transformation system based on transformation methods developed with R.M. Burstall. The programming languages used, and the formal transformation rules together with a brief description of the system, can be found in Burstall and Darlington [4]. In Darlington [7] we show how these same methods can be used to accomplish program synthesis, the conversion of non-executable program specifications into runnable programs. This paper concentrates on the more practical aspects of the system showing how it behaves at present, and describing some of the techniques used to achieve this behaviour. We have attempted to make this paper as self-contained as possible, but for a fuller description of the languages and formal transformations used the reader is referred to the earlier papers.

The system is under continuing development, it is viewed more as a research tool for the investigation of program transformation methodologies than a prototype programming assistant, however, the performance of the system at present gives some hope for the ultimate feasibility of such systems, and we

discuss several possible developments in Section 7. Section 2 describes the language used and gives the formal transformation rules the system is based upon. Section 3 outlines the basic structures of the system and gives some examples of its use for simple transformations. Section 4 concerns itself with synthesis, Section 5 shows how the system is able to generate auxiliary functions and synthesise functions from equations giving properties of the desired function, and finally Section 6 describes how several features that previously required user intervention have now been automated.

2. Languages and Formalism Used

2.1. The NPL language

We transform programs written in NPL, Burstall [9], a first order recursion equation language that grew out of our work on program transformation, and is being developed as a usable language by Burstall who has written an interpreter and type checker for it. The output of the transformation process is still an NPL program, but hopefully of a radically different form. It is a thesis of ours that a lot of the important transformations can be most easily expressed and achieved within the framework of recursion equations.

One of the novel features of NPL is the use of multiple left hand sides for the equations to eliminate the need for some conditionals and structure accessing functions. For example, for the traditional factorial function, instead of

$$fact(n) \Leftarrow if\ n = 0\ then\ 1$$
$$else\ n * fact(n-1)$$

one would write

$$fact(0) \Leftarrow 1$$
$$fact(n+1) \Leftarrow n+1 * fact(n)$$

The syntax of the main part of NPL is

Primitive functions: a set of primitive function symbols, with zero or more arguments; a subset of the primitive functions are the constructor functions.

Parameters: a set of parameter variables.

Recursive functions: a set of recursive function symbols.

Expressions: an expression is built in the usual way out of primitive function symbols, parameter variables and recursive function symbols.

Left hand expressions: a left hand expression is of the form $f(e1, \ldots, en)$, $n > 0$, where $e1, \ldots, en$ are expressions involving only parameter variables and constructor function symbols.

Right hand expressions: a right hand expression is an expression, or a list of expressions, qualified by conditions, or a where expression.

Artificial Intelligence **16** (1981), 1–46
North-Holland Publishing Company

Recursion equations: A recursion equation consists of a left hand expression and a right hand expression, written $E \Leftarrow F$. Thus an NPL program is a list of equations such as

$$member(x1, x :: X) \Leftarrow true \quad if\, x1 = x \quad (:: \text{ is an infix for cons})$$
$$member(x1, X) \quad if\, x1 \neq x$$

$$member(x1, nil) \Leftarrow false$$

Two defined functions are important for the transformation system. As an alternative to the *if* construct a three-placed conditional, cond, is defined,

$$member(x1, x :: X) \Leftarrow cond(x1 = x, true, member(x1, X))$$
$$member(x1, nil) \Leftarrow false$$

and a function Maketuple is provided to simulate the action of tuples (Maketuple should be thought of as variadic although it actually takes a list as argument).

$$maxandmin(x :: X) \Leftarrow maketuple([u1, u2]) \quad if\, x < u1\ and\ x > u2$$
$$maketuple([x, u2]) \quad if\, x > u1\ and\ x > u2$$
$$maketuple([u1, x]) \quad if\, x < u1\ and\ x < u2$$
$$where\ maketuple([u1, u2]) = maxandmin(X)$$

$$maxandmin(x :: nil) \Leftarrow maketuple([x, x])$$

In addition, NPL allows certain set and logic constructs to appear on the right hand side, for example

$$setofeven(X) \Leftarrow \langle :x: in\ X\ \&\ even(x): \rangle$$

$$even(0) \Leftarrow true$$
$$even(1) \Leftarrow false$$
$$even(n + 2) \Leftarrow even(n)$$

$$alleven(X) \Leftarrow forall\ x\ in\ X : even(x)$$
$$haseven(X) \Leftarrow exists\ x\ in\ X : even(x)$$

The deep structure of these expressions is rather interesting, but we postpone its discussion until Section 4.

NPL is a strongly typed language, but as at present the transformation system makes no use of the typing information we will ignore this aspect of NPL.

2.2. Transformation rules

The transformation rules operate on the equations and produce new equations. They are

(i) *Definition*: Introduce a new recursion equation whose left hand expression is not an instance of the left hand expression of any previous equation.

(ii) *Instantiation*: Introduce a substitution instance of an existing equation.

(iii) *Unfolding*: If $E \Leftarrow E'$ and $F \Leftarrow F'$ are equations and there is some occurrence in F' of an instance of E, replace it by the corresponding instance of E' obtaining F''; then add the equation $F \Leftarrow F''$.

(iv) *Folding*: If $E \Leftarrow E'$ and $F \Leftarrow F'$ are equations and there is some occurrence in F' of an instance of E', replace it by the corresponding instance of E obtaining F''; then add the equation $F \Leftarrow F''$.

(v) *Abstraction*: Introduce a *where* clause, by deriving from a previous equation $E \Leftarrow E'$ a new equation

$$E = E'[u_1/F_1, \ldots, u_n/F_n] \quad where \quad \langle u_1, \ldots, u_n \rangle = \langle F_1, \ldots, F_n \rangle.$$

(vi) *Laws*: Transform an equation by using on its right hand expression any laws we have about the primitives (associativity, commutativity, etc.) obtaining a new equation.

A rule similar to the folding rule was discovered independently by Manna and Waldinger in their work on program synthesis, Manna and Waldinger [13].

The basic strategy the system implements is based on the observation that a sequence of unfoldings, abstractions and applications of laws followed by foldings is bound to produce a dynamic improvement provided that the abstractions and law applications produce a static (textual) improvement.

3. System Structure

The system is written in POP-2, Burstall et al. [6] on the DEC 10 at Edinburgh University. It is written for clarity and flexibility rather than efficiency. Nevertheless it is not very large, occupying approximately 18K of which the NPL system and interpreter takes up 12K. At the moment it is set up as a semi-interactive system, the user supplying help and advice in certain key areas which will be outlined below.

Before describing the structure of the system and giving some examples of its performance we would like to correct any possible misconceptions about its nature. It is not designed as a prototype programmer's assistant that will enable users to develop their programs via transformations, rather it is a research tool for the development of program transformation methodologies. In several of the examples we shall see that some of the interactions require a knowledge of the internal workings of the system or the final program being aimed for. However, we are of the opinion that the best way to develop and test our understanding of such phenomena is by implementing them in working systems. What we would claim is that the behaviour of the present system demonstrates that the present transformation methodology is capable of making significant improvements in program behaviour without requiring excessive computer resources. All the examples shown have been typed directly from teletype output and although we apologise for the verbosity of some of them, we believe they illustrate our point better than suitably edited or invented dialogues. We have been able to do several larger examples on the system but we have not presented them here as the dialogues become rather long. The next stage in the development is to devise methods (both manual and automatic) whereby programmers could sensibly use these methods for program development. We are working on several ways to achieve this, putting more control with the user and these will be discussed briefly in Section 7.

The system has no quantitative means of evaluating the improvements made, relying on the user to accept or reject them, however, the system has an inbuilt bias towards improvement and, as will be seen in the examples, behaves quite purposefully.

We will display the system's basic behaviour by means of a very simple example. Consider the following program

$$append(nil, Y) \Leftarrow Y$$
$$append(x::X, Y) \Leftarrow x::append(X, Y)$$
$$g(X, Y, Z) \Leftarrow append(append(X, Y), Z)$$

g is slightly inefficient as it builds up an intermediate list that it then iterates along. Given that the user has input the above equations to the NPL system, he could affect an improvement by the following dialogue with the transformation system.

EXAMPLE 1. *Append.*

```
EQNLIST.PREXP;
APPEND([], Y) ⇐ Y                              —print out of original
APPEND(X1::Y, W) ⇐ X1::APPEND(Y, W)             equations, [] is the
G(X, Y, W) ⇐ APPEND(APPEND(X, Y), W):           empty list nil
:
START:                                         —user starts dialogue
TYPE IN INSTANTIATED L.H.S. BASE               —system's response
CASES FIRST.
G(NIL, Y, W) END                               —user
G([], Y, W) ⇐ APPEND(Y, W)                     —system
NOW TYPE IN RECURSIVE BRANCHES                 —system
G(X1::X, Y, W) END                             —user
HOW DOES
G(X1::X, Y, W) ⇐ X1::G(X, Y, W)                —system
LOOK TO YOU
OK                                             —user

FINISHED.CPU TIME TAKEN 0 MINS 2 SECS
:
.PREXP;                                        —print out of modi-
G([], Y, W) ⇐ APPEND(Y, W)                      fied equations
G(X1::X, Y, W) ⇐ X1::G(X, Y, W)                 handed back to
APPEND([], Y) ⇐ Y                               NPL system
APPEND(X1::Y, W) ⇐ X1::APPEND(Y, W)
```

The system exits with an indication that it has achieved an acceptable improvement and passes back to the NPL system the modified list of equations

$$append(nil, Y) \Leftarrow Y$$
$$append(x::X, Y) \Leftarrow x::append(X, Y)$$
$$g(nil, Y, Z) \Leftarrow append(Y, Z)$$
$$g(x::X, Y, Z) \Leftarrow x::g(X, Y, Z)$$

Thus we see that the main user responsibilities are to provide the correct instantiations for the functions he wants to improve, and to accept or reject proposed improvements. Each of the instantiations given above could have been a list of instantiations, the system attempting to find an acceptable equation for every instantiation given. In the above dialogue the system comes up with the 'correct' solution first time for each instantiation. If the user rejects any solution the system continues looking at this case until it runs out of improvements to suggest or a pre-set effort bound is exceeded. If no acceptable improvement is found for any case the system immediately exits with a signal of failure and the equation list remains unaltered.

For the base cases the system relies solely on evaluation. It selects the equation required, instantiates it as requested and unfolds the right hand side completely or until the pre-set effort bound is exceeded.

For the other cases the system implements the strategy outlined earlier, viz. sequences of unfoldings, rewritings and abstractions followed by sequences of foldings. This is embodied in the routine DEVELOP which takes the suitably instantiated equation and searches for a fold.

intelligent behaviour but for the moment the first method is preferred for simplicity and was used for most of the examples presented here.

allwaysofunfolding returns a list of the equation given plus all versions of the equation that can be produced by one unfolding using the equations on the present list. A switch enables the user to restrict this to call by value unfoldings if required.

tryfindfold is where most of the cleverness of the system resides. It attempts to find a fold between the developing equation and an equation on the equation list. There are several filters that reject obviously undesirable folds e.g. ones that lead to recursions that definitely do not terminate, or ones that lead to recursive patterns different from those being sought (more about this later). For any possible fold that passes all the filters the equation that would result is printed out for the user's inspection. The user can then do one of three things

(i) Reject this fold by typing NOGOOD whereupon the system ignores this possible fold and continues developing the equation.

(ii) Accept this fold but continue by typing CONTINUE, in this case the system makes the fold and carries on developing the equation.

(iii) Accept the fold as a final version of the equation by typing OK. The system makes the fold and exits directly from develop to select the next instantiation if any remain.

At its simplest, folding consists of searching through the equation list to find an equation an instance of whose right hand side occurs within the right hand side of the developing equation. More interesting behaviour occurs when tryfindfold looks for a forced fold, using information collected from a failure to achieve a simple fold to direct the development of the equation so that a fold can be achieved. The simplest form of this occurs when trying to fold the equation with an equation whose right hand side is a tuple. We will illustrate this by showing the optimisation of the fibonacci function, defined thus

$$\text{fib}(0) \Leftarrow 1$$
$$\text{fib}(1) \Leftarrow 1$$
$$\text{fib}(n+2) \Leftarrow \text{fib}(n+1) + \text{fib}(n).$$

The key to this optimisation lies in defining the auxiliary function

$$g(n) \Leftarrow \text{maketuple}([\text{fib}(n+1), \text{fib}(n)])$$

The system can now discover such definitions for itself as we shall see in Section 6, however, for the moment let us take it as given. The dialogue for the improvement goes as follows.

```
develop(eqn) =
    if toodeep( )
    then return
    else reduce (eqn)→eqn;
        forall eqn1 in allwaysofunfolding (eqn)
        do tryfindfold (eqn1)→eqn1
            develop (eqn1)
        od
    fi
```

toodeep controls how much effort is expanded down any particular branch of the recursion. It is true if the depth of recursion exceeds a pre-set depth bound, false otherwise

reduce applies a set of reduction rules to the equation. These reduction rules are supplied to the system as equations with the convention that they are only to be used in a left to right direction. The system has a kernel of reduction rules and these can be added by the user for particular problems. Amongst the ones used are

$$\text{Cond}(true, x, y) \Leftarrow x$$
$$\text{Cond}(false, x, y) \Leftarrow y$$
$$\text{append}(x, \text{append}(y, z)) \Leftarrow \text{append}(\text{append}(x, y), z)$$

We have experimented with various ways of using these reduction rules. In order of sophistication these have been.

(i) Applying each applicable reduction rule just once at each iteration. This simple method suffices for a lot of smaller examples but for larger ones one has to tailor the rules to fit the transformations required.

(ii) Using the rules to keep the developing equation in a normal form. This is not always successful as the form required is dictated more by the need to find a fold rather than any global criteria.

(iii) Using the rules in a 'means-end' fashion. The rewritings are used to direct the developing equation to a foldable form. Earlier versions of the system used a matching routine, due to Topor [15] whereby certain properties of functions such as commutativity, and associativity were built into the matching routine and only applied when necessary.

The last method is the one to be ultimately preferred giving the most

EXAMPLE 2. *Fibonacci.*

EQNLIST.PREXP;

$G(N) \Leftarrow$ MAKETUPL([FIB($N+1$), FIB(N)])   —original equations
FIB(($N+1$)+1) $\Leftarrow$ FIB($N+1$)+FIB(N)
FIB(1) $\Leftarrow$ 1
FIB(0) $\Leftarrow$ 1:

:. START;
TYPE IN INSTANTIATED L.H.S. BASE CASES FIRST.
G(0) END

G(0) $\Leftarrow$ MAKETUPL([1,1])

NOW TYPE IN RECURSIVE BRANCHES
FIB(($N+1$)+1), $G(N+1)$ END   —two cases to try
HOW DOES

FIB(($N+1$)+1) $\Leftarrow U1+U2$ WHEREP
          MAKETUPL([$U1$, $U2$]) $= = G(N)$ —fibonacci in terms of g

LOOK TO YOU
OK

HOW DOES

$G(N+1) \Leftarrow$ MAKETUPL([FIB((N+FIB(1))+FIB(1)), FIB(N)+FIB(1)])

LOOK TO YOU
NOGOOD

HOW DOES

$G(N+1) \Leftarrow$ MAKETUPL([FIB((N+FIB(0))+FIB(0)), FIB(N)+FIB(0)])

LOOK TO YOU
NOGOOD

HOW DOES

$G(N+1) \Leftarrow$ MAKETUPL([$U3+U4$, $U3$]) WHEREP
          MAKETUPL([$U3$, $U4$]) $= = G(N)$
          —recursion for g

LOOK TO YOU
OK

FINISHED CPU TIME TAKEN 0 MINS 11 SECS
: ...
: ...
:. PREXP;   —print out of resulting equations
FIB(0) $\Leftarrow$ 1
FIB(1) $\Leftarrow$ 1
FIB(($N+1$)+1) $\Leftarrow U1+U2$ WHEREP MAKETUPL([$U1$, $U2$]) $= = G(N)$
G(0) $\Leftarrow$ MAKETUPL([1,1])
$G(N+1) \Leftarrow$ MAKETUPL([$U3+U4$, $U3$]) WHEREP
          MAKETUPL([$U3$, $U4$]) $= = G(N)$

Forced folding comes into play during the optimisation of $g(n+1)$, simple unfolding produces the equation

$$g(n+1) \Leftarrow \langle \text{fib}(n+1)+\text{fib}(n), \text{fib}(n)\rangle \quad \text{Ⓐ}$$

and when tryfindfold attempts to fold this with

$$g(n) \Leftarrow \langle \text{fib}(n+1), \text{fib}(n)\rangle \quad \text{Ⓑ}$$

the matching routine fails to find a direct match but notices that all the components necessary to match Ⓑ are present within Ⓐ so it forces the rearrangement of Ⓐ to

$$g(n+1) \Leftarrow \langle u1+u2, u1\rangle \ where \ \langle u1, u2\rangle = \langle \text{fib}(n+1), \text{fib}(n)\rangle$$

which folds with Ⓑ giving

$$g(n+1) \Leftarrow \langle u1+u2, u1\rangle \ where \ \langle u1, u2\rangle = g(n)$$

as above.

This technique of forced folding, an application of means end analysis, contributes greatly to any sense of purpose the system possesses. Forced folding is also used in the automatic generation of sub-functions, but we will postpone this discussion until Section 5, after synthesis, as it is used in both transformation and synthesis. As mentioned earlier, forced folding was also used to restrict the application of rewrite rules to those that were immediately beneficial in achieving folds, but for the moment this has been dropped in favour of a simpler method.

EXAMPLE 3. *Conversion to iterative and bottom up form. Sum.*

3.1. *Normal recursion to iteration*
The transformation system enables us to convert normal recursive forms to iterative forms that use an accumulator. The user has to supply a definition for the iterative form in terms of the recursive.

EQNLIST.PREXP:

SUMIT(I, ACC) = ACC + SUM(I)   original equations
SUM($N + 1$) = ($N + 1$) + SUM(N)   including definition
SUM(0) = 0:   of iterative form

$$\text{sum}(N) = \sum_{i=0}^{N} i$$

: START;
TYPE IN INSTANTIATED L.H.S. BASE CASES FIRST.
SUMIT(0, ACC) END
SUMIT(0, ACC) = ACC
NOW TYPE IN RECURSIVE BRANCHES.
SUMIT($I + 1$, ACC), SUM($N + 1$) END
HOW DOES

SUMIT($I + 1$, ACC) = SUMIT(I, ($I + 1$) + ACC)
LOOK TO YOU
OK

HOW DOES

SUM($N + 1$) = SUMIT(N, $N + 1$)
LOOK TO YOU
OK
FINISHED. CPU TIME TAKEN 0 MINS 3 SECS

:.PREXP;
SUM(0) $\Leftarrow$ 0
SUM($N + 1$) $\Leftarrow$ SUMIT(N, $N + 1$)
SUMIT($I + 1$, ACC) $\Leftarrow$ SUMIT(I, ($I + 1$) + ACC)
SUMIT(0, ACC) $\Leftarrow$ ACC
:

3.2. *Top down recursion to bottom up recursion*
We can also convert the normal 'going down' recursion to a 'going up' form, again

by supplying a definition

EQNLIST.PREXP;
SUMUP(I, N) $\Leftarrow$ SUM(N) − SUM(I)
SUM($N + 1$) $\Leftarrow$ ($N + 1$) + SUM(N)
SUM(0) $\Leftarrow$ 0:
:
:START;
TYPE IN INSTANTIATED L.H.S. BASE CASES FIRST.
SUMUP(N, N) END

SUMUP(N, N) $\Leftarrow$ 0

NOW TYPE IN RECURSIVE BRANCHES.
SUMUP(I, N), SUM($N + 1$) END

HOW DOES

SUMUP(I, N) $\Leftarrow$ (SUM(N) − SUM($I + 1$)) + ($I + 1$)

LOOK TO YOU
CONTINUE

HOW DOES

SUMUP(I, N) $\Leftarrow$ SUMUP($I + 1$, N) + ($I + 1$)

LOOK TO YOU
OK

HOW DOES

SUM($N + 1$) $\Leftarrow$ ($N + 1$) + (SUM(N) − SUM(0))

LOOK TO YOU
CONTINUE

HOW DOES

SUM($N + 1$) $\Leftarrow$ ($N + 1$) + SUMUP(0, N)
LOOK TO YOU
OK

FINISHED CPU TIME TAKEN 0 MINS 4 SECS
:PREXP;
$SUM(0) \Leftarrow 0$
$SUM(N+1) \Leftarrow (N+1) + SUMUP(0,N)$
$SUMUP(I,N) \Leftarrow SUMUP(I+1,N) + (I+1)$
$SUMUP(N,N) \Leftarrow 0$
:

4. Synthesis

As mentioned previously, NPL allows certain set and logic constructs on the right hand side of equations. The concrete syntax of these constructs is

setexpression   ::= ⟨:expression:generator*:⟩

existsexpression :: = *exists* generator* : expression

forallexpression :: = *forall* generator* : expression

generator   :: = variable *in* expression (range)

& expression (condition).

The NPL interpreter evaluates the list of generators in a left to right fashion so conditions can mention any bound variables that occur to their left. The interpreter is able to run many programs written using these facilities, but some programs written are horrendously inefficient while others are not runnable as they stand.

For example a function begins(a,b) to check whether the list a forms the initial segment of list b can be defined thus begins(a,b)$\Leftarrow$ *exists* c in universofists( ): equallist($a \langle \rangle c, b$) where universofists( ) can either be uninterpreted or return the set of all possible lists up to a certain size given a set of atoms, the former makes the definition unrunnable, the latter makes it very inefficient. The transformation system is able to convert these sorts of definitions to efficient recursions removing the set or logic constructs. For example

EXAMPLE 4. *Begins.*

EQNLIST.PREXP;
BEGINS(L,M)$\Leftarrow$EXISTS $L1$ IN UNIV:$L \langle \rangle L1 == M$ ($\langle \rangle$ is infix for append)

$A::L \langle \rangle M \Leftarrow A::(L \langle \rangle M)$
$[ ] \langle \rangle M \Leftarrow M$
$A::L == B::M \Leftarrow (A = B)$ AND $(L == M)$
$[ ] == B::M \Leftarrow$ FALSE
$A::L == [ ] \Leftarrow$ FALSE

$[ ] == [ ] \Leftarrow$ TRUE
:
:START;
TYPE IN INSTANTIATED L.H.S. BASE CASES FIRST.
BEGINS (NIL, M), BEGINS ($A::L$, NIL) END

BEGINS ($[ ], M$)$\Leftarrow$TRUE
BEGINS ($A::L$, $[ ]$)$\Leftarrow$FALSE

NOW TYPE IN RECURSIVE BRANCHES.
BEGINS ($A::L$, $B::M$) END
HOW DOES
BEGINS ($A::L$, $B::M$)$\Leftarrow$($A = B$) AND BEGINS (L, M)
LOOK TO YOU
OK
FINISHED.CPU TIME TAKEN 0 mins 4 secs
:
:

:PREXP;
BEGINS ($[ ], M$)$\Leftarrow$TRUE
BEGINS ($A::L$, $[ ]$)$\Leftarrow$FALSE
BEGINS ($A::L$, $B::M$)$\Leftarrow$($A = B$) AND BEGINS (L, M)

The system behaves towards these new constructs exactly as it does towards the more normal expressions shown earlier. However, the concept of unfolding has to be extended as often these constructs obviate the need for recursively defined functions to appear on the right hand side of equations. We have developed a set of reduction rules that are used on these constructs, for example

$$\langle :f(x): x \text{ in } \emptyset \ \& \ P(x): \rangle \Leftarrow \emptyset$$

$$\langle :f(x): x \text{ in } x1 + X \ \& \ P(x): \rangle \Leftarrow \langle :f(x1): \rangle \cup \langle :f(x): x \text{ in } X \ \& \ P(x): \rangle \ \textit{if } P(x1)$$

$$\langle :f(x): x \text{ in } X \ \& \ P(x): \rangle \ \textit{otherwise}$$

$$\textit{exists } x \text{ in } \emptyset \ \& \ P(x): Q(x) \Leftarrow \text{False.}$$

These are applied allwaysofundolding (not reduce) always in a left to right manner.

This task has been greatly simplified by use of a unifying deep structure for these constructs that reduces the number of separate reduction rules needed. To illustrate this let us first rewrite our constructs

$$\langle:f(x): x\ in\ X\ \&\ P(x):\rangle \equiv \bigcup_{x\ in\ X\ \&\ P(x)} \langle:f(x):\rangle \quad \text{(union)}$$

$$forall\ x\ in\ X\ \&\ P(x): Q(x) = \bigwedge_{x\ in\ X\ \&\ P(x)} Q(x) \quad \text{(conjunction)}$$

$$exists\ x\ in\ X\ \&\ P(x): Q(x) = \bigvee_{x\ in\ X\ \&\ P(x)} Q(x) \quad \text{(disjunction)}$$

and we see the underlying similarity. Each construct consists of a predicated generation process ($x\ in\ X\ \&\ P(x)$), an expression for each element so generated ($\langle:f(x):\rangle$, $Q(x)$) and an operation to combine these expressions ($\cup, \wedge, \vee$). Each operator has associated identifiers and zeros forming a monoid. These structures are represented by iterative expressions which have the following abstract syntax.

iterative expression ::= ⟨monoid, generator*, expression⟩

generator ::= ⟨variable, range, condition⟩

monoid ::= ⟨operator, identity, zero⟩

The monoids for our various constructs are

set = ⟨union, $\emptyset$, $\perp$⟩

forall = ⟨and, true, false⟩

exists = ⟨or, false, true⟩

Thus for example

$$\langle:f(x,y): x\ in\ X \cup Y\ \&\ P(x), y\ in\ Y\ \&\ Q(x,y):\rangle$$

is represented as

⟨setmonoid, [gen1, gen2], $\langle:f(x, y):\rangle$⟩

where

gen1 = ⟨x, $X \cup Y$, $P(x)$⟩

gen2 = ⟨y, Y, $Q(x,y)$⟩

Thus our rewrite rules are expressed in terms of these iterative expressions.

Some of the ones available to the system at present are

(i) ⟨monoid, ⟨bv, $x1 + X$, Cond⟩::genlist, exp⟩ $\qquad$ ($x1 + X \equiv \langle:x1:\rangle \cup X$)
$\Leftarrow$⟨monoid, genlist$\{bv/x1\}$[1], exp$\{bv/x1\}$⟩
$\quad$ monoid.operatorof ⟨monoid, genlist, exp⟩ $\qquad$ *if* Cond$\{bv/x1\}$
$\quad$ ⟨monoid, genlist, exp⟩ $\qquad\qquad\qquad\qquad$ *otherwise*

For example

$$forall\ x\ in\ x1 + X\ \&\ P(x), y\ in\ Y\ \&\ Q(x, y): R(x, y)$$

reduces to

$$forall\ y\ in\ Y\ \&\ Q(x1, y): R(x1, y)$$
and
$$forall\ x\ in\ X\ \&\ P(x), y\ in\ Y\ \&\ Q(x, y): R(x, y) \quad \text{if } P(x1)$$
$$forall\ x\ in\ X\ \&\ P(x)\ y\ in\ Y\ \&\ Q(x, y): R(x, y) \quad \text{otherwise}$$

(ii) ⟨monoid, nil, exp⟩
$\Leftarrow$ exp

In conjunction with (i) this reduces

$$\langle:x: x\ in\ x1 + X\ \&\ P(x):\rangle$$

to

$$\langle:x1:\rangle \cup \langle:x: x\ in\ X\ \&\ P(x):\rangle \quad \text{if } P(x1)$$
$$\langle:x: x\ in\ X\ \&\ P(x):\rangle \qquad\qquad \text{otherwise}$$

(iii) ⟨monoid, ⟨x, $\emptyset$, Cond⟩::genlist, exp⟩
$\Leftarrow$ monoid.identityof

This reduces

$$\langle:x: x\ in\ \emptyset\ \&\ P(x):\rangle \text{ to } \emptyset$$
$$forall\ x\ in\ \emptyset\ \&\ P(x): Q(x) \text{ to true}$$
and $exists\ x\ in\ \emptyset\ \&\ P(x): Q(x)$ to false

(iv) ⟨monoid, ⟨x, $S1 \cup S2$, Cond⟩::genlist, exp⟩
$\Leftarrow$⟨monoid, ⟨x, $S1$, Cond⟩::genlist, exp⟩
$\quad$ monoid.operatorof ⟨monoid, ⟨x, $S2$, Cond⟩::genlist, exp⟩

This reduces

$$exists\ x\ in\ X1 \cup X2: R(x)$$

to

$$exists\ x\ in\ X1: R(x) \text{ or } exists\ x\ in\ X2: R(x)$$

[1] $g\{bv/x1\}$ means g with all occurrences of bv replaced by x1.

(v) $\langle$monoid, genlist, $e1$ op $e2\rangle$
$\Leftarrow \langle$monoid, genlist, $e1\rangle$ op $\langle$monoid, genlist, $e2\rangle$

provided op and the monoid operator distribute, i.e. if the monoid operator is opm we need

$$(a \text{ op } b) \text{ opm } (c \text{ op } d) \equiv (a \text{ opm } c) \text{ op } (b \text{ opm } d)$$

This reduces

$$exists \ x \text{ in } X: P(x) \text{ or } Q(x)$$

to $exists \ x \text{ in } X: P(x) \text{ or } exists \ x \text{ in } X: Q(x)$

and

$$forall \ x \text{ in } X: P(x) \ \& \ Q(x)$$

to $forall \ x \text{ in } X: P(x) \ \& \ forall \ x \text{ in } X: Q(x)$

and

$$\bigcup_{x \text{ in } X} f(x) \cup g(x)$$

to

$$\bigcup_{x \text{ in } X} f(x) \cup \bigcup_{x \text{ in } X} g(x)$$

(vi) $\langle$monoid, genlist, $e1$ op $e2\rangle$
$\Leftarrow e1$ op $\langle$monoid, genlist, $e2\rangle$

provided that $e1$ contains no variables bound in genlist. This reduces

$$forall \ x \text{ in } X: P(y) \text{ or } Q(x, y)$$

to $P(y) \text{ or } forall \ x \text{ in } X: Q(x, y)$

5. Generalisation and Sub-function Synthesis

In all the examples shown so far, the recursions introduced have been calls to previously defined functions. An important attribute of the system is its ability to invent new functions for itself, through various forms of generalisation. Switches enable the user to switch the various generalisation facilities on and off.

5.1. Simple generalisation

The simplest form of generalisation used is when a new function is defined to compute some part of the developing equation. For example if we define the

Cartesian product of two sets thus

$$\text{Cart}(X, Y) \Leftarrow \langle\langle x y\rangle: x \text{ in } X, y \text{ in } Y:\rangle$$

and proceed with a synthesis we get

$$\text{Cart}(\emptyset, Y) \Leftarrow \emptyset$$

and

$$\text{Cart}(x1 + X, Y) \Leftarrow \langle\langle x1 y\rangle: y \text{ in } Y:\rangle \cup \langle\langle x y\rangle: x \text{ in } X, y \text{ in } Y:\rangle$$

Using reduction rules (iii) and (i).

The system spots that $\langle\langle x1 y\rangle: y \text{ in } Y:\rangle$ is going to need computing and asks the user if it can go ahead and define a new function by

$$newf1(u1, u2, u3, u4) \Leftarrow \langle\langle u1 y\rangle: y \text{ in } u3:\rangle \cup \langle\langle x y\rangle: x \text{ in } u2, y \text{ in } u4:\rangle$$

If this is accepted by the user, the system postpones consideration of Cart and turns its attention to $newf1$. It asks the user to provide instantiations as before, base cases and main recursions (this time the form of input is slightly different as the system already knows what function is to be so instantiated) and proceeds to evaluate these as before. If it is successful in finding acceptable forms for all the instantiations of the new function it adds these equations to the equation list and returns to working on Cart. If it succeeds with Cart the equations for $newf1$ are retained. If no acceptable forms can be found for $newf1$ the system abandons this generalisation and returns to working on Cart. In this example the system succeeds and the final equations produced are

$$cart(\emptyset, Y) \Leftarrow \emptyset$$
$$cart(x1 + X, Y) \Leftarrow newf1(x1, X, Y, Y)$$
$$newf1(u1, u2, \emptyset, u4) \Leftarrow cart(u2, u4)$$
$$newf1(u1, u2, y1 + u3, u4) \Leftarrow \langle\langle u1 y1\rangle:\rangle \cup newf1(u1, u2, u3, u4)$$

This system of recursion is rather idiosyncratic. A more orthodox pattern is

$$cart(\emptyset, Y) \Leftarrow \emptyset$$
$$cart(x1 + X, Y) \Leftarrow newf1(x1, Y) \cup cart(X, Y)$$
$$newf1(u1, \emptyset) \Leftarrow \emptyset$$
$$newf1(u1, y1 + u2) \Leftarrow \langle\langle u1 y1\rangle:\rangle \cup newf1(u1, u2)$$

which can be achieved by defining

$$newf1(u1, u2) \Leftarrow \langle\langle u1 y\rangle: y \text{ in } u2:\rangle$$

We can produce this pattern also and in Section 5.3 we show how it is achieved. Martin Feather wrote much of the code to enable the system to achieve this form of generalisation.

EXAMPLE 5. *Multiple Cartesian product.* In this example we convert the definition of the Cartesian product of three sets to a recursion involving three loops.

In this example the switch NOSETEXPRS is set. This restricts the use of the set and logic constructs to the specification stages and does not allow them in the final versions, cf. the specification and target languages used by Manna and Waldinger [13]. This enables the system to suggest the 'right' version every time.

EQNLIST.PREXP;
CART3(X, Y, Z) ⇐ ⟨: MAKETUPL([$X1, X2, X3$]): $X1$ IN X $X2$ IN Y $X3$ IN Z:⟩;

:START;
TYPE IN INSTANTIATED L.H.S. BASE CASES FIRST.
CART3(NILSET, Y, Z) END

CART3(⟨:⟩, Y, Z) ⇐ ⟨:⟩

NOW TYPE IN RECURSIVE BRANCHES.
CART3(CONSSET($X4, X$), Y, Z) END

COULD GENERALISE FOLLOWING EXPRESSION:
HOW DOES

⟨: MAKETUPL([$X4, X2, X3$]): $X2$ IN Y $X3$ IN Z:⟩ + ⟨: MAKETUPL([$X1, X2, X3$]):$X1$ IN X $X2$ IN Y $X3$ IN Z:⟩

LOOK TO YOU
OK

AN ATTEMPTING TO SYNTHESISE A FUNCTION NEWF1 DEFINED IMPLICITLY BY THIS EQUATION

NEWF1 ($U6, U5, U4, U3, U2, U1$) ⇐ ⟨:MAKETUPL([$U3, X2, X3$]): $X2$ IN $U1$ $X3$ IN $U2$:⟩ + ⟨:MAKETUPL([$X1, X2, X3$]): $X1$ IN $U4$ $X2$ IN $U5$ $X3$ IN $U6$:⟩

HOW DOES

NEWF1 ($U6, U5, U4, U3, U2, U1$) ⇐ ⟨:MAKETUPL([$U3, X2, X3$]): $X2$ IN $U1$ $X3$ IN $U2$:⟩ + ⟨:MAKETUPL([$X1, X2, X3$]): $X1$ IN $U4$ $X2$ IN $U5$ $X3$ IN $U6$:⟩

LOOK TO YOU
OK

(There is avoidable redundancy here, having accepted the generalisation the new function will always be accepted.)

WOULD YOU TYPE IN SUITABLE INSTANTIATION PAIRS BASE CASES FIRST.
:END
NOW THE RECURSIONS   —'base' case involves a recursion

:$U1$, NILSET END $U1$, CONSSET($X5, U1$) END END

HOW DOES

NEWF1($U6, U5, U4, U3, U2$, ⟨::⟩) ⇐ CART3($U4, U5, U6$)

LOOK TO YOU
OK

COULD GENERALISE FOLLOWING EXPRESSION:
HOW DOES

(⟨: MAKETUPL([$U3, X5, X3$]): $X3$ IN $U2$:⟩ + ⟨: MAKETUPL([$U3, X2, X3$]): $X2$ IN $U1$ $X3$ IN $U2$:⟩) + ⟨: MAKETUPL([$X1, X2, X3$]): $X1$ IN $U4$ $X2$ IN $U5$ $X3$ IN $U6$:⟩

LOOK TO YOU
OK

AM ATTEMPTING TO SYNTHESISE A FUNCTION NEWF2 DEFINED IMPLICITLY BY THIS EQUATION

NEWF2($U15, U14, U13, U12, U11, U10, U9, U8, U7$) ⇐ (⟨: MAKETUPL([$U8, U9, X3$]): $X3$ IN $U7$:⟩ + ⟨: MAKETUPL([$U12, X2, X3$]): $X2$ IN $U10$ $X3$ IN $U11$:⟩) + ⟨: MAKETUPL([$X1, X2, X3$]): $X1$ IN $U13$ $X2$ IN $U14$ $X3$ IN $U15$:⟩

HOW DOES

NEWF2($U15, U14, U13, U12, U11, U10, U9, U8, U7$) ⇐ (⟨: MAKETUPL([$U8, U9, X3$]): $X3$ IN $U7$:⟩ + ⟨: MAKETUPL([$U12, X2, X3$]): $X2$ IN $U10$ $X3$ IN $U11$:⟩) + ⟨: MAKETUPL([$X1, X2, X3$]): $X1$ IN $U13$ $X2$ IN $U14$ $X3$ IN $U15$:⟩

```
:.PREXP;
NEWF1(U6, U5, U4, U3, U2, ⟨::⟩)⇐CART3(U4, U5, U6)
NEWF1(U6, U5, U4, U3, U2, CONSSET(X5, U1))⇐NEWF2(U6, U5,
          U4, U3, U2, U1, X5, U3, U2)
NEWF2(U15, U14, U13, U12, U11, U10, U9, U8, CONSSET(X6,
U7))⇐⟨: MAKETUPL([U8, U9, X6]):⟩+ NEWF2(U15, U14, U13, U12,
          U11, U10, U9, U8, U7)
NEWF2(U15, U14, U13, U12, U11, U10, U9, U8, ⟨::⟩)⇐NEWF1(U15,
          U14, U13, U12, U11, U10)
CART3(CONSSET(X4, X), Y, Z)⇐NEWF1(Z, Y, X, X4, Z, Y)
CART3(⟨::⟩, Y, Z)⇐⟨::⟩
..
```

EXAMPLE 6. *Double Sum.* This example illustrates generalisation at work in a transformation example. Every element of a two level list is doubled by the function double and the resulting two level list summed by the function sum. Both double and sum use subsidiary functions db and sm to iterate along the component lists. This loop structure is collapsed to produce a more efficient version that traverses the list only once using an invented subsidiary function.

```
EQNLIST.PREXP;
G(XLL)⇐SUM(DOUBLE(XLL))                    e.g. G([[1, 2], [3]]) = 12
DOUBLE(XL::XLL)⇐DB(XL)::DOUBLE(XLL)
DOUBLE([])⇐[]
DB(X::XL)⇐2*X::DB(XL)
DB([])⇐[]
SUM(XL::XLL)⇐SM(XL)+SUM(XLL)
SUM([])⇐0
SM(X::XL)⇐X+SM(XL)
SM([])⇐0: START;
TYPE IN INSTANTIATED L.H.S. BASE CASES FIRST.
G(NIL) END
G([])⇐0
NOW TYPE IN RECURSIVE BRANCHES.
G(XL::XLL) END
COULD GENERALISE FOLLOWING EXPRESSION:
HOW DOES

SUM(DOUBLE(XL::XLL))

LOOK TO YOU
NOGOOD

HOW DOES
```

```
LOOK TO YOU
OK

WOULD YOU TYPE IN SUITABLE INSTANTIATION PAIRS. BASE
CASES FIRST.

: END
NOW THE RECURSIONS

: U7, NILSET END U7, CONSSET (X6, U7) END END

HOW DOES

NEWF2(U15, U14, U13, U12, U11, U10, U9, U8, ⟨::⟩) = NEWF1(U15,
U14, U13, U12, U11, U10)

LOOK TO YOU
OK

HOW DOES

NEWF2(U15, U14, U13, U12, U11, U10, U9, U8, CONSSET(X6, U7))
⇐⟨: MAKETUPL([U8, U9, X6]):⟩+ NEWF2(U15, U14, U13, U12,
U11, U10, U9, U8, U7)
                                         —system climbs back up

LOOK TO YOU
OK

HOW DOES

NEWF1(U6, U5, U4, U3, U2, CONSSET(X5, U1))⇐NEWF2(U6, U5,
                U4, U3, U2, U1, X5, U3, U2)

LOOK TO YOU
OK

HOW DOES

CART3(CONSSET(X4, X), Y, Z)⇐NEWF1(Z, Y, X, X4, Z, Y)

LOOK TO YOU
OK

FINISHED.CPU TIME TAKEN 0 MINS 33 SECS

..
```

$G(XL :: XLL) \Leftarrow \mathrm{SUM}(\mathrm{DOUBLE}(XL :: XLL))$

LOOK TO YOU
NOGOOD

COULD GENERALISE FOLLOWING EXPRESSION:
HOW DOES

$\mathrm{SM}(\mathrm{DB}(XL) :: \mathrm{DOUBLE}(XLL))$

LOOK TO YOU
NOGOOD

COULD GENERALISE FOLLOWING EXPRESSION:
HOW DOES

$\mathrm{SM}(\mathrm{DB}(XL)) + \mathrm{SUM}(\mathrm{DOUBLE}(XLL))$

LOOK TO YOU
OK

AM ATTEMPTING TO SYNTHESISE A FUNCTION   —again redundant
NEWF1 DEFINED IMPLICITLY BY THIS EQUATION

$\mathrm{NEW}F1(U2, U1) \Leftarrow \mathrm{SM}(\mathrm{DB}(U1)) + \mathrm{SUM}(\mathrm{DOUBLE}(U2))$

HOW DOES

$\mathrm{NEW}F1(U2, U1) \Leftarrow \mathrm{SM}(\mathrm{DB}(U1)) + \mathrm{SUM}(\mathrm{DOUBLE}(U2))$

LOOK TO YOU
OK

WOULD YOU TYPE IN SUITABLE INSTANTIATION PAIRS.
BASE CASES FIRST.
: END   (newf2(u2, nil) involves a recursion)
NOW THE RECURSIONS

U1, NIL END U1, X :: U1 END END

HOW DOES

$\mathrm{NEW}F1(U2, [\,]) \Leftarrow \mathrm{SM}(\mathrm{DB}([\,])) + G(U2)$

LOOK TO YOU
NOGOOD

HOW DOES

$\mathrm{NEW}F1(U2, [\,]) \Leftarrow \mathrm{SM}(\mathrm{DB}(\mathrm{DOUBLE}([\,]))) + \mathrm{SUM}(\mathrm{DOUBLE}(U2))$

LOOK TO YOU
NOGOOD

HOW DOES

$\mathrm{NEW}F1(U2, [\,]) \Leftarrow \mathrm{SM}(\mathrm{DB}(\mathrm{DB}([\,]))) + \mathrm{SUM}(\mathrm{DOUBLE}(U2))$ (nearly there!)

LOOK TO YOU
NOGOOD

HOW DOES

$\mathrm{NEW}F1(U2, [\,]) \Leftarrow \mathrm{SUM}([\,] :: \mathrm{DOUBLE}(U2))$

LOOK TO YOU
NOGOOD

COULD GENERALISE FOLLOWING EXPRESSION:

HOW DOES

$\mathrm{SM}([\,]) + \mathrm{SUM}(\mathrm{DOUBLE}(U2))$

LOOK TO YOU
NOGOOD

HOW DOES

$\mathrm{NEW}F1(U2, [\,]) \Leftarrow G(U2)$

LOOK TO YOU
OK

HOW DOES

$\mathrm{NEW}F1(U2, X :: U1) \Leftarrow \mathrm{SM}(\mathrm{DB}(X :: U1)) + G(U2)$ main recursion for newf1

LOOK TO YOU
NOGOOD

HOW DOES

NEW(U2, X :: U1) ⇐ SUM(DB(X :: U1) :: DOUBLE(U2))

LOOK TO YOU
NOGOOD

COULD GENERALISE FOLLOWING EXPRESSION:

HOW DOES

SM(DB(X :: U1)) + SUM(DOUBLE(U2))

LOOK TO YOU
NOGOOD

HOW DOES

NEWF1(U2, X :: U1) ⇐ SM(DB(X :: U1)) + SUM(DOUBLE(U2))

LOOK TO YOU
NOGOOD

HOW DOES

NEWF1(U2, X :: U1) ⇐ SUM((2 * X :: DB(U1)) :: DOUBLE(U2))

LOOK TO YOU
NOGOOD

COULD GENERALISE FOLLOWING EXPRESSION:

HOW DOES

SM(2 * X :: DB(U1)) + SUM(DOUBLE(U2))

LOOK TO YOU
NOGOOD

HOW DOES

NEWF1(U2, X :: U1) ⇐ (2 * X) + NEWF1(U2, U1)

LOOK TO YOU
OK

HOW DOES   *back to top level*

G(XL :: XLL) ⇐ NEWF1(XLL, XL)

LOOK TO YOU
OK

FINISHED.CPU TIME TAKEN 0 MINS 23 SECS

.PREXP;   *(resulting equations)*

NEWF1(U2, X :: U1) ⇐ (2 * X) + NEWF1(U2, U1)
NEWF1(U2, []) ⇐ G(U2)
SM([]) ⇐ 0
SM(X :: XL) ⇐ X + SM(XL)
SUM([]) ⇐ 0
SUM(XL :: XLL) ⇐ SM(XL) + SUM(XLL)
DB([]) ⇐ []
DB(X :: XL) ⇐ 2 * X :: DB(XL)
DOUBLE([]) ⇐ []
DOUBLE(XL :: XLL) ⇐ DB(XL) :: DOUBLE(XLL)
G(XL :: XLL) ⇐ NEWF1(XLL, XL)
G([]) ⇐ 0:
.

5.2. Forced folding leading to sub-function definition

A more sophisticated method of introducing new functions arises from extending the notion of forced folding. We will illustrate this technique using the following example that employs binary trees.

Given

flatten(atom(a)) ⇐ [a]
flatten(consbt(X, Y)) ⇐ flatten(X)(>)flatten(Y)
nil(>)Y ⇐ Y
(x :: X)(>)Y ⇐ x :: (X(>)Y)
length(nil) ⇐ 0
length(x :: X) ⇐ 1 + length(X)

can we optimise

g(X) ⇐ length(flatten(X))

The system proceeds as follows; straight evaluation gives

$$g(\text{atom}(a)) \Leftarrow 1$$

but trying to evaluate $g(\text{consbt}(X, Y))$ it gets as far as

$$g(\text{consbt}(X, Y)) \Leftarrow \text{length}(\text{flatten}(X)\rangle\text{flatten}(Y)) \quad Ⓐ$$

and no further unfolding or immediate folds are possible. However, on attempting to fold the above with $g(X) \Leftarrow \text{length}(\text{flatten}(X))$ the system automatically synthesises an equation defining a new subsidiary function that can be used to rewrite the above into a form that will fold. In this case the equation produced is

$$\text{newf1}(\text{length}(u1), \text{length}(u2)) \Leftarrow \text{length}(u1\rangle u2) \quad Ⓑ$$

We call these new style equations with complicated left hand sides (which cannot be run in NPL) *implicit* equations. Using Ⓑ the system can rewrite Ⓐ as

$$g(\text{consbt}(X, Y)) \Leftarrow \text{newf1}(\text{length}(\text{flatten}(X)), \text{length}(\text{flatten}(Y)))$$

which will fold immediately giving

$$g(\text{consbt}(X, Y)) \Leftarrow \text{newf1}g(X), g(Y))$$

But first the system must synthesise proper recursions for newf1. It firsts asks the user to accept or reject this proposed new function and if it is accepted asks for suitable instantiations. In this example the system performs the following deductions.

$$\text{newf1}(\text{length}(\text{nil}), \text{length}(u2)) \Leftarrow \text{length}(\text{nil}\rangle u2)$$
$$\Leftarrow \text{length}(u2) \quad \text{Unfolding the right hand side}$$

$$\text{newf1}(0, \text{length}(u2)) \Leftarrow \text{length}(u2) \quad \text{Unfolding the left hand side}$$

$$\text{newf1}(0, u3) \Leftarrow u3 \quad \text{Generalising}$$

and

$$\text{newf1}(\text{length}(x::u1), \text{length}(u2)) \Leftarrow \text{length}((x::u1)\rangle u2)$$
$$\Leftarrow 1 + \text{length}(u1\rangle u2) \quad \text{Unfolding the right hand side}$$
$$\Leftarrow 1 + \text{newf1}(\text{length}(u1), \text{length}(u2)) \quad \text{Folding with } Ⓑ$$
$$\text{newf1}(1 + \text{length}(u1), \text{length}(u2)) \Leftarrow 1 + \text{newf1}(\text{length}(u1), \text{length}(u2)) \quad \text{Unfolding the left hand side}$$
$$\text{newf1}(1 + u3, u4) \Leftarrow 1 + \text{newf1}(u3, u4) \quad \text{Generalising.}$$

Thus the system has synthesised a recursion for $+$. This could be tidied up by

applying the schemata reduction rule

$$f(b, c) \Leftarrow d$$
$$f(a1 \text{ op } a2, b) \Leftarrow a1 \text{ op } f(a2, b)$$
reduces to
$$f(a, b) \Leftarrow a \text{ op } b, \text{ provided } d = b \text{ op } c \text{ and op is associative.}$$

Thus in the above $u3 = 0 + u3$ and $+$ is associative so $\text{newf1}(g(X), g(Y))$ is $g(X) + g(Y)$.

Discovery of implicit equations. How does the system come up with the implicit equation of Ⓑ? The mechanism is rather complex but basically relies on mismatching and forced folding. To view the process in a little more detail let us look more closely at the example above. The implicit equation Ⓑ arose from attempting to fold Ⓐ with $g(X) \Leftarrow \text{length}(\text{flatten}(X))$ in particular in trying to match $\text{length}(\text{flatten}(X))$ with $\text{length}(\text{flatten}(X)\rangle\text{flatten}(Y))$. The matching routine proceeds top down and succeeds at the first recursion matching length with length. At the next recursion it attempts to match flatten and gets instead $\langle\rangle$, however, it does not give up but looks if the remaining expression it is trying to match, $\text{flatten}(X)$, occurs within the rest of the other expression, which it does, twice. These remaining instances of the sought for sub-expression are then replaced by new variables and the implicit equation constructed to 'move' these variables to the correct position to allow the match to succeed and achieve the fold. Any remaining sub-expressions are also generalised out to get the implicit equation in its simplest form.

Alternative forms. Many solutions involving new sub-functions require the form

$$g(x) \Leftarrow g(\text{newf1}(x))$$
$$\text{newf1}(x) \Leftarrow \text{newf1}(k(x))$$

Methods have been developed to achieve this form identical to the one given above except that in this case the implicit equation is of the form

$$Ⓑ1(\text{newf1}(u)) \Leftarrow Ⓑ2(u)$$

This method has not been implemented yet, although it is actually computationally simpler than the previous method, so we will not discuss it here. All these patterns can also be achieved using pattern directed generalisation which we discuss in Section 5.3.

EXAMPLE 8. *Reverse flatten.* In this example the frontier of a binary tree is produced and then reversed. This is first transformed to a version that walks over the tree in reverse order and joins the resulting frontiers together. This new version involves an invented subsidiary function which is simply append.

Given that we can recognise this we can go on to convert this to a semi-iterative version, see Burstall and Darlington [4, Section 7], which accumulates the result an element at a time while walking over the tree.

EQNLIST.PREXP;
$G2(X) \Leftarrow$ REVERSE(FLAT(X))
REVERSE($X1::XL$) $\Leftarrow$ REVERSE(XL)$\langle\rangle$[$X1$]
REVERSE([]) $\Leftarrow$ []
$A::L\langle\rangle M \Leftarrow A::(L\langle\rangle M)$
$[]\langle\rangle M \Leftarrow M$
FLAT(CONSBT(X, Y)) $\Leftarrow$ FLAT(X)$\langle\rangle$FLAT(Y)
FLAT(ATM($X1$)) $\Leftarrow$ [$X1$]:
..
:START;
TYPE IN INSTANTIATED L.H.S. BASE CASES FIRST.
$G2$(ATM($X1$)) END

$G2$(ATM($X1$)) $\Leftarrow X_1::$[]

NOW TYPE IN RECURSIVE BRANCHES.
$G2$(CONSBT(X, Y)) END

AM ATTEMPTING TO SYNTHESISE A FUNCTION NEW$F1$ DEFINED
IMPLICITLY BY THIS EQUATION

NEW$F1$(REVERSE($U2$), REVERSE($U1$)) $\Leftarrow$ REVERSE($U1\langle\rangle U2$)

HOW DOES

NEW$F1$(REVERSE($U2$), REVERSE($U1$)) $\Leftarrow$ REVERSE($U1\langle\rangle U2$)

LOOK TO YOU
OK

WOULD YOU TYPE IN SUITABLE INSTANTIATION PAIRS.
BASE CASES FIRST.
:$U1$, NIL END $U1$, $X1$::NIL END END

NEW$F1$($U3$, []) $\Leftarrow U3$

NEW$F1$($U4$, $X1::$[]) $\Leftarrow U4\langle\rangle X1::$[]

NOW THE RECURSIONS

:$U1$, $X1::U1$ END END

AM ATTEMPTING TO SYNTHESISE A FUNCTION NEW$F2$ DEFINED
IMPLICITLY BY THIS EQUATION

NEW$F2$($U7$, REVERSE($U6$)) $\Leftarrow$ REVERSE($U7::U6$)

HOW DOES

NEW$F2$($U7$, REVERSE($U6$)) $\Leftarrow$ REVERSE($U7::U6$)

LOOK TO YOU
NOGOOD

HOW DOES

NEW$F1$(REVERSE($U2$), REVERSE($X1::U1$)) $\Leftarrow$ NEW$F1$(REVERSE($U2$),
REVERSE($U1$)$\langle\rangle X1::$[]

LOOK TO YOU
OK

HOW DOES

$G2$(CONSBT(X, Y)) $\Leftarrow$ NEW$F1$($G2$(Y), $G2$(X))

LOOK TO YOU
OK

FINISHED.CPU TIME TAKEN 0 MINS 11 SECS

.PREXP;
NEW$F1$($U3$, []) $\Leftarrow U3$
NEW$F1$($U4$, $X1::$[]) $\Leftarrow U4\langle\rangle X1::$[]
NEW$F1$($U8$, $U9\langle\rangle U10$) $\Leftarrow$ NEW$F1$($U8$, $U9$)$\langle\rangle U10$
REVERSE($X1::XL$) $\Leftarrow$ REVERSE(XL)$\langle\rangle$[$X1$]
REVERSE([]) $\Leftarrow$ []
$A::L\langle\rangle M \Leftarrow A::(L\langle\rangle M)$
$[]\langle\rangle M \Leftarrow M$
FLAT(CONSBT(X, Y)) $\Leftarrow$ FLAT(X)$\langle\rangle$FLAT(Y)
FLAT(ATM($X1$)) $\Leftarrow$ [$X1$]
$G2$(CONSBT(X, Y)) $\Leftarrow$ NEW$F1$($G2$(Y), $G2$(X))
$G2$(ATM($X1$)) $\Leftarrow X1::$[]

If we recognise that newf1 is ⟨⟩ and give an extra definition for git we can convert this further.

EQNLIST.PREXP;
G2(CONSBT(X, Y)) ⟸ G2(Y)⟨⟩G2(X)
G2(ATM(X1)) ⟸ [X1]
GIT(X, ACC) ⟸ G2(X)⟨⟩ACC
A::L⟨⟩M ⟸ A::(L⟨⟩M)
[]⟨⟩M ⟸ M:
..
START;
TYPE IN INSTANTIATED L.H.S. BASE CASES FIRST.
: GIT(ATM(X1), ACC) END

GIT(ATM(X1), ACC) ⟸ X1::ACC

NOW TYPE IN RECURSIVE BRANCHES.
GIT(CONSBT(X, Y), ACC) END

HOW DOES

GIT(CONSBT(X, Y), ACC) ⟸ G2(Y)⟨⟩GIT(X, ACC)

LOOK TO YOU
CONTINUE

HOW DOES

GIT(CONSBT(X, Y), ACC) ⟸ GIT(Y, GIT(X, ACC))

LOOK TO YOU
OK

FINISHED.CPU TIME TAKEN 0 MINS 9 SECS

PREXP;
G2(CONSBT(X, Y)) ⟸ G2(Y)⟨⟩G2(X)   (G2(X) is GIT(X, NIL))
G2(ATM(X1)) ⟸ [X1]

A::L⟨⟩M ⟸ A::(L⟨⟩M)
[]⟨⟩M ⟸ M
GIT(CONSBT(X, Y), ACC) ⟸ GIT(Y, GIT(X, ACC))
GIT(ATM(X1), ACC) ⟸ X1::ACC

EXAMPLE 9. *Descending.* Ascending checks whether a list of numbers is in

ascending order. We define descending as ascending of the reverse list and convert this to a simple recursion.

EQNLIST.PREXP;
DESCENDI(X) ⟸ ASCENDIN(REVERSE(X))
ASCENDIN(X1::(X2::X)) ⟸ X1 < X2 AND ASCENDIN(X2::X)
ASCENDIN(X1) ⟸ TRUE
ASCENDIN([]) ⟸ TRUE
A::L⟨⟩M ⟸ A::(L⟨⟩M)
[]⟨⟩M ⟸ M
REVERSE(X1::XL) ⟸ REVERSE(XL)⟨⟩[X1]
REVERSE([]) ⟸ []:

:START;
TYPE IN INSTANTIATED L.H.S. BASE CASES FIRST.
DESCENDING(NIL), DESCENDING(X1::NIL) END

DESCENDI([]) ⟸ TRUE
DESCENDI([X1]) ⟸ TRUE

NOW TYPE IN RECURSIVE BRANCHES.
DESCENDING(X3::(X4::X)) END

HOW DOES

DESCENDI(X3::(X4::X)) ⟸ ASCENDIN(REVERSE(([]⟨⟩X3)::
                                         (([]⟨⟩X4)::([]⟨⟩X))))

LOOK TO YOU
NOGOOD

HOW DOES

DESCENDI(X3::(X4::X)) ⟸ ASCENDIN(REVERSE(([]⟨⟩X4)::([]⟨⟩X))
                                         ⟨⟩([]⟨⟩X3)::([]⟨⟩[]))

LOOK TO YOU
NOGOOD

HOW DOES

DESCENDI(X3::(X4::X)) ⟸ ASCENDIN(REVERSE(X3::(X4::X)))

LOOK TO YOU
NOGOOD

HOW DOES

$DESCENDI(X3::(X4::X)) \Leftarrow ASCENDIN(REVERSE(X4::X)\langle\rangle X3:: REVERSE([]))$

LOOK TO YOU
NOGOOD

AM ATTEMPTING TO SYNTHESISE A FUNCTION NEWF1 DEFINED IMPLICITLY BY THIS EQUATION

$NEWF1(U3, U2, ASCENDIN(U1)) \Leftarrow ASCENDIN((U1\langle\rangle U2)\langle\rangle U3)$

HOW DOES

$NEWF1(U3, U2, ASCENDIN(U1)) \Leftarrow ASCENDIN((U1\langle\rangle U2)\langle\rangle U3)$

LOOK TO YOU
OK

WOULD YOU TYPE IN SUITABLE INSTANTIATION PAIRS. BASE CASES FIRST.

$: U1, NIL END END$

$NEWF1(U3, U2, TRUE) \Leftarrow ASCENDIN(U2\langle\rangle U3)$

NOW THE RECURSIONS

$U1, X3::(X4::U1) END END$

HOW DOES

$NEWF1(U3, U2, ASCENDIN((\langle\rangle X3)::((\langle\rangle X4):: \Leftarrow ASCENDIN((([\,]\langle\rangle X3)::(([\,]\langle\rangle X4)::([\,]\langle\rangle U1))\langle\rangle([\,]\langle\rangle U2))\langle\rangle([\,]\langle\rangle U3))$

LOOK TO YOU
NOGOOD

HOW DOES

$NEWF1(U3, U2, ASCENDIN(X3::(X4::U1))) \Leftarrow ASCENDIN((X3::(X4::U1)\langle\rangle U2)\langle\rangle U3)$

LOOK TO YOU
NOGOOD

HOW DOES

$NEWF1(U3, U2, ASCENDIN(X3::(X4::U1))) \Leftarrow ASCENDIN(X3::(X4::((U1\langle\rangle U2)\langle\rangle U3)))$

LOOK TO YOU
NOGOOD

HOW DOES

$NEWF1(U3, U2, ASCENDIN(X3::(X4::U1))) \Leftarrow X3<X4 \text{ AND } ASCENDIN(X4::((U1\langle\rangle U2)\langle\rangle U3))$

LOOK TO YOU
CONTINUE

HOW DOES

$NEWF1(U3, U2, ASCENDIN(X3::(X4::U1))) \Leftarrow (([\,]\langle\rangle X3)<([\,]\langle\rangle X4) \text{ AND } ASCENDIN(([\,]\langle\rangle X4)::$
$\langle\rangle([\,]\langle\rangle U2))\langle\rangle([\,]\langle\rangle U3))$

LOOK TO YOU
NOGOOD

HOW DOES

$NEWF1(U3, U2, ASCENDIN(X3::(X4::U1))) \Leftarrow X3 < X4 \text{ AND } ASCENDIN((X4::U1\langle\rangle U2)\langle\rangle U3)$

LOOK TO YOU
CONTINUE

HOW DOES

$NEWF1(U3, U2, ASCENDIN(X3::(X4::U1))) \Leftarrow (([\,]\langle\rangle X3)<([\,]\langle\rangle X4 \text{ AND } ASCENDIN((([\,]\langle\rangle X4)::([\,]\langle\rangle U1)$
$\langle\rangle([\,]\langle\rangle U2))\langle\rangle([\,]\langle\rangle U3))$

LOOK TO YOU
NOGOOD

HOW DOES

NEWF1(U3, U2, ASCENDIN(X3::(X4::U1)))
⇐ X3 < X4 AND NEWF1(U3, U2, ASCENDIN(X4::U1))
                    Cleaned up will be recursion for and!

LOOK TO YOU
OK

HOW DOES

DESCENDI(X3::(X4::X)) ⇐ NEWF1(X3::[], X4::[], DESCENDI(X))

LOOK TO YOU
OK

FINISHED.CPU TIME TAKEN 1 MINS 39 SECS

.PREXP;
NEWF1(U3, U2, TRUE) ⇐ ASCENDIN(U2⟨⟩U3)
NEWF1(U3, U2, U13 AND U14) ⇐ U13 AND NEWF1(U3, U2, U14)
            (newf1(x, y, t) ⇐ y < x and t)

ASCENDIN(X1::(X2::X)) ⇐ X1 < X2 AND ASCENDIN(X2::X)
ASCENDIN([X1]) ⇐ TRUE
ASCENDIN([]) ⇐ TRUE
A::L⟨⟩M ⇐ A::(L⟨⟩M)
[]⟨⟩M ⇐ M
REVERSE(X1::XL) ⇐ REVERSE(XL)⟨⟩[X1]
REVERSE([]) ⇐ []
DESCENDI(X3::(X4::X)) ⇐ NEWF1(X3::[], X4::[], DESCENDI(X))
DESCENDI([]) ⇐ TRUE
DESCENDI([X1]) ⇐ TRUE
:

5.2.1. Synthesis of inverses

The ability to synthesise functions defined by implicit equations enables the system to produce recursions for functions defined by their properties. In particular, it can synthesise the inverse of given functions. For example, given a function, double, that doubles every element of a list

double(nil) ⇐ nil
double(x::X) ⇐ 2 * x::double(X)

we can define the inverse of double, doubleinv,

doubleinv(double(X)) = X   ⊗

and a recursion for doubleinv can be synthesised thus

doubleinv(double(nil)) ⇐ nil   Unfolding right hand sides
doubleinv(nil) ⇐ nil
doubleinv(double(x::X)) = x::X
doubleinv(2 * x::double(X) = x::doubleinv(double(X))   Unfolding the left hand side,
                                                        folding the right hand side.

doubleinv(2 * x::u1) = x::doubleinv(u1)
                                        Generalising

A function, tryfindinverse, is provided for the user. This takes an equation such as ⊗ and then uses the same mechanism that is used to derive recursions from the implicit equations as in Section 5.2. This ability to synthesise inverses enables us to mechanise more of the data representation technique outlined in Burstall and Darlington [4, Section 8 and the second example following shows the 'twistree' example given there].

EXAMPLE 10. Inverse of reverse.

EQNLIST.PREXP;
REVERSE(X1:X) ⇐ APPEND(REVERSE(X), [X1])   equations for reverse

REVERSE([]) ⇐ []
APPEND([], Y) ⇐ Y
APPEND(X1::X, Y) ⇐ X1::APPEND(X, Y):

(Needs fact on reduction rule list, that reverse(append(X, Y)) ⇐ append(reverse(Y), reverse(X)))

EQ1.PREXP;
REVINV(REVERSE(X)) ⇐ X:

EQ1.TRYFINDINVERSE;

AM ATTEMPTING TO SYNTHESISE A FUNCTION REVINV DEFINED IMPLICITLY BY THIS EQUATION   —definition of inverse of reverse

                    —function provided for user

REVINV(REVERSE(X)) ⇐ X   —redundant print out (uses same part of system as used for subsidary functions)

HOW DOES

REVINV(REVERSE(X))⇐X

LOOK TO YOU
OK

WOULD YOU TYPE IN SUITABLE INSTANTIATION PAIRS. BASE CASES FIRST.

:X, NIL END END

REVINV([])⇐[]

NOW THE RECURSIONS

X, APPEND(X, [X1]) END END

HOW DOES

REVINV(REVERSE(APPEND(X, [X1])))
⇐APPEND(REVINV(REVERSE(X)),
REVINV(REVERSE(X1))::
REVINV(REVERSE([])))   *printed out in uncleaned up form to save (compu-tation) time*

LOOK TO YOU
OK
: ...

:.PREXP;

REVINV(X1::U0)⇐APPE   REVINV(U0), X1::[]   —cleaned up form

REVINV([])⇐[]

EXAMPLE 11. *Twistree* (see [4, Section 8]).

EQNLIST.PREXP;
REP(CONSP(A, CONSP(B, C)))
⇐CONSTREE(A, REP(B), RE?(C))
REP(NILP)⇐NILTRE
CONCTWIS(A)⇐REPINV(TWIST(REP(A)))
TWIST(CONSTREE(A, T1, T2))⇐
CONSTREE(A, TWIST(T2), TWIST(T1))
TWIST(NILTRE)⇐NILTRE: *equations for twist and representation function (mapping pairs onto trees)*

Stage 1: Production of inverse of representation function.

EQ1.PREXP;
REPINV(REP(A))⇐A :
:
:EQ1.TRYFINDINV;

AM ATTEMPTING TO SYNTHESISE A FUNCTION REPINV DEFINED IMPLICITLY BY THIS EQUATION

REPINV(REP(A))⇐A

HOW DOES

REPINV(REP(A))⇐A

LOOK TO YOU
OK

WOULD YOU TYPE IN SUITABLE INSTANTIATION PAIRS. BASE CASES FIRST.
:A, NILP END END

REPINV(NILTRE)⇐NILP
NOW THE RECURSIONS
A, CONSP(A, CONSP(B, C)) END END

HOW DOES

REPINV(REP(CONSP(A, CONSP(B, C))))⇐CONSP(REPINV(REP(A)), CONSP(REPINV(REP(B)), REPINV(REP(C))))

LOOK TO YOU
OK
: ...

:.PREXP;
REPINV(CONSTREE(A, U0, U1))⇐CONSP(A, CONSP(REPINV(U0), REPINV(U1)))
REPINV(NILTRE)⇐NILP:

Stage 2: Synthesis of concrete twist function, given inverse of representation function.

EQNLIST.PREXP;

5.3. Pattern directed generalisation

The transformation system is greatly assisted if it knows the form of acceptable solutions to the problem it is tackling. One rudimentary way of achieving this at present is via the switch ONLYTOPFOLD. If this is set by the user the system only looks for solutions of the form

$$g(X) \Leftarrow \mathcal{G}(\cdots g(k(X))\cdots)$$

where $\mathcal{G}$ may involve subsidiary recursive functions but these are similarly restricted to being defined by this pattern of recursion. If the user knows in advance that the solution is of this form the amount of searching the system has to do during folding is greatly reduced.

This idea of indicating solution patterns is being developed by a student, Martin Feather, and although it will be reported elsewhere when completed, I will give a brief account of it here. The facility is built on top of the present system and the dialogue follows the same pattern as before except that for each case the system asks the user to indicate the pattern of the anticipated result. The system then identifies which parts of the developing equation are to be associated with the components of the pattern and attempts to produce solutions to match this pattern. The patterns are expressions built up using existing function names and TOPFN and SYNFN. TOPFN matches with any function and SYNFN indicates that part of the developing expression is to be taken as the definition of a subsidiary function. This facility seems particularly useful during synthesis and approximates to a top down programming style.

EXAMPLE 13. *Cartesian product using pattern directed generalization. Cartesian product is specified as before, this time only for two sets.*

```
EQNLIST.PREXP;
CART(X, Y) ⇐ ⟨:MAKETUPL([X1::Y1]): X1 IN X
                                    Y1 IN Y:⟩;     —original equation

:START;
TYPE IN LIST OF SUITABLY INSTANTIATED LEFT HAND SIDES
(SEPARATED BY COMMAS, TERMINATED BY END)
..
:CART(NILSET, Y), CART(CONSSET(X3, X), Y) END

AM SEEKING SOLUTION FOR FOLLOWING EQUATION:
CART(⟨::⟩, Y) ⇐ ⟨::⟩             —system suggests pattern
AM TRYING FOLLOWING PATTERN           automatically
⟨::⟩
CART(⟨::⟩, Y) ⇐ ⟨::⟩:
```

```
REPINV(CONSTREE(A, T1, T2)) ⇐ CONSP(A, CONSP(REPINV(T1),
                              REPINV(T2)))

REPINV(NILTRE) ⇐ NILP
REP(CONSP(A, CONSP(B, C))) ⇐ CONSTREE(A, REP(B), REP(C))
REP(NILP) ⇐ NILTRE
CONCTWIS(A) ⇐ REPINV(TWIST(REP(A)))
TWIST(CONSTREE(A, T1, T2))
    ⇐ CONSTREE(A, TWIST(T2), TWIST(T1))
TWIST(NILTRE) ⇐ NILTRE:
.. .. .. ..

:START;
TYPE IN INSTANTIATED L.H.S. BASE CASES FIRST.
CONCTWIST(NILP) END
CONCTWIS(NILP) ⇐ NILP

NOW TYPE IN RECURSIVE BRANCHES:
CONCTWIST(CONSP(A, CONSP(B, C))) END

HOW DOES

CONCTWIS(CONSP(A, CONSP(B, C))) ⇐ CONSP(A, CONSP(CONCTWIS
                                   (C), CONCTWIS(B)))

LOOK TO YOU
OK

FINISHED.CPU TIME TAKEN 0 MINS 3 SECS

:PREXP;
REPINV(CONSTREE(A, T1, T2)) ⇐ CONSP(A, CONSP(REPINV(T1),
                              REPINV(T2)))

REPINV(NILTRE) ⇐ NILP
REP(CONSP(A, CONSP(B, C))) ⇐ CONSTREE(A, REP(B), REP(C))
REP(NILP) ⇐ NILTRE
TWIST(CONSTREE(A, T1, T2)) ⇐ CONSTREE(A, TWIST(T2),
                             TWIST(T1))

TWIST(NILTRE) ⇐ NILTRE
CONCTWIST(NILP) ⇐ NILP
CONCTWIST(CONSP(A, CONSP(B, C))) ⇐ CONSP(A, CONSP(CONCTWIS
                                   (C), CONCTWIS(B))):
```

NEWF1(X3, CONSSET(Y3, Y))⇐SGTON(MAKETUPL([X3, Y3]))
                                    + NEWF1(X3, Y)

NEWF1(X3, ⟨::⟩)⇐⟨::⟩
CART(CONSSET(X3, X), Y)⇐NEWF1(X3, Y)+CART(X, Y)
CART(⟨::⟩, Y)⇐⟨::⟩

EXAMPLE 14. *Diagonal Search.* We wish to find all pairs of members of a set that satisfy some reflexive, symmetric relation R. Using pattern directed generalisation the system is able to optimise a simple specification to a set of equations that perform diagonal search. As the equations as typed out are rather hard-going, we have departed from our policy of presenting the telytype output unedited. However, the dialogue is just as presented, we have only 'pretty-printed' the equations.

EQNLIST.PREXP;
$G(X) \Leftarrow \{\langle x1, y1 \rangle \mid x1 \in X, y1 \in X \ \& \ R(x1, y1)\}$

        (the facts about R are given by the redlist)

:START;
TYPE IN LIST OF SUITABLE INSTANTIATED LEFT HAND SIDES
(SEPARATED BY COMMAS, TERMINATED BY END)
: G(nilset), G(conset(x2, X)) END
AM SEEKING SOLUTION FOR FOLLOWING EQUATION
G({})⇐{}
HAVE FOUND BASECASE
G({})⇐{}

AM SEEKING SOLUTION FOR FOLLOWING EQUATION:

$G(conset(x2, X)) \Leftarrow \{\langle x2, x3 \rangle\}$
$\qquad\qquad + \{\langle x2, y1 \rangle \mid y1 \in X \ \& \ R(y1, x2)\}$
$\qquad\qquad + \{\langle x1, x2 \rangle \mid x1 \in X \ \& \ R(x1, x2)\}$
$\qquad\qquad + \{\langle x1, y1 \rangle \mid x1 \in X, y1 \in X \ \& \ R(x1, y1)\}$

TYPE IN SUITABLE PATTERN (END WITH END)
:TOPFN(G(X), SYNFN(X2, X)) END
HAVE FOUND FOLLOWING SOLUTION

$G(conset(x2, X)) \Leftarrow \{\langle x2, x2 \rangle\} + (u1 + u2 + G(X))$
$\qquad$ wherep $\langle u1, u2 \rangle = = newf2(x2, X)$

AND HAVE THE FOLLOWING NEW FUNCTIONS TO SYNTHESISE

$newf2(x2, X) \Leftarrow \langle\{\langle x2, y1 \rangle \mid y1 \in X \ \& \ R(y1, x2)\}$
$\qquad\qquad\{\langle x1, x2 \rangle \mid x1 \in X \ \& \ R(x1, x2)\}\rangle$

AM SEEKING SOLUTION FOR FOLLOWING EQUATION:
CART(CONSSET(X3, X), Y)⇐(:MAKETUPL([X3, Y1]): Y1 IN X Y1 IN Y :)+
⟨MAKETUPL([X1, Y1]): X1 IN X Y1 IN Y :⟩
TYPE IN RECURSIVE CASES (END WITH END)
:NIL END   —rejected by giving no pattern
TRY ANOTHER PATTERN?
:YES
TYPE IN SUITABLE PATTERN (END WITH END)
:TOPFN(CART(X, Y), SYNFN(X3, Y)) END—user

CART(CONSSET(X3, X), Y)⇐NEWF1(X3, Y)+CART(X, Y)
AND HAVE THE FOLLOWING NEW FUNCTION TO SYNTHESIZE:

NEWF1(X3, Y)⇐(:MAKETUPL([X3, Y1]): Y1 IN Y:)
NOW TACKLING FOLLOWING EQUATION:

NEWF1(X3, Y)⇐(:MAKETUPL([X3, Y1]): Y1 IN Y:)
TYPE IN A LIST OF SUITABLY INSTANTIATED LEFT HAND SIDES
(SEPARATED BY COMMAS, TERMINATED BY END)
:NEWF1(X3, NILSET), NEWF1(X3,   —user
                        CONSSET(Y3, Y)) END

AM SEEKING SOLUTION FOR FOLLOWING EQUATION:

NEWF1(X3, ⟨::⟩)⇐⟨::⟩
AM TRYING FOLLOWING PATTERN
⟨::⟩

NEWF1(X3, ⟨::⟩)⇐⟨::⟩
AM SEEKING SOLUTION FOR FOLLOWING EQUATION:

NEWF1(X3, CONSSET(Y3, Y))⇐SGTON(MAKETUPL([X3, Y3]))
            + ⟨:MAKETUPL([X3, Y1]):
                        Y1 IN Y:⟩

TYPE IN RECURSIVE CASES (END WITH END)
:NEWF1(X3, Y) END
AM TRYING FOLLOWING PATTERN
TOPFN(Y3, NEWF1(X3, Y), X3)

NEWF1(X3, CONSSET(Y3, Y))⇐SGTON(MAKETUPL([X3, Y3]))
            + NEWF1(X3, Y)

: ...
:EQNLIST.PREXP;

TYPE IN LIST OF SUITABLY INSTANTIATED LEFT HAND SIDES SEPARATED BY COMMAS TERMINATED BY END

:newf2(x2, nilset), newf2(x2, consset(x3, X)) END

AM SEEKING SOLUTION FOR FOLLOWING EQUATION

newf2(x2, {}) ⇐ ⟨{}, {}⟩

HAVE FOUND BASECASE

newf2(x2, {}) ⇐ ⟨{}, {}⟩

AM SEEKING SOLUTION FOR FOLLOWING EQUATION

$$newf2(x2, consset(x3, X)) \Leftarrow$$
$$if\ R(x2, x3)$$
$$then\ \langle\langle x2, x3\rangle\rangle + \{\langle x2, y1\rangle \mid y1 \in X\ \&\ R(y1, x2)\}$$
$$\langle\langle x3, x2\rangle\rangle + \{\langle x1, x2\rangle \mid x1 \in X\ \&\ R(x1, x2)\}\rangle$$
$$else\ \langle\{\langle x2, y1\rangle \mid y1 \in X\ \&\ R(y1, x2)\}$$
$$\{\langle x1, x2\rangle \mid x1 \in X\ \&\ R(x1, x2)\}\rangle$$

TYPE IN SUITABLE PATTERN (END WITH END)

:topfn(newf2(x)) END

HAVE FOUND FOLLOWING SOLUTION

$$newf2(x2, consset(x3, X)) \Leftarrow$$
$$if\ R(x2, x3)$$
$$then\ \langle\langle x2, x3\rangle\rangle + u3, \{\langle x3, x2\rangle\} + u4\rangle$$
$$wherep\ \langle u3, u4\rangle == newf2(x2, X)$$
$$else\ newf2(x2, X)$$

FINISHED ALL FUNCTIONS

:EQNLIST.PREXP;

$$newf2(x2, consset(x3, X)) \Leftarrow$$
$$if\ R(x2, x3)$$
$$then\ \langle\langle x2, x3\rangle\} + u3, \{\langle x3, x2\rangle\} + u4\rangle$$
$$wherep\ \langle u3, u4\rangle == newf2(x2, X)$$
$$else\ newf2(x2, X)$$

newf2(x2, {}) ⇐ ⟨{}, {}⟩
$$G(consset(x2, X)) \Leftarrow \langle\langle x2, x2\rangle\rangle + (u1 + u2 + G(X))$$
$$wherep\ \langle u1, u2\rangle == newf2(x2, X)$$
$$G(\langle\{\}\rangle) \Leftarrow \{\}$$

6. Eureka Elimination

In Burstall and Darlington [4], several of the examples required the user to provide auxiliary definitions of 'eurekas' to assist the system. Since then we have mechanised the invention of auxiliary functions involving tuples such as we used in the fibonacci example. Here the key lay in introducing the auxiliary definition

$$g(n) \Leftarrow \langle fib(n + 1), fib(n)\rangle$$

A function findclevertuple is now provided for the user which when given the main equation for fibonacci

$$fib(n + 2) \Leftarrow fib(n + 1) + fib(n)$$

produces just the equation above.

EXAMPLE 15. *Invention of auxilary fibonacci function.*

E3.PREXP;
FIB((N + 1) + 1) ⇐ FIB(N + 1) + FIB(N):
:E3.FINDCLEVERTUPLE;
:

HOW DOES

NEWF3(N) ⇐ MAKETUPLE([FIB(N + 1), FIB(N)])

LOOK TO YOU
OK
:.

The system achieves this by implementing the process described in Burstall and Darlington [4], that is looking for matching tuples in the expanding computation tree for fib(n + 2). An interesting point is that when it has achieved the definition for fib(n + 2) it has done most of the work required for the complete optimisation of fibonacci. However, we have not as yet merged these two processes.

Of the other areas of user assistance still required, I feel that it should be fairly easy to remove from the user the task of giving the correct instantiations. The system could store a number of well-orderings with appropriate base cases, for example $x::X$ and nil, $x1::x2::X$, $x::$nil and nil and $n+1$ and 0, and could then use the typing information that NPL provides to select those appropriate. Using this process it should be possible, in the majority of cases, to ensure that the algorithms produced definitely terminate. However, this would involve the system in extra search for no useful purpose at the moment. Of the other 'eurekas' the main one is involved in supplying auxiliary definitions to enable the translation of recursive definitions to iterative form. These auxiliary definitions are closely related to the invariants required in the proofs of iterative programs and although much promising work has been done in this area [1, 14] we are not yet in a position to be able to automate their invention, although we now have enough experience to produce them without too much thought when required.

7. Conclusion

The conclusion of this report gives the state of the system as of Summer 1977. As stated the system is regarded as an experimental tool and will continue to develop.

We hope that program transformation techniques can be utilised to provide a practical programming tool and have started the design of systems to accomplish this. These systems will put more control back with the user requiring him to have an intuitive idea of the development of his algorithm leaving to the system of task of implementing this development correctly. At the moment we see the progression from specification to efficient algorithm in two stages, firstly a top-down production of a tree structured program and a transformation process that optimises this program, intertwining the various computations that take place.

ACKNOWLEDGMENTS

The transformations and the basic system were developed during joint work with R.M. Burstall at Edinburgh University and I am grateful to him for the years of fruitful and enjoyable collaboration. We benefited greatly from interactions with R. Boyer and J. Moore whose LISP theorem prover provided many ideas for the transformation system and Manna and Waldinger whose work on program synthesis encouraged us to continue with this aspect of our work. I would like to thank all my colleagues in the Department of Artificial Intelligence, Edinburgh University for their help and encouragement. Special thanks are due to M. Feather for his work on the system. The studies of R. Kowalski and K. Clark at Imperial College into the use of predicate logic as a programming language has provided valuable new insights into our work. The excellent typing was done by Eleanor Kerse at Edinburgh and by Elizabeth Larch at Imperial College. The work was supported by grants from the Science Research Council.

REFERENCES

1. Aubin, R., Some generalisation heuristics in proofs by induction, *Proc. IRIA Symposium on Proving and Improving Programs*, Arcet-Senans, France (1975) pp. 197–208.

2. Boyer, R.S. and Moore, J.S., Proving theorems about LISP functions, *J. Assoc. Comput. Mach.* 22 (1) (1975) 129–144.

3. Burstall, R.M., Design considerations for a functional programming language, *Proc. Infotech State of the Art Conf.*, Copenhagen (1977).

4. Burstall, R.M. and Darlington, J., A transformation system for developing recursive programs, *J. Assoc. Comput. Mach.* 24 (1) (1977) 44–67.

5. Burstall, R.M. and Goguen, J.A., Putting theories together to make specifications, invited paper Fifth International Joint Conf. on Artificial Intelligence, Boston, MA. (August 1977).

6. Burstall, R.M., Collins, J.S. and Popplestone, R.J., *Programming in POP-2 Edinburgh* (Edinburgh University Press, 1971).

7. Darlington, J., Application of program transformation to program synthesis, *Proc. IRIA Symposium on Proving and Improving Programs*, Arc-et-Senans, France (1975) pp. 133–144.

8. Darlington, J., A synthesis of several sorting algorithms, Research Report No. 23, Department of Artificial Intelligence, University of Edinburgh (1976).

9. Darlington, J., The formal development of a priority queue algorithm, in preparation.

10. Goguen, J.A., Thatcher, J.W. and Wagner, E.G., An initial approach to the specification, correctness and implementation of abstract data types, in: R.T. Yeh, Ed., *Current Trends in Programming Methodology, Vol. 3, Data Structuring* (Prentice-Hall, Englewood Cliffs, NJ, 1977).

11. Guttag, J.V., The specification and application to programming of abstract data types, CSRG-S9, University of Toronto (1975).

12. Kowalski, R., Predicate logic as a programming language, in: *Proc. of IFIP Congress 1974* (North-Holland, Amsterdam, 1974) pp. 569–574.

13. Manna, Z. and Waldinger, R., Knowledge and reasoning in program synthesis, *Artificial Intelligence* 6 (2) (1975) 175–208.

14. Moore, J.S., Introducing iteration into the pure LISP theorem prover, CSL-74-3, Xerox Palo Alto Res. Center, Palo Alto, CA (1975).

15. Topor, R.W., Interactive program verification using virtual programs, Thesis, Department of Artificial Intelligence, University of Edinburgh (1975).

Received 21 May 1979

Program Development as a Formal Activity

MANFRED BROY AND PETER PEPPER

Abstract—A methodology of program development by transformations is outlined. In particular, ways of representing the transformation rules are discussed, and the relationship between notions of their correctness and the semantic definition of programming languages is studied. How transformation techniques are complemented by the use of abstract data types and assertions is described. In the resulting calculus of transformations, the single rules not only represent design or optimization techniques, but they also incorporate verification principles. To illustrate this approach, the Warshall algorithm is developed by successive applications of transformations.

Index Terms—Abstract data types, correctness of transformation rules, program transformations, transformational semantics.

I. INTRODUCTION

IT seems reasonable to organize the activity of writing computer programs in the form of a development process leading through a series of more and more detailed versions. A number of ways for carrying out such developments have been suggested ranging from Wirth's "stepwise refinement" to Dijkstra's "discipline of programming." We consider here a most rigorous approach where the transition between the successive versions is done according to strictly formal rules called "program transformations."

This idea took shape in the middle of the 1970's. At this time, several groups started a systematic research on the subject. In Munich, working plans for a project called CIP ("Computer-Aided Intuition-Guided Programming") were fixed in 1975 under the joint guidance of F. L. Bauer and K. Samelson after two years of exploration (cf. [1]). This project comprises the design of an (abstract) programming language and of a support system for carrying out transformations.

Manuscript received June 30, 1980. This work was performed within the Sonderforschungsbereich 49, Programmiertechnik, Munich, Germany.

M. Broy is with the Institut für Informatik, Technische Universität München, D-8000 Munich, Germany.

P. Pepper is with the Institut für Informatik, Technische Universität München, D-8000 Munich, Germany, on leave at Stanford University, Stanford, CA 94305.

As a consequence of this approach programs are considered as formal objects ("formulas") which can be manipulated by transformation rules ("deduction rules"). These considerations lead to a sound mathematical basis for program transformations and their correctness.

Of course, it is also important to discuss the software engineering aspects, i.e., questions concerning the methodology of software construction which allows us to make the best use of transformation techniques. This includes the problems of the transformation systems and the degree to which they shall provide automated support for the programmer. Such systems usually comprise catalogs of transformation rules, a manipulation system, a user interface, and possibly some kind of heuristics.

However, in this paper we want to concentrate on the basic idea and the formal background of the program development by transformations.

For a first impression of a transformation process, we give a little toy-example.

Example—Natural number approximation of dual logarithm:
1) Specification of the problem

$$\underline{\text{funct}}\ \text{blog} \equiv (\underline{\text{nat}}\ n : n > 0)\ \underline{\text{nat}} : \underline{\text{that}}\ \underline{\text{nat}}\ y :$$
$$n \div 2 < 2^y \leqslant n;$$

2) Recursive version

$$\underline{\text{funct}}\ \text{blog} \equiv (\underline{\text{nat}}\ n : n > 0)\ \underline{\text{nat}} : \underline{\text{if}}\ n = 1\ \underline{\text{then}}\ 0$$
$$[\!]\ n > 1\ \underline{\text{then}}$$
$$\text{blog}(n \div 2) + 1\ \underline{\text{fi}};$$

3) Recursive version after the introduction of an auxiliary function

$$\underline{\text{funct}}\ \text{blog} \equiv (\underline{\text{nat}}\ n : n > 0)\ \underline{\text{nat}} : \text{aux}(n, 0),$$
$$\underline{\text{funct}}\ \text{aux} \equiv (\underline{\text{nat}}\ x, \underline{\text{nat}}\ y : x > 0)\ \underline{\text{nat}} :$$
$$\underline{\text{if}}\ x = 1\ \underline{\text{then}}\ y$$
$$[\!]\ x > 1\ \underline{\text{then}}\ \text{aux}(x \div 2, y + 1)\ \underline{\text{fi}};$$

4) Iterative version

$$\underline{\text{funct}}\ \text{blog} \equiv (\underline{\text{nat}}\ n : n > 0)\ \underline{\text{nat}}\ :$$
$$\lceil(\underline{\text{var}}\ \underline{\text{nat}}\ x,\ \underline{\text{var}}\ \underline{\text{nat}}\ y) := (n, 0)\ ;$$
$$\quad\underline{\text{while}}\ x > 1\ \underline{\text{do}}\ (x, y) := (x \div 2, y + 1)\ \underline{\text{od}}\ ;$$
$$\quad y \qquad\qquad\qquad\qquad\qquad\qquad\qquad\rfloor$$

* 5) Version after sequentialization, using (conditional) jumps

$$\underline{\text{funct}}\ \text{blog} \equiv (\underline{\text{nat}}\ n : n > 0)\ \underline{\text{nat}}:$$
$$\lceil\underline{\text{var}}\ \underline{\text{nat}}\ x := n\ ;\ \underline{\text{var}}\ \underline{\text{nat}}\ y := 0\ ;$$
$$\quad\underline{\text{if}}\ \neg x > 1\ \underline{\text{then}}\ \text{goto}\ l2\ \underline{\text{fi}};$$
$$l1 : x := x \div 2\ ;$$
$$\quad y := y + 1\ ;$$
$$\quad\underline{\text{if}}\ x > 1\ \underline{\text{then}}\ \text{goto}\ l1\ \underline{\text{fi}}\ ;$$
$$l2 : y \qquad\qquad\qquad\qquad\qquad\rfloor$$

It is intuitively clear that these five versions represent an evolution in small steps from a problem description towards a machine-oriented program. Although all five versions represent the same mathematical function, they are of increasing comprehensive complexity for a person who wants to find out which function is described. Of course, our notion of intelligibility is formed by our habits. But in spite of this we claim that version 1) is most easily understood and that even version 2) is more comprehensible than, e.g., version 5).

The example also indicates a requirement for the programming languages used in connection with transformation systems. Such languages should range over a sufficiently wide spectrum of programming styles. But these styles have to coexist in a unique syntactic frame, since transformations are usually applied locally and thus change only small parts of a program.

II. Transformation Rules

A transformation is the transition from one program to another one. A *transformation rule* thus is a mapping from programs to programs. In general, these mappings are partial ones since they are only defined for particular kinds of programs.

In principle, there are two possibilities of representing a transformation rule.

1) It can be described in the form of an algorithm that takes the given program as input and produces an equivalent one as output—provided that the input program is in the domain of the rule (compilers behave in this way).

2) It can be given as an ordered pair of *program schemes*, the *input template a* and the *output template b* (corresponding to the premise and conclusion of a postproduction rule).

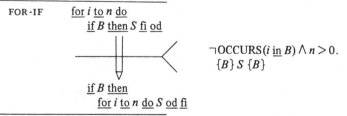

FOR-IF $\underline{\text{for}}\ i\ \underline{\text{to}}\ n\ \underline{\text{do}}$
$\underline{\text{if}}\ B\ \underline{\text{then}}\ S\ \underline{\text{fi}}\ \underline{\text{od}}$

$\underline{\text{if}}\ B\ \underline{\text{then}}$
$\underline{\text{for}}\ i\ \underline{\text{to}}\ n\ \underline{\text{do}}\ S\ \underline{\text{od}}\ \underline{\text{fi}}$

We will concentrate here on the second variant which seems to be preferable at least when dealing with extensive collections of transformations (e.g., [14]). The first variant is only reasonable for small sets of special rules such as UNFOLD (replacement of the call of a function/procedure by the right-hand side of its declaration) and FOLD (the inverse operation), cf. [10].

We represent our transformation rules here in the form

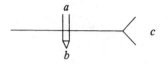

where a and b are the input and output templates, and c is a condition, called the *enabling condition*, mandatory for the applicability of the rule. The domain of such a rule, i.e., the set of programs to which it may be applied, is determined by the form of the input template ("success of the matching process") and by the enabling condition.

Simple examples are given by the following rules for conditional expressions:

CUT IF

$$\underline{\text{if}}\ B\ \underline{\text{then}}\ E\ \underline{\text{else}}\ E\ \underline{\text{fi}}$$

DEFINED(B)

$$E$$

SEQUENTIALIZE OR

$$B' \quad \vee \quad B$$

DEFINED(B).

$$\underline{\text{if}}\ B'\ \underline{\text{then}}\ \underline{\text{true}}\ \underline{\text{else}}\ B\ \underline{\text{fi}}$$

We distinguish three kinds of enabling conditions: the *syntactic conditions* simply state that particular scheme variables stand for certain syntactic entities. (We will be very informal here and indicate syntactic conditions only by our use of letters, e.g., "E" stands for an expression, "S" for a statement, x for an identifier, "$\underline{\text{m}}$" for a mode, etc.) The *context conditions* usually are predicates such as OCCURS($x\ \underline{\text{in}}\ E$) stating that the identifier x occurs freely in the expression E. An example for *semantic conditions* is given by DEFINED(E) stating that the evaluation of the expression E yields a defined value.

Remark: In general semantic conditions cannot be checked automatically and need interaction from the programmer's side. Therefore we are very liberal here and allow any suitable form of conditions. For instance, the following rule is only applicable if the statement S leaves the predicate B invariant.

$$\neg\text{OCCURS}(i\ \underline{\text{in}}\ B) \wedge n > 0.$$
$$\{B\}\ S\ \{B\}$$

The application of a transformation rule to a given concrete program (part) P obviously needs the three steps: *matching* with the input template, *test* of the enabling condition, *in-*

stantiation of the output template to generate the new program (part) P'. Since transformation rules may also be applied to program schemes, one can compose new transformation rules from existing ones in this way (cf. [18]).

III. CORRECTNESS OF TRANSFORMATIONS

The notion of the "correctness of transformations" has to be based on suitable relations between programs. Given such a relation φ, the transition from a program P to another program P' then is said to be *correct* iff $P\varphi P'$ holds. There are various relations which are reasonable in connection with program transformations (cf. [8]). A few examples follow.

1) P and P' have to be "equivalent."

2) Weakening condition 1) the equivalence of P and P' is only required if P is defined (i.e., we do not care what our transformations do to erroneous programs).

3) For nondeterminate programs, it may suffice that P' is "included" in P, i.e., that the possible results of P' form a subset of the possible results of P.

Any relation φ which is used here has to fulfill the following requirements: It has to be *reflexive*, since the identity should be a valid transformation. It also has to be *transitive* in order to allow the successive application of several transformations. A slightly more subtle point comes from the local application of a transformation to a (small) part Q of a program P. Then the validity of $Q\varphi Q'$ only implies the validity of $P\varphi P'$, if the relation φ is *monotonic* for the constructs of the language (where $P' = P[Q'/Q]$).

The formalization of such relations has to refer to the actual semantic definition of the programming language under consideration. For instance, in denotational semantics the meaning of a program is specified with the help of a function $\mathfrak{M}$ mapping programs to semantic objects. Two programs P_1 and P_2 then can be defined to be equivalent iff $\mathfrak{M}(P_1) = \mathfrak{M}(P_2)$. Taking Dijkstra's approach, two programs P_1 and P_2 may be considered equivalent iff they specify the same predicate transformer, i.e., iff $\forall R: wp(P_1, R) = wp(P_2, R)$. (Note that in general these two notions of equivalence do not coincide, cf. [7].) Finally, in operational semantics, two programs may be regarded equivalent iff they lead to the same sequences of "elementary actions" (cf. [5]; since most transformations aim at gaining operational efficiency, this equivalence relation usually is too restrictive for program developments).

For nondeterministic and for parallel programs, inclusion relations are of great importance. In a mathematical semantics we may use a "breadth function" $\mathfrak{B}$ giving the set of all possible results of a program. Then we may say that a program P_2 is included in the program P_1 iff $\mathfrak{B}(P_2) \subseteq \mathfrak{B}(P_1)$. In Dijkstra's approach, the inclusion could be stated as $\forall R: wp(P_1, R) \Rightarrow wp(P_2, R)$ which means that the program P_1 needs a stronger precondition in order to establish the postcondition R than P_2 does. (Again the two notions do not coincide.) Operational semantics becomes very interesting here, since we may model problems of parallelism using sets of possible action sequences (cf. [5]). Here we get an inclusion relation between two programs P_1 and P_2 by requiring that every possible action sequence of P_2 is also a possible action-sequence of P_1.

We distinguish between equivalence and inclusion rules by using the two notations

Note: Also in the case of an equivalence rule, we use an asymmetric notation to indicate that the application is directed.

The *verification* of a transformation rule $T = (a, b, c)$ can be done essentially in two ways.

1) "Model-Theoretic" Proof: Using the properties of the semantic model the equivalence/inclusion of a and b is proved. (Note that one has to deal here with a universal quantification over all instantiations of the scheme variables occurring in a and b.)

2) "Deduction-Oriented" ("Transformational") Proof: One has to show that T can be deduced from a sequence of already verified transformation rules $T_1, \cdots, T_n$ such that $a \overset{T_1}{\longmapsto} a_1 \overset{T_2}{\longmapsto} \cdots \overset{T_n}{\longmapsto} a_n = b$. (Note that the enabling condition c has to be derived from $c_1, \cdots, c_n$—cf. [18].)

The second approach fits better into the philosophy of program transformations, but it has to be enhanced by induction methods in order to make it powerful enough. One example of an induction principle, which is based on the computational induction of Scott and Park, can be described as follows. Let p and q be two recursive functions or procedures with the bodies $\tau[p]$ and $\sigma[q]$, respectively. Then every call $p(x)$ can be transformed into a call $q(x)$, if there is a transformation rule $\tau[y] \to \sigma[y]$. (This principle may be called *transformational induction*, cf. [5]).

IV. TRANSFORMATIONAL SEMANTICS

The correctness of transformation rules as it has been viewed in the previous section relies heavily on the semantic description of the programming language, and consequently one cannot start with transformation proofs without having first verified at least a few rules by means of model-theoretic methods. This leads to the idea of considering such basic rules as "axioms." The resulting method for defining the meaning of a language may be called *transformational semantics*.

To give an idea of how transformational semantics works, we present two rules which define the differences between call-by-name and call-by-value in Algol 60.

where the substitution operation $S[E/x]$ of course resolves name clashes by a renaming of local identifiers.

$$\underline{\text{procedure}}\, f(x)\; ;\underline{\text{value}}\, x\; ;\underline{\text{m}}\, x; \underline{\text{begin}}\, S\, \underline{\text{end}}\; ;$$
$$f(E)$$

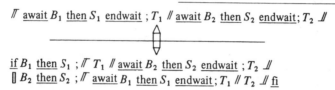

$$\neg\text{OCCURS}(x\, \underline{\text{in}}\, E).$$

$$\underline{\text{procedure}}\, f(x)\; ;\underline{\text{value}}\, x\; ;\underline{\text{m}}\, x\; ; \underline{\text{begin}}\, S\, \underline{\text{end}}\; ;$$
$$\underline{\text{begin}}\quad \underline{\text{m}}\, x\; ;x := E\; ; S\, \underline{\text{end}}$$

For a programmer, such a description will probably be easier to comprehend than, say, a denotational specification. In [16], it has been shown that in this way large parts of a language can be reduced to a small kernel language with the help of a few transformation rules, and in [9] also this kernel language has been described with the help of transformations.

This approach even allows to explain parallel programs in terms of nondeterministic sequential programs. For instance, in [5] the following transformation rule is used to specify the meaning of the $\underline{\text{await}}$- construct

$$\mathbin{\mathit{\text{/\!/}}} \underline{\text{await}}\, B_1\; \underline{\text{then}}\, S_1\; \underline{\text{endwait}}\; ;T_1\; \mathbin{\mathit{\text{/\!/}}} \underline{\text{await}}\, B_2\; \underline{\text{then}}\, S_2\; \underline{\text{endwait}};T_2\; \mathbin{\mathit{\text{/\!/}}}$$

$$\underline{\text{if}}\, B_1\; \underline{\text{then}}\, S_1\; ;\mathbin{\mathit{\text{/\!/}}} T_1\; \mathbin{\mathit{\text{/\!/}}} \underline{\text{await}}\, B_2\; \underline{\text{then}}\, S_2\; \underline{\text{endwait}}\; ;T_2\; \mathbin{\mathit{\text{/\!/}}}$$
$$[\!]\, B_2\; \underline{\text{then}}\, S_2\; ;\mathbin{\mathit{\text{/\!/}}} \underline{\text{await}}\, B_1\; \underline{\text{then}}\, S_1\; \underline{\text{endwait}};T_1\; \mathbin{\mathit{\text{/\!/}}} T_2\; \mathbin{\mathit{\text{/\!/}}} \underline{\text{fi}}$$

The generalization to n branches is obvious.

In the rest of this section, we will give a rough overview of the theoretical background of transformational semantics as it is viewed in [16] and [9]. First, the syntax of a language can be considered as the "signature" of a type: every nonterminal of the grammar stands for a carrier set ("syntactic domain") and every production of the grammar is regarded as a function between such syntactic domains (cf. [13]).

Thus the programming language is considered as an *algebra of terms*. (This is what we call "abstractness of the language.") The intuitive notion of the "equivalence of programs" then is formalized by *congruence relations* on this algebra (or by quasi-orderings in the case of nondeterministic programs).

These congruence relations are established by a set of (conditional) transformation rules which can be interpreted as (conditional) equations. Taking these equations as *axioms*, the whole language is specified as an "abstract data type." Since there are, in general, many congruence relations which are compatible with the given axioms, this approach defines a class of possible semantic models of a language and leaves enough freedom for choosing suitable implementations. If the "input/output" behavior of the programs is specified sufficiently complete, then the "functional meaning" of the language is uniquely determined.

Furthermore, all transformation rules can now be verified by deduction-oriented methods only, i.e., by combining already verified rules and by using certain induction principles like the aforementioned "transformational induction."

The Wide Spectrum Language (cf. [2]) which is designed in the course of the project CIP is being described exactly in this way.

V. The Role of Abstract Data Types

In the previous section we have shown that the whole programming language can be viewed as an abstract data type. Of course, it is then reasonable to specify the data structures occurring in a program by abstract data types, too. This establishes a natural hierarchy for the programming language.

Since it is our intention to discuss the interrelationship between types and transformations, we content ourselves here with a most simple and well-known example, viz., stacks. This example should be self-explanatory enough to prevent us from going deeper into details of the theory and notation of abstract data types. Nevertheless it will suffice to make our point clear.

$\underline{\text{type}}$ STACK $\equiv$ ($\underline{\text{sort}}$ m) stack, emptystack, empty, append, top, rest :

$\underline{\text{sort}}$ stack,
$\underline{\text{stack}}$ emptystack　　　　　　　　　　denote emptystack by 0,
$\underline{\text{funct}}$(stack) $\underline{\text{bool}}$ empty ,
$\underline{\text{funct}}$(stack, m) stack append　　　denote append(s, x) by $s + x$,
$\underline{\text{funct}}$(stack s : $\neg$empty(s)) $\underline{\text{m}}$ top　denote top(s) by top s,
$\underline{\text{funct}}$(stack s : $\neg$empty(s)) stack rest　denote rest(s) by rest s,

$\forall$　stack s, $\underline{\text{m}}$ x :

(S1) empty(0) = $\underline{\text{true}}$,
(S2) empty$(s + x)$ = $\underline{\text{false}}$,
(S3) top$(s + x)$ = x ,
(S4) rest$(s + x)$ = s ,
(S5) $\neg$empty(s) $\Rightarrow$ rest s + top s = s

endoftype

In the previous section, we considered particular transformation rules as conditional equations representing the axioms of an abstract type. Now we can go the other way round and use the axioms of an abstract data type as transformation rules. A law "LHS = RHS" gives rise to a rule (valid everywhere in the scope of the type):

LHS

RHS

(*A note of caution:* The laws of an abstract data type contain free variables which become scheme variables of the rule standing for expressions. In general we therefore have to guarantee that these are "good" expressions, i.e., defined, determinate and without side effects.)

To illustrate the way of using the laws of an abstract type in connection with transformations we are going to develop a "stack implementation" for recursive functions which fit into the program scheme

$$\underline{\text{funct}}\ F \equiv (\underline{m}\ x)\ \underline{r} : \underline{\text{if}}\ b(x)\ \underline{\text{then}}\ F(e(x)) \circ g(x)$$
$$\underline{\text{else}}\ h(x) \qquad \underline{\text{fi}}.$$

It should be noted that the development given below constitutes a completely formal proof of the techniques which are generally used in compilers. (It is shown in [17] that this approach is not restricted to linear recursion but works with any kind of recursive function schemes.) The heart of the whole development is the following transformation rule which turns a linear recursion into two tail-recursions by inverting the decrementing function on the parameter position (this rule goes back to [11] and may be proved using transformational induction).

INVERSION

$$\underline{\text{funct}}\ f \equiv (\underline{m}\ x)\ \underline{r} : \underline{\text{if}}\ B(x)\ \underline{\text{then}}\ G(f(E(x)), x)$$
$$\underline{\text{else}}\ H(x) \qquad \underline{\text{fi}}$$

$\forall \underline{m}\ x : \overline{E}(E(x)) = x$

$$\underline{\text{funct}}\ f \equiv (\underline{m}\ x)\ \underline{r} :$$
$$\lceil\ \text{up}(\text{down}(x), H(\text{down}(x)))\ \underline{\text{where}}$$
$$\underline{\text{funct}}\ \text{down} \equiv (\underline{m}\ y)\ \underline{m} : \underline{\text{if}}\ B(y)\ \underline{\text{then}}\ \text{down}(E(y))$$
$$\underline{\text{else}}\ y \qquad \underline{\text{fi}},$$
$$\underline{\text{funct}}\ \text{up} \equiv (\underline{m}\ y, \underline{r}\ z)\ \underline{r} : \underline{\text{if}}\ y \neq x\ \underline{\text{then}}\ \text{up}(\overline{E}(y), G(z, \overline{E}(y)))$$
$$\underline{\text{else}}\ z \qquad \underline{\text{fi}}\ \rceil$$

We first define the new function

$$\underline{\text{funct}}\ F^* \equiv (\underline{\text{stack}}\ s : \neg\text{empty}(s))\ \underline{r} : F(\underline{\text{top}}\ s).$$

For this function we can prove by applying UNFOLD and the law (S3)

$$(*)\quad \forall\ \underline{\text{stack}}\ s, \underline{m}\ x : F^*(s + x) = F(\text{top}(s + x)) = F(x).$$

On the other hand, UNFOLDING of the call $F(\underline{\text{top}}\ s)$ in the body of F^* gives

$$\underline{\text{funct}}\ F^* \equiv (\underline{\text{stack}}\ s : \neg\text{empty}(s))\ \underline{r} :$$
$$\underline{\text{if}}\ b(\underline{\text{top}}\ s)\ \underline{\text{then}}\ F(e(\underline{\text{top}}\ s)) \circ g(\underline{\text{top}}\ s)$$
$$\underline{\text{else}}\ h(\underline{\text{top}}\ s) \qquad \underline{\text{fi}}.$$

The application of (*) to $F(e(\underline{\text{top}}\ s))$ now yields

$$\underline{\text{funct}}\ F^* \equiv (\underline{\text{stack}}\ s : \neg\text{empty}(s))\ \underline{r} :$$
$$\underline{\text{if}}\ b(\underline{\text{top}}\ s)\ \underline{\text{then}}\ F^*(s + e(\underline{\text{top}}\ s)) \circ g(\underline{\text{top}}\ s)$$
$$\underline{\text{else}}\ h(\underline{\text{top}}\ s) \qquad \underline{\text{fi}}.$$

The law (S4) of the type STACK now provides the enabling condition required for the application of the rule INVERSION. The functions down and up obviously can be converted into loops, and thus we have finally constructed the new transformation rule (using the abbreviations $\underline{\text{pop}}\ s$ for $s := \underline{\text{rest}}\ s$ and $s\ \underline{\text{push}}\ x$ for $s := s + x$).

$$\underline{\text{funct}}\ F \equiv (\underline{m}\ x)\ \underline{r} : \underline{\text{if}}\ b(x)\ \underline{\text{then}}\ F(e(x)) \circ g(x)\ \underline{\text{else}}\ h(x)\ \underline{\text{fi}}$$

$$\underline{\text{funct}}\ F \equiv (\underline{m}\ x)\ \underline{r} :$$
$$\lceil \underline{\text{var}}\ \underline{\text{stack}}\ s := \text{empty and}\ x\ ;$$
$$\underline{\text{while}}\ b(\underline{\text{top}}\ s)\ \underline{\text{do}}\ s\ \underline{\text{push}}\ e(\underline{\text{top}}\ s)\ \underline{\text{od}}\ ;$$
$$\lceil \underline{\text{var}}\ \underline{r}\ z := h(\underline{\text{top}}\ s)\ ;$$
$$\underline{\text{while}}\ \neg\text{empty}(\underline{\text{rest}}\ s)\ \underline{\text{do}}\ \underline{\text{pop}}\ s\ ; z := z \circ g(\underline{\text{top}}\ s)\ \underline{\text{od}}\ ; z\ \rfloor\rfloor$$

(End of example).

Decidedly, the most challenging connections between abstract data types and transformations occur when the types are to be transformed themselves. But such "changes of type" (e.g., [3], [15], [19]) have to be handled carefully. A closer look at the theoretics behind abstract data types shows immediately that one actually has to construct homomorphisms between algebras, a task which is by no means trivial. Transformations may well assist in carrying out the single steps of such a transition, but the main effort lies in backing the overall proceeding from the theoretical side (and this certainly goes beyond the scope of this paper).

VI. The Role of Assertions

The laws of an abstract data type are globally valid within the whole scope of the type. But there are also properties which hold only locally at certain points of the program. If such a local property is required for the applicability of a transformation rule, we encounter several problems. For instance, in a rule like

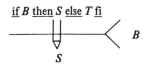

$$\underline{if}\ B\ \underline{then}\ S\ \underline{else}\ T\ \underline{fi}$$

$$B$$

$$S$$

the meaning of the enabling condition and its dependence from the environment of the conditional are rather implicit. Furthermore, it is not precisely expressed where the condition B has to hold. Hence, such local properties should be

ENUMERATE

$$\underline{funct}\ f \equiv (\underline{nat}\ n)\ \underline{r} : E(n)$$

$$\forall\ \underline{nat}\ i : \text{DEFINED}(f(i+1)) \Rightarrow \text{DEFINED}\ (f(i))$$

$$\underline{funct}\ f \equiv (\underline{nat}\ n)\ \underline{r} :$$
$$\lceil \underline{var}\ \underline{r}\ v\ ;$$
$$\underline{for}\ i\ \underline{from}\ 0\ \underline{to}\ n\ \underline{do}\ v := E(i)\ \{v = f(i)\}\ \underline{od}\ ; v$$
$$\rfloor.$$

expressed by assertions. The above rule then reads

$$\{B\}\ \underline{if}\ B\ \underline{then}\ S\ \underline{else}\ T\ \underline{fi}$$

$$\{B\}\ S$$

In analogy to the laws of abstract data types, the assertions can be used in two ways: Either they provide the enabling condition required for the application of a transformation rule or they have the form of equations and therefore may serve

TABULATE

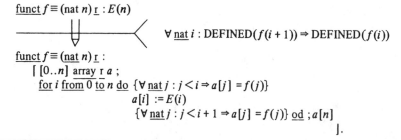

$$\underline{funct}\ f \equiv (\underline{nat}\ n)\ \underline{r} : E(n)$$

$$\forall\ \underline{nat}\ i : \text{DEFINED}(f(i+1)) \Rightarrow \text{DEFINED}(f(i))$$

$$\underline{funct}\ f \equiv (\underline{nat}\ n)\ \underline{r} :$$
$$\lceil\ [0..n]\ \underline{array}\ \underline{r}\ a\ ;$$
$$\underline{for}\ i\ \underline{from}\ 0\ \underline{to}\ n\ \underline{do}\ \{\forall\ \underline{nat}\ j : j < i \Rightarrow a[j] = f(j)\}$$
$$a[i] := E(i)$$
$$\{\forall\ \underline{nat}\ j : j < i+1 \Rightarrow a[j] = f(j)\}\ \underline{od}\ ; a[n]$$
$$\rfloor.$$

as transformation rules themselves (cf. [12]). The latter use is frequently found in approaches where an auxiliary variable (or parameter) is introduced in order to substitute it for another variable having the same, but less efficiently computed, value.

How do assertions get into programs? One way is that the programmer uses them as (hopefully proven) statements of facts. But there is also the possibility that transformations are used to generate or to propagate information in the form of assertions (cf. [6]). The following rules shall illustrate this way of proceeding (the extended example of Section VII will make heavy use of such rules).

FLATTEN

$$\underline{for}\ i\ \underline{from}\ a\ \underline{to}\ b\ \underline{do}\ S\ \{p(i)\}\ \underline{od}$$

$$\underline{if}\ a \leqslant b\ \underline{then}\ \underline{nat}\ i \equiv a\ ; S\ \underline{fi}\ ;$$
$$\underline{for}\ i\ \underline{from}\ a + 1\ \underline{to}\ b\ \underline{do}\ \{p(i - 1)\}\ S\ \{p(i)\}\ \underline{od}$$

The assertion $\{p(i - 1)\}$ now may be used to simplify S. It often will be interesting to prepare FLATTEN by first applying a rule like

Of course, the application of the rule ENUMERATE leads to a less efficient program, since for every call $f(n)$ the results of $f(0), \cdots, f(n - 1)$ are computed although we do not make use of them. But ENUMERATE may prepare a further development. When the body E of f contains recursive calls $f(i - 1)$, the transformations ENUMERATE and FLATTEN will allow to replace these calls simply by v thus leading to a considerable gain in efficiency. If, however, more general recursive calls appear in E, one usually has to store the values $f(i)$ in an array. This can be done by

Transformations like ENUMERATE and TABULATE are particularly interesting, as they reflect general implementation techniques and usually constitute major steps in a development. For instance, TABULATE simplifies the control structure by transferring information onto suitable data structures.

Remark: We get a modified notation of correctness now. When an assertion is used to establish a necessary enabling condition, then the transformed program is only equivalent to (included in) the original program if the assertion is indeed valid for that program. In [4], Blikle even considers transformations which change the semantics of the program but guarantee that the (also modified) assertions still hold.

VII. An Extended Example: The Warshall Algorithm

To round off this paper, we will discuss a not too small example. The Warshall algorithm seems a good choice here for the following reasons. First, the problem itself is quite easily understood. Nevertheless the development of the algorithm is by no means trivial (to our knowledge it is still judged a real challenge for all proof methodologies). Second, the derivation covers several language styles, from specifications using existential quantifiers via recursive functions to assignments and for-loops. And third, we can show how transformations and assertions may act together. In addition, one may see how, according to a proper "separation of concerns," some mathematical theorems are employed in the development.

The problem can be specified as follows. Let G be a finite directed graph with n nodes. It may be described by its characteristic function:

funct edge $\equiv$ (node x, node y) bool:
$\ll$ there is an edge leading from x to $y \gg$

A sequence of nodes is called a path, if for any two successive nodes x, y in the sequence the predicate edge (x, y) holds, i.e.,

funct ispath $\equiv$ (sequ node s)bool:
$\forall$ sequ node s_1, sequ node s_2, node x, node y :
$\quad s = s_1 \circ x \circ y \circ s_2 \Rightarrow$ edge(x, y).

Here "$\circ$" denotes the concatenation both of sequences (of nodes) and of nodes. The specification of the transitive closure then is straightforward:

funct trans $\equiv$ (node x, node y) bool :
$\quad \exists$ sequ node p : ispath$(x \circ p \circ y)$.

Now the essential task consists of finding a (recursive) algorithm that computes the function "trans." We use here the basic idea of approximating the transitive closure such that in the ith step only paths are considered the inner nodes of which are not greater than i. Therefore we have to number the nodes from 1 through n, i.e., we define

submode node $\equiv$ nat $[1 .. n]$.

The above idea is realized by the function

funct tc $\equiv$ (nat i, node x, node y) bool :
$\quad \exists$ sequ node p : (ispath$(x \circ p \circ y)$
$\quad\quad \wedge \forall$ node $z : z \in p \Rightarrow z \leq i$).

In order to connect this newly introduced function to the earlier function "trans"—which is our contract—we consider the following assertion.

Lemma 1: $tc(n, x, y) =$ trans(x, y). The proof of this equation can be done by means of transformations: UNFOLDing, simplifications (for all nodes z the predicate $z \leq n$ holds!) and FOLDing yield, successively

$tc(n, x, y) =$
$\exists$ sequ node p : (ispath$(x \circ p \circ y)$
$\quad \wedge \forall$ node $z : z \in p \Rightarrow z \leq n) =$
$\exists$ sequ node p : ispath$(x \circ p \circ y)$ $=$
trans (x, y).

According to this assertion, the function trans is embedded into tc:

funct trans $\equiv$ (node x, node y) bool : $tc(n, x, y)$.

Now we are aiming at a recursive formulation of tc by a case analysis.
Lemma 2: $tc(0, x, y) =$ edge(x, y).
Lemma 3: $tc(i + 1, x, y) = tc(i, x, y) \vee (tc(i, x, i + 1) \wedge tc(i, i + 1, y))$.

The proof of Lemma 2 is analogous to that of Lemma 1. To verify Lemma 3 we also start with UNFOLD, do some logical manipulations and finally apply FOLD :

$tc(i + 1, x, y) =$
$\exists$ sequ node p : (ispath$(x \circ p \circ y) \wedge$
$\quad \forall$ node $z : z \in p \Rightarrow z \leq i + 1) =$
¢.

We distinguish two cases.
1) There is a path p all nodes of which are already $\leq i$.
2) There is a path p containing the node $i + 1$ at least once; then there is also a path where the node $i + 1$ occurs exactly once (for we can disregard inner cycles). This path has the form $x \circ p_1 \circ i + 1 \circ p_2 \circ y$, and all nodes in p_1, p_2 are $\leq i$ ¢.

1) $\exists$ sequ node p : (ispath$(x \circ p \circ y) \wedge \forall$ node z :
$\quad (z \in p \Rightarrow z \leq i)) \vee$
2) $(\exists$ sequ node p_1 : (ispath$(x \circ p_1 \circ (i + 1)) \wedge \forall$ node z
$\quad (z \in p_1 \Rightarrow z \leq i)) \wedge$
$\quad \exists$ sequ node p_2 : (ispath$((i + 1) \circ p_2 \circ y) \wedge \forall$ node z :
$\quad (z \in p_2 \Rightarrow z \leq i))) =$
$tc(i, x, y) \vee (tc(i, x, i + 1) \wedge tc(i, i + 1, y))$.

From Lemma 3 we immediately get two corollaries by the logical rule $A \vee (A \wedge B) = A$.
Corollary 1: $tc(i, x, i + 1) = tc(i + 1, x, i + 1)$.
Corollary 2: $tc(i, i + 1, y) = tc(i + 1, i + 1, y)$.
Lemmas 2 and 3 give rise to the (terminating) algorithm

funct tc $\equiv$ (nat i, node x, node y) bool :
$\quad$ if $i = 0$ then edge(x, y).
$\quad [\!]$ $i > 0$ then $tc(i - 1, x, y) \vee (tc(i - 1, x, i)$
$\quad\quad\quad\quad\quad\quad \wedge tc(i - 1, i, y))$ fi

which can be derived by transformations directly from the specifications by applying the same rules as in the proofs of Lemmas 2 and 3.

Our next goal is to avoid the extensive recursive computations in the function tc. As a first step, we pass over to the well-known matrix representation for finite graphs. Using the (informal) complex notation $A := $ matrix(tc, i) for expressing the fact that all components $A[x, y]$ are assigned the values $tc(i,x,y)$ the transformation ENUMERATE (cf. Section VI) yields

```
funct trans ≡ (node x, node y) bool :
  ⌈ matrix A ;
    for i from 0 to n do A := matrix(tc, i)
      {∀ node r, s : A[r, s]
         = tc(i, r, s)} od ; A[x, y] ⌋.
```

FLATTENing produces

```
funct trans ≡ (node x, node y) bool :
  ⌈ matrix A;  A := matrix(tc, 0);
    for i from 1 to n do {∀ node r, s :
      A[r, s] = tc(i - 1, r, s)}
      A := matrix(tc, i)    od ; A[x, y] ⌋.
```

Of course, the complex assignment to a whole matrix has to be done by individual assignments to the single components of the matrix. The complex notations used above therefore stand for nested loops which are introduced by a generalized version of the rule TABULATE (cf. Section VI).

```
funct trans ≡ (node x, node y) bool :
  ⌈ [1..n, 1..n] array bool A ;
    for j to n do
      for k to n do A[j, k] := tc(0, j, k) od od ;
    for i to n do
  for j to n do
  for k to n do {∀ node r, s :
         (r, s) < (j, k) ⇒ A[r, s] = tc(i, r, s) ∧
         (r, s) ≥ (j, k) ⇒ A[r, s] = tc(i - 1, r, s)}
         A[j, k] := tc(i, j, k)          od od
  od ; A[x, y]                                    ⌋.
```

(The assertions here have been derived from those introduced by FLATTEN and by TABULATE.) As a next step the rule UNFOLD is applied to the calls $tc(i, j, k)$. The main loop now becomes

```
for i to n do
for j to n do
for k to n do {∀ node r, s :
       (r, s) < (j, k) ⇒ A[r, s] = tc(i, r, s) ∧
       (r, s) ≥ (j, k) ⇒ A[r, s] = tc(i - 1, r, s)}
       A[j, k] := tc(i - 1, j, k) ∨
            (tc(i - 1, j, i) ∧ tc(i - 1, i, k)) od od
  od.
```

The assertion now allows to replace the call $tc(i - 1, j, k)$ by $A[j, k]$. For the call $tc(i - 1, j, i)$ Corollary 1 and the first part of the assertion yield for $i < k$: $tc(i - 1, j, i) = tc(i, j, i) = A[j, i]$. If $i \geq k$ then the second part of the assertion directly gives $tc(i - 1, j, i) = A[j, i]$. Analogously Corollary 2 allows the replacement of $tc(i - 1, i, k)$ by $A[i, k]$. We have thus arrived at the version

```
funct trans ≡ (node x, node y) bool :
  ⌈ [1..n, 1..n] array bool A ;
    for j to n do
      for k to n do A[j, k] := edge(j, k) od od ;
    for i to n do
      for j to n do
        for k to n do
          A[j, k] := A[j, k] ∨ (A[j, i]
                          ∧ A[i, k]) od od
    od ; A[x, y]                                    ⌋.
```

Now the expensive recursive computation has been avoided by introducing a matrix for storing the intermediate results. But we can speed up the algorithm further by optimizing the innermost loop for which $A[j, i]$ is constant.

By the transformation SEQUENTIALIZE OR the assignment becomes

$$A[j, k] := \text{if } A[j, i] \wedge A[i, k] \text{ then true else } A[j, k] \text{ fi}$$

which can be simplified to

$$\text{if } A[j, i] \wedge A[i, k] \text{ then } A[j, k] := \text{true fi}.$$

This can be transformed further into

$$\text{if } A[j, i] \text{ then if } A[i, k] \text{ then } A[j, k] := \text{true fi fi}.$$

The inner loop now has the form

```
for k to n do
  if A[j, i] then if A[i, k] then A[j, k] := true fi fi
                                                      od.
```

Obviously the assertion $\{A[j, i] = \text{true}\}$ is left invariant by the conditional statement. Therefore we can apply the rule FOR IF (cf. Section II) and thus get the final result

```
funct trans ≡ (node x, node y) bool :
  ⌈ [1..n, 1..n] array bool A ;
    for j to n do
      for k to n do A[j, k] := edge(j, k) od od ;
    for i to n do
      for j to n do
        if A[j, i] then for k to n do
                          if A[i, k] then A[j, k] := true fi
                        od
        fi
      od
  od ; A[x, y]                                    ⌋.
```

The correctness of this program is guaranteed by the development—"the program is correct by construction." Clearly a postconstruction verification would be very hard to do. The assertions for such a proof had to be obtained from the lemmas used in the above development process. This shows the close connection between assertion methods and program development by transformations.

VIII. CONCLUDING REMARKS

In the previous sections we have tried to outline how the development of programs can be considered as a completely formal discipline, which is based on a calculus of transformation rules. Such rules serve either as axioms or as theorems and usually represent particular implementation or optimization techniques. So they act both as carriers of programming knowledge and as verification tools.

Of course, the construction of software by applying only formally verified rules is a time-consuming and highly sophisticated activity even for an expert programmer. If, however, high-quality software is required, then such an expensive approach may be justified. Moreover, the transformational approach seems to be the most promising way which allows mechanical support both for the construction and the verification of software.

Apart from these practical points, we can find several other interesting aspects of transformation techniques. One of them is the language issue. No methodology in software engineering can ignore this question since its influence may be decisive. For instance, both Dijkstra's approach and the transformation system of Burstall and Darlington owe their attractiveness and elegance to a great extent to the simplicity of the languages they use.

Of course, the principal techniques of program development by transformations depend neither on a particular language nor on a specific notation. The underlying ideas of most transformation rules can even be expressed in natural language. If, however, the development process is to be done by only applying formal rules, then formal languages are needed for representing the rules as well as the programs.

If we want to deal with "real-life" languages instead of small toy languages, then the advantages of transformational semantics become decisive. First of all, we can base all valid transformation rules upon a small set of "axiomatic" rules. These axiomatic rules also specify the semantic models (up to isomorphism) or at least describe their functional ("input/output") behavior; thus they provide a very abstract definition of the programming language. Furthermore, this specification technique allows us to modularize the description of the language in a natural way as a hierarchy of types. And finally, the data structures occurring in a program are incorporated into that hierarchy as the base layer. In this way, we have developed a unique algebraic frame for handling data types, transformation rules and the semantics of programming languages.

Acknowledgment

All the material presented in this paper results mainly from the work of the CIP Research Group in Munich. The authors gratefully acknowledge the work of Prof. F. L. Bauer and Prof. K. Samelson, and of W. Dosch, F. Geiselbrechtinger, R. Gnatz, W. Hesse, U. Hill, B. Krieg-Brückner, A. Laut, B. Möller, H. Partsch, M. Wirsing, H. Wössner, and the other Munich colleagues.

References

[1] F. L. Bauer, "Programming as an evolutionary process," in *Language Hierarchies and Interfaces*, F. L. Bauer and K. Samelson, Eds. Berlin, Heidelberg, New York: Springer, 1976, LNCS vol. 46, pp. 153–182.

[2] F. L. Bauer, M. Broy, R. Gnatz, W. Hesse, B. Krieg-Brückner, H. Partsch, P. Pepper, and H. Wössner, "Towards a wide spectrum language to support program specification and program development," *SIGPLAN Notices*, vol. 13, no. 12, pp. 15–24, 1978.

[3] F. L. Bauer and H. Wössner, *Algorithmic Language and Program Development*. Berlin, Heidelberg, New York: Springer, 1981.

[4] A. Blikle, "Specified programming," in *Proc. Int. Conf. Mathematical Studies of Information Processing*, Kyoto, Japan, Aug. 1978.

[5] M. Broy, "Transformation parallel ablaufender Programme," Tech. Univ. München, Faculty of Mathematics, dissertation, Feb. 1980.

[6] M. Broy and B. Krieg-Brückner, "Derivation of invariant assertions during program development by transformation," *TOPLAS*, vol. 2, no. 2, pp. 321–337, 1980.

[7] M. Broy, H. Partsch, P. Pepper, and M. Wirsing, "Semantic relations in programming languages," in *Proc. IFIP Congr. 80*, S. H. Lavington, Ed., Tokyo/Melbourne. New York: North-Holland, 1980, pp. 101–106.

[8] M. Broy, P. Pepper, and M. Wirsing, "On relations between programs," in *Proc. 4th Int. Symp. Programming*, B. Robinet, Ed., Paris, Apr. 1980, LNCS vol. 83. Berlin, Heidelberg, New York: Springer, 1980, pp. 59–78.

[9] M. Broy and M. Wirsing, "Programming languages as abstract data data types," in *Proc. Les Arbres en Algébre et en Programmation, 5th Colloque de Lille*, M. Dauchet, Ed., Feb. 1980, pp. 160–177.

[10] R. M. Burstall and J. Darlington, "Some transformations for developing recursive programs," in *Proc. 1975 Int. Conf. Reliable Software*, Los Angeles, CA, 1975, pp. 465–472; revised version, *J. Ass. Comput. Mach.*, vol. 24, no. 1, pp. 44–67, 1977.

[11] D. C. Cooper, "The equivalence of certain computations," *Comput. J.*, vol. 9, pp. 45–52, 1966.

[12] E. Deak, "Source-to-source transformations with SETL case study: Nodal spans parsing algorithm," presented at the Program Transformation Workshop, Boston, MA, Sept. 1975; also in this issue, pp. 23–31.

[13] J. A. Goguen, J. W. Thatcher, E. G. Wagner, and J. B. Wright, "Initial algebra semantics and continuous algebras," *J. Ass. Comput. Mach.*, vol. 24, no. 1, pp. 68–95, 1977.

[14] D. F. Kibler, "Power, efficiency and correctness of transformation systems," Ph.D. dissertation, Comput. Sci. Dep., Univ. California, Irvine, 1978.

[15] H. Partsch and M. Broy, "Examples for change of types and object structures," in *Program Construction*, F. L. Bauer and M. Broy, Eds. Berlin, Heidelberg, New York: Springer, 1979, LNCS vol. 69, pp. 421–463.

[16] P. Pepper, "A study on transformational semantics," dissertation, Munich Univ., 1979; also in *Program Construction*, F. L. Bauer and M. Broy, Eds. Berlin, Heidelberg, New York: Springer, 1979, LNCS vol. 69, pp. 322–405.

[17] P. Pepper, H. Partsch, H. Wössner, and F. L. Bauer, "A transformational approach to programming," in *Program Transformations, Proc. 3rd Int. Symp. Programming*, B. Robinet, Ed. Paris: Dunod, 1978, pp. 248–262.

[18] R. Steinbrüggen, "The composition of schemes for local program transformations," presented at the 3rd Hungarian Comput. Sci. Conf., Jan. 1980.

[19] D. S. Wile, "Type transformations," Univ. Southern California, draft, Sept. 1978; also in this issue, pp. 32–39.

Manfred Broy received the Dipl.-Math. degree and the Ph.D. degree in 1980, both from the Technical University of Munich, Munich, Germany.

Since 1976 he has been a member of the CIP Research Group at the Institut für Informatik, Technical University of Munich. His professional interests concentrate on programming languages, parallelism, and theory of abstract data types.

Peter Pepper received the Dipl.-Math. degree in mathematics in 1974 and the Ph.D. degree in 1979, both from the Technical University of Munich, Munich, Germany.

Since 1975 he has been working as a Research Assistant in the project CIP at the Institut für Informatik, Technical University of Munich. Currently, he is spending a year as visitor at Stanford University, Stanford, CA. His work centers on programming language design, abstract data types, and program transformations.

An Experiment in Knowledge-based Automatic Programming

David R. Barstow*

Yale University, New Haven, CT 06520, U.S.A.

Recommended by Bruce Buchanan

ABSTRACT

Human programmers seem to know a lot about programming. This suggests a way to try to build automatic programming systems: encode this knowledge in some machine-usable form. In order to test the viability of this approach, knowledge about elementary symbolic programming has been codified into a set of about four hundred detailed rules, and a system, called PECOS, has been built for applying these rules to the task of implementing abstract algorithms. The implementation techniques covered by the rules include the representation of mappings as tables, sets of pairs, property list markings, and inverted mappings, as well as several techniques for enumerating the elements of a collection. The generality of the rules is suggested by the variety of domains in which PECOS has successfully implemented abstract algorithms. In each case, PECOS's knowledge of different techniques enabled the construction of several alternative implementations. In addition, the rules can be used to explain such programming tricks as the use of property list markings to perform an intersection of two linked lists in linear time. Extrapolating from PECOS's knowledge-based approach and from three other approaches to automatic programming (deductive, transformational, high level language), the future of automatic programming seems to involve a changing role for deduction and a range of positions on the generality-power spectrum.

1. Introduction

1.1 Motivation

The experiment discussed here is based on a simple observation: human programmers seem to know a lot about programming. While it is difficult to state precisely what this knowledge is, several characteristics can be identified. First, human

* This research was conducted while the author was affiliated with the Computer Science Department, Stanford University, Stanford, California, 94305. The research was supported by the Advanced Research Projects Agency of the Department of Defense under Contract MDA 903-76-C-0206. The views and conclusions contained in this document are those of the author and should not be interpreted as necessarily representing the official policies, either expressed or implied, of Stanford University, ARPA, or the U.S. Government.

programmers know about a wide variety of concepts. Some of these concepts are rather abstract (e.g., set, node in a graph, sorting, enumeration, pattern matching), while others are relatively concrete (e.g., linked list, integer, conditional, while loop). Second, much of this knowledge deals with specific implementation techniques (e.g., property list markings to represent a set, bucket hashing to represent a mapping, quicksort, binary search). Third, programmers know guidelines or heuristics suggesting when these implementation techniques may be appropriate (e.g., property list markings are inappropriate for sets if the elements are to be enumerated frequently). In addition to these kinds of rather specific knowledge, programmers also seem to know several general strategies or principles (e.g., divide and conquer), which can be applied in a variety of situations. Finally, although programmers often know several different programming languages, much of their knowledge seems to be independent of any particular language.

Is this knowledge precise enough to be used effectively by a machine in performing programming tasks? If not, can it be made precise enough? If so, what might such an automatic programming system be like? The experiment discussed here was designed to shed some light on questions like these. The experimental technique was to select a particular programming domain, elementary symbolic programming, and a particular programming task, the implementation of abstract algorithms, and to try to codify the knowledge needed for the domain and task. For reasons to be discussed later, the form used to express the knowledge was a set of rules, each intended to embody one small fact about elementary symbolic programming. A computer system, called PECOS, was then built for applying such rules to the task of implementing abstract algorithms.

The resulting knowledge base consists of about 400 rules dealing with a variety of symbolic programming concepts. The most abstract concepts are collections[1] and mappings, along with the appropriate operations (e.g., testing for membership in a collection, computing the inverse image of an object under a mapping) and control structures (e.g., enumerating the objects in a collection). The implementation techniques covered by the rules include the representation of collections as linked lists, arrays (both ordered and unordered), and Boolean mappings, the representation of mappings as tables, sets of pairs, property list markings, and inverted mappings (indexed by range element). PECOS writes programs in LISP (specifically, INTERLISP [29]); while some of the rules are specific to LISP, most (about three-fourths) are independent of LISP or any other target language. In addition to the rules concerned with details of the different implementation techniques, PECOS has about a dozen choice-making heuristics dealing with the appropriateness and relative efficiency of the techniques. None of PECOS's rules are concerned with general strategies such as divide and conquer.

The utility of the rules is suggested by the variety of domains in which PECOS

[1] The term "collection" is used since the rules do not distinguish between multisets, which may have repeated elements, and sets, which may not.

Artificial Intelligence 12 (1979), 73–119

was able to implement abstract algorithms, including elementary symbolic programming (simple classification and concept formation algorithms), sorting (several versions of selection and insertion sort), graph theory (a reachability algorithm), and even simple number theory (a prime number algorithm). PECOS's knowledge about different implementations of each algorithm, often with significantly different efficiency characteristics.

PECOS has also been used as the Coding Expert of the PSI (Ψ) program synthesis system [13]. Through interaction with the user, Ψ's acquisition phase produces a high level description (in PECOS's specification language) of the desired program. The synthesis phase, consisting of the Coding Expert (PECOS) and the Efficiency Expert (LIBRA [17]), produces an efficient LISP implementation of the user's program. In this process, PECOS can be seen as a "plausible move generator", for which LIBRA acts as an "evaluation function". The nature of the search space produced by PECOS, as well as techniques for choosing a path in that space, will be discussed further in Section 6.1.

1.2. Representations of programming knowledge

Unfortunately, most currently available sources of programming knowledge (e.g., books and articles) lack the precision required for effective use by a machine. The descriptions are often informal, with details omitted and assumptions unstated. Human readers can generally deal with the informality, filling in the details when necessary, and (usually) sharing the same background of assumptions. Before this programming knowledge can be made available to machines, it must be made more precise: the assumptions must be made explicit and the details must be filled in.

Several different machine-usable forms for this knowledge are plausible. Some kind of parameterized templates for standard algorithms is one possibility, and would work well in certain situations, but would probably not be very useful when a problem does not fit precisely the class of problems for which the template was designed. In order to apply the knowledge in different situations, a machine needs some "understanding" of why and how the basic algorithm works. Alternatively, one could imagine some embodiment of general programming principles, which could then be applied in a wider variety of situations. However, such a technique loses much of the power that human programmers gain from their detailed knowledge about dealing with particular situations. The form used in this experiment is something of a middle ground between these two extremes: the knowledge is encoded as a large set of relatively small facts. Each is intended to embody a single specific detail about elementary symbolic programming. Ultimately, of course, automatic programming systems will need knowledge from many places on the power-generality spectrum.

There are still several possible forms for these facts, ranging from explicit formal axioms about the relevant concepts and relations, to explicit but less formal symbolic rules such as those of MYCIN [26], to the implicit form of code embedded within a program designed to perform the task. For this experiment, the form of symbolic rules was selected.[2] Several rules from PECOS's knowledge base are given below (for clarity, English paraphrases of the internal representation are used; the internal representation will be discussed in Section 5.2):

A collection may be represented as a mapping of objects to Boolean values; the default range object is FALSE.

If the enumeration order is linear with respect to the stored order, the state of an enumeration may be represented as a location in the sequential collection.

If a collection is input, its representation may be converted into any other representation before further processing.

If a linked list is represented as a LISP list without a special header cell, then a retrieval of the first element in the list may be implemented as a call to the function CAR.

An association table whose keys are integers from a fixed range may be represented as an array subregion.

The primary reason for using the symbolic rule representation, as opposed to a mathematical axiomatization of the relevant concepts and relations, is simply that the relevant concepts and relations are not well enough understood (in many cases, not even identified) for an axiomatization to be possible. Ultimately, it may be possible to axiomatize the concepts and relations, but a necessary first step is to identify and understand them. A second reason is that most of the human-oriented sources of programming knowledge are not particularly mathematical in nature, and these sources are the first places to try when looking for programming knowledge. Finally, the development of other rule-based systems has provided considerable knowledge engineering experience that greatly facilitated PECOS's development.

1.3. The value of an explicit rule set

A large part of this experiment involved developing a set of rules about symbolic programming. The rule set itself provides several benefits. First, precision has been added to the human-oriented forms of programming knowledge, in terms of both the unstated assumptions that have been made explicit and the details that have been filled in. For example, the rule given above about representing a collection as a Boolean mapping is a fact that most programmers know; it concerns the characteristic function of a set. Without knowing this rule, or something similar,

---

[2] Actually, "fact" may be a better term than "rule", but "rule" will be used throughout because of the similarity between PECOS and other "rule-based" systems.

it is almost impossible to understand why a bitstring (or even property list markings) can be used to represent a set. Yet this rule is generally left unstated in discussions of bitstring representations; the author and the reader share this background knowledge, so it need not be stated. As another example, consider the rule given above about representing an association table as an array subregion. The fact that an array is simply a way to represent a mapping of integers to arbitrary values is well known and usually stated explicitly. The detail that the integers must be from a fixed range is usually not stated. Yet if the integers do not satisfy this constraint, an array is the wrong representation, and something like a hash table should be used.

A second major value of PECOS's rule set is the identification of useful programming concepts. Consider, for example, the concept of a sequential collection: a linearly ordered group of locations in which the elements of a collection can be stored. Since there is no constraint on how the linear ordering is implemented, the concept can be seen as an abstraction of both linked lists and arrays. At the same time, the concept is more concrete than that of a collection. One benefit of such intermediate-level concepts is a certain economy of knowledge: much of what programmers know about linked lists and arrays is common to both, and hence can be represented as rules about sequential collections, rather than as one rule set for linked lists and one for arrays. For example, the following two pieces of LISP code are quite similar:

```
(PROG (L)
    (SETQ L C1)
RPT (COND ((NULL L)
          (RETURN NIL)))
    (RPLACA L (IPLUS (CAR L) 1))
    (SETQ L (CDR L))
    (GO RPT))
```

```
(PROG (I)
    (SETQ I 1)
RPT (COND ((IGREATERP I (ARRAYSIZE C2))
          (RETURN NIL)))
    (SETA C2 I (IPLUS (ELT C2 I) 1))
    (SETQ I (IPLUS I 1))
    (GO RPT))
```

Each adds 1 to every element of a collection. In the first, the collection C1 is represented as a linked list; in the second, the collection C2 is represented as an array. The code is similar because both involve enumerating the objects in a sequential collection. The state of the enumeration is saved as a location in the sequential collection (here, either a pointer L or integer I). The remaining aspects depend

on the representation of the enumeration state: an initial location (here, either C1, a pointer, or 1, an index), a termination test (either (NULL 1) or (IGREATERP I (ARRAYSIZE C2))), an incrementation to the next location (either (CDR L) or (IPLUS I 1)), and a way to find the object in a given location (either the CAR of L or the array entry for I in C2). Other than the differences based on the representation of locations, all of the knowledge needed to write these two pieces of code is independent of the way the sequential collection is represented.

This example also illustrates the identification of particular design decisions involved in programming. One of the decisions involved in building an enumerator of the objects in a sequential collection is selecting the order in which they should be enumerated. In both of the above cases, the enumeration order is the "natural" order from first to last in the sequential collection. This decision is often made only implicitly. For example, the use of the LISP function MAPC to enumerate the objects in a list implicitly assumes that the stored order is the right order in which to enumerate them. While this is often correct, there are times when some other order is desired. For example, the selector of a selection sort involves enumerating the objects according to a particular ordering relation.

A final benefit of PECOS's rules is that they provide a certain kind of explanatory power. Consider, for example, the well-known (but little documented) trick for computing the intersection of two linked lists in linear time: map down the first list and put a special mark on the property list of each element; then map down the second collecting only those elements whose property lists contain the special mark. This technique can be explained using the following four of PECOS's rules (in addition to the rules about representing collections as linked lists):

The intersection of two collections may be implemented by enumerating the objects in one and collecting those which are members of the other.

If a collection is input, its representation may be converted into any other representation before further processing.

A collection may be represented as a mapping of objects to Boolean values; the default range object is FALSE.

A mapping whose domain objects are atoms may be represented using property list markings.

Given these rules, it can be seen that the trick works by first converting the representation of one collection from a linked list to property list markings with Boolean values, and then computing the intersection in the standard way, except that a membership test for property list markings involves a call to GETPROP rather than a scan down a linked list.[3]

[3] Since a new property name is created (via GENSYM) each time the conversion routine is executed, there is no need to erase marks after the intersection is computed, except to retrieve the otherwise wasted space.

As another example, consider the use of association lists: lists whose elements are dotted pairs (generally, each CAR in a given list is unique). In some situations such a structure should be viewed simply as a collection represented as a list; in others it should be viewed as a way to represent a mapping. The following rule clarifies the relationship between these two views:

A mapping may be represented as a collection whose elements are pairs with a "domain object" part and a "range object" part.

Thus, in general an association list should be viewed as a mapping, but when implementing particular operations on the mapping, one must implement certain collection operations. For example, retrieving the image of a given domain object involves enumerating the elements of the list, testing the CAR of each pair for equality with the desired domain object. In turn, implementing this search involves rules about sequential collections, enumeration orders, and state-saving schemes such as those mentioned above. Thus, PECOS's rules are sufficient for writing the definition of the LISP function ASSOC.

1.4. Program construction through gradual refinement

PECOS constructs programs through a process of gradual refinement. This process may be simply illustrated as a sequence of program descriptions:

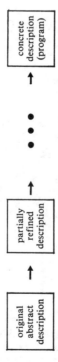

Each description in the sequence is slightly more refined (concrete) than the previous description. The first is the program description in the specification language and the last is the fully implemented program in the target language. Each refinement step is made by applying one of the rules from PECOS's knowledge base, thereby transforming the description slightly. When several rules are relevant in the same situation, PECOS can apply each rule separately. In this way PECOS can construct several different implementations from one specification. This capability for developing different implementations in parallel is used extensively in the interaction between PECOS and LIBRA in Ψ's synthesis phase.

2. Overview of the Knowledge Base

A detailed discussion of PECOS's entire rule set is beyond the scope of this paper and the interested reader is referred elsewhere [3]. Nevertheless, a brief overview may help to clarify what PECOS can and cannot do.

2.1. General rules and LISP rules

The rules can be divided into "general" and "LISP-specific" categories, where the latter deal with such concepts as CONS cells and function calls. Of PECOS's four hundred rules, slightly over one hundred are LISP-specific.[4] Most of the LISP rules are quite straightforward, merely stating that specific actions can be performed by specific LISP functions. Note that knowledge about LISP is associated with the uses to which the LISP constructs can be put. That is, rather than describing the function CAR in terms of axioms or pre- and post-conditions, as is done in most automatic programming and problem solving systems, PECOS has rules dealing with specific uses of CAR, such as returning the item stored in a cell of a "LISP list" or returning the object stored in one of the fields of a record structure represented as a CONS cell. Thus, there is never a necessity of searching through the knowledge base of facts about LISP in order to see whether some function will achieve some desired result; that information is stored with the description of the result. This representation reduces searching significantly, but also lessens the possibilities of "inventing" some new use for a particular LISP function.

The rest of this overview will be concerned only with the "general" rules. Three major categories of implementation techniques are covered by the rules: representation techniques for collections, enumeration techniques for collections, and representation techniques for mappings. The rules also deal with several lower-level aspects of symbolic programming, but they will be omitted completely from this discussion.

2.2. Representation of collections

Conceptually, a collection is a structure consisting of any number of substructures, each an instance of the same generic description. (As noted earlier, PECOS's rules do not distinguish between sets and multisets.) The diagram in Fig. 1 summarizes the representation techniques that PECOS currently employs for collections, as well as several (indicated by dashed lines) that it does not. Each branch in the diagram represents a refinement relationship. For example, a sequential collection may be refined into either a linked list or an array subregion. These refinement relationships are stored in the knowledge base as refinement rules. Of course, the diagram doesn't indicate all of the details that are included in the rules (e.g., that an array subregion includes lower and upper bounds as well as some allocated space).

As can be seen in the diagram of Fig. 1, PECOS knows primarily about the use of Boolean mappings and sequential collections. Both of these general techniques will be illustrated in the derivation of the Reachability Program in Section 4. Although "distributed collection" occurs in a dashed box, PECOS can implement a collection using property list markings by following a path through a Boolean mapping to a distributed mapping. The most significant missing representations

[4] In a preliminary experiment, the LISP-specific rules were replaced by rules for SAIL (an ALGOL-like language [24]), and PECOS wrote a few small SAIL programs [22]. The programs were too simple to justify definite conclusions, but they are an encouraging sign that this distinction between "general" and "language-specific" rules is valid and useful.

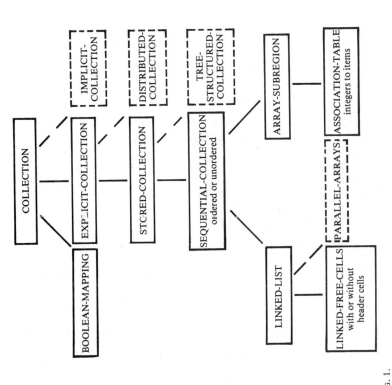

Fig. 1.

are the use of trees (such as AVL trees or 2–3 trees) and implicit collections (such as lower and upper bounds to represent a collection of integers). Codification of knowledge about these techniques would be a valuable extension of PECOS's knowledge base.

Note the extensive use of intermediate-level abstractions. For example, there are four concepts between "collection" and "linked cells". As noted earlier, such intermediate levels help to economize on the amount of knowledge that must be represented, and also facilitate choice making.

2.3. Enumerations over stored collections

In its most general form, enumerating the elements of a collection may be viewed as an independent process or coroutine. The elements are produced one after another, one element per call. The process must guarantee that every element will be produced on some call and that each will be produced only once. In addition, there must be some way to indicate that all of the elements have been produced,

as well as some way to start up the process initially. The process of constructing an enumerator for a stored collection involves two principal decisions: selecting an appropriate order for enumerating the elements, and selecting a way to save the state of the enumeration.

There are several possible orders in which the elements can be produced. If the enumeration order is constrained to be according to some ordering relation, then clearly that order should be selected. If it is unconstrained, a reasonable choice is to use the stored (first-to-last) order, either from the first cell to the last (for linked lists) or in order of increasing index (for arrays). In some cases, it may be useful to use the opposite (last-to-first) order.

The enumeration state provides a way for the enumerator to remember which elements have been produced and which have not. There are many ways to save such a state. Whenever the enumeration order is first-to-last (or last-to-first), an indicator of the current position is adequate: all elements before (or after, for last-to-first) the current position have been produced and all elements after (before) the position have not. PECOS's rules handle these cases, as well as the case in which the enumeration order is constrained and the collection is kept ordered according to the same constraint, in which case a position indicator is also adequate for saving the state.

The situation is somewhat more complex for nonlinear enumerations (i.e., the enumeration order is not the same as the stored order or its opposite); finding the next element typically involves some kind of search or scan of the entire collection. During such a search, the state must be interrogated somehow to determine whether the element under consideration has already been produced. There are basically two kinds of nonlinear enumeration states, destructive and nondestructive. PECOS's rules deal with one destructive technique, the removal of the element from the collection. A technique not covered by the rules is to overwrite the element. The rules also do not cover any nondestructive techniques.

2.4. Representation of mappings

A mapping is a way of associating objects in one set (range elements) with objects in another set (domain elements).[5] A mapping may (optionally) have a default image: if there is no stored image for a particular domain element, a request to determine its image can return the default image. For example, when a Boolean mapping is used to represent a collection, the default image is FALSE.

The diagram of Fig. 2 summarizes representation techniques for mappings. As with collection representations, there are several intermediate levels of abstraction for mappings. Note that an association list representation is determined by following the path from "mapping" to a "collection" whose elements are domain/range pairs; the refinement path in the collection diagram given earlier then leads to a

[5] PECOS's rules only deal with many-to-one mappings and not with more general correspondences or relations.

3. Sample Programs

As an indication of the range of topics covered by PECOS's rules, five sample programs will be presented in this section.[6] The next section gives a detailed look at a sixth. The first four of these were selected as target programs early in the research, in order to have a focus for the development of the rules. After most of the rules were written, the last two were selected as a way of testing the generality of the rules. About a dozen rules (dealing primarily with numeric operations) needed to be added for the last two programs to be constructed.

3.1. Membership test

The variety of implementations that PECOS can produce is illustrated well by a simple membership test. PECOS can implement such a test in about a dozen ways, differing primarily in the way that the collection is represented. If a sequential collection is used, there are several possibilities. In the special case of a linked list, the LISP function MEMBER can be used. In addition, there are various ways of searching that are applicable for either linked lists or arrays. If the collection is ordered, the search can be terminated early when an element larger than the desired element is found. If the collection is unordered, the enumeration must run to completion. A rather strange case is an ordered enumeration of an unordered collection, which gives a membership test whose time requirement is $O(n^2)$. If the collection is represented as a Boolean mapping, a membership test is implemented as the retrieval of the image of the desired element. For each way to represent a mapping, there is a way to retrieve this image. The LISP functions GETHASH, GETPROP, and ELT apply to hash arrays, property list markings, and arrays respectively. In addition, a collection of pairs can be searched for the entry whose CAR is the desired element and the entry's CDR can be returned. PECOS has successfully implemented all of these cases.

3.2. A simple concept classification program

The second target program was a simple classification program called CLASS. CLASS inputs a set (called the concept) and then repeatedly inputs other sets (called scenes) and classifies them on the basis of whether or not the scene fits the concept. A scene fits a concept if every member of the concept is a member of the scene. The specification given to PECOS is paraphrased below[7]:

Data structures

CONCEPT   a collection of integers
SCENE   a collection of integers or "QUIT"

Algorithm

```
CONCEPT ← input a list of integers;
loop:
      SCENE ← input a list of integers or the string "QUIT";
      if SCENE = "QUIT" then exit the loop;
      if CONCEPT is a subset of SCENE
            then output the message "Fit"
            else output the message "Didn't fit";
      repeat;
```

[7] Integers were used as the elements of the scenes and concept to facilitate the use of ordered collections. A different set of implementations would be possible with different types of elements in the sets.

linked list of atoms. Property lists give a distributed mapping whose domain is the set of atoms. A plex (or record structure) with several fields would constitute a mapping whose domain is the set of field names. The most significant mapping representations missing from PECOS's rules are implicit mappings (such as function collections) and discrimination nets. As with the use of trees to represent several collections, codifying knowledge about discrimination nets will certainly involve several aspects of graph algorithms. The rules currently deal with only one small aspect of hash tables: the use of INTERLISP's hash arrays. This is clearly another area where further codification would be valuable.

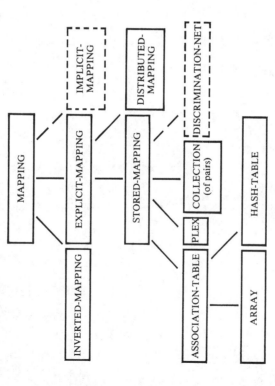

Fig. 2.

[6] Theoretically PECOS can implement any algorithm that can be described in its specification language. In practice, however, PECOS cannot handle specifications much longer than "a page" before space limitations become prohibitive.

The major variations in implementations of CLASS involve different representations for SCENE and the role they play in the subset test. The test is refined into an enumeration of the elements of CONCEPT, searching for one that is not a member of SCENE.[8] In the simplest case, the internal representation of SCENE is the same as the input representation, a linked list. The other cases involve converting SCENE into some other representation before performing the subset test. The major motivation for such a conversion is that membership tests for other representations are much faster than for unordered linked lists. One possibility is to sort the list, but the time savings in the membership test may not be sufficient to offset the time required to perform the sorting.[9] Other possibilities include the use of Boolean mappings such as property list markings and hash tables. PECOS has successfully constructed all of these variations.

3.3. A simple formation program

The third target program was TF, a rather simplified version of Winston's concept formation program [32]. TF builds up an internal model of a concept by repeatedly reading in scenes which may or may not be instances of the concept. For each scene, TF determines whether the scene fits the internal model of the concept and verifies the result with the user. The internal model is then updated based on whether or not the result was correct. The internal model consists of a set of relations, each marked as being necessary or possible. A scene fits the model if all of the necessary relations are in the scene. The updating process is divided into four cases: (1) if the model fit the scene and this was correct (indicated by user feedback), all relations in the scene that are not in the model are added to the model and labelled "possible"; (2) if the model fit but this was incorrect, any relation marked "possible" but not in the scene is picked and relabelled as "necessary"; (3) if the model did not fit and this was incorrect, all relations marked "necessary" that are not in the scene are relabelled as "possible"; (4) otherwise, there is no change.

The most interesting variations in the implementation revolve around the representation of the mapping CONCEPT. Inverting this mapping gives two sets to be represented, NECESSARY and POSSIBLE. Since "any" and "all" operations are applied to these sets, a stored collection is appropriate (although for some distributions of input data Boolean mapping representations may be better). Since elements will be added and removed from both sets, linked lists are reasonable representations. The computation of the domain of CONCEPT is fairly interesting in that the domain set does not exist explicitly with inverted mappings, but must be computed (in this case by a union of NECESSARY and POSSIBLE).

[8] For some representations that PECOS cannot handle, other forms for the subset test are appropriate. For example, if CONCEPT and SCENE are both represented as bit vectors, "CONCEPT ∧ ¬ SCENE" is zero if and only if CONCEPT is a subset of SCENE.

[9] PECOS cannot currently use the technique of sorting both lists so that they can be scanned in parallel, thereby greatly increasing the savings.

Note, however, that the only operation applied to the domain is a membership test. In such a case, the test can be refined into a disjunction of two membership tests, one on NECESSARY and one on POSSIBLE, and there is no need to explicitly compute the domain of CONCEPT. This is the implementation that PECOS constructed.

3.4. Sorting

PECOS's development originally began as an investigation into the programming knowledge involved in simple sorting programs [14–16]. PECOS's current rule set is sufficient to synthesize a variety of sorting algorithms within the transfer paradigm, in which sorting is viewed as a process of transferring the elements from the (unordered) input collection one at a time to the (ordered) output collection. Under this view, the part of the program that selects the next element to transfer is simply an enumerator over the elements of the input set. If the enumeration order of this selector is the same as the stored order of the input, the resulting sort program does an insertion sort. If the enumeration order of the selector is the same as (or the opposite of) the sorted order, the program is a selection sort. PECOS has implemented selection and insertion sort programs using both arrays and lists for the input and output collections. Thus, PECOS can carry out (approximately) the reasoning required for what was earlier described as a "hypothetical dialogue" [15].

3.5. Primes

The following problem is taken from Knuth's textbook series [18]:

7.1–32. [22] (R. Gale and V. R. Pratt.) The following algorithm can be used to determine all odd prime numbers less than N, making use of sets S and C.

P1. [Initialize] Set $j \leftarrow 3$, $C \leftarrow S \leftarrow \{1\}$. (Variable j will run through the odd numbers 3, 5, 7, ... At step P2 we will have

$$C = \{n \mid n \text{ odd}, 1 \leq n < N, n \text{ not prime, and } \mathrm{gpf}(n) \leq p(j)\},$$
$$S = \{n \mid n \text{ odd}, 1 \leq n < N/p(j), \text{ and } \mathrm{gpf}(n) \leq p(j)\},$$

where $p(j)$ is the largest prime less than j and $\mathrm{gpf}(n)$ is the greatest prime factor of n; $\mathrm{gpf}(1) = 1$.)

P2. [Done?] If $j \geq N/3$, the algorithm terminates (and C contains all the nonprime odd numbers less than N).

P3. [Nonprime?] If $j \in C$ then go to step P5.

P4. [Update the sets.] For all elements n in S do the following: If $nj < N$ then insert nj into S and into C, otherwise delete n from S. (Repeat this process until all elements n of S have been handled, including those which were just newly inserted.) Then delete j from C.

P5. [Advance j.] Increase j by 2 and return to P2.

Show how to represent the sets in this algorithm so that the total running time to determine all primes $< N$ is O(N). Rewrite the above algorithm at a lower level (i.e., not referring to sets) using your representation.

[Notes: The number of set operations performed in the algorithm is easily seen to be O(N), since each odd number $n < N$ is inserted into S at most once, namely when $j = gpf(n)$, and deleted from S at most once. Furthermore we are implicitly assuming that the multiplication of n times j in step P4 takes O(1) units of time. Therefore you must simply show how to represent the sets so that each operation needed by the algorithm takes O(1) steps on a random-access computer.]

Since PECOS's rules do not cover enumerations over collections that are being modified during the enumeration, a slightly modified version of the original algorithm was given to PECOS. In this version, the set S has been replaced by two sets $S1$ and $S2$, and the set P is created to output the set of primes (the complement of C).

Data structures

C a set of integers
P a set of integers
$S1$ a set of integers
$S2$ a set of integers
J an integer
K an integer
N an integer

Algorithm

```
N ← input an integer;
J ← 3;
C ← {1};
S1 ← {1};
loop:
  if 3*J ≥ N then exit;
  if J is not a member of C then
    S2 ← S1;
    S1 ← { };
    loop until S2 is empty:
      for any X in S2:
        remove X from S2;
        if J*X < N then
          add X to S1;
          add J*X to S2;
          add J*X to C;
```

Algorithm (*continued*)

```
    remove J from C;
  J ← J+2;
  repeat;
  K ← 3;
  P ← { };
  loop:
    if N < K then exit;
    if K is not a member of C
      then add K to P;
    K ← K+2;
  repeat;
  output P as a linked list.
```

The only operations being performed on $S2$ are addition, removal, and taking "any" element. The "any" operation suggests that a Boolean mapping may be inappropriate and the frequent destructive operations suggest that an array may be relatively expensive. Thus, an unordered linked list is a reasonable selection. Since the value of $S1$ is assigned to $S2$, a representation conversion can be avoided by using the same representation for both sets. This is especially useful here, since the only operation applied to $S1$, the addition of elements, is relatively simple with unordered linked lists. The only operations applied to C are addition, removal, and two membership tests. Such operations are fairly fast with Boolean mappings. Since the domain elements of the mapping are integers with a relatively high density in their range of possible values, an array of Boolean values is a reasonable representation of C. PECOS has implemented the Primes Program in this way, as well as with a linked list representation for C. To check the relative efficiency of the two implementations, each was timed for various values of N, see Table 1. (Note the approximately linear behaviour of the Boolean array case and the distinctly nonlinear behavior of the linked list case.)

TABLE 1. (Times are given in milliseconds)

N	C as linked list	C as Boolean array
10	0.05	0.04
50	0.28	0.20
100	0.63	0.40
500	6.40	2.02
1000	21.21	4.08

4. A Detailed Example

Perhaps the best way to understand how PECOS works is to see an example of the use of programming rules and the refinement paradigm to construct a particular program. This example also demonstrates that the rules enable PECOS to deal with the program at a very detailed level and that the same rules may be used in several different situations.

In order to focus on the nature of the rules and the refinement process, the example will be presented in English. After a description of the abstract algorithm to be implemented, several specific aspects of it will be discussed in detail. For each of these aspects, the abstract description of that part of the algorithm will be presented, followed by a sequence of rules, together with the refinements they produce in the original description. The result of this sequence of rule applications will be a LISP implementation of the original abstract description.

4.1. The reachability problem

The example is based on a variant of the reachability problem [30]:

Given a directed graph, G, and an initial vertex, v, find the vertices reachable from v by following zero or more arcs.

The problem can be solved with the following algorithm:

Mark v as a boundary vertex and mark the rest of the vertices of G as unexplored. If there are any vertices marked as boundary vertices, select one, mark it as explored, and mark each of its unexplored successors as a boundary vertex. Repeat until there are no more boundary vertices. The set of vertices marked as explored is the desired set of reachable vertices.

Note that the algorithm's major actions involve manipulating a mapping of vertices to markings.

Based on this observation, the algorithm can be expressed at the level of PECOS's specification language. The following is an English paraphrase of the specification given to PECOS when this example was run. (As a notational convenience, $X[Y]$ will be used to denote the image of Y under the mapping X and $X^{-1}[Z]$ will be used to denote the inverse image of Z under X.)

Data structures

VERTICES	a collection of integers
SUCCESSORS	a mapping of integers to collections of integers
START	an integer
MARKS	a mapping of integers to {"EXPLORED", "BOUNDARY", "UNEXPLORED"}

Algorithm

```
VERTICES ← input a list of integers;
SUCCESSORS ← input an association list of ⟨integer, list of integers⟩ pairs;
START ← input an integer;
for all X in VERTICES:
    MARKS[X] ← "UNEXPLORED";
MARKS[START] ← "BOUNDARY";
repeat until MARKS⁻¹["BOUNDARY"] is empty:
    X ← any element of MARKS⁻¹["BOUNDARY"];
    MARKS[X] ← "EXPLORED";
    for all Y in SUCCESSORS[X]:
        if MARKS[Y] = "UNEXPLORED" then MARKS[Y] ← "BOUNDARY";
output MARKS⁻¹["EXPLORED"] as a list of integers.
```

The specification is abstract enough that several significantly different implementations are possible. For example, MARKS could be represented as an association list of ⟨integer, mark⟩ pairs or as an array whose entries are the marks. The relative efficiency of these implementations varies considerably with several factors. For example, if the set of vertices (integers) is relatively sparse in a large range of possible values, then implementing MARKS as an array with a separate index for each possible value would probably require too much space, and an association list would be preferable. On the other hand, if the set of vertices is dense or the range small, an array might allow much faster algorithms because of the random-access capabilities of arrays. For the remainder of this discussion, it will be assumed that the range of possible values for the vertices is small enough that array representations are feasible. Note also that concrete input representations are specified for VERTICES (a linked list), SUCCESSORS (an association list), and START (an integer), and that an output representation is specified for MARKS⁻¹["EXPLORED"] (a linked list). These constrain the input and output but not the internal representation. They are intended to reflect the desires of some hypothetical user and PECOS could handle other input and output representations equally well.

When PECOS was run on the Reachability Algorithm, there were several dozen situations in which more than one rule was applicable. In most of these cases, selecting different rules would result in the construction of different implementations, and PECOS has successfully implemented the algorithm in several different ways. In the following discussion, one particular implementation is synthesized. About two-thirds of the choices made during the synthesis were handled by PECOS's choice-making heuristics, and in the remaining third, a rule was selected interactively in order to construct this particular implementation.

4.2. SUCCESSORS

Under the SUCCESSORS mapping, the image of a vertex is the set of immediate successors of the vertex:

$$\text{SUCCESSORS}[v] = \{x \mid v \rightarrow x \text{ in } G\}$$

SUCCESSORS is constrained to be an association list when it is input, but such a representation may require significant amounts of searching to compute SUCCESSORS[X]. Since this would be done in the inner loop, a significantly faster algorithm can be achieved by using an array representation with the entry at index k being the set of successors of vertex k. In the rest of this section, the derivation of this array representation will be considered in detail.

4.2.1. Representation of SUCCESSORS

SUCCESSORS is a mapping of integers to collections of integers. An English paraphrase of PECOS's internal representation is given below:

SUCCESSORS:
MAPPING (integers → collections of integers)

The selection of an array representation for **SUCCESSORS** involves four distinct decisions: that each association in the mapping be represented explicitly, that the associations be stored in a single structure, that a tabular structure be used, and that an array be used for the table. These four decisions are made by applying a sequence of four rules (corresponding to the path from "mapping" to "array" in the diagram of mapping representations given earlier). Each rule results in a slight refinement of the abstract description of SUCCESSORS:

A mapping may be represented explicitly.

SUCCESSORS:
EXPLICIT MAPPING (integers → collections of integers)

An explicit mapping may be stored in a single structure.

SUCCESSORS:
STORED MAPPING (integers → collections of integers)

A stored mapping with typical domain element X and typical range element Y may be represented with an association table whose typical key is X and whose typical value is Y.

SUCCESSORS$_{table}$:
ASSOCIATION TABLE (integers → collections of integers)

(Subscripts, as in SUCCESSORS$_{table}$, are used to distinguish between representations at different refinement levels.)

An association table whose typical key is an integer from a fixed range and whose typical value is Y may be represented as an array with typical entry Y.

SUCCESSORS$_{array}$:
ARRAY (collection of integers)

The final step involves selecting a particular data structure in the target language, in this case INTERLISP's array representation:

An array may be represented directly as a LISP array.

SUCCESSORS$_{lisp}$:
LISP ARRAY (collection of integers)

The objects stored in the array must also be represented. Through a sequence of six rule applications, tracing the path in the collection diagram from "collection" to "linked free cells", followed by a LISP-specific rule, a LISP list representation is developed:

SUCCESSORS$_{lisp}$:
LISP ARRAY (LISP LIST (integer))

4.2.2. *SUCCESSORS[X]*

Determining the set of successor vertices for a given vertex involves computing the image of that vertex under the SUCCESSORS mapping. The abstract specification of this operation is:

compute the image of *X* under SUCCESSORS

The construction of the program for computing SUCCESSORS[X] follows a line parallel to the determination of the representation of SUCCESSORS:

If a mapping is stored as an association table, the image of a domain element X may be computed by retrieving the table entry associated with the key X.

retrieve the entry in SUCCESSORS$_{table}$ for the key *X*

If an association table is represented by an array, the entry for a key X may be retrieved by retrieving the array entry whose index is X.

retrieve the entry in SUCCESSORS$_{array}$ for the index *X*

If an array is represented as a LISP array, the entry for an index X may be retrieved by applying the function ELT.

(ELT SUCCESSORS$_{lisp}$ X)

4.2.3. *Converting between Representations of SUCCESSORS*

Recall that the input representation for **SUCCESSORS** is constrained to be an association list of ⟨integer, list of integers⟩ pairs:

SUCCESSORS$_{input}$:
LISP LIST (CONS CELL (DOMAIN . RANGE))
DOMAIN: integer
RANGE: *LISP LIST* (integer)

Since the input and internal representations differ, a representation conversion must be performed when the association list is input. The description for the input operation is as follows:

SUCCESSORS ← input a mapping (as an association list);

The following rule introduces the representation conversion:

If a mapping is input, its representation may be converted into any other representation before further processing.

SUCCESSORS$_{input}$ ← input a mapping (as an association list);
SUCCESSORS ← convert SUCCESSORS$_{input}$

The conversion operation depends on the input representation:

If a mapping is represented as a stored-collection of pairs, it may be converted by considering all pairs in the collection and setting the image (under the new mapping) of the "domain object" part of the pair to be the "range object" part.

for all X in SUCCESSORS$_{input}$:
  set SUCCESSORS[X:DOMAIN] to X:RANGE

(Here X:DOMAIN and X:RANGE signify the retrieval of the "domain object" and "range object" parts of the pair X.) Since the pairs in SUCCESSORS$_{input}$ are represented as CONS cells, the X:DOMAIN and X:RANGE operations may be implemented easily through the application of one rule in each case.

If a pair is represented as a CONS cell and part X is stored in the CAR part of the cell, the value of part X may be retrieved by applying the function CAR.
If a pair is represented as a CONS cell and part X is stored in the CDR part of the cell, the value of part X may be retrieved by applying the function CDR.

for all X in SUCCESSORS$_{input}$:
  set SUCCESSORS[(CAR X] to (CDR X)

The implementation of the "set SUCCESSORS[(CAR X)]" operation is constructed by applying a sequence of rules similar to those used for implementing SUCCESSORS[X] in the previous section, resulting in the following LISP code:

for all X in SUCCESSORS$_{input}$:
  (SETA SUCCESSORS$_{lisp}$ (CAR X) (CDR X))

In constructing the program for the "for all" construct, the first decision is to perform the action one element at a time, rather than in parallel:

An operation of performing some action for all elements of a stored collection may be implemented by a total enumeration of the elements, applying the action to each element as it is enumerated.

enumerate X in SUCCESSORS$_{input}$:
  (SETA SUCCESSORS$_{lisp}$ (CAR X) (CDR X))

Constructing an enumeration involves selecting an enumeration order and a state-saving scheme:

If the enumeration order is unconstrained, the elements of a sequential collection may be enumerated in the order in which they are stored.
If a sequential collection is represented as a linked list and the enumeration order is the stored order, the state of the enumeration may be saved as a pointer to the list cell of the next element.

The derivation now proceeds through several steps based on this particular state-saving scheme, including the determination of the initial state (a pointer to the first cell), a termination test (the LISP function NULL), and an incrementation step (the LISP function CDR):

```
STATE ← SUCCESSORS input;
loop:
if (NULL STATE) then exit;
X ← (CAR STATE);
(SETA SUCCESSORS lisp (CAR X) (CDR X));
STATE ← (CDR STATE);
repeat;
```

The complete LISP code for this part is given below, exactly as produced by PECOS. The variables V0074, V0077, V0071, and V0070 correspond to SUCCESSORS$_{input}$, STATE, X, and SUCCESSORS$_{lisp}$, respectively.

```
(PROG (V0077 V0075 V0074 V0071 V0070)
      (PROGN (PROGN (SETQ V0074 (PROGN (PRIN1 "Links:")
                                       (READ)))
                    (SETQ V0070 (ARRAY 100)))
             (SETQ V0077 V0074))
G0079 [PROGN (SETQ V0075 V0077)
             (COND
               ((NULL V0077) (GO L0078)))
             (PROGN (PROGN (SETQ V0071 (CAR V0075))
                           (SETA V0070 (CAR V0071)
                                       (CDR V0071)))
                    (SETQ V0077 (CDR V0077]
      (GO G0079)
L0078 (RETURN V0070)))
```

4.3. MARKS

MARKS is the principal data structure involved in the Reachability Algorithm. At each iteration through the main loop it represents what is currently known about the reachability of each of the vertices in the graph:

MARKS[X] = "EXPLORED"
⇒ X is reachable and its successors have been noted as reachable
MARKS[X] = "BOUNDARY"
⇒ X is reachable and its successors have not been examined
MARKS[X] = "UNEXPLORED"
⇒ no path to X has yet been found

In the rest of this section, E, B, and U will denote "EXPLORED", "BOUNDARY", and "UNEXPLORED" respectively. The abstract description for MARKS is as follows:

MARKS:
$MAPPING$ (integers → {E, B, U})

Note that the computation of the inverse image of some range element is a common operation on MARKS. In such situations, it is often convenient to use an inverted representation. That is, rather than associating range elements with domain elements, sets of domain elements can be associated with range elements.

A mapping with typical domain element X and typical range element Y may be represented as a mapping with typical domain element Y and typical range element a collection with typical element X.

MARKS$_{inv}$:
$MAPPING$ ({E, B, U} → collections of integers)

At this point, the same two rules that were applied to SUCCESSORS can be applied to MARKS$_{inv}$:

A mapping may be represented explicitly.
An explicit mapping may be stored in a single structure.

MARKS$_{inv}$:
$STORED\ MAPPING$ ({E, B, U} → collections of integers)

When selecting the structure in which to store the mapping, we may take advantage of the fact that the domain is a fixed set (E, B, and U):

A stored mapping whose domain is a fixed set of alternatives and whose typical range element is Y may be represented as a plex with one field for each alternative and with each field being Y.

MARKS$_{plex}$:
$PLEX$ (UNEXPLORED, BOUNDARY, EXPLORED)
EXPLORED: collection of integers
BOUNDARY: collection of integers
UNEXPLORED: collection of integers

A plex is an abstract record structure consisting of a fixed set of named fields, each with an associated substructure, but without any particular commitment to the way the fields are stored in the plex. In LISP, the obvious way to represent such a structure is with CONS cells:

MARKS$_{lisp}$:
$CONS\ CELLS$ (UNEXPLORED BOUNDARY . EXPLORED)
EXPLORED: collection of integers
BOUNDARY: collection of integers
UNEXPLORED: collection of integers

Notice that we are now concerned with three separate collections which need not be represented the same way.
Since MARKS is inverted, the inverse image of an object under MARKS may be computed by retrieving the image of that object under MARKS$_{inv}$. If the domain object (e.g., B) is known at the time the program is constructed, this operation may be further refined into a simple retrieval of a field in the plex:

retrieve the BOUNDARY field of MARKS$_{plex}$

Likewise, the image of a domain object may be changed from one value to another (for example, from B to E) by moving the object from one collection to another:

remove X from the BOUNDARY field of MARKS$_{plex}$;
add X to the EXPLORED field of MARKS$_{plex}$;

4.4. BOUNDARY

BOUNDARY is the set of all vertices that map to B under MARKS. Since MARKS is inverted, this collection exists explicitly and a representation for it must be selected. The abstract description of BOUNDARY is as follows:

BOUNDARY:
$COLLECTION$ (integer)

The operations that are applied to BOUNDARY include the addition and deletion of elements and the selection of some element from the collection. A linked list is often convenient for such operations. To derive a representation using cells allocated from free storage, we apply a sequence of five rules, which lead from "collection" to "linked free cells" in the collection diagram given earlier:

> *A collection may be represented explicitly.*

> *An explicit collection may be stored in a single structure.*

> *A stored collection with typical element X may be represented as a sequential arrangement of locations in which instances of X are stored.*

> *A sequential arrangement of locations with typical element X may be represented as a linked list with typical element X.*

> *A linked list may be represented using linked tree cells.*

BOUNDARY$_{cells}$:
> *LINKED FREE CELLS (integer)*

It is often convenient to use a special header cell with such lists, so that the empty list need not be considered as a special case:

> *A special header cell may be used with linked free cells.*

BOUNDARY$_{cells}$:
> *LINKED FREE CELLS (integer) with special header cell*

Any use of cells allocated from free storage requires allocation and garbage collection mechanisms. In LISP, both are available with the use of CONS cells:

> *Linked free cells may be represented using a LISP list of CONS cells.*

BOUNDARY$_{lisp}$:
> *LISP LIST (integer) with special header cell*

4.4.1. Any Element of MARKS^{-1}["BOUNDARY"]

The main loop of the Reachability Algorithm is repeated until MARKS^{-1}-["BOUNDARY"] (i.e., the BOUNDARY collection) is empty. At each iteration, one element is selected from the collection:

> *retrieve any element of BOUNDARY*

The first refinement step for this operation depends on the earlier decision to represent BOUNDARY as a sequential collection:

> *If a collection is represented as a sequential collection, the retrieval of any element in the collection may be implemented as the retrieval of the element at any location in the collection.*

> *retrieve the element at location L of BOUNDARY$_{seq}$*
> *L is any location*

The next step is then to select the location to be used. The two most useful possibilities for sequential collections are the front and the back. Of these, the front is generally best for linked lists; although the back can also be used, it is usually less efficient:

> *If a location in a sequential collection is unconstrained, the front may be used.*

> *retrieve the element at the front of BOUNDARY$_{list}$*

The remaining steps are straightforward:

> *If a linked list is represented using linked free cells with a special header cell, the front location may be computed by retrieving the link from the first cell.*

> *If linked free cells are implemented as a LISP list, the link from the first cell may be computed by using the function CDR.*

> *If linked free cells are implemented as a LISP list, the element at a cell may be computed by using the function CAR.*

The result of these three rule applications, when combined with the code for computing MARKS$_{inv}$[B], is the following LISP code for computing "any element of MARKS^{-1}["BOUNDARY"]":

> (CAR (CDR (CAR (CDR MARKS$_{lisp}$))))

4.4.2. Remove X from MARKS$_{inv}$["BOUNDARY"]

Recall that one of the operations involved in changing the image of X from B to E is the removal of X from MARKS$_{inv}$[B]:

> *remove X from BOUNDARY*

The first refinement step is similar to that of the "any element" operation:

> *If a collection is represented as a sequential collection, an element may be removed by removing the item at the location of the element in the collection.*

> *remove the item at location L of BOUNDARY*
> *L is the location of X*

Normally, determining the location of an element in a sequential collection involves some kind of search for that location. In this case, however, the location is already known, since X was determined by taking the element at the front of BOUNDARY:

If an element X was determined by retrieving the element at location L of a sequential collection C, then L is the location of X in C.

remove the item at the front of BOUNDARY

(Testing the condition of this rule involves tracing back over the steps that produce the particular element X and determining that, indeed, the location of X in BOUNDARY is the front.) From this point on, the program construction process is relatively straightforward, and similar to the "any element" derivation. The end result is the following LISP code:

(RPLACD (CAR (CDR MARKS_lisp))
        (CDR (CDR (CAR (CDR MARKS_lisp)))))

4.5. UNEXPLORED

The UNEXPLORED collection contains all of those vertices to which no path has yet been found. The initial description of UNEXPLORED is the same as that of BOUNDARY:

UNEXPLORED:
    COLLECTION (integer)

The only operations applied to this collection are membership testing, addition, and deletion. For such operations, it is often convenient to use a different representation than simply storing the elements in a common structure (as was done with the BOUNDARY collection):

A collection may be represented as a mapping of objects to Boolean values; the default range object is FALSE.

UNEXPLORED_map:
    MAPPING (integers $\rightarrow$ {TRUE, FALSE})

Having decided to use a Boolean mapping, all of the rules available for use with general mappings are applicable here. In particular, the same sequence of rules that was applied to derive the representation of SUCCESSORS can be applied with the following result:

UNEXPLORED_lisp:
    LISP ARRAY ({TRUE, FALSE})

Thus, UNEXPLORED is represented as an array of Boolean values, where the entry for index k is TRUE if vertex k is in the UNEXPLORED collection and FALSE otherwise.

The implementation of the "change MARKS[Y] from U to B" operation involves removing Y from the UNEXPLORED collection. Since UNEXPLORED is represented differently from BOUNDARY, removing an element must also be done differently. In this case, four rules, together with the LISP representation of FALSE as NIL, give the following LISP code:

(SETA UNEXPLORED_lisp Y NIL)

4.6. Final program

The other aspects of the implementation of the Reachability Algorithm are similar to those we have seen. The following is a summary of the final program. (Here, $X[Y]$ denotes the Yth entry in the array X and $X{:}Y$ denotes the Y field of the plex X.)

Reachability Program

```
VERTICES ← input a list of integers;
SUCCESSORS_input ← input an association list of ⟨integer, list of
                                                integers⟩ pairs;

SUCCESSORS ← create an array of size 100;
for all X in the list SUCCESSORS_input;
    SUCCESSORS[X:DOMAIN] ← X:RANGE;
START ← input an integer;
MARKS:UNEXPLORED ← create an array of size 100;
MARKS:BOUNDARY ← create an empty list with header cell;
MARKS:EXPLORED ← create an empty list with header cell;
for all X in the list VERTICES:
    MARKS:UNEXPLORED[X] ← TRUE;
MARKS:UNEXPLORED[START] ← FALSE;
insert START at front of MARKS:BOUNDARY;
loop:
    if MARKS:BOUNDARY is the empty list then exit;
    X ← front element of MARKS:BOUNDARY;
    insert X at front of MARKS:EXPLORED;
    remove front element of MARKS:BOUNDARY;
    for all Y in the list SUCCESSORS[X];
        if MARKS:UNEXPLORED[Y] then
            MARKS:UNEXPLORED[Y] ← FALSE;
            insert Y at front of MARKS:BOUNDARY;
    repeat;
output MARKS:EXPLORED.
```

5. Implementation

There are three important aspects to PECOS's implementation: the representation of program descriptions in a refinement sequence, the representation of programming rules, and the control structure. In this section, each of these will be considered briefly.

5.1. Representation of Program Descriptions

Each program description in a refinement sequence is represented as a collection of nodes, with each node labelled by a particular programming concept. For example, a node labelled IS-ELEMENT represents an operation testing whether a particular item is in a particular collection. Each node also has a set of links or properties related to the node's concept; for example, an IS-ELEMENT node has properties (named ELEMENT and COLLECTION) for its arguments. Although property values may be arbitrary expressions, they are usually links to other nodes (as in the IS-ELEMENT case). Fig. 3 shows part of the internal representation for the expression IS-ELEMENT(X,INVERSE(Y,Z)).[10] Each box is a node. The labels inside the boxes are the concepts and the labelled arrows are property links. The argument links of an operation all point to other operations.

conditions both on the data structure it produces and on the data structures produced by its operands, the refinement of this COLLECTION node enables the refinements of the IS-ELEMENT and INVERSE nodes to be coordinated. Thus, for example, the refined inverse operation does not produce a linked list when the refined membership test expects a Boolean mapping. This explicit representation of every data structure passed from one operation to another is perhaps the most important feature of PECOS's representation of program descriptions.

5.2. Representation of Programming Rules

PECOS's rules all have the form of condition–action pairs, where the conditions are patterns to be matched against subparts of descriptions, and the actions are particular modifications that can be made to program descriptions. Based on the action, the rules are classified into three types:

Refinement rules refine one node pattern into another. The refined node is typically created at the time of rule application. These are the rules which carry out the bulk of the refinement process, and are by far the most common type.

Property rules attach a new property to an already existing node. Property rules are often used to indicate explicit decisions which guide the refinements of distinct but conceptually linked nodes.

Query rules are used to answer queries about a particular description. Such rules are normally called as part of the process of determining the applicability of other rules.

The internal representation of the rules is based on this classification:

(REFINE ⟨*node pattern*⟩⟨*refinement node*⟩)
(PROPERTY ⟨*property name*⟩ ⟨*node pattern*⟩ ⟨*property value*⟩)
(QUERY ⟨*query pattern*⟩ ⟨*query answer*⟩)

where REFINE, PROPERTY, and QUERY are tags indicating rule type. In the REFINE and PROPERTY rules, each ⟨*node pattern*⟩ consists of a ⟨*concept*⟩ and an ⟨*applicability pattern*⟩. For example, the following rule

A sequential arrangement of locations with typical element X may be represented as a linked list with typical element X.

is represented as a refinement rule:

(REFINE (SEQUENTIAL-COLLECTION
        (GET-PROPERTY ELEMENT (BIND X)))
        (NEW-NODE LINKED-LIST
                 (SET-PROPERTY ELEMENT X)))

SEQUENTIAL-COLLECTION is the ⟨*concept*⟩ and (GET-PROPERTY ELEMENT (BIND X)) is the ⟨*applicability pattern*⟩.

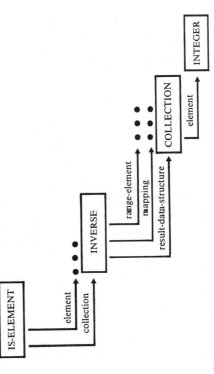

Fig. 3.

For example, the COLLECTION operand of the IS-ELEMENT node is the INVERSE node. The value computed by an operation is indicated by the RESULT-DATA-STRUCTURE property. Thus, the COLLECTION node represents the data structure passed from the INVERSE operation to the IS-ELEMENT operation. (Note that this collection is only implicit in the corresponding English description.) Since refinement rules for an operation have

[10] Read "Is X an element of the inverse image of Y under the mapping Z?".

Several other issues have arisen in the design of the rule base organization, including an indexing scheme for efficient rule retrieval, the design of a pattern matcher, and the breakdown of the condition patterns into separate parts for different uses. Detailed discussions of these issues may be found elsewhere [3]. It should also be noted that several kinds of rules are not easily expressed in the current formalism. For example, more general inferential rules (such as the test constructor used by Manna and Waldinger [23]) and rules about certain kinds of data flow (such as merging an enumeration over a set with the enumeration that constructed it) can not be described conveniently with the current set of rule types. It is not clear how difficult it would be to extend PECOS to handle such cases.

5.3. Control Structure

PECOS uses a relatively simple agenda control structure to develop refinement sequences for a given specification: in each cycle, a task is selected and a rule applied to the task. While working on a given task, subtasks may be generated; these are added to the agenda and considered before the original task is reconsidered. There are three types of tasks:

- (REFINE n) specifies that node n is to be refined.
- (PROPERTY p n) specifies that property p of node n is to be determined.
- (QUERY rel arg1 arg2 ···) specifies that the query (rel arg1 arg2 ···) must be answered.

When working on a task, relevant rules are retrieved and tested for applicability. For example, if the task is (REFINE 72) and node 72 is an IS-ELEMENT node, then all rules of the form (REFINE (IS-ELEMENT ··) ··) will be considered. When testing applicability, it may be necessary to perform a subtask. For example, an argument may need to be refined in order to determine if it is represented as a linked list. This is, in fact, quite common: the refinement of one node is often the critical factor making several rules inapplicable to a task involving another node.

When several rules are applicable, each would result in a different implementation. When a single rule cannot be selected (either by the choice-making heuristics the user, or LIBRA), a refinement sequence can be split, with each rule applied in a different branch. As a result, PECOS creates a tree of descriptions in which the root node is the original specification, each leaf is a program in the target language, and each path from the root to a leaf is a refinement sequence. With the current knowledge base, most refinement sequences lead to complete programs. For the few that do not, the cause is generally that certain operation/data structure combinations do not have any refinement rules. For example, there are no rules for computing the inverse of a distributed mapping, since this might require enumerating a very large set, such as the set of atoms in a LISP core image. If

PECOS encounters a situation in which no rules are applicable, the refinement sequence is abandoned.

Further details of the control structure and the context mechanism used for the tree of descriptions may be found elsewhere [3].

6. Discussion

6.1. A Search space of correct programs

The problem of choosing between alternative implementations for the same abstract algorithm is quite important, since the efficiency of the final program can vary considerably with different implementation techniques. Within the framework of Ψ's synthesis phase, this problem has been broken into two components:

(1) constructing a search space whose nodes are implementations (possibly only partial) of the abstract algorithm, and
(2) exploring this space, making choices on the basis of the relative efficiency of the alternatives.

The first is provided by PECOS's rules and refinement paradigm; the second is provided by LIBRA [17], Ψ's Efficiency Expert. PECOS can thus be viewed as a "plausible move generator" for which LIBRA is an "evaluation function".

6.1.1. Refinement trees

The space of alternative implementations generated by PECOS can be seen as a generalization of refinement sequences. Whenever alternative rules can be applied (and hence, alternative implementations produced), a refinement sequence can be split. Thus, we have a refinement tree, as illustrated in Fig. 4. The root of such a tree is the original specification, the leaves are alternative implementations, and each path is a refinement sequence.

Experience, both with PECOS alone and together with LIBRA, has shown that a refinement tree constitutes a fairly "convenient" search space. First, the nodes (program descriptions) all represent "correct" programs.[11] Each node represents a step in a path from the abstract specification to some concrete implementation of it. When paths cannot be completed (as happens occasionally), the cause is generally the absence of rules for dealing with a particular program description, rather than any inherent problem with the description itself. Second, the refinement paradigm provides a sense of direction for the process. Alternatives at a choice point represent reasonable and useful steps toward an implementation. Third, the extensive use of intermediate level abstractions makes the individual refinement steps fairly small and "understandable". For example, the efficiency transformations associated with the rules for use by LIBRA (see Section 6.1.3) are simpler than they would be if the intermediate levels were skipped.

[11] Assuming correctness of the rules, of course; see Section 6.3.

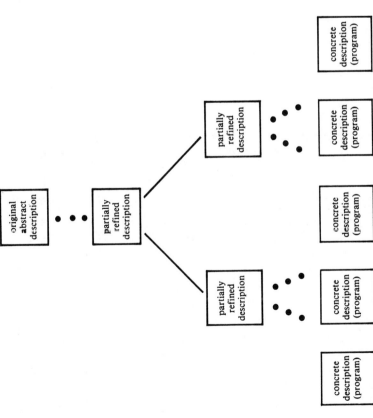

FIG. 4.

6.1.2. Techniques for reducing the space

The size of refinement trees (i.e., the total number of rule applications) may be reduced without eliminating any of the alternative implementations by taking advantage of the fact that many of the steps in a refinement sequence may be reordered without affecting the final implementation: the only absolute ordering requirement is that one task must be achieved first if it is a subtask of another. For example, if a program involves two collections, the refinement steps for each must occur in order, but the two subsequences may be intermingled arbitrarily. PECOS postpones consideration of all choice points until the only other tasks are those for which some choice point is a subtask.[12] As a result, refinement trees

tend to be "skinny" at the top and "bushy" at the bottom. Experience has shown that a considerable reduction in tree size can result. For example, the size of the tree for the four implementations of CLASS (see Section 3) was reduced by about one third by using this technique.

When two choice points are sufficiently independent that a choice for one may be made regardless of what choice is made for the other, a simple extension of the choice point postponement technique permits further pruning. For example, suppose there are two choice points (A and B), each having two applicable rules. The four leaves of the entire tree represent the cross-product of the alternatives for each of the choices. If one (say A) is considered first, then several further refinement steps (for which A had been a subtask) may be made before B needs to be considered. Since A is independent of B, the two paths for A can be carried out far enough that a preference for one path over the other can be determined before B is considered. Thus, the alternatives for B along the other path need not be considered at all. In the tree shown below, the branches inside the box need not be explored if A_2 can be selected over A_1 independently of what choice is made for B.

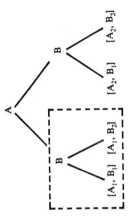

6.1.3. Techniques for making choices

When PECOS is running alone, choices between alternative rules are made either by the user or by a set of about a dozen choice-making heuristics. Some of these heuristics are intended to prune branches that will lead to dead ends (situations in which no rules are applicable). For example, PECOS has no rules for adding an element at the back of a linked list. One of the heuristics (for selecting a position at which an element should be added to a sequential collection) tests whether the sequential collection has been refined into a linked list, and if so rejects "back" as a possibility. One interesting feature of such heuristics is that they embody knowledge about the capabilities of the system itself, and thus should be changed as rules are added and the system's capabilities change.

Other heuristics deal with decisions that can be made on a purely "local" basis, considering only the node being refined and the alternative rules. Sometimes one alternative is known a priori to be better than another; if both are applicable the better alternative should be taken. For example, one of PECOS's heuristics

[12] With the current rule set, choice points are relatively infrequent. In the Reachability Program, for example, there were about three dozen choice points in a refinement sequence that involved about one thousand rule applications.

prefers PROGN to PROG constructs: (PROGN··) is better than (PROG NIL··). In other cases, the cost difference between two alternatives isn't very great, but one is more convenient for most purposes. For example, PECOS has a heuristic that suggests always using special headers for linked free cells, since the extra cost is low (one extra cell) and they are often more easily manipulated.[13]

Experience with programs such as those in Section 3 suggests that PECOS's heuristics are capable of handling a majority of the choice points that arise in refinement sequences. About two-thirds of the three dozen choice points involved in developing the Reachability Program were handled by the heuristics. For example, the front/back heuristic for linked lists handled the selection of the front position of BOUNDARY for the "any" operation. On the other hand, the selection of the array representation for SUCCESSORS was beyond the capabilities of the heuristics, since it involved global considerations, such as the size of the set of integers that might be nodes, the density of nodes within that set, and the cost of conversion.

When PECOS and LIBRA are used together, LIBRA provides the search strategy and makes all choices. LIBRA's search strategy includes the choice point postponement technique described earlier, as well as techniques for identifying critical choice points and allocating resources. LIBRA's choice-making techniques include local heuristics, such as PECOS's, as well as global heuristics. When the heuristics are insufficient, or when a choice point is determined to be especially important, analytic methods are applied. Using cost estimates for the intermediate level constructs, LIBRA computes upper and lower bounds on the efficiency of all refinements of a node in the refinement tree. Then standard search techniques (such as branch and bound) can be used to prune the tree. The efficiency estimates also rely on specific information about the user's algorithm, such as set sizes and branching probabilities. These are provided as part of the original abstract description, and are computed for refinements by efficiency transformations associated with PECOS's refinement rules. PECOS and LIBRA's behavior together has been fairly good. For example, they constructed the linear implementation of the prime number algorithm given by Knuth. The reader is referred elsewhere for further details of LIBRA's operation [17], and for a detailed example of PECOS and LIBRA operating together [4].

6.2. Rule generality

One of the critical issues involved in this knowledge-based approach to automatic programming is the question of rule generality: will many (or even some) of PECOS's rules be useful when other programming domains are codified? If so,

[13] Note that the heuristic doesn't take into account whether or not the extra cell actually helps in the particular case under consideration. And, indeed, it may be difficult to tell at the time the choice is made.

there is some hope that a generally useful set of rules can eventually be developed. If not, then the knowledge base required of such a system may be prohibitively large. While it is too early to give a definitive answer, there are several encouraging signs. First, as described in Section 3, PECOS has successfully implemented programs in a variety of domains, ranging from simple symbolic programming to graph theory and even elementary number theory. As mentioned earlier, very few additional rules (about a dozen out of the full 400) needed to be added to the knowledge base in order to write the reachability and prime number programs. Second, the fact that LISP-specific rules could be replaced by SAIL-specific rules, leaving most of the knowledge base unchanged, also suggests a degree of generality in the rules.

In the long run, the question of rule generality can only be resolved by trying to extend the rule set to cover new domains. Work is underway at Yale to codify the programming knowledge needed for elementary graph algorithms [2]. The early signs again suggest the utility of knowledge about sets and mappings. For example, the notion of an enumeration state seems important for enumerating the nodes in a graph, just as it is important for enumerating the elements of a set. The MARKS mapping used in the abstract algorithm in Section 4 encodes the state of the enumeration of the reachable nodes in the graph. As another example, consider the common technique of representing a graph as an adjacency matrix. In order to construct such a representation, only one rule about graphs need be known:

A graph may be represented as a pair of sets: a set of vertices (whose elements are primitive objects) and a set of edges (whose elements are pairs of vertices).

The rest of the necessary knowledge is concerned with sets and mappings and is independent of its application to graphs. For example, in order to derive the bounds on the matrix, one need only know that primitive objects may be represented as integers, that a set of otherwise unconstrained integers may be represented as a sequence of consecutive integers, and that a sequence of consecutive integers may be represented as lower and upper bounds. To derive the representation of the matrix itself, one need only know PECOS's rules about Boolean mappings and association tables, plus the fact that a table whose keys are pairs of integers in fixed ranges may be represented as a two-dimensional matrix.

6.3. Issues of correctness

It seems plausible that access to a large base of programming knowledge would help reduce the search involved in program verification. Consider, for example, the problem of determining the loop invariant in the following program for adding 1 to every entry in an array A:

```
(PROG (I)
     (SETQ I 1)
RPT  (COND ((IGREATERP I N)
            (RETURN NIL)))
     (SETA A I (IPLUS (ELT A I) 1))
     (SETQ I (IPLUS I 1))
     (GO RPT))
```

The invariant, to be attached "between" the RPT label and the COND expression, is as follows:

$$\forall k(1 \leqslant k < I \supset A[k] = A_0[k]+1) \wedge (I \leqslant k < N \supset A[k] = A_0[k])$$

where $A[k]$ denotes the current kth entry of A and $A_0[k]$ denotes the initial kth entry. Knowing the sequence of rule applications that produced this code gives us the invariant almost immediately. The $\forall k$ is suggested by the fact that the loop implements an enumeration over a sequential collection represented as an array subregion. Since the enumeration order is the stored order, and the enumeration state is held by I, we know that the action should have been done for all and only those indices less than I. And since the enumeration is total and the bounds on the subregion are 1 and N, we know the indices of concern are those between 1 and N.

But on another level, we might ask whether PECOS's rules are themselves correct. For refinement rules such as these, a reasonable definition of correctness might be: a rule is correct if, for all programs to which the rule may be applied, all relevant properties of the program are preserved under rule application. Thus, if the original abstract algorithm is correct (i.e., has the properties desired by the user), and if all rules that are applied are correct in this sense, then the final implementation is a correct one. What properties are the relevant ones? Clearly, the same kinds of properties that have been considered in the traditional approaches to program verification: that the value returned by a refined operation be the same as the value returned by the abstract operation under the same conditions, and that the side effects of a refined operation be the same as those of the abstract operation. But note that the question of side effects is complicated by the fact that some of the side effects at a refined level cannot even be discussed at an abstract level. For example, the fact that list cells are being modified when a new object is added to a list doesn't have any relevance at the more abstract level of adding an object to a sequential collection.

Although it would clearly be useful, no formal proofs of PECOS's rules have yet been made. In fact, the relevant properties of the abstract operators have only been specified informally. The goal of this research was rather to lay the groundwork by identifying the useful concepts and relationships, as a necessary precursor to a complete formalization. Nonetheless, some of the issues mentioned above have come up in the process of developing a set of rules that seems at least informally to be correct. As a simple example, consider the operation of inserting a new cell after a given cell in a linked list. PECOS's representation of this operation is approximately (INSERT-AFTER-CELL ⟨cell⟩ ⟨new-object⟩). The obvious refinement rule here indicates that a new cell should be created (for ⟨new-object⟩) and the link from ⟨cell⟩) and that a link to this new cell should be stored in the link field of ⟨cell⟩. Implementing this as a simple macro expansion gives roughly (REPLACE-LINK ⟨cell⟩ (CREATE-CELL ⟨new-object⟩ (GET-LINK ⟨cell⟩))). But notice that, if ⟨cell⟩ is an expression (possibly with side effects), rather than simply the value of a variable, the expression is evaluated twice, which might then violate the correctness criteria discussed above, or at least be somewhat inefficient. Thus, the correct refinement involves storing the value of ⟨cell⟩ before performing the above operations.

7. Approaches to Automatic Programming

The term "automatic programming" is rather difficult to define. In part the problem lies in the long history of the term: it was used over twenty years ago in discussions about early programming languages [1]. Nonetheless, for the sake of this discussion, let us define automatic programming rather loosely as an attempt to automate some part of the programming process. A variety of approaches have been taken in facing this problem, including extending language development to higher level languages [21, 25], formalizing the semantics of programming languages [5, 9], and many attempts involving the application of artificial intelligence techniques [8, 12, 27, 28, 31]. PECOS is an attempt to apply yet another artificial intelligence paradigm, knowledge engineering, to the same goal of automatic programming.

While it is too early to tell how far any of these approaches will lead, insight may be gained by comparing them. In the rest of this section, we will consider four systems, each of which exemplifies a different approach, and compare them with respect to certain fundamental issues of automatic programming. The four systems are DEDALUS [23], based on a *deductive* approach; Darlington and Burstall's system [8], involving a *transformational* approach; Low's system [21], based on *high level languages*; and PECOS, based on a *knowledge-based* approach. Of course, there are aspects of each approach in each of the systems, and, as will become clearer, the differences are less than they might seem at first. But nonetheless, each system will serve to illustrate one approach.

7.1. Summaries of three other automatic programming systems

Before comparing these systems, let us briefly review DEDALUS, Darlington and Burstall's system, and Low's system.

Although DEDALUS employs transformation rules extensively, it is classified as an example of the deductive approach to automatic programming because of the use of deduction in developing the control structure of the target program.

Briefly, DEDALUS takes a program specified non-algorithmically in terms of sets (and lists) of integers, and tries to apply various transformations that introduce primitive constructs in the target language. In the process, conditionals and recursive calls may be introduced when their need is recognized by the deductive system. For example, consider implementing a program to compute $x < all(l)$, that is, whether x is less than every member of l, where x is an integer and l is a list of integers. There are two transformation rules for the all construct. The first transforms $P(all(l))$ into true if l is the empty list; the second transforms $P(all(l))$ into $P(head(l))$ and $P(all(tail(l)))$, if l is not empty. Since l cannot be proved to be either empty or not empty, the original construct is transformed into if $empty(l)$ then true else $(x < head(l))$ and $(x < all(tail(l)))$. DEDALUS then notices that $x < all(tail(l))$ is an instance of the original goal $x < all(l)$, suggesting the use of a recursive call to the function being defined. In this way, various control constructs can be introduced into the program by the deductive mechanism. Among the programs which DEDALUS has successfully constructed are programs for computing the maximum element of a list, greatest common divisor, and cartesian product.

Darlington and Burstall developed a system (which we will refer to as DBS) for improving programs by a transformation process. Programs are specified in the form of recursive definitions in the domain of finite sets, and are transformed into an imperative language which includes constructs such as "while" and assignment, as well as recursion. The transformation process goes through four stages: procedure removal, elimination of redundant computation, replacement of procedure calls by their bodies, and causing the program to reuse data cells when they are no longer needed. In addition, DBS could implement the set operations with either bitstring or list representations. Among the programs optimized by DBS are an in-place reverse from its recursive definition and an iterative Fibonacci from its doubly recursive definition. In a later system [6], they incorporated various strategies for developing recursive programs (e.g., a "folding" rule which is similar to Manna and Waldinger's recursion introduction rules).

Low has developed a system (which will be referred to here as LS) for automatically selecting representations for sets. LS accepts programs specified in a subset of SAIL which includes lists and sets as data types, and uses a table of concrete (at the machine code level) implementations for these data types and the associated operations, together with information about the efficiency of the implementations. The available implementation techniques include sorted lists and arrays, balanced trees, bitstrings, hash tables, and attribute bits. LS first partitions the various instances of sets and lists into groups that should be implemented uniformly, then analyzes the frequency of use of the various constructs, both statically and dynamically with sample data, and finally uses a hill-climbing technique to find an optimal implementation. LS has been applied to such programs as insertion sort, merge sort, and transitive closure.

7.2. Techniques of program specification

Programs are specified to the four systems in basically two ways: DEDALUS accepts specifications such as the following:

compute $x < all(l)$
where x is a number
and l is a list of numbers

This can be seen as simply another way of giving input and output predicates, where the input predicate is the "where" clause and the output predicate is the "compute" clause. The other three systems all accept specifications as abstract algorithms in terms of set operations; PECOS also allows operations on mappings. However, the difference is perhaps less than it might seem, since an abstract operator is simply a shorthand for some implicit input and output predicates. For example, $inverse(x, y)$ is simply another way of saying the following (assuming the domain and range of y are integers):

compute $\{z \mid y(z) = x\}$
where y is a mapping from integers to integers
and x is an integer

The main advantage of the input/output form over the abstract algorithm is increased generality: there may not be a concept whose implied input/output predicates are precisely those desired. On the other hand, the algorithmic form often seems more natural.

There are other specification techniques that one could imagine, such as example input/output pairs, natural language, and even dialogue. In the long run, it seems that a mixture of all of these techniques (and probably more) will be needed— perhaps the prime criterion should be the "naturalness" of the technique to the person specifying the program and the domain under consideration.

7.3. Side effects

The problem of side effects has long been a difficult one for problem-solving and automatic programming systems. HACKER [28], for example, was unable to solve certain kinds of robot problems because the side effects of operations to achieve one goal might interfere with previously achieved goals. Consequently, many automatic programming systems deal with side effects in only limited ways. DBS, for example, only accepts programs specified in an applicative (i.e., without side effects) language, although assignments to variables are allowed in the target language. In addition, the final stage of transformation involves attempting to reuse discarded list cells, instead of calls to CONS. DEDALUS allows only a few target language operations that have side effects (basically, different kinds of assignment), along with specification language constructs like "only z changed", meaning that z is the only variable that may be modified. The problem of interfering goals is faced by labelling certain goals as "protected", and requiring that those which cannot be proved to hold must be re-achieved. LS and PECOS both allow a richer set of specification operators with side effects, such as adding to and removing elements from sets (and, in PECOS's case, operators such as changing the image of an object under a mapping). In each case, the knowledge base (i.e., LS's implementation table and PECOS's rules) include techniques for implementing the specific operators. As mentioned earlier, the nature of side effects sometimes requires that PECOS's rules not be implemented as simple macro expansion: the rule for inserting an object into a list requires that the insertion location be saved, since a call to (REPLACE-LINK ⟨cell⟩ (CREATE-CELL ⟨new-object⟩ (GET-LINK ⟨cell⟩))) would involve computing ⟨cell⟩ twice. In any case, it seems that the problem of side effects is likely to plague automatic programming systems for some time. The problem is, unfortunately, unavoidable, since efficient implementations often require explicit and deliberate use of side effects.

7.4. Abstraction and refinement

Just as abstraction and refinement have become increasingly important in programming methodology [20, 33], they have also begun to play a role in automatic programming. In DEDALUS, the role is relatively minor: some of the specification language constructs can be viewed as abstractions. For example, the all construct, as in FOR-ALL-TRUE, is essentially the same as PECOS's abstract control structure FOR-ALL-TRUE, as in (FOR-ALL-TRUE y l (LESS x y)). Abstraction and refinement are much more important in DBS, LS, and PECOS. Each accepts programs specified in abstract terms involving sets (and, in PECOS's case, mappings) and produces a concrete program which is essentially a refinement of the abstract program. For DBS and PECOS the target language is LISP, and for LS the target language is PDP-10 machine code. Perhaps the greatest distinction between the systems is PECOS's use of multiple levels of abstraction. While DBS and LS both refine in one step from the abstract concepts to the target language constructs, PECOS may go through as many as a half dozen levels between the specification level and the target level. This seems to offer several advantages. First, multiple levels contribute to an economy of knowledge. The example noted earlier, sequential collections, illustrates this well: much of the knowledge about linked lists and arrays is common to both and can be stored once rather than once for linked lists and once for every other kind of sequential collection). Second, multiple levels facilitate the use of different representations in different situations. This was a major problem with LS: the sets to be represented were partitioned into equivalence classes such that all arguments of any operator were in the same equivalence class. The effect, in the case of a transitive closure program, was that

all of the sets were represented in the same way. The motivation for this partitioning was that the tables would have to be prohibitively large to allow each of the operators to take different kinds of arguments or to include representation conversions between them. In PECOS, the intermediate levels of abstraction provide convenient hooks for knowledge about converting between representations. For example, the BOUNDARY and UNEXPLORED collections of the Reachability Program are represented differently, while in LS's implementation of transitive closure the corresponding sets were forced to have the same representation. In fact, not only can PECOS avoid the requirement that several related data structures have the same representation, but the same data structure can even have different representations. For example, the SUCCESSORS mapping was input as an association list but converted into a Boolean array, which was more efficient in the inner loop. A third benefit of the muliple levels of abstraction, and perhaps this is the cause of the benefits just described, is that there is room for a rich interplay between the programming concepts involved. The single rule about representing collections as Boolean mappings, for example, leads to a variety of different collection representations because of the knowledge already known about mappings.

7.5. Dealing with alternative implementations

The ultimate goal of an automatic program synthesis system is to produce the best (or at least an adequate) target language program that satisfies the user's specifications. Thus, in a sense, the problem involves search in the space of all legal target programs. This space is obviously too large to be explored exhaustively, so all automatic synthesis systems incorporate (at least implicitly) some way of reducing this space. But notice that there are two aspects of the desired program: it must satisfy the user's requirements, and it should be the best such satisfactory program. Earlier systems (e.g., the Heuristic Compiler [27] and the theorem-prover based systems [12, 31]) basically faced only the first aspect: they were concerned with finding any program that worked. DEDALUS shares this concern: its goal is to find some program in the target language that satisfies the user's specifications. The only sense in which it faces the second aspect is that the user may disable certain rules in the hope that the program found using the remaining rules (if any is found) will be better. DBS, LS, and PECOS all focus on the second aspect, in that there is an explicit space of alternative implementations. DBS allows the user to choose between two alternative implementations of the basic set constructs, lists and bitstrings. LS has its table of seven alternative implementations for set operations, and chooses among them automatically. PECOS's rules deal with about a dozen representations for collections (although not as varied as LS's representations), about a half dozen representations for mappings, and essentially two different enumeration techniques (ordered and unordered). There are several questions that one may ask about such a space of alternative implementations:

Does it include the desired implementation? Are there any dead-end or incorrect paths? How easy is it to explore? LS includes implementation techniques that PECOS does not (e.g., AVL trees). On the other hand, PECOS includes global considerations that LS does not. As noted above, PECOS avoids the restriction that all operands to a set operator must be represented in the same way, and even allows the same set to be represented in different ways in different places in the program. Thus, both LS's and PECOS's spaces include a variety of implementations for a given abstract algorithm, but the spaces seem to differ along slightly different dimensions. With respect to dead-end or incorrect paths, LS clearly has none. As discussed earlier (see Section 6.1), PECOS occasionally has a few dead-ends but no incorrect paths. How easy are the spaces to explore? In LS, after the partitioning restriction is made, the space is searched with a hill-climbing technique that seems both natural and convenient, although the possibility remains that the optimal program may be missed. As discussed in Section 6.1, PECOS's use of intermediate-level abstractions seems to facilitate greatly the process of making choices. PECOS has about a dozen choice-making heuristics that seem able to handle about two-thirds of the cases that arise in practice. LIBRA, Ψ's Efficiency Expert, uses more analytic methods, again taking advantage of the intermediate-level abstractions. In several test cases, LIBRA has performed quite well, although space limitations have prevented PECOS and LIBRA from being applied together to programs as large as the Reachability Algorithm. In the long run, it seems that the problem of choosing among alternative implementations will grow in importance for automatic programming systems, and that better techniques will be required, both for generating spaces that include the desired target programs and are convenient for exploration, and for choosing from among alternatives in such spaces. As far as the choice-making process is concerned, it seems a good guess that heuristic methods will become increasingly important, and that analytic methods (largely because of the cost of using them) will be reserved for cases in which the heuristics are inapplicable.

7.6. The role of deduction

In the earliest attempts to apply AI techniques to automatic programming, deduction (that is, the use of some kind of relatively general purpose theorem prover or problem solver) played a central role. The Heuristic Compiler was based on problem solving within the GPS framework [27]. The work of Green [12] and Waldinger [31] both involved extracting a program directly from a proof of a predicate calculus theorem derived from the input/output specifications of the program. In the more recent systems discussed here, the role of deduction seems less central. In DEDALUS, deduction is used for three purposes. First, some of the transformation rules have conditions associated with them, and these rules cannot be applied unless the conditions have been proven true in the current context. Second, in cases where the conditions have not been proven, a conditional control structure may be introduced in order to provide contexts in which the conditions are provable (and hence, the rule can be applied). Finally, in trying to prove or disprove "protected" conditions, deduction plays an important role in DEDALUS's handling of side effects. In DBS, a simple equality-based theorem prover plays an auxiliary role, similar to the first use of deduction in DEDALUS. Each recursive-to-iterative transformation rule has an associated set of equations over the primitives (e.g., equations satisfied only by associative operators); the rule can only be applied if the equations are satisfied. Deduction plays no role at all in LS. In PECOS, deduction plays a role only in a very limited sense: the QUERY subtasks of a task can be viewed as conditions in the DEDALUS sense described above, and the QUERY rules can be viewed as specialized deduction rules for handling particular situations (as opposed to giving the condition to a more general theorem prover).[14] In the Reachability Program, for example, the "deduction" that the front of BOUNDARY is the location of X was handled by QUERY rules. In the long run, it seems clear that the knowledge-based approach will require access to a more general deductive mechanism than simply a set of QUERY rules. First, it will be impossible to put in rules for all of the kinds of conditions that will need to be tested. For example, consider the following rule:

If it is known that an object is larger than all the elements of an ordered sequence, then the object may be added to the sequence by inserting it at the back.

The "it is known that ..." should clearly be tested by calling a deductive mechanism. And second, it will also be impossible to put in refinement and transformation rules to handle all possible cases that may arise in program specifications, and a general mechanism may provide the backup capability to handle the extra cases. Nonetheless, the appropriate role for a general deductive mechanism seems to be as an adjunct to the synthesis process, rather than as the driving force behind it.

7.7. Generality vs. power

It has often been stated (e.g., see [10, 11, 19]) that there is a trade-off between generality and power: techniques that are general will not help much in specific complex situations, and techniques that are powerful in particular complex situations will not be applicable in very many. We can see the same trade-off in the four automatic programming systems being discussed here. DEDALUS seems to occupy a point near the "general" end of the spectrum: It is designed to apply a general deductive framework to a wide variety of different problems specified with input/output predicates, but has not yet been successfully applied to very

[14] In fact, the transformation rules of DEDALUS, LS, and PECOS can all be seen as specialized (or perhaps even "compiled") deduction rules; and under this view the control structures serve as special-purpose deductive mechanisms.

complex programs. LS seems to be at the "power" end of the spectrum: it does extremely well at selecting data structure representations for sets, but is inapplicable to other programming problems; even to enable it to choose representations for a machine other than a PDP-10 would require redoing the tables completely. Yet even in these two cases, one can see traces of the other end of the spectrum. DEDALUS includes a large number of specific transformations that increase its power, and LS's control structure, including the partitioning and hill-climbing, could clearly be applied to other situations. DBS and PECOS seem to occupy the middle ground of the spectrum. While DBS's transformations are not universally applicable, they are certainly more general than those of LS. And while PECOS's rules are relatively specific to collections and mappings (and fairly powerful when they can be applied), they seem to possess a degree of generality, as suggested by the different domains in which they have been successfully applied (see Section 3). But note that this "generality" is concerned with a set of rules, rather than with individual rules. This does not necessarily mean that generality can be achieved by incorporating larger and larger numbers of specific rules, but my own belief about the future of automatic programming systems is that, in order to be useful and powerful in a variety of situations, they must necessarily incorporate a large number of rather specific detailed rules (or facts, or frames, or ...), together with fairly general mechanisms (deductive, analytic, ...) that can handle the situations in which the rules are inapplicable. And I would suggest that the organization will not be one driven by the general mechanism, with guidance from the rules, but rather one driven by the rules, with the general mechanisms for problem cases.

One of the critical issues involved in the knowledge-based approach to automatic programming is the question of rule generality: will many (or even some) of PECOS's rules be useful when other programming domains (e.g., graph algorithms) are codified? A definitive answer to this question must wait for other domains to be codified, but PECOS's successful application to the varied algorithms described in Section 3 is an encouraging sign.

In the long run, perhaps the greatest benefit of the knowledge-based approach lies in the rules themselves. Most knowledge about programming is available only informally, couched in unstated assumptions. While such knowledge is usually understandable by people, it lacks the detail necessary for use by a machine. For part of the domain of elementary symbolic programming, PECOS's rules fill in much of the detail and many of the unstated assumptions. Taken together, the rules form a coherent body of knowledge that imposes a structure and taxonomy on part of the programming process.

8. Assessment

The development of PECOS represents the final stage in an experiment investigating a knowledge-based approach to automatic programming. The essence of this approach involves the identification of concepts and decisions involved in the programming process and their codification into individual rules, each dealing with some particular detail of some programming technique. These rules are then represented in a form suitable for use by an automatic programming system.

As seen in Section 4, the process of constructing an implementation for an abstract algorithm involves considering a large number of details. It seems a reasonable conjecture that some kind of ability to reason at a very detailed level will be required if a system is to "understand" what it is doing well enough to perform the complex tasks that will be required of future automatic programming systems. PECOS's ability to deal successfully with such details is based largely on its access to a large store of programming knowledge. Several aspects of PECOS's representation scheme contribute to this ability. The refinement paradigm has proved convenient for coping with some of the complexity and variability that seem inevitable in real-world programs. The use of several levels of abstraction seems particularly important.

ACKNOWLEDGEMENTS

Cordell Green, my thesis adviser, and the other members of the Ψ project have been a source of motivation and focus for this work. Interaction with Elaine Kant and her work on LIBRA has been especially beneficial. Juan Ludlow's development of rules for SAIL exposed some of the hidden assumptions in my rules. Brian McCune contributed greatly to the design of the specification language. Randy Davis, Jorge Phillips, Drew McDermott, and Richard Waldinger have provided very helpful comments on drafts of this paper. The referees comments were also quite valuable.

REFERENCES

1. Automatic coding: *Proceedings of a Symposium at the Franklin Institute*, Philadelphia, Pennsylvania, April 1957.
2. Barstow, D. R., *Codification of programming knowledge: graph algorithms* (Yale University, Department of Computer Science, TR 149, December 1978).
3. Barstow, D. R., *Knowledge-based Program Construction* (Elsevier North-Holland, New York, 1979).
4. Barstow, D. R. and Kant, E., Observations on the interaction of coding and efficiency knowledge in the PSI program synthesis system. *Proceedings of the Second International Conference on Software Engineering*, San Francisco, California, October 1976, 19-31.
5. Buchanan, J. and Luckham, D., *On automating the construction of programs* (Stanford University, Computer Science Department, AIM-236, May 1974).
6. Burstall, R. M. and Darlington, J., A transformation system for developing recursive programs. *Journal of the ACM* **24** (January 1977) 44-67.
7. Dahl, O.-J., Dijkstra, E. W. and Hoare, C. A. R., *Structured Programming* (Academic Press, New York, 1972).
8. Darlington, J. and Burstall, R. M., A system which automatically improves programs. *Acta Informatica* **6** (1976) 41-60.
9. Dershowitz, N. and Manna, Z., The evolution of programs: a system for automatic program modification. *IEEE Transactions on Software Engineering* (November 1977) 377-385.
10. Feigenbaum, E. A., The art of artificial intelligence: I. Themes and case studies of knowledge engineering. *Proceedings of the Fifth International Joint Conference on Artificial Intelligence*, Cambridge, Massachusetts, August 1977, 1014-1024.

11. Goldstein, I. and Papert, S., Artificial intelligence, language, and the study of knowledge. *Cognitive Science* **1** (January 1977) 54–123.

12. Green, C. C., *The application of theorem proving to question-answering systems* (Stanford University, Computer Science Department, AIM-96, August 1969).

13. Green, C. C., The design of the PSI program synthesis system. *Proceedings of the Second International Conference on Software Engineering*, San Francisco, California, October 1976, 4–18.

14. Green, C. C. and Barstow, D. R., Some rules for the automatic synthesis of programs. *Advance Papers of the Fourth International Joint Conference on Artificial Intelligence*, Tbilisi, Georgia, USSR, September 1975, 232–239.

15. Green, C. C. and Barstow, D. R., A hypothetical dialogue exhibiting a knowledge base for a program understanding system, in: Elcock, E. W. and Michie, D. (Eds.), *Machine Representations of Knowledge* (Ellis Horwood Ltd. and John Wylie, 1977) 335–359.

16. Green, C. C. and Barstow, D. R., On program synthesis knowledge, *Artificial Intelligence* **10** (November 1978) 241–279.

17. Kant, E., A knowledge based approach to using efficiency estimation in program synthesis. *Sixth International Joint Conference on Artificial Intelligence*, Tokyo, Japan (1979).

18. Knuth, D. E., *The Art of Computer Programming, Combinatorial Algorithms* (Vol. 4) (Addison-Wesley, 1977). (Preprint).

19. Lenat, D. B., The ubiquity of discovery, *Artificial Intelligence* **9** (December 1977) 257–286.

20. Liskov, B., Snyder, A., Atkinson, R. and Schaffert, C., Abstraction mechanisms in CLU. *Commun. ACM*, **20** (August 1977) 564–576.

21. Low, J., *Automatic coding: choice of data structures* (Stanford University, Computer Science Department, AIM-242, August 1974).

22. Ludlow, J., Masters Project (Stanford University, 1977).

23. Manna, Z. and Waldinger, R., Synthesis: dreams ⇒ programs. (SRI International, Technical Note 156, November 1977).

24. Reiser, J. F. (Ed.) SAIL Reference Manual (Stanford University, Computer Science Department, AIM-289, August 1976).

25. Schwartz, J. T., On programming: an interim report on the SETL project (New York University, Courant Institute of Mathematical Sciences, Computer Science Department, June 1975).

26. Shortliffe, E. H., *MYCIN: Computer-Based Medical Consultations* (American Elsevier, New York, 1976).

27. Simon, H. A., Experiments with a heuristic compiler. *Journal of the ACM* **10** (April 1963) 493–506.

28. Sussman, G. J., *A Computer Model of Skill Acquisition* (American Elsevier, New York, 1975).

29. Teitelman, W., INTERLISP Reference Manual (Xerox Palo Alto Research Center, Palo Alto, California, December 1975).

30. Thorelli, L-E., Marking algorithms. *Behandling Informations-tidskrift for Nodisk* **12** (1972) 555–568.

31. Waldinger, R. J. and Lee, R. C. T., A step toward automatic program writing. *Proceedings of the International Joint Conference on Artificial Intelligence*, Washington, D.C., 1969, 241–252.

32. Winston, P. H., Learning Structural Descriptions from Examples, in: Winston, P. H. (Ed.), *The Psychology of Computer Vision* (McGraw-Hill, 1975).

33. Wulf, W., London, R. and Shaw, M., An introduction to the construction and verification of ALPHARD programs. *IEEE Transactions on Software Engineering* (December 1976) 253–265.

Received 20 December 1977; revised version received 26 February 1979

On the Efficient Synthesis of Efficient Programs*

Elaine Kant

Computer Science Department, Carnegie-Mellon University, Pittsburgh, PA 15213, U.S.A.

Recommended by R.M. Burstall

ABSTRACT

Efficiency is a problem in automatic programming—both in the programs produced and in the synthesis process itself. The efficiency problem arises because many target-language programs (which vary in their time and space performance) typically satisfy one abstract specification. This paper presents a framework for using analysis and searching knowledge to guide program synthesis in a stepwise refinement paradigm. A particular implementation of the framework, called LIBRA, is described. Given a program specification that includes size and frequency notes, the performance measure to be minimized, and some limits or synthesis resources, LIBRA selects algorithms and data representations and decides whether to use 'optimizing' transformations. By applying incremental, algebraic program analysis, explicit rules about plausible implementations, and resource allocation on the basis of decision importance, LIBRA has guided the automatic implementation of a number of programs in the domain of symbolic processing.

1. Introduction

Is automatic program synthesis really possible? The technology is progressing, though slowly. Most people agree that it is easier to specify programs in higher level languages but complain that default implementations are unsatisfactory. One serious problem area in automatic programming is therefore efficiency, both in the programs produced and in the synthesis process itself.

* The research reported here was conducted while the author was at Stanford University. The work was supported by a National Science Foundation Fellowship, by a Fannie and John Hertz Foundation Fellowship, by the Stanford Artificial Intelligence Laboratory under ARPA Order 2494, Contract MDA903-76-C-0206, and by Systems Control, Inc. under ARPA Order 3687, Contract N00014-79-C-0127. The views and conclusions contained in this paper should not be interpreted as necessarily representing the official policies, either expressed or implied, of any funding agency.

Artificial Intelligence **20** (1983) 253–305

0004-3702/83/$03.00 © 1983 North-Holland

This paper describes a framework for making efficiency decisions and discusses the design and implementation of a system, called LIBRA, that guides the construction of programs from abstract descriptions. The framework embodied in the system is also one model for how people combine program analysis with implementation. As an automatic system, LIBRA weighs the merits of alternate program implementations, using both algebraic program analysis and knowledge-based techniques from artificial intelligence. In comparison with optimizing compilers, LIBRA works from a more abstract specification and considers a wider range of target programs. Many choices of algorithms and data structures must be made, and making a good decision depends on a global view of the program. LIBRA has guided the automatic implementation of programs that classify relations, retrieve information, sort integers, and generate prime numbers.

The efficiency problem arises because many target-language programs (which vary in their time and space performance) typically satisfy one abstract specification. The framework discussed here covers the ground between the extremes of choosing standard implementations for all high-level constructs (results not efficient) and a complete search for the most efficient of all possible programs (search too expensive). Many points along this spectrum can be achieved by heuristic search through a set of increasingly detailed program descriptions generated by stepwise refinement. LIBRA extends an interactive program synthesis system [3] that generates this space with *coding rules*—refinements and transformations of program descriptions. In LIBRA, sets of *efficiency rules* choose from among applicable coding rules to generate a tree of plausible program descriptions and eventually produce an efficient program. The coding and efficiency rules together function both as the synthesis phase of the PSI system [6] and as an independent synthesis system. The general approach is summarized in Fig. 1.1.

LIBRA avoids explicitly constructing and comparing alternate implementations whenever possible. Both searching knowledge (heuristic planning rules) and

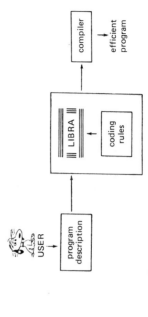

FIG. 1.1. A LIBRA's eye view of program synthesis.

analysis knowledge (estimates of the execution costs of program implementations) help accomplish this goal. The search strategy is a modified best-first search with look-ahead; it resembles both dynamic programming and the B* algorithm (but was developed independently and is successful in different types of search spaces).

Searching knowledge includes rules that
- identify plausible (as opposed to merely legal) implementations,
- group related decisions to reduce search and make cost tradeoffs more obvious,
- schedule tasks and allocate resources to reflect the importance of a coding decision in the effort expended in making the choice.

When choices remain, alternate implementations are partially refined and compared according to global execution costs estimated by symbolic, incremental program-analysis rules. Although costs can be estimated at any stage, those for more refined programs are generally more accurate. LIBRA computes upper and lower bounds on the costs to prune program implementations (with a form of branch and bound) and to identify parts of the program that might become bottlenecks (to concentrate resources on those parts). Prototypes for individual programming constructs, for types of constructs, and for cost-estimation simplify the analysis rules.

One goal of this research was to examine the interactions of heuristic and analytic techniques. For example, LIBRA's heuristics determine when analysis is cost effective and suggest particular cost-estimation techniques. Rules about plausible implementations use partial analysis information to evaluate alternatives, in effect making less precise cost comparisons. Human algorithm designers mix techniques, so a formalization should benefit people as well as automatic programming systems.

The rule-based approach (like many highly modular approaches) facilitates adding and modifying knowledge about new implementations, about efficiency, and about search strategies. Although knowledge acquisition was not a design goal in LIBRA, its usefulness as a system development tool soon became apparent. When new high-level programming constructs (e.g., trees or merge sort) are added to LIBRA, new efficiency knowledge is needed to analyze them (find their subparts, running times, and data structure accesses). Semi-automated acquisition routines inspect the coding rules and create specific construct prototypes (sometimes questioning the user about missing information). LIBRA also provides a semi-automatic procedure to help write functions to estimate running time based on a set of functions for the target-language constructs.

Section 2 of this paper gives some background for the program synthesis problem and Section 3 gives a framework for its solution. Section 4 briefly describes the research context in which LIBRA was developed and defines some basic terms. Section 5 presents an example of how the LIBRA system guides the implementation of a program specification. Search-reduction techniques are described in Section 6, prototypes in Section 7, algebraic cost-estimation in Section 8, and techniques for adding new efficiency knowledge in Section 9. Section 10 describes a number of actual runs of the system. Section 11 surveys other efficiency systems, and Section 12 presents some conclusions and future directions.

2. Background

2.1. The problem

The question addressed here is how to *automatically* select an efficient implementation for a high-level program specification, given a set of refinement rules that can gradually generate a large set of implementations. The following example illustrates the type of problem that LIBRA solves. The problem is to synthesize a retrieval program with the following behavior:

The program first reads a database of news stories. It then loops, accepting a keyword and printing a list (alphabetized by story name) of all stories in the database that contain that keyword. At the special keyword 'xyzzy', the program halts.

The user may include in the program specification the estimated number of times a keyword command will be given, the expected number of stories in the database, and the average number of keywords per story. Variations of this example are developed further in later sections.

2.2. Implementation issues and tradeoffs

In implementing a high-level program description, several issues must be considered:
- choosing a cost function,
- choosing data structure representations and operation implementations,
- applying optimizing transformations.
Some of the major difficulties in resolving these issues arise from the need to consider:
- time and space tradeoffs in program performance,
- dependencies among decisions,
- efficiency of final program versus efficiency of synthesis,
- ensuring progress towards a solution.
These issues are outlined below.

Choosing a cost function. Part of a program specification is a cost function that includes
- a target-program cost based on space use and program response time and their relative weights (possibly different cost functions for different parts of a program),

implementation choice depends on a global analysis of the impacts of the decisions, taking into account the relative frequency of retrieval operations and also the data structure sizes.

Efficiency of final program versus efficiency of synthesis. Traditional compiler optimization is based on local recognition of program constructs that are transformed into equivalent (and hopefully more efficient) forms. Only a few alternate implementation techniques are considered, and the optimization process is relatively efficient. At the other extreme, a system can synthesize programs from a knowledge base of constructive rules or can use theorem proving with axioms.

Combining the leftmost extremes in Fig. 2.1 is costly, but potentially produces a more efficient program. An intermediate possibility is large-grained, library-routine programming, which has the advantage of simplicity for programs of only moderate complexity. The payoff in designing more detailed rules is the ability to construct new combinations for unanticipated uses.

The research described in this paper assumes that compromise is the best long-range solution and that rules of a suitable level of detail can be developed. Medium-sized chunks of programming knowledge (refinement stages) provide islands in the search space and reduce search time. The insights that lead to the identification of a few good techniques in the traditional approaches are explicitly represented in plausibility rules. At the risk of finding non-optimal programs, search time can be reduced by using less reliable heuristics. For example, multiple representations can be forbidden, or data structures appearing as arguments to the same operation can be forced to have the same implementation. Another possibility is to relax the accuracy required of the cost estimates. In LIBRA, such synthesis speed-ups are explicitly represented in rules that are applied only when quick decisions are required.

Ensuring progress towards a solution. Progress toward a solution is easier to measure for pure data structure selection than when 'optimizing' transformations are considered. The measure is simplified when the known representations form a partially ordered set or directed acyclic graph so that all refinement steps are in the direction of more complete implementations. This is the case when all implementations are stored in a library of representations or, as in LIBRA, are constructed by refinement rules that embody the knowledge of a specific set of representations. If the transformations include sets that are inverses, cycles must be avoided. Fortunately, the current coding rules do not include such sets. Determining whether progress is being made is more difficult in algorithm design from non-procedural specifications.

construct everything ------------------ a few good choices
large search tree ---------------- linear in program size
global decisions ------------- local decisions

FIG. 2.1. Dimensions in program synthesis.

- a tradeoff function between the efficiency of the target program and the resources spent to find a good target program, for example an upper bound on the time to produce a solution or a time limit per expected percentage of improvement.

LIBRA allows the target-program cost to be any single polynominal function of running time and storage space (not including code length). The cost function includes upper bounds on the time and space for synthesis.

Choosing data structure representations and operation implementations. Abstract data structures often have no ideal implementation because of space-time tradeoffs, though conflicting demands can occasionally be resolved by using more than one representation. The coding rules allow multiple representations only if the modifications made to one representation need not be reflected in another. While the implementation of an operation is sometimes determined by the representation of the data structures it references, there are a variety of implementations for some high-level operations (such as sorting and searching), LIBRA's efficiency rules select combinations of data structure and high-level operation implementations but do not design algorithms for complex reasoning tasks such as prime number generation.

Applying 'optimizing' transformations. Transformations of program segments consisting of more than one operation or data structure, though commonly called optimizations, do not always improve program efficiency. Program costs before and after a sequence of transformations must be compared to evaluate utility. LIBRA supplements its general practice of comparing costs with heuristic rules about when to consider and when to apply transformations.

Time and space tradeoffs in program performance. When space-time tradeoffs arise, LIBRA compromises between choosing less efficient implementations for the less frequent accesses and using multiple representations for data structures. The latter technique exponentially increases the size of the search space, and the resulting program may require more storage and more time for changing between representations and maintaining consistency. LIBRA's efficiency rules limit the cases in which such a decision is considered and allow implementation of more than one representation only if the additional costs are outweighed by the improved efficiency of access (according to the cost estimates).

Dependencies among decisions. When a program has several data structures, it may not be possible to analyze the costs of implementation decisions independently. Under most cost functions, the cost expression will contain cross-product terms involving the space from one data structure and the time from an operation on another data structure. For example, this happens if the cost function is the product of (1) execution time of a statement, (2) number of executions, and (3) total storage in use during statement execution (assuming dynamic storage allocation with garbage collection), with the products summed over all statements in the program. For a given cost function, the best

2.3. Some subproblems

In summary, to find efficient implementations automatically, a large body of efficiency information must be codified. LIBRA addresses three subtasks of this general problem by explicating several different types of knowledge:

- resource-management knowledge to concentrate improvement effort on important parts of the program,
- plausibility knowledge to store and apply the results of previous analyses,
- analysis knowledge to symbolically estimate and compare execution costs.

These knowledge sources, along with some others describing program implementation techniques, are integrated into a rule-based system as described in the following section.

3. A Framework for Efficient Program Synthesis

Program synthesis is approached here as a knowledge-based tree search with coding, analysis, and search knowledge represented in rules and prototypes. The space is defined by a set of coding rules and is explored under the control of efficiency rules about program analysis and searching.

3.1. The search space

The space of programs is searched by generating a tree of possible implementation descriptions, as illustrated in Fig. 3.1. For a sample tree generated in implementing a news-retrieval program, see Fig. 5.2. The root of the search tree is the original program specification; intermediate nodes represent partially specified implementations. The leaf nodes are complete, alternate target-language implementations. Each arc represents the application of one or more coding rules when no choices of rules are considered in detail; the tree branches when alternate coding rules are applied to the same program part. Associated with each node in the search tree are estimates of the cost of running the target-language program, more accurate for more fully implemented program descriptions.

Many trees with the same root can be drawn. Each can be viewed as a subtree of one complete tree in which all possible refinements are expanded and in which all orders of making decisions are considered. Which tree is actually generated depends on the order in which *choicepoints* (decisions with more than one applicable coding rule) are considered and on whether any coding rules are eliminated by efficiency rules.

3.2. Coding rule sequence

One path through the tree represents a sequence of coding rule applications that construct one target-language program. The rules produce more and more concrete program implementation descriptions by filling in details. For example, a coding rule can refine a mapping (such as in the specification of the database of news stories) into explicit mapping indexed by domain elements (as opposed to other representations such as inverted mappings). Another coding rule refines the explicit mapping into a hash table in LISP. The paradigm includes both refinement from abstract to more detailed program descriptions and transformations such as combining nested blocks of code or nested loops, with the emphasis on the former. Most coding rules are not specific to the target language; for example, five rules might refine a mapping into a hash table and then a few language-specific rules would refine the hash table into target-language constructs. The target language to machine language translation is left to existing compilers and assemblers since there are very few implementation choices to be made.

3.3. Search control techniques

Two major techniques control search. One is program cost analysis, which provides an evaluation function for the search. The other is the use of specific searching heuristics, both domain independent ones such as branch and bound, and domain specific ones that embody programming knowledge such as plausible data structure representations.

A tree of partial program implementations, each with an agenda of synthesis tasks, is the workspace for recording the state of the search (see Fig. 3.2). When several rules are applicable to a task, other sets of rules (dependent on the type of task) prune and order the first set.

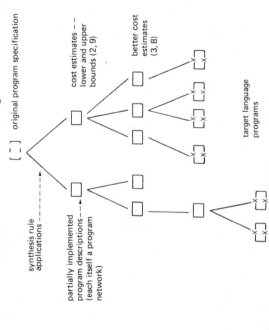

[:] original program specification

synthesis rule applications ------

partially implemented program descriptions --- (each itself a program network)

cost estimates — lower and upper bounds (2, 9)

better cost estimates (3, 8)

target language programs

FIG. 3.1. Efficient implementation selection by tree search.

4. An Overview of the LIBRA Implementation

4.1. The PSI system context

A PSI user specifies a program in a restricted-English dialogue with the system. During the dialogue, the acquisition phase builds up a *program model* that is a high-level-language specification of a program. This program model is passed on to the *synthesis phase*, which consists of LIBRA and the coding rules. The synthesis phase then chooses a reasonable implementation of the program model from among those that can be constructed by the coding rules. LIBRA controls the decision making in this phase. A program can also be specified directly in a high-level language with a more conventional syntax and translated into a program model. For a summary of the PSI system, see [7].

4.2. Program-model specifications

An implementation request is specified to LIBRA as a program model that describes the basic control and data structures and constraints on input or output representations. The model language is similar in some ways to SETL [21], and also includes structured control constructs. A program model can include efficiency specifications: data structure sizes, probabilities of execution of branches of conditional expressions, a cost function for comparing implementations, and bounds on the resources for producing the target-language program. If necessary efficiency information is not specified in the model, LIBRA will prompt the user for it early in the synthesis process, or make default decisions if so requested.

4.3. Coding rules

A collection of approximately 400 rules provides LIBRA with a variety of techniques for representing data and implementing algorithms in the domain of symbolic processing. For example, sets and mappings can be represented as linked lists or arrays (ordered or unordered), hash tables, property list markings, and mappings indexed by range elements. Several types of sorting algorithms and enumerations, including multiple exit loops, can be constructed. Other manipulations include removing and inserting elements in sets and mappings and testing Boolean predicates on sets. Values can be stored in variables and recomputed. A data structure can be represented in more than one way within a program. The coding rules are part of Barstow's PECOS system (which includes its own control structure in which a person is responsible for making decisions with the aid of some simple heuristics). Figs. 4.1 and 4.2 show a subset of the refinement paths for collections and mappings that are permitted by the coding rules. The term 'collection' refers to data structures that may be either sets (in

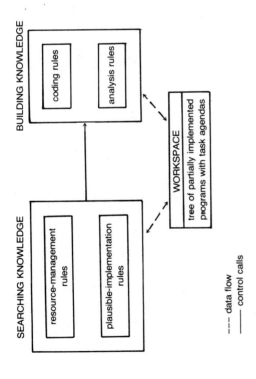

FIG. 3.2. Overview of efficiency framework.

A simplified description of the search strategy is: pick a program implementation to work on, pick a refinement task within that implementation, pick a coding rule to achieve that task, and finally apply the coding rule and any associated analysis rules. This strategy is implemented by three interacting types of efficiency rules: resource-management rules, plausible-implementation rules, and cost-analysis rules.

Resource-management rules choose a program implementation (node in the search tree) to expand and then a part of that program to work on. These rules assign resources and priorities to tasks and ensure that the tasks are carried out within the limits of the resources.

When refining a part of a program, all relevant coding rules are retrieved and tested for applicability. At choicepoints (where more than one coding rule is applicable), *plausible-implementation rules* help pick a coding rule based on precomputed analyses of what is reasonable in a given program situation.

When several coding rules seem plausible, separate program descriptions are set up and refined, then compared using the cost estimates determined by *cost-analysis rules*. Resource-management and plausible-implementation rules may call on the cost-analysis rules for program analyses, including data structure size and statement execution frequency information, and symbolic cost estimates (for all or part of a program). Some analysis rules are always applied during refinement to simplify later analyses, but the major cost estimates are prepared only as needed.

the network around the construct instance to be refined. When refining a program construct, all coding rules relevant to that construct (usually five or fewer) are retrieved. The applicability checks then determine which of the rules (typically one to three) are legal in the current situation. The target language is a subset of INTERLISP [25]. However, over two thirds of the coding rules are not specific to any target-language.

4.4. Efficiency rules: searching and analysis knowledge

4.4.1. *Resource-management knowledge: assigning priorities to decisions*

Since all implementations cannot be considered in equal detail, the quality of the decisions depends on the order in which they are considered and the depth to which the consequences of alternatives are explored before making a commitment. LIBRA has several types of resource-management rules.

(1) *Priority-setting rules* limit the resources available to test a particular branch in the refinement tree and decide which branches should be pursued in which order. These rules, which are not specific to program synthesis applications, enforce global search strategies; in LIBRA, these are branch and bound and best-first search with look-ahead. The rules, combined with a plausible-implementation rule that eliminates implementations that are worse in space *and* worse in time than their alternatives, produce behavior similar to a dynamic programming algorithm. (See [26] for a good discussion of dynamic programming in implementation selection.)

(2) *Task-ordering rules* determine an order for attempting refinement tasks *within* a particular branch of the search tree. Ordering principles include postponing choices of coding rules while working on more clear-cut refinements (to gather additional information), exposing choices by early expansion of complex programming constructs such as 'subset', and postponing low-level coding until major decisions are made.

(3) *Choice-ordering rules* find an order for considering the decisions (choice-points) with a branch. One rule suggests allocating the most resources to the decisions that are likely to lead to bottlenecks and making those decisions first. Section 4.4.3 describes how these *high potential impact* decisions are identified. The values are adjusted to reflect the accuracy of cost estimates at the current stage of program development and the expected cost of completing refinement. Without this, a highly refined implementation might be abandoned in favor of a very abstract description with a slightly better optimistic estimate that is probably not achievable.

(4) *Grouping rules* reduce the number of alternatives constructed by considering related implementation decisions together. This reduces both the number of decisions and number of interactions between decisions. Better decisions can be made at a lower cost since, for example, all uses of a data structure are considered at one time.

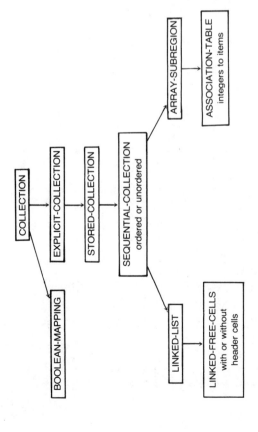

FIG. 4.1. Overview of collection representations.

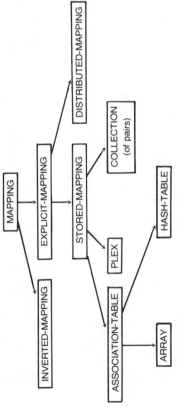

FIG. 4.2. Overview of mapping representations.

which elements may not be repeated) or multisets (in which they may). Mappings are correspondences between elements in a domain and elements in a range. For a detailed description of the coding knowledge, see [3].

Coding rules highlight the important decisions at each stage and suppress secondary considerations until later refinement steps. The rules either refine one instance of a programming *construct* into a more concrete one or add information in the form of a *property* to an existing construct instance. Coding rules have applicability checks that match the rule condition (a pattern) with estimated by assuming optimistic costs for each program construct and by assuming that no representation conflicts occur.

The importance of a decision is measured by its *potential impact*. This is the difference between the achievable-bound cost and the execution cost estimated when optimistic values are used for all parts of the program involved in the decision (and achievable costs for the rest).

The top-down, incremental analysis produces cost estimates for programs that would be difficult to analyze automatically if only the target program were given. An advantage of combining stepwise refinement with incremental analysis is that *classes* of implementations can be compared according to cost estimates for intermediate programs rather than generating and comparing target-language programs. For example, a collection can be refined to a mapping (leading to a hash table, bit vector, or property list) or to a sequential collection (leading to a linked list or array, ordered or unordered). If the collection's primary use is in membership tests, it can be estimated that any mapping representation will give a faster execution time than any sequential collection, so the mapping rule can be applied without explicitly considering the list and array representations.

5. An Example of LIBRA in Operation

To illustrate the efficiency framework, this section presents an example of LIBRA's selection of data structures on the basis of global efficiency criteria and heuristic rules (variety in algorithms is not stressed here). The example, a simple retrieval program called NEWS, uses a *database* of news stories that is a

```
                   NEWS

DATA STRUCTURES
database: mapping from story to keywords;
story: string;
keywords: collection of key;
key: string;
command: alternative 'xyzzy' or key;

ALGORITHM
input(database);
loop
  repeating
    input(command);
    if command = 'xyzzy' then assert-exit quitloop;
    forall S in domain-of(database) when command in database[S] do output(S);
  exits
    quitloop;
end;
```

FIG. 5.1. Initial program description for NEWS.

4.4.2. *Plausibility knowledge: suggesting implementations with stored analyses*

Approximately forty plausible-implementation rules describe the situations under which data structure representations are or are not appropriate, under which different operations implementations are plausible, and under which more than one representation for a data structure should be considered. Some typical rules are shown below; others are given in Sections 5.2 and 6.3.

In refining a set with more than 30 elements that is used only for membership tests and adding and deleting elements, the hash-table representation is a good choice.

In refining a sequence in which elements are frequently inserted and deleted in the middle, use a linked list rather than an array (to avoid shifting).

Plausible-implementation rules are condition–action rules. Conditions state critical uses of a data structure that make a rule applicable and check any analysis facts (such as the size of a data structure and the number of executions of a statement). Rule actions can prune coding rules directly (based on the type of constructs produced or the space and/or time costs of the constructs), postpone the choice, or set a Boolean combination of constraints for a set of program parts. Constraints are checked in a three-valued propositional logic in which conditions are satisfied, possible, or impossible.

Some plausible-implementation rules are always applied. A second set of less reliable (according to the system designer) rules are used only for quick decisions (when more accurate comparisons require too much resources or are not potentially profitable). These rules also identify the standard implementation choices; for example, to use lists rather than arrays to represent sequences in LISP.

4.4.3. *Analysis knowledge: estimating execution costs*

The user specifies basic information in terms of the original specification and the system keeps the analysis updated for the rest of the refinement process, making analysis transformations in parallel with refinements to associate more accurate cost estimates with succeeding nodes in the tree. The rules maintain information about data flow, data structure sizes and storage use, and statement running times and execution frequencies.

Analysis rules compute two bounds on the execution cost. An upper bound, or *achievable* estimate, is based on a standard (default) implementation for each programming construct and assumes that standard implementation choices are made for the rest of the refinement process. An *optimistic* cost estimate is a lower bound for implementations known to the coding rules, not a theoretical lower bound and not a best-case value. Global optimistic costs are mapping from the stories to collections of *keywords* associated with each story. The program's behavior is to be as follows:

> Read in a database of news stories. Then repeatedly accept a keyword and print out a list of the names of the stories in the database that contain that keyword. If the special keyword 'xyzzy' is given, then halt.

The program description for NEWS is shown in Fig. 5.1. This version is a mechanical translation of the actual specification given to LIBRA; the internal representation is a semantic net with hash links, property lists, and some additional cross-referencing information. The syntax of the loop allows for multiple exits and exit actions, but there is only one exit in this example.

5.1. Alternate implementation paths for NEWS

Under different assumptions about the size of the database or the cost function to be used, LIBRA selects different implementations for NEWS. A refinement tree showing several implementations and critical decision points is presented in Fig. 5.2. Achievable and optimistic cost estimates are given in parentheses. Costs are in millisecond-pages (since the cost function is the product of running time measured in milliseconds and space measured in pages) and have been rounded for convenience of explanation. As the figure shows, the major choices to be made are the representation for the mapping from stories to keywords and the representation for the keywords.

One refinement sequence, leading to node *G* in the search tree of Fig. 5.2, is explained in more detail in the following sections. It involves representing *database* internally as a hash table of stories, with each *story* mapping to another hash table of keywords. The cost function is the product of running time and number of pages is use. LIBRA chooses a hash-table representation for *keywords* because there are many keywords for each story. The time to convert the input list of keywords into a hash table is balanced by the time savings from the membership test, which is faster as a hash-table look-up than as a search through a list (for large keyword collections). The *database* representation decision is similar. Both choices are reinforced by the fact that the main loop is executed many times before exiting with 'xyzzy'. In this case, the default of dynamic storage allocation is assumed.

Under other assumptions, a path through node *B* is taken and a linked-list representation is selected for *database*. For example, if the loop is executed only a few times or if the number of keywords associated with a story is small, then the time required to convert the database from the list of pairs ((story, keywords)) representation to a hash-table representation is not outweighed by the fast hash-table look-up operations. If space is a critical factor in the cost function, another path through *B* might be taken in which the original

representation of a list of pairs can be preserved. This avoids using any more space than necessary, but at a cost in time.

A different tree than the one pictured in Fig. 5.2 is searched under other assumptions. If there are only a few keywords per story, many stories, and a cost function dominated by running time, then the representation of the *database* mapping is a more critical (and hence earlier) decision than the *keywords* representation because the time for the membership test is similar for both representations. (The importance of decision ordering is discussed in Section 6.2.4.) The tree searched also differs if fewer resources are available for synthesis and some choices are made by heuristic rules rather than efficient computations. For example, nodes *F* and *H* are not considered if a plausible-implementation rule that prefers hash-table representations to property-list entries is applied because a quick decision is needed.

The implementations that LIBRA chooses in these examples are about the best possible with the given set of coding rules.

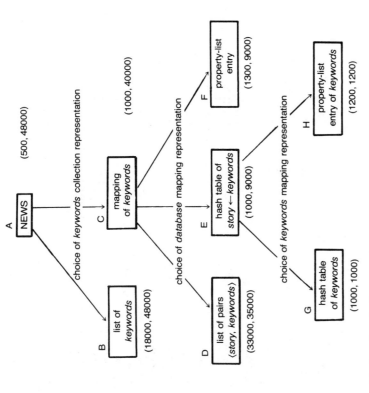

FIG. 5.2. Overview of refinements of NEWS.

5.2. Initial refinements in NEWS

The following sections show more details of the refinement sequence leading to node G. In this run, LIBRA questions the user and determines that the expected number of stories in the database is 80, the average number of keywords per story is 100, the expected number of iterations of the loop is 300, and the probability that the command is a keyword of the average story is 0.01. LIBRA then calls on the coding rules to make refinements that do not involve any decisions. For example, the input database is refined to the standard input format for mappings, a list of pairs (story, keywords), and the input collection of keywords is refined into a linked list.

5.2.1. Applying plausible-implementation rules

LIBRA applies plausible-implementation rules that suggest considering additional representations for keywords and database within the loop body. Next, the 'forall' statement enumerating the domain of database (inside the loop) is refined into an explicit enumeration of the items of domain since only one coding rule is applicable. Before refining the enumeration further, more information about the representation of the domain is needed.

LIBRA does not consider all representations of the database domain explicitly; the following plausible-implementation rules about collections (from Section 6) constrain the choice to a single possibility:

COLL 1. If the only references to a collection A are enumerations over A, and if B is another representation for A that is easily enumerable, then use the same representation for A and B.

COLL 2. If all references to a collection are its enumerations, pointers to positions in it, or tests of the state of the enumeration, and if the target language is LISP, then refine the collection into a linked list.

The domain collection satisfies these rules and therefore should be refined into a linked list. Constraints on the domain collection are established, and it is eventually refined into a sequential collection and then into a list (rather than an array).

5.2.2. Postponing choicepoints

Several choices that arise and cannot be resolved by plausible-implementation rules are postponed until other useful refinements are finished. Also, details of the construction of the domain list and its enumeration are postponed by resource-management rules because LIBRA predicts that no decisions will be involved (based on a precomputed analysis of possible refinements of constructs) and therefore that the cost estimate for these parts of the program will not change significantly.

5.3. Identifying the most important decision

All of the changes above take place before node A of Fig. 5.2 is reached. The choices postponed during this refinement are (1) how to refine the database representation used inside the 'forall', and (2) how to refine the keywords collection within that mapping. What are the effects of the two choices?

5.3.1. Comparing potential impacts

An additional representation of database, called db1, is being considered within the scope of the 'forall'. It is used to retrieve the map value (keyword collection) once per story per command. Possible implementations for mappings range from a linked-list format that makes retrieval linear in the number of stories to associative structures that have constant expected retrieval time.

The keyword collections in db1, called keywords1, are referenced by a 'member(command, keywords1)' test once per each story for each iteration of the loop. Possible implementations give membership tests with times ranging from linear in the number of keywords to constant. The achievable estimate for a membership test assumes that the default implementation of a collection is a list (when LISP is the target language) and that the average running time is therefore a constant times $n(1 - 0.5p)$, where p is the probability that the test succeeds and n is the size of the set. For the membership test in NEWS (with a constant of 0.015), this is $0.015(100(1-0.005))$, which is approximately 1.5 milliseconds. The lower bound or optimistic cost estimate for the membership test is a small constant (0.01) because representing the set with a mapping such as a hash table is a possibility.

LIBRA's cost-computation rules estimate that the achievable cost of the program is $(a + 300(b + 80(c + d)))$, where a is the achievable cost to read in the database and find its domain, b is the cost to input and test the command, c is the cost for the membership test inside the enumeration, and d is the cost to find the keywords corresponding to the command. (Since space is measured in pages and in this example everything fits on one page, cost is the same as time.) Other rules estimate that a is approximately 10; b, 0.05; c, 1.5 (the achievable time for a membership test as described above); and d, 0.5 (for reasons similar to the membership test analysis). The global time (and cost) is therefore $10 + 300(0.05 + 80(2))$, or about 48000. Similarly, substituting $(0.01 + 0.01)$ for $(c + d)$ gives an optimistic time (cost) of about 500. Recall that the potential impact is the difference between the achievable cost estimate and the execution cost estimate when optimistic costs are used for all parts of the program involved in the decision. From the cost expression given above, the potential impact of keywords is about $24000(2 - 0.51)$, or 35760 millisecond-pages (ignoring differences in the optimistic and achievable estimates of a and b, which are small; LIBRA does not compute the exact value). A similar calculation for the effect of how the database is represented yields $24000(2 - 1.51)$ or 11760, so the keywords decision is more likely to be a bottleneck in the final program if care is not taken in the representation choice.

According to the resource-management rule about making high-potential-impact decisions first, the next step is to look at the possible refinements of keywords1.

5.3.2. Assigning resources

As a first step in making the keywords1 decision, search resources (maximums for CPU time and number of construct-instances) are assigned in proportion to the decision's importance. The resources needed to complete a program with default implementations are estimated and subtracted from the total available resources. Decision-making resources from the remainder are assigned in proportion to the estimated importance. If resources were low, the decision would be made by plausible-implementation rules, but in this case, separate program descriptions are set up in which each of the alternate coding rules are applied. In this decision, the applicable rules allow either refining the keyword collection into an explicit collection, leading to search node B, or into an explicit mapping, leading to node C.

5.4. Exploring two implementations for keywords1

LIBRA's goal is to refine the alternatives (B and C) enough for an informative comparison. The resources previously allocated give upper limits on the time and space to be spent on getting more accurate cost estimates for the implementations being explored. As part of the resource-management strategies, each program description has a 'purpose' to be fulfilled (to test whether the refinement task has been achieved) and a 'focus set' of program parts to be the center of attention of processing—in this case, the keywords1 data structure, the conversion from the input representation, and the membership test.

5.4.1. Preliminary look-ahead

The two competing program descriptions each use a small portion of the assigned resources for a quick check of their efficiencies (to see if any effects of the decision are immediately apparent). During this look-ahead, resource-management rules prevent consideration of other decisions and ensure that only tasks related to the focus set are attempted. Processing of the program description continues until the resources run out or until there are no more relevant tasks.

In node B, the explicit-collection rule is applied and refinement proceeds until all relevant tasks are satisfied—the synthesis resources are generous in this example. At the conclusion, the keyword collection for each story is refined (after the application of several coding rules) into a LISP list, and the membership operation is refined into a list search.

Refinement of node C (the program description with the explicit-mapping) also halts after all relevant tasks are accomplished. Here the keyword collection is refined to a mapping and membership is tested by seeing if there is mapping for the given key. The keyword collection representation is converted to a mapping from the list format of the input.

5.4.2. Applying branch and bound

Next, LIBRA estimates the total cost for each program description. In the linked-list implementation of node B, the optimistic estimate is 18000 millisecond-pages, and the achievable bound is 48000. For C, the bounds are 1000 and 40000 respectively. Branch and bound is applied to eliminate any implementations with optimistic estimates worse than the achievable estimate of some other implementation. No implementation is eliminated in this case, but later this technique will be fruitful.

5.4.3. Making a preliminary choice for keywords1

The remaining decision-making resources are divided among the surviving alternatives, nodes B and C, for the purpose of choosing which rule to apply, and refinement continues until resources or relevant tasks are exhausted. Processing then continues in the program description with the lowest optimistic bound, which is the explicit-mapping in node C. This comparison includes all active program descriptions, not just those involved in the most recent decision. The purpose of the best program description (node C) is then restored to the original one of continued refinement to a target-language program. If resources are running out in a continued-refinement situation, the user is asked if more resources should be spent. If not, LIBRA produces a program as quickly as possible by making standard refinement choices for each programming construct.

5.5. Refining the rest of NEWS

The remaining decisions in node C include choosing a refinement for the explicit-mapping of keywords1 and choosing a refinement for db1. The database decision (db1) is chosen by the potential impact method as the most important decision to be made.

5.5.1. Refining db1

Three program descriptions are set up to consider the three applicable refinement rules—one to consider refining the db1 mapping to a list of pairs (node D), one to consider a stored mapping (node E), and one to consider a distributed mapping (node F). The relevant parts of the program, those related to the db1 decision, are then refined in each program description. For example, the resulting program descriptions are compared with each other and with other program descriptions that have been temporarily abandoned, such as the node B. As Fig. 5.2 shows, nodes B and D can be eliminated from further consideration because even their optimistic bounds are worse than the achievable bound on node E. The most promising implementation, node E, is then chosen for further refinement.

5.5.2. Refining keywords1

The final decision to be made is how to represent the *keywords*1 collection, which has been refined into a mapping. As in the refinement of node C, there are three applicable coding rules. However, a plausible-implementation rule about mappings eliminates one of the possibilities (the 'collection of pairs'). This mapping rule states:

MAP 5. If an explicit mapping has already been refined from a collection, then do not refine it into a collection of pairs.

Thus, only two coding rules are considered. These rules are tested in nodes G and H, and the stored mapping, leading to the hash-table representation (node G), proves to be the best choice. At this point, the cost estimate is precise enough to eliminate all other possibilities.

5.5.3. And finally, LISP code

Thus, the best possibility is to implement both the keyword collection and the database mapping as hash tables. As refinement continues, several other choices of coding rules are resolved by plausible-implementation rules. The program description is finally refined into the one page LISP program shown in Fig. 5.3.

6. Methods for Controlling Search in Program Refinement

Several regularities in LIBRA's search space influence the search strategies. The space is large because more than one representation of the same type of data structure or operation is allowed (as well as combinations of implementations). In addition, most implementations are reachable (perhaps requiring representation conversion however), so refinement failure occurs only in the rare cases when no coding rules apply. Finally, the fixed set of programming constructs generated by the coding rules can be partially ordered by level of abstraction. This ordering allows the plausible-implementation rules to predict good paths. Because most of the implementations are reachable and because the potential refinements of abstract constructs can be predicted from the partial ordering, the analysis rules compute reasonably tight cost bounds. When an implementation requires representation changes, the cost is often higher than the first prediction, but a small amount of refinement will expose the true cost.

```
(NEWS [LAMBDA NIL
(PROG (DDB DB)
[SETQ DB (CONS (QUOTE 'HEAD)
(PROGN (PRIN1 'DATABASE?) (TERPRI) (READ)]
(SETQ DDB (PROG (G1 C1)
(SETQ C1 (CONS (QUOTE 'HEAD') (QUOTE NIL)))
(SETQ G1 DB)
RPT1 (COND ((NULL (CDR G1)) (GO L1))
(RPLACD C1 (CONS (CAR (CDR G1))) (CDR C1)))
(SETQ G1 (CDR G1))
(GO RPT1)
L1 (RETURN C1)))
(PROG (DB1)
(SETQ DB1 (PROG (G2 C2)
(SETQ C2 (HARRAY 100))
(SETQ G2 DB)
RPT3 (COND ((NULL (CDR G2)) (GO L2)))
(PUTHASH (CAR (CAR (CDR G2)))
(PROG (G3 X C3)
(SETQ C3 (HARRAY 100))
[SETQ G3 (CDR 'CAR (CDR G2]
RPT4 (COND ((NULL G3) (GO L3)))
(SETQ X (CAR G3))
(PUTHASH X T C3)
(SETQ G3 (CDR G3))
(GO RPT4)
L3 (RETURN C3))
C2)
(SETQ G2 (CDR G2))
(GO RPT3)
L2 (RETURN C2)))
RPT2 (PROG (KEY COM)
(SETQ COM (PROGN (PRIN1 'COMMAND?)(TERPRI)(READ)))
(COND ((EQ COM (QUCTE XYZZY)) (GO L4)))
(SETQ KEY COM)
(PROG (G4 Y)
(SETQ G4 DDB)
RPT4 (COND ((NULL (CDR G4)) (GO L5)))
(SETQ Y (CAR (CDR G4))
(COND ((GETHASH KEY (GETHASH Y DB1))
(PRINT Y)))
(SETQ G4 (CDR G4))
(GO RPT4)
L5 (RETURN)))
(GO RPT2)
L4 (RETURN])
```

FIG. 5.3. The final LISP program for NEWS.

Resource-management rules (filter sets of coding rules)
* priority-setting rules (allocate resources, set strategies, enforce branch and bound, best-first)
* task-ordering and choice-ordering rules (order sets of coding rules)
* grouping rules (group parts of programs and therefore sets of coding rules)

Plausible-implementation rules (filter coding rules) (can check global context and set global constraints)
* decision rules
* plausibility rules

Fig. 6.1. Search control rules.

This section discusses the types of search-control rules that LIBRA applies and how they fit together to organize an efficient search. Fig. 6.1 summarizes the types of rules, which can be considered as layers of metarules that control the coding rules; this is more apparent if the list is read from the bottom up (although those at the top of the list are usually applied earlier). Fig. 6.2 summarizes the search policy that the current efficiency rules enforce and matches the search steps with the types of rules applied. The analysis-maintenance and cost-estimation rules mentioned in this summary are discussed in Section 8.

1. Compare the cost estimates of all competing program implementations. Prune unlikely prospects; choose the most promising candidate as the focus for further refinement (priority-setting rules, cost-estimation rules).

2. Select a part of the program implementation description for refinement. If no parts remain, go to step 5 (resource-management rules).
   (a) If possible, divide the program into independent blocks, refine separately, and then recombine (grouping rules).
   (b) Postpone consideration of program parts according to constraints set by search strategies (task-ordering rules).
   (c) Postpone program parts that involve difficult choices (task-ordering rules).

3. Eliminate and suggest possible refinements for the program part under consideration (plausible-implementation rules).
   (a) Apply decision rules if indicated by search strategies.
   (b) If more than one refinement rule remains, postpone the decision so that other refinements can be made and more analysis information can be collected (task-ordering rules). Then return to step 2.

4. Apply the chosen coding rule and apply analysis-maintenance rules to update analysis properties. Go back to step 2.

5. Select the most important of the pending choices and allocate resources accordingly (choice-ordering rules, priority-setting rules).

6. Consider the chosen task more carefully now; do not postpone it.
   (a) If the decision is to be made quickly, apply plausibility rules to make the choice or to narrow the options severely. If only one rule remains, go to step 4.
   (b) If resources are sufficient, explore the alternatives in detail. Set up a program description for each coding rule. Set strategies to focus on the parts of the program that are related to the current decision, and divide up the decision-making resources. Within the limits of the resources, explore the effects of applying the chosen rule, starting over from step 2 for each possibility (priority-setting rules).

7. Go to step 1.

Fig. 6.2. Search policy summary.

6.1. Program-status descriptions and the task agenda

The state of the search is recorded in a tree of *program-status descriptions*. Each description includes:
- a *program-implementation description* (describing a partially implemented program),
- a *task agenda* for refinement of the partial program,
- a 'purpose'—why the program-status description was created and a goal (such as refining part of the program and comparing it with an alternate implementation of the same part),
- the resources available to achieve the overall goal,
- estimates of the target-program cost for the implementation.

A program-implementation description is a network of *program-nodes*. Each node is labelled with a programming construct (such as 'is-subset') and a unique identification number to distinguish instances of constructs. Between five and twenty coding and efficiency properties are typically added to each node by coding and efficiency rules. Coding properties point to structural parts of a construct and record design decisions (for example, that a list will be ordered by 'less-than'). Efficiency properties record time and space costs of program parts, numbers of occurrences of data structures and executions of enumeration constructs, and parts of the program where data structures are created, referenced, and modified (for analysis of information flow). Different types of properties have different inheritance schemes.

The top level goal of the system is to select and refine one of the competing program implementations (leaf nodes of the search tree that haven't been pruned). The tasks on the agenda associated with each description are the subtasks of refining the individual parts of the program-implementation description. These tasks and their associated control information are summarized in Fig. 6.3. Tasks are selected from the agenda by resource-management rules. Selection criteria are discussed in Section 6.2.

Most tasks on an agenda are coding tasks such as 'refine collection N' or 'find an ordering relation for list M'. Coding tasks are satisfied by applying coding rules, which may add subtasks to the agenda. Analysis rules are invoked after coding rules are successfully applied and may also add subtasks, including those of refining competing program status descriptions.

Analysis tasks such as 'find the probability that condition C is true' or 'calculate the frequency of execution of this loop' also appear on the agenda. Most analysis rules are applied immediately, but if a coding construct must be

Coding tasks
  *state
  *constraints
  *subtasks
  *supertasks
  *applicable rules
Program description tasks (search tasks)
  *purpose, strategies
  *focus
  *resources
  *parent and child links to other program descriptions
  *coding and analysis task agenda
Analysis tasks
  *subtasks
  *supertasks

FIG. 6.3. Summary of task types with associated information.

refined before an analysis question can be answered, the analysis task is added to the agenda with the refinement as a subtask.

A task has a number of properties that help determine when and how to satisfy it. One important property is state: 'potential' when a task is first proposed but there is no reason to work on it, 'getrules' when the process of finding applicable rules begins, 'pickrule' when several rules are applicable but none has been chosen, 'applyrule' while the rule application is in progress, and 'succeed' or 'fail' after the process is finished. The task-ordering rules use state to determine the priority of the task.

Other properties that are associated with each task are a list of subtasks (all of which must be accomplished) and a list of supertasks. Tasks are added to the agenda when they arise as subgoals of other tasks and sometimes when new program parts are created. When a subtask is created, the parent task is suspended. When a task succeeds, its supertasks are informed; if they have no other pending subtasks, then they are enabled. When a task fails, the supertasks are also informed. Further action depends on the type of task that failed.

Coding tasks have properties that list the rules under consideration and the rule chosen to accomplish the task. Coding tasks may also have constraints attached that are used to determine which of the applicable rules to choose. For example, certain rules may be forbidden, perhaps because they have already been tried in an alternate program description.

6.2. Resource-management rules

LIBRA's resource-management rules assume that the most expensive part of the synthesis process is making alternative sets of refinements. Grouping rules divide the program into parts to be considered together, task-ordering and

cost-estimation rules identify the decisions that potentially have the greatest impact on the overall program cost, priority-setting rules to allocate resources in proportion to the potential impact, and choice-ordering rules start work on the highest-impact decisions first. The goal in the ordering of non-choicepoint tasks is to provide maximum information about existing decisions and to avoid redundant satisfaction of identical tasks in different contexts. To this end, the task-ordering rules try to force tasks to be satisfied either in a program description before a choicepoint split or in the alternative that is finally chosen.

6.2.1. Grouping rules

Grouping related decisions reduces the size of the search space and enables a better group of decisions to be made at a lower computational cost.

Costwise-independent blocks. LIBRA attempts to factor programs into disjoint parts that are independent in effect on global program cost and can be refined separately. One grouping technique uses syntactic data flow analysis to identify statically independent blocks. An independent block contains all data structures referenced by statements within the block, and all references to any data structures in the block are also in the block (for example, a procedure with arguments passed by value). This definition assumes dynamic storage allocation with garbage-collection costs factored into the cost for the block. Not all programs can be factored; the original specification of NEWS, for example, can not. A more general grouping technique would symbolically analyze program and factor based on cost-expressions, but this has not been implemented.

Information-structure groupings. More commonly, LIBRA groups information structures, which means that decisions about the representation of a data structure and the implementation of all operations that reference it are considered together. Information-structure groupings are not always disjoint; an operation that accesses two data structures is part of two groupings. Whenever there is a decision about a program part, its whole group is considered: the global cost impact of the group is computed to make cost tradeoffs more explicit, plausible-implementation rules applicable to any part of the group are used, and when alternate implementations are refined, the first pass of look ahead is limited to tasks relevant to the operations and data structures in the related group.

6.2.2. Priority-setting rules

Order the search nodes. One rule chooses the next program-description to work on by first applying branch and bound to eliminate nodes with optimistic estimates that are worse than the default estimates of other nodes. The program description with the lowest cost estimate is then selected. Bounds are estimated by first computing achievable and optimistic values for the *program* costs and then adding a constant times the difference between remaining *synthesis* resources and estimated synthesis resources necessary to complete the program; this favors more complete plans when synthesis resources are low.

Assign resources. Another rule assigns the planning resources to make a decision in a program description based on a form of decision theory that uses potential impacts. (The relation of decision theory to heuristic methods is discussed in [23].) The factors in the function used to compute the value of planning are: (1) the total extra resources (the difference between total remaining resources and the estimated resources needed to complete writing the program in the standard fashion), and (2) the ratio of potential gain from this decision (its potential impact) to potential gain for the whole program (the difference between the achievable and optimistic estimates for the whole program).

6.2.3. *Task-ordering rules*

The goal in ordering tasks on the agenda is to avoid redundant computations. The most important rules delay choicepoints, focus on one decision at a time, and expand complex constructs early.

Delay choicepoints. Choicepoints (identified by the task state 'pickrule') are postponed until all other tasks allowed by the ordering rules are considered. Thus, more information can be collected before making a decision and can be collected once in the parent program description rather than many times in the program descriptions created to check alternate coding rules.

Focus on one decision at a time. Because of decision grouping, it costs less to look at one decision group in some detail and then at another than to explore the second decision in the context of different possibilities for the first. One task-ordering rule therefore completely bypasses choicepoint tasks when a program description's purpose is exploratory (quick look-ahead), enabling preliminary comparison of the possibilities before new program descriptions are created to try other sets of choices. A related rule postpones all tasks (even when a choice is not involved) that are *not* related to the decision group of an exploratory program description.

Expand complex constructs early. Other task-ordering rules expand user-defined constructs before other constructs and expand the most abstract constructs first to expose their components to see what decisions need to be made. Refinement of less abstract constructs might prove to be less important than or unnecessary because of the decisions in the refinement of complex constructs. Abstraction is measured by the number of implementations reachable from the construct to be refined (MLEVEL). This measure is a crude approximation of the number of decisions to be made, which is in turn an approximation of the potential impact of the decisions.

Order tasks by state of computation. Tasks are ordered by state so that nearly-complete tasks are finished before new ones are attempted. Tasks that have succeeded and only need cleanup actions (such as releasing subtasks or applying efficiency rules) are handled first. Tasks for which only one rule is applicable are attempted next. Those tasks that are the prime focus of attention for decisions between alternative implementations are given preference over the rest of the tasks with applicable rules. Tasks that have rules needing applicability tests are next in line, followed by tasks that still need the set of relevant rules retrieved. Tasks for which more than one rule is applicable (choicepoints) are postponed until after all tasks in the preceding states have been considered. There is also a very low priority state for tasks that are to be delayed until no choicepoints remain. For example, constructs which can be straightforwardly refined without changes to their cost estimates are left alone to prevent redundant task satisfaction in different contexts.

Order tasks of the same state. Tasks of the same state are currently ordered by the complexity of the construct being refined (MLEVEL). However, it is not clear whether it is worth the expense of maintaining this ordering of tasks. A simpler ordering such as a LIFO stack might work equally well.

Create tasks as needed. When to create a task is also an ordering decision. Subtasks of other tasks are always set up and enabled. Tasks could also be set up when a new instance of a construct is created, since that instance often needs to be refined. Several empirically determined conditions are incorporated in rules that decide when such tasks should *not* be created, the default being to set up the task of refining a new construct instance as soon as the construct is created.

6.2.4. *Choice-ordering rules*

A general ordering principle is to consider the most important decisions, in terms of effect on global program cost, first. In the coding rules, this principle is applied by having design decisions that have far reaching effects be explicit refinement decisions. In the resource-management rules, this principle is applied by deciding when to consider choicepoints. About ten or twenty non-trivial decisions have to be made in a program that is 10 lines of specification (and leads to about 80 lines of code). With the current set of task-ordering rules, about half of these choices show up early in the refinement process and half gradually throughout the remaining refinement.

The rule for ordering choicepoint tasks says that the decision with the highest estimated global potential impact is made first. Selecting high-impact choices ensures that if the first decision cannot be made decisively, the more important or more costly set of refinements does not have to be made twice. Consider the case where decision A is between $a1$ and $a2$ and decision B is between $b1$ and $b2$. Then if decision A is considered before B, the four programs $a1b1$, $a1b2$, $a2b1$, and $a2b2$ are produced at a cost of $c(a1) + c(a2) + 2*(c(b1) + c(b2))$. If B is considered first, the same four programs are produced at a cost of $c(b1) + c(b2) + 2*(c(a1) + c(a2))$. If the costs of considering decision A are greater than the costs of considering B, then A should be considered first, otherwise the costlier decision A will have to be considered in each of the options generated by B.

Other choice-ordering rules could include considering algorithm decisions before data structure decisions under certain circumstances, but such rules have not been implemented.

6.3. Plausible-implementation rules

Plausible-implementation rules are indexed by the coding constructs to be refined or property values to be determined (a few rules apply to all constructs). When trying to refine a particular coding construct C, LIBRA first finds the applicable coding rules, then applies all the plausible-implementation rules relevant to C's decision group. Sets of plausible-implementation rules for a construct may be partially ordered. The input to each plausible-implementation rule is a task and a set of applicable coding rules. The applicability test for the plausible-implementation rule can specify a set of operations on a data structure that must be a subset of the program parts in the decision group and/or a set that must be a superset of all operations in the decision group. Unless noted otherwise, plausible-implementation rules are applicable only when more than one coding rule is being considered. The result of a rule can be to filter the set of applicable coding rules, to set up a constraint expression, and/or to set up a back-up point. Constraints can be set on *combinations* of program parts, which reduces the exponent in the number of implementations considered.

6.3.1. Constraining refinement choices

Three types of constraints can be attached to program constructs.

(1) The construct constraint specifies a Boolean combination of constructs and properties which refinements may be required or forbidden to match.

(2) The similarity constraint specifies that one data representation is to be the same as some other, without specifying what the representation is to be.

(3) Two instances of a data structure can be forced to be identical. This possibility only arises after considering multiple representations for one data structure.

Constraints can also be attached to tasks. For example, a set of explicitly forbidden rules (usually some that have been tried elsewhere and discarded) may also be associated with each task. The constraints currently record the actual rule names.

The construct and task constraints are applied *before* any other plausible-implementation rules. No particular ordering of the constraint-checking rules is required.

Construct constraints. Constraints on combinations of program parts are specified by attaching pointers to the complete constraint expression on all affected construct instances. Each constraint expression consists of pieces pointing to a program part and a desired construct type or property value for refinements of the part. The pieces are joined by logical connectives that are forms of 'and', 'or', and 'not' that evaluate in a three-valued logic to determine whether a constraint has been satisfied, is possibly satisfiable, or cannot be satisfied. The constraints are checked whenever those instances or any of their refinements are refined and whenever properties are added to them. Checking constraints is not difficult since the set of coding constructs to which a construct can be refined (in one or more steps) is on record (determined automatically and updated if the rules are changed). Most of the coding rules result in a known set of constructs, but 'unknown' is also a legal refinement construct within the constraint mechanism. If the construct or property listed in the constraint is a member of the set of possible refinements, then the rule satisfies the constraint. If the result of a rule is 'unknown', then the rule may possibly satisfy. Otherwise, the rule fails to satisfy.

Similarity constraints. LIBRA can constrain two data structures to have the same implementation, without knowing what it will be, if the original constructs and their constraints are consistent. For example, one plausible-implementation rule (about collections referenced only by enumeration constructs) constrains elements of sets that are both arguments to the same subset test to have the same representation. Once data structures A and B are constrained to be similarly refined, 'references to B' or to 'references to A' in the plausible-implementation rules mean references to *both* A and B. When the same refinements are applied to A and B, all the substructures and properties of A and B are similarly refined by applying the same rules to A-related constructs as B-related constructs.

6.3.2. Some examples

This section gives a representative sample of LIBRA's plausible-implementation rules. The complete system has more rules about the constructs mentioned here and also rules about some constructs that are not mentioned.

6.3.2.1. Decision rules

Decision rules are always applied; they can set constraints as described in Section 6.3.1 and return either a subset of the applicable coding rules or a special value indicating that some other efficiency decision should be made before reconsidering the original decision.

6.3.2.1.1. *Rules about collections* (COLL). The following rules about refining collections are applied in the order shown.

The first rule avoids needless representation change.

COLL 1. If the only references to a collection *A* are enumerations over *A*, and if *B* is another representation for *A* that is easily enumerable, then use the same representation for *A* and *B*.

One use of this rule is after a 'subset(*A*, *C*)' test is refined into an enumeration of the elements of *A*, testing each for membership in *C*, where *A* is read in as a linked list, *B*. At first, *A* is allowed to have a different representation from *B* so the subset test can be implemented using bit maps or some other efficient way. But if the subset test is refined into an 'enumerate-and-test', there is no point in considering another representation for *A* since the linked list of *B* is quite satisfactory.

COLL 2. If all references to a collection are its enumerations, pointers to positions in it, or tests of the state of the enumerations, and if the target language is LISP, then refine the collection into a linked list.

The rule above is applied in the NEWS program to refine the representation of the domain of the database mapping. Since the rule is applied only after the preceding rule has failed, it does not cause any unnecessary representation changes.

COLL 3. If a collection is used as the collection argument of a membership test, and if all uses of the collection are as the collection argument of membership tests, enumerations, and element insertions, then refine the collection to a mapping if condition *A* below is met and into a list if condition *B* below is met. No recommendation is made if neither condition is met.

First compute the product *P* of the number of elements in the collection and the difference between the frequency of the membership test and a conversion-time coefficient (depending on any other representations of the collection and the target language).

Condition *A* is that *P* is greater than constant *C1*, and condition *B* is that *P* is less than constant *C2*.

6.3.2.1.2. *Rules about mappings* (MAP). The following rule tells when a mapping should not be inverted.

MAP 4. If a mapping is not used to find inverse images or if the product of the frequency of operations finding inverse images and the size of the domain set is less than the product of the frequency of operations finding images of domain elements and the size of the range set, then do not consider an inverted mapping.

This rule is derived from the approximate lower bound costs of each type of operation in both explicit and inverse mapping representations. Setting and changing images and enumerating the domain are not significantly different in cost for this level of analysis. Note that this rule does not eliminate the explicit-mapping representation, so if it is cheaper, it eventually will be chosen.

When a collection is refined into a mapping, the domain is the elements in the collection and the range is 'true' or 'false'. While refining this mapping into an array can speed up inserting and deleting elements and membership tests in some cases, refining it into a list of pairs would not save any time or space and is therefore discouraged by the following rule.

MAP 5. If an explicit-mapping has already been refined from a collection, then do not refine it into a collection of pairs.

6.3.2.1.3. *Rules membership tests* (MEMB). The following two rules about refining membership tests must be applied in the order given.

MEMB 6. In refining a test of whether an element is stored in a sequential collection, if the linked list has an ordering (in addition to the positional ordering in the list) then refine the test into an ordered enumeration of elements. Postpone the membership decision until the ordering decision is made.

MEMB 7. In refining a test of whether an element is stored in a linked list, if there is no ordering of the elements (except the positional one), and if the language is LISP, then use the LISP function MEMBER.

If the rule above were not present, the coding rules could construct a membership test by enumerating the list items and testing each for equality. Since this is no more efficient than the LISP function, the plausible-implementation rule saves time and space in the synthesis process.

6.3.2.1.4. *A rule about enumerations* (ENUM).

ENUM 8. If there is a choice about what position in a sequential collection to use for inserting elements, set the constraints that either (1) the position is the front and the sequential collection is refined into a list, or (2) the position is the front and the collection is refined into an array that is growing from the front, or (3) the position is the back and the collection is refined into an array that is growing from the back.

6.3.2.1.5. *A rule picking a storage scheme* (STOR). The coding rules for the storage scheme for local variables allow the value of a variable to be 'stored' and sometimes to be 'recomputed'.

STOR 9. If a variable can be recomputed, and if the value is referenced in only one place and never changed or if the value computation is simply the retrieval of the value of some other variable or if total computation cost (taking into account the number of times the value-referencing statement is executed) is less than computing once, storing, and retrieving, then use the recompute scheme.

In this rule, some of the conditions are special cases of others, but they are stated explicitly because they are much cheaper to compute.

6.3.2.1.6. Rules for representation change (REP). Plausible-implementation rules also determine when to consider redundant data structure representations or representation changes between parts of the program. The database of stories in NEWS, for example, can have one representation in the input format, another in the main body of the program, and another in the loop where keyword commands are requested. The current coding rules can not maintain consistency between parallel representations, so plausible-implementation rules forbid parallel representations where modifying a data structure would cause consistency problems. LIBRA applies data-flow analysis rules (a subset of the analysis-maintenance rules) to find the legal places where changes can be inserted. The default is to consider a new representation unless a rule explicitly recommends otherwise; the new representation can be constrained to be the same as the original one at a later stage. The following rules about whether to consider a new representation are applied in the order listed until no choice remains.

REP 10. If the program block to which this instance of the data structure is local contains operations that modify the data structure, then do not use a new representation.

REP 11. If a data structure has had constraints imposed by other plausible-implementation rules, then consider a new representation.

REP 12. If the representation of a complex data structure is changed from A to A', and if some substructure B, of A is not used in operations on representation A', use the identical representation for B' in A' as for B in A.

REP 13. Use a new representation.

6.3.2.1.7. Rules applicable to refining any construct (ANY). LIBRA applies the following rules (and some others) *after* all other decision rules and only when more than one coding rule is still being considered. If a choice remains after the rules in this section are applied, then a branch is created in the search tree to consider the remaining alternatives.

ANY 14. Apply quick decision rules if a search strategy indicates continuing the refinement process indefinitely (rather than just performing a quick look-ahead), and if either there are few construction resources available or if a decision between the most optimistic cost estimate and the achievable cost estimate makes difference of less than 10 percent of the total cost.

ANY 15. If one implementation choice dominates all others in terms of both space and time, then choose that one (since it will dominate for any space-time cost function).

6.3.2.2. Plausibility rules

If LIBRA decides that a quick decision should be made, less reliable heuristics are used. These rules include the standard implementation choices and are applied until only one coding rule remains. Some sample rules for making quick decisions are:

QUICK 16. When refining a sequential collection, if the target language is LISP, use a linked list.

QUICK 17. Use a header cell on linked lists.

QUICK 18. Implement transfer-element sorts as insertion sorts; the enumeration order of the source collection should be the stored order of that collection.

6.3.3. Coping with refinement failures

If coding rules are missing or if some plausible-implementation rules are unreliable, then there may be no coding rules applicable to refining a program part. For example, no coding rule creates a hash function for non-atomic arguments, but an early plausible-implementation rule assumed that a hash table was a good representation for *all* large sets when membership was tested frequently. Plausible-implementation rules that 'know' about missing coding rules have been added, but LIBRA does not automatically add such rules or disable them if a 'missing' coding rule is later added.

The present set of coding rules seldom fails, so it is not critical to performance to be very smart about backing up. Currently, LIBRA returns to the most recent back-up point that involved a choice related to the decision that failed. Related means that the construct is a refinement of a back-up point construct or has a constraint on the back-up point construct or one of its refinements. The plausible-implementation rules that were applied at the back-up point are temporarily disabled for that task while the decision is attempted once again.

Coding constructs are divided into three major classes—data structure (DS), control structure (CS), and operation (OP). Each construct prototype includes slots specific to its class, a standard refinement height (SHEIGHT) indicating the number of refinements to be made to reach the standard implementation in the target language, and a maximum refinement index (MLEVEL) indicating the total number of implementations that are possible from the current construct. LIBRA allocates resources and orders tasks based in part on these values, which approximate the expected work to complete the refinement and the complexity of a construct.

Data structure constructs. A data structure prototype includes a list of the subparts of the construct (and their formats) and the name of a function for computing the size of a data structure (given a particular instance). This is illustrated in the collection prototype:

COLLECTION

```
TYPE:      DS
PARTS:     (element)
SIZEFN:    collection/size
SHEIGHT:   6
MLEVEL:    10
```

Operation constructs. Associated with operation constructs are a list of arguments (and properties of each) and a function that computes the operation's running time. For example, 'is-element' has the prototype:

IS-ELEMENT

```
TYPE        OP
ARGUMENTS   ((element one value) (collection one value))
SHEIGHT:    5
MLEVEL:     10
```

IS-ELEMENT/OPTIME:
optimistic bound is C1
achievable bound is $C2 * length(collection) * (1 - (0.5 * prob\text{-}true(\text{IS-ELEMENT})))$

The ARGUMENTS property shows that the 'is-element' operation takes two arguments, an element to test and a collection against which the element is checked. As indicated by the 'one', both arguments are single nodes in the program network (as opposed to lists) and both are used by 'value'. LIBRA uses this information to mark the data structure instances pointed to by the element and collection arguments as being referenced, but not modified, by the 'is-element' instance.

The function for computing the running time, IS-ELEMENT/OPTIME, has constant factors, C1 and C2, and symbolic expression length(collection), which represents the size of the collection node at the time the operation is executed.

6.4. Rejected search control rules

Since it is easy to add and remove rules, some rules that were tried were discarded as not useful. One of these was to order tasks within a particular state by the number of supertasks the tasks would satisfy. This takes some time to compute, and it was seldom important since all of the tasks eventually needed to be done. Aside from postponing trivial refinements and exposing choices, the ordering of non-choicepoint tasks did not seem critical. Another rule that was rejected for making quick decisions (a plausibility rule) was to use the coding rule that had the shortest path to a target-language construct. This did not lead to especially efficient programs.

6.5. Discussion

I believe that synthesis systems using heuristic search, as opposed to limited-alternative algorithmic decision making, should be further developed, at least as research tools. Plausible-implementation and resource-management rules similar to those described here seem to be crucial to controlling search in such systems, and the process of writing the rules is itself a good way to codify efficiency knowledge. Efficiency rules allow classes of implementations to be tested and can represent self-knowledge in the sense of knowing what a system is and is not good at doing. In the research systems, search techniques such as dynamic programming can be varied by resource-management rules, and eventually methods for 'compiling' a performance version of such systems should be developed. Global constraints were implemented in LIBRA with little overhead and proved to be very useful. The cost of maintaining constraints is very small compared to the cost of performing all the refinements, storing history information, and maintaining other efficiency information such as running times and data structure cross-referencing. The overhead from all of the plausible-implementation and ordering rules is only about twenty percent of the whole system, and seems well worth the price.

7. Prototypes

Prototypes of program construct classes (such as a general control structure that includes loops) and specific prototypes for each construct (such as 'forall') organize the analysis and knowledge-acquisition processes. They describe data substructures, operation arguments the initialization or body of a loop, and other information that allows cost-estimation rules to trace out program structure without many construct-specific analysis rules and is also used to print out the internal state of refinement (for debugging). Prototypes for cost estimation strategies (discussed in Section 8.2) allow a standard cost-computation process to share subroutines between rules for estimating different types of properties and different levels of detail of analysis.

The 'prob-true' expression is the probability that the 'is-element' test is true, which is an efficiency property whose value is filled in by analysis rules.

Control structure constructs. Control structure constructs are characterized by the ability to store local (temporary) data and to control enumerations or conditional statement evaluations. Control structure prototypes may have any subsets of the slots LOCAL-MEMORY, ARGUMENTS, INITIALIZATION, LOOPBODY parts, and EXIT-UNITS. The LOOPBODY slot identifies the actions in the body of the loop to help the analysis rules compute execution frequency and time. An example of a control structure prototype is:

ENUMERATE-ITEMS

TYPE:	CS
ARGUMENTS:	((collection one reference))
LOCAL-MEMORY:	((referent one reference))
INITIALIZATION:	((inital-action one))
LOOPBODY:	((action one) (abandon-test one))
EXIT-UNITS:	((early-exits list) (termination-exit one)).

One procedure computes the running time of any control structure construct (another computes cost expressions) by inspecting the prototype entries for individual constructs.

8. Estimating Execution Costs

To provide execution-cost estimates and global information-flow analysis, LIBRA analyzes program implementations at all stages of development and with varying precisions and costs of analysis. The accuracy of the cost estimates can be improved as more details of the implementation are determined, but costs can be approximated if detailed calculations are too expensive. There are several reasons why performance is estimated by program analysis rather than by interpreting the specification on sample data. If large data structures are expected, it may take a long time to run the program with realistic sample data (and possibly to gather the data). In many cases, analysis is faster since during interpretation the cost of each high-level operation is recomputed whereas in analysis a loop is executed (symbolically) only one time. Analysis may take longer, however, if there are complex expressions that are expensive to simplify. Finally, although there is an interpreter for PSI's program-model language [15], there is none for program descriptions at arbitrary stages of refinement, and writing one could be fairly complex.

Analysis rules determine optimistic and achievable cost estimates to provide data for the branch-and-bound strategy and for the identification of important decisions by potential impacts. The optimistic estimate is based on optimistic costs for individual parts of the program, without considering whether all are simultaneously achievable. The individual optimistic estimates are bounds on the best implementation available from the coding rules; they are not costs for the best known implementation or theoretical, minimum-complexity costs. The achievable costs are estimates of the time for the standard representations. Both bounds are estimates of the expected time, not best-case or worst-case estimates. The symbolic, incremental analysis is similar to methods people use, but such analysis has not been previously applied in automatic programming systems. LIBRA demonstrates that costs estimated by symbolic analysis are sufficiently accurate to guide search. The cost estimates in the current version may be more precise than needed, but the symbolic nature of the estimates is useful and should be emphasized in future systems.

The major steps in cost estimation are acquiring the initial analysis information, updating that information, and preparing execution cost estimates. These steps are summarized below and explained in more detail in [8].

8.1. Acquiring and updating analysis information

The user can report an initial set of data-structure sizes and probabilities and a cost function in the original specification, can ask the system to prompt for information as needed, or can ask the system to use default values. Some of the task-ordering rules encourage LIBRA to ask the necessary questions at the beginning of the sessions so that the user does not have to be present throughout the synthesis process.

From the initial information, LIBRA computes an execution frequency, which is the average (expected value) number of executions, for each statement in the program description. Also, the creation, references and modifications of data structures are recorded with the data structures. As refinement proceeds, *analysis-maintenance rules* update the probabilities, data-structure properties, and execution frequencies of modified or new program parts. (Cost estimates or information flow summaries are computed only when needed.) Rules are associated with both coding constructs and refinement rules.

Probabilities and sizes do not have to be specified numerically in LIBRA. For example, a probability can be a function of the current size of set X or the number of iterations of loop Y. Currently, however, the system cannot handle specifications of inequalities such as 'the probability is between 0.2 and 0.5', and it assumes uniform distributions of all probabilities and independence of probabilities in Boolean combinations. To handle the symbolic analysis, LIBRA has its own simplifier that includes some simple recurrence relation solving. However, comparisons currently are made after numeric substitutions due to limitations in the symbolic manipulation system; ideally the comparison step should be symbolic with only the critical parameters determined numerically.

The analysis-maintenance rules have analyzed programs with set membership and subset tests and with element insertion and deletion in hash tables, property lists, and ordered and unordered sequences and have computed execution frequencies of programs with multiple-exit loops. LIBRA has analyzed insertion and selection sorts in detail as well as made approximate analyses for less completely understood program areas such as prime number generation. With the incremental approach, new analysis knowledge can be added to the system whenever new coding knowledge is added (domain specific analysis information may need to be added when new types of programs are written). Thus, although general program analysis is an unsolvable problem, incremental analysis of synthesized programs seems tractable.

8.1.1. An example: analyzing an insertion sort

To have LIBRA analyze a sorting program, the user need only specify the approximate number of elements to be sorted. Suppose the coding rules have refined a sort specification into a transfer of elements from a *Source* sequence to a *Target* sequence that is ordered by the 'greater-than' relation (an insertion sort). We will look at LIBRA's analysis of the program after two coding rules have refined the transfer operation into the enumeration shown below. The first rule refines the transfer into an enumeration of *Source*, inserting each item *S* into the appropriate 'position in ordered collection'. The second refines the position-locating construct into an enumeration of the positions in the *Target* until reaching the position where the value of *S* is greater than the value of the item at *TT*.

```
enumerate-items S of Source
  :repeating
    insert S into Target at position
      enumerate position TT of Target
        :repeating
          if S > valueat(TT) then assert-exit quit1;
          on exhaustion assert-exit quit1;
        exits
          quit1: return position TT
        end;
  end;
```

An analysis rule associated with the second coding rule states that for a uniform distribution of elements, the probability of being the desired position is the same for all positions, namely $1/(T + 1)$, where T is the size of the target collection of the sort. These probabilities can take several forms, which are converted into others needed.

Most analysis information is associated with individual coding constructs rather than with a particular coding rule. For example, a rule attached to the insert-element prototype says that inserting an element into a collection such as *Target* increases the size of the collection by one. Also, when enumerations are set up, analysis rules augment the internal representation with a loop index variable and set bounds on the number of enumerations in the loops. In this example, the enumeration of the *Target* collection is assigned a loop index tt, a lower bound of 1 iteration, and an upper bound of the size of *Target*. Since sizes and probabilities are expressed symbolically, the fact that the insert-element operation increases the size the *Target* collection can be represented.

Given the analysis information derived above, LIBRA computes the number of executions of loops (analyzing inner loops first since they sometimes determine the number of executions of an outer loop). As noted, the (conditional-form) probability that a loop exit occurs is $1/(T + 1)$ for any iteration that is reached. The probability that iteration tt occurs is then computed to be

$$1 - \sum_{1 \le ss \le tt-1} \frac{1}{T+1} = 1 - \frac{tt-1}{T+1}.$$

The expected number of executions of the inner loop, where ss is the index for the outer loop, is then

$$\sum_{1 \le tt \le ss} \left(1 - \frac{tt-1}{T+1}\right) = ss - \frac{ss*(ss+1)}{2*(T+1)}.$$

Since T, the size of the *Target* collection on entrance to the inner loop enumerating *Target*, is computed to be $(ss-1)$ on the iteration ss of the outer loop, the expression for the expected number of executions of the inner loop simplifies to $\frac{1}{2}(ss + 1)$.

8.2. Computing and updating execution costs

LIBRA's *cost-estimation rules* provide symbolic descriptions of storage use, operation run-time, or overall execution costs for a program or program section. Global information flow is derived as needed from basic usage information that is accumulated incrementally. The cost-estimation process is guided by prototypes of cost-estimation techniques.

Cost estimation is expensive if accurate estimates are critical (for example, to optimize inner loops or real-time programs). LIBRA approximates exact cost expressions, which could be integrals of space-time products over time, in several ways. One way is approximating the integrals by sums. Another difficulty is that as more details are added to a program implementation, cost expressions are more complex (they can incorporate dependencies on changing data structure sizes and so on). LIBRA can ignore the new information and apply a simpler cost-estimation function for a more abstract version of the programming construct, can use special-purpose estimation functions concentrating on a particular cost aspect, or can average storage costs over larger intervals.

Prototypes of cost estimation procedures allow variants to be constructed by combining basic cost parameters. Each analysis property (for example, achievable and optimistic bounds on run time, average or maximum total space use, total execution cost) is computed by several functions that give more details for more effort. One pass of symbolic execution over the program description (which includes the efficiency properties built up incrementally) collects summary information.

The symbolic execution procedure augments an initial command list of properties to compute with additional ones needed to compute the request. For example, the achievable time property must be on the command list to compute an achievable cost bound if the cast function includes time. Each name on the command list refers to a cost-estimation prototype that tells the symbolic execution procedure how to compute that property for programming constructs in general. If necessary, prototypes for individual constructs are consulted to trace through the substructures of each construct.

8.2.1. Cost-estimation prototypes

Cost-estimation prototypes are illustrated by the example of ATIME, the expected achievable implementation time. The capitalized slot names in Fig. 8.1 are common to all cost-estimation prototypes; lower case names are the functions used in ATIME computations.

The SCHEME of a cost-estimation prototype controls time-space tradeoffs in the cost estimation process itself by indicating when to store intermediate results. In this case, the SCHEME is 'store', so the running time value is stored for each operation or control structure. The scheme could also be 'recompute', or 'storecs' (only store control structure values). If refinements are made to a program part, the corresponding values are recomputed no matter what the SCHEME is.

The DOTHISNODE slot holds a function (dotime, in this example) that computes the property for a programming construct. The value of the property for substructures of the construct are determined by recursive calls to DOTHISNODE controlled by a general construct-walking function.

The COMBINE function describes how to combine results. For time, the function is timeadd, which just adds together the running times for a construct's arguments or substructures.

ATIME

SCHEME:	store
DOTHISNODE:	dotime
COMBINE:	timeadd
LOOPSUM:	ntime
EXCEPTION:	otime

FIG. 8.1. A prototype of a cost-estimation strategy.

The LOOPSUM function tells what special actions to take to summarize the body of the loop. The 'ntime' function multiplies the expression for the running time of one execution of the loop body by the number of times the loop is executed. There is a more exact function that sums an expression with variables based on the loop index over all possible iteration values of the loop index.

The EXCEPTION slot, used in computing potential impacts, names a prototype that matches the accuracy of the main cost computation and is to be used on program parts marked as involved in a decision. Here, 'otime', which is the optimistic time property, is used.

8.2.2. Computing individual efficiency properties

One construct-walking function computes the property value of any simple operation construct. For example, the running time of an operation is the sum of the time to retrieve the arguments of the operation and the time returned by the estimation function in the prototype for the operation construct. The time function may have the size of some set or the probability of some condition as parameters. Another construct-walking functions is used for control structures. Here, the running time is the sum of times for all subparts, each of which is the product of running time of a statement (based on the specific prototype for the control-structure in question) and the number of executions of that statement. For example, consider the analysis of a sort when it is refined into:

enumerate-items S of Source
store-element-in-collection Target

A partial prototype for enumerate-items is shown below with bracketed items indicating the statements in the program fragment above that correspond to the slot of the enumerate-items.

ENUMERATE-ITEMS

ARGUMENTS:	((collection . . .))	[SOURCE]
LOCAL-MEMORY:	((referent . . .))	[S]
LOOPBODY:	(action . . .)	[store-element-in-collection].

In this example, the time to compute the value of the arguments is simply the time to access the value of a variable, estimated as a small constant. The time to initialize the one local memory location is also estimated as a small constant. As specified by the LOOPSUM slot function 'ntime', the time for the ACTION store-element in collection is computed by a recursive call, then multiplied by the number of executions of the loop and added to the running time for program parts outside the loop. The running time is estimated by the time function attached to the store prototype as a constant times half the length of the target collection. The number of executions of the enumerate-items was previously determined to be the size of the source set. Thus, the total running time for this program fragment is size($Source$)*(C1*size($Target$)/2) where C1 is a constant and the sizes of the source and target sets are represented symbolically since they may change.

9. Adding New Efficiency Knowledge

When new coding knowledge (constructs and rules) is added to LIBRA, related efficiency knowledge (prototypes and run-time estimates) is also added or modified with the help of some knowledge-acquisition tools. Typically, new coding rules describe how to implement some existing constructs in terms of a new construct or how to implement a new construct in terms of old constructs. The acquisition tools were designed primarily to build up the efficiency system, and would require more human engineering before anyone not familiar with LIBRA and the coding rules could easily use them. They would need improvement if very different sorts of coding rules were added, but could probably be used as is to add coding rules for a new language such as Pascal.

9.1. Incorporating new coding constructs

A routine to modify efficiency knowledge is called when a new construct is defined or when LIBRA encounters a prototype that is missing or is missing information needed for efficiency analysis. The routine prompts for the information required to build up the prototype if it cannot supply it by examining the coding rules that refine the new construct. Examining the rules is often helpful because the rule text always lists all coding properties (substructures, arguments, design decisions, etc.) of the construct being refined. The SHEIGHT and MLEVEL values associated with constructs are automatically updated when new constructs are added or if the standard implementation is changed. Also, when LIBRA is running and notices that a probability value is missing from a program part where it is expected (such as on the condition of a test or exit-unit of a loop), the refinement rule and resulting coding construct are retrieved and presented to the user along with the type of probability information that is missing. The user may then define the missing transformation.

LIBRA first guesses the type of the coding construct (data structure, operation, or control structure), based on regularities in the constructs and rules, and then checks with the user. For example, the 'local-memory' property is unique to control structures, and in all enumerations, the name of the property specifying what to enumerate is 'collection'. This rather brittle technique worked well because the original rules were written by one person with additions and modifications by people who tried to be consistent. However, there should be a rule editor based on prototypes that enforces such conventions.

Once the construct type is known, the corresponding prototype instance is instantiated. If the new construct is a data structure, the properties listed in the rule text are offered to the user as possible substructures. Not all properties describe substructures—one property of sequential collections is an ordering on the collection. The user identifies the valid ones and responds to prompts about their format. Finally, the user is asked to define a function for estimating the space use of the new data structure. Similarly, when the new construct is an operation, the user must verify whether the properties in the rules are arguments, specify whether data structure references are creations or possible modifications, and note if the operation adds or deletes from its arguments. A function for computing the running time on the operation is determined semi-automatically, as discussed in the next section. Adding new control structure prototypes is usually easy since the names of the properties in the rules provide clues. Local memory is called 'local-memory' or 'referent' or 'position', exit units are called xxx-exit, and so on. The user is asked to verify the system's guesses.

9.2. Time estimators for new constructs

The time (and space) estimates of the coding constructs must be kept consistent so that, for example, the optimistic estimate for an abstract construct such as a 'collection' is not greater than the optimistic estimate for less abstract constructs such as 'linked list'. Similarly, achievable cost estimates must be consistent with the default implementations.

The process of writing time estimating functions for coding constructs has been largely automated in the Costassistant subsystem of LIBRA. Using the task agenda, Costassistant delays creating estimators for higher level constructs until the estimators for the constructs into which they can be refined are created or updated. Since the coding constructs form a partial ordering, the process of computing estimators terminates.

When a construct is reached, Costassistant retrieves the time estimators for all constructs into which the new construct can be refined. The achievable estimate for a new construct is the achievable estimate of the construct which is its standard implementation. The optimistic estimate for a new construct is based on the optimistic estimators of the constructs into which a given construct can be refined. If the estimates are all numeric, Costassistant can determine the proper value. For symbolic estimates, however, 'most optimistic' may depend on some of the parameters to the various functions, so the exact definition is currently left to the user. A better symbolic manipulation system would enable Costassistant to compute intersection points and do more of the work itself.

Operation constructs are sometimes refined into other operation constructs, sometimes into control structures, and infrequently into data structure accesses. In the first and last cases, Costassistant uses the time estimating functions of the more concrete constructs to define a time estimate for the operation construct as described above. If an operation refines into a control structure, however, the computation is more difficult. An instance of the operation construct (similar to those used in the program descriptions but with dummy arguments) is created. Then, the refinement rule leading to control structure is applied. This enables new symbolic arguments (for example, to represent list lengths) to appear in the cost expression. Finally the general rule for estimating running time for control structures is applied.

10. Results

In addition to the NEWS and SORT programs described earlier, LIBRA has guided the synthesis of several variants of classification and retrieval programs and has also chosen data structures for a prime number generating algorithm that make the program run in linear rather than quadratic time. The longest synthesis took 20 minutes of CPU time.

The classification program reads a sample set of items (e.g., a list of job requirements), then repeatedly reads a trial set (e.g., the applicant qualifications), tests whether the sample set is a subset of the trial set and prints 'Fit' or 'Didn't fit' accordingly. The input format of the sample is a list of strings and the input format for the trial set is either a list of strings or the special string 'Quit'.

In several cases LIBRA chooses linked-list representations for requirements and for applicant, for example when the specification is 10 requirements, 20 applicant qualifications, 100 loop executions, and a 0.1 probability of an applicant's qualifications matching the requirements. In this case plausible-implementation rules make some initial decisions: to consider different internal representations for requirements and for applicant lists (since both are used in the subset test), to refine requirements into an explicit collection rather than a Boolean mapping, to pick an enumeration state, and to pick a representation conversion scheme. On the other hand, LIBRA uses analytic cost estimation to decide how to represent the applicant qualifications set, which is used in the membership test. Converting the linked-list representation of the applicant set to a mapping costs about the same as enumerating the set several times in the list representation (plus additional storage costs). Also, since the applicant is not likely (0.1) to have all the necessary requirements, the outer enumeration of the requirements will only be executed about 4 times. This combination of assumptions makes the sequential representation (which has no representation conversion costs) more cost-effective than the mapping representation. Similar cost computations dictate that the sequential representation be refined into a linked list rather than an array (to avoid representation conversion costs—both have similar costs for testing membership on unordered sequences). Several plausible-implementation rules complete the refinement to LISP code in a single branch of the search tree. The rules select the LISP function 'member' rather than generating code for a membership test (since an ordered test is not possible), decide when to store and when to recompute several values (using some cost information), and decide to combine several blocks of code.

For other specifications, such as 100 requirements, 3000 applicant qualifications, 100 loop executions, and a 0.8 probability of the applicant meeting the job requirements, LIBRA chooses a hash table implementation for applicant. As in the previous example, a linked list implements the requirements set. But for the applicant set, neither explicit-collection nor mapping representations are ruled out by the plausible-implementation rules. Since the achievable cost estimate is 1800 times that of the optimistic estimate, both alternatives are examined. The explicit-collection is refined into a sequential collection and the mapping alternative is refined until there is a choice between distributed and stored mappings. LIBRA then estimates optimistic and achievable implementation costs for the alternatives. The sequential representation is eliminated by branch and bound, and refinement continues in the mapping representation. After some refinement, the distributed mapping (property list entry) is eliminated because it is more costly than the stored mapping (hash table). The remaining decisions are made by plausible-implementation rules about enumeration states, positions in linked lists, representation conversion, block combining, and store vs. recompute.

LIBRA has also implemented classification programs with relations rather than simple items. Because of limitations in the coding rules, this difference imposes some constraints on the target-language programs that can be produced. The plausible-implementation rules include enough self-knowledge in this case so that the branches that would lead to failures are not followed.

Another classification program was specified with integer items rather than string items. This allows the applicant set to be represented as a sorted sequential collection. (If the coding rules allowed alphabetizing, sorting would have been possible in the JOBS example.) With the current implementations of sorting (roughly quadratic time) and ordered searching (linear time, smaller coefficient than unordered search), LIBRA's cost estimates rule out a sorted collection because the presort cost is not made up for by the savings in the membership-test time.

Another variant reverses the arguments to the subset test from 'subset(R, A)' to 'subset(A, R)'. Since R is read in only once, and A is the changing set, converting the representation of R becomes cost-effective for small as well as large sets. Since A is used only for enumeration, it is implemented as a linked list to match the input format.

Finally, LIBRA was tested on choosing data structures for a prime-number generating algorithm. The problem, taken from Exercise 7.1-32 of Knuth's textbook series [9], describes a prime finding algorithm that steps through the odd numbers less than a given integer, finding those that are not in a set C of nonprimes, and multiplying each by the numbers in an auxiliary set S. The resulting numbers are added to the set of nonprimes C. The problem states that the number of set operations performed in the algorithm is $O(N)$, since each odd number $n < N$ is inserted into S at most once and deleted from S at most once. Insertion into C is also $O(N)$. (Multiplication is assumed to. take a constant time.) These set operations are the only major operations in the algorithm, so the running time of the whole algorithm is linear if the set operations can be done in approximately constant time.

In the specification of this algorithm to LIBRA, the set S is split into two sets, $S1$ and $S2$, because the coding rules do not handle enumerations over collections that are modified during the enumeration process. LIBRA cannot analyze this algorithm precisely since it does not know anything about prime numbers, but it makes approximations that are sufficient to choose a linear algorithm in this case. The set $S2$ is used for the insertion, removal, and choosing an arbitrary element. An unordered linked list is chosen to represent $S2$ since choosing an arbitrary element is very easy, and since the frequent destructive operations make array manipulations relatively expensive. The value of $S1$ is assigned to $S2$, and the only operation on $S1$ is the insertion of elements, which is easy with an unordered linked list, so a representation conversion is avoided by using the same representation for $S2$ and $S1$. The operations applied to C are insertion and removal of elements, and membership tests. These operations take approximately constant time with Boolean mappings. Since the domain elements of the mapping are integers with a relatively high density in their range of possible values, an array of Boolean values is chosen as the representation of C.

11. Related Research

Only some of the types of efficiency knowledge described here have been codified for machine automation. The primary research has been in data-structure selection systems. Some verification and theorem proving systems can proved facts about the execution performance of programs, but they do not use this information to guide program synthesis. The use of efficiency knowledge in automatic programming has not been addressed by debugging or analogy approaches.

A logical extension of historical attempts to automate programming is to 'compile' a very high level language. This is perhaps best exemplified by work on SETL [2]. SETL's specification language contains primarily mathematical concepts similar to PSI's sets and mappings. The implementation involves choosing from a small number of parameterized implementations by an algorithmic procedure based on sophisticated analysis of data flow and subset relations between sets. Adding new implementations requires a complete system rewrite in this approach.

A wider variety of implementations is allowed in systems designed by Low [12], and Rovner [19], with choices based on partitioning data structures into equivalence classes and using hill-climbing to select combinations of implementations. Programs are analyzed by monitoring default implemen-

tations. These approaches use only one level of refinement from the high-level construct to code in the target language. Rovner's system allows multiple representations and uses heuristics about cost tradeoffs; the heuristics are built in but clearly identified. Tompa [26] discusses a dynamic programming search for another one-level system.

Support for gradual implementation (as well as for verification) is provided by languages such as CLU [11] and Alphard [29], in which the programmer can define intermediate types or encapsulations. However, only one implementation of a type is allowed in each program. There has also been some work on automatic implementation selection systems with a few intermediate levels of refinement. For example, [20] and [18] attempt to match modelling structures to a user's needs, and PROTOSYSTEM [14] chooses file system organizations and orders the flow of processing operations with a dynamic programming algorithm specially tailored for management information systems.

In the area of program analysis, research includes a program that analyzes the performance of recursive LISP programs with constant branch probabilities [27], and several paper and pencil systems for specifying and verifying performance properties of programs ([10, 17, 22]).

There has been much recent work on transformations as a method for developing programs [4, 5, 1], but most do not automate the choice of transformations. Work by Wegbreit [28], however, included goal-directed transformations that explicitly used theoretical lower bounds to drive search. Another approach to automatic programming involves the use of theorem proving (for example, by Manna and Waldinger in [13]). Axiomatic definitions of program properties, rather than rules, are used to describe implementation techniques. This approach has been reasonably successful with the addition of some programming and domain-specific knowledge to the mathematical axioms.

12. Conclusions

The remainder of the paper clarifies LIBRA's contributions, noting the lessons learned along the way and some limitations and directions for future research.

12.1. Lessons

One definite conclusion from work on this and earlier versions of LIBRA and the coding rules is that the interaction between coding, analysis, and searching knowledge is inherently complex and requires a high bandwidth for communication between the different types of knowledge. A previous version had a lower bandwidth and was not as successful. There, the coding rules called on an efficiency module to decide between special efficiency-oriented descriptions of programs. The cost of constructing the large, specialized efficiency descriptions was high, and the time and space savings of incremental analysis were not possible. Also, search control mechanisms had to be embedded in the coding module rather than the efficiency module, which made it difficult to set up look-ahead or backtracking search strategies. Details of the previous system are given in [2].

The design of a synthesis system must include careful consideration of how to handle multiple data representations, alternate views of data structures, user-defined abstract types, complex argument binding and argument passing for procedure calls, recursion as well as iteration, and data-flow analysis. Although the temptation to start with a manageable subset of programming knowledge is great, ignoring the harder issues has long term costs: simplicity and clarity of design will be sacrificed. Also, given the framework used in LIBRA, the early design of prototypes, analysis and search-control languages, and rule and prototype editors seems advisable.

12.2. Limitations and future directions

One limitation of the current framework is that it says nothing about how to decompose large systems into loosely coupled modules or reorganize a set of modules specified by the user. Similarly, when the specification is changed, the entire synthesis process is repeated rather than computing the scope of the change and making local modifications.

The implementation itself has many problems: the form and content of the plausible-implementation rules could be improved, more use could be made of domain-knowledge, and the symbolic manipulation system is minimal. The programs synthesized by the current system are relatively small, but nevertheless use up most of the INTERLISP core image and have a 5–20 minute CPU time for synthesis, which is frustrating but not unbearable. The system would certainly have to be optimized before synthesizing larger programs.

Plausible-implementation rules. Since plausible-implementation rules reflect the capabilities of the coding rules as well as general knowledge of good implementation techniques, they can save synthesis resources but could prevent the choice of good implementations if the coding rules were changed. Recording the assumptions on which such a rule depends and automatically removing the rule and warning LIBRA's maintainer if the assumptions are violated would be a useful extension to the current system. Techniques for analyzing refinement failures to determine missing coding rules and to predict hidden interactions (say between different constraints) are needed. Perhaps a concept formation program could compare an after-the-fact analysis with the prediction program to clarify the circumstances under which a proposed heuristic is truly applicable.

The current crude split into decision and plausibility rules could be refined by adding a certainty factor or reliability index to each plausible-implemen-

tation rule. These values could be matched against a threshold for each decision to determine when to apply the rules. The threshold for the more important decisions would be higher so that only the most reliable rules would be used.

A program-synthesis language with better integration of prototypes. A language formalizing the conventions about how rules and tasks are written and interfaced to the prototypes is needed. The language should be able to express that a rule is to be applied before/after a construct *C* is refined, or before/after all other efficiency rules that apply to that construct or to generalizations of that construct and should allow rules about using prototypes to check for consistency and completeness in the coding rules. The language should extend the constraint mechanism described in Section 6.3.1 to cover analysis rules (for example, to constrain two probabilities to be identical). Some of these topics are being explored in the CHI system [16], which is based on experiences with PECOS and LIBRA.

Prototypes should record more information, such as the standard implementation for a construct, a list of all operation constructs that can operate on a data structure, and all types that are legal arguments to an operation. Type-checking information could be moved from the coding rules to the prototypes, eliminating redundancy. When new coding rules such as refining a set into a tree are added, checks whether all of the operations on the set can carry over to the tree can be made and new rules added if necessary or if desired. Prototypes should be in a tangled hierarchy describing different classes of coding, analysis, and searching rules, and also tasks and agendas.

Analysis and symbolic manipulation capabilities. The current symbolic analysis capabilities are quite limited; they only handle average-case analysis, not best-case or worst-case, only uniform distributions are considered, cost approximation techniques are not very general, and representation conversion costs are only crudely predicted. Domain-knowledge (such as about prime number generation) and better symbolic manipulation for recurrence relation and simultaneous equation solving are also necessary for a more complete system.

The Costassistant program should find the *symbolic* cross-over points at which different implementations become less time consuming (these could depend on the cost function). With Costassistant, analyses can be made even in the absence of specific programs. A set of operations and relative frequencies can be given to the system, which then conducts an exhaustive search to find and record the best combinations of implementations.

The implementations that LIBRA considers depend on the possibilities allowed by the coding rules and, when resources are limited, on the *ordering* of constructs that those rules impose. An improved Costassistant subsystem could be used by system developers to evaluate the structure defined by the coding rules. For example, one criterion for an intermediate operation construct might be that the lower-level operations that implement it should have similar running times. A Costassistant program with additional symbolic manipulation capabilities could be applied in a bottom up fashion to suggest alternate clusterings of constructs based on similarities in efficiency.

Generalize the search techniques. To what extent can the search-control techniques used in LIBRA be generalized to other domains? Preliminary investigations [24] indicate that the general framework is applicable in the area of algorithm design if more powerful deductive problem solving methods and rules about general programming principles are added. A goal-oriented approach such as means-ends analysis with an ordered set of differences and a history of what has been tried so far could be handled by the task agenda mechanism. The system should be able to predict the synthesis times; for example, it should know that applying a theorem prover rather than coding from a known set of choices is likely to take longer as well as (potentially) produce a better target program.

What about domains other than program synthesis? The notions of analysis, plausibility, and search knowledge seem general enough to help plan chemistry or genetics experiments, for example. Cost functions could involve the time for reactions to occur, the amount of enzymes needed to catalyze a reaction, and so on. LIBRA's resource-management rules and symbolic manipulation rules would be still applicable, but new plausibility and analysis-maintenance rules would be needed since the current ones are specific to the programming domain.

Investigate human models of efficiency knowledge. The framework for efficiency knowledge described in this paper may also prove helpful for teaching people about algorithm design and analysis. One way to test this would be to build a more interactive tool (an algorithm design assistant) that could serve both as an instructor and apprentice for making decisions about algorithms and data structures.

12.3. Contributions

Efficient program synthesis is a problem that draws on program synthesis technology, artificial intelligence, and analysis of algorithms. What does the LIBRA system and the framework on which it is based have to say in return to these areas?

As an exercise in *program synthesis*, the efficiency framework offers a focus on using analysis to automatically guide the production of efficient programs. It allows global optimizations based on an overall view of the uses to which structures are put and allows more than one representation for the same type of construct within a program. The framework introduces codifications of efficiency knowledge into new classes of rules about plausible implementations, analysis, and resource management. The most critical features of the system

are explicit plausible-implementation-rules for global planning and constraint setting, automatic symbolic and incremental cost analysis (which includes the ability to analyze multiple-exit loops), optimistic and achievable cost estimates for identifying critical decisions based on their potential impact, and resource allocation based on potential impact to control the size of the search tree. LIBRA is a working system that demonstrates the feasibility of the approach and is successful in a limited but important domain.

As an example of a particular *expert system* in artificial intelligence, LIBRA indicates that an organized structure that includes some self-knowledge is important. LIBRA successfully combines rules and prototypes to help achieve this goal. It also makes a start on representing search strategies in rules that can be used by the system itself to enforce different strategies under different conditions.

The main contribution in the area of applied *algorithm analysis* is showing the value of keeping algorithm analysis closely tied to algorithm design, with both proceeding in a top-down fashion. By enunciating the principles behind classes of algorithms and their analyses, there is a good potential for building a program efficiency assistant that can suggest appropriate techniques.

While many potential improvements to the system are now painfully obvious and much remains to be discovered, even in the current version LIBRA has successfully guided the application of coding rules in the synthesis of a number of moderate-sized programs.

ACKNOWLEDGMENT

I owe thanks to many people for helpful discussions and suggestions during this research. Notable among them are Dave Barstow, Cordell Green, Brian McCune, Steve Tappel, Nancy Martin, Don Knuth, Richard Waldinger, Terry Winograd, Dick Gabriel, Tom Pressburger, Jorge Phillips and Jan Aikins, Jon Bentley, Jaime Carbonell, and the referees provided helpful comments on drafts of this paper.

REFERENCES

1. Blazer, R., Transformational implementation: an example, *IEEE Trans. Software Engrg.* 7(1) (1981) 3–14.
2. Barstow, D.R. and Kant, E., Observations on the interaction between coding and efficiency knowledge in the PSI synthesis system. Proceedings of the Second International Conference on Software Engineering, Computer Society. Institute of Electrical and Electronics Engineers, Inc., Long Beach, CA (1976) 19–31.
3. Barstow, D.R. *Knowledge-based Program Construction.* (North-Holland, Amsterdam, 1979).
4. Burstall, R. and Darlington, J., A transformation system for developing recursive programs. *J. ACM* 24 (1977).
5. Cheatham, T.E., Townley, J.A. and Holloway, G.H., A system for program refinement. Proceedings of the 4th International Conference on Software Engineering (1979) 53–63.
6. Green, C.C., The design of the PSI program synthesis system. Proceedings Second International Conference on Software Engineering, Computer Society. Institute of Electrical and Electronics Engineers, Inc., Long Beach, CA (1976) 4–18.

7. Green, C.C., Gabriel, R., Kant, E., Kedzierski, B., McCune, B., Phillips, J., Tappel, S. and Westfold, S., Results in knowledge-based program synthesis, Proceedings of the Sixth International Joint Conference on Artifical Intelligence, Tokyo, Japan (1979) 342–344.

8. Kant, E., Efficiency considerations in program synthesis: a knowledge-based approach, Tech. Rept. STAN-CS-79-755, Stanford University, Computer Science Department, 1979 (Ph.D. Thesis).

9. Knuth, D.E., Bit manipulation, Draft of Section 7.1 of The Art of Computer Programming.

10. Kozen, D., Semantics of probabilistic programs, Tech. Rept. T. J. Watson Research Report, Computer Science RC 7581 (32819), IBM, Yorktown Heights, NY, 1979.

11. Liskov, B., Snyder, A., Atkinson, R. and Schaffert, C., Abstraction mechanisms in CLU, Comm. ACM 20(8) (1977) 564–576.

12. Low, J.R., Automatic data structure selection: an example and overview, Comm. ACM 21(5) (1978) 376–387.

13. Manna, Z. and Waldinger, R., Synthesis dreams $\Rightarrow$ programs, IEEE Trans. Software Engrg. 5(4) (1979) 294–328.

14. Morgenstern, M., Automated design and optimization of management information system software, Ph.D. Thesis, Massachusetts Institute of Technology, Laboratory for Computer Science, 1976.

15. Nelson, B., The PSI interpreter, Unpublished masters project, Stanford University, Computer Science Department.

16. Phillips, J.V., Self-described programming environments, Ph.D. Th., Stanford University, Computer Science Department, 1983.

17. Ramshaw, L., Formalizing the analysis of algorithms, Tech. Rept. STAN-CS-79-741, Stanford University, Department of Computer Science, 1979 (Ph.D. Thesis).

18. Rosenschein, S.J. and Katz, S.M., Selection of representations for data structures, Proceedings of the Symposium on Artifical Intelligence and Programming Languages (1977) 147–154; Joint SIGPLAN Notices 12(8) and SIGART Newsletter 64.

19. Rovner, P.D., Automatic representation selection for associative data structures, Tech. Rept. TR10, The University of Rochester, Computer Science Department, 1976.

20. Rowe, L.A., A formalization of modelling structures and the generation of efficient implementation structures, Ph.D. Thesis, Computer Science Department, University of California at Irvine, 1976.

21. Schwartz, J.T., On programming: an interim report on the SETL project, revised, New York University, Computer Science Department, Courant Institute of Mathematical Sciences, 1975.

22. Shaw, M., A formal system for specifying and verifying program performance, Tech. Rept. CMU-CS-79-129, Carnegie-Mellon University, Department of Computer Science, 1979.

23. Sproull, R.F., Strategy construction using a synthesis of heuristic and decision-theoretic methods, Tech. Rept. CSL-77-2, Xerox Palo Alto Research Center, Palo Alto, CA, 1977.

24. Tappel, S., Some algorithm design methods, Proceedings of the First Annual National Conference on Artificial Intelligence (1980) 64–67.

25. Teitelman, W., INTERLISP Reference Manual. Xerox Palo Alto Research Center, Palo Alto, CA, 1978.

26. Tompa, F. and Ramirez, R., An aid for the selection of efficient storage structures, Tech. Rept. CS-80-46, University of Waterloo, Department of Computer Science, 1980.

27. Wegbreit, B., Mechanical program analysis, Comm. ACM 18(9) (1975) 528–537.

28. Wegbreit, B., Goal-directed program transformation, Third Annual Symposium on Principles of Programming Languages, ACM SIGPLAN/SIGART, 1976.

29. Wulf, W.A., London, R.L. and Shaw M., Abstraction and verification in Alphard: an introduction to language and methodology, Carnegie-Mellon University, Department of Computer Science, 1976.

Received August 1980; revised version received May 1981

Reusability Through Program Transformations

THOMAS E. CHEATHAM, JR.

Abstract—We describe a methodology and supporting programming environment that provide for reuse of abstract programs. Abstract programs are written using notations and constructs natural to the problem domain in a language realized by syntactic extension of a base language. Program transformations are employed to refine an abstract program into its concrete counterpart. We discuss the use of the methodology in the setting of *rapid prototyping* and *custom tailoring*.

Index Terms—Programming environments, program transformations, rapid prototyping, reusability, specification languages.

I. INTRODUCTION

THE reuse of programming has a number of obvious payoffs--reduction of costs, increased reliability, increased ease of maintenance and enhancement of software systems, and so on. However, with the exception of a few well-defined "mathematical" functions and programmers' personal libraries there is relatively little programming that is actually reused without considerable reworking. And, correctly or not, many programmers perceive that it is better to start afresh rather than to rework existing programs for some new application.

Some will argue that the fault lies with the structure of most of the existing programming languages in that programs do not end up sufficiently modularized that parts of them are readily susceptible to reuse. Indeed, one of the claims for Ada is that through its package and separate compilation mechanisms one will be able to reuse programming in Ada. There are now ongoing studies to detemine how to provide for libraries of Ada programming.

It is our belief that, even with the relatively advanced modularization facilities provided by Ada, the extensive reuse of *concrete* Ada programs is unlikely. The problem is that programs in any concrete high-level programming languages are the result of mapping from some conceptual or abstract specification of what is to be accomplished into very specific data representations and algorithms which provide an *efficient* means for accomplishing the task at hand. Simple abstractions are eliminated in favor of complex but efficient concrete realizations. In this optimization process constructs that are conceptually independent at a sufficiently abstract level tend to become distributed throughout the resulting concrete program, often making it very difficult to change the program, even in minor ways, to be suitable for use in some new setting.

Manuscript received August 1, 1983; revised May 14, 1984.

The author is with the Center for Research in Computing Technology, Harvard University, Cambridge, MA 02138 and Software Options, Inc., Cambridge, MA 02138.

In this paper we will describe a programming methodology and a supporting programming environment that fosters the reuse of *abstract* programs through refining a single abstract program to a *family* of distinct concrete programs.

Section II discusses our approach to developing abstract programs. In Section III we describe how we derive concrete programs from abstract programs using program transformations. In Section IV we discuss our experience in using our methodology and environment to develop several families of programs. Section V provides an overview of the programming environments that have evolved to support our methodology. We close with a discussion of some of the future directions our work is expected to take.

II. ABSTRACT PROGRAMS

If we are to write abstract programs we clearly need some programming language in which to write them. There have been a number of very high level languages (VHLL's) that have been proposed as possible candidates: SETL [3], GIST [2], and V [1] are three that have been implemented and used and there are several others that have been discussed in the literature. Each provides a number of very high-level constructs (for example sets, tuples, bags, queues, and so on) and operations (for example, generalized iteration, nondeterministic choice (with backtracking) and the like). And, each provides means for execution of programs written in them after some kind of "compilation" activity. Each also provides the means for controlling the choice among a variety of alternate concrete realizations of the high-level constructs.

To this point, we have not been comfortable with accepting a *fixed* programming language in which to write abstract programs. There are two basic reasons for this. First, while a fixed VHLL may offer a wide variety of constructs, it may not provide just the construct that is exactly appropriate for the task at hand—and we believe that the kinds of choices (both explicit and implicit) that are made when we have to "shoe-horn" a problem into a fixed language are a good part of the reusability problem. The second reason is that there are often a number of apparently "low-level" constructs that we may want to realize in nonstandard ways. Examples would include constructs like

$$A[i] \leftarrow E$$
$$x.foo$$

when, for example, in the concrete realization A was represented by a linked list of sparse array elements and x was a binary tree with x.foo denoting the leaf named "foo" to be located, say, by a binary search.

We believe that a critical aspect of abstract programs is that they be machine representable and that there exist tools to syntactically and semantically analyze them. We would, however, reject a restriction that forced us to use purely functional notation to capture the abstract constructs, employing, say,

    AssignSparseElement (A, i, E)
    LocateLeaf (x, "foo")

to denote the sample fragments above. That is, we believe that form is very important—a designer should be able to choose the notation that is most natural to the problem domain. Also, with procedural abstraction alone it is difficult to realize constructs that include bound variables (for example, iterators) or sets of constructs that need to interact at the concrete level even though they are conceptually orthogonal. An example of the kind of interaction that might be difficult to realize would be process control records that were described as queues in the high-level description of an operating system but which, at the concrete level, needed to be threaded through extra components of the records themselves instead of being handled by the general-purpose queue implementation. This would be difficult to achieve with procedures or type encapsulation facilities alone.

The method that we have used to provide a language for writing abstract programs is to use the notations provided in a base language (in our case, the EL1 programming language, a high-level language containing a reasonably rich inventory of built-in notations) plus syntactic extensions to provide new notations for various high level constructs. The programmer can declare the symbols of his choice to act as infix or prefix operators, or both, and he may specify precedence and associativity attributes for them. We also have a category of operator pairs called *matchfix* operations. The declaration *Matchfix* ("{", "}"), for instance, adds a new bracketing construct to the language. Subsequent to this declaration, the expression {x, $y + 2$, $A [j]$} would be a legal utterance and when evaluated would be equivalent to a call on the left brace operation ({}) with the operands shown.

Longer phases, such as the notation supporting the construct

    WhileExists I In 1..$|A| - 1$
        SuchThat A[I] $>$ A[I + 1]
            Do Exchange (A[I], A[I + 1]) End

are added by analogy with existing ones. Notation appropriate for this example could be introduced by the declaration

    EquatePhrases ("WhileExists -- In -- SuchThat
                        -- Do -- End",
            "For   -- From -- To
                        -- Repeat -- End")

This declaration ensures that each terminal symbol of the new phrase will be treated by the parser like the corresponding token from the old phrase. The internal form produced by the parser contains the tokens actually used so that the conversion from internal to external representation (that is, "unparsing" or "pretty printing") can be done correctly.

For the above example, we would argue that if one understands the meaning of the notation, then it is clear that it defines a correct bubble sort algorithm.

For further elaboration of our argument for such syntactic extension facility we refer the interested reader to [5].

We argued above that we should be able to semantically analyze abstract programs in addition to analyzing them syntactically. Although we are working on analysis tools that will do a deep analysis of some program contruct (see [6]) for a preliminary account of that work), the analysis tool that we have in daily use does relatively weak analysis—essentially discovering undefined constructs and propagating (constant) modes. The mechanism we have used to "extend" this analyzer to "understand" new notations that have been invented to describe high-level constructs introduced into abstract programs is a so-called *analogy*. In essence, an analogy provides the interpretation of some new construct in terms of more concrete (ultimately, base language) constructs. This (weak) interpretation is specifically, with respect to the analysis tool, telling it just what it needs to know in order to do its job. Consider the example:

    WhileExists $i In $r SuchThat $p Do ? body End <~>
        For $i From $r Repeat $p; ?body End

is an analogy with a *subject* and *target* separated by the "is analogous to" operator (<~>). The prefix dollar ($) and question (?) operators identify match variables; $i matches an expression and ?body matches a list of statements. The interpretation of this analogy is that any program fragment matching the subject is to be treated, by the analyzer, as an occurrence of the target. In EL1 an iteration variable is entered into the environment for the scope of the body of the iteration and then removed. Thus the analogy indicates that the program fragments matching $p and ?body are evaluated in a context that has the variable matching $i defined as a local variable. Considering the bubble-sort fragment discussed above, this is just what we would wish the analyzer to do. As another example:

    Insert $e Into $q <~> Defined($e, $q)

says that a program fragment which inserts $e into $q is defined if the expressions matching $e and $q are defined.

III. REFINEMENT OF ABSTRACT PROGRAMS TO CONCRETE PROGRAMS

Given that we have developed an abstract program for some application, its refinement to a concrete program that can actually be executed is accomplished using two mechanisms: definition and transformation. The refinement may be done in several stages, successively deriving a "more concrete" representation. By "definition" we mean simply providing a binding (or value) for a procedure, type, data object, or what have you. By "transformation" we mean replacing some high-level construct by a (more) concrete construct that realizes the intended function.

A transformation rule consists of a syntactic pattern part, optionally augmented by a semantic predicate, and a replacement part. The symbol <-> separates the pattern (including any predicate) from the replacement. All three parts may include match variables just as with an analogy. Thus, a general transformation rule has the form

> pattern Where predicate <-> replacement

The most common kind of transformation rule that we use is one that carries no semantic predicate and simply serves to implement some abstract notion. For example, the following rule provides an implementation for notation designating the addition of an element to the end of a queue:

```
Insert $e Into $Q <->
    Begin
        $Q.count <- $Q.count + 1;
        $Q.rear <-
            CreateQueueMember ($e, $Q.rear)
    End
```

Further examples of the kinds of transformations that we have employed are contained in [5].

We have a tranformation tool that is supplied with a collection of (abstract) program entities, a set of transformations, and a sequence of instructions. The instructions direct the tool to apply various of the transformations to sets of program entities (P) and transformations (T) into a new set of program entities (P'):

$$P \times T \to P'$$

The final concrete program may result from several rounds of transformations. The instructions may be as simple as "apply all applicable transformations to all program entities" or may specify a sequence of local transformations of particular entities or sets of entities.

IV. SOME EXPERIENCE WITH REUSING ABSTRACT PROGRAMS

Our reuse of abstract programs is achieved by varying the definitions and transformations that are used to derive a concrete program from its abstract counterpart. There are two different settings in which we have done a number of experiments in varying the transformations in order to derive new implementations; we term them *rapid prototyping* and *custom tailoring*. We now discuss some of our experiences in these two settings.

Rapid Prototyping

We have done a number of experiments in (our version of) rapid prototyping. Given an abstract program for some application, it is often useful to devise definitions and transformations that enable us to (reasonably quickly) derive a concrete program that has little concern for efficiency but does exhibit the functionality (or, perhaps, a subset of the functionality) desired. There are several reasons for doing this. For one, it enables us to assess whether or not the abstract program actually captures what its user *thought* he wanted. To the extent that it does not, we must, of course, modify the abstract program and try again. In one particular example that involved devising a user interface using high resolution graphics and pointing mechanisms, we went through several cycles of respecification.

We believe this only occurred because at each stage we produced an operational interface that we explored to expose awkward or unsatisfactory behavior. It would have been difficult, if not impossible, to discover this without being able to actually use it.

Another reason for developing a prototype rapidly is to enable gathering of data that permits the choice of representations of data and algorithms that prove to be efficient. That is, with sufficiently complex programs it may be difficult or impossible to do sufficient formal analysis of the ultimate behavior of the program to enable making good choices—it is much easier to produce a prototype where behavior can actually be observed and measured.

A third reason that we have had for such prototyping has occurred in developing various tools that were ultimately to be integrated into the programming support environment that we will discuss in Section V. We often found it very useful to first develop a tool that functioned in a simple testbed that was not integrated into the environment. Only when the testbed version operated satisfactorily did we develop the refinements that provided for its integration.

Custom Tailoring

By *custom tailoring* we refer to the development of refinements that permit us to derive from a single abstract program a family of concrete programs, each appropriate for a specific target environment. We have done a number of experiments with custom tailoring; we will discuss two of the larger ones, termed MSG and ECL.

MSG was the first large experiment that we have carried out to test our custom tailoring ideas and methodology. MSG is a component of the National Software Works (NSW) (see [4]) that provides for process-to-process communication between two processes operating in the NSW; the processes may be on the same computer or may be on two distinct computers communicating via the ARPANET.

Fig. 1 depicts an instance of MSG; we will not attempt here to discuss MSG in any detail but simply note that it includes a number of queues, I/O with processes and the network, authentication mechanisms, timeout mechansims, and so on. MSG makes a particularly good candidate for custom tailoring. At a sufficiently abstract level, every MSG must clearly be identical while at the concrete level two MSG's may differ drastically because they depend upon the particular host computer and operating system. For example, in our experiment two of the target hosts were the PDP-10 under the Tenex operating system and the PDP-11 under Unix; with the PDP-10, communication between MSG and host processes was most efficiently accomplished using shared pages while with the PDP-11, "pipes" were employed for the same function.

Our MSG experiment involved four target systems: the two aforementioned DEC targets plus an IBM 370/158 and a simulation testbed. The simulation testbed provides an implementation that permits us to test the functionality of MSG with user processes and the network being simulated.

A single abstract MSG program was refined to derive the four distinct target MSG's. There were three stages in the refinement of abstract MSG to the three actual targets. The first

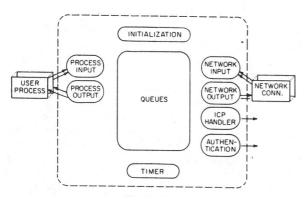

Fig. 1. MSG.

stage of refinement was independent of the eventual target; it provided for the introduction of a number of constructs that were concerned purely with efficiency. As an example, the first refinement provided for a number of threads running through the queue elements to enable efficient access to them. While deemed necessary for efficiency reasons, their inclusion in the most abstract model of MSG would have added nothing conceptually but, rather, detracted from the abstract model because of the complexity they engendered.

The second stage of refinement was concerned with the overall architecture of the target. As an example, the introduction of shared memory as versus some kind of channel for communication between MSG and a user process was introduced at this stage. The third and final stage of refinement takes into account the details of the target including the specific system calls required to realize the various interfaces.

The MSG experiment produced concrete programs for the four target systems. Because of limited funds and the lack of a compiler producing PDP-11/70 or IBM 370 code, the three MSG's for actual targets were never compiled and tested; the simulation MSG was run satisfactorily. In spite of the fact that we did not produce operational programs, a great deal was learned from the MSG experiment. For example, we believe that the experiment demonstrated the feasibility of custom tailoring of a single abstract model to produce widely disparate concrete implementations (see [7] for more details of this). It also showed that developing an abstract model and determining the stages appropriate for refinement were not trivial tasks. Indeed, we went through several iterations before settling on the final abstract program and the stages to use in the refinement.

A second major experiment with custom tailoring is currently in progress. Termed the ECL experiment, it involves (re)developing ECL systems for several target computers. An ECL system includes a parser and interpreter for the EL1 programming language plus a rich run-time system including a compactifying garbage collector, unparser, hash package, debug facilities, I/O primitives, and so on. For present purposes, let us focus on the EL1 interpreter itself, one of the larger components of the ECL system.

The current ECL system runs on a PDP-10 and was implemented several years ago in a reasonably conventional fashion (that is, the basic interpreter was implemented directly in machine language and most of the run-time facilities were implemented by compiling EL1 representations of them; the

compiler itself was bootstrapped by being run interpretively to compile itself.

There are, at present, six target realizations that we wish to derive from an abstract model for an EL1 interpreter. These six are pairs of targets for three different computers: the PDP-10, the Apollo Domain, and the VAX. One member of each pair is a testbed simulation that can be executed interpretively and that provides an implementation in which the basic functionality of the ECL interpreter for the particular target can be validated. The other member of each pair is the stand-alone code that implements the ECL interpreter on that particular target computer. This code is produced by a cross-compiler (running on the PDP-10) that compiles EL1 programs that are constrained from using any part of the ECL run-time system and produces text that can be assembled on each of the targets.

The PDP-10 was included as a target in order to provide a benchmark by comparison with the original ECL implementation. The Apollo and VAX targets will enable us to use ECL on those computers as we phase out the PDP-10. Thus, implicit in the project is the need for efficient final products—we want the resulting interpreters to compare favorably with hand-coded versions.

The refinement of the abstract EL1 interpreter to one of the six targets is accomplished in two stages. One stage is concerned with refining the high-level constructs that describe the behavior of the interpreter into the constrained subset of EL1 that is handled by the cross-compiler. A second stage introduces refinements that are specific to the particular target computer.

At the present time, the pairs of implementations are operational on the PDP-10 and Apollo computers. The PDP-10 implementations were thoroughly tested prior to attempting the Apollo implementation with the result that the time that elapsed between the first successful compilation of the Apollo stand-alone code and the Apollo interpreter being operational was about one week. Testing of the stand-alone versions of the interpreter was carried out by executing the interpreter on some input and, if it failed, presenting the same input to the testbed simulation and letting it proceed to the same failure point. Since it was running interpretively, all the facilities of the interpreter system were available to explore the reasons for the failure. This was particularly important when testing the Apollo version since we had no machine level debug facilities on the Apollo.

There is a seventh target that we are going to explore at some future date, namely a *symbolic interpreter* that deals with tokens and formulas rather than "values."

At the present time, the simulation testbed implementation is operational as are the PDP-10 and Apollo implementations. It is anticipated that the VAX target will be quite straightforward and involve a very few man-months of work since a lot of what needs be done is "replaying" what we have done before.

V. The Programming Support Environment

The methodology we have been advocating demands, we believe, a supporting programming environment if it is to be practicable. That is, a "program," in our view, exists at several levels—abstract, concrete, and, perhaps, several levels in between. In addition, a given abstract program may be the progenitor of a family of custom tailored variants and each of these may involve several cycles of prototyping before the final result is achieved. Thus, for bookkeeping reasons alone, we have found it necessary to use the computer to manage the various components of a program and the interrelationships among them. In fact, the environment that we are presently using and will describe briefly below is the result of several evolutionary steps that started in 1975 with a very simple "file editor" whose function was to help us keep track of program entities and transformations and a "transform tool" that applied the transformations within a "file" to the program entities it contained.

Our present programming environment is called the Program Development System (PDS). It is an integrated programming support environment that has three major components: a software database, a user interface, and a collection of tools that can be called via the user interface to manipulate the software modules stored in the software database. We discuss these components in turn.

The Software Database

The elements of the software database are called *modules* and are containers for a collection of *program entities*. Each module has a name, a partition, a version number, a derivation number, and a derivation history. A module name is an identifier and the partition, if any, is a list of identifiers and/or identifier pairs separated by "is." The name-partition pair is an "extended name" in a multidimensional naming space that aids in creating names in a rapid prototyping and custom tailoring setting. Examples are:

Foo
CodeGen (target is Apollo)
M (debug)
M (production)

Modules are either abstract or derived. Abstract modules are created by people using the so-called module editor whereas derived modules are created by a tool from one or more *parent* modules. The derivation number of an abstract module is zero and that of a derived module is the maximum derivation number of its parents plus one. The version number is, essentially, a time stamp and increases by one each time a module is modified (via the module editor, if it is abstract, and via (re)derivation from its parent by some tool otherwise). The derivation history of an abstract module is null and that of a derived module identifies the tool and parents that were involved in its derivation.

Each program entity within a module has a name and a set of attributes—essentially type-value-version triples. Early on we had only three types of attributes: definitions, transformations, and comments. One of our early evolutionary steps was to generalize the notion of attribute; the present PDS has some 25 distinct attribute types and the set is open-ended. An attribute (type) exists either because there is some tool that can produce it or some tool that can consume it. Attributes now include descriptors, data types, analogies, syntax specification, annotations (the results of analyzing some attribute), and so

on. Each attribute bears a version number. When a new module is created from an old module by the module editor, those attributes added or edited receive new version numbers while those unchanged bear their old version number. Thus, the version number of an abstract module is the maximum of the version numbers of the attributes of its entities. If a derivation tool is called to derive some module, it does this by first locating the previous result and producing a new module whose version number is one greater than that of the previous result and ascribing this new version number to each attribute it must derive anew (because of changes in the parents) and retaining the old version number for each attribute that is unchanged (because the relevant attributes in the parent were unchanged). Thus the derivation tools are actually incremental rederivation tools.

The User Interface

The user interface for the operational PDS essentially offers the user the ability to invoke the various tools, to monitor the progress as some tool does its job, to inspect the current directory of modules and their interrelationships, and to delete modules that are outdated.

The Tool Set

The tool set is open-ended and presently includes the following tools.

• *Module Editor:* Permits the user to peruse the entities and attributes of some module and invoke one of several editors (text, structure, and so on) to create or edit some particular attributes.

• *Transform:* Derives a module by collecting a set of attributes and transforming them.

• *Merge:* Derives a module by merging selected parts of existing modules

• *Analyze:* Derives a module that contains the results of analysis of some given module, citing undefined constructs in various attributes and so on.

• *Package:* Derives a module in which the attributes are ordered so that an item is defined before use (as a prelude to loading for interpretive execution or for compilation).

• *Compile:* Derives a "load" module by compiling one or more subject modules.

• *Fix:* Provides a "quick fix" by editing one or more abstract entities and rederiving just those concrete entities that depend upon them. Use of this tool avoids the usual "patching" to repair bugs quickly.

• *Aggregate:* Derives a module that "aggregates" one or more modules to define a module set. Its major use is to do configuration management.

In addition, there are various utilities to deal with the software database.

We commented earlier that the PDS was in "integrated" support environment. The sense in which it is integrated is that there is a set of *policies* that each tool must adhere to. These include the following.

• *Version Control:* Each tool is responsible for maintaining version control by ensuring that the version number of each attribute of a module derived correctly reflects the changes since the previous derivation.

• *Access Control:* Each tool deals with the modules they use or generate via utilities provided in the software database to ensure proper authorization, maintain correct derivation histories, and the like.

• *Common Representation:* There are a small set of representations provided for modules and attributes contained therein and a collection of utilities to deal with these. While it is not impossible that some new tool would require the introduction of a new representation tailored to its use, the general principle is that tools deal with the representations provided.

VI. CONCLUSIONS AND FUTURE DIRECTIONS

Our experience to date using the methodology we have described to do rapid prototyping and custom tailoring of program families by the reuse of abstract programming has given us considerable confidence in proposing it as a variable alternative to the conventional programming paradigm. We do not, however, propose that at this point we have a "package" that is ready for widespread use. Rather, we believe that we have concluded a feasibility demonstration and that we have mapped out a course of action that will result in a viable methodology and supporting environment in a few years time.

Several of the threads that we are following are worth a brief comment.

• *Documentation:* Our methodology and its supporting systems are poorly documented. We have recently mounted a significant effort to produce the kinds of primers, examples, and the like that will permit the use of them on other than an "apprentice" basis. However, even with excellent documentation of the system there still remains the question of teaching people how to develop an abstract program, how to stage the refinements, and so on. It may take a good deal of trial and error before we can produce a "guide to abstract programming" that will enable "anyone" to use our methodology and system.

• *A Lifecycle Support System:* We are presently in the early stages of developing a successor to the PDS. Termed LISUS (for LIfecycle SUpport System) it will augment the PDS to deal with multiple simultaneous users and, eventually, provide facilities that let us experiment with knowledge-based mechanisms that provide for coordination of ongoing activities and assist in overall project management. In addition, we are replacing the present user interface that uses "dumb" terminals with a new user interface that uses high resolution graphics terminals, multiple windows, pointing devices, menu-driven interaction, and so on.

• *Improved Compilation Facilities:* There is a problem with our methodology in terms of getting production quality products if we use conventional compiling techniques. This arises because the concrete programs we produce tend to have large numbers of small and/or sparsely used procedures. The overhead with conventional compilers that use standard calling sequences that are expensive (if the called procedure is small) is too high. Thus, we are designing a new compiler that will be able to do quite sophisticated interprocedural analysis that will enable the generation of code tailored to particular uses of procedures and thereby significantly reduce (or eliminate) procedure call overhead.

• *A Wide-Spectrum Language:* As we noted earlier, we rejected the idea of a fixed VHLL as the language for writing abstract programs. At the same time we do recognize that the base language we presently use to host high-level constructs and notations would be easier to use if it did provide a collection of very high level facilities—sets, tuples, bags, and so on—that could be used, say, early-on in developing a prototype when efficiency of their implementation was not a foremost concern. Our strategy is to develop a two-level language containing a very high-level (VHLL) component plus a reasonably conventional base-level component. The whole will enjoy formal semantics and will be interpretable; only the base-level component will be compilable, so that at some point it will be necessary to refine the VHL constructs into equivalent base level constructs. Even with the VHL constructs available, we will still permit the user to define new constructs and notations that he feels particularly germane to the problem at hand.

• *Program Analysis:* We continue to seek program analysis tools that can do "deep" analysis of programs to enable various tools to "reason" about various aspects of a program (for example, to find faults, validate the applicability of a transformation, ensure absence of unwanted side-effects, and so on). Given our methodology, a concommitant problem is therefore to "extend" the analysis to new high-level constructs introduced by the programmer. It is our hope that some variant of the analogy mechanism now used to "explain" high-level constructs to the present (simple) analyzer can be developed to "explain" them to a more sophisticated analyzer.

REFERENCES

[1] C. Green *et al.*, "Research on knowledge-based programming and algorithm design—1981," Kestrel Inst., Palo Alto, CA, 1981.
[2] R. M. Balzer *et al.*, "Operational specification as the basis for rapid prototyping," Inform. Sci. Inst., Univ. Southern California, Marina del Rey, 1981.
[3] R. B. K. Dewar *et al.*, "Higher level languages: Introduction to the the use of the set-theoretic programming languages—SETL," Courant Inst. Math. Sci., Dep. Comput. Sci., New York University, New York, NY, 1981.
[4] "MSG Design Specification," in *Third Semi-Annual Technical Report for the National Software Works*, Massachusetts Comput. Assoc., Inc., Wakefield, MA: 1977.
[5] T. E. Cheatham, G. H. Holloway, and J. Townley, "Program refinement by transformation," in *Proc. 5th IEEE Int. Conf. Software Eng.*, San Diego, CA, 1981.
[6] ——, "Symbolic evaluation and the analysis of programs," *IEEE Trans. Software Eng.*, vol. SE-5, pp. 402–417, 1979.
[7] G. H. Holloway W. R. Bush, and G. H. Mealy, "Abstract model of MSG: Fist phase on an experiment in software development," Center Res. Comput. Technol., Harvard Univ., Cambridge, MA, Tech. Rep. 25-78, 1978.

Thomas E. Cheatham, Jr. received the B.S. and M.S. degree in mathematics from Purdue University, Lafayette, IN, in 1951 and 1953, respectively.

Since 1969 he has been Gordon McKay Professor of Computer Science and Director of the Center for Research in Computing Technology at Harvard University, Cambridge, MA. As of 1981 he has been Chairman of the Board of Software Options, Inc., Cambridge, MA. His current research interests include symbolic evaluation of programs, mechanical theorem proving for program verification, and the construction of systems for program development and maintenance.

Professor Cheatham is a Fellow of the American Academy of Arts and Sciences and a member of Sigma Xi and the Association for Computing Machinery.

RESEARCH
CONTRIBUTIONS

Programming
Techniques and
Data Structures

Ellis Horowitz
Editor

Program Developments: Formal Explanations of Implementations

DAVID S. WILE   *USC/Information Sciences Institute*

Author's Present Address:
David S. Wile,
USC/Information Sciences
Institute, 4676 Admiralty
Way, Marina del Rey, CA
90291.

This research was supported
by the National Science
Foundation under Contract
No. MCS-7918792. Views and
conclusions contained in this
report are the author's and
should not be interpreted as
representing the official
opinion or policy of NSF, the
U.S. Government, or any
person or agency connected
with them.

1. INTRODUCTION: TRANSFORMATIONAL IMPLEMENTATION

The programming paradigm considered here involves implementing a very high-level specification through the use of *correctness-preserving transformations*. The implementor—a person—chooses different transformations on the basis of his knowledge of the domain in which the program will ultimately run and appropriateness. The computer actually applies the transformations and displays the results so that he can consider further transformations.

These transformations accomplish two separate tasks [34]: 1) implementation—selecting realizations of abstract constructs in terms of more concrete ones; and 2) optimization—rearranging a set of operations so as to minimize their execution cost. To get around the confusion between implementation of the specification and optimization of the implementation in the programming language, it has become common to simply speak of "optimization of programs" in a "wide-spectrum language" [8]. Such a language encompasses both specifications and programs. To do so, every construct must be operational, i.e., even the highest level constructs are executable (though very inefficiently). Hence, all transformations are potential optimizations. Throughout this report, we will call the person performing the optimization and implementation the "implementor"; his task is "implementation of specifications" or equivalently, "optimization of programs."

Although proponents of this paradigm have been active for several years [5, 7, 10, 32, 39], no production-level system for transformational optimization has been designed [35]. Several problem areas for the paradigm have become evident:

- Constructing a library of transformations that adequately captures most useful optimizations (for any specification/programming language). Standish [39], Barstow [6], and Rich [36] have done pioneering work in this area.

- Indexing such a library so that one can browse through it to find transformations suitable to the purpose at hand. This is an essential component recently considered by Neighbors [34] as a classification issue. A different approach to the problem is to develop *generic* transformations, encapsulating some large chunk of knowledge about several different, but related, transformations.

- Verifying and validating transformations to be correctness-

ABSTRACT: Automated program transformation systems are emerging as the basis for a new programming methodology in which high-level, understandable specifications are transformed into efficient programs. Subsequent modification of the original specification will be dealt with by reimplementation of the specification. For such a system to be practical, these reimplementations must occur relatively quickly and reliably in comparison with the original implementation. We believe that reimplementation requires that a formal document—the program development—be constructed during the development process explaining the resulting implementation to future maintainers of the specification. The overall goal of our work is to develop a language for capturing and explaining these developments and the resulting implementations. This language must be capable of expressing: 1) the implementor's goal structure; 2) all program manipulations necessary for implementation; and 3) optimization and plans of such optimizations. We discuss the documentation requirements of the development process and then describe a prototype system for constructing and maintaining this documentation information. Finally, we indicate many remaining, open issues and the directions to be taken in the pursuit of adequate solutions.

preserving. Work by Gerhart [23] and Broy and Pepper [9] has provided a technology for transformation verification, though its adequacy has yet to be tested on any significant set of transformations.

- Designing a mechanism for dynamically verifying that conditions in the program pertain, enabling the application of transformations. In its worst guise, this is the automatic theorem-proving problem; it may suffice to use flow-analysis techniques developed for traditional compilers [2, 25] along with specialized *predicate pushing mechanisms* developed in program verification efforts [18, 19] and transformation system designs [13].

- Automating large parts of the transformation process. Enormous chains of primitive transformation applications are necessary to optimize even the most trivial specifications. *Simplification* [30] and *conditioning* [22] (getting the program into shape for a desired transformation) are two approaches to this problem. These are tied together by the work of Feather [20], in which the implementor describes how he would like the resulting program to look, along with some key (insightful) transformations the system should use in obtaining it. Naturally, all work on optimizing compilers is relevant here [1, 37, 45].

- Describing what the implementor did in optimizing the program, i.e., describing the design decisions as well as the particular steps he went through in producing the final program. Such information must be available for modifiers to an optimization design to be able to maintain the original specification. Feather [20], Feather and Darlington [16], and Sintzoff [38] have laid the groundwork for this largely unexplored problem.

- Scaling up—problems of *size*. For realistic applications, enormous numbers of transformations, transformation applications, intermediate program states, intermediate predicate states, etc., must be dealt with quickly. This makes size the most crucial problem to be solved.

However, not all problems need to be solved to obtain a useful, albeit incomplete, system. Currently, it is possible to maintain predicates correctly (or approximately correctly) with considerable success. Thus, it does not appear that proofs of programs or transformations are crucial; we can (temporarily) continue to rely on people to perform these tasks informally. Also, it is quite reasonable to expect that the automation problems—simplification and conditioning—will become more tractable and that an acceptable level of automation can be achieved through techniques such as preprocessing sets of transformations, using the ideas of Kibler [30] and Knuth and Bendix [31]; automatic data structure optimization, as begun by Low [33]; and automation of conditioning transformations, as begun by Feather [20] and developed by Fickas [22]. While these capabilities are being developed, a useful transformation system must rely on more intervention by the user. Hence, arriving at a useful, large catalog of transformations, supporting its perusal, and documenting the development process itself seem to be the unsolved problems most critical to realizing a practical transformation system.

We focus on the last of these problems—documenting the development of optimization for the purpose of maintaining specifications and subsequently reimplementing them. What we call a *program development* is a formal document explaining the implementation of a specification for subsequent use by maintainers. The efforts of Feather and Darlington [16, 17, 20] expose the fundamental principle: If the application of transformations is expressed in a way that captures the *structure* or *optimization strategy* being pursued, it may be read later to understand how subsequent specification changes might impinge on the original optimization, and whether or not the original implementation strategy is still valid. (N.B.: Feather and Darlington made the crucial observation that a *formal* structure representing the optimization has the potential to be *replayed* automatically—reapplied to a changed specification.) Sintzoff [38] precisely defines the notion of design decision and develops several commonly used structuring facilities. Cheatham [14] provides a mechanism for replaying the *historical* development of the program on subsequent versions. Swartout [40] has designed a system to generate explanations automatically, given appropriate formal documentation of the primitives from which a program is constructed and the goals which they accomplish. The relationship of these bodies of work to ours will be detailed in the relevant sections which follow.

Our work concerns the nature of the formal object we call *development structure*, which is *applied* to specifications to produce implementations. The characterization of development structures as objects applied to produce other programs allows our development structures to encompass the related notions of developments, strategies, transformations, and editors. Transformations obviously satisfy this characterization. Editors are simply programs (usually interactive) for applying sequences of transformations (not necessarily equivalence- or correctness-preserving). Strategies represent the intent, or plan, behind such sequences, and developments are the combination of all these capabilities into a coherent structure.

Below we list the properties required of a development description language and relate this language to the development process itself and its use in replay. We then describe POPART [44], a prototype system we have built for experimenting with developments, transformations, and other program manipulations.

2. DEVELOPMENT LANGUAGE PROPERTIES

Recall that the principal reason for the development language is to enable future (re)implementors to understand how the original implementation was made. This does not actually necessitate a *formal* development language in and of itself. As we mentioned above, the desire arises from the observation that developments expressed in a formal language could be reapplied to changed specifications (automatically) and, in some cases, would produce an appropriate reimplementation. Hence, it is not the formal properties of the language that determine the desired characteristics for the development, but rather those properties of the language that will allow suitable explanation for reimplementation purposes.

In particular, the primary property of the development language is that it should allow the optimizer (human) to clearly explain (to the human reimplementer) the motivations and design decisions made in the original development of a program. At the very least, this implies a *structuring* of goals and explanations into goals with subordinate goals or ways of achieving them. Hence, some mechanism for *subordination* will be required: traditional mechanisms achieving these include *named subfunctions* and *explicit refinements* ("do *X* by doing *Y* and *Z*").

In addition, goals at the same conceptual level must be related to one another; hence, the need for mechanisms conveying *goal dependencies* as perceived by the implementor. For example, it will certainly be essential to understand that two subgoals are independent. The maintainer should be able to ignore independent subgoals that deal with sections of the specifications unaffected by a change.

The particular goal structures we have foreseen include the following:

- Sequential dependency (composition): Goal *A* must be achieved before Goal *B*.
- Goal independence: Goal *A* may be achieved in parallel with Goal *B*.
- Choice: Goal *A* was chosen from a set of possible goals {*A*, *B*, ...} all of which supported the same overall goal.
- Conditional goals: Goal *A* need only be achieved if Goal *B* could not be achieved.
- Repetitive goals: Achieve a set of goals {A_1, A_2, A_3 ...}.

Other primitive goals structures may become important as we gain more experience with developments and development languages.

More complex goal structures should also be expressible and, most importantly, *definable*, for these correspond to *plans*, or *strategies*, in design activities. Certainly they need to be parameterizable as well. We see a spectrum of plan-like objects spread along the axis of "completeness" or "degree of parameterization." In particular, a low-level, single-purpose transformation is a complete plan that is quite certain to succeed with little intervention from the implementor. Transformations with "free parameters" are a little less transformation-like and a little more strategic—for example, a transformation that introduces an arbitrary predicate to break out a special case. At the "less complete" end of the spectrum, a plan for "divide and conquer" that reads "split off parts, apply function to parts, and then combine results" is a highly parameterized, incomplete plan. It is clear that the implementor must be able to define and invoke the whole spectrum of plan types.

Interestingly enough, Sintzoff has independently arrived at essentially the same goal structuring facilities for recording design decisions. He includes an *inductive* decision type; we substitute several forms of conditionality, including loops and recursive plan invocation, to achieve the same ends. It would be surprising if any great differences were exhibited in such a minimal-semantics, decision-structuring language! The main source of differences lies in the primitives filling the structure and the interpretation of the structure.

Until now the discussion has not required any properties of the development language dependent on the choice of specification/programming language. Appropriately so, for the whole notion of implementation strategy and documentation is primarily language independent, relying only on "programming knowledge" (currently) locked inside the experts' heads. The only real constraint on the development language that relates to the programming language is that all commands necessary to describe program manipulation be expressible in the language. This requires that the development language be grounded in some language for manipulating programs and program properties. If an extremely powerful underlying mechanism were present, this could be as simple as the single command "*achieve* goal." For our experiments, we have chosen a quite basic editing language, but other quite different (primitive) languages could have been chosen and used successfully within our development language.

To summarize, the overall goal is to explain the implementation using a formal development language which is capable of expressing: a) a rich goal structure; b) *all* program manipulations necessary to optimization; and c) plans for optimization, as well as detailed optimizations.

3. THE DEVELOPMENT LANGUAGE
The development language we have designed and imple-

mented (called **Paddle**[1]) primarily emphasizes *structure*. The structural aspects of the language seem almost independent of the programming/specification language whose objects are being transformed. That independence is emphasized below, where the structural facilities are introduced first, followed by the actual primitives that manipulate the specifications.

3.1 Definition and Refinement
The need for definition facilities for transformations, strategies, plans, etc., was mentioned above. Although there may be strict distinctions between these various definable entities, we are not yet sure where to draw the boundaries. Hence, our development language currently supports only a single definition facility: the *command*, consisting of a name, a set of parameters, and a body. Let's define the well known problem-solving paradigm "divide and conquer." We would like to capture the essence of this paradigm in an abstract plan. We begin by defining the following Paddle command:

```
command DivideAndConquer(function, set) =
  begin
    split set into subsets, s₁, s₂, . . .;
    compute a related function, f₁, on the subsets;
    combine values of f₁ on subsets via a new function, f₂;
    note You must insure that function applied to set = f₂
      applied to {f₁(s₁), f₁(s₂), . . .}
  end
```

The **begin/end** pair indicates the *sequential composition* of goals to be satisfied by the implementor, i.e., the goals must be satisfied in the order stated. "Split," "compute," and "combine" are not understood by the development system as predefined commands. Rather, the user must *refine* these "stubs" to deal with the situation at hand when the command is actually invoked. In particular, we could refine the "split" stub into a binary decomposition of the set using the following syntax for *refinement* (a refinement is simply an in-place definition):

```
split set into subsets s₁, s₂, . . .
  by
    binary partitioning into s₁ = {e₁ . . . e_{k/2}} and
                             s₂ = {e_{k/2+1} . . . e_k};
```

The use of the reserved word **by** indicates that what follows the description is what was actually meant by the commentary before it. This will be indented and, thus, appropriately subordinate to the concept it implements. Thus, as with Caine and Gordon's Program Design Language [11], our development language provides a skeletal structure for English description leading ultimately to primitive Paddle commands.

3.2. Goal Structures
The examples above already illustrate two different goal structures: *sequential composition* and *refinement subordination*. Another goal type that arises frequently is an *and* goal: the optimizer wishes to convey independence of subgoals. Paddle allows this using the *each* construct. There are at least two varieties of *and* goal: each must be *achieved* independently or each must be *achievable* independently (but the order chosen may be relevant). The latter interpretation has been adopted in Paddle; the former may have to be introduced later.

---

[1] From POPART's Development Language: a homonym.

Another Paddle goal type is a *choice* goal. For example, the transformation/plan designer may wish to convey more information about the alternative possible methods for doing the split above. This is accomplished using the **choose from** construct:

split set = $\{e_1, e_2, \ldots\}$ into subsets $s_1, s_2, \ldots$;
  by
    choose from
      partitioning into $s_1 = \{e_1\}$ and $s_2 = \{e_2, e_3, \ldots\}$;
      binary partitioning into $s_1 = \{e_1 \ldots e_{k/2}\}$ and
                                $s_2 = \{e_{k/2+1} \ldots e_k\}$;
      basis partition $s_0, s_1, s_2, s_4, \ldots s_2^i$,
      where each e_n is a linear combination of the s_2^j
    end

Presently, such choices are not made automatically; the implementor decides in each situation what the appropriate selection should be.

Conditional structures, are used to make automatic choices. Currently the only conditional structure, **first of**, is like LISP's COND, in which the first goal to succeed is the one chosen.[2] For example, the following indicates successively worse implementations (slower or requiring more space) for sequences:

first of
  ArrayImplementation;
  LinkedListImplementation;
  DoublyLinkedListImplementation;
  HashedImplementation
end

If each of the "implementations" is a transformation, then the first one to be usable in the current situation will be the goal achieved. The failure of each goal is the conditionality for the attempt of the next alternative.

Finally, there is a loop goal structure that enables the body to be executed (achieved) repeatedly *while* (or *until*) another goal is satisfied. An example of such a loop structure is one that implements all sets by repetitively applying the above conditional set implementation transformation to each unimplemented set.

These goal structures provide Paddle with a general programming capability so that arbitrary developments can be constructed. Our goal is to make such developments both convenient and understandable.

3.3. Relationship with the Program Manipulation System

Paddle is a language for structuring goals. How these goals are achieved is an orthogonal issue dependent entirely on how the terminal nodes of the goal structures are defined. As we mentioned earlier, a single primitive command, **achieve**, could be used as the terminal node for all goal statements, which would leave to the transformation system the choices of how to achieve the primitive goals. We could be slightly less ambitious and allow "hints" to the transformation system by introducing Feather's **using** statement:[3] the goal is to be accomplished automatically, but it must **use** a set of named transformations in its achievement [20].

Alternatively, a large set of primitive commands could be used to describe very particular ways of achieving goals; some may appear to be actions rather than goals. Although all of

these options are acceptable, we have chosen the last, in the form of an editing language, as the primitive Paddle node language expressing how to accomplish the goals stated in the development. This choice was thought to be both universal and easily implementable; further, as higher levels of automation are achieved (as is planned), more abstract "primitives" can be added. In the meantime, we will continue to have a functioning, usable system.

Notice that the process is potentially recursive in two ways: conditioning the program may require that further subgoals in the process be met, and applying the strategy itself may require modification of several pieces of the program (as in the divide-and-conquer example above). This recursive structure must eventually be reflected in the development. It can be incorporated wholly beforehand (*a priori*) or afterward (*a posteriori*) as the explanation of that development.

An implementor normally switches back and forth between these two modes during any single session.

3.4 Operational Interpretation

In fact, the set of primitive commands is actually a parameter to Paddle; however, the fact that the goal structure is given an *operational interpretation* is fixed and crucial to the actual kinds of problem solving/design activity that can be expressed. In particular, the overall model of program manipulation used by Paddle is as follows: there is at all times a specification/program affected by Paddle expressions. This specification/program, together with the active goal structure(s), forms the data and control portion of the state of the "abstract Paddle machine." The development structure is applied to an initial state to produce a new state. That application is a relatively straightforward interpretation of the development language as though it itself were a programming language. In particular, it is a depth first, left-to-right tree traversal of the goal structure represented by the development.

The state into which the initial state is transformed depends on whether the development process contains any errors or is incomplete. In such situations, the new state represents "progress so far"; facilities are provided for fixing the Paddle "program" and continuing. When there are no errors, the development is entirely automatic, and the Paddle program indeed represents the entire implementation history of the specification: the final state is the implementation. N.B.: It is the *automatic* application of a development structure to a specification to yield the final implementation which guarantees the fidelity of the implementation explanation.

We emphasize that Paddle is executed as a programming language; we have no facilities to interpret Paddle breadth-first or in some other nonoperational manner. To illustrate the significance of this decision, consider the problem of choosing two different data structures in different parts of the program. An implementor may interactively decide which choices to make "in any order," using whatever strategy he feels is appropriate (breadth-first examination of alternatives, for example). The system, when it is *applying* the development to the program (for example, during a replay), will completely elaborate one of the choices and its dependencies even before introducing the other choice.

This distinction involves the differences between the development *process* and the development *structure*, to be described presently.

4. THE DEVELOPMENT PROCESS

Although the development structure is applied like a program to a specification to yield an implementation, the process of

---

designing the implementation and its explanation is by no means so stylized. In general, the following scenario captures the normal activity of the implementor:

- Focus on a program fragment;
- Find an appropriate implementation strategy;
- Get the program into "condition" to allow application of the strategy;
- Apply the strategy;
- Simplify the resulting program.

4.1 *A Priori* Explanations

An *a priori* explanation corresponds to planning, or using an existing implementation strategy. This is certainly a frequent initial implementation approach, for high-level specifications are usually so intrinsically inefficient that previous experience with similar problems suggests an overall implementation design. For example, while text-processing systems are best specified as multiple pass algorithms, most programmers will implement such systems as single-pass algorithms. Hence, most implementors will choose multiple-pass merging as their topmost strategy.

To produce an *a priori* explanation using our system, the implementor must indicate the focus of attention on the program in the development, as well as the actual implementation plan. He generally creates a piece of development structure to express both the implementation plan and the focus of attention. He then applies the development structure to the specification.

When using an *a priori* explanation, and therefore, applying a development to a specification, the implementor needs feedback as to exactly what is happening to the specification, in case his expectations are not met. Hence, in our system, the application of the development structure is *traced*. This gives the implementor exactly the same feedback as he would have had if he had done the transformations *a posteriori*.

Normally, something goes wrong during *a priori* development. Either the development plan contains undefined steps or a transformation's pattern or enabling conditions fail to match. When this happens the implementor becomes problem-driven rather than strategy-driven: he will produce an *a posteriori* explanation.

4.2 *A Posteriori* Explanations

When the implementor is not sure what transformation to apply next, or what portion of the program to focus on, or when problems arise with a planned development, he will switch his attention to the program itself. He may change the program, using editing commands and transformations. Often, such commands are used to condition the program for the transformation that was being attempted. When this happens, he may want the editing steps to be "bundled up" and inserted into the development structure, or he may want to make a new transformation which generalizes his editing steps and insert a call to it in the development. Support for both of these processes is provided in our system.

We emphasize that ultimately, it is the entirely automatic application of a development to a program to produce the resulting implementation that gives credence—and self-confidence— to the optimizer. Despite excursions into *a posteriori* explanations, the final implementation must appear to subsequent maintainers to have been produced entirely *a priori*.

5. REPLAY OF DEVELOPMENTS

Of course, the reason for having the development structure as a formal object in the first place is so that replaying the

development (in part) on changed specifications is the normal mode of operation. Unfortunately, simply having the explanation for the implementation does not guarantee the ability to replay developments accurately. There are two basic problems: (a) replaying the development and getting errors when it was expected to work; and (b) replaying the development and getting no error when the replay should not work. Naturally, the latter problem is the most insidious, for the implementor will not know that the new development is flawed. These can arise from insufficient identification of assumptions in the original development or implicit assumptions in the system.

5.1 Unexpected Errors

We have no real-world experience with replay, since we have not "maintained" (i.e., changed) any of the example specifications yet. Nevertheless, a fair amount of it occurs even in a normal design: midstream in the design, one often decides to try the whole thing "from scratch," as though the entire development were designed *a priori*, in order to test the accuracy of our development structure. From this experience, it is clear that the problems related to the development failing when we thought it would work are often problems of *focus*. The language we use is inadequate for expressing exactly which portion of the specification or development is being transformed. Generally, the language is simply too low level— it does not identify the pieces being transformed by using labeled program segments or high-level descriptions, e.g., "the loop over characters." High-level editing notions as suggested by [43] must be incorporated to avoid this problem.

5.2 Unreported Errors

We have begun to use conventions to forestall problems of the second type above. First, we often express a "map" or "template" of what we believe the implementation looks like at different, key stages in the development.

Second, we have started identifying key stages in the development structure where a dynamic snapshot of the implementation should be presented to the implementor. In particular, although the tracing facility is extremely useful during the design of the development, it is just like any other tracing facility when the traced object becomes large: it is overwhelming. Hence, looking back to it for information during reimplementation would be time consuming.

We have found it quite useful to identify *major steps* in the development and print out the entire implementation state before and after those steps. Subsequent maintenance versions can be compared with the original major steps to decide on new strategies. Basically, this is one mechanism which allows the maintainer to check that his newly created development is "on track" with the old one when he intends for it to be.

Of course, the major issue of checking that (implicit) assumptions match is most difficult. Recent work on semantic matching by [15] has solved part of the problem; systems can automatically compare two implementations and present semantic explanations of their differences to the user. However, this area remains completely open for solutions.

6. THE UNDERLYING PROGRAM MANIPULATION SYSTEM: POPART

POPART[4] [44] is a system developed in Interlisp [42] to provide the basis for a programming environment for *arbitrary*

---

[4] Producer of Parsers and Related Tools.

programming languages—in fact, for arbitrary languages describable in BNF.[5] The tools provided for objects described in BNF grammars[5] include a parser, an editor, a pretty printer, a lexical analyzer, and a language-independent, pattern-matching and replacement mechanism. In fact, the transformation system itself is one of these language-independent tools! A "pure" parser was produced intially as a reaction of systems that embed semantic processing in the syntactic parsing mechanism [27]—LISP itself seemed to be a preferable medium for expressing the semantics of parsed sentences. In fact, to support the set of tools mentioned, an abstract representation of all the information in the source language must be maintained, i.e., a "pure" parser *must* be used for such systems. The idea to provide tools for manipulating expressions in these languages arose from proposals by Balzer [3, 4] and Yonke's Ph.D. dissertation establishing its feasibility [46]. POPART is certainly related to recent efforts on programming language environments, such as Gandalf [28, 21] and the environments for PL/CS [41] and Pascal [29]. It also defines a language for program manipulation, and is thus related to the recent work of Cameron and Ito on grammar-based metaprogramming systems [12].

A BNF grammar is used to generate an *abstract syntax* for the language; expressions are subsequently parsed by POPART into this abstract syntax. Thereafter, no other representation of the program exists, i.e., no stream of lexemes or characters. All tools work with the abstract syntax, variously converting strings into it and it into strings when communication with the user is necessary: the user always views and enters *source language*—he never sees the abstract syntax representation itself. This is quite different from the Gandalf system, but is consonant with Kahn's Pascal system, Mentor. POPART is embedded in the Interlisp interactive environment: it is a set of "commands" invoked just like any other Interlisp commands (EVALQUOTE). Hence, we should think of POPART not as a system, but as a set of augmentations to the already extensive Interlisp environment, provided to deal uniformly with objects described in BNF grammars.

POPART itself is intended to be a set of tools from which a *system designer* constructs and customizes a system. The default mechanism provided to the designer support an environment in which a single object is always being edited (for each grammar known to POPART). The *user* of the editor has commands for moving about in the abstract representation of the object; he may go in, out, forward, and backward in the structure. He also can change the object, but only in ways that maintain the grammatical integrity of the object.

It is not the intent of this report to describe the POPART system in detail. Those portions relevant to understanding the transformation system (component) will be dealt with as they are encountered.

7. STRUCTURES EXPRESSED IN THE PADDLE LANGUAGE

The single most powerful feature of the POPART/Paddle system is that since Paddle itself is described as a language with a formal syntax, Paddle developments themselves may be manipulated by the user using the POPART primitives! This is the nature of the synergism derived from using generic, tool-based systems rather than pat encapsulations isolating users from the environment system.

The fact that the Paddle language is independent of the programming language means that the development structure

mechanism can be a POPART tool. As was mentioned above, POPART editing *commands* can be written using Paddle's program manipulation facilities. Introducing Paddle comes full circle: we use POPART on Paddle, and then use Paddle in POPART.[6]

The Paddle development language is used to describe four different structures to POPART: Global Commands, Simplifications, Conditioners, and the Development.

7.1. Global Commands

The global commands are simply parameterized macros that can be used in any of these POPART structures and that may be explicitly invoked as editing instructions when editing the program itself. For example, if one wanted an abbreviated way to find a conditional statement, he might define the command:

command FindIf( ) =
    Find !ConditionalStatement

This innocuous definition represents much of the complexity of the Paddle/POPART marriage, so we will belabor it a bit. First, there are conceptually three different languages involved here:

- the language of the development system, Paddle;
- the primitive commands of the development system (chosen to be POPART's editing commands);
- the programming language that represents the program being transformed.

Font Conventions   Different font conventions have been adopted for each of the different languages to help the reader differentiate them, as follows:

Paddle
    Development Language—optimize body, comments, and so forth
    Development Keywords—**each, by, first**. . .
    Global Command Names—MERGELOOPS, FINDCALL. . .

Popart
    Primitive Command Names—*Find, Top, ReplaceAll*. . .

Programming Language
    Programming Language—text, character, vary3. . .
    Programming Language Keywords—***begin, end, procedure***. . .

Notice that the Paddle global command FINDIF above is defined to be the POPART editor *Find* command of a pattern in the programming language: !ConditionalStatement. It is necessary for POPART to support switching between grammars for such expressions to be parsed. The expression !ConditionalStatement indicates that anything syntactically derivable from the grammar nonterminal "Conditional-Statement" should match. ConditionalStatement represents a pattern variable in the pattern language used for the *Find* and *Replace* commands.

What are normally considered to be transformations are also definable as commands. For example, to replace a conditional whose predicate is the constant ***true*** with its ***then*** clause one could write the following:

```
command REPLACEWITHTHEN( ) =
  begin
    first of
      Match  if true
                then !Statement;
      Match  if true
                then !Statement
                else !Statement#
    end;
    Replace !Statement
  end
```

The POPART editing commands *Match* and *Replace* are the primitives of the Paddle development language. Notice that here in a simple transformation we have used the conditional goal satisfaction mechanism of the Paddle language—the **first of** command.[7] Either pattern may match (an **if** statement with or without an **else** clause). The *Match* command differs from the *Find* command in that it is an "anchored search" for the pattern. The statement matched will subsequently be replaced by the **then** part. This replacement will only occur if (some option within) the **first of** command succeeded. Otherwise, the **first of** command will fail.

Finally, plans or strategies as described above may be included among the global commands;

```
command DIVIDEANDCONQUER(function, set) =
  begin
    split set={e_1, e_2, . . . } into subsets s_1, s_2, . . . ;
      by
        choose from
          partitioning into s_1 = {e_1} and s_2 = {e_2, e_3, . . . };
          binary partitioning into s_1 = {e_1 . . . e_{k/2}} and
                                  s_2 = {e_{k/2+1} . . . e_k};
          basis partition s_0, s_1, s_2, s_4, . . . s_2^i,
            where each e_n is a linear combination of the s_2^i
        end
    compute a related function, f_1, on the subsets;
    combine values of f_1 on subsets via a new function, f_2;
    note  You must insure that function applied to set =
          f_2 applied to {f_1(s_1), f_1(s_2), . . . }
  end
```

Notice, in this command, the only predefined command is the *note* command!

7.2 Simplifications

Paddle is also used to describe **simplifications** to the editor. Each time a *Replace* command is called in the editor, the resulting expression is checked for various simplifications. Some of these are described by the grammar designer to POPART, such as automatic removal of extra parentheses when nested constructs replace expressions in which the nesting is unnecessary. In addition, a single Paddle **Simplification** command is always applied to the modified program when a replacement is made. For example, the REPLACE-WITHTHEN command defined above would be a reasonable simplification command to try. If we had an analogous command, REPLACEWITHELSE,

```
command REPLACEWITHELSE( ) =
  begin
    Match  if false
             then !Statement
             else !Statement#;
    Replace !Statement#
  end
```

we might include these in the simplification structure:

```
first of
  REPLACEWITHTHEN;
  REPLACEWITHELSE
  * * *
end. . .
```

7.3 Conditioning

During the transformation process, it is frequently the case that a transformation's pattern will fail to match when the implementor thought it would (or should). He will then have to divert his attention from transforming to "getting the program into condition" to be transformed. Normally, this process of conditioning[8] the program will merely involve the application of a simple, equivalence-preserving transformation to the program.

POPART provides conditioning at the syntactic level within the *Find* and *Match* commands. The system builder builds tables which direct this activity by classifying productions as having associative, commutative, or nested fields. POPART will then automatically rewrite expressions using this information to condition it to match.

Conditioning is also provided for in the Paddle language in a manner analogous to simplification: A conditioning command is applied to the current expression to attempt to change it so that it will match a pattern that has failed to match.[9] For efficiency reasons, this will require preprocessing of the conditioning commands, to see if the pattern being matched could be produced by a *Replace* command in the conditioning command. For example, if the following conditioning commands were given to the system

```
begin
  command INTRODUCETHEN( ) =
    begin
      Match !Statement
      Replace  if true
                  then !Statement
    end;
  command INTRODUCEELSE( ) =
    begin
      Match !Statement;
      Replace  if false
                  then null
                  else !Statement
    end
end
```

and the user attempted

> *Match* **if** !Predicate **then** !ActionInvocation

when the current expression was

> TextRemove[text, character]

---

[7] Lack of an "option" in the pattern language forces the use of the first of command. We contemplate the future use of POPART's BNF to specify patterns, thus eliminating this difficulty.

[8] We previously called this "jittering," but find the connotation distasteful.
[9] This is not yet implemented.

the conditioner would have to notice that the INTRODUCETHEN command produces a conditional statement with the same format as the pattern being matched (the argument to the *Match*). It would then attempt to execute the command. If it succeeded, and the resulting expression matches, it is done.

if true then TextRemove[text, character]

Otherwise, it has a choice: it can either attempt to make the command succeed or try other conditioning commands. We will probably implement this mechanism as a breadth-first search with a very early cutoff (depth 2). This mechanism is significant because Paddle is used to express all program manipulations and because much of the conditionality currently embedded in plans and developments to handle local variability can be factored out and put into the conditioning mechanism. This will greatly simplify and clarify the plans and developments while insuring that this conditioning capability is uniformly applied.

7.4 The Development Process: A Simple Example
Of course, the development structure itself is the major focus of attention here. However, it is instructive to examine actual transcripts of the development process to understand the relationship between it and the resulting development structure. Hence, a set of four (lengthy) appendices to this article is available from the author, illustrating this relationship in considerable detail.

Appendix II is an actual transcript of a development of an implementation for the toy specification designed in Appendix I. The two transcripts together—Appendix I and Appendix II—have been constructed to be "self-explanatory"; many details of the POPART/Paddle system can be gleaned from careful reading of them.

The development process described in the Appendix typifies the nature of interactive program and development manipulation. Two characteristics stand out: (a) The development process is much more verbose and tedious than the final development explanation. (b) The development process is quite error-prone. Both argue strongly that a transcript of the development process is inappropriate documentation of the optimization itself.

7.5 Text Compression: An Extended Example Development
The actual development structure arrived at in the above example was too trivial to actually demonstrate most of the interesting issues involved in structuring explanations for later consumption. Hence, a related but considerably longer example development has been presented in its final form in Appendix III. This describes the partial implementation of the program

begin
   action
      savet[text | list of character, pred | predicate]
      definition *loop*(*any* character) *suchthat* character *in* text
      unless pred(character)
      do removet[text, character];
   relation
      redundant space(character, seq | list *of* character)
      definition successort(seq, *, character) *isa* space
          and character *isa* space;
      loop(*any* linefeed) *suchthat* linefeed *in* text
      do atomic insert linefeed *isa* space;
        delete linefeed *isa* linefeed
      end atomic;

      savet[text, '*a* character ‖ character *isa* alphanumeric **or**
          character *isa* space];
    loop(*any* space) *suchthat* space *in* text **and** redundant ←
        space (space, text)
      do removet[text, space]
end . . .

This example was first worked out (manually, without system aids) in [5]. In that paper, approximately the same development strategy as we are now able to describe formally was suggested as the desirable way of accomplishing the optimization. Our formal representation of that strategy is now[10]

begin
   Pretty;
   MajorStep substitute savet definition for call
      by Unfold savet;
   MajorStep obtain a single loop
      by !POTAndCommands;
   MajorStep optimize loop body
      by !POTSeqCommands;
   MajorStep pick data representations
end . . .

The primitive command *MajorStep* causes the program to be printed out after its refinement has been executed. As was mentioned above, the verbatim trace of the executed primitive commands is not very valuable after-the-fact documentation. It is much more informative for the development structure to dynamically identify key steps which subsequent optimizers should use as "checkpoints" that the maintenance they perform is "on track" with the previous optimization. Thus, Appendix IV is included as an important (though easily regenerated) adjunct to the formal development. It represents the actual application of the development in Appendix III to the initial program. The tracing of the primitive commands has been turned off, yielding a much clearer picture of the development process itself.

8. PROBLEMS AND FUTURE RESEARCH
We believe we are in an excellent position to begin to do experimental research on development styles and the fundamental support necessary to make transformation systems realistic. The POPART and Paddle facilities are all implemented and function as described. Extensions to the system will arise from extensive experiments with large, realistic examples. I expect future experience to duplicate the past: Paddle commands are defined to approximate some facility that seems desirable. Experimentation with it leads to its inclusion as a primitive command or its rejection.

We are aware that these specific areas still need considerable attention.

8.1 A. Separate Goal Structure
Some goals cannot actually be expressed as independent, even though there appear to be two separate tasks being accomplished. For example, in the divide-and-conquer plan above, f_1 and f_2 are neither independent nor sequentially dependent. This defect may require that a separate goal structure be maintained (a noninterpretable structure). This is actually necessary for any reasonable interpretation of codependent goals or even entirely independent goals: the operational-

---

[10] The summarization of this development has been produced automatically using the POPART pretty-printer's level control mechanism. The references to !POTAnd Commands and !POTSeqCommands have been inserted automatically; they are merely "stubs" whose values are printed subsequently in the transcript.

ity of the development structure is too constraining to express these concepts adequately.

8.2 Styles to Support Maintenance

Exactly what mechanisms—like checkpoint snapshots of the optimization in progress—are necessary to facilitate maintenance activities on the specifications? How should the optimizer describe the editor's focus of attention on the program so as to remain general enough so that simple changes do not cause the attention to "drift," and yet be specific enough that replays do not work with just any new specification?

Although we described the development structure as "an explanation" of the development, there are other explanatory styles of more utility. For example, [40] uses a similar structure to produce answers to individual questions (about programs); the same might be used to justify development steps on a more localized basis.

8.3 Generic Transformations

The sequential composition, refinement subordination, and choice constructs provide the basis for creating packages that encapsulate a structured knowledge base of interrelated decisions. Their use results in selection of an implementation for some higher level goal (for example, "divide and conquer"). Packaging development strategies in ways that exhibit intelligent reaction to information provided by the user is an important issue for future research: how to describe or suggest the appropriateness of certain choices and to order dynamically the consideration of decisions.

8.4 Increased Automation

It is clear that automatic facilities are necessary for a useful system. Two major areas need work: predicate maintenance—flow analysis as well as domain dependent "predicate pushing," and automatic conditioning—including choosing appropriate transformations based on hints from the user.

8.5 Developments in Other Domains

We mentioned above that the set of primitive commands underlying Paddle need not be an editing language. We have two applications to quite different domains in which we wish to study the use of Paddle. First, we have already experimented with the use of Paddle in Affirm. Affirm [24] is a program verification/theorem proving system. Its command set has been used as a Paddle primitive node language. In that context, Paddle provides a mechanism for defining and invoking proof strategies. Paddle developments are applied to a state consisting of a set of theorems to be proved and a set of program specifications to be verified. The developments (may) represent entire program validations. A language-dependent version of some of these same Paddle development notions is captured in the proof metalanguage for LCF [26].

Another application in which Paddle may be useful is for specification design. In particular, the design decisions used in arriving at an initial specification should be documented as thoroughly as those used to arrive at an implementation. With a primitive node language devoted to describing the goals achieved when features are introduced into specifications we expect Paddle to provide a suitable framework for such design documentation. This will not be like Caine and Gordon's PDL [11], but will instead document the design process; i.e., the final development structure will not contain the program pieces in the leaves, but rather will tell how the specification changes between design stages.

We must emphasize that the directions taken for the future work will be based principally on the necessities demanded by a large example. If predicate maintenance does not seem to be a significant bottleneck, we will ignore it to the benefit of other areas. We believe we have laid the groundwork for extensive experimentation into the appropriate facilities for realistic transformation systems of the future.

Acknowledgments. Many thanks to Bob Balzer, Steve Fickas, Susan Gerhart, Neil Goldman, and Bill Swartout for their helpful comments on early drafts of this report. I would also like to thank Martin Feather and Phil London for helping to debug the Paddle system (as guinea pigs, of course). Most of the ideas in this report arose from discussions with these individuals, and Don Cohen and Lee Erman. Thanks to Nancy Bryan for her critical corrections to the final draft of this report. And finally, particular thanks to the *CACM* referee who suggested major structural improvements to this report.

REFERENCES

1. Allen, F.E. Bibliography on program optimization. Tech. Rep. RC 5767, IBM Research, Yorktown Heights, New York, 1975.
2. Babich, W.A., and Jazayeri, M. The method of attributes for data flow analysis: Parts I and II. *Acta Inf.* 10, 3 (1978), 245–264, 265–272.
3. Balzer, R.M. EXDAMS—extendable debugging and monitoring system. Spring Joint Computer Conference, IFIP, 1969, pp. 567–580.
4. Balzer, R.M. Language-independent programmer's interface. Tech. Rep. RR-73-15, USC/Information Sciences Institute, Marina del Ray, California, 1973.
5. Balzer, R., Goldman, N., and Wile, D. On the transformational implementation approach to programming. *Proc. 2nd International Conf. Softw. Eng.,* 1976, pp. 337–343.
6. Barstow, D.R., *Knowledge-based Program Construction.* Elsevier, North Holland, 1979.
7. Bauer, F.L. Programming as an evolutionary process. *Proc. 2nd International Conf. Softw. Eng.,* 1976, pp. 223–234.
8. Bauer, F.L., Broy, M., Partsch, H., Pepper, P. et al. Report on a Wide Spectrum Language for Program Specification and Development. Tech. Rep. TUM-18104, Technische Universitaet Muenchen, May 1981.
9. Broy, M., and Pepper, P. Program development as a formal activity. *IEEE Trans. Softw. Eng.* 1 (January 1981), 14–22.
10. Burstall, R.M., and Darlington, J. A transformation system for developing recursive programs. *J. ACM* 24, 1 (1977), 44–67.
11. Caine, S.H., and Gordon, E.K. PDL—a tool for software development. In *Proc. National Computer Conference,* AFIPS, 1975.
12. Cameron, R.D., and Ito, M.R. Grammar-based definition of meta-programming systems. University of British Columbia, Vancouver, January 1982.
13. Cheatham, T.E., Holloway, G.H., and Townley, J.A. Symbolic evaluation and the analysis of programs. *IEEE Trans. Soft. Eng.* 5, 4 (July 1979), 402–417.
14. Cheatham, T.E., Holloway, G.H., and Townley, J.A. Program refinement by transformation. *Proc. 5th Int. Conf. Softw. Eng.,* IEEE, March 1981, pp. 430–437.
15. Chiu, W. *Structure Comparison and Semantic Interpretation of Differences.* Ph.D. Th., University of Southern California, 1981.
16. Darlington, J., and Feather, M. A Transformational Approach to Modification. Tech. Rep. 80/3, Imperial College, London, 1979.
17. Darlington, J. The structured description of algorithm derivations. Algorithmic Languages: Proc IFIP TC-2 International Symposium, 1982.
18. Deutsch, L. P. *An Interactive Program Verifier.* Ph.D. Th., University of California, Berkeley, June 1973.
19. Dijkstra, E.W., *A Discipline of Programming.* Englewood Cliffs, New Jersey: Prentice-Hall, 1976.
20. Feather, M.S. *A System for Developing Programs by Transformation.* Ph.D. Th., University of Edinburgh, Department of Artificial Intelligence, 1979.
21. Feiler, P.H., and Medina-More, R. An Incremental Programming Environment. Carnegie-Mellon University, April 1980.

22. Fickas, S. Automatic goal-directed program transformation. *Proc. 1st Annual Nat. Conf. Artif. Intell.*, The American Association for Artificial Intelligence, 1980, pp. 68–70.

23. Gerhart, S.L. Knowledge about programs: A model and a case study. *Proc. Int. Conf. Reliable Softw.*, IEEE, 1975, pp. 88–95.

24. Gerhart, S.L., et al. An overview of *Affirm*: A specification and verification system. Proceedings IFIP 80, Australia, October, 1980, pp. 343–348.

25. Geschke, C.M. *Global Program Optimizations.* Ph.D. Th., Carnegie-Mellon University, 1972.

26. Gordon, M., Milner, R. et al. A metalanguage for interactive proof in LCF. In *Proc. Conference Symp. Principles of Programming Languages*, 1978, pp. 119–130.

27. Griss, C., Griss, M., and Marti, J. META/LISP. Tech. Rept. Operating Note No. 24, University of Utah, Utah Computational Physics Group, 1976.

28. Habermann, A.N. An overview of the Gandalf project. In *CMU Computer Science Research Review 1978–79*, Carnegie-Mellon University, 1980.

29. Donzeau-Gouge, V., Huet, G., Kahn, G., Lang, B., and Levy, J.J. A structure-oriented program editor: A first step towards computer assisted programming. International Computing Symposium, 1975, 1975, pp. 113–120.

30. Kibler, D.F. *Power, Efficiency, and Correctness of Transformation Systems.* Ph.D. Th., University of California, Irvine, 1978.

31. Knuth, D.E., and Bendix, P.B., Simple word problems in universal algebras. In Leech, J., Ed., *Computational Problems in Abstract Algebra*, New York: Pergamon Press, 1970, pp. 263–297.

32. Loveman, D.B. Program improvement by source to source transformation. *J. ACM 24*, 1 (Jan. 1977), 121–145.

33. Low, J.R. Automatic Coding: Choice of Data Structures. Tech. Rep. 1, University of Rochester, Computer Science Department, 1974.

34. Neighbors, J.M. *Software Construction Using Components.* Ph.D. Th., University of California at Irvine, 1980.

35. Partsch, H., and R. Steinbrueggen. A comprehensive survey on program transformation systems. Tech. Rep. TUM 18108, Technische Universitaet Muenchen, July, 1981.

36. Rich, C. A formal representation for plans in the Programmer's Apprentice. In *Proc. 7th Int. Joint Conf. Artif. Intell.*, August 1981.

37. Schwartz, J.T. On Programming, An Interim Report on the SETL Project. New York University, Courant Institute of Mathematical Sciences, June 1975.

38. Sintzoff, M. Suggestions for composing and specifying program design decisions. In *4th Int. Symp. Progr.*, Paris, April 1980.

39. Standish, T.A., Harriman, D.C., Kibler, D.F., and Neighbors, J.M. Improving and refining programs by program manipulation. ACM National Conference Proceedings, ACM, 1976, pp. 509–516.

40. Swartout, W.R. Explaining and justifying expert consulting programs. *Proc. 7th Int. Joint Conf. Artif. Intell.*, August 1981.

41. Teitelbaum, T., and Reps, R. The Cornell program synthesizer: A syntax-directed programming environment. *Comm. ACM 24*, 9 (September 1981), 563–573.

42. Teitelman, W. *Interlisp Reference Manual.* Xerox Palo Alto Research Center, 1978.

43. Waters, R.C. "The Programmer's apprentice: Knowledge based program editing." *IEEE Trans. Soft Eng 8*, 1 (January 1982), 1–12.

44. Wile, D.S. *POPART: Producer of Parsers and Related Tools, System Builder's Manual.* USC/Information Sciences Institute, TM-82-21, 1982.

45. Wulf, W.A., Johnsson, R.K., Weinstock, C.B., Hobbs, S.O., and Geschke, C.M. *The Design of an Optimizing Compiler.* American Elsevier, New York, 1975.

46. Yonke, M.D. A knowledgeable, language-independent system for program construction and modification. Tech. Rep. RR-75-42, USC/Information Sciences Institute, October 1975.

CR Categories and Subject Descriptors: 4.12 [**Compilers and generators**], 4.20 [**Programming languages**]: general, 4.43 [**Program maintenance**], 5.23 [**Formal languages**]: grammars

Additional Key Words and Phrases: program design, program development, program optimization, program transformation, programming environments, replay, structure editors

Received 6/81; revised 11/81; accepted 11/82

IV / Natural Language Specifications

During the 1970s, there were a number of research projects aimed at developing automatic programming systems that started with natural language input. [Heidorn, Chapter 11] reviews four such projects at MIT, IBM, the Naval Post Graduate School, and the University of Southern California Information Sciences Institute (ISI). Heidorn also provides a general discussion of the problems involved in using natural language input.

Protosystem I (the project at MIT) is discussed in detail in [Ruth, Chapter 12]. Protosystem I was divided into two parts. The upper part was intended to generate a program specification based on natural language dialog with the user. This part of the work turned out to be more difficult than expected and was not carried beyond the point of initial experimentation. The lower part of the system, however, which generated PL/I code to implement the given specification, was much more successful and resulted in a working prototype.

There are a number of parallels between Protosystem I and the PSI system at Stanford. First, both systems were divided into the same two basic subtasks—PECOS [Barstow, Chapter 7] and LIBRA [Kant, Chapter 8] together correspond to the lower part of Protosystem I. Second, both projects ended up showing that the subtask of converting natural language into a specification was much harder than the subtask of converting a specification into code.

A contrast between the lower part of Protosystem I and the PECOS/LIBRA part of PSI is that Protosystem I is implemented along the lines of an ordinary compiler, rather than being based on transformations. Protosystem I is thus an important counterbalance to the papers in Section III. [Schonberg, Schwartz, and Sharir, Chapter 14] and [Rowe and Tonge, Chapter 15] describe other systems, which are not based on transformations.

[Balzer, Goldman, and Wile, Chapter 13] comes out of the automatic programming project at ISI. Specifically, this paper investigates the kinds of informality that exist in natural language program specifications and describes how an automatic system can compensate for these deficiencies by bringing domain knowledge to bear.

Since the end of the 1970s, there has been an (assumedly temporary) reduction in automatic programming research oriented toward directly utilizing natural language input. For the moment, it seems that very high level languages have become the input medium of choice (see Section V).

G. E. Heidorn

Automatic Programming Through Natural Language Dialogue: A Survey

Abstract: This paper describes and compares four research projects whose goal is to develop an automatic programming system that can carry on a natural language dialogue with a user about his requirements and then produce an appropriate program. It also discusses some of the important issues in this research area.

Introduction

Since the early days of computing, effort has been put into automating more and more of the programming process. (Reference [1] describes some of the most recent work.) The ultimate objective in automatic programming is a system that can carry on a natural language dialogue with a user (especially a nonprogrammer) about his requirements and then produce an appropriate program for him. Although the basic idea of "programming in English" has often been expressed in the literature [2–4], only in recent years have any serious attempts been made toward producing such a system.

Three major research efforts of this sort are currently in progress. One is at the Information Sciences Institute (ISI) of the University of Southern California; another is at Project MAC at the Massachusetts Institute of Technology (MIT), and the third is at IBM's Thomas J. Watson Research Center. A fourth effort of interest, although it has been discontinued, was at the Naval Postgraduate School (NPGS) in Monterey, California. Whereas the broadly stated objectives of these projects are the same and their techniques are similar, they do differ markedly in the details.

This paper describes and compares these four projects. The NPGS work is presented first and in the greatest detail because to date it is the only one for which there is a complete running system. Then the ISI and MIT projects are discussed, followed by a description of the work being done at IBM. After a brief comparison of the four projects, some of the important research issues are considered. (See note [5] and references [6–8].)

NPGS

The NPGS work was actually begun at Yale University in 1967 as a doctoral dissertation and then was completed at NPGS during the years 1968-1972 [9–11]. The goal of this project was to develop a system that would generate a GPSS simulation program after carrying on an English dialogue with a user about a simple queuing problem. A general purpose natural language processing system called NLP was developed and was then used to develop the automatic programming system for queuing problems, called NLPQ, by furnishing it with an appropriate grammar and information about queuing.

A sample problem presented to NLPQ and taken from [10] is shown in Tables 1-3. The dialogue has been divided into three parts to illustrate the main steps required to produce a program. All lower case typing was

Figure 1 Portion of a semantic network (NPGS).

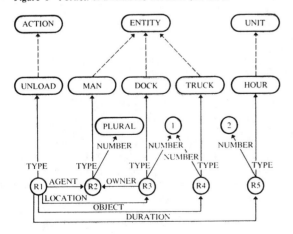

done by the user and all upper case typing by the computer. Table 1 shows the dialogue through which the system acquired a description of the problem. It can be seen that the user can make statements, give commands, answer questions, and ask questions, and that the system can ask and answer questions and respond to commands. Table 2 shows an English description of the complete problem "in the computer's own words," which can be helpful to the user for checking the computer's "understanding." Table 3 shows the GPSS program produced, complete with English comments and meaningful symbolic names. This sample problem used about 3½ minutes of virtual CPU time on an IBM System 360/model 67 and about 350 K bytes of virtual storage. (On an IBM 370/168, it uses only about 33 seconds of virtual CPU time.)

The data structure used by NLP is a form of semantic network. It consists of a collection of objects called records, each of which is just a list of attribute-value pairs. These records represent such things as concepts, words, physical entities, and probability distributions. The attributes of a particular record depend upon what it represents. The value of an attribute is usually a pointer to another record, but it may be simply a number or a name.

The processing to be done by NLP is specified by rules written in a rule language designed especially for this system. "Decoding" rules specify how strings of text are to be converted into records, and "encoding" rules specify how records are to be converted into text. These rules are basically phrase structure grammar rules, but they are augmented with arbitrary conditions and structure building actions.

Prior to a dialogue, NLP is given a set of about 300 "named" records containing information about some words and concepts relevant to simple queuing problems. Also, it is furnished with a set of about 300 English decoding rules and 500 English and GPSS encoding rules. (NLP augmented with these records and rules is in fact NLPQ.) As the dialogue progresses, the system uses the information it obtains from the user to build a subnetwork called the Internal Problem Description (IPD).

Basically an IPD describes the flow of mobile entities, such as vehicles, through a system consisting of stationary entities, such as pumps, by specifying the actions that take place there and their interrelationships. Each action is represented by a record whose attributes furnish such information as the type of action, the entity doing the action (i.e., the agent), the entity that is the object of the action, the location where it happens, its duration, its frequency of occurrence, and what happens next. For example, the action "The men unload the truck at a dock for two hours" could be represented (approximately) by the record:

Table 1   Problem acquisition (NPGS).

1. when a vehicle arrives at a station, it leaves there immediately if the length of the line at a pump in the station is not less than 2.
2. 75 percent of the vehicles are cars and a fourth are trucks.
3. there is just 1 pump.
4. a simulation run time of 8 hours is desired.
5. ask questions for further info.
6. HOW OFTEN DO THE VEHICLES ARRIVE AT THE STATION?
7. the arrivals of vehicles are normally distributed with a mean of 8 minutes.
8. WHAT IS THE STANDARD DEVIATION OF THE NORMAL DISTRIBUTION?
9. 1 minute.
10. OTHERWISE, WHAT DO THE VEHICLES DO?
11. what?
12. AFTER ARRIVING AT THE STATION, IF THE LENGTH OF THE LINE AT THE PUMP IN THE STATION IS NOT LESS THAN 2, THE VEHICLE WILL LEAVE THE STATION. OTHERWISE, WHAT DO THE VEHICLES DO?
13. they are serviced.
14. WHERE ARE THE VEHICLES SERVICED?
15. at the pump.
16. HOW LONG ARE THE VEHICLES SERVICED AT THE PUMP IN THE STATION?
17. vehicle service times are exponential.
18. THE TIME FOR THE VEHICLES TO BE SERVICED AT THE PUMP IN THE STATION IS EXPONENTIALLY DISTRIBUTED. WHAT IS THE MEAN OF THE EXPONENTIAL DISTRIBUTION?
19. 5 minutes for cars and 9 minutes for trucks.
20. AFTER BEING SERVICED AT THE PUMP IN THE STATION, WHAT DO THE VEHICLES DO?
21. leave the station.
22. WHAT IS THE BASIC TIME UNIT TO BE USED IN THE MODEL?
23. 30 seconds.
24. THE PROBLEM STATEMENT IS COMPLETE.
25. how often does a vehicle arrive at the station?
26. THE TIME BETWEEN ARRIVALS OF THE VEHICLES AT THE STATION IS NORMALLY DISTRIBUTED, WITH A MEAN OF 8 MINUTES AND A STANDARD DEVIATION OF 1 MINUTE.
27. the standard deviation of the time between arrivals should be 2 minutes.
28. are vehicles serviced at the pump?
29. YES, THE VEHICLES ARE SERVICED AT THE PUMP IN THE STATION.

R1:	Type	unload
	Agent	men
	Object	truck
	Location	dock
	Duration	2 hours

In the usual graphical notation for semantic networks, a record is depicted as a node with a set of arcs emanating from it. The attribute names appear as labels on the arcs, and the attribute values appear at the arc termini. A portion of such a semantic network for the action just stated is shown in Fig. 1. The nodes in the top two rows

Table 2 Model verification (NPGS).

30. state the complete problem in english.
31.   THE VEHICLES ARRIVE AT THE STATION. THE TIME BETWEEN ARRIVALS OF THE VEHICLES AT THE STATION IS NORMALLY DISTRIBUTED, WITH A MEAN OF 8 MINUTES AND A STANDARD DEVIATION OF 2 MINUTES. 75 PERCENT OF THE VEHICLES ARE CARS, AND THE REST ARE TRUCKS. AFTER ARRIVING AT THE STATION, IF THE LENGTH OF THE LINE AT THE PUMP IN THE STATION IS LESS THAN 2, THE VEHICLE WILL BE SERVICED AT THE PUMP IN THE STATION. OTHERWISE, THE VEHICLE WILL LEAVE THE STATION. THE TIME FOR THE VEHICLES TO BE SERVICED AT THE PUMP IN THE STATION IS EXPONENTIALLY DISTRIBUTED, WITH A MEAN OF 5 MINUTES FOR THE CARS, AND 9 MINUTES FOR THE TRUCKS. AFTER BEING SERVICED AT THE PUMP IN THE STATION, THE VEHICLES LEAVE THE STATION.
    THE SIMULATION IS TO BE RUN FOR 8 HOURS, USING A BASIC TIME UNIT OF 30 SECONDS.

of the figure show some of the named records that must be available prior to a dialogue. The dotted arcs imply that one or more nodes representing concepts intermediate to those shown have been left out (e.g., mobile entity between truck and entity). The nodes in the lower part of the figure (i.e., R1, R2, etc.) are part of the IPD built during a dialogue. The owner arc between nodes R3 and R2 indicates that: "The men own the dock."

The English dialogue for specifying the problem must furnish all of the information needed by the system to enable it to build a complete IPD. The flow of mobile entities through the queuing system must be described by making statements about the actions that take place in the system and how these actions are related to one another. Each mobile entity must "arrive" at or "enter" the system. Then it may go through one or more other actions, such as "service," "load," "unload," and "wait." Then, typically, it "leaves" the system. The order in which these actions take place must be made explicit by the use of subordinate clauses beginning with such conjunctions as "after," "when," and "before," or by using the adverb "then." If the order of the actions depends on the state of the system being simulated, an "if" clause may be used to specify the condition for performing an action. Then a sentence with an "otherwise" in it is used to give an alternative action to be performed when the condition is not met.

The English dialogue must also furnish other information needed to simulate the system, such as the various times involved. It is necessary to specify the time between arrivals, the time required to perform each activity, the length of the simulation run, and the basic time

unit to be used in the GPSS program. Inter-event and activity times may be given as constants or as probability distributions, such as uniform, exponential, normal, or empirical. The quantity of each stationary entity should also be specified, unless 1 is to be assumed.

The user may either state the complete problem immediately, or he may state just some part of it and then let the system ask questions to obtain the rest of the information, as was done in Table 1. The latter method results in a scanning of the partially built IPD for missing or erroneous information and the generation of appropriate questions. Each time the system asks a question, it is trying to obtain the value of some specific attribute that will be needed to generate a GPSS program. A question may be answered by a complete sentence or simply by a phrase to furnish a value for the attribute. The user may ask the system specific questions also to check on specific pieces of information in the IPD. Answers are generated from this information. In order to check the entire IPD as it exists at any time the user may request that an English problem description be produced, as was done in Table 2.

The user of NLPQ is constrained to using words and grammatical constructions known to the system. Part of the vocabulary has words for about 25 actions and entities. In addition to grammatical information about each word, such as its part of speech and how the plural or past participle is formed, semantic information is furnished. This primarily specifies whether an entity is mobile or stationary and whether an action is an event or an activity. The vocabulary also includes about 200 other words, such as attribute names, time units, certain prepositions, pronouns, conjunctions, and forms of to be. This information is entered in the form of named records.

The grammar for the system, embodied in the decoding and encoding rules, has both syntactic and semantic aspects, with the syntactic reflecting general English usage and the semantic being more narrowly oriented toward queuing problem jargon. For instance, verb phrase syntax has been treated fairly thoroughly, including various tenses, passives, negatives, and interrogatives. Most reasonable orderings of phrases in clauses and clauses in sentences are accommodated.

It is important to realize, however, that even though NLPQ can handle a fairly wide range of inputs, there are many more that it does not handle. As a specific example, the following are *some* of the ways in which statement 17 in Table 1 *could* have been made to NLPQ for that problem:

Vehicle service times are exponential.
Service times are exponentially distributed.
The time to service vehicles is exponential.

The time for vehicles to be serviced is exponential.
The time to service vehicles at the pump is exponential.

In the above, "exponential" and "exponentially distributed" are interchangeable. The following are *some* of the ways in which statement 17 *could not* have been made to NLPQ:

Vehicle service times have an exponential distribution.
Service times are distributed exponentially.
Service times may be described by an exponential distribution.
Service times are drawn from an exponential distribution.
The service times of vehicles are exponential.

To extend the system to handle these forms would require furnishing it with additional English decoding rules. Whereas syntactic extensions of this sort would be fairly straightforward, arbitrary semantic extensions generally would be more difficult.

An English problem description such as in Table 2 is essentially a "dump" of the information in the IPD put out by the English encoding rules. The overall flow of the process is for the system to make one or more statements about each action. For an action with no predecessor, a new paragraph is begun with a simple action sentence containing information about the type of action, its agent and/or object, and its location. This may be followed by a statement about the inter-event time or duration. Then, a statement beginning with "after" is produced from the successor attribute. A conditional successor may result in two sentences, with the first one having an if clause in it and the second one beginning with otherwise. After all of the actions have been described, a separate one-sentence paragraph is produced with the values of the run time and the basic time unit.

The GPSS program shown in Table 3 was produced from the IPD using the GPSS encoding rules. Definitions are put into the beginning of the GPSS program for the stationary entities, mobile entities, and distributions. Then for each action a comment consisting of a simple English action sentence is produced, followed by the GPSS statements appropriate to this action. For example, an "arrive" usually produces a GENERATE and an ASSIGN, a "leave" produces a TABULATE and a TERMINATE, and most activities produce a sequence like QUEUE, SEIZE, DEPART, ADVANCE, and RELEASE. These are usually followed by some sort of TRANSFER, depending upon the type of value the action's successor attribute has. Finally a standard "timing loop" is produced to govern the run length of the simulation.

Although this project was "completed," a system ready for production use was not developed. The NLPQ

Table 3   Automatic coding (NPGS).

```
32.    produce the gpss program.
33.           SIMULATE
              RMULT       277, 423, 715, 121, 655, 531, 999, 813
STAT1 EQU                 1, F, Q
PUMP2 EQU                 2, F, Q
CAR2  EQU                 2, T
2     TABLE               M1, 1, 1, 2
TRUC3 EQU                 3, T
3     TABLE               M1, 1, 1, 2
1     FUNCTION            RN1, C24
0.0, 0.0/0.100, 0.104/0.200, 0.222/0.300, 0.355/
0.400, 0.509/0.500, 0.690/0.600, 0.915/0.700, 1.200/
0.750, 1.390/0.800, 1.600/0.840, 1.830/0.880, 2.120/
0.900, 2.300/0.920, 2.520/0.940, 2.810/0.950, 2.990/
0.960, 3.200/0.970, 3.500/0.980, 3.900/0.990, 4.600/
0.995, 5.300/0.998, 6.200/0.999, 7.000/1.000, 8.000/
2     FUNCTION            RN2, C29
0.0, -3.000/0.012, -2.250/0.027, -1.930/0.043, -1.720/
0.062, -1.540/0.084, -1.380/0.104, -1.260/0.131, -1.120/
0.159, -1.000/0.187, -0.890/0.230, -0.740/0.267, -0.620/
0.334, -0.430/0.432, -0.170/0.500, 0.0/0.568, 0.170/
0.666, 0.430/0.732, 0.620/0.770, 0.740/0.813, 0.890/
0.841, 1.000/0.869, 1.120/0.896, 1.260/0.916, 1.380/
0.938, 1.540/0.957, 1.720/0.973, 1.930/0.988, 2.250/
1.000, 3.000/
3     FUNCTION            RN3, D2
0.750, CAR2/1.000, TRUC3/
4     FUNCTION            P1, D2
CAR2, 10/TRUC3, 18/
1     FVARIABLE           16 + 4*FN2
*
*             THE VEHICLES ARRIVE AT THE STATION.
              GENERATE    V1
              ASSIGN      1, FN3
              TEST L      Q$PUMP2, 2, ACT2
              TRANSFER    .ACT3
*
*             THE VEHICLES LEAVE THE STATION.
ACT2          TABULATE    P1
              TERMINATE
*
*             THE VEHICLES ARE SERVICED AT THE PUMP.
ACT3          QUEUE       PUMP2
              SEIZE       PUMP2
              DEPART      PUMP2
              ADVANCE     FN4, FN1
              RELEASE     PUMP2
              TRANSFER    .ACT2
*
*             TIMING LOOP
              GENERATE    960
              TERMINATE   1
              START       1
              END
```

prototype has been demonstrated several times on a variety of problems, but usually with the author as the user. Although the capabilities of the system implemented are limited, the research did establish an overall framework for such a system, and useful techniques were developed. Enough details were worked out to enable the system to perform in an interesting manner, as evidenced by the sample problem in Tables 1-3.

This project was about a five man-year effort and was partially supported by the Information Systems Program of the Office of Naval Research. The primary documentation is a 376-page technical report [9], but introductory papers are available also, e.g., [10, 11].

ISI

The ISI work began in 1972 with a large report [12] describing the form that an automatic programming system could take. Such a system would have four phases: problem acquisition, process transformation, model verification, and automatic coding. The first phase would consist of a natural language dialogue in problem domain terms. In the second phase the system would manipulate the information obtained during the first phase to transform it into a high level process for solving the problem. The third phase would be used to verify that this process was the one desired and that it was adequate for the problem solution. Finally, the fourth phase would optimize the process and produce the actual code to solve the problem. (The titles on Tables 1-3 were chosen to show how NLPQ fits within this framework.)

By early 1974 a prototype implementation of such a system was underway [13]. A key feature of this work is its emphasis on "domain-independence." This means that prior to the dialogue the system has *not* been primed with information about a specific problem area (e.g., queuing simulation or accounts receivable) but must obtain all of this information. The dialogue consists of the user initially stating his problem, from which the system constructs a "loose model." Then the system, through a process called "model completion," attempts to transform this loose model into an operational, interpretable form called the "precise model." The model completion process usually requires further dialogue with the user.

In this system knowledge is represented as stored tuples, which may be considered to be a form of semantic network. The processing is specified in AP/1 (an extension of the list processing language LISP) developed specifically for this project [14]. The language AP/1 supports associative relational data bases, strongly typed variables, compound pattern matches, and failure control.

In late 1974 this group decided to limit their implementation efforts to a very specific task domain, i.e., military message distribution [15], and one year later succeeded in generating their first program [16]. The example that their system handled is shown in Table 4. The program generated consists of about 6 pages of AP/1 code and took about one hour of CPU time on a Digital Equipment Corp. PDP/10 to produce.

So far this group has been concentrating their efforts on the processing required to convert an imprecise functional description of a task into a precise program rather than on the initial acquisition of the task description in natural language. Consequently, at this time, each input sentence must be *manually* translated into a parenthesized format that segments each clause and noun phrase. Table 5 shows this input form for the example in Table 4. Workers on this project intend to eventually replace the use of this form with an "off-the-shelf" natural language interface.

The processing that this system does is driven by trying to produce a viable program. First the system extracts intra-sentence information about the domain and the actions that occur there; it then builds a semantic network to represent this information. Next it does inter-statement processing to organize the actions into an appropriate control structure. This whole process requires 1) the filling in of omitted details and 2) the recognition of what is being referred to by the various phrases and clauses in the problem description. To do this the processor makes heavy use of both static and dynamic program well-formedness criteria.

Although the ISI group has been concentrating on the particular task domain of military message distribution, they are still concerned with domain independence and have made a strong effort to keep information about the domain separate from the more general information. By mid-1976 they hope to have done examples in several different domains to test their techniques. They are presently not concerned with generating optimized programs.

This project is sponsored by ARPA. The group at ISI currently consists of three people, although it has had as many as six. The references already cited give a reasonably good idea of what this group is trying to do and how they are going about doing it. Reference [17] provides an especially good, concise progress report.

MIT

In 1972 work was begun at MIT's Project MAC toward the goal of a natural language automatic programming system for business applications. In the first progress report [18], an overview of Protosystem I, a partially implemented system, was given. The user's interaction with this system begins with a questionnaire, but one that allows constructive responses rather than just multiple-choice answers. The user's particular application is constrained to being an instantiation of a general model of a business procedure, such as billing, constructed in a relational modeling language called MAPL. After acquiring the user's description of his application, the system guides him in the construction of an appropriate block diagram. He is then allowed to explore the resulting procedure through simulation. Finally, the block diagram is translated into an optimized PL/1 program.

MAPL was intended to be a language in which relational models of the world could be built and was designed especially for this system. This form of knowledge representation is basically a semantic network also. A routine for translating natural language text into a MAPL expression was also designed. It uses an aug-

Table 4 Message distribution example (ISI).

MESSAGES RECEIVED FROM THE AUTODIN-ASC ARE PROCESSED FOR AUTOMATIC DISTRIBUTION ASSIGNMENT.

THE MESSAGE IS DISTRIBUTED TO EACH AS-SIGNED OFFICE.

THE NUMBER OF COPIES OF A MESSAGE DIS-TRIBUTED TO AN OFFICE IS A FUNCTION OF WHETHER THE OFFICE IS ASSIGNED FOR ACTION OR INFORMATION.

THE RULES FOR EDITING MESSAGES ARE (1) REPLACE ALL LINE FEEDS WITH SPACES (2) SAVE ONLY ALPHANUMERIC CHARACTERS AND SPACES AND THEN (3) ELIMINATE ALL REDUNDANT SPACES.

IT IS NECESSARY TO EDIT THE TEXT PORTION OF THE MESSAGE.

THE MESSAGE IS THEN SEARCHED FOR ALL KEYS.

WHEN A KEY IS LOCATED IN A MESSAGE, PER-FORM THE ACTION ASSOCIATED WITH THAT TYPE OF KEY.

THE ACTION FOR TYPE-0 KEYS IS: IF NO ACTION OFFICE HAS BEEN ASSIGNED TO THE MESSAGE, THE ACTION OFFICE FROM THE KEY IS ASSIGNED TO THE MESSAGE FOR ACTION. IF THERE IS AL-READY AN ACTION OFFICE FOR THE MESSAGE, THE ACTION OFFICE FROM THE KEY IS TREATED AS AN INFORMATION OFFICE. ALL INFORMA-TION OFFICES FROM THE KEY ARE ASSIGNED TO THE MESSAGE IF THEY HAVE NOT ALREADY BEEN ASSIGNED FOR ACTION OR INFORMATION.

THE ACTION FOR TYPE-1 KEYS IS: IF THE KEY IS THE FIRST TYPE-1 KEY FOUND IN THE MESSAGE THEN THE KEY IS USED TO DETERMINE THE AC-TION OFFICE. OTHERWISE THE KEY IS USED TO DETERMINE ONLY INFORMATION OFFICES.

Table 5 Actual input for message distribution example (ISI).

* ((MESSAGES ((RECEIVED) FROM (THE "AUTO-DIN-ACS"))) (ARE PROCESSED) FOR (AUTOMATIC DISTRIBUTION ASSIGNMENT))

* ((THE MESSAGE) (IS DISTRIBUTED) TO (EACH ((ASSIGNED)) OFFICE))

* ((THE NUMBER OF (COPIES OF (A MESSAGE) ((DISTRIBUTED) TO (AN OFFICE)))) (IS) (A FUNC-TION OF (WHETHER ((THE OFFICE) (IS ASSIGNED) FOR (("ACTION") OR ("INFORMATION"))))))

* ((THE RULES FOR ((EDITING) (MESSAGES))) (ARE) (: ((REPLACE) (ALL LINE-FEEDS) WITH (SPACES)) ((SAVE) (ONLY (ALPHANUMERIC CHARACTERS) AND (SPACES))) ((ELIMINATE) (ALL REDUNDANT SPACES))))

* (((TO EDIT) (THE TEXT PORTION OF (THE MES-SAGE))) (IS) (NECESSARY))

* (THEN (THE MESSAGE) (IS SEARCHED) FOR (ALL KEYS))

* (WHEN ((A KEY) (IS LOCATED) IN (A MESSAGE)) ((PERFORM) (THE ACTION ((ASSOCIATED) WITH (THAT TYPE OF (KEY))))))

* ((THE ACTION FOR (TYPE-0 KEYS)) (IS) (: (IF ((NO OFFICE) (HAS BEEN ASSIGNED) TO (THE MESSAGE) FOR ("ACTION")) ((THE "ACTION" OFFICE FROM (THE KEY)) (IS ASSIGNED) TO (THE MESSAGE) FOR ("ACTION"))) (IF ((THERE IS) AL-READY (AN "ACTION" OFFICE FOR (THE MES-SAGE))) ((THE "ACTION" OFFICE FROM (THE KEY)) (IS TREATED) AS (AN "INFORMATION" OFFICE))) (((LABEL OFFS1 (ALL "INFORMATION" OFFICES FROM (THE KEY))) (ARE ASSIGNED) TO (THE MESSAGE)) IF ((REF OFFS1 THEY) (HAVE (NOT) (ALREADY) BEEN ASSIGNED) FOR (("AC-TION") OR ("INFORMATION"))))))

* ((THE ACTION FOR (TYPE-1 KEYS)) (IS) (: (IF ((THE KEY) (IS) (THE FIRST TYPE-1 KEY ((FOUND) IN (THE MESSAGE)))) THEN ((THE KEY) (IS USED) TO ((DETERMINE) (THE "ACTION" OFFICE)))) (OTHERWISE (THE KEY) (IS USED) TO ((DETER-MINE) (ONLY "INFORMATION" OFFICES)))))

mented transition network approach and pays special attention to verb case frames. The process of PL/1 code generation and optimization is described in this report too, using an inventory system example.

From the second year's progress report [19] it be-came apparent that the emphasis had shifted from trying to build a single integrated system to studying the pieces somewhat independently. Currently there are basically three prototypes being constructed. One is OWL, which is intended to be a very general system for dealing with knowledge representation and natural language process-ing. Another is a system for putting together packages of programs configured according to answers a user gives to a multiple choice questionnaire, for the domain of planning and scheduling in production and distribution systems. The third prototype deals with automatically

optimizing data organization and accessing procedures for data processing systems operating on large keyed files [20].

A related effort, which was completed in 1974, dealt with understanding how a user might interact with a knowledge-based application system [21]. A series of experiments were performed in which a manager was given a problem to solve by obtaining information in unrestricted English from a data base about a hypotheti-cal small company. The experimenter would intercept the questions and answer them with the aid of a more restricted system. By recording and analyzing these dia-logues, much was learned about the capabilities required of an actual system of this sort.

Table 6 Hypothetical dialogue with Susie software (MIT).

HELLO. I AM SUSIE. WHAT IS YOUR NAME?

bill. i need a program written to manipulate blocks.

I CAN HELP YOU SOLVE THE PROBLEM OF WRITING A PROGRAM WHICH BUILDS A SCENE USING THE BLOCKS FROM ANOTHER SCENE.

that is what i want.

OK. I NEED A DESCRIPTION OF THE INITIAL AND FINAL SCENES.

the final scene contains 3 blocks: B1. B2, B3

OK.

what else do you want to know about the final scene?

WHAT ARE THE POSITIONS OF B1, B2, and B3 WITH RESPECT TO EACH OTHER?

B1 is on top of B2 and B3 is on top of B1.

OK.

initially, all of them are on the ground.

DO YOU MEAN IN THE INITIAL SCENE?

yes. can you write a program from that?

I HAVE ENOUGH INFORMATION TO START WRITING THE PROGRAM. I CAN'T DETERMINE ALL OF THE INFORMATION WHICH I WILL NEED UNTIL I WRITE THE PROGRAM.

ok. start writing it.

DO YOU WANT ME TO DECIDE IMPLEMENTATION ISSUES SUCH AS WHAT TO GRASP A BLOCK WITH?

yes, if i can ask you about them later.

YOU CAN. IS THERE A BLOCK ON TOP OF B2 IN THE INITIAL SCENE?

the initial scene only contains B1, B2, and B3.

I SEE. I HAVE FINISHED THE PROGRAM. DO YOU WANT ME TO DESCRIBE THE PROCEDURE?

yes

FIRST I MOVE B2 WITH MY LEFT HAND, THEN I PUT B1 ON TOP OF B2 WITH MY LEFT HAND, THEN I PUT B3 ON TOP OF B1 WITH MY LEFT HAND.

how did you decide to use your left hand to move B2?

I NEEDED TO CHOOSE A HAND WITH WHICH TO GRASP B2. BOTH OF MY HANDS ARE FREE AT THAT POINT IN THE PROBLEM. YOU TOLD ME TO DECIDE THE IMPLEMENTION ISSUES. I CHOSE THE FIRST HAND WHICH I THOUGHT OF.

OWL is considered to be central to the MIT project and has been described in considerable detail [22–24]. The OWL language, which has replaced MAPL for representing knowledge, has as its major feature that English has been used as a guide in the definition of its data structures. It is still basically a form of semantic network, however.

Table 7 Definition of PUT-ON-TOP in OWL (MIT).

```
(LEARN (DEFINE PROCEDURE (PUT-ON-TOP-OF BLOCK-1))
   (AGENT (PUT-ON-TOP-OF BLOCK-1) PERSON-1)
   (INSTRUMENT (PUT-ON-TOP-OF BLOCK-1) HAND-1)
   (PART AGENT HAND-1)
   (SPECIFIC-POSITION (PUT-ON-TOP-OF BLOCK-1)
          (ON-TOP-OF BLOCK-2))
   (PRINCIPAL-RESULT (PUT-ON-TOP-OF BLOCK-1)
          (POSITION OBJECT SPECIFIC-POSITION))
   (METHOD (PUT-ON-TOP-OF BLOCK-1) (FIND SPACE-1))
   (POSITION SPACE-1 SPECIFIC-POSITION)
   (BENEFICIARY SPACE-1 OBJECT)
   (THEN (FIND SPACE-1) (GRASP OBJECT))
   (THEN (GRASP OBJECT)
          (MOVE (INSTRUMENT-1 (GRASP OBJECT)))
   (DESTINATION (MOVE INSTRUMENT-1) POSITION-1)
   (RESULT (MOVE INSTRUMENT-1)
          (POSITION OBJECT SPECIFIC-POSITION))
   (THEN (MOVE INSTRUMENT-1) (LET-GO-OF OBJECT))
   (Y-COORDINATE POSITION-1
          (PLUS 2
          (Y-COORDINATE (POSITION (OBJECT (FIND SPACE-1))))
          (MEASURE (HEIGHT OBJECT))))
   (X-COORDINATE POSITION-1
          (X-COORDINATE (POSITION (OBJECT (FIND SPACE-1))))))
```

Two basic structural devices are used in the OWL formalism: specialization and restriction. Specialization says essentially that one concept is a-kind-of another concept (e.g., a dog is a kind of animal). Restriction has to do with giving properties to a concept (e.g., a dog has four legs). The use of case relations, such as agent, object, location, and duration, is basic to OWL also.

Effort has been put into building an augmented transition network parser [25] for translating English sentences into OWL data structures [19, 22]. For debugging purposes, this group is attempting to write a program in OWL capable of carrying on the dialogue shown in Table 6. The OWL language also provides for the specification of procedures in such a manner that they can be executed for their effect or merely inspected for their information. Table 7 shows an OWL procedure relevant to the dialogue of Table 6.

This project also is sponsored by ARPA and currently involves 12 faculty members and students. In addition to the cited references, there are a number of internal memos and student papers describing various aspects of the work.

IBM

The work in this area of automatic programming at IBM took on project status in 1974, although much of the groundwork was laid prior to that [26]. The long range goal of the Computer Assisted Application Definition Group is to develop a system that will permit users to create business application programs by holding an informal, interactive dialogue with the computer. Currently under development is a more modest system that will help a user to customize a set of highly parameterized application programs for business accounting by means of a natural language dialogue.

An example of the sort of dialogue that this system is expected to support is shown in Table 8. It can be seen that this dialogue has similar characteristics to the ones shown in Tables 1 and 6, namely that both the user and the computer make statements and ask and answer questions. There is also some verification included. It is intended that the user also be able to request a simulated execution of his application program to explore its behavior under various conditions.

The data structure used by this system is a form of semantic network too [27]. This network is considered to have basically three parts, called the program model, the application model, and the linguistic model. The program model furnishes an abstract description of the parameterized programs available to be customized, including information about the various options, using concepts from the Business Definition System, BDS [28, 29]. The application model provides information about concepts relevant to business, such as that invoices and statements are kinds of documents that normally are sent to customers. The linguistic model provides information about the words of the English language and how they are used. The interrelationship of these models is important. Each object in the program model is linked to its "related application object," which serves as a sort of conceptual explanation for it, and each object in the application model (and possibly some in the program model) is linked to its "related linguistic object," which is used for communicating in natural language.

A simplified example of a very small portion of such a semantic network is shown in Fig. 2. Each node represents an object and has a name in it for reference purposes. The relationships among objects are shown as directed arcs, sometimes labeled. All of the arcs are actually two-way links, but the label names shown are meaningful only in the direction shown.

The unlabeled arcs in the figure represent the "instance" relation, which serves the same purpose as the type relation in Fig. 1, although it is drawn in the opposite direction. For example, F1 is an instance of Field (i.e., the type of F1 is Field), and Field is an instance of POB (Program OBject). Because of the transitivity of the instance relation, every object in the program model is ultimately an instance of POB. Similarly, every object in the application model is ultimately an instance of AOB (Application OBject), and every object in the language model is ultimately an instance of LOB (Language OBject). In the full network there tends to be many more levels between the most general objects at the top and the most specific objects at the bottom than appears in this small example.

The portion of program model shown in the figure may be interpreted as saying that some field F1 is derived by performing an operation OP3 using fields F2 and F3 as operands. By following the RAO (Related Application Object) arcs it can be seen that in terms of application concepts this calculation is EXT-PR =

Table 8 Hypothetical customizing dialogue (IBM).

IN ORDER FOR ME TO CREATE A BILLING PROGRAM FOR YOU I WILL NEED TO GET CERTAIN INFORMATION FROM YOU ABOUT WHAT YOU WANT. FEEL FREE TO ASK QUESTIONS AS WE GO ALONG.

WOULD YOU LIKE YOUR SYSTEM TO BE TRANSACTION ORIENTED OR BATCH ORIENTED?

what is a transaction oriented system?

IN A TRANSACTION ORIENTED SYSTEM AN INVOICE IS PRODUCED IMMEDIATELY WHEN AN ORDER ARRIVES.

i want invoices to be produced just once a day at 5 p.m.

DO YOU WANT A SEPARATE INVOICE FOR EACH ORDER OR DO YOU WANT THE ORDERS GROUPED BY CUSTOMER?

separate invoices.

ARE THE CUSTOMER'S NAME AND ADDRESS FURNISHED ON EACH ORDER OR MUST THEY BE LOOKED UP IN THE CUSTOMER MASTER FILE?

looked up; is it possible to specify a different address on an order?

NO, NOT IF THEY ARE TO BE LOOKED UP IN THE CUSTOMER MASTER FILE.

how would i handle an order from a new customer?

BY "NEW CUSTOMER" DO YOU MEAN ONE WHO IS NOT IN THE MASTER FILE?

yes.

YOU WOULD HAVE TO MAKE AN ENTRY FOR HIM IN THE CUSTOMER MASTER FILE BEFORE THE ORDER IS PROCESSED.

okay.

DOES THE SAME TAX RATE APPLY TO ALL CUSTOMERS?

yes, 5%.

TO SUMMARIZE YOUR REQUIREMENTS:
  INVOICES ARE TO BE PRODUCED IN A BATCH AT 5 PM EACH DAY.
  A SEPARATE INVOICE WILL BE PRODUCED FOR EACH ORDER.
  THE CUSTOMER'S NAME AND ADDRESS WILL BE LOOKED UP IN THE CUSTOMER MASTER FILE.
  A TAX RATE OF 5% APPLIES TO ALL CUSTOMERS.

DO YOU HAVE ANY FURTHER QUESTIONS?

what does an invoice look like?

(SYSTEM PRINTS A SAMPLE INVOICE)

how is extended price calculated?

THE EXTENDED PRICE FOR AN ITEM IS CALCULATED BY MULTIPLYING THE UNIT PRICE BY THE QUANTITY.

that's all.

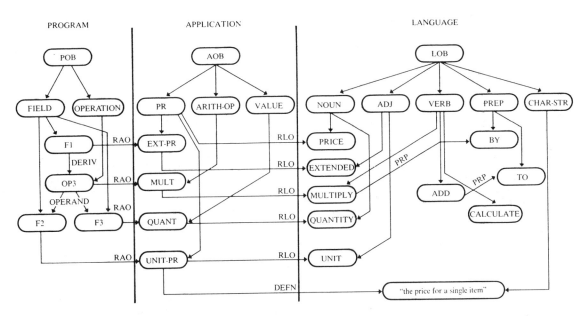

Figure 2   Portion of a semantic network (IBM).

UNIT-PR * QUANT. By making use of the relationships given in the program and application models, along with the RAO's and RLO's (Related Language Objects) given, it is possible to generate the sentence, "Extended price is calculated by multiplying unit price by quantity." The semantic network for this system is still in its early stages of development, and undoubtedly its final form will be somewhat different from that shown here.

The dialogue is driven by the options given in the program model. In its simplest form this is not much different from providing the user with a questionnaire of the sort that is central to the Application Customizer Service, ACS [30]. However, in this case the questioning is dynamic, with later questions being dependent upon information supplied by the user earlier in the conversation. Also, the user may ask questions about terms he does not understand and about the effects of making certain choices.

The natural language processing in this system is being done by an expanded version of NLP. Whereas the original version of NLP used for the queuing problem application described earlier was implemented in FORTRAN, this new version has been implemented in LISP so that the facilities of this more powerful list processing language may be taken advantage of. In order to support the large amount of network manipulation required by the system described here, a companion special purpose language, called THINKER, which has some of the same features as ISI's AP/1, has been implemented in LISP also [27]. The business application programs are written in the BDS language.

To observe the kinds of questions a user of this system might ask, a series of actual dialogues with a manually simulated system have been recorded and analyzed [31, 32]. This manual system is also providing a framework for building the actual system. As appropriate techniques are developed, parts of the system are automated, with the eventual goal being to completely eliminate the need for manual intervention.

This project is funded internally by IBM and currently has six people on it. In addition to the references already cited, an overview is also available [33].

Comparison

It should be apparent by now that none of these groups is trying to develop what might be called "an English-like programming language." (After all, that is what some people would say COBOL is.) Rather, what they are trying to do is develop knowledge-based systems that can "understand" a user's statement of a problem or a procedure in his own terms and convert it into a computer program. As stated by Balzer [13], "the main distinction between conventional and automatic programming is the latter's use of a semantic model of a domain to structure the dialogue between the system and the user, to understand the user's responses, and to translate the user's responses into actions."

A tabular summary of information about the four projects just described is presented in Table 9 for quick reference and comparison. The philosophy underlying all of these projects is that the ultimate automatic programming system is one that carries on a natural language

Table 9 Summary of the four projects.

	NPGS	ISI	MIT	IBM
Location	Monterey, CA.	Marinadel Rey, CA.	Cambridge, MA.	Yorktown Heights, NY.
Sponsor	ONR	ARPA	ARPA	IBM
Principal investigator	George Heidorn	Robert Balzer	William Martin	Irving Wladawsky
Time period	1968-72	1972-	1972-	1974-
People currently on project	0	3	12	6
Problem domain	queuing simulations	any	business applications	accounting applications
Task	generate progs.	generate progs.	gen. or cust. progs.	customize progs.
Data structure	semantic network	semantic network	semantic network	semantic network
Nat. lang. technique	aug. phrase struc.	none yet	aug. trans. net.	aug. phrase struc.
Computer used	360/67	PDP-10	PDP-10	370/168
Language used	FORTRAN	LISP	LISP	LISP
Language developed	NLP	AP/1	MAPL, OWL	THINKER
Target language	GPSS	AP/1	PL/1	BDL
Current status	completed prototype	completed prototype for message distribution	implementing three prototypes	implementing prototype
Relevant references	9-11	12-17	18-25	26-33

dialogue with a user about his requirements and then produces an appropriate program for him. They also share the philosophy that the way to bring this about is by trying to build extendable prototype systems that will support this processing for at least a limited class of applications.

Except for the NPGS project, detailed documentation about the techniques being used is lacking. Also, that which does exist becomes out-of-date pretty quickly because this work is constantly breaking new ground. Consequently, it would be difficult and probably not very useful to compare these projects in great detail at this time. However, some general comments can be made.

Of the three current projects, two (IBM and MIT) are concerned with business applications, and the other (ISI) is striving to be "domain independent." (However, the ISI group has been concentrating on a military message distribution application.) The ISI system is intended to *generate* programs "from scratch," whereas the IBM system is intended initially just to *customize* parameterized programs. The MIT system is intended to do both.

All three of the current projects are using LISP as their basic implementation language, but each is also developing a higher level language embedded in LISP to make the processing easier to specify. All are using basically some form of semantic network representation for their knowledge base and some form of procedural specification for their natural language processing. Because each of these groups is in its early stages of prototype implementation, nothing can be said yet about their relative performance.

Research issues

As implementation progresses these researchers are faced with many problems. For instance, saying that a

semantic network representation is being used is a rather general statement. What is the specific form that is best for the system? What are the specific concepts that must be represented? How are these concepts related to each other? How many might there be? Will this form of representation support the large number of inductive and deductive inferences likely to be required? Some interesting work on a formalism for semantic networks (or "conceptual graphs") that eventually may be useful in projects of this sort is described by Sowa [34]. An excellent discussion of many of the issues involved with the use of semantic networks appears in [35].

The natural language processing to be done by these systems requires techniques that are more advanced than those currently available, and it is likely that the only way these techniques are going to be developed is by work on such systems. A communication view of language must be taken, rather than being concerned with parsing and interpreting sentences in isolation as is done in most query systems [e.g., 36, 37]. In an automatic programming system the user and the computer engage in a dialogue with the mutual goal of finding a match between the user's requirements and what the system can provide. They must enter into the conversation with a certain amount of knowledge in common, and then each must help the other to know more. In any conversation the actual words and sentences uttered provide only a very small part of new information. Primarily they serve as keys that enable the listener to open up new paths through information he already has.

The important point is that a dialogue takes place for a purpose. This sets the overall context. As the dialogue progresses, many sub-purposes are established and satisfied, each setting its own local context. (Actually, this may be multi-layered.) By knowing these purposes at each point in time, a listener is able to set up expectations that help him to understand what is being said. Making this notion of context operational would seem to be crucial for supporting a truly natural language dialogue in an automatic programming system. In our work at IBM we feel that this will be possible because we are dealing with a very restricted domain of discourse and a system with a very specific purpose. Also, because the dialogue is driven by options in the program model, we have a good basis for establishing local contexts throughout the dialogue. A technique for dealing with context in task-oriented dialogues is described in [38].

In addition to devising an operational notion of context, another problem to be faced in the natural language processing part of such a system has to do with giving the user freedom in the way he expresses himself, which is especially important when the need for training him is to be minimized. Ultimately this means that the system should be able to process completely, both syntactically and semantically, every user utterance (i.e., it would "understand" anything that was said). Clearly this would be extremely difficult, if not impossible, to bring about. What is needed is a technique for partially processing utterances, to make it possible for the system to get something out of an utterance when it is not able to do a complete syntactic and semantic analysis. To do this, it would have to be able to recognize some words and phrases and make assumptions about the unrecognized portions. The idea would be for the system to get enough information out of such an utterance to be able to respond in a manner that the user would feel is reasonable. In many cases this response could take the form of one or more fairly specific clarifying questions [39].

Debugging can be a major difficulty with any program generator. How could we ever be sure that all of the huge number of programs that might be produced would be correct? The usual approach is to test each piece independently and then put them together "very carefully," performing some tests on their interaction. When the input is in natural language, there is an additional level of difficulty. How can we be sure that the computer interprets correctly each of the essentially infinite number of different statements that the user might make? It would seem essential to provide facilities to enable a user to readily check for himself the programs produced but without requiring him to have an intimate knowledge of the programming language. The computer-produced English verification and the comments and symbolic names in the GPSS program from NLPQ are considered to be initial steps in this direction, but additional facilities, such as the computer-assisted running of test cases, will have to be provided.

This debugging issue is not of such great concern in our initial work at IBM because of the fact that the sys-

tem under development will customize programs rather than generate them. This makes it possible to completely check out the various programs that can result beforehand. Also, as Mikelsons has pointed out [27], in this system the burden of matching a procedure to a task is being placed more on the user than on the machine, and he is better suited for doing it. The planned capability of the system to do simulated execution of an application program should be helpful to the user in this regard, too.

There will probably always be the danger that a computer conversing in English may give the appearance of being more knowledgeable than it actually is, thus instilling false confidence on the user's part. It might be able to discuss an application beautifully, but produce an erroneous program that would be accepted simply because "it came from the computer." Higher level considerations such as this will have to be dealt with in addition to the more technical issues discussed above before natural language automatic programming can become a practical reality.

Acknowledgments

This paper benefitted from discussions with R. Balzer, A. Brown, C. Green, A. Malhotra, W. Martin, M. Mikelsons, J. Sammet, P. Sheridan, N. Sondheimer, and I. Wladawsky.

References and notes

1. A. W. Biermann, "Approaches to Automatic Programming," *Advances in Computers* 15, Academic Press, New York. 1975.
2. J. E. Sammet, "The Use of English as a Programming Language," *Commun. ACM* 9, 228 (March 1966).
3. M. Halpern, "Foundations of the Case for Natural-Language Programming," *AFIPS Conf. Proc., Fall Jt. Comput. Conf.*, Spartan Books, Washington, D.C., 1966, p. 639.
4. J. E. Sammet, *Programming Languages: History and Fundamentals*, Prentice-Hall, Englewood Cliffs, New Jersey, 1969.
5. There is another project at the Artificial Intelligence Laboratory of Stanford University that should be mentioned here, too. This group is currently building a system for automatically generating concept formation programs through natural language dialogue. Although this work is very much in line with the topic of this survey, it was begun only recently and has not yet been described in any published documents. References [6–8] describe earlier related work.
6. C. C. Green, et al, "Progress Report on Program-Understanding Systems," *Memo AIM-240*, Artificial Intelligence Laboratory, Stanford University, Stanford, California, August 1974.
7. C. C. Green and D. R. Barstow, "A Hypothetical Dialogue Exhibiting a Knowledge Base for a Program-Understanding System," *Memo AIM-258*, Artificial Intelligence Laboratory, Stanford University, Stanford, California, January 1975.
8. C. C. Green and D. R. Barstow, "Some Rules for the Automatic Synthesis of Programs," Advance Papers of the Fourth International Joint Conference on Artificial Intelligence, 1975, p. 232.

9. G. E. Heidorn, "Natural Language Inputs to a Simulation Programming System," *Technical Report NPS-55HD72101A*, Naval Postgraduate School, Monterey, California, October 1972.
10. G. E. Heidorn, "English as a Very High Level Language for Simulation Programming," Proc. Symp. on Very High Level Languages, *Sigplan Notices* 9, 91 (April 1974).
11. G. E. Heidorn, "Simulation Programming through Natural Language Dialogue," *North-Holland/Tims Studies in the Management Sciences* 1, *Logistics*, edited by M. A. Geisler, North-Holland Publishing Co., Amsterdam, 1975, p. 71.
12. R. M. Balzer, "Automatic Programming," *Technical Report RR-73-1*, USC/Information Sciences Institute, Marina del Rey, California, September 1972.
13. R. M. Balzer, et al., "Domain-Independent Automatic Programming," *Information Processing* 74, North-Holland Publishing Co., Amsterdam, 1974, p. 326.
14. R. M. Balzer, et al, "AP/1—A Language for Automatic Programming," *Technical Report RR-73-13*, USC/Information Sciences Institute, Marina del Rey, California, 1974.
15. R. M. Balzer, "Imprecise Program Specification," *Technical Report RR-75-36*, USC/Information Sciences Institute, Marina del Rey, California, June 1975.
16. R. M. Balzer, N. M. Goldman, and D. S. Wile, "Specification Acquisition from Experts," Presentation transparencies, USC/Information Sciences Institute, Marina del Rey, California, September 1975.
17. "Automatic Programming," *Annual Technical Report SR-75-3*, USC/Information Sciences Institute, Marina del Rey, California, June 1975, p. 24.
18. "Automatic Programming Group," *Project MAC Progress Report X*, Massachusetts Institute of Technology, Cambridge, Massachusetts, July 1973, p. 172.
19. "Automatic Programming Group," *Project MAC Progress Report XI*, Massachusetts Institute of Technology, Cambridge, Massachusetts, July 1974, p. 107.
20. G. R. Ruth, "Optimization in Protosystem I," Project MAC, Massachusetts Institute of Technology, Cambridge, Massachusetts, July 1975
21. A. Malhotra, "Design Criteria for a Knowledge-Based English Language System for Management: An Experimental Analysis," *Technical Report TR-146*, Project MAC, Massachusetts Institute of Technology, Cambridge. Massachusetts, February 1975.
22. W. A. Martin, "OWL, A System for Building Expert Problem Solving Systems Involving Verbal Reasoning," unpublished course 6.871 notes, Massachusetts Institute of Technology, Cambridge, Massachusetts, Spring 1974.
23. L. Hawkinson, "The Representation of Concepts in OWL," Advance Papers of the Fourth International Joint Conference on Artificial Intelligence, 1975, p. 107.
24. W. A. Martin, "Conceptual Grammar," *Automatic Programming Group Memo 20*, Project MAC, Massachusetts Institute of Technology, Cambridge, Massachusetts, October 1975.
25. W. A. Woods, "Transition Network Grammars for Natural Language Analysis," *Commun. ACM* 13, 591 (October 1970).
26. M. Mikelsons, "Computer Assisted Application Definition," Unpublished memo: IBM Thomas J. Watson Research Center, Yorktown Heights, New York, August 1973.
27. M. Mikelsons, "Computer Assisted Application Definition," *Proc. Second ACM Symp. on Principles of Programming Languages*, Palo Alto, California, January 1975.
28. W. G. Howe, V. J. Kruskal, and I. Wladawsky, "A New Approach for Customizing Business Applications," *Research Report RC 5474*, IBM Thomas J. Watson Research Center, Yorktown Heights, New York, March 1975.
29. M. Hammer, W. G. Howe, V. J. Kruskal, and I. Wladawsky, "A Very High Level Programming Language for Data Processing Applications," *Research Report RC 5583*, IBM Thomas J. Watson Research Center, Yorktown Heights, New York, August 1975.
30. *Application Customizer Service Application Description*, GH20-0628-5, IBM Data Processing Division, White Plains, New York, 1971.
31. J. C. Thomas, "A Method for Studying Natural Language Dialogues," *Research Report RC 5882*, IBM Thomas J. Watson Research Center, Yorktown Heights, New York, February 1976.
32. A. Malhotra and P. B. Sheridan, "Experimental Determination of Design Requirements for a Program Explanation System," *Research Report RC 5831*, IBM Thomas J. Watson Research Center, Yorktown Heights, New York, January 1976.
33. I. Wladawsky, "The Mentor for Business Applications (MBA): A Natural Language Automatic Programming System," Unpublished memo, IBM Thomas J. Watson Research Center, Yorktown Heights, New York, March 1975.
34. J. F. Sowa, "Conceptual Graphs for a Data Base Interface," *IBM J. Res. Develop.* 20, 336 (1976, this issue).
35. W. A. Woods, "What's in a Link?" *Representation and Understanding: Studies in Cognitive Science*, edited by D. G. Bobrow and A. Collins, Academic Press, New York, 1975.
36. W. J. Plath, "REQUEST: A Natural Language Question-Answering System," *IBM J. Res. Develop.* 20, 326 (1976, this issue).
37. S. R. Petrick, "On Natural Language Based Computer Systems," *IBM J. Res. Develop.* 20, 326 (1976, this issue).
38. B. G. Deutsch, "Establishing Context in Task-Oriented Dialogs, *Amer. Journ. Computational Linguistics*, Microfiche 35, 1975.
39. E. F. Codd, "Seven Steps to RENDEZVOUS with the Casual User," *Data Base Management*, edited by J. W. Klimbie and K. L. Koffeman, North-Holland Publishing Co., Amsterdam, 1974, p. 179.

Received November 25, 1975

The author is located at the IBM Thomas J. Watson Research Center, Yorktown Heights, New York 10598.

Protosystem I—An automatic programming system prototype

by GREGORY R. RUTH

Massachusetts Institute of Technology
Cambridge, Massachusetts

INTRODUCTION

Over the years people have come to understand certain functions of the programming process well enough to automate them—that is to replace those functions by programs. The most notable results were assemblers, compilers, and operating systems. Our knowledge and understanding of programming is once again reaching a level where a significant advance in automation is both necessary and possible. In particular, it is now possible (for certain simple application domains) to create a system that will take as input a specification for a user's application and will automatically design and code the desired data processing system. To demonstrate feasibility and gain insight into the issues and technology involved in creating such a system, a prototype automatic programming system (Protosystem I) for generating business data processing systems is currently being developed at MIT.

A MODEL OF THE PROGRAM WRITING PROCESS

The data processing system writing process may be conceived as a sequence of phases leading from the conception of a system to its implementation as executable machine code. A useful and plausible model for this sequence of phases is:

Phase 1: Problem Definition—The system specification is expressed in domain dependent terms in English that is understandable by the program developers.

Phase 2: General System Analysis and Design—The problem is reformulated in standard data processing terms and expressed as an instance of a known solvable problem class (in our case a subset of the class of all batch oriented dps's). Domain dependent policy and procedures are worked out in detail at this stage.

Phase 3: System Implementation—The system—the actual procedural steps and data representations and organizations—is constructed by intelligent selection from and adaptation of a number of standard implementation possibilities.

Phase 4: Code Generation—The design specifications are implemented in a high-level language (e.g., PL/I, COBOL) in a fairly straightforward, but not totally mechanical, way.

Phase 5: Compilation and Loading—A form is produced that can be "understood" and executed by the target computer.

These phases progress from a general notion of *what* is to be done by the desired system toward a detailed specification of *how* it can be accomplished. They also represent the classes of design and implementation problems involved in program writing, progressing from the most global and general considerations toward the most local and detailed issues.

Protosystem I seeks to automate the program writing process by automating and tying together the phases described in the model given above. That is, Protosystem I is designed in such a way that there are explicit parts or stages corresponding to each of the model phases. Each such stage embodies the knowledge and expertise of the human agent(s) for the corresponding phase, so that, given the same or similar input, it can intelligently produce comparable corresponding results.

The products of each stage should be sufficiently general and malleable so that further stages can have the maximum freedom in making their design contributions in the most effective and efficient ways. Consequently, we have chosen in Protosystem I to make the product of each stage a descriptive representation of the dps in terms of concepts and considerations appropriate for the next stage of development. In this way the programming process is conceived as the development of a succession of ever more precise system descriptions until, ultimately, a level is reached where every detail has been decided and the result is an executable computer program.

EFFICIENCY ENHANCEMENT IN SYSTEM DEVELOPMENT

To produce a credible and practical result an automatic programming system must perform a reasonable degree of optimization. Current formal optimization methods pertain mainly to the compilation level; when the entire program development process is automated, new, additional types of optimization will have to be included.

The various possible types of optimizations fall quite naturally into categories that correspond to the program writing levels in our model. For instance, the combination of computations (for the sake of I/O efficiency) is something that should be considered during Stage 3 (system implementation) where the data and computational interrelationships among conceptual processing units are most evident. Problems involving efficient loop construction should be handled in a Stage 4.

THE DEVELOPMENT OF PROTOSYSTEM I

The Protosystem I effort began in 1971. Because of the difference in the natures of the technologies involved the work was divided into two parallel efforts: (1) a top-part-of-the-system effort (Phases 1 and 2), essentially of an Artificial Intelligence nature, concerned with natural language comprehension, model formation and problem solving, (2) a bottom-part-of-the-system-effort (Phases 3 and 4) addressing the problems of implementation and optimization of a program given an abstract relational specification (ultimately to be passed down from the top part of Protosystem I). The bottom part of Protosystem I has been completely implemented in the MACLISP language and is operational on the MIT LCS PDP-10. Research and development on the top part, being considerably more ambitious and novel, is not expected to cross the threshold of practical applicability for another five years, and so will not be discussed further in this article.

A structural diagram of the bottom part of Protosystem I is shown in Figure 1. The following sections give an explanation of its workings.

THE PROTOSYSTEM I DATA PROCESSING SYSTEM MODEL AND THE SYSTEM SPECIFICATION LANGUAGE

Protosystem I handles a restricted but significant subset of all data processing applications: I/O intensive batch oriented systems. Such systems involve a sequence of runs or job steps that are to be performed at specified times. They are assumed to involve significant I/O activity due to repetitive processing of keyed records from large files of data. Systems such as inventory control, payroll, and employee or student record keeping systems are of this type.

A simple example of such a dps is a software system to perform the inventory and warehousing activities in the following case:

> The A&T Supermarket chain consists of 500 stores served by a centrally located warehouse. There are 4000 items, supplied by the warehouse, that these stores can carry.

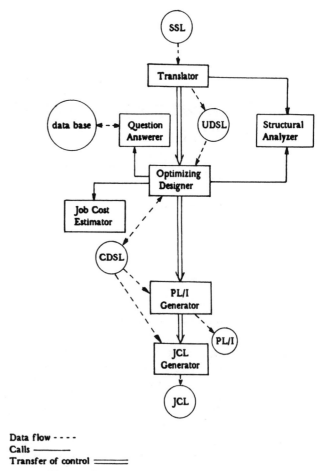

Data flow - - - -
Calls ————
Transfer of control ═════

Figure 1—Protosystem I—Structure of the bottom part

Every day the warehouse receives shipments from suppliers and updates its inventory level records accordingly.

It also receives orders from the stores for various quantities of items. If for a particular item there is sufficient stock to fill all of the orders for that item, the warehouse simply fills the orders as made; but if there is insufficient stock it ships partial orders proportional to fraction of the total quantity ordered that is on hand.

Inventory records are adjusted to reflect the decrease in levels.

Finally, a daily check is made on the inventory levels of all items. If the level of an item is lower than 100 the warehouse orders 1000 more units of that item from the appropriate supplier.

In order for the bottom part of Protosystem I to implement such a data processing system application the basic aggregate data entities and their interrelationships must be determined. Consider the inventory updating activity of the second paragraph. There are three aggregate data entities involved: (1) the set of quantities received from suppliers, (2) the set of closing inventory levels for the previous day, and (3) the set of the updated inventory levels to be used for filling store orders. Such collections of similar data that are processed in a similar way are termed *data sets*. In

Protosystem I a data set is assumed to consist of fixed format *records* (e.g., one for the level of each inventory item). Associated with each record is a *data item* (e.g., the level of an inventory item) and *keys*. The key values of a record uniquely distinguish it (e.g., the inventory data set can be keyed by item since there is only one level [record] per item) and so can be used to select it.* If we call these data sets SHIPMENTS-RECEIVED, FINAL-INVENTORY and BEGINNING-INVENTORY, the relationship between BEGINNING-INVENTORY and the others may be described as:

For every item:

> the beginning inventory level of that item
> (i.e. the value of the data item for the record in BEGINNING-INVENTORY for that item)
> is the closing inventory level of that item from the previous day
> (i.e. the value of the data item in the record of FINAL-INVENTORY for the same item)
> plus the quantity of that item received
> (i.e. the value of the data item in the record of SHIPMENTS-RECEIVED for the item in question),
> if any.

This relationship is expressed more succinctly in SSL (the System Specification Language):**

> BEGINNING-INVENTORY IS FINAL-INVENTORY(1 DAY AGO) + SHIPMENTS-RECEIVED

The repetitive application of an operation to the members of a data set or sets such as this is termed a *computation*. The order of applications of the operation to the records of its input data sets by a computation is assumed to be unimportant to the user; in fact, he may think of them as being performed in parallel. However, every computation does, in fact, process its input serially, according to a particular ordering (chosen by Protosystem I) on their keys. Computations typically *match* records from different data sets by their keys (as above) and operate on the matching records to produce a corresponding output record. A computation may also *group* the members of a data set by common keys and operate on each group to produce a single corresponding output. Returning to our example, note that item orders can come from different sources (stores), so that both the item and the source of an order are needed (as keys) to distinguish it. To form the total of all orders for each item, a computation must group the orders by item and sum over the order amounts in each group. In SSL this would be expressed as:

> TOTAL-ORDERS FOR EACH ITEM IS THE SUM OF THE QUANTITY-ORDERED-BY-STORE

Figure 2 shows the structure of the A&T inventory and warehousing data processing system in terms of computations (boxed) and data sets (unboxed). The complete SSL

description of A&T dps is given in Figure 3. Note that in addition to the relational statements a list of data sets must be included to indicate the keys by which they are accessed.

THE TRANSLATOR AND THE DATA SET LANGUAGE

For the dps's which Protosystem I proposes to treat the calculations themselves are easily dealt with; the structuring and manipulation of the masses of data involved forms the major part of the Stage 3 implementation activity. Consequently, the development process at Stage 3 is data set oriented. Therefore, to facilitate the design process the SSL dps description is first analyzed from this point of view and re-expressed in a more appropriate medium, DSL (the **Data Set Language**). This reformulation is performed by the Translator module.

The determination of dps characteristics that can aid in the development of the dps design is made with the aid of the Structural Analyzer and included in the Translator's output description. This output is called the UDSL (Unconstrained **Data Set Language**) description, because most design details remain unbound (undecided) in it. As such it forms the skeleton of the dps description ultimately to be produced by Stage 3.

One useful piece of information determined by the Structural Analyzer is the set of *driving data set* candidates for each computation. A driving data set is an input data set that is guaranteed to have a data item for every tuple of key values for which the computation can produce an output. The computation, then, instead of having to loop over all possible combinations of values for the keys of the inputs, can be driven by the driving data set in that it only has to consider those key value combinations for which the driving data set contains records.

Another type of information the Structural Analyzer determines is directly related to our desire to specify data set organizations and orders and computation accessing methods and orders in such a way as to minimize the cost of operating the dps. Because a dps typically involves the repetitive application of *simple* calculations to large quantities of data we make the first-order approximation that the cost of operation is due entirely to data accessing (reading and writing). Our design, therefore, focuses on minimizing the total number of I/O events.

Accordingly, the Structural Analyzer also determines predicates that are the conditions under which a data item will be generated and under which a data item will be used by a computation. For example, a store will be shipped an item if (it is true that) that store ordered that item and there was sufficient inventory to fill the order; the order allocation step will use the inventory level for a particular item if some store ordered it. These predicates, together with basic information concerning the sizes of data sets in the dps, are used by the Question Answerer to determine the average and maximum sizes of files (proposed by the Optimizing Designer) and the average number of a file's records a computation will access.

---

* Thus, a data set is essentially the same as a Codd relation and its keys are what Codd calls primary keys.

** Implicit in this statement is that the addition operation is performed for each item and that if one of the operands is missing (e.g., if no chicken noodle soup was received today) it is treated as having a zero value.

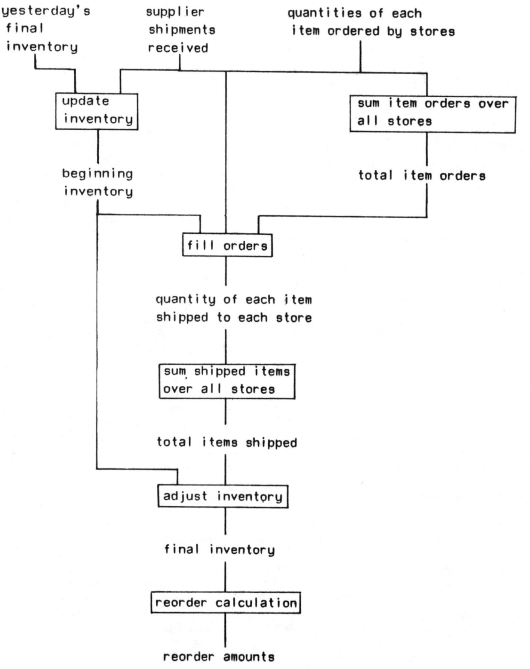

Figure 2—A&T inventory and warehousing system

THE DESIGN CRITERION AND THE JOB COST ESTIMATOR

The design criterion for Protosystem I is the minimization of the dollars and cents cost of running the final dps program on the target machine/operating system configuration. Because the dps's are assumed to be I/O intensive, as a first approximation, this can be equated with access minimization. An *access* in this sense is defined as the reading or writing of a single secondary storage block, which corre-

sponds to a single operating system I/O event. In Protosystem I, for a particular data set a *block* consists of a fixed number of records.

With this approximation the relative costs of alternative dps design configurations can often be assessed without knowledge of the particular target configuration. But sometimes actual cost estimates, provided by the Job Cost Estimator, are necessary. This module must thus contain knowledge of the charging scheme and operating characteristics of the target configuration (in our case the OS/360 configuration). Optimization with respect to a different configura-

DATA DIVISION

FILE SHIPMENTS-RECEIVED
    KEY IS ITEM
    GENERATED EVERY DAY

FILE BEGINNING-INVENTORY
    KEY IS ITEM
    GENERATED EVERY DAY

FILE TOTAL-ITEM-ORDERS
    KEY IS ITEM
    GENERATED EVERY DAY

FILE QUANTITY-SHIPPED-TO-STORE
    KEYS ARE ITEM, STORE
    GENERATED EVERY DAY

FILE QUANTITY-ORDERED-BY-STORE
    KEYS ARE ITEM, STORE
    GENERATED EVERY DAY

FILE TOTAL-SHIPPED
    KEY IS ITEM
    GENERATED EVERY DAY

FILE FINAL-INVENTORY
    KEY IS ITEM
    GENERATED EVERY DAY

FILE REORDER-AMOUNT
    KEY IS ITEM
    GENERATED EVERY DAY

COMPUTATION DIVISION

BEGINNING-INVENTORY IS FINAL-INVENTORY(1 DAY AGO) + SHIPMENTS-RECEIVED

TOTAL-ITEM-ORDERS IS SUM OF QUANTITY-ORDERED-BY-STORE FOR EACH ITEM

QUANTITY-SHIPPED-TO-STORE IS

    QUANTITY-ORDERED-BY-STORE   IF BEGINNING-INVENTORY IS GREATER
                                     THAN TOTAL-ITEM-ORDERS

    QUANTITY-ORDERED-BY-STORE
  * (BEGINNING-INVENTORY / TOTAL-ITEM-ORDERS)
                                IF BEGINNING INVENTORY IS NOT
                                GREATER THAN TOTAL-ITEM-ORDERS

TOTAL-SHIPPED IS SUM OF QUANTITY-SHIPPED-TO-STORE FOR EACH ITEM

FINAL-INVENTORY IS BEGINNING-INVENTORY - TOTAL-SHIPPED

REORDER-AMOUNT IS 1000 IF FINAL-INVENTORY IS LESS THAN 100

Figure 3—SSL relational description for the A&T data processing system

tion and/or charging scheme would require the substitution of a new appropriately tailored module.

THE QUESTION ANSWERER

The function of the Question Answerer is to supply answers to questions from the Optimizing Designer about the average sizes (in records) of abstract aggregate data entities. Two examples of such data aggregates are a file and the collection of records in a file that are accessed by a particular computation. Each "question" sent to the Question Answerer is in the form of a predicate describing the conditions under which a record will be in the data aggregate in question.

The Question Answerer maintains a data base of all of the event probability and size information given by the user. When asked a question it attempts to find the associated size or probability directly. Failing this, it will try to calculate the probability of the event in question happening from those of its sub-events and its knowledge of event independence and correlation within the dps. If the information on hand is insufficient to answer the question, the Question Answerer obtains enough additional information from the user (through a flexible line of questioning) to do so.

THE OPTIMIZING DESIGNER

The Optimizing Designer is the heart of Stage 3; all of the other modules in this stage exist merely to serve it. When the translation from SSL to UDSL has been completed, control passes to the Optimizing Designer. This module is responsible for constructing job steps to implement computations and files to implement data sets. In particular its job is to:

1. design each keyed file—in particular its

    a. contents (information contained)
    b. OS/360 organization (consecutive, index sequential, or regional(2))
    c. storage device
    d. associated sort ordering (by key values)
    e. blocking factor (number of records per block)

2. design each job step of the dps—namely

    a. which computations it includes
    b. its accessing method (sequential, random, core table)
    c. its driving data set(s)
    d. the order (by key values) in which it processes the records of its input data sets

3. determine whether sorts are necessary and where they should be performed
4. determine the sequence of the job steps

The Optimizing Designer performs dynamic analysis (analysis of the operating behavior) on the dps to propose and evaluate alternative design configurations. Occasionally, static analysis (analysis of system structure and interrelationships) of such tentative configurations is also necessary, and this is obtained through calls to the Structural Analyzer. When additional information is needed to make evaluations and decisions the Question Answerer and the Job Cost Estimator are called.

All design decisions are made in an effort to minimize the total number of accesses that must be performed in the execution of the dps. There are three major techniques that the Optimizing Designer uses toward this end:

1. *Designing files and job steps to take advantage of blocking*—Accesses can be reduced if files are given blocking factors greater than one and if processing and

file organizations are designed in such a way that the records of each block can be used consecutively.
2. *Aggregating data sets*—If two or more data sets that are accessed by the same computation are combined into one file (whose records have multiple data items) and processing is arranged so that a single record of the aggregate can be accessed where more than one record from each of the otherwise unaggregated files would have been accessed, accesses can be saved.
3. *Aggregating computations*—When two or more computations access the same data set and the orders in which they process the records of that data set are the same, it may be advantageous to combine them into a single job step. Then each record of the shared data set can be accessed once for all, rather than once for each computation.

These access minimizations techniques require that the key order of processing agree in a special way with the organization of the data being processed. Because different computations accessing the same data set may have different preferences for its organization, optimization of the type performed is necessarily a problem in global compromise.

The straightforward solution of evaluating the cost of every possible combination of assignments of sort order, device, organization, and access method for data sets and computations in every possible aggregation configuration to determine the least expensive is ruled out by the sheer combinatorics involved. Even with mathematical and special purpose tricks it would be impossibly slow.

To make optimization tractable a heuristic approach must be taken. First different kinds of decisions (e.g., choice of driving data sets, which objects to aggregate) must be decoupled wherever possible. Further decoupling must be judiciously introduced where it is not strictly possible, for the sake of additional simplicity. Such forced decoupling does not mean, though, that decisions that are in fact coupled are treated as if they were independent. The decoupled decisions are still made with a certain awareness of their effects on other decisions. Finally, as a first order approximation, the optimizer does what is reasonable locally, and then adjusts somewhat for global realities. While we make no claim that this approach will lead to the true optimum, it does produce good and usually near-optimal solutions for real and honest problems.

STAGE 4: CODE GENERATION

Stage 4 of Protosystem I consists of the PL/I and JCL Generator modules. The PL/I Generator takes the fully specified output of Stage 3 (the CDSL or Constrained Data Set Language description) as input and produces PL/I code for each job step. This involves the determination and arrangement of PL/I I/O specifics, the construction of the data processing loops, and the programming of the necessary calculations. The JCL Generator then writes IBM OS/360 JCL and ASP instructions for the I/O, administration **and** scheduling of the compilation and execution of the dps job and job steps.

CONCLUSION

A model of the data processing system implementation process has been presented and a blue-print, based on that model, for automating the entire process has been developed. Protosystem I is a project to exhibit the feasibility of these ideas. Already, two of the four heretofore manual phases of the software writing process have been automated and are capable of producing acceptable implementations. The automation of the remaining two phases should easily fall within the realm of presently developing technologies within the next decade.

ACKNOWLEDGMENTS

The author wishes to thank Bill Martin, the originator of many of the ideas in this paper, and Mike Hammer, whose numerous comments, criticisms and suggestions were indispensable.

BIBLIOGRAPHY

1. Balzer, R., "Automatic Programming," Institute Technical Memo, University of Southern California—Information Sciences Institute, 1973.
2. Codd, E. F., "A Relational Model of Data for Large Shared Data Banks," *Communications of the ACM*, 13,6, June 1970, pp. 377-387.
3. Early, J., "Relational Level Data Structures For Programming Languages," Computer Science Department, University of California, Berkeley, 1973.
4. Hammer, M., W. Howe, and I. Wladawsky, "An Overview of a Business Definition System," *ACM SIGPLAN Notices*, 9, 4, April 1974.
5. Hawkinson, L., "The Representation of Concepts In OWL," Fourth International Joint Conference on Artificial Intelligence, Sept. 1975.
6. Nunamaker, J. F. Jr., W. C. Nylin, Jr., and B. Konsynski, Jr., "Processing Systems Optimization through Automatic Design and Reorganization of Program Modules," *Information Systems* (Tou ed.), pp. 311-336, Plenum, 1974.
7. Ruth, G., "Automatic Design of Data Processing Systems," Third ACM Symposium on Principles of Programming Languages, Jan. 1976.
8. Ruth, G., "The New Question Answerer," Automatic Programming Group Internal Memo 21, MIT Laboratory for Computer Science, 1975.
9. Sussman, G., "A Computational Model of Skill Acquisition," MIT AI TR-297, MIT Artificial Intelligence Laboratory, August 1973.

Informality in Program Specifications

ROBERT BALZER, NEIL GOLDMAN, AND DAVID WILE

Abstract—This paper is concerned with the need for computer-based tools which help human designers formulate formal process-oriented specifications. It first determines some attributes of a suitable process-oriented specification language, then examines the reasons why specifications would still be difficult to write in such a language in the absence of formulation tools. The key to overcoming these difficulties seems to be the careful introduction of informality based on partial, rather than complete, descriptions and the use of a computer-based tool that uses context extensively to complete these descriptions during the process of constructing a well-formed specification. Some results obtained by a running prototype of such a computer-based tool on a few informal example specifications are presented and, finally, some of the techniques used by this prototype system are discussed.

Index Terms—Formal specification languages, informal languages, meta-evaluation, software specification, specification generator, symbolic execution.

I. INTRODUCTION

A CRITICAL step in the development of a software system occurs when its goal-oriented requirements specification is transformed into a process-oriented form that specifies how the requirements are to be achieved. Only after this transformation has occurred can the feasibility of the system be analyzed and the consistency of the process specification with the requirements be verified. The key to this transformation is expressing the process-oriented specification abstractly so that its functionality is completely determined while the class of possible implementations remains broad.

We believe that such abstract process-oriented specifications are the key to rationalizing the software development process. Such specifications are, in reality, programs written in a very high level abstract programming language. As such, they could provide an effective interface between the two major software concerns: functionality and efficiency. These concerns should be decoupled so that the functionality of a system can be addressed before its efficiency has been considered. Once functionality has been accepted, it can be preserved while the system is optimized. Thus, since the abstract process-oriented specification is a program, its consistency with the requirements could be formally verified, informally argued, or tested

Manuscript received May 23, 1977; revised October 3, 1977. This research was supported by the Defense Advanced Research Projects Agency (DARPA) under Contract DAHC15 72 C 0308. This paper is a revision and expansion of a paper of the same title presented at the 5th International Joint Conference on Artificial Intelligence, Boston, MA, August 1977.

The authors are with the Information Sciences Institute, University of Southern California, Marina del Rey, CA 90291.

by actually executing the specification. Furthermore, the end user could be given hands-on experience exercising the specification to see if it behaved as intended. Deviations and/or inconsistencies could be corrected in the specification before any implementation occurred.

Once the system's functionality has been accepted by the user, the efficiency of the system in meeting its performance requirements remains an issue. Such efficiency must be gained without altering the system's accepted functionality. We have argued elsewhere [1] that a computer-based tool can be built which guarantees maintenance of functionality while a program is optimized without sacrificing the programmer's ingenuity or initiative in determining how best to achieve efficiency.

In this paper we are concerned primarily with the need for computer-based tools which aid human designers formulate formal process-oriented specifications. We will begin by determining some attributes of a suitable process-oriented specification language, then examine why specifications would still be difficult to write in such a language in the absence of formulation tools. We will argue that the key to overcoming these difficulties is the careful introduction of informality based on partial, rather than complete, descriptions and the use of a computer-based tool which utilizes context extensively to complete these descriptions during the process of constructing a well-formed specification. We will then present some results obtained by a prototype of such a computer-based tool on a few informal example specifications. Finally, we will discuss some of the techniques used by this prototype system.

II. ATTRIBUTES OF SUITABLE PROCESS-ORIENTED SPECIFICATION LANGUAGES

As stated above, a suitable process-oriented specification must completely define functionality, represent a broad class of possible implementations, and be executable.

How can we obtain such a language? We begin by noting that a suitably abstract programming language is a specification language. Several recent languages almost meet the above requirements for an executable specification language. They have arisen from two separate disciplines:

1) *Specification languages:* Languages, such as RSL [2], PSL [3], etc., designed specifically for specification, describe a system in terms of data flows and processing units but do not functionally define the processing. Such languages can provide a simulation of the described system down to some level of detail, but cannot describe or simulate its full functionality.

2) *Abstract programming languages:* Spawned by Dijkstra's

notions of structuring, a generation of programming languages (CLU [4], Alphard [5], Euclid [6], Pearl [7]) has bloomed which isolate the definition of data objects, and the operations allowed on them, from their use and manipulation in the program. The result is the ability to use abstract program entities which model those that occur in the application being programmed. These entities are defined in terms of more computer-science-oriented entities, which are, in turn, defined in terms of more primitive ones, until the primitive objects and operations of the language are reached. Without the successive refinements of the abstract objects and operations, these languages would be suitable for specification, except that they would then lose their property of executability. Their executability has been gained at the expense of complete specification of implementation (down to the base level of the language).

What is clearly needed, then, is a language which can fully specify a system functionally without fully specifying its implementation. What are the required properties of such a language?

First, it must be able to define and manipulate application-oriented objects (as is done by the abstract programming languages). Second, the description of these objects and operations must be in terms of some formalism that does not require successive refinement to gain functionality and that does not overly constrain the implementation. This is the key issue that would enable specification and programming languages to be unified.

Three formalisms have been proposed for this role: sets, axiomatic specification, and relational data bases.

One of the earliest efforts is J. Schwartz's SETL [8] language. Sets are the single abstract type allowed for which multiple implementations exist. All the operations on sets can deal with any of the implementations. Thus, users need not be concerned with any of these implementations while specifying the manipulations to be performed on their sets. Because functionality was completely captured by the SETL definitions of sets, implementation did not have to be considered. However, such implementation-free functionality existed only for sets and was not extensible.

More recently, Guttag, Horowitz, and Musser [9] have discussed an axiomatic specification technique in which the functional behavior of new abstract objects are axiomatically defined by algebraic equations. These algebraic equations act as functional requirements which any implementation of the objects and operations upon them must satisfy. Furthermore, they provide a way of executing programs using the operations directly (assuming they act as unidirectional rewrite rules) without providing any implementation. Whenever an operation is performed on an object, the "state" of that object is transformed by applying the algebraic expression for that operation to the existing "state." The resulting state is just another expression in the algebra. As more and more operations are performed, these states become more complex. However, the states can be simplified by general rules of the algebra such as $\text{AND}(\text{A False}) \Rightarrow \text{False}$, or by using the equations for the abstract objects as rewrite rules, such as for a stack, $\text{POP}(\text{PUSH}(\text{A x})) \Rightarrow \text{A}$. Such equivalence rules are part of the functional definition of the operations on the abstract objects. If the axiomatic functional definitions are complete, then specifications in this language can be directly executed while no implementation need be selected and the choice of possibilities has not been constrained. These axiomatic functional definitions provide a user the capability of adding arbitrary new abstract types to the language that can be manipulated in an implementation independent way. This extensible capability is exactly analogous to SETL's built-in capability to manipulate sets in an implementation independent way.

Finally, we have languages in which the "state" is represented by a series of assertions in a relational data base, rather than by an expression, and in which the effects of an action are expressed as a series of additions or deletions to the data base rather than as an expression to be applied to the "state." The big difference between these two approaches is that in the axiomatic approach the functional definitions are expressed as interactions between the operations on a data type and hence do not rely on any more primitive notions. In the relational approach, as in SETL, each operation is functionally defined in terms of how it affects a built-in primitive notion, the relational data base.

The self-defining, or closed, property of axiomatic definitions would seem to favor that approach because each abstract object and its operations can be considered in isolation without relying on outside semantics and without specifying any constraints on the implementation. Unfortunately, this property comes at the expense of expressing the behavior of objects entirely in terms of the operations upon them and the need to express this behavior in the form of algebraic equations so that the equivalence of alternative sequences of operations can be formed (e.g., the $\text{POP}(\text{PUSH}(\text{A x})) \Rightarrow \text{A}$ equivalence cited earlier for stacks).

In the relational approach [10], [11], rather than stressing a closely knit set of types and operations on them, objects are perceived entirely in terms of their relationships with each other and a set of primitive operations which allow these relationships to be built and destroyed and to be extracted. Non-primitive operations exist on the objects, but they merely alter the set of relationships that exist between the objects. This view allows incremental elaboration of objects, their relationships with each other, and operations upon them. Most importantly, this approach enables objects and operations to be modeled almost exactly as they are conceived by the user in his application (as measured by how they are expressed in our most unconstrained form of communication—natural language).

This latter property is the reason we have selected the relational approach: we feel it minimizes the difficulty that a user would have in constructing an operational specification.

III. Why Operational Specifications are Hard to Construct

Unfortunately, even when the user's difficulties in constructing operational specifications are minimized by the use of the relational approach, the task remains burdensome and error-prone, primarily because although a suitable language has been chosen, it is still formal. Each reference to an object or action must be consistent and complete. The large number of interacting objects, actions, and relationships require the user to do a great deal of (error-prone) clerical bookkeeping which impedes his attention to the specification itself and reduces its reliability.

Suppose we constructed a computer aid which relieved the user of these clerical chores. How would the specification task be altered? We begin by considering how people specify software systems when unconstrained by computer formalisms.

IV. Semantic Constructs in Natural Language Specification

We studied many actual natural language software specifications. The main semantic difference between these specifications and their format equivalent is that partial descriptions instead of complete descriptions are used. When such partial descriptions are understood it is because they can be completed from the surrounding context. The partial descriptions focus both the writer's and the reader's attention on the relevant issues and condense the specification. Furthermore, the extensive use of context almost totally eliminates bookkeeping operations from the natural language specification. These are some of the properties we find so useful in natural language specifications and which we so sorely lack in formal specification languages.

We have evidence [see Sections V and VI] in the form of a running prototype system that these properties can be added to a previously formal specification language and that a computer tool can complete the partial description from the existing context. Such a capability is not totally new; it already exists in limited form.

Most programming languages use the context provided by declarations to complete partial descriptions of the operations to be performed on those objects (e.g., ADD becomes either INTEGER-ADD or FLOATING-ADD, depending on the declared attributes of its operands). The Codasyl DBDTG report [12] goes further in the use of context by completing partial references to an item by use of the "current" instance of that item as established by some other statement in the program. Data base declarations are also used to determine how various program variables are to be used in completing partial descriptions of data base items.

These uses of context in programming languages have been accepted, and even championed, because for each use, the context-providing mechanisms are well defined, the completion rules are simple and direct, and only a single interpretation is valid.

The context mechanisms we are proposing here are much more complex, the context generated much more diffuse, and a given partial description may produce zero, one, or several valid interpretations. Zero valid interpretations means that the partial description is inconsistent with the existing context. A single valid interpretation means that the partial description can be unambiguously completed through use of the existing context. Multiple valid interpretations indicate that sufficient context does not exist to complete the description and that interaction with the user is required to resolve the ambiguity.

Our work should be viewed as an effort to provide more general context mechanisms to resolve the ambiguity introduced in the specification by partial descriptions. If, as we believe, such mechanisms can be provided, would they be a beneficial addition to specification languages?

V. Desirability of Informality

We recognize that our approach is controversial and apparently opposes the current trend to make program specifications more and more formal and to introduce such formalisms earlier in the development cycle. We believe closer examination will reveal that our approach is not only compatible with the desire for increased formalism, but a necessary adjunct to it.

Attention has been focused on formalisms for program specification to the exclusion of concern with the difficulty and reliability of creating such formal specifications and with maintaining them during the program life cycle. Our approach specifically addresses these issues.

First, it should be recognized that informality will always exist during the formulation of a specification. The issue is whether the informal form is explicitly entered into the computer and transformed, with the user's help, into the formal specification, or whether it exists only outside the computer system in someone's head or written somewhere in unanalyzable form. We should consider, then, the feasibility and the desirability of a computer-based tool to aid in the transformation of an informal specification into a formal one.

Let us begin with the question of feasibility. While the results presented in the next section are preliminary and the examples chosen far smaller and simpler than real specifications, we are optimistic about continued progress and ultimate practicality of this approach. However, since these results are far from conclusive, we invite the reader to reach his own conclusions after considering the examples of the next section and the description of the prototype system which follows them.

Assuming for the moment that such a system is feasible, we consider its desirability. Informal specifications have three obvious advantages. First, they are more concise than formal specifications and focus both the specifier's and the reader's attention. They are more concise because only part of the specification is explicit; the rest is implicit and must be extracted from context. Attention is focused on the explicit information and, therefore, away from the implicit information, which increases both the readability and the understandability of the specification.

The second advantage is that informal specifications which employ partial rather than complete descriptions are a familiar, in fact normal, mode of communication. This reduces the training requirements of users, permits a wider set of users, and reduces dependence on the judgment and accuracy of intermediaries.

The final advantage deals with the maintainability of the system. Since about 70 percent of the total life cycle costs of large systems are for maintenance, any improved capabilities in this area are very significant. As we have argued elsewhere [1], the main deterrent to maintainability is optimization. Optimization spreads information throughout a program and increases its complexity through increased interactions among the parts. Both of these optimization effects greatly impede the ability to alter the program. An obvious solution is to alter an unoptimized specification and then reoptimize the program. No cost-effective and reliable technology currently exists for such reoptimization, though one has been proposed [1].

A similar situation exists between the informal and formal specifications. The creation of a formal specification involves spreading implicitly specified information throughout the specification and increasing the complexity by structuring the specification into parts and establishing the necessary interfaces between them. As before, both of these formalization effects greatly impede the ability to modify the specification. Again, a solution is obvious: modify the informal specification and retransform it into a revised formal specification. Under the assumed feasibility of our approach, this solution would be possible and would greatly simplify maintaining the formal specification of the system.

We now consider three possible disadvantages of a computer-based tool to aid in transforming an informal specification into a formal one. The first possible disadvantage is that the informal constructs will be misunderstood by the computer tool. This is entirely possible, just as it is when a human intermediary interprets an informal specification. While the computer tool cannot match human performance in understanding the informal specification, it operates much more methodically. It can question the user when it detects that there are alternative interpretations of some statement. It can record and make explicit all assumptions it makes in transforming the formal specification. It can paraphrase the informal specification to verify that its interpretation is accurate (the current prototype system records its assumptions and interacts with the user to determine the correct interpretation of unresolved ambiguities, but does not yet contain any paraphrase capabilities). Thus, feedback and interaction with the user can help eliminate the problem of possible misinterpretation of the informal specification.

The second possible disadvantage is that the computer-based tool will decrease the reliability of the transformation to a formal specification. If the informal specification exists only outside the computer system, then we must rely on the accuracy of the user or, more often, on some trained intermediary to accurately transform it into a formal specification. This transformation depends upon properly understanding the informal specification (see previous paragraph), then restating it in the required formalism. Once the proper understanding has been obtained, the restatement involves moving information from one place to another and changing its form. History would indicate that such clerical bookkeeping transformations are error prone and can always be done more reliably by a computer tool. Hence, once the correct interpretation has been obtained through the use of context and interaction with the user, the restatement of the informal specification into the required formalism can be more reliably performed by the computer-based tool than by the user or his intermediary. Therefore, reliability would be improved rather than reduced by such a tool once understanding was obtained.

Understanding, rather than reliability, thus emerges as the key feasibility issue. One way to improve understanding is to increase the interaction with the user. This leads to the third

possible disadvantage: that the required volume of interaction will abrogate the advantage of informality. We do not expect this to be an issue with the current system or its successors, since we feel that its current performance level, as evidenced in the following section, indicates that the required interaction rate would be sufficiently small to prevent annoying or sidetracking the user.

Thus, we conclude that the availability of such a computer-based tool would be highly desirable because it would simplify the creation of a formal specification while increasing the reliability of the formulation process; improve the maintainability of the formal specification; reduce special training requirements; and expand the base of potential users. The question of feasibility, which remains as the paramount issue, rests clearly on the ability to correctly interpret an informal specification. We therefore now present some preliminary results obtained by the prototype system and describe its operation so that the reader can observe its performance level and judge for himself the generality of its context resolution mechanisms and therefore its feasibility.

VI. RESULTS

This section presents three examples successfully handled by the prototype system (called SAFE). The examples were extracted from actual natural language specification manuals, and the results illustrate the power of the system's context mechanisms. However, our system is a prototype and, as such, it is far from complete. New examples currently expose new problems which are resolved by adding new capabilities to the system. Therefore, until some measure of closure is obtained, it should not be assumed that the prototype will correctly process new examples of the same "complexity" as earlier examples. Our goal is to add each new capability in as general a form as possible so that when it is used in new examples it will function correctly. In this way we expect to "grow" the system as more complex and varied examples are tried.

For each of the examples, we present three figures: the actual parenthesized version of the informal input currently used by the system (to avoid syntactic parsing problems) [13], a manually marked version which indicates some of the informalities to be resolved by the system, and a stylized version of the formal output program produced by the system. These programs are expressed (and run) in our own language (AP2) which uses a relational data base as the repository for all data manipulated by the programs.

The first example is a system which automatically distributes messages to offices on the basis of a keyword search of the text of the message. Fig. 1 gives the informal natural language description. Fig. 2 indicates some of the imprecisions contained in this example which must be resolved to obtain the system's formalization of this specification as an operational program (Fig. 3).

To give some measure of the amount of imprecision in this example and, therefore, the amount of aid provided by the system, we have compiled the following statistics:

number of missing operands	18
number of incomplete references	22

```
*((MESSAGES ((RECEIVED) FROM (THE "AUTODIN-ASC"))) (ARE
PROCESSED) FOR (AUTOMATIC DISTRIBUTION ASSIGNMENT))

*((THE MESSAGE) (IS DISTRIBUTED) TO (EACH ((ASSIGNED))
OFFICE))

*((THE NUMBER OF (COPIES OF (A MESSAGE) (((DISTRIBUTED) TO
(AN OFFICE)))) (IS) (A FUNCTION OF (WHETHER ((THE OFFICE) (IS
ASSIGNED) FOR (("ACTION") OR ("INFORMATION"))))))

*((THE RULES FOR ((EDITING) (MESSAGES))) (ARE) (: ((REPLACE)
(ALL LINE-FEEDS) WITH (SPACES)) ((SAVE) (ONLY
(ALPHANUMERIC CHARACTERS) AND (SPACES))) ((ELIMINATE)
(ALL REDUNDANT SPACES))))

*(((TO EDIT) (THE TEXT PORTION OF (THE MESSAGE))) (IS)
(NECESSARY))

*(THEN (THE MESSAGE) (IS SEARCHED) FOR (ALL KEYS))

*(WHEN ((A KEY) (IS LOCATED) IN (A MESSAGE)) ((PERFORM)
(THE ACTION ((ASSOCIATED) WITH (THAT TYPE) (OF (KEY))))))

*((THE ACTION FOR (TYPE-0 KEYS)) (IS) (: (IF ((NO OFFICE) (HAS
BEEN ASSIGNED) TO (THE MESSAGE)) FOR ("ACTION")) ((THE
"ACTION" OFFICE FROM (THE KEY)) (IS ASSIGNED) TO (THE
MESSAGE) FOR ("ACTION"))) (IF ((THERE IS) ALREADY (AN
"ACTION" OFFICE FOR (THE MESSAGE))) ((THE "ACTION" OFFICE
FROM (THE KEY)) (IS TREATED) AS (AN "INFORMATION"
OFFICE))) (((LABEL OFFS) (ALL "INFORMATION" OFFICES FROM
(THE KEY)) (ARE ASSIGNED) TO (THE MESSAGE)) IF ((REF OFFS)
THEY) (HAVE (NOT) (ALREADY) BEEN ASSIGNED) FOR
(("ACTION") OR ("INFORMATION"))))

*((THE ACTION FOR (TYPE-1 KEYS)) (IS) (: (IF ((THE KEY) (IS)
(THE FIRST TYPE-1 KEY (FOUND) IN (THE MESSAGE)))) THEN
((THE KEY) (IS USED) TO ((DETERMINE) (THE "ACTION" OFFICE)))
(OTHERWISE (THE KEY) (IS USED) TO ((DETERMINE) (ONLY
"INFORMATION" OFFICES)))))
```

Fig. 1. Actual input for message processing example.

Fig. 2. Specification deficiencies of message processing example (by conventional programming standards).

```
(WHENEVER (receive message FROM autodin-asc BY safe)
  DO(edit text OF message)
  (search text OF message FOR (CREATE THE SET OF keys))
  (distribute-process#1 message))

(distribute-process#1 (message)
  (FOR ALL (offices assigned TO message FOR ANYTHING)
    (distribute-process#2 message office)))

(distribute-process#2 (message office)
  (DO (function#1 (BOOLEAN (assigned office TO message FOR action))
    (BOOLEAN (assigned office TO message FOR information)))
  TIMES (distribute A copy WHICH IS A copy OF message AND located
    AT safe FROM safe TO location OF office)))

(edit (text)
  (FOR ALL line-feeds IN text
    (replace line-feed IN text BY (CREATE SET OF spaces)))
  (keep (union (CREATE THE SET OF alphanumberic characters IN text)
    (CREATE THE SET OF spaces IN text))
  FROM text)
  (FOR ALL spaces IN text AND redundant IN text
    (remove space FROM text)))

(WHENEVER (locate A key IN text OF message AT POSITION ANYTHING)
  DO(CASE (type OF key)
    (type-0 (type-0-action message key))
    (type-1 (type-1-action message key))))

(type 0-action (message key)
  (IF (NOT (EXISTS action office FOR message))
    THEN (assign THE action office#1 FOR key
      TO message FOR action)
    ELSE (treat action office#2 FOR key
      AS information office#2 FOR key
    IN (IF (NOT (assigned office#2 TO message
      FOR action OR information))
      THEN (assign office#2 TO message FOR information))))
  (FOR ALL (office#3 assigned TO key FOR information)
    (IF (NOT (assigned office#3 TO message
      FOR action OR information))
      THEN (assign office#3 TO message FOR information))))

(type 1-action (message key)
  (IF key = (key#1 WHICH IS (SEARCH HISTORY FOR FIRST
    (locate type 1 key#1 IN text OF message AT position ANY)))
    THEN (determine THE action office FOR message
      BY (type 0-action message key))
    ELSE (determine ONLY THE information office FOR message
      BY (IF (EXISTS action office FOR message)
        THEN (treat action office#1 FOR key
          AS information office#1 FOR key
        IN (IF (NOT (assigned office #1 TO message
          FOR action OR information))
          THEN (assign office#1 TO message FOR information))))
      (FOR ALL office#2 assigned TO key FOR information)
        (IF (NOT (assigned office#2 TO message
          FOR action OR information))
          THEN (assign office#2 TO message
            FOR information)))))))
```

Fig. 3. Program created by prototype system.

number of implicit type conversions	9
number of terminology changes	3
number of refinements or elaborations	2
number of implicit sequencing decisions	7

To illustrate how context is used to complete the partial descriptions in the example, we consider a few cases.

1) *Partial sequencing:* Distribution is never explicitly invoked in the informal specification. However, the first sentence indicates that Assignment is performed to enable the Distribution. Hence, Distribution should be explicitly invoked after Assignment.

2) *Missing operand:* Sentence two indicates that the message should be distributed to certain offices—those that are "assigned." But, as can be determined from other usages in the informal specifications, offices can be "assigned" to either messages or keys. This missing operand can be resolved by remembering that Assignment was performed to enable Distribution. Hence, Distribution must use some result of the assignment process. Assignment, from the last two input sentences, assigns offices to the current message. Hence, Distribution must use the offices assigned to that message.

3) *Incomplete reference:* Sentence four says to replace all

```
((THE SOL)
 (IS SEARCHED)
 FOR
 (AN ENTRY FOR (THE SUBSCRIBER)))

(IF ((ONE)
     (IS FOUND))
    ((THE SUBSCRIBER'S (RELATIVE TRANSMISSION TIME))
     (IS COMPUTED) ACCORDING-TO ("FORMULA-1")))

((THE SUBSCRIBER'S (CLOCK TRANSMISSION TIME))
 (IS COMPUTED) ACCORDING-TO ("FORMULA-2")))

WHEN ((THE (TRANSMISSION TIME))
      (HAS BEEN COMPUTED))
     ((IT)
      (IS INSERTED)
      AS (THE (PRIMARY ENTRY))
      IN (A (TRANSMISSION SCHEDULE))))

FOR (EACH RATS ENTRY)
    (PERFORM)
    (: ((THE RATS'S (RELATIVE TRANSMISSION TIME))
        (IS COMPUTED) ACCORDING-TO ("FORMULA-1"))
       ((THE RATS'S (CLOCK TRANSMISSION TIME))
        (IS COMPUTED) ACCORDING-TO ("FORMULA-2"))))

((THE RATS (TRANSMISSION TIMES))
 (ARE ENTERED)
 INTO (THE SCHEDULE))
```

Fig. 4. Actual input for link scheduling example.

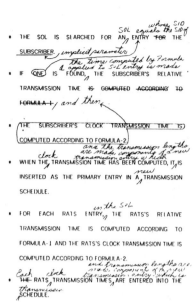

Fig. 5. Specification deficiencies of link scheduling example.

```
(build-transmission-schedule (sol subscriber)
 (CREATE transmission-schedule)
 (search sol FOR A subscriber-entry SUCH THAT
   sid OF subscriber EQUALS sid OF subscriber-entry)
 (IF (locate A subscriber-entry SUCH THAT
      sid OF subscriber EQUALS sid
        OF subscriber-entry IN sol)
   THEN
     (MAKE (RESULT-OF (FORMULA-1 subscriber-entry))
       BE THE relative-transmission-time OF subscriber)
     (MAKE (RESULT-OF (FORMULA-2 subscriber-entry))
       BE THE clock-transmission-time OF subscriber))
 (FOR ALL rats WHICH ARE IN sol
   DO (MAKE (RESULT-OF (formula-1 rats))
        BE THE relative-transmission-time OF rats)
      (MAKE (RESULT-OF (formula-2 rats))
        BE THE clock-transmission-time OF rats))
 (FOR ALL clock-transmission-time OF rats
   DO (MAKE clock-transmission-time BE THE
        transmission-time OF (CREATE transmission-entry))
      (ADD transmission-entry TO transmission-schedule)))

(WHENEVER (MAKE time BE THE clock-transmission-time
   OF subscriber)
 DO (MAKE time BE THE transmission-time
      OF (CREATE transmission-entry))
    (ADD transmission-entry TO transmission-schedule)
    (MAKE transmission-entry BE THE primary-entry
      OF transmission-schedule))
```

Fig. 6. Program created by prototype system.

line feeds with spaces. First, replace requires a third operand, some set in which the replacement will occur. Context indicates that this missing operand should be the text of the message parameter of Edit. Second, the use of a plural in the operand of an action which expects a singular operand, indicates an implicit loop. Hence, we have, "for all line feeds, replace the line feed by a space in the text of the message." Now, which line feeds are we concerned with? Only those in the text of the message because they are the only ones which can be replaced. Hence, completing the partial reference, we have "for all line feeds in the text of the message, replace the line feed by a space in the text of the message."

It should be noted that of the approximately 61 decisions which had to be made for this example, all but one were resolved correctly by the prototype system. The message it distributed is the edited one (with all punctuation removed) rather than the original unedited one. The cause of the error is that the system does not understand the difference between an object being changed and its participating in relations with other objects; therefore, it has no concept of the original state of an object and hence does not consider this as a possible completion of any partial reference.

This capability can clearly be added to the system, but the important point is that interpretation errors will occur, just as they do when human intermediaries are used to produce the formal specification. It is therefore essential to provide extensive feedback and assumption-testing facilities so that such errors, when made, can be discovered and corrected by the user.

The second example is from a system for scheduling a satellite communication channel by multiplexing it among several users (subscribers). It specifies the component of the system which receives a schedule (SOL) from the controller of the satellite channel and extracts from it the portion of the next transmission cycle which has been reserved for a particular subscriber and those portions available to any user (RATS). This information is placed in a transmission schedule used by another component to actually utilize the channel during the allowed periods. Fig. 4 gives the informal natural language description. Fig. 5 indicates some of the imprecisions contained in this example which must be resolved to obtain the system's

formalization of the specification as an operational program (Fig. 6). In addition to the process description of Fig. 4, we have assumed that the formulas referenced and a structural description of the objects of the domain have been separately specified.

The relevant portions of these specifications are that the SOL is an ordered set of subscriber and RATS entries. Each subscriber entry has subscriber identifier and transmission length fields, while a RATS entry has only the latter. The transmission schedule is a set of entries, each of which is composed of an absolute transmission time and a transmission length. One of these entries is the primary entry of the transmission schedule. Finally, formulas 1 and 2 both take an SOL entry as input and produce, respectively, a relative and an absolute transmission time.

Using the same measures of imprecision as in the first example, we find that this example has about half as many imprecisions.

number of missing operands	7
number of incomplete references	12
number of implicit type conversion	3
number of terminology changes	0
number of refinements or elaborations	0
number of implicit sequencing decisions	4

The example is interesting as a test of the generality of the mechanisms which worked on the first example, and because of the new issues it raises. We will examine each of these to illustrate the range of capabilities added to the prototype to enable it to correctly understand this example and produce the operational program of Fig. 6.

1) *Scope of conditional:* In natural language communication the end of a conditional is almost never explicit. Instead, context must be used to determine whether subsequent statements are part of the conditional. In sentence three of the example, the input to formula 2 is the SOL entry found in the previous sentence. Thus, sentence three is really part of the conditional statement.

2) *Implicit formation of relations:* In sentence two, the relative transmission time produced by formula 1 is supposed to be associated with the subscriber. Since that association is not established elsewhere, it is implicitly being established here. Hence this passive construct must be treated as an active one.

3) *Implicit creation of outputs:* In a similar fashion, various sentences establish associations with a transmission schedule (the output of this example) but an instance of one is never explicitly created. Such usage indicated that an implicit creation of the output is required.

4) *Expectation failure:* In addition to process and structural statements, a specification normally contains expectations about the state of the computation at some point which provide context for people to explain why something is being done or some properties of its result. They also provide some redundancy against which an understanding of the specification can be checked. In the example, one of these expectations (that all of the components of the entries of the output have been produced) fails, which indicates either a misunderstanding of the specification or an inconsistency or incompleteness. In this case, both our example and the actual specification from which it was drawn are incomplete; they fail to describe how the length field of the entries of the transmission schedule are calculated from the inputs.

The third example is from the same satellite communication system as the previous example. This portion specifies the component of the system which determines whether the entire text of a message received over the satellite channel should be printed or only its header. This determination is based on the type of message, for which several different cases are specified, and upon whether the message is "addressed" to the subscriber.

```
((The CGL) (is) (a list of (addressees)))).

((The NP) (is) (a list of (addressees)))).

((((Link messages)) ((first-run messages))
and ((normal mode) (rerun broadcast messages)))
(are screened) by ((comparing) (all addressees in
(the message)) with (the CGL)) in-order-to ((determine)
(whether ((the message) (is) ((addressed) to (the subscriber)).

(During ((screening)) (initially (compare) (an addressee)
with (the NP)))).

(If ((the addressee) (matches)) ((continue) ((screening))
with (the next (message) addessee)))).

((Messages with (an addressee ((matching) (a (CGL)
entry) (are) ((addressed) to (the subscriber)))).

(Context: (((Link messages)) and ((first-run broadcast
messages)).

((Messages ((addressed) to (the subscriber))) (are noted)
so-that ((the message) (will be printed)))).

((Messages (not ((addressed) to (the subscriber) (are
noted) so-that ((the (message heading)) (will be printed)))).

((((First-run RS messages)) and ((first-run OLE messages)))
(are noted) so-that ((the message) (will be printed)))).

(Not ((do screen) (((first-run RS messages)) and ((first-run
OLE messages)).

(((OLE messages)) (are output) on (the (utility punch)))).
```

Fig. 7. Actual input for narrative message analysis example.

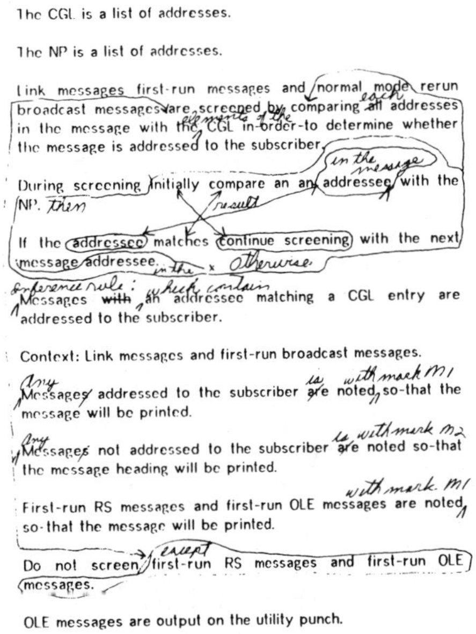
The CGL is a list of addresses.

The NP is a list of addresses.

Link messages first-run messages and normal mode rerun broadcast messages are screened by comparing all addresses in the message with the CGL in-order-to determine whether the message is addressed to the subscriber.

During screening initially compare an an addressee with the NP.

If the addressee matches continue screening with the next message addressee.

Messages with an addressee matching a CGL entry are addressed to the subscriber.

Context: Link messages and first-run broadcast messages.

Messages addressed to the subscriber are noted so-that the message will be printed.

Messages not addressed to the subscriber are noted so-that the message heading will be printed.

First-run RS messages and first-run OLE messages are noted so-that the message will be printed.

Do not screen first-run RS messages and first-run OLE messages.

OLE messages are output on the utility punch.

Fig. 8. Specification deficiencies of narrative message analysis example.

This, in turn, is determined by seeing if the message contains an addressee which is in one set (the CGL) but not in another (the NP).

The parenthesized informal specification used as the actual input for the third example is shown in Fig. 7. Fig. 8 shows some of the informal constructs contained in the input, and a

```
INFERENCE RULE:
        (message-addressee addressee IN message)
    AND    (match addressee addressee#1)
      WHERE (element addressee#1 cgl)
    IMPLIES
        (addressed message TO subscriber)
-----------------------------------------------------
Screen (message)
Loop1:
  FOR EACH (message-addressee addressee#1
            IN message)
        DO
          FOR EACH (element addressee#2 NP)
          DO (compare addressee#1 TO addressee#2
              BY eq)
          IF (match addressee#1 TO addressee#3 BY eq)
            WHERE (element addressee#3 np)
            THEN (continue loop1 with addressee#4)
            WHERE (message-addressee addressee#4
                   IN message)
              AND (successor addressee#4 OF addressee#1)
          FOR EACH (element addressee#5 cgl)
          DO (compare addressee#1 TO addressee#5 BY eq)
-----------------------------------------------------
Top-Level-Program (message subscriber utility-punch)
  IF (is message A first-run-message) OR (is message
      A normal-mode-rerun-broadcast-message)
  THEN IF (not (is message A first-run-rs-message)
       OR (is message A first-run-ole-message))
  THEN DETERMINE WHETHER (addressed message TO
                         subscriber)
       BY (screen message)
    IF (addressed message TO subscriber)
    THEN (mark message WITH mark#1)
      FOR PURPOSE (print message)
    ELSE IF (not (addressed message TO subscriber)
      THEN (mark message WITH mark#2)
      FOR PURPOSE (print header)
      WHERE (message-header header OF message)
    IF (is message A first-run-rs message) OR
    (is message A first-run-ole message)
    THEN (mark message WITH mark#1)
      FOR PURPOSE (print message)
    IF (is message A ole-message)
    THEN (output message ON utility-punch)
```

Fig. 9. Program created by prototype system.

stylized version of the format operational abstract program produced by the prototype system is contained in Fig. 9.

In addition to the types of informality described previously, this example also contains the following.

1) *Discovered parameters:* Normally, references to objects within a procedure body are resolved by equating them to some known objects (a parameter, iteration variable, or variable determined by a data base pattern match) or by finding a close association between one of the known objects and the reference. When both these methods fail, the prototype system recognizes that it is unable to resolve the reference in the current context. It therefore assumes that the reference must be resolved in some larger context (i.e., the context existing when the procedure is called). It ensures this resolution by making the unresolved reference a parameter of the routine and requiring that it be supplied in each call to that routine. The "subscriber" and "utility-punch" parameters to the top level program are discovered by this means.

2) *Dynamic reference:* Similarly, the inference rule (sentence 6) contains a reference to "subscriber" which cannot be resolved within the context of the inference rule itself. Instead, it must be resolved in the larger context in which the rule is invoked. The inference rule is fired during the compare operation inside of "screen" (which is called by the top level program) when (and if) a match occurs. Hence, its dynamic context is the active portions of those routines. Within this

dynamic context, resolving the "subscriber" reference is quite straightforward. It is simply a reference to the "subscriber" parameter of the top level program.

3) *Combination of separate conditional clauses:* Often, in informal descriptions a succession of IF-THEN statements (with no ELSE clause) specify the mutually exclusive actions to be performed for the various cases. Recognizing such mutual exclusion is, of course, critical to a semantic understanding of the specification and is dependent upon determining that the truthfulness of one of the predicates is sufficient to ensure that none of the others is simultaneously true. The prototype system has such a mechanism and is therefore able to combine the actions to be performed when the message is and is not addressed to the subscriber into a single IF-THEN-ELSE statement.

4) *Special action semantics:* We have attempted to remove all representation issues from the specification through our use of the relational data base. This has been highly successful, but some representation issues still remain. The notion of marking or noting something is such a case. Some value (the mark or notation) is associated with an object so that at some later point the existence of the association and particular value will trigger some action. Naturally, the correspondence between a particular value and an action or goal is a representation issue. To remove this problem, the prototype system maintains a set of goals (or purposes) to be achieved at some later time and a set of marking values associated with these goals. When the informal specification specifies a marking operation without indicating the marking value, then the purpose of the marking operation is used by the prototype system to determine the appropriate marking value. This construct occurs in the three marking operations in this example.

VII. DESCRIPTION OF THE PROTOTYPE SYSTEM

The prototype system is structurally quite simple. It has three phases (Linguistic, Planning, and Meta-Evaluation) which are sequentially invoked to process the informal specification. Each phase uses the results of the previous phases, but no capability currently exists to reinvoke an earlier phase if a difficulty is encountered. Hence, either ambiguity must be resolved within a phase or the possibilities passed forward to the next phase for it to resolve.

We will describe the prototype system by working backward from the goal through the phases (in reverse order) toward the input to expose the system design and provide context for understanding the operation of each phase.

The goal of the system is to create a formal operational specification from the informal input, which means that it must complete each of the partial descriptions in the input to produce the output. In general, each partial description has several different possible completions, and a separate decision must be made for each partial description to select the proper completion for it.

Based on the partial description and the context in which it occurs, an *a priori* ordered set of possible completions is created for each partial description. But one decision cannot be made in isolation from the others; decisions must be consistent with one another and the resulting output specification must make sense as a whole. Since the output is a program in the formal specification language, it must meet all the criteria for program well-formedness. Fortunately, programs are highly constrained objects (one reason they are so hard to write), so there are many well-formedness criteria which must be satisfied.

This provides a classical backtracking situation [13], since there are many interrelated individual decisions that in combination can be either accepted or rejected by some criteria (the well-formedness rules). In such situations, the decisions are made one at a time in some order. After each decision the object (program) formed by the current set of decisions is tested to see if it meets the criteria (well-formedness rules). If it does, then the next decision is made, and so on, until all the decisions have been made and the result accepted. If at any stage the partially formed result is rejected, then the next possibility at the most recent decision point is chosen instead and a new result formed and tested as before. If all possibilities have been tried and rejected for the most recent decision point, then the state of the decision-making process is backed up to that existing at the previous decision point and a new possibility chosen. This process will terminate either by finding an acceptable solution (formal specification) or by determining that none can be found. The resulting object (program) is an acceptable solution (formal specification) for the problem (informal specification).

The order in which decisions (rather than the order of alternatives within a decision) are made should be chosen to maximize early rejection of infeasible combinations of decisions. This requires that the rejection criteria can be applied to partially determined objects. The preferred decision order is clearly dependent on the nature of the acceptance/rejection criteria.

We now let the nature of the well-formedness criteria determine the structure of the prototype system so that the early rejection possibilities inherent in the criteria can be utilized. The criteria fall into three categories: dynamic state-of-computation criteria, global reference criteria, and static flow criteria. Each of these categories must be handled differently.

The dynamic state-of-computation criteria are based only on the current "state" of the program and its data base (e.g., "the constraints of a domain must not be violated" and "it must be possible to execute both branches of a conditional"). They require that all decisions that affect the computation to that point (but not beyond) must be made before the criteria can be tested. Thus, if decisions could be made as they are needed by the computation of the program and the program "state" examined at each stage of the computation, then the dynamic state-of-computation criteria could be used to obtain early rejection of infeasible decisions.

This is exactly the strategy adopted in the design of the prototype system. However, since no actual input data are available for the program to be tested, and since the program must be well-formed for a variety inputs, symbolic inputs rather than actual inputs are used. Instead of actual execution, the program is symbolically executed on the inputs, which provides a much stronger test of well-formedness than would execution on any particular set of inputs.

However, completely representing the state of the computation as a program is symbolically executed is very difficult (e.g., determining the state after execution of a loop or a con-

ditional statement) and more detailed than necessary for the well-formedness rules. Therefore, the prototype system uses a weaker form of interpretation, called Meta-Evaluation, which only partially determines the program's state as computation proceeds (e.g., loops are executed only once for some "generic" element, and the effects of THEN and ELSE clauses are marked as POSSIBLE, but are not conditioned by the predicate of the IF). This Meta-Evaluation process is much easier to implement and still provides a wealth of run-time context used by the acceptance/rejection criteria to determine program well-formedness.

The global referencing criteria (such as "parameters must be used in the body of a procedure") test the overall use of names within the program and thus cannot be tested until all decisions have been made. They are tested only after the Meta-Evaluation is complete.

The final category of criteria, static flow (e.g., "items must be produced before being consumed" and "outputs must be produced somewhere"), are more complex. The Meta-Evaluation process requires a program on which to operate, which may contain partial descriptions that the Meta-Evaluation process will attempt to complete by backtracking. This program "outline" is created from the informal input for the Meta-Evaluation process by the flow analysis, or Planning, phase, which examines the individual process descriptions and the elaborations, refinements, and modifications of them in the input, then determines which pieces belong together and how the refinements, elaborations, and modifications interact. It performs a producer/consumer analysis of these operations to determine their relative sequencing and where in the sequence any unused and unsequenced operations should occur. This analysis enables the Planning phase to determine the overall operation sequencing for the program outline from the partial sequencing information contained in the input. It uses the data flow well-formedness criteria and the heuristic that each described operation must be invoked somewhere in the resulting program (otherwise, why did the user bother to describe it?) to complete the partial sequence descriptions.

If the criteria are not sufficiently strong to produce a unique program outline, the ambiguity must be resolved either by interacting with the user or by including the alternatives in the program outline for the Meta-Evaluation phase to resolve as part of its decisionmaking process. In the prototype system, the Meta-Evaluation phase is prepared to deal with only minor sequencing alternatives such as the scope of conditional statements (if a statement following a conditional assumes a particular value of the predicate, it must be made part of one of the branches of the conditional) and demons (are all situations which match the firing pattern of a demon intended to invoke it or only those which arise in some particular context, and if so what context?). Major sequencing issues—such as whether one statement is a refinement of another or not—that cannot be resolved by the Planning phase must be resolved by the user before the Meta-Evaluation phase.

Both the Planning and Meta-Evaluation phases use a structural description of the application domain to provide context for their program execution, and inference rules which define relation interdependencies in the process domain. This structural base is the application-specific foundation upon which the Planning and Meta-Evaluation phases rest, and must be provided before they are invoked. It contains all the application-specific contextual knowledge. It augments the system's built-in knowledge of data flow and program well-formedness, and enables the system to be specialized to a particular application and to use this expertise in conjunction with its built-in program formation knowledge to formalize the input specification.

The construction of a suitable application-specific structural base is itself an arduous, error-prone task. Furthermore, our study of actual program specifications indicated that most of the structural information was already informally contained in the program specification. We therefore decided to allow partial descriptions in the specification of the structural base and to permit such descriptions to be intermixed with the program specification.

Since we are concerned only with the semantic issues raised by using partial descriptions in the program specification, the system uses a parenthesized version of the natural language specification as its actual input to avoid any syntactic parsing issues. This parenthesized input does not affect the semantic issues we have discussed.

The first tasks, then, of the system are to separate the process descriptions from the structural descriptions, to convert both to internal form, and to complete any partial structural descriptions. These tasks comprise the system's Linguistic phase, which precedes the other two.

If a formal structural base already exists for some application, then, of course, it is loaded first and is augmented by and checked for consistency with any structural statements contained within the program specification.

Thus, in chronological order (rather than the reverse dependence order used above), the system's basic mode of operation consists of reading an input specification; separating it into structural and processing descriptions; completing the structural descriptions and integrating the result into any existing structural base; determining the gross program structure by producer/consumer analysis during the Planning phase; and, finally determining the final program structure through Meta-Evaluation.

REFERENCES

[1] R. Balzer, N. Goldman, and D. Wile, "On the transformational implementation approach to programming," in *2nd Int. Conf. Software Eng.*, Oct. 1976, p. 337.

[2] T. E. Bell and D. Bixler, "An extendable approach to computer-aided software requirements engineering," in *2nd Int. Conf. Software Eng.*, Oct. 1976, p. 70.

[3] D. Teichroew and E. A. Hershey, III, "PSL/PSA a computer-aided technique for structured documentation and analysis of information processing systems," in *2nd Int. Conf. Software Eng.*, Oct. 1976, p. 2.

[4] B. Liskov, A. Snyder, R. Atkinson, and C. Schoffert, "Abstraction mechanisms in CLU," *Commun. Ass. Comput. Mach.*, vol. 20, pp. 564–577, Aug. 1977.

[5] W. A. Wulf and M. Shaw, "An introduction to the construction and verification of alphard programs," in *2nd Int. Conf. Software Eng.*, Oct. 1976, p. 390.

[6] B. W. Lampson, J. J. Horning, R. L. London, J. G. Mitchell, and G. J. Popek, "Report on the programming language Euclid," Xerox Res. Center, Palo Alto, CA, Aug. 1976.

[7] R. A. Snowdon, "PEARL: An interactive system for the preparation and validation of structured programs," Computing Lab., Univ. Newcastle Upon Tyne, Nov. 1971.

[8] J. T. Schwartz, "On programming, an interim report on the SETL project," Comput. Sci. Dep., Courant Inst. Math. Sci., New York Univ., 1973.

[9] J. V. Guttag, E. Horowitz, and D. R. Musser, "The design of data type specifications," in *2nd Int. Conf. Software Eng.*, Oct. 1976, p. 414.

[10] E. F. Codd, "A relational model of data for large shared data bases," *Commun. Ass. Comput. Mach.*, vol. 13, no. 6, June 1970.

[11] D. D. Chamberlin, "Relational data base management systems," *ACM Comput. Surveys*, vol. 8, no. 1, Mar. 1976.

[12] CODASYL, Data Base Task Group, Apr. 1971 Rep., ACM, NY.

[13] R. Elschlager, "Overview of a natural language programming system," unpublished Rep., Comput. Sci. Dep., Stanford Univ., Feb. 1977.

[14] S. L. Gerhart and L. Yelowitz, "Control structure abstractions of the backtracking programming technique," in *2nd Int. Conf. Software Eng.*, Oct. 1976, p. 391.

Robert Balzer received the B.S., M.S., and Ph.D. degrees in electrical engineering from the Carnegie Institute of Technology, Pittsburgh, PA, in 1964, 1965, and 1966, respectively.

He joined the Rand Corporation in June 1966 where he was concerned with reducing the effort required to utilize computers for problem solving, especially in on-line environments.

In April 1972 he left Rand to help form the Information Sciences Institute, University of Southern California, Marina del Rey, CA. He is currently Associate Professor of Computer Science and Project Leader of the Specification Acquisition From Experts (SAFE) Project. This project is attempting to aid users to compose precise and correct program specifications from informal natural language descriptions by resolving the ambiguity present through context provided by the system's knowledge of programs, programming, and the application domain.

Neil Goldman attended Stanford University, Stanford, CA, under a National Science Foundation Fellowship, where he received the B.S. degree in mathematics and the M.S. and Ph.D. degrees in computer science in 1969, 1971, and 1973, respectively.

He spent one year at the Institute for Studies in Semantics and Cognition in Lugano, Switzerland, and in September of 1974 he joined the University of Southern California/Information Sciences Institute, Marina del Rey, CA. His primary field of interest is artificial intelligence, particularly the mechanized understanding and generation of natural language.

David Wile received the Sc.B. degree in applied mathematics from Brown University, Providence, RI, in 1967, and the Ph.D. degree in computer science from Carnegie-Mellon University, Pittsburgh, PA, in 1974.

His professional interests center around programming language design and programming methodology. In December 1973 he joined the University of Southern California/Information Sciences Institute, Marina del Rey, CA, as a Research Associate on the Specification Acquisition from Experts (SAFE) Project, a project whose goal is the automated translation of informal program specifications to formal specifications. He also works with the Program Verification Group on a project to develop a methodology for the formal verification of program properties. Recently, he has begun work on the Transformational Implementation Project at ISI, a project to develop the basis for a system which aids a user in transforming high level, abstract programs into very efficient, concrete programs.

Dr. Wile is a member of the Association for Computing Machinery and Sigma Xi.

V / Very High Level Languages

Very high level programming languages can be viewed from two perspectives. From one perspective, they are the natural continuation of a trend that began with assembly languages and has continued through current high-level languages. This trend is toward programming language constructs that delegate an increasing amount of mundane programming details to a compiler. The SETL language described in [Schonberg, Schwartz, and Sharir, Chapter 14] and the V language described in [Green and Westfold, Chapter 16] are examples of this trend.

Another way to view very high level languages is as a very restricted form of natural language. From this perspective, the goal is to create an artificial language without the syntactic difficulties of natural language, while retaining some of the semantic informality of natural language. The GIST language described in [Feather and London, Chapter 17] takes this perspective.

SETL is the prototype of a general purpose very high level language. (Chapter 14 is a relatively recent paper. The basic outline of SETL, however, was put forward in the middle 1970s.) SETL supports logical quantifiers and the abstract data type *set* as the prominent high-level features of the language. Programmers are intended to use these features as much as possible and leave more specific data structure and control structure decisions to the SETL compiler. Most other very high level languages start by incorporating these same features.

A key question with regard to any very high level language is, how is the compiler going to make the design decisions that have been relegated to it? In particular, how can the compiler automatically select appropriate data structure implementations?

[Schonberg, Schwartz, and Sharir, Chapter 14] describes how the SETL compiler chooses data structure implementations. [Rowe and Tonge, Chapter 15] treats the topic of automatic data structure selection independent of any particular programming language. Neither of the approaches described in these papers is currently powerful enough to completely automate the data structure selection process. Systems based on these approaches are therefore best viewed as intelligent assistants, as in Section VII.

An interesting aspect of both the SETL compiler and the system proposed by Rowe and Tonge is that, like the compilers for conventional programming languages, they are procedural, as opposed to transformational, in nature. As such, they are a useful contrast to the transformational systems described in Section III. ([Ruth, Chapter 12] describes another very high level compiler, which is nontransformational in nature.) However, like a transformational system, both of these approaches depend on the existence of a library of standard data structure implementations (see [Green and Barstow, Chapter 26]).

[Green and Westfold, Chapter 16] describes the language V, which is the focus of the CHI project. V supports essentially the same basic features as SETL. In addition, it has a limited notion of global assertions. The discussion in [Green and Westfold, Chapter 16] revolves primarily around how the V compiler operates. The V compiler is a transformational system descended from PECOS [Barstow, Chapter 7]. Also, like the other systems above, the V compiler requires human assistance to perform complex implementation steps. The system therefore shows some of the features of the systems described in Section VII.

GIST [Feather and London, Chapter 17] grew out of the work described in [Balzer, Goldman, and Wile, Chapter 13]. In addition to all of the features of SETL and V, GIST provides a number of powerful additional features, such as arbitrary global assertions and reference to prior computational states. In light of this added power, it is not surprising that a workable compiler for GIST has not yet been constructed.

An Automatic Technique for Selection of Data Representations in SETL Programs

EDMOND SCHONBERG, JACOB T. SCHWARTZ, and MICHA SHARIR
New York University

SETL is a very-high-level programming language supporting set-theoretic syntax and semantics. It allows algorithms to be programmed rapidly and succinctly without requiring data-structure declarations to be supplied. Such declarations can be manually specified later, without recoding the program, to improve the efficiency of program execution. We describe a new technique for automatic selection of appropriate data representations during compile time for programs with omitted declarations and present an efficient data representation selection algorithm, whose complexity is comparable with those of the fastest known general data-flow algorithms of Tarjan and Reif.

Key Words and Phrases: very-high-level languages, program optimization, automatic data-structure selection, SETL
CR Categories: 4.12, 4.20, 4.22, 5.24

1. INTRODUCTION

The level of a programming language is determined by the power of its semantic primitives, which influence the ease and speed of programming in the language profoundly. (See [8] for an attempt at quantifying these abstract concepts.) Thus a language of very high level should provide high-level abstract objects and operations between them, high-level control structures, and the ability to select data representation in an easy and flexible manner. It is the third property of very-high-level languages that we address in this paper.

In relatively low-level programming languages, concrete data structures representing abstract types have to be selected in advance, before starting to code the program; the code to be written then depends heavily on this selection, and large sections of it are devoted solely to the manipulation of the selected data structures. These lengthy code sections constitute a significant source of bugs and become deeply embedded in the program logic to the extent that they have to be replaced or modified when we want to change the data representation.

The programming language SETL [4], being designed and implemented at New York University, serves in this paper as a prototype of a very-high-level language which treats the selection of data structures in a different way. We describe an automatic technique which enables the SETL programmer to code his program in a high level, relatively independently of specific data structure representations, and yet allows a reasonable level of efficiency to be achieved.

In the SETL system the data representation used to realize an algorithm depends on its code, and not vice versa. More specifically, algorithms are coded without specifying any nonabstract data structures at all. The objects appearing in a program are (dynamically) assigned appropriate abstract data types from among the basic data types supported by the language. In the optimizing version of SETL, each such data type is viewed as a generic indication representing a collection of more specific data structures, all of which are capable of representing the same abstract data type. Thus, the data type "set" can be represented as a hash table, a linked linear list, or a bit string, etc. However, the semantic features of the abstract SETL data types, as well as of the operations on them, are independent of any specific data-structure selection. Thus program code need not be modified when this selection is made.

Once an algorithm in SETL has been coded, debugged, and executed successfully (and in future endeavors, also proved correct), data representations can be selected in order to improve execution efficiency. Two selection techniques are provided. The more conservative technique is manual. In this technique the program text is supplemented with declarations specifying data-structure representation for some (or all) program variables to be used (cf. [5]). These representations should be consistent with the abstract data types actually acquired by the declared variables during execution. If they are, then the supplemented program will be equivalent to the original purely abstract one (in the sense that no operation result changes in any way visible to the SETL system user), but it can run much more efficiently.

In the second, more ambitious data-structuring mode, which is the one to be described in this paper, data-structure selection is performed automatically by an optimizing compiler. This is, in general, a complex task because each particular data structure will usually be more efficient for some instructions and less efficient for others. Consequently, in order to arrive at a realistic evaluation of the cost of using alternative data structures for a given program variable, we must perform an appropriate global analysis of the way in which program objects are used and related to each other.

Our main aim in this paper is to present an automatic data-structure choice algorithm. While this algorithm reflects the particular semantic environment of SETL and therefore cannot be regarded as a general-purpose automatic data-structure selection procedure, it does establish the possibility of performing automatic data-structure selection in a reasonably efficient manner in a language of very high level.

The possibility and importance of separating the choice of data representation from the specification of an algorithm has been noted by many authors, including Mealy [12], Balzer [3], d'Imperio [6], Earley [7], Senko et al. [21], and Low [11]. The present paper should be regarded as continuing and helping to complete this earlier work.

This work was supported by National Science Foundation grant no. MCS-76-00116 and U. S. Department of Energy Office of Energy Research contract no. EY-76-C-02-3077.
A preliminary version of this paper [15] appeared in the Proceedings of the Sixth ACM Conference on the Principles of Programming Languages, San Antonio, Texas, 1979.
Authors' addresses: E. Schonberg and J. T. Schwartz, Department of Computer Science, Courant Institute of Mathematical Sciences, New York University, 251 Mercer Street, New York, NY 10012; M. Sharir, Department of Mathematics, Tel Aviv University, Tel Aviv, Israel.
© 1981 ACM 0164-0925/81/0400-0126 $00.75

This paper is organized as follows: In Section 2 we briefly review SETL and its manual data-structuring system, which uses the concept of "basing." Section 3 describes our data representation selection algorithm in detail and includes examples illustrating the way in which this algorithm applies to sample programs.

2. THE SETL LANGUAGE AND ITS BASING SYSTEM

2.1 General Features of the SETL Language

The principal features of the SETL language and its basing system are described in [5], which also describes the manual data-structuring facilities of SETL. The language itself is described in detail in a forthcoming book [4]. For the sake of completeness we will summarize the features that are essential for the understanding of the automatic data-structuring methods described in this paper.

SETL admits finite set-theoretic objects, such as arbitrary finite sets, maps, and tuples, and supports most of the operations on these objects. The language also supports the major elementary data types found in most programming languages, in particular, integers, reals, and strings.

Tuples in SETL are arbitrary-length dynamically extensible ordered sequences of component values, which can be either primitive or themselves structured. Tuple concatenation, indexed retrieval and storage of components, subtuple retrieval and storage operations, and a tuple length operator are provided.

Sets in SETL are unordered collections of elements (these elements being primitive or structured) such that no element can appear in a set more than once. SETL provides the usual set-theoretic operations (union, intersection, etc.), general set-former expressions, universal and existential quantifiers, compound operators on sets, and similar high-level constructs.

Maps in SETL are simply sets of tuples of length 2 (called pairs) and can represent both functions and relations. SETL provides functional style constructs for map retrieval and storage, as well as several special operators such as **domain** and **range**, which compute the domain set and the range set of a map. Since maps are sets, all set-valued operators can also be used with maps. Data structures such as trees and graphs are represented in SETL using maps which give the relationships among the elements of the structure, without having to specify the detailed storage structure to be used.

A special value **om** (for omega) is used to indicate an undefined value. All variables are initialized to **om**, and certain operations can also yield **om** if domain constraints are not met. For example, $v(i)$ yields **om** if v is a tuple whose present length is less than i.

The SETL control structures are generally conventional and include the **if-then-else** clause, **case** statements, **while** loops, numerical iteration, etc., and a few additional very-high-level control structures, such as iteration over a set and universal and existential quantifiers.

SETL, like APL, has value semantics rather than pointer semantics. This means that the value of each program variable is essentially independent of the values of other variables and is not affected when other variables are modified. For storage efficiency, the language is implemented so that several variables can share a common value using an (internal) pointer mechanism, but care is always

taken to create new copies of that value whenever logically necessary. This value semantics also implies that subprocedure parameters are passed by value rather than by name and that no explicit reference to or manipulation of pointers is allowed.

2.2 Implementation Structures and the Basing System

Let us now describe the data representations which SETL supports. Tuples are represented as dynamic arrays of consecutive memory locations (which have to be reallocated if their length increases too much).[1] Sets are represented as "breathing" linked hash tables (i.e., these tables contract and expand to maintain optimal density), so that iteration over a set is fairly rapid, but most of the other set operations involve hashing into a set, an operation which can be expected to be relatively costly. In fact, as is seen later, the main optimization that our automatic selection of data structures aims to achieve is to minimize the number of hashing operations performed during the execution of a program.

The default representation of maps is either their standard set representation or, if it can be asserted during compilation that an object will always assume a map value, a linked hash table hashed on the domain elements of the map, where each entry in the table points to the range value of the corresponding domain element. This representation expedites map-related operations, such as map retrieval and storage, but makes global set operations, such as set union, slightly more cumbersome than they are for the default set representation.

In order to obtain a coherent extended class of efficient data representations, we introduce new program objects, called *bases*, which will be used as universal sets of program values (cf. [5] for a more detailed description). Bases are auxiliary data structures which enable us to access related groups of program variables in an especially efficient manner. This is the only use of bases; they are not explicitly manipulated by the program.

Once one or more bases have been introduced, the representation of other program variables can be described by the relationship of the variables to these bases. The set of these declarations determines the run-time value of these bases, as bases are constantly updated so that these relationships will always be true during execution. For example, we can declare a program variable x to be an element of a base B by writing

$$x : \in B;$$

If this declaration is made, then any value assigned to x during execution is automatically inserted into B unless this value is found to be in B already.

Internally, a base B is represented as a linked hash table of "element blocks." Each such block contains a program value (or a pointer to such a value) and additional fields needed to store (pointers to) certain program variables that have been declared to be based on B (see below for details). A variable x declared as $\in B$ is represented by a pointer to some element block of B, so that the actual value of x can be obtained simply by dereferencing this pointer. Whenever x is represented in this way, we say that x is *located* in B. Computation of such a

---

[1] Presently, no alternative representations for tuples are provided.

pointer, which may imply insertion of a new value into B, is called a *base locate* operation. A main aim of our data-structuring system is to minimize the number of these "search and insert" operations (normally realized as hashing operations) that are performed during program execution.

In addition to the "element of a base" representation described above, which can be declared for any program variable, related based representations are available for sets and maps. A set s can be declared as a subset of a base B by writing one of the following declarations:

s: **local set** $(\in B)$;

s: **indexed set** $(\in B)$;

s: **sparse set** $(\in B)$;

If the first declaration is used, a single bit position is reserved in each element block of B; this bit is on if and only if the element represented in the block belongs to s. This representation of s supports very fast insertion and deletion of elements from s and membership tests, operations that would have otherwise required hashing into s. The representation corresponds to the familiar notion of an attribute bit (or flag) in a plex structure.

If the second declaration is used, all these bits are grouped into a bit string stored somewhere else. In order to access this string via B, a unique index is assigned to each element block of B when this block is created. The bits of s are arranged in the order of these indices. Thus to perform the insertion operation "s **with**:= x" where x is declared as $\in B$, the following steps are taken:

(1) retrieve $i(x)$, the index of the element block to which x points;
(2) turn on the $i(x)$th bit of s.

Note that in both these cases the set insertion operation "s **with**:= x" is fast only if x is represented as an element of B. In any other case the value of x must first be hashed into B to find the corresponding element block (or a new element block must be created if the value of x is not yet in B). This observation suggests that based representations are profitable when consistent basings (i.e., basings all using the same base or bases) are given to all the variables involved in hashing operations. Even when this is done, hashing operations will still be required to create B; however, they will be fewer than in the unbased case. (See a more detailed remark in the beginning of the next section.)

The first two declarations have one common disadvantage. To iterate over s, we must iterate over B and perform a membership test in s for each element in B. This is certainly less efficient than a direct iteration over s, as would have been done in the unbased case, and is especially so if the cardinality of s is much smaller than that of B. When iteration over such a sparse set is performed often, we can use the third representation, in which s is represented by a linked hash table whose entries are pointers to element blocks of B. This representation supports fast iteration over s and is slightly more advantageous than the unbased representation for search, insertion, and deletion from s since equality of pointers can be checked rapidly, whereas equality of general values is much more expensive.

Note finally that in effect the **local** and **indexed** set representations use what is often called the characteristic function of the set to represent it as a subset of its base.

Similar alternative representations are available for maps. A map f whose domain is a subset of a base B can be declared in one of the following ways:

f: **local map** $(\in B)$ *;

f: **indexed map** $(\in B)$ *;

f: **sparse map** $(\in B)$ *;

where * denotes any representation for the range of f. We temporarily assume that f is single-valued to simplify the description of its corresponding representations. Thus, for example, "**map** $(\in B)$ **int**" denotes a map from some subset of B to some set of integers.

If the first declaration is used, a fixed field within each element block x of B is allocated and reserved for storing the value, or a pointer to the value, of $f(x)$ (or **om** if $f(x)$ is undefined). This makes map retrieval and storage operations very efficient. For example, the instruction "$y := f(x)$;", where x is represented as an element of B, can be implemented as a direct storage reference, and the need to hash on x in f is eliminated. This local map representation captures the familiar notion of data structures consisting of plexes (base element blocks) within which various fields contain either values (if the range of the corresponding map is unbased) or pointers to other plex nodes.

Local representation of sets and maps has one basic disadvantage. Since they are allocated in static fields within each element block of a base, their number must be predetermined at compile time. Also, no other variable can share their value without violating the value semantics of the language. Thus whenever such value is assigned to other variables, or incorporated within other composite objects, or passed as parameters to a procedure, their value must first be copied. Hence, if such a variable is frequently subjected to operations of this kind, its representation may be quite inefficient.

The indexed representation is provided to avoid such problems. If the indexed declaration is used for f, then an array V, disjoint from B, is allocated for f and contains the range values of f in the order of the element-block indices in B. Thus to retrieve $f(x)$, provided that x is represented as "$\in B$", two storage references are performed, as follows:

(1) retrieve $i(x)$, the index of the element block to which x points;
(2) retrieve $V(i(x))$.

The sparse map representation is completely analogous to the sparse set representation given above.

A multivalued map f is represented in a similar fashion, with the distinction that $f\{x\}$ is stored (instead of $f(x)$) for each x in the domain of f.

Remark. One potential disadvantage of bases is that they may be bulky, since each base B contains all elements that have ever been inserted into some set or map based on B. In a very dynamic situation, where elements enter these sets and then leave them and are continually replaced by new elements, B can become very large while the sets based on it remain small. (Such situations occur frequently in *external* data processing, where, for example, we read records from an input file, manipulating each record separately and writing it to an output file.) One possible remedy for this problem is a kind of garbage collection that would contract bases by removing dead elements from them (see [5]). However, this is expensive, and the more favorable situation for the introduction of a base is that in which a collection of objects is built up in an initial phase of the program and is then extensively manipulated, with most or all of these objects remaining active. This is typical for *internal* data manipulation, as is seen, for example, in the sample program which follows.

2.3 An Example

We now illustrate the preceding considerations by an example showing the process of declarative data-structure selection in SETL. The following program computes a minimum-cost path between two nodes in a directed graph. Statement numbers are given for later reference.

```
      Program MINPATH;
(1)   read(graph, cost, x, y);        $ read in graph and auxiliary information
                                      $ graph is a set of edges (which can also be interpreted
                                      $ as a map from nodes to their successors);
                                      $ cost is an integer-valued map on these edges;
                                      $ x is the source node, and y is the target
(2)   prev := {};                     $ prev is a map from each encountered node to its "cheapest"
                                      $ predecessor, initialized to the null set (map)
(3)   val := {};                      $ val maps each encountered node to the minimal cost of a path
                                      $ reaching it from x, initialized to the null set (map)
(4)   val(x) := 0;                    $ start node has zero cost path
(5)   newnodes := {x};                $ initially, only start node is newly reached
(6)   (while newnodes /= {})          $ while there exist newly reached nodes
(7)     n from newnodes;              $ select and remove such a node from newnodes
(8)     (∀m ∈ graph{n})               $ and for each of its successors
(9)       newval := val(n) + cost(n, m);   $ calculate new path cost
(10)      if val(m) = om or val(m) > newval then   $ cheaper path
(11)        val(m) := newval;         $ note path value
(12)        prev(m) := n;             $ and cheapest predecessor
(13)        if m /= y then            $ keep searching if goal not reached
(14)          newnodes with:= m;      $ and add m to set of newly reached nodes
            end if;
          end if;
        end ∀;
      end while;
    if val(y) = om then               $ y is not reachable from x
      print("y is not reachable from x");
    else
      path := [y];                    $ build up reversed path as a tuple
      z := y;                         $ starting with the last node
      (while (z := prev(z)) /= om     $ chain to preceding node
        path with:= z;                $ and add it to path
      end while;                      $ and now reverse path
      path := [path(#path + 1 - i) : i := 1 ... #path];   $ # is the cardinality
                                                          $ operator
      print(path);
    end if;
    end program MINPATH;
```

This is the "pure" SETL program in which no specification of data structures has been supplied. After this program has been coded and tested, we can select efficient data structures for its variables. A typical choice might be as follows: Introduce a base *nodes*, which will be the set of all nodes in the graph. Then declare

```
graph: local map (∈nodes) ∈nodes;
cost: local map (∈nodes) indexed map (∈nodes) int;
newnodes: local set (∈nodes);
prev: local smap (∈nodes) ∈nodes;        $ (i.e., single-valued map)
val: local smap (∈nodes) int;
x, y, m, n: ∈nodes;
path: tuple (∈nodes);
```

In the presence of these declarations, a hash table is generated for the base *nodes*. This hash table is filled in automatically as soon as the graph is read in by our program. Each block in this hash table contains several fields which store values, bits, and pointers to other entries in this table. After the input phase, the rest of the program is executed without performing a single hashing operation. We pay a very small price for this huge saving when we print *path*, since each component must be dereferenced to its actual value before being printed out. We stress the point that we can map our objects onto lower level data structures and generate code sequences quite close to those which would appear in a lower level variant of our algorithm (such as one written in PASCAL or PL/I), and we attain comparable efficiency without recoding the original form of our algorithm at all.

This example indicates that the trade-off between programming language level and execution efficiency need not be so unfavorable as is generally expected. Of course, in our example we lower the level of "pure" SETL somewhat by supplying the data-structure declarations. However, this program supplement is very small compared with the labor that would be involved in an actual recoding of the algorithm in a lower level language. Furthermore, as is shown in the following sections, the data structures that we have declared can be selected automatically, thus relieving the programmer of the task of specifying any data structures at all.

3. AN AUTOMATIC DATA REPRESENTATION SELECTION ALGORITHM

3.1 Informal Statement of Strategy

Now we turn to a discussion of automatic techniques for data-structure selection. As noted above, our main goal in introducing bases and based objects into a program is to reduce the number of hashing operations required during its execution. To illustrate this point, consider the case where several sets S_1, S_2, ..., S_n, with $n > 1$, are known to be (possibly overlapping) subsets of some universal set B, so that we can introduce B as a base and represent each S_i as a "set of elements of B." It is easily seen that the number N_u of hashing operations required when using the based representation never exceeds the number N_u of hashing operations required in the unbased case (and in typical cases N_b is considerably less than N_u) provided that B is introduced in such a way that no value becomes an element of B without being inserted into one of the sets or maps based on B. (Compare, e.g., with case (a) of phase (a) of the algorithm described below.) This is also true if we consider not just maps which are domain-based on B but also subsets of B.

Additional performance improvements can be obtained by using more refined data structuring in SETL; see [5, 14, 16]. A strategy common to these approaches, but initially we ignore this subtler issue. We also ignore the fact that hashing into a base may be a slightly more costly operation than hashing into a set or map, since creation of base element blocks is a bit slower than creation of set or map elements.

The algorithm sketched below is not our first attempt at performing automatic data structuring in SETL; see [5, 14, 16]. A strategy common to these approaches, and to our new algorithm as well, is to generate provisional bases and corresponding based representation for variables involved in operations otherwise requiring hashing. These provisional bases initially reflect only local information, and separate bases are generated for each hashing operation. For these "local" provisional basings to be integrated into an overall basing structure, they are propagated globally. During propagation individual bases are equivalenced whenever logically appropriate. We feel that the efficiency and simplicity of our present algorithm makes it our best candidate for performing automatic data structuring in SETL.

To illustrate the strategy that this algorithm employs, consider the following SETL code fragment (taken from the MINPATH program shown in the previous section):

```
(1) n from newnodes;
(2) prev(m) := n;
        .
        .
(3) newnodes with:= m;
```

In this code, instructions (2) and (3) implicitly require hashing operations. Thus we first generate two bases B_2, B_3 and provisionally establish the representations

$$prev_3: \quad \textbf{map}\ (\in B_2)\ *; \qquad m_2:\ \in B_2;$$
$$newnodes_3: \textbf{set}\ (\in B_3); \qquad m_3:\ \in B_3;$$

where v_i denotes the occurrence of a program variable v at instruction i and $*$ denotes any mode. Note that we generate representations for variable occurrences rather than for the variables themselves; the reason is that SETL is only weakly typed, so that each variable may assume more than one data type in the course of execution. (Various problems arising in view of this fact are addressed later on.) However, since there exists a data-flow link between m_2 and m_3 (i.e., there exists an execution path connecting these two occurrences along which m is not modified), it follows that m_2 and m_3 can assume the same value, which must therefore be an element of both B_2 and B_3. We therefore merge the representations of m_2 and m_3 into one common representation by identifying B_2 with B_3. We can then propagate the resulting basing to instruction (1), which is a retrieval operation whose execution speed is virtually independent of the representation of

its arguments. Then, in view of the data-flow link between $newnodes_1$ and $newnodes_3$, we give $newnodes_1$ the same representation as $newnodes_3$, and we put $n_1:\ \in B_3$. An additional propagation step, using the n_1-n_2 link, gives $prev_2$ the representation "$\textbf{map}\ (\in B_3)\ \in B_3$".

3.2 The Selection Algorithm

Our algorithm mechanizes the strategy that has been sketched above in a relatively efficient and simple manner. Before describing this algorithm, let us sketch the form of input it assumes. We suppose that the program to be analyzed has already undergone several other analyses and optimizations, including a modified version of the definition-use chaining analysis (cf. [2]) which computes a data-flow map, called BFROM, whose definition is as follows: Let VO_1, VO_2 be two occurrences of a variable V. Then $VO_1 \in \mathrm{BFROM}(VO_2)$ iff VO_2 is a use of V and there exists an execution path leading from VO_1 to VO_2 that is free of other occurrences of V (cf. [18] for more details).

We also assume that type analysis has been performed using Tenenbaum's approach [25], so that type information will have been assigned to each variable occurrence in a manner ensuring that the calculated type of each variable occurrence dominates every data type that the variable can acquire at that program point during execution.

Assuming all this, our algorithm consists of the following phases:

(a) base generation;
(b) representation merging and base equivalencing;
(c) base pruning and representation adjustment;
(d) conversion optimization.

(a) *Base Generation.* This phase performs a linear pass through the code being analyzed. For each instruction I we introduce enough bases and corresponding based representations for arguments of I to ensure that execution of I with these based representations for its arguments is not slower than execution of I with unbased arguments. For example,

(1) Suppose that I is "S with:= x;". Then we introduce a base B_I and provisionally assume the representations S: $\textbf{set}$ ($\in B_I$); x_I: $\in B_I$. Note that here the introduction of B_I speeds up the execution of I considerably.

(2) Next, suppose that I is "$f(x) := y$;". Here we introduce two bases B_I^1, B_I^2 and provisionally represent f: $\textbf{map}$ ($\in B_I^2$) $\in B_I^1$; x_I: $\in B_I^1$; y_I: $\in B_I^2$; here only B_I^1 is essential, since its introduction eliminates a hashing operation, and we refer to B_I^1 as an *effective* base. The introduction of B_I^2 does not speed up execution of I (but does not slow it down either), and we refer to B_I^2 as a *neutral* base. The utility of neutral bases will become clear in our description of the next phase of the data-structure choice algorithm.

(3) Next, suppose that I is "$x := v(j)$;", where v is a tuple. Here no speed-up is possible, but nevertheless we introduce a (neutral) base B_I, and provisionally establish the representations v_I: $\textbf{tuple}$ ($\in B_I$); x_I: $\in B_I$.

(4) Finally, suppose that I is "$x := x + 1$;". Here no base B can be introduced without running the risk of significantly slowing down I because of the

possible introduction of conversion operations for the newly created values of x between their **int** mode and their tentative ($\in B$) mode. Hence we introduce no base for I.

In this first phase we also build up a map EM, mapping each generated base to the mode of its elements. During this phase all these modes are unbased, but they may be transformed into based modes during phase (b).

(b) *Representation Merging and Base Equivalencing.* This phase executes a linear pass through the map BFROM. For each pair of variable occurrences $(VO_1, VO_2) \in$ BFROM such that both VO_1 and VO_2 have the same type, and supposing that VO_1 and VO_2 have both received based representations in phase (a), we perform the following representation merging operation (recursively).

Let R_1, R_2 denote the based representations of VO_1, VO_2, respectively. Three cases are possible:

(1) Both R_1 and R_2 are base pointers; that is, R_1 is $\in B_1$ and R_2 is $\in B_2$. In this case *equivalence B_1 and B_2*.

(2) One of these representations, say R_1, is $\in B_1$ and the other is a composite based representation. In this case *merge $EM(B_1)$ with R_2*, setting $EM(B_1)$ to R_2 if the former is an unbased mode.

(3) Both R_1 and R_2 are composite representations. Since the gross set-theoretic types of VO_1 and VO_2 are assumed to be equal, the composite structures specified by R_1 and R_2 must also have the same gross type (i.e., both must be sets, maps, or tuples, if one is). In this case *merge* the element mode of R_1 with that of R_2 (if R_1 and R_2 represent maps, merge their domain element modes and their range element modes separately; if R_1 and R_2 represent tuples of the same known length n, each component then having its own type and representation, perform n componentwise merges).

The element-mode map EM need be kept only for equivalence classes. Whenever two classes represented by B_1, B_2 are merged into one, we compute the map EM of the new class as follows:

(1) If both $EM(B_1)$ and $EM(B_2)$ are unbased, they must be equal, and this is the EM value of the new class.

(2) If one of them is based and the other is not, set EM of the new class to the based mode.

(3) If both are based, then assign either of the two basings to the new class, but *merge* them with one another.

Note that phase (b) uses the neutral bases introduced in phase (a) to transmit basing information between instructions without actually having to use any global propagation technique. This point is illustrated by the following example (where the objects involved are assumed to have data types as indicated):

(1) S **with**:= x;   \$ S is a set
(2) $V(i) := S$;   \$ V is a tuple (of sets)
(3) $T := V(j)$;   \$ T is a set
(4) y **from** T;   \$ T is a set

Phase (a) will have generated the following provisional representations:

$$
\begin{array}{ll}
S_1: \textbf{set }(\in B_1); & x_1: \in B_1 \\
V_2: \textbf{tuple }(\in B_2); & S_2: \in B_2 \\
V_3: \textbf{tuple }(\in B_3); & T_3: \in B_3 \\
T_4: \textbf{set }(\in B_4); & y_4: \in B_4
\end{array}
$$

Here only B_1 is effective, since it supports hashing (see case (1) of phase (a)). B_2 and B_3 are neutral (case (3) of phase (a)), as is B_4, since no hashing is required for operation (4). Using the S_1–S_2 link, phase (b) will set $EM(B_2) = \textbf{set }(\in B_1)$. By virtue of the V_2–V_3 link we then equivalence B_2 and B_3, setting EM of the new class to "**set** $(\in B_1)$". Then, by virtue of the T_3–T_4 link, we merge $EM(B_3 \equiv B_2)$ with "**set** $(\in B_4)$", that is, merge "**set** $(\in B_1)$" and "**set** $(\in B_4)$", causing B_1 and B_4 to be equivalenced. If B_2 and B_3 were unavailable, this deduction would have been more difficult, and a rather complex propagation of basing information through the code would have been required.

This merging/equivalencing process can be made highly efficient by using a compressed balanced tree representation for the set of all generated bases (cf. [24]). This representation allows execution of a sequence of equivalencing operations in almost linear time.

(c) *Base Pruning and Representation Adjustment.* When phase (b) terminates, the set of all initial bases will have been split into equivalence classes. Each such class corresponds to one *actual* base B, and the map EM maps this class to the common representation of the elements of B. However, it is possible that such a base B may be *useless*, in the sense that its introduction cannot speed up the execution of any instruction or, even if some instructions are made more efficient due to the introduction of B, all these instructions involve only the same composite object s based on B. In this latter case, introduction of B will simply replace the hash table of s by that of B, gaining us nothing. Such cases are detected and eliminated by phase (c), as follows:

(1) We find all actual bases which are useless according to the criterion stated above and flag them as such.

(2) We update all based representations of variable occurrences and the element modes of all actual bases, in the following recursive manner:

   (a) unbased modes are left unchanged;

   (b) each provisional base B appearing in a mode is replaced by the corresponding actual base $\hat{B}$ if $\hat{B}$ is not useless. If $\hat{B}$ is useless, we replace the submode $\in B$ by $EM(\hat{B})$.

(3) We enter all useful bases into the symbol table.

It can be shown that the preliminary type-analysis phase of the optimizer can be adjusted in such a way as to guarantee that this recursive adjustment operation involves no cycles. Note also that it is only after this adjustment that a variable occurrence can have a based representation involving more than one level of specification, for example, **set** (**tuple** $(\in B)$).

As an example, consider the case of an integer-valued bivariate map f. In compilation of SETL, each retrieval of the value $f(x, y)$ is expanded into the code sequence

(1) $t := f\{x\}$;
(2) $z := t(y)$;

Phase (a) of our algorithm will generate the following provisional representations:

$$t_1: \in B_2; \qquad f_1: \textbf{map}\ (\in B_1)\ \in B_2;$$
$$t_2: \textbf{map}\ (\in B_3)\ \in B_4;$$

Now we assume that (the equivalence class of) B_2 turns out to be useless (which is the case, e.g., if f is always accessed as a bivariate map) and that B_4 is useless (e.g., no set manipulation of the range of f occurs in the program being analyzed). Phase (b) will merge the representations of t_1 and t_2 to obtain $EM(B_2) = \textbf{map}\ (\in B_3) \in B_4$. Hence, phase (c) will update the representation of f_1 to "$\textbf{map}\ (\in B_1)\ \textbf{map}\ (\in B_3) \in B_4$" and again to "$\textbf{map}\ (\in B_1)\ \textbf{map}\ (\in B_3)\ \textbf{int}$", which is probably the representation that a programmer would have chosen manually and is the best representation for sparse multivariate maps defined on arbitrary domains.

(d) *Conversion Optimization.* This is the final phase of our data-structuring algorithm. At the end of phase (c), based representations, as well as type information, will have been computed for each variable occurrence, rather than for each variable. We use occurrences rather than variables because the weak typing of SETL allows a variable to assume more than one data type during execution; moreover, even objects with the same data type may be represented in different ways at different occurrences of the same variable. Nevertheless, the information collected by our algorithm must finally be stated on a per variable basis since subsequent compiler phases (e.g., our machine-code generator) cannot support more than one type or detailed representation per variable. Furthermore, the first three phases of our algorithm ignore the operations which actually insert elements into a base B. For example, consider the code

(1) $x := x + 1$;
(2) s with:= x;

The first three phases of our algorithm will assign "**int**" as the representation of x_1, and "$\in B$" as the representation of x_2, where B is some base. This means that the value of x is represented by a pointer into B, instruction (2) can assume that the value of x is represented by a pointer into B, but of course such a pointer must first be created.

These two problems of information integration and base insertion are solved simultaneously in phase (d) of our algorithm. In this phase we first scan all occurrences of each program variable x. For each representation R assigned to at least one of these occurrences, we generate a new symbol-table entry, which we denote as x_R and which is said to be *split* from x. We then replace all occurrences of x having the representation R by occurrences of x_R. If two occurrences of the same original variable x having different representations R_1, R_2 are linked by BFROM, then we must of course ensure that conversion of the value of x from representation R_1 to representation R_2 takes place as control advances from the first occurrence to the second one. To enforce this conversion, we insert an assignment "$x_{R_2} := x_{R_1}$" into the code at some optimal (low-frequency) place separating these two occurrences. Insertion of such conversions into the code is

accomplished using a simple data-flow analysis of the "bitvectoring" type [19], which is rather similar to expression availability and motion analyses [1, 9]. To describe the technique used, we first introduce the following terminology. Let R_1, R_2 be any two representations of some variable. We say that R_1 is a *subrepresentation* of R_2 (or that R_2 is a *superrepresentation* of R_1) if R_1 is more specific than R_2, so that conversion from R_1 to R_2 is a no-op. (For example, **set(int)** is a subrepresentation of **general**.) Each occurrence of a split variable x_R in the program code is treated as requiring a preliminary check/conversion, unless we can show that this conversion is *redundant*, in the sense that x must already have the representation R (or a subrepresentation of R) along all execution paths leading to that occurrence. It follows that we can treat each occurrence of a split variable x_R as *generating* all split variables x_{R_1} for which R_1 is a superrepresentation of R and as killing all other variables split from x (i.e., making the corresponding representations unavailable).

This rule allows us to proceed in standard fashion to determine the set of all split variables available at each program point and hence to eliminate redundant conversions, and to move these conversions out of loops, where possible.

The process of moving conversion operations deserves a few more comments, as it is governed by somewhat special profitability and safety criteria. It is *profitable* to move a conversion to x_R out of a loop I if there exists at least one such conversion within I which becomes redundant if (and only if) this conversion is available at entry to I. To discuss *safety* of conversion motion, it is appropriate to introduce a relation .*conv.* between representations, so that R_1.*conv.* R_2 if R_1 can always be converted to R_2 without producing an error. For example, **set(int)** .*conv.* **set**, **set** .*conv.* **general**, etc.; also, if B is a base of integers, **int** .*conv.* $\in B$, as well as $\in B$.*conv.* **int**. Then it is *safe* to insert a conversion of x_R at entry to a loop I if, along each path leading from that entry to any program exit, the first use of x has some representation R_1 such that R_1.*conv.* R. (This condition guarantees that if the inserted conversion to x_{R_1} were to fail, along each execution path some subsequent conversion (to x_R) would have failed anyway.)

To determine safety of conversion motion, we perform another preliminary data-flow analysis of the bitvectoring type, in which we determine the set of all split variables x_R which can safely appear at each program point. This analysis is rather similar to a standard live-variables analysis [1, 9] and can be handled by an interval-based elimination algorithm.

Once having carried out these analyses, we use their output in the following way: For each use of a split variable x_R we check whether x_R is already available at that point. If it is, no conversion or check is necessary; if it is not, a conversion of the form "$x_R := x_{R_1}$" is inserted, where R_1 is the disjunction of all representations R' such that $x_{R'}$ is available at the use of x_R.

It is important to note that the set of all program points at which there occur conversions to representations based on a base B is also the set of all points at which elements are added to B (by hashing operations). As noted in the beginning of this section, the execution frequency of these conversions is smaller (and for typical programs, substantially smaller) than the number of hashing operations which would have been required without the presence of B.

A comment on the complexity of our algorithm: Phases (a) and (c) are linear in the length n of the code. Phase (b) is almost linear in the number m of BFROM links, which for typical programs will be linear in n. Phase (d) is implemented as an interval-based bitvectoring data-flow analysis, so that its complexity is measurable in terms of the flow-graph parameters of the program; it is usually linear in these parameters. Thus, excluding phase (d), the overall complexity of our algorithm is of order $O(n + m\alpha(m))$, where α is an extremely slow-growing function (cf. [24] for details). This is comparable with the complexity of the fastest known general data-flow algorithms of Tarjan [22, 23] and Reif [13].

3.3 An Example

We now indicate the way in which our algorithm applies to the MINPATH program given earlier. For simplicity, we consider only the first section of the MINPATH program, which searches through the graph within which a path is sought.

The preliminary type analysis determines the types of the various objects appearing in this program. The graph nodes are given a general type in the absence of any specific declarations for the input objects. (In general, such declarations are very helpful and allow much more accurate type determination for all other objects; see [20] for an example.) The type finder can even detect that the ranges of the maps val and $cost$ consist of integers, by proper propagation of the type information from the initializing statements (3) and (4).

Phase (a) of the selection algorithm will then generate the following provisional based representations:

$graph_1, cost_1, x_1, y_1$: **general**;
$prev_2$:   **map** $(\in B_{21})$ $\in B_{22}$;[2]
val_3:   **map** $(\in B_{31})$ $\in B_{32}$;[2]
val_4:   **map** $(\in B_{41})$ $\in B_{42}$; x_4: $\in B_{41}$;
$newnodes_5$: **set** $(\in B_5)$; x_5: $\in B_5$;
$newnodes_6$: **set** $(\in B_6)$;
$newnodes_7$: **set** $(\in B_7)$; n_7: $\in B_7$;
$graph_8$:   **map** $(\in B_{81})$ $\in B_{82}$; n_8: $\in B_{81}$; m_8: $\in B_{82}$;

Instruction 9 of the MINPATH code expands into roughly the following sequence:

(91) $tcost := cost\{n\}$;
(92) $vcost := tcost(m)$;
(93) $vval := val(n)$;
(94) $newval := vval + vcost$;

and thus generates the following provisional representations:

$cost_{91}$: **map** $(\in B_{911})$ $\in B_{912}$; n_{91}: $\in B_{911}$; $tcost_{91}$: $\in B_{912}$;
$tcost_{92}$: **map** $(\in B_{921})$ $\in B_{922}$; m_{92}: $\in B_{921}$; $vcost_{92}$: $\in B_{922}$;
val_{93}:   **map** $(\in B_{931})$ $\in B_{932}$; n_{93}: $\in B_{931}$; $vval_{93}$: $\in B_{932}$;

(no bases are generated by instruction 94);

val_{10}: **map** $(\in B_{101})$ $\in B_{102}$; m_{10}: $\in B_{101}$; $newval_{10}$: **int**;
val_{11}: **map** $(\in B_{111})$ $\in B_{112}$; m_{11}: $\in B_{111}$; $newval_{11}$: $\in B_{112}$;
$prev_{12}$: **map** $(\in B_{121})$ $\in B_{122}$; m_{12}: $\in B_{121}$; n_{12}: $\in B_{122}$;
m_{13}, y_{13}: $\in B_{13}$;
$newnodes_{14}$: **set** $(\in B_{14})$; m_{14}: $\in B_{14}$;

Among the above bases, only B_{41}, B_5, B_{81}, B_{911}, B_{921}, B_{931}, B_{101}, B_{111}, B_{121}, and B_{14} are effective.

Phase (b) will perform the following merging and equivalencing: In view of the $prev_2$–$prev_{12}$ link, we equivalence B_{21} with B_{121} and B_{22} with B_{122}. In view of the val_3–val_4 link, we equivalence B_{31} with B_{41}, and B_{32} with B_{42}. In view of the x_4–x_5 link, B_{41} and B_5 are equivalenced, etc. Only one additional merge deserves extra comment, namely, the step which merges the representation of $tcost_{91}$ and $tcost_{92}$ and which belongs to case (2) of the general description of merging given above. This merge step causes us to set $EM(B_{912}) = $ **map** $(\in B_{921})$ $\in B_{922}$. The information thereby generated will be used by phase (c) to update representations containing $\in B_{912}$, which will turn out to be useless.

At the end of phase (b), the following equivalence classes of bases will have been formed:

$\hat{B}_1 = \{B_{912}\}$
$\hat{B}_2 = \{B_{922}\}$
$\hat{B}_3 = \{B_{32}, B_{42}, B_{932}, B_{102}, B_{112}\}$
$\hat{B}_4 = $ a class containing all the remaining bases,

with the following element nodes:

$EM(\hat{B}_1) = $ **map** $(\in \hat{B}_4)$ **int**
$EM(\hat{B}_2) = EM(\hat{B}_3) = $ **int**
$EM(\hat{B}_4) = $ **general** (i.e., general type, since no data type description for the nodes of the graph is provided).

Since only $\hat{B}_4$ is effective, the first three classes are useless. Phase (c) will thus eliminate any reference to bases in these classes; for example, the representation of $cost_{91}$ will be updated to

$$\text{\textbf{map} } (\in \hat{B}_4) \ \text{\textbf{map} } (\in \hat{B}_4) \ \text{\textbf{int}}.$$

As for $\hat{B}_3$, we simply replace the submode "$\in \hat{B}_3$" by "**int**", since, as is easily checked, $EM(\hat{B}_3) = $ **int** at the end of phase (b).

Phase (c) thus assigns the representations suggested in Section 2 to most of the occurrences of the variables $graph$, $cost$, $newnodes$, $prev$, val, x, y, m, and n. However, the occurrences $graph_1$, $cost_1$, x_1, and y_1 remain unbased. This causes phase (d) of our algorithm to split each of these variables into two symbol-table entries, a based one and an unbased one, and to insert four conversions from each of the unbased split variables to the corresponding based one before entering the **while** loop (but the conversion of x will precede instruction (4), as x_4 already has the based representation). The base $\hat{B}_4$ is built precisely at these places and then remains constant during execution of the remainder of the MINPATH program.

---

[2] The two decisions that make $prev_2$ and val_3 **map** rather than **set** follow from a special backward type propagation performed during the preceding type analysis which determines that these null values should be maps rather than sets.

4. CONCLUSION

We have presented an algorithm for the automatic generation of bases and the selection of based representations for objects appearing in a SETL program. The main advantage of this algorithm is that it can properly identify subcollections of the program's data as independent "universes" (bases) and describe the program objects in terms of their relationships to these "universes." It thus determines major features of representations to be used for the program objects but does not decide on finer representational details of the sort described in Section 2. Concerning such refinement of the coarse based representations selected by our algorithm, we note that a main goal of our algorithm is to speed up program execution by reducing the number of hashing operations performed by the program. Having achieved this optimization, we can expect a considerable speedup in the execution of the program. However, additional improvement is possible if we refine the based representations thereby selected, choosing suitable local, indexed, or sparse representation for based sets and maps. To choose refined data structures effectively may require frequency information, object size estimates, etc., which are unavailable during compile time (but cf. [11] for various interactive and run-time techniques which can help gather such information). Since our aim is to develop a fully automatic data-structuring technique, we abandon any attempt to collect and use such information and make do with a coarser and more modest approach, which can be summarized roughly as follows:

(1) If a based object A is iterated upon, choose the sparse representation for A.

(2) If not, but if A is involved in global set-theoretic operations, assigned to any variable, passed as a procedure parameter, incorporated into other objects, or used destructively in a manner requiring value copying, choose the indexed representation for A.

(3) In all other cases, A can have local representation.

The algorithm described in this paper has been implemented as the major phase of the SETL optimizer. It has been tested on several programs (including MINPATH) and has produced very satisfactory results. This implementation and experience are reported in [20].

ACKNOWLEDGMENTS

We take this opportunity to thank some other members of the SETL project at New York University, namely, Robert B. K. Dewar, Ssu-Cheng Liu, and Arthur Grand, for numerous suggestions concerning automatic data-structure selection. In particular, our work has been greatly influenced by earlier work by Liu [10].

REFERENCES

(Note. Reference [17] is not cited in the text.)

1. AHO, A.V., AND ULLMAN, J.D. *Principles of Compiler Design*. Addison-Wesley, Reading, Mass., 1977.
2. ALLEN, F.E. Control flow analysis. In Proc. Symp. Compiler Optimization, *SIGPLAN Notices 5* (1970), 1–19.
3. BALZER, R.M. Dataless programming. In *Proc. 1967 AFIPS Fall Joint Computer Conf.*, Thompson Books, Washington, D.C., pp. 535–544.
4. DEWAR, R.B.K. The SETL programming language. To appear.
5. DEWAR, R.B.K., GRAND, A., LIU, S.-C., SCHWARTZ, J.T., AND SCHONBERG, E. Programming by refinement, as exemplified by the SETL representation sublanguage. *ACM Trans. Program. Lang. Syst. 1*, 1 (July 1979), 27–49.
6. d'IMPERIO, M.E. Data structures and their representation in storage. *Annu. Rev. Autom. Program. 5* (1969), 1–76.
7. EARLEY, J. Toward an understanding of data structures. *Commun. ACM 14*, 10 (Oct. 1971), 617–627.
8. HALSTEAD, M.H. *Elements of Software Science*. Elsevier North-Holland, New York, 1977.
9. HECHT, M.S. *Flow Analysis of Computer Programs*. Elsevier North-Holland, New York, 1977.
10. LIU, S.C. Data-Structure Choice. Ph.D. Dissertation, Courant Inst. Mathematical Sciences, New York, 1979.
11. LOW, J.R. Automatic data structure selection: An example and overview. *Commun. ACM 21*, 5 (May 1978), 376–385.
12. MEALY, G.H. Another look at data. In *Proc. 1967 AFIPS Fall Joint Computer Conf.*, Thompson Books, Washington, D.C., pp. 525–534.
13. REIF, J.H. Combinatorial Aspects of Symbolic Program Analysis. Ph.D. Dissertation, Harvard Univ., Cambridge, Mass., 1977.
14. SCHONBERG, E., AND LIU, S.C. Manual and automatic data-structuring in SETL. In Proc. 5th Ann. Informal Implementors Interchange Conf., Guidel, France, 1977, pp. 284–304.
15. SCHONBERG, E., SCHWARTZ, J.T., AND SHARIR, M. Automatic data structure selection in SETL. In Conf. Rec., 6th Ann. ACM Symp. on Principles of Programming Languages, San Antonio, Texas, Jan. 29–31, 1979, pp. 197–210.
16. SCHWARTZ, J.T. Automatic data structure choice in a language of very high level. In Conf. Rec., 2d ACM Symp. on Principles of Programming Languages, Palo Alto, Calif., Jan. 20–22, 1975, pp. 36–40.
17. SCHWARTZ, J.T. On programming: An interim report on the SETL project, 2d ed. Courant Inst. Mathematical Sciences, New York, 1975.
18. SCHWARTZ, J.T. Use-use chaining as a technique in typefinding. *SETL Newsl.* 140, Courant Inst. Mathematical Sciences, New York, 1974.
19. SCHWARTZ, J.T., AND SHARIR, M. A design for optimizations of the bitvectoring class. Courant Computer Science Rep. No. 17, Courant Inst. Mathematical Sciences, New York, 1979.
20. SCHWARTZ, J.T., AND SHARIR, M. Experience with automatic data structure selection in the SETL system. Presented at 2d Program Transformation Workshop, Harvard Univ., Cambridge, Mass., Sept. 1979.
21. SENKO, M., ALTMAN, E., ASTRAHAN, M., AND FEHDER, P. Data structures and accessing in data base systems. *IBM Syst. J. 12* (1973), 30–93.
22. TARJAN, R.E. Fast algorithms for solving path problems. *J. ACM 28*, 3 (July 1981), to appear.
23. TARJAN, R.E. A unified approach to path problems. *J. ACM 28*, 3 (July 1981), to appear.
24. TARJAN, R.E. Efficiency of a good but not linear set union algorithm. *J. ACM 22*, 2 (April 1975), 215–225.
25. TENENBAUM, A.M. Type determination for very high level languages. Courant Computer Science Rep. No. 3, Courant Inst. Mathematical Sciences, New York, 1974.

Received February 1979; revised October 1980; accepted November 1980

Automating the Selection of Implementation Structures

LAWRENCE A. ROWE AND FRED M. TONGE

Abstract—An approach to automating the selection of implementations for the data representations used in a program is presented. Formalisms are developed for specifying data representations and implementation structures. Using these formalisms, algorithms are presented which will recognize the use in a program of known data representations (e.g., stacks, queues, lists, arrays, etc.) so that alternative implementations can be retrieved from a library and which will, for those representations not recognized, generate alternative implementations with a wide range of space–time tradeoffs. Experience with using these algorithms indicates they are reasonably successful, although there are several problems that must be solved before automatic implementation selection systems will be practical.

Index Terms—Data representations, data structures, implementation structure selection, modeling structures, modeling-structure recognition.

I. INTRODUCTION

A PROGRAMMER makes many decisions when designing and implementing a computer program that dictate how efficiently the program will execute. In this paper, work is presented on the development of a system for automating

Manuscript January 6, 1978; revised March 1, 1978.

L. A. Rowe was with the Department of Information and Computer Science, University of California, Irvine, CA 92717. He is now with the Computer Science Division, Department of Electrical Engineering and Computer Sciences, University of California, Berkeley, CA 94720.

F. M. Tonge is with the Department of Information and Computer Science, University of California, Irvine, CA 92717.

part of this decision-making process, followed by an evaluation of the potential of such systems.

During program development, decisions are made on the choice of data representations and the operations on those representations that comprise the algorithm for solving a given problem. In some cases, this choice requires that an appropriate algorithm already has been selected. Data representations may be chosen before, during, or after an algorithm is selected, and evidence exists that this choice has been made successfully at each of these times. The time at which the choice is made appears to depend on many factors including: the problem domain, the experience of the programmer, and the context within which the program is being developed. In any case, it makes little difference here because the system under consideration comes into play only after both the data representation and algorithm are chosen.

The choice among data representations is influenced by data relationships intrinsic to the problem (*problem structures*) and by their possible implementation in a computer (*implementation structures*). Often, in the process of devising data representations, various intermediate structures are used to model problem structures. These intermediate structures are suitable for analysis and expression of data representations and consequently are independent of specific implementation commitments. After D'Imperio, we call such structures *modeling structures* [5].

Our view of the programming process is that problem struc-

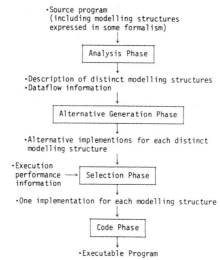

•Source program
(including modelling structures
expressed in some formalism)

Analysis Phase

•Description of distinct modelling structures
•Dataflow information

Alternative Generation Phase

•Alternative implementions for each distinct
modelling structure

•Execution
performance ⟶ Selection Phase
information

•One implementation for each modelling structure

Code Phase

•Executable Program

Fig. 1. Components of an implementation-structure selection system.

tures are reduced to implementation structures utilizing one or more layers of modeling structures. For example, to list a collection of items with a partial order defined on the collection in topological order (an item appears in the list before all items following it in the partial ordering), one might use the concept of a directed graph, where vertices correspond to items and edges correspond to the partial ordering between items. A computer program that finds such a list might represent the directed graph internally using "nodes" and "pointers." In this case, "collection of items" and "partial ordering" are problem structures, a "directed graph" with "vertices" and "edges" is a modeling structure, and "nodes" and "pointers" suggest an implementation structure. Modeling structures are independent of the problem domain (e.g., graphs are used for modeling programs when doing code optimization) and of commitments to underlying implementation (e.g., the topological sort program could use integers and an adjacency matrix to implement the graph).

Most programming languages provide features for describing implementation structures. Therefore, when writing a program, a programmer must choose both modeling and implementation structures. Research in data abstraction [1], [3], [4], [8], [9] [13], [22] has shown that separating abstract specification from implementation makes programs easier to understand, easier to show correct (either by formal proof or by testing), and more convenient for change of implementations. A natural extension of this work is to write programs in terms of modeling structures and to automate the selection of implementations. It must be emphasized that our concern is with choosing implementations that meet a specified efficiency criterion, given an appropriate modeling structure and not with how the modeling structure is chosen. In other words, we are concerned with the mapping from modeling to implementation structure and not the mapping from problem to modeling structure.

The principle components of the system, along with their inputs and outputs, are shown in Fig. 1. In the analysis phase,

the set of distinct modeling structures and information about their use are collected. Following this, alternative implementations for each modeling structure are generated. The selection phase takes this set of alternatives and, with predicted execution performance data, selects one implementation for each modeling structure which optimizes the given performance constraints. These constraints are expressed in terms of execution space and time. Finally, the code phase generates an executable program that implements the source program.

This paper presents formalisms for describing modeling and implementation structures and an algorithm for the alternative generation phase. The analysis and code phases are straightforward. The selection phase is complicated by the need for performance information. Obvious sources for this information are the programmer, automatic analysis programs, and sample executions. In practice, information given by programmers is highly unreliable [12] and automatic analysis is currently unable to handle complex programs. Thus we believe sample execution information will be the most useful in the near future. The collection and use of such information is not well understood and warrants more research. Nevertheless, a selection algorithm based on branch and bound searching given such information is discussed elsewhere [21].

The proposed system incorporates modeling and implementation structure formalisms. The modeling structure formalism provides the specification language a programmer uses to describe the chosen data representation. In this paper, we concentrate on the semantics of this formalism, as opposed to how it would be embedded into a new or existing programming language.

Any formalism must allow for the convenient description of a wide variety of structures. Thus a formalism based on a small fixed set of data structures, as suggested in [1], is unlikely to handle conveniently the variety of program structures found in complex program solving.

Liskov and Zilles survey five classes of specification languages ranging from less abstract methods based on a fixed domain of formal objects to more abstract methods based on algebraic relations [13]. Less abstraction generally means more representational detail is included in the specification of a structure, implying limitations on the range of possible implementations. Some researchers argue that because of this and because the more abstract methods explicitly represent relations between operations on data structures, data specifications should use the more abstract techniques.

However, because of the kind of detailed information needed to make intelligent choices among alternative implementation structures, we chose to use a specification technique that moves some of the invariant properties of the data structure from the description of operations into a "structure" description. Some examples of the information needed to choose implementations are as follows.

1) Whether an operator modifies one of its arguments or makes a copy of the argument and only modifies the copy.

2) Whether an operator modifies the membership relation between its arguments (i.e., does an operator insert or delete an entity from a structure?).

3) Whether an access to a structure is restricted (e.g., root of a tree or top of a stack).

4) Whether an entity can be a member of more than one structure at a time.

This kind of information is difficult to infer mechanically from a program-level description using either a more abstract specification technique (unless additional conventions on the interpretation of the specifications are made or supplementary information is included with the specification)[1] or a less abstract specification technique (e.g., a PL/1, ECL, or PPL program level description).

In any case, a library of commonly used modeling structures (e.g., stacks, trees, queues, and graphs) will undoubtedly be provided to the programmer. Alternative implementations are associated with each structure in the library. Systems for retrieving implementations from such a library for named modeling structures have been investigated previously [7], [15]. In the remainder of this paper, formalisms and algorithms are described for generating alternative modeling-structure implementations not selected by name from a library.

There are three steps to the generation of alternative implementations. In the first step, modeling-structure descriptions collected during the analysis phase are matched with the modeling-structure library. If a match occurs, alternative implementations from the library are used. This might happen if a programmer does not know about an appropriate modeling structure or does not realize that the structure being used is available in the library. The second step in the process is to generate alternative implementations for those structures not found in the library. Finally, an algorithm is needed to combine implementations in those cases where one modeling structure may be a member of another (e.g., a set of trees).

Since the completion of the work reported here, other approaches to related problems in implementation structure selection have been reported [11], [16], [17]. Because our work is similar in concept to that of Rosenschein and Katz, the same problem of joining together operation descriptions arises. This problem has not been solved and until it is implementation selection systems will require considerable human interaction.

In the next section the modeling- and implementation-structure formalisms are presented. The third section describes the generation of alternative implementation structures, including the modeling-structure library, the generate alternatives algorithm (called GENALT), and the process of combining implementations. Lastly, conclusions are presented with a discussion of the future prospects for automatic implementation selection. A complete system embodying the approach discussed here has not been implemented. However, the algorithms discussed have been implemented and the examples presented were generated by this implementation.

II. FORMALISMS

In this section, descriptions and examples are given of a modeling structure formalism for specifying data representations and an implementation structure formalism for specifying implementations for these data representations.

A. Modeling-Structure Formalism

Two goals for this formalism are: 1) it must be possible to represent commonly used structures (e.g., sets, graphs, trees, arrays, and stacks), and 2) the information needed to generate alternative implementations must be easily obtained from a program written in some language which uses the formalism to specify data representations. To illustrate these two points, consider the following structures: a one-dimensional array, a stack, and a binary tree. Arrays are often described by a mapping from the integers to a collection of entities (the elements of the array) where the mapping is a function [9]. Another way to look at this is that there are a collection of named slots capable of holding a value. The salient characteristics are that these slots be named by the integers (we call this "element number selection") and that only two operations can be performed on the structure: reference the value in a slot (read) and replace a value in a slot (assign).

A stack is a collection of entities with a relation between the entities that represents the order in which they were entered. This relation controls which single entity can be referenced (typically called the "stack top") and which entity will become the stack top if the current one is removed from the structure. This example illustrates several important features: explicit relations between elements of a structure, limitations on the operations that can be performed on a structure (delete and read an element may access only stack top), and implicit updating of the distinguished-element stack top.

The third example structure is a binary tree. A binary tree is a collection of elements, one of which is a distinguished element called the "root," with three relations defined: left, right, and ancestor. Each element has left- and right-related elements (the descendants) and a single ancestor. Because any element in a binary tree may be accessed, pointers, or external accesses to elements, are needed.

Formal specifications of these structures are given after the formalism description.

---

[1] This relates to the more general question of whether a uniform specification technique is used for the entire program development cycle in which later stages merely add more detail or whether different specification techniques are used in the different stages.

A modeling structure is defined by six properties involving its component elements, relations between elements, and operations upon them. These properties are described below.

1) Replication: Values in a structure may or may not be duplicated. For example, in sets there is no replication, while the examples just discussed allow replication.

2) Ordering: Elements in a structure may be linearly ordered by a specified predicate, this ordering being preserved by operations on the structure. For example, a collection of integers may be ordered by "less than." In practice, the maintenance of such an ordering is useful when later processing time can be decreased by matching the ordering of the elements in a structure to the order in which they are to be processed.

3) Relations: Elements in a structure may be structurally related by one or more named relations, each characterized by the following properties.

a) Degree—A relation is one-one (one element is related to only one other element), one-many (one element to many elements), many-one (many elements to one element), or many-many (many elements to many elements).

b) Scope of Domain—May be total (all elements are in the domain of the relation), unique (all but a single unique element is included), or partial (none or more elements are included).

c) Scope of Range—Same possibilities as domain (i.e., total, unique, or partial range).

d) Connected—A relation may be connected or not connected. A connected relation is one whose transitive closure and the transitive closure of its implied algebraic inverse is equal to the set of elements in the structure. Intuitively, a connected relation means there are no isolated components.

e) Reflexive—A relation may or may not be reflexive.

f) Symmetric—A relation may or may not be symmetric.

To specify a relation, all of these properties must be given for the relation. For example, the relation for representing a stack is one-one, unique domain, unique range, connected, not reflexive, and not symmetric. Using directed arcs to represent a relation between two elements, this relation would be pictured as

$$\cdot \rightarrow \cdot \rightarrow \cdot \rightarrow \cdots \rightarrow \cdot$$

Notice that the relation is unique domain (i.e., only one vertex does not have an arc emanating from it) and unique range (i.e., only one vertex does not have an arc entering it). A specific relation between two elements may have a value stored with it (called its "attribute"). This is useful for representing problems such as finding the shortest path between two nodes in a network where there is a distance associated with an arc between nodes.

4) Distinguished Element: One or more distinguished elements may be defined by predicates, typically upon the relations of a structure. Distinguished elements refer to that single element in the structure, if any, which satisfies the predicate. For example, the root of a binary tree is defined to be that element having no ancestor.

5) Referencing Methods: Elements in a structure may be referenced by some or all of the following access methods.

a) Distinguished Element—At the time of reference, that

```
Stack:    replication;
          no ordering;
          relations:  NEXT (1-1, unique domain, unique range, connected,
                            not symmetric, not reflexive);
          distinguished elements: (element such that NEXT(STACKTOP) is
                            undefined);
          referencing: distinguished element;
          operations: read(STACKTOP),
                      delete(STACKTOP,S),
                      relate(S,[<STACKTOP,NEXT,E>]);

Array:    replication;
          no ordering;
          relations: none;
          distinguished element: none;
          referencing: element number selection (n-dimensional);
          operations: read(E),
                      assign(E,E);

Binary Tree:
          replication;
          no ordering;
          relations: LEFT (1-1, partial domain, partial range, not connected,
                           not symmetric, not reflexive),
                     RIGHT (1,1, partial domain, partial range, not
                           connected, not symmetric, not reflexive),
                     ANCS (many-1, unique domain, partial range, connected,
                           not symmetric, not reflexive),
                     ANCS is (LEFT⁻¹ ∪ RIGHT⁻¹)

          distinguished elements: (element such that ANCS(ROOT) is undefined);
          referencing: distinguished element, external access;
          operations: read(E),
                      delete(E,S),
                      replace(E,E,S),
                      create-an-access(E,S),
                      relate(S,[<E,R,E>]),
                      related(E,S,R);
```

Fig. 2. Examples of modeling-structure definitions.

element satisfying the distinguished-element predicate is accessed.

b) External Access—A pointer refers to an element in a structure. An external access is restricted to a particular structure.

c) Selection—Individual elements may be named, either by numbers (element number selection), as shown by the array example, or by names (name selection) similar to Pascal records [10].

d) Quantification—Either universal quantification (e.g., <u>forall</u> x <u>in</u> structure <u>do</u> · · ·) or existential quantification (e.g., <u>first</u> x <u>in</u> structure <u>then</u> · · · <u>else</u> · · ·, as proposed for Alphard [20]) are allowed.

6) Operations: A structure may be operated upon by one or more of the following operations:

a) <u>read</u> the value of an element;
b) <u>replace</u> an element with another;
c) <u>insert</u> an element;
d) <u>delete</u> an element;
e) <u>assign</u> a value to an element;
f) <u>relate</u> two elements by a particular relation (implies insertion if either or both entities are not elements of the structure);
g) <u>unrelate</u> two elements;
h) find the element(s) <u>related</u> to an element by a particular relation;
i) <u>read-attribute</u> value of a relation;
j) <u>store-attribute</u> value of a relation; and
k) <u>create-an-access</u> to an element.

Parameters to these operations may be limited to specific elements. In a stack, for example, the only element that can be <u>read</u> is the distinguished-element stack top. A brief definition of each operation is given in the Appendix.

7) Examples and Discussion: Formal specifications for an array, stack, and binary tree are shown in Fig. 2.

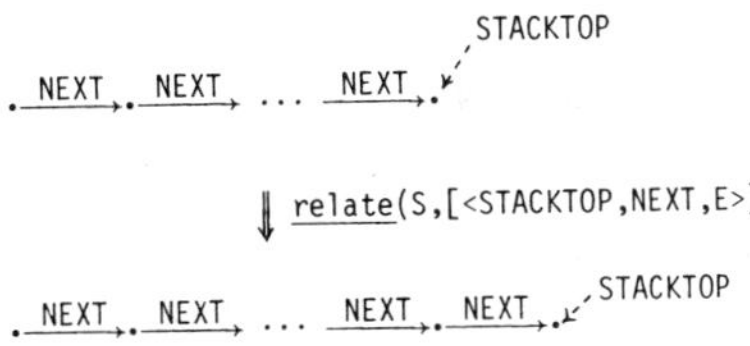

STACKTOP

.NEXT, NEXT ... NEXT, ↙

⬇ relate(S,[<STACKTOP,NEXT,E>])

.NEXT, NEXT ... NEXT, NEXT, ↙ STACKTOP

Fig. 3. Example of inserting an element into a stack.

```
begin
            {define modelling structures}
  declare
     A: (elements: char, noreplication,
         relations:
         SUC(many-many, partialdomain, partialrange, notconnected,
             notreflexive, notsymmetric)),
     x,s1,s2: char;

            {read related pairs}

  while not(eof(input))
     do begin
           read(input,s1,s2); {s2 follows s1}
           if s1 ≠ s2 then
              relate[SUC(s2) = s1] in A;
        end;
            {Remove maximal elements from A until it is empty or
             a cycle exists}

  while size(A) ≠ Ø do
     first x in A such that size(related(x,SUC)) = Ø
     then begin{found one}
        write(output,x);
        delete x from A
        end
     else begin {cycle exists in data}
        write(output, "cycle in data");
        stop
        end;

  end {Topological Sort}
```

Fig. 4. Topological sort program.

These definitions are arbitrary in that there are no generally agreed upon precise definitions for these modeling structures. Furthermore, there are many ways to capture the same abstract behavior in this formalism. The examples show how the salient characteristics discussed informally above are expressed in the formalism. The domain of each argument is either restricted to a particular value (as in the stack example where operations are restricted to the specified distinguished element) or is specified by the symbols for an arbitrary structure (S), relation (R), or entity (E).

In the specification of a stack, read and delete operations are restricted to the distinguished element STACKTOP. Note that relate only inserts a new element after the current STACKTOP and that after this operation the new element is the one that satisfies the predicate defining STACKTOP. This is shown pictorially in Fig. 3.

In the specification of a binary tree, the properties of the relations LEFT, RIGHT, and ANCS insure that there are no cycles and that each element has a unique ancestor. In this specification there is no restriction on the arguments to the operations.

sponding modeling-structure property description is used

<replication, ordering, relations, distinguished elements, referencing, operations>

where

replication   is rep or norep;
ordering   is ord or noord;
relations   is a set of seven-tuples, one for each relation, of the form <name of relation, degree, domain scope, range scope, connectedness, reflexivity, symmetry>;
distinguished elements   is a set of distinguished-element descriptions, a two-tuple giving the name and defining predicate;
referencing   is a set of referencing forms, taken from distElem, extAcc, nameSelect, elemNo, existQuant, and univQuant;
operations   is a set of operations.

For example, the stack described previously is denoted

<rep, noord, {<"NEXT", 1-1, udom, uran, conn, noref, nosym>}, {<"STACKTOP", undef("NEXT"("STACKTOP"))>},{distElem}, {read("STACKTOP"), delete("STACKTOP",s), relate(s,[<"STACKTOP","NEXT",E>])}>

A shorter notation is used in the remainder of the paper to specify a modeling structure. A six-tuple giving the corre-

Fig. 4 shows a program which prints a topological order for a set of related input items (in this case characters). A single modeling structure, bound to the variable A, with a relation named SUC, is declared. After a pair of characters are read, they are inserted into A (if not already members of the structure) and related by the operation

relate [SUC(s2) = s1] in A

The fact that A is declared *noreplication* insures that only one instance of a given character will be inserted. Size is a predefined function that returns a count of the number of elements in a structure. The *first*-statement is used to express the search for an element with no successors. Related(x, y) returns a set of elements related to x by relation y (x and y must refer to the same structure, i.e., x must be an element of a structure with a relation y defined).

The modeling-structure description for the structure bound to *A* is

$$\langle \underline{norep}, \underline{noord}, \{\langle \text{``SUC''}, \underline{many\text{-}many}, \underline{pdom}, \underline{pran}, \underline{noconn}, \underline{noref}, \underline{nosym}\rangle\},$$
$$\phi, \{\underline{existQuant}\}, \{\underline{relate}(\text{S},[\langle \text{E},\text{``SUC''},\text{E}\rangle]), \underline{related}(\text{E},\text{S},\text{``SUC''}),$$
$$delete(\text{E},\text{S})\}\rangle$$

B. Implementation-Structure Formalism

The implementation-structure formalism is used to describe implementations for a modeling structure at the level of main storage as addressed in assembly language.

An *implementation structure* is described by an arrangement of storage locations into a *storage structure*, *correspondences* between components of that storage structure and the modeling structure it implements, and *procedures* for operating upon the storage structure. These latter two are called an *interpretation* of the storage structure.

Storage structures are composed of *cells* (holding primitive values) and/or *groupings* of cells and storage structures. Groupings may be on the basis of *contiguity* (indexing and other forms of address arithmetic), *explicit linkage* (pointers), or *structure defining functions* (association and hashing).

A particular storage structure may have several possible interpretations, each representing the implementation of a different modeling structure.

An implementation structure, then, is defined by eight categories of information. These categories are described in the next sections followed by examples of implementation structures.

1) Storage Structure: Storage structures are composed of cells capable of representing primitive values. Storage-structure composition is expressed in the following syntactic notation. Given two entities (cells or compositions of cells), named e and f, there are three operators for composing them:

e + f   e and f appear contiguously in memory;
e @ f   e is linked to f;
e ? f   there exists a structure-defining function on e (based either on e's content or address, not specified here) which yields f's address.

Multiple instances of an entity are expressed by

n(e)   n distinct instances of e;
#(e)   an indeterminate number of instances of e.

A composition operator can be distributed over a collection of entity instances by

$$e \; op \; e \; op \cdots op \; e = \#(e)/op$$

Entities can be named, for example,

g: n(f)/+

names an entity g which is composed of n contiguous instances of f. For convenience, particular operators can be indexed (this is necessary for describing interpretations).

The linking operator (@) and associative operator (?) also serve as unary operators denoting a pointer or an associative link to an entity. For example, "@e" means a pointer to an e, implying that storage for a pointer is allocated.

There are two special symbols: one for describing a cell (labeled a "cell") and one describing a Boolean flag (labeled a "tag").

2) Relations: For each relation implemented, the following are given: the name of the corresponding modeling-structure relation (if any), Boolean flags indicating whether or not the relation is explicitly defined in the modeling structure (or implied by the need to maintain order, for example), whether the structure is ordered on this relation or not and whether or not for relations implemented by explicit links (@ in the storage structure) a head element is maintained, and finally a symbolic representation of the procedure for accessing related element(s) given an element. Thus there is for each relation a tuple of the form:

$$\langle name, explicit\text{-}flag, order\text{-}flag, head\text{-}flag, access\text{-}procedure\rangle.$$

3) Structure-Defining Functions: For each function, a procedure is given for finding the associated entity (i.e., the code for ? in the storage structure).

4) Order: A field indicating whether the implementation structure is unordered (norder), ordered at insertion (order), or ordered at access (sort).

5) Sizes: For each indeterminate size operator (#), a bounding value.

6) Elements: A field indicating whether actual values are stored (value) or pointers to values (pointer). For modeling structures referenced by name selection, an indicator is maintained for each separate field.

7) Descriptor: A set of symbols indicating which components of a run-time descriptor, if any, are to be generated. Examples of descriptor components are: type—generate run-time type information; insertFlag—generate a Boolean flag indicating whether an element has been inserted since the structure was last ordered, needed only if order is maintained by sort; extAcc, elemNo and distElem—generate run-time data needed to process external access, element number, and distinguished-element referencing (e.g., array descriptors for elemNo); and explicitSize—maintain explicit count of the number of elements in the structure.

8) Operations: Code generators for necessary operations, both those specified in the modeling structure and other

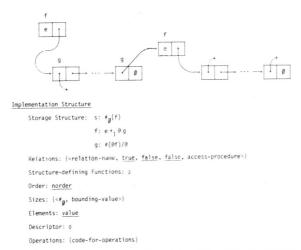

Implementation Structure

Storage Structure: s: $\#_\emptyset(f)$

f: $e +_1 @ g$

g: $\#(@f)/@$

Relations: {<relation-name, <u>true</u>, <u>false</u>, <u>false</u>, access-procedure>}

Structure-defining Functions: ◇

Order: <u>norder</u>

Sizes: {<$\#_\emptyset$, bounding-value>}

Elements: <u>value</u>

Descriptor: ◇

Operations: {code-for-operations}

Fig. 5. Explicit link from each element to a linked list of pointers to related elements.

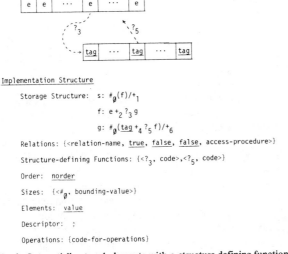

Implementation Structure

Storage Structure: s: $\#_\emptyset(f)/+_1$

f: $e +_2 ?_3 g$

g: $\#_\emptyset(\underline{tag} +_4 ?_5 f)/+_6$

Relations: {<relation-name, <u>true</u>, <u>false</u>, <u>false</u>, access-procedure>}

Structure-defining Functions: {<$?_3$, code>,<$?_5$, code>}

Order: <u>norder</u>

Sizes: {<$\#_\emptyset$, bounding-value>}

Elements: <u>value</u>

Descriptor: :

Operations: {code-for-operations}

Fig. 6. Sequentially stored elements with a structure-defining function to a Boolean adjacency vector.

primitive actions associated with an implementation (e.g., space allocation).

9) Examples and Discussion: Two examples of implementation structures are given in Figs. 5 and 6, together with informal diagrams of each structure. These examples are implementations of an unordered modeling structure with a single many–many relation.

In the first example, each element is stored independently together with a link to a list of pointers to related elements. The end of a list is represented by a null pointer, ∅.

In the second example, the elements are stored consecutively, and with each is associated (by structure-defining function $?_3$) a Boolean adjacency vector (one row of an adjacency matrix). Tag fields in the vector are associated back (by function $?_5$) to related elements. The storage-defining functions require no additional space in the storage structure.

In both examples, the flag fields in the relation tuple indicate that the relation is explicitly specified in the modeling structure, that the structure is not ordered on that relation, and that no list head for the relation need be maintained. In both implementations, no run-time descriptor is required.

III. ALTERNATIVE IMPLEMENTATION-STRUCTURE GENERATION

Given a modeling structure description derived from a program, this section describes how alternative implementations are generated either by matching the description with an entry in the modeling-structure library or by the GENALT algorithm.

During the execution of a program many distinct objects are created. For example, in the program segment

<u>while</u> <Boolean expression>
<u>do begin</u>
    ...
    x ← "create object";
    ...
<u>end</u>

each iteration of the loop creates a distinct object. Each of these objects will use the same implementation structure (that is, will be a particular instance of the same implementation). The set of distinct modeling structures in a program for which implementations must be generated is the set of lexical points at which objects are created.

A modeling structure description (as presented in Section II-A) is derived for each distinct structure during the analysis phase. Information is collected about the static properties of the structure from the type definition (i.e., replication, ordering, distinguished elements, and relations) and dynamic properties from the other part of the program (i.e., referencing mechanisms and operations).[2] One feature of the information-gathering strategy embodies an important aspect of the recog-

[2] We assume that the modeling-structure formalism is embedded in a strongly typed language.

```
<sequence,
 <rep,ord,φ,φ,{elemNo,existQuant,univQuant},
  {read(E),insert(E,S),delete(E,S),replace(E,E,S)}>,
 {implementations}>
<orderedSet,
 <norep,ord,φ,φ,{elemNo,existQuant,univQuant},
  {read(E),insert(E,S),delete(E,S),replace(E,E,S)}>,
 {implementations}>
<bag,
 <rep,noord,φ,φ,{existQuant,univQuant},
  {read(E),insert(E,S),delete(E,S),replace(E,E,S)}>,
 {implementations}>
<set,
 <norep,noord,φ,φ,{existQuant,univQuant},
  {read(E),insert(E,S),delete(E,S),replace(E,E,S)}>,
 {implementations}>
```

Fig. 7. Descriptions in modeling-structure library.

nition process. For many structures, constraints on arguments to the operations or limitations on which elements in a structure can be referenced are essential identifying characteristics. A stack illustrates this point very nicely. Note in the stack description given in Fig. 2 that arguments to each of the operations are constrained. This requires that the information-gathering process retains the actual argument in some cases while substituting an indicator that any argument is allowed (or used) in other cases. This is accomplished by substituting an "any argument" indicator (S, R, or E as noted earlier) in all cases except where a distinguished element or a relation name is used, in which case the identifier is substituted. For example, if the operation is 'DELETE TOP FROM X', and TOP is not a distinguished element, the operation delete(E,S) is included as an operation performed on the modeling structure. By contrast, if TOP is a distinguished element, delete("TOP",S) is included. Here the definition of the formalism and the mechanical recognition process are closely matched.

A. Modeling-Structure Library and Matching Algorithm

Each entry in the modeling-structure library is composed of a structure name, a description of the modeling structure, and alternative implementation structures. Modeling-structure descriptions are of the form described near the end of Section II-A-7. Several additional examples of library descriptions are given in Fig. 7. Alternative implementation structures are represented as described in the previous section.

A typical library might contain entries for, among others, modeling structures such as: array, vector, tuple, bag, sequence, ordered set, set, graph, digraph, tree, binary tree, 2-way list, 1-way list, dequeue, queue, stack, 2-way ring, and 1-way ring.

Modeling-structure descriptions derived from the program being implemented are matched with library entries, and all alternative implementations associated with successful matches provide possible implementation structures for the modeling structure under consideration.

Matching of derived descriptions (i.e., those deduced from a program) to library descriptions requires an exact match of the replication and ordering fields, and an exact match (up to renaming) of the sets composing the relations, distinguished elements, referencing methods, and operations fields in the derived description with a subset of the corresponding fields in the library description. (In some cases, a matching library description may be eliminated as being covered by other matching descriptions; e.g., if both 2-way and 1-way lists matched, only the 1-way list might be retained.)

An analysis of the number and property values of library entries in a particular case would indicate whether match efficiency could be increased by an organization more elaborate than a simple set of entries.

B. Generate Alternatives

In this section, an algorithm is presented for generating alternative implementations for a structure that is not covered by any entry in the modeling-structure library. Implementations are generated by focusing on the relations defined for a structure (a relation is added for structures without an explicitly defined relation). For each relation, alternative implementations for a modeling structure with just that relation are retrieved from a library of one-relation implementations. (Note: This is not the modeling-structure library; it is a small data base of implementations used by this algorithm.) Assuming the modeling structure has n relations, n one-relation implementations are joined together to form an n-relation implementation. After a set of alternative n-relation implementations are produced, other properties of the modeling structure (e.g., ordering, replication, and referencing) cause implementations to be changed, added, and removed from the set of alternatives.

An *enumeration relation* traverses, or enumerates, all elements in a modeling structure. Many implementations for modeling structures require that there be an enumeration relation. For example, enumeration is often required in implementations for structures with universal quantification (to generate all elements) or when an ordering predicate is specified (to represent the ordering between elements). Some implementations do not require an enumeration relation. The GENALT algorithm decides whether an enumeration relation is necessary based on the modeling-structure properties.

For those structures that require enumeration there may be an explicitly defined relation that can be used as the enumeration relation. In other cases, the relation is specified indirectly in the form of an ordering predicate. In these cases, an additional relation (1-1, unique domain and range, connected, not reflexive, and not symmetric), called an *assumed relation*, is added to the modeling-structure description. Fig. 8 shows the GENALT algorithm. The essential step in the algorithm is the call on the GEN procedure in step 3.0 which retrieves one-relation implementations from the implementation library and joins them together. The retrieval operation is straightforward. For each relation in the structure, a set of alternative implementations is retrieved based on the relation properties (i.e., mapping degree, domain and range scope, connectivity, reflexivity, and symmetry). Each alternative is checked for consistency with other requirements of the modeling structure (e.g., operations performed on the modeling structure must be defined for the implementation). These one-relation implementations are then joined together by repeated application of the operator JOIN(X,Y), where X and Y are implementa-

```
          GENerate ALTernatives (GENALT).  This algorithm generates implementations
          for a modelling structure (MS).  Relations(MS), references(MS), and operations(MS)
          are the sets of relations, references, and operations, respectively, defined
          for or performed on the modelling structure.  For an implementation x, order(x)
          and descriptor(x) are the order field and descriptor set of the implementation
          description.  ALT_IMP_STRUX is the set of alternative implementations generated.

     1.0  [Initialize.]  Let ALT_IMP_STRUX ← φ and
          ASSUMED_REL ← <"",1-1,udom,uran,conn,noref,nosym>.

     2.0  [Add assumed relation.]  If an enumeration relation is required and either
          MS is ordered or an enumeration relation does not exist, insert ASSUMED_REL
          into relations(MS).

     3.0  [Look up and join alternatives from the implementation library.]
          ALT_IMP_STRUX ← GEN(MS).

     4.0  [Add ordered implementations if no replication or existential referencing.]
          If MS not ordered and either no replication or existential referencing,
          for each x ∈ ALT_IMP_STRUX do
          4.1  Let y be a copy of x.
          4.2  Let order(y) ← order and order-flag for the assumed relation in y
               be true.
          4.3  Insert y into ALT_IMP_STRUX.

     5.0  [If the structure is ordered, add two cases for each implementation --
          sorted and implicit.]  If MS ordered, for each x ∈ ALT_IMP_STRUX do
          5.1  Let order(x) ← sort and order-flag for the assumed relation in x
               be true.
          5.2  Let y be a copy of x.
          5.3  Let order(y) ← sort.

          5.4  Insert insertFlag into descriptor(y).
          5.5  Insert y into ALT_IMP_STRUX.

     6.0  [Mark descriptor for distinguished element, external access, or element
          number referencing.]  If distElem, extAcc, or elemNo ∈ references(MS),
          insert it into descriptor(x) for each x ∈ ALT_IMP_STRUX.

     7.0  [Add explicit size.]  If size ∈ operations(MS), then for each
          x ∈ ALT_IMP_STRUX do
          7.1  Let y be a copy of x.
          7.2  Insert explicitSize into descriptor(y).
          7.3  Insert y into ALT_IMP_STRUX.

     8.0  [Done.]  Algorithm terminates.
```

Fig. 8. Generate alternative implementations algorithm.

tions, to produce an implementation for the desired modeling structure. The remainder of this subsection describes how JOIN combines two implementation-structure descriptions. First JOIN combines the storage structures for the implementations. All storage-structure descriptions for implementations in the library are of the form "s: $\#_\phi(x)/op$", where "$\#_\phi$" is the number of elements in the structure, x may be "e" (symbolizing the element) or the name of another construct (i.e., "f", where "f: ···" also appears), and "op" is from the set $\{+,?,@,\phi\}$. The top levels of the two storage structures to be joined are "s: $\#_\phi(x)/op_1$" and "s: $\#_\phi(y)/op_2$". There are sixteen possible joinings of the top-level operations of which four are not possible because either cell contiguity is used to represent two distinct relations ($op_1 = +$ and $op_2 = +$), cell contiguity interacts with associative linking ($op_1 = +$ and $op_2 = ?$ or vice versa), or associative linking is used for two relations ($op_1 = ?$ and $op_2 = ?$). In the other cases, the storage structures can be joined by subsuming op_2 into the top-level element of the first storage structure (x). The rule for joining storage structures is as follows.

1) Switch arguments so that op_1 precedes op_2 in the ordering $[+,?,@,\phi]$.

2) Let s: $\#_\phi(z)/op_1$ and z: $x + y + op_2 z$ (do not add $+op_2 z$ if $op_2 = \phi$ because there is no top-level relationship between y's).

3) Substitute for x and y in z their definitions, removing duplicate occurrences of e and replacing any occurrence of x or y by the symbol z (the new top-level element).

4) Copy all other constructs from the two storage structures replacing occurrences of x or y by the symbol z.

An example will make this clearer. Fig. 9 shows the joining of two storage structures: n contiguously stored entities and n

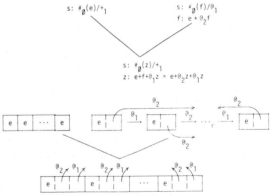

Fig. 9. Example of joining storage structures.

entities with two relations both represented by explicit pointers ($@_1$ represents a 1-1 relation, $@_2$ may represent another degree relation, depending on the operations definitions). The JOIN rule makes the 1-1 relation pointer part of the top-level entity so that the contiguity between top-level entities, defined in the other storage structure, can be retained. The same symbol, either identifier or subscripted operator, may appear in both storage structures. To resolve the naming conflict, unique identifiers and subscripts are substituted throughout the implementation-structure descriptions before joining.

After combining storage-structure descriptions, other parts of the implementation descriptions are joined by taking the union of the relations, structure-defining functions, descriptor, and size sets. The order field of the two implementations must be norder. The elements field is set to value or the name selection sequence is constructed with each name indicator set to value. Thus far, the join operator is characterized by:

a) Storage Structure: apply combine rule;
b) Relations: union;
c) Structure-Defining Functions: union;
d) Descriptor: union;
e) Order: norder;
f) Sizes: union;
g) Elements: value or [<name$_1$,value>, $\cdots$].

The operations set presents a problem. For some operations, such as related, read, and read-attribute, a general code generation procedure can be defined which produces the correct operation based on other parts of the implementation description (particularly the storage structure and relation set). For other operations, such as insert, delete, and relate, a general procedure cannot be defined because implementation specific knowledge must be encoded. The problem is that knowledge represented procedurally is difficult to combine. If, on the other hand, this knowledge could be represented as data, the possibilities for defining a suitable joining rule are improved. Our work with examples to date suggests that a joining rule can be devised. However, until more examples have been studied, particularly in the context of an operational system, it would be premature to state that the problem can be solved.

C. Example and Discussion of Implementation-Structure Generation

The topological sort program presented earlier (see Fig. 4) provides an example for implementation-structure generation. The single modeling-structure description derived from the program was

<norep, noord, {<"SUC", many-many, pdom, pran, noconn, noref, nosym>}, ϕ, {existQuant}, {delete(E,S), relate(S,[<E,"SUC",E>]), related(E,S,"SUC")}>.

(In practice, the description would match a library description of the modeling structure "directed graph," but it here serves as a convenient example of generation of alternative implementations.) This example was processed by an implementation of the GENALT algorithm in UCI Lisp [2]. Because of the existential quantification referencing, an enumeration relation was added to the structure previously given. Thus the structure had two relations when input to GEN. The one-relation implementations library available to GEN included two representations for a 1–1 relation (sequential or linked implementation) and five representations for a many–many relation. (Two of the many–many relation implementations are given as illustrations of implementation structures in Figs. 5 and 6. Of the other three, one differs from Fig. 5 only in that the pointers to other elements are stored contiguously rather than linked (i.e., g: #$_\phi$(@f)/+$_2$), and the other two store the top-level elements contiguously rather than independently. GEN returned seven implementations for the modeling structure (the other three could not be joined).

Fig. 10 gives the storage structure part of two of the returned implementations. The first implementation represents the enumeration relation by sequentially storing the z's. Associated with each z is a pointer to a linked list of pointers to

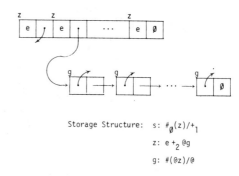

Storage Structure: s: #$_\phi$(z)/+$_1$
  z: e +$_2$ @g
  g: #(@z)/@

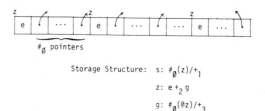

$\underline{\#_\phi}$ pointers

Storage Structure: s: #$_\phi$(z)/+$_1$
  z: e +$_2$ g
  g: #$_\phi$(@z)/+$_3$

Fig. 10. Example implementation storage structures returned by GEN.

(Case 1) s: #$_\phi$(z)/+$_1$
  z: e +$_2$ @g
  g: #(@z)/@

(Case 2) s: #$_\phi$(z)/+$_1$
  z: e +$_2$ g
  g: #$_\phi$(@z)/+$_3$

(Case 3) s: #$_\phi$(z)/@
  z: e +$_1$ g
  g: #$_\phi$(@z)/+$_2$

(Case 4) s: #$_\phi$(z)/+$_1$
  z: e +$_2$ g +$_3$ @z
  g: #$_\phi$(@z)/+$_4$

(Case 5) s: #$_\phi$(z)/@
  z: e +$_1$ @g
  g: #(@z)/@

(Case 6) s: #$_\phi$(z)/+$_1$
  z: e +$_2$ @g +$_3$ @z
  g: #(@z)/@

(Case 7) s: #$_\phi$(z)/+$_1$
  z: e +$_2$?$_3$g +$_4$ @z
  g: #$_\phi$($\underline{tag}$+$_5$?$_6$z)/+$_7$

Fig. 11. Storage structures for implementation returned by GEN.

elements related to this one by the relation SUC. The second implementation also represents the enumeration relation in sequential storage. The SUC relation is represented in that case by #$_\phi$ pointer fields stored with each element. The other implementations returned by GEN are variations of these based on whether the elements are stored contiguously or linked and how the connection relation SUC is stored. Storage structures for all seven implementations are shown in Fig. 11. The last implementation shown uses an adjacency (or connection) matrix to represent SUC, with structure-defining functions to refer from the set of elements to the matrix and back. Step 4.0 of the GENALT algorithm adds seven additional ordered implementations to improve existential referencing. (This step assumes that there exists an ordering predicate for the elements of the structure; otherwise, the ordered implementations are not added.) In this example, the ordered implementations will not necessarily be more efficient because the searching involved in the existential referencing is not related to an ordering among the elements in the structure (i.e., the characters). Thus, the algorithm returns 14 possible implementations.

Two comments on the generation procedure previously described are in order. First, the algorithm requires that for the resulting implementation all elements of a structure (except those with name-selection referencing) must either have values of the same type, values with descriptors giving type information, pointers to values of the same type, or pointers to descriptors. Some such constraints are to be expected with a general procedure intended to replace hand-coded implementations. The question is how well does the general procedure perform? Our limited experience to date suggests that it does reasonably well in generating a set of alternatives with a wide range of space–time tradeoffs, but a more systematic evaluation should be undertaken. Second, there are several questions concerning the introduction of an enumeration relation. In what cases do modeling structures not require an enumeration relation either because an alternative traversal scheme is available (perhaps as specific implementation knowledge, e.g., binary tree traversals) or because the elements of the structures need not be enumerated? Which relation should be designated the enumeration relation if several candidates are available? The generation algorithm could be improved by recognizing those cases in which an implementation for a relation explicitly defined in the modeling structure contains a sequential or linked representation of elements which could be used to implement the enumeration relation. This can be seen in Case 7 in Fig. 11. The implementation uses an extra pointer to represent the enumeration relation when the contiguity of elements required by the adjacency matrix implementation could be exploited. The current algorithm does not discover this, resulting in the generation of less efficient implementations.

D. Hierarchical Combination

In some programs a modeling structure may be inserted into other structures (e.g., an array of records). Consequently, a hierarchical combination algorithm is needed to adjust the implementations for those structures that during program execution might contain another as an element. The information used by the algorithm describes which modeling structures might be inserted into other structures. This is deduced from a program by what Schwartz calls value flow analysis [19].

The algorithm considers the following three situations.

a) Does a structure contain more than one type of entity?

b) Is an entity in more than one structure simultaneously,
more than once in the same structure, or require an existence outside a structure (called *separate existence*)?

c) Are elements of a sequentially implemented structure of fixed size?

In the first situation, each of the element implementations is modified to include a run-time descriptor with a type field so that the type of an arbitrary element can be determined.

The second situation is handled by using a pointer to the elements of a structure. Separate existence is an extremely important concept. Because an entity, at some point in the computation, might be accessed through a variable, but not be a member of any structure, or might be an element of more than one structure at the same time, it must be stored outside or separated from the structure. Thus the structure elements must be pointers to the actual elements.

The third situation relates to implementations with sequentially stored elements. If the number of elements in the structure varies and the element entities are different sizes, the implementation is changed so that pointers to the elements, rather than the elements themselves, are stored.

Unlike the generation algorithm, our experience with this algorithm indicates that it is not particularly successful at producing acceptable implementations. This poor performance is because the detailed input required to produce efficient implementations is not easily collected, and so the output of the algorithm is overly simplified. Two examples illustrate this. The first example relates to elements occurring simultaneously in several structures. Consider the case when an entity x is a member of S and S′ during execution. Now, if T_S is the set of time epochs during which x is a member of S, which of the following cases hold?

a) $T_S \cap T_{S'} = \phi$

b) $T_S \subseteq T_{S'}$ or $T_S \supseteq T_{S'}$, or

c) $T_S \cap T_{S'} \neq \phi$.

Cases a and c require x to have a separate existence (i.e., be stored outside of the structure). Case b, on the other hand, does not require that x have a separate existence.

The second example relates to an entity occurring more than once in a single structure. For example, suppose e_1 and e_2 are two entities. Value flow analysis can determine that many instances of e_1 are created and that more than one element of e_2 was created at e_1 (i.e., several entities created at e_1 were inserted into e_2). This form of analysis cannot, however, determine whether multiple occurrences of a single e_1 are inserted into e_2 or whether distinct entities were inserted. Because of the possibility of the former, an inefficient implementation for the latter (which is the more likely situation) must be used. This problem arises because the modeling-structures formalism allows multiple insertions of a single entity.

IV. Summary and Conclusions

In this paper, an approach was presented to automate the selection of implementations for data representations used in a program. In particular, we described formalisms for modeling and implementation structures and three algorithms that comprise the alternative generation phase (modeling-structure recognition, generation of alternative implementations, and hierarchical combination of implementations). The principal contributions of this work were the demonstration of the possibility of mechanical recognition of known modeling structures and the development of a general algorithm for generating alternative implementations with a wide range of space-time tradeoffs for those structures not recognized.

Two key features of the modeling-structures formalism make mechanical recognition possible: first, using binary relations to model "structure," and second, making explicit the distinction between references to elements in a structure based on structural relationships (distinguished elements) and references directed at a specific element (external access). This distinction has not been made in other models of data structures. The full formalism, as defined here, may be too complicated for programmers to use in a real-world programming environment. Nevertheless, it may be used as the internal representation for an implementation selection system.

Although a complete system based on the approach presented has not been developed, certain conclusions about the formalism and algorithms can be drawn.

The performance of the mechanical recognition algorithm cannot be accurately assessed because it depends on examining its application to a large number of example programs generated by different programmers. This is one direction for future research.

As stated previously, the alternative generation algorithm was quite successful at producing reasonable alternatives, assuming a well-stocked library of one-relation implementations and provided that the problem of joining operation code generators can be satisfactorily resolved. Because the modeling-structure formalism presented here emphasizes static structural relationships, it may be easier to devise an algorithm to combine the operation descriptions than in a system where structural relationships are embedded in the operations on the modeling structure (e.g., as in [16]). Nevertheless, this problem has not been solved and until it is an implementation selection system, such as that described here, will be only moderately successful.

The performance of the hierarchical combination algorithm was unsatisfactory because of the inability to deduce from a program enough detailed information about the dynamic interactions between the various entities created. The types of information required concern the necessity of separate existences for entities, the relationship between the times during which an entity is an element of various structures, and the existence of multiple occurrences of an entity in a single structure. Assuming that one is not willing to constrain the language for describing programs, there are three possible solutions.

a) A more complicated program-understanding system could be constructed to deduce the information.

b) The user could be asked for the information.

c) The actual running of the program could be monitored to gather the information.

Each of these alternatives has some disadvantages. The first solution, given current performance of knowledge-based sys-

tems, may not yield sufficient information to justify the additional processing. While the second solution is certainly possible, the volume and detail of information that is required would be both time-consuming to gather and tedious to provide. And lastly, the third solution, while again certainly possible, would not be acceptable if the program for which implementations are being generated were to be executed only a few times and/or it was exceptionally costly to execute.

As a result of these observations, the need for specific types of user interaction becomes more apparent. We see two distinct classes of users who would use such a system in different ways. Those users with programs which are prohibitively expensive to execute will likely want to interact with the system to provide the information needed to generate efficient implementations. On the other hand, those users with programs which are not prohibitively expensive to execute with inefficient implementations, but which will be run many times will likely want to monitor actual executions to gather the necessary information. Notice that whichever approach is taken, user interaction is not just desirable but necessary.

Three other comments about implementation selection systems are relevant. First, another kind of interaction between structures, not considered here, must be included in an implementation selection system. The interaction relates to how implementations are placed in various regions of memory. For example, given two stacks implemented sequentially a well-known programming practice is to place the stacks at opposite ends of a block of memory and have them grow towards the other. In this way, free space is shared between the two structures. In [18], we call this an *implementation coalescing*. A coalescing between two or more implementations can have a considerable impact on space and/or time efficiency.

Second, Low in his system uses the following heuristic to determine which data structures should use the same implementation:

Any pair of data structures which are operands to an operation should use the same implementation.

We believe this heuristic to be too restrictive. The heuristic we used was

Any structures of the same type created at the same place in a program should use the same implementation.

Then, depending on the relative run-time efficiencies, two structures that are operands to an operator may or may not use the same implementation. During the course of examining some programs, we discovered another heuristic which may prove useful in limiting the search space of alternative implementations.

Any structures of the same type which are simultaneously elements of the same structure should use the same implementation.

Finally, any progress on the problem of automating the selection of efficient implementations depends on the ability to predict a program's execution performance. Progress to date in this area has been limited. As a result, one should not expect to see practical use of such systems in the near future.

We believe, however, that economically viable systems allowing user interaction to choose alternatives from an implementation library are feasible and can be developed for practical use. This idea is being pursued in other work on data abstraction, see [6] and [13].

Appendix

In this Appendix a brief, informal description is given for the modeling-structures formalism primitive operations. The following notation is used:

s	a modeling structure;
x,y,z	references to entities;
R	a relation name;
I	an identifier.

The primitive operations are:

read(x)	return value of entity;
insert(x,s)	insert entity referenced by x into s;
delete(x,s)	delete entity referenced by x from s;
replace(x,y,s)	replace x by y in s;
assign(x,y)	copy value of y into x;
createaccess(x,s)	return an external access for x in s;
relate(s,{<x,R,y>, ···})	for each <x,R,y>, insert x or y into s, if not already a member, and relate them by R;
unrelate(s,{<x,R,y>, ···})	remove relation R between x and y, neither entity is deleted;
related(x,s,R)	return element or elements of s that are R related to x, i.e., $\{y\|<x,R,y>\}$;
readattr(s,<x,R,y>,I)	return attribute labeled I associated with xRy in s;
storeattr(s,<x,R,y>,<I,z>)	store z as attribute I with xRy in s.

Acknowledgment

The authors wish to thank S. Katz, O. Roubine, and an anonymous referee for their valuable comments on an earlier version of this paper.

References

[1] R. Balzer, "Dataless programming," in *Proc. 1967 Fall Joint Computer Conf.*, vol. 31, 1967, pp. 534–544.
[2] R. J. Bobrow *et al.*, *UCI Lisp Manual*, Dep. Inform. Comput. Sci., Univ. of California, Irvine, Tech. Rep. 21, Oct. 1973.
[3] O.-J. Dahl, E. W. Dijkstra, and C. A. R. Hoare, *Structured Programming*. New York: Academic, 1972.
[4] *Proc. Conf. Data: Abstraction, Definition and Structure (ACM SIGPLAN Notices)*, (Special Issue), vol. 11, Mar. 1976.
[5] M. E. D'Imperio, "Information structures: Tools in problem solving," *ACM-SIGMOD FDT Newsletter*, vol. 1, 1969.
[6] C. M. Geschke, J. M. Morris, Jr., and E. H. Satterthwaite, "Early experience with mesa," *Commun. Ass. Comput. Mach.*, vol. 20, pp. 540–553, Aug. 1977.
[7] C. C. Gotlieb and F. W. Tompa, "Choosing a storage schema," *Acta Inform.*, vol. 3, pp. 297–319, 1974.
[8] J. Guttag, "Abstract data types and the development of data structures," *Commun. Ass. Comput. Mach.*, vol. 20, pp. 396–404, June 1977.
[9] C. A. R. Hoare, "Notes on data structuring," in *Structured Programming*. New York: Academic, 1972.
[10] K. Jensen and N. Wirth, *PASCAL User Manual and Report*. New York: Springer, 1975.
[11] E. Kant, "The selection of efficient implementations for a high-level language," in *Proc. Symp. Artificial Intelligence and Programming Languages (ACM SIGPLAN Notices*, vol. 12, Aug. 1977), pp. 141–146.
[12] D. E. Knuth, "An empirical study of FORTRAN programs," *Software–Practice and Experience*, vol. 1, pp. 105–133, 1971.
[13] B. H. Liskov and S. N. Zilles, "Specification techniques for data abstraction," *IEEE Trans. Software Eng.*, vol. SE-1, pp. 7–19, Mar. 1975.
[14] B. H. Liskov *et al.*, "Abstraction mechanisms in CLU," *Commun. Ass. Comput. Mach.*, vol. 20, pp. 564–576, Aug. 1977.
[15] J. Low and P. Rovner, "Techniques for the automatic selection of data structures," in *Conf. Rec. 3rd ACM Symp. Principles of Programming Languages*, pp. 58–67, Jan. 1976.
[16] S. J. Rosenschein and S. M. Katz, "Selection of representations for data structures," in *Proc. Symp. Artificial Intelligence and Programming Languages (ACM SIGPLAN Notices*, vol. 12, August 1977), pp. 147–154.
[17] P. Rovner, "Automatic representation selection for associative data structures," Comput. Sci. Dep., Univ. of Rochester, Tech. Rep. 10, Sept. 1976.
[18] L. A. Rowe, "A formalization of modeling structures and the generation of efficient implementation structures," Ph.D. dissertation, Dep. Inform. Comput. Sci., Univ. of Calif., Irvine, June 1976.
[19] J. T. Schwartz, "Automatic data structure choice in a language of very high level," *Commun. Ass. Comput. Mach.*, vol. 18, pp. 722–728, Dec. 1975.
[20] M. Shaw, W. A. Wulf, and R. L. London, "Abstraction and verification in Alphard: Defining and specifying iteration and generators," *Commun. Ass. Comput. Mach.*, vol. 20, pp. 553–546, Aug. 1977.
[21] F. M. Tonge and L. A. Rowe, "A selection algorithm for coalesced implementation structures," Dep. Inform. Comput. Sci., Univ. of California, Irvine, Sept. 1976.
[22] W. A. Wulf, R. L. London, and M. Shaw, "An introduction to the construction and verification of alphard programs," *IEEE Trans. Software Eng.*, vol. SE-2, pp. 253–265, Dec. 1976.

Lawrence A. Rowe received the B.A. degree in mathematics and the Ph.D. degree in information and computer science from the University of California, Irvine, in 1970 and 1976, respectively.

He is currently an Assistant Professor of Electrical Engineering and Computer Science at the University of California, Berkeley. His research interests are in programming language design and implementation with special emphasis on language constructs for accessing data bases.

Dr. Rowe is a member of the Association for Computing Machinery.

Fred M. Tonge is Professor of Information and Computer Science and of Administration at the University of California, Irvine, where he has served as Director of Computer Facilities and Chairman of the Department of Information and Computer Science. He has been a faculty member at UCLA, Stanford, and the Carnegie Institute of Technology, and an employee of The RAND Corporation, Westinghouse Electric Corporation, and NCR.

Dr. Tonge is a member of the Association for Computing Machinery and The Institute of Management Sciences.

KNOWLEDGE-BASED PROGRAMMING SELF APPLIED

Cordell Green
Stephen Westfold*

Kestrel Institute
1801 Page Mill Road
Palo Alto, CA 94304

March, 1981

appeared in *Machine Intelligence 10*, published by
Ellis Horwood Limited, Halsted Press (John Wiley &Sons), 1982.

This work describes research done at Kestrel Institute and Systems Control Inc. This research is supported in part by the Defense Advanced Research Projects Agency Contracts N00014-79-C-0127 and N00014-81-C-0582, monitored by the Office of Naval Research. The views and conclusions contained in this paper are those of the authors and should not be interpreted as representing the official policies, either expressed or implied of KESTREL, SCI, DARPA, ONR or the US Government.

*Also with Computer Science Department, Stanford University

ABSTRACT

A knowledge-based programming system can utilize a very-high-level self description to rewrite and improve itself. This paper presents a specification, in the very-high-level language V, of the rule compiler component of the CHI knowledge-based programming system. From this specification of part of itself, CHI produces an efficient program satisfying the specification. This represents a modest application of a machine intelligence system to a real programming problem, namely improving one of the programming environment's tools — the rule compiler. The high-level description and the use of a programming knowledge base provide potential for system performance to improve with added knowledge.

§1 Introduction

This paper presents a specification of a program in a very-high-level description-oriented language. Such a specification is suitable for compilation into an efficient program by a knowledge-based programming system. The program specified is the rule compiler component of the CHI knowledge-based programming system [Green et al, 1981]. The language used for the specification is V, which is used in CHI to specify programs as well as to represent programming knowledge (see [Phillips 82] for a discussion of the V language). The compiler portion of CHI can produce an efficient program from this self description. The availability of a suitable self description allows not only self compilation, but also enhanced potential for the knowledge-based system to assist in its own modification and extension.

We use the term knowledge-based programming system to imply that most of the programming knowledge used by the system is expressed explicitly, usually in some rule form, and is manipulable in that form. This collection of programming rules is used by the system to help in selecting implementation techniques, and to help in other programming activities such as editing and debugging. By comparison a conventional compiler tends to use procedures that compile source language constructs into preselected choices for data and control structure implementations rather than exploring alternative implementations.

The programming knowledge base includes stepwise refinement or transformation rules for optimizing, simplifying and refining data structures and control structures. The synthesis paradigm of CHI is to select and apply these rules to a program specification, generating a space of legal alternative implementations. By applying different refinement rules from CHI's knowledge base in different orders one gets alternative implementations, whose efficiency characteristics can be matched to the problem. In general, refinement choices may be made interactively by the user or automatically by incorporating efficiency estimation knowledge (see [Kant 79] for a discussion of this important issue). It is our intent that strategies for rule selection and ordering will be expressed in the meta-rule language portion of V. But in this paper we just present a particular set of rules and an order of application rather than alternative synthesis rules and strategies for selecting among them.

The V language is used not only to specify programs but also to express the knowledge base of synthesis rules and meta-rules. The high-level primitives of V include sets, mappings, relations, predicates, enumerations and state transformation sequences. It is a wide-spectrum language that also includes low-level constructs. Both declarative and procedural statements are allowed. In this language there is little distinction between the terms "program specification," "program description" and just "program". We use the terms interchangeably. V is translated into Lisp by the compiler portion of CHI.

In choosing a program for use as a start on self modification, we decided to work with a program that is being used and modified, rather than a contrived example. We picked RC, a *rule compiler* written in Lisp that compiles the production rule subset of the V language into efficient Lisp code. Since the program refinement rules are expressed as production rules, the rule compiler allows refinement rules to be expressed in a simple, readable and concise syntax without loss of efficiency. By expressing refinement rules in a clean formalism, their content is more readily available for scrutiny, improvement and transfer to other systems. Since production rules are also a method of specifying programs, it is possible to specify the rule compiler using this production rule subset of V. Thus the very-high-level version of the compiler can be tested by compiling itself.

We have succeeded in creating a very-high-level description of RC in the V language. The remaining sections of this paper present this description. The adequacy of the description has been tested by having RC compile itself. More precisely, the original version of RC in Lisp compiled the V description of RC into Lisp. This newly-compiled Lisp program was then tested by having it compile its V description.

We decided that rather than attempting to create an ideal version of the rule compiler immediately, we would first create and present a V version that approximates the input-output performance of the original program. The original program was written in Lisp in 1979 as part of the first version of CHI and had some undesirable limitations in its input formats and optimizations. The V version is being extended to overcome the limitations.

The very-high-level V version proves to have several advantages over the Lisp version: size, comprehensibility and extensibility. The V version is less than 20% of the size of the Lisp version (approximately 2 pages versus 10 pages). The size improvement is due in part to a better understanding of the program, but is mainly due to the declaratively-oriented description and high-level constructs that are allowed in the very-high-level language, and the concomitant allowance of other general programming knowledge to fill in details that needed to be explicitly provided in the Lisp version. Rules compiled by the V version of RC are more efficient then those produced by the Lisp version of RC, due to some simplification rules in CHI.

Subjectively, we find RC in V much easier to understand and extend. In section 3 of this paper we present several possible extensions to the rule compiler, and discuss how our approach facilitates these extensions. Indeed, the difficulty of making frequently-required extensions was a reason for using the rule compiler in this study. A major step would be the extension of the description of the small compiler RC to a description of the entire V compiler portion of CHI. Then the rule compiler will not be a separate component, but will be merged with the knowledge-based compiler portion of CHI. Rules will then be compiled as is any other V program.

Is the self-application of CHI really different from that done in other systems? It appears to differ to an extent that may make a difference. Obviously self-referencing is possible in many languages, from machine language up, and bootstrapping is often done with compilers. The notion of a language with an accessible, sophisticated environment expressed in the same language already occurs in Smalltalk [Ingalls 78], InterLisp [Teitelman and Masinter 81] and other languages. These systems provided much of the inspiration for our work. But there does appear to be a difference, in that CHI is knowledge-based, and CHI's programs are described in a higher-level description-oriented language. The availability of a very-high-level description provides greater potential for the use of additional programming knowledge in program compilation and modification. The hope is that this self description and the knowledge base can lead to a set of programming tools that are more powerful not only for creating target end-user programs but also for extending the programming environment. Extending the environment can in turn further facilitate modifying target end-user programs. An example is in a new application where the program editor or pretty printer (part of the environment) must be extended to edit or print some new information structure (part of the target program). The tools provided by the programming environment can more easily assist in this modification process if the environment is itself described in terms that the modification tools can deal with. We have shown in this paper the feasibility of describing and implementing the programming environment in the system's own very-high-level language. See [Phillips 82] for an extended discussion of self-referential programming tools.

A drawback of knowledge-based systems is that the addition of new application-domain rules often slows down system performance. In our case, where the application domain is programming, the new knowledge that is introduced can be utilized to speed CHI up. The speed-up helps to mitigate the slowdown caused by the introduction of new alternatives to consider during program synthesis. The net result may well be that system performance improves as new programming knowledge is added. An example would be that as rules are introduced for implementing sets in some new form, say balanced trees, the new tree data structure would be used where appropriate by CHI to implement sets when CHI recompiles itself. In addition, smart self-compilation allows the possibility that new knowledge can be invoked only at reasonable times so that search time isn't increased. Another way the descriptive capability helps as new knowledge is added, is that different pieces of the environment are driven off the same internal representations. For example, when a new rule format is added, the reader, printer, editor and compiler all use the same description of the rule format so that consistency is maintained.

In a knowledge-based programming system it can be difficult to draw a boundary between a program specification and general programming knowledge. For example, the specification of RC contains several rules that are specific to RC, dealing with particular rule formats and names of CHI functions. Yet other rules are simplifications such as removing redundant nesting of conjunctions, or optimizations such as moving a test outside the scope of a quantifier where possible. The philosophy of a knowledge-based programming system is that general rules such as these are part of the knowledge base and are available to be used whenever appropriate, and are not part of any particular program. For clarity we have included all the general rules in this paper, but if we wished to claim further economy of expression we could argue that the general rules are not a proper part of RC and thus the specification is really less than half the size presented here. One reason most of the rules are general is that RC deals with the mapping of declarative logic into procedures; the necessary ideas tend to be rather fundamental to programming and are more plausibly classified as general.

1.1 Related Work

Situation variables in predicate calculus are used in this paper to formally state the input-output specifications of the desired target code to be produced by the rule compiler, and are also used to give the semantics of a refinement rule. However for convenience the high-level notation omits the explicit dependence on situations unless necessary. The method of introducing situation variables into the predicate calculus to describe state changes was first introduced in [Green 68] and expanded in [Green 69a]. Current progress in the use of this method is exemplified in [Manna and Waldinger 80].

Other knowledge-based programming systems are exemplified by the TI system [Balzer 81], and the Programmer's Apprentice [Rich 81], [Shrobe 79], and [Waters 78]. Very-high-level specification languages are exemplified by GIST [Goldman and Wile, 79] and SETL [Schonberg et al, 78]. GIST is currently compiled interactively with the TI transformation system and SETL contains some sophisticated compiler optimizations.

A very-high-level self description of part of a compiler to produce programs from a logic specification using situation variables was first given in [Green 69b]. A theorem prover was the method used to interpret and compile programs specified in the predicate calculus. The control structure of the theorem prover (the interpreter and compiler) was itself described in predicate calculus. But this engine was not powerful enough to either interpret or compile the program. A logic-based technique was used again, this time with an improved theorem prover and specification language in PROLOG to describe a compiler, and in this case PROLOG was able to interpret the compiler [Warren 80]. But the described program was not part of the PROLOG system itself. In the case of CHI, a system that was self-described using situation calculus was compiled. Another closely related work is that of Weyhrauch [Weyhrauch 80] in which he describes part of the FOL system in its own logic language. This description can be procedurally interpreted to control reasoning in FOL and aids in extending its areas of expertise. MRS [Genesereth and Lenat, 1980] also features a framework where self-description is used to control reasoning in the system.

§2 Specification of the Rule Compiler

The rules we are considering have the form:

$$P \to Q$$

which loosely means "if P is true in the current situation then transform the situation to make Q true." P and Q are conjunctions of predicates involving pattern variables. An example of a rule is:

$$class(a) = \text{set} \land element(a) = x$$
$$\to class(a) = mapping \land domain(a) = x \land range(a) = \text{boolean}$$

which transforms a set data structure into a boolean mapping data structure. This is easier to read in the equivalent form with pattern expressions:

$$a:\text{'}set\ of\ x\text{'}\ \rightarrow\ a:\text{'}mapping\ from\ x\ to\ \text{boolean'}$$

The input/output specification of the rule $P\ \rightarrow\ Q$ can be stated formally as:

$$\forall\, x_1, \ldots, x_n[P(s) \Rightarrow Q(succ(s))] \tag{*}$$

where x_i are the free variables of P, $P(s)$ means that P is true in situation s, and $succ(s)$ is the situation after the rule is applied to situation s. We assume frame conventions that specify, with certain exceptions, that what is true in the initial state is true in the successor or final state unless the rule implies otherwise.

A predicate can be instantiated with objects from our domain of discourse. Each instantiated predicate corresponds to a relation[1] being in the database. An instantiated left-hand-side predicate is satisfied if the corresponding relation is in the initial state of the database. An instantiated right-hand-side predicate is satisfied by putting the corresponding relation in the final state of the database. Thus the specification can be satisfied by enumerating all instantiations of the quantified variables and for each instantiation in which all the relations of the left hand side are in the initial state of the database, adding the relations of the right hand side to the final state of the database. The main task of the rule compiler is to use constraints in the left hand side of a rule to limit the number of instantiations that need to be enumerated. This optimization is done on the specification itself by reducing quantification.

RC has four main stages. The initial stage constructs the input/output specification (*) of the rule. The second stage applies optimizing transformations to the specification by bounding quantifiers and minimizing their scope. The third stage specifies how to satisfy logic expressions using standard high level programming constructs. The last stage converts database accesses to implementation-specific constructs. We shall be examining stages 2 and 3 in detail.

In order to make the specification cleaner we have presented a few of the rules in a form which RC cannot compile. In section 3 we show how RC can be extended to compile all the rules presented.

2.1 Guide to Rule Subset of the V Language

The rules are constructed from predicates that correspond to relations in the database. The

---

[1]In our system the relation $R\!:\!X \times Y$ is stored as a function of the form $f\!:\!X \mapsto Y$, where $y=f(x)$ iff $R(x,y)$ if R is one to one or many to one, or $f\!:\!X \mapsto set\ of\ Y$, where $y \in f(x)$ iff $R(x,y)$ if R is one to many or many to many. The inverse relation is represented by a function in a similar way. Functions may also be computed.

rules of RC transform logic expressions and program expressions, so we need to show how such expressions are represented as relations in the database. For example, the expression $if\ p(x,y)\ then\ f(x)$ is represented internally by an object w_1 with the following attribute-value relations:

$$class(w_1)=\text{conditional},\ condition(w_1)=w_2,\ action(w_1)=w_3$$

where w_1 and w_2 are objects with the following properties:

$$class(w_2)=\text{p},\ arg_1(w_2)=v_1,\ arg_2(w_2)=v_2,$$
$$class(w_3)=\text{f},\ arg_1(w_3)=v_1,$$
$$class(v_1)=\text{var},\ name(v_1)=\text{x},$$
$$class(v_2)=\text{var},\ name(v_2)=\text{y}.$$

One rule conjunction which matches this representation is:

$$class(a)=\text{conditional} \wedge condition(a)=P \wedge action(a)=Q$$

with instantiations: $a \leftarrow w_1$; $P \leftarrow w_2$; $Q \leftarrow w_3$. Because rule conjunctions refer to the representation of the expression to be matched rather than the expression itself, it can be difficult to understand them. Therefore, we introduce an alternate notation for rule conjunctions which we call pattern expressions. The pattern expression for the previous conjunction is:

$$a:\text{'}if\ P\ then\ Q\text{'}.$$

Pattern expressions are useful for the reader to see the form of the expressions that the rule refers to, but it is the conjunctive form that is compiled by RC.

In this paper we follow certain naming conventions for pattern variables. Variables starting with S stand for sets of objects. All other pattern variables stand for individual objects. Thus, in the pattern $a:\text{'}\forall S[C \Rightarrow P]$, S matches the set of quantifier variables of a, whereas in the pattern $a:\text{'}\forall x[C \Rightarrow P]\text{'}$, x matches the single quantifier variable of a. The other variable naming conventions do not affect the way the rules are compiled. They are: P, Q, R and C match boolean-valued expressions (C is used specifically for conjunctions); u, v and t match terms; p and q match predicates; f matches functions.

2.2   The Rule Compiler Rules

We first present the rules without examples of their use. Then, in section 2.3, we present the steps in the compilation of a rule, which involves applications of all the rules in the current section. It may be useful for the reader to read these two sections together.

Stage 1: Conversion to Input/Output Specification

Creating the specification of the rule involves determining the quantification of variables. The quantification convention is that variables that appear only on the right hand side are existentially quantified over the right hand side and variables on the left hand side are universally quantified over the entire rule. The reason for variables on the right being existentially quantified is that we want to create new objects in the new situation, and this can be expressed by stating existence.

The rule that does the conversion is:

$$a{:}`P \rightarrow Q` \wedge FreeVars(P){=}S_0 \wedge FreeVars(Q){-}S_0 = S_1$$
$$\rightarrow a{:}`Satisfy(\forall S_0[P \Rightarrow \exists S_1[Q]])` \qquad \text{(SatisfySpec)}$$

where $FreeVars(P)$ is the set of free variables in the expression P except for those declared to be bound global to the rule. Note that we have not specified that P refers to the initial state and Q refers to the succeeding state. This could be done by marking predicates as referring to either the initial state or the succeeding state. It turns out that in the current version of RC this marking is unnecessary because the initial separation of left- and right-hand-side predicates is maintained. At the end of stage 3, predicates that refer to the final state are marked as having to be *Satisf*ied. How RC can be extended to take advantage of situational tags is discussed in section 3.2.

Stage 2: Optimizing transformations

The rules in this stage do most of the optimizations currently in RC, using equivalence transformations. We do this within logic rather than on a procedural form of the rule because there is a well-understood repertory of logical equivalence transformations. The choice of equivalence transformations is made with a procedural interpretation in mind. The effect of these transformations is to explicate constraints on the evaluation order of the left hand side conjuncts. This reflects in the logic form as dependencies being explicit, for example an expression being outside a quantification rather than unnecessarily inside it.

To give an idea of the overall effect of stages 2 and 3, we show the compilation of the rule **SubstBind** before and after these stages. Its purpose is not important here.

$$a:\text{`}Satisfy(P/S_0)\text{'} \land y \in S_0 \land y:\text{`}x/t\text{'} \;\rightarrow\; a:\text{`}bind\ S_1\ do\ Satisfy(P)\text{'} \land z \in S_1 \land z:\text{`}x \leftarrow t\text{'}$$

(SubstBind)

We abbreviate the right hand side to RHS as we are concentrating on the left hand side. At the beginning of stage 2, the rule has been transformed to:

$$Satisfy(\forall\, S_0, y, x, t[class(a)=\text{substitute} \land satisfy(a) \land substexp(a)=P \land substset(a)=S_0$$
$$\land y \in S_0 \land class(y)=\text{subst} \land var(y)=x \land substval(y)=t$$
$$\Rightarrow RHS])$$

(2.1)

At the end of stage 2:

$$Satisfy(class(a)=\text{substitute} \land satisfy(a)$$
$$\Rightarrow (\forall y \in S_0[class(y)=\text{subst} \Rightarrow (RHS/\{x/var(y), t/substval(y)\})])$$
$$/ \{P/substexp(a), S_0/substset(a)\})$$

(2.2)

At the end of stage 3:

```
if Test(class(a)=substitute ∧ satisfy(a)) then
    bind P ← substexp(a), S₀ ← substset(a)
        do enumerate y in S₀
            do if Test(class(y)=subst) then
                    bind x ← var(y), t ← substval(y)
                do RHS
```

(2.3)

The rule compiler determines the order and manner in which each of the eight left-hand-side conjuncts of (2.1) is treated. The fate of the conjuncts can be seen in (2.3). The conjuncts $class(a)=\text{substitute}$ and $satisfy(a)$ can be tested immediately because they depend only on the variable a which is bound externally. The conjunct $substexp(a)=P$ requires that the value of the unknown variable P be equal to an expression in the known variable a, so it is selected next and used to compute the value of P. Similarly, the conjunct $substset(a)=S_0$ is used to compute the value of S_0. Of the remaining conjuncts, $y \in S_0$ is selected next because it contains only the unknown y and so can be used to compute the possible values of y, which is done using an enumeration. This leaves $class(y)=\text{subst}$ with no unknown variables so it is used as a test, and $var(y)=x$ and $substval(y)=t$ give known expressions equal to x and t respectively and so are used to compute values for x and t. Briefly, RC turns conjuncts with no unknown variables into tests and conjuncts with one unknown variable into computations to find the possible value(s) of this variable. At present RC cannot handle conjuncts with more than one unknown variable.

These structural changes, which reflect dependencies among the conjuncts, are performed in stage 2 within logic. In stage 3 implications "become" *if* statements, substitutions "become" variable bindings, and bounded universal quantifications "become" enumerations.

Note that for convenience we have given the conjuncts of the rule in the order in which they are used in the compiled rule, but this is not required by RC.

Another view of RC is that it produces a procedure to find the anchored matches of simple graph patterns. Variables are nodes of the graph and conjuncts are links. At any point there are known nodes and unknown nodes. An unknown node becomes known by following a link from a known node. The structure of variable binding in the target program (2.3) corresponds to a spanning tree of the graph pattern. Consider the expression $RHS/\{x/var(y), t/substval(y)\}$ which is matched when **SubstBind** itself is being compiled. a has the whole expression as its value (actually the object representing the expression); P has the value RHS; S_0 has the set $\{x/var(y), t/substval(y)\}$ as its value; y first has the value $x/var(y)$, x the value x, and z the value $var(y)$; y then has the value $t/substval(y)$, x the value t, and z the value $substval(y)$.

2a) Reducing quantification scope

The following rule, when applicable, moves expressions outside the scope of a quantification. If the quantification later becomes an enumeration, the evaluation will be done outside the enumeration instead of inside. The equivalence can be loosely stated: if p is not dependent on x then $(\forall x[p \wedge q \Rightarrow r]) \equiv (p \Rightarrow \forall x[q \Rightarrow r])$.

The corresponding rule expression of this is[2] :

$$a:`\forall S[C_0 \Rightarrow Q]' \wedge P \in conjuncts(C_0) \wedge NoVarsOf(P, S)$$
$$\rightarrow \quad a:`C_1 \Rightarrow \forall S[C_0 \Rightarrow Q]' \wedge class(C_1) = \text{conjunction} \qquad \text{(ReduceScope)}$$
$$\wedge\ P \in conjuncts(C_1) \wedge P \notin conjuncts(C_0)$$

where $NoVarsOf(P, S)$ is true when the expression P is not a function of any of the variables S. Note that there may be more than one conjunct P for which the left hand side is true, in which case C_1 will have more than one conjunct. Because of the later procedural interpretation of implication (**ImplIf**) the conjuncts added to C_1 will be tested before those remaining in C_0.

---

[2]We use the convention that the antecedent of an implication is always a conjunction, possibly with only one conjunct.

However, there is no necessary ordering among the conjuncts of C_1. Note also that we want C_1 to have *only* those conjuncts P such that $P \in conjuncts(C_0) \land NoVarsOf(P, S)$, but this is not explicitly stated. It is implicit that the compiled rule produces the minimal situation that satisfies the specification.

2b) Bounding quantifiers

The following two rules recognize explicit bounds on quantifier variables and move the quantification of these variables outside the quantification of any as-yet-unbounded quantifiers. This often enables these rules (and also **ReduceScope**) to be applicable to the inner quantification. This splitting explicates an implicit dependency of the internal quantification on the external quantifier variables.

The first rule uses the idea of the following logical equivalence:

$$\forall x[(x \in S \land p) \Rightarrow q] \equiv \forall x \in S[p \Rightarrow q]$$

The actual rule is more complicated mainly because there may be more than one quantification variable, and the bounded quantification is separated and moved outside any remaining unbound quantifiers. This allows the inner quantified expression to be manipulated independently.

$$
\begin{aligned}
y{:}\text{`}\forall S_0[C \Rightarrow Q]\text{'} &\land a \in conjuncts(C) \land a{:}\text{`}x \in t\text{'} \land x \in S_0 \land NoVarsOf(t, S_0) \\
\rightarrow \quad & y{:}\text{`}\forall S_1[\forall S_0[C \Rightarrow Q]]\text{'} \land x \in S_1 \land x \notin S_0 \land univset(x){=}t \\
& \land a \notin conjuncts(C)
\end{aligned}
\qquad \text{(BoundForall)}
$$

where $univset(x){=}t$ means that x can only take values in the set given by the term t.

The following rule is a special case where a quantifier variable can only take on one value because it is asserted to be equal to some term independent of the quantifiers. We express this by stating that the variable is substituted by this term in the expression, but we do not actually perform the substitution.

$$
\begin{aligned}
a{:}\text{`}\forall S_0[C \Rightarrow Q]\text{'} &\land y \in conjuncts(C) \land y{:}\text{`}x{=}t\text{'} \land x \in S_0 \land NoVarsOf(t, S_0) \\
\rightarrow \quad & a{:}\text{`}\forall S_0[C \Rightarrow Q]/S_1\text{'} \land z \in S_1 \land z{:}\text{`}x/t\text{'} \land x \notin S_0 \land y \notin conjuncts(C)
\end{aligned}
\quad \text{(ForallSubst)}
$$

Stage 3: Interpreting Input/Output Specification Procedurally

In this stage the rule is converted from predicate calculus to procedural language. We assume the initial situation is given and that actions necessary to create the successor situation from the initial situation must be performed so that the rule specification is satisfied. Each rule specifies a high-level procedural form for satisfying a particular logical form.

Implication becomes an *if* statement.

$$a\text{:}`Satisfy(C \Rightarrow R)\text{'} \rightarrow a\text{:}`if\ Test(C)\ then\ Satisfy(R)\text{'} \qquad \text{(ImplIf)}$$

$Test(C)$ is true if C is satisfied in the initial state. *Test* is not explicitly used by any of the following rules, but predicates which are not to be *Satisfied* are to be *Tested*.

The following rule says that "substitution" is actually done using variable binding rather than substitution.

$$a\text{:}`Satisfy(P/S_0)\text{'} \land y \in S_0 \land y\text{:}`x/t\text{'} \rightarrow a\text{:}`bind\ S_1\ do\ Satisfy(P)\text{'} \land z \in S_1 \land z\text{:}`x \leftarrow t\text{'}$$
$$\text{(SubstBind)}$$

An existential variable appearing in the new situation is handled by creating a new object with the specified properties.

$$a\text{:}`Satisfy(\exists\ S_0[P])\text{'} \land y \in S_0 \rightarrow a\text{:}`bind\ S_1\ do\ Satisfy(P)\text{'} \land x \in S_1 \land x\text{:}`y \leftarrow (New\ Object)\text{'}$$
$$\text{(ExistBindNew)}$$

A conjunction can be satisfied by satisfying each of the conjuncts. In this specification we assume that they can be satisfied independently.

$$a\text{:}`Satisfy(C)\text{'} \land class(C) = \text{conjunction} \land P \in conjuncts(C)$$
$$\rightarrow class(a) = \text{block} \land Q \in steps(a) \land Q\text{:}`Satisfy(P)\text{'} \qquad \text{(AndBlock)}$$

Bounded quantification becomes an enumeration:

$$a\text{:}`Satisfy(\forall\ x \in S[R])\text{'} \rightarrow a\text{:}`enumerate\ x\ in\ S\ do\ Satisfy(R)\text{'} \qquad \text{(ForallEnum)}$$

Stage 4: Refine to standard database access functions

4a) Rules for object-centered database implementation

The following rules convert references to functions into references to the database. The particular database representation we use is that the function value $f(u)$ is stored as the f property of the object u. Objects are thus mappings from function names to values. This arrangement may be thought of either as a distributed representation of functions or as the function being indexed by its argument.

$$a{:}`f(u)` \;\rightarrow\; a{:}`(GetMap\ u\ f)` \qquad\qquad \text{(MakeGetMap)}$$

$$a{:}`Satisfy(f(u){=}v)` \;\rightarrow\; a{:}`(ExtendMap\ u\ f\ v)` \qquad\qquad \text{(MakeExtMap)}$$

$$a{:}`Satisfy(p(u))` \;\rightarrow\; a{:}`(ExtendMap\ u\ p\ True)` \qquad\qquad \text{(MakeExtMapT)}$$

Note that we have not made all the preconditions for **MakeGetMap** explicit. It should only be applicable when **MakeExtMap** and **MakeExtMapT** are not applicable.

4b) System-specific transformations

The rules of this section are specific to the conventions we use to implement the abstract database. We only present the two of them that reflect issues particularly relevant to the problem of compiling logic specifications. The others convert accesses to abstract datatypes, such as mappings, into accesses to concrete datatypes. These are part of the standard CHI system.

The first rule is for the case where the class of an object gets changed. There are frame conventions which say which of the other properties of the object are still valid. The function *Ttransform* enforces these conventions at rule execution time.

$$a{:}`(ExtendMap\ u\ class\ v)` \;\rightarrow\; a{:}`(Ttransform\ u\ v)` \qquad\qquad \text{(MakeTtransform)}$$

Creating a new object in the database requires that its class be known; the object is created as an instance of its class.

$$a{:}`(ExtendMap\ u\ class\ v)` \wedge a \in steps(P) \wedge z{:}`u \leftarrow (NewObject)`$$
$$\rightarrow\; z{:}`u \leftarrow (Tinstance\ v)` \wedge a \notin steps(P) \qquad\qquad \text{(MakeTinstance)}$$

Simplification rules

The following are general simplification rules that are needed by RC to canonicalize expressions to ensure that other rules will be applicable when appropriate.

$$class(a){=}\text{conjunction} \wedge class(C){=}\text{conjunction}$$
$$\wedge\ a \in conjuncts(C) \wedge P \in conjuncts(a)$$
$$\rightarrow\; P \in conjuncts(C) \wedge a \notin conjuncts(C) \qquad\qquad \text{(SimpAndAnd)}$$

$$\dot{a}:`C \Rightarrow Q' \wedge Null(conjuncts(C)) \rightarrow Replace(a, Q) \tag{SimpImpl}$$

($Replace(a, P)$ causes a to be replaced by P in the expression tree. Formalizing $Replace$ is beyond the scope of this paper.)

$$a:`\forall S[P]' \wedge Null(S) \rightarrow Replace(a, P) \tag{SimpForall}$$

2.3 Sample Rule Compilation

We present the steps in compiling a representative rule, **ExistBindNew**:

$$a:`Satisfy(\exists S_0[P])' \wedge y \in S_0 \rightarrow a:`bind \; S_1 \; do \; Satisfy(P)' \wedge x \in S_1 \wedge x:`y \leftarrow (NewObject)'$$

Replacing pattern expressions by conjunctions:[3]:

$$class(a){=}\text{exists} \wedge satisfy(a) \wedge quantifiers(a){=}S_0 \wedge matrix(a){=}P \wedge y \in S_0$$
$$\rightarrow class(a){=}\text{bind} \wedge x \in bindings(a) \wedge body(a){=}P \wedge satisfy(P) \wedge class(x){=}\text{binding}$$
$$\wedge var(x){=}y \wedge initval(x){=}e_1 \wedge class(e_1){=}\text{NewObject}]])$$

We now apply **SatisfySpec** assuming that a is given as a parameter to the rule and so is not quantified within the rule:

$$Satisfy(\forall S_0, P, y[class(a){=}\text{exists} \wedge satisfy(a) \wedge quantifiers(a){=}S_0$$
$$\wedge matrix(a){=}P \wedge y \in S_0$$
$$\Rightarrow \exists x, e_1[class(a){=}\text{bind} \wedge x \in bindings(a) \wedge body(a){=}P \wedge satisfy(P)$$
$$\wedge class(x){=}\text{binding} \wedge var(x){=}y \wedge initval(x){=}e_1$$
$$\wedge class(e_1){=}\text{NewObject}]])$$

Note that $Satisfy$ is distinct from $satisfy$. Their relationship is not important for purposes of this example.

We next apply the stage 2 rules to the specification to reduce quantification. For now we abbreviate the existential expression to RHS as it does not influence anything for awhile, and concentrate on the universal quantification.

Apply **ReduceScope** to move $class(a){=}\text{exists}$ and $satisfy(a)$ outside the quantification:

---

[3]We have also eliminated the unnecessary variable S_1 by replacing $(bindings(a){=}S_1 \wedge x \in S_1)$ by $x \in bindings(a)$

$$class(a)=\text{exists} \land satisfy(a) \Rightarrow \forall S_0, P, y[quantifiers(a)=S_0 \land matrix(a)=P \land y \in S_0$$
$$\Rightarrow RHS]$$

Apply **ForallSubst** to fix values for S_0 and P in terms of a:

$$class(a)=\text{exists} \land satisfy(a) \Rightarrow (\forall y[y \in S_0 \Rightarrow RHS]/\{S_0/quantifiers(a), P/matrix(a)\})$$

Apply **BoundForall** to bound the remaining universal quantifier and simplify away the inner implication with **SimpImpl**:

$$class(a)=\text{exists} \land satisfy(a) \Rightarrow (\forall y \in S_0[RHS]/\{S_0/quantifiers(a), P/matrix(a)\})$$

Bring back RHS and focus on the universal quantification expression:

$$(\forall y \in S_0)(\exists x, e_1)[class(a)=\text{bind} \land body(a)=P \land satisfy(P) \land x \in bindings(a)$$
$$\land class(x)=\text{binding} \land var(x)=y \land initval(x)=e_1$$
$$\land class(e_1)=\text{NewObject}]$$

Moving expressions not depending on y, x and e_1 outside the quantifications (the rules that do this have not been shown before and will be defined in section 3.2):

$$class(a)=\text{bind} \land body(a)=P \land satisfy(P)$$
$$\land (\forall y \in S_0)(\exists x, e_1)[x \in bindings(a) \land class(x)=\text{binding} \land var(x)=y$$
$$\land initval(x)=e_1 \land class(e_1)=\text{NewObject}]$$

This brings us to the end of stage 2 rules.

(Note that we could have interleaved the following applications of stage 3 rules with those of stage 2 without affecting the final outcome.) The complete rule is:

$$Satisfy(class(a)=\text{exists} \land satisfy(a)$$
$$\Rightarrow (class(a)=\text{bind} \land body(a)=P \land satisfy(P)$$
$$\land (\forall y \in S_0)(\exists x, e_1)[x \in bindings(a) \land class(x)=\text{binding} \land var(x)=y$$
$$\land initval(x)=e_1 \land class(e_1)=\text{NewObject}]$$
$$)/\{S_0/quantifiers(a), P/matrix(a)\})$$

Applying **ImplIf**:

if $Test(class(a)=\text{exists} \;\wedge\; satisfy(a))$ **then**

$\quad Satisfy((class(a)=\text{bind} \;\wedge\; body(a)=P \;\wedge\; satisfy(P)$

$\qquad\qquad\qquad \wedge\; (\forall\, y \in S_0)(\exists\, x, e_1)[x \in bindings(a) \;\wedge\; class(x)=\text{binding} \;\wedge\; var(x)=y$

$\qquad\qquad\qquad\qquad\qquad\qquad \wedge\; initval(x)=e_1 \;\wedge\; class(e_1)=\text{NewObject}]$

$\qquad\quad)/\{S_0/quantifiers(a),\, P/matrix(a)\})$

Applying **SubstBind:**

if $Test(class(a)=\text{exists} \;\wedge\; satisfy(a))$ **then**

$\quad$ (**bind** $S_0 \leftarrow quantifiers(a),\; P \leftarrow matrix(a)$

$\qquad$ **do** $Satisfy(class(a)=\text{bind} \;\wedge\; body(a)=P \;\wedge\; satisfy(P)$

$\qquad\qquad\qquad \wedge\; (\forall\, y \in S_0)(\exists\, x, e_1)[x \in bindings(a) \;\wedge\; class(x)=\text{binding} \;\wedge\; var(x)=y$

$\qquad\qquad\qquad\qquad\qquad\qquad \wedge\; initval(x)=e_1 \;\wedge\; class(e_1)=\text{NewObject}])$

Applying **AndBlock:**

if $Test(class(a)=\text{exists} \;\wedge\; satisfy(a))$ **then**

$\quad$ (**bind** $S_0 \leftarrow quantifiers(a),\; P \leftarrow matrix(a)$

$\qquad$ **do** $Satisfy(class(a)=\text{bind})$

$\qquad\quad Satisfy(body(a)=P)$

$\qquad\quad Satisfy(satisfy(P))$

$\qquad\quad Satisfy((\forall\, y \in S_0)(\exists\, x, e_1)[x \in bindings(a) \;\wedge\; class(x)=\text{binding} \;\wedge\; var(x)=y$

$\qquad\qquad\qquad\qquad\qquad\qquad \wedge\; initval(x)=e_1 \;\wedge\; class(e_1)=\text{NewObject}])$

Applying **ForallEnum** to the last $Satisfy$ expression:

if $Test(class(a)=\text{exists} \;\wedge\; satisfy(a))$ **then**

$\quad$ (**bind** $S_0 \leftarrow quantifiers(a),\; P \leftarrow matrix(a)$

$\qquad$ **do** $Satisfy(class(a)=\text{bind})$

$\qquad\quad Satisfy(body(a)=P)$

$\qquad\quad Satisfy(satisfy(P))$

$\qquad\quad$ **enumerate** y **in** S_0

$\qquad\qquad$ **do** $Satisfy(\exists\, x, e_1[x \in bindings(a) \;\wedge\; class(x)=\text{binding} \;\wedge\; var(x)=y$

$\qquad\qquad\qquad\qquad\qquad \wedge\; initval(x)=e_1 \;\wedge\; class(e_1)=\text{NewObject}])$

Applying **ExistBindNew** to the last $Satisfy$ (it is here that we are applying the rule to part of itself):

if $Test(class(a)=\text{exists} \wedge satisfy(a))$ **then**
    (**bind** $S_0 \leftarrow quantifiers(a),\ P \leftarrow matrix(a)$
        do $Satisfy(class(a)=\text{bind})$
           $Satisfy(body(a)=P)$
           $Satisfy(satisfy(P))$
           enumerate y **in** S_0
               do (**bind** $x \leftarrow (NewObject),\ e_1 \leftarrow (NewObject)$
                    do $Satisfy(x \in bindings(a) \wedge class(x)=\text{binding} \wedge var(x)=y$
                            $\wedge\ initval(x)=e_1 \wedge class(e_1)=\text{NewObject})))$

Applying **AndBlock** to the last *Satisfy*:
if $Test(class(a)=\text{exists} \wedge satisfy(a))$ **then**
    (**bind** $S_0 \leftarrow quantifiers(a),\ P \leftarrow matrix(a)$
        do $Satisfy(class(a)=\text{bind})$
           $Satisfy(body(a)=P)$
           $Satisfy(satisfy(P))$
           enumerate y **in** S_0
               do (**bind** $x \leftarrow (NewObject),\ e_1 \leftarrow (NewObject)$
                    do $Satisfy(x \in bindings(a))$
                        $Satisfy(class(x)=\text{binding})$
                        $Satisfy(var(x)=y)$
                        $Satisfy(initval(x)=e_1)$
                        $Satisfy(class(e_1)=\text{NewObject})))$

This is the end of stage 3. After applying the stage 4 rules we get the following program which is LISP code except for certain function names and minor syntactical differences.

(**if** $(GetMap\ a\ '\text{class})='\text{exists}$ **and** $(GetMap\ a\ '\text{satisfy})$ **then**
    (**bind** $S_0 \leftarrow (GetMap\ a\ '\text{quantifiers}),\ P \leftarrow (GetMap\ a\ '\text{matrix})$
        do $(Ttransform\ a\ '\text{bind})$
           $(ExtendMap\ a\ '\text{body}\ P)$
           $(ExtendMap\ P\ '\text{satisfy}\ True)$
           (**for** y **in** S_0
               do (**bind** $x \leftarrow (Tinstance\ '\text{binding})$,
                        $e_1 \leftarrow (Tinstance\ '\text{NewObject})$

$$\mathbf{do} \; (AddElement \; x \; (GetMap \; a \; \text{'bindings}))$$
$$(ExtendMap \; x \; \text{'var} \; y)$$
$$(ExtendMap \; x \; \text{'initval} \; e_1)))))$$

2.4 Control Structure of Rule Compiler

We have largely succeeded in making the preconditions of the rule compiler rules explicit in the rules themselves, allowing the rules to be used in a wide variety of control structures. The choice of control structure can then concentrate on the issues of efficiency of compilation and efficiency of the target code produced by the compiler. At one extreme the user may interactively control the order of rule application in order to produce the most efficient code. At the other, the rules can be incorporated into a program which exploits their interrelations: commonalities in preconditions of rules can be used to produce a decision tree; dependencies between rules, such as the action of one rule enabling the preconditions of others, can be used to direct the order in which rules are tried.

There are some rules whose preconditions we have not made explicit. **MakeGetMap** should not be applied before **MakeExtMap** and **MakeExtMapT**. This constraint could be incorporated explicitly into **MakeGetMap** by adding negations of the distinguishing predicates of **MakeExtMap** and **MakeExtMapT**. The system could embody the general principle that a rule that has a weaker precondition than others should be applied after them, or, alternatively, distinguishing predicates could be added to the weaker rule by the system. This would give the user the choice of specifying the preconditions of a rule implicitly by reference to other rules rather than explicitly within the rule itself.

The control structure we are currently using to automatically compile rules is very simple but provides a reasonable compromise between efficiency of execution, efficiency of the code produced, and flexibility (changing one rule does not require that the entire rule compiler be recompiled). The expression tree for the rule being compiled is traversed depth-first applying each rule to each object on the way down. If an object is transformed by a rule then the traversal continues from this object. The order in which rules are applied to a particular node affects the efficiency of the code produced. In particular it is desirable to apply **ReduceScope** before **ForallSubst** and **ForallSubst** before **BoundForall**.

§3 Extensions to the Rule Compiler

One of the main tests of our high-level description of RC is how easy is it to extend. In this section we show how it can be extended along various dimensions: improving efficiency of the target code, augmenting the rule language, improving the user interface, and adapting to other system tasks.

3.1 Improving Efficiency

We give examples of adding rules in order to improve the execution efficiency of compiled rules. Adding rules will tend to slow down the rule compiler, but as RC is specified primarily in terms of rules, after recompiling its own rules RC may become substantially faster. This section considers a number of different areas where efficiency can be improved.

Frequently it is possible to express the same program in two ways where one way is simpler or more uniform, but compiles into more inefficient code. The trade-off can be circumvented by modifying a compiler so that it translates the simpler form into the more efficient form. For example, the LISP macro facility allows the user to do this to some extent. Adding new rules to RC provides a more general way of doing this in a more convenient language. A simple example is using a more specific access function for a special case of a general access function. The following rule would be useful if an object were stored as a list whose first element is the class of the object:

$$a\text{:'}(GetMap\ u\ \text{'class})\text{'}\ \rightarrow\ a\text{:'}(car\ u)\text{'}$$

Such a speed-up should be derived by CHI from knowledge of how objects are stored. That the rule compiler can be extended easily can be exploited by the rest of CHI as well as by the user directly.

A more extensive change to RC would be to use a different implementation for the database. In particular, a less general data structure could be used for representing the rules. If singly-linked lists were used, the compiled rules could no longer follow inverse links. To compensate for this, the control structure surrounding the rules would have to keep more context in free variables for the compiled rules to refer to. Rather than rewriting the rules that previously used inverse links, only the rules that compile uses of inverse relations need be rewritten.

A useful improvement in efficiency could be gained by combining sets of rules into a single function as indicated in section 2.4. There would be relative advantages in doing the combination using the original rule form or with the forms produced by stage 2. The changes necessary to RC would be modification of the control structure so that it could take more than one rule and a new set of rules to do the combining. Few changes to existing rules would be necessary.

A special case of combining rules is where one rule always follows another. This is true for a number of pairs of rules in RC: **BoundForall** is followed by **ForallEnum**; **ForallSubst** is followed by **SubstBind**. We could have specified RC with these rules combined at the cost of less clarity, and less generality of the individual rules. The combination of **BoundForall** and **ForallEnum** is:

$$y\text{:}'Satisfy(\forall S_0[C \Rightarrow Q])' \wedge a \in conjuncts(C) \wedge a\text{:}'x \in t' \wedge x \in S_0 \wedge NoVarsOf(t, S)$$
$$\rightarrow a\text{:}'enumerate\ x\ in\ t\ do\ Satisfy(\forall S_0[C \Rightarrow Q])' \wedge x \notin S_0 \wedge a \notin conjuncts(C)$$

which is comparable in complexity to **BoundForall** alone. However, it blurs the two things which are going on that are distinguished in the individual rules: a logical equivalence and how to procedurally satisfy a universal quantification. Having the two ideas in separate rules means that they can be applied separately elsewhere. However, it may well be desirable to compile them together to increase efficiency.

3.2 Extending the Rule Language

There are two classes of extensions to the rule language. New constructs and abbreviations can be incorporated by adding rules to stage 1 which translate the new constructs into standard logic constructs compilable by the lower part of RC. The second class of extension is the addition of rules to stage 2 and/or stage 3 to increase RC's coverage of logic constructs. An addition of the first class may require additions to lower parts of RC in order that the new pattern be compilable.

The following two rules free the user from having to decide whether it is necessary to use a particular relation or its inverse. They also loosen constraints on which variables may be chosen as parameters to the rule or as enumeration variables. They are required in order to compile a number of the rules without unnecessary enumerations, including **BoundForall** when a is the parameter.

$$y\text{:}'\forall S[C \Rightarrow Q]' \wedge a \in conjuncts(y) \wedge a\text{:}'f(u) = t' \wedge NoVarsOf(t, S)$$
$$\wedge OneToOne(f) \rightarrow a\text{:}'u = f^{-1}(t)'$$

$$y \colon \text{`}\forall\, S[C \Rightarrow Q]\text{'} \land a \in conjuncts(y) \land a \colon \text{`}f(u){=}t\text{'} \land NoVarsOf(t,S)$$
$$\land\; ManyToOne(f) \;\rightarrow\; a \colon \text{`}u \in f^{-1}(t)\text{'}$$

A number of rules, including **ExistBindNew**, require the following two rules in order to compile correctly. Like **ReduceScope**, they move expressions outside the scope of quantifications.

$$a \colon \text{`}\exists\, S[C]\text{'} \land class(C){=}\text{conjunction} \land P \in conjuncts(C) \land NoVarsOf(P,S)$$
$$\rightarrow class(a){=}\text{conjunction} \land P \in conjuncts(a) \land y \in conjuncts(a)$$
$$\land\; y \colon \text{`}\exists\, S[C]\text{'} \land P \notin conjuncts(C)$$

$$a \colon \text{`}\forall\, S[C]\text{'} \land class(C){=}\text{conjunction} \land P \in conjuncts(C) \land NoVarsOf(P,S)$$
$$\rightarrow class(a){=}\text{conjunction} \land P \in conjuncts(a) \land y \in conjuncts(a)$$
$$\land\; y \colon \text{`}\forall\, S[C]\text{'} \land P \notin conjuncts(C)$$

The main part of RC involves compiling the satisfaction of an input/output specification. In the remainder of this section we consider extensions to RC that increase the types of acceptable input/output specifications.

By explicitly marking functions as referring to either the initial or succeeding state we get more freedom in how to mix them in the specification and more freedom in how the specification can be manipulated in stage 2. We use the convention that functions or expressions marked with a single prime, as in f', refer to the initial state, and those marked with a double prime refer to the succeeding state, as in f''.

Consider the case where we allow disjunctions in the input/output specification. For example, consider the expression $Satisfy(A' \Rightarrow B'')$ in the disjunctive form $Satisfy(\neg A' \lor B'')$. To get from the latter to an expression similar to that obtained from applying **ImplIf** to the former expression, one can apply the rule:

$$a \colon \text{`}Satisfy(P \lor Q)\text{'} \;\rightarrow\; a \colon \text{`}if\; UnSatisfiable(P)\; then\; Satisfy(Q)$$

giving $if\, UnSatisfiable(\neg A')then\, Satisfy(B'')$. Comparing this with $if\; Test(A')\; then\; Satisfy(B'')$ we see that $Test(x)$ corresponds to $UnSatisfiable(\neg x)$. Note that we could also have derived the program $if\; UnSatisfiable(B'')\; then\; Satisfy(\neg A')$, but if we have no procedures for testing unsatisfiability in the final state or satisfying things in the initial state, then this choice will lead to a dead end.

In general, relaxing the restrictions on the form of the specification requires additional Stage 3 rules rather than changes to existing ones, but the rules may lead to dead ends, so a more sophisticated control structure is necessary. On the other hand, the Stage 4a rules do require the addition of preconditions concerning whether functions refer to the initial or final state. For example, **MakeExtMap** becomes:

$$a{:}`Satisfy(f''(u){=}v)` \; \rightarrow \; a{:}`(ExtendMap \; u \; f \; v)`$$

with restrictions also necessary on u and v if these are allowed to be expressions more general than variables.

RC in its present form can be used to compile rules that derive implications of the current state rather than transform it. The specification for such rules is exactly the same as (*) except that it is not necessary to distinguish the initial and succeeding states. This distinction is not actually used by RC so therefore RC can compile these rules. The rule **MakeTtransform** is not applicable to compiling such implication rules. Its preconditions being true would imply that the implication rule does not reflect a valid implication.

3.3 Improving User Interface

The user interface can be improved in a variety of ways. Extending the rule language, discussed above, is one way. Another is to put error detection rules which report problems in the rule or indicate when the rule is beyond the scope of the rule compiler. This is also useful as self-documentation of the rule compiler. The following rule can be used to detect any unbound quantifiers left after the application of stage 2 rules:

$$a{:}`Satisfy(\forall \, S[P])` \land x \in S \land \neg univset(x) \; \rightarrow \; Error(x, Unbound)$$

In another dimension, RC can be extended to produce target code that is oriented to the user's use of it. The main use of compiled rules outside the rule compiler is in refining high level programs under user guidance. At each decision point the user wants to know which rules are relevant. The system should help in providing such a list. We have added a set of rules to RC in V that extracts part of the left hand side to use as a filter. The rule language provides a convenient way for the user to express and experiment with heuristics for determining the relevant parts to test.

3.4 Relation to the Rest of the System

In this section we discuss specifically how the rule compiler can benefit the system and how the rest of the system can benefit the rule compiler, apart from the primary purpose of the rule compiler of compiling rules.

Some ways in which the rule compiler can benefit the system have already been covered, such as in providing filters to screen irrelevant rules from the user. The primary contribution of the rule compiler is the provision of a useful high level language that can be used elsewhere. One immediately applicable example is in compiling user database queries. These are exactly like rules except that they usually do not have any parameters and the actions are typically to display the matching objects (although editing could be performed if desired). An example query may be to print out all rules that apply to universal quantifications:

$$y:`C \rightarrow Q' \land P \in conjuncts(C) \land P:`class(x)=\text{forall}' \rightarrow Display(y)$$

Improvements in the rest of the system can have benefits for the rule compiler. As mentioned above, the whole program synthesis system may be brought to bear on compiling an important rule. General efficiency knowledge for determining which of several implementations is most efficient would carry over to rule compilation. Also, additions made to take advantage of dataflow or for manipulating enumerations could be applicable to the rule compiler. All the tools for maintaining programs written in V are applicable to maintaining the rule compiler program, including editors, consistency maintenance systems and the system for answering user queries about programs.

Acknowledgements

We would like to acknowledge Jorge Phillips for numerous key ideas in the design of CHI and V and for suggestions for describing the rule compiler in V. Sue Angebranndt helped implement and debug an initial version of RC in V. Tom Pressburger developed an implementation-independent description of CHI's knowledge base. Steve Tappel helped to define V and wrote the original version of RC in LISP. Bob Floyd and Bernard Mont-Reynaud provided considerable technical and editing assistance with this paper.

References

[Balzer 81] Robert Balzer, "Transformational Implementation: An Example," IEEE Transactions on Software Engineering, Jan. 1981, pp. 3-14.

[Genesereth and Lenat, 80] M.R. Genesereth and D.B. Lenat, "A Modifiable Representation System," Report HPP-80-26, Stanford University Computer Science Department, Dec. 1980.

[Goldman and Wile, 79] Neil M. Goldman and David S. Wile, "A Relational Data Base Foundation for Process Specifications," in: P. P. Chen (Ed.) *Int. Conf. on Entity-Relationship Approach to Systems Analysis and Design* 1979, pp. 413-432.

[Green 68] Cordell Green, "Theorem Proving by Resolution As a Basis for Question Answering Systems," in Bernard Meltzer and Donald Michie (eds) *Machine Intelligence 4*, Edinburgh University Press, Edinburgh, Scotland, 1969, pp. 183-205.

[Green 69a] Cordell Green, "Application of Theorem Proving to Problem Solving," in Donald E. Walker and Lewis M. Morton (eds), *Proceedings of the International Joint Conference on Artificial Intelligence*, Gordon and Breach Science Publishers, New York, New York, 1969, pp. 219-239.

[Green 69b] Cordell Green, "The Application of Theorem Proving to Question Answering Systems," Ph.D. thesis, Electrical Engineering Department, Memo AIM-96, Report STAN-CS-69-138, Artificial Intelligence Laboratory, Computer Science Department, Stanford University, CA, June 1969 [reprinted by Garland Publishing, Inc., New York, New York, 1979].

[Green et al, 81] Cordell Green, Jorge Phillips, Stephen Westfold, Tom Pressburger, Susan Angebranndt, Beverly Kedzierski, Bernard Mont-Reynaud, and Daniel Chapiro, "Towards a Knowledge-Based Programming System," Systems Control Inc. Technical Report KES.U.81.1 March 1, 1981.

[Ingalls 78] Daniel H. Ingalls, "The Smalltalk-76 Programming System: Design and Implementation," *Conference Record of the Fifth Annual ACM Symposium on Principles of Programming Languages*, Tucson, Arizona, Jan. 1978, pp. 9-16.

[Kant 79] Elaine Kant, Efficiency Considerations in Program Synthesis: A Knowledge Based Approach, Ph.D. thesis, Memo AIM-331, Report STAN-CS-79-755, Computer Science Department, Stanford University, Sept. 1979 [reprinted as 'Efficiency in Program Synthesis' by UMI Research Press, Ann Arbor, Michigan, 1981]

[Kowalski 79] Robert Kowalski, Logic for Programming, Elsevier North Holland, 1979.

[Manna and Waldinger 80] Zohar Manna and Richard Waldinger, "Problematic Features of Programming Languages: A Situational-Calculus Approach," Stanford Department of Computer Science Report No. STAN-CS-80-779, Sept. 1980.

[Phillips 82], Jorge Phillips, Self-Described Programming Environments: An Application of a Theory of Design to Programming Systems. Ph.D Thesis, Electrical Engineering and Computer Science Departments, Stanford University (forthcoming).

[Phillips and Green, 80] Jorge Phillips and Cordell Green, "Towards Self-Described Programming Environments," *SCI Technical Report*, SCI.ICS.L.81.3, June 1980.

[Rich 81] Charles Rich, Inspection Methods in Programming, Ph.D. thesis, MIT/AI/TR-604.

[Schonberg et al, 78] Schonberg, J.T. Schwartz and M. Sharir, "Automatic Data Selection in SETL," *Proc. Fifth ACM Symposium on Principles of Programming Languages*, Tucson, Arizona, Jan. 1978.

[Shrobe 79] Howard Shrobe, Dependency Directed Reasoning for Complex Program Understanding, Ph.D. thesis, MIT/AIM/TR-503, April 1979.

[Teitelman and Masinter, 81] Warren Teitelman and Larry Masinter, "The Interlisp Programming Environment," *Computer*, Vol. 14, 4, April 1981.

[Warren et al, 77] David H. D. Warren, Luis Pereira and Fernando Pereira, "PROLOG: the language and its implementation compared with LISP," in *Proc. Symposium on AI and Programming Languages*, SIGPLAN/SIGART, 1977.

[Warren 80] David H. D. Warren, "Logic Programming and Compiler Writing," *Software—Practice and Experience*, Vol. 10, (1980) pp. 97-125.

[Waters 1978] Richard Waters, Automatic Analysis of the Logical Structure of Programs, Ph.D. thesis, MIT/AI/TR-492, Dec. 1978.

[Weyhrauch 80] Richard W. Weyhrauch, "Prolegomena to a Theory of Mechanized Formal Reasoning," *Artificial Intelligence* 13 (1980) pp. 133-170.

IMPLEMENTING SPECIFICATION FREEDOMS*

Philip E. LONDON** and Martin S FEATHER***

Information Sciences Institute, University of Southern California, Marina del Rey, CA 90291, U.S.A.

Communicated by L. Lamport
Received June 1981
Revised October 1982

Abstract. The process of converting formal specifications into valid implementations is central in the development of reliable software. As formal specification languages are enriched with constructs to enhance their expressive capabilities and as they increasingly afford specificational freedoms by requiring only a description of intended behavior rather than a prescription of particular algorithms, the gap between specification and implementation widens so that converting specifications into implementations becomes even more difficult. A major problem lies in the mapping of high-level specification constructs into an implementation that effects the desired behavior. In this paper, we consider the issues involved in eliminating occurrences of high-level specification-oriented constructs during this process. Mapping issues are discussed in the context of our development methodology, in which implementations are derived via the application of correctness-preserving transformations applied to a specification language whose high-level expressive capabilities are modeled after natural language. After the general discussion, we demonstrate the techniques on a real system whose specification is written in this language.

1. Introduction

As formal specification technology continues to develop, the constructs available in specification languages will increasingly differ from those available in the various implementation languages. A problem then arises in the mapping between these disparate language levels. Implementation languages simply do not possess the ability to express directly concepts that are to be found in specifications. This is as it should be because the languages are designed for different purposes; implementation languages are for describing efficient algorithms, and specification languages are for describing behaviors.

* This research was supported by Defense Advanced Research Projects Agency contract DAHC15 72 C 0308. Views and conclusions contained in this document are those of the authors and should not be interpreted as representing the official opinion or policy of DARPA, the U.S. Government, or any other person or agency connected with them.
** Current address: Knowledge Engineering Group, Digital Equipment Corporation, 678 Andover Street, Lawrence, MA 01843, U.S.A.
*** Order not significant.

One goal in the design of formal specification languages is to ease the task of writing specifications. One approach to this involves using a specification language that reduces the burden in two ways. First, by enhancing expressiveness the specifier finds it easier to state his desires. Second, by requiring only a description of intended behavior rather than the detailed specification of a particular algorithm, the specifier is afforded the freedom to specify *what* is desired rather than *how* to achieve it.

This, however, makes more serious the problem of producing a correct implementation from the design specification. In this paper, we investigate a solution to this problem by presenting a number of implementation options for each of several high-level specification constructs. We then demonstrate that the *mappings* of these high-level specification constructs into implementations are derivable by sequential application of relatively straightforward correctness-preserving[1] transformations. The collection of high-level specification mappings can be viewed as the major conceptual steps in a 'Transformational Implementation'.

The work presented here should be viewed as being but part of a larger effort[2] investigating reliable software development by considering methods for automating aspects of the software development process. The methodology for developing reliable software that we have adopted is comprised of the following activities:

(1) system specification in a formal language designed for specification,
(2) elimination of high-level specification constructs by mechanical application of correctness-preserving transformations,
(3) selection and development of algorithms and abstract data types to effect behavior described in the specification (also by mechanical application of correctness-preserving transformations),
(4) transition into the target implementation language.

It is through the selection and application of appropriate transformations (from a pre-existing catalog) that the implementor maps the specification into an implementation. The programmer in this scenario has control over the implementation process, making many of the same decisions he would ordinarily. Our goal is to construct a system that will relieve some of the implementor's burden by performing the perfunctory tasks of bookkeeping and program source text maintenance. Specifically, the portions of this software development system to be automated are:

(1) tools to assist the implementor in deciding on the appropriateness and applicability of a given transformation,
(2) a mechanism for applying a chosen transformation to the developing program,
(3) support for the development process (e.g., automatic production of documentation, 'replay' facilities which allow a development to be repeated so as to reimplement a modified specification, etc.),

---

1 Since in our view a specification denotes a set of behaviors, our notion of a 'correct' transformation is one whose application results in a specification denoting a subset of those behaviors (a non-empty subset, provided that the original specification denoted a non-empty set of behaviors).
2 Being conducted by the Transformational Implementation (TI) group at ISI.

(4) the catalog of correctness-preserving source-to-source transformations, which embodies the knowledge of alternative implementations of particular specificational constructs,

(5) a mechanism for translating a fully developed program into a target implementation language.

The development of these high-level transformations, which we call *mappings*, presents a rich set of issues dealing with the translation of specifications into implementations. As it is often difficult to separate the activities of mapping high-level constructs and selection and development of algorithms and data types, the discussion of mapping transformations will also consider these issues.

The specification language itself is critical within this software development framework. Two basic characteristics are required of the specification language. The first of these is that the language provide the flexibility and ease of expression required for describing the full range of acceptable behaviors of the system under design. See Balzer and Goldman [2] for a description of the requirements for specification languages that will exhibit these characteristics. The second requirement for a specification language for our software development methodology is that it be wide-spectrum (Bauer et al. [8]). This means, in essence, that the same language can serve both as a specification language (for describing the full range of acceptable behaviors) and as an implementation language (for describing an efficient program whose behavior is true to the specification). In reality, the specification language need not be wide-spectrum only up to a point; after selection of algorithms and abstract data types, the 'implementation' can automatically be translated into a suitable implementation language.

Our group has developed such a language, called GIST (Goldman and Wile [26]), which permits expressibility by the provision of many of the constructs found in natural language specifications of processes. These expressive capabilities include *historical reference* (the ability to refer to past process states), *constraints* (restrictions on acceptable system behavior in the form of global declarations), a relational and associative model of data which captures the logical structure without imposing an access regime, *inference* (which allows for global declarations describing relationships among data), and *demons* (asynchronous process responding to defined stimuli), among others. Thus, the effort in GIST has been to provide the specificational expressiveness of natural language while imposing formal syntax and semantics.³

This paper focusses on the transformations used to eliminate these high-level specification constructs. Such elimination is obviously necessary because no target implementation language is expected to provide such facilities. More importantly, to the extent that the specification language is doing its job of describing intended behavior (*what*) without prescribing a particular algorithm (*how*) these constructs represent the freedoms offered by the specification language. How such freedoms are implemented determine in large part the efficiency of the resulting algorithm. Furthermore, as such constructs are just beginning to be incorporated into specification languages, consideration of alternative implementations of these constructs has received little attention. Absence of these constructs has forced systems analysts and designers to choose (normally unconsciously) one implementation as a precondition to expressing a specification.

³ Note that GIST syntax is ALGOL-like and not English-like!

2. Specification in Gist

A Gist specification describes the behavior of a closed-world system. Not only is the behavior of the process to be implemented described, but also described is the nature of the environment in which it resides. In this way, all constraints on the process by its environment are made explicit, as is all information on which it can rely.

As an example to illustrate this point, consider a routing system for distributing packages into destination bins.⁴ The complete specification in Gist appears in Appendix 1; Fig. 1 illustrates the routing network. This problem serves as our source of illustrative examples throughout the paper.

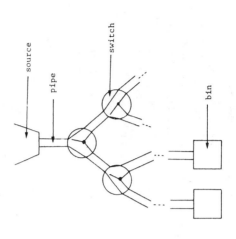

Fig. 1. Package router.

A specification of this system would describe the topology of the routing network (a binary tree whose nodes are switches). In addition, it would describe the behavior of the switches and conveyors. The specification would state that the switches must

⁴ This problem was constructed by representatives of the process control industry to be typical of their real-world applications. A study of various programming methodologies was done using this as the comparative example, Hommel [27].

These points are illustrated by small examples from the package router domain described in English; we adopt a convention of displaying such examples within italicized, indented paragraphs. Our primary intent here is to consider the general issues related to mappings of specification freedoms rather than to describe Gist syntax or the complexities of a large realistic example. In Sections 4 and 5, we examine GIST-related issues by considering the package router in more detail.

3.1. Relational model of information

We begin the discussion of mapping GIST's major features by focusing on its underlying data model. Information in Gist is modeled simply by typed objects and relations among them.

> *The package router domain involves objects of type package, objects of type switch, etc. Type hierarchies are possible; for example, a switch or a bin might more generally be considered a location.*

Relations among these objects model information about this domain.

> *The location of a package would be modeled by a relation between packages and locations.*

> *The setting of a switch (i.e., the outlet pipe into which the switch is currently directing packages) would be modeled by a relation between switches and pipes.*

The collection of objects and relations at any time during the interpretation of a specification comprises what we call a 'state'. Change in the domain is modeled by the creation and destruction of objects (e.g., the introduction of a new package), and by the insertion and deletion of relations (e.g., altering the setting of a switch may be modeled by relating the switch to a different outlet pipe). Each change is a transition from the current state into a new state.

3.1.1. Specification freedom

The relational model of information permits the specifier to use a descriptive reference to an object to refer to that object.

> *The pipe that this switch is set to.*

> *The bin that is the destination of this package.*

The relational data model is a very general data representation. The specifier need not be concerned about data access paths, for instance, because they are associatively accessible. Further, concern about the statistical distribution of these operations is unnecessary. The implementation process selects particular physical representations for information that are appropriate for anticipated patterns of data storage and access.

behave in a way that guarantees correct routing of packages whenever possible; an implementation must switch the switches in the proper direction at the correct time.

The conveyors, on the other hand, operate under the action of gravity, and are thus an environmental factor rather than an effector that the system may control. While the specification describes the range of desired interactions between conveyors and switches that give rise to acceptable system behavior, the process to be implemented is limited to controlling the switches. Implementation of a Gist specification, therefore, requires controlling the implementable portions of the specification so as to respond in acceptable ways to the specified environment.

In specifying a system, as in this example, we aim to make a clear and correct statement of the behavior the switches must exhibit in their interaction with each other and the environment. However, the specification strives to describe the behavior directly without resorting to an algorithm that effects that behavior; deriving such an algorithm is rightly part of the separate task of implementing the specification. Therefore, the emphasis in Gist specification is on *what* rather than *how*. This is important for making a clear distinction between specification and implementation; by describing *what*, we do not restrict the implementation freedoms available.

In a further effort to simplify the specification of intended behavior, Gist specifications assume perfect knowledge. That is, any information used to describe the behavior of a system is available to each of the component parts to describe its interactions with other parts. This assumption is often not satisfied in the actual system. In the package router example, the specification relies upon knowing the location and destination of each package. However, in the actual system the destination of a package is only accessible at the time it enters the network, and its location is only deducible from sensor data indicating the passage of packages through the network. In an implementation, the unavailable information must be deduced from other available information. Explicitly stating in the body of the specification what information is available to the implementable portion would complicate the description of the system behavior by substituting a *how* for a *what* description. For this reason, these separable issues have been decoupled; the specification uses the perfect knowledge assumption, while the information actually available in an implementation is described separately.

3. Mappings

In this section Gist's major constructs are considered in turn, and for each we
- informally describe the semantics of the construct,
- describe the freedoms it provides for specification,
- outline the alternatives available for mapping away instances of that construct,
- outline the considerations that influence the selection among those mappings.

3.1.2. Mappings

The most general solution to implementing information storage is to support an associative relational data-base and leave the specification's insertions and retrievals of information unchanged. In most cases, however, a specification does not indiscriminately insert or retrieve data; rather, it displays predictable data access patterns. These can be mapped into appropriate data structures (arrays, hash tables, etc.) to conserve space and time.

If the relation between a package and its destination bin is referenced in the specification only as Given the package, what is the bin?, then the destination information could be stored as a field of a record structure of information associated with each package.

It should be noted that many of the issues presented here relating to the relational data model are similar to those investigated by the SETL group (Dewar et al. [19], Schonberg, Schwartz and Sharir [37]) and by Rovner [36], Low [31], and Barstow [5].

3.1.3. Choice criteria

Concerns for efficiency of time and space dictate the selection of data structures. Probabilistic expectations of frequency of use are not explicitly described in GIST specifications. Clearly, for implementation purposes, such information will be of importance in selection.

3.2. Historical reference

Historical reference in GIST specifications provides the ability to extract information from any preceding state in the computation history.

Has this package ever been at that switch?,

What was the most recent package to have been in this switch?,

Was the bin empty when the package entered the network?

Note that the past can only be queried, not changed.

3.2.1. Specification freedom

Historical reference allows the specifier to easily and unambiguously describe *what* information is needed from earlier states without concern for the details of *how* it might be made available. Reference to the past has been studied in the database world, where the freedom has been called 'memory independence', and temporal logic has been applied to formally investigate the matter (see, e.g., Sernadas [39]).

3.2.2. Mapping away historical references

Two generally applicable methods exist for mapping historical reference into a reasonable implementation. These are

(1) save the information desired in the earlier state, then modify the historical reference to extract it from the saved information, or

(2) modify the historical reference to rederive the desired information from the current state.

To use the first method, it is necessary to introduce and maintain auxiliary data structures to store information that might be referenced in a later state, and modify the historical references to extract the desired information from those introduced structures when needed. The desire for economy of storage in an implementation encourages the implementor to determine just what information need be preserved, seek a compact representation facilitating both storage and retrieval, and discard the information once it is no longer useful.

To be prepared to answer the query "what was the destination of the last package to have passed through this switch?" we could choose to remember the time-ordered sequence of packages to have been in the switch, or more efficiently, only the destination of the immediately preceding package. This latter case would require storage space for the identity of only a single destination bin; upon arrival of a new package, the identity of its destination would be remembered in that space, overwriting the old information.

The alternative method for implementing historical reference is to rederive the desired information in terms of information available in the current state (without having to retain extra information from past states).

The identity of the previous package to have been at this switch might be derived by determining which package in the network is closest to and downhill from the switch.

3.2.3. Choice criteria

We suspect that rederivation is rarely an available option; the information desired is often not derivable from current available information. When both options are possible, they present the classic store/recompute tradeoffs. An implementor must compare the cost of the derivation with the cost of storage and maintenance of redundant information to permit simple access.

3.2.4. Idiomatic uses of historical reference

Certain patterns of historical reference recur frequently in Gist specifications. For example, evaluating

⟨predicate⟩ asof ⟨event⟩   or   ⟨expression⟩ asof ⟨event⟩

(of which *What was the setting of the switch at the time the package entered the network?* is an example). For an idiom like this we can construct special purpose mappings,[5] reducing the effort that would be required during implementation

---

[5] This idiom is mapped into an explicit relation between the objects that parameterize the event and the ⟨predicate⟩/⟨expression⟩, together with code to maintain this relation, namely to insert the relation whenever the event occurs and the ⟨predicate⟩ holds/there exists an object denoted by the ⟨expression⟩).

development if a general purpose mapping technique was applied. A general-purpose mapping technique would require application of further simplifications to tailor the result for the special case.

Other idioms that we deal with include:
- the **latest** object to satisfy a given predicate,
- the sequence of objects ordered by their time of creation or the time at which they satisfied a given predicate,
- did event$_1$ take place before event$_2$?

3.3. Non-determinism and constraints

Non-determinism within Gist occurs in two ways: When use is made of a descriptive reference that denotes more than one object,

Set the switch to one of the switch outlets,

or when some specifically non-deterministic control structure is used

Choose between "*Set switch*" and "*Release package*".

In terms of the behavior that a Gist specification denotes, non-determinism gives rise to a **set** of behaviors; an implementor is free to select any (non-empty!) subset[6] of those behaviors as the ones his implementation will satisfy.

The activity of setting switches is described non-deterministically by stating that at random times random switches set themselves to a random one of their outlet pipes.

Constraints within Gist provide a means of stating integrity conditions that must always remain satisfied.

A package cannot overtake another

A package must never reach a wrong bin (a bin other than its destination).

Within Gist, constraints are more than merely redundant checks that the specification always generates valid behaviors; constraints serve to *rule out* those behaviors that would be invalid.

The non-determinism of switch setting, in conjunction with the constraint on packages reaching correct bins, denotes only behaviors that route the packages to the proper destination bins.

3.3.1. Specification freedom

Where there are several equally acceptable alternatives in the resolution of a data reference or a control structure choice, non-determinism makes it easy to specify them all.

[6] I.e. there may be behaviors denoted by the specification not displayed by the implementation. Conversely, however, any behavior displayed by the implementation must be one of the behaviors denoted by the specification.

The freedom afforded by constraints is that the requirement that packages cannot overtake one another need be stated only once, rather than everywhere in the specification that locations of packages are changed. That is, constraints provide a concise statement of intents and limitations.

The conjunction of the two proves to be an extremely powerful specification technique; a specification denotes those and only those behaviors that do not violate constraints. In contrast, an implementation is characterized by the cunning encoding of its components to interact in ways guaranteed to result in only valid behaviors.

3.3.2. Mapping away constraints and non-determinism

A general mapping technique to eliminate constraints is to make each non-deterministic activity into a choice point, and to unfold global constraints so as to provide tests at all points in the program where the constraint might possibly be violated. When a violation is detected, a 'failure' results; this causes backtracking to the most recent choice point with an alternative choice.

To place 8 queens on a chessboard under the constraint that no queen may attack any other queen, simultaneously place all the queens on the board (64^8 non-deterministic choices!), and after doing so, check to see whether the no-capture constraint is violated—if so, try the next choice of placements. (Note that this is a most inefficient mapping.)

Two separate processes are required to implement this mapping:
(1) determining all locations in the specification at which the constraint might be violated, and
(2) inserting, at those points, code to do the checks and backtracking.

The first of these capabilities is of use in not only constraint mapping, but also, as we shall see in the next sections, in mappings for other Gist constructs. In general terms, given a predicate, this process identifies those locations in the specification where an action might result in a change in the truth of the predicate. Clearly this is a 'refinable' capability; we may begin with a crude mechanism that identifies many locations of potential change and later refine it to improve the identification process (i.e., eliminate some of those places which, with deeper analysis, can be shown to not cause any change in the predicate value).

The second capability mentioned above as required for mapping constraints and non-determinism implements the backtracking control mechanism. Our research suggests that it is possible to intermix Gist's non-determinism and constraints with explicit backtracking, permitting the incremental mapping of individual non-deterministic choice points, and of the constraints that impinge upon them (as opposed to having to simultaneously map away *all* the non-determinism and constraints at once). The task of building the backtracking mechanism itself is trivial if our intended target language supports backtracking (as does, for example, PROLOG (Clocksin and Mellish [13])).

over the behavior of the portion of the specification we are implementing. (See Section 2.) We assume that our mission is to implement this portion so that no constraints are violated. We have no control over the behavior of other portions of the system, though we can assume that they too behave according to specifications. Those other portions of the specification describe the environment in which our implementation will execute. The constraints in those portions of the specification are viewed as invariants upon which our implementation relies, rather than has to maintain. It is, however, our responsibility to implement our portion to react to any allowable behavior of the other portions of the specification so as to never cause any constraints to be violated.[8]

3.4. Derived relations

In specification, it is convenient to use information that is implicitly derived from other information. Derived information in Gist takes the form of 'derived relations'; this is consistent with Gist's relational data model. The declaration of such derived relations denote all the maintenance necessary to preserve the invariant between the derived relation and the relations upon which it depends.

Two queens may be said to 'attack' if they lie on the same row, column or diagonal. Thus attack is a derived relation between pairs of queens, derived in terms of queens, the squares they are located on, and the rows/columns/diagonals those squares lie on.

A switch may be said to be 'empty' if there is no package whose location is the switch.

3.4.1. Specification freedom

The specificational power of this construct comes from being able to state a derivation (that is, an invariant among several relations) in a single place, and make use of the derived information throughout the specification.

3.4.2. Mapping away derived relations

Since no corresponding construct is likely to be available in any implementation language we might choose,[9] we must map the derivation into explicit data structures

---

[8] Of course, such a one sided division of responsibility may not be possible in a given situation (i.e. the specification is unimplementable). Avoiding constraint violation may require cooperation among the portions of the system. If so, then the specification must be revised so that such cooperation is required from each portion and can therefore be relied upon.

[9] Many of the Artificial Intelligence programming languages *do* provide facilities for implementing derived relations in terms of inference processes. For example, an implementation of derived relations might be provided in CONNIVER (McDermott and Sussman [33]) in terms of IF-ADDED or IF-NEEDED methods. However, AI programming languages in which these facilities are present typically do not provide for the efficient execution one would desire for an optimized implementation, nor do these facilities provide precisely the semantics desired without the inclusion of satisfactory 'truth maintenance' capabilities (Doyle [20], London [30]).

Backtracking, however, presupposes the ability to undo actions that have been executed since the last choice point. Since this is often not possible, strict backtracking is not always an option for mapping to an implementation of non-determinism.

In controlling the switches in the routing network, we are constrained to ensure that the items being routed do not reach wrong destinations. Backtracking presupposes that we have the ability to return the items to the switching points after an error is detected, and then send them in different directions. Obviously, in the case of a package router whose package movement mechanism is not under our control, this is not an available option.

An alternative technique to mapping non-determinism into backtracking is a 'predictive' solution. Here, the constraints are pushed back to the choice points so that only those choices are made which guarantee no constraints will be violated. In other words, the generator of alternatives is modified to generate only non-violating choices.

To effect correct routing, set switches prior to the arrival of each package in the direction that leads to the package's destination.

Compromise between these two extremes is possible; we may employ a backtracking algorithm, but push some (though not all) of the unfolded constraint(s) into the choice generators.

In the 8-queens problem, split the non-determinism into several successive choices (place the first queen, place the second queen and check for capture, etc.), and incorporate some of the no-capture constraint into the placement (by not attempting to place a subsequent queen on a row already occupied by a queen). See Balzer [1] for a detailed development illustrating this.

3.3.3. Choice criteria

The choice between a backtracking implementation and a predictive implementation is determined very much by the nature of the domain of the specification. The capabilities of, and the control we have of, the effectors[7] (if there are any in the system being specified), the amount of information available for making decisions, and the desired amount of precomputation all affect the choice of algorithm. Typically, the interesting issue is to develop the specification toward an implementation that embodies an algorithm to perform the search efficiently, and not to assume that the result has been pre-calculated and make use of it.

3.3.4. Further remarks

The methods by which an implementation preserves the integrity of constraints is one of the more difficult mapping problems. At the specification level, constraints apply to the whole specification. As implementors, however, we only have control

---

[7] E.g., in a routing network, the switches and conveyor.

and mechanisms to support all the uses of that information scattered throughout the program. A range of choices are available for this mapping.

At one extreme, we might simply unfold the derivation at all the places where a reference to the relation is made. Having done this, the relation and its derivation may be completely discarded.

Wherever the specification makes reference to 'attack' between queens, unfold the definition of 'attack'.

This approach is analogous to backward inference, where computation is performed on demand and at the site of the need.

At the other extreme we might retain the relation, but explicitly scatter throughout the program the code necessary to explicitly maintain the invariant between the derived information and the information upon which it depends.

To maintain the derived relation of switch 'empty', introduce explicit storage (a non-derived relation) to represent this information, and introduce the appropriate maintenance code everywhere in the specification that the locations of packages might change (more precisely, at the places where a package may become located at, or cease being located at, switches).

This approach is analogous to forward inference, where computation is performed whenever a modification to a relevant predicate occurs and at the site of the change. As with the mapping of constraints into backtracking, Section 3.3.2, there are two separate capabilities required by this mapping:

(1) detecting all those locations in the specification at which the derived information could possibly be changed, and

(2) inserting code to do the recalculation at those locations.

Note that the former capability is an instance of predicate maintenance, the general capability outlined in Section 3.3.2, wherein sites of potential change to a derived relation are exactly those at which the predicate defining the derived relation[10] might change in value.

The latter capability can be achieved by either recomputing the defined relation from scratch, or incrementally changing its present value; this we call 'incremental maintenance'.

To maintain the sequence of packages in a pipe, when a package enters the pipe, concatenate that package onto the end of the maintained sequence; when a package exits, remove the package from the front of the maintained sequence.

This is a technique derived from the work of other researchers in set-theoretic settings, particularly Paige and Schwartz [35], who call the technique 'formal differentiation,' and Earley [21], who calls it 'iterator inversion'.

[10] A derived relation is defined by declaring the types of the objects it relates, and declaring a predicate over those objects to serve as its definition. The derived relation is defined to hold among those objects, and only those objects, for which the predicate is true.

Unfolding a derived relation results in rederivation at points of use; maintaining it results in rederivation (incrementally or otherwise) at points of change. It is permissible to do the computation for maintaining the relation at other points, but it must have its correct value by the time it is used.

3.4.3. Choice criteria

The choices among the implementation alternatives suggest alternatives between storage and computation in the resulting program. Completely unfolding the derivation is tending towards complex recalculation with a minimum of stored data. Maintenance simplifies retrievals at the expense of the maintenance operations and the extra storage to hold the maintained information.

3.4.4. Idiomatic uses of derived relations

A derived relation defined to be the transitive closure of another relation exemplifies an idiom for which it is fruitful to construct special-purpose mappings. Indeed, a fully general mapping able to deal with arbitrarily recursive defined relations is probably of little practical use, so we are motivated to seek mappings for idiomatic uses of recursion. (We observe that the 'derived data' in Koenig and Paige [29] may not be recursively defined.)

Other idioms that we have considered include

- the cardinality of objects satisfying a predicate,
- sequences, ordered with respect to some idiomatic ordering,
- extrema, the worst/best of a set of objects with respect to some idiomatic ordering.

3.5. Demons

Demons provide Gist's mechanism for data-directed invocation of processes. A demon has a **trigger** and a **response**. The **trigger** is a predicate that triggers the demon's **response** whenever a state change induces a change in the value of the trigger predicate from false to true.

Whenever a new package arrives at the source station, open the gate and release the package into the network.

3.5.1. Specification freedom

Demons are a convenient construct for situations in which we wish to specify the execution as an asynchronous activity that arises from a particular change of state in the modeled environment. This eliminates the need to identify the individual portions of the specification where actions might cause such a change and the need to insert into such places the additional code necessary to invoke the response accordingly. The specificational power of the demon construct is enhanced by the power of Gist's other features; for example, the triggering predicate may make use of defined relationships or historical reference. This exemplifies one of Gist's strengths, namely the orthogonal combination of (not necessarily novel) features in such a manner as to emerge with a powerful specification language (in the sense that it reduces conceptual distance between intent and formal specification).

3.5.2. Mapping away demons

Mapping away a demon involves identifying all places in the program where a state change might cause a change of the value of the demon's trigger from false to true, and then inserting code at those places to make the determination and perform the demon's **response** when necessary.

To map away a demon which sends a signal every time a package reaches a wrong bin (some bin other than its intended destination), introduce code into the places where package movement occurs to check to see whether that package has moved into a bin other than its destination; in such a case, perform the signalling.

This is another mapping that makes use of the capability to identify locations in the specification where the value of a predicate (in this case the demon's trigger) might be affected (in this case changed from false to true). Here the action to be taken upon detecting such a change is to invoke the demon's response.

Demons are a potent source of non-determinism in the behaviors denoted by a specification. This is because our semantics for demon 'response' are that a new 'line of control' to perform that response is begun, and that line of control runs in parallel with the already active line(s) of control, permitting any arbitrary interleaving that does not violate constraints.

*In the package router, specify the behavior of a switch via a demon that has a **random** trigger,[11] and whose response is to set the switch to any of its outlets (further non-determinism). Together with a constraint to prohibit items from being routed to incorrect destinations, this would suffice to denote behaviors in which switches are set at the appropriate times and in the appropriate directions to effect correct routing, while denoting complete freedom of switch behavior when their settings are not crucial to the routing of any packages.*

Our experience with both specifying and mapping this form of non-determinism is somewhat limited. We anticipate that in many cases it will be preferable to map this form of non-deterministic control structure while expressed concisely as demons, rather than first to unfold those demons throughout the specification and then to have to manage the resulting disparate instances of non-determinism. Our hope is that control non-determinism provided by demons, constrained by constraints which prune out the undesired effects of arbitrary interleaving, will occur in commonly occurring styles of usage, for which we will be able to build idiomatic mappings.

3.6. Total information

For specification purposes it is convenient to reference information about the world described by the specification arbitrarily. Since the development task is to implement only a portion of that world, there are typically restrictions on what information will be available to the implementation and how much it can control the surrounding environment.

In the routing system, we assume for specification purposes that the identity and intended destination of every package are always available. The implementation, however, may not have access to this information. Perhaps the destinations of items may only be read from each item as they enter the system; perhaps the only indication of the passage of items within the network comes from the signalling of sensors placed strategically throughout the network, which indicate merely the passage of an item, but not its identity.

3.6.1. Specification freedom

Total information provides the freedom to use any and all information about the system and its environment to specify desired behaviors. It is left to the development of the implementation to determine just what information is necessary and derive it from what is available.

3.6.2. Mapping away reliance on total information

Mapping away this reliance is similar to mapping historical reference; the implementation can either introduce and maintain auxiliary data structures to hold information that might be needed, or it can find ways to derive the required information from other information that is available.

3.6.3. Choice criteria

As with mapping away other constructs, the context in which unobservable information is used, and the nature of its use may impact our decisions on how to do the mapping.

4. Concrete examples of Gist

This section introduces the syntax of Gist through small examples set in the package router domain; in each case, an informal English description set in italics precedes the Gist formalism. In Section 5, we return to our main goal of demonstrating mappings on the full package router problem.

4.1. Types and relations used to describe the domain

The package router domain contains objects of type package and location, the latter subdivided into source, pipe, switch and bin. These types are declared as follows:

---

[11] Indicating that in any state each such demon has the non-deterministic choice of triggering or not triggering.

type PACKAGE( );

type LOCATION( ) **supertype of**(SOURCE( ); PIPE( ); SWITCH( ); BIN( ))

Relations among the objects serve to model the information within this domain, and must be similarly declared:

The destination of a package – represented as a relation between objects of type BIN and PACKAGE:
    relation Destination(BIN,PACKAGE)

The location a package is currently at – represented as a relation between objects of type LOCATION and PACKAGE:
    relation At(LOCATION,PACKAGE)

Since binary relations are a frequently used form of *n*-ary relations, we find it advantageous to use a syntactic shorthand to more easily declare and access such relations. This shorthand takes the form of 'attributes' associated with types, for example Destination, a binary relation between types BIN and PACKAGE, becomes an attribute of type PACKAGE (note that because of the non-directional nature of relations, Destination could equally well be made an attribute of type BIN). The simultaneous declaration of types and attributes becomes:

Type package with attributes Destination (*type* BIN) *and* At (*type* LOCATION):
    type PACKAGE(Destination|BIN, At|LOCATION)[12]

Type location, one of
– *source, with attribute* Source_Outlet (*type* PIPE)
– *bin,*
– *pipe, with attribute* Pipe_Outlet (*type* SWITCH *or* BIN), *or*
– *switch, with attributes* Switch_Outlet (*type* PIPE) *and* Switch_Setting (*type* PIPE):

    type LOCATION( ) **supertype of**
      ⟨SOURCE(Source_Outlet|PIPE);
      BIN( );
      PIPE(Pipe_Outlet|SWITCH **union** BIN);
      SWITCH(Switch_Outlet|PIPE, Switch_Setting|PIPE)⟩

The current state of the domain is modeled by the collection of (typed) objects and relations among these objects.

4.2. Predicates and expressions

Information about the current state may be retrieved via predicates and expressions denoting objects in the current state.

[12] *Notation*: The special symbol | should be read as "which is of type ...".

Expressions:
A package in the domain:
    a package
A switch in the domain:
    a switch
The destination of package p:
    p:**Destination**[13]
The location package p is at:
    p:**At**
A package destined for bin b:
    a package ‖ (package : **Destination** = b)[14]

Predicates:
Is package p at its destination?
    p:**At** = p:**Destination**

Existential and universal quantification over objects of a given type is permitted:
Is there a package at every switch?
    all switch ‖ (**exists** package ‖ (package : **At** = switch))

4.3. Change in the domain

Change is modeled in the domain by the creation and destruction of objects, and the insertion and deletion of relations among objects. Each such primitive change causes a 'transition' to a new state. A Gist specification denotes 'behavior' – a sequence of states connected by transitions.

Create a new package:
    create package
Assign bin b as destination of package p:
    insert p:**Destination** = b

To include within a single transition several such primitive changes, embed them inside Gist's 'atomic' construct:

Change the location of package p from loc1 to loc2:
    atomic
      delete p:**At** = *loc1*;
      insert p:**At** = *loc2*
    end atomic

[13] *Notation*: ⟨expression⟩:⟨attribute name⟩ denotes the object(s) related to the object(s) denoted by the expression by that attribute.
[14] *Notation*: The special symbol ‖ should be read as "such that". The construct used here takes the form **a** ⟨typename⟩‖⟨predicate⟩ and denotes the object(s) of that type satisfying the predicate.

4.4.   Historical reference

The sequence of states connected by transitions leading to the current state is a 'history'. By default, a predicate or expression is evaluated in the current state. Evaluation in some arbitrary state in the history is possible. As with reference to objects, specifying the state(s) in which to do the evaluation is done by description – provide a predicate which, when true of a state in the history, indicates that state is to be used for evaluation.

(The predicate describing) states in which package p2 is at the source:

> p2 : At = **the** source

The location of package p1 **when package p2 was at the source:**

> (p1 : At) **asof** (p2 : At = **the source**)[15]

Has package p ever been at switch s?

> (p : At = s) **asof** true

The time-ordered sequence of packages ever at the source:

> (a package) **ordered wrt** package : At = **the source**

4.5.   Derived relations

In Gist relations are used to model information, hence derived relations serve as the means to define information in terms of objects in the domain and relations among them.

Define a relation In_Correct_Bin to hold between package and bin whenever a package is at its destination bin:

> **relation** In_Correct_Bin(package,bin)[16]
>
> **definition** package : Destination = bin **and** package : At = bin ;

Derived relations may be accessed within expressions and predicates in just the same way as any standard relation.

Is package p in a correct bin?

> **exists** bin ||| In_Correct_Bin(p, bin)

They may not, however, be explicitly inserted or deleted – their definitions serve to denote precisely when they hold.

In each case the evaluation takes place in the state(s) in the history (i.e. now or before) in which predicate₂ held. For the predicate, the result will be true if predicate₁ held in any of the selected states. For the expression, the result will be the object(s) (non-deterministic if multiple objects) denoted by the expression in any of the selected states.
16 Notation: A derived relation consists of a name, list of formal parameters, and a definition consisting of a predicate over those parameters; the relation is defined to hold between those and only those objects (of the same types as the parameters) which, when substituted for the parameters into the predicate, make the predicate evaluate to true.

4.6.   Demons

It is often convenient to describe when to perform some activity in terms of the changes to the domain. Demons are Gist's means of providing data-triggered activity; their definition includes a 'trigger', some arbitrary predicate, and a 'response', some arbitrary statement. The trigger predicate is used to recognize transitions when the activity, the response statement, is to be performed. Any transition which causes a state change from an old state in which the trigger predicate was false, to a new state in which it is true, is such a transition.

... when a package reaches a bin:

> **exists** package,bin ||| (package : At = bin

Signal the arrival of a package at a bin:

> **demon** SIGNAL_UPON_ARRIVAL[package,bin][17]
>
> **trigger** package : At = bin
>
> **response** SIGNAL_ARRIVAL[package,bin][18]

4.7.   Non-determinism and constraints

4.7.1.   Non-determinism

Gist's form of reference to objects, because of its 'descriptive' nature, may result in several objects satisfying the description. In such a case we say the expression is non-deterministic.

Any package whatsoever:

> a package

Any package at a bin:

> a package ||| (package : At = (a bin))

An outlet pipe of switch s:

> a pipe ||| (s : Switch_Outlet = pipe)

(more concisely)   s : Switch_Outlet

Non-deterministic behavior results when such a non-deterministic reference is used in a transition. The alternative transitions give rise to distinct continuations of the behavior. Hence a Gist specification denotes a **set** of behaviors (and a valid implementation is one that gives rise to a non-empty subset of those behaviors).

Set the switch s (non-deterministically) to one of its outlets:

> **insert** s : Switch_Setting = s : Switch_Outlet

Non-determinism may also be introduced through the use of non-deterministic control constructs.

Furthermore, since this case is typical of many attributes, the default is to assume: **unique** and **:: any**, so the declaration simplifies to:

type PACKAGE(Destination | BIN, At | LOCATION)

Prohibit a package from being in a bin other than its destination:

always prohibited MISROUTING
  exists *package* ||(*package* : At **isa** BIN **and**
    not *package* : Destination = *package* : At)

4.7.3. Combination of non-determinism and constraints

The conjunction of non-determinism and constraints serves as a powerful specification technique; non-determinism denotes a set of behaviors, constraints rule out those behaviors containing anomalous states. Hence a Gist specification denotes the set of only valid behaviors.

Switches set at random (SET_SWITCH demon) in such a way as to cause correct routing of packages, always avoiding routing a package to a wrong bin (MISROUTING constraint). Hence the behaviors denoted by the package router specification are all the ways of setting switches that cause the correct routing of packages.

4.8. Closed specification

Gist specifications are closed, in the sense that in addition to describing the portion to be implemented, they also describe (in as much detail as necessary) the environment in which that portion is to operate. Thus the behaviors specified are those required of the entire world. The portion to be implemented must act in such a manner as to interact with its environment to produce a non-empty subset of those behaviors.

The package router is described in a closed world in which packages are created at the source, and are caused to move down through the network. The portions to be implemented (and hence over which we have control) are the source, where packages are released into the network, and the switches. These must perform in such a manner as to cause the correct routing of packages, whatever their destination, and however they might move through the network.

Movement of packages through the router is not within the control of the portion we are to implement, yet must be described in sufficient detail to express the behaviors required of that portion. Movement is modeled by a (non-deterministic) demon that at random causes a random package to move (if possible) to the next location in the router.

demon MOVE_PACKAGE[*package,location.next*]
  trigger Random()
  response if CONNECTED_TO(*package* : At, *location.next*)
    then update[22] : **At of** *package* **to** *location.next*

[22] *Notation*: **update**:(attribute) **of** (expression) **to** (expression') changes the attribute value of expression to expression', i.e. does a delete of the old value and an insert of the new value in an atomic transition.

Assign bin b as destination of every package:

loop (**a** *package*) **do insert** *package* : Destination = *b*[19]

At random times, set switches to one of their outlets:

demon SET_SWITCH(*switch*)
  trigger Random()[20]
  response insert *switch* : Switch_Setting =
    switch : Switch_Outlet

4.7.2. Constraints

Constraints are used to describe the limitations of the domain and of the desired behaviors. Constraints serve to rule out anomalous states; Gist specifications denote only those behaviors containing only valid states.

There cannot exist more than one source:

always prohibited exists *s1* | SOURCE, *s2* | SOURCE ||(**not** *s1* = *s2*)

more precisely, there cannot arise a state in which there exists an object *s1* which is of type source and *s2* which is of type source such that *s1* does not equal *s2*.

Every package has precisely one destination bin:

always required all *package* ||
  ((**exists** *bin* ||(*package* : Destination = *bin*)) **and**
  not exists *b1* | BIN, *b2* | BIN ||(*package* : Destination = *b1* **and**
    package : Destination = *b2* **and**
    not *b1* = *b2*))

Constraints of this form (on the cardinality of attributes and relations) are common, hence we apply a notational shorthand and declare them at the same time as we make type and attribute declarations:

A package has two attributes
– Destination, a unique bin; a bin may be the Destination of any number of packages, and
– At, a unique location; a location may be the At of any number of packages:

type PACKAGE(Destination | BIN : **unique** :: **any**[21],
    At | LOCATION : **unique** :: **any**)

[19] *Notation*: **loop** (expression) **do** (statement) does the statement for each object denoted by the expression – the non-determinism arises from the non-specified ordering in which to consider the objects.
[20] *Notation*: Random() here denotes the non-deterministic choice of either triggering or not triggering the demon on a transition.
[21] *Notation*: the keyword following ':', in this case **unique**, constrains how many objects of the attribute type (BIN) may be attributed to the type being defined (PACKAGE); the keyword following '::' in this case **any**, constrains how many objects of the defined type (PACKAGE) may have as their attribute an object of the attribute type (BIN).

An abstraction specification states which details of the whole system are to be included in the behaviors the specification is to denote. (Details abstracted away are analogous to construction lines in geometry.)

abstraction
  types
    LOCATION, SOURCE, PIPE, SWITCH, BIN, PACKAGE;
  attributes
    Source_Outlet, Pipe_Outlet, Switch_Outlet,
    Switch_Setting, At, Destination;
  actions
    DISPLAY_MISROUTING, WAIT
end abstraction

Action DISPLAY_MISROUTING *is included in the abstraction specification, i.e. invocation of this action is part of the behavior denoted by the specification, hence transformations must retain these invocations. Conversely, derived relation* SWITCH_IS_EMPTY *is not included in the abstraction specification, hence the freedom to unfold all uses of this relation and discard it, should we wish to do so.*

4.9. Total information

In specifying the behaviors required of the system, it is convenient to make arbitrary retrievals from relations, quantification over all objects of a given type, etc., in order to achieve a straightforward specification. Typically, however, the portion to be implemented will be restricted in the queries it may make of its surrounding environment.

To describe the desired behavior of the package router, the constraints, demons, etc. make use of knowledge about the destinations and locations of packages anywhere within the routing network. Physical reality of the package router limits observation of the destination of a package to the time at which the package is at the source (there is a bar code reader), and hence an implementation may explicitly read each package's intended destination only while it is at the source. If the implementor decides this information is required, say to control the switches, then the implementation must save the information when it is available.

The implementation specification describes what the portion to be implemented may observe and what it may effect.

implement PACKAGE_ROUTER
  observing
    predicates
      exists package ‖ (package : Destination = bin and
                        package : At = the source);

The package router may observe the destination bin of a package located at the source.

5. Case study

In this section, we present three examples of mappings applied to the package router specification that appears in Appendix 1. Our focus here is analogous to that of an implementer; we consider the ramifications of the implementation decisions necessary for effectively mapping the specification. We have suppressed the details of how each mapping is accomplished by the application of transformations. However, each has actually been performed by the sequential application of low-level source to source transformations. The interested reader should refer to Feather and London [24].

5.1. Derived relations

The following derived relation is used by the constraint that enforces appropriate routing of packages (and, as we shall see, in the realization of the constraint by algorithmic means):

relation PACKAGES_TO_BE_ROUTED_BY_SWITCH
    (*packages* | **sequence of** PACKAGE, *switch*)
  definition *packages* =
    (**a** *package* ‖
      (BELOW(*switch,package* : At) **and**
       BELOW(*package* : Destination,*switch*) **and**
       not PACKAGE_IN_CORRECT_SWITCH_WRONGLY_SET(*package*))
) **ordered wrt** PACKAGES_EVER_AT_SOURCE(∗);

For any particular switch, the sequence of packages due to be routed by the switch consists of those for which:
– the switch lies below the package's current location in the network,
– the package's destination lies below the switch, and
– the package is not in a correct switch that is wrongly set (which would imply the package is doomed to be misrouted).

The ordering puts packages in sequence ordered by the time at which they were located at the source.[23]

The mapping choice is between unfolding or maintaining this relation. An incremental maintenance mapping is selected because the frequent retrievals of the information required to maintain this information can be made inexpensive; by performing incremental maintenance, the explicit sequences of packages may be updated as packages start to, or cease to, require routing by a switch. By contrast, unfolding would imply repeated complex recalculations of this maintained information.

[23] Observe that the structure of the network (a tree with the source at the root) and the property that packages cannot overtake one another combine to ensure that packages will arrive at switches in the same order in which they were located at the source.

The value of the maintained relation may potentially change upon:

(1) Changes to the attributes At and Destination of packages, which occur when a new package is created at the source, and when movement of a package occurs.

(2) Changes to the derived relation PACKAGE_IN_CORRECT_SWITCH_WRONGLY_SET, which occur on changes to the attributes At and Destination of packages (as before), and also on changes to the Switch_Setting attribute of switches.

(3) Changes to the derived relation PACKAGES_EVER_AT_SOURCE, which occur when a new package is created at the source.

(Note that derived relation BELOW, a property of the static structure of the routing network, is not changed by any activity in the specification.)

At these identified points of change, code is introduced to maintain the sequences of packages defining the PACKAGES_TO_BE_ROUTED_BY_SWITCH relation. The incremental nature of this calculation is embodied in the introduced maintenance code, which modifies the sequences of packages defining the relation. However, the modifications are of a restricted type. These changes are restricted to addition of new packages to be routed onto the end of sequences, and the removal of old packages from the front; the interior of the sequences always remaining unchanged. This greatly simplifies the maintenance code.

An example of a site at which maintenance code need be introduced is within the RELEASE_PACKAGE_INTO_NETWORK demon, which notices a new package at the source. The introduced code (marked at the side by ▶) adds the new package to the end of the sequences associated with each switch on that package's route to its destination.

After mapping:

```
demon RELEASE_PACKAGE_INTO_NETWORK[package.new]
  trigger package.new : At = the source
  response
  begin
▲   loop switch ||BELOW(package : Destination,switch)
▲   do update packages in
▲       PACKAGES_TO_BE_ROUTED_BY_SWITCH(packages,switch)
          to packages concatenate package.new;

    if package.new : Destination ≠ (etc. as before);
    update : At of package.new to (the source) : Source_Outlet
  end;
```

5.2. Historical reference

One example of historical reference in the Package Router specification is in determining the destination of the preceding package. This is necessary to decide whether to delay release into the network of a newly arrived package at the source:

```
relation PACKAGES_EVER_AT_SOURCE(packages | sequence of PACKAGE)
  definition packages = (a package) ordered
    wrt package : At = (the source);

demon RELEASE_PACKAGE_INTO_NETWORK[package.new]
  trigger package.new : At = the source
  response
  begin
    if package.new : Destination ≠
      (a package.previous ||
        package.previous immediately < package.new
          wrt PACKAGES_EVER_AT_AT_SOURCE(*)) : Destination
    then WAIT[ ];
    update : At of package.new to (the source) : Source_Outlet
  end;
```

Determination of when to release a package into the network commences when a new package becomes located at the source station. If the new package's destination differs from that of the previous package (that is, the package immediately preceding the new package in the sequence of packages to have been located at the source (defined below)), then wait.

The sequence of packages ever located at the source is defined by non-deterministically referring to packages, and ordering them by the order in which they were located at the source.

To map away this historical reference we must be prepared to save some information (as opposed to attempting to compute it from the current state since there is no way (in general) to deduce from the locations of packages in the router which was the previous package). The mapping decision is one of selecting what information to remember – we could remember the entire sequence of packages ever to have been at the source, or the sequence of their destinations, or only the previous package to have been there, or that package's destination. We select the latter based on the principle that it minimizes the amount of information to be remembered, and permits simple maintenance.

After mapping:

```
▶ relation PREVIOUS_PACKAGE_DESTINATION(ppdest | BIN);

demon RELEASE_PACKAGE_INTO_NETWORK[package.new]
  trigger package.new : At = the source
  response
  begin
    if package.new : Destination ≠
        PREVIOUS_PACKAGE_DESTINATION(*)
      then WAIT[ ];
▲
```

▲ **update** ppdest **in** PREVIOUS_PACKAGE_DESTINATION($)
  to *package.new* : Destination;
▲ **update** : **At of** *package.new* **to** (**the** *source*) : Source_Outlet
end;

5.3. Non-determinism and constraints

Package routing behavior is specified by a combination of non-determinism and constraint:

demon SET_SWITCH[*switch*]
trigger Random( )
response
 begin
  require SWITCH_IS_EMPTY(*switch*);
  update : Switch_Setting **of** *switch* **to** *switch* : Switch_Outlet
 end;

always prohibited DID_NOT_SET_SWITCH_WHEN_HAD_CHANCE
exists *package, switch* ∥
 (PACKAGE_IN_CORRECT_SWITCH_WRONGLY_SET(*package*)
 and
 ((SWITCH_IS_EMPTY(*switch*) **and** *package* =
  first(PACKAGES_TO_BE_ROUTED_BY_SWITCH(*,*switch*)))**as of true**)
 );

The SET_SWITCH demon expresses switch setting in a very non-deterministic fashion, requiring only that the switch be empty when it be set. The DID_NOT_SET_SWITCH_WHEN_HAD_CHANCE constraint prunes this non-determinism so as to require correct routing whenever possible. For convenience of specification, this is stated in a backward-looking manner –

prohibit being in a state in which a package is in a correct switch wrongly set when there has been some opportunity in the past to set the switch correctly for that package (i.e., a state in which the switch was empty and that package was the first of those due to be routed by that switch).[24]

This combination of non-determinism and constraint is convenient for specification in that it allows the behavior to be stated succinctly, yet does not force the specification to commit that behavior to any particular implementation.

The backtracking technique for mapping them away is not an available option here, since the mechanism that moves packages through the routing network is not under our control (and backtracking would require us to be able, upon recognizing that a package has entered a correct switch wrongly set, to move the package backwards out of the switch and reset the switch).

The alternative technique is to find a predictive implementation. That is, we desire an algorithm for controlling the setting of switches that ensures the constraint will never be violated. The end result of this mapping process is a modified SET_SWITCH demon, which is deterministic. The constraint has been deleted altogether.

After mapping:

demon SET_SWITCH[*switch*]
▶ **trigger** SWITCH_IS_EMPTY(*switch*) **and**
▶ **exists** *package* ∥ *package* =
▶ **first**(PACKAGES_TO_BE_ROUTED_BY_SWITCH(*,*switch*))
response
 update : Switch_Setting **of** *switch*
  to (**the** *pipe* ∥ (*pipe* = *switch* : Switch_Outlet **and**
   BELOW(*package* : Destination,*pipe*)));
▶
▶

5.4. Summary

In this section, we have briefly presented some mappings applied to an actual specification. The emphasis in the discussion has been on the decision-making process involved in deriving a good implementation from a specification. Our purpose here has been to suggest the reasonableness of our approach, both in the mechanics of producing implementations via application of transformations and in the focusing of attention on implementation concerns provided by the concept of *mapping*.

6. Related work

6.1. Transformational methodology

The transformational methodology that we follow is one of several approaches to improving software development. The research we have described relates most closely to those efforts involving some form of mapping between constructs on different levels of programming. We comment on several such efforts:

Burstall and Darlington: Their early schema based transformations, Darlington [14], Darlington and Burstall [18], served to do optimization tasks of recursion removal, common subexpression elimination, loop combination, in-line procedure expansion and introduction of destructive operations to re-use released storage.

[24] Note that a straightforward constraint that prohibits a package reaching a wrong bin would be impossible to satisfy without control of the movement mechanism or the ability to delay arbitrarily the release of a package into the network. The specification presented is a compromise in that some misrouting of packages is tolerated, but we must operate our portion to cause correct routing when possible.

These techniques were built into a system which allowed the user to select the optimization process to be attempted next. They made the observation that manipulations are better done on the higher level programs before mappings down to the next level (recursion to iteration, procedure expansion etc.) are performed.

Their later work concentrated upon manipulation of recursion equations, and achieved efficiency improvements by altering the recursion structure, Burstall and Darlington [11]. The changes were primarily radical restructuring of algorithms, achieving efficiency at the expense of modularity and clarity. These ideas were embodied in an experimental system that relied upon a semi-automatic approach. The system proposed steps to take and the user selected or rejected avenues for exploration (Darlington [17]). Another system based on these same ideas was developed to tackle larger scale examples by requiring (and permitting) the user to provide guidance in a more high-level fashion, Feather [22], Feather [23]. Darlington extended the underlying approach to be able to go from specifications initially containing set and sequence constructs into recursion equations, Darlington [15], Darlington [16]. Darlington's research along these and related directions continues.

We see many of the issues crucial to the overall transformational methodology being pursued in this research. The most significant difference (from our own efforts) lies in the nature of the specification language. Their language, HOPE (Burstall, MacQueen and Sannella [12]) (formerly NPL), is purely applicative in nature, and although they are able to investigate many of the issues in transformational development of software within this applicative framework, we believe that an applicative specification language is limited in the nature of the problems to which it is suited. In contrast our language, Gist, has been constructed explicitly to express a wide range of tasks.

Manna and Waldinger: their DEDALUS system, Manna and Waldinger [32], comprised a fully automated approach to deriving algorithms in some target language from specifications in some specification language rich with constructs from the subject domain of the application. The examples they have tackled involve specifications using set theoretic constructs; these become synthesised into recursive procedures, and in turn into iterative procedures (in a LISP-like language). In their investigations the scale of the examples tackled has been rather small because of the desire to do the synthesis in a fully automatic fashion. In contrast, the emphasis of our research has been to investigate tools which will assist a skilled developer in deriving implementations from specifications. Our hope is that as we gain more experience with this activity, we will incrementally introduce more automation into our tools.

CIP: The CIP (Computer-aided Intuition-guided Programming) group at Munich, Bauer [6], Bauer et al. [7], advocate using machine support to do the bookkeeping tasks in development and documentation, with a human user providing the intuition to guide this process. Their specification language is built upon a kernel of recursive functions together with transformations to manipulate these.

Language extensions can be defined in terms of the kernel by application of the transformations. Thus, new constructs can be defined for both implementation (e.g., loops, assignments, blocks) and specification (e.g., 'descriptive expressions', corresponding to Gist's (**the** $x \| P(x)$), abstract data types, non-deterministic expressions which could denote zero, one or more objects) (Bauer et al. [8]). In order to transform programs making use of these introduced constructs, the defining transformations are used to convert them into recursive procedures, where substantial efficiency improvements may be achieved by applying the kernel transformations, before mapping back into the desired constructs. As with the Burstall and Darlington work, we see much overlap in the approach and the research avenues being explored.

The SETL work has been based upon the idea of augmenting specifications with guidance to a sophisticated compiler to suggest data representations, etc., Schwartz [38], Dewar et al. [19]. SETL is based around liberal use of tuples, sets and functions (and operations upon them). User-provided declarations direct the compiler to select appropriate data structures (from a pre-existing library), and the sophisticated compiler is to automatically generate the code to implement the operations on these representations. The group continues to investigate the usefulness of this approach and the extent to which currently user-made decisions can be automated (Schonberg, Schwartz and Sharir [37]). As mentioned in the mappings section, we are able to incorporate into our framework their techniques for dealing with some 'data' freedoms, which should save us from the 'reinventing the wheel' syndrome.

Neighbors [34] advocates a methodology based on picking some domain of tasks, developing a set of reusable components for that domain, and then when faced with a specific problem in that domain, combining and tailoring those components for that problem. While this differs from the methodology we follow, parallels can be drawn between some of the details of, and observations drawn from, each approach. Neighbors' 'refinements' (which convert 'components' – objects and/or operations – in one domain into another domain closer to implementation correspond to our mappings to eliminate Gist constructs. The constructs expressed in the components of domains he has so far considered are not as rich as those within Gist, yet he has been led to similar observations, e.g. that optimizations (his 'customising' by transformation) are best done at the appropriate levels, that retaining the refinement record is helpful to maintenance, and that the choice of 'refinement' (mapping to us) for one component may influence and interact with the refinement of other components.

6.2. Specification

We believe that the approach to constructing our specification language, and the resulting combination of features, is new. Analogies of individual features can be found in other languages, however:

- The relational data base model – espoused by Smith and Smith [40].
- Temporal logic, at least in its use to talk and reason about the past. Gist's use

specifications can be readily constructed and manipulated, and that the result of our mappings (a Gist specification with all uses of its high-level constructs mapped away) can readily be converted into an efficient program in a conventional implementation language. Our group is involved in continuing research in these areas.

We have described techniques for mapping away each of Gist's high-level constructs, have suggested criteria for selecting one technique over another in terms of the specification and the desired nature of the implementation, and have demonstrated that the mappings are derivable by the application of low-level equivalence-preserving transformations. However, some major tasks remain. Important among these are the tasks of actually compiling a sizable library of transformations for use in mapping activities, and development of mechanisms to assist an implementor in carrying out the mappings. We are now confident, however, that it will indeed be possible to both describe and collect such transformations, and make use of them in actual developments.

While pursuing the research described in this paper, several issues were confronted that bear further investigation:

– The order in which constructs are mapped away seems to be important. We do not expect there to be a 'best' order independent of the problem. There seems to be an opportunistic component to transformational program development.

– Although there might be standard mappings to convert uses of one construct into uses of another, we do not think that a viable approach could be based on converting uses of all types of constructs into uses of just one type, and then concentrating on mapping away that construct.

– The need to map two separate constructs occurring in disparate sections of the specification may lead to sharing of data structures or procedures. Thus, the selections of mappings cannot be made independently; each might derive an optimal implementation for its instance, yet together they provide a suboptimal implementation for both. It is unlikely that we will be able to foresee all the ramifications of mapping decisions. Hence, we may expect to cycle back through the development process to adjust some of our earlier choices. This further highlights the need for machine support during the development process. With such support, exploratory development should be a relatively painless activity.

– Dealing with the distinction between system (the portion of the specification to be implemented) and environment (the remaining portions of the specification which establish the framework within which the system will operate) is very difficult. Often, mappings distribute code not only through the system portion of the specification, but also through the description of the environment – thus modifying its behavior. This indicates that the implementation chosen requires cooperation from the environment. Since such cooperation cannot be assured (because it was not part of the specification), either another implementation must be chosen or the specification must be renegotiated (as is often necessary when implementation problems arise).

of historical reference is very close to the approach of Sernadas in his temporal process specification language, DMTLT (Sernadas [39]).
– Automatic demon invocation – seen in the AI languages PLANNER and Qlisp (Bobrow and Raphael [10]).
– Non-determinism in conjunction with constraints – closest to non-deterministic automata theory, Hopcroft and Ullman [28].
– Operational semantics and closed system assumptions – as seen in simulation languages, Birtwistle et al. [9], Zave's executable specification language PAISLEY (Zave and Yeh [44], Zave 43]).

6.3. Group efforts at ISI

We outline the efforts that our group at ISI has performed. References to these occur earlier in this paper, we gather them together here to clarify the relation of the mapping component to the whole.
– Methodology: An outline of our overall approach is given in Balzer, Goldman and Wile [3]. A detailed case study of a single development (of the 8-queens problem) is presented in Balzer [1].

– Specification language: Some requirements of a specification language suitable for system specification can be found in Balzer and Goldman [2], and Goldman and Wile [26] provides a description of Gist, the language we are developing to satisfy those requirements.
– Supporting system for development: The POPART system, which produces tools to support our development process, is described in Wile [41], and a detailed discussion of issues relating to making the development process itself a formal object in Wile [42]. A mechanism for automatically producing ('jittering') the many mundane steps that occur in a development is discussed in Fickas [25].
– Construction of specifications: Research aimed at supporting the construction of formal specifications from informal natural language expositions is reported in Balzer, Goldman and Wile [4].

7. Conclusions

The primary goal of the research described in this paper has been the investigation of how to map away uses of Gist's high-level specificational constructs. An example specification provides the underlying motivation for, and illustration of, our efforts. However, we have considered the task in more general terms; in so doing, we have provided a further illustration of the utility of Gist's constructs for specification.

The usefulness of our efforts can only be judged within the larger framework of the Transformational Implementation approach to software development. As but part of this overall methodology for developing software, our efforts depend on the success of that methodology. It remains to be demonstrated that Gist

Appendix 1. Package router specification

A.1. English description of package router problem

The package router is a system for distributing packages into destination bins. A source station at the top feeds packages one at a time into the network, which is a binary tree consisting of switches connected by pipes. The terminal nodes of the binary tree are the destination bins.

When a package arrives at the source station, its intended destination (one of the bins) is determined. The package is then released into the pipe leading from the source station. For a package to reach its designated destination bin, the switches in the network must be set to direct the package through the network and into the correct bin.

Packages move through the network by gravity (working against friction), and so steady movement of packages cannot be guaranteed; so they may 'bunch up' within the network and thus make it impossible to set a switch properly between the passage of two such bunched packages (a switch cannot be set when there is a package or packages in the switch for fear of damaging such packages). If a new package's destination differs from that of the immediately preceding package, its release from the source station is delayed a (pre-calculated) fixed length of time (to reduce the chance of bunching). In spite of such precautions, packages may still bunch up and become misrouted, ending up in the wrong bin; the package router is to signal such an event.

Only a limited amount of information is available to the package router to effect its desired behavior. At the time of arrival at the source station but not thereafter, the destination of a package may be determined. The only means of determining the locations of packages within the network are sensors placed on the entries and exits of switches, and the entries of bins; these detect the passage of packages but are unable to determine their identity. (The sensors will be able to recognize the passage of individual packages, regardless of bunching.)

A.2. Gist specification of package router

A.2.1. Key to font conventions and special symbols used in Gist

symbol	meaning	example
		of type	obj|T – object obj of type T
=	such that	(an integer||(integer > 3)) – an integer greater than 3
-	may be used to build names, like this.name	
.	concatenates a type name with a suffix to form a variable name, e.g. integer.1 with the semantics that such variables with distinct suffixes denote distinct objects.	

fonts	meaning	example
bold	key word	**begin, definition, if**
SMALL CAPITALS	type name	INTEGER

fonts	meaning	example
lower case italics	variable	x
UPPER CASE SANS SERIF	action, demon, relation and constraint names	SET_SWITCH
Mixed Case Sans Serif	attribute names	Destination

A.2.2. Package router specification in Gist

The network

type LOCATION( )**supertype of**

⟨SOURCE⟨Source_Outlet|PIPE⟩;

    Gist comment – the above line defines SOURCE to be a type with one attribute, Source_Outlet, and only objects of type PIPE may serve as such attributes. **end comment**

PIPE(Pipe_Outlet|(SWITCH **union** BIN)) :: **unique**);

SWITCH(Switch_Outlet|PIPE : 2, Switch_Setting|PIPE)
where always required
    switch : Switch_Setting = switch : Switch_Outlet **end**;
BIN( )
);

    Spec comment – of the above types and attribute, only the Switch_Setting attribute of SWITCH is dynamic in this specification, the others remain fixed throughout. **end comment**

    Gist comment – by default, attributes (e.g. Source_Outlet) of types (e.g. SOURCE) are functional (e.g. there is one and only one pipe serving as the Source_Outlet attribute of the SOURCE). The default may be overridden, as occurs in the Switch_Outlet attribute of SWITCH – there the ':2' indicates that each switch has exactly 2 pipes serving as its Switch_Outlet attribute. **end comment**

always prohibited MORE_THAN_ONE_SOURCE
exists source.1, source.2;

    Gist comment – constraints may be stated as predicates following either **always required** (in which case the predicate must always evaluate to true), or **always prohibited** (in which case the predicate must never evaluate to true). The usual logical connectives, quantification, etc. may be used in Gist predicates. Distinct suffixes on type names after **exists** have the special meaning of denoting distinct objects. **end comment**

always required PIPE_EMERGES_FROM_UNIQUE_SWITCH_OR_SOURCE
for all pipe ||(**count**(a switch_or_source|(SWITCH **union** SOURCE)||
       (pipe = switch_or_source : Switch_Outlet **or**
       pipe = switch_or_source : Source_Outlet)) = 1);

    Gist comment – the values of attributes can be retrieved in the following manner: if obj is an object of type T, where type T has an attribute Att, then obj : Att denotes any object serving as obj's Att attribute. **end comment**

relation IMMEDIATELY_BELOW(*ib1* | LOCATION, *ib2* | LOCATION)
definition
  ib1 = (**case** *ib2* **of**
    a *pipe* =)*ib2* : Pipe_Outlet;
    a *switch* =)*ib2* : Switch_Outlet;
    the *source* =)*ib2* : Source_Outlet
  end case)
;

  Gist comment – the predicate of a defined relation denotes those tuples of objects participating in that relation. For any tuple of objects of the appropriate types, that tuple (in the above relation, a 2-tuple of LOCATIONS) is in the defined relation if and only if the defining predicate equals true for those objects. **end case**

relation BELOW(*b1* | LOCATION, *b2* | LOCATION)
definition
  IMMEDIATELY_BELOW(*b1,b2*) **or**
  (**exists** *b3* | LOCATION || (BELOW(*b1,b3*) **and** BELOW(*b3,b2*)));

always required SOURCE_ON_ROUTE_TO_ALL_BINS
  for all *bin* || BELOW(*bin*, **the** *source*);

Packages – the objects moving through the network
type PACKAGE(At | LOCATION, Destination | BIN);

always prohibited MULTIPLE_PACKAGES_AT_SOURCE
  exists *package.1, package.2* || (*package.1* : At = **the** *source* **and**
                                        package.2 : At = **the** *source*);

Our portion

  Spec comment – the portion over which we have control, and are to implement. **end comment**

agent PACKAGE_ROUTER( ) **where**

relation PACKAGES_EVER_AT_SOURCE(*packages* | **sequence of** PACKAGE)
definition *packages* = (a *package*) **ordered**
  wrt *package* : At = (**the** *source*) ;

The source station

demon RELEASE_PACKAGE_INTO_NETWORK[*package.new*]
trigger *package.new* : At = **the** *source*
response
  begin
  if *package.new* : Destination ≠
    (a *package.previous* ||
    package.previous **immediately** < *package.new*
    wrt PACKAGES_EVER_AT_SOURCE(*)) : Destination
  then WAIT[ ];

  Spec comment – must delay release of the new package if its destination differs from that of the previous package (the immediately preceding package to have been at the source). **end comment**

update : At of *package.new* **to** (**the** *source*) : Source_Outlet
end
;

  Gist comment – a **demon** is a data-triggered process. Whenever a state change takes place in which the value of demon's **trigger** predicate changes from false to true, the demon is triggered, and performs its **response**. **end comment**

action WAIT[ ];

The switches

relation SWITCH_IS_EMPTY(*switch*)
definition not exists *package* || (*package* : At = *switch*) ;

demon SET_SWITCH[*switch*]
trigger Random( )
response
  begin
    require SWITCH_IS_EMPTY(*switch*);
    update : Switch_Setting **of** *switch* **to** *switch* : Switch_Outlet
  end
;

  Spec comment – the non-determinism of when and which way to set switches is constrained by the always prohibited that follows shortly: **end comment**

relation PACKAGES_TO_BE_ROUTED_BY_SWITCH
  (*packages* | **sequence of** PACKAGE,*switch*)
definition *packages* =
  (a *package* ||
  (BELOW(*switch, package* : At) **and**
  BELOW(*package* : Destination,*switch*) **and**
  not PACKAGE_IN_CORRECT_SWITCH_WRONGLY_SET(*package*))
) **ordered wrt** PACKAGES_EVER_AT_SOURCE(*);

  Spec comment – packages to be routed by a switch are those packages for whom (i) the switch lies below them, (ii) the switch lies on their routes to their Destinations, and (iii) they are not in some switch set the wrong way. The sequence is ordered by the order in which they were at the source. Note that this excludes packages that are already misrouted; there may be such packages on their way to this switch, but since they are already misrouted, the switch will not have to route them in any particular direction. **end comment**

relation PACKAGE_IN_CORRECT_SWITCH_WRONGLY_SET(*package*)
definition
  exists *switch* ||
  (*package* : At = *switch* **and**

BELOW(package : Destination,switch) and
not BELOW(package : Destination,switch : Switch_Setting));

Spec comment – A package is in a correct switch that is wrongly set if the switch lies on the route to that package's destination, but the switch is currently set the wrong way. (This is how a package becomes misrouted.) end comment

always prohibited DID_NOT_SET_SWITCH_WHEN_HAD_CHANCE
exists package,switch ||
(PACKAGE_IN_CORRECT_SWITCH_WRONGLY_SET(package)
and
((SWITCH_IS_EMPTY(switch) and
package = first(PACKAGES_TO_BE_ROUTED_BY_SWITCH
(*,switch)))asof true)
);

Spec comment – must never reach a state in which a package is in a wrongly set switch, if there has been an opportunity to set the switch correctly for that package, i.e. at some time that package was the first of those due to be routed by the switch and the switch was empty. end comment

Indicating arrival of misrouted package in bin

demon DETECT_MISROUTED_ARRIVAL[package.misrouted,
bin.reached,bin.intended]

trigger package.misrouted : At = bin.reached and
package.misrouted : Destination = bin.intended
response DISPLAY_MISROUTING[bin.reached,bin.intended];

action DISPLAY_MISROUTING[bin.reached,bin.intended];
end

The environment

agent ENVIRONMENT( ) where

Arrival of packages at source

demon CREATE_PACKAGE[ ]
trigger Random( )
response
create package.new ||(package.new : Destination = a bin and
package.new : At = the source);

Spec comment – for the purposes of defining the environment in which the package router is to operate, packages with some random bin as their Destination appear at random intervals (subject to the prohibition on there being multiple packages at the source) at the source. end comment

Movement of packages through network

relation CONNECTED_TO(location.1,location.2)
definition
location.2 = (case location.1 of
a pipe = > location.1 : Pipe_Outlet;
a switch = > location.1 : Switch_Setting
end case);

demon MOVE_PACKAGE[package,location.next]
trigger Random( )
response
if CONNECTED_TO(package : At, location.next)
then update : At of package to location.next;

Spec comment – modelling of the unpredictable movement of packages through the network is achieved by having this demon at random move a random package from one location to the next CONNECTED_TO location. end comment

always prohibited
MULTIPLE_PACKAGES_REACH_LOCATION_SIMULTANEOUSLY
exists package.1, package.2,location ||
((start package.1 : At = location) and
(start package.2 : At = location);

Gist comment – start ⟨predicate⟩ is true if the predicate has just changed in value from false to true. end comment
Spec comment – the mechanical construction of the router is such that although packages may bunch up, the passage of each individual package may be detected. This we model by constraining the 'granularity' of movement to be that of individual packages. end comment

always prohibited PACKAGES_LEAVE_OUT_OF_ORDER
exists package.1,package.2, common_location |LOCATION||
((start package.1 : At = common_location <
start package.2 : At = common_location) and
package.1 : At = common_location and
not package.2 : At = common_location);

Spec comment – prohibited that package.1 enters before package.2 yet still be there when package.2 has left. end comment

Abstraction specification

Gist comment – the behaviors denoted by the specification are an abstraction of the detailed behaviors of the preceding system. This section states just which of those details are to be included in the abstracted behaviors. end comment

abstraction
types

Acknowledgment

We wish to thank the other members of the ISI Transformational Implementation group: Bob Balzer, Wellington Chiu, Don Cohen, Lee Erman, Steve Fickas, Neil Goldman, Bill Swartout, and Dave Wile. They collectively have defined the context within which this work lies, and individually have improved this paper through frequent discussions about the research and helpful comments on the drafts. We also wish to thank the referees for their insightful comments and guidance.

References

[1] R. Balzer, Transformational implementation: An example, *IEEE Trans. Software Engrg.* **7** (1) (1981) 3–14.

[2] R. Balzer and N. Goldman, Principles of good software specification and their implications for specification languages, in: *Specification of Reliable Software* (IEEE Computer Society, New York, 1979) 58–67.

[3] R. Balzer, N. Goldman and D. Wile, On the transformational implementation approach to programming, *Proc. 2nd IEEE International Conference on Software Engineering*, San Francisco, CA (1976) 337–344.

[4] R. Balzer, N. Goldman and D. Wile, Informality in program specifications, *IEEE Trans. Software Engrg.* **4** (2) (1978) 94–103.

[5] D.R. Barstow, *Knowledge-Based Program Construction* (North-Holland, Amsterdam, 1979).

[6] F.L. Bauer, Programming as an evolutionary process, *Proc. 2nd IEEE International Conference on Software Engineering*, San Francisco, CA (1976) 223–234.

[7] F.L. Bauer, H. Partsch, P. Pepper and H. Wössner, Notes on the project CIP: Outline of a transformation system, Institut für Informatik, Technische Universität München, Technical Report TUM-INFO-7729 (1977).

[8] F.L. Bauer, M. Broy, R. Gnatz, H. Partsch, P. Pepper and H. Wössner, Towards a wide spectrum language to support program specification and program development, *SIGPLAN Notices* **13** (12) (1978) 15–23.

[9] G.M. Birtwistle, O. Dahl, B. Myrhaug and K. Nygaard, *SIMULA Begin* (Auerbach, Philadelphia, PA, 1973).

[10] D. Bobrow and B. Raphael, New programming languages for artificial intelligence, *ACM Comput. Surveys* **6** (3) (1974) 153–174.

[11] R.M. Burstall and J. Darlington, A transformation system for developing recursive programs, *J. ACM* **24** (1) (1977) 44–67.

[12] R.M. Burstall, D.B. MacQueen and D.T. Sannella, HOPE: An experimental applicative language, *Proc. 1980 LISP Conference*, Stanford, CA (1980) 136–143.

[13] W.F. Clocksin and C.S. Mellish, *Programming in Prolog* (Springer, Berlin, 1981).

[14] J. Darlington, A semantic approach to automatic program improvement, Ph.D. thesis, Department of Artificial Intelligence, University of Edinburgh, Edinburgh (1972).

[15] J. Darlington, Applications of program transformation to program synthesis, *Proc. International Symposium on Proving and Improving Programs*, Arc-et-Senans, France (1975) 133–144.

[16] J. Darlington, A synthesis of several sorting algorithms, *Acta Informat.* **11** (1) (1978) 1–30.

[17] J. Darlington, An experimental program transformation and synthesis system, *Artificial Intelligence* **16** (1) (1981) 1–46.

[18] J. Darlington and R.M. Burstall, A system which automatically improves programs, *Acta Informat.* **6** (1) (1976) 41–60.

[19] R.B.K. Dewar, A. Grand, S. Liu and J.T. Schwartz, Programming by refinement, as exemplified by the SETL representation sublanguage, *ACM Trans. Programming Languages and Systems* **1** (1) (1979) 27–49.

LOCATION, SOURCE, PIPE, SWITCH, BIN, PACKAGE;

attributes

Source_Outlet, Pipe_Outlet, Switch_Outlet, Switch_Setting, At, Destination;

actions

DISPLAY_MISROUTING, WAIT

end abstraction

Implementation specification

Gist comment – this section states what the portion to be implemented may observe and what it may effect. **end comment**

implement PACKAGE_ROUTER

observing

types

LOCATION, SOURCE, PIPE, SWITCH, BIN, PACKAGE;

attributes

Source_Outlet, Pipe_Outlet, Switch_Outlet, Switch_Setting;

predicates

start (a *package*) : At = **the** *source*,

start (a *package*) : At = *switch*,

finish (a *package*) : At = *switch*,

start (a *package*) : At = *bin* ;

exists *package* ‖ *package* : Destination = *bin* **and** *package* : At = **the** *source*);

Spec comment – the router is limited to observing: the routing network, the arrival of packages at the source and their movement into and out of switches and into bins, and the destination of a package while it is located at the source. **end comment**

effecting

attributes

switch : Switch_Setting

package : At **asof** *package* : At = **the** *source* ;

Spec comment – the router is limited to effecting the setting of switches, and the release of packages at the source. **end comment**

end implement

[20] J. Doyle, A truth maintenance system, *Artificial Intelligence* **12** (3) (1979) 231–272.

[21] J. Earley, High level iterators and a method for automatically designing data structure representation, *Comput. Languages* **1** (4) (1975) 321–342.

[22] M.S. Feather, 'ZAP' program transformation system primer and users manual, Department of Artificial Intelligence, University of Edinburgh, Edinburgh, Technical Report DAI 54 (1978).

[23] M.S. Feather, A system for assisting program transformation, *ACM Trans. Programming Languages and Systems* **4** (1) (1982) 1–20.

[24] M.S. Feather and P.E. London, Implementing specification freedoms, ISI, Marina del Rey, CA 90291, Technical Report RR-81-100 (1982).

[25] S. Fickas, Automatic goal-directed program transformation, in: *AAAI80*, Palo Alto, CA (1980) 68–70.

[26] N. Goldman and D. Wile, A relational data base foundation for process specification, in: P.P. Chen, Ed., *Entity-Relationship Approach to Systems Analysis and Design* (North-Holland, Amsterdam, 1980).

[27] G. Hommel, Vergleich verschiedener Spezifikationsverfahren am Beispiel einer Paketverteilanlage, Kernforschungszentrum Karlsruhe, Technical Report (1980).

[28] J.E. Hopcroft and J.D. Ullman, *Formal Languages and Their Relation to Automata* (Addison-Wesley, Reading, MA, 1969).

[29] S. Koenig and R. Paige, A transformational framework for the automatic control of derived data, *Proc. 7th International Conference on Very Large Data Bases* (1981) 306–318.

[30] P.E. London, A dependency-based modelling mechanism for problem solving, *AFIPS Conference Proceedings* **47** (1978) 263–274.

[31] J.R. Low, *Interdisciplinary Systems Research, Vol. 16: Automatic Coding: Choice of Data Structures* (Birkhauser, Basel, 1976).

[32] Z. Manna and R. Waldinger, Synthesis: dreams $\Rightarrow$ programs, *IEEE Trans. Software Engrg.* **5** (4) (1979) 294–328.

[33] D. McDermott and G.J. Sussman, The CONNIVER reference manual, MIT, Technical Report Memo 259a (1974).

[34] J.M. Neighbors, Software construction using components, Ph.D. thesis, University of California, Irvine (1980).

[35] R. Paige and J. Schwartz, Expression continuity and the formal differentiation of algorithms, *Proc. 4th ACM POPL Symposium*, Los Angeles (1977) 58–71.

[36] P. Rovner, Automatic representation selection for associative data structures, *Proc. AFIPS National Computer Conference*, Anaheim, CA (1978) 691–701.

[37] E. Schonberg, J.T. Schwartz and M. Sharir, An automatic technique for selection of data representations in SETL programs, *ACM Trans. Programming Languages and Systems* **3** (2) (1981) 126–143.

[38] J.T. Schwartz, On programming, an interim report on the SETL project, Courant Institute of Mathematical Sciences, New York University, Technical Report (1975).

[39] A. Sernadas, Temporal aspects of logical procedure definition, *Information Systems* **5** (3) (1980) 167–187.

[40] J. Smith and D. Smith, Database abstractions: aggregation and generalization, *ACM Trans. Database Systems* **2** (2) (1977) 105–133.

[41] D.S. Wile, POPART: Producer of parsers and related tools, Systems builders' manual, ISI, Marina del Rey, CA 90291 (1981).

[42] D.S. Wile, Program developments as formal objects, ISI, Marina del Rey, CA 90291, Technical Report RR-81-99 (1981).

[43] P. Zave, An operational approach to requirements specification for embedded systems, *IEEE Trans. Software Engrg.* **8** (3) (1982) 250–269.

[44] P. Zave and R.T. Yeh, Executable requirements for embedded systems, *Proc. 5th IEEE International Conference on Software Engineering*, San Diego, CA (1981) 295–304.

VI / Programming by Example

Programming by example systems seek to synthesize programs based on examples of their behavior. This is an attractive approach because of the naturalness and simplicity of the user interface in comparison with systems that operate on natural language specifications (see Section IV) or very high level languages (see Section V).

Programming by example has been successfully demonstrated in a number of simple situations. Unfortunately, the techniques used in these situations do not appear to scale up effectively to programs of realistic size and complexity. As a result, although there was significant activity in this area during the 1970s, there is not much work going on at the current time.

The key problem with using examples of behavior as a program specification is appropriately generalizing them. It would be trivial to create a program that supported the examples and nothing more. What is desired is a program that can operate on whole classes of data in a manner which is analogous to the examples.

[Summers, Chapter 18] presents the fundamental theoretical results on which most subsequent programming-by-example systems are based. Although several different kinds of behavior examples are discussed by Summers, his demonstration system, called THESYS, accepts only input/output pairs. Input/output pairs have the advantage of being the most straightforward kind of behavior example. However, they are less informative than partial program traces and are therefore harder to generalize.

[Bauer, Chapter 19] focuses on the idea of using partial traces of program behavior on example inputs as a specification technique. Bauer has developed a language for expressing these traces and an algorithm for generalizing sets of traces into a program.

A Methodology for LISP Program Construction from Examples

PHILLIP D. SUMMERS

IBM Thomas J. Watson Research Center, Yorktown Heights, New York

ABSTRACT. An automatic programming system, THESYS, for constructing recursive LISP programs from examples of what they do is described. The construction methodology is illustrated as a series of transformations from the set of examples to a program satisfying the examples. The transformations consist of (1) deriving the specific computation associated with a specific example, (2) deriving control flow predicates, and (3) deriving an equivalent program specification in the form of recurrence relations. Equivalence between certain recurrence relations and various program schemata is proved. A detailed description of the construction of four programs is presented to illustrate the application of the methodology.

KEY WORDS AND PHRASES: automatic programming, LISP, program synthesis, inductive inference, programming languages, sample computations, recursive programs

CR CATEGORIES: 3.61, 4.12, 4.20, 5.24

1. Introduction

This paper reports on a system, THESYS, that synthesizes LISP recursive programs from examples of what they do. There has been recent interest in this form of program specification [1, 4, 5, 9]. The theory of such inductive systems has been investigated by Blum and Blum [2], Kugel [6], and Summers [11]. In this paper we describe the practical results of an investigation into the problem of program synthesis from examples. The methodology to be presented is based on a firm theoretical foundation, which may provide a basis for generalizing the results to other kinds of program synthesis systems. The various theoretical models for computation and data that comprise the theory are not described in detail in this paper but may be found in [11].

As part of the methodology we describe two processes used in constructing LISP recursive programs from examples. The first is a method for discovering and encoding the relationships or differences between pairs of examples used to specify a program. The multiple-example approach permits implicit relationships rather than infer them from a single example. The multiple-example approach permits the construction of a greater variety of programs than does the single-example approach. If the algorithm for difference discovery is successful, the relationship between examples is encoded as a kind of recurrence relation. Derivation of such relations effectively determines the program to be constructed since one may prove equivalence between certain recurrence relations and various program schemata.

The second method to be described involves a process for the systematic introduction

of local variables to programs being constructed. For a given set of examples it is not always possible to find a recurrence relation that characterizes the examples and leads to such a program. Often, if the program specification is generalized, it is possible to find such a recurrence relation. A given recursive function may be considered to have been generalized by means of the addition of a local variable if it is defined in terms of a second recursive program with one additional variable such that the second program has execution properties identical to those of the first program when the added variable is assigned some fixed value. The technique of solving a particular problem by first solving a more general problem is called the *insane heuristic* by Siklossy [10]. The approach has been used by Boyer and Moore [3] to prove properties of LISP programs and by Siklossy [10] in a program generation system. The procedure is also similar in idea to that of *accumulator generalization* in [8]. Almost all interesting (nontrivial) programs that are synthesized by the THESYS system rely on introducing a local variable into the program being constructed.

Difference discovery is informally presented in Section 2 as part of a sample derivation of a recursive function. It is formally described in Section 3 along with a statement of the equivalences between recurrence relations and program schemata. Variable addition is defined and used in Section 4 to generate the program **reverse**. Section 5 contains the derivation of two additional functions. Section 6 discusses capabilities and limitations of the approach by comparing the results with other similar works. The remainder of the introduction will discuss the example and target languages used by the system.

It is assumed that the reader is familiar with Lisp 1.5 as described in [7]. Programs are to be synthesized by using the primitive functions **car**, **cdr**, **cons**, and **atom** and control structures of recursion, functional composition, and the McCarthy conditional. It may be shown that this subset of the Lisp language is computationally complete [11] even though it does not contain the usual primitive **eq**.

The expression "programming by example" will be taken to mean the act of specifying a program by means of a set of examples of the program's behavior. An example will consist of S-expressions representing an input and an output. For example, if the program to return the last element of a list is to be specified, an example might be $(A B C) \rightarrow C$, where the arrow separates the input from the output. Examples convey information about the program in two ways. First, a single example indicates a specific transformation or computation that must be duplicated by any program defined by the example. A second source of information is derived from the relations that exist among the examples in a set specifying a function.

In the language of examples it is assumed that each atom acts as a representative instance of any element from the domain of S-expressions. In this way one may consider an example to be a form of assertion about the existence of entities which may be transformed in a particular way. The more conventional form of program specification by assertion is illustrated by the following example from Waldinger's thesis [12] for specifying a program to extract the second element from a list:

$$(\forall a)(\exists y)(\exists z z) equal[a:list[w:y:zz]].$$

The set of examples

$$\{(A B) \rightarrow B, (A B C) \rightarrow B, (A B C D) \rightarrow B\}$$

specifies the same program in a way that is easier to understand. Three examples are used to indicate that the program is to work for lists of all lengths, a fact that is supplied by the universal quantifier in the assertion.

In general examples are a useful way of describing large or infinite objects only when the objects have repetitive properties that may be demonstrated by means of a finite number of examples. When the object being described is a program, the examples represent a finite number of instances of the possibly infinite set of computations

An earlier version of this paper appears in the Conference Record of the Third ACM Symposium on the Principles of Programming Languages, January 1976, pp. 68-76.
This work was presented as part of a dissertation for the Ph.D. at Yale University, New Haven, Conn.
This work was supported by an IBM Resident Study Fellowship.
Author's address: IBM Thomas J. Watson Research Center, Yorktown Heights, NY 10598.

representing the program. In addition, for any finite set of examples there are an infinite number of programs that behave like the examples. We say that a program satisfies or is defined by a set of examples if it produces the example's output when applied to the example's input for all examples in the specifying set. The system produces the simplest program which satisfies the examples; i.e. it creates the most general hypothesis to explain the examples. If the system is able to detect a repetitive phenomenon in the examples, it attempts to encode this phenomenon as a recursive program; otherwise it produces a simple noniterative program that is defined for just the set of examples. Indeed, there is no reasonable way to do more.

2. A Sample Synthesis

To illustrate the basic synthesis procedure, we consider the problem of generating the function unpack[x]. The program is to unpack the list x into a list of constituents of x, where each constituent is a list containing a single element from x. A set of examples that might be given to the system is

$\{( ) \rightarrow ( ),$
$(A) \rightarrow ((A)).$
$(A\ B) \rightarrow ((A)\ (B)).$
$(A\ B\ C) \rightarrow ((A)\ (B)\ (C)).$

Each example represents a transformation that is to be encoded as a function formed from an appropriate composition of the primitive functions **car**, **cdr**, and **cons**. In order to arrive at this function algorithmically (in contrast to the heuristic searches by theorem-prover-oriented synthesizers), it is necessary to note a particular property of S-expressions. Any nonatomic S-expression is uniquely constructed from the function **cons** and two less complex S-expressions. The functions **car** and **cdr** provide for the unique decomposition of any nonatomic S-expression. This property leads us to an algorithm for encoding the transformation indicated by an example into a function which we call a *program fragment*. For the examples given above we have the following four fragments:

$f_1[x] = nil;$
$f_2[x] = cons[x;nil];$
$f_3[x] = cons[cons[car[x];nil];cons[cdr[x];nil]];$
$f_4[x] = cons[cons[car[x];nil];cons[cons[cadr[x];nil];cons[cddr[x];nil]]].$

We illustrate the algorithm by deriving a representative fragment $f_3[x]$ from the example (A B) → ((A) (B)). The approach is to enumerate all possible subexpressions of the example's input, then combine these expressions to form the output. Remembering the functions needed to produce the subexpressions (combinations of **car**'s and **cdr**'s) and remembering how the subexpressions were combined to create the output (**cons**'s), one is able to construct the function that will transform the input to the output.

Let x be associated with the input (A B); then a set of all subexpressions of the input with the functions that produce them are

$\{\langle x. (A\ B)\rangle.$
$\langle car[x]. A\rangle.$
$\langle cdr[x]. (B)\rangle.$
$\langle cadr[x]. B\rangle,$
$\langle cddr[x]. ( )\rangle\}.$

We combine these expressions in the following way:

$$((A)\ (B)) = cons[(A) : ((B))] = cons[cons[A : ( )];cons[(B) : ( )]].$$

We see that A may be derived from the input by the function car[x] and (B) by the function cdr[x]. Replacing these values by the associated functions yields the expression

cons[cons[car[x]; ( )];cons[cdr[x]; ( )]]. As a rule, ( ) is never derived from the input but takes it value from the evaluation of the niladic function **nil**. Substitution for ( ) produces the fragment $f_3[x]$ given above.

The set of fragments corresponding to the set of examples may be thought of as instances of computations for functions we are trying to generate. If we embed these fragments in the McCarthy conditional expression, we have the following straight-line program:

$F_L[x] \leftarrow [p_1[x] \rightarrow nil;$
$\qquad\qquad p_2[x] \rightarrow cons[x;nil];$
$\qquad\qquad p_3[x] \rightarrow cons[cons[car[x];nil];cons[cons[cadr[x];nil];cons[cddr[x];nil]]];$
$\qquad\qquad T \rightarrow cons[cons[car[x];nil];cons[cons[cadr[x];nil];cons[cddr[x];nil]]].$

Defining an appropriate set of predicates for $p_i[x]$, $i = 1, 3$, will produce a function that satisfies the set of specifying examples.

To determine the predicates needed for $F_L[x]$, we look at the four S-expressions ( ), (A), (A B), and (A B C) that are the inputs of the examples. These expressions will be taken to be representative of the kinds of inputs for which the function is defined. Recalling that our set of primitives does not contain the function **eq**, we observe that it is impossible to distinguish between two S-expressions on the basis of differences between atoms they might contain. Therefore all semantic information must be conveyed in an S-expression by means of the structure of that expression. For the examples given we observe that each expression is structurally more complex than the preceding one.

There exists a mathematical model for the set of all S-expressions which reveals the structural relationships between elements of the set. For any S-expression we define the *form* of that expression to be the expression with each atom replaced by the indistinguishable or indeterminate atom ω. For example, if

$$x = (A\ (B\ C)\ D) = (A . ((B . (C . ( ))) . (D . ( )))).$$

then $form[x] = (ω . ((ω . (ω . ω)) . (ω . ω)))$. The set of forms corresponding to the set of S-expressions will be called SF. There is a poset relation ≤ over SF defined by ω ≤ α for all α ∈ SF and (a . b) ≤ (c . d) if and only if a ≤ c and b ≤ d. In addition it may be shown that SF is a lattice. The first four levels of the lattice SF are shown in Figure 1.

The definition of the form of an S-expression specifies an effective procedure for mapping S-expressions into the lattice SF. The four S-expressions ( ), (A), (A B), and (A B C) correspond to the four points labeled A, B, C, D in Figure 1. We may now formalize the observation about (A B)'s having less structure than (A B C) by saying that form[(A B)] ≤ form[(A B C)]. This relation induces an ordering on the examples and was in fact the basis for ordering the examples given above. It should be pointed out that THESYS accepts examples in any order since it is able to sort them using the relation ≤ if they are totally ordered by ≤.

The lattice SF is a useful model of the data domain for the functions being synthesized. With this model we may make precise some of the intuitive notions about the way LISP programs behave when applied to S-expressions. As a first observation, consider the four points in SF referred to as A–D in Figure 1. By associating with each of these points the appropriate fragment generated above, we define an approximation to the sought after function $F_L[x]$. One set of predicates defined by such an association is $p_1[x] = equal[form[x];ω]$, $p_2[x] = equal[form[x];(ω . ω)]$, etc. For example, $p_2[x]$ is true for any dotted pair of atoms and not just for the dotted pair of the example, e.g. $p_2[(A . B)] = T$. This definition for the predicates generalizes the function $F_L[x]$ from a domain consisting of the example inputs to a domain of expressions having the same form as the examples.

From the rules for writing examples, we know that an atom may stand for any legal S-expression. From this it follows that the function $F_L[x]$ should work on lists whose inferring a recursive program whose set (possibly infinite) of computations will be an inferred generalization of the computations $f_i[x]$, $1 \le i \le 3$.

As a first step toward finding such a recursive program, we try to derive a formula for generating additional predicates and fragments that will extend the program to larger and larger domains. If the sequences of fragments and predicates were sequences of integers, we might set up equations that would characterize the difference between elements of the sequences and permit the extrapolation of new elements. There is an analogue to the integer difference that we call *differencing*. We say that a difference exists between two functions $f_i[x]$ and $f_{i+k}[x]$ if $f_{i+k}[x]$ may be expressed as a composition of the primitive functions and the expression $f_i[x]$. There is an algorithm, somewhat akin to unification as used in resolution theorem provers, for finding all possible differences, if any exist, between two fragments. For the program $F_L[x]$ we find the following differences:

$$f_2[x] = cons[x;f_1[x]].$$
$$f_3[x] = cons[cons[car[x];nil];f_2[cdr[x]]].$$
$$f_4[x] = cons[cons[car[x];nil];f_3[cdr[x]]].$$

$$p_2[x] = p_1[cdr[x]],$$
$$p_3[x] = p_2[cdr[x]],$$
$$p_4[x] = p_3[cdr[x]].$$

We observe that we may rewrite these differences as a set of recurrence relations:

$$f_1[x] = nil,$$
$$f_2[x] = cons[x;nil],$$
$$f_{k+1}[x] = cons[cons[car[x];nil];f_k[cdr[x]]], \quad k = 2, 3.$$

$$p_1[x] = atom[x],$$
$$p_{k+1}[x] = p_k[cdr[x]], \quad k = 1, 2, 3.$$

Since the recurrence relations are defined for $k = 2, 3$, we *infer* that the same relationship holds for *all k*. The sets of recurrence relations become a means of generating new sets of examples and therefore a means for defining a program that satisfies these examples. By applying one of the theorems from Section 3, we are able to move from the recurrence relation characterization of the function to a recursive program that satisfies the examples. The program for **unpack** becomes

$$unpack[x] \leftarrow [atom[x] \rightarrow nil;$$
$$T \rightarrow u[x]]$$
$$u[x] \leftarrow [atom[cdr[x]] \rightarrow cons[x;nil];$$
$$T \rightarrow cons[cons[car[x];nil];u[cdr[x]]]].$$

3. Synthesis Theorems

In this section we make more precise the sequence of steps taken by the system in going from a set of fragments and predicates to a recursive program. Assume that a function $F[x]$ is specified by a set of examples $\{e_1, \ldots, e_k\}$, where $input[e_1] \le \cdots \le input[e_k]$.
Definition. We define

$$F_k[x] \leftarrow [p_1[x] \rightarrow f_1[x];$$
$$\cdots$$
$$p_{k-1}[x] \rightarrow f_{k-1}[x];$$
$$T \rightarrow \omega]$$

to be the kth approximating function to $F[x]$, where ω is undefined and the $p_i[x]$ and $f_i[x]$ are generated from the examples by the methods of Section 2.
Definition. If there exists an initial point j and an interval n such that $1 \le j < k$ in a kth-approximation $F_k[x]$ defined by a set of examples such that the following fragment differences exist:

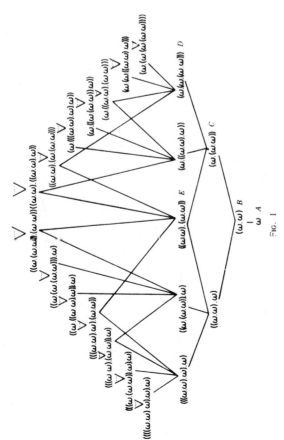

FIG. 1

elements have arbitrary structure. For example, we expect the list ((A) B) to be transformed by the function to (((A)) (B)); i.e. it should be transformed in the same way as the example, (A B) → (A) (B). If we look again to Figure 1 we see that form[(((A) B)] is at point E. Points in SF less than E may be thought of as approximating the structure of E. In the set {A, B, C, D} only A, B, and C are less than E. Of these C is the greatest and therefore has a structure most like E. We call C the *best approximation* of E in the set {A, B, C}. Point C corresponds to the example whose associated fragment will transform E in a way corresponding to our intuition about the meaning of the examples. What are needed to complete our function $F_L[x]$ are predicates $p_i[x]$ which are true iff the input of the ith example is the best approximation to x.

For a set of examples $E = \{e_1, \ldots, e_k\}$ totally ordered by $\le$, we denote the input of the ith example to be $input[e_i]$. There exists an algorithm, not stated here (see [11]), for deriving a sequence of predicates $p_1[x], \ldots, p_{k-1}[x]$ from E such that $p_i[x] = T$ if and only if $form[input[e_i]] \le form[x]$ and it is not true that $form[input[e_j]] \le form[x]$ for $j > i$; i.e. $p_i[x] = T$ iff $input[e_i]$ is a best approximation to x. A series of such predicates for the four S-expressions given above would be $p_1[x] = atom[x]$, $p_2[x] = atom[cdr[x]]$, $p_3[x] = atom[cddr[x]]$, and $p_4[x] = T$. The first three predicates may be thought of as testing for the differences between successive example inputs; i.e. $p_3[x]$ is able to distinguish between $input[e_3] = $ (A B) and $input[e_4] = $ (A B C) by testing where the structures of the two expressions differ.

Having generated a set of predicates to select the computations represented as fragments, we may write out the completely defined function $F_L[x]$ that satisfies the examples:

$$F_L[x] \leftarrow [atom[x] \rightarrow nil;$$
$$atom[cdr[x]] \rightarrow cons[x;nil];$$
$$atom[cddr[x]] \rightarrow cons[cons[car[x];nil];cons[cdr[x];nil]];$$
$$T \rightarrow cons[cons[car[x];nil];cons[cons[cadr[x];nil];cons[cddr[x];nil]]]].$$

Note that the order of the predicates and fragments is determined by the ordering of the examples by $\le$.

The goal now becomes one of trying to generalize this program into a form that will yield appropriate calculations for other S-expressions; i.e. we are looking for a way of

$$f_{j+n}[x] = a[f_j[b_1[x]];x].$$
$$f_{j+n+1}[x] = a[f_{j+1}[b_1[x]];x].$$
$$\cdots$$
$$f_{k-1}[x] = a[f_{k-n-1}[b_1[x]];x],$$

and such that the following predicate differences exist:

$$p_{j+n}[x] = p_j[b_2[x]],$$
$$p_{j+n+1}[x] = p_{j+1}[b_2[x]],$$
$$\cdots$$
$$p_{k-n}[x] = p_{k-n-1}[b_2[x]],$$

then we define the *functional recurrence relation* for the example to be

$$f_1[x],\ldots,f_j[x],\ldots,f_{j+n-1}[x],f_{i+n}[x] = a[f_i[b_1[x]];x], \quad j \le i \le k - n - 1,$$

and we define the *predicate recurrence relation* for the examples to be

$$p_1[x],\ldots,p_j[x],\ldots,p_{j+n-1}[x],p_{i+n}[x] = p_i[b_2[x]], \quad j \le i \le k - n - 1.$$

Inference. If a functional recurrence relation and a predicate recurrence relation exist for a set of examples such that $k - j \ge 2n$, then we *inductively infer* that these relationships hold for all $i \ge j$. The recurrence relations may be used to produce new examples and corresponding fragments leading to new approximating programs. The mth approximating program, $m \ge j$, is of the form

$$F_m[x] \leftarrow [p_1[x] \to f_1[x];$$
$$p_2[x] \to f_2[x];$$
$$\cdots$$
$$p_k[x] \to f_k[x];$$
$$p_{k+1}[x] \to f_{k+1}[x];$$
$$\cdots$$
$$p_m[x] \to f_m[x];$$
$$T \to \omega].$$

where the $p_i[x]$ and $f_i[x]$, $j \le i \le n$ are defined in terms of the recurrence relations. We call the set $\{F_m[x]\}$, $m \ge j$, the set of *approximating functions* for the function defined by the examples. Note that each new predicate-fragment pair in $F_m[x]$ provides an effective way of computing other examples for the inferred function.

LEMMA. *The set of approximating functions, if it exists, is a chain with partial order $\le_F$, where $F[x] \le_F G[x]$ if it is true that, for all x for which $F[x]$ is defined, $F[x] = G[x]$.*

PROOF. We define $D_m = \{x \mid p_1[x]\}\cup\cdots\cup\{x \mid p_m[x]\}$ to be the domain of the approximating function $F_m[x]$. From this it is clear that $F_i[x] \le_F F_{i+1}[x]$ for all i since D_i is a subset of D_{i+1}. □

Intuitively each function in the approximating set is an approximation to the function being generated from the set of original examples. The recurrence relations define arbitrarily large sets of examples for which one may derive programs for the approximating function set. As the size of the example set approaches infinity, the number of computations in the greatest (with respect to the relation $\le_F$) program in the set likewise approaches infinity. This then is the motivation for defining the function defined by the examples $F[x]$ to be $\sup\{F_m[x]\}$ or the limit as m approaches infinity of $F_m[x]$.

Definition. If a set of examples define the chain $\langle\{F_m[x]\},\le_F\rangle$, we define $F[x]$, the function defined by the examples, to be the $\sup\{F_m[x]\}$ or the limit as m approaches infinity of $F_m[x]$.

The simplest kind of recursive program synthesis is specified by the basic synthesis theorem. The proof of the theorem relies on material from the fixpoint theory of program language semantics. During the early 1970s, there developed a theory of recursive program semantics based on the first recursion theorem of Kleene. The purpose of such a development was to try to formalize what partial function was defined by a particular recursive program. The basic synthesis theorem represents the converse of this problem; i.e. it attempts to find a recursive program from a recurrence relation characterization of a partial function.

THEOREM (Basic Synthesis). *If a set of examples defines* $\mathbf{F}[x]$, *with recurrence relations*

$$f_1[x],\ldots,f_n[x],f_{i+n}[x] = a[f_i[b[x]];x],$$
$$p_1[x],\ldots,p_n[x],p_{i+n}[x] = p_i[b[x]] \quad \text{for } i \ge 1,$$

then $\mathbf{F}[x]$ *is equivalent to the following recursive program:*

$$F[x] \leftarrow [p_1[x] \to f_1[x];$$
$$\cdots$$
$$p_n[x] \to f_n[x];$$
$$T \to a[F[b[x]];x]].$$

PROOF.   To prove the theorem we show that the function calculated by $F[x]$, i.e. the least fixpoint of the functional τ, defined as

$$\tau[F][x] \leftarrow [p_1[x] \to f_1[x];$$
$$\cdots$$
$$p_n[x] \to f_n[x];$$
$$T \to a[F[b[x]];x],$$

is identical to $\mathbf{F}[x] = \sup\{F_n[x]\}$.

First we show that $\tau^k[\Omega][x] = F_{kn}[x]$ for all k, where $\tau^k[F][x] = \tau[\tau^{k-1}[F]][x]$ and $\Omega[x]$ is the function that is everywhere undefined, i.e. $\Omega[x] = \omega$ for all x. From this equality we conclude that $\sup\{F[x]\}$ equals the limit as i approaches infinity of $\tau^i[\Omega][x]$ equals the least fixpoint of $\tau[F][x]$.

Prove the equivalence by induction. The basis ($k = 1$):

$$\tau^1[\Omega][x] = [p_1 \to f_1[x];$$
$$\cdots$$
$$p_n[x] \to f_n[x];$$
$$T \to \omega]$$
$$= F_n[x].$$

Induction hypothesis:

$$\tau^k[\Omega][x] = [p_1[x] \to f_1[x];$$
$$\cdots$$
$$p_{kn}[x] \to f_{kn}[x];$$
$$T \to \omega]$$
$$= F_{kn}[x].$$

To prove the induction we need the semantic property that
$$f[[p_1[x] \to e_1[x];\ldots;p_k[x] \to e_k[x]]] = [p_1[x] \to f[e_1[x]];\ldots;p_k[x] \to f[e_k[x]]]$$ if and only if $f[x]$ is undefined if x is undefined.

$$\tau[\tau^k[\Omega]][x] = [p_1[x] \to f_1[x];$$
$$\cdots$$
$$p_n[x] \to f_n[x];$$
$$T \to a[[p_1[b[x]] \to f_1[b[x]];$$
$$\cdots$$
$$p_{kn}[b[x]] \to f_{kn}[b[x]];$$
$$T \to \omega];x]]$$

PROOF. Let

$$F_i[x] \leftarrow [p_1[x] \rightarrow f_1[x];$$
$$\cdots$$
$$p_1[x] \rightarrow f_1[x];$$
$$T \rightarrow \omega].$$

be an approximating program for $F[x]$. The $p_i[x]$ and $f_i[x]$ are defined from the initial fragments and the recurrence relations. We now define a diadic approximating function $G_i[x;y]$ which is identical to $F_i[x]$ whenever $y = x$.

$$G_i[x;y] \leftarrow [p_1[y] \rightarrow f_1[x];$$
$$\cdots$$
$$p_1[y] \rightarrow f_1[x];$$
$$T \rightarrow \omega].$$

We can show that $G_{i \times n}[x;y] = \tau^i[G[[x;y]$, where $G[[x;y]$ is defined to be the recursive function of the corollary. This may be demonstrated by using a proof technique similar to that used for the basic synthesis theorem. □

COROLLARY. *If a set of examples define* **F**[x] *with the recurrence relations*

$$f_1[x], \ldots, f_{j-1}[x], \ldots, f_{j+n-1}[x], f_{j+n}[x4 = a[f_i[b[x]]:x], \quad i \geq j,$$
$$p_1[x], \ldots, p_{j-1}[x], \ldots, p_{j+n-1}[x], p_{i+n}[x] = p_i[b_2[x]], \quad i \geq j,$$

then the recursive program F[x] defined below is identical to **F**[x]:

$$F[x] \leftarrow [p_1[x] \rightarrow f_1[x];$$
$$\cdots$$
$$p_{j-1}[x] \rightarrow f_{j-1}[x];$$
$$T \rightarrow G[x;x]],$$

where

$$G[x;y] \leftarrow [p_j[y] \rightarrow f_j[x];$$
$$\cdots$$
$$p_{j+n-1}[y] \rightarrow f_{j+n-1}[x];$$
$$T \rightarrow a[G[b_1[x]:b_2[y]]:x]].$$

PROOF. Immediate from previous corollaries. □

The basic synthesis theorem and the three corollaries provide the link between the function specified as a set of recurrence relations and a recursive program. These results are not sufficient to generate all of the programs that the system is capable of handling. Generating the more interesting programs requires use of the results of this section with the technique of variable addition presented in the next section.

4. Variable Addition

We recall that the synthesis results of the previous section require the existence of characterizing recurrence relations for the predicate and fragment portions of the program. Existence of these recurrence relations is not always insured; indeed, the ability to find a difference expression among all the elements of a set of fragments is not always possible. Application of the variable addition heuristic transforms a set of fragments into a more general set for which a recurrence relation may exist. The new set is more general in that each of the fragments of the new set is a function of two variables. Substituting a common expression for the added variable in the new set will produce a set of fragments identical to the original set.

We illustrate the technique by attempting the synthesis of the LISP function **reverse**. Note that unlike other systems [4, 5, 9] the following synthesis does not rely on the function **append**. We omit discussion of the early construction steps.

$$= [p_1[x] \rightarrow f_1[x];$$
$$\cdots$$
$$p_n[x] \rightarrow f_n[x];$$
$$p_1[b[x]] \rightarrow a[f_1[b[x]]:x]:$$
$$\cdots$$
$$p_{kn}[b[x]] \rightarrow a[f_{kn}[b[x]]:x];$$
$$T \rightarrow \omega]$$

$$= [p_1[x] \rightarrow f_1[x]; \quad \text{from the recurrence definition}$$
$$\cdots$$
$$p_{(k+1)m}[x] \rightarrow f_{(k+1)m}[x];$$
$$T \rightarrow \omega]$$

$$= F_{(k+1)m}[x]. \qquad \square$$

The basic synthesis theorem provides the foundation for recursive program synthesis from a finite set of examples. It should be noted that the theorem specifies the generation of a recursive program based on the existence of functional and predicate recurrence relations that satisfy a particular set of conditions. The conditions, as stated in the theorem, are far too strict for most applications. Three corollaries will be presented below that will define recursive program equivalents for recurrence relations with simpler conditions than those of the basic synthesis theorem. The first corollary relaxes the condition that the recurrence relations must define the relationship among all the fragments. By exempting some finite set of initial fragments from the set of fragments characterized by a recurrence relation, many more functions may be synthesized. The second corollary relaxes the condition that the $b[x]$ in the functional recurrence be the same as the $b[x]$ in the predicate recurrence relation. The third corollary relaxes both conditions.

COROLLARY. *If a set of examples define* **F**[x] *with the recurrence relations*

$$f_1[x], \ldots, f_{j-1}[x], f_j[x], \ldots, f_{j+n-1}[x], f_{j+n}[x] = a[f_i[b[x]]:x], \quad i \geq j,$$
$$p_1[x], \ldots, p_{j-1}[x], p_j[x], \ldots, p_{j+n-1}[x], p_{i+n}[x] = p_i[b[x]], \quad i \geq j,$$

then the recursive program F[x] defined below is identical to **F**[x].

$$F[x] \leftarrow [p_1[x] \rightarrow f_1[x];$$
$$\cdots$$
$$p_{j-1}[x] \rightarrow f_{j-1}[x];$$
$$T \rightarrow G[x]].$$

where

$$G[x] \leftarrow [p_j[x] \rightarrow f_j[x];$$
$$\cdots$$
$$p_{j+n-1}[x] \rightarrow f_{j+n-1}[x];$$
$$T \rightarrow a[G[b[x]]:x]].$$

PROOF. Immediate from the basic synthesis theorem. □

COROLLARY. *If a set of examples define* **F**[x] *with the recurrence relations*

$$f_1[x], \ldots, f_n[x], f_{i+1}[x] = a[f_i[b_1[x]]:x], \quad i \geq 1,$$
$$p_1[x], \ldots, p_n[x], p_{i+n}[x] = p_i[b_2[x]], \quad i \geq 1,$$

then the program F[x] is equivalent to **F**[x]. *F*[x] ← G[x;x], *where*

$$G[x;y] \leftarrow [p_1[y] \rightarrow f_1[x];$$
$$\cdots$$
$$p_{j+n-1}[x] \rightarrow f_{j+n-1}[x];$$
$$T \rightarrow a[G[b[x]]:x]].$$

$$G[x;y] \leftarrow [p_j[x] \rightarrow f_j[x];$$
$$\cdots$$
$$p_n[y] \rightarrow f_n[x];$$
$$T \rightarrow a[G[b_1[x]:b_2[y]]:x]].$$

Examples. {( ) → ( ), (A) → (A), (A B) → (B A), (A B C) → (C B A)}.

Fragments.

$f_1[x] = $ nil,
$f_2[x] = $ cons[car[x];nil],
$f_3[x] = $ cons[cadr[x];cons[car[x];nil]],
$f_4[x] = $ cons[caddr[x];cons[cadr[x];cons[car[x];nil]]].

Differences.

$f_2[x] = $ cons[car[x];$f_1[x]$],
$f_3[x] = $ cons[cadr[x];$f_2[x]$],
$f_4[x] = $ cons[caddr[x];$f_3[x]$].

Had all of the differences been of the same form, we would have generalized or inferred that this form represented the relationship among *all* computations of the function and thus we could have encoded the relationship as a recurrence relation and thus a recursive program as in the last section. Since the differences are not of the same form, we apply the following procedure to introduce a local variable into the program for **reverse**.

VARIABLE ADDITION

1. Given a set of fragments $\{f_i[x]\}$, $1 \le i \le k$, search the set for a common subexpression a that is common to all fragments.
2. Rewrite the fragments as $g_i[x;a] = f_i[x]$.
3. Abstract (generalize) the set as $\{g[x;y]\}$.
4. Derive, if possible, a recurrence relation to describe $\{g[x;y]\}$.
5. If step 4 did not result in a recurrence relation, return to step 1 and select another subexpression.
6. If step 4 was successful, generate the program G[x;y].
7. Define the program for $\{f_i[x]\}$ to be F[x] ← G[x;a].

Observing that **nil** exists as a subexpression common to all of the fragments and by abstracting this expression to the variable y, we have the following set of more general fragments for the function **reverse**:

$g_1[x;y] = y$,
$g_2[x;y] = $ cons[car[x];y],
$g_3[x;y] = $ cons[cadr[x];cons[car[x];y]],
$g_4[x;y] = $ cons[caddr[x];cons[cadr[x];cons[car[x];y]]].

Two differences exist for for each pair of the generalized fragments:

$g_2[x;y] = \{$cons[car[x];$g_1[x;y]$], $g_1[\alpha;$cons[car[x];y]]}, $\quad \alpha = $ anything.
$g_3[x;y] = \{$cons[cadr[x];$g_2[x;y]$], $g_2[$cdr[x];cons[car[x];y]]}},
$g_4[x;y] = \{$cons[caddr[x];$g_3[x;y]$], $g_3[$cdr[x];cons[car[x];y]]}}.

The second of the two differences are of the same form, so they may serve as a basis for the characterizing recurrence relations

$f_i[x] = g_i[x;$nil$]$, $\quad i \ge 1$,
$g_1[x;y] = y$,
$g_{k+1}[x;y] = g_k[$cdr[x];cons[car[x];y]]$, $\quad k \ge 1$.

Predicate recurrence relation may be derived to be

$p_1[x] = $ atom[x],
$p_{k+1}[x] = p_k[$cdr[x]]$ (note that the predicate is independent of the added variable y).

From these relations the following program may be produced:

reverse[x] ← r[x;nil],
r[x;y] ← [atom[x] → y;
$\quad$ T → r[cdr[x];cons[car[x];y]]].

The first program definition follows directly from the procedure for variable addition. The second definition follows from the theorems of the previous section.

5. Two Additional Examples

To further illustrate the application of the techniques of this paper we consider the construction of two additional programs. The first, **half**, demonstrates application of the second synthesis corollary.

Function.

half[x] = function that returns the first half of the even length list x.

Examples.

{( ) → ( ),
(A B) → (A),
(A B C D) → (A B),
(A B C D E F) → (A B D)}.

Fragments.

$f_1[x] = $ nil,
$f_2[x] = $ cons[car[x];nil],
$f_3[x] = $ cons[car[x];cons[cadr[x];nil]],
$f_4[x] = $ cons[car[x];cons[cadr[x];cons[caddr[x];nil]]].

Predicates.

$p_1[x] = $ atom[x],
$p_2[x] = $ atom[cddr[x]],
$p_3[x] = $ atom[cddddr[x]].

Functional recurrence relation.

$f_1[x] = $ nil,
$f_{i+1}[x] = $ cons[car[x];$f_i[$cddr[x]]]$, $\quad i \ge 1$.

Predicate recurrence relation.

$p_1[x] = $ atom[x],
$p_{i+1}[x] = p_i[$cddr[x]]$, $\quad i \ge 1$.

Program generated.

half[x] ← h[x;x],
h[x;y] ← [atom[y] → nil;
$\quad$ T → cons[car[x];h[cdr[x];cddr[y]]]].

The second program illustrates the application of the methodology to a diadic function **pairs**.

Function. pairs[x;y] returns a list of dotted pairs of the elements of the two lists x and y. The two lists must be of the same length.

Examples.

{( ) ( ) → ( ),
(A) (X) → ((A . X)).
(A B) (X Y) → ((A . X) (B . Y)).
(A B C) (X Y Z) → ((A . X) (B . Y) (C . Z))}.

Fragments.

$f_1[x;y]$ = nil,
$f_2[x;y]$ = cons[cons[car[x];car[y]];nil],
$f_3[x;y]$ = cons[cons[car[x];car[y]];cons[cons[cadr[x];cadr[y]];nil]],
$f_4[x;y]$ = cons[cons[car[x];car[y]];cons[cons[cadr[x];cadr[y]];
           cons[cons[caddr[x];caddr[y]];nil]]].

Predicates. The difficulty in handling diadic functions comes in the determination of which variable or variables is to determine the flow of control in the program. In the current example, the analysis needed for predicate determination should take place in terms of the projection of the example inputs into the lattice SF × SF (the Cartesian product of the lattice with itself). One way of interpreting this is to derive predicates for each projection and then conjoin them to get the predicates for the program:

$p_1[x;y]$ = and[atom[x];atom[y]].
$p_2[x;y]$ = and[atom[cdr[x]];atom[cdr[x]].
$p_3[x;y]$ = and[atom[cddr[x]];atom[cddr[y]]].

Note that such an assumption about the predicates leaves the function undefined for any pair of arguments x and y that are lists of different length.

Functional recurrence relation.

$f_1[x;y]$ = nil,
$f_{i+1}[x;y]$ = cons[cons[car[x];car[y]];f_i[cdr[x];cdr[y]]].

Predicate recurrence relation.

$p_1[x;y]$ = and[atom[x];atom[y]].
$p_{i+1}[x;y]$ = p_i[cdr[x];cdr[y]].

Program generated.

pairs[x;y] ← [and[atom[x];atom[y]] → nil;
             T → cons[cons[car[x];car[y]];pairs[cdr[x];cdr[y]]]].

6. System Capabilities and Limitations

It would be nice to conclude this paper with a formal characterization of the class of programs that may be generated by THESYS. Such a formal description does not exist. However, some insight into the capabilities and limitations of the system may be seen by contrasting THESYS to other systems for synthesizing Lisp programs [4, 5, 9].

The most obvious difference between THESYS and other systems is THESYS's use of a set of examples rather than a single example to specify a program. The advantage of multiple example specification over single example specification is easily illustrated by considering an example from Hardy [5]. The input/output specification is

(A B C D E F) → (A B B C D D E F).

The program derived by Hardy is

F[x] ← [or[atom[x];atom[cdr[x]]] → nil;
        T → cons[car[x];cons[cadr[x];cons[cadr[x];F[cddr[x]]]]]].

This same program will be produced by THESYS with the following set of examples:

{() → (),
(A B) → (A B B),
(A B C D) → (A B B C D D),
(A B C D E F) → (A B B C D D E F F)}.

A discussion of the synthesis of programs from examples which are not consecutive may be found in [11]. Note that if this function is applied to a list of odd length, it behaves as if it were operating on a list with one less element, e.g.

F[(A B C D E)] = (A B B C D D) = F[(A B C D)].

Another possible interpretation for the single example is the function specified by the set of input/output examples

{() → ().
(A) → (A),
(A B) → (A B B),
(A B C) → (A B B C),
(A B C D) → (A B B C D D),
(A B C D E) → (A B B C D D E)}.

THESYS will produce the following different program satisfying this specification:

G[x] ← [atom[x] → nil;
        atom[cdr[x]] → cons[car[x];nil];
        T → cons[car[x];cons[cadr[x];cons[cadr[x];G[cddr[x]]]]]].

Comparing THESYS with other systems [4, 5], one observes a number of functions for which THESYS is unable to synthesize a program. The increased function of these systems is due in part to the approach taken by their authors. In both of the reported systems there is a heavy reliance on heuristics based on knowledge of Lisp programming to drive the synthesis mechanism. In particular Hardy relies on a library of schemata and associated heuristics to generate the appropriate control structure for the program being generated. In contrast to this it was an objective of the THESYS system to base the synthesis on algorithms for deriving the control structure from the set of examples, thus avoiding searches of a program space. As a result the current state of the theory enables THESYS to derive programs with control structures involving at most a single recursive call. It is believed that future work will extend this to more complicated control structures.

To compare the power of the various approaches, the THESYS methodology was applied to the list of programs generated by Green [4] and Hardy [5]. THESYS is able to generate eleven of the sixteen programs listed by Green and five of the twelve listed by Hardy. The programs not yielding to the current THESYS methodology either involve control structures using two recursive calls or else use the function **append** in a way that is not possible to duplicate in THESYS without the use of nested function calls. Extentions to the theory along these lines are under investigation.

7. Conclusion

We have presented a methodology for Lisp recursive program construction from examples. The methodology defines a systematic program construction procedure that is based on a theoretical analysis of the problem. Two techniques were described that are crucial to this methodology, difference discovery and local variable addition. Four synthesis theorems were given for relating a function specified by recurrence relations to a program for calculating that function. These procedures may find application in other areas of program synthesis or manipulation, particularly those having to do with program behavior characterized by examples.

ACKNOWLEDGMENTS. The thesis work on which this paper is based was done under the supervision of Professor Alan Perlis of Yale University. My committee at Yale and colleagues at IBM have helped to clarify many of the ideas in the work. Special thanks must go to Professor Larry Snyder of Yale University for his ideas and support during the evolution of this work.

REFERENCES

1. BIERMANN, A.W., AND KRISHNASWAMY, R. Constructing programs from example computations. Rep. OSU-CISRC-TR-74-5, Comptr. and Inform. Sci. Res. Ctr., The Ohio State U., Columbus, Ohio, 1974.

2. BLUM, L., AND BLUM, M. Toward a mathematical theory of inductive inference. *Inform. and Control 28* (1975), 125–155.

3. BOYER, R.S., AND MOORE, JS. Proving theorems about LISP programs. *J. ACM 22*, 1 (Jan. 1975), 129–144.

4. GREEN, C.C., ET AL. Progress report on program understanding systems. Rep. STAN-CS-74-444, Comptr. Sci. Dep., Stanford U., Stanford, Calf., 1974.

5. HARDY, S. Synthesis of LISP functions from examples. Proc. Int. Joint Conf. on Artif. Intel., 1975, pp. 240–245.

6. KUGEL, P. A theorem about automatic programming. SIGART Newsletter (ACM) *51* (April 1975), 5–8.

7. McCARTHY, J., ET AL. *LISP 1.5 Programmer's Manual.* M.I.T. Press, Cambridge, Mass., 1962.

8. MOORE, JS. Introducing PROG into the pure LISP theorem prover. Rep. CSL-74-3, Xerox Palo Alto Res. Ctr., Palo Alto, Calf., 1974.

9. SHAW, D.E., ET AL. Inferring LISP programs from examples. Private communication, 1974.

10. SIKLOSSY, L. The synthesis of programs from their properties and the insane heuristic. Proc. Third Texas Conf. on Comptr. Syst., Austin, Tex., 1974, paper 5-2.

11. SUMMERS, P.D. Program construction from examples. Ph.D. Th., Dep. Comptr. Sci., Yale U., New Haven, Conn. 1975.

12. WALDINGER, R.J. Constructing programs automatically using theorem proving. Ph.D. Th., Dep. Comptr. Sci., Carnegie-Mellon U., Pittsburgh, Pa., 1969.

RECEIVED MARCH 1976; REVISED JULY 1976

Programming by Examples

Michael A. Bauer

Department of Computer Science, The University of Western Ontario, London, Ont., Canada

Recommended by S. Amarel

ABSTRACT

In this paper, examples of how an algorithm behaves on particular input are considered as possible means of describing the algorithm. In particular, a simple language for examples (a Computational Description Language) is presented and an algorithm for the synthesis of a procedure from a set of such example computations is described. The algorithm makes use of knowledge about variables, inputs, instructions and procedures during the synthesis process to guide the formation of a procedure. Several examples of procedures actually synthesized are discussed.

1. Introduction

A programmer's assistant [1, 15, 16] can involve various facilities to aid a programmer. These facilities might include a clever editor or, possibly, a language understanding subsystem. An assistant might also include a facility for program synthesis where input to the synthesizer might be natural language [10, 11, 13], input/output predicates [12] or input/output lists [7, 8]. Another form of input consists of sequences of instructions describing in a step-by-step manner, the execution of a particular algorithm on specific inputs. Such descriptions might be the sole form of input to a synthesizer or might provide additional input to a system in which a program was initially described in natural language or specified by input/output predicates.

In the following we describe initial work on a "specialist" capable of accepting sequences of instructions and synthesizing a procedure from the sequences. The algorithm described uses no knowledge of what the intended program is to compute. However, "common sense" knowledge about the use of variables, the use of inputs within descriptions, the use of parameters and instructions is incorporated into the algorithm. Thus, this specialist can be used to create procedures at varying levels of detail and for a variety of uses. In one instance, it can be used to synthesize a program to compute a specific value. At another time it may be used to form a procedure consisting of sub-procedures which remain to be defined. This latter procedure could then be used as a "skeleton" indicating the overall flow of control, and, hence, used as a basis to guide the formation of a complete procedure previously described in natural language.

To motivate a number of aspects of our model of instruction sequences, let us briefly consider an English description of how a list of names, treated as a 1-dimensional array, can be sorted. The example describes the algorithm on an array of three elements.

Let the list of names be Jones, Doe, Smith. First, compare Jones and Doe. Since Jones does not precede Doe alphabetically, we interchange the names, making the list Doe, Jones, Smith. Now, compare Doe and Smith. Since they are in alphabetic order, we do not interchange. Next, we compare Jones and Smith and again do not interchange since they are in alphabetic order. This completes our sort and the result is the list Doe, Jones, Smith.

This example suggests certain characteristics about sequences of instructions and procedures to be synthesized. Inherent in the description are such programming concepts as variables (the "list"), assignments (the "list" is assigned an initial list of Jones, Doe, Smith), predicates or tests ("precedes") and subprocedures ("interchange"). The "input" is used within the description (i.e., the input list Jones, Doe, Smith) and components (Jones, etc.) of the array are used directly in the description. Anyone attempting to form a general procedure from this specific example must also have certain knowledge of procedures, their components and the data structures involved. In particular, one must determine what the "input" is, which actions are specific cases of more general ones (e.g., "...Jones does not precede Doe..." and "...compare Doe and Smith..." are specific cases of comparisons between the components of the array), what variables are the same (the "list" in the first and last lines are the same) or are different. One must also know about arrays, how to retrieve their elements and how to access their elements sequentially.

The algorithm which we shall describe deals with examples having a subset of these characteristics. The algorithm can group instructions to form loops, resolve the use of different variables in different examples of the same algorithm, replace constants in the description by parameters and cope with certain extraneous introductory statements.

This work is based upon the work of Biermann, who has dealt with the inference of Turing Machines [3] and with the formation of procedures from sequences of instructions [4, 5]. This work extends Biermann's ideas to permit more variation and flexibility in the class of examples handled by the synthesis algorithm. It also describes how information about procedures can be incorporated into such a synthesis algorithm. Finally, through the use of a language for examples, the work illustrates how language can be used as a means of describing examples of algorithms.

This latter facet of the work is indirectly related to work by Zloof and DeJong

Artificial Intelligence **12** (1979), 1–21

[17, 18] who have used examples as a means of specifying what information was to be retrieved from a data base and what operations should be performed on the data. The examples of the operation to be executed or the data retrieved are described in a tabular format. The work here suggests a more language-oriented approach for the description of these examples.

2. A Computation Description Language

A Computation Description Language (CDL) is similar to a conventional programming language in that it has a well-defined syntax. It is unlike a programming language in two respects. First, the language is used to describe a computation of an algorithm on some specific input, rather than a complete program defining the algorithm. Second, unlike a programming language in which programs are translated into code to be executed, descriptions are transformed into data structures representing the computation to be used in the synthesis of a program.

Such a language was created for two reasons. First, regardless of whether the examples are in natural language or some formal language, techniques for the synthesis of procedures from examples must be available and understood. Thus, since our primary concern is with the development of such techniques, a usable, well-defined means of description seemed a reasonable first step. Second, a well-defined and restricted class of examples provides a concrete basis for considering how knowledge of procedures can be represented and utilized within the synthesis process.

We shall use a simple CDL throughout our discussion to illustrate various aspects of such a language. A BNF description of such a language can be found in Appendix I. The above example of how to sort a 1-dimensional array expressed in this CDL occurs in Fig. 1. An alternative description of a sort, using a procedure to find the alphabetically first name in a sequence, is presented in Fig. 2.

The current descriptions of example computations in this language must include every action and test involved in the computation. Of course, an action or test may be the call of some subprocedure which may or may not have been defined (e.g., INTERCHANGE or FIRST need not be defined in order to present either description of SORT). This is especially useful in a "top-down" definition of a procedure.

Constants (see below) within the description must either be actual constants (e.g., 1 in the description of Fig. 1) or be inputs — the SORT procedure described has a single input, ARRAY(JONES,DOE,SMITH). The input value of a parameter can be used in place of the parameter within an instruction involving that parameter providing, in the example, that the parameter has not been assigned to prior to the execution of the instruction. This simply enables one to use the value of a parameter instead of the parameter before its value is changed. Also, we shall assume that if a constant is used in an instruction instead of a parameter, then it will be used wherever possible in the example. Such a constant simplifies some

definitions and is not unreasonable since if one used such a constant once, then one would likely use it whenever possible. Other variables may not be replaced by their values nor may components of composite objects be used within the description. In the current framework we have concentrated solely on parameters and their values in order to develop some basic approaches to handling occurrences of constants.

```
TO SORT ARRAY(JONES,DOE,SMITH) DO:
LET L BE ARRAY(JONES,DOE,SMITH).
LET N BE LENGTH OF L.
LET I BE 1.
I IS NOT EQUAL-TO N SO LET EL1 BE ELEMENT I OF L.
LET J BE I PLUS 1.
J IS NOT GREATER-THAN N SO LET EL2 BE ELEMENT J OF L.
EL1 IS NOT LESS-THAN EL2 SO INTERCHANGE I AND J OF L.
LET EL1 BE EL2.
ADD 1 TO J.
J IS NOT GREATER-THAN N SO LET EL2 BE ELEMENT J OF L.
EL1 IS LESS-THAN EL2 SO ADD 1 TO J.
J IS GREATER-THAN N SO ADD 1 TO I.
I IS NOT GREATER-THAN N SO LET EL1 BE ELEMENT I OF L.
LET J BE I PLUS 1.
J IS NOT GREATER-THAN N SO LET EL2 BE ELEMENT J OF L.
EL1 IS LESS-THAN EL2 SO ADD 1 TO J.
J IS GREATER-THAN N SO ADD 1 TO I.
I IS EQUAL-TO N SO THE RESULT IS L.
```

FIG. 1. Description of a sort in a CDL.

```
TO SORT ARRAY(JONES,DOE,SMITH) DO:
LET L BE ARRAY(JONES,DOE,SMITH).
LET N BE LENGTH OF L.
LET I BE 1.
LET P BE FIRST OF L FROM I TO N.
I IS NOT EQUAL-TO P SO INTERCHANGE I AND P OF L.
ADD 1 TO I.
I IS NOT EQUAL-TO N SO LET P BE FIRST OF L FROM I TO N.
I IS EQUAL-TO P SO ADD 1 TO I.
I IS EQUAL-TO N SO THE RESULT IS L.
```

FIG. 2. Alternative description of a sort.

Finally, a number of "initialization" statements are permitted in a description. In Fig. 1 the statement "LET L BE..." is such a statement. These may be used to assign a variable a particular input value.

2.1. Translation of descriptions

A computation is represented as a 3-component structure which we call a computation-tree (c-tree). The first component is the name of the algorithm being described. The second component is its input list — the list of the specific values used in the particular computation. Both of these components are obtained from the first line of the description. The third component is an ordered, directed tree. The nodes of the tree are the instructions included in the description.

Let $t, t_1, \ldots, t_n$ be variables (denoted X, Y, Z) or constants. We shall assume for our discussion that constants are either numbers, strings (enclosed in single quotes) or composite objects. We treat composite objects, such as arrays, as record structures with appropriate functions for defining, accessing and updating the particular structure. In the previous examples, ARRAY(...) defines an "array", and ELEMENT is the accessing and updating function for arrays (see POP-2 [6] for the use of updaters in an existing programming language). This approach permits the language, with very little syntax, to accommodate procedures involving complex data structures and not just integers. More importantly, it enables the synthesis algorithm to handle such structures in the same way functions, predicates, etc. are handled with only slight extensions.

An *instruction* in a c-tree will be one of the following:

(a) *assignment* — either a simple assignment or a record assignment,

(1) a simple assignment is $X \leftarrow t$ or $X \leftarrow f(t_1, \ldots, t_n)$, where f is an n-ary function or predicate, $n \geq 0$. We shall call $f(t_1, \ldots, t_n)$ a *function application*,

(2) a *record assignment* is $U(X, t_1, \ldots, t_m) \leftarrow t$ or $U(X, t_1, \ldots, t_m) \leftarrow f(t_1, \ldots, t_n)$, where f is an n-ary function or predicate and U is an updater. We shall assume that X is the variable whose value is being updated by U,

(b) *predicate* — $p(t_1, \ldots, t_n)$, where p is an n-ary predicate, $n \geq 0$,

(c) *procedure call* — $P(t_1, \ldots, t_n)$, where P is a procedure of $n \geq 0$ arguments,

(d) RETURN or RETURN$(t_1, \ldots, t_n)$, $n \geq 0$.

The formation of the tree is straightforward except for a few special cases. The construction is done incrementally, growing the tree as each statement is processed. All assignments, predicates, procedure calls and RETURN's yield a single node. Each node is added as a successor of the previous node unless the previous one was a predicate which was untrue (indicated by the keyword NOT). In this case, the node is added as the next successor of the node which is the predecessor of the predicate. This means that the successors of any node in a c-tree are ordered. (We shall assume that the successors are ordered counter-clockwise in figures.) The c-tree of Fig. 3 is the tree formed from the description of Fig. 1.

This particular structure enables details arising from arcs labelled by True and False to be avoided in the synthesis algorithm. This structure also permits backtracking procedures to be described as well (see Bauer [2]).

The only exception to the formation of a c-tree as described above is the case in which the first statement is a predicate. In this case, a procedure of no arguments, NOOP, is used as the root: it has no effect on the computation. Finally, the words

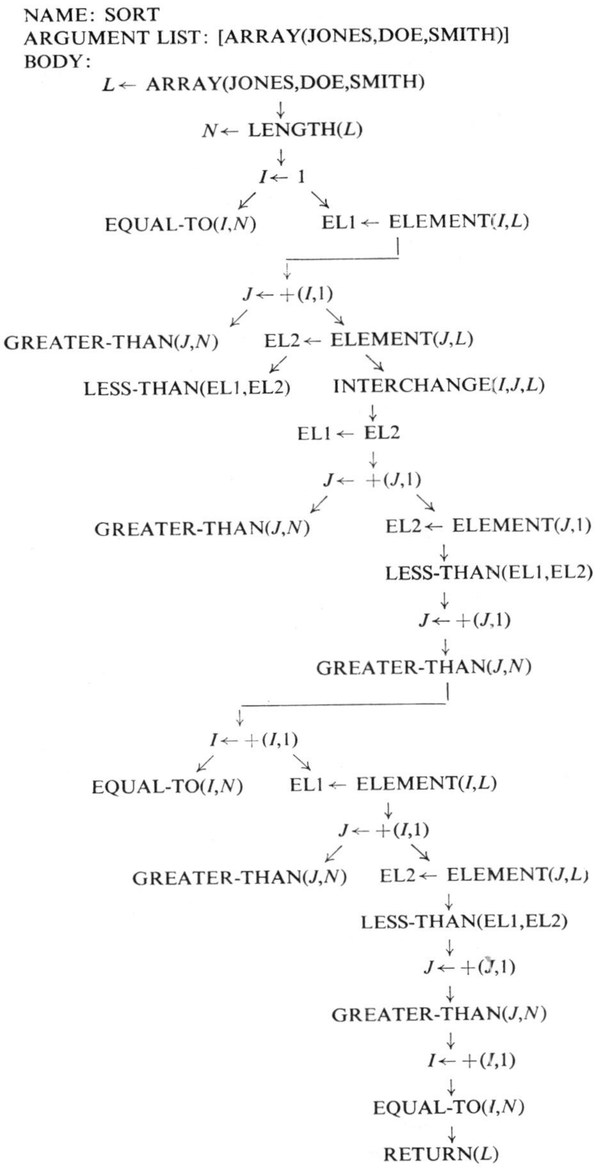

```
NAME: SORT
ARGUMENT LIST: [ARRAY(JONES,DOE,SMITH)]
BODY:
    L ← ARRAY(JONES,DOE,SMITH)
    N ← LENGTH(L)
    I ← 1
    EQUAL-TO(I,N)
        EL1 ← ELEMENT(I,L)
        J ← +(I,1)
        GREATER-THAN(J,N)     EL2 ← ELEMENT(J,L)
        LESS-THAN(EL1,EL2)    INTERCHANGE(I,J,L)
                              EL1 ← EL2
                              J ← +(J,1)
                              GREATER-THAN(J,N)     EL2 ← ELEMENT(J,1)
                              LESS-THAN(EL1,EL2)    J ← +(J,1)
                                                    GREATER-THAN(J,N)
                    I ← +(I,1)
                    EQUAL-TO(I,N)
                        EL1 ← ELEMENT(L)
                        J ← +(I,1)
                        GREATER-THAN(J,N)     EL2 ← ELEMENT(J,L)
                        LESS-THAN(EL1,EL2)    J ← +(J,1)
                                              GREATER-THAN(J,N)
                              I ← +(I,1)
                              EQUAL-TO(I,N)
                                  RETURN(L)
```

Fig. 3. A computation tree.

TO, FROM and BY have been included to provide some common uses of binary functions. In the case of TO and FROM the expression "Function *t* TO/FROM Variable" becomes Function(Variable, *t*). The expression "Function Variable BY *t*" becomes Function(Variable,*t*).

3. The Synthesis Algorithm

We shall describe the algorithm in terms of c-trees. Intuitively, one should think of a c-tree as an example computation and a node as an instruction. We shall also rely on some common graph-theoretic notions, such as root, path, tree, successor, predecessor (see Harary [9]).

Let us briefly examine how a person might form a procedure from a number of examples of computations. The first task might be to locate instructions or computations which appear to do the same thing. Once a number of possibly related actions have been located, the person attempts to verify the relationships by examining the variables and constants involved, how corresponding variables are used, what instructions follow, etc.

Our synthesis algorithm proceeds in a similar manner, although at a more detailed level. Knowledge of procedures, use of variables, etc., is incorporated into the synthesis algorithm in the form of constraints.

```
TO FIND-ROOT OF 5 DO:                TO FIND-ROOT OF −1 DO:
5 IS GREATER-THAN 0 SO                   −1 IS NOT GREATER-THAN 0
   LET R BE 1.                               SO THE ANSWER IS 0.
   LET S2 BE S TIMES S.
   S2 IS NOT GREATER-THAN 5
      SO LET R BE S.
   ADD 1 TO S.
   LET S2 BE S TIMES S.
   S2 IS GREATER-THAN 5 SO
      THE ANSWER IS R.
```

FIG. 4. Description of computations of a procedure to find the integer square root.

Given a set of c-trees, say $\mathcal{T} = \{T_1, \ldots, T_k\}$, the algorithm attempts to group nodes into classes. Nodes of the same class are, supposedly, occurrences of the same instruction in the algorithm being illustrated. This is analogous to an individual loosely relating instructions or actions which appear to do the same thing. Once a suitable set of classes (defined below) has been constructed, the set is examined to guarantee that certain consistency conditions are satisfied. One set of conditions involves verifying that variables in the same position of nodes within the same class are used in a similar manner in their respective computations. The second set involves the existence and construction of a parameter list. These conditions constitute certain "common sense" knowledge about procedures, use of variables, use of parameters, etc.

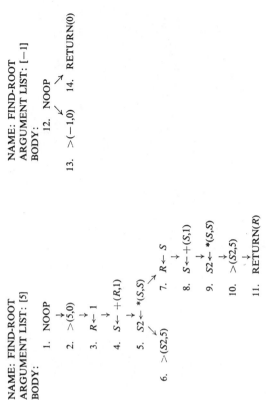

NAME: FIND-ROOT
ARGUMENT LIST: [5]
BODY:

1. NOOP
2. >(5,0)
3. $R \leftarrow 1$
4. $S \leftarrow +(R,1)$
5. $S2 \leftarrow *(S,S)$
6. >(S2,5)
7. $R \leftarrow S$
8. $S \leftarrow +(S,1)$
9. $S2 \leftarrow *(S,S)$
10. >(S2,5)
11. RETURN(R)

NAME: FIND-ROOT
ARGUMENT LIST: [−1]
BODY:

12. NOOP
13. >(−1,0)
14. RETURN(0)

FIG. 5. Computation trees for descriptions in Fig. 4.

To illustrate the concepts and definitions involved we shall consider the synthesis of a procedure from two c-trees as we describe the steps involved. Fig. 4 contains two descriptions of a procedure which computes the integer square root ($\lfloor\sqrt{n}\rfloor$) of a positive integer n. For input of less than 1, the result is 0. The c-trees of these descriptions are presented in Fig. 5. We have numbered the nodes for reference throughout the text and the ordering of successors is counter-clockwise from a node. For simplicity we have used common mathematical symbols for predicates and functions (e.g., >, +, *).

3.1. Classifying nodes which "look alike"

The first step of the synthesis algorithm is to try to class nodes which seem to do the same thing. One straightforward approach is to class only those nodes which are identical. This is obviously too constraining since one may also wish to class together nodes which differ only in the variables involved. Because input arguments may also be used within instructions one should allow such variations as well.

To illustrate why one must be concerned with the variables and constants in instructions, assume that an instruction $X \leftarrow f(Y,X)$ exists in one c-tree. Suppose further that Y is a parameter, i.e., is assigned an input. In another c-tree, perhaps describing the same computation, this same instruction might be $Z \leftarrow f(3,Z)$, where Z had been used instead of X and 3, the input for Y, was used directly in the instruction. In terms of the CDL these two instructions might be:

LET X BE F OF Y AND X,
LET Z BE F OF 3 AND Z,
respectively.

Thus, a reasonable criterion for nodes to be classed together would be that they are identical except for the use of variables and constants within them. These, in turn, must satisfy additional constraints based upon the use of variables and constants within procedures (to be described).

Note that instructions involving predicates and functions of different names but which are equivalent will never be classed together under this paradigm. A reasonable alternative in general would involve solutions to equivalence problems. To do so in general would involve solutions to equivalence problems. A reasonable alternative would be to consider functional synonyms — for example, ADD and PLUS, SUBTRACT and MINUS, or SORT and ORDER. In this case, a dictionary of such "synonyms" would exist for use during the synthesis process.

Intuitively, we can class two instructions if they can be formed from the same instruction by replacing variables within that instruction by variables and constants. Such substitutions must be consistent with certain "common sense" conditions. For example, all occurrences of a variable must be replaced by at most one other variable in any instruction of an example. Similarly, a variable can be replaced by at most one constant representing an input.

Let us define a *substitution* σ to be a set of pairs $\{(W_i \mid t_i)\}$ where the following hold:

(a) W_i is a variable,

(b) t_i is a variable other than W_i or is a constant,

(c) for pairs $(W_i \mid t_j)$, $(W_i \mid t_j)$ in σ, $t_i = t_j$ (W_i can be replaced by at most one variable or constant),

(d) for pairs $(W_i \mid t_i)$, $(W_j \mid t_i)$ in σ and t_i a variable, $W_i = W_j$ (a variable t_i can replace at most one variable).

Let s be a function application, predicate or procedure call. We *apply a substitution* σ to s (denoted $\sigma \circ s$) by simultaneously replacing each W_i by t_i in s.

Assignment statements introduce special problems — the same variable might be replaced by a constant on the right-hand side and be assigned to on the left-hand side. In order to deal with this, we extend the idea of a substitution to a pair of substitutions, one for each side, with constraints between the two substitutions.

A *mapping* π (map π) is:

(a) a substitution, if the instruction is a predicate, procedure call, or function application,

(b) a pair of substitutions (σ_L, σ_R), if the instruction is an assignment, where
(1) if $(W_i \mid t_j)$ is in σ_R, t_i a variable, then if $(W_i \mid t_j)$ is in σ_L, then $t_i = t_j$,
(2) if $(W_i \mid t_i)$ is in σ_R, t_i a variable, then if $(W_j \mid t_i)$ is in σ_L, then $W_i = W_j$.

A *mapping* π *applied to an instruction* s ($\pi \circ s$) is:

(a) $\sigma \circ s$, if s is a predicate, procedure call or function application and $\pi = \sigma$,

(b) $\sigma_L \circ (\mathrm{Lhs}(s)) \leftarrow \sigma_R \circ (\mathrm{Rhs}(s))$, if s is an instruction and $\pi = (\sigma_L, \sigma_R)$ (where $\mathrm{Lhs}(s)$ and $\mathrm{Rhs}(s)$ yield the left and right hand sides of the assignment s, respectively).

Let $s_1, \ldots, s_n$ be instructions, $\pi_1, \ldots, \pi_n$ be maps and let s be an instruction. Call s a *least generalization* of $s_1, \ldots, s_n$ if $\pi_i \circ s = s_i$, $i = 1, 2, \ldots, n$. Call s a *generalization* of $s_1, \ldots, s_n$ if for any generalization s' of $s_1, \ldots, s_n$, there is a mapping π' such that $\pi' \circ s' = s$.

Finally, call $s_1, \ldots, s_n$ *similar* if they have a least generalization. The concept of least generalization for terms involving variables and constants was introduced by Plotkin [14] in the context of Predicate Calculus, but extended here to deal with instructions and, in particular, assignment statements. Intuitively, a mapping characterizes "common sense" knowledge about the use of variables and constants within different instructions.

In Fig. 5, nodes 2, 6 and 13 are similar since we can let s be $>(X, Y)$ with substitutions $\pi_2 = \{(X \mid 5), (Y \mid 0)\}$, $\pi_6 = \{(X \mid S2), (Y \mid 5)\}$ and $\pi_{13} = \{(X \mid -1), (Y \mid 0)\}$. Consider, instead, nodes 4 and 8. Their least generalization must be of the form $X \leftarrow +(Y, 1)$ and, in node 4, S and R must replace distinct variables (condition (b(1)) of a mapping). But then a mapping for node 8 would have to be $\{(X \mid S), (Y \mid S)\}$ which would violate condition (b(2)). Thus nodes 4 and 8 are not similar.

In the latter case, we obviously do not wish nodes 4 to 8 to be classed together and so similarity provides a good criterion. In the former case, we do not wish node 6 to be classed with nodes 2 and 13. As we shall see, this classification will ultimately be rejected by subsequent constraints.

Similarity provides one condition for possibly classifying nodes together. A second condition, however, must also be met — namely, we also wish that the computations from nodes "look alike", i.e., corresponding nodes are also similar.

Let S be a set of instructions $(s_1, \ldots, s_n)$. Since the successors of any node in a c-tree are ordered, we can define the sets of ith successors of nodes in a given set S. Let $\mathrm{Succ}(S, i) = \{s \mid s$ is the ith successor of $s_j \in S\}$. Call a set S *0-identifiable* (0-id) if the nodes of S are similar. Call S *M-identifiable* (M-id) if the nodes of S are similar and $\mathrm{Succ}(S, 1), \ldots, \mathrm{Succ}(S, k)$ are $(M-1)$-identifiable, where k is the maximum number of successors of any node in S. Finally, call S *identifiable* if S is M-identifiable and M is the length of the longest path in any c-tree of T.

The set of nodes $S = \{5, 9\}$, in Fig. 5, are identifiable. Clearly, they are similar. The set $\mathrm{Succ}(S, 1)$ is $\{6, 10\}$ and the set $\mathrm{Succ}(S, 2)$ is just $\{7\}$ (recall that in figures successors are ordered left to right). Both sets of nodes are obviously similar: $\mathrm{Succ}(S, 2)$ satisfies the conditions trivially. A singleton set is always identifiable and hence so is $\{5, 9\}$.

On the other hand, even though nodes 2, 10 and 13, of Fig. 5, are similar, they do not form an identifiable set. The definition of identifiable nodes provides the basis for classifying nodes from a set of c-trees. To make this precise, we define an identifiability cover.

A *cover* C is a set of sets $\{S_1, \ldots, S_k\}$, the S_i are called *classes*, such that the following hold:

(a) if a node $s \in S_i$, then each successor of s is in some S_j of C.
(b) any node s of a c-tree not in a class S_i of C is of the form Variable $\leftarrow$ constant, and the constant appears in the argument list of the c-tree.

Call C an *identifiability cover* (id-cover) if:

(a) C is a cover,
(b) each S in C is an identifiable set of nodes,
(c) for any S in C, then Succ$(S, i) \subseteq S_j$, S_j is in C, for $i = 1, 2, \ldots, k$, k is the maximum number of successors of any node in S.

Intuitively, nodes which are identifiable are those which involve the same functions and are followed by computations which involve the same kinds of instructions. An id-cover is a partition of nearly all nodes into identifiable classes. Nodes not included would be those hypothesized to be nodes added as introductory assignments.

Several id-covers based upon the nodes of Fig. 5 are pictured in Fig. 6.

$\{\{1,12\}, \{2,13\}, \{14\}, \{3\}, \{4\}, \{5\}, \{6\}, \{7\}, \{8\}, \{9\}, \{10\}, \{11\}\}$ — (1).
$\{\{1,12\}, \{2,6,13\}, \{11,14\}, \{3\}, \{4\}, \{5\}, \{7\}, \{8\}, \{9\}, \{10\}, \{11\}\}$ — (2).
$\{\{1,12\}, \{2,13\}, \{11,14\}, \{3\}, \{4\}, \{5,9\}, \{6,10\}, \{7\}, \{8\}\}$ — (3).
$\{\{1,12\}, \{2,13\}, \{14\}, \{3\}, \{4\}, \{5,9\}, \{6,10\}, \{7\}, \{8\}, \{11\}\}$ — (4).

FIG. 6. Several id-covers from c-trees of Fig. 5.

3.2. Constraints on the use of variables

The discovery of an id-cover determines a plausible grouping of instructions — essentially using only knowledge of instruction similarity. The mappings constructed for each node of each set of the cover relate the variables within instructions of each class. Ultimately the least generalization of each class will become a single instruction in the synthesized procedure.

However, variables in any least generalization cannot be treated as independent. For example, suppose a variable X appeared in two instructions of the same example. Then in the least generalizations corresponding to these instructions, the variables in the same positions as X must also be the same. Similarly, if a variable W in some least generalization replaces a constant c in one instruction, then in any other instruction of the same example, the only constant it can replace is c.

This information about the use of variables and arguments within examples, as opposed to only within instructions of the same class, is formalized as follows. Let S be a set of nodes $s_1, \ldots, s_n$ whose least generalization is s. Let $\pi_1, \ldots, \pi_n$ be maps such that $\pi_i \circ s = s_i$. Call map π_i the *map associated with* s_i.

Let $\mathscr{I}$ be an id-cover of nodes from the c-trees of $\mathscr{T}$. Let $s_1, \ldots, s_n$ be the nodes of a c-tree that are in any class of $\mathscr{I}$. Let $\Gamma = \{\pi_1, \ldots, \pi_n\}$, where π_i is the map associated with s_i. Call Γ *consistent* if the following hold:

(a) for any pair $(W \,|\, t_i)$ in π_i, t_i a variable, then
  (1) there does not exist $(W \,|\, t_j)$ in π_j, t_j a variable, such that $t_i \neq t_j$, and
  (2) there does not exist $(W' \,|\, t_i)$ in π_j, $W \neq W'$,
(b) for any pair $(W \,|\, t_i)$ in π_i, t_i a constant, then
  (1) t_i occurs in the argument list of the c-tree, and
  (2) if a pair $(W \,|\, t_j)$ is in π_j, s_i and s_j are in the same class, t_j a variable, then t_j is not assigned to on the path to s_i, from a node of the c-tree in some class.

Condition (a) guarantees that any variable in a least generalization of a class of the cover is associated with at most one variable in each c-tree. This condition corresponds to one aspect of our knowledge about variables — a variable of the example is a renaming of at most one variable in the algorithm being illustrated. The second condition captures certain information about variables which may be parameters. It simply ensures that if a variable in a least generalization replaces a constant, i.e., is to be a parameter, then that constant is an input of the example and the variable in the least generalization can become a parameter.

The least generalization of $\{2, 13\}$ in id-cover (1) is $>(X, 0)$ with maps $\pi_2 = \{(X \,|\, 5)\}$ and $\pi_{13} = \{(X \,|\, -1)\}$. Since 5 is an argument in the first c-tree and -1 is an argument in the second, the conditions are satisfied. The least generalization of $\{2, 6, 13\}$ in id-cover (2) is $>(X, Y)$. In this case, π_6 must be $\{(X \,|\, S2), (Y \,|\, 5)\}$ if π_2 is as above in order not to violate condition (a(2)). Even so, S2 is assigned to in node 5 and condition (b(2)) is violated. Hence id-cover (2) would be rejected since the maps of the first c-tree would be inconsistent.

The previous constraints apply to mappings associated with nodes within a c-tree. If a variable W in a least generalization is to be considered as a parameter, then its usage as a parameter must make sense in other c-trees. In particular, if W replaced c in one c-tree and c was the second input, then any constant that W replaced in any other c-tree must also be the second input. This provides an additional constraint across c-trees and embodies certain knowledge about variables which can be considered parameters.

Now let Γ_i, $i = 1, 2, \ldots, r$ be the sets of maps for each c-tree T_i in T. Let us call the set of these sets of maps *consistent with respect to* $\mathscr{I}$ if both of the following hold:

(a) each Γ_i is consistent,
(b) for every pair $(W \,|\, t_j)$ in π_j of Γ_i, such that t_j is a constant, then $\bigcap_{k=1,r}$ POS$((W \,|\, t_j), k) \neq \emptyset$, where POS$((W \,|\, t_j), k) = \{p \,|\,$ either

(1) $(W | t_k)$ is in π_k of Γ_t, t_k a constant and occurs in argument position p of T_i,

or

(2) $W \leftarrow t_k$ is an instruction of T_i, is not in any class of $\mathcal{I}$ and t_k occurs in argument position p of T_i.

The class $\{11, 14\}$ is a member of id-covers (2) and (3). Its least generalization is RETURN(X) with maps $\pi_{11} = \{(X | R)\}$ and $\pi_{14} = \{(X | 0)\}$. Since Γ_1 is not consistent (R is assigned to before node 11) the set $\{\Gamma_1, \Gamma_2\}$ is not consistent with respect to $\mathcal{I}$. Suppose that R was not assigned to before node 11. Then $\{\Gamma_1, \Gamma_2\}$ would still fail to be consistent since, in π_{14}, 0 does not occur in the argument list of T_2 and so $\bigcap_{k=1,2} POS((X | 0), k) = \emptyset$.

The above consistency conditions provide necessary conditions for the mappings across the entire set of c-trees whereas the previous conditions are local to each c-tree.

Providing that $\Gamma_1, \ldots, \Gamma_r$ is consistent with respect to $\mathcal{I}$, the id-cover is a potential basis for a procedure. Should the maps fail to be consistent for any reason the selected cover is rejected and a new one sought. Fig. 7 contains two possible covers and the sets of maps associated with each.

id-cover = {{1,12}, {2,13}, {14}, {3}, {4}, {5,9}, {6,10}, {7}, {8}, {11}}:
$\Gamma_1 = \{\pi_1 = \{ \}, \pi_2 = \{(X | 5)\}, \pi_3 = \{Y | R)\}, \pi_4 = \{(Z | S), (Y | R)\},$
$\pi_5 = \pi_9 = \{(W | S2), (Z | S)\}, \pi_6 = \pi_{10} = \{(W | S2)\},$
$\pi_7 = \{(Y | R), (Z | S)\}, \pi_8 = \{(Z | S)\}, \pi_{11} = \{(Y | R)\}\}.$
$\Gamma_2 = \{\pi_{12} = \{ \}, \pi_{13} = \{(X | -1)\}, \pi_{14} = \{ \}\}.$

id-cover = {{1,12}, {2,13}, {14}, {3}, {4}, {5}, {6}, {7}, {8}, {9}, {10}, {11}}.
Γ'_1 = same as Γ_1 above.
Γ'_2 = same as Γ_2 above.

FIG. 7. Two id-covers and sets of associated maps.

After successfully determining that the maps are consistent, the algorithm forms a procedure body from the id-cover and maps and then attempts to form a parameter list. The procedure is represented as directed graph (see Bauer [2] for the execution of digraphs as procedures) where each node is an instruction and the edges determine the execution sequence. Each class of the cover yields one instruction — the least generalization of the class. The successor relationship between instructions is determined from the successor relationships of nodes in the corresponding classes. For purposes of presentation, we shall present the synthesized procedures in an ALGOL-like language.

3.3. The parameter list and the use of parameters

Once the body of the procedure, its nodes and edges, has been constructed, the next step is the determination of a parameter list. The existence of a parameter list is a necessary condition for the id-cover selected to be considered adequate.

A *parameter list* is an n-tuple of unique variables. A parameter list $\langle Y_1, \ldots, Y_n \rangle$ is consistent with respect to $\mathcal{I}$, an id-cover $\mathcal{I}$ and sets of mappings $\Gamma_1, \ldots, \Gamma_r$ if

(a) each c-tree has n-arguments, and

(b) for any pair $(W_i | c) \in \pi_i$, $W_i = Y_k$, for some k, $1 \leq k \leq n$,

(c) for a node $X \leftarrow c$ in a c-tree T_i, but not in any class of $\mathcal{I}$,
(1) if $(W | X) \in \pi_j$ of Γ_i, then $W = Y_k$ for some k, $1 \leq k \leq n$, or
(2) otherwise, $X = Y_k$ for some k, $1 \leq k \leq n$.

Clearly, any arbitrary list of variables in the constructed body will not suffice as a parameter list. Hence, one must capture what conditions are necessary for a list of variables to be a parameter list — consistency. A parameter list is consistent, intuitively, if it contains all the variables of the least generalizations which must, in our framework of examples, be considered parameters. These variables are characterized by conditions (b) and (c). In the former, any variable which replaces a constant must be a parameter. In the latter condition, any node not included in a class of $\mathcal{I}$ must be of the form Variable $\leftarrow$ constant. If not in a class, then it must be that such a node is considered to be one added in order to assign an input value to a variable. Hence, that variable must become a parameter.

The discovery of a parameter list is essentially an enumerative procedure. However, because of constraints (b) and (c), certain variables from the mappings can be immediately assigned to positions in the parameter list. This reduces the positions to be filled and the possible choices. Likewise, it is also possible to determine the lack of any parameter list because of these conditions. For example, if two distinct variables are forced to be in the same parameter position then the search can fail immediately.

Note that the variables in a parameter list are not forced to be variables of the procedure, except under conditions (b) and (c). Such a requirement is too severe and in some cases leads to serious problems. A simple case is when one parameter is used in one particular instruction and no occurrence of the instruction is included in any example. Using a new variable is the correct approach while using an existing one could lead to a procedure which might not work on the input of the given examples.

As in the case of mappings, the failure to find a consistent parameter list causes the id-cover under consideration to be rejected.

In the covers and maps of Fig. 7, we have pairs $(X | 5)$ in π_2 of Γ_1 and $(X | -1)$ in π_{13} of Γ_2. In both cases X must be the first (and only) parameter of each. Hence the parameter list becomes $\langle X \rangle$.

Once a consistent parameter list has been discovered, the procedure is complete — a list of parameters and a body.

The final step is to try to replace constants occurring in the newly formed procedure by parameters. A constant c in a node n can be *replaced by the kth parameter Y_k providing*

(a) c occurred in the kth argument position of each c-tree having a node in the class forming n, and

(b) Y_k is not assigned to on some path from the root to n.

Based upon the id-covers and maps of Fig. 7, the two procedures in Fig. 8 could be formed. In both cases, the 5 in several instructions could, and would, be replaced by X. In both cases the 0 in RETURN(0) would not be replaced.

```
PROCEDURE FIND-ROOT(X):
NOOP:
IF X > 0 THEN BEGIN
    Y := 1;
    LABEL1: Z := Y+1;
    W := Z * Z;
    IF W > X THEN RETURN(Y)
        ELSE BEGIN
            Y := Z;
            GOTO LABEL1 END
        END
    ELSE RETURN(0)
END.

PROCEDURE FIND-ROOT(X):
NOOP:
IF X > 0 THEN BEGIN
    Y := 1;
    Z := Y+1;
    W := Z * Z;
    IF W > X THEN ??
        ELSE BEGIN
            Y := Z;
            Z := Y+1;
            W := Z*Z;
            IF W > X THEN RETURN(Y)
                END
        END
    ELSE RETURN(0)
END.
```

FIG. 8. Two possible procedures.

Note that in this case two "procedures" are possible. The second is not a complete procedure since the operations after one of the THEN's is missing. Such "partial procedures" must be allowed, since it is possible that the given examples do not involve certain sequences of instructions. The execution rule for digraphs can, however, still operate successfully on such partial procedures.

The synthesis algorithm produces a procedure or partial procedure having the fewest instructions. This is done by searching for an id-cover having the fewest classes (see Section 3.4). The user may reject the synthesized procedure causing the algorithm to resume its search. Of the two procedures in Fig. 8, the first would be the one synthesized.

3.4. Search for an id-cover

The discovery of an id-cover is the most time consuming aspect of the algorithm outlined. Using a straightforward "generate-and-test" approach, where possible covers are generated and then tested to see if they are id-covers, is possible, but quite unreasonable.

By taking advantage of some local information and performing some preliminary computations, the formation of an id-cover can be formulated in terms of a state-space search and made less time consuming. Because each example is from the same procedure and because we are assuming that no steps have been omitted, the first node (leftmost) of each c-tree involving a function, predicate or procedure must originate from the same instruction in the procedure being described. Therefore, we wish these nodes to be in the same class. Let us call these nodes the *start nodes*. Since we are seeking an id-cover, corresponding successors of nodes already in the same class must also be in the same class. Thus we can determine other nodes which must be in the same class once the start nodes have been determined.

In the previous examples of Fig. 5, nodes 1 and 12 would be the start nodes (recall that NOOP is a procedure). Since 1 and 12 must be in the same class, so must nodes 2 and 13. Hence, the initial set is $\{\{1, 12\}, \{2, 13\}\}$.

Let C' be a set of sets $\{S_1, \ldots, S_n\}$. Call C' a *partial id-cover* if

(a) each S_i is a set of similar nodes, and

(b) for any S in C',

(1) either Succ $(S, i) \subseteq S_j$, $S_j \in C'$, for $i = 1, k$, where k is the maximum number of successors of any node in S,

(2) or, Succ $(S, i) \not\subseteq S_j$, for any $S_j \in C'$, $i = 1, k$.

The initial set $\{\{1, 12\}, \{2, 13\}\}$ in the example is a partial id-cover since both $\{1, 12\}$ and $\{2, 13\}$ are each a similar set of nodes and the sets of successors of $\{2, 13\}$ (namely, $\{3\}$) is not contained in any set of the initial cover.

Let us treat the initial partial id-cover as the start state in a state-space. We determine the successors of any state by considering each class of the state whose successors are not yet in any class of the state. Given such a class and the partial id-cover, a number of partial id-covers (possibly 0) are computed in which the successors of the chosen class are in some class of the newly formed state.

By adopting this approach, one only constructs sets that could become id-covers. Sets of classes which would yield covers which are not id-covers would not be considered as possible states. In essence, such sets would be rejected as soon as it was discovered that they fail to be id-covers.

Finally, the choice of which state to expand next is made by choosing the one

4. Concluding Remarks

The synthesis algorithm has been implemented in POP-2 and has been tested on a number of examples. A simple interchange sort for 1-dimensional arrays has been synthesized from two examples illustrating the sort procedure on the 1-dimensional arrays ARRAY(6, 7) and ARRAY(7, 6). The number of elements in each array constituted the second input (i.e., 2 in both cases) and was used directly within the descriptions. The same sort was also synthesized from a single example illustrating the sort on the input [ARRAY(2, 7, 6), 3]. It is interesting to note that the latter example required quite a bit more time (a factor of 5) than the two examples, even though the total number of nodes involved only differed by 1 in the two situations. This difference was apparently due to the redundancy of information (nodes) in the case of the two example computations.

When the instructions involved in a procedure are all nearly unique (i.e., the successors are not identifiable), one can determine which pairs of nodes are not identifiable before beginning the search for an id-cover.

Additional preprocessing can yield other information to aid in the rapid rejection of an id-cover having no consistent mappings or consistent parameter lists. This has not been done in the current implementation of the algorithm.

To summarize the steps involved, an ALGOL-like description of the synthesis algorithm is presented in Fig. 9. Only the major steps have been included.

with the fewest classes. Such a choice leads to procedures having the fewest instructions and, more importantly, encourages the formation of loops.

Once an id-cover has been selected some additional computation is done to see if nodes occurring before the start nodes can be included. This phase can also take advantage of mappings already computed, if it is postponed until after a consistent set of maps is discovered. Of course, if no set of maps is found, then the cover is rejected.

Implicit in the formation of states is the determination of whether or not a constructed set of classes is actually an id-cover. This testing can be made more efficient by some preprocessing of the nodes. Given the nodes in all the c-trees, one can determine for any pair whether they are similar or not. Using these results and the fact that two nodes are not identifiable if any two of their corresponding procedure contains very few instructions which are identical) the search space considered by the synthesis algorithm on a few examples is usually small. The search for an id-cover is then relatively short. This could probably be reduced if a better selection procedure was adopted. Nevertheless, it seems that in practice, the search space will be tractable for many procedures.

We did, however, test the synthesis algorithm on examples from a "Turing Machine procedure" for recognizing sentences of the form 0^n1^n. The procedure involved only four instructions — READ(X), WRITE(X), MOVER(TAPE) and MOVEL(TAPE); X could be 0 or 1. This creates many similar nodes within the examples. The procedure was correctly synthesized from two examples based upon the inputs 01 and 0011.

A summary of several procedures synthesized is presented in Tables 1 and 2. Table 1 contains a description of the algorithm to be synthesized. Table 2 includes the number of examples used to synthesize the indicated procedure and the inputs which were used to form the examples. Also included is the number of nodes in the examples and the execution time (in seconds, including garbage collection). In all cases the first procedure synthesized was the correct one.

The existing synthesis system is still very primitive. Currently the synthesis algorithm obtains the c-trees to process from a user specified file. Also the system never "understands" the examples that are presented. Rather it "understands" certain aspects of procedures, variables, instructions and programming, even though these have been rather formally defined.

The formality of the concepts may seem excessive, but their precision has made it possible to show (Bauer [2]) that this synthesis algorithm is sound and complete. The soundness of the algorithm guarantees that regardless of the procedure synthesized, it will produce the same result as the examples used to synthesize it. This is true whether the procedure is equivalent to the one intended or not. The completeness of the algorithm guarantees that for any procedure if one continues to present examples, then the algorithm eventually synthesizes a procedure which

```
PROCEDURE SYNTHESIZE(EXAMPLES,NEW-PROC):
(* EXAMPLES is a set of c-trees *)
INITIAL-STATE := FIND-INIT-STATE(EXAMPLES);
ALL-STATES := {INITIAL-STATE};
(* Choose the next, i.e., partial id-cover, and delete from set of possible states *)
SELECT-STATE: STATE := CHOOSE-STATE(ALL-STATES);
IF IS-ID-COVER(STATE) THEN BEGIN
    IF NOT(CONSISTENT-MAPS(EXAMPLES,STATE,MAPS))
        THEN GOTO SELECT-STATE;
    (* Maps contain the consistent mappings if found *)
    BODY := FORM-BODY(EXAMPLES,STATE,MAPS);
    IF NOT(CONSISTENT-PLIST(EXAMPLES,STATE,MAPS,PARAM-LIST))
        THEN GOTO SELECT-STATE;
    (* PARAM-LIST is the consistent list of parameters if one is found *)
    NEW-PROC := REPLACE-CONSTANTS(EXAMPLES,STATE,MAPS,BODY,
        PARAM-LIST);
    (* Form a new procedure by replacing constants when possible *)
END
ELSE BEGIN
    ALL-STATES := GEN-STATES(ALL-STATES,EXAMPLES,STATE);
    (* Fail if no more partial id-covers exist *)
    IF EMPTY(ALL-STATES) THEN FAIL
        ELSE GOTO SELECT-STATE
    END;
END.
```

FIG. 9. The synthesis procedure.

always produces the same results as the original on any input for which the original halts.

The techniques used to define an example of a computation appear to be generalizable, that is, they suggest ways to extend the class of examples. In particular, it seems reasonable to consider examples for which the synthesis algorithm requires certain knowledge about particular programming structures and techniques. Such information may involve, for example, techniques for accessing elements of arrays, functions involved in such accesses (such as "increment by 1"), how elements of arrays are used in descriptions rather than their positions, etc. Moreover, it may be possible to examine such extended synthesis algorithms for their soundness and completeness.

with a particular instruction and involving the instructions to another under some initial assignment of values to the variables involved. For example, it may begin with a predicate which evaluates to True and describes a computation along this "branch" of the program. In an interactive environment, the synthesis system could request such descriptions from a program designer whenever it detects an undefined branch. The classification process and search for an id-cover described can be used in these cases without modification.

Appendix I

A BNF Description of a Computation Description Language.

$\langle$Description$\rangle$ ::= TO $\langle$Verb Phrase$\rangle$ DO: $\langle$Actions$\rangle$ $\langle$End$\rangle$
   | TO SEE IF $\langle$Test Phrase$\rangle$ DO: $\langle$Actions$\rangle$ $\langle$End$\rangle$

$\langle$END$\rangle$ ::= . . . . . .

$\langle$Actions$\rangle$ ::= $\langle$Action$\rangle$. $\langle$Actions$\rangle$ | $\langle$Action$\rangle$
$\langle$Action$\rangle$ ::= $\langle$Imperative$\rangle$ | $\langle$Conditional$\rangle$ | $\langle$Assignment$\rangle$
   | $\langle$Result$\rangle$

$\langle$Imperative$\rangle$ ::= $\langle$Verb Phrase$\rangle$ | $\langle$Test Phrase$\rangle$
$\langle$Conditional$\rangle$ ::= $\langle$Test Phrase$\rangle$ SO $\langle$Do Something$\rangle$
   | $\langle$Test Phase$\rangle$ ETC.

$\langle$Do Something$\rangle$ ::= $\langle$Imperative$\rangle$ | $\langle$Assignment$\rangle$ | $\langle$Result$\rangle$
   | DO AS BEFORE

$\langle$Assignment$\rangle$ ::= LET $\langle$Variable$\rangle$ BE $\langle$Object Phrase$\rangle$
   | LET $\langle$Variable$\rangle$ BE $\langle$Imperative$\rangle$

$\langle$Result$\rangle$ ::= THE ANSWER IS $\langle$Object$\rangle$
$\langle$Verb Phrase$\rangle$ ::= $\langle$Function$\rangle$ $\langle$Object Phrase$\rangle$
$\langle$Test Phrase$\rangle$ ::= $\langle$Object Phrase$\rangle$ $\langle$Be$\rangle$ $\langle$Predicate$\rangle$
   $\langle$Object Phrase$\rangle$

$\langle$Be$\rangle$ ::= IS | ARE | IS NOT | ARE NOT
$\langle$Object Phrase$\rangle$ ::= $\langle$Objects$\rangle$ | $\langle$Function$\rangle$ OF $\langle$Objects$\rangle$
$\langle$Objects$\rangle$ ::= $\langle$Object$\rangle$ $\langle$Separator$\rangle$ $\langle$Objects$\rangle$ | $\langle$Objects$\rangle$
$\langle$Separator$\rangle$ ::= , | TO | FROM | BY | AND
$\langle$Object$\rangle$ ::= $\langle$Variable$\rangle$ | $\langle$Constant$\rangle$
$\langle$Variable$\rangle$ ::= $\langle$Identifier$\rangle$ | $\langle$Record Variable$\rangle$
$\langle$Record Variable$\rangle$ ::= $\langle$Creation Function$\rangle$
   | $\langle$Access Function$\rangle$

$\langle$Creation Function$\rangle$ ::= $\langle$Function$\rangle$ ($\langle$Args$\rangle$)
$\langle$Access Function$\rangle$ ::= $\langle$Function$\rangle$ $\langle$Args$\rangle$ OF $\langle$Identifier$\rangle$
$\langle$Args$\rangle$ ::= $\langle$Constant$\rangle$ | $\langle$Identifier$\rangle$
   | $\langle$Constant$\rangle$, $\langle$Args$\rangle$
   | $\langle$Identifier$\rangle$, $\langle$Args$\rangle$

$\langle$Function$\rangle$ ::= $\langle$Identifier$\rangle$
$\langle$Predicate$\rangle$ ::= $\langle$Identifier$\rangle$

TABLE 1. Description of procedures synthesized

Procedure	Description
MULT(X,Y)	Multiply X by Y using repeated addition.
SORT(A,N)	Sort array A of N elements using an interchange sort.
P01(T)	Recognizes strings of the form 0^n1^n using a Turing Machine algorithm (4 instructions; READ(X,T), WRITE(X,T), MOVEL(T), MOVER(T)— X is a symbol; T is a tape).
PROP(L,VAL)	Given a list L of the form [[Item$_1$ value$_{11}$ . . . value$_{1n_1}$] . . . [Item$_k$ value$_{k1}$ . . . value$_{kn_k}$]], search L and return the first item having a value = VAL. Return NIL otherwise.
ROOT(A,B,C)	Find the real roots of a quadratic equation: Ax^2+Bx+C. Return "I" if the roots are imaginary.

TABLE 2. Some procedures synthesized, number of instructions and computation time

Procedure	Examples	No. Instr's	Time(sec)
MULT(X,Y)	MULT(3,2)	15	12
	MULT(2,0)		
SORT(A,N)	SORT(ARRAY(6,7),2)	32	34
	SORT(ARRAY(7,6),2)		
SORT(A,N)	SORT(ARRAY(2,4,3),3)	33	224
P01(T)	P01(01)	50	208
	P01(0011)		
PROP(L,VAL)	PROP([[A 1]],0)	31	24
	PROP([[B 2 3]],3)		
ROOT(A,B,C)	ROOT(1,4,4)	19	22
	ROOT(1,6,9)		

It should also be noted that the techniques used in the synthesis algorithm are not restricted to "complete" examples. That is, partial examples fit into this framework equally well. A partial example may be just a computation beginning

ACKNOWLEDGMENTS

The author would like to acknowledge the suggestions of the referees which helped to improve the readability of this paper. The financial support of the National Research Council of Canada, Grant S193A1, in the preparation of this paper is greatly appreciated.

REFERENCES

1. Balzer, R., Goldman, N. and Wile, D., Informality in program specification, *Fifth IJCAI* (1977).
2. Bauer, M., A basis for the acquisition of procedures, Thesis, University of Toronto (1978).
3. Biermann, A., On the inference of Turing Machines from sample computations, *Artificial Intelligence* 3 (3) (1972).
4. Biermann, A. and Krishnaswamy, R., Construction programs from example computations, Techn. Rep. OSU–CISRC–TR–74–5, Ohio State University Computer and Information Science Research Center, Columbus (1974).
5. Biermann, A., Automatic indexing in program synthesis, Techn. Rep., CS–1976–4, Dept. of Computer Science, Duke University, Durham, NC (1976).
6. Burstall, R., Collins, J. and Popplestone, R., *Programming in POP-2* (University Press, Edinburgh, 1971).
7. Green, C., Shaw, D. and Swartout, W., Inferring LISP programs from examples, *Fourth IJCAI*, Tbilisi, USSR (1974).
8. Hardy, S., Automatic induction of LISP functions, *AISB Summer Conference* (1974).
9. Harray, F., *Graph Theory* (Addison-Wesley, Reading, MA, 1969).
10. Heidorn, G., English as a very high level language for simulating programming, *Proc. Symp. on Very High Level Languages* (1974).
11. Heidorn, G., Natural language inputs to a simulation programming system, Techn. Rep. NPS–55HD72101A, Naval Postgraduate School, Monterey, CA (1972).
12. Manna, A. and Waldinger, R., Toward automatic program synthesis, *Comm. ACM* 14 (3) (1971).
13. Martin, W., Ginzburg, M., Krumland, R., Mark, B., Morgenster, M., Niamir, B. and Sunguroff, A., Internal Memos, Automatic Programming Group, MIT (1974).
14. Plotkin, G., A note on inductive generalization, in: Michie, D. (Ed.), *Machine Intelligence* 5 (Edinburgh University Press, Edinburgh, 1969).
15. Smith, C. B., Towards a programming apprentice, *IEEE Trans. Software Engineering* (1) (1975).
16. Winograd, T., Breaking the complexity barrier again, *Proc. ACM SIGPLAN-SIGIR Interface Meeting* (1973).
17. Zloof, M. Query-by-example: A data base management language, IBM Res. Rep. (December 1976).
18. Zloof, M. and DeJong, P., The system for business automation (SBA): Programming language, *Comm. ACM* 20 (6) (1977).

Received June 1978; revised version received December 1978

VII / Intelligent Assistants

Most of the experimental programming tools described in this volume seek to completely automate some aspect of the programming problem. However, because of the difficulties involved, most of these tools fail to reach this goal and require human guidance. (See in particular, [Smith, Chapter 2], [Good, Chapter 3], [Boyer and Moore, Chapter 4], [Wile, Chapter 10], [Schonberg, Schwartz, and Sharir, Chapter 14], and [Neighbors, Chapter 30].)

There are basically three possible reactions to the need for human guidance: eliminate it by simplifying the tool, grudgingly tolerate it while waiting for advances in research, or intentionally design the tool to be an intelligent assistant. The tools described in [Cheatham, Chapter 9] and to a lesser extent [Green and Westfold, Chapter 16] have taken the simplification route. The other tools mentioned above have taken a mixture of the latter two approaches.

The papers in this section cover the intelligent assistant approach in depth. [Floyd, Chapter 20] is probably the earliest published description of an intelligent programming assistant. It describes an imagined interaction between a computer programmer and an intelligent program verifier assistant and predicts that such systems will be feasible within the following decade (the paper appeared in 1971).

[Moriconi, Chapter 21] in 1979 describes an implemented system that is very much like Floyd's early vision. Moriconi's system, called the Designer/Verifiers Assistant, shares many features in common with the program verification systems described in Section II. It is, however, more wholeheartedly intended to be an assistant. It is also oriented toward supporting incremental modification of a large data base of information about a program.

The Knowledge-Based Editor in Emacs (KBEmacs) [Waters, Chapter 22] is the current demonstration system implemented as part of the Programmer's Apprentice project at MIT. KBEmacs allows a programmer to construct a program rapidly and reliably by combining standard algorithmic fragments. An interesting aspect of KBEmacs is that, unlike most of the systems in Sections III, IV, and V, it is not specifications oriented. Instead, KBEmacs emphasizes the process of program composition and modification.

Like Floyd's early paper, [Green et al., Chapter 23] is a thought experiment. It presents a vision of the Knowledge-Based Software Assistant that would be used throughout the programming process—from requirements through implementation to later modification. The primary contribution of this paper is to identify the intermediate research milestones along the way to this long-term goal.

TOWARD INTERACTIVE DESIGN OF CORRECT PROGRAMS

Robert W. FLOYD

Computer Science Department, Stanford University,
Stanford, California 94305, USA

I want to describe to you an imagined interaction between a computer programmer and his machine, which I think might be made feasible within the next decade. The programmer is at an interactive console, designing a program, first in its overall outline, then by successive developments in detail. The computer is, of course, serving its customary role as syntactic analyzer, code generator, program executor, prompter, and file handler. In addition, the computer is continually checking the program, at each level of specification, for consistency with the programmer's stated intentions. The computer is expected to carry the burden of proving the logical, or semantic, correctness of whatever level of specification of the program it has [1,2,4]. It is further expected to prove termination of iterations and to provide counterexamples to incorrect programs by supplying data for which the programmer's stated expectations are not met.

For the sake of the example, I shall write as if communication between programmer and computer were going on in stylized English; one need not assume that such a communication language is achievable. The point is to make the interchange intelligible without introducing an elaborate grammar. I am not describing an automatic program writer; I do not think that pragmatically satisfactory automatic program writers will be constructed in the near future.* The novel features of the system I shall describe embody skilled mathematical manipulation of a rather pedestrian type, but no particular creative ability.

We find the programmer preparing to write a procedure which will locate a symbol in a sorted table of known size. He calls the symbol X, the table $A_1, A_2, ..., A_N$. The man speaks first. I enclose my own comments on the interaction in square brackets.

Man: I want to design a program I shall call "Locate X in table $A_1...A_N$", or P_1 for short. [The name is

---

* For an account of the current development of automatic program writing, see Manna and Waldinger [5,7].

simply for the programmer's convenience; the system makes no attempt to interpret or understand it.] In P_1, X is a symbol, N and L are integers, and A is an array of symbols. The values of X, N, and A may not change in P_1. We assume the following true at the start of P_1 (its *antecedent* condition):

For all integers i, j, $1 \leqslant i \leqslant j \leqslant N \supset A_i \leqslant A_j$. (1.1)

I will abbreviate this by "A monotone".

There is an integer k, $1 \leqslant k \leqslant N$, for which $A_k = X$. (1.2)

I will abbreviate this by "$X \in A_{1:N}$".
After execution, P_1 must guarantee (its *consequent* condition) that

$$1 \leqslant L \leqslant N \qquad (1.3)$$

$$A_L = X . \qquad (1.4)$$

[Note that, since (1.3) is satisfiable only by a finite number of values of L, and since (1.4) could be coded as a test, it would be trivial to generate an iteration to satisfy these conditions. The resulting program would not, however, be efficient if N were large.]

Computer: To design P_1, with antecedent

$$A \text{ monotone}, X \in A_{1:N}$$

and consequent

$$1 \leqslant L \leqslant N, \quad A_L = X .$$

The consequent does not logically follow from the antecedent (as I can demonstrate by counterexample), so P_1 must apparently change L. [Recall that A, N, and X are protected from change.]

Man: Let P_1 be an iteration. [He has the idea of keeping pointers B and C, bounding the region of A where the symbol X will be found.] Let P_1 be

ITERATE UNTIL $B = C$: P_2 .

Computer: What conditions do you want to assume before and after P_2?

Man: (2.1) B and C are integer variables of P_1.
(2.2) $1 \leqslant B \leqslant C \leqslant N$
(2.3) There is an integer k, $B \leqslant k \leqslant C$, for which $A_k = X$, abbreviated $X \in A_{B:C}$.

Computer: Why does P_2 terminate?

Man: $C - B$ is a non-negative integer, decreasing at each cycle of the iteration. [Another standard termination proof would be based on the Archimedian property of the real numbers; if x is always positive in an iteration, and d is a fixed positive value, and x is decreased by d at each cycle, the iteration must terminate. Because of rounding error, this method is not reliable, however, unless an exact floating-point axiom system is used for proofs.]

Computer: The antecedent of P_2 does not follow from the antecedent of P_1 and the iteration-non-terminated condition $B \neq C$. Do you want to initialize the iteration later? [This suggestion is usually good programming practice.]

Man: Yes.

Computer: The consequent of P_2, with the iteration termination condition, does not seem to imply the consequent of P_1. Do you want to finalize the iteration later?

Man: Yes.

Computer: Do you want to design P_2 now?

Man: Yes.

Computer: In P_2, A, X, and N are invariant; B, C, and N are integers.
Antecedent condition is:
(3.1) $1 \leqslant B \leqslant C \leqslant N$
(3.2) $X \in A_{B:C}$
(3.3) A monotone
[The computer does not mention that $X \in A_{1:N}$, since that logically follows from (3.1) and (3.2).]
Consequent condition is:
(3.4) $1 \leqslant B' \leqslant C' \leqslant N$
(3.5) $X \in A_{B':C'}$
(3.6) $C' - B' < C - B$
You must change C or B.
[The computer does not mention "A monotone" as a consequent condition, since it is a part of the antecedent condition, and the programmer may

not change any of the variables mentioned in it. Primes denote values of potentially changed variables after execution of P_2.]

Man: Define P_2 as
$$D := (B+C) \div 2; \text{ [Integer division]}$$
$$\text{IF } X \leqslant A_D \text{ THEN } C := D$$
$$\text{ELSE } B := D$$
[This statement sequence must appear, syntactically, as a block in the finished program, but the necessary punctuation will be automatically added on assembly.]

Computer: Well, suppose $B = 1$, $C = 2$, $N = 2$, $X = 0$, $A_1 = -1$. P_2 becomes
$$D := (1+2) \div 2 \ (=1);$$
$$\text{IF } 0 \leqslant -1 \ (\equiv \text{FALSE}) \text{ THEN } ... \text{ ELSE }$$
$$B := 1$$
resulting in $B' = 1$, $C' = 2$. This violates the condition needed for termination, that $C' - B' < C - B$. [See Appendix for a sketch of how the computer found the counterexample.]

Man: Sorry. Let's try modifying the third line of P_2; call it P_3.

Computer: Antecedent is
(4.1) $1 \leqslant B < C \leqslant N$ [Note that $B = C$ is not possible.]
(4.2) $X \in A_{B:C}$
(4.3) A monotone
(4.4) $D = (B+C) \div 2$
(4.5) $X > A_D$
Consequent is
(4.6) $1 \leqslant B' \leqslant C' \leqslant N$
(4.7) $X \in A_{B':C'}$
(4.8) $C' - B' < C - B$

Man: What must P_3 do if
$$B = 1, C = 2, N = 2, X = 0, A_1 = -1?$$

Computer: Consequent is then
$$B' = 2$$
$$C' = 2$$

Man: Check whether $B < D + 1 \leqslant C$ follows from antecedent of P_3.

Computer: True.

Man: Define P_3 as $B := D + 1$.

Computer: That works. Would you like to design the initialization for P_2?

Man: Yes.

Computer: Antecedent is
(5.1) A monotone
(5.2) $X \in A_{1:N}$
Consequent is
(5.3) $1 \leqslant B \leqslant C \leqslant N$
(5.4) $X \in A_{B:C}$

Man: Initialization of P_2 is

$$B := 1; \quad C := N$$

Computer: That works. Would you like to design the finalization of P_2?

Man: Yes.

Computer: Antecedent is

(6.1) $1 \leqslant B = C \leqslant N$

(6.2) $A_B = X$

Consequent is

(6.3) $1 \leqslant L' \leqslant N$

(6.4) $A_{L'} = X$

May I try?

Man: Yes.

Computer: $L := B$

Man: That works. May I see the complete program?

Computer: BEGIN

INVARIANTS A, N, X; INTEGER B, C, D;

(ASSERT $N \geqslant 1$, A MONOTONE, $X \in A_{1:N}$);

$B := 1; C := N$;

ITERATE (ASSERT $1 \leqslant B \leqslant C \leqslant N$, $X \in A_{B:C}$)

UNTIL $B = C$:

    BEGIN

    $D := (B+C)$ DIV 2;

    IF $X \leqslant A_D$ THEN $C := D$

                    ELSE $B := D + 1$

    END

$L := B$;

(ASSERT $1 \leqslant L \leqslant N$, $A_L = X$)

END

CONCLUSION

The above example illustrates several points. One is that the antecedent and consequent which a program must satisfy do not determine the program; a large part of the programmer's activity consists in exploring for computationally feasible methods, while maintaining assurance that the semantic specifications of the program are met. Another is that it is feasible to have the computer itself deductively generate counterexamples to a program, rather than search at random through the data space. Another is that some logical errors (such as the initial failure to initialize the iteration) can be detected even when only the outline of a program has been specified; indeed, it would be conceivable to have a system which would determine, within the limits of its theorem-proving power, whether a given partially specified program could be completed consistently with the specifications given for it.

The Appendix shows how a counterexample to the incorrect program is found, using proof methods based on the laws of ordering relations, equality, and linear properties of the integers. The proof is feasible because a proof system can be built which embodies knowledge about the subject matter; rather than randomly generate consequences of what is known, the system must have a strong sense of direction and must aim for simplification. Current work in mathematical manipulation by computer is developing such mechanized knowledge in polynomial manipulation, symbolic integration and linear algebra; in order to provide adequately for automatic proofs of program correctness, it will probably be necessary to develop similar machine skills in proofs in elementary set theory, concatenation of finite sequences, bounded quantification, and graph theory, at least.

APPENDIX

To find the flaw in the original design of P_2, the computer assumes the antecedent, in the form

(1) $B, C, D, N, K, B', C', D' \in J$ (the set of integers)

(2) $1 \leqslant B$

(3) $B + 1 \leqslant C$ [for integers, this is a useful form of $B < C$]

(4) $C \leqslant N$

(5) $B \leqslant K$

(6) $K \leqslant C$

(7) $X = A_K$

(8) $(\forall_{i,j})(i \leqslant 0 \vee j \leqslant i-1 \vee N \leqslant j-1 \vee A_i \leqslant A_j)$

and that the program follows the path in the program on which

$$D := (B+C) \div 2$$
$$\neg(X \leqslant A_D)$$
$$B := D$$

so that

(9) $D' = (B+C) \div 2$, or $0 \leqslant B + C - 2D' \leqslant 1$

(10) $A_{D'} < X$

(11) $B' = D'$

(12) $C' = C$.

It further assumes the falsehood of one of the consequents, so that

(13) $C' - B' \geqslant C - B$

and attempts to simultaneously satisfy all of these predicates. Using (7), (11), and (12) to eliminate X, B', and C' from the other lines, we have

(1') $B, C, D, N, K, D' \in J$

(2') $1 \leqslant B$

(3') $B + 1 \leqslant C$

(4') $\quad C \leqslant N$

(5') $\quad B \leqslant K$

(6') $\quad K \leqslant C$

(8') $\quad (\forall_{i,j})(i \leqslant 0 \vee j \leqslant i-1 \vee N \leqslant j-1 \vee A_i \leqslant A_j)$

(9') $\quad 2D' - B \leqslant C \leqslant 2D' - B + 1$

(10') $\quad A_{D'} < A_K$

(13') $\quad D' \leqslant B$.

By systematic application of the transitive laws of ordering,

$$B + 1 \leqslant C \leqslant 2D' - B + 1 , \quad \text{or} \quad B \leqslant D'$$

so that $D' = B$.

$$C \leqslant B + 1 \leqslant C$$

so that $C = B + 1$

$$B \leqslant K \leqslant B + 1$$

so that $K = B$ or $K = B + 1$.

The former results in (10') $A_B < A_B$, absurd, so

$$K = B + 1 ,$$

We can now restate the known facts as

(1") $\quad B, N \in J$

(2") $\quad 1 \leqslant B$

(4") $\quad B \leqslant N - 1$

(8") $\quad (\forall_{i,j})(i \leqslant 0 \vee j \leqslant i-1 \vee N \leqslant j-1 \vee A_i \leqslant A_j)$

(10") $A_B \leqslant A_{B+1}$.

Now, by resolution [6], (10") is eliminated as redundant. Then $B = 1$ satisfies (1'), (2"), and (4") if anything does:

(1''') $\quad N \in J$

(4''') $\quad 2 \leqslant N$

(8''') $= (8")$.

A simple argument shows that $N = 2$ satisfies the above if anything does; thus

(8'''') $(\forall_{i,j})(i \leqslant 0 \vee j \leqslant i-1 \vee 3 \leqslant j \vee A_i \leqslant A_j)$.

By case analysis, this is reduced to $A_1 \leqslant A_2$, which is satisfiable. Back substitution yields the counterexample. All of the manipulation above is readily programmed; most of it is already embodied in the Verifying Compiler [2,3]. Many of the proofs required to verify programs seem to be similarly mechanizable.

REFERENCES

[1] R.W.Floyd, Assigning meaning to programs, in: Proc. Symposia in Applied Mathematics, Vol. 19, American Mathematical Society, (1967) 19-32.

[2] J.King, A program verifier, Ph.D. Thesis, Carnegie-Mellon University, Pittsburgh, Pa. (1969).

[3] J.King and R.W.Floyd, Interpretation oriented theorem prover over integers, Second Ann. ACM Symp. on Theory of Computing, (Northampton, Mass. 1970).

[4] Z.Manna, The correctness of programs, J. Computer and System Sciences, 3, 2 (1969) 119-127.

[5] Z.Manna and R.Waldinger, Toward automatic program synthesis, Comm. ACM, 14, 3 (1971) 151-165.

[6] J.Robinson, A machine-oriented logic based on the resolution principle, J. ACM, 12, 1 (Jan. 1965) 23-41.

[7] R.J.Waldinger, Constructing programs automatically using theorem proving, Ph.D. Thesis, Carnegie-Mellon University, Pittsburgh, Pa. (1969).

A Designer/Verifier's Assistant

MARK S. MORICONI, MEMBER, IEEE

Abstract—Since developing and maintaining formally verified programs is an incremental activity, one is not only faced with the problem of constructing specifications, programs, and proofs, but also with the complex problem of determining what previous work remains valid following incremental changes. A system that reasons about changes must build a detailed model of each development and be able to apply its knowledge, the same kind of knowledge an expert would have, to integrate new or changed information into an existing model.

This paper describes a working computer program called the designer/verifier's assistant, which is the initial prototype of such a system. The assistant embodies a unified theory of how to reason about changes to a design or verification. This theory also serves as the basis for answering questions about the effects of hypothesized changes and for making proposals on how to proceed with the development in an orderly fashion. Excerpts from a sample session are used to illustrate the key ideas.

Index Terms—Automated program verifier, automated programmer assistance, design of incremental systems, effects of incremental changes, incremental program design and verification, maintenance, program design, program specifications, program verification, proofs of programs, question answering.

I. INTRODUCTION

DEVELOPING and maintaining formally verified programs, especially large ones, is an incremental activity. Specifications, programs, and proofs are gradually built up and frequently revised. Consequently, one is faced not only with the problem of constructing this data, but also with the complex problem of determining the effects of incremental changes to it.

Consider the task of developing a formally verified operating system. A good strategy is first to decompose the system into its functional parts, then to design and verify each part separately. The file system, for example, can be broken down into files and directories, each of whose design and verification involves developing a large, highly interrelated collection of specifications, programs, verification conditions, and proofs. Certainly, numerous revisions—e.g., to correct an error in a program or to augment or reformulate a specification—would

be made in getting this myriad of detailed information to fit together properly. Each revision can raise a variety of complex issues. If, for example, some specifications and programs dealing with files are changed to allow blocks of file storage to be scattered throughout memory, instead of allocated sequentially as originally planned, some of the key issues are: Do any previous proofs about files remain valid? Does any code for directories need to be recompiled? Do all established properties of the file system still hold? Is the rest of the operating system affected? If so, how? These are just some of the questions that must be answered to avoid excessive redoing of still-valid work.

The same problems arise when maintaining verified software, whether it be recoding programs to increase efficiency, extending specifications, or changing design decisions. However, it may be even more difficult to determine the effects of these "after-the-fact" changes because of the time that may have elapsed since the original development.

Much research has focused on the problem of constructing specifications, programs, and proofs. Several programming and specification languages and structuring and proof techniques, as well as tools to support them, have been developed to aid in the construction process. For example, there are several program verification systems (including [2], [3], [5], [7], [10], [11], and [17]) capable of parsing programs and specifications and of generating and proving verification conditions.[1] They support a variety of languages (such as subsets of Algol, Jovial, Lisp, and Pascal) and proof methods (such as inductive assertions and structural induction).

The next step is to develop a highly incremental system—one that 1) parses programs and specifications and generates and proves verification conditions (like previous systems) and 2) has an *understanding* of the kinds of structures that can be changed and added, and the ways they can interact. This new system must be able to build a detailed *model* of each development. The model must contain information about key parts of a program's design and verification and their relationships. The system must be able to apply its *knowledge*—the same kind of knowledge an expert would have—to integrate new

Manuscript received November 6, 1978; revised March 5, 1979. This research was supported in part by the Defense Advanced Research Projects Agency under Contract DAHC 15-72-C-0308 (at the University of Southern California Information Sciences Institute), by the National Science Foundation under Grant MCS74-12866 (at the University of Texas at Austin), and by the Rome Air Development Center under Contract F30602-78-C-0031 (at SRI International).

The author is with the Computer Science Laboratory, SRI International, Menlo Park, CA 94025.

[1]The question of whether a program is consistent with its specifications can be reduced to proving a set of logical formulas called *verification conditions*. These formulas are derived directly from the program and its specifications. This paper presumes only a general familiarity with the area of formal program verification. Detailed knowledge, such as how to derive verification conditions, is not required.

or changed information into an existing model in a way that keeps intact previous work that remains valid. For example, if the specification of a function is changed, the system should be able to deduce what parts of the verification are unaffected.

A working system that has this kind of understanding is the *designer/verifier's assistant*. The assistant actively assists and cooperates with the user throughout a design and verification by accepting and reasoning about new or changed information, by proposing actions, and by answering questions. Programs and specifications can be constructed using a top-down, bottom-up, or mixed strategy, verified in parallel or any desired order, and revised at any time. The assistant is useful not only during a design and verification, but also afterwards for maintenance purposes.

The assistant has been implemented in a version of Lisp (developed at the University of California at Irvine) and runs on a PDP-10 computer under TOPS-10 at The University of Texas at Austin. All transcripts presented in this paper were actually produced by this running program. In order to test the validity of the ideas to be described, it was necessary to integrate the assistant into a program verification system, which is described in [12]. Like the assistant, this verification system reflects an incremental philosophy and has several capabilities that complement those of the assistant. It supports the combined programming and specification language Gypsy [1], which is Pascal based and includes features for data abstraction, error handling, and limited forms of concurrency. Another version of the assistant is currently being developed, again in the context of a verification system, at SRI International. It is being implemented in a release of Interlisp that runs on a PDP-10 computer under TOPS-20. This version of the assistant will handle programs written in any of several programming languages (namely, significant subsets of Jovial, Modula, and Pascal) and formally specified in a revised version of the specification language SPECIAL [16].

The work described here relates two areas of research: automated verification and automated programmer assistance. The first topic to be considered is how the designer/verifier's assistant represents a contribution to the area of automated verification. Traditional program verification systems (e.g., [2], [3], [5], [7], [10], [11], and [17]) can be viewed as consisting of a translator, a verification condition generator, and a theorem prover. As mentioned above, the assistant has been integrated into such a verification system [12]. In this augmented verification system, the human designer/verifier communicates with the assistant, which in turn calls the traditional verification system only as needed. When a program or specification is changed, the assistant determines what parts of the overall design and verification could possibly be affected, then uses the verification system to reverify only those parts. The assistant, in effect, decides how to use the verification system efficiently. This is extremely important due to the high cost of formally verifying programs of even moderate size and complexity.

The other important aspect of the assistant is its ability to provide useful assistance throughout the evolution of a consistent set of specifications, programs, and proofs. Specifically,

the assistant can provide the human designer/verifier with an explanation of the effects of possible revisions (before they are actually made) and with guidance on how to proceed with the development in an orderly fashion. Early work on facilities for assisting in the development of programs was done by Teitelman [19]. From this work evolved a set of useful tools (e.g., an editor, a cross-reference facility, a spelling corrector, and a specialized error corrector) that are part of the Interlisp system [18]. Two other extensively used systems that assist in program development are the ECL programming system [20] and the Programmer's Workbench [9], and a system that reasons about certain incremental changes to proofs is described by Doyle [4]. An imagined scenario illustrating several ways in which the computer might assist during the design and the verification of a program is found in [6]. A proposal for how one might construct a similar elaborate programming system has been made by Hewitt and Smith [8], and more recently a similar proposal, which stops short of formal verification, has been made by Rich and Shrobe [14].

The next section presents a brief excerpt from a session to illustrate the kinds of things the assistant does to facilitate incremental design and verification, and subsequent sections describe how the assistant works. Section III explains how the assistant can guide the user through an entire development, and Section IV describes how it answers "what" and "why" questions about the effects of hypothesized changes. These sections will show that both of these capabilities are relatively straightforward to provide once a theory for reasoning about incremental changes has been elaborated. This underlying theory is presented in Section V, which discusses important design issues, the model of a program's design and verification, and the knowledge used to analyze changes to any specific model. This material is then used to explain the reasoning done by the assistant throughout the scenario of Section II. Section VI concludes with a brief recounting of our experience in using the assistant and an outline of future plans.

II. Brief Scenario

The scenario described in this section, taken from the middle of an actual session, is a very simple illustration of some of the ways the assistant helps the user in incrementally designing and verifying programs. This includes allowing both the assistant and user to take the initiative in directing the development, using the assistant to preview the effects of intended changes, adding various kinds of new and changed information to an existing model, and automatically retaining still-valid work following changes.

The scenario starts in the middle of a session in which a sorting program is being incrementally designed and verified. Taken from the session is a sequence of three events that typically occur for each set of revisions. Before actually making any revisions, the user first engages in a conversation with the assistant to gain an understanding of the effects of the changes he might make. Guided by this interchange, the user makes the desired changes. The assistant then fits these changes into the current model, keeping intact previous work that remains valid. It should be reemphasized that the pur-

(1)   Suggest fully defining ExchangeSort ⟶ <u>Explain</u>

(2)   ⟵ <u>What are the effects of fully defining ExchangeSort?</u>
      ExchangeSort may have additional VCs.

(3)   ⟵ <u>What are the effects of changing the exit assertion of ValueOfMax?</u>
      No effects on ValueOfMax. The verification of other programs is not affected.

(4)   ⟵ <u>Why?</u>
      No effects on ValueOfMax because it is for specifications only and does not
      have VCs. No external effects because properties from ValueOfMax have not been
      used in proving any VCs.

(5)   ⟵ <u>What are the effects of changing the exit of IsPerm?</u>
      No effects on IsPerm. The verification of other programs is not affected if the formula
      $$\textit{Changed exit specification} \Rightarrow \text{all } Z : \text{IntArray}, \text{IsPerm}(Z, Z)$$
      is true. If not, the change invalidates the verification of ExchangeSort.

(6)   ⟵ <u>Why?</u>
      No effects on IsPerm because it is for specifications only and does not have
      VCs. Invalid verification because a property from IsPerm has been used in proving
      ExchangeSort#1.

(7)   ⟵ <u>Done</u>

(8)   Suggest fully defining ExchangeSort ⟶ <u>Edit</u>

Fig. 1. An actual dialog with the assistant.

pose of the scenario is to illustrate what the assistant does and how it is used; specific details of the sorting program are unimportant.

Fig. 1 joins the session just after the program ExchangeSort has been partially defined and proved. ExchangeSort is currently of the form

    function ExchangeSort . . . = begin . . . pending . . . end;

The completed part of ExchangeSort has already been verified; the keyword "pending" identifies the part of ExchangeSort that has not yet been defined. In all figures, the parenthesized numbers are for reference in the text and underlining designates lines typed by the user to distinguish them from the computer's response. Throughout the scenario, the assistant and user intermittently exchange initiative in directing the course of the development. To eliminate the risk of impeding progress, the assistant assumes the dominating position only when the user intentionally relinquishes it, and retains it until it is unlikely that its guidance will be helpful. At line (1), the assistant has the initiative. The user can either accept the suggestion by typing "$", or he can issue a command. Rather than going ahead and completing the definition of ExchangeSort as suggested, the user decides to use the assistant to preview the effects of some intended changes. Typing the command "Explain" in line (1) initiates a conversation with the *explanation facility*, whose prompting symbol for input is "⟵" in line (2).

The following dialog provides a sample of the kinds of in-

teraction possible.[2] ValueOfMax in (3) and IsPerm in (5) are functions introduced only for specifying ExchangeSort and are not intended to be implemented. Thus, any change to their exit assertions[3] cannot affect their (nonexistent) verification. The dialogue also illustrates some useful characteristics of the explanation facility. It shows how remembering the immediately preceding "what" questions makes it easy to state questions such as the ones at (4) and (6). It shows how answers not only tell the user about the potential effects of different kinds of changes, but also give hints about how to make the changes. For example, the response to (5) describes the exact formula that must hold for revisions to the exit specification of IsPerm not to have effects. (The current exit specification of IsPerm is "all Z:IntArray, IsPerm(Z,Z).") Of course, different formulas and combinations of formulas are described in different situations. No relationships are described when revisions cannot have effects, as in the answer to (3). This is also illustrated when the assistant says "No effects on IsPerm" in the first part of the answer to (5). The dialog also shows how answers are given at two levels of detail. Answers to "why" questions refine answers to "what" questions. The potential effects of the change indicated at (5) are narrowed down from ExchangeSort in the response to (5) to the single

---

[2] In transcripts, the term "verification conditions" is abbreviated as "VCs."

[3] An *exit assertion* is a specification that is intended to hold if the associated program terminates.

verification condition called ExchangeSort#1 in the response to (6).

Knowing the potential effects of intended changes, the user types "Done" in line (7) to indicate a readiness to continue working with the assistant toward a problem solution. Upon leaving the explanation facility, the suggestion initially given at (1) is reproposed at (8) since it still makes sense. Typing "Edit" in (8) invokes a standard text editor.

Fig. 2 rejoins the session immediately after the editing is finished. At line (9) the assistant is directed to read the just-edited file into the system. The file contains Gypsy programs and specifications[4] that are echoed as they are parsed and type checked. All type checking is done in the existing context. For example, the previously defined type IntArray is used in type checking the exit specification of IsPerm. Notice that the changes explored in Fig. 1 have all been made, and also that several new programs have been introduced. The assistant figures out how to fit all this information into the existing model, while keeping intact previous work that remains valid. This requires, for example, assembling and proving the formula described in the response to the question at (5). After all the necessary reasoning has been done, the assistant [by printing "Exec⟶" at line (10)] asks for user direction, instead of offering a suggestion. The assistant observes that there are many reasonable courses of action following all these revisions. It therefore wants the user to at least initiate a line of attack by giving the appropriate command. (Had the user accepted the suggestion at (8), the assistant would have offered a suggestion about ExchangeSort.)

Fig. 3 completes the scenario by showing how the replacement of the "pending" in ExchangeSort by two new statements had the effects described in the response to the question at line (2). After the suggestion at (11) is accepted, the changed path through the loop of ExchangeSort is traced and some new verification conditions are generated. Three previously generated verification conditions (which came from the unchanged paths) were unaffected by the change. Proving the first new verification condition is suggested at (12), and the rest of the development proceeds from there.

III. Suggesting What To Do Next

Throughout a development, one is continually faced with the problem of recalling what tasks remain to be done and then choosing which one to do next. Initially, the number of choices is very limited. But, as a program's design and verification is evolved, the choices increase in number and become more varied. This is due not only to the gradual in-

---

[4]Notice that Gypsy specifications are included directly in Gypsy programs. The keywords "entry," "exit," and "assert" all designate specifications to be proved about the associated program. A proof shows that the entry assertion always implies the exit assertion if the program terminates. The assert statements supply the intermediate assertions for a proof by inductive assertions, and each loop in a program must contain at least one assert statement. Also notice that some functions are implemented as programs (e.g., ExchangeSort), while others are solely for specification purposes (e.g., ValueOfMax). The latter have "null" bodies. These general observations provide all the needed background on Gypsy. Its syntax is important here only insofar as it defines the overall structure of a program.

---

(9) Suggest fully defining ExchangeSort ⟶ Read FileOfChanges.Sort

```
function ExchangeSort(A:IntArray):IntArray =
begin
    entry N ge 1;
    exit (all I:int,
          I in [1..N] ⟹ ExchangeSort(A)[I]
                        = ValueOfMax(ExchangeSort(A),1,I))
    and IsPerm(A, ExchangeSort(A));
    var B:IntArray := A;
    var K:int := N;
    keep K in [1..N];
    loop
        assert (all I:int, I in [K + 1..N] ⟹ ValueOfMax(B,1,I))
            and K in [1..N] and IsPerm(A,B);
        if K = 1 then leave end;
        B := Exchange(B,LocationOfMax(B,1,K),K);
        K := K-1;
    end;
    result := B;
end;


function ValueOfMax(A:IntArray; I,J:int):int =
begin
    exit (all k:int, k in [I..J] and I in [1..N] and J in [1..N]
        ⟹ A[k] le ValueOfMax(A,I,J)) and ... ;
end;


function IsPerm(X,Y:IntArray) : boolean =
begin
    exit (all Z:IntArray, IsPerm(Z,Z))
    and (all Z:IntArray,
        IsPerm(X,Z) and IsPerm(Z,Y) ⟹ IsPerm(X,Y));
end;


function LocationOfMax(A:IntArray; I,J:int):int =
begin
    entry I in [1..N] and J in [1..N] and I le J;
    exit LocationOfMax(A,I,J) in [I..J]
        and A[LocationOfMax(A,I,J)] = ValueOfMax(A,I,J);
    pending
end;


function Exchange(A:IntArray; I,J:int):IntArray = ... ;

function IsExchanged(A,B:IntArray;I,J:int):boolean = ... ;
```

(10) Exec ⟶ Suggest

Fig. 2. The assistant incorporates several changes, some of which were discussed in Fig. 1, into the existing model. These changes are indicated by brackets.

---

crease in size (i.e., the building up of more and more programs, specifications, verification conditions, etc.), but also to the impact of revisions. Changing a specification, for example, can invalidate several parts of the verification, all of which must eventually be redone. To help in remembering these kinds of things, the assistant displays, on request, a detailed

(11)   Suggest generating new VCs for ExchangeSort $\longrightarrow$ <u>$</u>

Tracing new path in loop
Assume loop assertion
$$(\text{all } I\#1 : \text{INT}, I\#1 \text{ in } [K + 1..N]$$
$$\Rightarrow B[I\#1] = \text{ValueOfMax}(B, 1, I\#1))$$
and K in [1..N]
and IsPerm(A, B)

$\cdots$

Generating new verification condition ExchangeSort#4

$\cdots$

End of path

Unaffected VCs: ExchangeSort#1, ExchangeSort#2, ExchangeSort#3

(12)   Suggest proving VC called ExchangeSort#4 $\longrightarrow$

Fig. 3. Impact of changes in Fig. 2 on ExchangeSort. Some new verification conditions are generated, while three existing ones (along with their proofs) have been kept intact by the assistant.

summary of what has been done and what remains to be done. However, status summaries are lists of alternatives; the user must figure out which alternative to pursue. Consequently, a mechanism was developed that actively assists the user in making such decisions by always having available a reasonable suggestion for the next step in a design and verification.

Although this mechanism can be very helpful, it may at times "get in the way." If the scenario being suggested is different from what the user wants, a suggestion mechanism can hinder, rather than enhance, progress. Therefore, the assistant embodies a dual-mode philosophy, giving the user the option of directing the system by giving commands, or being guided through the system by accepting suggestions, or a combination of both. Suggestions are based on the current state of development. The remainder of this section describes the suggestion mechanism and how it works.

The suggestion mechanism maintains an *agenda* of tasks that need to be done, each one having an assigned priority based on its relation to a particular development strategy. The *scheduling policy* is to find the highest priority task on the agenda, and then suggest it to the user. Agenda entries that have the same priority are handled on a first-come first-serve basis. If the user accepts a suggestion, the corresponding task is removed from the agenda and executed. Its execution may cause new tasks to be merged into the agenda, or existing ones to be deleted.

Each entry on the agenda is of the form (operation object priority). An example is (GENERATE-VCS ExchangeSort 5) which gets translated into the suggestion "Suggest generating VCs for ExchangeSort." The main problem, of course, is determining what should be on the agenda and how agenda entries should be ordered. This is done by applying heuristics that revise the agenda when built-in operations (such as parsing or generating verification conditions) are executed and when revisions are made to the design or verification. Each heuristic is represented as a *production rule* consisting of a condition/action pair. The condition on the left side of a rule tests whether

the rule is applicable; if it is, the action on its right side is a list of things to do.

At the beginning of the scenario in Fig. 1, the only entry on the agenda is (FULLY-DEFINE ExchangeSort 4), causing the scheduler to make the suggestion "Suggest fully defining ExchangeSort." A heuristic rule is applied to determine the impact on the agenda of each new or revised *program unit*, defined to be a program and its specifications, in Fig. 2. The rule is

if program unit X was successfully parsed
then delete all entries about X
  and if X has type errors **then** add (CORRECT-TYPE-ERRORS X 5)
    elseif X has a pending body **then** add (FULLY-DEFINE X 3)
    elseif X is new and has a body **then** add (GENERATE-VCS X 5)
  and for every change C that was made to X and that has effects,
    execute the rule associated with C

Starting with ExchangeSort, this rule removes (FULLY-DEFINE ExchangeSort 4) from the agenda, then its last conjunct handles the change to the body of ExchangeSort. The theory described in Section V is used to determine that this change has effects, causing the rule

if the body of program unit X has changed
then if X already has one or more verification conditions
    then add (GENERATE-NEW-VCS X 5)
    else add (GENERATE-VCS X 5)

to be selected and executed. Since ExchangeSort already has some verification conditions, (GENERATE-NEW-VCS ExchangeSort 5) is added to the agenda. Next, ValueOfMax and IsPerm are determined not to affect the agenda. Both have "null" bodies, instead of "pending" ones, indicating that the user intends to use them solely for specification purposes and not implement them. Therefore, entries of the form (FULLY-DEFINE $\cdots$) are inappropriate. Also, the changes to their specifications do not cause the agenda to be changed, since no existing verification work is invalidated. An entry for

LocationOfMax is then added to the agenda, which now looks like

```
((GENERATE-NEW-VCS ExchangeSort 5)
 (FULLY-DEFINE LocationOfMax 3) . . .)
```

The first entry is removed when the user accepts the first suggestion "Suggest generating new VCs for ExchangeSort" in Fig. 3. Next, the rule

> **if** verification conditions were generated for program unit X
> **then** for each new verification condition V, add (PROVE V 5)
>> and for each unaffected verification condition V,
>>> re-add every just-deleted entry about V
>> and **if** X has a pending path **then** add (FULLY-DEFINE X 4)

determines how generating verification conditions affects the agenda. Executing this rule makes (PROVE ExchangeSort#4 5) the highest priority item on the agenda, as evidenced by the last suggestion in Fig. 3.

It should be emphasized that the implemented rules work best for a top-down development strategy, such as the one illustrated in the scenario. The top-level program unit Exchange-Sort was completely designed and verified before lower-level ones, such as LocationOfMax, were completed. Attention was properly kept on ExchangeSort even after LocationOfMax was partially defined and specified. LocationOfMax was introduced solely to allow ExchangeSort's external reference to it to be resolved and to allow its specifications to be used in the proof of ExchangeSort. But what if the user wanted to work on LocationOfMax, instead of going back to Exchange-Sort? He could simply have ignored the suggestion and issued the appropriate commands. Suppose, for example, that the user chose to define LocationOfMax and to prove some of its verification conditions. Rather than adapting to this diversion and making suggestions about LocationOfMax's remaining verification conditions, the suggestion mechanism would retain ExchangeSort as the highest priority item. It assumes that diversions are not intended to alter the basic top-down strategy. The suggestion mechanism can be modified to take the alternate view of adapting to certain diversions by handling agenda entries on a last-in-first-out basis. The fundamental top-down strategy modeled by the rules can be changed to a bottom up or mixed strategy by adjusting the priority ratings.

IV. Previewing the Effects of Changes

One of the most difficult problems in designing and verifying programs is trying to understand the effects of a change. Before changing the type of an argument in the parameter list of a function, for example, it helps to know what programs or specifications could have type conflicts, what part of the verification could be invalidated, why it could be invalidated, etc. The purpose of the explanation facility is to make this kind of information available in order to give the user a general understanding of the potential effects of revisions before they are actually made.

All "what" and "why" questions answered by the explanation facility are variants of a few basic kinds of questions. A sample of each is given below:

> What are the effects of fully defining X?
> What are the effects of changing its exit assertion?
> What are the effects of changing the header of X?
> What are the effects of changing X's body?
> What is affected if lemma X is modified?
> What does altering type definition X affect?
> Why is X affected?
> Why?

Questions like the second one can be asked about any Gypsy specification, not just exit assertions. Answers to these questions vary in form and content according to context.

A user's question is processed in three stages:

1) **Understanding the question.** A simple pattern-matching scheme that looks for keywords works well for the limited domain of discourse. Context is used only in resolving pronoun references. These patterns of keywords are translated into calls to functions responsible for answering the question. If a question is not understood, the user is informed of the options for the missing or incorrect sentence fragments.

2) **Getting the answer.** This involves two interleaved processes—deducing what could be affected if the indicated change were made and formatting the answer for English output. The formatted, English answer is generated by dynamically assembling and filling in language templates (which represent part of the answer) with actual, problem-specific data, such as the name ExchangeSort. The theory described in the next section is used at each step to guide the choice of templates and to supply actual data for filling them in.

3) **Reporting the answer.** A set of routines for formatted printing of templates is used for typing the English answer on the terminal.

It is worth noting that the explanation facility could have been implemented to answer questions about specific changes, instead of "classes" of changes. The intention, however, was to avoid involved language-understanding issues and to have a smooth interface with the techniques in the next section, while still providing an effective question-answering facility. The current design seems to meet these criteria.

V. Reasoning About Changes

This section explains how the assistant reasons about incremental changes to a program's design or verification, then shows how this theory was applied in the scenario of Section II.

A. Overview of the Approach

1) A General Strategy

It is important to distinguish the user's conception of *what* an incremental system does from *how* the system does it. From the user's viewpoint, an incremental system responds to changes by keeping intact previous work that remains valid, *without* any unnecessary reprocessing. But, a system can convey this impression even though it does a certain amount of reprocessing. In fact, there is a spectrum of strategies a system could employ. At one end of the spectrum is the most straightforward strategy—reprocess everything completely, then bring to the user's attention any information that is not currently correct. This is the way traditional compilers work. If a source file is changed, the entire file is recompiled, and the user is informed of any errors that are detected. The approach at the other end of the spectrum is to isolate the exact impact of changes, thereby avoiding all unnecessary reprocessing. A compiler based on this approach would never recompile unaffected parts of a changed file.

As a general strategy, both of these approaches to reasoning about incremental changes can be highly inefficient. Complete reprocessing, although generally acceptable in compilers, is too costly in program verifiers, mostly because of the expense involved in redoing proofs. Determining the exact effects of changes is too costly since it can take as much effort (or more) to figure out how to keep from redoing still-valid work as it would take to redo it.

An efficient general strategy lies somewhere between these endpoints. The idea is to *localize the effects of changes to a small amount of information, redo everything in that locality, then bring to the user's attention only that which is actually affected.* If applied properly, this strategy can minimize the amount of effort spent determining the effects of incremental changes. The main problem, of course, is in achieving the right balance between the amount of effort invested in approximating the effects of a change and the amount of unnecessary reprocessing. The discussion below will show how the assistant attempts to achieve this balance.

2) The Theory Embodied in the Assistant

The assistant expends much more effort trying to avoid unnecessary reprocessing of the verification than the design. In fact, the costly activity of reproving still-valid theorems is nearly always avoided, while a limited amount of retranslation (which, unlike proving theorems, is entirely automated) is accepted. The scenario for determining the effects of changes is as follows. If a program is changed, the assistant first approximates the affected part of the design and verification. Then, it retranslates the *potentially* affected part of the design and logically analyzes the *potentially* affected verification conditions to determine the *actual* effects of the change. This two-stage approach seems to be considerably more efficient than directly analyzing changes to programs on a case-by-case basis. In contrast, changes to specifications are analyzed without a preliminary approximation of their effects. The assistant performs certain logical analyses on the changed specification, often establishing that the change has no, or only limited, effects on the verification.

Let us now consider some of the key ideas used by the assistant in determining the effects of changes to programs. The main problem is that of quickly making a good initial approximation of what is affected, whereas the subsequent reprocessing needed to isolate the actual effects of the change is relatively straightforward. The assistant divides a program unit into an *external part* that defines its interface with its external environment and an *internal part* that gives details not visible to its callers. As an illustration, consider the definition of

ExchangeSort:

```
      function ExchangeSort(...):IntArray =
      begin
          entry ... ;
          exit ... ;
(1)       ... Exchange(...) ... ;
      end;
```

Its internal part is its body at line (1), and its external part is everything else. This distinction was brought about by the observation that only a change to the external part of a program unit can have global effects; or conversely, a change to an internal part can have only local effects.

The assistant can use this fact to significantly limit the amount of information that is reprocessed following a change to a program. As a simple illustration, consider the following definitions:

```
      function Exchange(...):IntArray =
      begin
(2)       exit ... IsExchanged(...);
      ...
      end;

(3)   function IsExchanged(...):boolean = ... ;
```

Now suppose that the parameter list of IsExchanged, in line (3), is revised. Since this is a change to an external part of IsExchanged, it may affect Exchange. Specifically, the exit specification of Exchange, line (2), may contain a *design inconsistency*, defined to be a syntactic or type error in a program or specification. Exchange may also have a *verification inconsistency*, a situation in which a verification condition does not correspond to a *design-consistent* part of the *current* design. (Note that this definition singles out verification conditions that 1) contain design-inconsistent information or 2) reflect a previous, instead of the current, version of the design.) ExchangeSort, on the other hand, can only be verification inconsistent. Since the design-inconsistent specification at line (2) is in an external part of Exchange, it appears in ExchangeSort's verification condition across the call at line (1). Since this call is from an internal part of ExchangeSort, the effects of the original change *cannot* propagate any further. Thus, any design changes needed to correct the exit specification of Exchange at line (2) must be balanced by changes to the verification of only Exchange and ExchangeSort.

Notice that the specific change in line (3) was not mentioned. The strategy is to determine whether an internal or external part of IsExchanged has been changed, and then approximate what *might* be affected accordingly. Once the effects of a change are approximated, the assistant next must determine its actual effects. Rather than reprocessing the potentially inconsistent parts of the development immediately, the assistant *delays reprocessing until necessary*. Immediate reprocessing is often fruitless, since a sequence of changes to the design is often made, the last of which resolves all intermediate inconsistencies. When the reprocessing is finally done, the assistant isolates the actual design inconsistencies and any verification conditions causing a verification inconsistency. These verification conditions are identified by generating new verification conditions and then logically comparing them with the old verification conditions. The logical technique employed is similar to the one described next for analyzing changes to specifications.

Changes to specifications often can be shown not to have effects with just one simple proof. When a specification is changed, the assistant figures out what logical relationship must hold between the changed specification and its preceding version in order for the change not to have effects. This is illustrated by the following interchange:

←What are the effects of changing the exit specification of LocationOfMax?

This change does not affect LocationOfMax if the formula

LocationOfMax(A, I, J) in [I..J] ... $\Rightarrow$ *Changed exit specification*

is true .... The verification of other programs is not affected if the formula

Changed exit specification $\Rightarrow$ LocationOfMax(A, I, J) in [I..J] ...

is true ....

If the exit specification of LocationOfMax is actually modified, the assistant forms the designated implications and invokes the proof system to attempt an automatic proof. If the attempted proof fails, the formula is assumed to be false and, guided by internal/external calling relationships, the assistant identifies those program units that are verification inconsistent.

The remaining problem is that of resolving confirmed inconsistencies. When can inconsistencies in the development be resolved? And how do they get resolved? The answer to the first question is that inconsistencies can be resolved in any intermediate stage in the development. This significantly enhances incremental development. The user, for example, can define programs that call as yet undefined programs, then define the callees whenever convenient. In short, the assistant's ability to retain and reason about temporarily inconsistent information gives the user the freedom to evolve a development according to any strategy that is convenient. In answer to the second question, the user and the assistant share the responsibility for removing inconsistencies. The assistant detects design inconsistencies which the user must correct (since the assistant does not embody a theory of automatic debugging), while the assistant removes verification inconsistencies by replacing irrelevant verification conditions with the appropriate new ones.

A final remark is in order concerning the use of the assistant. Despite its ability to reason about incremental changes, if misused, the assistant can suffer from the same kind of inefficiency as traditional verifiers suffer from—namely, excessive and unnecessary redoing of still-valid previous work. The problem for the assistant, however, is on a much smaller scale (since only a small portion of the development is usually reprocessed) and can easily be circumvented. The source of the problem is the iterative nature of the process of making revisions. Traditional verifiers can provide little, if any, assistance in helping the user avoid costly iterations. The assistant, on the other hand, can effectively assist the user via its explanation facility. The user can ask about the effects of an intended change, then ask about the effects of changing the affected information, etc., until an understanding of the total impact of the original change is gleaned. With this knowledge, all needed changes can be made at once.

The next two sections give the specifics of the ideas just presented. A model for describing a program's design and verification is given, followed by a discussion of the knowledge used in approximating, isolating, and resolving inconsistencies that result from a change to any specific model. The discussion assumes that programs and their specifications can be type checked at compile time and that programs do not have side effects except through call-by-reference parameters.

B. Model of a Program's Design and Verification

In general, a model will contain information about individual parts of a design and verification and information about how they interrelate. This information is represented as a network of nodes and relations. Suppose there is a program A that calls another program B, as in Fig. 4. Programs A and B are represented by the nodes labeled A and B, and the fact that A has a call to B is carried by the labeled pointer between the nodes. Individually, A and B can have properties like the one indicated by the HAS-STATUS-OF pointers in the second part of Fig. 4.

Let us now look at a sample model that the model-building programs would construct. A model of a program's development is really a collection of models—one model for each major task performed by the overall design and verification system. Recall that the major tasks performed by the overall system are translation (specifically, parsing and type checking), verification condition generation, and theorem proving. So there are three models, each of which can initially be viewed as an independent entity.

The parser/type-checker model is shown in the first part of Fig. 5. (From now on, all nodes labeled with individual letters represent program units.) Notice that calls in external parts of a program (i.e., those parts that are visible to its callers) are distinguished from calls in internal parts of programs (i.e., those parts that are not visible to its callers). Further observe that calling relationships are described with inverse pointers such as HAS-CALL-IN-INTERNAL-PART-TO and HAS-CALL-FROM-INTERNAL-PART-OF. The second part of Fig. 5 shows a model of the verification condition generation process. Naturally, the information contained in this model is different from the information contained in the parser/type-checker model. The focus is on the program paths traced by the verification condition generator and the verification conditions associated with each path. The proof system model, which describes certain proof dependencies, is in the third part of Fig. 5.

While it is easier to think of these models as independent

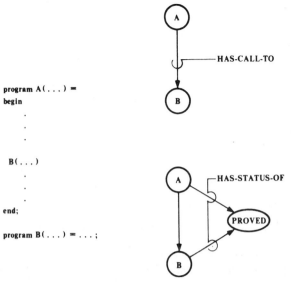

program A(. . .) =
begin
    .
    .
    .
  B(. . .)
    .
    .
    .
end;

program B(. . .) = . . . ;

Fig. 4. The first network shows that program A has a call to program
B; the second shows that both have been proved.

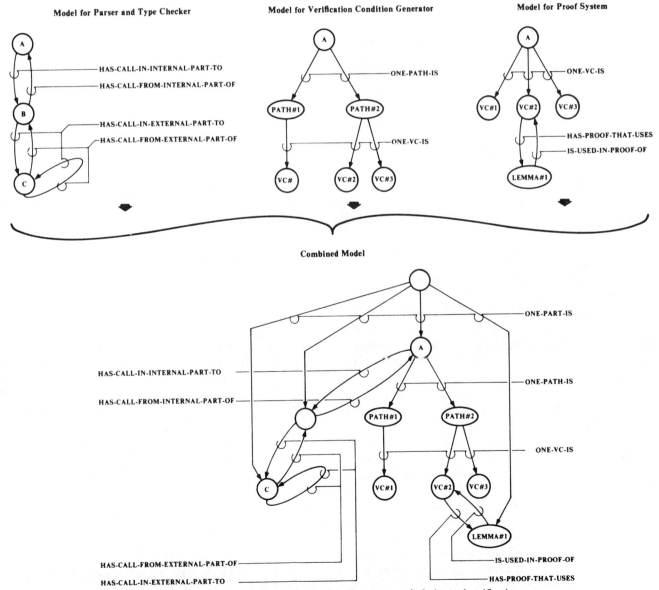

Fig. 5. Different models combine to describe a program's design and verification.

entities, there are, in fact, important ties among them that must be made apparent in order to handle incremental changes. For example, a change to a program in the parser/type-checker model may need to be reflected in the program's verification conditions in the verification condition generator model. There are several ways to represent model connections. The assistant does it by integrating all models into a single, unified model as shown in Fig. 5. The algorithms given in the next section reason about changes to this combined model.

Consider now the generation of a development's description. The starting point is a file containing programs and their specifications, and the end result is a network relating and describing various objects with pointers such as HAS-CALL-IN-EXTERNAL-PART-TO, ONE-PATH-IS, HAS-STATUS-OF, and HAS-PROOF-THAT-USES.

The first step in processing a file is to parse and type check all programs and specifications on the file, using the context supplied by the existing model to resolve external references. Processed entities that either have no errors or have only type errors are incorporated into the model by the algorithms described in the next section, whereas entities containing syntax errors are not. Typically, a single file contains only a small part of an entire design. As the design is evolved and refined, and as verification conditions are generated and proved, the model is gradually filled in. The final model describes a completed design and verification with all effects of incremental changes compensated for. Any subsequent changes made for maintenance purposes cause the model to be adjusted just as if the changes were made during the development.

C. Knowledge for Reasoning About Changes to Any Specific Model

This section further explains the main procedures introduced earlier in the overview. It elaborates on 1) how the assistant approximates the effects of a change and 2) how, by refining this approximation, the actual inconsistencies are eventually isolated. The algorithms described use the logical techniques described below.

1) Determining Whether Changes to Specifications Affect the Verification

To show that changes to specifications do not have effects, it suffices to establish certain logical relationships between the changed specification and its previous version. What these relationships are depends on how the specification in question has been used in proofs.

Specifications are used in well-defined ways, as prescribed by the program proof techniques employed. The assistant is given a set of templates that describe, for each kind of specification, which formula to prove in order to show that a change has no effects. There are two classes of relationship templates—those for showing that a change does not have global effects and those for showing that a change does not have local effects. Changes to external specifications (e.g., traditional entry and exit assertions) can have global and local effects, while changes to internal specifications (e.g., inductive assertions) can have only local effects.

Consider what the relationship templates would be for entry and exit specifications. The relationships for deciding

if a change does not have local effects are obtained by observing that Hoare's rule of consequence

$$\frac{P \Rightarrow Q, Q \{S\} R, R \Rightarrow T}{P \{S\} T}$$

can be instantiated as

$$\frac{entry' \Rightarrow entry, entry \{program\text{-}body\}exit, exit \Rightarrow exit'}{entry'\{program\text{-}body\}exit'}$$

The notational convention of designating changed information with a prime symbol is adopted throughout. For example, the revised version of the specification called exit is $exit'$. The notation $entry\{program\text{-}body\}exit$ means that if entry holds before executing the program, and if execution terminates, then exit will hold afterwards. The rule says that if it can be shown that $entry' \Rightarrow entry$, $entry\{program\text{-}body\}exit$, and $exit \Rightarrow exit'$, then the consequent $entry'\{program\text{-}body\}exit'$ can be inferred. We are interested here in the question of what happens when entry and exit are revised after $entry\{program\text{-}body\}exit$ has been proved. If $entry' \Rightarrow entry$ and $exit \Rightarrow exit'$ can be proved, then $entry'\{program\text{-}body\}exit'$ can be inferred, meaning that neither change invalidates any part of the verification of the associated program. The case when only entry or only exit is changed is handled in the obvious way.

Globally, entry and exit specifications of a program can arise in verification conditions of its callers in several ways. Suppose the program proof techniques handle subprogram calls 1) by proving that entry specifications hold at all calling sites and 2) by adding formulas of the form $entry \Rightarrow exit$ from callees to verification conditions of callers. Just as Hoare's rule of consequence was used in the derivation of local relationship templates, the *derived inference rule*

$$\frac{P \Rightarrow Q, Q \wedge R \Rightarrow S}{P \wedge R \Rightarrow S}$$

can be used in the derivation of global relationship templates. P, Q, R, and S are arbitrary logical formulas that are instantiated to give

$$\frac{P \Rightarrow entry, entry \Rightarrow entry'}{P \Rightarrow entry'}$$

where true has been substituted for R. This instantiation shows what to do if a verification condition of the form $P \Rightarrow entry$ has been proved, and subsequently entry is changed to $entry'$. If $entry \Rightarrow entry'$ can be established, then $P \Rightarrow entry'$ follows.

For the second case, let us start out by assuming that just exit, instead of $entry \Rightarrow exit$, is added to verification conditions at calling sites. Consider the following instantiation of the derived rule:

$$\frac{exit' \Rightarrow exit, exit \wedge R \Rightarrow S}{exit' \wedge R \Rightarrow S}$$

If $exit' \Rightarrow exit$ can be established, then proofs of verification conditions of the form $exit \wedge R \Rightarrow S$ also hold for those of the form $exit' \wedge R \Rightarrow S$. Similarly, if $((entry' \Rightarrow exit') \Rightarrow (en\text{-}$

try $\Rightarrow$ exit)) can be established, then proofs of verification conditions of the form (entry $\Rightarrow$ exit)$\wedge$R $\Rightarrow$ S also hold for those of the form (entry$'$ $\Rightarrow$ exit$'$)$\wedge$R $\Rightarrow$ S.

Even if verification conditions are always of the last form, the assistant can often take the shortcut of attempting to prove only exit$'$ $\Rightarrow$ exit, as is described by the following rule:

if entry = entry$'$ **then** exit$'$ $\Rightarrow$ exit

else (entry$'$ $\Rightarrow$ exit$'$) $\Rightarrow$ (entry $\Rightarrow$ exit)

This kind of rule allows the assistant to take advantage of its knowledge about what has changed. If the entry has not changed and the exit has, the test is true and a proof of the simpler formula on the then-branch is attempted. This simplification surfaces to the user level during explanations, as is evident in the following interchange:

$\longleftarrow$**What are the effects of changing the exit specification of LocationOfMax?**

. . . The verification of other programs is not affected if the formula

Changed exit specification $\Rightarrow$ **LocationOfMax(A, I, J) in [I . . J] . . .**

is true . . .

The answer refers only to the exit specification of LocationOfMax because the user did not hypothesize changing its entry specification too.

The scenario for applying the relationship templates is as follows. When a specification is changed, the assistant selects and instantiates the appropriate templates. It then invokes a fully automatic portion of the proof system in an effort to prove the desired formula without involving the user. In practice, the formula can often be established automatically with propositional inferences. For example, it is commonplace in top-down development to conjoin additional exit assertions onto a program before it has been implemented or verified. This was illustrated in the sample scenario when the proof of Exchange-Sort required adding a new conjunct to the exit specification of the lower-level program IsPerm. The formula exit$\wedge$"new conjunct" $\Rightarrow$ exit was easily proved. But what if it could not be proved automatically? If the attempted proof fails, the unproved formula is brought to the attention of the user, who can choose to invoke the more powerful capabilities of the interactive theorem prover or indicate that the formula should be treated as if it were false. How to identify what is affected when such attempted proofs fail and the conditions under which such proofs cannot even be attempted will be explained later.

Changes to verification conditions can be analyzed in much

which can be made automatically, is used to make this determination—two verification conditions must be the same syntactically within a uniform change of variables and they must be the same semantically symbol for symbol. Uniform variable renaming is considered as a special case so that the common source code change of uniformly renaming an identifier will not necessitate any reverifying. When checking the semantic criteria for equivalence, the types of free variables are found in the appropriate symbol tables.

This section has presented *sufficient* conditions for showing that a change to an entry or exit specification or to a verification condition has no effects. Any scheme for doing this is subject to certain theoretical limitations. Since the formula to be proved is typically a statement in number theory, Godel's Incompleteness Theorem says that there will be some true theorems that cannot be proved, meaning that the *exact*

effects of changes cannot always be determined. Thus, no matter how clever a scheme is employed, some previous work may need to be redone unnecessarily.

2) Isolating and Resolving Inconsistencies

The assistant combines the process of isolating inconsistencies (i.e., refining its initial approximation of the effects of a change) and the process of resolving verification inconsistencies (i.e., discarding verification conditions that no longer apply). The choice of when and on what part of the design and verification to initiate these processes centers around what might be thought of as an *invariant* at a particular point in a development.

This invariant, which is often (and perhaps incorrectly) assumed to hold, describes an important relationship between a particular part of the design and a particular program's verification conditions. The invariant states a condition under which newly generated verification conditions will be "well formed"—namely, when design inconsistencies are not contained in the program of interest, its specifications, or specifications that would be imported from other program units. This invariant guides the assistant's search for *relevant* design errors and *irrelevant* verification conditions. For example, suppose that the user issues a command to verify the function ExchangeSort. If the invariant does not hold for ExchangeSort, the assistant rejects the command:

Exec$\longrightarrow$**VCs ExchangeSort**

****Verification conditions cannot be generated for ExchangeSort,
because there is a type mismatch in the exit specification of IsExchanged.

---

the same way as changes to specifications. If a verification condition for a particular program is changed, the assistant loops through all the program's at least partially proved verification conditions to see if any of their proofs hold for the new verification condition. A simple "equivalence" test,

For now, observe only that the assistant detected a relevant design inconsistency, which must be corrected before verification conditions can be generated for ExchangeSort. (The reasons for this rejection are explained later in this section.) Suppose, on the other hand, that the invariant had been satisfied. In this case, the assistant would generate well-formed verification conditions for ExchangeSort and perform the logical equivalence test described in the preceding section to keep intact previous proofs that still apply. As was illustrated in Fig. 3, all this detailed reasoning is hidden from the user.

Let us now consider the issue of how the assistant tests the invariant. Before considering the algorithm, the model will be augmented to associate special variables with every program unit for recording whether it has inconsistencies. CHECK-DESIGN-FLAG is a boolean variable that is True if the associated program unit is thought to have a design error. Similarly, a variable called CHECK-VERIFICATION-FLAG is used to record verification inconsistencies. The algorithms described in the next section assign truth values to these flags so that the model properly reflects the development.

A nice property of the model is that the invariant is guaranteed to hold for a particular program if both of its flags are False. If either flag is True, the assistant must examine certain calling relationships to make its determination. A slightly more detailed view of the programs referred to earlier will be used to illustrate the general procedure:

```
      function ExchangeSort(. . .):IntArray =
      begin
          entry . . . ;
          exit . . . ;
(1)       . . . Exchange(. . .) . . . ;
      end;
      function Exchange(. . .):IntArray =
      begin
(2)       exit . . . IsExchanged(. . .);
          . . .
      end;
(3)   function IsExchanged(A,B:IntArray;I,J:int):boolean =
      begin
(4)       exit  (IsExchanged(A,B,i) iff . . . A[I] = B[J] and A[J] = B[I]);
      end;
```

The calling relationships among these programs are reflected by internal/external calling pointers in the model (as illustrated by the parser/type checker model of Fig. 5 with the substitutions of ExchangeSort for A, Exchange for B, and IsExchanged for C), CHECK-DESIGN-FLAG is True for IsExchanged, and CHECK-VERIFICATION-FLAG is True for all three functions. Recall that "HAS-CALL-FROM" pointers were traced in propagating the effects of changes. In contrast, "HAS-CALL-TO" pointers are traced in testing the invariant. The general procedure is illustrated by following the assistant as it determines whether the invariant holds for ExchangeSort. The assistant first observes that, since the CHECK-DESIGN-FLAG of ExchangeSort is False, Exchange-Sort does not contain any design inconsistencies. The next step is to determine whether there is an inconsistency in some other part of the design that would appear in ExchangeSort's verification conditions. For generality, assume that hierarchies of specifications are fully expanded in verification conditions.

Then, the search for a relevant design error traces sequences of pointers $p_1, p_2, \cdots, p_n$, where p_1 is any "HAS-CALL-TO" pointer and $p_2, \cdots, p_n$ are HAS-CALL-IN-EXTERNAL-PART-TO pointers. (The tracing algorithm must, of course, handle cycles properly.) Only program units encountered in tracing these sequences can contain relevant design inconsistencies. In the example being considered, the calls at lines (1) and (2) indicate that Exchange and IsExchanged must be considered. The assistant immediately knows that Exchange does not contain a design inconsistency because its CHECK-DESIGN-FLAG is False, but it must reanalyze IsExchanged because its CHECK-DESIGN-FLAG is True. IsExchanged is, in fact, found to have a design inconsistency, because the recursive call in line (4) has only three arguments [instead of four as required by line (3)]. Consequently, verification conditions cannot be generated for ExchangeSort until this error is corrected.

3) Approximating the Effects of Changes

The process of approximating the effects of a change to a program or its specifications culminates in certain truth value assignments to the special variables. CHECK-DESIGN-FLAG and CHECK-VERIFICATION-FLAG. No further background is needed to understand how the assistant makes these assignments. The algorithm is roughly as follows.

1) If the header of program unit X has changed, then assign the value True to both flags of all callers of X and to the CHECK-VERIFICATION-FLAG of all programs whose verifications use a specification that calls X.

2) If there is a change to an externally visible specification of X that has global effects, then assign the value True to the CHECK-VERIFICATION-FLAG of all programs that have used the preceding version of the changed specification in their verification.

3) If X contains design inconsistencies, then assign the value True to both of its flags. Otherwise, assign its CHECK-VERIFICATION-FLAG the value True if a) its body has changed, b) there is a change in one of its specifications that has local effects, or c) the invariant described in the immediately preceding section does not hold for X.

The first two steps approximate the global effects of a change, while the last step focuses on local effects. One additional point is that the logical reasoning needed to show that a change to a specification does not have effects cannot be done unless the changed specification and its preceding version are free of design inconsistencies and cannot depend on other design inconsistent specifications. If either condition is violated, the change is simply assumed to have effects.

The one kind of change left to consider is that of adding entirely new program units to the model. The local truth value assignments are very similar to those in step 3) above. Both flags are assigned the value True if the new program unit contains design inconsistencies; if it does not, its CHECK-VERIFICATION-FLAG is assigned the value True if the invariant does not hold. However, no global truth value assignments are ever required. To illustrate why, suppose the program units ExchangeSort and IsExchanged are defined before Exchange. When Exchange is defined, both of ExchangeSort's flags would already be True, and IsExchanged could not possibly be affected because the effects of defining Exchange propagate through "HAS-CALL-FROM" pointers.

For expository purposes, this discussion has not considered data type definitions or certain logical properties that are not part of a program unit's specifications. An example of such a property is rewrite rules that are used in proofs. The implementation handles both kinds of constructs, using straightforward extensions of the ideas already discussed. Appendix A gives a tabular summary of the key relations in the complete model.

D. The Scenario Revisited

As implemented, the assistant does not adopt the "worst case" view of completely expanding verification conditions during their generation because imported specifications, especially lower-level ones in a specification hierarchy, are not always needed in proofs. Only references to specifications of called programs, instead of the specifications themselves, are added to verification conditions during their generation. Then, complete specifications, or parts of specifications, are expanded as needed during proofs. A record of these expansions is then used to identify what proofs must be redone following changes to specifications or changes that affect specifications.

Let us now return to the scenario of Section II and see how the assistant reasons about the hypothesized and actual changes. In the dialog in Fig. 1, the explanation facility answers questions by querying the model directly or by invoking one of the assistant's main algorithms. The answer to the question "What are the effects of fully defining ExchangeSort?" requires only an interpretation of the status of ExchangeSort. The value of its HAS-STATUS-OF pointer is "waiting for body to be fully defined." So the assistant immediately concludes that "ExchangeSort may have additional VCs." (The word "may" allows for the possibility of replacing the "pending" in the body of ExchangeSort with the "null statement," which would not cause any new verification conditions to be generated.) More complex reasoning is done, for example, in answering the question "What are the effects of changing the exit of IsPerm?" The assistant selects and instantiates a relationship template that describes the logical implication that must hold. Pointers from IsPerm tell the assistant that the verification of ExchangeSort, specifically the proof of ExchangeSort#1, will be invalidated if the displayed implication cannot be proved.

Next, the revisions in Fig. 2 are reflected in the model by executing the appropriate reasoning programs. The assistant, observing that some new verification conditions need to be generated for ExchangeSort, assigns its CHECK-VERIFICATION-FLAG the value True. It also deduces that the changed exit specifications of ValueOfMax and IsPerm do not invalidate previous verification work, and incorporates new programs (such as LocationOfMax) into the existing model.

Finally, Fig. 3 shows the generation of the new verification conditions for ExchangeSort, with the assistant working in the background to formally establish that the change to Exchange-Sort did not affect previous proofs. Appendix B shows the resulting model.

VI. Conclusion

This paper has explained how to build a computer program that provides several useful kinds of assistance to the human designer/verifier and that also interfaces with traditional program verifiers to significantly increase their performance in working situations. A theory for determining the effects of incremental changes to a design or verification has been presented, and it has been shown how this theory can serve as the basis for answering questions about the effects of hypothesized changes and for making proposals for how to proceed with the design and verification in an orderly fashion. Since attention has been primarily on how the assistant works, only a glimpse of how it is used in a real working situation has been seen. A transcript illustrating the role of the assistant at each stage in the development of a message switching network (which allows secure, asynchronous message transfer among a fixed number of users) is presented in [13].

Experience in using the designer/verifier's assistant is very encouraging. As expected, its utility grows proportionately with the size and complexity of the program being developed. This is particularly evident when the assistant is used to obtain explanations of the effects of hypothesized changes. In all but the simplest cases, it is totally impractical to carry out the requisite calculations reliably by hand. This is true not only during a development, but even more so afterwards when confronted with the problem of "maintaining" formally verified software. A common problem is that of determining how to change specifications and programs to reflect new design constraints. If the human designer/verifier has forgotten relevant details about the development, the assistant is used to regain the necessary understanding—namely, to get explanations of the potential effects of any intended revisions and to get hints about how to make them. Similarly, as the tasks that remain to be done increase in number and variety, the importance of the assistant's ability to suggest a next logical step in the development also becomes more and more evident.

The amount of computational efficiency gained by using the assistant also grows proportionately with the size and complexity of the program being developed. When incremental changes are made, the assistant typically limits the scope of their effects to a relatively small fraction of the overall development, thereby generally avoiding unnecessary reapplication of the program verifier to unaffected parts of the development. As a result, the total savings in processing increases rapidly as the development evolves. This overall improvement in efficiency emanates from the cumulative impact of several design decisions. The fundamental ones of allowing a certain amount of unnecessary reprocessing in specific instances and of expending more effort trying to avoid unnecessary reverification than retranslation appear to have been very sound. The way in which these desiderata were reflected in the theory for reasoning about changes has resulted in the general avoidance of the costly activity of reproving still-valid theorems

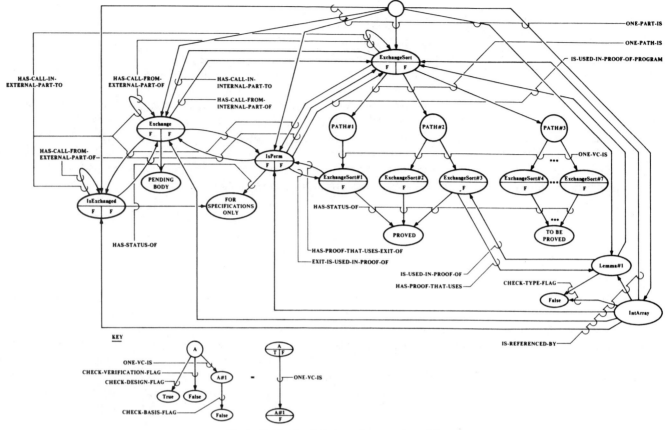

Fig. 6. Fairly detailed view of an actual model.

and in only a limited amount of the much cheaper activity of retranslation. The balance achieved between the amount of effort invested in approximating the effects of a change and the amount of unnecessary reprocessing generally appears to be appropriate for interfacing with traditional program verifiers. Another impact of the fundamental design decisions has been the simplifications they have allowed in both the model for representing a design and verification and the codified knowledge used for reasoning about changes to any specific model.

The assistant represents a beginning step towards the construction of an incremental system for use in developing and maintaining formally verified programs. Experimentation with the current version of the assistant suggests that, although it generally seems to reason at the appropriate level of detail, there are times when it would be better to analyze design changes individually, rather than by category as it does now. It also suggests a need for more structuring in explanations, specifically for the assistant to make available a hierarchy of explanations, ranging from very high level to very detailed. These issues are, in fact, closely related and are being actively explored. Further research is also being carried out to broaden the scope of the assistant to handle multiple version systems, additional programming languages, a hierarchical development methodology [15], and to eventually support a complete environment which includes editors, interpreters, etc. Another complementary line of investigation being conducted is the exploration of the principles which underlie any kind of incremental system. The goal is to evolve a general mathematical framework that explains how to build and extend incremental systems, such as the assistant.

APPENDIX A

RELATIONS IN A MODEL

The tables below summarize the key relations used in modeling a program's design and verification. The term *basis property* refers to logical properties, which are not part of a program's specifications, that are assumed in proofs (e.g., rewrite rules).

TABLE I
KEY RELATIONSHIPS BETWEEN NODES

Relationship Pointer	Meaning
CALLS	Points from a basis property to a function it calls
HAS-CALL-FROM	Inverse of CALLS
HAS-CALL-FROM-EXTERNAL-PART-OF	Inverse of HAS-CALL-IN-EXTERNAL-PART-TO
HAS-CALL-FROM-INTERNAL-PART-OF	Inverse of HAS-CALL-IN-INTERNAL-PART-TO
HAS-CALL-IN-INTERNAL-PART-TO	Points from program A to program B if B is called from a part of A that is not visible to callers of A
HAS-CALL-IN-EXTERNAL-PART-TO	Points from program A to program B if B is called from a part of A that is visible to callers of A
HAS-PROOF-THAT-USES	Points from a verification condition to a basis property used in its proof
IS-REFERENCED-BY	Points from type definition A to program B if B uses A
IS-USED-IN-PROOF-OF	Inverse of HAS-PROOF-THAT-USES
IS-USED-IN-PROOF-OF-PROGRAM	Points from basis property B to program A if B IS-USED-IN-PROOF-OF at least one verification condition of A
ONE-PATH-IS	Associates paths with programs
ONE-PART-IS	Ties together the "main" parts of a program's design and verification
ONE-VC-IS	Associates verification conditions with paths
REFERENCES	Inverse of IS-REFERENCED-BY

TABLE II
KEY PROPERTIES OF NODES

Property Pointer	Meaning
CHECK-DESIGN-FLAG	Set to True if a program or basis property may be design inconsistent and to False otherwise
CHECK-VERIFICATION-FLAG	Set to True if a program may be verification inconsistent and to False otherwise
HAS-STATUS-OF	Associated with all programs and logical formulas to describe their state of development
CHECK-BASIS-FLAG	Set to True if the proof of a logical formula depends on a potentially incorrect basis property and to False otherwise

APPENDIX B
A SAMPLE MODEL

Fig. 6 shows the model resulting from the scenario of Section II. It is given in a fair amount of detail to convey a feeling for the complexity dealt with even at an early stage in a development. The primary simplification in this rendition of the model is the omission of all information about Location-OfMax and ValueOfMax.

There is one new relation, along with its inverse, shown in the model. HAS-PROOF-THAT-USES-EXIT-OF, along with EXIT-IS-USED-IN-PROOF-OF, were added because the assistant does not always expand specifications from called programs into verification conditions. These additional relations keep track of those proofs in which the associated exit specification has actually been used.

ACKNOWLEDGMENT

This research was initiated as my Ph.D. dissertation at The University of Texas at Austin and partially carried out at the University of Southern California Information Sciences Institute. I would like to thank my advisors and committee members: W. W. Bledsoe, D. Good, R. London, and R. Yeh. In addition, I would like to thank D. Wile for his helpful suggestions on how to reason about incremental changes. This presentation has been improved by valuable comments from L. Flon, S. Katz, K. Levitt, L. Robinson, and one of the referees.

REFERENCES

[1] A. L. Ambler, D. I. Good, J. C. Browne, W. F. Burger, R. M. Cohen, C. G. Hoch, and R. E. Wells, "Gypsy: A language for specification and implementation of verifiable programs," in *Proc. ACM Conf. Language Design for Reliable Software, SIGPLAN Notices*, vol. 12, Mar. 1977, pp. 1-10.

[2] R. S. Boyer and J S. Moore, "A lemma driven automatic theorem prover for recursive function theory," in *Proc. 5th Int. Conf. Artificial Intelligence*, vol. 1, Aug. 1977, pp. 511-519.

[3] L. P. Deutsch, "An interactive program verifier," Ph.D. dissertation, Univ. California, Berkeley, 1973; also, Xerox Palo Alto Res. Center Rep. CSL-73-1, May 1973.

[4] J. Doyle, "Truth maintenance systems for problem solving," M.S. thesis, MIT Artificial Intelligence Laboratory Rep. AI-TR-419, Jan. 1978.

[5] B. Elspas, R. E. Shostak, and J. M. Spitzen, "A verification system for Jocit/J3 programs (Rugged Programming Environment—RPE/2)," SRI International Comput. Sci. Lab. Rep., Apr. 1977.

[6] R. W. Floyd, "Toward interactive design of correct programs," in *Proc. IFIP Congr. 71*. Amsterdam, The Netherlands: North-Holland, 1972, pp. 7-10.

[7] D. I. Good, R. L. London, and W. W. Bledsoe, "An interactive program verification system," *IEEE Trans. Software Eng.*, vol. SE-1, pp. 59-67, Mar. 1975.

[8] C. E. Hewitt and B. Smith, "Towards a programming apprentice," *IEEE Trans. Software Eng.*, vol. SE-1, pp. 26-45, Mar. 1975.

[9] E. L. Ivie, "The programmer's workbench—A machine for software development," *Commun. Ass. Comput. Mach.*, vol. 20, pp. 746-753, Oct. 1977.

[10] J. C. King, "A program verifier," Ph.D. dissertation, Carnegie-Mellon Univ., 1969.

[11] D. C. Luckham, "Program verification and verification-oriented programming," in *Proc. IFIP Cong. 77*. Amsterdam, The Netherlands: North-Holland, 1977, pp. 783-793.

[12] M. S. Moriconi, "A system for incrementally designing and verifying programs," Ph.D. dissertation, The University of Texas at Austin, Dec. 1977; also, SRI International Comput. Sci. Lab. Rep. CSL-73 and CSL-74.

[13] —, "Interactive design and verification: A message switching network example," SRI International Comput. Sci. Lab. Rep. CSL-90, May 1979; also, to appear in *Lecture Notes in Computer Science* (Springer-Verlag).

[14] C. Rich and H. E. Shrobe, "Initial report on a Lisp programmer's apprentice," *IEEE Trans. Software Eng.*, vol. SE-4, pp. 456-467, Nov. 1978.

[15] L. Robinson and K. N. Levitt, "Proof techniques for hierarchically structured programs," *Commun. Ass. Comput. Mach.*, vol. 20, pp. 271-283, Apr. 1977.

[16] O. Roubine and L. Robinson, *Special Reference Manual*, SRI International Comput. Sci. Lab. Rep. CSL-45, Jan. 1977.

[17] N. Suzuki, "Verifying programs by algebraic and logical reduction," in *Proc. Int. Conf. Reliable Software*, pp. 473-481, Apr. 1975, pp. 473-481.

[18] W. Teitelman, *Interlisp Reference Manual*, Xerox Palo Alto Res. Center, Oct. 1978.

[19] —, "Toward a programming laboratory," in *Proc. Int. Joint Conf. Artificial Intelligence*, May 1969, pp. 1-8.

[20] B. Wegbreit, "The ECL programming system," in *AFIPS Conf. Proc.*, vol. 39, Nov. 1971, pp. 253-262.

Mark S. Moriconi (S'74-M'76) was born in Pittsburg, KS, on May 7, 1948. He received the B.S. degree with honors in mathematics from Wichita State University, Wichita, KS, in 1970, and the Ph.D. degree in computer science from The University of Texas, Austin, in 1977.

He has been a Research Staff Member in the Computer Science Laboratory at SRI International (formerly Stanford Research Institute), Menlo Park, CA, since 1978. Prior to this appointment he conducted his doctoral research as a Research Assistant at The University of Texas, Austin, from 1974-1977 and at the University of Southern California Information Sciences Institute, Marina del Rey, CA, from 1975-1977. His current research interests are in the theory and development of incremental systems and in program verification, particularly in computer systems which assist in developing verified programs and programming methodologies which reduce the difficulties of verification.

Dr. Moriconi is a member of the Association for Computing Machinery and Sigma Xi.

The Programmer's Apprentice: A Session with KBEmacs

RICHARD C. WATERS, MEMBER, IEEE

(Invited Paper)

Abstract—The Knowledge-Based Editor in Emacs (KBEmacs) is the current demonstration system implemented as part of the Programmer's Apprentice project. KBEmacs is capable of acting as a semiexpert assistant to a person who is writing a program—taking over some parts of the programming task. Using KBEmacs, it is possible to construct a program by issuing a series of high level commands. This series of commands can be as much as an order of magnitude shorter than the program it describes.

KBEmacs is capable of operating on Ada and Lisp programs of realistic size and complexity. Although KBEmacs is neither fast enough nor robust enough to be considered a true prototype, both of these problems could be overcome if the system were to be reimplemented.

Index Terms—Computer-aided design, program editing, programming environments, reusable software components, Programmer's Apprentice.

I. INTRODUCTION

THE long term goal of the Programmer's Apprentice project is to develop a theory of programming (i.e., how expert programmers understand, design, implement, test, verify, modify, and document programs) and to automate the programming process. Recognizing that fully automatic programming is very far off, the current research is directed toward the intermediate goal of developing an intelligent computer assistant for programmers called the Programmer's Apprentice (PA). The intention is for the PA to act as a junior partner and critic, keeping track of details and assisting with the easy parts of the programming process while the programmer focuses on the hard parts of the process.

The Knowledge-Based Editor in Emacs (KBEmacs) is the current demonstration system implemented as part of the PA project. KBEmacs falls short of the PA because it focuses only on the task of program construction and because the depth of its understanding of a program is quite limited. However, KBEmacs demonstrates several of the capabilities of the PA and is a useful tool in its own right. The principle benefit of KBEmacs is that it makes it possible to construct a program rapidly and reliably by combining algorithmic fragments stored in a library.

The heart of this paper is a scenario (in Section II)

Manuscript received May 1, 1985; revised June 19, 1985. This work was supported in part by the Advanced Research Projects Agency of the Department of Defense under Office of Naval Research Contract N00014-80-C-0505, in part by the National Science Foundation under Grants MCS-7912179 and MCS-8117633, and in part by the International Business Machines Corporation.

The author is with the M.I.T. Artificial Intelligence Laboratory, 545 Technology Square, Cambridge, MA 02139.

showing the currently running KBEmacs system in action. The scenario shows a 58 line Ada [1] program being constructed using 6 simple KBEmacs commands. The remainder of this section discusses the basic goals of the PA project and the key AI ideas behind KBEmacs.

Goals of the PA Project

The PA project is pursuing two goals in parallel. On the one hand, the project uses programming as a domain in which to investigate human problem solving behavior. On the other hand, the project seeks to improve programmer productivity by developing programming tools based on AI techniques.

Dramatic improvements in programmer productivity have been frustratingly hard to achieve. One reason for this is that programming is a complex task which consists of a variety of subtasks (e.g., requirements analysis, design, implementation, testing, and maintenance). Since each of these subtasks is a significant part of the process as a whole, it is impossible to get a dramatic increase in productivity without addressing at least most of these subtasks.

Looking back over the history of programming, only one development stands out as truly dramatic—the introduction of high level languages. High level languages have had a positive impact on almost every phase of the programming process by representing programs in a more concise and understandable way. They do this by delegating a variety of low level programming decisions (e.g., register allocation) to a compiler.

Using AI techniques, it may soon be possible to get a second dramatic improvement in programmer productivity by developing programming tools which can automatically perform middle level programming decisions (e.g., data structure selection). AI techniques make it possible to represent a great deal of knowledge about programming in general and then use this knowledge to understand particular programs. As has been demonstrated in other areas where AI techniques have been applied, this approach opens the door to intelligent behavior.

Although AI techniques hold considerable promise as the basis for advanced programming tools, a great deal more work has to be done. The PA projects seeks both to develop the additional techniques which will be needed and to build demonstration systems which illustrate the potential for AI-based tools.

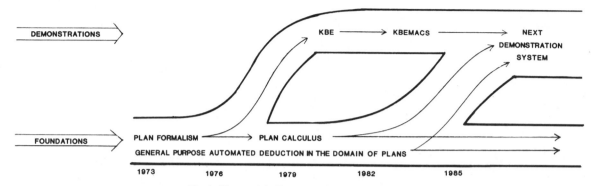

DEMONSTRATIONS

KBE ⟶ KBEMACS ⟶ NEXT
DEMONSTRATION
SYSTEM

FOUNDATIONS

PLAN FORMALISM ⟶ PLAN CALCULUS

GENERAL PURPOSE AUTOMATED DEDUCTION IN THE DOMAIN OF PLANS

1973   1976   1979   1982   1985

Fig. 1. History of the Programmer's Apprentice project.

History of the PA Project

Fig. 1 shows how KBEmacs fits into the PA project as a whole. The project consists of two principal lines of research: *foundations* and *demonstrations*. The first line seeks to develop new representation and reasoning techniques which can serve as the foundation for the PA. The second line of research seeks to construct demonstration systems based on these techniques and to experiment with how the PA might assist a programmer.

Besides laying out the basic concept of the PA, the most important contribution of the initial phase of the PA project (up to 1976) was the design of the *plan formalism* for representing knowledge about particular programs and about programming in general (see [32], [33], [46]). The plan formalism serves as the "mental language" of KBE-macs.

The first demonstration system constructed as part of the PA project was the Knowledge-Based Editor (KBE). KBE (see [49]) was a program editor which made it possible to operate directly on the algorithmic structure of a program rather than on its textual or syntactic structure. Like KBEmacs, the power of KBE came principally from the ability to construct a program out of algorithmic fragments.

The topic of this paper is KBEmacs, the second demonstration system. As the name Knowledge-Based Editor *in Emacs* is intended to imply, the most obvious difference between KBEmacs and KBE is that KBEmacs is tightly integrated with a standard Emacs-style [42] program editor. The integration makes it possible for the programmer to freely intermix knowledge-based program editing with text-based and syntax-based program editing. As discussed in Section VI, KBEmacs extends KBE in a number of other ways, coming a step closer to the PA. In particular, it increases the range of algorithmic fragments which can be manipulated; it allows a programmer to define new fragments; it supports the language Ada in addition to Lisp; and it can assist in the construction of program documentation.

During the implementation KBE and then KBEmacs, work has continued in parallel on the fundamental underpinnings of the PA. The central part of this work has been the refinement and extension of the plan formalism. This has resulted in the development of the *plan calculus* [28], [29] which extends the plan formalism by providing a firmer semantic basis and by increasing the range of in-

formation about programs and programming which can be represented. Work has also proceeded on the development of general purpose automated deduction methods which are appropriate for use in the domain of plans (see [30], [31], [39]).

There has been a significant amount of interaction between the work on foundations and the work on demonstrations. Several of the improvements in plans have been incorporated into demonstration systems and experience with the demonstration systems has motivated several of the improvements in plans. However, as highlighted by Fig. 1, the two lines of research have been largely separate. In particular, the magnitude of the implemetation required has forced there to be a large delay between the time when new fundamental concepts are developed and the time when they are incorporated into a demonstration system. Implementation has already begun on a new demonstration system which will incorporate all of the fundamental ideas developed to date.

Key AI Ideas Underlying KBEmacs

Three basic AI ideas—the assistant approach, cliches, and plans—underlie the PA project as a whole and KBEmacs in particular. These ideas define the approach taken and are the basis for the capabilities of the system. A fourth idea—general purpose automated deduction—is an important aspect of the project as a whole, but is not used by KBEmacs.

The Assistant Approach: When it is not possible to construct a fully automatic system for a task, it is nevertheless often possible to construct a system which can assist an expert in the task. In addition to being pragmatically useful, the assistant approach can lead to important insights into how to construct a fully automatic system.

Fig. 2 shows a programmer and an assistant interacting with a programming environment. Although presumably less knowledgeable, the assistant interacts with the tools in the environment (e.g., editors, compilers, debuggers) in the same way as the programmer and is capable of helping the programmer do what needs to be done. It is assumed that the programmer will not be able to delegate all of the work which needs to be done to the assistant and therefore will have to interact with the programming environment directly from time to time in order to do things which the assistant is not capable of doing.

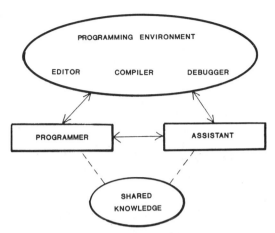

Fig. 2. A programming assistant.

The key issue in using an assistant effectively is *division of labor*. Since the programmer is more capable, the programmer will have to make the hard decisions about what should be done and what algorithms should be used. However, much of programming is quite mundane and can easily be done by an assistant. The key to cooperation between the programmer and the assistant is effective two-way communication—whose key in turn is *shared knowledge*. It would be impossibly tedious for the programmer to explain each decision to the assistant from first principles. Rather, the programmer needs to be able to rely on a body of intermediate-level shared knowledge in order to communicate decisions easily.

The discussion in the last two paragraphs applies equally well to human assistants and automated assistants. KBEmacs is intended with a programmer in the same way that a human assistant might. The long range goal of the PA is to create a "chief programmer team" wherein the programmer is the chief and the PA is the team.

An important benefit of the assistant is that it is nonintrusive in nature. The assistant is available for the programmer to use, but the programmer is not forced to use it. Note that this contrast sharply, for example, with program generators which completely take over large parts of the programming task and do not allow the programmer to have any control over them. A key goal of KBEmacs is to provide assistance to the programmer without preventing the programmer from doing simple things in the ordinary way. The intent is for the programmer to use standard programming tools whenever that makes things easy and to use KBEmacs only when doing so delivers real benefits.

A key part of the assistant approach as described above is the assumption that the assistant is significantly less knowledgeable than the programmer. There are situations where one might want an assistant system which was more knowledgeable than the programmer (e.g., a system which assists end users or neophyte programmers). However, KBEmacs does not attack these kinds of problems. The goal of KBEmacs is to make expert programmers superproductive rather than to make bad programmers good.

Cliches: The term *cliche* is used in this paper to refer to a standard method for dealing with a task—a lemma or

partial solution. In normal usage, the word cliche has a pejorative sound which connotes overuse and lack of creativity. However, it is not practical to be creative all the time. For example, when implementing a program, it is usually better to construct a reasonable program rapidly, than to construct a perfect program slowly.

A cliche consists of a set of *roles* embedded in an underlying *matrix*. The roles represent parts of the cliche which vary from one use of the cliche to the next but which have well defined purposes. The matrix specifies how the roles interact in order to achieve the goal of the cliche as a whole.

As an example of a cliche in the domain of programming, consider searching a one-dimensional structure. One way to do this is to use the cliche *sequential search*. This cliche enumerates the elements of a structure one at a time, tests each element to see if it satisfies the goal of the search, and returns the first element which passes the test. If no element passes the test, then a special value signifying the failure of the search is returned.

The cliche sequential search has three roles: the structure to be searched, the enumerator to use when searching the structure, and the test which defines the goal of the search. The matrix of the cliche specifies several different kinds of information. First, it specifies various pieces of fixed computation (i.e., nonvarying sets of operations). Second, it specifies the control flow and data flow which connect the roles with each other and with the fixed computation. For example, data flow connects the output of the enumerator with the input of the test and control flow specifies that the first time the test succeeds, the search should be terminated. Third, the matrix specifies various constraints on the roles (e.g., the constraint that the enumerator must be compatible with the data type of the structure to be searched).

When a cliche is used, it is *instantiated* by filling in the roles with computations which are appropriate to the task at hand. This creates an instance of the cliche which is specialized to the task. For example, in order to use the cliche sequential search to find the first negative element of a vector of integers, the vector would be used as the structure to be searched, the enumerator would be filled with computation which enumerates a vector, and the test would be filled with a test for negativity.

Given a particular domain, cliches provide a vocabulary of relevant intermediate and high level concepts. Having such a vocabulary is essential for effective reasoning and communication in the context of the domain. It is important to note that this is just as important for human thought as it is for machine-based thought.

Both men and machines are limited in the complexity of the lines of reasoning they can develop and understand. In order to deal with more complex lines of reasoning, intermediate level vocabulary must be introduced which summarizes parts of the line of reasoning. Once this intermediate vocabulary is fully understood, it can be used to express the full line of reasoning in a sufficiently straightforward way.

Men and machines are similarly limited in the complexity of the descriptions they can communicate. Just as it is in general never practical to reason about something from first principles, it is in general never practical to describe something in full detail from first principles. Effective communication depends on the shared knowledge of an appropriate vocabulary between speaker and hearer.

An essential part of the cliche concept is *reuse*. Once something has been thought out (or communicated) and given a name, then it can be reused as a component in future thinking (communication). There is an overhead in that something must be thought out very carefully in order for it to serve as a truly reusable component. However, if successful, this effort can be amortized over many instances of reuse.

A corollary of the cliche idea is that a library of cliches is often the most important part of an AI system. In KBEmacs, a large portion of the knowledge which is shared between man and machines is in the form of a library of algorithmic cliches. This library can be viewed as being a machine understandable definition of the vocabulary programmers use when talking about programs.

Plans: Selecting an appropriate knowledge representation is the key to applying AI to any task. As a practical matter, the only way to perform a complex (as opposed to merely large) operation is to find a knowledge representation in which the operation can be performed in a relatively straightforward way. To this end, many AI systems make use of the idea of a *plan*—a representation which is abstract in that it deliberately ignores some aspects of a problem in order to make it easier to reason about the remaining aspects of the problem.

To be useful, a knowledge representation must express all of the information relevant to the problem at hand. As discussed in detail in Section V, the plan formalism used by KBEmacs is designed to represent two basic kinds of information: the structure of particular programs and knowledge about cliches. The structure of a program is expressed essentially as a flowchart where data flow as well as control flow is represented by explicit arcs. In order to represent cliches, added support is provided for representing roles and constraints.

Equally important, a knowledge representation must facilitate the operations to be performed. The two key operations performed by KBEmacs are simple reasoning about programs (e.g., determining the source of a data flow) and combining cliches together to create programs. The plan formalism is specifically designed to support these operations. For example, the fact that data flow is expressed by explicit arcs makes it easy to determine the source of a given data flow.

An important aspect of the plan formalism is that it abstracts away from the syntactic features of programming languages and represents the semantic features of a program directly. Besides facilitating the manipulation of programs, this has the collateral advantage of making the internal operations of KBEmacs substantially programming language independent.

One of the most powerful ideas underlying AI systems is the idea of a *representation shift*—shifting from a representation where a problem is easy to state but hard to solve to a representation which may be less obvious but in which the problem is easy to solve. Much of the power of KBEmacs is derived more or less directly from the representation shift from the representation shift from program text to the plan formalism.

II. SCENARIO

This section uses a scenario to illustrate the various ways KBEmacs can be used. This scenario (which is an excerpt form a much larger scenario presented in [52]) shows the construction of an Ada program which prints out a report of information stored in a simple database. The database contains information about repairs performed on instructions sold by an imaginary marketing company. The company sells and maintains these instruments but does not build them. As illustrated in Fig. 3, the database is composed of four files: MODELS, DEFECTS, UNITS, and REPAIRS.

The MODELS file contains records specifying the name and maker of each model of instrument the company sells. The DEFECTS file specifies the defects which are known to occur on the various models. The UNITS file contains records corresponding to each instrument ever sold. Each unit record points to a chain of records in the REPAIRS file which describes the repairs which have been performed on the unit.

In addition to illustrating the structure of the database, Fig. 3 shows an example of the kind of data that might be placed in the database. For example, the second unit GA2-342 is a model GA2 (a gas analyzer) which has had three repairs performed on it (the fourth, second, and first repair records). The most recent repair (the fourth repair record) fixed an instance of defect GA-32 (a clogged gas injection port) which, in the repairman's opinion, was due to the fact that the port diameter was smaller than it should be.

In the interest of brevity, the database has been simplified to its barest essentials. A real database would probably contain more files, and would certainly have many more fields in each record. However, these simplifications do not alter the basic nature of the scenario. Adding more files or fields would make the program constructed in the scenario bigger, but it would not make it fundamentally more complex.

The scenario assumes that an Ada package MAINTENANCE_FILES defining the files in the example database has already been implemented (see Fig. 4). The package has a stereotyped structure which reflects the way in which the programmers at the marketing company prefer to do file I/O. Consider the file MODELS. Like the other files it is defined in five steps. A variable MODELS_NAME is defined which holds the external name of the file. A type MODELS_KEY_TYPE is defined so that other files can point to records in the file MODELS. A record type MODEL_TYPE is defined which specifies the fields of a record in the file. A package MODEL_IO is created which defines the I/O operations needed to operate on the file. This is done by instantiating a generic package KEYED_IO (defined in the package FUNCTIONS). Finally, a variable MODELS is defined which can hold an instance of the file.

The extended scenario in [52] shows that KBEmacs can

```
       the file MODELS

KEY    NAME        MAKER
OS1  Opal Sorter   Perth Mining
GA2  Gas Analyzer  Benson Labs


       the file DEFECTS

KEY          NAME              MODEL
OS-03  Power supply thermistor blown  OS1
GA-11  Control board cold solder joint GA2
GA-32  Clogged gas injection port     GA2


       the file UNITS

 KEY    MODEL REPAIR
OS1-271 OS1    3
GA2-342 GA2    4


       the file REPAIRS

INDEX  DATE   DEFECT      COMMENT              NEXT
  1  9/14/82  GA-32  Probably caused by humidity.  0
  2  1/23/84  GA-11  Took two days to find.        1
  3  2/25/84  OS-03  Sorter arm got stuck.         0
  4  3/19/84  GA-32  Port Diameter seems below specs. 2
```

Fig. 3. The example database.

```
with CALENDAR, FUNCTIONS;
use CALENDAR, FUNCTIONS;
package MAINTENANCE_FILES is
  MODELS_NAME: constant STRING := "models.data";
  type MODEL_KEY_TYPE is STRING(1..3);
  type MODEL_TYPE is
    record
       NAME: STRING(1..16);
       MAKER: STRING(1..16);
    end record;
  package MODEL_IO is new KEYED_IO(MODEL_TYPE, MODEL_KEY_TYPE);
  MODELS: MODEL_IO.FILE_TYPE;

  DEFECTS_NAME: constant STRING := "defects.data";
  type DEFECT_KEY_TYPE is STRING(1..5);
  type DEFECT_TYPE is
    record
       NAME: STRING(1..32);
       MODEL: MODEL_KEY_TYPE;
    end record;
  package DEFECT_IO is new KEYED_IO(DEFECT_TYPE, DEFECT_KEY_TYPE);
  DEFECTS: DEFECT_IO.FILE_TYPE;

  REPAIRS_NAME: constant STRING := "repairs.data";
  subtype REPAIR_INDEX_TYPE is INDEX_TYPE;
  type REPAIR_TYPE is
    record
       DATE: TIME;
       DEFECT: DEFECT_KEY_TYPE;
       COMMENT: STRING(1..32);
       NEXT: REPAIR_INDEX_TYPE;
    end record;
  package REPAIR_IO is new CHAINED_IO(REPAIR_TYPE, REPAIR_INDEX_TYPE);
  REPAIRS: REPAIR_IO.FILE_TYPE;

  UNITS_NAME: constant STRING := "units.data";
  type UNIT_KEY_TYPE is STRING(1..7);
  type UNIT_TYPE is
    record
       MODEL: MODEL_KEY_TYPE;
       REPAIR: REPAIR_INDEX_TYPE;
    end record;
  package UNIT_IO is new KEYED_IO(UNIT_TYPE, UNIT_KEY_TYPE);
  UNITS: UNIT_IO.FILE_TYPE;
end MAINTENANCE_FILES;
```

Fig. 4. The Ada definition of the example database.

be used to assist in the implementation of a declarative package such as MAINTENANCE_FILES just as it can be used to assist in the implementation of an ordinary program. More importantly, KBEmacs is able to understand the package which results. As will be illustrated below, KBEmacs can use its understanding of the structure of a file in order to assist a programmer who is writing a program which uses the file.

Cliches

The heart of KBEmacs is a library of programming cliches. These cliches provide the basic vocabulary used

in the communication between man and machine and embody most of the knowledge which is shared between the programmer and KBEmacs. One of the basic assumptions underlying KBEmacs is that the knowledge of cliches is indeed shared between man and machine—i.e., that the programmer is aware of at least the basic features of the various cliches. In consonance with this, it is important for the reader to develop an understanding of what these cliches are like before looking at the scenario below.

As a simple example of a cliche, consider the cliche equality_with_epsilon shown in Fig. 5. This cliche compares two numbers and returns a Boolean value which specifies whether or not the numbers differ by less than a given epsilon. Like any cliche, the cliche equality_with_epsilon specifies some standard computation (e.g., computing the absolute value of a difference), some roles to be filled in (e.g., the inputs x and y), and the data flow and control flow which combine them together. A constraint is used to specify that a default value of 0.00001 should be used for epsilon.

In order to support the definition of cliches, Ada syntax is extended slightly. A new defining form "cliche" is introduced in analogy with an Ada procedure definition. This form specifies the name of the cliche, some declarations describing the cliche, and the computation corresponding to the cliche. The body is the same as the body of an Ada procedure definition. The roles of a cliche are represented by $\{\cdots\}$. In Fig. 5, the roles are the two input numbers and the value epsilon.

When communicating with KBEmacs, an instance of a cliche is referred to by using an indefinite noun phrase—e.g., "an equality_within_epsilon of A and B". Such a phrase specifies the name of the cliche and may specify values which fill roles of the cliche. The "primary roles" declaration specifies which roles can be specified in such a noun phrase and the order in which they must be specified.

The "comment" declaration in the cliche definition is used for generating brief descriptions of instances of the cliche. Role references (represented by $\{\cdots\}$) in the comment string are replaced by descriptions of the actual computations filling the roles. For example, the cliche instance referred to in the last paragraph would be briefly described by saying that it "determines whether A and B differ by less than 0.00001". The "described roles" declaration is used for generating in-depth descriptions of instances of the cliche. As will be discussed in conjunction with Fig. 9 below, this declaration specifies which roles should be described in detail when constructing a comment for a program.

The "constraints" declaration is used to specify constraints which are part of the cliche. Constraint expressions are specified as a combination of ordinary Ada code and $\{\cdots\}$ annotation referring to roles. Here a simple constraint specifies a default value which will be used if no other value is specified for the epsilon role. More complex constraints will be discussed below.

Machine Understandable Annotation

Before looking at additional cliches it is useful to look

```
cliche EQUALITY_WITHIN_EPSILON is
   primary roles X, Y;
   described roles X, Y, EPSILON;
   comment "determines whether {the x} and {the y}
             differ by less than {the epsilon}";
   constraints
      DEFAULT({the epsilon}, 0.00001);
   end constraints;

begin
   return abs({the input x} - {the input y}) < {the epsilon};
end EQUALITY_WITHIN_EPSILON;
```

Fig. 5. The cliche equality_within_epsilon.

at the notation {···} in more detail. The most common use of {···} is to represent roles; however, it is not the only use. This extension to Ada syntax is provided to represent a variety of machine understandable program annotation.

There are two basic forms of the notation {···}. The first form is {*code, annotation*} which describes some feature of an existing part of a program. The second form is {*annotation*} which describes a nonexistent part of the program. In the latter case, the form acts as a place holder which specifies how the nonexistent part fits into the computation as a whole.

If the annotation in a {···} form begins with the word "the" then it specifies the name of a role (e.g., {the input x}). If code is provided as part of the annotation (e.g., {44, the input x}) then this indicates that the role is already filled in.

If a role name contains the word "input" then it is treated as logically being an input to the containing cliche. Similarly, if a role name contains the work "output" then it is treated as logically being an output of the containing cliche. Information about logical inputs and outputs is used to help determine the data flow between cliches when they are combined together. Most roles are neither inputs nor outputs but rather correspond to some internal part of the computation.

The name of a role can either by a simple noun phrase (e.g., {the input x}) or a compound phrase (e.g., {the empty_test of the enumerator}). A compound phrase implicitly specifies a higher level compound role (e.g., the enumerator) which contains the indicated subrole.

When {···} annotation acts as a place holder for a role, it is analogous to a function call. Often, as in Fig. 5, it will be analogous to a zero argument function call (e.g., {the input x}). However, one or more arguments can be specified. For example, the form {the operation}(DATA) specifies that the function filling the operation role should use as an input the value of the variable DATA.

A kind of annotation unrelated to roles is illustrated by the form {DATA,modified}. This specifies that the given instance of the variable DATA is being side-effected. For example, in the form F(X, {Y, modified}) the annotation specifies that the function F side-effects its second argument. This kind of annotation is used by KBEmacs as part of the basis for understanding the side-effects in a program.

The Cliche File_Enumeration

The cliche equality_within_epsilon is very simple in na-

```
cliche FILE_ENUMERATION is
   primary roles FILE;
   described roles FILE;
   comment "enumerates the records in {the file}";
   constraints
      RENAME("DATA_RECORD", SINGULAR_FORM({the file}));
      DEFAULT({the file_name}, CORRESPONDING_FILE_NAME({the file}));
   end constraints;

   FILE: {};
   DATA_RECORD: {};
begin
   FILE := {the input file};
   OPEN(FILE, IN_FILE, {the file_name});
   while not {END_OF_FILE, the empty_test}(FILE) loop
      {READ, the element_accessor}(FILE, DATA_RECORD);
      {DATA_RECORD, the output data_record};
   end loop;
   CLOSE(FILE);
exception
   when DEVICE_ERROR | END_ERROR | NAME_ERROR | STATUS_ERROR =>
      CLOSE(FILE); PUT("Data Base Inconsistent");
   when others => CLOSE(FILE); raise;
end FILE_ENUMERATION;
```

Fig. 6. The cliche file_enumeration.

ture and could have been represented as a subroutine. A key feature of cliches is that they are capable of representing algorithmic fragments which cannot be usefully expressed as subroutines. For example, the cliche file_enumeration (see Fig. 6) captures the concept of reading the records in a file, enumerating them sequentially. This cliche can be combined together with other looping cliches in order to efficiently perform various operations on files.

The cliche file_enumeration is a member of a class of cliches referred to as *enumerators*. In general, enumerators have five roles. An input role corresponds to the aggregate structure to be enumerated. An *empty_test* determines whether all of the elements in the aggregate structure have been enumerated and therefore whether the enumeration should be terminated. An *element_accessor* accesses the current element in the aggregate. A *step* steps from one element of the aggregate structure to the next. An output role identifies the individual elements enumerated so that they can be conveniently referred to when communicating with KBEmacs.

In the cliche file_enumeration, the input role is the file to be enumerated. The empty_test is the function END_OF_FILE. The procedure READ corresponds to both the element_accessor and the step. (Stepping occurs as a side-effect of the procedure READ. In addition to reading a record from a file and returning it in the variable which is its second argument, the procedure READ moves from one record to the next.) The output role specifies that the variable DATA_RECORD contains the enumerated records.

The cliche file_enumeration specifies a number of things in addition to how to enumerate the records in the file. The cliche takes care of opening and closing the file. The exception handlers at the end of the begin block specify what to do when an interrupt occurs during the execution of the block. If the interrupt occurs when accessing the file then an error message is printed and the exception suppressed; otherwise, the exception is passed on to be handled at a higher level. In either case, the file is closed. The cliche also specifies what declarations to use. (The notation {} is used to represent things which must be present for syntactic completeness, but which are not important enough to be given names as explicit roles—e.g., the data types of the variables FILE and DATA_RECORD.)

An important issue underlying cliches in general is that they are not designed in isolation. Rather, they must be carefully designed to fit together with each other and with whatever programming conventions are in effect. Several programming conventions used by the marketing company are evident in the cliche file_enumeration.

The strong typing in Ada requires that there be different I/O functions for each type of file. In the cliche file_enumeration, it is assumed that overloading will be used so that these functions can always be referred to by their standard names (e.g., OPEN, CLOSE, READ).

Another convention revolves around the handling of exceptions. Each program written is required to be complete in that it explicitly checks for every kind of abnormal condition which could occur. However, programs are allowed to assume that the database files are in a consistent state. For example, while the cliche file_enumeration explicitly checks for the end of the file being enumerated, it does not check that the file actually exists before opening it. Rather, it is assumed that the cliche will only be used to operate on files which are known to exist when the data base is consistent. In order to deal with the fact that, in extraordinary circumstances, the database might not be in a consistent state, a single blanket exception handler is included as part of the outermost block of every program that accesses any files. This exception handler is included in the cliche file_enumeration (see Fig. 6) and discussed above.

The first constraint specified as part of the cliche file_enumeration suggests a name to use for the variable holding the records being enumerated. The name chosen reflects a convention governing the way files are named— the name of a file and the name of a variable holding a record in that file should be the plural and singular forms, respectively, of the same word. For example, if a variable is needed in order to hold a record in the file MODELS, it will be given the name MODEL.

The constraint RENAME is textual in nature. It replaces all instances of its first parameter with its second parameter. For example, if the file were specified to be the variable MODELS then the identifier DATA_RECORD would be changed MODEL. In addition to whole identifiers, parts of identifiers are also changed—if there were an identifier DATA_RECORD_KEY it would be changed to MODEL_KEY. It should be noted that renaming is convenient, but not a fundamental issue. It merely makes it easier for KBEmacs to generate aesthetic program code.

The second constraint specifed as part of the cliche file_enumeration specifies a default value for the file_name role. The function CORRESPONDING_FILE_NAME determines the appropriate external name to use when opening the file. This function depends on the convention that whenever a file is defined, a variable is defined which holds the name. The function CORRESPONDING_FILE_NAME works by looking at the package where the file is defined.

The Cliche Simple_Report

A cliche of central importance to the scenario is the cliche simple_report (see Fig. 7). This cliche specifies the

```
with CALENDAR, FUNCTIONS, TEXT_IO;
use CALENDAR, FUNCTIONS, TEXT_IO;
cliche SIMPLE_REPORT is
    primary roles ENUMERATOR, PRINT_ITEM, SUMMARY;
    described roles FILE_NAME, TITLE, ENUMERATOR, COLUMN_HEADINGS,
                    PRINT_ITEM, SUMMARY;
    comment "prints a report of
            {the input structure of the enumerator}";
    constraints
        DEFAULT({the file_name}, "report.txt");
        DERIVED({the line_limit},
                66-SIZE_IN_LINES({the print_item})
                  -SIZE_IN_LINES({the summary}));
        DEFAULT({the print_item},
                CORRESPONDING_PRINTING({the enumerator}));
        DEFAULT({the column_headings},
                CORRESPONDING_HEADINGS({the print_item}));
    end constraints;

    use INT_IO;
    CURRENT_DATE: constant STRING := FORMAT_DATE(CLOCK);
    DATA: {};
    REPORT: TEXT_IO.FILE_TYPE;
    TITLE: STRING(1..{});
    procedure CLEAN_UP is
    begin
        SET_OUTPUT(STANDARD_OUTPUT);
        CLOSE(REPORT);
    exception
        when STATUS_ERROR => return;
    end CLEAN_UP;
begin
    CREATE(REPORT, OUT_FILE, {the file_name});
    DATA := {the input structure of the enumerator};
    SET_OUTPUT(REPORT);
    TITLE := {the title};
    NEW_LINE(4); SET_COL(20); PUT(CURRENT_DATE); NEW_LINE(2);
    SET_COL(13); PUT(TITLE); NEW_LINE(60);
    while not {the empty_test of the enumerator}(DATA) loop
        if LINE > {the line_limit} then
            NEW_PAGE; NEW_LINE; PUT("Page: "); PUT(INTEGER(PAGE-1), 3);
            SET_COL(13); PUT(TITLE);
            SET_COL(61); PUT(CURRENT_DATE); NEW_LINE(2);
            {the column_headings}({CURRENT_OUTPUT, modified});
        end if;
        {the print_item}({CURRENT_OUTPUT, modified},
                         {the element_accessor of the enumerator}(DATA));
        DATA := {the step of the enumerator}(DATA);
    end loop;
    {the summary};
    CLEAN_UP;
exception
    when DEVICE_ERROR | END_ERROR | NAME_ERROR | STATUS_ERROR =>
        CLEAN_UP; PUT("Data Base Inconsistent");
    when others => CLEAN_UP; raise;
end SIMPLE_REPORT;
```

Fig. 7. The cliche simple_report.

high level structure of a simple reporting program. The cliche has seven roles. The *file_name* is the name of the file which will contain the report being produced. The *title* is printed on the title page and, along with the page number, at the top of each succeeding page of the report. The *enumerator* enumerates the elements of some aggregate data structure. The *print_item* is used to print out information about each of the enumerated elements. The *line_limit* is used to determine when a page break should be inserted in the report. The *column_headings* are printed at the top of each page of the report in order to explain the output of the print_item. The *summary* prints out some summary information at the end of the report. Note that the print_item, column_headings, and summary are all computations which side-effect the report file (which is used as the value of STANDARD_OUTPUT) by sending output to it.

The enumerator is a compound role which has the subroles typical of an enumerator (i.e., an input structure, empty_test, element_accessor, and step). These subroles can be filled individually, or they can be filled together as a unit by using an enumeration cliche (such as the cliche file_enumeration) which specifies values for each of them.

The most interesting feature of the cliche simple_report

is its constraints. The first constraint specifies a default value for the file_name role. The second constraint specifies that the line limit should be derived as 66 minus the number of lines printed by the print_item and the number of lines printed by the summary. Under the assumption that there is room for 66 lines (numbered 1 through 66), the constraint guarantees that, whenever the line number is less than or equal to the line limit, there will be room for both the print_item and the summary to be printed on the current page. Because the line_limit role is derived by this constraint the programmer never has to fill it in explicitly, and the role will be automatically updated whenever either the print_item or the summary is changed.

The final two constraints specify default values for the print_item and column_headings roles. The function CORRESPONDING_PRINTING determines what should be used to fill in the print_item role based on the type of object which is being enumerated. The function CORRESPONDING_HEADINGS determines what headings should be used based on the way the print_item is filled in.

The functions CORRESPONDING_PRINTING and CORRESPONDING_HEADINGS operate in one of two modes. In general, cliches will have been defined which specify how to print out a given type of object in a report, and how to print the corresponding headings. If this is the case, then the functions CORRESPONDING_PRINTING and CORRESPONDING_HEADINGS merely retrieve the appropriate cliches. However, if there are no such cliches, then the functions CORRESPONDING_PRINTING and CORRESPONDING_HEADINGS use a simple program generator in order to construct appropriate code based on the definition of the type of object in question.

Limits to the Power of Constraints

The power of a constraint follows directly from the power of the functions used in the constraining expression. Constraining expressions can utilize any of the standard Ada functions and operators, and the programmer is free to write additional functions. Therefore, theoretically, there are no limitations placed on the computation which can be performed by a constraint expression.

However, as a practical matter the power of constraints is limited by the fact that writing new functions to use in constraints is not particularly easy. A major problem is that instances of {···} annotation in constraint expressions evaluate to direct pointers into the internal knowledge representation used by KBEmacs. This allows for great flexibility in what can be done by constraint functions, but requires that the writer of a constraint function be conversant in this internal representation. In contrast, when defining the body of a cliche the programmer need not understand anything other than Ada and {···} annotation.

It is expected that the typical programmer will not write new functions to use in constraints, but rather will only write expressions which use predefined functions. As a result, the power of constraints is, in effect, limited by the constraint functions provided by the designer of the basic cliche library.

Viewed from this perspective, the constraints in the cliches above fall into three categories. It is expected that simple constraints such as the one deriving the line_limit role in the cliche simple_report (see Fig. 7) will be common. They depend only on standard functions and a few general purpose constraint functions such as SIZE_IN_LINES. There is no reason why such constraints could not be included as part of idiosyncratic cliches defined by programmers.

The constraint function CORRESPONDING_FILE_NAME (see Fig. 6) is at an intermediate level of complexity. It is plausible that such a function would be defined by a system programmer as part of defining an important group of cliches. It is even plausible that an ordinary programmer might use the function when defining a new cliche to add to the group. However, the constraint function is of no use outside of the group of cliches and it is not plausible that the typical programmer would define additional constraint functions at this level of complexity.

Finally, the inclusion of constraint functions such as CORRESPONDING_PRINTING and CORRESPONDING_HEADINGS (see Fig. 7) would seem to be an unusual event. Writing such a function not only requires an understanding of the internal knowledge representation used by KBEmacs, but is difficult in its own right. These constraint functions are included in the cliche simple_report in order to demonstrate the full power of constraints and to illustrate the way constraints can be used as an interface between KBEmacs and other programming tools—e.g., in this case a program generator.

Directions for a Human Assistant

In the following scenario, KBEmacs is used to construct a program UNIT_REPAIR_REPORT which prints out a report of all the repairs that have been performed on a given unit. Suppose that an expert programmer were asked to write the program UNIT_REPAIR_REPORT and decided to delegate the task to an (inexperienced) assistant. In order to tell the assistant what to do, the expert programmer might give directions like these:

Define a simple report program UNIT_REPAIR_REPORT. Enumerate the chain of repairs associated with a unit record, printing each one. Query the user for the key (UNIT_KEY) of the unit record to start from. Print the title ("Report of Repairs on Unit " & UNIT_KEY). Do not print a summary.

A key feature of these directions is that they refer to a significant amount of knowledge that the assistant is assumed to possess. In particular, they assume that the assistant understands the phrases "simple report," "enumerate the chain," and "query the user for the key." They also assume an understanding of the structure of the database of units and repairs. As we shall see, by using cliches such as simple report, a programmer can tell KBEmacs how to produce the program UNIT_REPAIR_REPORT by giving directions as a similar level of detail to the directions shown above.

Knowledge-Based Editing

The scenario below consists of a sequence of Lisp Machine screen images. These screens show snapshots of the Emacs-style Lisp Machine editor in which KBEmacs is embedded. Each of these screens has two parts [see Screen 1 (Fig. 8)]. The first two lines show a set of commands. The box which makes up most of the screen shows the Emacs buffer which is the result of these commands.

Boldface italics is used to highlight the changes in the buffer (in comparison to the previous screen) caused by the commands. Highlighting changed portions of the editor buffer is not currently supported by KBEmacs. However, whenever KBEmacs modifies the editor buffer, it positions the editing cursor (indicated by □ in the screens) at the beginning of the first significant change in the buffer.

Except for the boldface italics highlighting, the buffer images are shown exactly as they appear on the screen of the Lisp Machine when running KBEmacs on the example in the scenario.

Before beginning to construct the program UNIT_RE-PAIR_REPORT the programmer uses a standard Emacs command in order to create a file which will contain the program (see Screen 1). KBEmacs is implemented so that it is tightly integrated with Emacs. KBEmacs adds a variety of new editor commands without interfering with any of the standard commands. As a result, the scenario presented here uses standard editor commands in order to perform standard operations.

KBEmacs supports a new set of commands referred to as knowledge-based commands. These commands are specified in an extremely simple pseudo-English command language. Each knowledge-based command is a verb followed by one or more noun phrases. Automatic word completion is used to facilitate typing of the command language.

In order to begin the construction of the program UNIT_REPAIR_REPORT, the programmer uses the knowledge-based command "Define". The command "Define a simple_report program UNIT_REPAIR_REPORT." (see Screen 1) specifies both the name of the program and the cliche which should be used as the top level structure of the program. (If a word in a command is typed using capital letters (e.g., "UNIT_REPAIR_REPORT" as opposed to "program") it is assumed to be a literal name or a code fragment and is interpreted without regard for any special meaning it may have in the command language.)

KBEmacs communicates the results of a knowledge-based command to the programmer (and to the rest of the Lisp Machine system) by directly modifying the text in the editor buffer. In this case, an instance of the cliche simple_report is inserted in the buffer.

For the most part, the code in Screen 1 is exactly the same as the code in the definition of the cliche simple_report (see Fig. 7). However, there are several key differences. For example, the file_name and line_limit roles have been filled in, since they are specified by constraints. (The line_limit role has been given the value 64 under the default assumption, made by the function SIZE_IN _LINES, that the print_item and summary will each take up one output line.)

Another difference between the code in Screen 1 and the code in the definition of the cliche is that the {···}

A file is created using a standard Emacs command.
`Define a simple_report program UNIT_REPAIR_REPORT.`

```
□ith CALENDAR, FUNCTIONS, TEXT_IO;
use CALENDAR, FUNCTIONS, TEXT_IO;
procedure UNIT_REPAIR_REPORT is
    use INT_IO;
    CURRENT_DATE: constant STRING := FORMAT_DATE(CLOCK);
    DATA: {};
    REPORT: TEXT_IO.FILE_TYPE;
    TITLE: STRING(1..{});
    procedure CLEAN_UP is
        begin
            SET_OUTPUT(STANDARD_OUTPUT);
            CLOSE(REPORT);
        exception
            when STATUS_ERROR => return;
        end CLEAN_UP;
begin
    CREATE(REPORT, OUT_FILE, "report.txt");
    TITLE := {the title};
    SET_OUTPUT(REPORT);
    NEW_LINE(4); SET_COL(20); PUT(CURRENT_DATE); NEW_LINE(2);
    SET_COL(13); PUT(TITLE); NEW_LINE(60);
    DATA := {the input structure of the enumerator};
    while not {the empty_test of the enumerator}(DATA) loop
        if LINE > 64 then
            NEW_PAGE; NEW_LINE; PUT("Page: "); PUT(INTEGER(PAGE-1), 3);
            SET_COL(13); PUT(TITLE);
            SET_COL(61); PUT(CURRENT_DATE); NEW_LINE(2);
            {the column_headings}({CURRENT_OUTPUT, modified});
        end if;
        {the print_item}({CURRENT_OUTPUT, modified},
                         {the element_accessor of the enumerator}(DATA));
        DATA := {the step of the enumerator}(DATA);
    end loop;
    {the summary};
    CLEAN_UP;
exception
    when DEVICE_ERROR | END_ERROR | NAME_ERROR | STATUS_ERROR =>
        CLEAN_UP; PUT("Data Base Inconsistent");
    when others => CLEAN_UP; raise;
end UNIT_REPAIR_REPORT;
```

Fig. 8. Screen 1.

annotation marking the file_name and the line_limit roles has been suppressed. Once a role is filled in, the annotation indicating where it is located is, in general, no longer displayed.

Suppressing the annotation of filled roles is an aesthetic choice. For the task of program construction, suppressing such annotation is helpful because it reduces visual clutter and highlights the roles which are not yet filled in. In other situations (e.g., documentation) it might be beneficial for KBEmacs to redisplay this annotation.

Although KBEmacs does not display annotation for filled in roles, it remembers this information as part of its understanding of the program. In addition, KBEmacs remembers what cliches have been used to build up a program. As will be illustrated shortly, there are a number of ways in which KBEmacs can use each of these types of information to assist the programmer.

The above discussion brings up the interesting question of exactly what the purpose of the code produced by KBEmacs is. Clearly it is not a complete representation for everything that KBEmacs knows about a program. Rather, it fulfills two quite distinct purposes.

The first purpose of the code is to serve as the medium of communication between KBEmacs and the rest of the programming environment. For example, KBEmacs must create ordinary Ada code for a program so that it can be compiled by a standard Ada compiler. This purpose requires only that the code produced correctly represent the algorithms being used.

The second purpose of the code is to serve as the primary medium of communication between KBEmacs and the programmer. At each moment, the code summarized the net effect of the knowledge-based commands given so far. This purpose requires that the code produced be reasonably aesthetic so that it will be easily readable. In addition, note that since the programmer can freely edit the code at any time, the code is a two-way communication channel.

Propagation of Design Decisions

The central design decision in any report program is deciding what values are to be reported. When using the cliche simple_report, this decision is specified by selecting an appropriate enumerator. In Screen 2 (Fig. 9), the programmer uses the command "Fill the enumerator with a chain_enumeration of UNITS and REPAIRS." in order to specify that the enumerator should be a chain_enumeration which enumerates a chain of records in the file REPAIRS pointed to from a record in the file UNITS.

The knowledge-based command "Fill" specifies that an instance of a cliche is to be used to fill in an unfilled role. It should be noted that definite noun phrases in knowledge-based command are disambiguated with respect to the position of the cursor. As a result, the phrase "the enumerator" in the knowledge-based command is interpreted to mean the enumerator of the program UNIT_REPAIR_REPORT because the cursor was positioned in this program when the command was typed (see Screen1).

An important thing to notice about Screen 2 is that all of the subroles which are part of the enumerator of the program have been filled in at once. The cliche chain_enumeration (like the cliche file_enumeration in Fig. 6) specifies these roles as a logical unit even though the roles are distributed through the program. (KBEmacs places the cursor in Screen 2 on the read of the file UNITS on the theory that changes to the body of a procedure are more interesting than changes to the declarations or to the code which opens files.)

Another thing to notice about the program in Screen 2 is that it no longer uses the variable DATA but rather the more informative variable name UNIT. The readability of a program depends to a surprising extent on how the data flow is implemented and, in particular, on what variable names are used. Therefore, KBEmacs works hard to use nesting of expressions where appropriate and to pick the best variable names possible. In this case, the variable name UNIT is chosen because it is specifically suggested by a constraint in the cliche chain_enumeration.

Once the enumerator has been specified, the constraints (described above) in the cliche simple_report fill in most of the rest of the program UNIT_REPAIR_REPORT. It is assumed that two cliches (PRINT_REPAIR and PRINT_REPAIR_HEADINGS) have already been defined which specify how to print a repair record and the associated column headings. The scenario in [52] shows how these cliches are defined as a semiautomatic consequence of using KBEmacs to implement the package MAINTENANCE_FILES.

When the print_item is filled in in Screen 2, the line_limit is changed from 64 to 63 since the code used to fill the print_item generates two lines of output, whereas the default assumption used by the constraint function SIZE_IN_LINES in Screen 1 was that the print_item would produce one line of output. This automatic updating of the line_limit role is a good example of the way KBEmacs can

Fill the enumerator with a chain_enumeration of UNITS and REPAIRS.

```
with CALENDAR, FUNCTIONS, MAINTENANCE_FILES, TEXT_IO;
use CALENDAR, FUNCTIONS, MAINTENANCE_FILES, TEXT_IO;
procedure UNIT_REPAIR_REPORT is
    use DEFECT_IO, REPAIR_IO, UNIT_IO, INT_IO;
    CURRENT_DATE: constant STRING := FORMAT_DATE(CLOCK);
    DEFECT: DEFECT_TYPE;
    REPAIR: REPAIR_TYPE;
    REPAIR_INDEX: REPAIR_INDEX_TYPE;
    REPORT: TEXT_IO.FILE_TYPE;
    TITLE: STRING(1..{});
    UNIT: UNIT_TYPE;
    procedure CLEAN_UP is
        begin
            SET_OUTPUT(STANDARD_OUTPUT);
            CLOSE(DEFECTS); CLOSE(REPAIRS); CLOSE(UNITS); CLOSE(REPORT);
        exception
            when STATUS_ERROR => return;
        end CLEAN_UP;
begin
    OPEN(DEFECTS, IN_FILE, DEFECTS_NAME);
    OPEN(REPAIRS, IN_FILE, REPAIRS_NAME);
    OPEN(UNITS, IN_FILE, UNITS_NAME);
    CREATE(REPORT, OUT_FILE, "report.txt");
    TITLE := {the title};
    SET_OUTPUT(REPORT);
    NEW_LINE(4); SET_COL(20); PUT(CURRENT_DATE); NEW_LINE(2);
    SET_COL(13); PUT(TITLE); NEW_LINE(60);
    READ(UNITS, UNIT, {the main_file_key});
    REPAIR_INDEX := UNIT.REPAIR;
    while not NULL_INDEX(REPAIR_INDEX) loop
        READ(REPAIRS, REPAIR, REPAIR_INDEX);
        if LINE > 63 then
            NEW_PAGE; NEW_LINE; PUT("Page: "); PUT(INTEGER(PAGE-1), 3);
            SET_COL(13); PUT(TITLE);
            SET_COL(61); PUT(CURRENT_DATE); NEW_LINE(2);
            PUT("  Date    Defect   Description/Comment"); NEW_LINE(2);
        end if;
        READ(DEFECTS, DEFECT, REPAIR.DEFECT);
        PUT(FORMAT_DATE(REPAIR.DATE)); SET_COL(13); PUT(REPAIR.DEFECT);
        SET_COL(20); PUT(DEFECT.NAME); NEW_LINE;
        SET_COL(22); PUT(REPAIR.COMMENT); NEW_LINE;
        REPAIR_INDEX := REPAIR.NEXT;
    end loop;
    {the summary};
    CLEAN_UP;
exception
    when DEVICE_ERROR | END_ERROR | NAME_ERROR | STATUS_ERROR =>
        CLEAN_UP; PUT("Data Base Inconsistent");
    when others => CLEAN_UP; raise;
end UNIT_REPAIR_REPORT;
```

Fig. 9. Screen 2.

enhance program reliability. The main leverage KBEmacs applies to the reliability problem is that each cliche is internally consistent. The use of constraints can help maintain this consistency.

It is interesting to note that if KBEmacs had not updated the line_limit role, the programmer might not have realized that it needed to be updated. The bug which would result, although minor, would have the pernicious quality of being rather hard to detect during program testing since the bug only manifests itself when the program attempts to print the summary as the last line of a page.

Taking Care of Details

Another thing to note about the code in Screen 2 is that a number of variable declarations and the like have been added to the program. This is an example of the fact that KBEmacs can automatically take care of several kinds of programming details. It is interesting to note that the data types in these declarations are not specified as part of the cliches used. Rather, KBEmacs computes what data types should be used based on the definitions of the relevant files and the specifications for the procedures which operate on the variables.

After specifying the enumerator in Screen 2, the only roles which are left unfilled are the title, the main_file_key, and the summary. In Screen 3 (Fig. 10), the programmer specifies that the user of the program UNIT_REPAIR_REPORT should be queried in order to determine what main file key to use. This is done with the command "Fill

Fill the main_file_key with a query_user_for_key of UNITS.

```
with CALENDAR, FUNCTIONS, MAINTENANCE_FILES, TEXT_IO;
use CALENDAR, FUNCTIONS, MAINTENANCE_FILES, TEXT_IO;
procedure UNIT_REPAIR_REPORT is
   use DEFECT_IO, REPAIR_IO, UNIT_IO, INT_IO;
   CURRENT_DATE: constant STRING := FORMAT_DATE(CLOCK);
   DEFECT: DEFECT_TYPE;
   REPAIR: REPAIR_TYPE;
   REPAIR_INDEX: REPAIR_INDEX_TYPE;
   REPORT: TEXT_IO.FILE_TYPE;
   TITLE: STRING(1..{});
   UNIT: UNIT_TYPE;
   UNIT_KEY: UNIT_KEY_TYPE;
   procedure CLEAN_UP is
      begin
         SET_OUTPUT(STANDARD_OUTPUT);
         CLOSE(DEFECTS); CLOSE(REPAIRS); CLOSE(UNITS); CLOSE(REPORT);
      exception
         when STATUS_ERROR => return;
      end CLEAN_UP;
begin
   OPEN(DEFECTS, IN_FILE, DEFECTS_NAME);
   OPEN(REPAIRS, IN_FILE, REPAIRS_NAME);
   OPEN(UNITS, IN_FILE, UNITS_NAME);
   CREATE(REPORT, OUT_FILE, "report.txt");
   TITLE := {the title};
   SET_OUTPUT(REPORT);
   NEW_LINE(4); SET_COL(20); PUT(CURRENT_DATE); NEW_LINE(2);
   SET_COL(13); PUT(TITLE); NEW_LINE(60);
   loop
      begin
         NEW_LINE; PUT("Enter UNIT Key: "); GET(UNIT_KEY);
         READ(UNITS, UNIT, UNIT_KEY);
         exit;
      exception
         when END_ERROR => PUT("Invalid UNIT Key"); NEW_LINE;
      end;
   end loop;
   READ(UNITS, UNIT, UNIT_KEY);
   REPAIR_INDEX := UNIT.REPAIR;
   while not NULL_INDEX(REPAIR_INDEX) loop
      READ(REPAIRS, REPAIR, REPAIR_INDEX);
      if LINE > 63 then
         NEW_PAGE; NEW_LINE; PUT("Page: "); PUT(INTEGER(PAGE-1), 3);
         SET_COL(13); PUT(TITLE);
         SET_COL(61); PUT(CURRENT_DATE); NEW_LINE(2);
         PUT("  Date       Defect     Description/Comment"); NEW_LINE(2);
      end if;
      READ(DEFECTS, DEFECT, REPAIR.DEFECT);
      PUT(FORMAT_DATE(REPAIR.DATE)); SET_COL(13); PUT(REPAIR.DEFECT);
      SET_COL(20); PUT(DEFECT.NAME); NEW_LINE;
      SET_COL(22); PUT(REPAIR.COMMENT); NEW_LINE;
      REPAIR_INDEX := REPAIR.NEXT;
   end loop;
   {the summary};
   CLEAN_UP;
exception
   when DEVICE_ERROR | END_ERROR | NAME_ERROR | STATUS_ERROR =>
      CLEAN_UP; PUT("Data Base Inconsistent");
   when others => CLEAN_UP; raise;
end UNIT_REPAIR_REPORT;
```

Fig. 10. Screen 3.

the main_file_key with a query_user_for _key of UNITS." In addition to getting a key from the user, the cliche query_user_for_key checks the key to determine whether the key is valid. In order to check the key, the cliche attempts to read the corresponding record from the file. If the read fails, then the user is asked for a different key.

Both the code in Screen 2 and the cliche query_user _for_key specify that the file UNITS should be opened and closed. If nothing more were said this would cause the file UNITS to be opened twice and closed twice in Screen 3. In order to prevent this from happening, KBEmacs determines which files are required to be open and makes sure that each file is opened only once. This is another example of the way KBEmacs can help a programmer by taking care of details. Special provision is made for the opening and closing of files because this is an important efficiency issue in file oriented I/O.

Modification

The code in Screen 3 is inefficient in that it reads the same record of the file UNITS twice. The record is read twice because it is read for two different reasons by two different cliches. The cliche query_user_for_key reads the record in order to determine that the key is a valid key and the cliche chain_enumeration reads the record in order to obtain the index of the first repair record.

The existence of this problem illustrates that, although KBEmacs is capable of automatically sharing multiple opens and closes of a file, it is not capable of automatically sharing redundant code in general. However, KBEmacs provides a knowledge-based command "Share" which can assist a programmer in sharing code.

From the point of view of KBEmacs, the most difficult thing about sharing two computations is detecting where sharing might be useful. On the other hand, it is quite easy for KBEmacs to check that two computations can be shared and to modify a program in order to effect a given sharing.

From the point of view of the programmer, the most difficult thing about sharing two computations is verifying that the two computations are in fact identical and can therefore actually be shared. The problem is that the existence of side-effects and the like can prevent the sharing of computations which otherwise appear identical.

The divergence in abilities between the programmer and KBEmacs with regard to sharing provides an opportunity for a useful division of labor. In Screen 4 (Fig. 11), the programmer determines that the two calls on READ of the file UNITS should be shared and asks KBEmacs to change the program so that they are shared. KBEmacs checks that the two calls on READ are in fact reading the same record and that they can be shared. It then modifies the program by removing the second call on READ.

The sharing shown in Screen 4 is a relatively trivial example. KBEmacs is capable of handling much more complicated cases. There are two ways in which things can become more complex. First, if side-effects are involved, it can be much harder to determine whether the two computations to be shared can indeed be shared. KBEmacs is able to deal with side-effects because the system understands which functions have side-effects and the data flow in a plan takes side-effects into account. Second, sharing two computations can require more extensive changes in the program text. In particular, once one of the two computations has been removed, a variable usually has to be introduced so that the value created by the remaining computation can be used in two places. Here the changes are very simple because, in Screen 3, the procedure READ already forces the use of a variable and KBEmacs used the same variable for both READS. (KBEmacs tries to reuse variable names in logically related contexts in order to reduce the number of variables in a program.)

KBEmacs supports a second knowledge-based command ("Replace") which facilitates program modification. This command makes it easy for a programmer to change the way a role is filled. For example the programmer might say "Replace the enumerator with a file_enumeration of REPAIRS." This would change the program UNIT_REPAIR_REPORT so that it printed out every repair record. The key underpinning of the "Replace" command is the fact that KBEmacs remembers the positions of roles in a program even after they are filled in.

Share the first READ and the second READ.
Direct editing is performed with standard Emacs commands.

```
with CALENDAR, FUNCTIONS, MAINTENANCE_FILES, TEXT_IO;
use CALENDAR, FUNCTIONS, MAINTENANCE_FILES, TEXT_IO;
procedure UNIT_REPAIR_REPORT is
    use DEFECT_IO, REPAIR_IO, UNIT_IO, INT_IO;
    CURRENT_DATE: constant STRING := FORMAT_DATE(CLOCK);
    DEFECT: DEFECT_TYPE;
    REPAIR: REPAIR_TYPE;
    REPAIR_INDEX: REPAIR_INDEX_TYPE;
    REPORT: TEXT_IO.FILE_TYPE;
    TITLE: STRING(1..{});
    UNIT: UNIT_TYPE;
    UNIT_KEY: UNIT_KEY_TYPE;
    procedure CLEAN_UP is
        begin
            SET_OUTPUT(STANDARD_OUTPUT);
            CLOSE(DEFECTS); CLOSE(REPAIRS); CLOSE(UNITS); CLOSE(REPORT);
        exception
            when STATUS_ERROR => return;
        end CLEAN_UP;
begin
    OPEN(DEFECTS, IN_FILE, DEFECTS_NAME);
    OPEN(REPAIRS, IN_FILE, REPAIRS_NAME);
    OPEN(UNITS, IN_FILE, UNITS_NAME);
    CREATE(REPORT, OUT_FILE, "report.txt");
    TITLE := "Report of Repairs on Unit " & UNIT_KEY;
    SET_OUTPUT(REPORT);
    NEW_LINE(4); SET_COL(20); PUT(CURRENT_DATE); NEW_LINE(2);
    SET_COL(13); PUT(TITLE); NEW_LINE(60);
    loop
        begin
            NEW_LINE; PUT("Enter UNIT Key: "); GET(UNIT_KEY);
            READ(UNITS, UNIT, UNIT_KEY);
            exit;
        exception
            when END_ERROR => PUT("Invalid UNIT Key"); NEW_LINE;
        end;
    end loop;
    REPAIR_INDEX := UNIT.REPAIR;
    while not NULL_INDEX(REPAIR_INDEX) loop
        READ(REPAIRS, REPAIR, REPAIR_INDEX);
        if LINE > 63 then
            NEW_PAGE; NEW_LINE; PUT("Page: "); PUT(INTEGER(PAGE-1), 3);
            SET_COL(13); PUT(TITLE);
            SET_COL(61); PUT(CURRENT_DATE); NEW_LINE(2);
            PUT("  Date     Defect   Description/Comment"); NEW_LINE(2);
        end if;
        READ(DEFECTS, DEFECT, REPAIR.DEFECT);
        PUT(FORMAT_DATE(REPAIR.DATE)); SET_COL(13); PUT(REPAIR.DEFECT);
        SET_COL(20); PUT(DEFECT.NAME); NEW_LINE;
        SET_COL(22); PUT(REPAIR.COMMENT); NEW_LINE;
        REPAIR_INDEX := REPAIR.NEXT;
    end loop;
    {the summary};
    CLEAN_UP;
exception
    when DEVICE_ERROR | END_ERROR | NAME_ERROR | STATUS_ERROR =>
        CLEAN_UP; PUT("Data Base Inconsistent");
    when others => CLEAN_UP; raise;
end UNIT_REPAIR_REPORT;
```

Fig. 11. Screen 4.

Remove the summary.
The program is compiled using a standard Emacs command.

```
with CALENDAR, FUNCTIONS, MAINTENANCE_FILES, TEXT_IO;
use CALENDAR, FUNCTIONS, MAINTENANCE_FILES, TEXT_IO;
procedure UNIT_REPAIR_REPORT is
    use DEFECT_IO, REPAIR_IO, UNIT_IO, INT_IO;
    CURRENT_DATE: constant STRING := FORMAT_DATE(CLOCK);
    DEFECT: DEFECT_TYPE;
    REPAIR: REPAIR_TYPE;
    REPAIR_INDEX: REPAIR_INDEX_TYPE;
    REPORT: TEXT_IO.FILE_TYPE;
    TITLE: STRING(1..33);
    UNIT: UNIT_TYPE;
    UNIT_KEY: UNIT_KEY_TYPE;
    procedure CLEAN_UP is
        begin
            SET_OUTPUT(STANDARD_OUTPUT);
            CLOSE(DEFECTS); CLOSE(REPAIRS); CLOSE(UNITS); CLOSE(REPORT);
        exception
            when STATUS_ERROR => return;
        end CLEAN_UP;
begin
    OPEN(DEFECTS, IN_FILE, DEFECTS_NAME);
    OPEN(REPAIRS, IN_FILE, REPAIRS_NAME);
    OPEN(UNITS, IN_FILE, UNITS_NAME);
    CREATE(REPORT, OUT_FILE, "report.txt");
    loop
        begin
            NEW_LINE; PUT("Enter UNIT Key: "); GET(UNIT_KEY);
            READ(UNITS, UNIT, UNIT_KEY);
            exit;
        exception
            when END_ERROR => PUT("Invalid UNIT Key"); NEW_LINE;
        end;
    end loop;
    TITLE := "Report of Repairs on Unit " & UNIT_KEY;
    SET_OUTPUT(REPORT);
    NEW_LINE(4); SET_COL(20); PUT(CURRENT_DATE); NEW_LINE(2);
    SET_COL(13); PUT(TITLE); NEW_LINE(60);
    REPAIR_INDEX := UNIT.REPAIR;
    while not NULL_INDEX(REPAIR_INDEX) loop
        READ(REPAIRS, REPAIR, REPAIR_INDEX);
        if LINE > 64 then
            NEW_PAGE; NEW_LINE; PUT("Page: "); PUT(INTEGER(PAGE-1), 3);
            SET_COL(13); PUT(TITLE);
            SET_COL(61); PUT(CURRENT_DATE); NEW_LINE(2);
            PUT("  Date     Defect   Description/Comment"); NEW_LINE(2);
        end if;
        READ(DEFECTS, DEFECT, REPAIR.DEFECT);
        PUT(FORMAT_DATE(REPAIR.DATE)); SET_COL(13); PUT(REPAIR.DEFECT);
        SET_COL(20); PUT(DEFECT.NAME); NEW_LINE;
        SET_COL(22); PUT(REPAIR.COMMENT); NEW_LINE;
        REPAIR_INDEX := REPAIR.NEXT;
    end loop;
    CLEAN_UP;
exception
    when DEVICE_ERROR | END_ERROR | NAME_ERROR | STATUS_ERROR =>
        CLEAN_UP; PUT("Data Base Inconsistent");
    when others => CLEAN_UP; raise;
end UNIT_REPAIR_REPORT;
```

Fig. 12. Screen 5.

Direct Editing

After sharing the two reads, the programmer uses ordinary Emacs commands to fill in the title role (see Screen 4). The programmer could have used a knowledge-based command in order to fill in the title. However, the programmer judged that ordinary editing would be simpler.

In addition to filling in roles, the programmer can prune away unneeded ones. In general, cliches (such as simple_report) are defined so that they include a wide variety of features on the theory that it is easier for the programmer to prune things away than to think them up. In Screen 5 (Fig. 12), the programmer uses the knowledge-based command "Remove" in order to get rid of the summary role. (The line_limit role is automatically changed for 63 back to 64 since it is now clear that zero lines are required for the summary.)

The biggest change in Screen 5 has nothing to do with the knowledge-based command "Remove" *per se*. Before executing any knowledge-based command, KBEmacs first analyzes the effects of any editing which the programmer has performed. Here, KBEmacs concludes that the code added by the programmer in Screen 4 is intended to fill the title role since the only change in the program is

that the new code replaces the title role textually. KBEmacs waits until the next knowledge-based command is used in order to avoid analyzing partially edited programs which are in inconsistent states.

A very interesting aspect of the direct editing performed in Screen 4 is that it created an incorrect program. The problem is that the variable UNIT_KEY is referenced before it is given a value. This situation arose because in Screen 3, the title role happened to precede the GET of the UNIT_KEY. (These two computations were not ordered by control flow or data flow and KBEmacs chose to put the title first.)

When analyzing Screen 4, KBEmacs detects that the variable UNIT_KEY is being used before it has been given a value and tries to fix the problem. KBEmacs reasons that since the title role is not required to precede the GET of UNIT_KEY, the program can be fixed by reordering these operations as shown in Screen 5.

Another interesting change in Screen 5 is that once the computation of the title has been specified KBEmacs can compute the length of the string which stores the title. This is done based on the length of the literal string supplied by the programmer and on the fact that KBEmacs knows how long a UNIT_KEY is (by looking at the package MAINTENANCE_FILES).

The fact that KBEmacs can determine the appropriate declaration for the variable TITLE shields the programmer from an irritating detail of Ada. Since there is no varying length string data type in standard Ada, the declaration of a local string variable such as TITLE must include the exact length of the string.

After removing the summary in Screen 5, the programmer uses a standard Emacs command in order to compile the program. Once this is done the programmer can test the program. (An interpreter for a subset of Ada was implemented as part of KBEmacs.) Fig. 13 shows the result of using the program UNIT_REPAIR_REPORT to generate a report based on the test data in Fig. 3.

Documentation

Documentation is another area where KBEmacs can assist a programmer. In particular, the knowledge-based command "Comment" can be used to create a summary comment describing a program. Fig. 14 shows the comment which would be produced for the program UNIT _REPAIR_REPORT. This is an example of one way in which KBEmacs can use the information it maintains about the structure of a program in order to assist a programmer in understanding the program.

The comment is in the form of an outline. The first line specifies the top level cliche in the program. The subsequent lines describe how the major roles in this cliche have been filled in. The comment is constructed based on the cliches that were used to create the program. The "described roles" declaration in the definition of the top level cliche (i.e., simple_report, see Fig. 7) specifies what roles to describe and what order to describe them in.

Each role is described in one of three ways. If the role has been removed, then it is reported as missing (e.g., the summary). If the role is filled by a cliche then this cliche is named (e.g., the enumerator). Further, a brief one line description showing how the roles of this subcliche are filled in is included. (This description is generated from the "comment" declaration in the definition of the subcliche.) If a role is filled with noncliched computation which is short enough to fit on a single line then the corresponding code is displayed (e.g., the title). The individual lines of the comment are written in the same style as the knowledge-based commands. In particular, variable names and code fragments are rendered in upper case.

The comment generation capability currently supported by KBEmacs is only intended as an illustration of the kind of comment that could be produced. There are many other kinds of comments containing either more or less information that could just as well have been produced. For example, KBEmacs could easily include a description of the inputs and outputs of the program in the comment. The form of comment shown was chosen because it contains a significant amount of high level information which is not explicit in the program code. As a result, it should be of genuine assistance to a person who is trying to understand the program.

A key feature of the comment in Fig. 14 is that, since it

```
4 blank lines
                    7/27/1984

            Report of Repairs on Unit GA2-342
59 blank lines
page break
Page:   1   Report of Repairs on Unit GA2-342          7/27/1984

   Date    Defect   Description/Comment

3/19/1984  GA-32   Clogged gas injection port
                   Port Diameter seems below specs.
1/23/1984  GA-11   Control board cold solder joint
                   Took two days to find.
9/14/1982  GA-32   Clogged gas injection port
                   Probably caused by humidity.
```

Fig. 13. Example output produced by UNIT_REPAIR_REPORT.

```
-- The procedure UNIT_REPAIR_REPORT is a simple_report:
--   The file_name is "report.txt".
--   The title is ("Report of Repairs on Unit " & UNIT_KEY).
--   The enumerator is a chain_enumeration.
--       It enumerates the chain records in REPAIRS starting from the
--       the header record indexed by UNIT_KEY.
--   The column_headings are a print_repair_headings.
--       It prints headings for printing repair records.
--   The print_item is a print_repair.
--       It prints out the fields of REPAIR.
--   There is no summary.
```

Fig. 14. Automatically generated comment for UNIT_REPAIR_REPORT.

is generated from the knowledge underlying the program, it is guaranteed to be complete and correct. In contrast, much of the program documentation one typically encounters has been rendered obsolete by subsequent program modifications. Although it is not currently supported, it would be easy for KBEmacs to generate a new program comment every time a program was modified. Using this approach, it might be possible for such commentary to augment (or even partially replace) program code as the means of communication between KBEmacs and the programmer.

Discussion of the Commands Used

The set of knowledge-based commands which were used in order to construct the program UNIT_REPAIR_REPORT are summarized below with the direct editing recast as an equivalent use of the knowledge-based command "Fill".

Define a simple_report program UNIT_REPAIR_REPORT. Fill the enumerator with a chain_enumeration of UNITS and REPAIRS. Fill the main_file_key with a query _user_for_key of UNITS. Share the first READ and the second READ. Fill the title with ("Report of Repairs on Unit " & UNIT_KEY). Remove the summary.

It is interesting to compare these commands to the hypothesized set of directions for an inexperienced assistant programmer (reproduced below).

Define a simple report program UNIT_REPAIR_REPORT. Enumerate the chain of repairs associated with a unit record, printing each one. Query the user for the key (UNIT_KEY) of the unit record to start from. Print the title ("Report of Repairs on Unit " & UNIT-_KEY). Do not print a summary.

The two sets of directions are quite similar. They differ in grammatical form, but not in semantic content. This is not surprising in light of the fact that the hypothesized commands were in actuality created by restating the knowledge-based commands in more free flowing English.

The purpose of this translation is to demonstrate that although the commands may be syntactically awkward, they are not semantically awkward. The commands are neither redundant nor overly detailed. With the exception of the "Share" command, they specify only the basic design decisions which underlie the program. There is no reason to believe that any automatic system (or for that matter a person) could be told how to implement the program UNIT_REPAIR_REPORT without being told at least most of the information in the commands shown.

III. EVALUATION

The most obvious benefit derived by using KBEmacs is that using cliches makes it possible to construct a program more quickly. The exact increase in speed is difficult to assess. However, given that programmers seem to be able to produce more or less a constant number of lines of code per day independent of the programming language they are using, one way to estimate the increase is to compare the number of commands the programmer has to type in order to construct a program using KBEmacs with the number of lines of code in the program produced. For example, the scenario shows the construction of a 58 line program using 6 KBEmacs commands.

The scenario in [52] shows the construction of several Ada programs. The productivity gains attained vary from a factor of 3 (15 commands are required to construct the package MAINTENANCE_FILES shown in Fig. 4) to a factor of 10 (a 110 line program is constructed using only 11 commands). The most important reason for this variance is that programs vary in the extent to which they contain idiosyncratic computation as opposed to computation corresponding to cliches. For example, the program UNIT_REPAIR_REPORT is composed almost exclusively of cliches while the package MAINTENANCE_FILES is composed primarily of idiosyncratic record declarations.

Another important advantage of KBEmacs is that using cliches enhances the reliability of the programs produced. Since cliches are intended to be used many times, it is economically justifiable to lavish a great deal of time on them in order to ensure that they are general purpose and bug-free. This reliability is inherited by the programs which use the cliches. When using an ordinary program editor, programmers typically make two kinds of errors: picking the wrong algorithms to use and incorrectly instantiating these algorithms (i.e., combining the algorithms together and rendering them as appropriate program code). KBEmacs eliminates the second kind of error.

In order to get the full benefit of cliches, the programmer has to make a few compromises. In particular, the programmer has to try to think as much as possible in terms of the cliches available so that cliches can be used as often as possible. Similar kinds of accommodations have to be make in order to fully benefit from a human assistant.

Problems

KBEmacs is a research experiment. Rapid prototyping and rapid evolution have been the only goals of the current implementation. As a result, it is hardly surprising that KBEmacs is neither fast enough, robust enough, nor complete enough to be used as a practical tool.

Knowledge-based operations on large programs can take longer than 5 minutes. Even simple operations on small programs take 5–10 seconds. In contrast, experience with interactive systems in general suggests that in order for a system to be judged highly responsive, operations must be performed in at most 1–2 seconds. In order to approach this goal, the speed of KBEmacs would have to be increased by a factor of 100.

KBEmacs is fraught with bugs. The system has not been extensively tested and there has been no visible diminution in the rate at which bugs have been discovered during this testing. This suggests that many bugs remain to be found.

KBEmacs is incomplete in two primary ways. First, the system handles only 50 percent of Ada. (It handles 90 percent of Lisp.) In order to be a practical tool, KBEmacs would have to be extended to deal with the complete target language in at least a minimal way.

Second, KBEmacs knows only a few dozen cliches. Several lines of research (see [3], [28]) suggest that hundreds of cliches are required for an understanding of even a small part of programming and that thousands of cliches would be required for a comprehensive understanding of programming.

Fortunately, although the problems above are quite serious, it appears that they could be overcome by reimplementing KBEmacs from scratch with efficiency, robustness, and completeness as primary goals. In particular, [52] presents an experiment which shows that the central operations of KBEmacs could be straightforwardly speeded up by a factor of 30.

Unfortunately, since KBEmacs is quite large (some 40 000 lines of Lisp code) reimplementation would be an arduous task. As a result, it would probably be most practical to reimplement the system initially for a small language such as Pascal or basic Lisp rather than for a large language such as Ada. Further, although there is no fundamental barrier to defining additional cliches, designing the exact cliches to use would be a lengthy task.

One might comment that it would not be sufficient to make KBEmacs run acceptably on a Lisp Machine, because machines of this power are too expensive to use as programmer work stations. However, if the reduced cost of such computers coupled with the increased cost of programmers has not yet made such computers economical, it soon will. A basic goal of the PA project is to look forward into the future when computers 10 or even 100 times as powerful as the Lisp Machine will be economical and investigate how this power can be harnessed to assist a programmer.

IV. CAPABILITIES

This section compares the capabilities supported by KBEmacs to the capabilities the PA is intended to support. It begins by summarizing the capabilities supported by

KBEmacs and then outline the additional capabilities which will be supported by the next demonstration system.

Strongly Demonstrated Capabilities

Several of the capabilities which the PA is intended to support are strongly demonstrated by KBEmacs. Saying that a capability is *strongly demonstrated* is intended to imply two things. First, restricted to the domain of program construction, essentially the full capability that the PA is intended to possess is supported. Second, the capability is supported in a general way which demonstrates the efficacy of the key ideas underlying the PA (i.e., the assistant approach, cliches, and plans).

Rapid and Reliable Program Construction in Terms of Cliches: The dominant activity in the scenario is the construction of a program by combining algorithmic cliches. As discussed in Section III, cliches make it possible to construct programs both more rapidly and more reliably.

Editing in Terms of Algorithmic Structure: The knowledge-based commands make it possible for the programmer to operate directly on the algorithmic structure of a program. The essence of this is the ability to refer to the roles of the various cliches used to construct the program. This in turn depends on the fact that KBEmacs remembers what these cliches are, and where the roles are, even after the roles are filled in. Commands are provided for filling, removing, and replacing these roles.

Editing in terms of algorithmic structure elevates the level of interaction between the programmer and KBEmacs to a fundamentally higher plane than text-based or syntax-based editing. Such editing makes it possible to state straightforward algorithmic changes to a program as simple commands even when the algorithmic changes require widespread textual changes in the program. For example, the command "Fill the enumerator with a chain_enumeration of UNITS and REPAIRS." in Screen 2 causes changes throughout the program UNIT_REPAIR_RE-PORT.

User Extendable Library of Cliches: Although it is not illustrated in the scenario, a programmer can define new cliches as easily as new subroutines. This is done by simply creating cliche definitions analogous to the ones shown in Figs. 5–7. It should be noted that defining new cliches is also just as hard as defining new subroutines—i.e., there is nothing at all easy about deciding exactly what cliches should be defined.

The ability to easily define new cliches has two benefits. First, a programmer can readily extend KBEmacs into new domains of programming. Second, a programmer can tailor KBEmacs so that it fits in better with a given style of programming.

Escape to the Surrounding Environment: The programmer is free to operate on the program being edited with any of standard Lisp Machine programming tools. In particular, text-based (or syntax-based) editing can be applied to the program at any time.

Escape to the surrounding environment is of particular importance because it gives the KBEmacs system the property of *additivity*. New capabilities are added to the programming environment without removing any of the standard capabilities.

Programming Language Independence: As discussed in Section V, the internal operation of KBEmacs is substantially language independent. This is illustrated by the fact that it can operate on both Ada programs and Lisp programs. (Extensive Lisp scenarios are shown in [52].)

Weakly Demonstrated Capabilities

KBEmacs demonstrates a number of capabilities which the PA is intended to support in addition to the ones discussed above. However, these additional capabilities are only weakly demonstrated. Saying that a capability is *weakly demonstrated* is intended to imply two things. First, even restricted to the domain of program construction, only parts of the capability are supported. Second, the capability is not supported in a general way. However, the weakly demonstrated capabilities are better than mere mockups because, like the strongly demonstrated capabilities, they are based on the key ideas underlying the PA and their implementation illustrates the leverage of these ideas.

Reasoning by Means of Constraints: KBEmacs uses simple constraint propagation in order to determine some of the consequences of the programmer's design decisions. When defining a cliche the programmer can specify various constraints between the roles. As shown in the scenario, these constraints can be used both to reduce the number of roles which have to be specified by the programmer and to enhance the reliability of the programs produced.

As discussed in the beginning of Section II, there is an unfortunate weakness in the way constraints are implemented in KBEmacs. As a practical matter, the fact that constraints are represented procedurally by functions which operate directly on the internal implementation of the plan formalism severely limits the constraints which can be stated.

Taking Care of Details: One of the ways in which KBEmacs can be particularly helpful to a programmer is by taking care of details. This is an area where KBEmacs can take over parts of the programming task completely. A good example of this is the fact that the system can generate most of the variable declarations in an Ada program. Another example is the support the system provides for making sure that each data file in a program is opened and closed exactly once.

KBEmacs' support for taking care of details is weak for two reasons. First, it is not supported in any general way. Rather, each kind of detail supported is taken care of by a special purpose procedure. Second, only a few examples of taking care of details are supported.

Program Modification: KBEmacs supports two commands ("Share" and "Replace") which support program modification. In addition, constraints and editing in terms of algorithmic structure facilitate modification. However, KBEmacs' support for program modification can really only be said to have scratched the surface. In particular, KBEmacs is not able to reason about the effects of of changes in any general way. Rather, each modification command is implemented on an ad hoc basis.

Program Documentation: KBEmacs is able to create a simple comment describing a program. Again, this capability only scratches the surface of what could be done. In this area, the goal of KBEmacs is to illustrate the fact that the plan formalism represents a significant amount of imformation which could be useful in producing documentation.

Capabilities of the Next System

The next demonstration system will differ from KBEmacs in two crucial ways. First, it will be based on the plan calculus developed by Rich [28],[29] rather than the simple plan formalism used by KBEmacs. Second, the new system will incorporate a fourth key AI idea—general purpose automated deduction.

As discussed at the end of Section V the key advantage of the plan calculus is that it represents three kinds of information about programs which are not represented by the plan formalism: knowledge about data structures, specifications, and interrelationships between cliches and design decisions.

General purpose automated deduction is best understood in contrast to reasoning performed by special purpose procedures. In a general purpose automated deduction system not only the facts being reasoned about but also various theorems and other reasoning methods are represented as data objects. Only a few very basic reasoning methods (e.g., reasoning about equality) are built into the system. This makes it possible for a general purpose automated deduction system to reason about a wide range of problems and to flexibly use a wide range of knowledge when doing so. In addition, such a system can be straightforwardly extended by adding a new theorems and new kinds of knowledge. In contrast, special purpose reasoning systems typically embed theorems in procedures. Such procedures are fundamentally restricted in that each one solves a narrowly defined problem using a limited amount of knowledge. In order to attack a new problem or use additional knowledge, a new procedure has to be written.

In the new system, general purpose automated deduction will be supported by a reasoning module [30],[31] specially designed to work in conjunction with the plan calculus. Together, the reasoning module and the plan calculus will make it possible to strongly demonstrate the capabilities which are only weakly demonstrated by KBEmacs. In addition, they will make it possible for the new system to demonstrate two key capabilities which are not demonstrated by KBEmacs.

Contradiction Detection: The most important use of the reasoning module will be *contradiction detection*. In contrast to automatic verification (which seeks to prove that a program satisfies a complete set of specifications), contradiction detection starts with whatever partial specifications are available for a program and locates bugs in the program by discovering any obvious contradictions.

Data type checking (e.g., as performed by an Ada compiler) is a simple example of contradiction detection. A data type checker locates contradictions based on specifications for the data types of various quantities. The new system will be much more powerful than a type checker because it will be able to utilize a much wider variety of specifications. The system will also be more flexible than current type checkers because it will not require that every contradiction detected by immediately fixed. It is often important to be able to temporarily ignore minor problems so that more serious problems can be investigated (e.g., through testing).

As an example of the utility of contradiction detection, consider the following. Since KBEmacs does not support any contradiction detection, the system has no way to determine whether a set of commands is reasonable. Rather, it just does whatever the programmer says. For example, if the programmer had told KBEmacs to implement the enumerator in the program UNIT_REPAIR_REPORT as a vector_enumeration of REPAIRS, KBEmacs would have gone right ahead and done it. In contrast, the next demonstration system will be able to complain that such a command does not make any sense.

Interaction in Terms of Design Decisions: The fundamental level of interaction between a programmer and KBEmacs is in terms of specific algorithms (cliches). An important goal of the next demonstration system is to go beyond this level of interaction and support interaction in terms of design decisions. For example, when constructing the program UNIT_REPAIR_REPORT, the programmer had to specify the use of the cliche chain_enumeration. In the new system the programmer will instead merely have to say that the repair records are in a chain file. The system will be able to conclude that in order to print a simple_report of repairs, the cliche chain_enumeration must be used.

Design decisions will be introduced into the new system by making them the basis for the organization of the cliche library. Cliches will be referred to by the relevant design concepts rather than by specific names. A major benefit of this is that while there are several thousand important cliches, there are probably only a few hundred important design concepts—large numbers of cliches, correspond to elements of cross products of various sets of design concepts (for example, there is an enumerator for every kind of aggregate data structure). It is the design concepts which form the key vocabulary which the programmer and the system must have a mutual understanding of.

V. Implementation

This section briefly outlines the way KBEmacs is implemented. The discussion focuses on the plan formalism which is the foundation of the implementation. All of the aspects of the implementation of KBEmacs are discussed in much greater detail in [47],[52].

KBEmacs is implemented on the Symbolics Lisp Machine [22]. Fig. 15 shows the architecture of the system. KBEmacs maintains two representations for the program being worked on: program text and a plan. At any moment, the programmer can either modify the program text or the plan. In order to modify the program text, the programmer can use the standard Emacs-style Lisp Machine

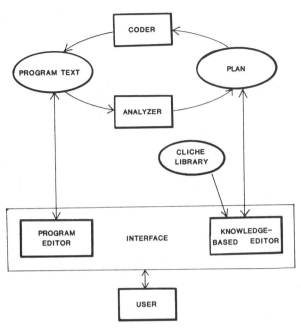

Fig. 15. Architecture of KBEmacs.

editor. This editor supports both text-based and syntax-based program editing.

In order to modify the plan, the programmer can use the *knowledge-based editor* implemented as part of KBEmacs. This editor supports a dozen different knowledge-based commands. Six of the most important commands ("Define", "Fill", "Share", "Replace", "Remove" and "Comment") are discussed in conjunction with the scenario in Section II. Each command is supported by a special purpose procedure which operates directly on the plan formalism. (The "Comment" command is based on the work of Cyphers [12].)

An interface (implemented by Pitman [26]) unifies ordinary program editing and knowledge-based editing so that they can both be conveniently accessed through the standard Lisp Machine editor. The knowledge-based commands are supported as an extension of the standard editor command set and the results of these commands are communicated to the programmer by altering the program text in the editor buffer. The effect is the same as if a human assistant were sitting at the editor modifying the text under the direction of the programmer.

An important adjunct of the knowledge-based editor is the *cliche library*. The library acts as a simple repository for cliches (represented by plans) which can be referenced by their names. New cliches can be defined by simply creating a cliche definition analogous to the ones shown in Figs. 5-7 (via ordinary and/or knowledge-based editing) and then using the standard editor command for compiling a definition in the editor buffer. A special compiler creates a plan corresponding to the textual representation of the cliche and inserts this plan into the cliche library. The main component of this compiler is the analyzer module described below.

The most important feature of the knowledge-based ed-

itor is the ability to create instances of cliches and integrate them with an existing program. For example, consider the command "Fill the enumerator with a chain_enumeration of UNITS and REPAIRS" from Screen 2. The knowledge-based editor first instantiates the cliche chain_enumeration. This is done by copying the appropriate plan from the cliche library and filling in the indicated roles with the values UNITS and REPAIRS. After this, the constraint functions specified for the cliche chain_enumeration are run. (They are rerun any time the value of a role is changed.) Once the specified cliche instance is created, it is inserted into the enumerator role and connected up to the rest of the program UNIT_REPAIR_REPORT. The only complexity here is locating appropriate sources for the data flow specified by the variables UNITS and REPAIRS. Filling the enumerator role triggers constraints in the cliche simple_report which leads to other changes in the program as shown in Screen 2.

Whenever the plan is modified, the *coder* module is used to create new program text. The coder operates in three steps. First, it examines the plan in order to determine how the control flow should be implemented—i.e., determining where conditional and looping constructs should be used. Second, it determines how the data flow should be implemented—i.e., when variables should be used and what names should be used for them. Third, it constructs program text based on the decisions above and then applies various transformations in order to improve the readability of the result. The complexity of the coder stems not from the need to create correct code (this is relatively easy) but from the need to create aesthetic code.

Whenever the program text is modified, the *analyzer* module is used to create a new plan. The analyzer is similar to the front end of an optimizing compiler. It operates on a program (or cliche) in four stages. First, the program is parsed. Second, macro expansion is used to express the various constructs of the language in terms of primitive operations. For example, all control constructs are expanded into GOTO's. Third, the resulting intermediate form is processed to determine the basic functions called by the program, the roles in the program, and the data flow and control flow between them. This results in the construction of a simple plan (see the discussion of the plan formalism below). Fourth, the plan is analyzed in order to determine the structure of the program in terms of conditionals and loops, and in order to locate compound roles such as enumerators.

Although the analyzer is able to construct a plan for a program based on the program text, it is not able to recognize what cliches could have been used to construct the plan. As a result, modifying a program textually reduces the programmer's ability to subsequently use knowledge-based commands. The problem is that when the text is modified, KBEmacs is forced to forget the cliches which were used to construct the program (since they may no longer accurately reflect the structure of the program) and is unable to determine what other cliches are appropriate. The only information about cliches and roles which KBEmacs is able to retain, is information about the roles which are unfilled and therefore textually visible. As a result, although the programmer can use a knowledge-based command after modifying a program textually, the command can only refer to the unfilled roles. (It should be noted that this is a definite weakness in KBEmacs' support for escape to the surrounding environment.)

There is one situation where KBEmacs is able to avoid the problem above. If (as in Screen 4) KBEmacs is able to recognize that the only effect of a textual modification is to fill in a role, then KBEmacs converts the textual modification into an equivalent "Fill" command and is able to maintain its knowledge of how the program was built up out of cliches.

An important difference between KBEmacs and the next demonstration system will be that the new system will contain an analyzer (based on the work of Brotsky [7]) which will be able to recognize the cliches used in a program.

Language Independence

An important virtue of KBEmacs is that the implementation is substantially programming language independent. As will be discussed below, the plan formalism is inherently language independent. This makes it possible for the knowledge-based editor and all but the last phase of the coder and the first two phases of the analyzer to be language independent.

In order to extend KBEmacs so that it can be used to operate on a new programming language, one must do four things. First, the syntax of the language has to be extended to support { · · · } annotation and cliche definition. This is done in analogy with the way function calls and function definitions are represented in the language.

Second, the coder and analyzer have to be given an understanding of the syntax and semantics of the language in question. This is done by writing appropriate functions to replace the language dependent parts of these modules. At the current time, the coder and analyzer work on both Ada and Lisp programs. In the past, analysis has been supported for Fortran and Cobol, and coding has been supported for PL/I and Hibol [35].

Third, if support for syntax-based editing is desired, then the Lisp Machine editor has to be given an understanding of the syntax of the new language. As part of the implementation of the KBEmacs interface, the standard editor was extended slightly so that it could perform basic operations on Ada programs.

Fourth, a library of cliches which are appropriate for writing programs in that language must be provided. Since cliches are represented as plans, they are inherently independent of programming language syntax. However, a separate library of cliches is required for each language because programming languages differ semantically as well as syntactically. For example, in the language Lisp the cliche simple_report has to be tailored to suit the I/O facilities provided by the Lisp run-time environment. Example cliche libraries have been created for both Ada and Lisp. (It should be noted that some cliches, particularly very abstract ones, are semantically language independent

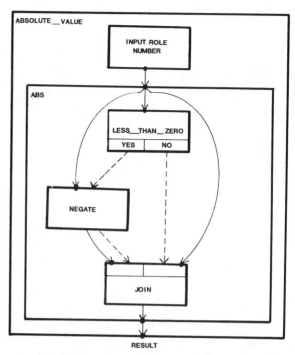

Fig. 16. A plan for the cliche absolute_value.

and therefore could be represented in a language independent cliche library.)

The Plan Formalism

The most important part of the implementation of KBEmacs is the plan formalism. A plan is like a hierarchical flow chart wherein both the control flow and data flow are represented by explicit arcs. Fig. 16 shows a diagram of a simple example plan—the plan for the cliche absolute_value.

The basic unit of a plan is a *segment* (drawn as a box in a plan diagram). A segment corresponds to a unit of computation. It has a number of *input ports* and *output parts* which specify the input values it receives and the output values it produces. It has a name which indicates the operation performed. A segment can either correspond to a primitive computation (e.g., the segment NEGATE) or contain a subplan which describes the computation performed by the segment (e.g., the segment ABS). All of the computation corresponding to a single program or cliche is grouped together into one outermost segment. The roles of a cliche are represented as specially marked segments (e.g., the segment NUMBER).

As in any flowchart, control flow from one segment to another is represented by an explicit arc from the first segment to the second (drawn as a dashed arrow). Similarly, data flow is represented by an explicit arc from the appropriate output port of the source segment to the appropriate input port of the destination segment (drawn as a solid arrow). It should be noted that like a data flow diagram, and unlike an ordinary flowchart, data flow is the dominant concept in a plan. Control flow arcs are only used where they are absolutely necessary. In Fig. 16, control flow arcs are necessary in order to specify that the operation NEGATE is only performed if the input number is negative.

An important feature of the plan formalism is that it abstracts away from inessential features of a program. Whenever possible, it eliminates features which stem from the way things must be expressed in a particular programming language, keeping only those features which are essential to the actual algorithm. For example, a plan does not represent data flow in terms of the way it could be implemented in any particular programming language—e.g., with variables, or nesting of expressions, or parameter passing. Rather, it just records what the net data flow is. Similarly, no information is represented about how control flow is implemented. One result of this abstraction is that plans are much more canonical than program text. Programs (even in different languages) which differ only in the way their data flow and control flow is implemented correspond to the same plan.

A second important feature of the plan formalism is that it tries to make information as local as possible. For example, each data flow arc represents a specific communication of data from one place to another and, by the definition of what a data flow arc is, the other data flow arcs in the plan cannot have any effect on this. The same is true for control flow arcs. This locality makes it possible to determine what the data flow or control flow is in a particular situation by simply querying a small local portion of the plan.

The key benefit of the locality of data flow and control flow is that it gives plans the property of *additivity*. It is always permissible to put two plans side by side without their being any interference between them. This makes it easy for KBEmacs to create a program by combining the plans for cliches. All KBEmacs has to do is just paste the pieces together. It does not have to worry about issues like variable name conflicts, because there are no variables.

A third important feature of plans is that the intermediate segmentation breaks a plan up into regions which can be manipulated separately. In order to ensure this separability, the plan formalism is designed so that nothing outside of a segment can depend on anything inside of that segment. For example, all of the data flow between segments outside of an intermediate segment and segments inside of an intermediate segment is channeled through input and output ports attached to the intermediate segment. As a result of this and other restrictions, when modifying the plan inside of a segment one can be secure in the knowledge that these changes cannot effect any of the plan outside of the segment.

Representing Loops

A final interesting aspect of plans is that loops are represented in a way which increases locality. Rather than representing loops by means of cycles in data flow and control flow, the plan is represented as a composition of computations applied to series of values (see [48]). For example, Fig. 17 shows a plan for summing up the positive elements of a vector. It is composed of three subsegments. The first enumerates the elements in the input vector creating a series (or stream) of values. The second selects the positive elements of this series. The third sums up the selected values.

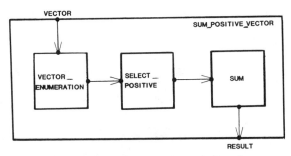
Fig. 17. A plan for summing up the positive elements of a vector.

Representing a loop as a composition of computations on series has two important advantages. First, it increases locality. For example, it makes it possible to modify one of the computations without disturbing the others (e.g., the vector enumeration could be replaced by a list enumeration). Second, it highlights the similarity between related loops. For example, it makes explicit the fact that exactly the same summation cliche is used in a program which sums the positive elements of a vector as in a program which sums the lengths of a list of queues.

Problems with the Plan Formalism

The plan formalism is capable of representing a wide variety of basic information about algorithms—e.g., data flow, control flow, inputs, outputs, loops, recursion, subroutine calling, etc. However, there are some limits to what it can represent in these areas. For example, the plan formalism cannot represent nonlocal flow of control such as interrupts. In addition, it does not represent multiple-entry loops or multiple recursion in any useful way.

A much more fundamental limitation of the plan formalism is that it cannot represent information about data structures. In particular, it is not capable of representing data cliches (as opposed to computational cliches). As a result, it cannot represent the way in which complex data structures are built up out of simple ones. (It should be noted that KBEmacs' support for Ada data declarations is provided by special purpose procedures.)

An equally fundamental limitation of the plan formalism is that it does not represent any information about specifications for either primitive operations, programs, or cliches. (To a certain extent KBEmacs' support for constraints can be used to make up for a lack of understanding of specifications—e.g., by explicitly specifying something that should follow generally from some specification.)

Finally, the plan formalism does not represent information about interrelationships between cliches or between cliches and design decisions. Together with the lack of specifications, this fundamentally limits the reasoning which KBEmacs can perform in order to determine which cliches are appropriate to use in a given situation.

The plan calculus [28], [29] extends the plan formalism so that it can represent information about data structures, specifications, and interrelationships. Using the plan calculus will give the next demonstration system a fundamentally better understanding of the program being constructed. In addition, by allowing a richer set of cliches to be defined, the plan calculus will be the basis for a better understanding of programming in general. However, it should be noted that the plan calculus does not remedy the defects in the plan formalism with regard to understanding nonlocal control flow, multiple-entry loops, and multiple recursion.

VI. RELATED WORK

This section compares KBEmacs to other approaches to improving programmer productivity. The comparison focuses on tools and projects which are either similar in their capabilities or based on closely related ideas. Projects which share ideas with KBEmacs in that they have intentionally used ideas from KBEmacs (or the PA project as a whole) are discussed in Section VII.

KBE

As discussed in Section I, KBEmacs is the second in a series of demonstration systems which are heading in the direction of the PA. The first demonstration system was the Knowledge-Based (KBE). KBEmacs is implemented as an extension of KBE, and for the most part, the capabilities of KBE (see [49]) are a subset of the capabilities of KBEmacs.

Rapid program construction in terms of cliches and editing in terms of algorithmic structure were the main focus of KBE. In these areas, KBE supported essentially the same capabilities as KBEmacs in essentially the same way. In addition, KBE provided the same weak support for program modification that KBEmacs provides.

The most obvious difference between KBE and KBEmacs is that while KBE was a stand-alone system, KBEmacs is embedded in the standard Lisp Machine Emacs-style program editor. As part of this change, KBEmacs provides much better support for escape to the surrounding environment. (Although a programmer could apply text-based editing to a program constructed using KBE this could not be done until after all of the roles had been filled in.)

KBEmacs supports a number of capabilities which were not supported by KBE at all. For example, KBEmacs supports a syntactic representation for cliches which allows a programmer to easily define new cliches. The most important part of this is the ability to use { · · · } annotation for input from the programmer as well as output to the programmer. In addition, KBEmacs introduces support for constraints and program documentation.

Another advance of KBEmacs is that it introduces support for Ada. (KBE only supported Lisp.) As part of this, KBEmacs provides greatly increased support for taking care of details. The speed and robustness of the system was also increased in order to make it possible to operate on Ada programs of realistic size. (Whereas the largest program ever constructed using KBE was only about 15 lines long, KBEmacs has been used to construct programs more than 100 lines long.)

It is interesting to note that KBE supported few features which are no longer supported by KBEmacs. For example,

```
     PROGRAM EDITOR       |     LEVEL of UNDERSTANDING
----------------------------------------------------------------
       Text Editor        |        Character Strings
                          |
      Syntax Editor       |          Parse Trees
                          |
        KBEmacs            |       Algorithmic Structure
                          |
 Next Demonstration System |        Design Decisions
          :                |                 :
                          |
```

Fig. 18. Levels of understanding exhibited by program editors.

KBE was able to draw a diagram showing the plan which corresponded to the program being constructed. It turned out that these diagrams were not very helpful because they were hard for people to read and understand. The basic problem is that while simple diagrams are very easy to understand (perhaps easier than the corresponding program), complicated diagrams are almost impossible to understand (much harder than the corresponding program). As an example of this problem, consider data flow. Explicit data flow arcs have very nice semantics and are very easy to comprehend in isolation. However, if a diagram contains a large number of data flow arcs, then the diagram has to be drawn with extraordinary care in order for the reader to be able to identify and follow the individual arcs (particularly when they cross). In order to render the various arcs legibly, the typical plan diagram requires from 100 to 1000 times the space of the corresponding program text. All in all, experience revealed that program text was a much more useful user interface than plan diagrams.

The argument above should not be taken to imply that graphical output is never useful. People seem to have a great affinity for structure diagrams and the like. However, note that these diagrams achieve simplicity because an enormous amount of information is left out. In the realm of documentation it would probably be very useful for KBEmacs to be able to create simple diagrams which represent various subsets of the information in a plan.

Program Editors

KBEmacs is essentially a program editor and every effort has been taken to ensure that programmers can think of it as an additive extension to a state-of-the-art program editor. However, this extension is a very powerful one. As a result, KBEmacs is quite different from other program editors.

A key dimension on which to compare program editors is their level of understanding of the programs being edited (see Fig 18). The level of understanding is important because it determines the kinds of operations an editor can perform.

The simplest program editors are merely ordinary text editors which are used for editing programs. These editors have no understanding of programs at all. The operations supported by these editors are limited to operations on characters—e.g., inserting, deleting, and locating character strings.

Some program editors incorporate an understanding of the syntactic structure of the program being edited (see for example [13], [23], [42], [45]). This makes it possible to support operations based on the parse tree of a program—

e.g., inserting, deleting, and moving between nodes in the parse tree.

An important aspect of syntax-based editors is that they can ensure that the program being edited is always syntactically correct. It has been shown [27] that syntax-based editors can succeed in utilizing essentially all of the information which has traditionally been expressed in terms of syntax (e.g., data type constraints).

KBEmacs goes beyond existing program editors by incorporating an understanding of the algorithmic structure of the program being edited. By means of the plan formalism, KBEmacs understands what cliches were used to construct the program as well as the basic operations, data flow, and control flow in the program. This understanding makes it possible for KBEmacs to support operations based on algorithmic structure—e.g., instantiating cliches and filling roles. In addition, via constraints, KBEmacs can ensure certain aspects of the semantic correctness of the program being edited.

The next demonstration system will take a step further by incorporating an understanding of the design decisions which underly the choice of algorithms in a program. This will make it possible for the programmer to converse with the system in terms of these decisions instead of in terms of specific algorithms. Levels of understanding much higher than those shown in Fig. 18 are possible—e.g., understanding the tradeoffs which underly design decisions. Reaching these higher levels is a long term goal of the PA project.

An unfortunate aspect of syntax-based editors is that (with the notable exceptions of Emacs [42]) early syntax-based editors significantly (if not totally) restricted the programmer's ability to use text-based editing commands. As discussed in detail in [50], such restrictions are frustrating in many ways. Syntax-based commands are more convenient than text based commands in many situations; however, there is no reason why programmers should be forced to use syntax-based commands when they are not more convenient.

Although most syntax-based editors still do not support text-based commands, at least one recent syntax-based editor (SRE [8]) fully supports them. In keeping with the assistant approach, KBEmacs pays scrupulous attention to fully supporting text-based and syntax-based commands.

An interesting aspect of syntax-based editors is the extent to which they support cliches. Almost every syntax-based editor provides cliches corresponding to the various syntactic constructs in the programming language being used. However, almost no syntax-based editor supports any other kind of cliche. To a certain extent this seems to be a missed opportunity (see the discussion of the Tempest editor [43] in Section VII). However, one cannot support more complex cliches in the same way that simple cliches corresponding to syntactic constructs are supported. In particular, in order to be able to flexibly combine complex cliches, an editor must have an understanding of the semantic structure of the cliches. For example, if two cliches use the same variable, then one of the uses of this variable will, more than likely, have to be renamed before the cliches can be combined. The primary advantage of KBE-macs over syntax-based editors is that, due to its understanding of semantic structure, KBEmacs can support the manipulation of complex cliches.

Program Generators

Program generators have the same overall goal as KBEmacs—dramatically reducing the effort required to implement a program. Further, they are in essence similar to KBEmacs in the way in which they reduce programmer effort—they embody knowledge of the cliched aspects of a class of programs. Where program generators are applicable, they are significantly more powerful than KBEmacs. However, program generators are only applicable in certain narrow domains.

In its purest form, a program generator obviates the need to have any programmer at all. An end user describes the desired results in a special problem-oriented language (or through some interactive dialog with the generator) and a program is produced automatically. A key aspect of this is that no one ever looks at the program produced—all maintenance is carried out at the level of the problem-oriented language.

There is ample evidence that a program generator can be created for any sufficiently restricted domain. An area where program generators have been particularly successful is database management systems. Dozens of program generators in this area exist, perhaps the most successful of which is Focus [17].

The problem with program generators is their narrowness of scope. Even a tiny bit outside of its scope, a given program generator is nearly useless. In order to get the flexibility they need, programmers sometimes resort to using a program generator to make an approximately correct program and then manually modifying the code produced in order to get the program desired. Unfortunately, there are two major problems with this. First, even the smallest manual change forces further maintenance to be carried out at the level of the code instead of the level of the problem-oriented language. Second, since the code created by a program generator is usually not intended for human consumption, it is typically quite difficult to understand and therefore modify.

The principal advantage of KBEmacs over program generators is that it has a wide range of applicability. The prime domain of applicability of KBEmacs is defined by the contents of the cliche library. Within this prime domain, KBEmacs is somewhat similar to a program generator although its interface is very different—the key information which has to be specified to KBEmacs in order to create a program is similar to what must be specified to a program generator. Beyond the edge of its prime domain of applicability, KBEmacs is very different from a program generator—it continues to be useful because the programmer can freely intermix cliched and noncliched computation. Instead of an abrupt reduction in utility, the utility of KBEmacs is reduced gradually as one moves farther and farther from the prime domain. In addition, the prime domain can be extended by defining new cliches.

The research on program generators is pursuing the goal of increasing the size and the complexity of the domains which can be handled. The PHI-nix system [4] is an interesting example of a program generator in a complex domain. Given a description which is primarily composed of mathematical equations, PHI-nix is capable of generating complex mathematical modeling programs in the context of petroleum geology. In order to do this, the system combines a variety of techniques including symbolic manipulation of mathematical expressions.

The CAP system [5] uses a few of the same ideas as KBEmacs in order to increase the size of the domain of applicability. In particular, CAP makes use of what is effectively a library of cliches rather than being solely procedurally based. Using CAP a programmer can build a program by combining *frames* (cliches) which have *breakpoints* (roles) that can contain custom code which becomed part of the generated program. The key weakness of CAP is that it does not have any semantic understanding of its frames and therefore is limited in its ability to manipulate and combine them.

It should be noted that KBEmacs is not really in competition with the program generator approach. Although KBEmacs has some fundamental advantages over program generators, it does not render them obsolete. Similarly, anything short of an all encompassing program generator would not render KBEmacs obsolete. Rather, program generators and KBEmacs can be synergistically combined. Program generators incorporated into KBEmacs can be used to generate special purpose sections of code and KBEmacs can integrate this code into the program being constructed. This makes it possible for the programmer to get the benefit of the program generator without being unduly limited by its narrow focus. (This is illustrated by the constraint function CORRESPONDING_PRINTING.

Transformations

Program transformations have important similarities to the cliches supported by KBEmacs. A program transformation takes a part of a program and replaces it with a new (transformed) part. Typically, a program transformation is *correctness preserving* in that the new part of the program computes the same thing as the old part. The purpose of a transformation is to make the part *better* on some scale (e.g., more efficient or less abstract). For example, a transformation might be used to replace "$X**2$" with "$X*X$".

As usually implemented, transformations have three parts. They have a pattern which matches against a section of a program in order to determine where to apply the transformation. They have a set of applicability conditions which further restrict the places where the transformation can be applied. Finally, they have a (usually procedural) action which creates the new program section based on the old section.

There are two principal kinds of transformations: *vertical* and *lateral*. Vertical transformations define an expression at one level of abstraction in terms of an expression at a lower level of abstraction—for example defining how to enumerate the elements of a vector using a loop. Lateral transformations specify an equivalence between two expressions at a similar level of abstraction—for example specifying the commutativity of addition. Lateral transformations are used principally to promote efficiency and to set things up properly so that vertical transformations can be applied.

The most common use of transformations is as the basis for *transformational implementation systems.* Such systems are typically used to convert programs expressed in a high level nonexecutable form into a low level executable form. In many ways, a transformational implementaion system can be looked at as a special kind of a program generator. The principal difference between transformational implementation systems and program generators is that the knowledge of how to implement programs is represented in a database of transformations rather than in a procedure. This makes it easier to extend and modify a transformational implementation system; however, it brings up a new problem: controlling the application of transformations.

The difficulty is that, in a typical situation, many different transformations are applicable and different results will be obtained depending on which transformation is chosen. With regard to vertical transformations, the problem is not too severe because usually only a few transformations will be applicable to a given abstract expression. However, the selection of lateral transformations typically has to rely on manual control.

Existing transformational implementation systems can be divided into two classes: those that are relatively limited in power but require no user guidance and those which are capable of very complex implementation but only under user guidance. TAMPR [6] and PDS [10] use simple control strategies and restrictions on the kinds of transformations which can be defined in order to obviate the need for user guidance. PDS is particularly interesting due to its emphasis on having the user define new abstract terms and transformations as part of the programming process.

PSI was one of the first systems to use a transformational implementation module for complex implementation. PSI's transformational module [3] operated without guidance, generating all possible low level programs. It was assumed that another component [20] would provide guidance as to which transformations to use. Work on complex transformational implementation systems is proceeding both at the USC Information Sciences Institute [2], [53] and the Kestrel Insititute [19]. A key focus of both these efforts has been attempting to automate the transformation selection process [16].

An interesting system which bridges the gap between transformational implementation systems and more traditional program generators is Draco [25]. Draco is a transformational framework in which it is easy to define special purpose program generators. When using Draco to define a program generator for a domain, a "domain designer" follows the classic program generator approach of designing a problem-oriented language which can be used to conveniently describe programs in the domain and then specifying how to generate programs based on the problem-oriented language. The contribution of Draco is that it provides a set of facilities which make it possible to specify the program generation process in a way which is primarily declarative as opposed to procedural. BNF is used to define the syntax of the problem-oriented language while lateral and vertical transformations are used to define its semantics. Procedures are used only as a last resort. When a program is being implemented by a Draco-based program generator, the user is expected to provide guidance as to which transformations to use.

In their essential knowledge content, KBEmacs' cliches are quite similar to vertical transformations. However, cliches are used differently. Instead of appying correctness preserving transformations to a complete high level description of a program, the user of KBEmacs builds a program essentially from thin air by applying noncorrectness preserving transformations. This supports an evolutionary model of programing wherein key decisions about what a program is going to do can be deferred to a later time as opposed to a model where only lower level implementation decisions can be deferred.

A more important difference between cliches and transformations is that cliches operate in the domain of plans rather than program text or parse trees. This raises the level at which knowledge is specified from the syntactic to the semantic. In addition, cliches are completely declarative whereas the action of a transformation is typically procedurally specified. Although KBEmacs does not make much use of this feature, the next demonstration system will. In particular, the new system will be able to reason about the action performed by a cliche in order to reduce the need for user guidance.

Very High Level Languages

The greatest increase in programmer productivity to date has been brought about by the introduction of high level languages. The advantage of high level languages is that they significantly reduce the size of the code which is required to express a given algorithm by allowing a number of low level details (e.g., register allocation) to go unstated. The key to this is the existence of a compiler which takes care of the low level details.

A logical next step would be the introduction of a very high level language which would provide a further significant reduction in the size of program code by allowing a number of middle level details (e.g., data structure selection) to go unstated. The key to this in turn would be the existence of a very powerful compiler which could take care of these middle level details.

The most persistent problem encountered by developers of very high level languages is that the more general purpose the language is, the harder it is to create a compiler which generates acceptably efficient low level code. This problem exists for high level languages as well. However, the inefficiencies have been reduced to a relatively low level and programmers have, for the most part, learned to live with them.

Program generators can be looked at as compilers which support special purpose very high level languages. Several lines of research are directed toward developing more general purpose very high level languages. For example, Hi-bol [35] and Model [11] are very high level languages which are useful in business data processing applications. SETL [36] achieves wide applicability while supporting several very high level operations. Significant progress has recently been made toward compiling SETL efficiently (see[18]).

Much of the current research on transformations is derected toward the support of very high level languages—in the case of the USC Information Sciences Institute the language Gist [2] and in the case of the Kestrel Institute the language V [19]. Neither of these systems is complete. However, they hold the promise eventually supporting truly general purpose very high level languages.

The most important thing to say about the relationship between KBEmacs and general purpose very high level languages is that there is no competition between the approaches. Rather, they are mutually reinforcing. As soon as a general purpose very high level language is developed, it can be used as the target language of KBEmacs. The net productivity gain will be the product of the gains due to the language and due to KBEmacs. The basic claim here is that no matter how high level a language is, there will be cliches in the way it is used and therefore KBEmacs can be usefully applied to it.

Intelligent Design Aids

The basic approach taken by KBEmacs transcends the domain of programming. KBEmacs is an example of a general class of AI systems which could be termed *intelligent design aids*. These programs are expert systems in the sense that they attempt to duplicate expert behavior. However, they are quite different from the more familiar kinds of expert systems which perform diagnostic tasks.

A diagnostic expert system typically takes a relatively small set of input data and derives a relatively simple answer. For example, it might take a set of symptoms and derive the name of a disease. In order to derive the answer the system performs relatively complex deductions utilizing a knowledge base of rules. The emphasis in such a system is on how to control the operation of the rules so that the required deductions can be reliably and efficiently performed without human intervention.

In an intelligent design aid the various components are the same but the emphasis is quite different. In particular, instead of generating a simple answer, a design aid generates a very complex answer—a complete design for the desired artifact. Just representing this design is, of necessity, an important focus of the system. The knowledge base of rules contains various pieces of knowledge about how to design things. However, due both to gaps in this knowledge and lack of adequate control strategies, design aids are not capable of very much automatic design. As a result, the major emphasis of a design aid is on how the user can control the selection of rules and provide specific aspects of the design when the rules are inadequate.

A good example of intelligent design aids outside of the domain of programming are VLSI design systems. As discussed in [44] the key ideas of the assistant approach, cliches, and plans can be used to support VLSI design in basically the same way that they can be used to support programming. For example, the Vexed VLSI design system [24] is startlingly similar to KBEmacs. The interface is different and the domain is of course very different, however the basic capabilities are very much the same. The dominant activity is building up a circuit by means of implementation rules (cliches) chosen from an extendable library. While this is going on, Vexed automatically takes care of a number of details centering around combining the rules correctly. In addition, the user is always free to modify the circuit directly.

VII. FUTURE DIRECTIONS

Work in the PA project is continuing in several areas. The largest amount of effort is going into the construction of the next demonstration system. As discussed in Section IV, this new system will go beyond KBEmacs primarily by supporting contradiction detection and interaction in terms of design decisions rather than specific algorithms.

Another area of activity centers around various applications of the ideas behind KBEmacs. A particularly interesting application is the Tempest editor implemented by Sterpe [43]. This editor is inspired by KBEmacs as a whole. It has a user extendable library of cliches (called templates) and makes it easy to combine these templates together. The key difference between Tempest and KBEmacs is that Tempest is purely text based. This greatly reduces the power of the system. However, it vastly simplifies the system and reduces the amount of computation which has to be performed by three to four orders of magnitude—Tempest runs with acceptable speed on an IBM PC. The power of Tempest is fundamentally limited by the fact that Tempest has essentially no understanding of the text it is operating on. However, for this same reason, Tempest has a very wide range of applicability. Instead of being restricted to operations on programs, Tempest is applicable to anything which can be represented as text.

An interesting application of one of the ideas behind KBEmacs is the programming language extension described in [51]. This extension is inspired by the way loops are represented in the plan formalism. The extension makes it possible to express computations of functions on series of values and uses some of the same algorithms which are used by the coder module of KBEmacs in order to compile the computations into efficient iterative loops.

Several researchers outside of the PA project have been able to make use of some of the ideas in KBEmacs. For example, Soloway [41] has done experiments which show that the kinds of cliches used by KBEmacs do in fact correspond to the way programmers think. Both Soloway [40] and Eisenstadt [21] have used the concepts of plans and cliches in order to implement systems which can assist novice programmers. Shapiro [38] has incorporated some of the ideas from KBEmacs into a more traditional program editor. In this editor, program analysis is used to help a programmer locate the parts of a program which are relevant to a given task.

A final area of activity centers around expanding the scope of the PA project beyond program implementation. Several pilot studies have already been done investigating how the ideas behind the PA can be applied to other phases of the programming process. For example, [34] discusses how the PA could assist with rapid prototyping. The idea here would be to build up a program very quickly by using cliches which omitted a lot of details (such as error checking) and then substitute more complete cliches when it became time to construct a full program. Shapiro [37] demonstrated a tool which helps a programmer to debug a program. The heart of this tool is a knowledge base of cliches describing particular bugs. Chapman [9] built a tool which assists with program testing. This tool keeps track of all the test cases which are used in conjunction with a set of programs and automatically reruns the appropriate tests when programs are modified. Zelinka [54] investigated how a PA-like tool might assist with the task of maintaining documentation. The key to this is a knowledge base which links parts of the documentation to relevant parts of the program.

A particularly interesting pilot study involved program translation. Faust [15] built a demonstration system based on components of KBE which was able to translate Cobol programs to Hibol [35] programs. The basic idea behind this system can be described as follows. First, the Cobol program is analyzed in order to determine what Cobol cliches could have been used to implement the program. Second, a new plan is created by replacing the Cobol cliches with equivalent Hibol cliches. Third, Hibol code is created based on the new plan. Duffey [14] proposed a system which used a similar paradigm in order to compile Pascal programs into extremely efficient machine code.

Currently, work has begun on the design of a Requirements Analyst's Apprentice. The intention is to focus on the opposite end of the programming process from program implementation and apply the basic ideas of the assistant approach, cliches, plans, and general purpose automated deduction to the task of acquiring and modifying requirements.

Once a system has been constructed which captures requirements in a machine understandable form it should be possible to construct a system which bridges the gap between requirements analysis and implementation by supporting the process of program design. Eventually it should be possible to build a true Programmer's Apprentice which can assist in all phases of the programming process.

ACKNOWLEDGMENT

I would particularly like to acknowledge the assistance of my partner C. Rich who has made important contributions to every aspect of my work for a decade.

KBEmacs is the result of a group effort which began with the original Programmer's Apprentice proposal of C. Rich and H. Shrobe. Over the years, many other people have contributed to that effort. G. Sussman has been an inspiration and mentor for us all. K. Pitman implemented the user interface for KBEmacs and assisted with many other aspects of the system. D. Cyphers developed the initial program documentation facilities. D. Brotsky. D. Chapman, R. Duffey, G. Faust, D. Shapiro, P. Sterpe, and L. Zelinka contributed ideas to KBEmacs while working on related parts of the Programmer's Apprentice project.

Special thanks are due R. Racine (of the C.S. Draper Laboratory) for his assistance with regard to Ada.

REFERENCES

[1] "Military Standard Ada Programming Language," U.S. Dep. Defense, Rep. ANSI/MIL-STD-1815A, Jan. 1983.
[2] R. Balzer, "Transformational implementation: An example," *IEEE Trans. Software Eng.*, vol. SE-7, 1981.
[3] D. R. Barstow, "Automatic construction of algorithms and data structures using a knowledge base of programming rules," Ph.D. dissertation, Stanford Univ., Stanford, CA, Rep. AIM-308, Nov. 1977.
[4] D. R. Barstow, R. D. Duffey, S. Smoliar, and S. Vestal, "An automatic programming system to support an experimental science," in *Proc. 6th Int. Conf. Software Eng.*, Sept. 1982.
[5] P. Bassett, "Design principles for software manufacturing tools," in *Proc. ACM*, Oct. 1984.
[6] J. M. Boyle, "Program reusability through program transformation," *IEEE Trans. Software Eng.*, vol. SE-10, Sept. 1984.
[7] D. Brotsky, "An algorithm for parsing flow graphs," M.S. thesis, Rep. MIT/AI/TR-704, Mar. 1984
[8] F. Budinsky, R. Holt, and S. Zoky, "SRE—A syntax recognizing editor," *Software Practice and Experience*, 1985.
[9] D. Chapman, "A program testing assistant," *Commun. ACM*, vol. 25, no. 9, Sept. 1982.
[10] T. E. Cheatham, "Reusability through program transformations," *IEEE Trans. Software Eng.*, vol. SE-10, Sept. 1984.
[11] T. T. Cheng, E. D. Lock, and N. S. Prywes, "Use of very high level languages and program generation by management professionals," *IEEE Trans. Software Eng.*, vol. SE-10, Sept. 1984.
[12] D. S. Cyphers, "Automated program explanation," Rep. MIT/AI/WP-237, Aug. 1982.
[13] V. Donzeau-Gouge et al., "A structure-oriented program editor; A first step towards computer assisted programming," in *Proc. Int. Comput. Symp.* Antibes, France, 1975.
[14] R. D. Duffey, II, "Formalizing the expertise of the assembler language programmer," Rep. MIT/AI/WP-203, Sept. 1980.
[15] G. G. Faust, "Semiautomatic translation of Cobol into Hibol," M.S. thesis, Rep. MIT/LCS/TR-256, Mar. 1981
[16] S. F. Fickas, "Automating the transformational development of software," Ph.D. dissertation, Inform. Sci. Inst., Univ. Southern California, Rep. ISI/RR-83-108, Mar. 1983.
[17] *Focus General Information Guide*, Information Builders Inc., New York, 1985
[18] S. M. Freudenberger, J. T. Schwartz, and M. Sharir, "Experience with the SETL optimizer," *ACM Trans. Program. Lang. Syst.*, vol. 5, no. 1, Jan. 1983.
[19] C. Green et al., "Research on knowledge-based programming and algorithm design—1981," Kestrel Inst., Palo Alto, CA, 1981.
[20] E. Kant, "Efficiency considerations in program synthesis: A knowledge-based approach," Ph.D. dissertation, Stanford Univ., Stanford, CA, Rep. AIM-331, Sept. 1979.
[21] J. Laubsch and M. Eisenstadt, "Domain specific debugging aids for novice programmers," in *Proc. IJCAI-81*, Aug. 1981.
[22] *Lisp Machine Documentation* (release 4), Symbolics, Cambridge, MA, 1984.
[23] R. Medina-Mora and P. Feiler, "An incremental programming environment," *IEEE Trans. Software Eng.*, vol. SE-7, Sept. 1981.
[24] T. M. Mitchell, L. I. Steinberg, and J. S. Shulman, "A knowledge-based approach to design," Rutgers Univ., New Brunswick, NJ, Rep. LCSR-TR-65, Jan. 1985.
[25] J. M. Neighbors, "The Draco approach to constructing software from reusable components," *IEEE Trans. Software Eng.*, vol. SE-10, Sept. 1984.
[26] K. M. Pitman, "Interfacing to the programmer's apprentice," Rep. MIT/AI/WP-244, Feb. 1983.
[27] T. Reps, T. Teitelbaum, and A. Demers, "Incremental context-dependent analysis for language-based editors," *ACM Trans. Program. Lang. Syst.*, vol. 5, no. 3, July 1983.
[28] C. Rich, "Inspection methods in programming," Ph.D. dissertation, Rep. MIT/AI/TR-604, June 1981.
[29] ——, "A formal representation for plans in the programmer's apprentice," in *Proc. IJCAI-81*, Aug. 1981.
[30] ——, "Knowledge representation languages and predicate Calculus: How to have your cake and eat it too," in *Proc. AAAI-82*, Aug. 1982.
[31] ——, "The layered architecture of a System for reasoning about programs," in *Proc. IJCAI-85*, Aug. 1985.
[32] C. Rich and H. E. Shrobe, "Initial report on a Lisp Programmer's Apprentice," M.S. thesis, Rep. MIT/AI/TR-354, Dec. 1976.
[33] ——, "Initial report on a Lisp programmer's apprentice," *IEEE Trans. Software Eng.*, vol. SE-4, Nov. 1978.
[34] C. Rich and R. C. Waters, "The disciplined use of simplifying assumptions," in *Proc. ACM SIGSOFT 2nd Software Eng. Symp. Workshop Rapid Prototyping*, (ACM SIGSOFT Software Engineering Notes vol. 7, no. 5), Dec. 1982.
[35] G. Ruth, S. Alter, and W. Martin, "A very high level language for business data processing," Rep. MIT/LCS/TR-254, 1981.
[36] J. T. Schwartz, "On programming," Interim Rep. SETL Project, Courant Inst. Math. Sci., New York Univ., June 1975.
[37] D. Shapiro, "Sniffers: A system that understands bugs," M.S. thesis, Rep. MIT/AIM-638, June 1981.
[38] D. Shapiro and B. McCune, "The intelligent program editor," in *Proc. IEEE Trends and Appl. Conf.*, May 1983.
[39] H. E. Shrobe, "Dependency directed reasoning for complex program understanding," Ph.D. dissertation, Rep. MIT/AI/TR-503, Apr. 1979.
[40] E. Soloway et al., "MENO-II: An intelligent programming tutor," *J. Comput.-Based Instruction*, vol. 10, no. 1, Summer 1983.
[41] E. Soloway and K. Ehrlich, "Empirical studies of programming knowledge," *IEEE Trans. Software Eng.*, vol. SE-10, Sept. 1984.
[42] R. Stallman, "Emacs the extensible, customizable, self-documenting display editor," in *Proc. ACM SIGPLAN-SIGOA Symp. Text Manipulation*, (ACM SIGPLAN Notices vol. 16, no. 6), June 1981.
[43] P. J. Sterpe, "Tempest—A template editor for structured text," M.S. thesis, Rep. MIT/AI/TR-843, May 1985.
[44] G. J. Sussman, J. Holloway, and T. Knight, "Computer aided evolutionary design for digital integrated systems," Rep. MIT/AIM-526, May 1979.
[45] T. Teitelbaum and T. Reps, "The Cornell program synthesizer: A syntax-directed programming environment," *Commun. ACM*, vol. 24, no. 9, Sept. 1981.
[46] R. C. Waters, "A system for understanding mathematical Fortran programs," Rep. MIT/AIM-368, May 1976.
[47] ——, "Automatic analysis of the logical structure of programs," Ph.D. dissertation, Rep. MIT/AI/TR-492, Dec. 1978.
[48] ——, "A method for analyzing loop programs," *IEEE Trans. Software Eng.*, vol. SE-5, May 1979.
[49] ——, "The programmer's apprentice: Knowledge based program editing," *IEEE Trans. Software Eng.*, vol. SE-8, Jan. 1982.
[50] ——, "Program editors should not abandon text oriented commands," *ACM SIGPLAN Notices*, vol. 17, no. 7, July 1982.
[51] ——, "Expressional loops," in *Proc. ACM SIGACT-SIGPLAN Symp. Principles of Program. Lang.*, Jan. 1984.
[52] ——, "KBEmacs: A step toward the programmer's apprentice," Rep. MIT/AI/TR-753, May 1985.
[53] D. S. Wile, "Program developments: Formal explanations of implementations," Inform. Sci. Inst., Univ. Southern California, Rep. ISI/RR-82-99, Aug. 1982.
[54] L. M. Zelinka, "An empirical study of program modification histories," Rep. MIT/AI/WP-240, Feb. 1983.

Richard C. Waters (M'78) received the B.S. degree magna cum laude in applied mathematics (computer science) from Brown University, Providence, RI, in 1972, the M.S. degree in computer science from Harvard University, Cambridge, MA, in 1973, and the Ph.D. degree in computer science with a minor in linguistics from the Massachusetts Institute of Technology, Cambridge, in 1978.

Since then, he has worked in the Artificial Intelligence Laboratory at the Massachusetts Institute of Technology and is currently a Principal Research Scientist. He is working on the Programmer's Apprentice project. This project is developing a system which can assist programmers to develop and maintain programs. His other interests include programming languages and engineering problem solving.

Dr. Waters is a member of the Association for Computing Machinery and the American Association for Artificial Intelligence as well as the IEEE Computer Society.

Kestrel Institute

REPORT ON A
KNOWLEDGE-BASED SOFTWARE ASSISTANT

Prepared by

CORDELL GREEN (Co-Chairman)

DAVID LUCKHAM (Co-Chairman)

ROBERT BALZER

THOMAS CHEATHAM

CHARLES RICH

Prepared for

ROME AIR DEVELOPMENT CENTER
Griffiss AFB, New York 13441
June 15, 1983

This research is supported by Rome Air Development Center through the University of Dayton, Ohio Order No. RI-23321 under United States Government contract #F30602-81-C-0206. This report has appeared as RADC #TR 83-195. The views and conclusions contained in this paper are those of the authors and should not be interpreted as representing the official policies, either expressed or implied, of Kestrel Institute or Rome Air Development Center. Additional copies are available from Kestrel Institute.

KESTREL INSTITUTE • 1801 PAGE MILL ROAD • PALO ALTO CA • (415) 493-6871

Contents

ABSTRACT

This report presents a knowledge-based, life-cycle paradigm for the development, evolution, and maintenance of large software projects. To resolve current software development and maintenance problems, this paradigm introduces a fundamental change in the software life cycle – maintenance and evolution occur by modifying the specifications and then rederiving the implementation, rather than attempting to directly modify the optimized implementation. Since the implementation will be rederived for each change, this process must be automated to increase its reliability and reduce its costs. Basing the new paradigm on the formalization and machine capture of all software decisions allows knowledge-based reasoning to assist with these decisions. This report describes a knowledge-based software assistant (KBSA) that provides for the capture of, and reasoning about, software activities to support this new paradigm. This KBSA will provide a corporate memory of the development history and act throughout the life cycle as a knowledgeable software assistant to the human involved (e.g., the developers, maintainers, project managers, and end-users. In this paradigm, software activities, including definition, management, and validation will be carried out primarily at the specification and requirements level, not the implementation level. The transformation from requirements to specifications to implementations will be carried out with automated, knowledge-based assistance. The report presents descriptions for several of the facets (areas of expertise) of the software assistant including requirements, specification validation, performance analysis, development, testing, documentation, and project management. The report also presents a plan for the development of the KBSA, along with a description of the necessary supporting technology. This new paradigm will dramatically improve productivity, reliability, adaptability, and functionality in software systems.

§1 EXECUTIVE SUMMARY

1.1 Objectives

The purposes of this report are:

1.　To propose a formalized computer-assisted paradigm for the development, evolution, and long-term maintenance of very large software application programs.

2.　To describe the knowledge-based software assistant (KBSA) needed to support that paradigm.

3.　To outline a long-term development plan designed to realize such a knowledge-based assistant.

1.2 The Problem

The existence of a software problem for large systems and its relevance to the military, which is becoming ever more reliant on software in its weapon systems, its planning, its logistics, its training, and its command and control has long been recognized and is well chronicled　. To date, attempts to resolve this problem have yielded only modest gains (a factor of 2-4 compared with the thousand fold increase in hardware performance) arising primarily from use of higher level languages and improved management techniques (software engineering).

Although further modest gains can still be achieved by continuing and accelerating this current technology, a fundamental flaw in the current software life cycle precludes larger qualitative improvements. The **process** of programming (conversion of a specification into an implementation, requirement into specification, etc.) is informal and largely undocumented. It is just this information, and the rationale behind each step, that is crucial, but unavailable, for maintenance. The current paradigm fails to recognize the general need to capture all life-cycle activities and the rationale behind them.

In order to capture the programming process and use knowledge-based tools appropriately, we must formalize **all** levels of activities as well as the transformations between them. Consider the current situation in which only the source code (implementation level) is available, but the specification and the mapping from it to the source code is not. In this situation, maintenance can be performed only on the source code (i.e., the implementation) which has already been optimized by the programmers. These optimizations spread information (take advantage of what is known elsewhere) and substitute complex but efficient realizations for simpler abstractions. Both of these effects exacerbate the maintenance problem by making the system harder to understand, by increasing the dependencies among the parts, and by delocalizing information. Similar situations hold for the mappings between requirement and specification, or requirement and testing levels.

1.3 Solution: A New Computer-Assisted Paradigm

We propose to shift the current informal person-based software paradigm into a formalized computer-assisted paradigm and to provide the knowledge-based software assistant (KBSA) required to support the paradigm.

The goals are more reliable and rapid development of systems with greater functionality and the build-up of a computerized corporate memory which, through the KBSA, will aid the continued evolution and adoption of the system, especially in the face of personnel turnover. The processes targeted for such assistance constitute the entire life cycle of major software development: project management, requirements definition, validation, implementation, testing, documentation, and maintenance. Thus, KBSA clearly parallels the DoD Software Initiative [1] and is a natural, long-term complement to it.

The basic KBSA paradigm can be summarized as "machine-in-the-loop", where **all software life-cycle activities are machine mediated and supported**. Initially, the KBSA will automatically document the occurrence of every activity and ensure the proper sequencing and coordination of all the activities performed by the individuals involved in a large project. Then, as the various activities are increasingly formalized, more sophisticated knowledge-based support will be provided.

In addition to mediating and supporting all life-cycle activities, all decisions (whether they concern requirements, validation, implementation, testing, or maintenance) must also be recorded together with their rationale. All these data must be machine readable and machine manipulable, so that the system can utilize programming and application knowledge bases as well as inference-based methods to explain complex aspects of the program and support its maintenance. Eventually – on the basis of understanding the relationships between the goals and the code of the application program – KBSA should be able to suggest plausible strategies for the design of program modifications and bear an appreciable portion of the burden of implementing and testing those strategies.

Because KBSA is mediating all development activities, it can support not only those individual activities, but also the development as a whole. It can coordinate one activity with another to maintain consistency; it can alert management if resources are, or are about to be, exceeded; it can help prevent maintainers from reexploring unfruitful implementations. In short, by mediating all of the development activity and by being knowledgeable about that development, KBSA can help people bring to bear whatever knowledge is relevant for their particular task. This is especially important on large projects where it is currently difficult, if not impossible, for people to comprehend and assimilate all the relevant information, which may be fragmented, incomplete, or inconsistent.

Rather than being merely a collection of capabilities, the KBSA would be an intelligent assistant that interfaces people to the computerized "corporate memory," aids them in performing their tasks, and coordinates their activities with those of other members of the team.

1.4 Areas of Assistance

We plan to incrementally formalize, and provide knowledge-based support for, all aspects of the software life cycle. In this section we highlight three areas that readily distinguish the KBSA paradigm from incremental improvements to the current paradigm. The first such area is "development," which encompasses both implementation and maintenance. We propose to formalize it so that implementations are the result of a series of transformations of the specifications. This formalization of the development process will enable maintenance to be performed by **altering the specification and replaying the previous development process** (the series of transformations), slightly modified, rather than by attempting to patch the implementation.

Such a capability will have profound effects. Systems will be larger, more integrated, longer lived, and will be the result of a large number of relatively small evolutionary steps. Software systems will finally reach their potential of remaining "soft" (modifiable) rather than becoming ossified, hardware-like, with age.

Another important life-cycle area is specification validation. Rather than validating already implemented systems which are difficult and expensive to change when problems are detected, validation will be performed by **using the specification itself as an executable prototype**. Specification errors detected will be much simpler and cheaper to correct, and systems will normally undergo several such specification/validation cycles (to get the specification "correct" and to get the end-users to completely state their requirements) **before** an implementation is produced.

A third life-cycle area is perhaps the most important: project management. The formalization, mediation, and support of life-cycle activities includes project management itself. Protocols will define the interaction between successive activies of a single agent and the concurrent activities of multiple agents. These activities will be mediated by an "activities coordinator." New management techniques will have to be developed for such a formalized and partially automated environment.

The other areas of assistance discussed in this report include requirements, performance, testing, and documentation.

1.5 Usage

As the KBSA evolves, it will be able to serve the needs of all participants in the program development, from the program manager to the journeyman coder. As it serves those needs, it will also serve as the repository of corporate knowledge, making possible both effective coordination of a large number of programmers and smooth transitions without serious setbacks as programming personnel change. While the KBSA will support all programming activities, it will present very different faces to different participants, depending on their roles in the program development process. To the project manager, it will appear as a planning assistant to help allocate tasks, and as a crisis monitor, warning of significant changes in system requirements or schedules and serving as a recording communications channel to the echelon of managers below. To the programmer in charge, for example, of testing a particular module, it will also serve as a news wire informing him/her of relevant program changes. But, in this case, it will further bring to bear its knowledge of program dependencies and of the rationale of prior test designs in order to assist the programmer in both the design and execution of the consequent retesting.

The application programs targeted include the very large (more than one million instruction) programs, such as those associated with command and control or weapons systems, that today require teams of more than a hundred programmers working several years on the original development and at least a decade on system maintenance.

1.6 The Development Plan

The KBSA development plan calls for the study and construction, over approximately a 10- to 15-year period, of individual mechanized facets of the assistant knowledgeable in program management, requirements analysis, implementation, validation, performance optimization, testing, and portability. At first, most of these facets will serve primarily as advanced documentation systems, recording the rationale for all design and implementation decisions. The first major technical efforts must be to formalize the representation of the subject matter and strategies in the domain of each facet. Next, inference mechanisms must be introduced to support the mechanical exploitation of the formal system development databases. Finally, knowledge bases specific to each facet, e.g., heuristic knowledge about the circumstances under which various choices of program transformations induce performance efficiencies, must be compiled. The true strength of KBSA will emerge as these knowledge-based methods provide greater levels of automation for the individual domain facets. KBSA must, just as importantly, provide a full life-cycle program development environment – a matrix in which the several facets may be integrated and which can serve as the all-important communication and coordination channel between them. The development of such advanced program coordination and a new form of project management appropriate for such an environment is an integral part of the KBSA proposal.

To achieve these goals one must:

1. Incrementally formalize each software life-cycle activity (with particular emphasis on project management, development, and validation) and create knowledge-based

tools and automated aids to support their use.

2. Formalize the coordinations and dependencies that arise in large software projects, create a language for stating project management policy in terms of these coordinations and dependencies, and an "interpreter" which coordinates all project activity in accordance with these rules.

3. Construct a framework in which all the tools and capabilities can be integrated (i.e., a life-cycle support environment) as they are incrementally created.

We believe that these requirements necessitate the use, and further development, of knowledge-based artificial intelligence techniques. Toward this end, our plan includes a major thrust of fundamental work in the supporting technologies of integrated knowledge representation, knowledge base management, and inference.

In the short term, the plan calls for several parallel efforts to construct the system framework, including activities coordination. The more successful will lead to the standards into which the formalized activities and automated aids will be integrated as they mature. Several such separate, unintegrated formalizations and automation efforts will be started. These development efforts are illustrated in Figure 1.

In the mid term, the separate formalization and automation efforts will be integrated into the standard frameworks to produce demonstrable prototypes. Meanwhile, the separate formalization and automation efforts will continue.

In the long term, one or more integrated prototypes will be production engineered for real use and transferred.

The plan distinguishes between varying degrees of automation and promises a certain amount of near- and mid-term technological "fallout." It also provides for a crucial mid-term attempt at system integration, the watershed test of whether the evolving KBSA meets the goals of rapid re-prototyping and retained software flexibility. Only if it does will knowledge-base managed system development and maintenance go beyond a brave new paradigm to become a reality.

The plan calls for a steering committee to help in further planning and to oversee the development of the KBSA.

§2 PROBLEMS AND SOLUTIONS

2.1 Statement of the Problem

The existence of a software problem and its relevance to the military, which is becoming ever more reliant on software in its weapon systems, its planning, its logistics, its training, and its command and control has long been recognized. The multitude of problems with the existing software development and maintenance life cycle, and their particular acuteness for the military, have been well chronicled elsewhere [1]. As pointed out in the DoD Software Initiative [1], merely doubling current productivity would result in yearly DoD savings of $2.5 to $3 billion and a payoff factor of over 200 on the investment.

Yet, attempts to date to resolve this problem have yielded only modest gains arising primarily from use of higher-level languages and improved management techniques. These improvements, which by the most optimistic estimates, have resulted in far less than an order-of-magnitude gain over the last 15 to 20 years, have in no way kept pace with the astounding thousand-fold increase that has occurred in hardware performance over the same period. Because the hardware revolution apparently will continue at this pace for at least the rest of this decade, it is clear that the utility of computers to the military, and to society as a whole, will be limited primarily by our ability to construct, maintain, and evolve software systems.

Continuation of existing efforts to improve the current software paradigm, broadly characterized as software engineering, will undoubtedly yield further incremental improvements more or less commensurate with those previously obtained, subject to the law of diminishing returns.

Rather than discuss problems with the current software paradigm here, we instead examine the underlying causes of these problems and suggest that qualitative improvements cannot be made until these underlying causes are removed. Unfortunately, the current software paradigm, which arose in an era when machines rather than people were expensive and in limited supply, is fundamentally flawed in a way that precludes larger qualitative improvements.

The flaw is that there is no technology for managing the knowledge-intensive activities that constitute the software development processes. The process of programming (the conversion of a specification into an implementation) is informal and largely undocumented.

It is just this information, and the rationale behind each step of this process, that is crucial, but unavailable, for maintenance. As a consequence, maintenance is performed on the implementation (i.e., the source code) because this is all that is available. All of the programmer's skill and knowledge have already been applied in optimizing this source code. These optimizations spread information. That is, they take advantage of what is known elsewhere and substitute complex but efficient realizations for (simple) abstractions.

Both of these effects exacerbate the maintenance problem by making the system harder to understand, by increasing the dependencies among the parts, and by delocalizing information.

Requirements analysis, specification, implementation, documentation, and maintenance are all knowledge-intensive activities. **But the current paradigm precludes the use of automated tools to aid these processes because it deals only with the products of these processes rather than with the processes themselves.**

Thus, the current software paradigm must be changed to explicitly represent and support these knowledge-intensive processes. The rest of this report is a description of such a knowledge-based approach to software support, and an identification of the technology needed to achieve it.

2.2 Proposed Solution

This section describes the long range objective of this effort in terms of a shift from the current informal, person-based software paradigm to a formalized, computer-assisted software paradigm and the knowledge-based software assistant that it both facilitates and requires. A more detailed view of the KBSA and its various facets is given in Section 3. The technology needed to support this paradigm is discussed in Section 4, and our incremental approach toward obtaining the goal KBSA system described here is presented in Section 5.

2.2.1 The Basis for a New Knowledge-Based Software Paradigm

The knowledge-based software paradigm of the future will provide a set of tools and capabilities integrated into an "assistant" that directly supports the human developers in the requirements analysis, specification, implementation, and maintenance processes. It will be characterized by the fact that "the machine is in the loop."

• All software life-cycle activities are machine mediated and supported

by the knowledge-based assistant as directed by the developers. These activities will be recorded to

• provide the "corporate memory" of the system evolution

and will be used by the assistant to determine how the parts interact, what assumptions they make about each other, what the rationale behind each evolutionary step (including implementation steps) was, how the system satisfies its requirements, and how to explain all these to the developers of the system.

This knowledge base will be dynamically acquired as a by-product of the development of each system. It must include not only the individual manipulation steps which ultimately lead to an implementation, but also the rationale behind those steps. Both pieces may initially have to be explicitly stated by the developers. Alternatively, explicit statement of the rationale by the developer may enable the automated assistant to select and perform a set of manipulations which achieve that objective for the developer. To make the process possible, it will be necessary to

- formalize all life-cycle activities.

For the knowledge-based assistant to begin to participate in the activities described above, and not just merely record them, the activities must be at least partially formalized. Formalization is the most fundamental basis for automated support; it creates the opportunity for the assistant to undertake responsibility for the performance of the activity, analysis of its effects, and eventually deciding which activities are appropriate. Not only will the individual development activities become increasingly formalized, but so, too, will coordinated sets of them which accomplish larger development steps. In fact, the development process itself will be increasingly formalized as coordinated activities among multiple developers.

2.2.2 Major Changes in Life-Cycle Phases

We have described three major differences between the knowledge-based software paradigm and the current software paradigm – the role of the history of system evolution, the formalization of life-cycle activities, and the automation it will enable – but we have not yet described the changes that will occur in the various phases of the software life cycle itself.

We are shifting from an informal person-based paradigm to a formalized computer-assisted paradigm. This formalization and computer support will alter and improve each life-cycle activity. But our intent is not to incrementally improve the current life-cycle activities, nor even to attempt to make large quantum improvements in them via advanced knowledge-based support. As we have argued, the current paradigm is fundamentally flawed and even large quantitative improvements will not correct those flaws.

Instead, our goal is to alter the current life cycle to remove the flaws and take advantage of the formalized computer-assisted paradigm described above. We therefore focus here on four life-cycle activities that differ in kind, rather than just degree, from current practice. They serve to distinguish the KBSA from incremental improvement of the current life cycle.

2.2.2.1 The Development (Implementation) Phase

First and foremost among these changes will be the emergence of formal specifications (expressed as machine-understandable descriptions) as the linchpin around which the entire software life cycle revolves.

In contrast to current practice, in which a specification serves only as an informal description of functionality and performance, which implementers and testers use as a guideline for their work,

- the actual implementation will be derived from the formal specification.

This will occur

- via a series of formal manipulations, selected by the developer and applied by the automated assistant

which convert descriptions of **what** is to happen into descriptions of **how** it is to happen efficiently. To the extent that these formal manipulations can be proved correct, the validation paradigm will be radically altered. Rather than testing the resulting implementation against the (informal) specification,

- the validity of the implementation will arise from the process by which it was developed.

That is, the development and the proof of correctness will be co-derived.

2.2.2.2 The Maintenance Phase

In order to maintain a program, it will be necessary only to

- modify the specification and/or refinement decisions and reimplement

  by "replaying" the development.

- Systems are not static;

even ones that, via prototyping (see below) match the user's original intent, and are validly implemented via automated assistance require updating. They evolve because the user's needs evolve, at least in part in response to the existence and use of the implemented system. Today, such evolution is accomplished by modifying (maintaining) the implementation. In the knowledge-based software paradigm, such evolution will occur by modifying (maintaining) the formal specification (rather than the implementation) and then reimplementing the altered specification by modifying and "replaying" the previously recorded implementation **process** (the sequence of formal manipulations that converted the specification into the implementation).

This represents another major shift from current practice.

- Rather than consisting of attempts to "patch" the optimized implementation,

- the maintenance activity will much more closely parallel the original development.

That is, first the specification will be augmented or revised (just as it is modified as a result of feedback from the prototyping/specification-revision cycle). Such modifications should be much simpler because they more closely approximate the conceptual level at which managers understand systems and for which their perception is that such modifications are trivial (it is the highly intertwined, delocalized, and sophisticated optimizations that make modification of implementations so difficult). The second step in maintenance is reimplementing the specification. This is another situation in which recording the development process provides leverage. Rather than recreating the entire implementation process, the developer will identify and modify those aspects of the previous development which either must be altered because they no longer work, or should be altered because they are no longer appropriate (i.e., no longer lead to an efficient implementation). Then, this altered development will be "replayed" by the automated assistant to obtain a new implementation.

• Increased development automation facilitates the "replay."

To the extent that automation has been used to fill in the details of the implementation process, as described earlier, the need to modify the development will be lessened as these details can be automatically adjusted to the new situation. In any case, the effort required to reimplement a specification is expected to be a small percentage of that required for the initial implementation, which in turn is expected to be a small percentage of that required for current conventional implementation.

Thus, in the knowledge-based software paradigm, the effort (and corresponding time delay) required both for implementation of the initial specification and especially for incremental modification (maintenance) of that specification, will be greatly reduced. This will allow that saved energy to be refocused on improved specification (matching the user's intent), on increased functionality in the specification (because implementation costs and complexity restrictions have been mitigated), and on increased evolution of that specification as the user's intent changes over time (at least in part because of the existence of the implemented system).

This will produce three of the most profound effects of the knowledge-based software paradigm:

• Systems will be larger, more integrated, longer lived, and will be the result of a large number of relatively small evolution steps.

• Software systems will finally reach their potential of remaining "soft" (modifiable) rather than becoming ossified, hardware-like, with age.

• Evolution will become the central activity in the software process.

In fact, rather than being limited to maintenance after the initial release,

• evolution will also become the means by which the "initial" specification is derived.

The current "batch" approach to specification in which the specification emerges full-blown all at once (often as a several-hundred-page tome) will be replaced by an "incremental" approach in which a very small formal specification is successively elaborated by the developer into the "initial" specification. These elaborations will occur via semantic manipulations (rather than "text editing") which capture the various types of elaboration (i.e., adding exceptions to a "normal" case, augmenting the functionality of a process, revising an earlier description, and so on). Thus, specifications will undergo a development just as the implementations they describe. Maintenance of the specification, whether after initial release of the implemented system or as part of the elaboration of the initial specification will occur by modifying this development structure rather than "patching" the specification.

2.2.2.3 Specification Validation Phase

Current testing supports more than just the comparison of the implementation with the (informal) specification, it also provides the means, through hands-on experience with the working implementation, to compare actual behavior to the user's intent. Often, if not usually, mismatches are detected and the implementation must be revised.

This second function of current testing will be replaced in the knowledge-based software paradigm by

- treating the specification as a testable prototype.

To make this possible, a subclass of formal specifications, called

- executable specifications must be employed.

Furthermore, some form of

- automatic or highly automated "compilation" must be used to provide reasonable (though not production quality) efficiency for running test cases.

Thus, the formal specification will be used as a prototype of the final system.

- This prototype will be tested against the user's intent.

Once it matches that intent, it will be developed into that final production implementation.

As opposed to current practice, in which prototyping is the exception,

- prototyping will become standard practice

in the new software paradigm because of its ready availability (via automatic or highly automated "compilation"). In fact,

- most systems will go through several prototyping or specification-revision cycles before implementation is undertaken.

2.2.2.4 Project Management

Project management has the responsibility for controlling, and therefore monitoring, all the software life-cycle activities. Currently project managers are severely hampered in this objective by the informal and undocumented nature of these activities and by the fragmentary, obsolete, and inconsistent data now available. In the KBSA paradigm, the situation will be very different. All the life-cycle activities will be formalized, their operation will be mediated and supported by the KBSA, and their progress will be recorded in the "corporate memory."

Thus, all the data needed for effective management will be available through the KBSA.

- Management must define what information it needs for on-line management

in terms of these data.

Furthermore, since the KBSA is mediating all life-cycle activities, the opportunity exists to

- formalize the coordination of activities.

- Management must define the project policies and procedures

to be implemented as protocols between the activities. These policies and procedures describe the operation of the project as a whole in terms of differentiated management styles. They define project organization, resource allocation, states and choices, transition between those states, and authorization of those transitions.

It should be noted that two desirable capabilities have been explicitly omitted from the knowledge-based software paradigm: fully automatic program synthesis (the automatic generation of production quality code from a formal specification) and natural language specification (the translation of an informal description into a formal specification). The rationale behind these omissions is described in Section 5.

To summarize, the knowledge-based software paradigm will differ markedly from the existing paradigm. The basis for this new paradigm will be capturing the entire development process (the identification of requirements, the design of the specification, the implementation of that specification, and its maintenance) and supporting it via an automated knowledge-based assistant. The development process will revolve around machine-understandable descriptions. Capabilities will exist to develop an "initial" specification incrementally from a kernel via a series of formal manipulations, to test the specification against the user's intent by treating it as a prototype (because the specification is executable), to develop an efficient implementation from that specification via further formal manipulations (which co-derive its proof of correctness), and to maintain the system by further developing the specification and its implementation and then replaying that implementation development. This will result in evolution as the central development activity and will produce systems that are longer lived, larger, more highly integrated and which remain pliable to further modification as user needs themselves evolve.

2.2.3 An Automated Assistant

In describing the knowledge-based software paradigm, frequent reference was made to an automated assistant. This paradigm both facilitates and requires the existence of such an assistant, as a consequence of having the whole development processes (requirements analysis, specification, implementation, and maintenance) machine mediated and supported. Thus, these development processes must be broken up into individual activities.

The KBSA will participate in all the coordinated development activities (including the coordination itself) to aid the developers. The existence of such an assistant will, in turn, fundamentally alter the software life-cycle activities, as described in Section 2.2.2, as its capabilities alter the feasibility and cost of these various development activities.

- The KBSA will support the new software paradigm by recording the development activities, performing some of them, analyzing their effects, and aiding their selection.

It is because of the sophistication of the capabilities involved and the fact that several different sources of knowledge will be involved (knowledge of requirements, specification, implementation, evolution, validation, analysis, etc.) that this assistant is called the knowledge-based software assistant or KBSA.

Because KBSA is mediating all development activities, it can support not only those individual activities, but also the development as a whole. It can coordinate one activity with another to maintain consistency; it can alert management if resources are, or are about to be, exceeded; it can help prevent maintainers from reexploring unfruitful implementations. In short, by mediating all of the development activity and by being knowledgeable about that development, KBSA can help people bring to bear whatever knowledge is relevant for their particular task. This is especially important on large projects where it is currently difficult, if not impossible, for people to comprehend and assimilate all the relevant information, which is often fragmented, incomplete, or inconsistent.

The KBSA is an intelligent assistant that interfaces people to the computerized "corporate memory," aids them in performing their tasks, and coordinates their activities with other members of the team.

- The evolutionary creation of the KBSA and the incremental formalization of the development activities upon which it is based is the central theme of our research plan.

As we learn to formalize the various life-cycle activities, we will build KBSA capabilities to perform, analyze, select, and/or coordinate them. Over time, this will allow developers to concentrate more and more on the higher level aspects of the development process and turn more and more of the low-level details over to the KBSA. That is,

- as the development process is incrementally formalized, it can be increasingly automated.

Because, for the foreseeable future, we intend to keep the developer, as well as the machine, in the loop, provision of suitable interfaces are necessary so that the developers and the KBSA can work effectively together.

To summarize, we begin with the commitment to having "the machine in the loop." This will cause the development processes of requirements, specifications, design, implementation, and maintenance to be divided into a larger number of smaller, more formalized steps. This finer granularity and increased formality will enable the emergence of a KBSA that aids developers in coordinating and performing of all of the activities and records those activities as the documentation of the system's development. This incremental approach to formalizing the individual development activities and their coordination, and to providing automated assistance to the developers through the KBSA, is the foundation of the shift from the current informal person-based software paradigm to the new formalized computer-assisted KBSA paradigm.

Related Work

Since surveys are available,and to limit the scope of this planning effort, we have intentionally not prepared a survey of related work. We refer the reader to three references. The first book [2] covers knowledge-based systems in general, and the referenced chapter specifically covers applications of knowledge-based systems to software assistance. The second two references, [3] and [4], review software engineering environments.

§3 KBSA INTERNAL STRUCTURE

In Section 2, we described the KBSA as a single unified knowledge-based assistant that mediated and supported all the life-cycle activities, recorded them to provide a "corporate memory" of the development, and coordinated the activities of the individual project members. Here we consider the internal structure needed to realize such capabilities.

The KBSA is a complex, highly interconnected system. Nevertheless, it is necessary to divide it, both for explanation and creation purposes, into its major functional blocks. There are four of these, as illustrated in Figure 2. The central foundation of the KBSA is the framework, which includes an activities coordinator and a knowledge-base manager.

The job of the KBSA is to validate each activity as it is performed, record that activity, and coordinate it with other activities as defined by formal protocols.

Project management policies and procedures establish those protocols. Its documentation requirements are satisfied by the recorded activity, and its tasking (resource allocation) is handled as a coordinated activity.

The other activities which are coordinated in the KBSA could be grouped in many different ways. We have chosen to group them according to the familiar software life-cycle phases to make them more understandable and to present one feasible decomposition. While this grouping helps us describe the evolutionary staged development of automated support we envision in each area, it is important to remember that major change in the life cycle (as described in Section 2.2.2) will result from the KBSA. Therefore, other groupings may well be more appropriate for the construction of the KBSA. Our choice of groupings and their evolutionary development must be considered illustrative and is not meant to restrict the selection of other groupings or development scenarios.

Eventually, as the integration between these activities becomes tighter, we expect them to lose their individual identity and to become the single knowledge-based assistant described in Section 2. Only then will we have fulfilled the promise of the new software paradigm.

To prevent misinterpretation, we feel it is important to reiterate that although the rest of this section describes the facets separately, the users will see but a single entity, the KBSA, with many capabilities. Instead of a multitude of interfaces, languages, and conventions, users will experience a single KBSA, expert in all aspects of software development.

Finally, there is the support environment upon which such a system is built. It includes version and access control, an inference engine, and user interface capabilities.

This KBSA internal structure is further described in the following subsections. At the end of each section we have provided a set of short and mid-term goals for each facet.

The long-term goals are given in the description of each facet, and in some sections, certain long-term goals have also been included in the list of goals at the end of the section.

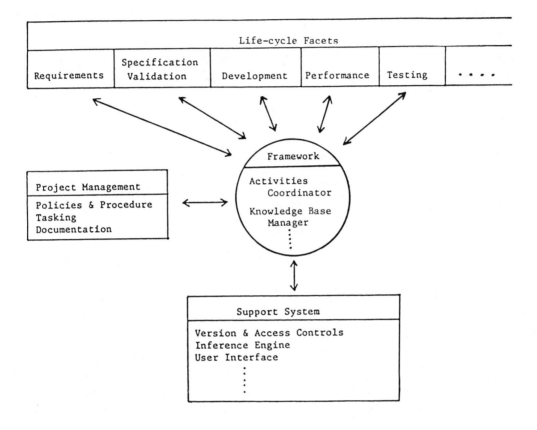

Figure 2. GENERALIZED KBSA STRUCTURE

3.1 Activity Coordination

The facets of the KBSA must be embedded in a large framework and support system, which includes an activities coordinator, knowledge base manager, inference mechanisms, program analyzer, version and access control, user interfaces, etc. In this subsection we have singled out for discussion the novel concept of the activities coordinator; the more familiar supporting components of knowledge-based systems are discussed in Section 3.4, "KBSA Support System," and Section 4, "Supporting Technology."

The development and subsequent maintenance of a large application program or family of related application programs often involve a considerable number of agents – analysts, programmers, test engineers, managers, documentation specialists, users, and so on. The activities being carried on by these agents require various kinds of coordination. For example, suppose that some agent has the task of modifying some program module. Before incorporating the result of the modification into a new release, project management policy may require that certain tests have been performed satisfactorily, that the changes have been logged appropriately, and that relevant documentation has been updated. Furthermore, the approval of some manager may be required before the result can be distributed.

How can such policies and procedures be formalized so that automated support can be provided? Modern programming environments, with their software data bases and integrated tool sets, often already provide some preliminary coordination capablities. For example, they usually provide mechanisms for version control so that one can determine those elements of the software data base that are up to date and those that are not. In addition to being part of a version, a program module derived by some tool (e.g., a compiler) often has a derivation history that relates it to the parent modules involved in its derivation. If one or more of these parents is subsequently modified, resulting in a new version, then the derived module also requires updating.

These environments also include lock and key mechanisms to ensure that only those agents having the requisite authority (the key) are permitted to take certain actions, like modifying certain modules or invoking certain tools.

While such version control and locking mechanisms are certainly necessary, they are not sufficient for the kinds of protocols needed to describe other software development and maintenance activities. Instead, we need a language to describe the types of coordination (i.e., protocols) that exist between the software development agents and an interpreter of that language. This would provide the basis for the formalization not only of the types of coordination, but also of the software development activities being coordinated. As described earlier, such formalization is the basis for the entire KBSA approach to computer-assisted support. Such a language would enable the wide range of idiosyncratic policies and procedures that have successfully been used by managers to be expressed. The interpreter could then monitor and facilitate project development in compliance with these policies and procedures. As with other aspects of the

KBSA, staged incremental introduction of knowledge-based capabilities would enable increasingly sophisticated support from the KBSA with less explicit user direction.

In addition to knowing about the elements of the software data base and the tools available in the tool set, this extended system would have knowledge of agents, both human and mechanized, that participate in the development and maintenance activities and the relationships among them. Rather then being limited to the current mode in which users explicitly invoke separate discrete tools, the extended system would support a collection of ongoing activities with each activity having an underlying protocol that specifies the coordination with other activities. Thus, the environment would be active rather then passive. It would ensure the validity of each agent's actions and instigate further activity from other agents as defined by the coordination protocols.

Communication among the agents and activities would be via messages. These messages would not just be text but would be formal objects in the system that included references to other formal objects – the modules, agents, organizations, activities, other messages, etc. Examples would include queries regarding some element (e.g., a "bug" report), replies to specific queries, requests for permission to take some action, grants and/or denials of such requests, and so on. The movement of a message (plus other messages generated on account of that message) would generate an audit trail that would, for example, enable the determination of the status of or prognosis for some activity that was generated in accordance with a query (for example, the repair of a problem in accordance with some "bug" report).

Each activity ongoing in the system would, at any point in time, be in some state. For each state there would be a set of choices that were possible, some of which could result in the transition to a new state. The inter- and intra-coordination of activities would be accomplished by controlling the choices that were possible at each state of an activity. There could be a number of ways of controlling these choices. One would most certainly be through the usual lock and key mechanisms; an agent could choose a certain action because he had the right (the key) to do so. Another means of control would be to require the agent to obtain formal permission from another agent or organization that had the right to authorize the action proposed. The request for a permission and the grant of the permission would be via formal message objects that were so interpreted by the system. A third means of control would entail a collection of rules that dynamically described the relationships among the various elements of the system.

That a particular choice was permitted or denied would result from demonstrating that the predicate enabling the choice could or could not be inferred from the current state of the activities within the system.

3.2 Project Management and Documentation

This section describes two facets – project management and documentation – that are called out for treatment here in a separate section from the other facets because they have strong, across-the-board interaction with all the other facets. That is, the power of these two facets contributes to the power of each of the other facets, and is derived from the existence of each of the other facets. For example, the project management facet helps to manage tasks being carried out with the assistance of the development assistant and also derives information from the development assistant. The documentation facet helps to explain specifications, requirements, performance, etc., using information from these facets.

3.2.1 Project Management Facet

The long-term goal of the project management facet is to provide knowledge-based help to users and managers in project communication, coordination, and management tasks that range from simple inquiries about tasks to reorganization of project plans. The goals are to reduce project costs, speed project development and maintenance, manage more effectively, provide greater project continuity, improve project communication, increase software reliability, and improve responsiveness to change. The management facet will assist throughout the life cycle from inception through maintenance. It will provide assistance to all KBSA users, not just managers.

The project management facet (PMF) consists of a formalism, a knowledge base and message manager, and an accompanying set of knowledge-based tools and procedures. All important (designated) project information, communication, and decisions will be formally expressed, recorded in the knowledge base, and available through these tools.

The project management facet uses the coordination and message handling capabilities of the activities coordinator to carry out its work. It is distinguished from the activities coordinator by its domain of discourse and types of decision making (task assignment, etc.). The PMF will use other general KBSA inference and knowledge-base management tools where appropriate. A tutoring system will help human agents (designers, users, and managers) learn how to use the assistant system.

The knowledge base, including the set of scripts and procedures, forms a **semantic model** of the entire project, including its history, and its procedures and policies. The **power** of the PMF derives from being able to use this semantic model or knowledge source to **reason** about the project rather than just act as a data management system. Most activities will have at least an underlying protocol that provides the means for internal coordination with other activities. More complex management activities will have more complex protocols and inference procedures to provide means for reasoning about management decisions, implementing policies, weighing evidence, etc. A uniform interface will allow human or automated agents to make requests for management assistance without having to know details about all the tools.

Short-Term Goals

- Project Management Formalism

  The first step is to develop a machinable formalism for project management knowledge.

  This formalism is the framework that will be used to implement all knowledge base operations, message handling, inference procedures, and other facet capabilities. To the extent that messages, tasks, etc. are not described within this formalism, the PMF will not be able to do intelligent things with them. At first there will be more free-form text associated with these entities, largely incomprehensible to machines, but as the PMF grows, more of this text will be expressed as knowledge in the PMF formalism.

- Knowledge Base and Message Handling

  Using the above formalism and the activities coordinator, the PMF knowledge base manager and message handler will deal with all formalized aspects of PMF knowledge. They will store and retrieve PMF knowledge and send and receive PMF messages. All messages and knowledge base entries will either include descriptors within the formalism or be entirely within the formalism. All important communications and decisions can be recorded, but at first their formalization (which allows indexed entry into the knowledge base) will be manual.

  The knowledge base of project tasks will let managers and other agents keep track of the tasks to be done and keep records of what is completed. (At first, completion will be explicitly reported to the KBSA; later the PMF facet will recognize completion automatically.) Managers will be able to look at the set of tasks and organize and assign them. The task structure will reflect the development of the system and the tasks completed, and those remaining will be explicit and available for study when the project is reviewed.

  An initial set of message-handling capabilities will be developed to allow agents to be assigned tasks and report their progress and to allow human agents to communicate. In the early stages, the arbitration of messages will be entirely by human designer or manager, but human arbitration will gradually receive increasing knowledge-based assistance. An interface will allow people to understand and monitor the formal messages to and from automated agents.

- Task Tracking

  The above formalism, knowledge-base system, and message-handling system together lay the necessary groundwork so that the PMF can be extended by the addition of simple project management procedures and deductive inferences. For convenience, we will group these simple procedures and inference capabilities under the heading of **task tracking**. The inferences will require that dependency links, messages, and other items can be traced through the knowledge base.

Scripts for project management disciplines or paradigms will be developed and used to guide or enforce these management disciplines.

Mid-Term Goals

- Suggesting Simple Management Decisions

  Using all the above tools, the capability of the PMF will then be extended so that it will suggest simple management decisions. The inferences made in this decision making differ from those inferences made in the task tracker, in that the decisions here require weighing of evidence and more detailed models of tasks and agents. The decisions will still be limited to relatively local decisions about particular tasks or agents, however.

- Plan and Procedure Creation and Modification

  Using all the above tools, the PMF will be extended to generate or modify plans and procedures. At this stage the PMF will deal with entire plans and procedures and carry out significant refinements and transformations of them. Transformational methods developed in the development facet could be brought to bear on the problem.

- Knowledge Acquisition

  Extensions of the above tools will allow simple knowledge aquisition by having PMF knowledge available and all transactions capturable and manipulable within the formalism.

3.2.2 Documentation

The long range goal of the KBSA is to provide the project manager and each project member with the equivalent of an expert on personal call to answer specific questions on any aspect of the project or the software being developed. For example, a user may inquire about the possible arguments to a command. A system developer/maintainer may inquire about the purpose of a particular line of code. The project manager may want to know the testing status of a particular module. In all these cases, the KBSA could answer their questions because the relevant knowledge has been captured and formalized as part of the software development process. In a sense, all of the knowledge used in each of the KBSA's activities is available for explanation and documentation.

Given adequate underlying knowledge, the main issues in documentation have to do with how to communicate this information cogently. For example, what constitutes a good explanation? How and when is it appropriate to summarize information? One good way to explain something is to identify it as an instance of some familiar general class, such as "this is a temporary variable" or "this is a kind of directory listing command." Another effective type of explanation is to describe the role of a thing in some causal or goal structure, such as "the setting of this flag causes the following actions to occur" or "the purpose of this test is to guarantee that the input satisfies the following condition." The feasibility of automatically generating explanations to unforeseen queries about the internal workings of a complicated program is being explored in current research.

An example of the use of the documentation facet is in project management. Maintaining up-to-date and accurate documentation is crucial to the management of any large software product, as well as in providing help and tutoring facilities for the users of the project management facet. The initial documentation facet will be for experienced managers, designers, and programmers. The help facilities initially will be for these experienced people and will be similar to current help facilities. Once the KBSA has evolved enough, it will have an environment that includes naive users as well as designers and managers with a range of experience. The KBSA will include many automated agents and will be used for production systems and maintenance. Therefore, tutoring capabilities will be added that go far beyond the original help system. The tutoring will allow new (and old) team members to learn about the assistant itself (and about other agents) and about the state of the project (task structure as well as design decisions and code state).

The most obvious benefit of this kind of explanation as compared to current documentation practices is that the information delivered is more focused and directed to the specific needs of the person inquiring at the time. However, the greatest benefit of this technique results from the fact that the underlying knowledge from which explanations are drawn is necessarily kept up to date because the KBSA mediates and supports all project activities. In the best current practice, most of the underlying decisions are lost from the beginning.

Short Term Goals

- On-Line Documentation

  There are many fairly standard kinds of documentation for various different audiences that are now in common use: " A, B, and C specs," hierarchical flowcharts, user reference manuals, "help" files, and so on. In the short term, it will not be possible to formalize much of the knowledge in these documents; most of it will have to remain in the form of text strings to be read and interpreted by the user. However, it will be a step in the right direction to provide a central data base with a defined (and possibly extensible) vocabulary of structuring primitives available to all agents in the software development process throughout the entire life cycle (this is an instance of KBSA's "corporate memory"). Furthermore, by cross-indexing this documentation to other parts of the software that are also kept on-line, such as the code or the requirements, it will be possible to automatically monitor whether the documentation is being kept up to date. Finally, it will be possible to automatically generate various kinds of standard-format documents using specially written procedures that read the appropriate subset of information out of the data base. Examples already exist in which a simple hierarchical data base (with text files at each node) is used to maintain the status of all modules for project management purposes. Final deliverable documents could then be automatically generated from the same data base by combining the text files with standard boiler-plate.

- Partially Formalized Documentation

To effectively increase the degree of formalization of the documentation, we propose to reduce the "chunk" size in the data base and extend the vocabulary of keywords describing the chunks and their relationships. At this stage, the chunks of unformalized text should not exceed the size of paragraphs and might often be smaller, such as a single line describing the purpose of a variable. One benefit of this fine-grain structure is to allow an incremental change in the software to require only incremental effort in revising the documentation. The pointers between the software and the documentation help to localize those parts of the documentation that are affected by a particular modification to the software. Also at this point, one could begin to design protocols for accessing and perusing the documentation which adjusted to the user's level of expertise, prior knowledge, and so on. With these facilities the emphasis begins to shift from "documentation," which suggests static pre-formatted text, to an "explanation" dynamically generated in answer to specific questions in an interactive relationship.

Mid-Term Goal

- Partially Automated Knowledge Acquisition

In mid-development of the KBSA, the system developer's burden of being the sole source of documentation information will begin to be lessened by having the KBSA automatically gather and record the knowledge needed for explanation and documentation as a by-product of other system development activities. For example, a natural by-product of using the KBSA is the knowledge about design decisions which is needed for reference during future modifications. Another general source of information is various kinds of program analyses, such as those performed for performance optimization.

3.3 KBSA Facets

This subsection describes an example set of KBSA facets selected to aid comprehension by their correspondence to current life-cycle phases. By selecting and describing these specific facets, one particular view is provided in sufficient detail to define what would suffice as a KBSA.

3.3.1 Requirements

The long-term goal of the requirements facet is to provide the following: comprehensive requirements management, intelligent editing of requirements, testing of requirements for completeness and consistency (both self-consistency and consistency with application domain models), performing requirements reviews, maintaining and transforming requirements in response to changes, decomposing and refining requirements into executable specification languages, and acquiring requirements knowledge. The knowledge base available for these actions will include both general and application-specific knowledge.

Requirements will be acquired by KBSA via dialog with end-users (systems analysts will have to be used until the level of this dialog becomes sufficiently high-level and application-specific). These end-users will define and modify the requirements and behavior of their desired system by a combination of high-level, domain-specific requirements languages, examples, traces, state-transition diagrams, graphics, and so on, in whatever mix they find comfortable. The process will be a mixed-initiative dialog, where the sequence of statements need not correspond to the organization of the final program. KBSA's role is to have enough knowledge about requirement analysis and about specific application domains to be able to accept and process these descriptions. The requirements facet will organize the stated requirements and incorporate them into existing descriptions. It will notice inconsistencies and missing parts of the requirements, and suggest remedies, fill in pieces, and point out trade-offs whenever it can. The facet will also, on request, describe the current state of the requirements specifications in natural language, graphically, or by simulating the behavior of the system as much as possible. The facet will help integrate new requirements into an existing requirements specification and will use knowledge-based program refinement techniques to help transform these requirements into executable specification languages.

Knowledge-based tools for the requirements facet will have a high payoff. Because the lower-level program development and management tasks will be increasingly automated and will take place in the background with less and less human intervention, requirements definition and specification will be of increasing importance, with most of the human effort in software development eventually going into this process.

Software development efforts today do not approach such an ideal. In most projects, requirements are largely unformalized and stated in natural language. Current requirements languages do allow some formalization, principally in the characterization of dependencies, but requirements are rarely machine comprehensible to any significant extent. An additional consequence of informal requirements statements is that requirements usually cannot be executed in any conventional sense.

A formal requirements language will allow, and in fact will demand, knowledge-based requirements processing. The reason is that formal requirements are incomplete; they only partially describe the intended behavior of any system. For them to be understood and processed in some meaningful sense, these partial descriptions must be integrated and completed in some reasonable manner. Such inference capabilities are prototypical of the type of assistance required by the KBSA facets. This formal language might also be executable to allow rapid prototyping (see "Specification Validation" Section 3.3.2, for a more complete description of rapid prototyping). It is important to note that it is unlikely in the near future either extreme of machine understanding of natural language requirements descriptions or formal languages for complete requirements specifications will be realizable. However, a knowledge-based facet could provide capabilities that allow requirements to be combinations of formalized specifications, machine-understandable but restricted natural language, keyword recognition, and unparsed text strings. The KBSA effort might use whatever natural language comprehension technology becomes available, but it is not committed to, or dependent upon, advances in this area.

A few knowledge-based software systems have been built that dealt with requirements specifications and have helped determine the consistency of these descriptions. They demonstrated the basic feasibility of formal requirements analysis, despite the added difficulty of working with restricted natural language.

Since generation of natural language is a more tractable problem than comprehension, paraphrasing or summarizing requirements definitions from multi-format presentations is possible. This is an achievable and valuable capability for helping people to handle the complexity of large systems and could be especially useful in validation activities.

Domain models for different application areas will facilitate requirements definition. These models give the requirements facet more knowledge to help understand user descriptions, to notice inconsistencies, and to suggest missing parts of descriptions. Since the potential range of applications areas is quite broad (and includes research topics such as reasoning about time and space), it is unlikely that a complete set of domain models can be supplied in advance. However, some simple and frequently used domain models are likely to be available.

Requirements definition can also be viewed as a knowledge-acquisition problem. The requirements activities will consist not only of acquiring new requirements descriptions, but also of acquiring models of new application areas. These activities will draw from the research areas of knowledge acquisition (including mixed initiative acquisition of domain models from experts), problem reformulation, rule-acquisition, inductive inference of requirements from examples, etc. Some practitioners of the requirements analysis art feel that a very important part of their task is generalizing and structuring the user's ill-defined needs. As the lower levels of software production are increasingly automated, requirements acquisition will become the main interface between the user and the programming environment. This is an exciting and high payoff area of research.

Short-Term Goals

- Analysis of Requirements Problem Definition

  There has been less research on knowledge-based tools for the requirements level than for the later phases of the software development life cycle. Accordingly, less is known and further problem definition should occur in the early phase of the KBSA project. The first year of work on the knowledge-based requirements facet should include a planning phase to review and refine the short-, mid-, and long-term goals.

- A Formal Requirements Language

An initial requirements language will be designed that allows a combination of formal specifications and text strings. This very high level language (VHLL) will probably be an extension of the very high level specification languages being developed today. In the early stages of the KBSA project, new insights will arise about the KBSA life cycle and its effect on this facet. By the mid-term, these should be incorporated into a revised VHLL for requirements. The language will also describe histories of requirements modifications and refinements.

- Smart Editing and Managing of Requirements

Knowledge-based editing and management capabilities for the requirements facets, including help facilities and a friendly user interface, are important aids to the requirements definition activity. A variety of specification fragments, including both a formal language for requirements and text strings, need to be managed. For convenience, even text strings will be handled in simple ways such as storage, retrieval, keyword analysis, etc. Dependencies among requirements will be specifiable.

An intelligent editor will be used to create and modify requirements definitions. At first, the editor will ensure only that the syntactic structure of the formal requirements language is followed. Next, the editor will be used to trace through the connections of related requirements during editing to ensure consistency. Later, generic requirements descriptions (for example, an input-process-output sequence) will be stored in the knowledge base. Such descriptions can be used as models to fill in and can be matched against a user-created description. These models will be used to check completeness and may provide additional consistency tests.

- Reviewing Requirements Definitions for the User

Getting the user to view the requirements in a new light and possibly see problems or opportunities is an important capability for producing requirements descriptions. Review methods could include paraphrase in natural language, graphic displays of domain models in the knowledge base, executing the specification, writing stubs or facades that demonstrate the format, if not the content, of the specified system, and rapid prototyping to help determine behavioral requirements.

- Requirements Testing

Simple inferences can be used to help determine the adequacy of requirements. One source of help in requirements definition is the adaptation of capabilities and paradigms from lower levels of the KBSA. Some activities can be carried out without any domain knowledge—consistency checking, analysis, and explanation, for example. The first set of requirements tools will therefore check for a simple heuristic kind of completeness and consistency. These inference procedures can extend the requirements editor's ability to either fill in details or test against stored general knowledge. In addition, by employing traditional, non-knowledge-based analysis, the requirements tools will detect entities that are undefined, entities defined but never referenced, data flow anomalies, etc. Later, for suitably limited domains, we can include the performance facet at the requirements level to help in assessing the cost of desired features.

Mid-Term Goals

- Incorporating Domain Knowledge into the Requirements Capabilities

Simple models of frequently used domains will be developed. The first model will be for a fairly narrow domain or application (e.g., simple classification programs). The models will supply the knowledge base that will be used for domain-specific support of the requirements capabilities.

As domain models are added, the requirements capabilities will be augmented to take advantage of the new knowledge. For example, domain knowledge will be used by the intelligent editor/manager to retrieve application-specific, previously described, or generic requirements descriptions from the knowledge base that match the user's current needs. These descriptions will serve as useful models to be compared to the specified requirements to check consistency and completeness. By employing more sophisticated techniques such as symbolic evaluation of the requirements language and some inductive inference, more application-specific inconsistencies can be inferred.

- An Automated Structured Walk-Through System for Requirements Engineering

Many of the capabilities described above will be combined in a script (process description) and applied with a form of symbolic interpretation. For example, a structured walk-through tool based on a fault model representation and on a requirements language will aid an expert systems analyst to keep track of loose ends and problem areas. It accepts requirements as input, together with other management information (e.g., who should approve it, who heads up the prime user groups, who heads the implementor group). Such a tool will be able to perform some useful background analysis for missing or incompatible requirements.

- Requirements Transformation and Refinement

At this stage, techniques from knowledge-based program synthesis could be extended to allow transformations of requirements. For example, if a program is set up for monthly reports, and weekly reports are required, the knowledge base could supply descriptions of the necesary changes to make. Depending on the level of difficulty, the facet might either suggest and remind the user of the kinds of changes, or actually carry out the transformations automatically. Requirements refinement is the other type of transformation. In this case the requirements are brought through successively more detailed stages until they reach the level of executability. This type of decomposition and filling in of detail is exactly what happens in program refinement discussed in the development facet (Section 3.3.3), but higher-level knowledge is needed here. The facet suggests alternative refinements and decompositions. The transformations may be manual, interactive, or automated as fits the situation.

- A Requirements Tutor

  Tutoring capabilities at the requirements level will help new members of the software design team to start contributing sooner. For example, tutoring will help them learn to use the software assistant's capabilities. It also will help them to understand the current configuration of requirements specifications and the previous decisions that provide the context for new requirements decisions.

3.3.2 Specification Validation

Eventually, formal specifications will be developed using KBSA and starting from informal requirements. Specifications will be the first formal representation of the system to be built. As in all other areas, this representation must be formal for KBSA participation and support. Furthermore, it is crucial for the KBSA paradigm that the specification language be executable so that the specification can be used as a testable prototype and so that source-to-source program transformations can be used to convert it into an efficient implementation.

As the first formal representation of the system to be built, the question arises as to whether this formal statement matches the user's original intent. Even though the specification is much more abstract than the implementation, it is still complex for real systems. Therefore, the first formal specification will usually be wrong and will have to be "debugged." In fact, several debugging cycles will normally be needed to get the specification correct.

Since we are dealing with a specification rather than an implementation, we use the term "validation" rather than "debugging" to describe this process. Because the formal specification is being compared to the user's informal intent, only the user can make this comparison.

Three techniques exist for validating the specification: prototyping, static validation, and dynamic validation. They are complementary and will be intermixed in practice.

Prototyping consists of running test cases on the specification. This is theoretically possible since the specification is executable. However, to achieve reasonable efficiency (so that test cases can be run), considerable optimization must be achieved. This would either be done via a partial interactive development or, preferably, by a smart compiler capable of producing testable, rather than production-quality, code. Such prototyping has all the strengths and weaknesses of current testing. Specific cases can be tried quickly and easily and can expose some bugs rapidly, but such probing is far from comprehensive.

The second validation technique is static validation, which consists of paraphrasing the formal specification in natural language so that an easily read form is available for the end-user to conduct a design review (as is being done with manually produced B5 specifications). Two advantages arise from such paraphrasing: first, formal specifications in any language are hard to read and comprehend; second, by regrouping the elements, a different view or perspective is presented which also aids comprehension.

The last validation technique is dynamic validation, which is an extension of the prototyping technique. Rather than running specific test cases, symbolic execution will be used to characterize all the behaviors produced for an entire class of test cases. In order to understand the set of such behaviors, an explanation must be produced which characterizes the "main line" and then details the exceptions and/or augmentations that are test-case specific. A mixture of natural language and graphic animation will be the medium of such an explanation.

Short-Term Goals

- Executable Specification Language

  We propose to develop a high level specification language that is still capable of being executed (albeit extremely slowly). Note that interaction with the development facet will occur via the specification language. The KBSA specification language must be both executable and wide spectrum.

- Specification Wellformedness Checking

  This would include the capability to check for internal consistency within a specification (e.g., all types and actions used are defined, number and type of actual arguments agree with the formal argument).

- Specification Testing

  It would be important to develop the capability to run test cases, both concrete and symbolic, on the specification.

- Specification Paraphraser

  The capability to automatically paraphase a formal specification in natural language (to make it more comprehensible, especially to end users) should include the ability to identify which portion or portions of the specification to emphasize.

Mid-Term Goals

- Rapid Prototyping

  This would entail developing the capability to automatically (or at least nearly automatically) compile a formal specification to an efficiency level that permits realistic testing of the specification as a prototype.

- Self Consistency Checker

  This would include verification of satisfaction of formal requirements, establishment of pre and post conditions, and detection of deadlock and starvation.

- Behavior Explanation

  We propose to develop the capability to explain in natural language the behavior of a specification (as opposed to just the result produced) on both concrete and symbolic test cases.

Long-Term Goals

- Summarize Behavior

  The idea is to develop the capability to automatically summarize specification behavior in natural language for different audiences and experience levels (e.g., highlight surprising results or normal case behavior).

3.3.3 Development

The job of this KBSA facet is to aid the creation of a production quality implementation. Since the full functionality of the intended system has been captured in the formal specification, that specification "merely" needs to be compiled to accomplish this task. Unfortunately, even smart, knowledge-based compilers, may not be capable of producing production-quality implementations. The reason is that to the extent that the specification language is fulfilling its purpose as a description of <u>what</u> rather than <u>how</u>, the gap between the formal specification and an efficient implementation is too wide to bridge totally automatically. Therefore, we will need to keep people, the developers, in the implementation loop. What should their role be and how can we aid them in that role?

These questions can best be answered by considering a related question: what implementation functions are difficult to automate (and hence will be performed by the developers)? The answer is simply, the decision-making portion. The implementation process consists of numerous implementation decisions such as how to represent some information, what algorithm to employ to obtain some result, what information to save, when and how to recompute that information not saved, etc..

There are three difficulties in automating these decisions. First, the decisions are not independent. The choice made for one decision often affects which choice should be made for another. Second, techniques for evaluating the relative values of different choices in the presence of other unmade decisions are quite limited or nonexistent (partly because of the interactions among these decisions). Finally, little is known about the order in which these decisions should be considered (good designers are observed to employ very different orderings).

These difficulties argue for a continuing role for the developer as decisionmaker in the implementation process. But what of the rest of the process? It consists of carrying out these decisions. Currently this is done all at once, after most (or all) of the decisions have been made, by incorporating them in the code of the implementation (the first and only formal representation of the system).

In the knowledge-based software paradigm, this process will proceed very differently. First, each decision will be captured as it is made to document the development process. Next, it will be realized in the "specification." That is, portions of the specification will be replaced with pieces of "implementation." As later decisions get made and realized, other pieces of the specification will be replaced, or the replacements themselves may undergo further refinement. Many such levels of implementation may occur before the final efficient implementation is obtained. Thus, through realizing the decisions as they get made, implementation will become a process of gradually replacing the constructs in the specification language by those in the implementation language. Since this replacement is gradual, the specification constructs must coexist with the implementation constructs. This requires a "wide-spectrum" language that contains both the specification and implementation languages as subsets.

The gradual refinement of the specification is accomplished via formal manipulations that realize the implementation decision chosen by the developer. Such formal manipulations are possible because the specification, and all its refinements, are formal (i.e., expressions in the wide spectrum language), and are necessary because such manipulations can be quite complex (as sophisticated algorithms replace simpler ones) and quite distributed (as information is spread through optimization). Automation is needed both to ensure that the manipulations are correctly performed (this presupposes that the transformations have been formally verified) and performed everywhere that is required and because the sheer magnitude of the task would be overwhelming otherwise. Fortunately, such automation of the formal manipulations required to realize decision making appears quite feasible and several prototype systems exist that accomplish implementation in this manner. Furthermore, the codification of programming knowledge in catalogs of such formal manipulations has already begun.

But experience with incremental implementation systems has shown that in addition to the implementation decisions, many other formal manipulations are required which either "prepare" the specification for the decision being realized or "simplify" the result of that realization. These low-level manipulations are much more numerous than the decisions made by the developer, and their employment must also be automated. In fact, the set of developer decisions forms a rich hierarchy (actually a heterarchy) of preparatory and simplification manipulations for each other. This raises the possibility of having the developer make only the "conceptual" or "strategic" implementation decisions with a knowledge-based problem-solving tool filling the remaining "tactical" implementation decisions automatically. Advanced versions of the knowledge-based software paradigm will employ such capabilities.

In this incremental implementation process, the automation of the formal manipulation will ensure that the resulting implementation is correct (i.e., is functionally equivalent to the specification). This means that the current phase of testing the implementation can be eliminated. The energy thus saved will be shifted to validating the specification (ensuring that it matches the user's intent, as described in Section 3.3.2) and evolving the system as the user's requirements change.

This brings us to the question of reimplementation. In the knowledge-based software paradigm, maintenance will be performed by modifying the specification (which is normally straightforward and simple) and then reimplementing that specification. But rather than repeating the incremental implementation process from scratch, the KBSA will help the implementer modify (normally only slightly) the previous incremental implementation, which will have been automatically recorded, and then replay it to obtain the new implementation. This reimplementation facility is another powerful automated tool for the developer. Furthermore, to the extent that the original (or previous) incremental implementation was achieved by the KBSA that filled in the "strategic" developer decisions with the remaining "tactical" ones, this development will tend to be automatically self adapting to changes in the specification and/or any changes the developer wishes to make in the decisions previously made.

Short-Term Goals

- Wide Spectrum Language

  We will develop a wide spectrum language capable of representing the design of a system in all stages from formal specification through optimized implementation.

- Transformation Language

  This language should be capable of describing transformations from the more abstract constructs within the wide spectrum language to the more concrete.

- Property Language

  This should be a language capable of describing the properties of program segments (such as the variables set and referenced, the module involved, the criteria under which it is reachable, the effects it creates, and the invariants it maintains.)

- Interactive Mechanical Development

  The idea is to develop a system capable of performing and documenting the development steps selected by the user. This requires the creation of a catalog of transformations.

- Automated Property Proving

  The aim is to develop an inference facility to automatically prove (or disprove) properties as they are needed during development.

Mid-Term Goals

- Automated Development

  We propose a system capable of taking a simple goal stated by the user and creating a short sequence of development steps to achieve that goal.

- Automated Replay

  We propose a system capable of adapting a previous development to an altered specification with a degree of automation commensurate with that available in the original development.

Long-Term Goal

- Enhance Replay

This would mean extending replay capability so that, in addition to changing those designer decisions that had to be changed for correctness, the system also detects those which ought to be changed for performance reasons and suggests appropriate changes. Notice that this entails interaction with the performance facet.

3.3.4 Performance

The long term goal of the performance facet is to help to create and maintain efficient programs that meet their performance requirements. The performance facet will guide performance decisions at many levels from requirements specifications to very-high level programs to low-level code. Performance assistance capabilities are critical for making practical tools of very-high-level, executable specification languages. Because the key disadvantage of such specifications is their lack of efficiency when executed straightforwardly, the important factor in their utility is being able to find efficient implementations. During development, efficiency estimation will be used to predict and compare the costs of proposed alternative data structure choices. With this capability, either a programmer or an automated program synthesizer can select a data structure. KBSA will also give performance advice about what control structures to use, what optimizing transformations to apply, and what algorithms to use. Thus, program analysis includes not only data flow and control flow analysis, but also higher-level analysis, such as algorithm analysis, to determine the time and space efficiency of programs, to suggest modularizations, and to find bottlenecks. It also involves augmenting application domain models to include some cost information. At the requirements level, advice will be given about the relative costs of different proposed features.

Currently, most efficiency estimation and optimization is performed by designers and programmers without much automated assistance. There are a few tools for estimating program timing information, and some data flow information is derived by compilers. However, the information is usually neither available in machine-understandable form nor available outside the compiler.

Performance advice can be given regardless of the degree of automation in the development phase. We assume that some combination of the following three development methods will be used: manually implementing programs from specifications; interactively synthesizing programs by applying transformations; and automatically synthesizing programs by a system that selects and uses transformations, simplifications, and inferences. In the case of automated synthesis, it is the efficiency estimator that bridges the gap from interactive synthesis to automated synthesis.

In all these cases the user, programmer, or knowledge-based assistant searches a space of possible combinations of implementations and decides among them on the basis of knowledge and their relative efficiency. Other factors come into play, such as the amount of effort (human or machine) available to implement the program and the relative importance of the particular part of the program being implemented. For example, a human programmer or a synthesis program might well try to find the most important bottleneck in a program and allocate the largest optimization effort to that portion.

Efficiency analysis facts can be gathered in several ways: rule of thumb estimations, algorithm analysis, or simulation coupled with statistics-gathering. By simulation we mean either directly executing the specification or executing an automatically compiled prototype implementation. By having default implementations for all levels of refinement, we could ensure that, at any time during program development, the program can be quickly implemented (even if it has been only partially refined or optimized). These multiple-level executable specifications can be used for both validation and collecting performance statistics. When analysis and simulation both fail, the fallback position will be to implement various versions and measure their performance. The feasibility of this technique will be dependent upon the cost of creating multiple implementations, which will in turn depend strongly upon the degree of automation of the development phase.

Efficiency estimation is also valuable in the knowledge-based project management and requirements activities, for example, a bottleneck analyzer can locate causes of delays in implementation. As with processor allocation, projects could be reallocated to the most efficient implementors, taking into account their workload and cost.

Short-Term Goals

- Symbolic Evaluation

  Symbolic evaluation (see Section 4.3.1) is a basic analysis technique that is useful in many of the KBSA facets described. However, it is crucial for the performance facet. The performance facet needs to be able to propagate and integrate efficiency estimations and to perform symbolic analysis on partial specifications.

- Data Structure Analysis and Advice

  A short-term target for the performance facet will be a set of estimators for data structure selection that are reasonably robust when handling conventional data structures (probably excluding external memory devices). These estimations could be used for automatic data structure selection or for advice to manual implementors. Efficiency estimation activities will be limited to those necessary for data structure selection, including the use of both rules of thumb and heuristic algorithm analysis. As an initial target, efficiency estimation will provide approximate, average-case performance analysis. The agents will compute and transform annotations about efficiency characteristics as programs are transformed, and will record cost analysis decisions for the benefit of future users. Some bottleneck finding also should be feasible in the short term; it is valuable for both automated and manual systems, and is a fairly straightforward extension of the basic performance analysis capability. By limiting the performance facet initially to data structure selection advice, we take a conservative position and increase the likelihood of success. It may be necessary, if certain applications are undertaken, to include other optimization decisions.

- Subroutine and Module Decomposition Advice

One class of performance decision is when to create new subroutines or modules. Given a definition of a potential subroutine, the decision about whether it should be kept as a subroutine or compiled in line is relatively easy, and such a capability will be developed as a useful adjunct for the manual programmer. However, the ability to logically find or formulate subroutines or modules that share substantially the same function is a more complex task and may require inductive inference. Such advice may not be available until later in the project.

Mid-Term Goals

- Domain Models for Analysis

Once domain models have been developed to help with other activities such as requirements definition, they will be augmented to cover performance or other analysis information. This domain information will be an inexpensive replacement for information that would otherwise have to be gathered by some form of simulation and monitoring.

- Algorithm Design Analysis and Advice

The data structure analysis and advice capability will be extended to include the ability to analyze control structures and other classes of optimizations. Some optimizations are almost always performed when possible (such as combining two enumerations through the same set) and thus are not especially interesting for efficiency analysis, but their effects need to be understood so efficiency characteristics can be updated. Also, combinations of optimizations sometimes need to be compared (say to determine file aggregation). Determining how to apply some of these transformations and deciding which combinations are really most efficient is a difficult problem.

We could also consider the effects of simplifying the cost function the user specifies. For example, additive cost functions are much easier to compute and may be sufficient for the user's needs.

- Real-Time Performance Advice

Real time systems are an important application domain. To achieve analysis and advice in these domains, the degree of completeness and accuracy of performance estimation will be improved to deal with worst-case performance. Better analyses will be available, and the ability to specify different accuracy goals for analysis will be provided. While in many cases a fast, approximate estimation is sufficient, for important cases (bottlenecks, real-time critical response programs) a more expensive analysis, taking closer account of interactions, should be available.

In the longer term, even more sophistication might be attempted, such as taking into account statistical distributions on input data.

3.3.5 Testing

In current software practice, program testing is a haphazard activity, generally not supported by sophisticated tools. In the best current practice, a set of test cases is defined at the beginning of the project, before detailed design has taken place, and put aside to be run after the final implementation is complete. More typically, test cases are generated after implementation has taken place with a view toward "exercising" all parts of the code. Test cases are almost never kept up to date during the long-term maintenance and evolution phase of the typical software life cycle.

In the long term, program testing will disappear as a separate activity in an automated, knowledge-based software development process. Most of what we now think of as program testing will be redistributed into the validation and development activities discussed in preceding sections. To understand this redistribution, we need to reexamine what a test case is and how it functions in the program development process. Fundamentally, a test case has two features: it is a small fragment of the total behavior of a system, and there is some sense in which that behavior can be judged correct or incorrect. The purpose of a test case differs, depending on whether it is primarily concerned with the specifications or with the implementation of a system.

From the point of view of specifications, the fragments of the total possible system behavior selected for test cases are determined by knowledge of the application task. The purpose of defining a set of test cases and their correctness conditions is to help clarify what the user desires. In the mid term, program testing should therefore begin to be coordinated and integrated with requirements and specification validation (see Sections 3.3.1 and 3.3.2). For example, the emergence of executable specifications will make it possible not only to define and record test cases early in the development process, but actually to run test cases before the bulk of the implementation is begun. The benefits of this methodology will be both in the area of helping users figure out what they actually want, and avoiding effort wasted in implementing what turn out to be incorrect specifications.

Automatic generation of test cases based on specific knowledge about the user and the application is also a possibility. This knowledge may be either in the form of domain-specific test generation procedures or precompiled, but highly parameterized, test cases for specific types of applications. For example, the KBSA will have knowledge about how to generate test data for specific computer-controlled hardware devices, such as a radio scanner or a motor mount.

A number of automatic test generation tools already exist which, given a complete program in some high level language, produce test input data guaranteed to satisfy some form of completeness property over the program, such as traversing each branch point in each direction. The main weakness in this approach is that the tools are in a sense too general – they treat all parts of the program the same, and at the code level. There is no way to incorporate specific knowledge of either the application domain or the software design. Given that program testing is inherently a partial process (i.e., in real software one can never test all possible input data), the advantage of the knowledge-based approach over uniform test generation algorithms is the use of specific knowledge to increase the density of tests in the areas of most relevance.

The second major purpose of current program testing has to do with the implementation process. The purpose of test cases from this point of view is to compensate for the fact that implementing a large and complicated software design is an error-prone process. Here, the fragments of the total system behavior selected for test cases are determined from knowledge of the software implementation design. In the long term, most of this kind of program testing will become unnecessary because a more formal program development methodology (see Section 3.3.3) will allow the interacting properties of different implementation steps to be explicitly managed and checked by automatic or semi-automatic tools.

Knowledge-based methods will also be applicable to the generation of test cases which address program implementation needs. In this area, the specific knowledge has to do with how to properly test specific kinds of software design structures, such as a multi-level interrupt system or a hash-sorted data base. As with application-specific test generation, this will be achieved through a combination of design-specific test generation procedures and libraries of parameterized test cases.

Short-Term Goal

- Test Case Maintenance Assistant

  The first step toward more automated, knowledge-based program testing is to provide tools that better support the current best practices. What is called for immediately is a uniform mechanism for associating test data with every unit of a software project (e.g., a requirement, specification, module). The purpose of a test (which may initially be only a keyword meaningful to the user) should also be recorded with the test itself. The main functions of the KBSA at this level will be to accept changes in test data, to schedule the running of relevant tests automatically when units undergo changes, and to give notification of problems. Such a facility will make it easier and therefore more likely for the system developer to define a test case at any point in the software development process at which it naturally comes to mind. Also, with more detailed knowledge about the relationship between specific test cases and features of the requirements, design, and implementation, testing will become much less of an all-or-none business, as it is today. A knowledge-based test-case maintenance system will allow incremental rerunning of test cases appropriate to the particulars of the modification.

Mid-Term Goal

- Knowledge-Based Test Generation

  In the mid term, it will be possible to begin to move from simply maintaining user-provided test cases to some automatic generation of test cases. The same underlying test case maintenance facilities can then be used to keep track of a mixture of user-defined test cases, test cases generated by uniform, automatic procedures, and those generated from specific domain and design knowledge. One of the first knowledge sources to exploit for automatic test case generation may be software "fault models," which are accumulations of heuristics, based on past experience, for the kinds of errors that correlate with specific kinds of tasks and programming structures.

Long-Term Goal

Testing will disappear as a separate activity; it will be redistributed into the validation and development activities.

3.3.6 Reusability, Functional Compatibility, and Portability

Many costly problems in present software production are essentially special cases of a general problem which we refer to as **compatibility** between modules. For example, a software module is **reusable** if it can be used as a component in differing systems; the facilities it **exports** must meet the requirements of a component and the facilities it **imports** must be provided by other components of the system. A module is **portable** to a new installation if the facilities it requires (imports) are provided by that installation. In the long term, complex systems will be hierarchically specified in wide spectrum specification languages (see previous sections); interface specifications will be separated from implementation details; the various VHLL's will eventually be rich enough to express all manner of complex details such as timing and I/O requirements, so that one may expect to have available the design of a complete system (hardware and software). At this time, many of our current problems will boil down to checking the compatibiliy of module interface specifications.

This section proposes a spectrum of KBSA facilities that provide assistance in determining compatibility of modules. These components could be developed in the short- and mid-term phases of the project and could become useful tools in production-quality programming support environments in the mid term. The long-term focus is to develop support technology for automating aids to the general modular interface compatibility problem. The long-term tools evolving from this effort will provide components for other KBSA facilities in requirements, validation, and testing.

Short-Term Goal

- ### An Automated Structured Walk-Through System for Software Portability

This capability will help check the transportability of software packages between different installations and machines. It will accept and record information about various computer installations, and give advice on the system constraints on software currently in force at a particular installation when asked.

The capacity for ensuring portability will accept interface specifications about various computer installations. Initially, these interface specifications will be highly restrictive, but they will include I/O requirements and limits, file access and privacy conventions, memory limitations, and run-time scheduler interface specifications. Later, more complete and formal interface specifications will be used. Based on such information about an installation, the assistant will build up a set of constraints to which a program running on that installation must conform. If a software specialist is tailoring a module for that installation and requests the portability walk through, he will get a checklist of constraints that his program must meet in order to run there. Items on the checklist will be displayed one at a time and will require an answer. The actual sequence of items displayed will probably depend on his previous answers.

Such portability assistants could be very useful in the short term and could probably be implemented using very simple facts about installations and rather simple rule-based reasoning to generate sequences of constraint checks.

Mid-Term Goals

Construction of a sophisticated mid-term version of a portability facet should focus research on (and take advantage of) several basic technology areas:

- **Knowledge domains** – Facts about an installation that affect the running of a software package will have to be represented together with dependencies.

- **Fault models** – The assistant, in some versions, may use a model of previous experience reports in reasoning about portability.

- **Specification languages** – As program design languages become more powerful, the information required by the portability facet will become precise and well defined, depending only on the formal specification of an installation (operating system and hardware). Construction of portability facets should promote research on specification in a precise high-level specification language of conventional operating systems in particular, and complete installations in general.

Mid-term development of portability facets should therefore take advantage of advances in specification languages, the existence of more complete modular specifications of systems (installations), and the development of complete glossaries of keyword concepts affecting portability (together with logical interrelations between those concepts expressed in a form suitable for automated reasoning including rules, special purpose deduction packages, etc.). The mid-term assistance would also be in the form of generated checklists. However, these would encompass a much more complete set of parameters affecting portability. Using associations with analysis of installation interface parameters, the assistant may also track histories of previous reports of software portability attempts to the installation in question. It may then issue advice during a portability walk through, e.g., who to contact about a particular interface requirement.

Long-Term Goals

Long-term development of a sophisticated reusability facet may involve a highly integrated KBSA. Reusability could be made a factor in requirements planning and refinement, module histories and documentation, and in activities coordination during system implementation. The reusability facet would track particular facts relevant to flexible use of a module and specification changes of system components.

3.4 KBSA Support System

This subsection identifies the lower-level utilities needed in the support system for the development, evolution, and eventual integration of the KBSA facets. Higher-level support utilities that require more sophistication, such as inference systems or symbolic evaluators, are discussed in Section 4, "Supporting Technology Areas."

The KBSA support system will be an integrated programming support environment that provides facilities for a number of agents to pursue a variety of simultaneous activities concerned with program development, testing, and maintenance, as well as with project management. The environment will be integrated in the sense that several policies must be adhered to by each of the many tools available in the environment; these policies are enforced through a set of system utilities. The two most important policies are those of version control and access control:

- Version control–

  The version control policy derives from a desire to minimize the amount of work each tool must do in order to account for the changes made since the last time that tool did the same job. To implement this, each program entity (for example, a procedure, a type, a data object, a fragment of documentation, a collection of program entities) will bear a version number. The version number will change only when that entity changes, thus enabling a tool like a symbolic evaluator to know what has (and what has not) changed since the last time it did an analysis of some collection of entitities. In addition, each program module that is derived by some tool will have a derivation history that relates it to the particular version of the parent modules and the particular version of the tool that contributed to its derivation.

- Access control –

  Access to all the elements of the KBSA development environment will be strictly controlled. The user (whether involved in developing/maintaining some software product or in modifying or augmenting the KBSA development environment itself) will be constrained to deal with the environment through the activity coordinator, which will ensure that any action that is taken is appropriately authorized.

The KBSA support system has three major components: the data base, the tool set, and the user interface; we discuss these in turn.

- Data base–

The data base maintained by the KBSA development environment consists of three functionally distinct major components: the administrative data base, the software data base, and the knowledge base. The administrative data base will be a data base that contains a variety of information to do with the agents and organizations that are known to the KBSA. Various administrative and management agents will be able to query and update this data base in order that the relationships among the organizations and personnel currently engaged in the projects under way are correctly reflected.

The software data base will contain a set of modules–collections of program entities that, together, embody all aspects of the set of products currently being developed or maintained by some instance of a KBSA development environment. The creation and manipulation of the program modules is done by various tools, whose use is mediated by the activity coordinator.

The knowledge base contains all the various kinds of knowledge acquired by and available to the collection of knowledge-based facets that will be integrated into the KBSA environment as well as by the activity coordinator.

A set of data-base utilities will be provided by the KBSA to deal with the addition and deletion of various data-base elements, with backup and archiving, and with organizing and reorganizing the various contained databases to ensure a timely response to a query or update.

- Tool set–

The set of tools available in the KBSA development environment will grow as new tools that provide assistance in various aspects of the life cycle of some software product are integrated into the KBSA. Initially, however, there will be a basic set of (standard) tools including tools for editing, compiling, and program transformation; debugging aids; tools for analysis, query, project management; for creating, dispatching, and responding to messages; for data base management and so on. It is assumed that the initial tool set will be developed by modifying various existing tools to adhere to the version and access control policies that are enforced by the KBSA. This initial tool set will later be superseded by the KBSA facets.

- User Interface–

The user interface to the KBSA will be through the activities coordinator. It is assumed that this interface will be realized through a work station that provides high-resolution graphic output plus a keyboard and various kinds of pointing mechanisms for input. It is further assumed that, at any time, there will be a number of windows into displays concerned with various aspects of one or more activities in which each agent is engaged.

A number of utilities will be provided to enable various tools to create and manage a variety of displays and to permit the user to control the positions, size, and other aspects of the windows currently open.

§4 SUPPORTING TECHNOLOGY AREAS

The KBSA facets must support problem-solving activities at all stages in the software life cycle. These automated facets depend on the application of different technologies, which we call supporting technology areas. These areas fall principally within software technology and artificial intelligence technology. For example, within software technology, the development of machine processable languages for formalizing programming activities and knowledge is a supporting technology area. Within artificial intelligence, the area of knowledge-based expert systems is a supporting technology area. The ultimate success of the KBSA depends very strongly on the development of the supporting technology areas.

In the past several years, the relevant supporting technology areas have been developing rapidly. There has, for example, been much research activity in the areas of requirements languages, knowledge-based expert systems, automated program verification, and sophisticated program management systems. Some of this activity has led to prototype experimental tools and in some cases to commercially applicable products.

These recent advances in the relevant supporting technology areas have created a sound foundation for the short-term goals of the proposed KBSA plan. However, further advances are required in these supporting technology areas to achieve the KBSA's mid- and long-term goals. It is expected that the relationship between the KBSA plan and the supporting technology will be symbiotic. The KBSA effort will produce growth in the supporting areas, and innovations in the supporting areas will contribute directly to KBSA. The overall effect should be a vigorous program of technology development followed by prototyping of and experimentation with advanced software support tools.

In this section, we discuss the major areas of technology required to support the KBSA.

4.1 Wide-Spectrum Languages

Work on all aspects of programming languages and high-level specification languages needs to be strongly encouraged. Language design and underlying formal semantics should be particularly emphasized. Languages concerned with distributed and parallel processing require special attention. It should be noted that our use of "language" here is intended to cover graphic and schematic representations of systems as well as conventional written representation. It is intended to cover the spectrum from requirements to implementation, from management to maintenance.

The importance of language design lies in providing the human user with natural methods of expressing different aspects of a computational system and focusing only on relevant details at any given life-cycle stage. Many languages, each somewhat suitable for different stages of software development, currently exist. These languages, although useful, are far from adequate for their intended use in the software development process, and the existing support tools for one language have not been designed with a view to interfacing with the tools for any other language or system. The aim of this support technology area should be development of a wide-spectrum language suitable for all stages.

At this time, research in the design of very-high-level formal specification languages should be emphasized. There is an immediate demand for specification languages that extend and complement current programming languages, for use as program design languages (PDL's) as well as for formal documentation. Later on, specification languages can be expected to provide the stepping stone for better systems design languages. By the mid-term period, new specification languages may well be developing as the new programming languages of the future. At that time, it should be possible to formulate a detailed research and development plan to produce a wide spectrum language suitable for KBSA needs.

4.1.1 Formal Semantics

Languages need a formal semantics to provide a basis for the construction of tools supporting activities such as error checking, consistency and compatibility analysis, and program transformation.

A great deal of progress has been made in the past few years in developing formal semantic models for programming languages, but much still remains to be done. For example, many of the conventional sequential high-level programming language constructs are quite reasonably modelled with denotational or Hoare-style models. Others, such as various aspects of memory management, are not yet modelled completely satisfactorily. As we consider adding certain very-high-level constructs and various notions of parallelism to our programming languages, we must extend the formal semantic models to encompass these new constructs.

4.1.2 Advanced Systems Analysis Tools

Support tools for activities carried out in a wide spectrum language must be developed. These tools will be based on the formal semantics of the wide spectrum language, and on expert systems techniques. This support area must be developed in conjunction with the language design effort. Current approaches to advanced program analysis tools can be placed in two broad categories. The first, often termed "smart compilation," seeks to gather certain facts about a program – use/set information about program variables (essentially syntactic) common subexpression information, dead/live regions of program flow for variables and so on. Much of this work is reasonably ad hoc and the mechanisms for doing it are usually embedded deep within a compiler with the information neither saved nor available to any other tool. This area of smart compilation tools needs to be expanded and the analyses they perform made available to other tools in standardized form. It can be expected to produce useful products in the short to mid term.

The second category is often termed "inference-based" and includes symbolic evaluators, transformation of specifications into run time error checks, and program verifiers. Tools in this area utilize not only the semantics of the underlying language but also user-supplied knowledge about the system itself (e.g., formal specifications, knowledge about the problem domain of the system). Development in this area of expert analysis tools needs to be vigorously encouraged and the results of these analyses made available in standardized form. This area will produce sophisticated KBSA facets in the mid to long term.

4.2 General Inferential Systems

A general inferential system is a system that supports automated inference from user-supplied inference rules applied to the modeled semantic properties of a user-defined data base. (This generally includes first-order logical operators but may also include other structural elements, e.g., operators and connectives from modal or temporal logics.) Such systems are applicable to all problem domains. This support technology area needs to be strongly supported with special emphasis placed on KBSA needs.

Important aspects in the implementation of such systems are:

1. Efficient implementation of inference rules and data representation for general logics. The inference rules are usually derived from the semantics of the language in which the data are represented. Such logics include first-order logic but also extensions and variants that may be useful in reasoning about programs such as first-order logics of partial functions, time logics, and nonmonotonic logics.

2. Structural modular facilities for expansion to include domain specific inference modules or efficient decision procedures.

3. User interface facilities specifically focused on making the system useful in practical applications. For example, an area where general inferential systems have lacked development so far is provision of facilities for explaining why a statement cannot be derived from the given data.

4. Efficient decision procedures for subclasses of logical formulas.

Much of this work will depend on theoretical advances and basic research in such areas as inference systems for various first-order logics, time logics, and decidable first-order theories. This basic research should be encouraged whenever it is relevant to KBSA facets.

4.3 Domain-Specific Inferential Systems

A major thrust of the KBSA is to provide facets that aid in the reasoning required concerning specific problem domains at various stages in the software production and maintenance process. There is a wide variety of specific problem domains for which the development of automated reasoning support is essential to KBSA facets. These domains include the domain of programming languages, application-specific domains, and the domain of project organization and the coordination of the activities ongoing within a software project.

For each individual problem domain, special rules of reasoning and solution finding will apply. Inferential systems based on the special rules are much more efficient than the application of general inferential systems to an encoding of special domain within, say, first-order logic. Specialized inferential and problem-solving systems will be essential components of individual KBSA facets. Therefore, research in this area focused on special problem domains related to proposed KBSA facets should be strongly supported. This research can be divided into three areas outlined in the subsections below.

4.3.1 Formal Semantic Models

A formal semantic model for a problem domain is a system of definitions and rules that permit a human being to reason about the objects in that domain, and their interrelations. Such a model is a most desirable, and perhaps necessary, precursor to any techniques for mechanical reasoning and problem solving in that domain.

4.3.2 Knowledge Representation and Management

The knowledge concerning each domain must, at least conceptually, be available in a knowledge base that is used by the various tools reasoning about that domain. This knowledge is represented in a fashion appropriate for external use and is also represented internally in such a way that it can be accessed, updated, and efficiently maintained. Several external representations will often be desired. For example, the form in which an expert in the domain presents knowledge to the knowledge base may differ drastically from the form in which we wish the system to represent this information to someone who is not a domain expert – a user, programmer, or manager, for example. For the nonexpert, we typically wish to explain, in lay terms, some aspect of the knowledge about certain objects or situations.

Data (knowledge) about a problem domain may be of various forms. Some data may be applicable to the knowledge base; these are generally called (inference) rules since their function is to deduce (new) facts about the domain from the existing data. Other data may take the form of heuristics for deciding when rules can be usefully applied.

Knowledge management concerns analysis of the knowledge data base. The knowledge base for a problem domain may change as a function of the activity in that domain. For example, a project progresses from a prototyping stage, during which the coordination may be mostly informal, to a production stage and then a maintenance stage during which the coordination may be highly formalized.

Support technology for knowledge management in KBSA must address the problems of change and explanation. For example, in KBSA, the following examples of knowledge management aids will be required:

- There must be mechanisms to "explain" the rules (appropriate to some situation) to, for example, managers who are not particularly adept at dealing directly with first-order logic or some variant thereof.

- It must be easy to add, remove, and modify rules. The use of relations in a relational data base to represent certain (ground) rules and a reasonable management system for the relational data base would be most helpful here.

- There should be mechanisms for checking the consistency of the data, noting redundant facts, and so on.

4.3.3 Specialized Inference Systems

Efficient inference systems for a given problem domain will need to be developed based on (and in conjunction with) the semantic model and data representation for that domain. Such systems may be close enough to standard general inference systems (resolution, equational rules, implicational rules, PROLOG schemes, etc.) to be implementable using general techniques. However we must also encourage research into specialized inference systems in order to explore all possibilities for efficiency. (This situation is somewhat analogous to a current situation where, in the context of current Von Neumann machines and programming languages built on top of them, research in alternative data flow machines is being pursued.) Efficient inference systems for a given problem domain are likely to be realized by building much of the inference mechanisms into the data representation.

4.4 Integration Technology

A fundamental premise in the KBSA plan is that various facets can be integrated into uniform (from the user's point of view) environments in the mid to long term. The ability to achieve this goal will depend on development of a supporting technology for integrating separate facets. Integration technology covers both the underlying KBSA support system itself (Section 3.4) and the integration of separately developed facets.

4.4.1 KBSA Support System Technology

Adequate technology for implementing the basic facilities required of the KBSA support system itself (Section 3.4) must be developed. This may be categorized as basic management facilities. While technology in this area is already well developed so that implementation of initial KBSA support systems can be undertaken now, experience will almost certainly demonstrate weaknesses and areas where further research and development is required.

4.4.2 Interfaces and Standards

As the KBSA progresses, our experience with initial integration experiments should be used to develop guidelines and standards for interfaces between KBSA facets. Experience has already shown that such standards are difficult undertakings . Research must be encouraged in investigating such support areas as

1. Definition of standard abstract data structure representations for internal forms of broad spectrum languages (Section 4.1).

2. Standard interface facilities to be supplied by knowledge data bases.

3. A universal user command language for all KBSA facets.

ACKNOWLEDGMENTS

Guidance and impetus for this study came from Northrup Fowler, Donald Roberts, Douglas White, Samuel DiNitto, and William Price. Larry Druffel, William Riddle, and Winston Royce all provided technical input to the study. Judy Tollner was administrator of this project. Assistance in formulating the facet descriptions was provided by Beverly Kedzierski and Elaine Kant. Carl Engelman helped formulate Section 1.

§6 REFERENCES

1. Software Technology for Adaptable Reliable Systems (STARS) Program Strategy: DoD Report, *ACM-SIGSOFT Engineering Notes, Vol.8,* No.2, April 1983, pp. 56-84.

2. Barr, Avron and Feigenbaum, Edward A., *The Handbook of Artificial Intelligence, Volume 2,* Chapter X, William Kaufmann, Inc., Los Altos, 1982, pp. 295-379.

3. Hünke, Horst (Ed.), *Software Engineering Environments,* North-Holland, New York, 1981.

4. Special Issue on Programming Environments, *IEEE Computer, Vol.14,* April 1981, pp. 7-45.

VIII / Programming Tutors

The goal of an intelligent programming tutor is to help novice programmers learn programming. A key activity of any tutoring system is to identify errors in students' work and then explain these errors in a way that facilitates learning. The programming tutors described in this section are similar in many ways to the intelligent assistant systems described in Section VII. In particular, both assistants and tutors must understand and manipulate programs in an effective way.

Ruth's intelligent tutoring system [Ruth, Chapter 24] is an early landmark in the field of computer-assisted instruction for teaching programming. Ruth's system finds errors in a student program on the basis of a grammar (constructed by the teacher) that describes all possible correct programs for a particular exercise. Anything in a student program that cannot be generated by this grammar is reported as an error. The main difficulty with this approach is that programs that are in fact correct can fail to match the grammar either because they use novel algorithms or novel syntactic embodiments of an algorithm.

The PROUST system [Johnson and Soloway, Chapter 25] also matches student programs against a description of the correct solutions to an exercise. PROUST, however, has specific knowledge of what can go wrong as well as of what is right. Also, the description of correct solutions in PROUST is more flexible and less syntactic than Ruth's grammar. This allows PROUST to match a wider class of correct programs. Nevertheless, PROUST is still susceptible to false negative responses. Better intelligent tutors will need to have yet a deeper understanding of programs.

Intelligent Program Analysis

Gregory R. Ruth

Project MAC, Massachusetts Institute of Technology, Cambridge, Mass. 02139, U.S.A.

Recommended by Bernard Meltzer

ABSTRACT

In order to examine the possibilities of using a computer as an aid to teaching programming, a prototype intelligent program analyzer has been constructed. Its design assumes that a system cannot analyze a program unless it can "understand" it; understanding being based on a knowledge of what must be accomplished and how code is used to express the intentions.

It was found that a one-page description of two common sorting algorithms or of some common approximation problems was sufficient for the computer to understand and analyze a wide variety of programs and identify and describe almost all errors.

1. Introduction

The idea of using computers to teach programming has long been an appealing one. Computer-assisted instruction (CAI) systems for teaching a variety of subjects have been widely implemented, but many are just automations of drill and practice lessons or, at best, on-line programmed textbooks. However, a more ambitious concept of CAI is now emerging. Alpert and Bitzer have proposed using the computer in "adapting the selection and presentation of instructional material to the pace and style of individual students and in acquiring and processing data relating to the effectiveness of the teaching and learning processes" [1]. The keystone of a system developed along these lines will be a capability to appraise the student's progress at each step along the way; that is, to understand and evaluate what a student has learned. In the domain of teaching programming the current empirical methods of grading students' programs are inadequate to this purpose. An analytic approach is needed.

To exhibit the feasibility of an intelligent program analyzer I have constructed a prototype that is implemented in CONNIVER and that runs on the MATHLAB PDP-10 at MIT's Project MAC. This analyzer's design is based on the premise that a system cannot satisfactorily analyze a program unless it can "understand" what it is examining; and further that this understanding can be built on a (user provided) description of the task that the program is to accomplish and a (built-in) body of knowledge concerning how intentions can be realized through code. The task description provides a broad delineation of the strategies that can be used in solving the problem that the program is to address but leaves their implementations open. The analyzing system's knowledge is in the form of programming "experts" that know how universal actions can be organized and coded to form a program and what the common sources of error in program writing are. The analyzer, advised by the task description and directed by the structure of the observed code, marshals the talents of its programming experts to comprehend, verify, and, if need be, correct the given program.

It was found that a one-page description of two common sorting algorithms and their variations provided enough knowledge for the analyzer to understand and analyze a wide variety of sorting programs. To check its generality and versatility, the same analyzer was further tested on a series of programs (written by students in an introductory programming course) to find approximations to the zeros of given functions. Again it was found that a description of their tasks less than a page in length was sufficient knowledge to enable the analyzer to identify and describe almost all of their errors and to recognize correct programs when they were finally written.

2. Finding the Plan

The basis for analysis of the type presented here lies in the simple observation that in writing a program the student is guided by a general plan of attack or strategy for effecting the desired purpose. As the usual computational environment admits only the sequential and deterministic execution of operations, such a plan must take the form of a finite set of well-defined steps with unambiguous rules at every point in the execution for determining which step is to be performed next. That is, the plan must be an algorithm.

Now if every program is in this way the manifestation of an algorithm (however, imperfectly conceived by its author) the top level activity of an analyzer is necessarily algorithm determination. More precisely, since it is often the case that something is lost in the transition from the true algorithm to the programmer's perception of it, and again in the translation of his ideas to code, the analyzer must attain its primary understanding of a program by discovering the *intended* algorithm associated with it.

The most basic way to find the intended algorithm is to deduce it directly from the task description (a specification of the end result) and the program to be analyzed. With this approach the system must be able in general to determine from the task description how it can be achieved and to reinvent, guided by the code of the observed program, the intended algorithm. For this the system requires a thorough knowledge of the context of its task and

Artificial Intelligence **7** (1976), 65–85

of how to procedurally achieve the stated goals (see Goldstein for a discussion of a system of this type).

Unfortunately there are many tasks whose end results do not suggest algorithms to the analyzer not already familiar with these tasks. A more practical approach to finding the intended algorithm involves providing to the analyzer knowledge of known algorithms for the task, or at least of the principles on which such algorithms are founded. This approach restricts the set of understandable programs to those whose algorithms (and their variations) are known. But in so doing it beneficially diminishes the degree of uncertainty. The algorithm search space is made finite. A program can be recognized as an instance (possibly corrupted by error "noise") of a particular algorithm or class or algorithms. Once it has been so recognized it can be described in terms familiar to the user (e.g. "This is an interchange sort with a test for early completion"). And semantics-directed matching with variations of the intended algorithm can locate sources of error.

This algorithm recognition method will be useful only where the number and variety of possible task algorithms is small enough so that they can be practically anticipated and readily organized into a relatively small number of classes. But this kind of task is by no means rare. It is the task that is sufficiently difficult, complex, or abstract that in order to have any chance of performing it correctly the programmer is virtually forced to use the concepts of known solution procedures. Examples are: sorting the elements of an array, finding the zeros of well-behaved functions and calculating the finite Fourier transform. Likewise, when a human grader analyzes programs for such tasks he proceeds as suggested above. If he has a sorting program he rarely attempts to construct an algorithm similar to the program's procedure using only sorting theorems and programming knowledge. Instead he quickly compares the program with the repertoire of sorting algorithms known to him. Unlikely matches are cast aside and those that remain are varied and manipulated until one is found that fits the program writer's apparent intention.

The algorithm description given to the program analyzer should be general enough to cover the broadest possible range of programs. But it must be sufficiently specific so that there is no ambiguity concerning the intended procedures and effects. These conflicting needs are met by expressing the task algorithms in terms of universal constructs and mechanisms (e.g. loops, conditionals, flags, calculation of expressions) and embedding in the analyzer knowledge of these, of how they can be realized procedurally, and how they can be woven together to form a program. That is, the analyzer knows how the algorithm steps can be rearranged and reorganized to produce functionally equivalent variations, how the common constructs can be coded, and how to recognize algorithm parts in the given program's code.

In this way the system user (say, an instructor in a programming course) need only supply descriptions of the algorithms relevant to achieving the task in terms of construct specifications (e.g. "loop N times through the following steps: ..."). He is relieved of implementation analysis, the responsibility for which is borne entirely by the analyzer.

3. Program Synthesis

There are many possible ways of describing the program task algorithmically. I chose one that effectively represents the decision making process involved in writing a program to perform the task. This representation is termed a program generation model (PGM). The idea is to capture the essence of the program writing *process* and formalize it, so that program analysis can be performed by reverse synthesis (much as the parsing of strings in a formal language is the reverse of string derivation). The actual process that a human goes through is not, however, of central importance here. The primary goal is to model the program writing process in such a way that the model will be most useful in understanding programs and their errors.

A particular program is a collection of code that is the result of syntactic choices made in generating it. But influencing these choices is a series of implementation or design decisions to perform the task at hand. Such decisions are: which algorithm to use, which variations to use, whether to exploit special situations, etc. Since the ultimate goal here is analysis and understanding of programs a model is used in which these decisions are primary. Realization rules that produce the necessary code are secondary (in fact, since they are the same for all tasks, they are built into the analyzer and so need not appear in the PGM at all). In this way, the semantic features of a program generation are made explicit and they appear near the top of the corresponding derivation tree, rather than being implicit and buried in a syntactic tangle.

If a program is derivable through the PGM, the derivation completely describes it semantically: so if the analyzer can determine a program's derivation, it will understand how it does what it does. If it is not derivable, the analyzer knows that it is incorrect; it then assumes that it is an unsuccessful attempt to implement some intended derivable program and will try to find the intended derivation. The derivation of the intended program will describe how the given program was supposed to work and the similarities and differences between them will show where and to what extent the given program was correct and in error, respectively.

4. Program Generation Models

Consider the bubble sorting algorithm in Fig. 1. This sorts an array A of N numbers. A is scanned from the top (beginning) to the bottom, comparing adjacent pairs of entries and "bubbling" any out of place entries up to their proper position in the array. An example of a correct program using

Step 1: Start at the top of the array. Set $i \leftarrow 1$.

Step 2: If $i > (N-1)$ stop; otherwise test adjacent entries $A(i)$ and $A(i+1)$.

Step 3: If $A(i) \leq A(i+1)$, $A(i+1)$ is in its correct place so far; go to step 9 (increment i and loop).
  Otherwise interchange $A(i+1)$ with preceding entries until it occupies its proper place.
  That is:

Step 4: Set $j \leftarrow i+1$

Step 5: If $j < 2$ we have reached the top of the list and the old $A(i+1)$ is in its proper place.
  Go to step 9 (increment i and loop).
  Otherwise test entries $A(j)$ and $A(j-1)$.

Step 6: If $A(j) > A(j-1)$ then the original $A(i+1)$ has found its proper place. Go to step 9 (increment i and loop).

Step 7: Otherwise interchange $A(j) \leftrightarrow A(j-1)$

Step 8: Set $j \leftarrow j-1$ and go to step 4

Step 9: Set $i \leftarrow i+1$ and go to step 2.

FIG. 1. A bubble sort algorithm.

this algorithm is shown in Fig. 2. (The simple LISP-like language used here is explained in the Appendix.) The common activities that occur in the bubble sort algorithm are looping, conditional branching, assignment, inter-changing the values of two variables, and iteration termination. These ACTION's can be represented by the following algorithm description primitives:

(LOOP parameter-list ACTION-list) where parameter-list is of the form (dummy-iteration-counter-variable, counter-initialization, counter-limit, counter-increment). This means: perform the ACTION's in ACTION-list

in sequence over and over again, adding the increment to the control variable on each iteration; stop when the value of this variable exceeds the counter limit. Parameter-list is optional.

(TEST predicate (ACTION's-if-true) (ACTION's-if-false): test the truth of predicate and perform the corresponding ACTION's.

(ASSIGN var expr): the variable var gets the value of the expression expr.

(INTERCHANGE var_1 var_2): the values of variables var_1 and var_2 are interchanged.

(LEAVE): cease iteration in the immediately superior loop.

Thus the algorithm can be described as

$$\text{BUBBLE} = (\text{LOOP } (I\ 1\ (-N\ 1)\ 1)$$
$$(\text{B-ITER}(I)))$$

where

$$\text{B-ITER}(I) = (\text{TEST } (\leq A(I)\ A(+\ I\ 1))$$
$$(\text{NIL})$$
$$((\text{LOOP } (J\ (+\ I\ 1)\ 2\ -1)$$
$$((\text{TEST } (\geq A(J)\ A(-\ J\ 1))$$
$$(\text{LEAVE})$$
$$(\text{NIL})$$
$$(\text{INTERCHANGE}(A(J)$$
$$A(-\ J\ 1)))))))$$

```
((REPEAT (I 1. (−N 1.) 1.)
  ((IF (< (A I) (A (+I 1.)))
  (THEN)
  (ELSE (REPEAT (J (+I 1.) 2. −1.)
    ((IF (> = (A J) (A (−J 1.)))
    (THEN (EXIT))
    (ELSE (S F (A J))
      (S (A J) (A (−J 1.)))
      (S (A (−J 1.))
      F)))))))))
```

FIG. 2. A sample bubble sort program.

(NIL represents an empty ACTION list). A more general PGM for this algorithm that allows the array scan to be either top-down or bottom-up and which includes a variation in array entry shifting is given in Fig. 3. A vertical line (meaning "or" as in formal grammars) indicates high level alternate design decisions. To avoid the sometimes unnatural and inconvenient inflexibility of a strict replacement rule format (which, for example, often requires the development of parallel subsets of rules for different cases) procedural rules (written in LISP) are allowed.

For example, ORDERP expands to a predicate that is true if the array elements indexed by its arguments are in the correct order. INDEX(I) expands to the index of the Ith element from the top or bottom of the array, depending on the top-down bottom-up decision. FIRST-INDEX makes that decision and then expands its argument via INDEX.

Three things are worth noting here. First, the use of the global variable TDBU explicitly shows how the top-down bottom-up decision affects the sorting procedure. Second, by using ORDERP the PGM shows what does not change in the basic procedure; namely, that regardless of the direction of the scan, the tests are to determine whether adjacent items are in their proper order. Finally, this PGM reflects the fact that the observed loop parameters in themselves contain no information about the top-down bottom-up decision. What determines this choice is the relationship between the loop parameters and the indices of A used. That is to say, one can think of the loop parameters as being arbitrary and the top-down bottom-up decision being made only when the programmer writes his first A( ). This is modeled by FIRST-INDEX. If a pure replacement rule format had been used, these observations would have remained implicit.

```
1. BUBBLE = (LOOP (I 1 (— N 1) 1)
             (B—ITER(I)))

2. B-ITER(I) = EXCH-BUB(I) | SHIFT-BUB(I)

3. EXCH-BUB(I) = (TEST ORDERP(FIRST-INDEX(I) INDEX(+ I 1))
               (NIL)
               ((LOOP (J (+ I 1) 2 —1)
                  ((TEST ORDERP (INDEX(J)
                                INDEX(— J 1))
                         (LEAVE)
                         (NIL))
                   (INTERCHANGE(A(INDEX(J))
                               (A(INDEX(— J 1)))))))))

4. FIRST-INDEX(I) = (SETQ TDBU 'TD) INDEX(I) | (SETQ TDBU 'BU) INDEX(I)

5. INDEX(I) = (COND ((EQ TDBU 'TD) I)
                    ((EQ TDBU 'BU) (— (+ N 1) I)))

6. ORDERP(X Y) = (COND ((GREATERP X Y) (>A(X) A(Y))
                        (T (> A(Y) A(X))))

7. SHIFT-BUB(I) = ((ASSIGN J I)
               (LOOP (TEST (> A(+ I 1) A(J))
                          (LEAVE)
                          (NIL))
                    (ASSIGN A(+ J 1) A(J))
                    (ASSIGN J (— J 1))
                    (TEST > J 0) (NIL) (LEAVE))
                (ASSIGN A(+ J 1) A(+ I 1)))
```

FIG. 3. A bubble sort PGM with scan decision and an entry moving variation.

As illustrated, the PGM describes algorithms in a computationally oriented way. The program writing process is modeled by a system of design decision rules. These rules embody the process of organizing the ACTION's and control structure of a program through a series of choices. As such they comprise the model's (and thus the analyzer's) knowledge of the task.

5. Analysis Policy

As already explained analysis of a program will be performed by reverse synthesis. Of course there will be a boundary beyond which the analyzer cannot find derivations for correct programs. This marks the limit of the analyzer's understanding. Correct programs for which no derivation can be found will either be misunderstood or not understood at all. As some consistent policy was necessary in this regard, a conservative one was chosen: unless after every attempt has been made the program is not thoroughly understood, it is declared incorrect. In this way no incorrect program is ever judged correct, but some correct programs may be ruled incorrect.

6. The Analysis Process

Since both the algorithm specifications and the program to be analyzed are essentially lists of ACTION's, the top-level driver for the analyzer is basically an ACTION list matcher (ALM). The analyzer proceeds in top-down fashion attempting to match the top-level ACTION's, calling itself recursively to match conditional clauses and loop bodies, which are ACTION lists themselves.

The ALM is entered with a list of ACTION's and a list of program statements to be matched against the ACTION list. The code given to the ALM is presumed to be an implementation of the desired ACTION's. At the top level the code and ACTION lists are the entire program and the entire algorithm specification, respectively. Generally the ALM begins matching by calling the analysis module for the first ACTION on the ACTION list, passing along the parameters given for that ACTION and the entire code list. For example, if at the top level the first item on the ACTION list is

(TEST (<B 1) ((S B 3)) (NIL))

the TEST analysis module is called with the entire program as its code list argument, (< B 1) as its predicate argument, ((S B 3)) as its true arm argument, and (NIL) as its false arm argument. The analysis module returns either FAIL, an indication that no match was possible, or the portion of the code list that was not used up in matching. If FAIL is received, the matching effort is aborted and the ALM returns a failure message to its caller.

If the ACTION match succeeds, the ALM calls the expert for the next ACTION on the ACTION list with the parameters given for that ACTION, and the remaining code. Matching continues in this incremental fashion until there is a failure or the ACTION list has been exhausted. In the latter event the ALM's job is done and it returns the remaining code, if any, to its caller (the caller can handle it more ably than the ALM since the former has the better vantage point).

The degree to which analysis in this style will be successful depends on the ability of the analyzer to establish the equivalence or non-equivalence of the input program actions to those in the task PGM. The equivalence problem may be divided into two parts: value equivalence and construct equivalence.

7. Value Equivalence

Every non-trivial program must calculate and manipulate values, for, in a broad sense, that is all that is left when execution is completed. Furthermore, in the execution of a program assignments manipulate variables, and the flow of control in loops and conditionals is dependent on the evaluation (either arithmetic or logical) of expressions. Consequently ACTION matching frequently requires value equivalence determination.

The analyzer can make such a determination only if it knows the values of the variables involved in the context in which they appear. For this it maintains an environment (a collection of variable value facts) at every step in its analysis. This environment is similar to the one that must be kept by the run-time system at every step in the execution of the program. But as the system is to analyze the program for the general case (i.e. for arbitrary inputs) rather than for a specific case, its environment is one not of numerical values, but instead of generalized assertions about values. Nevertheless, these assertions should embody such a complete knowledge of the value of each variable that given a specific set of input values one could, without executing the program, determine the value of any variable at any time (e.g. given that A = (3 5 11 2 5) initially, after the second statement is executed in the fourth iteration of the inner loop, the value of A(3) will be 2).

The analyzer scans the program code from left to right and from the top down. Since the absence of goto's insures that this is the order of execution the environment may be maintained along the way in a fairly straightforward manner. When an assignment statement of the form (S var expr) is encountered in the course of the analysis scan the analyzer modifies the environment to reflect what will happen when this statement is encountered in the course of execution. The fact that var now gets the value of expr must be added. If there is no value for a variable, it should be a "given" variable (like the formal parameters in a procedure). For example, in the sorting example the variable N and the array A are given. Given variables evaluate to themselves.

Accordingly, the fact (= var (VALUE expr)) is added to the environment and any other facts explicitly mentioning var (e.g. the previous value assertion for var, if any) are deleted, as they are now superseded by the new information. Conditional statements give rise to qualified value assertions. For example

$$(IF (> X\ Y) (THEN (S\ A\ 3)) (ELSE (S\ A\ 4)))$$

yields the assertion

$$(= A\ (*IF\ ((> (VALUE\ X)\ (VALUE\ Y))\ 3)$$
$$((< (VALUE\ X)\ (VALUE\ Y))\ 4)))$$

which means that henceforth the value of the variable A is 3 if $X > Y$ in the environment current when the assertion was made; otherwise it is 4. Note that while inside the THEN clause of the conditional the predicate may be asserted as true and there is no need for qualified values. Similarly in the ELSE clause the predicate is assumed false.

Inside a loop body, the value of a variable depends in general on the iteration number. For all iterations but the first a variable's value can depend on previous iterations, that is, on the executions of statements that follow it in the written code. So to determine the state of affairs at the top of the loop body, the analyzer must immediately upon entry scan the entire loop body. Let VAR(n) denote the value of the variable VAR at the beginning of the nth iteration. Then VAR(1) is the pre-loop value of VAR. Positing that all variables VAR, VAR2, VAR3, ... have the respective values VAR(n), VAR2(n), VAR3(n), ... at the beginning of the nth iteration (and that it is in the nth iteration) the analyzer scans the loop body, maintaining its environment as it goes. When it has reached the end, the value of VAR in he data base is an expression for VAR($n+1$) in VAR(n) and other variables, VAR2(n), VAR3(n), ... Thus, it has the recursive definition of VAR(n):

(Basis) $VAR(1) = \langle$pre-loop value of VAR$\rangle$,

(Induction) $VAR(n+1) = f(VAR(n), VAR2(n)\ ...)$.

where f is a rational polynomial (because the only arithmetic operations the simple input language are $+$, $-$, $*$, QUO, and $\sim$). The appropriate value assertion for VAR at the beginning of the loop body is thus

$$(= VAR\ (*RD\ \langle\text{pre-loop value of VAR}\rangle$$
$$\langle\text{induction expr}\rangle))$$

where $\langle$induction expr$\rangle = f(VAR, VAR2, ...)$. This assertion, together with those for VAR2, VAR3, etc, provide all of the necessary information to determine the value of VAR in the loop body. On leaving the loop the value of such a variable is made conditional (by a qualified value assertion) on the possible exit conditions.

To determine the equivalence of an expected expression E to an expression E' found in the input program the analyzer forms the difference $E - E'$ and evaluates it (by substituting the value in the current environment for each variable in it). The expressions are equivalent if the result is zero after algebraic simplification (performed by the MACSYMA rational function package [3]).

Equivalence in the presence of qualified values is handled by showing simplification to zero for each case. Where the difference is recursively defined the analyzer proves its equivalence or non-equivalence to zero by simple induction, using simplification to prove the basis and induction steps. The equivalence of an expected predicate p to a predicate p' found in the observed code is determined by trying to prove that $p \rightarrow p'$ and $p' \rightarrow p$. If such is the case the predicates are equivalent. These subproofs could be attempted using a classical theorem proving methodology as in [4]. However, a more deterministic, but heuristic, mathematical programming approach is used. To prove that, say $E > 0 \to E' > 0$ the mathematical programming problem to minimize E' subject to the assertions in the current environment plus $E > 0$ as constraints is set up. Then $E > 0 \to E' > 0$ iff the minimal value for E' under these conditions is greater than zero. The sub-theorem $E' > 0 \to E > 0$ can be tested similarly. It is easy to see how this proof technique can be applied, *mutatis mutandis*, to any pair of predicates using the logical operators of the model input language.

This description is intended only to provide a general outline of the environment maintenance and expression equivalence mechanisms. The details of these are far too complex to present here. A thorough discussion may be found in [12].

8. Construct Equivalence

The analyzer's capability for determining construct equivalence resides in ACTION experts. These are separate specialized modules, one for each type of ACTION. When called an expert checks whether the current ACTION that the ALM is trying to match is present and properly implemented at the current point in the observed code scan. If it is it returns the remaining code as in indication of success (this effectively moves the scanner to the beginning of the next observed ACTION); otherwise it returns the message "FAIL". These experts are briefly described in the following paragraphs.

The assignment expert is sent a sequence of ASSIGN and INTERCHANGE ACTION specifications. It determines whether the variables whose values are to be updated in accordance with the ACTION sequence get their new values before the first non-ASSIGN ACTION (i.e. a LOOP, TEST, or LEAVE) in the code list. First, the assignments in the given ACTION list are performed symbolically in order to generate expressions (in terms of the current environment) that the values of the affected variables are to have after the ACTION's are performed. For example, the ACTION list

```
(INTERCHANGE A B)
(ASSIGN B (+ B C))
```

gives rise to the association list

```
((A B) (B (+ A C)))
```

which means: after the ACTION's are performed, A will have the value that B had before they were done, and B will have the value that the expression A+C had before they were done. Likewise the code list is symbolically executed to produce an association list for the variables in the observed program. This execution continues until a REPEAT, EXIT, or non-degenerate IF (one whose predicate is neither a tautology nor the negation

of one in its context) is encountered. Each variable updated as specified in the desired association list is matched against the result produced by the observed program. If a variable that is to be updated has no pair on the observed code association list, it may be that it already has the desired value, so its value in the current environment is compared with the value of its desired associated expression in the current environment. If there is a corresponding pair on the observed code association list, the corresponding expressions are compared by value as described above.

The TEST expert first checks whether the desired conditional is degenerate. If so it calls the ALM with the ACTION's of the branch that will always be taken and returns the result of that match attempt. Otherwise it scans down the code list in search of the first non-degenerate IF, updating the environment as appropriate. If it finds a REPEAT or EXIT statement first, the observed control structure is clearly not as expected and it fails.

When an IF is found the TEST expert compares the expected predicate with the one found. If they are neither equivalent nor complementary failure occurs. In the case that one is the complement of the other the expected clause ACTION lists are interchanged before matching continues. The TEST expert completes verification by checking the observed THEN and ELSE clauses for equivalence to the corresponding expected ACTION lists by calls to the ALM.

The LOOP expert tries to find at the current point in the observed code scan a segment of statements that implements the iteration construct as specified. This segment need not begin with a REPEAT statement nor even contain one at the top level. The reason for this is that the LOOP ACTION represents a list of ACTION's that is to be cycled through, in general, an indefinite number of times. This cyclical nature means that if the ACTION's comprising a loop body are rotated as a circular list and proper modifications are made outside the loop, functional equivalence can be preserved. For example, the following two program fragments are equivalent:

```
(S I 1)                      (S I 1)
(REPEAT (S (A I) I)          (S (A I) I)
 (S I (+ I 1))               (REPEAT (S I (+ I 1))
 (IF (> I 3)                  (IF (> I 3)
  (THEN (EXIT))                (THEN (EXIT))
  (ELSE)))                     (ELSE))
                              (S (A I) I))
```

The body of the left loop has been rotated left once to obtain the body of the right loop. To maintain equivalence the statement that went to the end of the body had to be added to the code just before the loop. Such rotation requires only the addition of statements before the loop (a *prologue*) to

9. Error Analysis

The program analyzer as described so far is designed in such a way that errors are found where they occur and in a context in which they can be understood. Whatever explanations and descriptions of errors that an expert discovers can thus be made available both internally for the enlightenment of interested routines at a higher level, and externally for the benefit of the frustrated programmer.

Errors can be classified as either recoverable or non-recoverable. Recoverable errors are those which could be fixed without substantial change to the observed code. These include the expression whose value differs from what it should be by a constant, and the REPEAT that loops one too many times. Non-recoverable errors are chiefly those where something vital is missing or something unwanted is present. Usually these cannot be fixed without a significant overhaul of the parts of the program in which they appear. Examples of such errors are extra or missing control structures (exception: the missing EXIT is easily fixed) and missing ASSIGN ACTION's.

By this definition a recoverable error is insufficient reason to discontinue a line of investigation, although a mounting number of them will begin to cast doubt on the line's appropriateness. So the analyzer should be allowed to proceed ahead tentatively when such errors are encountered. On the other hand, an attempt to continue forward in the face of a non-recoverable error would require a great and questionable assumption about the programmer's real intentions that is not substantiated by the immediately available evidence. These errors should thus be treated as fail conditions; they are just the sort one would expect to occur when trying to match the wrong things.

The following are the match preference criteria that the analyzer uses to decide which of alternative explanations for the intended workings of a program should be chosen.

(1) A match that is completely successful is better than one that generates errors.

(2) A match with recoverable errors only is better than one with a non-recoverable error.

(3) If two matches have recoverable errors the one with the fewer errors is the better match.

(4) If two matches fail because of a non-recoverable error, the one that has proceeded farther in the observed code is deemed better.

The analysis scheme has been described to this point as if all errors were non-recoverable. Recoverability is introduced by making the analyzer aware of common errors and their manifestations. This knowledge enables it to maintain functionality; nothing has to be done to fix up the end of the last cycle of statements, for the EXIT will take care of that.

When the loop body's first statement is an IF with an EXIT, it is not correct to merely add that statement as a prologue before the loop since the meaning of its EXIT changes when it is moved outside the loop. If the EXIT is in the top level of the clause in which it appears (i.e. it is not buried in a nested IF) equivalent fragments are

```
(REPEAT                    (IF p
  (IF p                      (THEN sl_1)
    (THEN sl_1               (ELSE sl_2
      EXIT))                   (REPEAT
    (ELSE sl_2))                 sl_3
  sl_3                          (IF p
                                  (THEN sl_1
                                    (EXIT))
                                (ELSE sl_2))))
```

where sl_i denotes a statement list (and similarly for the case where the EXIT is in the ELSE clause). So when a loop body having as its first statement an IF containing an EXIT is rotated right, it must be replaced by a modification of that IF. The non-exiting clause of that IF contains its original code followed by the loop with its body rotated. The EXIT clause contains its original code less the final EXIT statement.

To handle these possible variations in loop implementation the LOOP expert begins by finding the first REPEAT after the position of the observed code scanner. If this REPEAT is a proper implementation of the expected loop, or a rotation of such an implementation, the intervening code is checked against the corresponding expected prologue. Otherwise the LOOP expert reports failure. The analysis of the REPEAT itself is straightforward. If the expected loop has iteration parameters the found loop must have the same implied number of iterations. If the found loop has parameters, the expected loop body is rewritten in terms of the observed loop's loop control variable. Otherwise the entire expected loop ACTION is recast as a parameterless loop specification. The expected loop body is matched against the observed body and its rotations by calling the ALM. If a match is found ACTION specifications for the associated prologue are formed and the observed pre-loop code is checked against these, also via the ALM.

The LEAVE expert merely passes over any assignment statements that may be at the beginning of the code list (modifying the environment as appropriate) until it reaches the EXIT statement it seeks. Intervening REPEATs or non-degenerate IFs cause failure.

understand and hypothetically fix them. Only a few common errors are included here but they cover a multitude of sins.

10. Expression Errors

When the analyzer cannot show the equivalence of its desired expression ED and the found expression EF there are several error types it can check for. One common and simple programming error is to write an expression that differs from the correct one by a constant. Another simple case is equivalence except for sign. So the analyzer checks $ED-EF$ and $ED+EF$ (unevaluated) for simplifying to a constant. Since expressions that are not comparable in a literal sense may still have comparable values in the context in which they appear, the analyzer also tries this test with $ED-EF$ and $ED+EF$ evaluated.

If these tests fail the unevaluated expression EF is checked for being off by an expression of a single variable (as might be the case where the programmer writes $(+\ I\ 1)$ for $(+\ (*\ 2\ I)\ 1)$ or $(+\ A\ B)$ for $(+\ A\ B\ C)$). Finally, if there is a single variable VF that appears in EF but not in ED and a single variable VD that appears in ED but not in EF, VD is substituted for VF in EF and expression analysis as described above is tried recursively. All divergences that cannot be explained in these ways are (arbitrarily) considered non-recoverable errors.

11. Conditional Clause Reversal

A simple mistake that can be made by the programmer is the inadvertent interchange of the arms of a conditional. This can be easily picked up by the TEST expert. If the attempted analysis of either clause of an observed IF fails, the TEST expert tries matching the expected true arm with the ELSE clause and the expected false arm with the THEN clause. If both of these matches succeed the error is recoverable.

12. Predicate Errors

The TEST expert can also check for two simple types of predicate errors when predicates fail to match. The desired and observed predicates are transformed from their original forms

$$(rel_1\ ED_1\ ED_2) \quad \text{and} \quad (rel_2\ EF_1\ EF_2)$$

to the equivalent forms

$$(rel_1\ ED_1\ ED_2) \quad \text{and} \quad (rel_1\ EF_1'\ EF_2')$$

respectively, if possible. Then they are further normalized to the forms

$$(rel_1\ ED\ 0) \quad \text{and} \quad (rel_1\ EF\ 0)$$

where $ED = ED_1 - ED_2$ and $EF = EF_1' - EF_2'$. Expression analysis can then

be performed on ED and EF (as above) and the results interpreted and acted on as appropriate.

When the observed predicate cannot be rewritten as a predicate in rel_1, a substitution of logical operator can be tried and predicate analysis applied as above. Success in the continued analysis is then taken as a vindication of the tentative substitution, which can then be confidently noted as an error, and TEST analysis can continue.

13. Loop Iteration Errors

As discussed above the LOOP expert checks for equivalence of the implied number of iterations when it is matching a parametered LOOP specification against a parametered observed REPEAT. To treat the possibly recoverable error of an incorrect number of iterations, it can compare expressions for the implied numbers of iterations in the found and specified loops. The case of exact equivalence generates no error message and analysis continues. When a single variable substitution can produce equivalence, the error is noted by the LOOP expert and analysis can continue as if the correct expressions had appeared in the observed parameter list.

The other describable errors are handled in a more heuristic way. If the compared expressions are of equal magnitude but opposite sign, the problem could either be that increment should have its sign reversed, or that init and limit should be interchanged. The LOOP expert tries both fixes, and chooses as the more likely explanation the one that leads to the better subsequent match of the specified LOOP body ACTION list with the observed REPEAT body code. (The criteria for match preferences are given above).

If the compared expressions differ by a constant the LOOP expert considers only the cases where either init or limit is modified to make the difference vanish. Again, the better explanation is chosen.

14. The Missing EXIT Statement

When an EXIT statement cannot be found at the end of the code list passed to the LEAVE expert, and the code list is otherwise unobjectionable, the LEAVE expert adds a missing-EXIT message to the analysis report and returns success to its caller.

15. An Example

A simple example will serve at once to clarify and illustrate the analysis mechanism. Consider the program in Fig. 4. From the PGM for bubble sorts the analyzer knows that the program should basically be a loop with exactly $N-1$ iterations. So it first finds the necessary REPEAT statement and checks that the implied number of iterations is correct. This verified, it substitutes the variable name D for I in the PGM's sub-pattern for the loop body of the bubble sort's outer loop and tries to match this with the observed loop body. This sub-pattern consists of a correct-order test with a null branch and a branch to bubble up array entries that are out of order. The corresponding IF statement is found and it is easily determined that the specified predicate is equivalent to the observed predicate and that the observed THEN clause is empty as expected.

```
((REPEAT (D 1. (- N 1.) 1.
    ((IF (> = (A (+ 1 D)) (A D))
       (THEN)
       (ELSE (S E (+ D 1.))
       (REPEAT ((IF (> = (A E) (A (- E 1.)))
          (THEN (S F (A E))
              (S (A E)
                 (A (- E 1.)))
              (S (A (- E 1.)) F))
              (ELSE (EXIT))
          (S E (- E 1.))
          (IF (< E 2.)
             (THEN (EXIT))
             (ELSE)))))))))
```

FIG. 4. Bubble sort attempt.

The bubble branch pattern is expected to be a loop whose body has order test and interchange mechanisms. The loop expert, finding a REPEAT without parameters replaces its expected parametered loop specification with an equivalent parameterless version. In analyzing the body it finds that a one statement right rotation of the observed body would be a correct implementation of the specified ACTION's if THEN and ELSE clauses of the first IF were interchanged. This is the best possible match. It is a recoverable error so analysis continues.

Because of the rotation the analyzer expects the REPEAT to be the ELSE clause of an IF statement, thus

```
(IF (< E 2)
    (THEN)
    (ELSE (REPEAT . . .))
```

or the equivalent. Finding that this is not the case it tries proving that the expected IF would be degenerate; that is, that (< E 2) is always false in the environment immediately preceding the REPEAT. It finds that this is in fact the case, so that the expected IF need not be present.

The LOOP expert is satisfied, returns success to the ALM, which returns success to the ELSE clause checker of the TEST expert, etc, until th

sequence of calls is completely unwound. Thus, analysis is completed and the analyzer can report that the program is a bubble sort and it is correct except for the offending IF, whose clauses should be interchanged.

16. Experience

As a check on the validity of these ideas the analyzer was applied to programs written by actual novices for an introductory programming course at MIT. Their assignment was to write a program in PL/I that would find the zeros of a given function in a specified interval. The suggested methods of solution were the binary search algorithm and Newton's method. The author wrote a short (less than a page) new PGM for this assignment but the analyzer itself was left unchanged. Several attempts for each of five students were intercepted, automatically translated into the 4-statement language, and given to the analyzer. For 4 out of the 5 students the analyzer correctly determined the algorithm and variation used and located and described any program errors that existed. (The failure in analyzing the programs of the fifth was due not to a fault in the PGM or the programming understanding abilities of the analyzer, but merely to the weakness of its linear programming based theorem prover—a non-linear programming based version would have succeeded). The fact that the analyzer performed so well on real programs written in a language other than the one it was intended for and for a task other than the one that was used to motivate its development (viz. sorting) is evidence of the generality and robustness of its algorithm description driven approach and of the universality of the computational constructs and the prevalence of the common error types it knows about.

17. Applications

An analyzer that would report directly to the teaching system instead of to the student could provide the kind of information necessary for selective adaptation of a CAI system's course of instruction as suggested at the behinning of this paper. For example, if the student has difficulty with setting up loops, the system will see this from his errors and can concentrate on this aspect of programming until the student's performance improves. Moreover, enough information is supplied so that the automated instructor can help the student see and understand his mistakes in the context in which they were made. And the analysis methods presented here need not be confined to use in teaching programming. They can easily be applied in many other problem solving situations, such as algebraic equation solving.

Program verification is another area in which the analysis principles presented here could be of use. The approach of this paper it would have two significant advantages over the current program proving approach: (1)

it would pin-point and describe implementation errors, and (2) it would use more natural descriptions than predicates. The program proving approach fails to provide fully satisfactory analysis because it does not know about common errors and hence cannot isolate and explain them in programming terms. It can only come up with a "yes" or "no" verdict and, at best, possibly a counterexample. It might seem that no description could be simpler or more natural than those of the program proving approach, which in principle requires only two predicates: one for the input (initial state) and one for the output (final state) of a program. However, this impression is misleading. The fact is that the program verification problem is difficult to solve in most cases (impossible in the general case) and that no matter what technique is used some degree of overspecification will usually be necessary to increase the chances of finding a proof when there is one. The user must guess (or take the time to figure out, if possible) exactly which predicates and suggestions are necessary for an effective proof and where they should be. It could take considerable effort to determine precisely what each predicate should be in order to avoid false acceptance or rejection.

On the other hand, I believe that the programmer would be more comfortable writing task descriptions in the style associated with the brand of analysis described in this paper, for these are in terms (mainly procedural) in which he, as a programmer, would be accustomed to thinking. The user could minimize the danger of rewriting his errors into the specification by giving a simple plan (that he can easily see the correctness of) of which his submitted program is a more efficient and complicated variation. The job of the analyzer would then be to establish the correspondences and to determine whether his intentions carry over without corruption.

Finally, the principles and methods described here can find application not only in the world of computers, but wherever procedures must be analyzed. It is often the case that tasks specified in semi- or non-procedural form require the generation of procedures whose complexity makes a capability for analysis desirable. For example, consider an aircraft assembly firm that has determined (through critical path analysis, say) the optimal (cost minimizing) scheduling and allocation of human and machine resources for the fabrication of special jet fighters of proven design. If the completed craft all seem to be manifesting a common failure it may wish (or be compelled) to analyze the assembly procedure for errors. There is a definite need for procedure analysis of this sort and the investigations of this paper could be the first step in developing the necessary technology.

Appendix. A Simple Programming Language Model

Rather than use an existing language (or a subset of such) for experimental program analysis, with all of its warts and wrinkles, a new language was

created—a simple expository tool without goto's, functions, subroutines, or recursion, but similar to many algebraic in syntax and semantics and with the same power. The language is a simple four-statement language with a LISPish looking syntax. The statements briefly described are:

(S var expr) assigns the value of the expression expr to the variable var.

(IF pred (THEN stmt-list$_1$) (ELSE stmt-list$_2$)) performs the statements in stmt-list$_1$ if the predicate pred is true; otherwise, it performs the statements in stmt-list$_2$.

(REPEAT stmt-list) performs the statements in stmt-list in sequence over and over again.

(REPEAT (lcv init limit increment) stmt-list) sets the loop control variable lcv to init, performs the statements in stmt-list in sequence and increments lcv by increment. If increment is positive (negative) and lcv is now greater than (less than) limit, the iteration is terminated and control passes to the next statement; otherwise the statements in stmt-list, the incrementing and the test are repeated. Reassignment to the loop control variable within the loop body is not permitted. The loop control variable is unknown outside the loop.

(EXIT) causes termination of the immediately enclosing REPEAT's stmt-list; control passes to the statement following the REPEAT.

The arithmetic operators $+$, $-$, $*$, QUO (division), ABS (absolute value), and $\wedge$ (exponentiation), and the logical operators $>$, $<$, $\Rightarrow$ ($\geq$), $\Leftarrow$ ($\leq$), and $=$ have their accustomed interpretations. These are prefix operators as in LISP.

Variables are allowed to have 0 (simple variables), 1 (arrays), or 2 subscripts (matrices). Array and matrix bounds are "declared" implicitly. That is, they are assumed to be as large as required by the program.

REFERENCES

1. Alpert, D. and Bitzer, D. L. Advances in computer-based education. *Science* **167** (March 1970).
2. Balzer, R. Automatic programming. USC-ISI Technical Memo 1 (September 1972).
3. Bogen, R. et al. *MACSYMA User's Manual.* M.I.T. Project MAC (February 1973).
4. Deutsch, L. P. An interactive program verifier. Ph.D Thesis, University of California, Berkeley (1973).
5. Goldstein, I. Understanding simple picture programs. MIT AI TR–294 (September 1974).
6. Knuth, D. E. *The Art of Computer Programming, Volume 3: Sorting and Searching.* Addison-Wesley, Reading, Mass. (1973).
7. Martin, W. A. Sorting. *Computing Surveys* **3** (4) (December 1971).
8. McCarthy et al. LISP 15 *Programmer's Manual.* MIT Press, Cambridge, Mass. (1965).

9. McDermott, D. V. and Sussman, G. J. The CONNIVER reference manual. AI Memo 259, MIT-AI Laboratory (July 1973).
10. Minsky, M. L. Matter, mind, and models. IFIP (1965).
11. Minsky, M. L. Steps toward artificial intelligence. *Proceedings of the IRE* **49** (1) (1961).
12. Ruth, G. R. Analysis of algorithm implementations. Ph.D Thesis, MIT Project MAC (October 1973).
13. Sussman, G. J. A computational model of skill acquisition. MIT AI TR–297, MIT–AI Laboratory (August 1973).
14. Winston, P. H. Learning structural descriptions from examples. MIT AI TR–231 (1970).

Received April 1975

PROUST: Knowledge-Based Program Understanding

W. LEWIS JOHNSON, STUDENT MEMBER, IEEE, AND ELLIOT SOLOWAY

Abstract—This paper describes a program called PROUST which does on-line analysis and understanding of Pascal written by novice programmers. PROUST takes as input a program and a nonalgorithmic description of the program requirements, and finds the most likely mapping between the requirements and the code. This mapping is in essence a reconstruction of the design and implementation steps that the programmer went through in writing the program. A knowledge base of programming plans and strategies, together with common bugs associated with them, is used in constructing this mapping. Bugs are discovered in the process of relating plans to the code; PROUST can therefore give deep explanations of program bugs by relating the buggy code to its underlying intentions.

Index Terms—Artificial intelligence, program debugging, programmer training, program understanding.

I. INTRODUCTION: MOTIVATION AND GOALS

OUR goal is to build a tutoring system which helps novice programmers to learn how to program. This system will have two components: a *programming expert* which can analyze and understand buggy programs, and a *pedagogical expert* that knows how to effectively interact with and instruct students. We have focused our attention on the first component, with the objective of building a system that can be said to truly understand (buggy) novice programs.[1] In this paper, we will describe the theory and processing techniques by which our analysis system PROUST understands buggy and correct programs.

Bugs in programs are sections of code whose behavior fails to agree with the program specification. Although the presence of bugs may be indicated by various kinds of anomalous program behavior, in general bugs are not properties of programs, but rather *are properties of the relationship between programs and intentions* [9]. For example, consider the program in Fig. 1. The programmer has written a program that reads in a number and then computes the average of all the numbers between it and 99 999, in integer increments. This is not what the stated problem requires; presumably the programmer was trying to solve the problem, but a bug has altered the program's behavior. How do we determine what this bug is? Note that the programmer first does a Read into the variable New, and then increments it by 1.

Based on our theory of programming knowledge, [1], [11], [16], [17] we would hypothesize that the student thought

Manuscript received January 31, 1984. This work was supported in part by the Personnel and Training Research Groups, Psychological Sciences Division, Office of Naval Research and the Army Research Institute for the Behavioral and Social Sciences, under Contract N00014-82-K-0714.

The authors are with the Department of Computer Science, Yale University, New Haven, CT 06520.

[1]Miller's SPADE-0 [10] is another example of a programming tutor; unlike PROUST, it constrains the program construction process so that less machinery is required for understanding and more effort can be devoted to pedagogy.

```
Problem:  Read in numbers, taking their sum, until
the number 99999 is seen.  Report the average.  Do
not include the final 99999 in the average.

  1      PROGRAM Average( input, output );
  2      VAR Sum, Count, New, Avg: REAL;
  3      BEGIN
  4         Sum := 0;
  5         Count := 0;
  6         Read( New );
  7         WHILE New<>99999 DO
  8           BEGIN
  9              Sum := Sum+New;
 10              Count := Count+1;
 11              New := New+1
 12           END;
 13         Avg := Sum/Count;
 14         Writeln( 'The average is ', avg );
 15      END;
```

PROUST *output:*

It appears that you were trying to use line 11 to read the next input value. Incrementing NEW will not cause the next value to be read in. You need to use a READ statement here, such as you use in line 6.

Fig. 1. Example of analysis of a buggy program.

that incrementing the variable New would return the next value of New; if incrementing Count gets the next INTEGER value, then incrementing New should get the next input value! The student has thus made an overgeneralization: adding one to a variable returns the next value of that variable. The key element of the above analysis is the construction of a relationship from a piece of code to a problem goal; the mechanism for that construction was knowledge about how programs are typically constructed, together with knowledge about novice misconceptions.

While we have not built a pedagogical expert yet, it would certainly need the type of information produced in the above analysis. That is, an intelligent tutoring system would need to know

• what the bugs in the student's program are, and where they occur;

• what the student was intending to do with the buggy code; and

• what misconceptions the student might have which would explain the presence of the bugs.

What is an appropriate method for deriving information such as this from a program? One way might be to compare the input–output behavior of the program to the expected input–output behavior. The information which this approach would provide is insufficient, particularly with larger programs, because a number of bugs might result in the same input/output behavior.[2] For example, many different bugs can cause a program to go into an infinite loop, so simply knowing that a program goes into an infinite loop is insufficient for determining what the bug is. Enhancing input–output analysis with

[2]BIP [20] makes use of input/output behavior in its program analysis; consequently it only deals with small programming problems.

dataflow analysis or other compiler analysis techniques will not help in cases where the code does not have any obvious structural anomalies,[3] such as in the preceding example.

What is missing in the above methods is a *detailed understanding of the relationship between the program text and the program's intentions.* We suggest that a method for building such a description involves 1) recreating the goals that the student was attempting to solve (i.e., what problem the student thought he was solving), and 2) identifying the functional units in the program that were intended to realize those goals. In effect, *the programming expert needs to analyze the buggy program by reconstructing the manner in which it was generated.* The claim is that the trace generated by the programming expert does actually correspond to what the student was thinking, although not necessarily to the utmost detail; the pedagogical expert would then use that trace in subsequent tutoring activity.[4] In this paper, we briefly highlight the theoretical basis for reconstructive program analysis, and we detail how PROUST goes about building the reconstruction.

II. THE ROLE OF PLANS IN PROGRAM UNDERSTANDING

Knowledge about what implementation methods should be used in programming is codified in PROUST in the form of *programming plans*. A programming plan is a procedure or strategy for realizing intentions in code where the key elements have been abstracted and represented explicitly. It is our position that expert programmers make extensive use of programming plans, rather than each time building programs out of the primitive constructs of a programming language. This claim is based on a theory of what mental representations programmers have and use in reading and writing programs. In [6], [16], [18], and [19] we describe various empirical experiments which support our theory. Thus, PROUST is directly based on a plausible psychological theory of the programming process. Note that codifying programming knowledge in terms of plans is not unique to PROUST; the Programmer's Apprentice [11], for example, also makes extensive use of plans.[5]

Fig. 2 is an illustration of how plans are realized in programs. The figure shows a correct implementation of the problem shown in Fig. 1, together with four plans that this program uses. Two of them, the RUNNING TOTAL VARIABLE PLAN and the COUNTER VARIABLE PLAN, are *variable plans*, i.e., they are plans which generate a result which is usually stored in a variable. Such plans typically have an initialization section and an update section, and carry information about what context they must appear in, e.g., whether or not they must be enclosed in a loop. The other two plans, the RUNNING TOTAL LOOP PLAN and the VALID RESULT SKIP GUARD, are *control plans*; their main role is not to generate results but to regulate the generation and use of data by other plans. The RUNNING TOTAL LOOP PLAN is a method for constructing a loop which

```
Problem:  Read in numbers, taking their sum, until
          the number 99999 is seen.  Report the average.  Do
          not include the final 99999 in the average.

                  PROGRAM Average( INPUT, OUTPUT );
                  VAR Sum, Count, New, Avg: REAL;
Counter           BEGIN
Plan      ------->  Count := 0;
          |  --->   Sum := 0;              Running Total Loop Plan
          |  |      Read(New); <--------------------
Running   |  |      WHILE New <> 99999 DO <-------|
Total     |  |      BEGIN                         |
Variable  |  ------->  Sum := Sum + New; <-------|
Plan      ---------->  Count := Count + 1;       |
                    Read(New);           <--------
                  END;              Valid Result Skip Guard
                  IF Count > 0 THEN <----------------------
                    BEGIN <-----------------------------|
                      Avg := Sum/Count; <---------------|
                      Writeln( Avg); <------------------|
                    END <-----------------------------|
                  ELSE <----------------------------|
                    Writeln( 'no legal inputs'); <---------|
          END
```

Fig. 2. Programming plans.

controls the computation of a running total; in this program it also controls the operation of the COUNTER VARIABLE PLAN. The VALID RESULT SKIP GUARD plan is an example of a skip guard, i.e., a control plan which causes control flow to skip around other code when boundary conditions occur. In this case it prevents the average from being computed or output when there is no input.

Recognition of plans in programs forms the basis of our approach to program understanding. But plan recognition alone is insufficient. Novices often use plans that would never occur to an expert because they do not have a good sense of what is a good plan and what is not. PROUST's knowledge base of plans has therefore been extended in order to include many stylistically dubious plans.[6] Unfortunately, the more alternative plans there are in the system, the harder it is to determine which plans the programmer was using. Furthermore, program behavior depends not only upon what plans are used, but how they are organized; it is thus possible for a program to use correct plans yet still have bugs. In order to cope with these problems a method is needed for relating plans to other plans and to the programmer's underlying intentions. This process, and the way it is used to search for the right interpretation of the program, is described in Section IV.

III. A TYPICAL PROBLEM IN PROUST'S DOMAIN

PROUST's knowledge base is currently tailored to analyze the programming problem in Fig. 3.[7] This problem (hereafter referred to as the Rainfall Problem) is a more complex version of the averaging problem shown in Fig. 1. Among other computations, a program that solves this problem must

1) count the number of valid inputs (i.e., days on which there was zero or greater rainfall); and

2) count the number of positive inputs (i.e., days on which rain fell).

Novices attempt to realize these two goals in a variety of correct and buggy ways. Since coping with variability is one of PROUST's main objectives, examining how PROUST handles

---

[3]One area in which many compilers do a reasonable job is analyzing *syntactic* errors. Although it would be worthwhile to construct a parser which produces error reports aimed at novices, this is outside of the scope of our current work.

[4]Most intelligent tutoring systems at least tacitly assume such a correspondence, e.g., [3], [7], [8].

[5]Sniffer [14] is a prototype of a debugging system which is based upon the Programmer's Apprentice.

[6]The process of collecting novice programs and analyzing them is described in [2] and [9].

[7]We are currently extending PROUST to handle a range of introductory programming problems.

Noah needs to keep track of rainfall in the New Haven area in order to determine when to launch his ark. Write a program which he can use to do this. Your program should read the rainfall for each day, stopping when Noah types "99999", which is not a data value, but a sentinel indicating the end of input. If the user types in a negative value the program should reject it, since negative rainfall is not possible. Your program should print out the number of valid days typed in, the number of rainy days, the average rainfall per day over the period, and the maximum amount of rainfall that fell on any one day.

Fig. 3. The Rainfall Problem.

this specific set of goals should be illustrative. Thus, in what follows, we will focus on PROUST's techniques for processing fragments of code that implement these goals.

IV. RELATING GOALS TO CODE VIA PLANS

In order to relate the plans in a program to the program requirements, PROUST makes explicit the *goal decomposition* underlying the program. A goal decomposition consists of

- a description of the hierarchical organization of the subtasks in a problem,
- indications of the relationships and interactions among subtasks, and
- a mapping from subtask requirements (goals) to the plans that are used to implement them.

The plans which a goal decomposition specifies are matched against the program; this results in a mapping from program requirements to individual statements.

In attempting to understand all except the most trivial programming problems, two issues must be squarely faced:

- the goal decomposition of a problem may not be unique, and
- one program may be associated with more than one goal decomposition.

We deal with each issue in turn in the next two sections.

A. The Space of Goal Decompositions and Programs

Fig. 4 illustrates how alternative goal decompositions can lead to different implementations. A single problem description, at the top, can result in several different goal decompositions, which in turn result in a number of different programs, depending upon which plans are used. Some of these programs may be correct, others buggy. Buggy programs are either derived from incorrect goal decompositions or from incorrect implementations of correct goal decompositions. Each path from the problem description down to an individual program is a *program interpretation;* we call this set of possible derivation paths the *interpretation space* associated with a problem.

Figs. 5 and 6 illustrate two different solutions of the Rainfall Problem (Fig. 3) and their corresponding goal decompositions. We focus here on two specific aspects of the problem:[8] 1) counting the valid inputs (daily rainfall greater than or equal to zero), and 2) counting the number of rainy days (daily rainfall strictly greater than zero).

Fig. 5 shows a fragment in which these two goals are realized directly. First, a COUNTER VARIABLE PLAN is used to count the valid inputs; this is realized in the code that computes the value of the variable Valid. Second, the GUARDED COUNTER

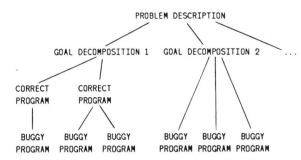

Fig. 4. Search space of possible programs.

VARIABLE PLAN is used for counting the positive inputs; the variable Rainy is used in this plan.

While the program in Fig. 6 also prints out the number of valid inputs and the number of positive inputs, the goal decomposition in this program is different. Instead of the two goals of counting the valid inputs and counting the positive inputs, the program in Fig. 6 uses three goals to achieve the same end: 1) count the zero inputs, 2) count the positive inputs, and 3) add these two counters together to derive the valid day total. The goal of counting the positive inputs is implemented with a GUARDED COUNTER VARIABLE PLAN, operating on the variable Rainy. The goal of counting the zero inputs is also implemented with a GUARDED COUNTER VARIABLE PLAN, operating on the variable Dry. The counters are combined with an ADD PARTIAL RESULTS PLAN, resulting in the variable Valid.

B. Resolving Ambiguous Interpretations

If the mapping from problem descriptions to programs is to be rich enough to generate a sufficiently wide variety of programs, ambiguity is an unavoidable consequence, i.e., two different paths in the interpretation space can lead to the same program. This situation is exacerbated when buggy programs are allowed: bugs add uncertainty to the analysis. For example, if one encounters a statement New := New + 1 in a correct program, one can be fairly certain that it is part of a counter plan. But if the program is buggy, as in Fig. 1, one must also consider the possibility that this statement is intended to input new values; the only way of determining which is the proper role is by looking at the program as a whole and determining which interpretation is more consistent with the interpretations of the other parts of the program. The ability to enumerate and evaluate alternative interpretations is a key processing technique for a system that attempts to understand buggy programs.

In Fig. 7 we give an example of the results of PROUST's attempt to resolve ambiguous interpretations. Fig. 7 shows a fragment of code which might appear in a novice solution to the Rainfall Problem in Fig. 3. We have focused on the counter variables in the program, Valid and Rainy; the rest of the main loop of the program is shown so that the surrounding context may be seen. Instead of counting the positive inputs (Rain>0) and the valid inputs (Rain>=0), this program counts the positive inputs and the zero inputs, and does not count the valid inputs.

There are two possible interpretations for this code, each of which results in a different explanation for the bugs. According to one interpretation, shown on the left side of the figure, the programmer intended to implement the valid input goal and the positive input goal directly. The plans used are COUNTER

---

[8] There are other differences in the goal decompositions of these programs besides the ones mentioned here. However, we will not analyze them in this discussion.

Plans

Goal Decomposition

Plan: RUNNING TOTAL LOOP PLAN

1. *Get input, stopping at 99999*
2. *Check that input is non-negative*
   ...

Plan: COUNTER VARIABLE PLAN
Plan: GUARDED COUNTER VARIABLE PLAN

6. *Count valid inputs*
7. *Count positive inputs*
   ...

```
PROGRAM Rain1 (INPUT, OUTPUT);
  CONST STOP=99999;
  VAR Sum,Rain,Max,Ave: REAL;
      Valid,Rainy: INTEGER;
  BEGIN
    Writeln('Enter rainfall');
    Sum:=0;
    Valid:=0;
    Rainy:=0;
    Max:=0;
    Readln;
    Read(Rain);
    WHILE Rain<>STOP DO
      BEGIN
        IF Rain<0 THEN
          Writeln(Rain:0:2,' is not a possible rainfall, try again')
        ELSE
          BEGIN
            Sum:=Sum+Rain;
            Valid:=Valid+1;
            IF Rain>Max THEN Max:=N;
            IF Rain>0 THEN
              Rainy:=Rainy+1;
          END;
        Writeln('Enter rainfall');
        Readln;
        Read(Rain)
      END;
    Writeln(Valid:0,' valid rainfalls were entered.');
    IF Valid>0 THEN
      BEGIN
        Ave:=Sum/Valid;
        Writeln('The average rainfall was ',Ave:0:2,' inches PER DAY.');
        Writeln('The highest rainfall was ',Max:0:2,' Inches.');
        WRITELN('There were ',Rainy:0,' rainy days in this period. ')
      END
  END.
```

COUNTER VARIABLE PLAN ← *Count valid inputs*

GUARDED COUNTER VARIABLE PLAN ← *Count positive inputs*

Fig. 5. Simple goal decomposition.

VARIABLE PLAN and GUARDED COUNTER VARIABLE PLAN; the resulting variables are Valid and Rainy, respectively. Valid appears to count only the zero inputs because the programmer intended to *modify* the COUNTER VARIABLE PLAN so that a copy of the counter update appears in both the THEN branch and the ELSE branch of the inner IF statement, and then left out one of the copies. The failure to update Valid in both branches thus appears to be a low-level slip, such as a mistake in editing the source file.

In the other interpretation, on the right side of the figure, the program is assumed to arise from a goal decomposition where the positive values and the zero values are counted separately and then added together. The programmer uses the variable Valid to refer to the count of zero values and Rainy to refer to the count of positive values. The plan to add Valid and Rainy together is missing. We could claim that the plan is missing because of an editing slip. However, the context in which the counter plans appear weighs agains this hypothesis: the average computation uses Valid in the denominator of the division, implying that Valid is the valid input counter as well as the zero input counter. We call variables which are used in contradictory ways such as this *mushed variables*. Mushed variables are very serious bugs; they reflect radical deficiencies in the programmer's ability to design programs. Therefore this goal decomposition is less highly valued than the previous goal decomposition. PROUST has a number of heuristics for deciding among alternative interpretations such as these.

V. THE UNDERSTANDING PROCESS: AN EXAMPLE OF PROUST IN ACTION

In the preceding sections, we 1) described what difficulties a program understanding system must overcome in order to analyze a program accurately, and 2) gave an example of the *results* of PROUST's analysis. In this section we will illustrate PROUST's *processing* capabilities. First we will describe the overall strategy by which PROUST searches through the space of potential interpretations for one that best accounts for the student's program, and then we will describe how PROUST actually produces the analysis depicted in Fig. 7.

A. Searching the Interpretation Space

Clearly, one cannot possibly enumerate beforehand the space

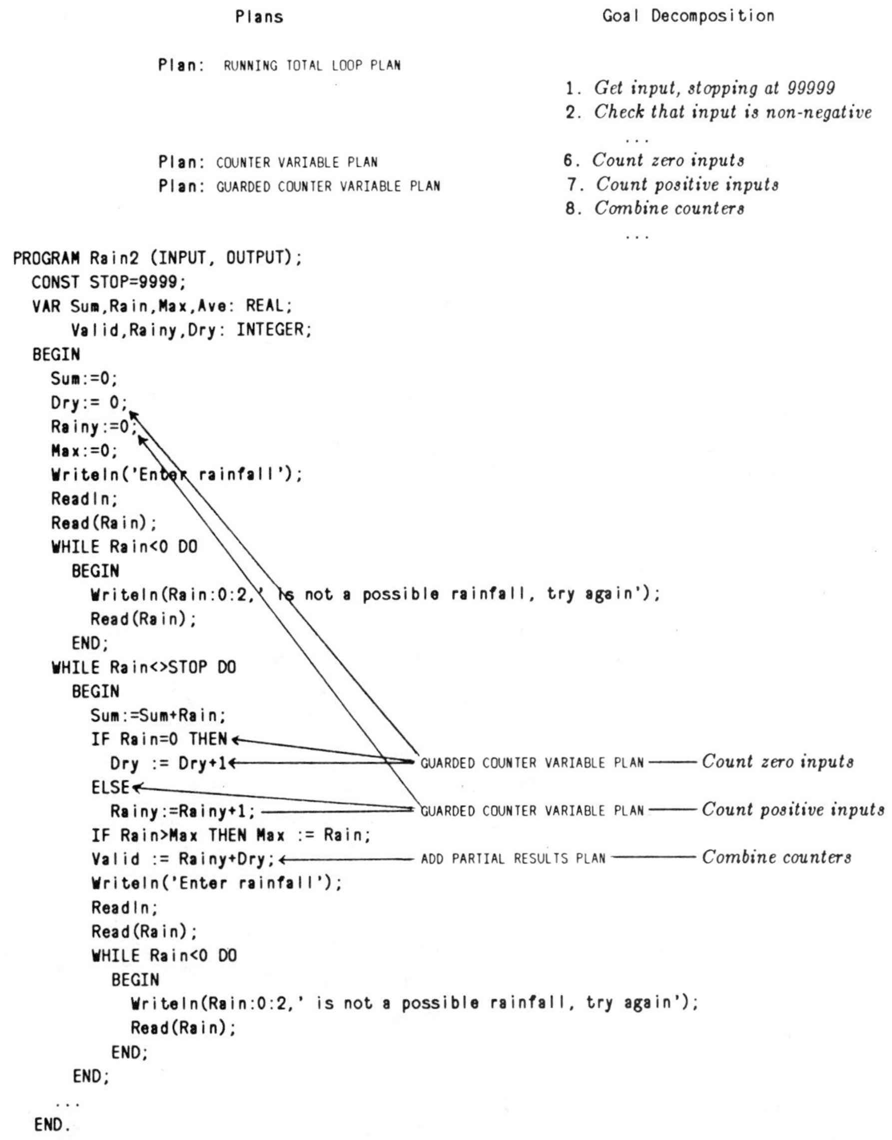

Plans

Goal Decomposition

Plan: RUNNING TOTAL LOOP PLAN

1. *Get input, stopping at 99999*
2. *Check that input is non-negative*
   . . .

Plan: COUNTER VARIABLE PLAN
Plan: GUARDED COUNTER VARIABLE PLAN

6. *Count zero inputs*
7. *Count positive inputs*
8. *Combine counters*
   . . .

```
PROGRAM Rain2 (INPUT, OUTPUT);
  CONST STOP=9999;
  VAR Sum,Rain,Max,Ave: REAL;
      Valid,Rainy,Dry: INTEGER;
  BEGIN
    Sum:=0;
    Dry:= 0;
    Rainy:=0;
    Max:=0;
    Writeln('Enter rainfall');
    Readln;
    Read(Rain);
    WHILE Rain<0 DO
      BEGIN
        Writeln(Rain:0:2,' is not a possible rainfall, try again');
        Read(Rain);
      END;
    WHILE Rain<>STOP DO
      BEGIN
        Sum:=Sum+Rain;
        IF Rain=0 THEN
          Dry := Dry+1
        ELSE
          Rainy:=Rainy+1;
        IF Rain>Max THEN Max := Rain;
        Valid := Rainy+Dry;
        Writeln('Enter rainfall');
        Readln;
        Read(Rain);
        WHILE Rain<0 DO
          BEGIN
            Writeln(Rain:0:2,' is not a possible rainfall, try again');
            Read(Rain);
          END;
      END;
    ...
  END.
```

GUARDED COUNTER VARIABLE PLAN —— *Count zero inputs*
GUARDED COUNTER VARIABLE PLAN —— *Count positive inputs*
ADD PARTIAL RESULTS PLAN —— *Combine counters*

Fig. 6. Alternative goal decomposition.

of program interpretations: there are just too many ways to construct correct and buggy programs. Rather, starting with the problem specification and a database of correct and buggy plans, transformation rules, and bug-misconception rules,[9] PROUST constructs and evaluates interpretations for the program under consideration. In effect, the goal decomposition and the plan analysis of the program evolve simultaneously. To constrain the generation process, PROUST employs heuristics about what plans and goals are likely to occur together.

The evaluation process is *prediction driven:* based on the current candidate interpretation for the program, how well do other parts of the program conform to PROUST's expectations? For example, if, in a program that attempts to solve the Rainfall Problem, PROUST has assumed that the variable Count is keeping track of the number of valid days, PROUST would expect to see Count in the denominator of the average daily rainfall calculation. If this expectation is confirmed, then PROUST is more confident of its interpretation, and vice versa. PROUST employs heuristics that evaluate matches, near-misses,

and misses of its expectations. Example of construction and evaluation processes will be given in the next section.

The fact the PROUST constructs and evaluates interpretations anew for each program, and does not rely on a prestored set of possible interpretations, provides it with an important capability: PROUST readily generates interpretations for programs that it (and we) have not seen previously. That is, unlike some diagnostic systems that effectively choose a fault from a set of predefined faults [4], [15], PROUST actively constructs diagnoses. Given the variability in programs, PROUST needs such a capability in order to be effective.[10]

B. Putting It All Together: Two Examples

In this section we will illustrate how PROUST actually goes about analyzing a program. We will show two examples; one is a correct program and the other is a buggy program.

1) Analysis of a Correct Program: Our first example, in Fig. 8, is an excerpt from a correct solution to the Rainfall Problem

[9] These entities will be explained shortly.

[10] FALOSY [13] is also capable for recognizing novel faults; however, it assumes that there is only one fault, which the programmer must describe beforehand.

Buggy Program Fragment

```
WHILE Rain<>99999 DO
  BEGIN
    IF Rain<0 THEN
      Writeln( 'Input not valid' )
    ELSE
      BEGIN
        IF Rain=0 THEN
          Valid := Valid+1
        ELSE
          BEGIN
            Rainy := Rainy+1;
          END;
        Sum := Sum+Rain;
        ...
      END;
    Writeln( 'Enter next value:' );
    Read( Rain );
  END;
  ...
Avg := Sum/Valid;
```

Goal Decomposition 1

goal: count all items
goal: count positive items

Bug:

Missing copy of duplicated plan segment

Explanation to student:

This program will not count the number of inputs correctly. You increment "Valid" when the input is zero, but not when it is positive.

Goal Decomposition 2

goal: count zero
goal: count positives
goal: combine partial counts

Bugs:

Mushed variables
Missing plan

Explanation to student:

You are using the variable "Valid" both to count the total number of inputs and the number of zero inputs. Each variable should be used to mean one and only one thing. Also, you are going to have to add the zero count and the positive count together.

Fig. 7. Alternative explanations for bugs.

```
Sum := 0;
Rainy := 0;
Valid := 0;
Max := 0;
Read( Rain );
WHILE Rain<>99999 DO
  BEGIN
    IF Rain<0 THEN
      Writeln( 'Input not valid' )
    ELSE
      BEGIN
        IF Rain=0 THEN            (a)
          Valid := Valid+1        (b)
        ELSE
          BEGIN
            Valid := Valid+1;     (c)
            Rainy := Rainy+1;
          END;
        Sum := Sum+Rain;
        IF Rain>Max THEN
          Max := Rain;
      END;
    Writeln( 'Enter next value:' );
    Read( Rain );
  END;
Avg := Sum/Valid;
```

Fig. 8. Excerpt of Rainfall Program.

in Fig. 3; it is based on the program fragment shown in Fig. 7. Although this program functions correctly, there is one construction which is unusual; the valid input counter Valid is updated in two places instead of one. That is, Valid is updated in each branch of the conditional statement at (a); the update at (b) is executed when Rain is zero, and the update at (c) when Rain is positive. The program in this figure illustrates the variability possible in programs; coping with this type of situation requires additional machinery, as will be seen shortly.

Assume the PROUST has carried out a partial plan analysis

of this program already, and has made the following tentative assumptions.

- The variable Sum is the running total variable.
- The variable Valid keeps tracks of the number of valid days.
- The update on Valid should be in the loop, embedded inside a test for negative rainfall (IF Rain < 0 THEN···).

The processing that continues from this point is illustrated in Fig. 9. PROUST maintains an agenda of goals that remain to be worked on; at this point in the analysis the agenda includes the Count goal for valid inputs, the Sum goal, and the Count goal for positive inputs, to name a few. PROUST selects the first goal on the agenda, as shown at (a), checks that it is ready for analysis, and then determines whether or not it needs to be decomposed. The entry in the knowledge base for Count stipulates that it is most commonly implemented in an undecomposed fashion, so Proust consults the plan database looking for appropriate plans for realizing this goal. It finds only one plan plan: the COUNTER VARIABLE PLAN, at (b). It then makes tentative bindings for the plan variables, and determines where each segment of the plan should be found. The resulting structure, shown at (c), can then be matched against the student's program.

Fig. 10 shows the results of matching the instantiated plan against the code. There is a unique match for the initialization step of the plan, but instead of there being one match for the update step, there are *two* matches. Furthermore, PROUST expects the update to be at "top level" inside the loop, i.e., it should not be enclosed inside code which might disrupt its function. Instead it discovers that each update is enclosed in an IF statement which restricts its application. PROUST treats the plan as a near-match for the program, but the plan cannot be accepted until the match discrepancies are accounted for.

PROUST has a number of different methods for explaining a plan difference; one of them is to use *transformation rules* to relate the code to the plan. One such transformation is shown in Fig. 11.[11] Each transformation rule has a test part and an action part. The test part consists of a conjunction of microtests, each testing various aspects of the program; the action part usually indicates how to modify the code in order to nullify the effect of the transformation. In this case the Distribution Transformation Rule applies. This is a rule for recognizing plans in situations where a set of computations have been divided into parts using a CASE statement or an IF-THEN-ELSE construct, and where the plan update is duplicated so that a copy appears in each branch. The control flow branches in this case are the two branches in the IF-THEN-ELSE construction which test for Rain=0 and Rain>0. The rule checks to see whether there is exactly one Valid:= Valid + 1 statement for each possible branch of the test. It then combines the two updates and moves the result to an appropriate place outside of the test. Once this is done the counter plan matches successfully.

2) A Buggy Example: We will now show how PROUST analyzes the buggy program shown in Fig. 7; a more complete version is given in Fig. 12. When PROUST analyzes buggy programs such as this, it goes through much the same process that

---

[11]PROUST currently has 15 such transformation in its database. Some rules, such as the Distribution Transformation Rule, are quite general; others, such as the transformation which changes Valid <>0 into Valid>0 if Valid is a counter variable, are plan specific.

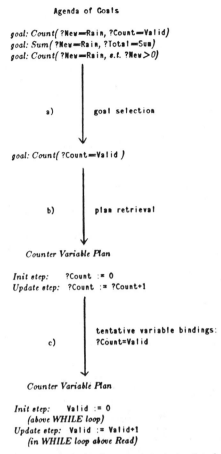

Agenda of Goals

goal: Count(?New=Rain, ?Count=Valid)
goal: Sum(?New=Rain, ?Total=Sum)
goal: Count(?New=Rain, s.t. ?New>0)

a)   goal selection

goal: Count(?Count=Valid)

b)   plan retrieval

Counter Variable Plan

Init step: ?Count := 0
Update step: ?Count := ?Count+1

c)   tentative variable bindings:
          ?Count=Valid

Counter Variable Plan

Init step: Valid := 0
          (above WHILE loop)
Update step: Valid := Valid+1
          (in WHILE loop above Read)

Fig. 9. Simple mapping from goals to instantiated plans.

```
IF Rain=0 THEN                          Valid := Valid+1;
    Valid := Valid+1                    IF Rain=0 THEN
ELSE BEGIN;                                 {}
    Valid := Valid+1;                  ELSE BEGIN;
    Rainy := Rainy+1;                      {}
END;                                       Rainy := Rainy+1;
                                        END;
```

Fig. 11. Program transformation.

```
Sum := 0;
Rainy := 0;
Valid := 0;
Max := 0;
Read( Rain );
WHILE Rain<>99999 DO
    BEGIN
    IF Rain<0 THEN
        Writeln( 'Input not valid' )
    ELSE
        BEGIN
        IF Rain=0 THEN
            Valid := Valid+1
        ELSE
            BEGIN
            Rainy := Rainy+1;
            END;
        Sum := Sum+Rain;
        IF Rain>Max THEN
            Max := Rain;
        END;
    Writeln( 'Enter next value:' );
    Read( Rain );
    END;
Avg := Sum/Valid;
```

Fig. 12. A buggy program.

```
Sum := 0;
Valid := 0;  ◄──────────Valid := 0  Init step:
Rainy := 0;                          EXACT MATCH
Max := 0;
Read( Rain );
WHILE Rain<>99999 DO
    BEGIN
    IF Rain<O THEN
        Writeln( 'Input not valid' )
    ELSE
        BEGIN
        IF Rain=0 THEN
            Valid := Valid+1◄──Valid := Valid+1  Update step:
        ELSE                     predicted by distribution transformation
            BEGIN
            Rainy := Rainy+1;
            END;               Valid := Valid+1 Update step:
        Sum := Sum+Rain;       transformation condition violated
        IF Rain>Max THEN         EXPLANATION: low-level slip
            Max := Rain;
        END;
    Writeln( 'Enter next value:' );
    Read( Rain );
    END;
Avg := Sum/Valid;
```

Fig. 13. Transformation with bugs.

```
Sum := 0;
Valid := 0;  ◄────────────Valid := 0  Init step:
Rainy := 0;                            EXACT MATCH
Max := 0;
Read( Rain );
WHILE Rain<>99999 DO
    BEGIN
    IF Rain<0 THEN
        Writeln( 'Input not valid' )
    ELSE
        BEGIN
        IF Rain=0 THEN◄
            Valid := Valid+1◄
        ELSE◄
            BEGIN              Valid := Valid+1  Update step:
            Valid := Valid+1;  TWO MATCHES; BOTH INSIDE
            Rainy := Rainy+1;       UNEXPECTED CODE
        END;
        Sum := Sum+Rain;
        IF Rain>Max THEN
            Max := Rain;
        END;
    Writeln( 'Enter next value:' );
    Read( Rain );
    END;
Avg := Sum/Valid;
```

Fig. 10. Plan matching.

it goes through in analyzing correct programs; the main difference is that PROUST must consider more alternative interpretations in order to find the most plausible explanation for the bug.

Fig. 13 shows what happens when the COUNTER VARIABLE PLAN is matched against this program. This time there is one good match for the counter update; unfortunately it is inside of an unexpected IF statement. The Distribution Transformation Rule is invoked to explain the plan difference, but

it predicts that there should be two updates, so it does not fully explain the problem. PROUST therefore looks for another rule which will explain the difference between the prediction made by the Distribution Transformation Rule and the observed code. A rule applies which states that if a single instance of duplicated code is missing, it is explainable as a low-level slip. This completes the mapping from the plan to the code.

Whenever an interpretation presumes the presence of a bug, it is necessary to make sure that there are no other interpretations which presume fewer or less severe bugs. PROUST therefore goes back and looks for another way of implementing the *Count* goal. PROUST has in its knowledge base an alternative method for decomposing *Count* goals, namely to implement counters for particular intervals and then combine the partial counts. One of these subgoals can be unified with the *Count positives* goal that already exists in the agenda. The two *Count* goals are thus transformed into a set of three goals. Plans can then be chosen and instantiated for each of these goals, as was done in Fig. 9. The resulting plans, and the results of matching them, are shown in Fig. 14. This time two match errors are found. First, Valid is the counter for zero values, but the average predicts that Valid is the main counter; Valid is a mushed variable. Second, the ADD PARTIAL RESULTS PLAN is missing altogether. PROUST ranks bugs according to their severity; missing plans that do not pertain to some boundary condition are moderately severe bugs, and mushed variables are extremely severe bugs. Therefore this interpretation is less highly valued, and the analysis involving the transformation holds.

VI. Performance: Preliminary Results

As a preliminary test of PROUST's capabilities, we tested PROUST on 206 different novice solutions to the Rainfall Problem shown above. We collected these programs by modifying the Pascal compiler used by the students in an introductory programming course so that each syntactically correct version of the program was stored on tape [2]. We ran PROUST on the first syntactically correct version from each student, so that we could see how PROUST behaves when faced with a large number of bugs.

In Fig. 15 we see how PROUST performed on this corpus of programs. After PROUST analyzes such program, it evaluates the goodness of the analysis, and assigns the analysis to one of three categories: complete, partial, and unsatisfactory. A complete analysis is one which accounts for all the important aspects of the specification, and which does not leave any code unanalyzed which might interfere with the behavior of the analyzed code. A partial analysis is one where goals in the specification were unaccounted for and parts of the program could not be interpreted, but where a significant portion of the program was understandable. An unsatisfactory analysis is one which leaves most of the program uninterpreted, or which contains programming constructs, such as GOTO's, which PROUST cannot analyze. Of the 206 programs in the sample, PROUST constructed complete analyses for 161 of them (79 percent). On those programs that it did feel confident of its analysis, it was correct almost[12] 95 percent of the time! Thirty-five of the programs (17 percent) received partial analyses. When PROUST comes up with a partial analysis, it throws out the more dubious parts of the analysis, and reports only those bugs that are unrelated to the parts of the program that PROUST could not understand. It tells the student explicitly that the analysis is a partial one, and that he or she should take it with a grain of salt. Nevertheless, we expect students to be able to make use of these partial bug reports, and get their programs into a form where PROUST is more likely to be able to generate a complete analysis. There remains a small number (4 percent) of programs that PROUST was unable to interpret. We would like this number to be smaller, but we do not think that it is practical to reduce it below 3–4 percent. The best thing that PROUST could do in these cases is to have the student get assistance from his/her instructor.

[12]There were still 55 "false alarms:" cases where PROUST misinterpreted a bug, or erroneously labeled correct code as buggy.

```
Sum := 0;                              Guarded Counter Variable Plan
Valid := 0;                                (dry day counter)
Rainy := 0;
Max := 0;                              Init step:    ?Cnt := 0
Read( Rain );                          Guard step:   IF Rain=0 THEN
                                       Update step:  ?Cnt := ?Cnt+1
WHILE Rain<>99999 DO                         MUSHED VARIABLES!
  BEGIN
    IF Rain<0 THEN
      Writeln( 'Input not valid' )    Guarded Counter Variable Plan
    ELSE                                  (rainy day counter)
      BEGIN
        IF Rain=0 THEN                 Init step:    ?Cnt := 0
          Valid := Valid+1            Guard step:   IF Rain>0 THEN
        ELSE                           Update step:      ?Cnt := ?Cnt+1
          BEGIN
            Rainy := Rainy+1;
          END;
        Sum := Sum+Rain;              Add Partial Results Plan
        IF Rain>Max THEN
          Max := Rain;                 Update step: Valid := ?Sum1+?Sum2
      END;                             [?Sum1←Valid, ?Sum2←Rainy]
    Writeln( 'Enter next value:' );        MISSING PLAN!
    Read( Rain );
END.
```

Fig. 14. Matching alternate plans.

```
Total number of programs:                206

PROUST gave complete bug reports for 161 programs (79%)

Total number of bugs (from 161 programs) 570
  Bugs recognized correctly:             533  (94%)
  Bugs not reported:                      37   (6%)
  False alarms:                           55

Number of partially analyzed programs: 35 (17%)

Total number of bugs in 35 programs:    191
  Bugs recognized correctly:             71   (37%)
  Bugs intentionally not reported:       70   (37%)
  Bugs not recognized:                   50   (26%)
  False alarms:                          35

Number of programs Proust did not analyze: 9 (4%)
```

Fig. 15. Preliminary results.

In looking at the cases where PROUST failed, we see no fundamental obstacle to getting PROUST up to the 80–85 percent overall correct rate. We can characterize the kinds of programs which will *always* cause problems for PROUST as follows: 1) very unusual bugs, which occur too infrequently to justify inclusion in PROUST's knowledge base; 2) programs which contain novel plans which PROUST has no means for predicting; and 3) ambiguous cases which can only be resolved through dialog with the student. For these cases, we would suggest that the student see a human teacher.

VII. Concluding Remarks

Is all the machinery described in this paper necessary in order to understand buggy and correct programs—programs that are only about one page in length? The answer, in our minds at least, is: undeniably yes. If anything, PROUST is the minimum that is required! The basis for this conclusion is twofold:

1) In artificial intelligence research, systems have been built to understand stories of moderate length that require machinery similar to that employed by PROUST, e.g., [5], [12]. Certainly, programs are as complicated an entity as are stories.

2) We attempted to build a bug finding system that used a database of bug templates in a *context-independent* fashion to analyze programs similar to those analyzed by PROUST.

That system, MENO [15], failed miserably: in order to cope with the variety and variability in actual programs, a system must be able to understand how the pieces of the program fit together—which is a highly *context-dependent* process.

Finally, all programmers intuitively know that the mapping from problem specifications to code is a complex process. What PROUST has done—which we feel is its major contribution—is lay that mapping process open to inspection; since PROUST constructs a program in its attempt to understand the program under analysis, we can "see" the programming process in action. By making the programming process explicit, our work joins with that of the software engineering community to change programming from an ethereal art to an object of scientific inquiry.

REFERENCES

[1] J. Bonar and E. Soloway, "Uncovering principles of novice programming," presented at the SIGPLAN-SIGACT 10th Symp. Principles of Programming Languages, 1983.

[2] J. Bonar, K. Ehrlich, and E. Soloway, "Collecting and analyzing on-line protocols from novice programmers," *Behavioral Res. Methods Instrum.*, vol. 14, pp. 203–209, 1982.

[3] J. S. Brown, R. R. Burton, and J. de Kleer, "Pedagorgical, natural language and knowledge engineering techniques in SOPHIE I, II, and III," in *Intelligent Tutoring Systems*, D. Sleeman and J. S. Brown, Eds. New York: Academic, 1981.

[4] W. J. Clancey, J. S. Bennett, and P. R. Cohen, "Applications-oriented AI research: Education," Stanford Heuristic Programming Project, Tech. Rep. HPP-79-17, July 1979.

[5] M. Dyer, "In-Depth Understanding," Dep. Comput. Sci., Yale Univ., New Haven, CT, Tech. Rep. 219, May 1982.

[6] K. Ehrlich and E. Soloway, "An empirical investigation of the tacit plan knowledge in programming," in *Human Factors in Computer Systems*, J. Thomas and M. L. Schneider, Eds. Norwood, NJ: Ablex, to be published.

[7] M. R. Genesereth, "The role of plans in intelligent teaching systems," in *Intelligent Tutoring Systems*, D. Sleeman and J. S. Brown, Eds. New York: Academic, 1981.

[8] I. P. Goldstein, "The genetic graph: A representation for the evolution of procedural knowledge," *Int. J. Man–Machine Studies*, vol. 11, pp. 51–77, 1979.

[9] L. Johnson, S. Draper, and E. Soloway, "Classifying bugs is a tricky business," in *Proc. NASA Workshop Software Engineering*, 1983.

[10] M. L. Miller, "A structured planning and debugging environment for elementary programming," *Int. J. Man–Machine Studies*, vol. 11, pp. 79–95, 1978.

[11] C. Rich, "A formal representation for plans in the programmer's apprentice," in *Proc. 7th Int. Joint Conf. Artificial Intelligence*, Aug. 1981, pp. 1044–1052.

[12] R. Schank and R. Abelson, *Scripts, Plans, Goals, and Understanding.* Hillsdale, NJ: Erlbaum, 1977.

[13] R. L. Sedlmeyer and P. E. Johnson, "Diagnostic reasoning in software fault localization," in *Proc. SIGSOFT Workshop High-Level Debugging*, Asilomar, CA, 1983.

[14] D. G. Shapiro, "Sniffer: A system that understands bugs," M.I.T. Artificial Intelligence Lab., Tech. Rep. AI Memo 638, June 1981.

[15] E. Soloway, E. Rubin, B. Woolf, J. Bonar, and W. L. Johnson, "MENO-II: An AI-based programming tutor," *J. Comput.-Based Instruction*, vol. 10, p. 1, 1983.

[16] E. Soloway, K. Ehrlich, J. Bonar, and J. Greenspan, "What do novices know about programming," in *Directions in Human-Computer Interactions.* Norwood, NJ: Ablex, 1982.

[17] E. Soloway, K. Ehrlich, and J. Bonar, "Tapping into tacit programming knowledge," in *Proc. Conf. Human Factors in Computing Systems*, Gaithersburg, MD, 1982.

[18] E. Soloway, K. Ehrlich, and E. Gold, "Reading a program is like reading a story (well, almost)," in *Proc. Cognitive Science Conf.*, Cognitive Science Society, Rochester, NY, 1983.

[19] E. Soloway, J. Bonar, and K. Ehrlich, "Cognitive strategies and looping constructs: An empirical study," *Commun. ACM*, vol. 26, Nov. 1983.

[20] K. T. Wescourt, M. Beard, L. Gould, and A. Barr, "Knowledge-based CAL: CINS for individualized curriculum sequencing Stanford Inst. Mathematical Studies in the Social Sciences, Psychology and Education Series, Tech. Rep. 290, Oct. 1977.

W. Lewis Johnson (S'84) received the A.B. degree in linguistics from Princeton University, Princeton, NJ, in 1978, and the M.S. degree in computer science from Yale University, New Haven, CT, in 1980.

He is currently completing the Ph.D. degree, also at Yale. His research interests include program synthesis and understanding, intelligent computer-aided instruction, and software error diagnosis and correction.

Mr. Johnson is a member of the Association for Computing Machinery and the American Association for Artificial Intelligence.

Elliot Soloway received the B.A. degree in philosophy from Ohio State University, Columbus, in 1969, and the M.S. and Ph.D. degrees in computer science from the University of Massachusetts, Amherst, in 1976 and 1978, respectively.

He is an Assistant Professor of Computer Science at Yale University, New Haven, CT, and a Vice President of Compu-Tech, Inc., New Haven, an educational software company.

His research interests include the cognitive underpinnings of programming, artificial intelligence, and computer science education.

Dr. Soloway is a member of the Association for Computing Machinery and the Cognitive Science Society.

IX / Programming Knowledge

The heart of any intelligent programming tool is knowledge about programming. The papers in this section are therefore strongly relevant to all the other work in this volume.

[Green and Barstow, Chapter 26] lays out a body of basic programming knowledge about array operations, divide-and-conquer algorithms, and representing and manipulating sets. The paper emphasizes the way the knowledge fits together. In particular, it discusses how large families of related algorithms can be constructed by combining a relatively small number of basic ideas in different ways. As an example of this, the paper discusses the relationships between various sorting algorithms.

In addition to describing the knowledge itself, Green and Barstow also show how the knowledge can be encoded as transformation rules. This encoding was used in the PECOS system described in [Barstow, Chapter 7].

[Dershowitz, Chapter 27] explores the question of how programming knowledge is to be acquired. In particular, Dershowitz presents formal methods for abstracting a given set of programs into a program schema that captures the knowledge shared by those programs. These methods are closely related to the program verification techniques described in Section II. Dershowitz also discusses how the program schemas he derives can be used as to support deductive program synthesis (see Section I).

[Rich, Chapter 28] defines a formal representation for programming knowledge called the Plan Calculus, which is used in the Programmer's Apprentice system (see [Waters, Chapter 22]). The Plan Calculus combines features of both program schemas and program transformations, which Rich argues have advantages over either approach alone. The paper also suggests how the Plan Calculus can be used to represent a body of knowledge similar to that discussed in [Green and Barstow, Chapter 26].

The papers discussed above focus on programming knowledge and how it can be represented in a machine. Another obvious concern is how programmers represent knowledge in their own heads. [Soloway and Ehrlich, Chapter 29] reports on a number of experiments that explore the knowledge programmers actually possess. These experiments tend to support the view that programming knowledge is chunked into planlike structures as described in [Rich, Chapter 28]. The experiments also indicate that this is more true of expert programmers than of novices.

On Program Synthesis Knowledge*

Cordell Green**

Systems Control, Inc., Palo Alto, CA 94304, U.S.A.

David Barstow

Computer Science Department, Yale University, New Haven, CT 06250, U.S.A.

Recommended by Nils Nilsson

ABSTRACT

This paper presents a body of program synthesis knowledge dealing with array operations, space reutilization, the divide-and-conquer paradigm, conversion from recursive paradigms to iterative paradigms, and ordered set enumerations. Such knowledge can be used for the synthesis of efficient and in-place sorts including quicksort, mergesort, sinking sort, and bubble sort, as well as other ordered set operations such as set union, element removal, and element addition. The knowledge is explicated to a level of detail such that it is possible to codify this knowledge as a set of program synthesis rules for use by a computer-based synthesis system. The use and content of this set of programming rules is illustrated by the methodical synthesis of bubble sort, sinking sort, quicksort, and mergesort.

1. Introduction

In this paper, we present a body of program synthesis knowledge and suggest that a computer can be programmed to use this knowledge to write several very good

* This research was supported in part by the Advanced Research Projects Agency under ARPA Order 2494, Contract MDA903-76-C-0206, and in part by the National Science Foundation under NSF Grant MCS 77-05740. A major portion of the work described herein was done while the authors were in the Computer Science Department of Stanford University. The views and conclusions contained in this document are those of the authors and should not be interpreted as necessarily representing the official policies, either expressed or implied, of Stanford University, Yale University, Systems Control Inc. or the U.S. Government.
** Cordell Green is currently in the Computer Science Department, Stanford University, Stanford, Calif. 94305.

sort programs, such as quicksort and mergesort, as well as related programs such as set union and basic enumeration operations.

This paper is an extension of two earlier papers [8, 9], parts one and two of this series on our *theory of programming*, or a codification of programming knowledge. The first paper presented rules as English statements, and the second showed how these rules could be translated into computer usable form. The earlier papers discussed the rules for iterative transfer paradigm sorting programs—selection and insertion sorts. This paper presents programming knowledge, again in English, about the divide-and-conquer paradigm, space reutilization, and other ordered set operations. This paper allows the synthesis of the previously synthesized sorts but also allows recursive sorts such as quicksort and mergesort. Another addition in this paper is the discussion of arrays as data types, which, combined with space reutilization knowledge, allows the synthesis of in-place insertion, selection, sinking, and bubble sorts, as well as quicksort, and mergesort.

1.1. Why a paper on program synthesis knowledge?

An automatic programming system that has a comprehensive set of programming abilities will require a large body of programming knowledge. Such a system would also require sophisticated planning methods, problem-solving methods, inference methods, etc., but at this time we feel that the most limiting factor is that of codifying the large body of programming knowledge. Since program synthesis is a young field, still an art rather than a science, this body of knowledge has not yet been structured for use by machines, and it is the proper domain of artificial intelligence research to begin the structuring of this knowledge at a detailed level. Accordingly, we feel it is most appropriate to look at programming knowledge bases at this time.

The programming knowledge presented in this paper, combined with that of our earlier two papers, extends well beyond sorting. The subject of sorting provides an excellent vehicle for the discussion of program synthesis knowledge. Knuth [11] has stated that "virtually *every* important aspect of programming arises somewhere in the context of sorting or searching," reflecting the generality of rules used for the synthesis of sort programs. Note that the sort programs discussed herein include as parts other programs for simple searching, ordered set union, removal of an element from a set, addition of an element to a set, etc. Much of what occurs in programs consists of set enumeration operations in the form of loops or recursions on arrays or lists. Thus our low-level programming rules for enumeration and other operations on lists and arrays and for space reutilization should be widely applicable. The higher-level transfer paradigm, recursive paradigm, and divide-and-conquer paradigm will be used less frequently than the low-level rules, but are certainly applicable outside the sorting context.

There is now empirical evidence confirming that this approach and the rules have wider utility. We have expressed a subset of these rules in a programming formalism [9]. These were used in a rule-testing system that included about 150 rules and produced a variety of sort programs. Further rules were tested in a larger program synthesis system [1, 2] that included about 400 rules. The system synthesized simple learning programs, linear prime-finding algorithms, reachability algorithms and information storage and retrieval programs. The basic rules showed considerable carryover to new applications.

We do not address the issue of how one might best build a system where one is interested in *only* the question "How do I find a good sort program?" One method might be to have stored a few sort routines and a questionnaire to help the user select the appropriate one. Of course, such an approach wouldn't help much if the user wanted some program other than a sort program, say a concept formation program. We will not discuss the generality vs. power issue except to note that it is very complex, depending upon the class of application programs synthesized and the larger context in which the synthesis system is used.

We neither claim nor believe that the particular synthesis rules and paradigms expressed here are "optimal" in any sense. Instead, we hope we have provided a starting point and that other researchers will introduce better rules and further refinements of those presented here. We especially wish to make no claims for the *synthesis paths* or particular derivations given. The particular synthesis paths we give were chosen to better explicate the programming rules, but it is likely that a synthesis system would make choices in different orders or even follow totally different synthesis paths.

For the reader who has missed our earlier papers, we summarize in the appendix a subset of the earlier rules, the enumerator rules, and indicate how they may be programmed. These rules cover enumeration of elements and positions in stored sets, according to given ordering relations. They cover lists and arrays as data structures and include enumerator constructs such as initialization, termination tests, and methods of saving or marking the state of an enumeration as it progresses. In this paper we will not descend to the detailed level, such as assignments and low-level list and array operations, as these were covered earlier.

1.2. On this approach

Our method of program synthesis can be viewed as detailed stepwise refinement or, alternatively, logical program synthesis by special rules of inference. One comment we have received is that it is a programming theory that could be taught to students so that they can synthesize programs by learning these rules and paradigms. Perhaps it is a good theory for humans to use, but it has been designed for computers to use, and we've not tested it as a teaching method. The reason we present most of the knowledge in English, rather than in a computer formalism, is to make it easier to follow rather than to claim it as a teaching method. Although we will primarily follow the stepwise refinement paradigm, we also invoke a hypothesize and test method, and an inferential capability for simplifying tests and producing speedups. The use of these methods allows more sophisticated syntheses, but makes the subsequent transformation into rules more complex and less deterministic.

The search for an efficient program is guided by several mechanisms. The synthesis rules themselves limit the search to plausibly correct programs, i.e., at each level of refinement the candidate synthesis paths will yield a correct program given the knowledge available at that level. There is no need to check whether a program at a given level is correct, since the refinement paths either lead to correct programs (assuming correctness of the rules, of course) or are not completable. One may thus view the refinement rules as a planning mechanism that structures and reduces the search to an orderly generation of reasonable programs.

Search is also guided by knowledge of the efficiency of different implementation techniques. There are some simple optimization heuristics that avoid complex efficiency estimation in clear-cut cases. In general, at any level of refinement, the time and space cost efficiency of the proposed synthesis path can be estimated by algorithm analysis. Upper and lower bounds on overall program cost are computed and used by branch and bound techniques to eliminate clearly inferior implementations. Since the global effect of a local decision is of importance, interactions among decisions could cause combinatorial problems. The combinatorics can be minimized by factoring the program being refined into cost-wise independent pieces and by using global interaction information to clump together relevant local refinement decisions. To insure that the search for an efficient program is itself reasonably efficient, searching efforts can be concentrated on decisions estimated to have high global impact. These techniques have been developed by Elaine Kant and embodied in an efficiency analysis program described elsewhere [10]. A more detailed discussion of the interaction between refinement and efficiency considerations is given by Barstow and Kant [2].

Much of the program synthesis knowledge and the general approach presented here are embodied in a program which is the "coder," and are also embodied to some extent in the "efficiency expert," of the much larger PSI program synthesis system [6, 7]. The PSI system consists of two phases: an acquisition phase and a synthesis phase. The acquisition phase constructs a high-level model of the desired program and information structures from a dialogue with the user. The dialogue contains English as well as examples and traces. The acquisition phase consists of a parser-interpreter written by Jerrold Ginsparg [5], a trace and examples inference system and domain expert by Jorge Phillips [16], a dialogue moderator by Lou Steinberg, an explainer by Richard Gabriel, and a model builder by Brian McCune [15]. The synthesis phase consists of the coder by David Barstow [1] and the efficiency expert by Elaine Kant [10]. These two modules interact to refine the high-level program model into executable and efficient code.

The most closely related work to that presented here is that of John Darlington

3. The Divide-and-conquer or Partitioning Paradigm

The top-level technique we shall consider is to split the set to be sorted (the input) into parts, sort the parts, and then put the parts back together to form the output. The three operations split, sort and join must be done cooperatively in such a manner that the whole set is sorted. We see that this method is naturally recursive, for we may use the same sorting algorithm to sort each of the parts. This general paradigm has several names including recursive sorts, partitioning sorts and divide-and-conquer sorts.

The set to be sorted may be divided into any number of parts. We shall assume in this paper that the set will be divided into *two* parts. The method may be diagrammed as shown. The set S is split into two disjoint sets S_1 and S_2. These are sorted into S'_1 and S'_2, which are then joined to form the sorted set S'.

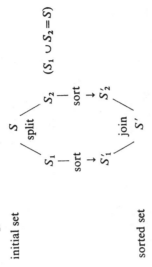

$$\text{initial set}$$
$$S$$
$$\text{split}$$
$$S_1 \qquad S_2 \qquad (S_1 \cup S_2 = S)$$
$$\text{sort} \qquad \text{sort}$$
$$S'_1 \qquad S'_2$$
$$\text{join}$$
$$S'$$
$$\text{sorted set}$$

Two instances of this paradigm would be mergesort and quicksort, as illustrated below:

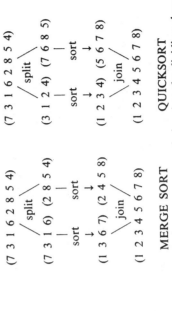

$$(7\ 3\ 1\ 6\ 2\ 8\ 5\ 4)$$
$$\text{split}$$
$$(7\ 3\ 1\ 6)\quad(2\ 8\ 5\ 4)$$
$$\text{sort}\qquad\text{sort}$$
$$(1\ 3\ 6\ 7)\quad(2\ 4\ 5\ 8)$$
$$\text{join}$$
$$(1\ 2\ 3\ 4\ 5\ 6\ 7\ 8)$$
$$\text{MERGE SORT}$$

$$(7\ 3\ 1\ 6\ 2\ 8\ 5\ 4)$$
$$\text{split}$$
$$(3\ 1\ 2\ 4)\quad(7\ 6\ 8\ 5)$$
$$\text{sort}\qquad\text{sort}$$
$$(1\ 2\ 3\ 4)\quad(5\ 6\ 7\ 8)$$
$$\text{join}$$
$$(1\ 2\ 3\ 4\ 5\ 6\ 7\ 8)$$
$$\text{QUICKSORT}$$
(using 4 as the dividing element)

Note that in mergesort the set is split into a left and right half, according to the position of the elements. The join or merge operation does some sorting-like work

---

[4]. He also presents a formalism for the synthesis of essentially the same class of sorting programs. His formalism is quite different, and is based upon an algebraic characterization of program transformations. Darlington and Burstall [3] present other techniques for recursive-to-iterative program transformations. Manna and Waldinger [14] and Laaser [12] investigate alternative techniques for synthesizing programs for finding the extreme of a set; their techniques include finding recursive programs through problem reduction.

2. Overview of Programming Knowledge

To help provide an overview, we present below a summary of some of the key program synthesis constructs used in this paper. These will be elaborated through the vehicle of tracing the synthesis of the various sort programs.

Divide-and-conquer paradigm
    correctness conditions
    uniform recursive
    choice of partitioning method
        singleton, equal-size
Transfer paradigm
    recursive-to-iterative transformation
    hypothesize and test method
    sufficient conditions
In-place operations
    feasibility
    reuse of "no longer referenced" sets, locations
    in-place element addition and deletion
    shifts, ordered and unordered
Sets stored in contiguous regions of arrays
    fixed and movable boundaries
    minimal shifting for insertions and deletions
    positions for placement of sets
Simplifications of insertions, deletions, position and element testing
Enumerate and process
    positions, elements
    selection of enumeration orders
        left-right, right-left, binary chop, largest first, alternating
Enumeration simplifications
    early stop, late start
    use of transitivity, reuse of earlier comparisons
    enumeration merging
        compares and shifts
    compare and shift by exchanging
    finding best by candidate replacement
Ordered set union
    insertion union, selection union

PROGRAM SYNTHESIS CONSTRUCTS USED

to merge the two parts. In quicksort the split does more work, dividing the set into all elements less than or equal to 4, and all elements greater than 4. The join operation is simpler, being just an append. In both cases the split is intended to produce sets of approximately equal size. Mergesort is somewhat analogous to insertion sort and quicksort is somewhat analogous to selection sort. For insertion and selection sorts, the split produces one subset with one element and another subset with all the rest. The analogy carries over to produce the taxonomy summarized in the following diagram:

	SINGLETON SPLIT	EQUAL SIZE SPLIT
WORK DONE BY JOIN	INSERTION (OR SINKING)	MERGESORT
WORK DONE BY SPLIT	SELECTION (OR BUBBLE)	QUICKSORT

A TAXONOMY OF SOME SORT PROGRAMS

In our paradigm, exchange sorts such as sinking and bubble sort are seen as minor variations on other forms of sorts.

One may state precise mathematical conditions that are sufficient for this partition, sort, and join technique to work. For the purposes of this discussion, we will assume that no elements are repeated. As in the case above, we let S be the initial set, and S_1 and S_2 be the subsets obtained by the split operations, $\text{split}_1(S)$ and $\text{split}_2(S)$. Thus the final set S' is the set join(sort($\text{split}_1(S)$), sort($\text{split}_2(S)$)). Let the predicate ORDERED mean that the order in which the sets are stored corresponds to the ordering which is to be achieved by the sorting operation. We will use "=" to mean that the sets have the same elements. Then one way to state sufficient conditions is to state that the split, sort, and join operations do not gain or lose elements inappropriately, i.e.

$$S = \text{split}_1(S) \cup \text{split}_2(S) \text{ and join } (S_1, S_2) = S_1 \cup S_2$$

Also, the split must divide the set into smaller subsets, and the sort operation must appropriately order the elements, i.e.

$$\text{ORDERED}(\text{sort}(S_1))$$

and the join must preserve that ordering, i.e.

$$\text{ORDERED}(S_1) \text{ and } \text{ORDERED}(S_2) \Rightarrow \text{ORDERED}(\text{join}(S_1, S_2)).$$

Note that we have not stated how each subset is to be sorted. Indeed, it is possible, within the framework given so far, for a different algorithm to be used to sort the subsets, and so forth. If one is repeatedly performing an operation, as in the recurrent sort operations performed on the smaller subsets, and the same mechanism is used, then a *uniform* method results. For more optimal algorithms, a different method may be selected, either in advance or dynamically for subsequent occurrences of the same operation. In fact, a very good sort is to use a uniform recursive quicksort until the subsets reach a certain size, then use an insertion sort for the subsets [17]. In rule form, our first rule is as follows:

In order to write a sort program:

(1) *choose the number of partitions into which the set shall be split*
(2) *choose a split operation*
(3) *write a sort program for each subset*
(4) *choose a join operation*

all subject to the conditions stated above.

If the same sort mechanism is chosen for each level, then we have a recursive technique, uniform at each level, except possibly for the end cases when the sets are reduced to singleton or empty sets. For the rest of this discussion, we will be concerned only with such uniform recursive sorting techniques. For such algorithms, we may use an inductive form of the correctness specification. The inductive form states that:

(1) the empty set is sorted, and
(2) the split subsets are sorted implies that the join of the sorted subsets is sorted, then
(3) the recursive paradigm works properly, i.e. the recursive sort

$$\text{sort}(X) \leftarrow \text{join}(\text{sort}(\text{split}_1(X)), \text{sort}(\text{split}_2(X)))$$

(with appropriate termination test) is correct.

Note again that these conditions allow different forms of split and join, as long as together they do the right thing. Obviously this technique may be extended to allow the set to be partitioned into more than two subsets.

4. Internal Representation of Sets

Before we begin the synthesis of insertion and selection sorts, let us briefly discuss the internal representation of ordered sets. Until now all sets have existed as abstract entities, and we have not stated how they are represented in the computer. Assume that all sets are *ordered* and all elements are *explicitly represented* rather than computed by some algorithm.
Both the ordering relationship and the members of the set must be represented.

Often the ordering is implicit and may be easily computed from the stored representation. For example the elements may be stored in a linked list and the traversal order of the list provides an ordering relation. Or the set may be stored in an array, with one member per array element, where the normal array ordering (first to last, say) provides an ordering relation. Thus the set is put in a correspondence with the integers, the i-th array element being i-th in the ordering. This correspondence can be separate, as in the case of a separate index array the same size as the set, where the i-th element holds the integer position in the ordering of the i-th element of the original array. There are many other representations such as bit maps or tree representations. In this paper we will discuss algorithms that place sets in explicit order, where the "natural" storage order will hold the ordering relation. Furthermore, we will speak as if the elements are all numbers and that the final order desired is that the numbers be in increasing order. We will also assume that no elements are repeated. These assumptions simplify the discussion, but do not significantly affect generality.

5. Singleton Split

The first case we will consider is that in which the split operation results in one set with a single member and a second set with the remaining elements of the original set. For example, one possibility is:

$$S = \langle 4\ 1\ 3\ 2 \rangle$$
$$\text{split}_1\ (S) = S_1 = \langle 4 \rangle$$
$$\text{split}_2\ (S) = S_2 = \langle 1\ 3\ 2 \rangle$$

or shown graphically:

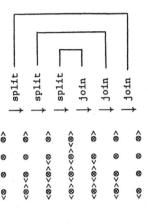

In this special case, only the second of the two subsets (S_2), must be sorted before the two are joined as the final step in the sorting operation. As mentioned above, we will consider only the case where the sorting operation for this subset is the same as the top-level sorting operation. The general paradigm may be simplified, thus

$$\text{sort}(X) \leftarrow \text{join}(\text{sort}(\text{split}_1\ (X)), \text{sort}(\text{split}_2(X)))$$

becomes

$$\text{sort}(X) \leftarrow \text{join}'\ (\text{split}_1'\ (X), \text{sort}(\text{split}_2(X))).$$

where join′ and split$_1'$ may be further simplified to deal with single elements rather than singleton sets.

Let us first look rather closely at the operation of programs within this paradigm, as illustrated in the following diagram.

```
⟨⊗ ⊗ ⊗⟩            → split
⟨⊗⟩·⟨⊗ ⊗⟩           → split
⟨⊗⟩·⟨⊗⟩·⟨⊗⟩          → split
⟨⊗⟩·⟨⊗⟩·⟨⊗⟩          → join
⟨⊗⟩·⟨⊗⟩·⟨⊗⟩          → join
⟨⊗⟩·⟨⊗ ⊗⟩           → join
⟨⊗ ⊗ ⊗⟩
```

According to the above recursive formulation the split operations are all performed first, followed by the join operations. Notice also the center line of the diagram. Here we see that all of the elements of the original set have been separated from each other. In effect, the stack used by the successive calls to the sort routine is a kind of intermediate storage or buffer. Notice also that the order in which the elements are added to the buffer by the split operation is the opposite of that in which they are removed by the join operation. We will later see that the split and join operations can be interleaved, and there is no need for the stack.

The diagram also illustrates that there is a sequence of input and output sets, beginning with the full input set and empty output set and concluding with the full output set and the empty input set. Each split operation produces a new input set with one fewer member. For example, a sequence might be

$$\{\langle 4\ 1\ 3\ 2 \rangle, \langle 1\ 3\ 2 \rangle, \langle 3\ 2 \rangle, \langle 2 \rangle, \langle\ \rangle\}$$

formed by the act of removing the first element each time. This sequence may be called the input sequence of sets, although we will sometimes refer to it as the "input set," hopefully without causing confusion. Note that the output is also formed through a sequence of sets of increasing size. For example,

$$\{\langle\ \rangle, \langle 4 \rangle, \langle 1\ 4 \rangle, \langle 1\ 3\ 4 \rangle, \langle 1\ 2\ 3\ 4 \rangle\}$$

is the output sequence of sets or just the "output set".

5.1. Insertion vs. selection

Sort programs in which the split always produces a singleton set can be classified into two types, depending on the nature of the split and join operations. These two types are generally referred to as *insertion* and *selection* sorts, and are illustrated in the following diagram storage buffer between them. The singleton divide and conquer paradigm is a type of produce-consume process in which the split is a producer and the join is a consumer. The recursive algorithm can be viewed as a series of "produce" (split) operations, followed by a series of "consume" (join) operations. The buffer is the recursion stack. If the elements can be produced one at a time and each element in the buffer can be consumed as soon as it is produced, then the buffer size can be

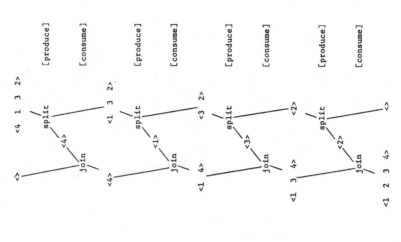

FIG. 1.

bounded to be of size one. In this case the produce and consume operations can be interleaved to form a sequence: produce, consume, produce, consume, etc. A straightforward implementation is a loop or iteration calling first the producer then the consumer. The interleaved sequence of operations for the insertion sort may be illustrated as shown in Fig. 1. (The iterative selection sort is analogous.)

Insertion sorts are characterized by split operations which take any convenient element (e.g., the first) from the input set and join operations which do an "insertion": the new element must be added to the output set in a position which is dependent on the values of the new element and the other elements of the output set. Selection sorts are characterized by simple or efficient join operations and split operations which do a "selection"; i.e. the chosen element is dependent on the values of all of the other elements.

What split operations are "efficient" for an insertion sort is, of course, dependent on the particular data structures used to represent the sets. It is efficient to minimize shifting in arrays and searching in lists. This efficiency typically occurs by selecting the first or last element. The insert (join) operation will typically require searching the output for the appropriate position for the new element (e.g., a linear scan or a binary search) followed by some kind of set modification to add the element at that position (e.g., shifting array elements by one or modifying pointers in a linked list).

For selection sorts, efficient join operations usually add the new element at the front or back of the output set. The corresponding selection (split) operations take the largest element or take the smallest element. In either case, the selection operation will usually require an enumeration of the elements of the set.

5.2. Transformation from recursive produce-consume to iterative transfer paradigm

We would like to show, for selection and insertion sorts, how the recursive partitioning paradigm presented in this paper can be reduced to the "transfer paradigm" presented in our earlier papers. The transfer paradigm consists of a selection operation which takes one element from the input and puts it into some buffer, and a construction operation which takes one element from the buffer and puts it into the output set in an appropriate position. This algorithm may be implemented as two concurrent processes, a producer (selector) and a consumer (inserter) with a

```
<4   1   3   2>  → split
<4><1   3   2>     split
<4><1><3   2>      split
<4><1><3><4>       join
<4><1><2   3>      join
<4><1   2   3>     join
<1   2   3   4>

recursive insertion sort          recursive selection sort
```

The transformation just described is that which is necessary to convert the recursive function:

$$sort(X) \leftarrow \textit{if } empty(X) \textit{ then } \langle \quad \rangle$$
$$\textit{else } join \,(split_1 \,(X), sort(split_2(X)))$$

into the loop:

$$sort(X) \leftarrow \textit{while } \neg \, empty(X) \textit{ do}$$
$$Y \leftarrow join' \,(split_1' \,(X) , Y)$$
$$X \leftarrow split_2' \,(X)$$

$$output \,(Y)$$

Note that different forms of $split_1$, $split_2$, and join may be needed in the iterative form (as indicated by $split_1'$, $split_2'$, and join').

We will use a "hypothesize and test" approach to recursive-to-iterative transformation rather than a set of program transformation rules. The transformation rule approach assumes that a set of syntactic transformations combined with some constraints is adequate to convert recursive to iterative programs. This is certainly true for simple recursion removal as is done in compilers, but in general the transformation process is quite complex, and closely interrelated with time and space efficiency issues. Furthermore, the iterative code may be considerably different from the recursive code.

We suggest that the system hypothesize the existence of components necessary for an iterative version (or a bounded buffer size version). Then the system attempts to synthesize these components but does not necessarily begin with existing recursive pieces of code. The synthesis system may answer that the components are too inefficient to pursue or too expensive to synthesize, or it may produce satisfactory code bearing little syntactic relation to the recursive code. This approach of meta-level hypothesis and test of iterative versions may also prove advantageous in the general case where the existence of an iterative version is undecidable, but one is willing to spend a certain amount of resources in an attempt to find one.

Let us exemplify this approach by suggesting a method by which a singleton-split partitioning paradigm can be reduced to an iterative transfer paradigm. This method may be formulated as constraints on the producer and consumer that are synthesized. Later in the paper we will follow the synthesis paths for these components.

First, we hypothesize the existence of a producer that can *produce the elements one at a time*. Obviously any singleton split operation produces the elements one at a time, and satisfies this condition. (A type of sort that does not effectively satisfy this condition is quicksort, since the efficiency of quicksort is derived by its splitting the elements off several at a time. See Section 8.1) Next, we hypothesize the existence of a consumer that can *consume the elements one at a time*. Any join

that takes a singleton and a set as its two arguments satisfies this condition. (A type of sort that does not effectively satisfy this condition is mergesort, which derives its efficiency by joining ever-larger ordered sets, using the ordered property to perform an efficient join. See Section 8.2) The producer and consumer so derived must not depend upon the identity or order of any elements already produced but not consumed. Such a dependence would require a buffer of size larger than one to hold these elements. The third condition is that it must be possible to *interleave the operations* of the producer and consumer which are

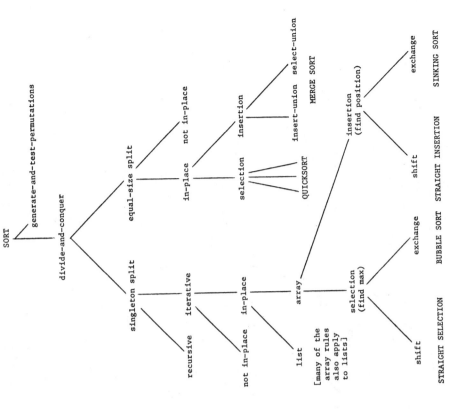

Fig. 2.

19

synthesized. That is, the elements must be consumed as soon as they are produced. For the sorting case, if the elements are consumed in the order they are produced, the induction correctness specifications must be satisfied, i.e. the output set must remain sorted after each produce-consume operation.

The insertion sort satisfies these conditions since the inserter works for any order of production of elements. For the selection sort to satisfy these conditions, it is necessary to match the producer and consumer, e.g. a largest-to-smallest selector and a right-to-left inserter would work. The derivation we will give later for the selection and insertion algorithms will synthesize producers and consumers that satisfy all of these conditions.

6. Refinement Diagram for Sorting Programs

At this point, let us introduce a summary of the refinement diagram we are following in this paper. Note that so far we have chosen the divide-and-conquer branch and the iterative branch. We are about to take the in-place branch. The reader is urged to refer back frequently to this refinement diagram to avoid getting lost (See Fig. 2).

7. In-place Sorting

7.1. Feasibility of an in-place sort

With respect to the selection of data structures to represent our sets, we have assumed only that the sets will be stored explicitly and will be sorted into ascending order. The ascending order will be exhibited by the implicit ordering of the data structure (called the storage order or stored order), e.g. first-to-last for a linked list or according to increasing index for an array. We have made no assumptions about which memory locations will be used and in particular about whether memory locations can be reused.

In synthesizing a sort algorithm it is important to find ways to conserve space, especially for very large sets. For example, if in the transfer sort we store one element of each set in one memory location, and each intermediate set in the input and output sequences consumes a new set of memory locations, then it would require $O(n^2)$ memory locations to sort n elements (we will use the $O(n^2)$ notation to mean approximately or "order" n^2). If we do not require that initial and intermediate sets be "saved," i.e. if we allow them to be "destroyed" by reusing their memory locations for the newly created sets then great space savings are possible and an n-element sort can be accomplished using only n memory locations (plus some overhead). Such sorts are referred to as *in-place* sorts. We shall now investigate in-place sorts and array representations in particular. We will consider in this section only the special case of in-place sorts where the split operation divides the set into a singleton and the rest. We will see that the classes of sorting programs which we have referred to as "selection" and "insertion" can

lead to in-place sorts that are often referred to as "bubble" and "sinking" sort programs [11].

We will now show that an in-place sort is possible. The first step is to show that the initial and intermediate sets may be destroyed, and the next is to show that only approximately n memory locations will be needed during the sorting process.

First, under what conditions is it possible to destroy the initial and intermediate sets? Let us assume that neither the initial set nor any intermediate set in the sorting process is needed after the sorting algorithm is complete. If for some reason the initial set is needed after it is sorted, then before sorting it can be saved by copying it over into a new position. For intermediate sets, after they are no longer referenced by any step of the algorithm, they can be destroyed and their memory locations can be recycled. Consider an arbitrary set in the input sequence. The only time it is referenced is during the split operation that splits the set into one element and the rest. One can verify that this is the only reference by examining all subsets in the split-sort-join paradigm and observing that each set is named only once. Similarly, each set in the output sequence is referenced only once (when the new element is added to it). Thus the initial and all intermediate sets may be destroyed after they are used.

Now consider the amount of computer memory that will be used to provide storage for a set having n elements. The memory required is that memory needed to indicate which are the elements of each set (a correspondence between each set and its elements) and to remember the ordering of the set. One unit of storage (e.g., one array element or one list cell) is adequate per element of each set represented. Next consider the total amount of space necessary at any step of the computation. In the iterative paradigm, the algorithm consists of a sequence of transfer operations, transferring one element from a set in the input sequence to a set in the output sequence. Before each transfer operation space is required only for the current input set and the current output set, i.e. space for n elements. During the transfer one space is needed to hold the element being transferred. Additionally, space will be required to store the state of enumerations of elements of the input set or of positions in the output sets, and some space could be required for bookkeeping in the set insertion or deletion operation. The exact amount of space for each of these memory requirements is dependent on the representation chosen. The new input set requires one less space and the new output set requires one more. Thus n spaces hold the old input and output set and n spaces hold the new input and output set. If no storage is reclaimed during the transfer, then $2n$ spaces plus some overhead are adequate. After the transfer the old input and output sets can be overwritten for the next transfer.

The $2n$ memory requirement can be reduced to n if the element addition and element deletion can be done "in-place," i.e. using all the old locations plus or minus one. Let us show that one element can be added to an ordered set stored in m contiguous locations to produce a new ordered set stored in $m+1$ using the where the three elements $\langle C\ D\ E \rangle$ are shifted to the right. There is an input sequence $\{\langle C\ D\ E \rangle, \langle C\ D \rangle, \langle C \rangle, \langle \rangle\}$ and an output sequence $\{\langle \rangle, \langle E \rangle, \langle D\ E \rangle, \langle C\ D\ E \rangle\}$. The "natural" divide-and-conquer recursive formulation would be to split off one element (say "C" first), transfer the rest, and then join the element back. The elements may be produced one at a time, and by producing elements right-to-left they may be consumed immediately and require no buffer storage.

We will not derive an in-place element deletion, as it is analogous to the element addition.

7.2. Array structures to represent sets

In the array representation, an ordered set is represented as a contiguous region of an array with increasing array indices giving the storage ordering on the set. There is a one-to-one, ordered correspondence between elements of the set and the contiguous array elements. This requires one array element or one memory location per set member. Additionally, the boundaries of the set must be marked. One method of boundary marking is to remember the indices of the initial and final elements. The storage of each index is of order $\log n$ bits but we will assume one computer "word" per index. We shall use the method of storing the two indices (an example of another boundary marking method is to store special elements just before and after the set), but note that if two regions are adjacent one boundary marker is sufficient where the boundary index marks the end element of the first set and one before the first element of the second set, so that it may be necessary to add or subtract one to find the first element of the second set. If it were the case that two sets overlapped (i.e., some elements belonged to each set), it would not be possible to merge boundary markers.

A set represented as a contiguous region of an array may be divided into three parts: the left boundary, the right boundary, and the interior. Each boundary may either be anchored to some array position and thus be immovable or else may move as the set in the sequence of sets grows or shrinks. We shall encounter cases where no boundary is movable, where only one boundary is movable and where both boundaries are movable. Suppose we wish to add an element to a set and reuse all storage locations belonging to the parent set. Then either the right or left boundary must expand outward by one position. If the element is inserted at a movable boundary, then that boundary marker is moved and no other elements in the set need to be moved. If the element is inserted in the interior of the set then all elements to either the right or left of the inserted element must be shifted. If only one boundary marker is movable, then all elements between the inserted element and the movable boundary marker must be shifted outward. An insertion at a fixed boundary requires the shift of all elements of the parent set. Thus, if shifting operations are to be minimized the element should be inserted as near to a movable boundary as possible. We may speak of a movable boundary as a

original m locations plus one adjacent location plus some overhead. The conditions that must be satisfied by the transfer are that no elements are lost or gained except for the added element. Also the order must be unchanged except for the new element. Suppose that the new element NEW is larger than all elements in the subset BEFORE and smaller than all elements in the subset AFTER. If there is a space to the right of AFTER (or to the left of BEFORE), we may add an element by shifting AFTER to the right (or BEFORE to the left) and placing the element in the vacant position as shown here:

```
        BEFORE              AFTER
   |------------------|-----------------|


   BEFORE      NEW          AFTER
   |--------------|----------|-----------------|
```

Note that elements are conserved in BEFORE and AFTER, and the new element is added. The ordering of BEFORE and AFTER and all orderings between the two sets are preserved. Finally, the stored order of NEW is correct. We assumed that the shift of AFTER preserved elements and orderings. Suppose that shift is not a primitive, and we must derive a suitable shift algorithm.

The shift may be stated as a divide-and-conquer where the sort does no re-ordering. It may be reformulated more simply as a singleton-split recursive total transfer, but if it is recursive, then a buffer is used to store the elements. However, it is feasible for the shift to be reduced to an iterative transfer by the following reasoning. Elements can be produced one at a time by a total scan. Elements can be stored one at a time by any total scan of positions and by writing into array locations. The ordering is preserved if both scans are the same (i.e. left-to-right). Can the elements be consumed as soon as they are produced? Use the facts that only one element can be stored in one location and it is all right to overwrite a location after the contents are no longer referenced. If a left-to-right scan is used, and we try to consume the first element as soon as it is produced, then the second element is overwritten. When the second element is referenced later it will not be available. (For a left-to-right scan, an "inchworm" style shift would be required, using a buffer to hold the element to be shifted next.) If a right-to-left scan is chosen then the elements can be consumed as soon as produced. An inductive argument suffices: the first element can be moved to the right, and after the i-th element is moved, its place is no longer needed and the $(i+1)$-st element can be moved into its location. The shift is illustrated in the example below.

```
A  B  C  D  E  ◇
A  B  C  D  ◇  E
A  B  C  ◇  D  E
A  B  ◇  C  D  E
```

growth point and the expansion direction as a growth direction. The case of deletion of an element is analogous to the addition case: all elements between the deleted element and a movable boundary must be shifted inward and the boundary reset.

7.3. Location of sets

Consider where the input and output set sequences will be located and how they will shrink and grow respectively. The analysis of the possibilities is very simple for the sinking and bubble sort (but becomes complicated for quicksort and merge sort). There are only two possibilities for the location of the two sets, input on the left and output on the right or vice-versa. One set cannot grow inside the other since sets must be represented by contiguous regions. Since the left-right distinction does not matter, assume input on the left and output on the right. Each set must have a fixed boundary on the outside and each must share a common movable boundary in the interior. In other words the output sequence will start at the right hand edge and grow toward the left, whereas the input sequence will begin by filling the entire space and shrink toward the left. As each element is transferred the common boundary marker (array index) will move one position to the left. The situation may be illustrated as follows:

```
input    output
⊗ ⊗ ⊗ ⊗ ⊗ ⊗
        ↑
        boundary moves left with each transfer
```

Without further decisions about the nature of the algorithm, we cannot say whether elements will be inserted or deleted at a fixed boundary, interior point, or the movable boundary. However note that insertions or deletions cause no shifting of elements if done at the movable boundary, some shifting if done at the interior of a set, and the most shifting if done at the outside, fixed boundaries. Accordingly we will strive to minimize shifts by either (a) adding elements at the shared boundary, or else (b) deleting elements at the shared boundary, when possible. We will see that case (a) is appropriate to a selection sort and case (b) to an insertion sort.

We have now laid the ground work for the in-place insertion sort and the in-place selection sort. In our derivation so far, we have created an in-place transfer sort, where array elements will be shifted appropriately as the elements are transferred from the input set sequence to the output set sequence. It appears that within this set of constraints, there are more than just the selection and insertion possibilities remaining. For example, the largest m elements might be selected out and put in their final position and an insertion sort performed on the next $n-m$ elements. However we have ruled out stranger possibilities such as selecting the first element, finding the final place (by comparing it against all others) inserting it there, finding the final place of the displaced element, etc. This algorithm would allow non-contiguous subset representations.

What constraints lead to a selection or insertion sort? One set of constraints that is adequate is either to always remove elements from the movable boundary or to always place elements at the movable boundary. This constraint says to allow shifting operations in only the producer or consumer but not both. It also is a uniform algorithm in that it is not a selection for several steps, then an insertion for the rest. Uniformity thus simplifies the resulting algorithm. Another form of constraint is to specify that either

(a) the producer re-orders the elements (finds the desired permutation) and the consumer merely stores the elements in that order, or

(b) the producer merely enumerates the elements and the consumer re-orders or finds the permutation. (One would then set up producer and consumer to minimize shifting.)

This form of constraint might arise from some simplicity criterion on the algorithm, i.e. either the producer or the consumer is very simple. The minimal shifting considerations are not applicable to sorting with list structures, but the simplicity consideration is applicable.

7.4. In-place insertion sort

Assume that an insertion sort will be synthesized. The producer must generate every element in the input set and transfer each to the output. We may satisfy the constraint of minimizing shifting in the input by removing elements from the boundary position, thus moving the boundary right to left across the input. This enumeration is total since each element is visited. This completes the producer.

The consumer or inserter must, according to the inductive hypothesis, keep the output set sorted at each step. Accordingly, the correct position of each new element relative to the other elements in the output must be found. After finding this position, elements to the left of this position are shifted left and the element is inserted. Each set in the output sequence is thus sorted and we have an in-place insertion sort.

Now consider the details of finding the correct position and shifting the elements to make room. The finding of the correct position means that the element must be larger than all to its left and smaller than all to its right. According to this definition each position is enumerated, and for each position the element is tested against all others. But since the output set is sorted, we know by transitivity that the element must be compared only against its two candidate neighbors. Then to enumerate all positions a linear scan is adequate and the simplest search.

Next a scan direction for the position finding must be selected. We know that a shift is required to make room for the inserted element and that a left-to-right enumeration will be used for the shift. A heuristic rule for selecting an enumeration direction is to consider the same direction as other scans of the same set. In this case, choosing the same direction as the shifting scan will lead to combining the two scans. Assume we choose a left-o-right scan for the position finding. The test against its two neighbors can be simplified to a test against only the element to the right since the new element must be larger then the element to the left or the scan would have ended.

The shifting operation entails shifting left by one all elements to the left of the inserted element. Recall that the shifting is itself a transfer operation that enumerates each element left-to-right and moves it left by one. Observe that exactly the same set must be enumerated, in exactly the same order if the transfer is iterative, for both the position finding operation and the insertion operation. This observation leads to a combining of the two operations and having only one enumeration; as each element in the output set is produced, it is compared against the inserted element and shifted left if it is smaller. When one is larger the element is inserted into the vacant position. The resulting algorithm is called an insertion sort.

```
5 3 1 6 2 4 7 8

        several steps later

5 3 1 6 2 4 7 8   hold 6 in temporary storage, compare to 2
6      output
5 3 1 2   4 7 8   shift 2, compare 6 to 4
6      output
5 3 1 2 4   7 8   shift 4, compare 6 to 7, insert 6
       output
5 3 1 2 4 6 7 8
.      output
.
.           finally
1 2 3 4 5 6 7 8
```

SERIES OF SHIFTS AND INSERTS

We observe that a binary chop algorithm for finding the correct position is possible since the output set is ordered. A binary chop would lead to $O(n \log n)$ comparisons but still require the same number of shifts, and the algorithm would be more complex.

One final modification brings us to the "sinking" sort: instead of holding the boundary element in any special temporary location, use the newly vacated position to hold it. Thus, at each step, the program performs a comparison to see if the correct position has been found, and if not interchanges the two elements. (This last modification might not necessarily result in a speed-up, but it clarifies

the way in which the insertion class of sorting programs includes the "sinking" sort as a special case.)

```
5 3 1 6 2 8 7 4

        several steps later

5 3 1 6 2 4 7 8   6 is to be inserted, compare to 2, interchange
       output
5 3 1 2 6 4 7 8   compare 6 to 4, interchange
       output
5 3 1 2 4 6 7 8   compare 6 to 7, completes insertion of 6
       output
5 3 1 2 4 6 7 8
.      output
.
.           finally
1 2 3 4 5 6 7 8
```

SINKING—SERIES OF INTERCHANGES

7.5. Rules for an in-place insertion sort

To illustrate how some of this can be expressed in a more rule-like form, we give here a summary for synthesizing the consumer (element inserter) of the in-place insertion sort. Similar rules have been given elsewhere [1, 9]. Low-level enumeration rules are given in the appendix, along with the internal representation we currently use. Some of the rules presented here are still rather sketchy. A similar set has recently been tested in a system that synthesized an in-place insertion sort, and, of course, all of the programming lore discussed in this paper has not yet been reduced completely to rules.

The first rule breaks the process of adding an element into two subparts (that will later be merged back together):

In order to add an element to an ordered sequential collection, find an appropriate position for the element and insert the element at that position.

As noted earlier, the process of finding an appropriate position involves enumerating potential positions:

In order to find an appropriate position for an element in an ordered sequential collection, enumerate all positions in the collection, testing each for appropriateness; if an appropriate position is found, halt the enumeration.

The enumeration process involves several design decisions, as indicated in the following four rules.

In order to enumerate all positions in a sequential collection, select an enumeration order and a state-saving scheme, then build a generator based on the enumeration order and the state-saving scheme.

One enumeration order for a sequential collection is the natural stored order.

If the enumeration order for a sequential collection is the stored order, the state may be saved by a position marker.

If a sequential collection is represented as a subregion of an array, a position marker may be represented by an index into the array.

(For more detail on the enumeration rules, see the appendix.)

The following rule describes the characteristics of an appropriate position in an ordered sequential collection:

If the ordering must be preserved, a position in an ordered sequential collection is appropriate for a new element if all elements preceding the position are less than (or equal to) the new element and all elements following the position are greater than (or equal to) the new element.

When such a test must be implemented, it can often be simplified somewhat. The best technique to use for such simplifications is an open question, but one possibility is to use specific (but rather complex) rules, such as the following:

If an enumeration of the positions in an ordered sequential collection is halted when an appropriate position for a new element is found and the enumeration order is the stored order, then all elements preceding a position being tested are less than the new element.

Applying this rule allows dropping the test against preceding elements, since it is guaranteed to return *True*. A different way of simplifying such tests involves somewhat more complex deductions, but is based on simpler facts of wider applicability, such as the following:

All elements of a set are greater than a given element if the set is empty or if the minimum element is less than the given element.

The minimum element in any subregion of an ordered sequential collection is the "front" element.

Using the above facts, the test can be simplified into a disjunction of a *null* test and a test on the first element after the position. Probably, both types of rules will be required.

The second part of the consumer involves shifting some of the elements in the array:

In order to insert an element at a position in a subregion of an array, shift all of the elements before the position toward the front by one and deposit the new element into the array at the given position.

(This is actually a slight simplification, since it does not take into account which boundary is movable, but rather assumes that the "front," or left, boundary is the movable one.)

As discussed above, shifting involves enumerating the positions to be shifted:

In order to shift all elements before a given position toward the front, enumerate the positions in the natural stored order, moving the element stored in each position toward the front by one location.

Note that this enumeration is constrained with respect to its enumeration order, while the enumeration for the position-finding was unconstrained. From this point, however, the same enumeration rules can be applied.

Finally, the following meta-rule suggests a simplification:

If two enumerations over the same locations have the same enumeration order, and they do not interfere with each other, they may be combined into a single enumeration.

Of course, defining "interfere" can be very difficult, but special case rules may be adequate for most purposes. In this case, a test will not affect a subsequent shift operation.

7.6. In-place selection sort

Assume that a selection sort will be synthesized. To minimize shifting operations, elements must be inserted into the output set at the movable boundary, so that they fill up the output set linearly, right to left. Also, the inductive hypothesis requires that the output set be sorted at each step as it is built up. Together, these force the elements to be produced, largest element first, then the rest in descending order. Thus the selection process is a series of operations, each having three steps: find the largest element, delete it from the input, then insert it into the output at the boundary between the sets.

First we will synthesize an algorithm to find the largest element. Our derivation will be very simple compared to an implemented version. The simplest "find" algorithm for an enumerable set is to generate each element and then test to see whether it is the largest element. This requires $O(m^2)$ comparisons per selection, where m is the number of elements in the current set of the input sequence, since each element must be compared against all others.

It is possible to speed up this algorithm to m comparisons. In the basic form of generate and test, each element is compared against all others and if it is not larger, the next element is attempted as a candidate. By the simple rule of stopping an enumeration once the answer is found, we need not compare the element with any more once a larger element is found. This is still an order $O(m^2)$ algorithm, but a little better. The refinement to $O(m)$ follows.

Assume that a fixed, left-to-right linear scan is chosen as the generation order of candidates. This is the obvious choice since it is the least complex total enumeration. Next, assume that the same fixed left-to-right enumeration order is chosen for enumerating the elements to which the candidate is compared. Any other fixed order would do as long as both are the same. Perhaps the strongest a priori reason for attempting to make both enumeration orders the same is the resulting uniformity, which sometimes results in a simpler algorithm. The heuristic of choosing the same enumeration order will also lead to combining two loops.

Next consider the step at which the candidate "a" is compared to an element, say "c", and found to be smaller. By the rule of stopping an enumeration as soon as possible, no other elements are compared to "a". According to our algorithm we select as next candidate the element "b" just to the right of "a".

$$\langle \ldots a\ b \ldots c \rangle$$

Here we invoke the rule of starting an enumeration as late as possible. By transitivity since "c" is larger than "a" and "a" is larger than "b", then "c" is larger than "b". Hence "b" need not be considered. This argument applies to all elements between "a" and "c", so that none need to be considered as candidates. However "c" is not known to be smaller than any element to its right, so "c" becomes the next candidate. This completes the derivation of an algorithm for finding the largest element in m steps. Note that we have effectively derived a special case of the more general rule "to find the extremum, perform one total enumeration and replace the candidate element each time a better element is found." The more general rule could have been used in this case, but we anticipate that the ability to derive it should also prove useful in other program synthesis situations.

The next operation is that of deleting the largest element from the input set. One deletion method is to remove the largest element and shift left all elements to its right. As before in the insertion sort, the shifting and the comparison operations are both linear, left-to-right. The only difference is that the element being rippled along changes when a new candidate for the largest element is found. This series of exchanges reorders the input set, but there is no constraint that the input order not be changed. Thus, as in the insertion sort, the shifting can be interleaved with the search for the largest element, to form a series of interchanges to both find the largest element and delete it by moving it to the right. The final position of the largest element is at the left side of the output set, thus also completing the insertion into the output set. This algorithm is called bubble sort or exchange selection. In this case where it is permissible to reorder the input set, another simple deletion and insertion method can be used. The largest element is just interchanged with the boundary element of the input set. This algorithm is called straight selection sort. We note that the bubble sort does more work than just selecting the largest element in each scan since more than one element may be moved toward its destination. The selection sort can be made with $O(n \log n)$ comparisons by using a tree-selection of the largest element as in heapsort.

8. Equal-size Split

And now we return to the partitioning sorts where the sets are divided into subsets that may each have more than one element. Suppose that we choose to divide the initial set into two subsets. The methods discussed for two subsets are probably extendable to several subsets. The next question is, "By what criterion shall we split the set into two parts?" We shall consider criteria which divide the set into two approximately equal sets. This often leads to faster algorithms, in particular the equal size split sometimes speeds up an algorithm from $O(n^2)$ to $O(n \log n)$ comparisons. The depth of recursion is reduced from n to $\log n$ and if the combined split and join operations are held to $O(n)$ comparisons, then this speedup is achieved. One way is to split the set into a left-part and right-part depending upon the position, but not the value, of the elements. Or it can be split into all elements larger than some size and all smaller than some size, which depends upon the value of the elements rather than the position. This choice is the major factor in determining what type of sort routine is produced.

If the set is divided into two sets each respectively having all elements larger than and smaller than a given size, the result is a class including quicksort. This class may be thought of as a general form of selection sort where the set having all elements larger (say) than a given size is being selected, i.e. a set rather than an element is being selected. Most of the burden falls on the split operation, to select out these sets. The join operation is a simple append (things may be viewed slightly differently for conventional in-place quicksorts).

If the set is divided arbitrarily, into two parts (say a left and right part for convenience) the split operation is simple, and the work of ordering the elements is done in the join operation. This method leads to mergesort and may be thought of as a general form of insertion sort (although, to complicate matters, a subpart of one form of the merge sort can be viewed as a selection sort).

8.1. Quicksort

Let us assume that we shall divide the set into all elements larger than some number and all less than or equal to that number. Let these two subsets be called LARGE and SMALL. Next, we must decide on the size of the dividing number. Our preferred choice is a number that divides the set so that LARGE and SMALL are of approximately equal size. If such a size is known then we may use it. If not, then we must make some estimate of this median. A random number might be a first guess. Better, we can select randomly but limited to any number within the range of the set being sorted (although not necessarily in the set, since it may fall between two numbers in the set). This at least increases the likelihood of it dividing the set equally. An easy way to find a number within the range spanned by the set is to choose an element of the set. Let us make this choice, but note that more effort could produce a better estimation of the mid-point by sampling some elements of the set. We will call the chosen element DIVIDER. Which element in the set shall be the DIVIDER? If there is no reason to believe the set is ordered in any way then pick the most convenient element. (If the set is perhaps somewhat ordered, then we might select from the middle of the set.) In many data structures, a convenient element to choose is the first or last element. Let us choose the first element, and let the rest of the set be called REST.

How shall this element be used to divide the set? The simplest method is to compare it against each of the other elements in the set. Those that are larger go into LARGE and those that are less than or equal go into SMALL. The splitting process requires a total enumeration over the finite set REST, or in other words a total generate and process algorithm where the process is the addition of the element to one of two subsets. Note that, as in the bubble and sinking sorts, the sets SMALL, LARGE, and REST are really sequences of sets, each growing or shrinking one element at a time. At this level of abstraction, we have completed the split operation. After completing the entire sort at this level, we shall continue in more detail. Most of the detail is concerned with efficiency and particular data structures.

Recall that the three top-level steps were to split, sort the subsets, and then join. Assume that the sorting of the subsets will be done recursively by the same algorithm. Now for the join. Since both subsets are sorted, and all the elements in LARGE are larger than those in SMALL, we may join the subsets with an append. So the join is quite simple. (In fact, if an in-place sort is used, then the two sets are already in their correct relative positions and no explicit join operation is required.) This completes the high-level description, as illustrated below:

```
        (7 3 1 6 2 8 5 4)
           /  split  \
     (3 1 2 4)     (7 6 8 5)
        sort          sort
         ↓             ↓
     (1 2 3 4)     (5 6 7 8)
           \   join   /
        (1 2 3 4 5 6 7 8)
```

8.1.1. *Details of the split operation*

This is the part of quicksort which is most interesting. We shall show a sequence of methods of doing the dividing, each of which typically results in greater efficiency. Each element of REST must be compared to DIVIDER, and put into its proper subset. What order of enumeration shall be used? Left-to-right or right-to-left linear scans are the easiest for most data structures.

As before we shall attempt to reuse space to produce an in-place sort. When the algorithm was described abstractly, no mention was made of whether the two sets LARGE and SMALL fit into the original space or were placed in new spaces. If every set in the sequences LARGE and SMALL is put into a new space, then the average space requirement is about $2n \log n$. But we will be able to achieve an in-place sort requiring roughly n locations. The argument that this is possible is the same as that given for singleton split and insertion sets. Examination of the algorithm shows that each set in the SMALL, LARGE, and REST sequences need be remembered only until the next set is produced. Thus after an element is produced from REST it can be placed in SMALL or LARGE and deleted from REST. The total number of spaces needed at any time is just n, plus some book-keeping overhead.

As before we shall assume that the sets will be placed in contiguous regions of arrays. Since each subset will be in a contiguous region of an array, each region can be marked by a left and right boundary rather than by marking each element. Also, two boundaries are adequate to mark the remainder of the original set. Where two regions touch, the two boundaries merge into one boundary and less marking space will be required. Some additional space will be needed to hold the element being transferred and to save the state of enumeration of elements of REST.

Now consider the process of enumerating the set and placing each element into its subset. There are several things needed; an enumeration order, e.g. left-to-right, or right-to-left, or something more complex, and a place for each subset. We will need to choose an initial position for each set, and growth directions for each boundary of each set. There are six possible relative positions for the three sets, LARGE, SMALL, and REST. Since an array can be accessed equally well from either direction, a left-right reversal of position is effectively the same structure. So, by symmetry, we need only consider 3 possibilities. If we also take advantage of the symmetry of SMALL and LARGE, two possibilities are left:

Case 1: SMALL LARGE REST
Case 2: SMALL REST LARGE

with all other cases essentially similar.

Recall that each element will be compared with the DIVIDER element and assigned to its subset. No delay is required to make the decision and place the element since the choice of a location to insert it is not dependent upon any element not yet transferred. Thus the produced element may be consumed as soon as it is produced. As soon as the produced element is removed, then a vacant space exists and there are enough places so that there is room, but the problem is to have that room occur at the right place to yield an efficient algorithm. There are no constraints on the order of elements in LARGE and SMALL so the element may be inserted any place. But in order to minimize shifting operations it should be inserted at a movable boundary. Also, insertion at a boundary minimizes search for an insertion position. But in order to minimize shifts by inserting at the boundary position there must be space made available at the boundary. What does it cost to make space available at the boundaries for each of the two cases?

Case 1: SMALL LARGE REST

There is no constraint on the enumeration order from REST, but if left-to-right is chosen then elements that need to be inserted into LARGE can be added at the LARGE–REST boundary and no shifting is required. Now consider, however, insertion of elements into SMALL. Any interior position or the left boundary position of SMALL necessitates shifts within SMALL and requires one new space on its right, so the best insertion position is at its right boundary. Since no element is given up from that boundary position, LARGE must be shifted right by one element. The obvious way is to shift all elements right by one, but this is expensive. By noting that there is no ordering constraint on LARGE, it can be shifted right by moving only its leftmost element to its rightmost boundary. This algorithm is illustrated below.

```
          7 3 1 6 2 8 5 4
          ↑↑
          7 3 1 6 2 8 5 4
          ↑↑↑
          3 7 1 6 2 8 5 4
          ↑ ↑
          3 1 7 6 2 8 5 4
          ↑ ↑
          3 1 7 6 2 8 5 4
          ↑ ↑
          3 1 2 6 7 8 5 4
              ↑ ↑
          3 1 2 6 7 8 5 4
              ↑ ↑
          3 1 2 6 7 8 5 4
                ↑ ↑
          3 1 2 4 7 8 5 6
                ↑ ↑

          SMALL LARGE REST
```

This is not a bad algorithm, but case 2 yields an interesting and possibly more efficient algorithm.

Case 2: SMALL REST LARGE

Both LARGE and SMALL share a boundary with REST. Any complete enumeration of the elements in REST will work. Merely take each element from rest and place it at the growth boundary of LARGE or SMALL respectively. Place the removed boundary element of REST into the vacated position. This strategy will in general reorder the set REST, which is allowable. In the cases where a boundary element in REST is next to its proper place in LARGE or SMALL no interchange takes place and only the boundary marker is moved.

Let us show one example

```
        SMALL   REST        LARGE
                7 3 1 6 2 8 5 4

Step 1          ↑                      exchange

                4 3 1 6 2 8 5 7
Step 2            ↑

                4 3 1 6 2 8 5 7
Step 3              ↑

                4 3 1 6 2 8 5 7
Step 4                ↑

                4 3 1 6 2 8 5 7
Step 5                  ↑              exchange

                4 2 1 6 3 8 5 7
Step 6                    ↑            exchange

                4 2 3 6 1 8 5 7
Step 7                      ↑          exchange

                4 2 3 1 6 8 5 7
                          ↑

                    SMALL  LARGE
```

The moving boundaries are marked by arrows. Our enumeration strategy was to enumerate from right to left, with SMALL to the left and LARGE to the right. The element "4" was the divider. At each step the element being compared to 4 is just to the left of the rightmost arrow. Note that after an interchange, the same *position* in REST had to be re-examined since it held a new element. When all of REST is enumerated, we are done. One way to check is to note that both SMALL and LARGE boundaries meet.

Next let us consider a change in the quicksort algorithm. Note that an element could sometimes be moved to a temporary location, then later examined and moved again. To see this, notice that in step 5 of the example, 2 and 3 were interchanged, although the element 3 was really in a suitable position. We could have just changed the boundary of small to include it, rather than moving it twice. Can this unnecessary move be avoided in general? So far we see no necessity for it in terms of the amount of space available to consume a produced element. A solution is to consider an alternative enumeration order for the set REST that allows the proper interchange spaces to become available as needed. The proper spaces occur at *both* boundaries of REST. So a good strategy is to enumerate both left-to-right.

and right-to-left in some reasonable manner. Suppose we move right-to-left. Sometimes just the boundary will change (when the element belongs to LARGE) and sometimes an element will have to be moved (when the element belongs to SMALL). When an element is to be moved, begin an enumeration from left-to-right, but don't make the exchange yet. Moving from left to right, again, sometimes an element will stay, as it is placed in SMALL by moving the boundary. But sometimes we will encounter an element that needs to be moved into LARGE. Then when both need to be moved, make an interchange and begin again. Whether we begin left-to-right or vice-versa doesn't matter as long as we make no interchanges until both elements need to be interchanged. We illustrate by example.

```
              REST
SMALL←  7 3 1 6 2 8 5 4        begin
        ↑
        →LARGE
        7 3 1 6 2 8 5 4        scan right to left, note 4 should be moved
        4 3 1 6 2 8 5 7        scan left to right, note 7 should be moved
        4 3 1 6 2 8 5 7        interchange 4 and 7
        4 3 1 6 2 8 5 7        scan right to left
        4 3 1 6 2 8 5 7        scan right to left
        4 3 1 6 2 8 5 7        scan right to left, note 2 should be moved
        4 3 1 6 2 8 5 7        scan left to right
        4 3 1 6 2 8 5 7        scan left to right
        4 3 1 6 2 8 5 7        scan left to right, note 6 should be moved
        4 3 1 2 6 8 5 7        interchange 2 and 6
```

So only two interchanges and no shifts were necessary with the new scanning strategy.

This synthesis path thus results in the standard quicksort algorithm (e.g., as given by Knuth [11]).

8.2. Mergesort

Recall that the work could be done in the split or in the join. In this section we shall assume that the work is done in the *join* and a simple split operation will be used. It does not matter which elements go into which of the two subsets. So the splitting method should be the easiest possible. If an array is used as the data structure, then a division into a right and left half requires storage space for only one boundary marker, an index. To find the value of this index only a division is required. If linked lists are used, the division into two sets requires one scan and possibly another scan to find the length.

We will assume that an array is divided into right and left halves. Each of these subsets, say S_1 and S_2, is then sorted. Now, how are the two to be joined? A simple append will not work since elements in either one may be larger than elements in the other one. Thus some merging technique will be required as illustrated below:

```
         (7 3 1 6 2 8 5 4)
                split
      (7 3 1 6)     (2 8 5 4)
        sort          sort
        ↓              ↓
      (1 3 6 7)     (2 4 5 8)
               merge-join
           (1 2 3 4 5 6 7 8)
```

In the quicksort case the union of the two sorted subsets reduced to a simple concatenation operation. For mergesort, we must find another technique. A form of the divide-and-conquer paradigm may be employed. Assume the two sorted subsets are S_1 and S_2. We wish to join them into S_3 by an ordered set union operation, i.e. $S_3 = S_1 \cup S_2$. By the divide-and-conquer paradigm, we may split $S_1 \cup S_2$ into two parts, form the union of the remainder, and then join them. Obviously a split into S_1 and S_2 leaves us with the same problem and we are no closer to a solution. So consider a singleton split of one element and the rest, say into $\{a\}$ and $(S_1-\{a\}) \cup S_2$. After forming the union of $S_1-\{a\}$ and S_2, $\{a\}$ is joined. Note that $\{a\}$ can be selected as the extremum, in which case the split is doing the work or else the element $\{a\}$ is chosen for the simplicity of the split and the join does the work.

One case appears to be a selection-style ordered union and one appears to be an insertion style ordered union. Also, both may be converted to an iterative transfer version, rather than a recursive version. We shall not discuss that conversion but we will trace the synthesis for both the insertion and the selection case, assuming an iterative transfer.

8.2.1. Insertion paradigm for merge

Consider the insertion process. Each element from $S_1 \cup S_2$ must be inserted into S_3. The order of selection of elements from S_1 and S_2 is not constrained. By observing that S_2 is sorted, just let $S_2 = S_3$ effectively transferring all elements from S_2 into S_3 at no cost. Then successive elements of S_1 must be inserted into S_2. The process of finding an efficient join or merge operation may be seen as a sequence of speed-ups of the various enumerations during the production of an element from S_1 and the generation of its correct position in S_2. As in our insertion sorts discussed earlier, use can be made of the knowledge that the element-consuming set, S_2, remains sorted during the insertion process. In addition we can use the information that the element-producing set is sorted to find still further speed-ups.

First consider the insertion of an element into S_2. Since S_2 is sorted, in general not every position need be examined. In fact, for a linear scan of positions, as soon as the first position is encountered in which the element to be inserted is larger than the element to its left and smaller than the element to its right, then no further searching is necessary, since that position is correct and the element may be inserted there. The correctness of this position follows from the transitivity of the sorted set. The test for correctness may also be slightly optimized, as discussed earlier.

Next consider the enumeration order of elements from S_1. If they are generated linearly, from, say left-to-right, then each successive element is larger than the last. This means that in scanning S_2, the scan need not begin to the left of the recently inserted element, since by transitivity it must be larger than all of those. So the scan need only begin at the position to the right of the inserted element. This method requires a state-saving scheme for the consuming set S_2 to remember the previous insertion position. This process turns out to be linear in the number of comparisons of elements. By observing that the depth of recursion is $\log n$, the total number of comparisons is of order $n \log n$.

The merge sort can be done in-place. The determination of the feasibility of an in-place sort is the same as shown for the other sorts discussed earlier. However, shifting will be required in S_2 since the elements are inserted into the interior of S_2. Suppose the sets are placed so that S_1 is on the left and S_2 is on the right. Then all elements in S_2 to the left of the inserted element must be shifted since S_2 cannot be reordered. The rule that says to minimize shifting by taking elements from the common boundary may be invoked to suggest a right-to-left descending order of elements in S_1. Since elements are taken from the boundary, no shifts are required. However, there may be as many as $n/2$ shifts of $n/2$ elements required for S_2. The insertion paradigm fits well with list representations of sets.

8.2.2. Selection paradigm for merge

We now present an alternate derivation path, a *selection* paradigm. In the selection paradigm the enumeration order is forced to select elements from both S_1 and S_2 according to the final ordering. Thus, first the largest is selected, then the next largest, and so on. These are then inserted in a linear order one after the other.

The two sorted subsets, S_1 and S_2, are the input to the selection process and the output, say S_3, will be the sorted set. If no a priori knowledge about the ordering relation on S_1 and S_2 is used, then all elements are enumerated to see which is the largest. As discussed earlier an inefficient way is to compare each against all others. A reasonably simple speed up is to carry a best-so-far candidate along, and replace it with any larger element. By transitivity, this finds the largest element in a number of comparisons equal to the size of the input, say n. Thus, a scan of the entire set produces one element. To produce all elements of S_3 requires about $n^2/2$ comparisons.

The fact that we know both S_1 and S_2 are sorted leads to one more speedup. The largest element in S_1 is its last element. The largest element in S_2 is its last element. The largest element in $S_1 \cup S_2$ must be either the largest in S_1 or the largest in S_2. If this is not clear, suppose that "e", the last element of S_1, is larger than the last element of S_2. We know that "e" is larger than all of S_1. Now, by transitivity, since it is larger than the last element of S_2, it is larger than all elements of S_2. So to find the largest element, only the two last elements need be compared. Now produce that element, remove it from its parent set, say S_1, and put it in the output set S_3. Again the same situation holds; the largest element is now either the new last element of S_1 or the last element of S_2. Compare these two elements to produce the second element and move it to the output set. We see that this results in one comparison per output element, so that the number of comparisons is reduced to $O(n)$, from $O(n^2)$. The speedup resulted from the use of the knowledge that the input sets were already sorted.

Note that two enumerations are being carried out simultaneously on S_1 and S_2, and the sequencing between the two enumerations depends on the data. We used removal of each element as the state-saving scheme, but other schemes such as marking elements or moving list pointers would also be adequate. The selection paradigm makes clear that if a second set of n locations is available, say S_3, then a sort with no shifting is possible since S_3 is created in order.

9. Conclusions

In this paper we have attempted to explicate the programming knowledge for space reutilization, ordered set enumeration, and the divide-and-conquer paradigm. With this knowledge converted into rule form one could synthesize efficient sort programs, ordered set unions and other programs.

The principal derivation path—divide-and-conquer, then singleton or equal size split, then recursive-to-iterative transfer, then in-place, then shifting or exchange—proved to be satisfactory. In particular we found this approach simpler than considering exchange sorts as a separate class. The paradigm could probably be reasonably extended to include heapsort, radix sort and others, with the introduction of trees and other primitives. However, while we felt the paradigm was adequate, we explored few other candidates except for transfer and exchange paradigms.

Much of the knowledge expressed here and in our previous papers has been implemented as rules and has been tested in programs that successfully synthesized many sorting and other programs. However, we have not yet implemented many of the higher-level rules and assume that further embellishments will be required.

An interesting and more global research question is that of the utility of this particular approach to program synthesis. At one extreme of the synthesis spectrum is the macro expansion of templates, or the instantiation of parameters into existing pieces of code. Those techniques are rigid but computationally cheap and are adequate for many purposes such as compiler code generators for medium-level languages. At the other extreme are more computationally expensive theorem proving techniques that search larger spaces of possible programs. Such techniques are more likely to create "new" algorithms, or at least unanticipated ones, but at the possibly prohibitive cost of considering many unusable programs. Our approach is more of a middle ground but as suits a particular application it may be combined with other techniques.

ACKNOWLEDGMENTS

We would like to acknowledge helpful discussions and suggestions from Elaine Kant, Bill Laaser, Juan Ludlow, Maarten van Emden, John Darlington, Bob Floyd, Don Knuth, Juan Bulnes, and Leo Guibas.

10. Appendix

In this appendix we illustrate how a few of the rules may be stated in more detail. In addition we will show how some of the rules may be written in the formalism used by PECOS, PSI's Coding Expert. Further details of the representation scheme may be found elsewhere [1].

A typical and widely-used rule is one which enumerates all the elements in an explicitly-stored set and performs some operation upon each element. An English level description of the rule is:

In order to write an enumerator for an explicitly stored set,
(1) *determine the order for generating the elements,*
(2) *select an appropriate scheme for saving the state of the enumeration between the production of the elements,*
(3) *based upon the enumeration order and the state-saving scheme, write the body, initializer, incrementer and termination test.*

This rule might be invoked by a higher level rule with certain constraints such as (a) "the enumeration is to be total," i.e. all elements must be processed or (b) a data structure may already have been selected or (c) an enumeration order may already have been imposed. Suppose that no enumeration order has been specified,

but the enumeration is constrained to be total and the set is stored in an array. Then one of the rules for enumeration orders must be chosen. We will assume that the rule for the natural order is selected:

An enumeration order for an enumeration of positions in a sequential collection is the stored order.

This rule is represented as follows:

```
(PROP←  ENUMERATION-ORDER
        (ENUMERATE-POSITIONS)
        (QUOTE STORED) )
```

Programs are represented using a fairly simple semantic network scheme. In the rule above, (ENUMERATE-POSITIONS) stands for the node representing the enumeration operation. The rule states that the ENUMERATION-ORDER attribute of the operation is to be set to STORED.

After the enumeration order has been chosen, a state-saving scheme must be selected. This involves the invocation of three rules. The first may be stated as:

The enumeration state of an enumeration whose enumeration order is the stored order may be represented as a position in the collection.

This rule is represented as follows:

```
(REF←   (ENUMERATION-STATE
          (#P ENUMERATION
            (#P ENUMERATION-ORDER (?#= STORED)))
          (#P COLLECTION (←← X)))
        (#NEW POSITION-IN-COLLECTION
          (←#P COLLECTION X)))
```

which specifies that: "an ENUMERATION-STATE node for an ENUMERA-TION where ENUMERATION-ORDER attribute is STORED may be represented as (refined into) a POSITION-IN-COLLECTION of the collection being enumerated (here denoted as X)".

The second rule gives a way to represent a position:

If a collection is represented as an array, a position in that collection may be represented as an index in that array.

This rule is represented similarly to the previous one, but note the #REF construct that tests whether the COLLECTION has been refined into an ARRAY:

```
(REF←   (POSITION-IN-COLLECTION
          (#P COLLECTION (←← X)
            (#REF ARRAY)))
        (#NEW ITEM-INDEX
          (←#P ARRAY X)))
```

Note also that this rule is applicable whenever one is concerned with portions in collections represented as arrays, not just when the collection is being enumerated.

The final rule is based on the assumption that the output code is to be in the LISP language:

An index in an array may be represented as a LISP integer.

More formally,

```
(REF←   (ITEM-INDEX)
        (#NEW LISP-INTEGER))
```

Other state-saving schemes can be pointers, bit strings, property list marks, hash table entries, list removal, element overwriting, etc. The rules must indicate which are suitable for non-destructive enumerations and which are for destructive enumerations, which are adequate for non-linear enumeration orders and which are not.

After choosing the state saving scheme, the body, initializer, incrementer and termination test must be written. For example, the termination test is written by invoking the following series of rules (all represented similarly to the rules given above):

A test of enumeration termination may be refined into a test on whether the state-saving scheme is in its final state.

If an enumeration is total, a test of whether a state-saving scheme is in its final state may be refined into a test of whether the state indicates that all elements have been enumerated.

Notice how this rule checks to see whether the range of the enumeration is constrained, as we assumed earlier. Were there no such constraint, then other rules to determine an appropriate range would have to be considered.

If the enumeration order is the stored order and the state is saved as a position in the collection, a test of whether the state indicates that all elements have been enumerated may be refined into a test of whether the position indicates the position after the last item in the collection.

If the collection is represented as an array and the position is represented as an index into the array, then a test of whether the position indicates the position after the last item may be refined into a test of whether the index is the index after the last item.

A test of whether an index is the index after the last item after the last item may be refined into a test of whether the index is greater than the upper bound of the array.

The final rule in the sequence produces a call to a LISP function:

A test of whether a LISP integer is greater than another LISP integer may be refined into a call to the LISP function IGREATERP.

Notice that it is still necessary to write the code which will retrieve the upper bound of the array. In most cases this would result in the retrieval of the value of a bound variable, so the final LISP expression would be: "(IGREATERP STATE UPPERBOUND)," where STATE is the variable which holds the state and UPPERBOUND is the variable which holds the upper bound of the array.

Despite the detail, the above derivation is itself a slight over-simplification, in that an array is simply a correspondence between integers and values, a fact which would be included in a complete derivation. Notice also, that for a list enumeration with arbitrary ordering, and using deletion as a state saving scheme, a very different piece of code would be produced.

The synthesis of the other parts of the enumerator follow similar lines. The body becomes a refinement of whatever operation is being applied to each element. The incrementer can be complex, as in the enumerator for the selector of a selection sort, or very simple as in the enumerator of the selector for an insertion sort. After the pieces of code for the various parts of the enumerator have been produced it is relatively straightforward to assemble them into a program and clean up the resulting code. Most of our programs have been produced in LISP but a small number of rules for producing SAIL code have been added by Juan Ludlow [13].

REFERENCES

1. Barstow, David R., Automatic construction of algorithms and data structures using a knowledge base of programming rules. Stanford University, Computer Science Department, AIM-308 (November 1977).
2. Barstow, David R. and Kant, Elaine, Observations on the interaction of coding and efficiency knowledge in the PSI program synthesis system. *Proceedings of the Second International Conference on Software Engineering*, San Francisco, CA (October 1976) 19–31.
3. Burstall, R. M. and Darlington, John, A transformation system for developing recursive programs, *Journal of the ACM* 24 (1977) 44–67.
4. Darlington, John, A synthesis of several sorting algorithms, *Research Report 23*, Department of Artificial Intelligence, University of Edinburgh, Scotland (July 1976).
5. Ginsparg, Jerrold M., Natural language processing in an automatic programming domain, Stanford University, Computer Science Department, A.I.M.-316 (June 1978).
6. Green, C. Cordell, The design of the PSI program synthesis system, *Proceedings of the Second International Conference on Software Engineering*, San Francisco, CA (October 1976) 4-18.
7. Green, C. Cordell, A summary of the PSI program synthesis system. *Proceedings of the Fifth International Joint Conference on Artificial Intelligence*, Cambridge, MA (August 1977) 380–381.
8. Green, C. Cordell and Barstow, David R., A hypothetical dialogue exhibiting a knowledge base for a program understanding system, in: Elcock, E. W., and Michie, D. (Eds.), Intelligence 8, *Machine Representations of Knowledge* (Ellis Horwood Ltd. and John Wiley, New York, 1976).
9. Green, C. Cordell and Barstow, David R., Some rules for the automatic synthesis of programs, Advance Papers of the *Fourth International Joint Conference on Artificial Intelligence*, Tbilisi, Georgia, U.S.S.R. (September 1975) 232–939.

10. Kant, Elaine, The selection of efficient implementations for a high level language, *Proceedings of ACM SIGART-SIGPLAN Symposium on Artificial Intelligence and Programming Languages*, SIGPLAN Notices, **12** (8) SIGART Newsletter, **64** (August 1977) 140–146.

11. Knuth, Donald E, Sorting and searching, *The Art of Computer Programming* **3** (Addison–Wesley, Reading MA, 1973).

12. Laaser, William, Synthesis of recursive programs, Personal communication.

13. Ludlow, Juan, Masters Project (Stanford University, 1977).

14. Manna, Zohar and Waldinger, Richard, The automatic synthesis of recursive programs, *Proceedings of ACM SIGART-SIGPLAN Symposium on Artificial Intelligence and Programming Languages*, SIGPLAN Notices, **12** (8) SIGART Newsletter, **64** (August 1977) 29–33.

15. McCune, Brian P., The PSI program model builder: synthesis of very high-level programs, *Proceedings of ACM SIGART-SIGPLAN Symposium on Artificial Intelligence and Programming Languages*, SIGPLAN Notices, **12** (8) SIGART Newsletter, **64** (August 1977) 130–139.

16. Phillips, Jorge, A framework for the synthesis of programs from traces using multiple knowledge sources, *Proceedings of the Fifth International Joint Conference on Artificial Intelligence*, Cambridge, MA (August 1977) pp. 812.

17. Sedgewick, Robert, Quicksort, Stanford University, Computer Science Department, CS–492, Stanford, CA (May 1975).

Received July 1977; revised version received March 1978

Program Abstraction and Instantiation

NACHUM DERSHOWITZ
University of Illinois

Our goal is to develop formal methods for abstracting a given set of programs into a program schema and for instantiating a given schema to satisfy concrete specifications. Abstraction and instantiation are two important phases in software development which allow programmers to apply knowledge learned in the solutions of past problems when faced with new situations. For example, from two programs using a linear (or binary) search technique, an abstract schema can be derived that embodies the shared idea and that can be instantiated to solve similar new problems. Along similar lines, the development and application of program transformations are considered.

We suggest the formulation of analogies as a basic tool in program abstraction. An analogy is first sought between the specifications of the given programs; this yields an abstract specification that may be instantiated to any of the given concrete specifications. The analogy is then used as a basis for transforming the existing programs into an abstract schema that represents the embedded technique, with the invariant assertions and correctness proofs of the given programs helping to verify and complete the analogy. A given concrete specification of the schema is compared with the abstract specification of the schema to suggest an instantiation of the schema that yields a correct program.

Categories and Subject Descriptors: D.2.2 [**Software Engineering**]: Tools and Techniques—*software libraries, structured programming*; D.2.4 [**Software Engineering**]: Program Verification—*correctness proofs*; D.2.6 [**Software Engineering**]: Programming Environments; F.2.2 [**Analysis of Algorithms and Problem Complexity**]: Nonnumerical Algorithms and Problems—*program transformation*; F.3.1 [**Logics and Meanings of Programs**]: Specifying and Verifying and Reasoning about Programs—*assertions, invariants*

General Terms: Design, Verification

Additional Key Words and Phrases: Abstraction, analogy, instantiation, program schemata

1. INTRODUCTION

Chaque vérité que je trouvais étant une règle qui me servait après à en trouver d'autres, non seulement je vins à bout plusieurs que j'avais jugées autrefois très difficiles, mais il me sembla aussi, vers la fin, que je pouvais déterminer, en celles même que j'ignorais, par quels moyens, et jusques où, il était possible de les résoudre.

—RENÉ DESCARTES, *Discours de la Méthode*

When confronted with a new task, humans often recognize some measure of resemblance between it and another, previously accomplished, task. Rather than "reinvent the wheel," they are prone to conserve effort by adapting the known solution to an old problem to the one now at hand. Later, after having solved several related problems, they might come to formulate a general paradigm for solving that *kind* of problem by highlighting shared aspects of the individual instances and suppressing inconsequential or idiosyncratic particulars. This process of formulating a general scheme from concrete instances is termed *abstraction*; that of applying an abstract scheme to a particular problem is termed *instantiation*.

Abstraction and instantiation are also important phases in the evolutionary cycle of many typical programs, a cycle that, in addition, often includes the debugging of early versions, modifications to meet amended specifications, and extensions for expanded capabilities. The more experience a programmer has had, the more programming methods are likely to have been assimilated, and the more judiciously they can be applied to new problems. Thus, after constructing a number of similar programs, a programmer is apt to formulate for himself or herself—and perhaps for others as well—an abstract notion of the underlying principle and to reuse it in new, but related, applications. Program *schemata* are a convenient form for remembering such programming knowledge. A schema may embody basic programming techniques (such as the "generate-and-test" paradigm) or specialized strategies for solving a class of problems; its specification is stated in terms of abstract predicate, function, and constant symbols. For example, the "binary-search" technique can be expressed as a schema that can be instantiated to compute roots or to search ordered arrays.

To formalize this aspect of programming, we develop methods for abstracting a given set of cognate programs into a program schema and for instantiating a schema to satisfy a given concrete specification. To date, there has been a limited amount of research on program abstraction. The STRIPS system [34] generalized the loop-free robot plans that it generated; the HACKER system [65] "subroutinized" and generalized the "blocks-world" plans it synthesized, executing the plan to determine which program constants could be abstracted. Dershowitz and Manna [25] suggested using the proof of correctness of a program to guide the abstraction process.

A number of researchers have described the use of program schemata. Dijkstra [28] maintains that theorems about schemata are unconsciously invoked by programmers; some programming textbooks [19, 73] have illustrated the use of basic schemata in the systematic development of programs. Gerhart [37] has advocated the use of schemata as a powerful programming tool; some illustrations of their use are given in [38, 55, 74]. Along similar lines, the Programmer's Apprentice project has led to suggestions that programs be analyzed in terms of "clichés" [11], and that a simplified abstract model of a program should be filled in and then debugged [60]. Related notions are "programming plans" (e.g., [6, 69]) and "generic program units" (e.g., [67]); plans are designed to contain more semantic information than schemata, generic facilities to contain less. In a somewhat similar vein, [59] and [23] demonstrate how abstractions may be used to guide theorem proving and problem solving, respectively. Some other examples of the use of abstract or simplistic algorithms as first steps in the development of programs are [4, 21, 27, 31, 47, 56]. An approach to the specification and verification of program schemata is given in [51].

An earlier version of this paper was presented at the Fifth Conference on Software Engineering, San Diego, Calif., March 1981.

This research was supported in part by the NSF under grants MCS 79-04897 and MCS 83-07755.

Author's address: Dept. of Computer Science, University of Illinois, Urbana, IL 61801.

We suggest the formulation of analogies as a basic tool in program abstraction. First, an analogy is sought between the specifications of the given programs. This yields an abstract specification that may be instantiated to any of the given concrete specifications. The analogy may then be used as a basis for transforming the existing programs into an abstract schema that represents the embedded technique. This methodology is applicable to all programming styles: iterative or recursive, declarative or applicative.

The importance of analogical reasoning has been stressed by many, from Descartes to Pólya. For a discussion of the role of analogy in the sciences, see [39]; for a review of psychological theories of analogical reasoning, see [64]. An early work on automating analogical reasoning is [33]; the use of analogy in automated problem solving in general, and theorem proving in particular, was proposed by Kling in [44]. Other works employing analogy as an implement in problem solving include [12, 13, 15, 17, 18, 32, 49, 52, 54, 72]. The use of analogies to guide the modification of programs is pursued in [26, 50, 66].

All our programs are assumed to be annotated with an *output specification* (stating the desired relationship between the input and output variables upon termination of the program), an *input specification* (defining the set of legal inputs on which the program is intended to operate), and *invariant assertions* (relations known to always hold at specific points in the program for the current values of variables) demonstrating its correctness. As we shall see, invariant assertions and correctness proofs play an important role in deriving analogies. The more information available regarding the underlying rationale of a program, the more directed the abstraction process can be. Additional advantages of maintaining a design history are enumerated in [53]. As Carbonell [16] has argued, looking for analogies between (program) derivations can be more fruitful than comparing final products.

A schema derived in this manner is usually not applicable to all possible instantiations of its specifications. For that reason, a schema is in general accompanied by an input specification containing conditions that must be satisfied by the instantiation in order to guarantee correctness. These *preconditions* are derived from a correctness proof of the schema. The abstract specification of the schema may then be compared with a given concrete specification of a new problem. By formulating an analogy between the abstract and concrete specifications, an instantiation is found that yields a concrete program when applied to the abstract schema. If the instantiation satisfies the preconditions, then the correctness of the new program is guaranteed. If not, analysis of the unsatisfied conditions may suggest modifications that will lead to a correct program.

Deriving a general correctness-preserving program transformation from a set of examples is similar to deriving a schema from a set of concrete programs; we show how the same approach works for both tasks. The importance of program transformations as a tool for program development has been pointed out by many, including [5, 9, 22, 36, 45, 63, 70, 71]. (For a survey, see [58]; for a more pessimistic view, see [30].) Gerhart [37] and others have recommended the hand-compilation of a handbook of program schemata. Such a collection of schemata, along with a catalog of correctness-preserving program transformations, could

serve as part of an interactive program development system. Some schemata that have appeared in the programming literature are collected in [24]; collections of transformations include [1, 2, 7, 42, 48, 61, 62].

In the next section we give an overview of the method. Section 3 presents a detailed example of abstraction and instantiation. Section 4 considers program transformations. It is followed by a discussion.

2. OVERVIEW

Abstracting a set of programs begins with finding their similarities and accentuating their differences. Based on this step, a set of transformations is applied to the programs. The result is a schema that can be instantiated to any of the given programs. In this section we give an outline of the abstraction process and consider correctness issues. We also describe the similar steps necessary to instantiate a schema when confronted with a new problem.

For example, one of the simplest programming schemata is the following [28]:

S_1: **begin** *linear-search schema*
  type $\xi \in N,\ \phi \in N \rightarrow B$
  B_1: **assert** $(\exists u \in N)\phi(u)$
  $\xi := 0$
  loop until $\phi(\xi)$
    $\xi := \xi + 1$
  repeat
  E_1: **assert** $\xi = \min\{u \in N \mid \phi(u)\}$
end

Given a predicate ϕ, this schema searches the nonnegative integers N one-by-one for the first to satisfy ϕ. The variable ξ is set to that integer. That is the meaning of the "output specification"

$$\text{assert } \xi = \min\{u \in N \mid \phi(u)\}.$$

The statement

type $\xi \in N,\ \phi \in N \rightarrow B$

is a global assertion to the effect that the program variable ξ is of type N and the input parameter ϕ is of type $N \rightarrow B$. That is, from the point at which ξ is first assigned a value until the end of execution, the value of ξ is in the set N of nonnegative integers, and ϕ is a predicate that takes a nonnegative integer (in N) as an argument and returns a Boolean value ($B = \{$**true**, **false**$\}$). The loop body is repeated (zero or more times) until the test

until $\phi(\xi)$

becomes true, at that point the loop is exited.[1] In general, to determine exactly under which conditions a schema is applicable, its correctness proof must be

---
[1] The **loop-until-repeat** construct is based on the suggestion of O.-J. Dahl in [45]. As a matter of convenience, we omit type declarations for interpreted symbols such as + and 0.

analyzed. The above schema, for example, will only terminate if there is some nonnegative integer for which ϕ is true. That is the meaning of the "precondition"

assert $(\exists u \in N)\phi(u)$.

2.1 Basic Method: Analogy

Two objects can be compared on many levels: external appearance, outward performance, and inner workings. Generally, the "external appearance" of a program (i.e., the code) can undergo dramatic changes without affecting the underlying algorithm. At the opposite end of the spectrum, input/output specifications, defining the "outward performance" of a program, but not how it accomplishes what it does, can be identical for very disparate programs. Between the two extremes, comments about the program's "inner workings," its correctness and efficiency, are often a better guide when looking for similarities between programs. It therefore makes sense to begin by formulating an analogy between program specifications, and then extending that analogy by examining how the different programs achieve their analogous desiderata. The more that is known about the "rhyme and reason" of a program, the better the chances of being able to profit from comparing it with other programs.

When the specifications for and documentation of programs are given formally, we can use formal means to compare them. For example, if one program is known to end with the condition $z \leq A[0]$ holding, and a second program halts with $B[p] \geq B[k]$, then we look for an analogy

$$z \leq A[0] \Leftrightarrow B[p] \geq B[k]$$

between the two. In this case, we could say that if $\leq$ in the first condition corresponds with $\geq$ in the second, then z and $A[0]$ in the first condition ought to correspond, respectively, with $B[p]$ and $B[k]$ in the second. Going a step further, we can say that where the former condition has $\leq$, z, A, and 0, the latter has $\geq$, $B[p]$, B, and k, respectively. This more detailed analogy is denoted

$$\leq \Leftrightarrow \geq$$
$$z \Leftrightarrow B[p]$$
$$A \Leftrightarrow B$$
$$0 \Leftrightarrow k.$$

In general, there are several possible ways in which an analogy

$$f(q, r) \Leftrightarrow h$$

between an expression of the form $f(q, r)$ and another expression h can be refined:

- If h is of the form $g(s, t)$, that is, if we are comparing

$$f(q, r) \Leftrightarrow g(s, t),$$

then the *imitating* mapping

$$f \Leftrightarrow g$$
$$q \Leftrightarrow s$$
$$r \Leftrightarrow t$$

suggests itself. These three correspondences may be broken down further, as long as the mappings remain consistent with each other.

- If f is an inverse in its first argument of some function f^-, that is, $f(f^-(x, y), y) = x$ (for all x and y), then an *inverting mapping*

$$q \Leftrightarrow f^-(h, r)$$

can be used.

- If f has an identity element f^0 in its first argument, that is, $f(f^0, v) = v$ (for all v), then a *collapsing* mapping

$$q \Leftrightarrow f^0$$
$$r \Leftrightarrow h$$

is possible.

- Another possibility is the *projecting mapping*

$$f(u, v) \Leftrightarrow u$$
$$q \Leftrightarrow h,$$

that is, f maps to a function that projects its first argument.[2]

For example, in comparing the expressions

$$z \leq A[0] \Leftrightarrow B[p] \geq B[k],$$

the imitating mapping

$$\leq \Leftrightarrow \geq$$
$$z \Leftrightarrow B[p]$$
$$A[0] \Leftrightarrow B[k]$$

is first used. To compare $A[0]$ with $B[k]$, another imitating mapping is used:

$$A \Leftrightarrow B$$
$$0 \Leftrightarrow k.$$

As another example, comparing the two expressions

$$c/d \Leftrightarrow \sqrt{a},$$

suggests numerous possibilities, including the imitating mapping

$$u/v \Leftrightarrow \sqrt{v}$$
$$d \Leftrightarrow a,$$

the collapsing mapping

$$d \Leftrightarrow 1$$
$$c \Leftrightarrow \sqrt{a},$$

[2] Similar mappings work for other than the first argument. For a discussion of a second-order pattern-matcher that uses imitating and projecting mappings, and its application to program manipulation, see [40]. The use of formal inverses in matching is described in [43].

or the projecting mapping

$$u/v \Longleftrightarrow u$$

The analogy

$$c \Longleftrightarrow \sqrt{a}.$$

can be inverted to give

$$c^2 \Longleftrightarrow a.$$

Note that the projecting mapping gives only partial information: it indicates how to get from c/d to $\sqrt{a}$; it does not, however, indicate how to go in the other direction, since the right-hand side u of the analogy $u/v \Longleftrightarrow u$ can match *anything*.

Give an analogy such as

$$\leq \Longleftrightarrow \geq$$
$$z \Longleftrightarrow B[p]$$
$$A \Longleftrightarrow B$$
$$0 \Longleftrightarrow k$$

we can define abstract entities for corresponding parts. Each pair in the analogy is denoted by an abstract variable. When the corresponding two parts are of the same type, their abstraction will also be of that type; when their types are incompatible, the abstract variable is given an abstract type. In our example, if the variable k is of type "integer," then the scalar constants 0 and k may be replaced by an abstract integer variable κ. If the variable z is a real number and the variable expression $B[p]$ is of type "string", say, then they would generalize to a variable μ of abstract type Γ. The array constants A and B act as functions from (subranges of) the integers to reals and strings, respectively, and generalize to a function Δ from the integers to Γ.[3] Finally, the predicate constants $\leq$ and $\geq$ are abstracted to a predicate variable α taking two arguments of type Γ. (We use Greek letters to distinguish *abstract* entities.)

Applying the transformations

$$\leq \Longrightarrow \alpha$$
$$z \Longrightarrow \mu$$
$$A \Longrightarrow \Delta$$
$$0 \Longrightarrow \kappa$$

to the predicate $z \leq A[0]$ yields the abstract condition $\alpha(\mu, \Delta[\kappa])$. Such a set of transformations is called an *abstraction mapping*. The other abstraction mapping,

$$\geq \Longrightarrow \alpha$$
$$B[p] \Longrightarrow \mu$$
$$B \Longrightarrow \Delta$$
$$k \Longrightarrow \kappa,$$

when applied to the condition $B[p] \geq B[k]$, yields the same abstract condition $\alpha(\mu, \Delta[\kappa])$.[4]

The first step in the abstraction process is the attempt to find a detailed analogy between the specifications of the given programs. Then, the tentative abstraction mapping may be applied to the corresponding program. The result is a program schema containing abstract symbols in place of the concrete entities that were in the original program. At other stages in the abstraction process, additional correspondences between the programs may be found, leading to further abstractions.

2.2 Correctness Considerations

To delineate when an abstraction mapping is sure to work, we need to distinguish between two types of symbols: a *constant* is any (interpreted) symbol appearing in a program with assumed properties, for instance, 0, **true**, +, and $\geq$; a *variable* is any (uninterpreted) symbol appearing in the program with no assumed properties other than those mentioned in the input specification. Variables that change value during program execution are termed *program variables*; any other variables are considered to be *input variables*. Those program variables that appear in the output specification are *output variables*.

A *global* transformation such as $A \Longrightarrow \Delta$, where an input variable is systematically replaced—in the assertions as well as in the code—by another input variable or by any function of only input variables, will yield a schema that satisfies the *transformed* input-output specification. Similarly, systematically replacing a program (or output) variable by a function of program (output) variables (e.g., $z \Longrightarrow \mu$ or $z \Longrightarrow \mu - 1$) preserves correctness with respect to the transformed specification.[5] Like simple "changes of variables" such transformations preserve the "meaning" of the program if applied systematically. But when, as usually happens, an abstraction mapping also involves transformations of constant symbols (e.g., 0 and $\leq$), the resultant schema will not necessarily be correct. That is because the correctness of the original programs presumably depends on specific properties of those constants. For example, were there a superfluous assignment $i := i + 0$ in a program, then an abstraction of 0 would overzealously change that assignment, as well as other, perhaps relevant, occurrences. Or, were some function symbol to appear in the specification, but not explicitly in the code, transforming that symbol would be ineffectual.

Hence, for some transformations, correctness must be verified. When an analysis of the abstracted program reveals that it is not necessarily correct, four remedies are available: localizing transformations, extending analogies, adding preconditions, and incorporating subgoals. The first thing to do is to try to identify exactly which occurrences of the various symbols in the given programs are analogous. Then, rather than apply an abstraction mapping blindly to all occurrences, transformations may be localized to the relevant ones only. For this to be possible, we need information about how the original programs were constructed, explaining which parts of the specifications are related to which

---

[3] When an array does not change value in a program, it is convenient to treat it as a function constant, taking an index as its argument; otherwise, an array can be treated as a variable, with array access as a function of both array and index.

[4] We should be careful and specify the order in which the individual mappings are applied. Were $B \Longrightarrow \Delta$ applied first, we would have to transform $\Delta[p] \Longrightarrow \mu$ instead of $B[p] \Longrightarrow \mu$.

[5] Replacement of a variable sometimes makes a program statement syntactically invalid, necessitating its rephrasing. See Section 2.2.

As an illustration, consider again the linear search schema S_1, and suppose we wish to find the "integer square-root" of a nonnegative integer input value n. That is, our goal is to construct a program that sets the value of a variable z to $\lfloor\sqrt{n}\rfloor$, where $\lfloor u\rfloor$ is the largest integer not larger than u:

R_1: **begin comment** *integer square–root specification*
type $n, z \in \mathbf{N}$
achieve $z = \lfloor\sqrt{n}\rfloor$ **varying** z
end

If z is to be the largest integer not greater than $\sqrt{n}$, then $z + 1$ must be the smallest integer greater than $\sqrt{n}$. It follows that the above goal will be attained if we can

achieve $z + 1 = \min\{u \in \mathbf{N} \mid u > \sqrt{n}\}$.

This version of the integer-square-root specification matches the abstract output specification

E_1: **assert** $\xi = \min\{u \in \mathbf{N} \mid \phi(u)\}$

of the schema. Applying the appropriate instantiation mapping

$$\xi \Rightarrow z + 1$$

$$\phi(u) \Rightarrow u > \sqrt{n}$$

to the schema, replaces the exit test

until $\phi(\xi)$

with

until $z + 1 > \sqrt{n}$.

After applying an instantiation mapping to a schema, we must make sure that all statements are executable. If we assume, as is reasonable, that the square-root function itself is not a primitive operation for this problem, then the above test is not executable. Fortunately, we can instead test

until $(z + 1)^2 > n$.

Similarly, applying the transformation

$$\xi \Rightarrow z + 1$$

to the initialization assignment

$$\xi := 0$$

results in the statement

$$z + 1 := 0,$$

which is not an executable assignment. But we can gain the same effect of making $z + 1$ equal to 0 via the assignment

$$z := -1.$$

parts of the programs. Ideally, all programs would come with detailed comments showing each stage in the refinement of the specifications step-by-step towards the final version of the program (as might be the case were programs constructed in a semiautomated environment, as suggested in [35], or formally, as described, for example, in [29]). Then the analogy can be made at the most appropriate level of refinement (cf. [16]). In the absence of such, we can attempt to derive invariants from the code, prove the program's correctness, and then extract the necessary data from the proof (see, for example, [41]).

Localizing transformations will avoid overzealousness, but it may also be the case that an analogy between specifications gives less than the "whole story." In that case, it may be possible to extend the analogy between the programs by examining them in more detail. When programs are solving similar problems in similar manners, it is likely that their major components will also have similar goals. Therefore, it should be possible to continue comparing the programs, level by level, down to the troublesome details of their code, until the analogy breaks down at fine points over which the programs really differ. With each extension of the analogy, abstract entities are added to the developing schema.

Usually, even after finding a complete analogy, it will not be possible to prove the schema correct. The reason is that the correctness of the original programs was in all likelihood based on certain properties of those constant, function, and predicate symbols that were abstracted. For an instance of the schema to work properly, those properties must also hold for the instantiation. What we need to do is to accompany each schema with *preconditions* that specify exactly under which circumstances an instantiation will yield a correct program. These conditions are derived from an analysis of the conditions necessary for a proof of correctness for the schema; they should, of course, hold for the given set of programs. (Verifying the correctness of schemata is no different than verifying programs.) Some amount of heuristic reasoning could also be used at this point to simplify preconditions (while ensuring that the given programs indeed satisfy the simpler conditions).

There may sometimes be no set of preconditions that ensures correctness of the complete schema. Nevertheless, those parts that are correct may be useful; those that are not can be replaced with unachieved subgoals. It may turn out, for example, that the abstracted initialization of a loop does not work as required, in which case the initialization part might be replaced by a subgoal stating, in terms of the schema's abstract entities, that variables appearing in the loop invariants must be set so that the invariants hold when the loop is first entered.

2.3 Instantiation

Given a collection of program schemata, we would like to be able to exploit them in the solution of new problems. This is accomplished by looking for a schema whose abstract specification matches the concrete specification of the desired goal. The comparison suggests an *instantiation mapping*, that, when applied to the schema, yields a concrete program for the given problem. If the instantiated preconditions hold in the new problem domain, the instantiated schema is a correct program.

that $\epsilon^-(\epsilon^-(y)) = y$). The desired effect of the transformed assignment is

achieve $\epsilon(y) = h(\epsilon(y'), z)$ **varying** y;

in other words, that the value of $\epsilon(y)$ equal $h(\epsilon(y'), z)$ for the prior value y' of y. That goal is attainable by assigning

$$y := \epsilon^-(h(\epsilon(y), z)).$$

(Of course, not all such equations can be solved for y; a heuristic approach to this problem may be found, for example, in [14].) Similarly, when ϵ does not contain y, but instead contains a *new* variable v, the effect

achieve $\epsilon(v) = h(\epsilon(v'), z)$ **varying** v

is obtained by assigning

$$v := \epsilon^-(h(\epsilon(v), z)).$$

When a global transformation replaces one variable with a function of two or more variables, the situation is more complicated. If ϵ is a function of both y and another variable v, say, then applying the transformation $y \Rightarrow \epsilon$ to a multiple assignment of the form

$$(y, v) := (g(y, v), h(y, v))$$

gives

$$(\epsilon, v) := (g(\epsilon, v), h(\epsilon, v)).$$

Thus we need to solve a system of equations:

achieve $\epsilon(y, v) = g(\epsilon', v'), v = h(\epsilon', v')$ **varying** y, v,

where ϵ' is short for $\epsilon(y', v')$ and y' and v' denote the prior values of the variables y and v, respectively. Assuming ϵ is an inverse (in the first argument) of some ϵ^- (i.e., $\epsilon^-(y, v), v) = y$ for all y and v), then we can achieve the desired relations by assigning

$$(y, v) := (\epsilon^-(g(\epsilon, v), h(\epsilon, v)), h(\epsilon, v))$$

instead. Note that the value of $\epsilon(y, v)$ changes when *either* y or v is assigned to. Therefore, any assignment $v := h(y, v)$ to v alone is also cause for updating the transformed y, and should be treated as though it were the multiple assignment $(y, v) := (y, h(y, v))$.

For example, the transformation

$$s \Rightarrow t - x$$

when applied in a straightforward manner to an assignment

$$(x, s) := (0, 1),$$

gives the illegal

$$(x, t - x) := (0, 1).$$

By the same token, applying that transformation to the loop-body assignment

$$\xi := \xi + 1$$

results in the "illegal"

$$z + 1 := z + 1 + 1,$$

which may be replaced by

$$z := z + 1.$$

Also

type $z + 1 \in \mathbf{N}$

can be replaced with

type $z \in \mathbf{N} - 1,$

where $\mathbf{N} - 1$ denotes the set of integers greater or equal to -1. The above changes provide us with the following integer square-root program:

R_1: **begin** *simple integer square-root program*
  type $n \in \mathbf{N}, z \in \mathbf{N} - 1$
B_1: **assert true**
  $z := -1$
  loop until $(z + 1)^2 > n$
  $z := z + 1$
  repeat
E_1: **assert** $z = \lfloor \sqrt{n} \rfloor$
end

Though not particularly inspiring, this program is correct, since this instance of ϕ satisfies the precondition

B_1: **assert** $(\exists u \in \mathbf{N})\phi(u),$

ensuring thereby that the instantiated program eventually terminates; that is, we have

$$(\exists u \in \mathbf{N})u + 1 > \sqrt{n}.$$

In general: suppose we wish to apply a transformation of the form

$$y \Rightarrow \epsilon$$

to a program variable y, where ϵ is an expression containing y. Replacing the occurrences of y in an assignment of the form

$$y := h(y, z)$$

results in an illegal statement

$$\epsilon := h(\epsilon, z)$$

since an expression now appears on the left-hand side of the assignment. This can be rectified when ϵ (as a function of y) is an inverse of some function ϵ^- (so

The desired effect of making the difference between the new values of t and x equal to 1, that is, for $t - 0 = 1$ (0 is the new value of x), can be achieved by the legal assignment $t := 1 + 0$. We then have

$$(x, t) := (0, 1).$$

Since the value of the difference $t - x$ also changes whenever x is assigned to, we must also look at an assignment like

$$x := x + s,$$

and view it as $(x, s) := (x + s, s)$, explicitly including a dummy assignment to the variable s. Transforming this augmented assignment gives $(x, t - x) := (x + t - x, t - x)$. Thus, x should get the value t, while t should get the value $t - x$ plus the *new* value of x, which happens to be the *old* value of t. The appropriate legal assignment is, therefore,

$$(x, t) := (t, 2 \cdot t - x).$$

3. A DETAILED EXAMPLE

The following example begins with two concrete programs, annotated with their specifications and invariant assertions. First, the programs are abstracted to obtain a more general program schema. Then, an analogy between the specifications of two essentially similar programs is used to transform one of them into an abstract schema. Analysis of the schema's verification conditions suggests another transformation and supplies preconditions that guarantee the correctness of an instantiation. Finally, we illustrate how the schema is instantiated to satisfy a third concrete specification.

The first program we are given is

P_2: **begin comment** *minimum-value program*
  type $n, i \in \mathbb{N}, z \in \mathbb{R}, A \in [0{:}n] \to \mathbb{R}$
  B_2: **assert true**
  $(z, i) := (A[0], 0)$
  loop L_2: **assert** $z \leq A[0{:}i], z \in A[0{:}i]$
    until $i = n$
    $i := i + 1$
    if $A[i] < z$ **then** $z := A[i]$ **fi**
  repeat
  E_2: **assert** $z \leq A[0{:}n], z \in A[0{:}n]$
end

The output specification of this program is given in the statement

E_2: **assert** $z \leq A[0{:}n], z \in A[0{:}n]$.

By $z \leq A[0{:}n]$, we mean that upon termination the value of z not be greater than the value of any element appearing in the array segment $A[0{:}n]$, that is,

$$(\forall u \in [0{:}n]) z \leq A[u].$$

By $z \in A[0{:}n]$, we mean that z should also be one of those array elements. The input specification $n \in \mathbb{N}$ of this program is included in the type specification

type $n, i \in \mathbb{N}, z \in \mathbb{R}, A \in [0{:}n] \to \mathbb{R}$,

where $\mathbb{R}$ is the set of "real" numbers. It states that the value of the input variable n must be a nonnegative integer (ensuring, thereby, that the assay segment $A[0{:}n]$ is nonempty), and also that the array A supplied to the program gives a real number (in $\mathbb{R}$) for each index in the range $[0{:}n]$. Furthermore, the program variable i is a nonnegative integer throughout execution, while the output variable z remains a real number. The statement

B_2: **assert true**

just means that there are no other restrictions on the values of the input variables n and A. The statement

L_2: **assert** $z \leq A[0{:}i], z \in A[0{:}i]$

at the head of the loop expresses invariant assertions that hold for the current values of the variables i and z each time control reaches that point in the program. These invariants are first made true by the multiple assignment

$$(z, i) := (A[0], 0)$$

of $A[0]$ to z and 0 to i. The two loop-body statements

$i := i + 1$
if $A[i] < z$ **then** $z := A[i]$ **fi**

maintain the truth of the invariants (i.e., assuming that the invariants are true before the statements are executed, the invariants remain true afterwards). When $i = n$ and the loop terminates, the output specification holds.

The following is a similar program which finds the position p of a *maximal* element in an array segment $B[b{:}c]$:

Q_2: **begin comment** *maximum-position program*
  type $b, c, p, j \in \mathbb{Z}, B \in [b{:}c] \to \Sigma^*$
  B_2: **assert** $b \leq c$
  $(p, j) := (c, c)$
  loop L_2: **assert** $B[p] \geq B[j{:}c], p \in [j{:}c]$
    while $j \neq b$
    $j := j - 1$
    if $B[j] > B[p]$ **then** $p := j$ **fi**
  repeat
  E_2: **assert** $B[p] \geq B[b{:}c], p \in [b{:}c]$
end

where Σ^* is the set of finite strings of letters from some alphabet Σ. Its output specification is

E_2: **assert** $B[p] \geq B[b{:}c], p \in [b{:}c]$,

meaning that the string $B[p]$ is (lexicographically) greater or equal to each of the elements $B[b]$ through $B[c]$, and its position p is in the range b through c, inclusive. The loop decrements j as long as the condition

while $j \neq b$

still holds. The input specification

B_2: **assert** $b \leq c$

requires that the initial value c of j not be smaller than b.

Both programs search for an extremum element within an array segment. Our task is to extract an abstract version of these two programs that captures the essence of the technique used, but that is not specific to either problem. The resultant schema could then be used as a model of such searches for the solution of future problems.

The first step in abstracting these two programs, P_2 and Q_2, is to find an analogy between (the first part of) their respective output specifications, $z \leq A[0:n]$ and $B[p] \geq B[b:c]$. A straightforward analogy (by imitation, see Section 2.1) is that where the specification of P_2 has 0, n, $\leq$, z, and A, the specification of Q_2 has b, c, $\geq$, $B[p]$, and B, respectively:

$$0 \Leftrightarrow b$$
$$n \Leftrightarrow c$$
$$\leq \Leftrightarrow \geq$$
$$z \Leftrightarrow B[p]$$
$$A \Leftrightarrow B.$$

Now abstract entities are substituted for analogous parts. For the scalar constant 0 in P_2 and the corresponding scalar input variable b in Q_2, we use an abstract input variable κ (of type $\mathbf{Z}$, like b). The corresponding input variables n (of type $\mathbf{N}$) and c (of type $\mathbf{Z}$) may be replaced by λ (of type $\mathbf{Z}$, since $\mathbf{Z}$ contains $\mathbf{N}$). The output variable z (of type $\mathbf{R}$) and the variable expression $B[p]$ (of type Σ^*) are generalized to a program variable μ (of abstract type Γ, since the types of z and $B[p]$ are different). The input arrays A and B (of reals and strings, respectively) generalize to an arbitrary function Δ, and the predicate constants $\leq$ and $\geq$ are replaced by an abstract predicate α. (The type of Δ is $[\kappa:\lambda] \to \Gamma$, since the ranges $[0:n]$ and $[b:c]$ for the indices of A and B, respectively, have been abstracted to $[\kappa:\lambda]$, while $B[p]$ has been abstracted to a variable of type Γ. The type of α is $\Gamma \times \Gamma \to \mathbf{B}$, since the arguments of $\leq$ and $\geq$ have been abstracted to objects of type Γ.) The corresponding abstraction mappings are

$$0 \Rightarrow \kappa \Leftarrow b$$
$$n \Rightarrow \lambda \Leftarrow c$$
$$\leq \Rightarrow \alpha \Leftarrow \geq$$
$$z \Rightarrow \mu \Leftarrow B[p]$$
$$A \Rightarrow \Delta \Leftarrow B,$$

where the leftmost column has symbols from P_2, the rightmost column symbols from Q_2, and the center column their abstract counterparts.

Applying the left set of transformations to the abstract specification

$$\mathbf{assert}\ \alpha(\mu, \Delta[\kappa:\lambda]), \mu \in \Delta[\kappa:\lambda].$$

For Q_2, to effect the transformation $B[p] \Rightarrow \mu$ followed by $B \Rightarrow \Delta$, we can apply $p \Rightarrow pos(\mu, \Delta)$, where pos denotes a formal inverse of the array access function; that is, $pos(v, U)$ returns the rightmost (say) occurrence of the element v in the array U, so that (as long as v occurs in U) we have $U[pos(v, U)] = v$. Applying these mappings to Q_2's specification yields

$$\mathbf{assert}\ \alpha(\mu, \Delta[\kappa:\lambda]), pos(\mu, \Delta) \in [\kappa:\lambda].$$

The second conjunct, $pos(\mu, \Delta) \in [\kappa:\lambda]$, implies that $\Delta[pos(\mu, \Delta)] = \mu \in \Delta[\kappa:\lambda]$, which is the same as what was obtained for P_2.

Now that both programs have the same abstract specification, the next step is to apply each of the mappings to the corresponding program itself. Applying the left set of transformations to P_2 yields

S_2: **begin comment** *tentative extremum schema*
type $i \in \mathbf{N}$, $\kappa, \lambda \in \mathbf{Z}$, $\mu \in \Gamma$, $\Delta \in [\kappa:\lambda] \to \Gamma$, $\alpha \in \Gamma \times \Gamma \to \mathbf{B}$
B_2: **suggest true**
$(\mu, i) := (\Delta[\kappa], \kappa)$
loop L_2: **suggest** $\alpha(\mu, \Delta[\kappa:i])$, $\mu \in \Delta[\kappa:i]$
    until $i = \lambda$
    $i := i + 1$
    if $\Delta[i] < \mu$ **then** $\mu := \Delta[i]$ **fi**
repeat
E_2: **suggest** $\alpha(\mu, \Delta[\kappa:\lambda])$, $\mu \in \Delta[\kappa:\lambda]$
end

Had all the transformations been of variables, as are $n \Rightarrow \lambda$, $z \Rightarrow \mu$, and $A \Rightarrow \Delta$, then applying the transformations to all occurrences of those variables in the annotated program would of necessity have resulted in a correct schema. But since the abstraction mapping involves the transformation of constant symbols as well, viz. 0 and $\leq$, the above schema is not necessarily correct. To signify that correctness is not guaranteed we have replaced the assertions with "suggestions" containing those relations that *might* hold for the schema (as they did for the concrete program they were derived from). As we shall see, suggestions that do not turn out to be invariants can be used to further refine the abstraction.

Before we try to determine under which conditions the suggestions are invariants, we check the type constraints. (Types can be thought of as "global" invariants that must hold throughout execution.) Since the variable i is of type $\mathbf{N}$, but is initially assigned the value κ of type $\mathbf{Z}$, we extend its type to $\mathbf{Z}$. The assignments to i now obey the type constraints, as do assignments to μ. The function Δ is required to take an argument in the range $[\kappa, \lambda]$. This imposes the restriction $i \in [\kappa, \lambda]$ on the occurrences of i in the conditional, which in fact is the case. The only remaining problem is that the symbol $<$, left over from P_2, now has arguments of type Γ, rather than $\mathbf{R}$ as in P_2. This suggests that $<$ needs to be abstracted to something of type $\Gamma \times \Gamma \to \mathbf{B}$. To what, will be determined below.

Next we check the verification conditions. Consider the loop-exit path

L_2: **assert** $\alpha(\mu, \Delta[\kappa:i])$, $\mu \in \Delta[\kappa:i]$
    assert $i = \lambda$
E_2: **suggest** $\alpha(\mu, \Delta[\kappa:\lambda])$, $\mu \in \Delta[\kappa:\lambda]$.

The first assertion has the transformed loop invariants, which we shall for the moment assume to be true whenever control is at the head of the loop; the second assertion declares that the exit test was true at that time, and therefore the loop was exited; the final suggestion contains the desired output relations with respect to which we are trying to prove this schema correct. For this path to be correct, the loop invariants in the first assertion, together with the exit test of the second, must imply that the desired output relation in the suggestion holds, that is, the verification condition for the exit path is[6]

$$\alpha(\mu, \Delta[\kappa{:}i]) \wedge \mu \in \Delta[\kappa{:}i] \wedge i = \lambda \rightarrow \alpha(\mu, \Delta[\kappa{:}\lambda]) \wedge \mu \in \Delta[\kappa{:}\lambda].$$

Indeed, if $\alpha(\mu, \Delta[\kappa{:}i])$ holds and $i = \lambda$, then $\alpha(\mu, \Delta[\kappa{:}\lambda])$ holds as well. So, too, $\mu \in \Delta[\kappa{:}\lambda]$. Thus, if only we can establish that $\alpha(\mu, \Delta[\kappa{:}i])$ and $\mu \in \Delta[\kappa{:}i]$ are in fact loop invariants, the schema will be proved correct.

Consider now the initialization path

B_2: **assert true**
   $(\mu, i) := (\Delta[\kappa], \kappa)$
L_2: **suggest** $\alpha(\mu, \Delta[\kappa{:}i]), \mu \in \Delta[\kappa{:}i];$

its verification condition may be written simply as

suggest $\alpha(\Delta[\kappa], \Delta[\kappa{:}\kappa]), \Delta[\kappa] \in \Delta[\kappa{:}\kappa].$

This condition is obtained from the path by "pushing" the suggestions $\alpha(\mu, \Delta[\kappa{:}i])$ and $\mu \in \Delta[\kappa{:}i]$ back over the assignment $(\mu, i) := (\Delta[\kappa], \kappa)$, substituting the new values $\Delta[\kappa]$ of μ and κ of i in the suggestions. The subterm $\Delta[\kappa{:}\kappa]$ simplifies to $\Delta[\kappa]$, and certainly $\Delta[\kappa] \in \Delta[\kappa]$, but there is no way of showing

$$\alpha(\Delta[\kappa], \Delta[\kappa])$$

(nor are there any possible abstractions that might help make it hold). This conjunct is therefore left as a precondition for applicability of the schema. For termination, we have the verification condition

$$(\exists u \in \mathbf{N})\kappa + u = \lambda,$$

that is, the exit test $i = \lambda$ will eventually hold for some value $\kappa + u$ of i, as i is being incremented from its initial value κ. Since $\kappa, \lambda \in \mathbf{Z}$ appears in the type specification, this termination condition is equivalent to just

$$\kappa \le \lambda.$$

This too is left as a precondition. (Note that it is, in fact, the abstracted input specification of Q_2.)

The verification condition for the loop-body path divides into two cases, one for each possible outcome of the conditional test. In the case in which the test fails, the **then**-branch is skipped, and the path taken is

L_2: **assert** $\alpha(\mu, \Delta[\kappa{:}i]), \mu \in \Delta[\kappa{:}i]$
   assert $\neg(i = \lambda)$
   $i := i + 1$
      assert $\neg(\Delta[i] < \mu)$
L_2: **suggest** $\alpha(\mu, \Delta[\kappa{:}i]), \mu \in \Delta[\kappa{:}i].$

To verify this path we must show that the loop invariants continue to hold if the

exit test is false, i is incremented, and the conditional test is false. The corresponding verification condition is

assert $\alpha(\mu, \Delta[\kappa{:}i]), \mu \in \Delta[\kappa{:}i], \neg(i = \lambda), \neg(\Delta[i+1] < \mu)$
suggest $\alpha(\mu, \Delta[\kappa{:}i+1]), \mu \in \Delta[\kappa{:}i+1].$

Clearly, if μ is in $\Delta[\kappa{:}i]$, it is in the longer $\Delta[\kappa{:}i+1]$. Furthermore, it is being assumed that $\alpha(\mu, \Delta[\kappa{:}i])$; thus all that needs to be shown is $\alpha(\mu, \Delta[i+1] < \mu)$. Of course, since α is an abstract predicate, there is no reason for $\neg(\Delta[i+1] < \mu)$ to imply $\alpha(\mu, \Delta[i+1])$. Accordingly, we look for an extension

$$\neg(\Delta[i+1] < \mu) \Rightarrow \alpha(\mu, \Delta[i+1])$$

to the abstraction mapping that will make this condition hold. Negating the two sides (i.e., inverting) gives

$$\Delta[i+1] < \mu \Rightarrow \neg\alpha(\mu, \Delta[i+1]),$$

for which it is only necessary (by imitation) to transform

$$u < v \Rightarrow \neg\alpha(v, u) \qquad loop\text{-}body.$$

This *local* transformation should only be applied to the loop body, as it was introduced for the loop-body verification condition. Applying this new transformation, we get the conditional statement

if $\neg\alpha(\mu, \Delta[i])$ **then** $\mu := \Delta[i]$ **fi**.

Note that the transformed verification condition and all the type constraints are satisfied.[7]

Now that the verification condition for the case in which the test is false carries through, it remains only to verify what happens when the abstract test $\neg\alpha(\mu, \Delta[i])$ holds true:

L_2: **assert** $\alpha(\mu, \Delta[\kappa{:}i]), \mu \in \Delta[\kappa{:}i]$
      assert $\neg(i = \lambda)$
   $i := i + 1$
      assert $\neg\alpha(\mu, \Delta[i])$
   $\mu := \Delta[i]$
L_2: **suggest** $\alpha(\mu, \Delta[\kappa{:}i]), \mu \in \Delta[\kappa{:}i].$

The verification condition for this case is

assert $\alpha(\mu, \Delta[\kappa{:}i]), \mu \in \Delta[\kappa{:}i], \neg(i = \lambda), \neg\alpha(\mu, \Delta[i+1]), \Delta[i+1] \in \Delta[\kappa{:}i+1]$
suggest $\alpha(\Delta[i+1], \Delta[\kappa{:}i+1]), \Delta[i+1] \in \Delta[\kappa{:}i+1].$

Clearly, $\Delta[i+1] \in \Delta[\kappa{:}i+1]$ is true. But since there is no way to prove $\alpha(\Delta[i+1], \Delta[\kappa{:}i+1])$ for arbitrary α (nor is there any way to extend the analogy so that it will be so),

$$\alpha(\mu, \Delta[\kappa{:}i]) \wedge \mu \in \Delta[\kappa{:}i] \wedge \neg(i = \lambda) \wedge \neg\alpha(\mu, \Delta[i+1]) \rightarrow \alpha(\Delta[i+1], \Delta[\kappa{:}i+1])$$

is left as a precondition.

---

[6] We use (from lowest to highest precedence) $\rightarrow$ for implication, $\wedge$ for conjunction, and $\neg$ for negation.

[7] Note the importance of not having simplified $\neg(\Delta[i+1] < \mu)$ to $\Delta[i+1] \geq \mu$ in the verification condition so as not to lose sight of the symbols as they appear in the code. In general, adding a transformation necessitates regenerating and checking anew all verification conditions covering paths containing a newly transformed symbol.

This precondition, and the previous two, $\kappa \leq \lambda$ and $\alpha(\Delta[\kappa], \Delta[\kappa])$, are sufficient to ensure correctness. Actually, they can be simplified to some extent, as long as the new conditions are satisfied by the given concrete programs. For example, we can replace the expression $\Delta[\kappa]$ in $\alpha(\Delta[\kappa], \Delta[\kappa])$ by (the universally quantified) u and require that

$$\alpha(u, u)$$

hold for all u, that is, α must be reflexive. Once we assume that α is reflexive, the new precondition can be simplified to

$$\alpha(\mu, \Delta[\kappa:i]) \wedge \mu \in \Delta[\kappa:i] \wedge \neg(i = \lambda) \wedge \neg\alpha(\mu, \Delta[i + 1]) \rightarrow \alpha(\Delta[i + 1], \Delta[\kappa:i]),$$

since $\alpha(\Delta[i + 1], \Delta[i + 1])$ must hold. This, in turn, can be generalized to

$$\alpha(w, u) \wedge \neg\alpha(w, v) \rightarrow \alpha(v, u)$$

by deleting the premises, $\mu \in \Delta[\kappa:i]$ and $\neg(i = \lambda)$, which do not involve α, and by replacing the subterms that appear on both sides of the implication with (universally quantified) variables u, v, and w. Note that this precondition holds when α is a transitive total relation.

The effect of these "simplifications" is to strengthen the preconditions: for example, α now needs to be reflexive for all values u, not just for $\Delta[\kappa]$. Although the stronger conditions do hold for both P_2 and Q_2, this may mean that an otherwise valid instantiation will be rejected. Had the programmer supplied the information that the program was based on the reflexivity of $\leq$, taking reflexivity of α as a precondition would have been more justified. But even without such information, it may pay to make simplifying assumptions, so that proofs will be easier. In that sense, this (optional) step is akin to the "generalization" heuristic in theorem proving (see [3, 10]).

Applying the complete abstraction mapping

$$0 \Rightarrow \kappa$$
$$n \Rightarrow \lambda$$
$$u \leq v \Rightarrow \alpha(u, v)$$
$$A \Rightarrow \Delta$$
$$z \Rightarrow \mu$$
$$u < v \Rightarrow \neg\alpha(v, u)$$

to program P_2, our final version of the schema is

```
S₂: begin comment extremum schema
  type i, κ, λ ∈ Z, μ ∈ Γ, Δ ∈ [κ:λ] → Γ, α ∈ Γ × Γ → B
  B₂: assert κ ≤ λ, α(μ, u), α(w, u) ∧ ¬α(w, v) → α(v, u)
  (μ, i) := (Δ[κ], κ)
  loop L₂: assert α(μ, Δ[κ:i]), μ ∈ Δ[κ:i]
    until i = λ
    i := i + 1
    if ¬α(μ, Δ[i]) then μ := Δ[i] fi
  repeat
  E₂: assert α(μ, Δ[κ:λ]), μ ∈ Δ[κ:λ]
end
```

Now that we have verified the conditions for each of the paths in the program, the suggestions have been replaced by assertions. The (simplified) preconditions

are given in the input assertion; any instantiation that satisfies them is guaranteed to yield a correct program. Of course, the predicate α that appears in the schema should be instantiated to a primitive predicate of the target language, or else it will need to be replaced for the program to be executable. Likewise, the constants Δ, κ, and λ must be replaced with primitives, or code must be prepended to set them.

Note that applying the corresponding abstraction mapping to Q_2, and going through the same steps as we did for P_2, results in an alternative schema. It differs from the schema S_2 only superficially, in that the search of the range $[\kappa, \lambda]$ proceeds from end to beginning, rather than from beginning to end. The form of programs and specifications can affect the abstraction process in other ways too. Were the two programs each specified in a different manner, we would first have to find equivalent, similar specifications before proceeding. And even if the specifications were similar, any true analogy between them may be disguised.[8]

Programs for finding the position or value of the minimum or maximum of an array (or of other functions with integer domain) are valid instantiations of this schema. For instance, say we want to find the position m of the minimum of some real function f for the first 50 odd integers. Comparing this goal,

```
R₂: begin comment function minimum specification
  type m ∈ N, f ∈ N → R
  achieve (∀u ∈ [1:100]) [odd(u) → f(m) ≤ f(u)] varying m
end
```

(meaning that m should be such that $f(m)$ is not greater than $f(u)$ for every integer u in the range [1:100] that is odd), with the (first conjunct of the) abstract output specification of the schema

assert $\alpha(\mu, \Delta[\kappa:\lambda])$

that is,

assert $(\forall u \in [\kappa:\lambda])\alpha(\mu, \Delta[u])$

suggests the (imitating) mappings

$$\kappa \Rightarrow 1$$
$$\lambda \Rightarrow 100$$
$$\alpha(\mu, \Delta[u]) \Rightarrow odd(u) \rightarrow f(m) \leq f(u).$$

The last of these mappings can be accomplished by the (projecting and imitating) mappings

$$\mu \Rightarrow m$$
$$\Delta[u] \Rightarrow u$$
$$\alpha(v, w) \Rightarrow odd(w) \rightarrow f(v) \leq f(w).$$

---

[8] Had P_2 and Q_2, for example, been specified to achieve $z = \min|A[0:n]|$ and $B[p] = \max|B[b:c]|$, respectively, then the analogy between $\leq$ and $\geq$ would have remained to be discovered from the analysis of the verification conditions. Had the specifications been $(\forall u \in \mathbf{Z}) (0 \leq u \leq n \rightarrow z \leq A[u])$ and $(\forall u \in \mathbf{Z}) (a \leq u \leq b \rightarrow B[p] \geq B[u])$, then the analogy between $\leq$ and $\geq$ would have to be restrained to apply to only some occurrences of $\leq$. To determine which occurrences in the program ought to be transformed would then require more detailed analysis.

Applying this instantiation mapping to the preconditions

$$\kappa \le \lambda$$
$$\alpha(u, u)$$
$$\alpha(w, u) \wedge \neg\alpha(w, v) \rightarrow \alpha(v, u)$$

yields

$$1 \le 100$$
$$odd(u) \rightarrow f(u) \le f(u)$$
$$[odd(u) \rightarrow f(w) \le f(u)] \wedge \neg[odd(v) \rightarrow f(w) \le f(v)] \rightarrow [odd(u) \rightarrow f(v) \le f(u)].$$

The first condition is obviously true; the second holds since ≤ is reflexive; the last follows from transitivity. Checking types reveals that i must be restricted to $\mathbf{N}$, since it is assigned to the nonnegative variable m. This poses no problem since i remains in the range [1:100]. Applying the instantiation mapping to the schema yields the program:

R_2: **begin comment** *function minimum program*
  type $i, m \in \mathbf{N}, f \in \mathbf{N} \to \mathbf{R}$
  B_2: **assert true**
   $(m, i) := (1, 1)$
  loop L_2: **assert** $(\forall u \in [1:i]) (odd(u) \rightarrow f(m) \le f(u))$
   until $i = 100$
    $i := i + 1$
   if $odd(i) \wedge f(m) > f(i)$ **then** $m := i$ **fi**
  repeat
  E_2: **assert** $(\forall u \in [1:100]) (odd(u) \rightarrow f(m) \le f(u))$
  end

where the transformed conditional test $\neg(odd(i) \rightarrow f(m) \le f(i))$ simplified to $odd(i) \wedge f(m) > f(i)$. Since the preconditions as well as the type constraints are satisfied by the instantiation, this program is guaranteed to be correct. Further improvements to the instantiated program could be made (e.g., incrementing i by two with each iteration) by a straightforward series of correctness-preserving program transformations.[9]

4. PROGRAM TRANSFORMATIONS

Designing and applying program transformations also fall into the abstraction/instantiation paradigm. The same methodology can be used for this purpose as was used in the previous section for designing and applying program schemata. For example, to design a recursion-elimination transformation (such as in [8, 20, 22, 68]), we could first write, and verify, iterative versions of several recursive programs; then, by abstracting those programs, and their proofs, a general recursion-to-iteration transformation schema may be obtained. As we shall see, very little information is gleaned just by a comparison of output specifications; instead, most of the analogy needs to be derived from the programs themselves.

Consider the recursive program

$P_3^*(m, n)$: **begin comment** *recursive factorial program*
  type $m, n \in \mathbf{N}$
  B_3^*: **assert true**
  if $n = 0$ **then** $m := 1$
        else $P_3^*(m, n - 1)$
           $m := m \cdot n$ **fi**
  E_3^*: **assert** $m = n!$
  end

for computing factorials. It can be transformed into the iterative program

P_3: **begin comment** *iterative factorial program*
  type $m, n, y \in \mathbf{N}$
  B_3: **assert true**
   $(m, y) := (1, n)$
  loop L_3: **assert** $m \cdot y! = n!$
   until $y = 0$
    $(m, y) := (m \cdot y, y - 1)$
  repeat
  E_3: **assert** $m = n!$
  end

In a similar manner, recursion may be eliminated from the program

$Q_3^*(k, s)$: **begin comment** *recursive summation program*
  type $k, l \in \mathbf{Z}, s \in \mathbf{R}, f \in \mathbf{Z} \to \mathbf{R}$
  B_3^*: **assert** $k \le l$
  if $k = l + 1$ **then** $s := 0$
          else $Q_3^*(k + 1, s)$
             $s := s + f(k)$ **fi**
  E_3^*: **assert** $s = \sum_{i=k}^{l} f(i)$
  end

for summing a function f over the range $k, k + 1, \ldots, l$, giving

Q_3: **begin comment** *iterative summation program*
  type $k, l, j \in \mathbf{Z}, s \in \mathbf{R}, f \in \mathbf{Z} \to \mathbf{R}$
  B_3: **assert** $k \le l$
   $(s, j) := (0, k)$
  loop L_3: **assert** $s = \sum_{i=k}^{j-1} f(i)$
   until $j = l + 1$
    $(s, j) := (s + f(j), j + 1)$
  repeat
  E_3: **assert** $s = \sum_{i=k}^{l} f(i)$
  end

What we would like to do is to use these four programs to design a program transformation schema of the form

S^*: recursive schema
S: iterative schema

meaning that a (correct) recursive program of form S^* may be replaced by the corresponding iterative program S, provided the preconditions of S are satisfied. In this case our object is to derive a schema for computing recursive functions

---

[9] In fact, applying the schema to the alternative specification $(\forall u \in [1:50]) f(m) \le f(2 \cdot u - 1)$ would have led immediately to a program with half the loop iterations.
[10] A formula of the form $(\forall x, y)[g(y) = f(x) \wedge \alpha(f(x), y) \rightarrow \beta(f(x), y)]$, where the only occurrences of x in α and β are within the same expression $f(x)$, is equivalent to $(\forall y)[\alpha(g(y), y) \rightarrow \beta(g(y), y)]$.

that are like factorial and summation. To that end, we begin with a comparison of the output specifications of the two programs:

$$m = n! \Leftrightarrow s = \sum_{i=k}^{l} f(i).$$

One possible analogy between them is

$$m \Leftrightarrow s$$
$$n \Leftrightarrow k$$
$$u! \Leftrightarrow \sum_{i=u}^{l} f(i).$$

The two output variables m (of type $\mathbf{N}$) and s (of type $\mathbf{R}$) generalize to the abstract output variable ζ (of type $\mathbf{R}$); the input variables n (of type $\mathbf{N}$) and k (of type $\mathbf{Z}$) generalize to v (of type $\mathbf{Z}$); the two functions $u!$ (of type $\mathbf{N} \to \mathbf{N}$) and $\sum_{i=u}^{l} f(i)$ (of type $\mathbf{Z} \to \mathbf{R}$) generalize to an abstract function variable $\psi(u)$ (of type $\mathbf{Z} \to \mathbf{R}$). Accordingly, the abstraction mappings are

$$m \Rightarrow \zeta \Leftarrow s$$
$$n \Rightarrow v \Leftarrow k$$
$$u! \Rightarrow \psi(u) \Leftarrow \sum_{i=u}^{l} f(i),$$

and the abstracted output specification is

suggest $\zeta = \psi(v)$.

So far, this analogy does not supply much information; it can, however, be extended by comparing the two recursive programs

$$P_3^* \Leftrightarrow Q_3^*.$$

(Later, we will concentrate on the iterative versions and see what conditions must be placed on the underlying recursive functions for the program transformation to be valid.) The conditional tests $n = 0$ of P_3^* and $k = l + 1$ of Q_3^*, after applying the abstraction mappings $n \Rightarrow v$ and $k \Rightarrow v$, respectively, provide the analogy

$$v = 0 \Leftrightarrow v = l + 1.$$

This suggests adding

$$0 \Rightarrow \theta \Leftarrow l + 1$$

to the abstraction mapping (where θ is of type $\mathbf{Z}$ as is $l + 1$); the base cases $m := 1$ and $s := 0$ map to

$$\zeta := 1 \Leftrightarrow \zeta := 0$$

and add

$$1 \Rightarrow \omega \Leftarrow 0$$

(where ω is of type $\mathbf{R}$, like s); the recursive calls $P_3^*(m, n - 1)$ and $Q_3^*(k + 1, s)$ abstract to

$$P_3^*(\zeta, v - 1) \Leftrightarrow Q_3^*(v + 1, \zeta)$$

and add

$$P_3^*(u, v) \Rightarrow S^*(u, v) \Leftarrow Q_3^*(v, u)$$
$$u - 1 \Rightarrow \delta(u) \Leftarrow u + 1$$

(making δ of type $\mathbf{Z} \to \mathbf{Z}$; and, lastly, the abstracted else-branch assignments

$$\zeta := \zeta \cdot v \Leftrightarrow \zeta := \zeta + f(v)$$

suggest (among other possibilities)

$$u \cdot v \Rightarrow \rho(u, v) \Leftarrow u + v$$
$$v \Rightarrow \sigma(v) \Leftarrow f(v)$$

(with ρ of type $\mathbf{R} \times \mathbf{R} \to \mathbf{R}$, like $+$, and σ of type $\mathbf{Z} \to \mathbf{R}$, like f). Note that the two kinds of $+$ in Q_3^* (integer increment and real addition) have been abstracted to two different functions (δ and ρ, respectively).

Were a programmer to supply additional information indicating which parts of the recursive programs led to which parts of the iterative programs, then these transformations could be localized to the relevant parts only. In particular, it would be absurd to apply the abstraction mapping $v \Rightarrow \sigma(v)$ throughout P_3^*; only those occurrences of expressions in P_3^* that can be found to correspond to occurrences of $f(v)$ in Q_3^* ought to be transformed.

Applying the mapping

$$s \Rightarrow \zeta$$
$$k \Rightarrow v$$
$$\sum_{i=u}^{l} f(i) \Rightarrow \psi(u)$$
$$l + 1 \Rightarrow \theta$$
$$0 \Rightarrow \omega$$
$$u + 1 \Rightarrow \delta(u)$$
$$u + v \Rightarrow \rho(u, v)$$
$$f(v) \Rightarrow \sigma(v)$$

to the recursive version Q_3^* of summation, yields the recursive schema

```
S_3*(v, ζ): begin comment recursive schema
  type v, θ ∈ Z, ω, ζ ∈ R, ψ, σ ∈ Z → R, δ ∈ Z → Z, ρ ∈ R × R → R
  B_3*: assert v ≤ θ
  if v = θ then ζ := ω
    else S_3*(δ(v), ζ)
      ζ := ρ(ζ, σ(v)) fi
  E_3*: assert ζ = ψ(v)
end
```

Applying the same mapping to the iterative version Q_3 yields the schema body

```
(ζ, j) := (ω, v)
loop L_3: suggest ζ = ∑_{i=v}^{j-1} σ(i)
  until j = θ
  (ζ, j) := (ρ(ζ, σ(j)), δ(j))
  repeat
```

There is, however, a serious problem with the correctness conditions for this iterative schema which shows up in the unprovable loop invariant

L_3: suggest $\zeta = \sum_{i=v}^{j-1} \sigma(i)$.

Were we given a detailed derivation of the summation program, we could follow it and determine that this form of the invariant depends on unstated properties of sums. Even without a derivation history, we can proceed by asking whether the abstracted loop invariant of the iterative factorial program is perhaps an invariant of the schema derived from the summation program. We also look at the programs themselves, in search of additional aspects of the analogy between P_3 and Q_3; the (abstracted) loop exit tests of the two iterative programs

$$y = \theta \Leftrightarrow j = \theta$$

suggest

$$y \Rightarrow \xi \Leftarrow j.$$

Applying the extended abstraction mapping

$$m \Rightarrow \zeta$$
$$n \Rightarrow v$$
$$u! \Rightarrow \psi(u)$$
$$0 \Rightarrow \theta$$
$$1 \Rightarrow \omega$$
$$u - 1 \Rightarrow \delta(u)$$
$$u \cdot v \Rightarrow \rho(u, v)$$
$$y \Rightarrow \xi$$

for P_3 to its invariant

L_3: assert $m \cdot y! = n!$

(and avoiding applying the overzealous abstraction $v \Rightarrow \sigma(v)$), yields

L_3: suggest $\rho(\zeta, \psi(\xi)) = \psi(v)$.

With this as the suggested loop invariant, we proceed to examine the verification conditions of the revised schema

S_3: **begin comment** *abstracted summation program*
type $v, \theta, \xi \in \mathbf{Z}, \zeta, \varsigma \in \mathbf{R}, \sigma, \psi \in \mathbf{Z} \to \mathbf{R}, \delta \in \mathbf{Z} \to \mathbf{Z}, \rho \in \mathbf{R} \times \mathbf{R} \to \mathbf{R}$
B_3: **suggest** $v \le \theta$
$(\zeta, \xi) := (\omega, v)$
loop L_3: **suggest** $\rho(\zeta, \psi(\xi)) = \psi(v)$
until $\xi = \theta$
$(\zeta, \xi) := (\rho(\zeta, \sigma(\xi)), \delta(\xi))$
repeat
E_3: **suggest** $\zeta = \psi(v)$
end

The type conditions are all satisfied. The initialization condition is

assert $v \le \theta$
suggest $\rho(\omega, \psi(v)) = \psi(v)$.

Making the more general

$$\rho(\omega, u) = u$$

into a precondition will insure the correctness of the initialization path. The loop-exit verification condition is

assert $\rho(\zeta, \psi(\xi)) = \psi(v), \xi = \theta$
suggest $\xi = \psi(v)$.

We replace this condition (i.e., $\rho(\zeta, \psi(\xi)) = \psi(v) \wedge \xi = \theta \to \zeta = \psi(v)$) with the equivalent[10]

$$\rho(u, \psi(\theta)) = u.$$

If we take into consideration the correctness condition $\omega = \psi(\theta)$ of the recursive schema S_3^*, then this precondition for the iterative schema can be simplified to $\rho(u, \omega) = u$. For the loop-body path, we have the condition

assert $\rho(\zeta, \psi(\xi)) = \psi(v), \neg(\xi = \theta)$
suggest $\rho(\rho(\zeta, \sigma(\xi)), \psi(\delta(\xi))) = \psi(v)$,

for which we use the equivalent precondition[10]

$$x \ne \theta \to \rho(z, \psi(x)) = \rho(z, \sigma(x)), \psi(\delta(x))).$$

Using the condition $x \ne \theta \to \rho(\psi(\delta(x)), \sigma(x)) = \psi(x)$ for correctness of the recursive schema, we can replace the precondition with

$$x \ne \theta \to \rho(z, \rho(\psi(\delta(x)), \sigma(x))) = \rho(z, \sigma(x), \psi(\delta(x))).$$

This, in turn, may be generalized to

$$\rho(u, \rho(v, w)) = \rho(\rho(u, w), v).$$

Finally, the verification condition for the termination of the abstracted program is

$$(\exists u \in \mathbf{N}) \delta^u(v) = \theta,$$

which must be true for the recursive schema to be terminating. Collecting all the preconditions, we obtain the schema

S_3: **begin comment** *associative recursion schema*
type $v, \theta, \xi \in \mathbf{Z}, \zeta, \varsigma \in \mathbf{R}, \sigma, \psi \in \mathbf{Z} \to \mathbf{R}, \delta \in \mathbf{Z} \to \mathbf{Z}, \rho \in \mathbf{R} \times \mathbf{R} \to \mathbf{R}$
B_3: **assert** $\rho(\omega, u) = u, \rho(u, \omega) = u, \rho(u, \rho(v, w)) = \rho(\rho(u, w), v)$
$(\exists u \in \mathbf{N}) \delta^u(v) = \theta$
$(\zeta, \xi) := (\omega, v)$
loop L_3: **assert** $\rho(\zeta, \psi(\xi)) = \psi(v)$
until $\xi = \theta$
$(\zeta, \xi) := (\rho(\zeta, \sigma(\xi)), \delta(\xi))$
repeat
E_3: **assert** $\zeta = \psi(v)$
end

In this manner we have obtained a general schema for computing a function $\psi(v)$. It applies to recursive programs of the form S_3^* that compute a function $\psi(x)$, such that $\psi(x) = \rho(x, \psi(\delta(x)))$ when x is not θ, and $\omega = \psi(\theta)$ is an identity element of the associative and commutative function ρ. This schema is similar to one of the recursion-to-iteration transformations in [22].

To see how the schematic transformation

> S_3^*: *recursion schema*
> S_3: *associative recursion schema*

may be applied to another problem, consider the recursive program

$R_3^*(n, z)$: **begin comment** *recursive minimum program*
  type $n \in \mathbf{N}$, $z \in \mathbf{R}$, $A \in [1:n] \to \mathbf{R}$
  B_3^*: **assert true**
  if $n = 0$ **then** $z := \infty$
      else $R_3^*(n - 1, z)$
          $z := \min(z, A[n])$ **fi**
  E_3^*: **assert** $z = \min\{A[1:n]\}$
end

for finding the minimum of an array of real numbers, where ∞ is (a "real" number) greater than "any" array value (so that it serves as the minimum of an empty array), and $\min(u, v)$ is a primitive binary operator (as opposed to $\min\{U\}$ which applies to arrays and is used solely for specification purposes). We wish to transform this program into an iterative one that finds the value of the smallest element.

An initial comparison of this program's output specification with the specification $\zeta = \psi(v)$ of our schema, suggests the possible instantiation

$$\psi(u) \Rightarrow \min\{A[1:u]\}$$
$$\zeta \Rightarrow z$$
$$v \Rightarrow n.$$

A comparison of R_3^* with the recursive pattern S_3^* suggests the added instantiations

$$\theta \Rightarrow 0$$
$$\omega \Rightarrow \infty$$
$$\delta(u) \Rightarrow u - 1$$
$$\rho(u, v) \Rightarrow \min(u, v)$$
$$\sigma(v) \Rightarrow A[v].$$

It remains to check the validity of the type constraints and preconditions. The instantiated type constraints

type $n, 0, \xi \in \mathbf{Z}$, $z, \infty \in \mathbf{R}$, $A \in \mathbf{Z} \to \mathbf{R}$, $\cdot - 1 \in \mathbf{Z} \to \mathbf{Z}$, $\min \in \mathbf{R} \times \mathbf{R} \to \mathbf{R}$

are satisfied. Applying the instantiation mapping to the four preconditions gives

$$\min(\infty, u) = u$$
$$\min(u, \infty) = u$$
$$\min(u, \min(v, w)) = \min(\min(u, w), v)$$
$$(\exists u \in \mathbf{N})\ n - u = 0.$$

Since they are all true, the following instantiation of S_3 is a correct iterative program for array minimum:

R_3: **begin comment** *iterative minimum program*
  type $n, \xi \in \mathbf{N}$, $z \in \mathbf{R}$, $z \in \mathbf{R}$, $A \in [1:n] \to \mathbf{R}$
  B_3: **assert true**
  $(z, \xi) := (\infty, n)$
  loop L_3: **assert** $\min(z, \min\{A[1:\xi]\}) = \min\{A[1:n]\}$
      until $\xi = 0$
      $(z, \xi) := (\min(z, A[\xi]), \xi - 1)$
      repeat
  E_3: **assert** $z = \min\{A[1:n]\}$
end

5. DISCUSSION

We have demonstrated a methodology for deriving an abstract schema from a given set of concrete programs. Once derived, the schema may be applied to solve new problems by instantiating the abstract entities of the schema with concrete elements from the problem domain. We have also seen how this methodology can be used to derive correctness-preserving program transformations and to guide their application.

Abstraction and instantiation complement other methods of program transformation. When faced with the task of developing a new program (or subprogram) to meet a set of specifications, a programmer ought to first search for an applicable schema. After instantiating that schema appropriately, various other transformations may be necessary to satisfy remaining specifications or increase efficiency. When no applicable schema can be found, one might still be able to find a program solving an analogous problem, and modify it (see [24, 26] and [66]). Those two programs together could then be used to formulate a schema for future use. Using a schema has the advantage over modifying a related program in that correctness is ensured by satisfying preconditions. The extraction of appropriate preconditions, however, is what makes abstraction more complex a task than either modification or instantiation.

The methods that we have described appear amenable to automation. Some steps we took in our examples were more intuitively obvious than others, and more easily implementable. Other steps would presumably require user interaction. One major hurdle is in deciding among alternative routes to follow at each point in the process. Thus, we envision the possibility of such methods being embedded in semiautomated program development environments in which the system would perform straightforward steps in a consistent manner, while the human would be left to guide the machine in the more creative steps. Though the illustrations we have provided are relatively small and limited in scope, "top-down programming" methodology favors small, easily comprehensible modules, each of which should be amenable to the kind of manipulations we have presented. In particular, general-purpose schemata should each embody only one programming technique. The larger a program, the more convoluted it is, or the deeper the ideas that went into it, the more difficult it would be—for human or machine—to reason about it.

The abstraction process begins with a set of programs. How many programs? On the one hand, it is conceivable that one might abstract a single program by somehow choosing specification symbols to be abstracted and proceeding to examine the consequences. (This is the approach taken, for example, in [25, 65].) This would be better than attempting to formulate a schema from scratch, since the program (with its proof) provides a means of specifying necessary properties of the abstract objects. On the other hand, using more programs reduces arbitrariness by insisting that only analogous parts be abstracted, on the presumption that they play similar roles in the different programs. It is the analogy, then, that suggests which "parameters" of a program are worthy of generalization. If additional programs become available, then there would be no reason not to attempt to generalize the derived schemata even more. By the same token, two schemata could themselves be abstracted. In such a manner, hierarchies of schemata would be created, each more abstract than its predecessors, as, for example, "binary search" is an instance of a more general "divide and conquer" strategem. The related question of which programs are *worthy* of abstraction is difficult to answer, let alone automate! One criterion might be the frequency with which a program is modified for tasks other than that which it was originally intended for. That is, the more a program is "cannibalized," the more worthy its skeleton of "immortalization." How many schemata are in the typical programmer's repertoire is difficult to guess.

As we have seen, there are some problems inherent in the use of analogies for program abstraction and instantiation. These include "hidden" analogies, "misleading" analogies, "incomplete" analogies, and "overzealous" analogies. Hidden analogies arise when given specifications (of existing programs in the case of abstraction, or of an abstract schema and concrete problem in the case of instantiation) that are to be compared with one another have little syntactically in common. It takes only small variations to make semantically similar objects appear unrelated. Since the pattern-matching ideas that we have employed are syntax-based, when the specifications are not syntactically similar, the underlying analogy would be disguised. In such a situation, before an analogy could be found, it would be necessary to rephrase the specifications in an equivalent manner, one that brings out the similarities. This is clearly a difficult problem in its own right; in general some form of "means-end" analysis [57] seems appropriate.

At the opposite extreme, a syntactic analogy may be misleading. The same symbol may appear in the specifications of two programs, yet play nonanalogous roles in them. Two programs might even have the exact same specifications, but employ totally different methods of solution. Situations such as these would be detected in the course of analyzing the correctness conditions for the abstracted programs. We have also seen how the proof of correctness of a program can be used to help avoid overzealously applying transformations to unrelated parts of a program, to complete an analogy between two programs (only part of which was found by a comparison of specifications), and to derive preconditions for applicability of a schema. For all these reasons, it is important that programs be accompanied by proofs, as would be the case if programs were developed formally from specifications, or if invariants were extracted from existing programs. It may be that logic-based programming languages (see [46]) will provide a relatively convenient environment for this kind of research. The identity of specification

and programming language, and the potential availability of suitable general-purpose theorem-provers, should aid the design of program-manipulation systems.

ACKNOWLEDGMENTS

I sincerely thank Zohar Manna and Richard Waldinger for their guidance in the early stages of this research, and also the referees for their perseverance.

REFERENCES

1. ALLEN, F. E., AND COCKE, J. A catalogue of optimizing transformations. In *Design and Optimization of Compilers*, R. Rustin, Ed., Prentice-Hall, Englewood Cliffs, N.J., 1972, 1–30.
2. ARSAC, J. J. Syntactic source to source transforms and program manipulation. *Commun. ACM 22*, 1 (Jan. 1979), 43–54.
3. AUBIN, R. Some generalization heuristics in proofs by induction. In *Proceedings IRIA Symposium on Proving and Improving Programs* (Arc-et-Senans, France, July 1975), 197–208.
4. BACK, R. J. R., MANILLA, H., AND RAIHA, K. J. Derivation of efficient dag marking algorithms. In *Proceedings 10th ACM Symposium on Principles of Programming Languages* (Austin, Tex., Jan. 1983), 20–27.
5. BALZER, R. M. Transformational implementation: An example. *IEEE Trans. Softw. Eng. SE-7*, 1 (Jan. 1981), 3–14.
6. BARSTOW, D. R. *Knowledge-Based Program Construction*. Elsevier North-Holland, New York, 1979.
7. BAUER, F. L. Programming as an evolutionary process. In *Proceedings 2nd International Conference on Software Engineering* (San Francisco, Oct. 1976), 223–234.
8. BIRD, R. S. Notes on recursion removal. *Commun. ACM 20*, 6 (June 1977), 434–439.
9. BLIKLE, A. Towards mathematical structured programming. In *Formal Descriptions of Programming Concepts*, E. J. Neuhold, Ed., North-Holland, Amsterdam, 1978, 9.1–9.19.
10. BOYER, R. S., AND MOORE, J. S. Proving theorems about LISP functions. *J. ACM 22*, 1 (Jan. 1975), 129–144.
11. BROTSKY, D. Program understanding through cliche recognition. Working Paper 224, Artificial Intelligence Laboratory, MIT, Cambridge, Dec. 1981.
12. BROWN, F. M., AND TÄRNLUND, S. A. Inductive reasoning on recursive equations. *Artif. Intell. 12*, 3 (Nov. 1979), 207–229.
13. BROWN, R. H. Reasoning by analogy. Working Paper 132, Artificial Intelligence Laboratory, MIT, Cambridge, Oct. 1976.
14. BUNDY, A., AND WELHAM, B. Using meta-level inference for selective application of multiple rewrite sets in algebraic manipulation. *Artif. Intell. 16*, 2 (1981), 189–212.
15. BURSTEIN, M. H. Concept formation by incremental reasoning and debugging. In *Proceedings 2nd International Workshop on Machine Learning* (Monticello, Ill., June 1983), 19–25.
16. CARBONELL, J. G. Derivational analogy in problem solving and knowledge acquisition. In *Proceedings 2nd International Workshop on Machine Learning* (Monticello, Ill., June 1983), 12–18.
17. CARBONELL, J. G. Learning by analogy: Formulating and generalizing plans from past experience. In *Machine Learning, An Artificial Intelligence Approach*, R. S. Michalski, J. G. Carbonell, and T. M. Mitchell, Eds., Tioga, Palo Alto, Calif., 1983, 137–162.
18. CHEN, D. T. W., AND FINDLER, N. V. Toward analogical reasoning in problem solving by computers. Tech. Rep. 115, Dept. of Computer Science, SUNY, Buffalo, Dec. 1976.
19. CONWAY, R., AND GRIES, D. *An Introduction to Programming: A Structured Approach*. 2nd ed., Winthrop, Cambridge, Mass., 1975.
20. COOPER, D. C. The equivalence of certain computations. *Computer J. 9* (1966), 45–52.
21. DARLINGTON, J. A synthesis of several sorting algorithms. *Acta Inf. 11*, 1 (1978), 1–30.
22. DARLINGTON, J., AND BURSTALL, R. M. A system which automatically improves programs. *Acta Inf. 6*, 1 (Mar. 1976), 41–60.
23. DECHTER, R., AND PEARL, J. A problem simplification approach that generates heuristics for

constraint satisfaction problems. In *Machine Intelligence 11*, D. Michie, J. E. Hayes, and J. Richards, Eds., 1985 (to appear).

24. DERSHOWITZ, N. *The Evolution of Programs*. Birkhäuser, Boston, 1983.

25. DERSHOWITZ, N., AND MANNA, Z. On automating structured programming. In *Proceedings IRIA Symposium on Proving and Improving Programs*. (Arc-et-Senans, France, July 1975), 167–193.

26. DERSHOWITZ, N., AND MANNA, Z. The evolution of programs: Automatic program modification. *IEEE Trans. Softw. Eng. SE-3*, 6 (Nov. 1977), 377–385.

27. DEUSSEN, P. One abstract accepting algorithm for all kinds of parsers. In *Proceedings 6th EATCS International Colloquium on Automata, Languages, and Programming* (Graz, Austria, July 1979), 203–217.

28. DIJKSTRA, E. W. Notes on structured programming. In *Structured Programming*, O. J. Dahl, E. W. Dijkstra, and C. A. R. Hoare, Eds., Academic Press, London, 1972.

29. DIJKSTRA, E. W. *A Discipline of Programming*. Prentice Hall, Englewood Cliffs, N.J., 1976.

30. DIJKSTRA, E. W. Why naive program transformation systems are unlikely to work. In *Selected Writings on Computing: A Personal Perspective*, Springer, Berlin, 1982, 324–328.

31. DUNCAN, A. G., AND YELOWITZ, L. Studies in abstract/concrete mappings in proving algorithm correctness. In *Proceedings 6th EATCS International Colloquium on Automata, Languages, and Programming* (Graz, Austria, July 1979), 218–229.

32. EGAN, D. E., AND GREEN, J. G. Theory of rule induction. In *Knowledge and Cognition*, L. Gregg, Ed., Lawrence Erlbaum, Hillsdale, N.J., 1973.

33. EVANS, T. G. A program for the solution of geometric-analogy intelligence test questions. In *Semantic Information Processing*, M. L. Minsky, Ed., MIT Press, Cambridge, Mass., 1968, 271–353.

34. FIKES, R. E., HART, P. E., AND NILSSON, N. J. Learning and executing generalized robot plans. *Artif. Intell 3*, 4 (Winter 1972), 251–288.

35. FLOYD, R. W. Toward interactive design of correct programs. In *Proceedings Information Processing Congress* (Ljubljana, Yugoslavia, Aug. 1971), 7–10.

36. GERHART, S. L. Correctness-preserving program transformations. In *Proceedings 2nd ACM Symposium on Principles of Programming Languages* (Palo Alto, Calif., Jan. 1975), 54–66.

37. GERHART, S. L. Knowledge about programs: A model and case study. In *Proceedings International Conference on Reliable Software* (Los Angeles, Calif., Apr. 1975), 88–95.

38. GERHART, S. L., AND YELOWITZ, L. Control structure abstractions of the backtracking programming technique. *IEEE Trans. Softw. Eng. SE-2*, 4 (Dec. 1976), 285–292.

39. HESSE, M. *Models and Analogies in Science*. University of Notre Dame Press, Notre Dame, Ind., 1966.

40. HUET, G., AND LANG, B. Proving and applying program transformations expressed with second-order patterns. *Acta Inf. 11* (1978), 31–55.

41. KATZ, S., AND MANNA, Z. Logical analysis of programs. *Commun. ACM 19*, 4 (Apr. 1976), 188–206.

42. KIEBURTZ, R., AND SHULTIS, J. Transformation of FP program schemas. In *Proceedings Conference on Functional Programming Languages and Computer Architecture*. (Portsmouth, Maine, 1981), 41–48.

43. KIRCHNER, C., KIRCHNER, H., AND JOUANNAUD, J. P. Algebraic manipulations as a unification and matching strategy for linear equations in signed binary trees. In *Proceedings 7th International Joint Conference on Artificial Intelligence* (Vancouver, B.C., Aug. 1981), 1016–1023.

44. KLING, R. E. A paradigm for reasoning by analogy. *Artif. Intell. 2* (1971), 147–178.

45. KNUTH, D. E. Structured programming with **go to** statements. *ACM Comput. Surv. 6*, 4 (Dec. 1974), 261–301.

46. KOWALSKI, R. A. *Logic for Problem Solving*. North-Holland, Amsterdam, 1979.

47. LEE, S., DE ROEVER, W. P., AND GERHART, S. L. The evolution of list-copying algorithms. In *Proceedings 6th ACM Symposium on Principles of Programming Languages* (San Antonio, Tex., Jan. 1979), 53–67.

48. LOVEMAN, D. B. Program improvement by source-to-source transformation. *J. ACM 24*, 1 (Jan. 1977), 121–145.

49. MCDERMOTT, J. Learning to use analogies. In *Proceedings 6th International Joint Conference on Artificial Intelligence* (Tokyo, Aug. 1979), 568–576.

50. MANNA, Z., AND WALDINGER, R. J. Knowledge and reasoning in program synthesis. *Artif. Intell. 6*, 2 (Summer 1975), 175–208.

51. MISRA, J. An approach to formal definitions and proofs of programming principles. *IEEE Trans. Softw. Eng. SE-4*, 5 (Sept. 1978), 410–413.

52. MOORE, J. A., AND NEWELL, A. How can MERLIN understand? In *Knowledge and Cognition*, L. Gregg, Ed., Lawrence Erlbaum, Hillsdale, N.J., 1973.

53. MOSTOW, J. Toward better models of the design process. *AI Mag. 6*, 1 (Spring 1985), 44–57.

54. MUNYER, J. C. Analogy as a heuristic for mechanical theorem-proving. In *Collected Abstracts of the Workshop on Automated Deduction*, Cambridge, Mass., Aug. 1977.

55. MURALIDHARAN, M. N. A methodology for algorithm development through schema transformations. Ph.D. dissertation, Computer Science Program, Indian Institute of Technology, Kanpur, India, Jan. 1982.

56. NAU, D. S., KUMAR, V., AND KANAL, L. General branch-and-bound, and its relation to A* and AO*. *Artif. Intell. 23*, 1 (May 1984), 29–58.

57. NEWELL, A., AND SIMON, H. A. *Human Problem Solving*. Prentice-Hall, Englewood Cliffs, N.J., 1972.

58. PARTSCH, H., AND STEINBRÜGGEN, R. Program transformation systems. *ACM Comput. Surv. 15*, 3 (Sept. 1983), 199–236.

59. PLAISTED, D. A. Theorem proving with abstraction. *Artif. Intell. 16*, 1 (1981), 47–108.

60. RICH, C., AND WATERS, R. C. Abstraction, inspection, and debugging in programming. Memo 634, Artificial Intelligence Laboratory, MIT, Cambridge, June 1981.

61. SCHWARTZ, J. T. Correct program technology. Rep. NSO-12, Courant Institute, New York Univ., Sept. 1977.

62. STANDISH, T. A., HARRIMAN, D. C., KIBLER, D. F., AND NEIGHBORS, J. M. The Irvine program transformation catalogue. Rep., Dept. Information and Computer Science, Univ. of California, Irvine, Jan. 1976.

63. STANDISH, T. A., KIBLER, D. F., AND NEIGHBORS, J. M. Improving and refining programs by program manipulation. In *Proceedings ACM National Conference* (Oct. 1976), 509–516.

64. STERNBERG, R. J. *Intelligence, Information Processing, and Analogical Reasoning*. Lawrence Erlbaum, Hillsdale, N.J., 1977.

65. SUSSMAN, G. J. *A Computer Model of Skill Acquisition*. American Elsevier, New York, 1975.

66. ULRICH, J. W., AND MOLL, R. Program synthesis by analogy. In *Proceedings ACM Symposium on Artificial Intelligence and Programming Languages* (Rochester, N.Y., Aug. 1977), 22–28.

67. United States Department of Defense. *The Programming Language Ada: Reference Manual*. Springer, Berlin, 1981.

68. WALKER, S. A., AND STRONG, H. R., JR. Characterizations of flowchartable recursions. *J. Comput. Syst. Sci. 7*, 4 (Aug. 1973), 404–447.

69. WATERS, R. C. The programmer's apprentice: Knowledge-based program editing. *IEEE Trans. Softw. Eng. SE-8*, 1 (Jan. 1982), 1–12.

70. WEGBREIT, B. Goal-directed program transformation. *IEEE Trans. Softw. Eng. SE-2* (1976), 69–80.

71. WILE, D. S. Program developments: Formal explanations of implementations. *Commun. ACM 26*, 11 (Nov. 1983).

72. WINSTON, P. H. Learning and reasoning by analogy. *Commun. ACM 23*, 12 (Dec. 1980), 689–703.

73. WIRTH, N. *Algorithms + Data Structures = Programs*. Prentice-Hall, Englewood Cliffs, N.J., 1976.

74. YELOWITZ, L., AND DUNCAN, A. G. Abstractions, instantiations, and proofs of marking algorithms. In *Proceedings ACM Conference on Artificial Intelligence and Programming Languages* (Rochester, N.Y., Aug. 1977), 13–21.

Received July 1981; revised August 1983 and August 1984; accepted April 1985

A Formal Representation For Plans In The Programmer's Apprentice

Charles Rich
Massachusetts Institute of Technology

ABSTRACT *A plan calculus is presented that is used to represent programs as well as a library of standard data and control abstractions in the Programmer's Apprentice. Important features of this formalism include programming language independence, additivity, verifiability, and multiple points of view. The logical foundations of the representation are specified formally by using a situational calculus in which side effects and overlapping mutable data structures are accounted for. The plan calculus is compared with other formalisms such as program schemas, and its advantages are pointed out.*

1. Introduction

This chapter reports on recent developments in a formalism called the *plan calculus* which is being used in the Programmer's Apprentice [RSW79] to represent and reason about programs. The plan calculus was originally developed by Rich and Shrobe [RS76] and was subsequently elaborated on by Shrobe [SHRO79] and Waters [WATE78]. Most recently the author has extended the plan calculus by adding data abstraction and multiple points of view, as well as by providing a formal semantics.

The goal of the Programmer's Apprentice project is to develop a knowledge-based tool for program development. The Programmer's Apprentice attacks the complexity barrier [WINO73] in programming in several ways:

1. By providing an on-line database of design decisions, documentation, and descriptions of a program's design at various levels of detail.

2. By reasoning about these descriptions to detect inconsistencies and to predict the influence of incremental changes.

3. By providing a library of standard forms for use in program construction and analysis.

This paper focuses on the representation used in building the library of standard forms. Reasoning about plans will not be discussed in detail (see [SHRO79]), other than to describe the formal system in which such reasoning takes place, nor will the detailed contents of the library be discussed except to show some examples.

The utility of a library of standard forms in program development is motivated by the observation that expert programmers (like experts in many other fields) are distinguished from novices by their use of a richer vocabulary of intermediate level programming concepts. The novice programmer thinks of constructing a program from assignments, tests, arrays, DO loops, *etc*, whereas the expert programmer works with larger, less language-specific concepts, such as searching, accumulation, hashing, *etc*. There are deep reasons for this having to do with managing the complexity of the design process [RSWS78]. To the extent that the Programmer's Apprentice can provide a library of such standard building blocks, the programmer benefits by a reduction in the amount he needs to say in order to construct a program.

The idea of developing libraries of standard software components in order to gain the same benefits that the use of standard components has provided in other areas of engineering is not new [SCHW75]. I believe that part of the reason that efforts in this direction have not been more successful is because of deficiencies in the formalisms used. The plan calculus is an attempt to remedy these deficiencies.

This chapter describes research done at the Artificial Intelligence Laboratory of the Massachusetts Institute of Technology. Support for the laboratory's artificial intelligence research has been provided in part by the Advanced Research Projects Agency of the Department of Defense under Office of Naval Research contracts N00014-75-C-0643 and N00014-80-C-0505, and in part by National Science Foundation grant MCS-7912179. The views and conclusions contained in this chapter are those of the author, and should not be interpreted as necessarily representing the official policies, either expressed or implied, of the Department of Defense, the National Science Foundation, or the United States Government. This chapter is reprinted with permission from the Proceedings of the Seventh International Joint Conference on Artificial Intelligence, Vancouver, BC, Canada, August 24-28, 1981.

2. The Plan Calculus

To a first approximation, the plan calculus may be thought of as unifying in one formalism ideas from flowchart schemas [MANN74], data flow schemas [DENN75], program transformations [CHEA81] [BALZ81] [BD77], and abstract data types [LZ77]. An example of a *plan* is shown in Figure 2.1. The details of the notation used in this figure can wait until later. For now the reader may note that a plan is basically a hierarchical structure made up of different kinds of boxes and arrows. The inner rectangular boxes denote operations and tests, while the arrows between boxes denote data flow (solid arrows) and control flow (hatched arrows). The chief features of this representation, as compared with previous formalisms, are as follows.

1. *Language Independence.* To achieve some measure of canonical form, the plan calculus suppresses features of a program that stem solely from the way an algorithm must be expressed in a particular programming language.

2. *Additivity.* For a library to be easy to use, the rules for combining forms must be straightforward and explicit. Combining forms in the plan calculus has the same formal properties as the union of axiom systems (*i.e.*, the result of combining two non-contradictory forms is always a form that satisfies the constraints of both of the original forms).

3. *Verifiability.* Simply having a library of standard forms addresses only the low productivity part of the software crisis. The plan calculus also provides leverage on the software reliability problem by providing a methodology (in this case, an axiomatic semantics) for verification of library components. Furthermore, this methodology provides a framework in which inconsistencies between uses of standard forms can be detected.

4. *Multiple Points Of View.* Multiple and overlapping points of view are represented in the plan calculus by *overlays* between plans. An example of an overlay is shown in Figure 2.2 (discussed further in the next section). Overlays are used to express the relationship between levels of implementation, to describe overlapping module hierarchies, and to decompose data and control structures in ways that make their relationship to the library more explicit.

An additional desideratum we set for representing the library of standard forms in the Programmer's Apprentice is that the formalism must be neutral between analysis, synthesis, and verification of programs. This turns out to be of great practical importance for building an interactive programming aid, since in real program design situations all three of these activities are intermingled. A neutral representation of standard forms is also theoretically more interesting since it is more likely *a priori* to capture significant features of human understanding of these forms than a representation tailored specifically for analysis, synthesis, or verification only.

2.1 Comparison With Other Formalisms

Past efforts to construct knowledge bases for automatic or partially automated programming have used one of the following formalisms: program schemas [GERH75], program transformations [CHEA81] [BALZ81] [BD77], program refinement rules [BARS77], or formal grammars [RUTH73]. Although each of these representations has been found useful in certain applications, none combine all of the important features of the plan calculus listed above. This section will serve both to contrast the plan calculus with these other formalisms, and as the preliminary to a more careful definition of the plan calculus to follow.

For example, program schemas (incomplete program texts with constraints on the unfilled parts) have been used by Wirth [WIRT73] to catalog programs based on recurrence relations, by Basu and Misra [BM76] to represent typical loops for which the loop invariant is already known, and by Gerhart [GERH75] and Misra [MISR78] to represent and prove the properties of various other common forms. Unfortunately, the syntax of conventional programming languages is not well suited for the kind of generalization needed in this endeavor. For example, the idea of a search loop (a standard programming form) expressed informally in English should be something like the following.

A *search loop* is a loop that has two exits in which a given predicate (the same one each time) is applied to a succession of objects until either the predicate is satisfied (in which case that object is made available for use outside the loop), or the objects to be searched are exhausted.

In Lisp, as in other languages, this kind of loop can be written in innumerable forms, many of which are syntactically (and structurally) very different. For example:

```
(PROG ()
  LP (COND (exhausted (RETURN NIL)))
     ...
     (COND ((predicate current) (RETURN current)))
     ...
     (GO LP))
```

This article originally appeared in Proc. of the 7th Int. Joint Conf. on Artificial Intelligence, Vancouver, Canada, 1981, 1044–1052. Reprinted here from On Conceptual Modeling, edited by Michael L. Brodie, John Mylopoulos, and Joachim Schmidt, New York: Springer-Verlag, 1984, by special arrangement.

or with only one RETURN instead of two,

```
(PROG ()
  LP (COND (exhausted NIL)
           (T ...
              (COND ((predicate current)
                     (RETURN current)))
              ...
              (GO LP))))
```

or even recursively, e.g.,

```
(DEFINE SEARCH ()
  (COND (exhausted NIL)
        (T ...
           (COND ((predicate current) current)
                 (T ...
                    (SEARCH))))))
```

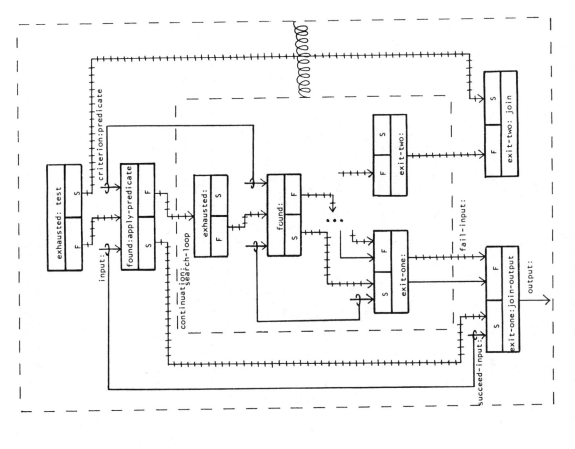

Figure 2.1 Plan for a Search Loop

The problem here is that conventional programming languages are oriented toward specifying computations in enough detail so that a simple local interpreter can carry them out. Unfortunately a lot of this detail is often arbitrary and conceptually unimportant. In the plan calculus, all three of the schemas above (and many other such variations) are expressed by the single plan shown in Figure 2.1.

A new generation of programming languages descended from Simula [DN66], such as CLU [LISK77] and Alphard [SWL77], provide a syntax for specifying standard forms (such as the search loop) in a more canonical way. However, there are two more fundamental difficulties with using program schemas to represent standard program forms, which Simula and its descendants do not solve. First, programs (and therefore program schemas) generally are not easy to combine, nor are they additive. Thus, when you combine two program schemas, the resulting schema is not guaranteed to satisfy the constraints of both of the original schemas, due to such factors as destructive interactions between variable assignments. Second, existing programming languages do not allow multiple views of the same program or overlapping module hierarchies. I believe the reason is that a program is still basically thought of, from the standpoint of these languages, as a set of instructions to be executed, rather than as a set of descriptions (e.g., blueprints) which together specify a computation.

Currently the most common way to represent relationships between standard forms (typically implementation/abstraction relationships) is via program transformations or program refinement rules [BARS77]. Compared with overlays, these formalisms have two serious problems that stem from their lack of neutrality between analysis and synthesis. An overlay in the plan calculus, as in Figure 2.2, is made up of two plans and a set of *correspondences* between the parts of the two plans. Each plan represents a point of view, and the correspondences express the relationship between the points of view. For example, in an implementation. Conversely, in a typical analysis step, the left hand plan serves as the pattern and the right hand plan is instantiated as a more abstract description. With both program refinement rules and knowledge-based[1] program transformations, this sort of symmetric use is not possible since the right hand side of a transformation or refinement rule is typically a sequence of substitutions or modifications to be performed rather than a pattern.

A second problem stemming from the asymmetry of program transformations and refinement rules is their lack of verifiability. The correctness of an overlay in the plan calculus is verified by proving essentially that the constraints of the plan on the left hand side, together with the correspondences (which are formally a set of equalities between terms on the left and terms on the right), imply the constraints of the plan on the right hand side. Neither Balzer's transformation language nor Green and Barstow's refinement tree notation has been adequately formalized to permit the question of correctness to be addressed. The recent work of Broy and Pepper [BP81c] is an improvement, since their transformations have program forms on both the left and right hand sides, with associated proof rules. Unfortunately, they use program schemas as the representation of the standard forms which have the difficulties discussed above.

Another formalism that some people have found attractive for codifying programming knowledge is formal grammars. For example, Ruth [RUTH73] constructed a grammar (that has global switches to control conditional expansions) that represented the class of programs expected to be handed in as exercises in an introductory PL/1 programming class. This grammar was used in a combination of top-down, bottom-up and heuristic parsing techniques in order to recognize correct and near-correct programs. Miller and Goldstein [MG77] also used a grammar formalism (implemented as an augmented transition network) to represent classes of programs in a domain of graphical programming using stick figures. The major shortcoming of these grammars is their lack of a clear semantics upon which a verification methodology can be based.

[1] As opposed to the folding-unfolding and similar transformations of Burstall and Darlington [BD77] which are intended to be a small set of very general transformations that are formally adequate but which must be composed appropriately to construct intuitively meaningful implementation steps.

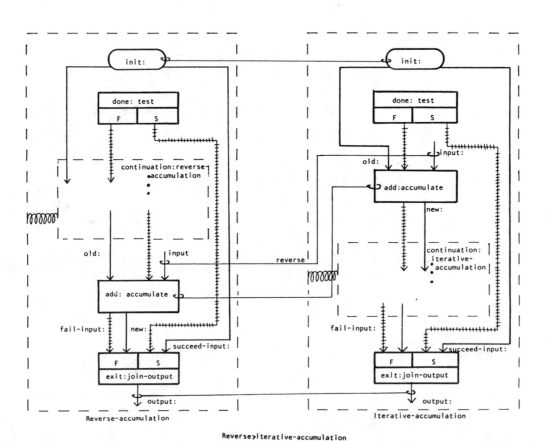

Figure 2.2 *Overlay Between Accumulation on the Way Down vs. Up*

implementation overlay the plan on the right hand side is the abstract description and the plan on the left hand side is an implementation. It is important, however, that either plan can be used as the "pattern." In a typical program synthesis step using overlays, the right hand plan is used as the pattern and the left hand plan is instantiated as a further

3. A Situational Calculus

Before defining the plan calculus more formally, we first need to introduce the underlying logical foundations using a *situational calculus* similar to the one developed by Green [GREE69b] and used by McCarthy and Hayes [MH69]. A situational calculus is a variant of predicate calculus in which certain variables and constants are interpreted as denoting *situations*. Situations can be thought of informally as "instants in time" or "states of the world."

3.1 Side Effects

One basic issue to be addressed in the logical foundations of the plan calculus is the description of *mutable objects*. In programming, as in the everyday world of physical objects, objects can change their behavior (or properties) over time without changing their identity. The approach taken by Green to this problem was to add an extra situational variable to the various function and relation symbols which described the time-dependent aspects of objects. So for example, for a mutable set A he would write $member(x,A,s)$ to assert that x is a member of A at time s. At some other time $t \neq s$, it then might be the case that $\neg member(x,A,t)$. We then say that A has been *modified* or that a *side effect* has occurred.

This situational notation becomes awkward, however, when one introduces defined relationships between objects. For example, suppose we wish to assert that between situations s and t some elements may have been removed from set A, but none have been added. The appropriate relation to use here is subset. In Green's approach we are forced to define subset as follows, adding two situational arguments:

$$subset\,(A,B,s,t) \equiv \forall x\,[\,member\,(x,A,s) \supset member\,(x,B,t)\,].$$

We then would then assert $subset\,(A,A,t,s)$ to specify the side effect discussed above.

This chapter proposes an alternative situational calculus that allows us to preserve the standard algebra of set relations. Mutable objects are treated formally here as functions from situations to *behaviors*. Behaviors are mathematical domains, such as sets, in which there are no side effects (*i.e.*, in which the usual axioms of extensionality apply).[2] A mutable set, such as A, is then formally a function from situations to sets. So for example we could write

$$A\,(s) = \{1,2,3\}$$
$$A\,(t) = \{1,2\} \text{ where } s \neq t.$$

and $A\,(t) \subseteq A\,(s)$ to specify the side effect discussed above. This is the most straightforward example of specifying side effects. Additional complexity enters in when side effects are combined with hierarchical objects (objects that have objects as parts) and multiple points of view. The representation of such side effects in the situational calculus in these more complex cases will be touched upon slightly in the sections on data plans and overlays. These topics are treated in detail in [RICH80]. Shrobe [SHRO79] also discusses some techniques for reasoning about such complex side effects.

3.2 Control Flow

Besides distinguishing the different behavior states of mutable objects, situations can be used to represent control information. This is achieved formally by introducing a primitive partial order on situations (called *precedes*). Intuitively, this relation captures the notion of states that occur before or after other states. This relation also makes it possible to talk about cyclic computations in which all objects return to the same state as at some earlier time.

Another basic feature of control flow that we need to deal with in the situational calculus is conditionals. To do so formally, we introduce a distinguished constant $\bot$ into the domain of situations, such that $\forall s \; precedes \; (s, \bot)$.

Intuitively, $\bot$ represents a situation that is never reached. As we shall see in the following section, $\bot$ appears in the axioms for tests as a way of saying that the two branches of a test are mutually exclusive. $\bot$ also gives us the power to talk about the termination of a loop.

3.3 Computations

Given objects and situations, we can by induction construct a domain of n-tuples (and n-tuples of n-tuples) in which the base components are objects and situations. We call each such n-tuple a *computation*. So for example, the 3-tuple $<A,s,t>$ is a computation involving the object A and situations s and t. If the assertions given in the example above for A, s, and t hold, then this computation involves a side effect to the mutable set A.

As we shall see in the next section, a plan is formally a *predicate* on computations (with the syntactic variation of referring to the components of an n-tuple by selector functions rather than by numerical index).

---

2 The axiom of extensionality for sets states that two sets are equal if and only if they have exactly the same members.

4. Plans

We are now in a position to give a formal definition of the plan calculus. In doing so, it is important to distinguish three levels of definition:

1. *Plan Diagrams*. This is the diagrammatic notation illustrated in Figure 2.1 and Figure 2.2. Historically this was the first level of the plan calculus to be developed and is still the notation used most by the author for intuition and explanation. It is also the abstract "mental language" of the Programmer's Apprentice, *i.e.*, the most natural language in which to describe its operations and strategies. (Of course there also has to be a concrete implementation of this language in computer memory, as discussed below.)

2. *Formal Semantics*. A systematic method is given to translate each form of plan diagram into the axiomatization of a predicate in the situational calculus. This axiomatization provides the rules of inference on plans, verifiability and additivity. Note also that for presentation purposes the actual formulae associated with some constraints in plans will often be omitted from plan diagrams, and the existence of a constraint just indicated by an arc between the constrained parts.

3. *Implementation*. Several different representations of the plan calculus as Lisp data structures have been implemented and used by the author, Shrobe, and Waters. Two early versions of the implementation used a general purpose fully inverted assertional database with pattern matching (similar to the one used in Conniver [MS73]), in which a separate assertion was stored in order to represent each feature (box, arrow, *etc.*) of a plan diagram. A subsequent re-implementation by Waters optimized this database by providing specific access paths tailored to the specific assertion types and pattern matching that was required by the current Programmer's Apprentice system. Most recently a third version was implemented using McAllester's truth maintenance system [MCAL80] in which the logical axioms are represented explicitly with additional extra-logical annotation that encodes the diagram level information. The implementation level will not be discussed further in this chapter, other than to show the external Lisp form in which plan definitions are entered in the most recent version.

The basic idea of a plan, as used in the Programmer's Apprentice, comes from an analogy between programming and other engineering activities [RSWS78]. "Plans" of various kinds are used by many different kinds of engineers. For example, an electrical engineer uses circuit diagrams and block diagrams at various levels of abstraction. A structural engineer uses large-scale and detailed blue prints that show both the architectural framework of a building and also various subsystems such as heating, wiring and plumbing. A mechanical engineer uses overlapping hierarchical descriptions of the interconnections between mechanical parts and assemblies.

Programming is viewed here as a process involving the construction and manipulation of specifications at various levels of abstraction. In this view, there is no fundamental distinction between specifications and programs. A program (*e.g.*, in Lisp) is merely a specification detailed enough to be carried out by some particular interpreter. This view is consistent with the current trend in computer science toward wide spectrum languages. The advantage of this approach is that various parts of a program design can be refined to different degrees without intervening shifts of formalism.

The current plan calculus is based on a very simple model of computation (some limitations of this model and possible future extensions are discussed in the final remarks). In this model all computations are composed of three types of primitives: operations, tests, and primitive data objects. Corresponding to each primitive type, there is a primitive specification form in the plan calculus. Operations are specified by input-output specifications (preconditions and postconditions). Tests are specified by a condition on the inputs that determines whether the test succeeds or fails. Primitive data objects are specified in an appropriate mathematical theory, such as numbers, sets, or functions.

Plans are composite specifications constructed by the uniform mechanism of defining parts (called *roles*) and *constraints*. Two kinds of plans are distinguished according to the types of the roles. *Data plans* specify data structures whose roles are primitive data objects or other data structures. Data plans thus embody a kind of data abstraction.

Temporal plans specify computations whose parts are operations, tests, data structures or other composite computations. The plan for a search loop in Figure 2.1 is an example of a temporal plan. In addition to arbitrary logical constraints between roles, temporal plans also include data flow and control flow constraints. Temporal plans thus embody a kind of control abstraction. Since temporal plans can have embedded data plans, and the same compositional mechanism is used for both, control and data abstraction are unified in the plan calculus. The following sections describe the diagrams and formal semantics for each kind of plan in detail.

4.1 Input-Output Specifications

In plan diagrams an input-output specification is drawn as a solid rectangular box that has solid arrows entering at the top and leaving at the bottom, as shown in Figure 4.1. Each arrow entering at the top represents an input; each arrow leaving at the bottom represents an output.

input-output specification is translated into a type predicate on computations, Set-add, defined as shown below.[3]

Note that each input and output name becomes a function symbol that is the selector function for a component of a computation. Such functions are called *role functions*. Thus input-output specifications (and also tests), although introduced as primitive above, are in fact composite from the standpoint of the formal semantics. Input and output names are treated as role names in other composite plans.

Note that two role functions in the definition above, In and Out, were implicit in the DEFIOSPEC form. These are situational roles that correspond intuitively to the situations immediately preceding and immediately following the execution of the specified operation. The constraint between them is that the In situation precedes the Out situation, and that they co-occur. Co-occur is an equivalence on situations which is defined as follows.

$$Co\text{-}occur(s,t) \equiv [s=\bot \lor t=\bot]$$

This means that if the In situation is reached, it follows that the Out situation is reached (*i.e.*, the operation terminates). Conversely, if the In situation does not occur (*i.e.*, $s=\bot$), then the Out situation does not occur. This converse implication, together with the axiomatization of tests shown in the next section, guarantees that none of the situations that follow in control flow from the failure side of a test occur.

Finally, note the terms $old(\alpha)(in(\alpha))$ and $new(\alpha)(out(\alpha))$ in the definition of Set-add. Input and output role functions return *objects* that must be applied to the appropriate situational arguments in order to talk about their behavior. Thus Old and New are mutable sets. However this specification makes no commitment about whether or not the Input object is added by side effect. (Note that we don't care about the behavior of the Input object here, only its identity.) Whether or not a side effect is allowed depends on the larger plan in which a particular use of Set-add appears, specifically on whether the Old set is used again after the operation. Formally, the specification of the side effect comes down to the question of equality between the Old and New objects. For example, a specialized form (the specialization mechanism used here will be explained further below) of Set-add can be defined by adding one more simple postcondition that stipulates that the addition be achieved by side effect.

[3] The axioms in this paper are slightly simplified by ignoring the fact that certain functions are partial. An axiom of extensionality for each plan type (*i.e.*, equality of instances follows from equality of all the parts) is also being omitted here. The complete axioms are given in [RICH80].

$Set\text{-}add(\alpha) \equiv$
$[precedes(in(\alpha),out(\alpha)) \land co\text{-}occur(in(\alpha),out(\alpha))$
$\land set(old(\alpha)(in(\alpha))) \land set(new(\alpha)(out(\alpha)))$
$\land member(input(\alpha),new(\alpha)(out(\alpha)))$
$\land \forall x[member(x,old(\alpha)(in(\alpha)))$
$\supset member(x,new(\alpha)(out(\alpha)))]$
$\land \forall x[member(x,new(\alpha)(out(\alpha))) \land x \neq input$
$\supset member(x,old(\alpha)(in(\alpha)))]]$

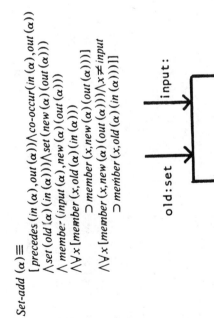

```
(DEFIOSPEC SET-ADD
 ((OLD SET) INPUT)          ;inputs
 ((NEW SET))                ;outputs
 ()                         ;preconditions
 ((MEMBER INPUT (NEW))      ;postconditions
 (FORALL X (IMPLIES (MEMBER X (OLD))
                    (MEMBER X (NEW))))
 (FORALL X (IMPLIES (AND (MEMBER X (NEW))
                         (NOT (= X INPUT)))
                    (MEMBER X (OLD)))))))
```

Figure 4.1 Input-output Specification for Adding to a Set

Constraints between inputs (preconditions) and between outputs and inputs (postconditions) are usually omitted in plan diagrams.

The definition of Set-add in the external format of the current database implementation is shown in Figure 4.1 next to the diagram. Set-add has two inputs: Old (constrained to be a set), and Input (which may be an object of any type), and no other preconditions. The only output of Set-add is named New (a set). The postconditions of Set-add specify that the New set has exactly the same members as the Old set, with the sole addition of the Input. In terms of its semantics, this

```
(DEFIOSPEC IMPURE-SET-ADD
         SPECIALIZATION SET-ADD
    (OLD INPUT)
    (NEW)
    ()
    ((= OLD NEW)))
```

The meaning of this definition is shown below. Note that whether or not the role function is to be applied to a situational argument is encoded in the database input notation by the presence or absence of parentheses around the role name in the constraint expression.

$$Impure\text{-}set\text{-}add\ (\alpha) \equiv [set\text{-}add(\alpha) \land old\ (\alpha) = new\ (\alpha)]$$

4.2 Test Specifications

In plan diagrams a test specification is drawn as a solid rectangular box that has a divided bottom part, as shown in Figure 4.2. The inputs and outputs of a test specification and their types are indicated in the same way that the inputs and outputs of an input-output specification are indicated. A test also has preconditions and postconditions, just like an input-output specification. A test specification differs from an input-output specification because two distinct output situations, named Succeed and Fail, are implicitly specified. Which one occurs depends on whether a given relation (called the *condition* of the test) holds true between the inputs. Control flow arcs originating from either the part of the test box marked S (for succeed), or the part marked F (for fail), are then used to indicate which other parts of a plan are executed, depending on the test.[4]

The definition of the test specification Apply-predicate, written in the format of the current database implementation, is also shown in Figure 4.2. Note that this is the test specification used in the Found role of the Search-loop plan of Figure 2.1. The two exit roles of Figure 2.1 illustrate *joins* that are the mirror images of tests in the plan calculus. Joins are required in conditional plans to specify what the output is in each case.

Apply-predicate has two inputs: Criterion (a predicate) and Input (any object to which the predicate is applicable), but it has no outputs. The test succeeds when the Criterion is true of the Input; otherwise it fails. In terms of its semantics, this test specification is translated into a type predicate on computations with three situational roles, In, Succeed, and Fail, as shown below.

---

[4] More complicated tests using more than two cases can be represented by composing binary tests. Alternatively, the test notation may be generalized to more than two cases.

$Apply\text{-}predicate\ (\alpha) \equiv$
$[precedes\ (in\ (\alpha), succeed\ (\alpha)) \land precedes\ (in\ (\alpha), fail\ (\alpha))$
$\land mutex\ (succeed\ (\alpha), fail\ (\alpha))$
$\land predicate\ (criterion\ (\alpha))\ (in\ (\alpha)))$
$\land member\ (input\ (\alpha), domain\ (criterion\ (\alpha))\ (in\ (\alpha)))$
$\land [apply\ (criterion\ (\alpha))\ (in\ (\alpha)), input\ (\alpha))$
$\qquad \supset co\text{-}occur\ (in\ (\alpha), succeed\ (\alpha))]$
$\land [\neg apply\ (criterion\ (\alpha))\ (in\ (\alpha)), input\ (\alpha))$
$\qquad \supset co\text{-}occur\ (in\ (\alpha), fail\ (\alpha))]]$

$Mutex\ (s,t) \equiv [s = \bot \lor t = \bot]$

From this way of defining tests it is possible to reason both backward and forward in time. For example, if the In situation is reached (*i.e.,* $in\ (\alpha) \neq \bot$) and the Criterion is true, it follows that the Succeed situation is reached. Conversely, if we know that the either the Succeed or Fail situation is reached, it follows that the In situation must have been reached.

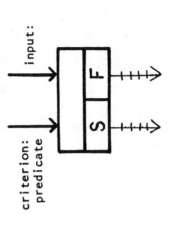

```
(DEFTEST APPLY-PREDICATE
    ((CRITERION PREDICATE) INPUT)      ;inputs
    ()                                 ;outputs
    ((MEMBER INPUT (DOMAIN (CRITERION))));preconds
    ()                                 ;postcondns
    (APPLY (CRITERION) INPUT))         ;test condn
```

Figure 4.2 *Test Specification for Applying a Predicate*

4.3 Data Plans

Data plans are plans whose roles are primitive data objects or other data plans. In plan diagrams primitive data objects are drawn as solid ovals. Data plans are drawn as dashed boxes. Data plans are used to represent standard data structure configurations that may be used in the implementation of more abstract data types. For example, the data plan Indexed-Sequence, shown in Figure 4.3, represents the common cliche of a sequence (typically implemented more concretely as an array) with an associated index pointer. This configuration is typically used to implement such things as buffers, queues, and stacks. (Implementation relationships are represented using overlays, discussed further in another section.)

The plan Indexed-sequence has two roles, Base (a sequence) and Index (an integer). There is the constraint that the Index is between zero and the length of the sequence. The definition of Indexed-sequence in the external format of the database is also shown in Figure 4.3.

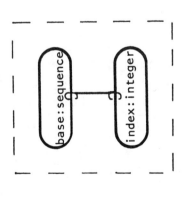

```
(DEFDATAPLAN INDEXED-SEQUENCE
  ((BASE SEQUENCE) (INDEX INTEGER))    ;roles
  ((GT (INDEX) 0)                      ;constraints
   (LE (INDEX) (LENGTH (BASE)))))
```

Figure 4.3   Data Plan for an Indexed Sequence

Data plans used as a mechanism for data abstraction are similar in certain ways to to algebraic axioms [GUTT77] [GTW78] and abstract data types [LZ77]. The constraints between roles of a data plan are similar to what is called the *invariant* in other formalisms. From this point of view, the semantic translation of a data plan can be thought of as a data type predicate. For example, Indexed-sequence is defined below.

$$\text{Indexed-sequence}(\delta) \equiv$$
$$\forall s \, [sequence\,(base\,(\delta)\,(s)) \wedge integer\,(index\,(\delta)\,(s))$$
$$\wedge gt\,(index\,(\delta)\,(s),0)$$
$$\wedge le\,(index\,(\delta)\,(s),length\,(base\,(\delta)\,(s)))]$$

Algebraic axioms and abstract data types, however, do not allow one to specify side effects on data structures. All operations are purely functional. In the plan calculus, we single out the primitive selector operations of the data abstraction, which become the role functions. Side effects are then specified in terms of changes to the roles of a data structure. Note that Indexed-sequence is defined as a predicate on behaviors not objects (i.e., δ above is meant to denote a 2-tuple with components named Base and Index). A mutable indexed sequence is an object D such that, for example, $D(s)=\delta$. Aspects of this formalization of mutable data structures are similar to the approaches taken by Earley [EARL71], by Reynolds [REYN79] for reasoning about arrays, and by Guttag and Horning [GH80].

The plan calculus also represents sharing (i.e., aliasing) in composite data objects, which is not the case with algebraic axioms or abstract data types. Space does not allow a full treatment of this topic here (see [RICH80]); the basic idea is that the parts of a composite data object can themselves be data objects (e.g., $base(D(s))$ above is a mutable sequence). In this formalization a side effect to $base(D(s))$ logically propagates to $D(s)$.

4.4 Temporal Plans

Temporal plans are the most general form of plan in which both data and control abstraction can be expressed. The roles of a temporal plan may be either primitive data objects, data plans, input-output specifications, or test specifications. The most typical constraints between input-output and test specification roles are data flow and control flow constraints. An example of the diagram for a temporal plan is shown in Figure 4.4 (note that Figure 2.1 also illustrates a temporal plan).

The Bump+update plan in Figure 4.4 has four roles: Bump, a subtract one operation; Update, an operation to change one term in a sequence; and Old and New, which are indexed sequence data structures. This plan captures the cliched pattern of operations on an indexed sequence in which the index is decremented and a new term is stored. (Among other things, this is the implementation of a Push operation if the Old and New indexed sequences are viewed as stacks. See the section on overlays.)

Solid arrows in a temporal plan diagram, such as between the Output of the Bump step and the Index input of the Update step, denote data flow (i.e., the Output of Bump becomes the Index input of Update).

This notion of data flow is intuitively one of the main sources of additivity in the plan calculus. An arbitrary amount of other computation may be added between Bump and Update as long as the stipulated data flow is not disturbed. As we shall see below, data flow constraints are formalized logically as equalities between terms that denote the respective input and output ports. The additional solid lines in Figure 4.4 denote equality constraints between parts other than the input and output ports of input-output specifications. For example, the Base of the Old indexed sequence becomes the Old sequence input to the Update step. The Base of the New indexed sequence is the New sequence output of the Update step.

A second feature of temporal plan diagrams introduced in Figure 4.4 is control flow (cross-hatched) arrows. The control flow arrow between Bump and Update means that the termination of the Bump step precedes (and implies) the initiation of the Update step. The external plan definition form for Bump+Update given in Figure 4.4 summarizes all of these features. Also shown below are the input-output specifications of the Subtract-one and Newterm, which are straightforward.

```
(DEFIOSPEC SUBTRACT-ONE
  ((INPUT INTEGER))
  ((OUTPUT INTEGER))
  ()
  ((= (OUTPUT)(- (INPUT) 1))))
```

```
(DEFIOSPEC NEWTERM
  ((OLD SEQUENCE)(INDEX INTEGER) INPUT)
  ((NEW SEQUENCE))
  ((GT (INDEX) 0)(LE (INDEX)(LENGTH (OLD))))
  ((= (LENGTH (NEW))(LENGTH (OLD)))
   (= (TERM (NEW)(INDEX)) INPUT)
   (FORALL I
     (IMPLIES (NOT (= I (INDEX)))
       (= (TERM (OLD) I)(TERM (NEW) I))))))
```

There are two further features of the Bump+update plan to note before looking at the semantic translation. First, like Set-add this plan makes no commitment to whether or not a side effect is involved. A specialized version of Bump+update can be specified in which the Update step is specialized to an impure Newterm specification, and in which the Old and New indexed sequences are constrained to be identical. Also note that the Input to Newterm (the value of the new term) is not constrained in this plan. Temporal plans are typically combined by providing data flow from and to such ports.

Shown below are the semantics of the temporal plan Bump+update which is defined, similar to input-output and test specifications, as a predicate on computations.

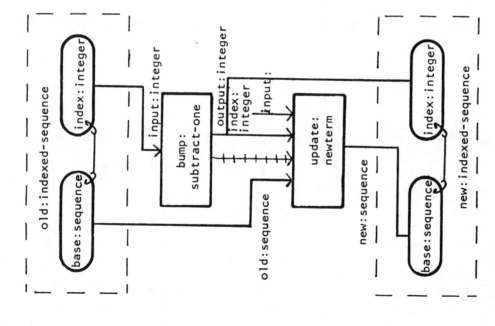

```
(DEFPLAN BUMP+UPDATE
  ;roles
  ((OLD INDEXED-SEQUENCE)(NEW INDEXED-SEQUENCE)
   (BUMP SUBTRACT-ONE)(UPDATE NEWTERM))
  ;constraints
  ((CFLOW (OUT (BUMP)) (IN (UPDATE)))
   (= ((INDEX (OLD))) ((INPUT (BUMP))))
   (= ((BASE (OLD))) ((OLD (UPDATE))))
   (= ((INDEX (BUMP))) ((INDEX (UPDATE))))
   (= ((OUTPUT (BUMP))) ((BASE (NEW))))
   (= ((OUTPUT (UPDATE))) ((BASE (NEW)))))))
```

Figure 4.4 *Temporal Plan for Updating an Indexed Sequence*

1. The primitive *actions* and *tests* of the language, such as CAR, CDR, CONS, NULL, and EQ in Lisp, are represented as input-output specifications and test specifications.

2. The primitive *connectives*, such as PROG, COND, SETQ, GO, and RETURN in Lisp, are represented as patterns of control and data flow constraints between operations and tests.

The translation from standard program text to an equivalent plan representation has been implemented for reasonable subsets of Lisp [RS76], Fortran [WATE79], and Cobol [FAUS81]. The translation from suitably restricted plans to Lisp code has also been implemented by Waters [WATE81].

5. Relations Between Plans

Figure 5.1 is a small excerpt from the current plan library that illustrates the the taxonomic structure of the library. An initial observation to make about the nodes of the library shown in this example is that they are a mixture of both data abstractions (*e.g.*, set, predicate, directed graph) and control abstractions. (Find and Thread-find are input-output specifications, and in general there are also temporal plans in the library, but none are shown here.)

The four types of relations that relate nodes of the library are named in the upper right hand corner of the figure next to an example of the type of line or arrow used to represent each relation in the body of the figure. The first relation, *component*, simply indexes which plans are used in the definition of other plans, as for example Indexed-sequence was used in the definition of Bump+update above. The next two relations are simple inheritance relationships by which a plan inherits the roles and constraints of another plan and then adds its own additional roles or constraints or both. *Specialization* is the relation in which only constraints are added; *extension* involves adding roles (and usually, constraints between new roles and inherited ones).

Overlays are the most important type of relation between plans in the library because overlays represent significant additional knowledge, such as the details of how one abstraction may be implemented in terms of another. The diagram notation and semantics for overlays are explained in the following section.

Starting with Set in Figure 5.1, a typical question we might want to ask in the course of program analysis or synthesis is, What plans (*e.g.*, input-output specifications) in the library use sets? This type of question is answered in general by looking up the composition relation (in this example from Set to Find). Find is an input-output specification

$Bump+update(\alpha) \equiv$
$[subtract-one(bump(\alpha)) \wedge newterm(update(\alpha))$
$\wedge cflow(out(bump(\alpha)), in(update(\alpha)))$
$\wedge output(bump(\alpha))(out(bump(\alpha)))$
$= index(update(\alpha))(in(update(\alpha)))$
$\wedge \exists s[indexed-sequence(old(\alpha)(s))$
$\wedge index(old(\alpha)(s))(s) = input(bump(\alpha))(in(bump(\alpha)))$
$\wedge base(old(\alpha)(s))(s) = old(update(\alpha))(in(update(\alpha)))]$
$\wedge \exists t[indexed-sequence(new(\alpha)(t))$
$\wedge index(new(\alpha)(t))(t) = output(bump(\alpha))(out(bump(\alpha)))$
$\wedge base(new(\alpha)(t))(t) = output(update(\alpha))(out(update(\alpha)))]]$

$Cflow(s,t) \equiv [precedes(s,t) \wedge co-occur(s,t)]$

The interpretation of this formal definition is left largely to the reader. The major complexity of translating temporal plans into their logical equivalent is in providing the appropriate situational arguments. In particular, for roles that are data plans, such as Old and New above, we posit the existence of some situation (*e.g.*, s and t above) in which the constraints of the data plan hold, and then assert constraints between the behavior of the parts in that situation and the input and output ports to which they are connected in the plan diagram. The default situational arguments for input and output ports here are assigned in the same way as the corresponding input-output specifications, namely In for input objects and Out for output objects.

The Bump+update plan does not illustrate an additional important feature of temporal plans, namely the use of recursion to represent loops. Recent work on Lisp interpreters [SS78b] and compilers [STEE78] suggests that the distinction between loops and singly recursive programs in which the recursive call is the last step of the program (so called "tail recursions") should be considered only a superficial syntactic variation. The plan calculus takes this point of view. Recursion in plan diagrams (data plans may also be recursively defined) is indicated by a spiral line as shown in Figure 2.1, the plan for a search loop, introduced earlier.

4.5 Programming Languages

The plan calculus makes it possible to build a Programmer's Apprentice which is concerned with the syntactic details of different programming languages only at its most superficial interface. In order to translate back and forth between a given programming language and the plan calculus, the primitives of the programming language are divided into two categories:

```
(DEFIOSPEC THREAD-FIND
  ((INPUT THREAD)(CRITERION PREDICATE))
  (OUTPUT)
  ((EXISTS X (AND (NODE (INPUT) X)
                  (APPLY (CRITERION) X))))
  ((NODE (INPUT) OUTPUT)
   (APPLY (CRITERION) OUTPUT)))
```

Finally, extension is a relation between plans that can be used to access useful variations of a plan. For example, in the figure an extension of Thread-find is Internal-thread-find. The input-output specifications of Internal-thread-find are shown below.

```
(DEFIOSPEC INTERNAL-THREAD-FIND
           EXTENSION THREAD-FIND
  (INPUT CRITERION)
  (OUTPUT PREVIOUS)
  ((NOT (APPLY (CRITERION)(ROOT (INPUT)))))
  ((SUCCESSOR (INPUT) PREVIOUS OUTPUT)))
```

Note that an additional output role, Previous, has been added with the constraint that it be the predecessor of the Output node in the Input thread. This is a very common kind of operation on directed graphs when splicing of nodes in and out is being performed. In order to be used properly, Internal-thread-find must also have the additional precondition (from which its name is suggested) that the Criterion is false for the root node of the Input thread.

5.1 Overlays

Overlays provide a mechanism in the plan calculus for representing the relationship between two different points of view, each of which is represented by a plan. Overlays are similar to Sussman's "slices" [SUSS78], which he uses to represent equivalences in electronic circuit analysis and synthesis. Formally, an overlay is a mapping from instances of one plan to instances of another. Such mappings are a very general mechanism. The intuitive import of various overlays depends on what kind of plans are involved, whether the mapping is many-to-one or one-to-one, and how the mapping is defined.

An example of an overlay between a temporal plan and an input-output specification is shown in Figure 5.2. Intuitively, this overlay expresses how a Push operation can be implemented by the Bump+update plan discussed above, given that the stack is implemented as an indexed sequence.

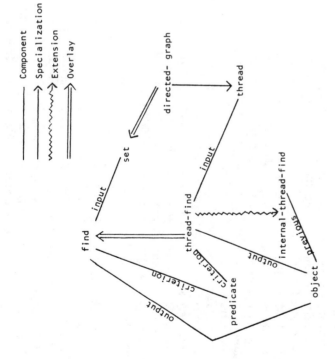

Figure 5.1   Excerpt from Plan Library Illustrating Taxonomic Relations

that has three roles, an Input set, a Criterion predicate, and an Output object. Its precondition is that an element of the Input set exists that satisfies the Criterion. Its postcondition is that the Output is such an element.

Overlays pointing to a node answer questions of the form, What implementations are available for Find operations? In this example, one answer is that Find may be implemented as Thread-find, where the Input set is implemented as a thread. (Note that Thread is a specialization of Directed-graph in which each node has at most one predecessor or successor and there are no cycles.) The input-output specifications of Thread-find are shown below. It has three roles similar to Find: an Input thread, a Criterion predicate, and an Output object. Its precondition is that a node of the Input thread exists that satisfies the Criterion. Its postcondition is that the Output is such a node.

```
(DEFOVERLAY BUMP+UPDATE>PUSH (BUMP+UPDATE PUSH)
  (= (OLD PUSH)
     (INDEXED-SEQUENCE>STACK (OLD BUMP+UPDATE)))
  (= (NEW PUSH)
     (INDEXED-SEQUENCE>STACK (NEW BUMP+UPDATE)))
  (= (INPUT PUSH) (INPUT (UPDATE BUMP+UPDATE)))
  (= (IN PUSH) (IN (BUMP BUMP+UPDATE)))
  (= (OUT PUSH) (OUT (UPDATE BUMP+UPDATE))))
```

Notice that each overlay has a name (*e.g.*, Bump+update>push)[5] that will become a function symbol in the formal semantics. Correspondences between roles are either simple equalities, as in

```
(= (INPUT PUSH) (INPUT (UPDATE BUMP+UPDATE))),
```

which says that the Input to Push (the object which becomes the head of the new stack) corresponds to the Input of the Update step in the Bump+update plan, or correspondences defined in terms of other overlays, as in

```
(= (OLD PUSH)
   (INDEXED-SEQUENCE>STACK (OLD BUMP+UPDATE))).
```

The overlay Indexed-sequence>stack is an example of a many-to-one overlay between data plans. The basic idea of this overlay is that an indexed sequence may be viewed as the implementation of a stack in which the head is the term of the sequence indexed by the current index, and the tail is, recursively, the sequence with index value one greater. The formal definition of this overlay will not be shown here because it is very similar to what is called an abstraction function in abstract data types. The formal semantics of the Bump+update>push overlay is the following function definition.

$$\beta = Bump+update > push\,(\alpha) \equiv$$
$$[old\,(\beta) = indexed\text{-}sequence > stack\,(old\,(\alpha))$$
$$\wedge new\,(\beta) = indexed\text{-}sequence > stack\,(new\,(\alpha))$$
$$\wedge input\,(\beta) = input\,(update\,(\alpha))$$
$$\wedge in\,(\beta) = in\,(bump\,(\alpha))$$
$$\wedge out\,(\beta) = out\,(update\,(\alpha))]$$

Implementation overlays such as Bump+update>push and Indexed-sequence>stack are typically many-to-one. There are also one-to-one overlays in the library, which are naturally thought of as providing alternative points of view or transformations of data or control structure. For example, a Lisp list can be viewed alternatively as a stack (*i.e.*, a

---

5 This symbol is intended to be read ''Bump and Update as Push''.

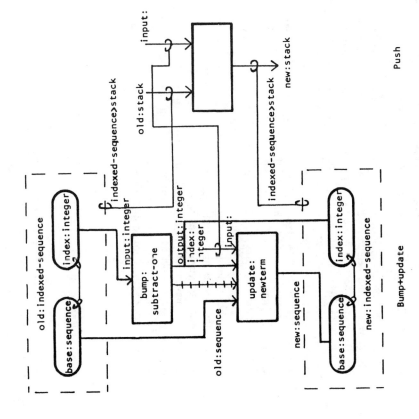

Figure 5.2 *Implementation Overlay for Push on Indexed Sequence*

Note that the diagram for an overlay is composed of a plan on the left hand side (which is the domain of the mapping), a plan on the right hand side (which is the range of the mapping), and a set of hooked lines showing a set of *correspondences* between roles of the two plans (which defines the mapping). In the external format of the current database, an overlay is defined as follows.

recursively defined data structure), as a labelled directed graph (in particular a thread) wherein the nodes are Cons cells connected by the Cdr relation and labelled by the Car relation, or as a sequence wherein the *i*th term is the Car of (*i*−1)th Cdr. Each of these data plans provides its own vocabulary for specifying properties of a data structure and a standard set of manipulations on it. There are one-to-one overlays in the library between them so that the appropriate point of view can be used depending on the properties and manipulations of interest. There are also one-to-one overlays in the library between temporal plans, such the overlay introduced earlier in Figure 2.2 that captures the relationship in general between singly recursive programs that accumulate "on the way down" (*e.g.*, reverse copying a list), and those that accumulate "on the way up" (*e.g.*, copying a list).

Other overlays of particular interest are those that map from temporal plans to data plans, in particular from recursive temporal plans to lists. These latter are called *stream* overlays and embody a kind of abstraction in which the objects filling a given role at all levels in a recursive plan are viewed as a single data structure. For example, there is a stream overlay in the library by means of which the succession of Inputs to the Found test in the Search-loop plan are viewed as a list. And if that overlay is composed with the overlay to view a list as the implementation of a set, then Search-loop can be viewed as the implementation of the Find specification discussed above. This method of abstraction provides a very powerful means of decomposing loops and recursions in a way that makes their behavior easier to understand than the standard invariant assertion method. For a further discussion of this idea see Waters [WATE79].

A final note regarding the use of overlays is that they are not only part of the taxonomic structure of the plan library, they are also used to construct the refinement tree of a particular program. This tree encodes the design history of a program at many levels of detail. A way in which overlays differ from other refinement tree notations is that overlays permit *overlapping* implementations [RICH81], and components that are distinct at one level of abstraction share parts at lower levels. This is a feature of good engineering design and is an important way in which overlays are an improvement over previous notations.

6. Final Remarks

The emphasis in this paper on representation rather than reasoning should not obscure an important dimension of the plan calculus. In the Programmer's Apprentice, reasoning about plans takes place within a

system [MCAL80] that maintains explicit dependencies between each assertion in the data base. These dependencies are crucial for supporting evolutionary design and debugging programs. Each overlay in the library has a precompiled network of dependencies between the specifications on the left and right hand sides (called its *teleological* structure) which is instantiated along with the parts, constraints, and correspondences when it is used.

There are several areas in which we have found the current plan calculus deficient, and we hope to extend it further in the future. Important among these are the following:

1. *Performance Considerations.* A way of formalizing time and space trade-offs is needed both for the library and for reasoning about particular programs.

2. *Error Handling.* The non-local flow of control typically involved in error handling code is not well represented in the current plan calculus.

3. *Global Shared Data.* Programs that communicate primarily by inserting and retrieving information in a global shared database are not well decomposed by the data flow ideas in the current calculus.

Finally, we intend to investigate the usefulness of the plan calculus in other planning contexts. In particular, I believe there is potential for a fruitful flow of ideas between program understanding (analysis, synthesis, and verification) and robot planning (*e.g.*, Abstrips [SACE74]). Many of the insights underlying the plan calculus originate from work in robot planning. I also believe that some of the techniques developed in the plan calculus for representing and reasoning about overlapping data structures and side effects have bearing on aspects of the classical "frame problem" [MH69] in robot planning.

References

[BALZ81]   R. Balzer, "Transformational Implementation: An Example", *IEEE Trans. on Software Eng.*, Vol. 7, No. 1, January, 1981.

[BARS77]   D.R. Barstow, "Automatic Construction of Algorithms and Data Structures Using A Knowledge Base of Programming Rules", Stanford AIM-308, Nov. 1977.

[BD77]   R.M. Burstall and J.L. Darlington, "A Transformation System for Developing Recursive Programs", *J. of the ACM*, Vol. 24, No. 1, January, 1977.

[BM76]   S. Basu and J. Misra, "Some Classes of Naturally Provable Programs", *2nd Int. Conf. on Software Eng.*, San Francisco, Cal., Oct., 1976.

[BP81c]   M. Broy and P. Pepper, "Program Development as a Formal Activity", *IEEE Trans. on Software Eng.*, Vol. 7, No. 1, January, 1980.

[CHEA81]   T.E. Cheatham, "Program Refinement by Transformation", *5th Int. Conf. on Software Eng.*, San Diego, Cal., March, 1981.

[DENN74]   J.B. Dennis, "First Version of a Data Flow Procedure Language", *Proc. of Symposium on Programming*, Institut de Programmation, U. of Paris, April 1974, pp. 241-271.

[DN66]   O.J. Dahl and K. Nygaard "SIMULA—An ALGOL-Based Simulation Language", *Comm. of the ACM*, Vol. 9, No. 9, September 1966, pp. 671-678.

[EARL71]   J. Earley, "Toward an Understanding of Data Structures", *Comm. of the ACM*, Vol. 14, No. 10, October 1971, pp. 617-627.

[FAUS81]   G. Faust, "Semiautomatic Translation of COBOL into HIBOL", (M.S. Thesis), MIT/LCS/TR-256, March, 1981.

[GERH75]   S.L. Gerhart, "Knowledge About Programs: A Model and Case Study", in *Proc. of Int. Conf. on Reliable Software*, June 1975, pp. 88-95.

[GREE69b]   C. Green, "Theorem Proving by Resolution as a Basis for Question-Answering Systems", *Machine Intelligence 4*, D. Michie and B. Meltzer, Eds., Edinburgh University Press, Edinburgh, Scotland, 1969.

[GTW78]   J.A. Goguen, J.W. Thatcher, and E.G. Wagner, "An Initial Algebra Approach to the Specification, Correctness, and Implementation of Abstract Data Types", *Current Trends in Programming Methodology, Vol. IV*, (ed. Raymond Yeh), Prentice-Hall, 1978.

[GUTT77]   J. Guttag, "Abstract Data Types and the Development of Data Structures", *Comm. of the ACM*, Vol. 20, No. 6, June 1977, pp. 396-404.

[GUTT80]   J. Guttag and J.J. Horning, "Formal Specification As a Design Tool", *7th Annual ACM Symposium on Principles of Programming Languages*, Las Vegas, January, 1980, pp. 251-261.

[LISK77]   B. Liskov *et al.*, "Abstraction Mechanisms in CLU", *Comm. of the ACM*, Vol. 20, No. 8, August 1977, pp. 564-576.

[LZ77]   B.H. Liskov and S.N. Zilles, "an Introduction to Formal Specifications of Data Abstractions", *Current Trends in Programming Methodology, Vol. I*, (ed. Raymond Yeh), Prentice-Hall, 1977.

[MANN74]   Z. Manna, *Mathematic Theory of Computation*, McGraw-Hill, 1974.

[MCAL80]   D.A. McAllester, "An Outlook on Truth Maintenance", MIT/AIM-551, August, 1980.

[MG77]   M.L. Miller and I. Goldstein, "Problem Solving Grammars as Formal Tools for Intelligent CAI", *Proc. of the Assoc. for Computing Machinery*, 1977.

[MH69]   J. McCarthy and P. Hayes, "Some Philosophical Problems from the Standpoint of Artificial Intelligence", *Machine Intelligence 4*, D. Michie and B. Meltzer, Eds., Edinburgh University Press, Edinburgh, Scotland, 1969.

[MISR78]   J. Misra, "Some Aspects of the Verification of Loop Computations", *IEEE Trans. on Software Eng.*, Vol. SE-4, No. 6, November 1978, pp. 478–485.

[MS73]   D. McDermott and G.J. Sussman, "The Conniver Reference Manual", MIT/AIM-259A, 1973.

[REY79]   J.C. Reynolds, "Reasoning About Arrays", *Comm. of the ACM*, Vol 22, No. 5, May 1979, pp. 290–298.

[RICH80]   C. Rich, "Inspection Methods in Programming", MIT/AI/TR-604, (Ph.D. thesis), December, 1980.

[RICH81]   C. Rich, "Multiple Points of View in Modeling Programs", *Proc. of Workshop on Data Abstraction, Data Bases and Conceptual Modeling,* ,pub(SIGPLAN), Vol. 16, No. 1, January, 1981, pp. 177–179.

[RS76]   C. Rich and H.E. Shrobe, "Initial Report On A LISP Programmer's Apprentice", (M.S. Thesis), MIT/AI/TR-354, December 1976.

[RSW79]   C. Rich, H.E. Shrobe, and R.C. Waters, "An Overview of the Programmer's Apprentice", *Proc. of 6th Int. Joint Conf. on Artificial Intelligence*, Tokyo, Japan, August, 1979.

[RSWS78]   C. Rich, H.E. Shrobe, R.C. Waters, G.J. Sussman, and C.E. Hewitt, "Programming Viewed as an Engineering Activity", (NSF Proposal), MIT/AIM-459, January, 1978.

[RUTH73]   G. Ruth, "Analysis of Algorithm Implementations", M.I.T. Project MAC Technical Report 130, (Ph.D. Thesis), 1973.

[SACE74]   E.D. Sacerdoti, "Planning in a Hierarchy of Abstraction Spaces", *Artificial Intelligence*, Vol. 5, No. 2, 1974, pp. 115–135.

[SCHW75]   J.T. Schwartz, "On Programming", An Interim Report on the SETL Project, Courant Institute of Mathematical Sciences, New York University, June 1975.

[SHRO79]   H.E. Shrobe, "Dependency Directed Reasoning for Complex Program Understanding", (Ph.D. Thesis), MIT/AI/TR-503, April, 1979.

[SS78b]   G.L. Steele and G.J. Sussman, "The Art of the Interpreter, or, The Modularity Complex (Parts Zero, One, and Two)", MIT/AIM-453, May 1978.

[STEEB78]   G.L. Steele, "Rabbit: A Compiler for Scheme (A Study in Compiler Optimization)", MIT/AI/TR-474, May, 1978.

[SUSS78]   G.J. Sussman, "Slices at the Boundary Between Analysis and Synthesis", *Artificial Intelligence and Pattern Recognition in Computer Aided Design*, Latombe, ed., North-Holland, 1978.

[SWL77]   M. Shaw, W.A. Wulf, and R.L. London, "Abstraction and Verification in Alphard: Defining and Specifying Iteration and Generators", *Comm. of the ACM*, Vol 20, No. 8, August 1977, pp. 553–563.

[WATE78]   R.C. Waters, "Automatic Analysis of the Logical Structure of Programs", MIT/AI/TR-492, (Ph.D. Thesis), December, 1978.

[WATE79]   R.C. Waters, "A Method for Analyzing Loop Programs", *IEEE Trans. on Software Eng.*, Vol. SE-5, No. 3, May 1979, pp. 237–247.

[WATE81]   R.C. Waters, "The Programmer's Apprentice: Knowledge Based Program Editing", *IEEE Trans. on Software Eng.*, Vol. SE-8, No. 1, January 1982.

[WINO73]   T. Winograd, "Breaking the Complexity Barrier (Again)", *Proc. of the SIGIR-SIGPLAN Interface Meeting*, November, 1973.

[WIRT73]   N. Wirth, *Systematic Programming, An Introduction*, Prentice-Hall, 1973.

Empirical Studies of Programming Knowledge

ELLIOT SOLOWAY AND KATE EHRLICH

Abstract—We suggest that expert programmers have and use two types of programming knowledge: 1) *programming plans*, which are generic program fragments that represent stereotypic action sequences in programming, and 2) *rules of programming discourse*, which capture the conventions in programming and govern the composition of the plans into programs. We report here on two empirical studies that attempt to evaluate the above hypothesis. Results from these studies do in fact support our claim.

Index Terms—Cognitive models of programming, novice/expert differences, program conprehension, software psychology.

I. Introduction: Motivation and Goals

WHAT is it that expert programmers know that novice programmers don't? We would suggest that the former have *at least* two types of knowledge that the latter typically do not.

• *Programming Plans:* Program fragments that represent stereotypic action sequences in programming, e.g., a RUNNING TOTAL LOOP PLAN, an ITEM SEARCH LOOP PLAN [16].

• *Rules of Programming Discourse:* Rules that specify the conventions in programming, e.g., the name of a variable should usually agree with its function; these rules set up expectations in the minds of the programmers about what should be in the program. These rules are analogous to discourse rules in conversation.

In our view, programs are composed from programming plans that have been modified to fit the needs of the specific problem. The composition of those plans are governed by rules of programming discourse. Thus, a program can be correct from the perspective of the problem, but be difficult to write and/or read because it doesn't follow the rules of discourse, i.e., the plans in the program are composed in ways that violate some discourse rule(s).

Our approach to programming borrows directly from at least two, converging sources: the research in text processing in artificial intelligence and psychology, and the research in problem solving with experts and novices. First, we base our claim that text comprehension research is appropriate to the task of understanding program comprehension on the following observation: programs have a dual nature—they can be *executed* for effect, and they can be *read* as communicative entities. Viewed in

Manuscript received August 1, 1983; revised May 14, 1984. This work was supported in part by the National Science Foundation, under NSF Grants MCS-8302382 and IST-8310659, and by a contribution from the Burroughs Corporation. However, the views expressed in this paper do not necessarily reflect those of the Burroughs Corporation. Portions of this paper appear in the *Proceedings of the Conference on the Nature of Expertise*, Carnegie-Mellon University, Pittsburgh, PA, October 1983.

E. Soloway is with the Department of Computer Science, Yale University, New Haven, CT 06520, and Compu-Tech, Inc., New Haven, CT.

K. Ehrlich is with Honeywell Information Systems, Inc. Waltham, MA 02154.

this light, we felt that the notion of *schemas*, one of the most influential notions to have emerged from recent research on text comprehension (e.g., [2], [3], [10], [16]) should be applicable to program comprehension.

"Schemas are generic knowledge structures that guide the comprehender's interpretations, inferences, expectations, and attention when passages are comprehended" [10].

Our notion of programming plan corresponds directly to this notion of schema.

Second, research with experts and novices in various technical domains (chess [4], [7], physics [14], electronic circuitry [8]) have shown that the former seem to develop *chunks* that represent functional units in their respective domains, while the latter do not. Similar results have been obtained in the programming domain [1], [16], [18]. The work reported in this paper builds on and extends the above research in the programming domain by examining whether or not programmers have and use specific programming plans and rules of programming discourse in the process of comprehending computer programs. Moreover, the work reported here extends our earlier studies on programming plans [9], [19] by presenting a broader, more systematic empirical examination of these concepts. Note too that this work is another example of our efforts to explore the cognitive underpinnings of programming: while in Soloway *et al.* [20] we examined the cognitive fit of a particular programming language construct (Pascal's WHILE loop) to people's natural cognitive strategies, here we examine the role that various types of programming knowledge play in the comprehension of programs.

In this paper we describe two empirical studies we conducted with programmers of varying levels of expertise. The goal of these studies was to evaluate the above claim: do expert programmers possess programming plans and discourse rules? Programs that do not conform to the plans and discourse rules should violate the programmers' expectations: for example, if they see a variable initialized to zero (N := 0) at the top of a program, they should be surprised to see it being changed via a read statement (READ(N)) later in the program. While this type of situation will not create an unrunnable program, it certainly violates the accepted conventions of programming: 1) variables are usually updated in the same fashion as they are initialized; thus we would expect N to be updated via an assignment statement, and 2) programmers do not like to include statements that have no effect: a READ statement destroys whatever is in the variable initially, and thus the initial setting of N to zero is superfluous. We claim that these violations in expectations—the surprises due to violations of conventions—can make such programs much more difficult to comprehend.

Thus, if advanced programmers have knowledge about plans and discourse rules then programs that do not conform to the rules of discourse (*unplan-like programs*) should be harder for them to understand than programs that do conform to these rules (*plan-like programs*). In contrast, we would not expect novice programmers to have acquired as many of the plans and conventions in programming: by definition a novice programmer has less knowledge than an advanced programmer. Thus, we would not expect novice programmers to be as sensitive to violations of conventions—since they don't know what the conventions are in the first place. Therefore, in a task that requires understanding a program, we expect 1) advanced programmers to do much better than the novice programmers on the programs that do conform to the plans and rules, while we expect 2) advanced programmers to perform at the level of novices when the programs violate the plans and the discourse rules.[1]

The organization of this paper is as follows. First, we present a brief description of our experimental studies; this section provides the needed motivation for why our "stimulus materials"—the computer programs used in our experiments—were constructed in the manner that they were. Next, we present a detailed description of how and why unplan-like programs can be generated from plan-like ones. In the following two major sections, we present detailed descriptions of each of our empirical studies, along with a discussion of the results from the studies. We close with implications from these studies for the practice of programming.

II. Brief Description of Both Experimental Techniques

The first stage in both experimental procedures is as follows. First, we construct a plan-like program, i.e., one that uses only typical programming plans and whose plans are composed so as to be consistent with rules of programming discourse. Next, we construct an unplan-like version of that program by violating one (or possibly two) of the discourse rules. We will refer to the plan-like version of the program as the Alpha version, while the unplan-like version will be referred to as the Beta version.[2] An example of an Alpha version with a Beta version for a programming problem is given in Fig. 1. (In Section III we describe in detail how these programs were constructed, and why we would consider the Beta version to be unplan-like.)

A. Brief Description of Study I: Fill-in-the-Blank

Our first study uses a "fill-in-the-blank technique": here we take out one line of code from the program and replace that line with a blank. The task we ask of our experimental subjects, who are novice and advanced student programmers, is to fill the blank line in with a piece of code that, in their opinion, best completes the program. An example of the programs with

blank lines is given in Fig. 1. Note carefully that we do *not* tell the subjects what problem the program is intended to solve. However, since there is only one blank line per program, a great deal of context is still left. If advanced programmers do have and use programming plans for stereotypic programming situations, then they should be able to recognize the program fragment in the plan-like versions as an example of programming plan X, and they should all fill in the blank line with the same piece of code. However, in the case of the unplan-like programs, advanced programmers should be more unsure of what plan is being indicated; thus, they should be less likely to complete the program in the correct fashion. On the other hand, novice programmers should not be as surprised by the unplan-like programs since they have not as yet acquired the programming conventions. Thus, we expect that the advanced programmers will be more affected by the unplan-like programs than will the novices.

Notice that both the Alpha version and the Beta version are runnable programs that in almost all cases compute the *same* values.[3] Moreover, to an untrained eye their differences may even not be apparent: they always only differ by a very few textual elements. Thus, our experimental materials are not random programs, as were used in previous studies [1], [16], [18]. While those studies demonstrated the basic effect—that advanced programmers have strategies for encoding and remembering programs better than do novice programmers—we see our work as focusing on the *detailed knowledge* that programmers have and use.

B. Brief Description of Study II: Recall

In our second study, we used essentially the same stimulus materials as in Study I. This time, however, the task was a recall one and all subjects were expert professional programmers. Subjects were presented with a complete program which they were asked to recall *verbatim*. Half the programs were plan-like and half were unplan-like. Each program was presented three times. On the first trial, subjects were asked to recall as much of the program as possible. On the second and third trials, they were asked to either add to their original recall or to change any part of their recall that they felt was in error. We tracked the progression of their recall by asking them to use a different color pencil on each of the three trials. This technique, of repeated presentation of the same program, was developed by Kahney [12] for research specifically on the comprehension of computer programs. If programming plans help programmers to encode a program more efficiently we should find that experts recall more of the program earlier. However, given sufficient time, they should be able to recall as much of the unplan-like programs as the plan-like ones. Again, while others have shown this basic effect our motivation is to identify specific knowledge units and to demonstrate the significant influence that planliness has on program comprehension: a change in just a few characters can result in significant differences in performance!

---

[1] In the second study we only used expert professional programmers as subjects, and thus we can not look for this type of interaction. Rather, we simply want to 1) evaluate our hypothesis with professional programmers, and 2) observe whether there is a difference in performance within the experts on programs that vary along the *plan-like* dimension.

[2] Clearly, the Beta versions are not totally unplan-like; in fact, they have many plans in common with the Alpha versions. The term "unplan-like" is thus meant for emphasis only.

[3] In only one program type, MAX (e.g., Fig. 1), do the Alpha and Beta versions compute different values.

Version Alpha

```
PROGRAM Magenta(input, output).           PROGRAM Magenta(input, output).
VAR Max, I, Num   INTEGER.                VAR Max, I, Num   INTEGER.
BEGIN                                     BEGIN
   Max = 0.                                  Max = 0.
   FOR I = 1 TO 10 DO                        FOR I = 1 TO 10 DO
      BEGIN                                     BEGIN
         READLN(Num).                              READLN(Num).
         If Num > Max THEN Max = Num               -------
      END.                                         If Num |  | Max THEN Max = Num
   WRITELN(Max).                                           |  |
END                                                        -------
                                              END.
                                           WRITELN(Max).
                                        END
```

Version Beta

```
PROGRAM Purple(input, output).            PROGRAM Purple(input, output).
VAR Max, I, Num   INTEGER.                VAR Max, I, Num   INTEGER.
BEGIN                                     BEGIN
   Max = 999999.                             Max = 999999.
   FOR I = 1 TO 10 DO                        FOR I = 1 TO 10 DO
      BEGIN                                     BEGIN
         READLN(Num).                              READLN(Num).
         If Num < Max THEN Max = Num               -------
      END.                                         If Num |  | Max THEN Max = Num
   WRITELN(Max).                                           |  |
END                                                        -------
                                              END.
                                           WRITELN(Max).
                                        END
```

```
      Program type 1

Basic plan        search plan (max, min)

Discourse rule    A variable's name should reflect its function (1)

How construct
Beta version      violate discourse rule (1)

Alpha case        variable name agrees with
                  search function

Beta case         variable name does NOT agree
                  with search function
```

Fig. 1. Example: Program type 1.

III. GENERATING PLAN-LIKE AND UNPLAN-LIKE PROGRAMS

What makes a program plan-like rather than unplan-like is the way in which plans are *composed* in a program. The composition is governed by *rules of programming discourse*, which are analogous to discourse rules in ordinary conversation or discourse rules that govern the structure of stories. In Fig. 2 we depict a set of programming discourse rules that we have identified. Individually, they look innocuous enough, and one could hardly disagree with them. While these rules typically are not written down nor taught explicitly, we claim that programmers have and use these rules in the construction and comprehension of programs. If programmers do use these rules

(1) Variable names should reflect function.

(2) Don't include code that won't be used.

(2a) If there is a test for a condition, then the condition must have the potential of being true.

(3) A variable that is initialized via an assignment statement should be updated via an assignment statement).

(4) Don't do double duty with code in a non-obvious way

(5) An IF should be used when a statement body is guaranteed to be executed only once, and a WHILE used when a statement body may need to be repeatedly executed.

Fig. 2. Rules of programming discourse.

and expect other programmers to also use these rules, then we would predict that programs that violate these rules should be harder to understand than programs that do not.

One key point to notice in the following sections is that the unplan-like version (the Beta version) is *only slightly* different than the plan-like version (the Alpha version). That is, the idea is to take a plan-like program and modify it ever so slightly, by violating a discourse rule, so as to create an unplan-like version. Both versions are executable programs that usually compute the same function. Moreover, both versions have about the same surface characteristics: about the same number of lines of code, about the same number of operands and operations, etc. Thus, while more traditional methods of calculating program complexity (e.g., lines of code, or Halstead metrics [11]) would predict no difference in the difficulty of understanding for the two programs (the Alpha version and the Beta version), we are looking for differences in actual performance on an understanding task.

In the following sections we will describe how and why we constructed the plan-like and unplan-like programs for use in our empirical studies. In each of the next four sections we will describe a different pair of programs, where the Beta version of the pair is generated by violating one (or possibly two) of the discourse rules given in Fig. 2. We will refer to a pair of programs as exemplifying a program type; thus, we will describe four different program types:[4] 1) MAX, 2) SQRT, 3) AVERAGE, and 4) IF/WHILE.

A. Program Type 1: MAX

In Fig. 1, version Alpha is the plan-like version of a program that finds the maximum of some numbers. In our plan jargon, it uses the MAXIMUM SEARCH LOOP PLAN which in turns uses a RESULT VARIABLE PLAN. Notice that the RESULT VARIABLE is appropriately named Max, i.e., the name of the variable is consistent with the plan's function. In contrast version Beta is unplan-like since it uses a MINIMUM SEARCH LOOP PLAN in which the RESULT VARIABLE is inconsistent with the plan's function: the program computes the minimum of some numbers using a variable name Max. To create the Beta version, we violated the first rule of programming discourse in Fig. 2: *variable names should reflect function.* (See also, Weissman [22], who did exploratory empirical studies on the role of variable names.)

The fill-in-the-blank versions of both these programs are also given in Fig. 1. Our hypothesis is that programmers will see the variable name Max and thus "see" the program as a MAXIMUM SEARCH LOOP PLAN. In other words, the name of the variable will color how they understand the rest of the program. Therefore, in the Beta version, where the function of the procedure is inconsistent with variable Max, we predict that programmers will fill in the blank with a >, rather than a <—indicating that they see the program as computing the maximum of a set of integers, instead of the minimum.

B. Program Type 2: SQRT

The Alpha and Beta programs in Fig. 3 are both intended to produce the square root of N. Since N is in a loop which will repeat 10 times, 10 values will be printed out. The question is:

[4] The names given to each of the four types carry no deep significance: they are meant only to aid the reader.

How should N be set? In version Alpha the DATA GUARD PLAN constrains what should be filled into the blank line. That is, the Sqrt function must be protected from trying to take the Sqrt of a negative number; thus, the immediately preceding IF test checks to see if the number is negative, and makes it positive if necessary. Besides protecting the Sqrt function, the DATA GUARD PLAN exerts influence on what could reasonably be filled into the blank. The very presence of the DATA GUARD PLAN implies that the numbers might be negative and thus the manner in which N is set *must allow for it to be negative.* A typical way of realizing this constraint is via a Read(N); the user decides what values should be entered. In contrast, setting N via an assignment statement, e.g., N := I, would *never* result in a negative number—thus making the DATA GUARD PLAN totally superfluous. The influence of the DATA GUARD PLAN over the blank line stems from a rule of programming discourse: *if there is a test for a condition, then the condition must have the potential of being true.* Thus, the blank line must be filled in with something that does not make the DATA GUARD PLAN superfluous, e.g., Read(N).

In version Beta, however, we have added an additional constraint on the blank line: the VARIABLE PLAN for N starts off with an assignment type of initialization (N := 0) and sets up the expectation that N will also be updated via an assignment statement, e.g., N := N + I, or N := N + 1. However, this expectation conflicts with the expectation set up by the DATA GUARD PLAN [namely, Read(N)]. Moreover, there is an additional level of conflict: the expectation of the DATA GUARD PLAN is now in conflict with the initialization of N to 0. This latter conflict is due to a violation of the following rule of programming discourse: *a variable that is initialized via an assignment statement should be updated via an assignment statement.*

C. Program Type 3: AVERAGE

The programs in Fig. 4 calculate the average of some numbers that are read in; the stopping condition is the reading of the sentinel value, 99999. Version Alpha accomplishes the task in a typical fashion: variables are initialized to 0, a read-a-value/process-a-value loop [20] is used to accumulate the running total, and the average is calculated after the sentinel has been read. Version Beta was generated from version Alpha by violating another rule of programming discourse: *do not do double duty in a nonobvious manner.* That is, in version Beta, unlike in Alpha, the initialization actions of the COUNTER VARIABLE (Count) and RUNNING TOTAL VARIABLE PLANs (Sum) in Beta serve two purposes:

• Sum and Count are given initial values.

• The initial values are chosen so as to compensate for the fact that the loop is poorly constructed and will result in an off-by-one bug: the final sentinel value (99999) will be incorrectly added into the RUNNING TOTAL VARIABLE, Sum, and the COUNTER VARIABLE, Count, will also be incorrectly updated.

We felt that using Sum and Count in this way was most nonobvious, and would prove very hard for advanced programmers to comprehend.

D. Program Type 4: IF/WHILE

The difference between an IF statement and a WHILE statement in Pascal is that the latter executes a body of statements

Version Alpha

```
PROGRAM Beige(input, output);
  VAR Num   REAL;
      I     INTEGER;
  BEGIN
     FOR I  = 1 TO 10 DO
        BEGIN
           Read (Num);
           IF Num < 0 THEN Num  = -Num;
           Writeln ( Num, Sqrt(Num) );
              (* Sqrt is a built-in
                 function which returns the
                 square root of its argument*)
        END;
  END
```

```
PROGRAM Beige(input, output);
  VAR Num   REAL;
      I     INTEGER;
  BEGIN
     FOR I  = 1 TO 10 DO
        BEGIN
        ------------------------------
        |                            |
        |                            |
        ------------------------------
           IF Num < 0 THEN Num  = -Num;
           Writeln ( Num, Sqrt(Num) );
              (* Sqrt is a built-in
                 function which returns the
                 square root of its argument*)
        END;
  END
```

Version Beta

```
PROGRAM Violet(input, output);
  VAR Num   REAL;
      I     INTEGER;
  BEGIN
     Num  = 0;
     FOR I  = 1 TO 10 DO
        BEGIN
           Read (Num);
           IF Num < 0 THEN Num  = -Num;
           Writeln ( Num, Sqrt(Num) );
              (* Sqrt is a built-in
                 function which returns the
                 square root of its argument*)
        END;
  END
```

```
PROGRAM Violet(input, output);
  VAR Num   REAL;
      I     INTEGER;
  BEGIN
     Num  = 0;
     FOR I  = 1 TO 10 DO
        BEGIN
        ------------------------------
        |                            |
        |                            |
        ------------------------------
           IF Num < 0 THEN Num  = -Num;
           Writeln ( Num, Sqrt(Num) );
              (* Sqrt is a built-in
                 function which returns the
                 square root of its argument*)
        END;
  END
```

```
        Program type 2

Basic plan       guard plan, variable plan

Discourse rule   Don't include code that won't be used  (2)

                 If there is a test for a condition,
                 then the condition must have the
                 potential of being true  (2a)

                 A variable that is initialized
                 via an assignment statement
                 should be updated via an assignment statement  (3)


How construct
Beta version     include two incompatible discourse rules  (2) and (3)

Alpha case       guard plan predicts read initialization

Beta case        guard plan predicts read update,
                 but initialization plan predicts
                 assignment update
```

Fig. 3. Example: Program type 2.

repeatedly, while the former only executes the body once; note both have a testing component. In looking at programs written by novice programmers, we found that novices sometimes used a WHILE statement when the body would only be executed once: it was as if novices have a rule such as *when a body needs to be executed only once*, then *either a* WHILE *or an* IF *could be used*. We felt that advanced programmers would be horrified by such a rule, and, moreover, would be confused in seeing a WHILE in a situation that "clearly" called for an IF.

The programs in Fig. 5 were developed to test the above hypothesis. Both these programs test to see if some variable contains a number that is greater than a maximum, and if so, the variable is reset to the maximum. The Alpha version uses an IF test; the Beta version uses a WHILE statement. The Beta

Version Alpha

```
PROGRAM Grey(input, output).
VAR Sum, Count, Num   INTEGER.
    Average  REAL.
BEGIN
    Sum  = 0.
    Count  = 0.
    REPEAT
        READLN(Num).
        IF Num <> 99999 THEN
                    BEGIN
                        Sum  = Sum + Num.
                        Count  = Count + 1.
                    END.
        UNTIL Num = 99999.
        Average  = Sum/Count.
        WRITELN(Average).
END
```

```
PROGRAM Grey(input, output).
VAR Sum, Count, Num   INTEGER.
    Average  REAL.
BEGIN
    Sum  = 0.
    --------------------------------
    |                              |
    |                              |
    --------------------------------
    REPEAT
        READLN(Num).
        IF Num <> 99999 THEN
                    BEGIN
                        Sum  = Sum + Num.
                        Count  = Count + 1.
                    END.
        UNTIL Num = 99999.
        Average  = Sum/Count.
        WRITELN(Average).
END
```

Version Beta

```
PROGRAM Orange(input, output).
VAR Sum, Count  Num   INTEGER.
    Average  REAL.
BEGIN
    Sum  = -99999.
    Count  = -1.
    REPEAT
        READLN(Num).
        Sum  = Sum + Num.
        Count  = Count + 1.
        UNTIL Num = 99999.
        Average  = Sum/Count.
        WRITELN(Average).
END
```

```
PROGRAM Orange(input, output).
VAR Sum, Count, Num   INTEGER.
    Average  REAL.
BEGIN
    Sum  = -99999.
    --------------------------------
    |                              |
    |                              |
    --------------------------------
    REPEAT
        READLN(Num).
        Sum  = Sum + Num.
        Count  = Count + 1.
        UNTIL Num = 99999.
        Average  = Sum/Count.
        WRITELN(Average).
END
```

Program type 3

Basic plan	read/process, running total loop plan
Discourse rule	don't do double duty in a non-obvious way (4)
How construct Beta version	violate discourse rule (4)
Alpha case	initialize to standard values
Beta case	initialize to non-standard values to compensate for poorly formed loop

Fig. 4. Example: Program type 3.

version was generated from the Alpha version by violating the following discourse rule: *An IF should be used when a statement body is guaranteed to be executed only once, and a WHILE used when a statement body may need to be repeatedly executed.* If the advanced programmers do have this rule, then we predict that they would not recognize the RESET PLAN in the Beta version nearly as often as they would in the Alpha version.

IV. DETAILED DESCRIPTION OF STUDY I:
FILL-IN-THE-BLANK

A. Subjects

A total of 139 students participated in the experiment. These students were recruited from programming classes and were paid $5 for participating in the experiment. There were 94 novice level programmers and 45 advanced level programmers.

Version Alpha

```
PROGRAM Gold(input,output),
    CONST
        MaxSentence=99,
        NumOfConvicts=5,
    VAR
        ConvictID, I, Sentence    INTEGER,

    BEGIN
        FOR I =1 TO NumOfConvicts DO
            BEGIN
                READLN(ConvictID, Sentence),
                IF Sentence > MaxSentence
                    THEN  Sentence  = MaxSentence,
                    WRITELN(ConvictID, Sentence),
            END,
    END
```

```
PROGRAM Gold(input,output),
    CONST
        MaxSentence=99,
        NumOfConvicts=5,
    VAR
        ConvictID, I, Sentence   INTEGER,

    BEGIN
        FOR I =1 TO NumOfConvicts DO
            BEGIN
                READLN(ConvictID, Sentence),
                IF Sentence > MaxSentence
                            -------------------------------
                    THEN  |                               |
                            -------------------------------
                    WRITELN(ConvictID, Sentence),
            END,
    END
```

Version Beta

```
PROGRAM Silver(input,output),
    CONST
        MaxSentence=99,
        NumOfConvicts=5,
    VAR
        ConvictID, I, Sentence    INTEGER,

    BEGIN
        FOR I =1 TO NumOfConvicts DO
            BEGIN
                READLN(ConvictID, Sentence),
                WHILE Sentence > MaxSentence
                    DO Sentence  = MaxSentence,
                    WRITELN(ConvictID, Sentence),
            END,
    END
```

```
PROGRAM Silver(input,output),
    CONST
        MaxSentence=99,
        NumOfConvicts=5,
    VAR
        ConvictID, I, Sentence   INTEGER,

    BEGIN
        FOR I =1 TO NumOfConvicts DO
            BEGIN
                READLN(ConvictID, Sentence),
                WHILE Sentence > MaxSentence
                            -------------------------------
                    DO  |                               |
                            -------------------------------
                    WRITELN(ConvictID, Sentence),
            END,
    END
```

Program type 4

Basic plan	reset to boundary condition
Discourse rule	An IF should be used when a statement body is guaranteed to be executed only once, and a WHILE used when a statement body may need to be repeatedly executed (5)
How construct Beta version	violate discourse rule (5)
Alpha case	use IF for testing and one time execution
Beta case	use WHILE for testing and one time execution

Fig. 5. Example: Program type 4.

Novice programmers were students at the end of a first course in Pascal programming. The advanced level programmers had completed at least 3 programming courses, and most were either computer science majors or first year graduate students in computer science; all had extensive experience with Pascal.

B. Materials

We created two pairs of programs (an Alpha version and a Beta version comprise one pair) for each of the 4 program types described in Section III; thus there were eight pairs of programs, two pairs of programs for each program type. One instance (an Alpha-Beta pair) of each of the four program types was presented in the preceding sections. Both instances of a program type were similar. For example, in Fig. 6 the second instance of the program type MAX is given; while the first instance of this type searched for the maximum (minimum) integer input (Fig. 1), the second instance searched from the maximum (minimum) character input.

Version Alpha

```
PROGRAM Green(input, output);          PROGRAM Green(input, output);
VAR I   INTEGER;                       VAR I   INTEGER;
    Letter, LeastLetter   Char;            Letter, LeastLetter   Char;
BEGIN                                  BEGIN
    LeastLetter = 'z';                     LeastLetter = 'z';
    FOR I  = 1 TO 10 DO                    FOR I  = 1 TO 10 DO
        BEGIN                                  BEGIN
          READLN(Letter);                        READLN(Letter);
          If Letter < LeastLetter                 -------
              THEN LeastLetter = Letter;      If Letter |     | LeastLetter
        END;                                          |- |
    Writeln(LeastLetter);                             -------
END                                              THEN LeastLetter = Letter;
                                           END;
                                       Writeln(LeastLetter);
                                   END
```

Version Beta

```
PROGRAM Yellow(input, output);         PROGRAM Yellow(input, output);
VAR I   INTEGER;                       VAR I   INTEGER;
    Letter, LeastLetter   Char;            Letter, LeastLetter   Char;
BEGIN                                  BEGIN
    LeastLetter = 'a';                     LeastLetter = 'a';
    FOR I  = 1 TO 10 DO                    FOR I  = 1 TO 10 DO
        BEGIN                                  BEGIN
          READLN(Letter);                        READLN(Letter);
          If Letter > LeastLetter                 -------
              THEN LeastLetter = Letter;      If Letter |   | LeastLetter
        END;                                          |   |
    Writeln(LeastLetter);                             -------
END                                              THEN LeastLetter = Letter;
                                           END;
                                       Writeln(LeastLetter);
                                   END
```

```
Program type 1 -- Instance 2

Basic plan        search plan (max, min)

Discourse rule    A variable's name should reflect its function (1)

How construct
Beta version      violate discourse rule (1)

Alpha case        variable name agrees with
                  search function

Beta case         variable name does NOT agree
                  with search function
```

Fig. 6. Example: Program type 1–instance 2.

C. Design: Independent and Dependent Variables

The three independent variables in this study were:

1) version—Alpha (plan-like), Beta (unplan-like)
2) program type—1 MAX, 2 SQRT, 3 AVERAGE, 4 IF/ WHILE
3) level of expertise—novice or advanced.

There were two dependent variables:

1) accuracy of the response; a correct response was one that completed the intended plan,[5] and
2) time to complete a problem.

[5] Strictly speaking filling in the blank line with an answer that differs from the plan-like one would not necessarily be *incorrect*. For example, filling in the blank line in Beta of Fig. 1 with a > would still result in a running program. However, it would be a strange program. Thus, by *correct* we actually mean the line of code that in our judgment best fulfills the overall intent of the program.

D. Procedure

Each subject was given eight programs. In four of the problems, the subject received the Alpha version of the program while in the other four problems, the subject received the Beta version of the program. We also counterbalanced versions within each of the four program types such that if a subject received an Alpha version for one program of a type then the subject would receive the Beta version for the other program of the same type. The test programs were presented as a booklet in which the order of the programs was randomized for each subject. Subjects were instructed to work through the booklet in the given order. As we mentioned earlier, each program was presented with one blank; subjects were not told what problems the programs were intended to solve. Subjects were given the following instruction: *fill in the blank line with a line of Pascal code which in your opinion best completes the program.* They were given as much time to do the test as they wanted; almost all finished within an hour.

E. Results and Discussion

The main results in this study were:

- the experts performed better than the novices (61 percent versus 48 percent, $F_{1,137} = 17.27, p < 0.001$),
- subjects answered the Alpha versions correctly more often than they did the Beta versions (88 percent versus 31 percent, $F_{1,137} = 375.22, p < 0.001$).
- the interaction between program version and expertise was significant ($F_{1,137} = 6.78, p < 0.01$).

Moreover, using a Newman-Keuls test the difference in performance between the novice and the advanced subjects for the Alpha versions was significant at the 0.05 level, while there was no significant difference between the two groups of subjects on the Beta versions. Thus, the statistical analyses support the visual effect of the graph in Fig. 7: the performance of the advanced students was reduced to that of the novices by the Beta versions!

The magnitude of the change in performance by the advanced programmers is impressive (Fig. 7): the advanced programmers performed about 50 percent worse on the Beta versions that they did on the Alpha versions. (This difference was significant at the 0.01 level using a Newman-Keuls test.) Given that the only difference between the two versions was a violation of one (or possibly two) rule of programming discourse, we are impressed with the enormous size of this difference. Clearly, discourse rules in programming have a major effect on programmers' abilities to comprehend programs.

A breakdown by version and program type is given in Table I. Here we see the percentage of subjects that correctly answered each program.

- There was a significant difference in accuracy for the four program types ($F_{3,411} = 26.81, p < 0.001$).
- Also, the differences between the Alpha and Beta programs was not constant over the four program types. This interaction between program type and version was significant ($F_{3,411} = 68.39, p < 0.001$).

While we had attempted to keep all the program types at about the same level of difficulty, apparently we were not successful in this regard.

There was also a significant three-way interaction between program type, version, and expertise ($F_{3,411} = 3.12, p < 0.05$). An intuition for this interaction can be gleaned from Table I: performance on the Beta version of the SQRT program type differed greatly from the performance on the Beta versions of the other program types. This difference was statistically significant at the 0.01 level using a Newman-Keuls test. Why was the performance on the Beta versions of this one program type so high? The most plausible explanation is based on a practice effect: since in every other program that the subjects saw, data were input via a READ statement, subjects simply did not even see the conflict and immediately filled in the blank line with a READ.

In Table II we display a breakdown of the number and type of errors that subjects made. There were of course, more errors made on the Beta versions (390) than on the Alpha versions (140) ($p < 0.001$ by a sign test).[6] More interesting, however, were the type of errors made on the Beta versions. Our theory makes a strong prediction about the type of incorrect response that subjects will make on the Beta versions: if subjects do not recognize that the Beta versions are unplan-like, and if subjects are simply using plans and discourse rules to guide their responses, then we expect them to perceive the Beta version as just being an Alpha version, *and provide the plan-like response for the Alpha version.* For example, as discussed earlier (Section III-A), Program Purple in Fig. 1 actually computes the minimum of a set of inputs; however, it appears, because of the key variable name MAX to compute the maximum of some input values. The correct fill-in-the-blank answer for the Program Purple was '<'. However, we predicted that those subjects who fill in the blank incorrectly would do so by saying '>'–which *is* the correct answer for the Alpha version.

The data do bear out the above prediction: the difference between the plan-like incorrect responses and the unplan-like incorrect responses on the Beta versions was significant ($p < .01$ by a sign test):[7] 66 percent (257/390) of the incorrect responses on the Beta versions were one specific response–the response that would have been appropriate for the corresponding Alpha version of the program.

Another view of the effect of the unplan-like Beta versions on our subjects' performance can be seen by examining the amount of time it took subjects to provide a *correct* response to the Alpha and the Beta versions. Fig. 8 depicts this relationship. The difference in response time for the correct answers between the Alpha and Beta versions was significant ($F_{1,288} = 35.1, p < 0.001$); it took approximately 50 percent more time to respond correctly to the Beta versions than it did to respond correctly to the Alpha versions. The difference between novice and advanced programmers was also significant ($F_{1,288} = 8.6$,

---

[6]The p value of 0.001 reduces the likelihood that we are affirming a chance result from having partitioned the data.

[7]The p value of 0.01 reduces the likelihood that we are affirming a chance result from having partitioned the data.

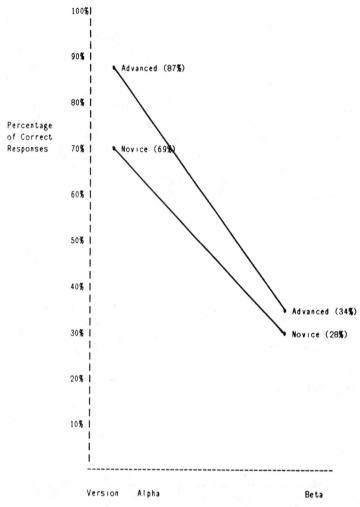

Fig. 7. Interaction: Expertise and program type.

TABLE I
PERCENTAGE OF CORRECTNESS BY PROGRAM TYPE

NOVICES (N = 94)		
Program Type	Alpha	Beta
1 MAX	78%	12%
2 SQRT	69%	61%
3 AVERAGE	80%	01%
4 IF/WHILE	48%	38%
ADVANCED (N = 45)		
1 MAX	93%	13%
2 SQRT	87%	84%
3 AVERAGE	96%	06%
4 IF/WHILE	73%	31%

TABLE II
ERROR DATA: FILL-IN-THE-BLANK STUDY

ERRORS on Alpha and Beta Versions:

Alpha Versions:
    Total number of errors by Novice and Advanced Subjects: 140
Beta Versions:
    Total number of errors by Novice and Advanced Subjects: 390

ERRORS on only Beta Versions:

Plan-like Errors:
    Total number on Beta versions by Novice and Advanced Subjects: 257
Unplan-like Errors:
    Total number on Beta versions by Novice and Advanced Subjects: 133

                                                                    390

$p < 0.01$); however, we did not find an interaction between expertise and program version in this situation ($F < 1$).

Our interpretation of these data is as follows: we conjecture that a correct response to the Alpha versions required only that programmers use their knowledge of programming plans and rules of programming discourse in a straightforward manner. However, in order to arrive at a correct answer to the Beta versions, subjects needed to employ additional processing techniques, e.g., trying to run the program on some sample numbers. This additional mental processing time corresponds to the increase in response time. Thus, not only do unplan-like pro-

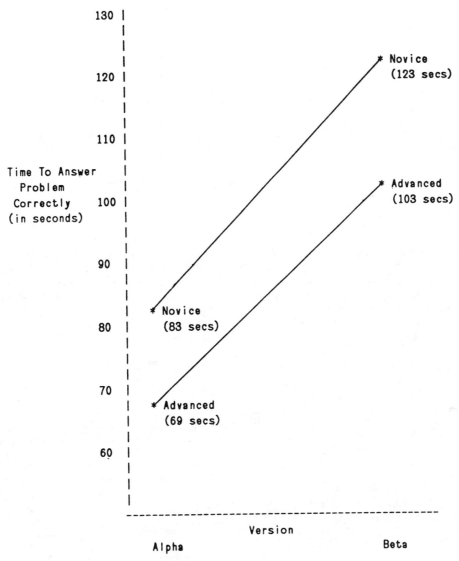

Fig. 8. Time to respond correctly: Alpha version versus beta version.

grams reduce the accuracy of programmers, their time to respond correctly to the unplan-like ones goes up dramatically since they need to bring in additional reasoning strategies in order to compensate for the unplanliness of the Beta versions.

V. DETAILED DESCRIPTION OF STUDY II: RECALL

A. Subjects

A total of 41 professional programmers participated in this study. The mean number of years experience was 7.5, with a standard deviation of 4.8. The minimum number of years of experience was 2 and the maximum was 20. The company for which these programmers worked gave them time off during the workday to participate in this study. Thus we did not have to pay subjects for their participation.

B. Materials

The programs we used in this study were essentially the same as those used in the study described above; the main differences were:

• the programs in this study were translated from Pascal into Algol, the language used by these subjects;

• program type SQRT was eliminated; in the Beta versions, these programs simply have an extra line of code, the initialization of N, which we felt was too mild a difference from the Alpha versions.

As described in Section III, each Alpha-Beta pair of programs was essentially identical[8] except for two critical lines (e.g., see lines 5 and 9 in the programs in Fig. 9.) We have called these lines critical because they carry the information that makes the programs plan-like or not. In the following analysis, we will focus on the two critical lines in assessing whether expert

[8]Programs of type AVERAGE were slightly different (see Fig. 4): the Alpha versions used a process/read loop structure, while the Beta conditions used a process/read structure [19]. However, the Alpha programs contain fewer lines than the Beta versions; thus, by more standard measures of program complexity (e.g., Halstead [11] or "lines of code") the Alpha programs should be harder to comprehend than the Beta ones.

```
Program Type MAX   Version Alpha              Program Type MAX   Version Beta

% PROGRAM MAGENTA,                             % PROGRAM PURPLE,
01 BEGIN                                          BEGIN
02    FILE REM (KIND = REMOTE, UNITS = CHARACTERS,   FILE REM (KIND = REMOTE, UNITS = CHARACTERS,
03           MAXRECSIZE = 1920, MYUSE = IO),             MAXRECSIZE = 1920, MYUSE = IO),
04    INTEGER MAX,I,NUM,                            INTEGER MAX,I,NUM,
05    MAX = 0,                                      MAX = 1000000,
06    FOR I = 1 STEP 1 UNTIL 10 DO                  FOR I = 1 STEP 1 UNTIL 10 DO
07       BEGIN                                         BEGIN
08          READ (REM,*/,NUM),                          READ (REM,*/,NUM),
09          IF NUM > MAX THEN MAX = NUM,                IF NUM < MAX THEN MAX = NUM,
10       END,                                          END,
11    WRITE(REM,*/,MAX),                            WRITE(REM,*/,MAX),
12 END                                            END
```

Fig. 9. Example: Critical lines in Algol programs. The critical lines in these programs—the lines that are different—are lines 05 and 09.

programmers recall plan-like programs better than unplan-like ones: we predict that the programmers should be able to recall the critical lines from the plan-like programs earlier than the critical lines from the unplan-like ones. The basis for this prediction is as follows: programmers will use their plans and discourse rules to encode a program when it is presented. In a plan-like program, the critical lines are the key representatives of the program's plans, and thus they should be recalled very early on. The fact that representatives of a category are recalled first is a recognized psychological principle [5]. However, in an unplan-like program, the critical lines do not represent the program's plans and as such should act no differently than the other lines in the program; thus, they should not be recalled first.

C. Design: Independent and Dependent Variables

In this study there were three independent variables:

- version—Alpha (plan-like), Beta (unplan-like)
- program type—MAX, AVERAGE, IF/WHILE
- trial—first, second, third presentation

As explained below, the dependent variable was correctness of recall of the critical lines.

D. Procedure

Subjects were presented with a complete program which they were asked to recall *verbatim*. The program was presented three times, each time for 20 s. On the first trial, subjects were asked to recall as much of the program as possible. On the second and third trials, they were asked to either add to their original recall or to change any part of their recall that they felt was in error. We tracked the progression of their recall by asking them to use a different color pencil on each of the three trials.

Just as in the previous study, there was two Alpha-Beta program pairs for each of three types of programs (MAX, AVERAGE, IF/WHILE). Each subject was shown a total of six programs: three Alpha and three Beta. We also counterbalanced version within each of the 3 program types such that if a subject received an Alpha version for one program of a type then the subject would receive the Beta version for the other program of the same type.

A critical line was scored as correct if and only if the line was recalled exactly as presented. If a subject recalled part of a critical line on the first trial and the rest of the line on the third trial, then the line would be scored as being recalled on the third trial. Similarly, if a subject recalled a whole line on the first trial but the recall was wrong, and if the subject corrected the line of the third trial, then again, this line would be scored as being correct on the third trial.

E. Results and Discussion

In Fig. 10 we present a summary of the results from the recall study. This figure shows the performance of programmers on the critical lines for all the programs. Shown are the cumulative percentages of recall for the critical lines for each of the three trials (presentations).[9] After the first trial, for example, 42 percent (101/240) of the critical lines on the Alpha versions were recalled correctly, while only 24 percent (58/240) of the critical lines on the Beta versions were recalled correctly. The effect of version was significant ($F_{1,40} = 9.05, p < 0.01$): more Alpha critical lines were recalled than Beta critical lines. The interaction of version and trial was also significant ($F_{2,80} = 4.72, p < 0.011$). The fact that the difference between the recall of the critical lines for the Alpha and the Beta versions changes over trials supports our hypothesis that the critical lines in the Alpha versions were recalled sooner than those in the Beta versions. Thus, just as in the study described previously (Section IV), we again see the significant, detrimental effect that unplan-like programs have on programmer performance.

In Table III we breakdown the errors and changes made by our three subjects. Of particular interest are the number of changes: programmers made almost three times as many changes on the Beta programs as they did on the Alpha programs.[10] Moreover, the changes made on the Beta programs were consistent with our theoretical predictions: subjects typi-

---

[9] The basis for this calculation is as follows: each subject was shown three Alpha programs and three Beta programs, there were two lines per program, and there were 40 subjects. Thus, there was a possible 240 critical lines in the Alpha programs, and 240 critical lines in the Beta programs.

[10] All changes on the Beta programs were from incorrect to correct; one subject changed from correct to incorrect on an Alpha program.

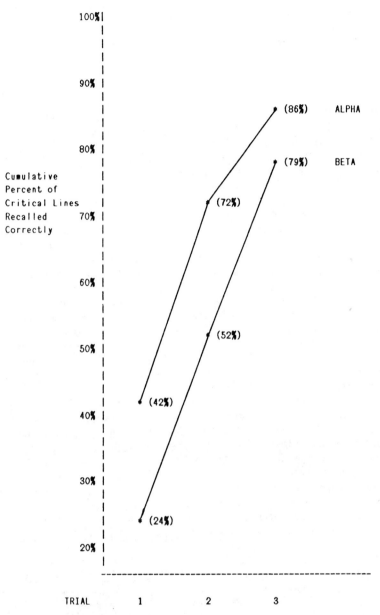

Fig. 10. Summary statistics of recall study.

cally incorrectly "recalled" the plan-like answer, and then changed their answer later to match what was actually being shown in the program. In particular, 22 out of 32 changes (69 percent) were from plan-like, but incorrect answers, to the correct answer. (This difference was significant $p < 0.025$ by a sign test.[11]) For example, on program PURPLE, which is a Beta version of type MAX (Fig. 9), of the eight subjects who made changes to the If line (line 9), seven of them initially wrote Num > Max—the response that would be correct if the program were actually finding the maximum value (see the Alpha version in Fig. 9)—and then changed their response on

[11] The p value of 0.025 reduces the likelihood that we are affirming a chance result from having partitioned the data.

TABLE III
BREAKDOWN OF THE ERRORS AND CHANGES THAT WERE MADE

	Correctly Recalled	Errors	Unrecalled	Changes
ALPHA (Out of 240)	206	17	23	12
BETA (Out of 240)	189	24	33	32

For BETA Programs Only

Changes Plan-like to Correct	Changes Otherwise
22	10

later trials to the correct Num < Max. Notice that these subjects were initially "recalling" something that *was not in the program.* Thus, just as in the fill-in-the-blank study, an analysis of incorrect responses is particularly telling: programmers expected to see plan-like programs and consistently behaved as if the programs at hand were plan-like.

VI. CONCLUDING REMARKS

The objective of these studies was to evaluate the claim that advanced programmers have and use 1) programming plans and 2) rules of programming discourse. The experiments discussed above were expressly designed to examine this question. The results of the experiments, as described above, support our initial claim.

- In Study I, when test programs were plan-like, advanced programmers did perform significantly better than novice programmers; however, when the test programs were *not* plan-like (i.e., the plan composition violated some rule of programming discourse), then the performance of the advanced programmers was reduced to essentially that of the novice programmers.

- In Study II, the performance of the expert programmers was significantly different on the plan-like programs as compared to the unplan-like ones: the critical lines in the plan-like programs were recalled earlier than those in the unplan-like ones.

On the one hand, the results point to the fragility of programming expertise: advanced programmers have *strong* expectations about what programs should look like, and when those expectations are violated—in seemingly innocuous ways—their performance drops drastically. On the other, the results support our claim that the plan knowledge and the discourse rule knowledge, upon which the expectations are built, do play a powerful role in program comprehension.

We hasten to point out that measures of surface characteristics, such as lines of code or Halstead metrics, would not predict the differences in performance we obtained. The Beta versions typically has either the same number of lines of code or slightly fewer lines of codes than did the comparable Alpha versions. We certainly do not dispute the results of earlier studies that show that such surface measures do correlate with program complexity (e.g., [6]). However, as our study vividly shows, surface feature measures do not necessarily predict complexity.

More importantly, our approach is to provide *explanations* for why a program may be complex and thus hard to comprehend. Towards this end, we have attempted to articulate the programming knowledge that programmers have and use. Thus, our intent is to move beyond *correlations* between programmer performance and surface complexity as measured by Halstead metrics, lines of code, etc., to a more principled, cognitive explanation (see also [20]).

A potential criticism of this work is that the programs we used in the experiments were unrealistic: while our experimental programs were short, the programs produced by experts are typically much longer. One major rationale for the use of short programs was experimental control: we wanted to keep as much constant as possible and only vary one (or possibly two) discourse rule. Given the range of results we obtained for the different program types (see Table I) we feel justified in our concern. Nonetheless, we are sensitive to the above criticism: while our intuition is that the effects we observed will in fact be more pronounced in longer programs, clearly, our studies need to be replicated with longer programs. While not discounting the value of this criticism, we feel that the magnitude of effects that we observed is too pronounced to simply be ignored.

In closing, then, our studies support the claim that knowledge of programming plans and rules of programming discourse can have a significant impact on program comprehension. In their book called *Elements of Style*, Kernighan and Plauger [13] also identify what we would call discourse rules. Our empirical results put teeth into these rules: it is not merely a matter of aesthetics that programs should be written in a particular style. Rather there is a psychological basis for writing programs in a conventional manner: programmers have strong *expectations* that other programmers will follow these discourse rules. If the rules are violated, then the utility afforded by the expectations that programmers have built up over time is effectively nullified. The results from the experiments with novice and advanced student programmers and with professional programmers described in this paper provide clear support for these claims.

ACKNOWLEDGMENTS

The authors would like to thank a number of colleagues who provided invaluable aid and comments on this research: B. Adelson, C. Seifert, D. Littman, E. Gold. We would also like to thank the reviewers for their helpful comments.

REFERENCES

[1] B. Adelson, "Problem solving and the development of abstract categories in programming languages," *Memory and Cognition*, vol. 9, pp. 422–433, 1981.
[2] F. C. Bartlett, *Remembering.* Cambridge, MA: Univ. Press, 1932.
[3] G. H. Bower, J. B. Black, and T. Turner, "Scripts in memory for text," *Cognitive Psychol.*, vol. 11, pp. 177–220, 1979.
[4] W. C. Chase, and H. Simon, "Perception in chess," *Cognitive Psychol.*, vol. 4, pp. 55–81, 1973.
[5] R. G. Crowder, "Principles of learning and memory," Lawrence Erlbaum Associates, Hillsdale, NJ, 1976.
[6] B. Curtis, S. Sheppard, and P. Milliman, "Third time charm: Stronger prediction of programmer performance by software complexity metrics," in *Proc. 4th Int. Conf. Software Eng.*, IEEE Comput. Soc., N. Denton, TX, 1979.
[7] A. D. deGroot, *Thought and Choice in Chess.* Paris, France: Mouton, 1965.
[8] D. Egan and B. Schwartz, "Chunking in recall of symbolic drawings," *Memory and Cognition*, vol. 7, pp. 149–158, 1979.
[9] K. Ehrlich and E. Soloway, "An empirical investigation of the tacit plan knowledge in programming," in *Human Factors in Computer Systems*, J. Thomas and M. L. Schneider, Eds. Norwood, NJ: Ablex Inc., 1984.
[10] A. C. Graesser, *Prose Comprehension Beyond the Word.* New York: Springer-Verlag, 1981.
[11] M. M. Halstead, *Elements of Software Science.* New York: Elsevier, 1977.
[12] J. H. Kaheny, "Problem solving by novice programmers," in *The Psychology of Computer Use: A European Perspective.* London, England: Academic, 1983.

[13] B. Kernighan and P. Plauger, *The Elements of Style*. New York: McGraw-Hill, 1978.

[14] J. Larkin, J. McDermott, D. Simon, and H. Simon, "Expert and novice performance in solving physics problems," *Science*, vol. 208, pp. 140-158, 1980.

[15] K. B. McKeithen, J. S. Reitman, H. H. Rueter, and S. C. Hirtle, "Knowledge organization and skill differences in computer programmers," *Cognitive Psychol.*, vol. 13, pp. 307-325, 1981.

[16] C. Rich, "Inspection methods in programming," M.I.T. Artificial Intell. Lab., Cambridge, MA, Tech. Rep. TR-604, 1981.

[17] R. C. Schank and R. Abelson, "Scripts, plans, goals, and understanding," Lawrence Erlbaum Associates, Hillsdale, NJ, 1977.

[18] B. Shneiderman, "Exploratory experiments in programmer behavior," *Int. J. Comput. Inform. Sci.*, vol. 5, no. 2, pp. 123-143, 1976.

[19] E. Soloway, K. Ehrlich, and J. Bonar, "Tapping into tacit programming knowledge," in *Proc. Conf. Human Factors in Comput. Syst.*, Nat. Bureau Standards, Gaithersburg, MD, 1982.

[20] E. Soloway, J. Bonar, and K. Ehrlich, "Cognitive strategies and looping constructs: An empirical study," *Commun. ACM*, vol. 26, pp. 853-861, 1983.

[21] E. Soloway, K. Ehrlich, and J. Black, "Beyond numbers: Don't ask "how many" ...ask "why", " in *Proc. SIGCHI Conf. Human Factors in Comput. Syst.*, SIGCHI, Boston, MA, 1983.

[22] L. Weissman, "Psychological complexity of computer programs: An experimental methodology," *SIGPLAN Notices*, vol. 9, June 1974.

He is an Assistant Professor of Computer Science at Yale University, New Haven, CT, and a Vice President of Compu-Tech, Inc., New Haven, an educational software company. His research interests include the cognitive underpinnings of programming, artificial intelligence, and computer science education.

Dr. Soloway is a member of the Association for Computing Machinery and the Cognitive Science Society.

Elliot Soloway received the B.A. degree in philosophy from Ohio State University, Columbus, in 1969, and the M.S. and Ph.D. degrees in computer science from the University of Massachusetts, Amherst, in 1976 and 1978, respectively.

Kate Ehrlich received the B.A. degree from the University of London, London, England, in 1973 and a Ph.D. degree from the University of Sussex, Sussex, England, in 1979.

She is a Human Factors Psychologist at Honeywell Information Systems, Inc., Waltham, MA. Her research interests include human-computer interaction, expert/novice difference in problem solving, artificial intelligence, and computers and education.

Dr. Ehrlich is a member of the Association for Computing Machinery, the American Association for Artificial Intelligence, the Cognitive Science Society, the Human Factors Society, and the Psychonomic Society.

X / Domain Knowledge

In a realistic automatic programming system, domain knowledge (i.e., knowledge about the particular application area of the program being written) is as important as programming knowledge. In particular, this kind of knowledge is essential to support the understanding of natural language and other user-oriented specifications (see Section IV).

Most of the experimental automatic programming systems described in Sections III, V, and VII do not contain much domain knowledge. They get away with this because they stop short of real end-user specifications. This section includes two relatively special-purpose systems that face up to the need for domain knowledge.

The DRACO system [Neighbors, Chapter 30] is a program generator generator. In order to create a program generator for a domain, a "domain designer" first defines a problem-oriented specifications language. The designer then uses DRACO to specify how to generate executable programs given the problem-oriented specifications as input. This approach is similar to the extensible language approach taken in PDS [Cheatham, Chapter 9], except that DRACO encourages even higher-level, domain-oriented, nonprocedural specifications. The mapping from specifications to implementation in DRACO is achieved primarily by transformations that encode domain knowledge, much as the transformations of the systems in Section III encode programming knowledge. Special-purpose procedures are used as a last resort.

The ΦNIX system [Barstow, Chapter 31] is a special-purpose automatic programming system that synthesizes programs related to oil well logging (determining how much oil is accessible from a given well). ΦNIX probably contains more (and more detailed) domain knowledge than any other automatic programming system in existence. Some of this knowledge is represented explicitly, such as via program transformations, but most of it is procedurally embedded.

[Borgida, Greenspan, and Mylopoulos, Chapter 32] treat the general topic of how to apply artificial intelligence techniques (such as frames and generalization hierarchies) to representing the domain knowledge underlying software requirements.

The Draco Approach to Constructing Software from Reusable Components

JAMES M. NEIGHBORS, MEMBER, IEEE

Abstract—This paper discusses an approach called Draco to the construction of software systems from reusable software parts. In particular we are concerned with the reuse of analysis and design information in addition to programming language code. The goal of the work on Draco has been to increase the productivity of software specialists in the construction of similar systems. The particular approach we have taken is to organize reusable software components by problem area or domain. Statements of programs in these specialized domains are then optimized by source-to-source program transformations and refined into other domains. The problems of maintaining the representational consistency of the developing program and producing efficient practical programs are discussed. Some examples from a prototype system are also given.

Index Term—Analysis, automatic programming, design, module interconnection languages, program generation, program refinement, program transformations, reusable software, software components.

I. INTRODUCTION

IN this paper we will outline an approach to software reusability which was developed through experiments with a prototype system called Draco[1] over the past several years.

Two basic approaches to the semiautomatic construction of software systems from reusable parts have been used. These approaches may be differentiated by the languages used to represent the developing program. In a *wide-spectrum language* approach one language suffices to represent the developing program from specification to final executable code. In a *narrow-spectrum language* approach there is a separate language for each phase of program development (e.g., specification language, design language, executable language) and the program progresses from being completely described in one language to being completely described in the next language. With both approaches the same language or set of languages is used to develop all programs.

The Draco approach described in this paper is neither a wide-spectrum language approach nor a narrow-spectrum language approach. Instead, we propose a different language called a *domain language* for describing programs in each different

Manuscript received August 1, 1983; revised May 14, 1984. This work was supported by the National Science Foundation under Grant MCS-81-03718 and by the Air Force Office of Scientific Research (AFOSR).

The author was with the Department of Information and Computer Science, University of California, Irvine, CA 92717. He is now with the CXC Corporation, Irvine, CA 92714.

[1] It has been a common practice to name new computer languages after stars. Since the approach described in this paper manipulates special-purpose languages it seemed only fitting to name it after a structure of stars, a galaxy.

problem area. The objects and operations in a domain language represent analysis information about a problem domain. Analysis information states *what* is important to model in the problem. This analysis information is *reused* every time a new program to be constructed is cast in a domain language. Further, we propose that the objects and operations from one domain language be implemented by being modeled by the objects and operations of other domain languages. These modeling connections between different domain languages represent different design possibilities for the objects and operations in the domains. Design information state *how* part of the problem is to modeled. *This design information is reused each time a new program to be constructed uses one of the given design possibilities.* Eventually, the developing program must be modeled in a conventional executable general-purpose language. These comprise the bottom level of the domain language modelling hierarchy.

The fine details, relevant work, and design tradeoffs of the Draco approach are discussed in more detail in [7]. The features and limitations of the current Draco implementation are given in the Draco manual [8].

II. THE ORGANIZATIONAL CONTEXT OF DRACO

Before we go into the technical details of a Draco program description and development it is helpful to understand the roles of people who interact with the system to supply these details. Fig. 1 shows the flow of information between people in different roles external to Draco.

Classically, during the system analysis phase of software construction a user with a desire for a certain type of system would interact with a systems analyst who would specify *what* the system should do based on the analyst's past experience with these types of systems. This would be passed on to system designers who would specify *how* the system was to perform its function.

With Draco we hypothesize two new major human roles: the domain analyst and the domain designer. A *domain analyst* is a person who examines the needs and requirements of a collection of systems which seem "similar." We have found that this work is only successfully done by a person who has built many systems for different customers in the same problem area. We refer to the encapsulation of this problem area as a *domain*. Once the domain analyst has described the objects and operations which are germane to an area of interest, then these are given to a *domain designer* who specifies different implementations for these objects and operations *in terms of the other*

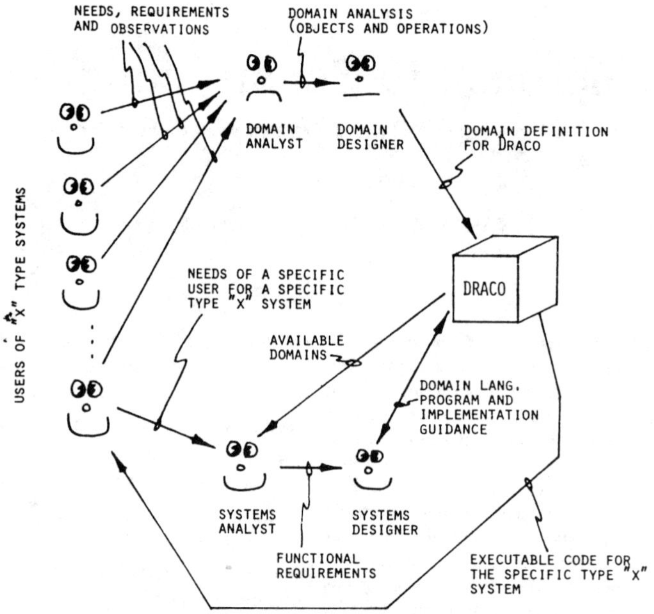

Fig. 1. Organizational context of Draco.

domains *already known to Draco.* The particular information needed to specify a domain is given in the following section.

Once a set of Draco domains has been developed by an organization in their area of software system construction, then new system requirements from users can be considered by the organization's *systems analysts* in the light of the Draco domains which already exist. If a Draco domain exists which can acceptably describe the objects and operations of a new system, then the systems analyst has a framework on which to hang the new specification. This is the *reuse of analysis information* and in our opinion it is the most powerful brand of reuse. Once the new system is cast as a domain language program, the *systems designer* interacts with Draco in the refinement of the problem to executable code. In this interaction the systems designer has the ability to make decisions between different implementations as specified by the domain designers of the Draco domains. This is the *reuse of design information* and it is the second most powerful brand of reuse.

Thus, Draco captures the experience of the "old hands" of the organization and delivers this experience in problem specific terms to *every* systems analyst in the organization for their education and use.

III. What Comprises a Domain Description?

In this section we will describe the results of domain analysis and domain design which must be given to the Draco mechanism to specify a complete domain. There are five parts to a domain description.

1) Parser: The parser defines the external syntax of the domain and the *prefix internal form* of the domain. The syntax is described in a conventional BNF notation which is augmented with control mechanisms such as parser error recovery and parser backtracking. The internal form is a tree with an at-

tribute name and data at each node. The internal form is the data actually manipulated by Draco.

2) Prettyprinter: The prettyprinter description tells Draco how to produce the external syntax of the domain for all possible *program fragments* in the internal form of the domain. This is necessary for the mechanism to be able to interact with people in the language of the domain and discuss incomplete parts of the developing program.

3) Transformations: The program transformations on a domain language program are *strictly source-to-source transformations* on the objects and operations of the domain. These transformations represent the rules of exchange between the objects and operations of the domain and are guaranteed to be correct independent of any particular implementation chosen for any object or operation in the domain.

4) Components: The *software components* specify the semantics of the domain. There is one software component for each object and operation in the domain. The software components make *implementation decisions.* Each software component consists of one or more *refinements* which represent the different implementations for the object or operation. *Each refinement is a restatement of the semantics of the object or operation in terms of one or more domain languages known to Draco.*

5) Procedures: Domain-specific procedures are used in circumstances where the knowledge to do a certain domain-specific transformation is algorithmic in nature. An example is the construction of LR(k) parser tables from a grammar description.

Thus, the basis of the Draco work is the use of *domain analysis* to produce *domain languages* which may be *transformed* for optimization purposes and implemented by *software components*, each of which contains multiple *refinements* which make implementation decisions by restating the problem in other domain languages.

IV. Differences in Definition from Other Approaches

Before we describe how these different parts are managed in the construction of a program it is important to point out the differences and similarities between the Draco approach and other approaches which use similar techniques.

In the Draco approach we use the term "program transformation" to denote only *source-to-source program transformations*. This means that all transformations consist of a left-hand side (LHS) which is a simple syntatic pattern which is replaced by a right-hand side (RHS) which is a simple syntatic rearrangement of the matched portions of the LHS. Since in the Draco approach the LHS and RHS of a transformation must be in the same domain language, then these transformations must be independent of any particular implementation for any object or operation in the domain. This is an important concept and different from the definition of program transformation used in the USC/ISI Transformational Implementation system [1] and the Harvard Program Development System [3]. In these wide-spectrum language based systems the program transformations may have procedural LHS's in addition to syntatic and the resulting RHS's may have made an implementation decision and also be procedural. This concept of program transformation combines the functions of Draco transformations and Draco refinements. Draco domain procedures are similar to the Draco transformations in that they only operate in one domain and never reach across domain boundaries to make implementation decisions. *Draco program transformations never make implementation decisions; they only represent optimizations at the domain language level.*

A Draco refinement at a high level of abstraction is similar to the concept of a plan in the M.I.T. Programmer's Apprentice system [15]. Each refinement of a component gives a plan for representing the semantics of that component. Refinements can be recursive to allow representations such as lists as arrays and arrays as lists.

V. An Example Domain Organization

Since each domain is implemented in terms of other domains the domain designers are really forming an organization of domains. Fig. 2 shows how some hypothetical domains might be connected together to build a "statistics reporting domain."

It is important to keep in mind that the "report format domain" might be used by many other domains other than the "statistics reporting domain" and this too is the reuse of analysis. It has been our experience that some domains such as a database domain are used in the design of many other domains. Thus in our figure we are not just discussing a reusable "statistics reporting domain," we are really discussing the reusable domains of "report formatting" and "statistical calculation." The "statistics reporting domain" is simply an instance of reuse.

While some domains sound very problem specific such as an "Air Defense System" domain where there is not a lot of demand for many systems, keep in mind that these domains are primarily built out of general and much more reusable do-

mains (e.g., database domain, graphics domain) which are tailored in the refinement process to the specific problem. We call general domains *modeling domains*.

Draco is a scheme where the problem is represented by many languages at once where the languages are not in a strict hierarchy. The person guiding the refinement decides which parts of a developing program are to be refined first. This fixes design decisions which will help to mechanically guide the refinement process later on.

A. A Domain Organization for the Examples Presented

To demonstrate the interactions between domain languages, refinements, and transformations for the examples in the rest of the paper we need an example domain organization. In addition, even though the most interesting domains are very problem specific, we need to choose a problem domain which will not slow the reader down in the details of a particular problem domain. We will attempt to solve this problem of examples by presenting an analogy. Assume we have the domain orgainization shown in Fig. 3.

In this simple domain organization SIMAL is an infix algorithmic general-purpose domain language we will invent for examples, ATN is an augmented transition network domain for describing natural language parsers, and LISP is a general-purpose prefix language. In this domain organization only the ATN domain represents the problem-specific concepts we really advocate. This is an actual domain with which we have experience and an example program statement in the domain is given in the Appendix. The reader can see that the ATN domain language differs vastly from general-purpose languages.

Within the ATN domain the concept of a "state" in a transition network is embodied as a software component since it is one of the objects and operations of the ATN problem domain. In the ATN example in the Appendix, SENTENCE is a state with two emanating arcs, one to the state Q1 and one to the state Q2. Within LISP there is no concept corresponding to an ATN state so the concept of an ATN state must be refined[2] by one of the refinements of the ATN component state into a collection of objects and operations in LISP.

For the sake of example only let us assume that the SIMAL domain has an operation for which there is no corresponding operator in the LISP domain. In our examples we have assumed that the SIMAL domain contains an exponentiation operator and that the LISP domain does not. The analogy we wish to draw is between the implementation of an ATN state in the LISP domain and the implementation of a SIMAL exponentiation in the LISP domain. When the reader becomes uncomfortable because we are discussing the simple implementation of an exponentiation operator in a single refinement, please keep in mind that by analogy we are discussing the implementation of a parallel executing ATN state through what could be many refinements in many domains. The goal here is to emphasize the process of the approach and not the particular domain being manipulated.

[2] Actually, in the prototype system an ATN state is refined into a statement in a collection of other domains such as the model of parallel execution of tasks (TSK domain); but for the examples this simple view is useful.

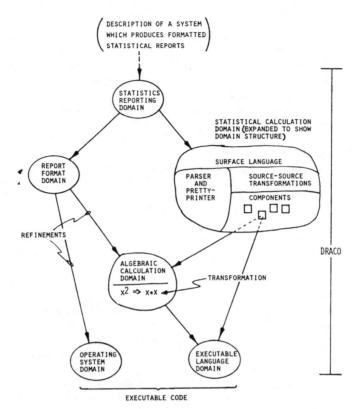

Fig. 2. An example domain organization.

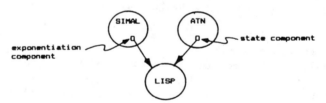

Fig. 3. Domain organization for example by analogy.

VI. SOFTWARE COMPONENTS AND THE REFINEMENT PROCESS

There is one software component for each object and operation in a domain and each software component consists of multiple refinements. Each refinement makes an implementation decision by restating the semantics of the object or operation in terms of other domains known to Draco. The *refinement process* is the process of restating the problem originally specified in one domain repetitively into other domains. Eventually, the level of abstraction of the developing program must decrease to an executable language. Each refinement must specify its implementation decisions explicitly so that Draco can *automatically maintain the consistency* of the developing program. As an example, if an operation in a domain manipulates an object in that domain, then the chosen refinements of these two components must agree on the underlying representation of the object. These decisions are manually specified by the domain designer, automatically kept by the Draco mech-

anism, and semiautomatically used by a systems designer in a form similar to that used in module interconnection languages (MIL's) which are discussed in [9].

An example software component for exponentiation in the SIMAL domain is shown in Fig. 4.

The example component has two refinements which refine the exponentiation operator in the SIMAL domain back into the SIMAL domain by making implementation decisions. Notice that the choice of one or the other of these refinements will cause the final programs to act differently even if all other implementation decisions are the same. The exception conditions for these two methods are different as are the acceptable types and ranges.

During the refinement process a *systems designer* would be responsible for making two different decisions with respect to this component. First it must be decided which *refinement* to use, and second it must be decided what kind of *modular structure* will result from the refinement.

```
COMPONENT: EXP(A,B)
PURPOSE:   exponentiation, raise A to the Bth power
IOSPEC:    A:number,B:number/number
DECISION:  The binary shift method is O(ln2(B)) and requires
           B integer=>0 while the Taylor expansion is an
           adjustable number of terms and requires A>0.

REFINEMENT: binary shift method
CONDITIONS: A a SIMAL number
            B a SIMAL integer
BACKGROUND: Knuth's SemiNumerical, Algorithm A, pg. 399
INSTANTIATION: FUNCTION, INLINE
CODE: SIMAL.BLOCK
       [[ IF B<0 THEN EXCEPTION ;
          POWER:=B ; NUMBER:=A ; ANSWER:=1 ;
          WHILE POWER>0 DO
             [[ IF POWER&1=1 THEN ANSWER:=ANSWER*NUMBER ;
                POWER:=POWER>>1 ;
                NUMBER:=NUMBER*NUMBER ]] ;
          RETURN ANSWER ]]
END REFINEMENT

REFINEMENT: Taylor expansion
CONDITIONS: A,B as SIMAL numbers
BACKGROUND: VNR Math Encyclopedia, pg. 490
INSTANTIATION: FUNCTION, INLINE
ADJUSTMENTS: TERMS[20] - number of terms, error is
             approximately (B*ln(A))^TERMS/TERMS!
CODE: SIMAL.BLOCK
       [[ IF A<=0 THEN EXCEPTION ;
          SUM:=1 ; TOP:=B*LN(A) ; TERM:=1 ;
          FOR I:=1 TO TERMS DO
             [[ TERM:=(TOP/I)*TERM ;
                SUM:=SUM+TERM ]] ;
          RETURN SUM ]]
END REFINEMENT
END COMPONENT
```

Fig. 4. An example software component.

The decision of which refinement to use must be made unless some of the refinements have been excluded by ASSERTIONS in previously used refinements. As an example, if it had previously been decided that all numbers in the domain would be represented in floating point notation, then the "binary shift method" would be automatically excluded from use by the Draco *refinement consistency checking*. ASSERTIONS specify implementation decisions if a refinement is used and CONDITIONS specify decisions which must have been made before a refinement may be used. Primarily the domain object refinements make ASSERTIONS and domain operation refinements check CONDITIONS.

Once a refinement for a component is chosen, the system designer must describe how the refinement is to fit into the modular structure of the developing program. The different possibilities are governed by the INSTANTIATION field of the refinement. By *modular structure* we mean the function-procedure call structure of the resulting program. If the refinement is used INLINE, then one can think of the refinement mechanism as simply expanding the refinement in the developing program as a macro.[3] If the refinement is used as a FUNCTION, then the body of the refinement is set aside as a function definition and the original use of the component is replaced with a call to the function.[4] Between these two extremes is PARTIAL instantiation where some of the arguments are instantiated inline and some are passed.[5]

If a single problem statement is refined with different modular structure and implementation decisions, then the resulting executable programs will exhibit drastically different execution speed and space characteristics [7].

The refinement and modular structure decisions must be considered by the systems designer for each and every component in every domain in the developing system. These are far too many decisions for a person to make or even consider for a large system. The refinement mechansim in Draco provides two primary mechansims for dealing with this complexity: *domains* and *tactics*.

A. Domains as an Aid to Refinement Complexity

Aside from the convenient encapsulation of a problem area that the concept of domains provides to the domain and systems analysts, the domain concept is also of use to the designers. The original problem is stated in the domain language of a single domain, but the instant the refinement process is invoked on the problem, it ends up as a statement in many domains at once. These domains are being used as *modeling domains* for the problem [14]. Fig. 5 graphically illustrates the refinement process from a statement in only the problem domain (ATN), through many modeling domains (ATN and TSK), and into the final target domain (LISP).

The systems designer works with the refinement mechanism in one domain at a time. In a developing program there may be multiple *instances* of a domain, the refinement mechansim may be directed to scan all instances during refinement or a single one. The concept of domain here is very useful in supplying a psychological set to the systems designer (i.e., the designer must only consider and think about the objects and operations of one domain at a time). The ability to provide a psychological set to the systems designer is lost if the underlying representation of the developing program is a wide-spectrum language.

---

[3]With variable renaming and access problems it is a bit more complex than a macro expansion, but this is a useful model of the process.
[4]The types and accesses to the passed parameters must be right, of course.
[5]In the PARTIAL case, Draco must keep track of different versions of the functions.

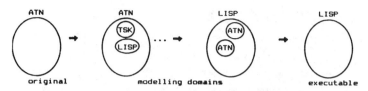

Fig. 5. Domains in the refinement process.

B. Tactics for Refinement

The domain instance concept limits the scope of what the systems designer has to think about. The *refinement tactics* limit the sheer number of decisions the systems designer must make.

The tactics are domain-independent rules for making refinement decisions about representation and modular structure. They are not guaranteed to make a decision and when they do not the systems designer must make the decision. Tactics must obey the refinement consistency checking just as the systems designer must. Some example tactics are summarized below.

1) If we have already defined a function which implements this component, then use that function.

2) If there is a refinement to this component which can be made into a function, then use it as a function.

3) Use the default refinement for the component (the first one specified) with the default instantiation (the first instantiation specified).

4) Use the refinement with the minimum number of assertions and conditions.

The Draco approach to rapid prototyping is to build tactics which use the default refinement under the default instantiation. These refinements are usually very general (i.e., few conditions and assertions) but expensive in time and space. Very little interaction is required from the systems designer in this case other than selecting the domains and using the rapid prototyping tactics.

We refer to this mechanism as tactics because policy decisions are made without respect to the global context and Draco domain organizational structure. We expect to investigate *refinement strategies* and will discuss these later.

C. Recording the Refinement Process

The refinement process does *not* proceed strictly top-down or from one language level to another. In fact, sometimes it is necessary to back-up the refinement process to remove an overly restrictive decision. As the process proceeds a *refinement history* is recorded which can supply a top-down derivation for each statement in the resulting executable program. There are two uses for this refinement history: to understand the resulting program and to guide the *refinement replay* of the problem if the original specification is changed and a new implementation is needed [16].

The refinement history tends to be much larger than the resulting program code.[6] This large amount of information is lost to someone attempting to reuse an existing piece of source code. To combine two existing pieces of executable source

[6]Our best estimate is that the refinement history is about ten times the size of the resulting source code.

code this information must be recreated to ensure that any exchanged representations are consistent. For this reason we expect the reuse of existing executable source code will have a limited long-term benefit where whole systems are built from reusable parts.

In general we have found the making of design decisions to proceed as shown in Fig. 6.

The number of decisions to be made rises initially as implementation decisions must be made in the modeling domains and decreases finally as the already made decisions constrain the remaining decisions to only one choice. The *intermediate modeling swell* of this graph is the largest barrier to refinement.

VII. DOMAIN SPECIFIC SOURCE-TO-SOURCE PROGRAM TRANSFORMATIONS

It should be possible to refine a statement in any domain without the use of program transformations. The transformations only state rules of exchange between statements in a domain language and statements in that same domain language (i.e., *source-to-source transformations*).

Transformations are used only to optimize a domain language program. In general, the transformations are simple enough that they are seldom of use on a domain language program written by a systems designer. The transformations are usually obvious statements. The following might be transformations in the low-level SIMAL language.

ADDx0:   ?x+0 => ?x

MPYx0:   ?x*0 => 0

IFTRUE: IF TRUE THEN ?s1 ELSE ?s2 => ?s1

The following is a transformation in the high-level ATN language.

REMOVESTATE:

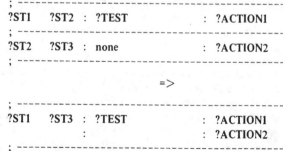

However, when a very general refinement of a component is used in a specific context the left-hand sides (LHS) of these simple rules of exchange tend to appear. Thus, the program

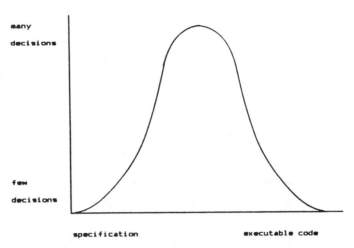

Fig. 6. Design decisions pending versus abstraction level.

transformations *specialize* the refinements of components to their use in a specific system at levels of abstraction far above that of executable code.

The transformations do not make or use implementation decisions but they do change the execution of the program. Certain side-effects must be checked or prohibited. The type and checking of these enabling conditions is discussed in [11]. As an example, the transformation MPYx0 above requires that the code fragment ?x does not write any data as a side-effect. Similarly, the ATN transformation REMOVESTATE requires that no other references to the state ?S2 exist.

A. The Transformation Naming Problem

A domain may easily have more than 2000 transformations and we do not believe that having the systems designer remember all the names or look them up in a catalog would be very successful. In the early program transformation systems the user would decide where to apply each transformation and which transformation to apply. This would be chaos in a Draco development with large programs and many domains.

In Draco all program fragments held in the internal form are annotated with all the program transformations which could apply. This includes domain language programs which have been parsed, refinement code bodies, and the RHS of all transformations. Thus, the systems designer never suggests transformations but instead *solicits suggestions* from Draco as to which transformations can be applied to a given program fragment. This technique coupled with the concept of *domain instances* discussed earlier keeps the system designer from having to examine too many suggested transformations.

As some tranformations are applied they suggest still other transformations which could apply. The scheme which keeps this process going is the interpretation of *transformation metarules*. The metarules relate the transformations of a domain to other transformations in that domain [6]. They are automatically produced as transformations are added to the transformation library of a domain. As an example metarule, the RHS of the transformation MPYx0 would contain a metarule which would suggest the transformation ADDx0 in an enclosing context because the LHS of ADDx0 contains a 0 and RHS of MPYx0 introduces a 0 into the program.

B. The Importance of Performing Source-to-Source Transformations at the Right Level of Abstraction

Assume that we have the transformation[7]

EXPx2: $?x\char`^2 => ?x*?x$

in the SIMAL language which converts an exponentiation to a multiply in a special case. This transformation is actually a manipulation of the exponentiation component presented in Fig. 4.

Given the above transformation and the Taylor expansion refinement from the EXP component in Fig. 4, then Fig. 7 presents the possible actions[8] to refine the SIMAL exponentiation operator into LISP which we have assumed has no exponentiation operator. Once the Taylor expansion has been used, no set of equivalence preserving program transformations can achieve the same effect as the EXPx2 transformation without *recognizing* that a Taylor expansion is the method being used. Such transformations would be far too specific to be useful. The problem is far more aggravated when we refine into a language such as LISP which we are assuming has no exponentiation operator. The designer of the LISP domain would not include transformations to recognize and deal with a Taylor expansion. Clearly this example is extreme in that we used an approximation, the Taylor expansion, to prove the point. If we had used the "binary shift method" of Fig. 4 many powerful SIMAL transformations would have been required to manipulate the results of the refinement into a simple multiply as EXPx2 does.

The ATN transformation REMOVESTATE removes states (the equivalent of parse rules) from parser descriptions. Extremely powerful transformations would be incapable of removing these same states from the resulting parallel executing LISP program.

The point here is that truly powerful optimization can be achieved with fairly simple mechanisms at the correct level of abstraction (i.e., at the domain language level). These optimi-

---

[7]EXPx2 requires the enabling condition that ?x be side-effect-free.
[8]Once again we must ask the reader to keep in mind the analogy between SIMAL and ATN we have drawn. This discussion also applies to the ATN transformation REMOVESTATE and the ATN component for state.

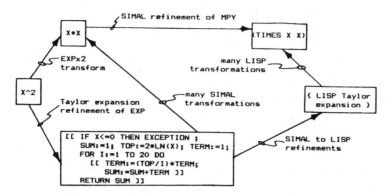

Fig. 7. Possible actions on a SIMAL exponentiation.

zations are far more powerful than all of the classical and more difficult optimizations (e.g., code motion, register allocation, reuse of temp space, data flow analysis, reduction in operator strength, etc.) which are applied to general-purpose low-level languages. *The use of source-to-source transformations on domain languages is the key to building efficient programs out of reusable and general software components.*

VIII. WHAT CAN BE SAID ABOUT THE POWER OF THE DRACO METHOD?

Given a collection of Draco domains with their interdependencies and their CONDITIONS and ASSERTIONS, we would like to know what we can do with them. In particular, given a specific domain language program, a set of domains, and a target domain (an executable language), we would like to be able to answer the following *reusability questions.*

1) Can we refine the domain language program completely into the target domain?

2) If so, can Draco provide an implementation for the given domain language program?

3) If not, what extra implementation knowledge is needed?

A Petri net model of the implementation decisions in the Draco domains can be constructed and the reusability questions can *be treated as the Petri net reachability problem* [7].

In particular, we were surprised to find that reusability questions 1 and 2 are *decidable*. It is unknown whether reusability question 3 is decidable or not.

Since reusability questions 1 and 2 are decidable, then the problem of *refinement deadlock* is decidable. The refinement deadlock problem plagues system designers and it occurs when the designer makes an implementation choice which will later on prohibit the program from being refinable into a given target domain. A program cannot be further refined when a consistent implementation is not possible with respect to the implementation decisions already made and the possible implementation choices in the given set of domains. After each decision the systems designer would like to know if a complete refinement of the problem into the target domain is still possible. Refinement deadlock primarily occurs when the designer is using elaborate refinements with many CONDITIONS and ASSERTIONS.

The decidability of questions 1 and 2 means that an algorithm can be constructed which will *automatically refine* any given problem with respect to a set of domains and their implementa-

tion restrictions if such an implementation exists. However, the complexity of the Petri net reachability problem prevents the straightforward use of the results. The complexity of answering the reusability questions for a medium-sized augmented transition network refined into only one other domain is approximately $O(2^{100})$. We do not regard this terribly high complexity as a insurmountable problem because in using full Petri nets we are using far too general a model. We suspect that a less general model and AI planning techniques will suffice as a basis for *refinement strategies* which are directly aimed at the reusability questions.

IX. CONCLUSIONS

The first Draco prototype became operational in 1979 [7], [8]. We have found experimenting with a complete prototype rewarding. The details and results of these experiments have been reported elsewhere [5], [7], [12], [13]. Our results and experience with the method is summarized in the following sections.

A. Reuse of Analysis, Design, and Code

We have found that the reuse of analysis and design is much more powerful than the reuse of code. We measure this power quite simply by the cost of these phases in the software life-cycle and the cost of correcting a mistake made in these phases. We realize that in the short term the reuse of code has the largest payoff and software producing organizations should start to exploit this technology now [4]. Code is very tricky to reuse. Many of the analysis, design, and implementation decisions which went into its construction are absent from the code itself. The fact that refinement histories may be more than 10 times the size of the final code speaks for the large amount of information missing in just the code itself. This loss of information will only become important when systems are built out of many reusable parts which must exchange information.

B. Domain Analysis and Design

Only about 10 or 12 full usable Draco domains have been built[9] and each has reenforced the idea that domain analysis and design is *very hard*. Typically, it takes an expert in a particular problem area four months to complete a first attempt at

---

[9] Our current research emphasis is on the instrumental use of Draco which will result in the production of more domains.

the domain. Even with well-documented work such as the ATN's it takes some time to read all the literature and extract an appropriate set of objects and operations. It takes further time to find an appropriate syntax for these structures. This is creative work and similar in scope to writing a survey paper on the area. As an example, a domain analysis of tactical display systems given by Sundfor [12] is over 100 pages long.

One sure way to make the Draco method fail is to have un-experienced people observe the work of the "old hands" to construct a domain. It is easy to construct a poor domain and very hard to construct a good one. The reasons are similar to the reasons for the failure of extensible languages [10] . Care-ful consideration over a long period of time is required to pro-duce a model of objects and operations in a problem area which is flexible enough to last through the 10–15 year lifespan of a large system.

C. Reusable Software and Efficiency

It is not true that software constructed from reusable soft-ware components must be inefficient. We have shown that, using the Draco method, systems with different implementa-tions and different modular structures can be created. Each of these has a different time–space execution characteristic.

In addition we discussed the use of domain-specific trans-formations to provide optimization at the correct level of ab-straction which results in more powerful optimizations than usually available to users of general-purpose languages. Neither source-to-transformations or domain languages by themselves will produce efficient programs. It is the combination of the two concepts which can produce efficient programs.

D. The Draco Method

The Draco method described here provides a context where source-to-source program transformations, module intercon-nection languages, software components, and domain-specific languages work together in the construction of similar systems from reusable parts. In fact, all of these techniques must be used if the draco method is to be successful.

APPENDIX

In the body of the paper we discuss Draco's manipulation of high-level languages in terms of analogies with low-level lan-guages like SIMAL. This Appendix presents program fragments from an actual high-level Draco domain in a form accepted by the current implementation.

A. Augmented Transition Network Example

This example taken from [7] presents a statement in the domain language of augmented transition networks.

```
ATN WOODS
NETWORK SENTENCE
; Example ATN from both Woods [17] and Burton [2].
; Abbreviations
;  NP      = noun phrase       NPR      = nomitive pronoun
;  PPRT    = past participle   ADJ      = adjective
;  ITRANS  = intransitive      AGNTFLG  = agent possible
;  TRANS   = transitive        DET      = determiner
;  PREP    = preposition       S-TRANS  = sentence object
;  PRO     = pronoun           AUXVERB  = auxiliary verb
;
; from    to  |      tests      |          actions
;-----------------------------------------------------------------
SENTENCE       |
      +Q1      | class AUXVERB ? | VERB:=word[ROOT]
               |                 | TENSE:=word[TENSE]
               |                 | TYPE:='QUESTION
;
       Q2      | none            | SUBJ<=NOUN-PHRASE
               |                 | TYPE:='DECLARE
;-----------------------------------------------------------------
Q1    Q3       | none            | SUBJ<=NOUN-PHRASE
;-----------------------------------------------------------------
Q2    +Q3      | class VERB ?    | VERB:=word[ROOT]
               |                 | TENSE:=word[TENSE]
;-----------------------------------------------------------------
Q3    Q3       | class VERB ?    | put SUBJ on hold as NP
               | is word PPRT ?  | SUBJ:=('NP ('PRO 'someone))
               | VERB='be        | AGNTFLG:='TRUE
               |                 | VERB:=word[ROOT]
;
       --------------------------------------------------------
```

	+Q3	class VERB is word PPRT ? VERB='have	TENSE:=TENSE+'PERFECT VERB:=word[ROOT]
;	Q4	is VERB TRANS ?	OBJ<=NOUN-PHRASE
;	Q4	holding NP? is VERB TRANS ?	OBJ::=remove NP from hold
;	exit	is VERB ITRANS ?	<=('S ('TYPE TYPE) ('SUBJ SUBJ) 　　　('VP ('TNS TENSE) ('V VERB)))
Q4	+Q7	word='by AGNTFLG='TRUE	AGNTFLG:='FALSE
;	+Q5	word='to is VERB S-TRANS?	none
;	exit	none	<=('S ('TYPE TYPE) ('SUBJ SUBJ) 　　　('VP ('TNS TENSE) 　　　('V VERB) ('OBJ OBJ)))
Q5	Q6	none	SUBJ::=OBJ TENSE::=TENSE TEMP:='DECLARE TYPE::=TEMP OBJ<=VERB-PHRASE
Q6	+Q7	word='by AGNTFLG='TRUE	AGNTFLG:='FALSE
;	exit	none	<=('S ('TYPE TYPE) ('SUBJ SUBJ) 　　　('VP ('TNS TENSE) ('V VERB) 　　　('OBJ OBJ)))
Q7	Q6	none	SUBJ<=NOUN-PHRASE
VERB-PHRASE	+Q3	class VERB ? is word UNTENSED?	VERB:=word[ROOT]
NOUN-PHRASE	+NP1	class DET ?	DET:=word[ROOT]
;	+NP3	class NPR ?	NPR:=word
NP1	+NP1	class ADJ ?	ADJS:=#ADJS+word[ROOT]
;	+NP2	class NOUN ?	NOUN:=word[ROOT]
NP2	exit	none	<=('NP ('DET DET) ('ADJ #ADJS) 　　　　　('NOUN NOUN))
NP3	exit	none	<=('NP ('NPR NPR))

REFERENCES

[1] R. Balzer, N. Goldman, and D. Wile, "On the transformational implementation approach to programming" in *Proc. 2nd IEEE Int. Conf. Software Eng.*, 1976, pp. 337-344.

[2] R. Burton, "Semantic grammar: A technique for efficient language understanding in a limited domain," Ph.D. dissertation, Dep. Inform. Comput. Sci., Univ. California, Irvine, 1976.

[3] T. E. Cheatham, G. H. Holloway, and J. A. Townley, "Program refinement by transformation," in *Proc. 5th IEEE Int. Conf. Software Eng.*, 1981, pp. 430-437.

[4] P. Freeman, "Reusable software engineering: Concepts and research directions," in *Proc. ITT Workshop on Reusability in Programming*, Sept. 1983, pp. 2-16.

[5] L. Gonzalez, "A domain language for processing standardized tests," Master's thesis, Dep. Inform. Comput. Sci., Univ. California, Irvine, 1981.

[6] D. Kibler, J. M. Neighbors, and T. A. Standish, "Program manipulation via an efficient production system," *SIGPLAN Notices*, vol. 12, no. 8, pp. 163-173, 1977.

[7] J. M. Neighbors, "Software construction using components," Ph.D. dissertation, Dep. Inform. Comput. Sci., Univ. California, Irvine, Tech. Rep. TR-160, 1980.

[8] J. M. Neighbors, "Draco 1.1 manual," Dep. Inform. Comput. Sci., Univ. California, Irvine, Tech. Rep. TR-156, 1980.

[9] R. Prieto-Diaz and J. M. Neighbors, "Module interconnection languages: A survey," Dep. Comput. Inform. Sci., Univ. California, Irvine, Tech. Rep. TR-189, 1982.

[10] T. A. Standish, "PPL—An extensible language that failed," Center Res. Comput. Technol., Harvard Univ., Cambridge, MA, Rep. 15-71, 1971.

[11] T. A. Standish, D. Harriman, D. Kibler, and J. M. Neighbors, "The Irvine program transformation catalogue," Dep. Inform. Comput. Sci., Univ. California, Irvine, Tech. Rep., 1976.

[12] S. Sundfor, "Draco domain analysis for a real time application: The analysis," Dep. Inform. Comput. Sci., Univ. California, Irvine, Tech. Rep. RTP 015, 1983.

[13] ——, "Draco domain analysis for a real time application: Discussion of the results," Tech. Rep., Dep. Inform. Comput. Sci., Univ. California, Irvine, RTP 016, 1983.

[14] F. Tonge and L. Rowe, "Date representation and synthesis," Dep. Inform. Comput. Sci., Univ. California, Irvine, Tech. Rep. TR-63, 1975.

[15] R. C. Waters. "The programmer's apprentice: Knowledge based program editing," *IEEE Trans. Software Eng.*, vol. SE-8, pp. 1-12, Jan. 1982.

[16] D. S. Wile, "Program developments: Formal explanations of implementations," *Commun. ACM*, vol. 26, pp. 902-911, Nov. 1983.

[17] W. A. Woods, "Transition network grammars for natural language analysis," *Commun. ACM*, vol. 13, pp. 591-606, Oct. 1970.

James M. Neighbors (S'78-S'80-M'80-M'81) received the B.S. degree in computer science in 1974, the B.A. degree in physics in 1974, and the Ph.D. degree in computer science in 1980, all from the University of California, Irvine.

He was an Adjunct Assistant Professor in Computer Science at the University of California, Irvine, from 1980 to 1983. Currently, he is specializing in understanding the structure and aiding the development of existing large (500 K lines and up) software systems at the CXC Corporation, Irvine.

Dr. Neighbors is a member of the Association for Computing Machinery, the IEEE Computer Society, and the American Association for Artificial Intelligence.

A Perspective on Automatic Programming

David Barstow

Schlumberger-Doll Research
Old Quarry Road
Ridgefield, Connecticut 06877

Abstract

Most work in automatic programming has focused primarily on the roles of deduction and programming knowledge. However, the role played by knowledge of the task domain seems to be at least as important, both for the usability of an automatic programming system and for the feasibility of building one which works on non-trivial problems. This perspective has evolved during the course of a variety of studies over the last several years, including detailed examination of existing software for a particular domain (quantitative interpretation of oil well logs) and the implementation of an experimental automatic programming system for that domain. The importance of domain knowledge has two important implications: a primary goal of automatic programming research should be to characterize the programming process for specific domains; and a crucial issue to be addressed in these characterizations is the interaction of domain and programming knowledge during program synthesis.

The perspective described here has resulted from the work of many people. Steve Smoliar, Stan Vestal, and especially Roger Duffey have been heavily involved in the design, implementation, and retrospective analysis of ϕ_0. Steve Smoliar and Roger Duffey have done detailed analyses of existing quantitative log interpretation software as well as several hypothetical syntheses. Paul Barth has been actively involved in the development of the model of programming for quantitative log interpretation described here; Steve Smoliar and Roger Duffey have contributed several key insights duringrr the process. Several of the interpretation developers at SDR have patiently and repeatedly explained the intricacies of log interpretation to us. Bruce Buchanan, Randy Davis, Elaine Kant, Tom Mitchell, and Reid Smith provided valuable feedback on earlier drafts of this paper.

MOST PREVIOUS WORK in automatic programming has focused on the roles played by deduction and programming knowledge in the programming process. For example, the work of Green (1969) and Waldinger and Lee (1969) in the late 1960s was concerned with the use of a theorem-prover to produce programs. This deductive paradigm continues to be the basis for much research in automatic programming (*e.g.*, Manna & Waldinger 1980, Smith 1983). In the mid 1970's, work on the PSI project (Barstow 1979, Green 1977, Kant 1981) and on the Programmer's Apprentice (Rich 1981) was fundamentally concerned with the codification of knowledge about programming techniques and the use of that knowledge in program synthesis and analysis. Work within the knowledge-based paradigm is also continuing (*e.g.*, Barstow 1982, Waters 1981).

This article is concerned with the role played by knowledge of the task domain, a role which seems to be at least as important. One of the reasons for this importance derives from the basic motivating assumption for work on automatic programming: there are many computer users who would prefer not to do their own programming and who would benefit from a facility that could quickly and accurately produce programs for them. The primary concern of these users is not computation — they generally are not interested in the idiosyncrasies of the programming process and certainly don't want to learn the strange notations computer scientists have developed. Rather, they are interested in some application domain — they have problems they wish solved and questions they wish answered. Computation is merely a tool to help solve the problems and answer the questions. Conventional programming is a hindrance to their use of that tool. It would be much more useful to them if they could communicate in the natural terms, concepts, and styles of their domain. For such interaction to be effective, the automatic programming systems must understand a great deal about the domain. Another reason for the importance of domain knowledge is that the problems to be solved and the questions to be answered are generally so complex that straightforward techniques are inadequate to write programs to solve them. Knowledge of the task domain can play a major role in helping a machine to cope with this complexity.

This perspective on the role of domain knowledge in automatic programming has evolved over the last two years during the course of a variety of studies by members of the Software Research group at Schlumberger-Doll Research [SDR]. These studies will be reviewed briefly, followed by a more detailed discussion of the perspective. An experimental research methodology will be illustrated by a project currently underway at SDR.

Logging an Oil Well.

Figure 1.

The Task Domain: Quantitative Log Interpretation

The task domain is the interpretation of well logs, an activity central to exploration for hydrocarbons. As illustrated in Figure 1, oil well logs are made by lowering instruments (called tools) into the borehole and recording the measurements made by the tools as they are raised to the surface. The resulting logs are sequences of values indexed by depth. (See Figure 2.) Logging tools measure a variety of basic petrophysical properties (e.g., the resistivity of the rock surrounding the borehole). Petroleum engineers, geophysicists and geologists are typically interested in other kinds of information which cannot be measured directly (e.g., water saturation — the fraction of the rock's pore space occupied by water rather than hydrocarbons). Log interpretation is the process of deriving the desired information from the measured data.

Log interpretation can be divided into two broad categories: qualitative interpretation is concerned with identifying geological attributes (e.g., lithology — the set of minerals which make up the rock around the borehole), while quantitative interpretation is concerned with numeric properties (e.g., the relative volumes of the minerals). Figure 2b shows a volumetric analysis based on the logs of Figure 2a. The studies described here have focused primarily on quantitative log interpretation.

Quantitative interpretation relies on models — statements of relationships between the measured data and the desired information. These statements may take many forms, such as graphs and equations. For example, the following equation relates water saturation (S_w), porosity (ϕ), the resistivity of the water (R_w), and the resistivity of the formation (R_t):

$$S_w^n = \frac{a \cdot R_w}{\phi^m \cdot R_t}$$

where a, m and n are parameters that describe certain formation characteristics (Archie 1942). Since the pore spaces must be occupied by either water or hydrocarbons, a low water saturation indicates the presence of oil or gas.

Although the interpretation models themselves are relatively simple, applying them to a particular problem involves a great deal of uncertainty. There are over one hundred qualitatively different lithologies. It's been estimated that it would require over four hundred numeric parameters, such as a, m and n, to fully characterize a formation. Since there are only about a dozen measurements, the situation is hopelessly underdetermined. Consequently, quantitative log interpretaion is a highly expert activity, based not only on a knowledge of a variety of relationships, but also of when and how to use them. This knowledge is the basic task domain knowledge for our automatic programming studies.

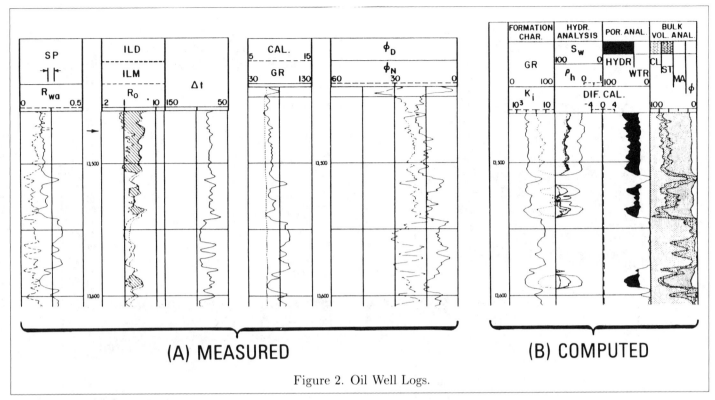

Figure 2. Oil Well Logs.

Initial Studies

Examination of Existing Software. The first study involved characterizing the nature of existing quantitative log interpretation software. The study was performed by examining, at various levels of detail, several programs in common use by Schlumberger. The programs all shared certain characteristics. They were moderate in size, ranging from 50 to 200 pages of FORTRAN, and had been written primarily by experienced log interpreters who had received some training in programming. They had gone through many major revisions as the result of testing and of growth in knowledge about log interpretation. They were intended for relatively wide use on a large number of wells with varying sets of tool readings as inputs. Since each was based on specific models, each program typically embodied significant assumptions about the geological nature of the formation around the well (e.g., that the lithology consists of a sequence of sand and shale layers). The programs were heavily parameterized to enable their application to individual wells with unique characteristics.

In a typical program the code which performs the calculations can be divided into two categories. About one fourth is related to the central calculations of the model. About three fourths deal with the wide variety of special situations that can arise when running the programs (e.g., adjusting inputs and outputs that seem unreasonable according to the assumed model, such as saturation greater than 100%). This division reflects certain characteristics of the domain. Given that one is willing to make assumptions about the formation, the appropriate mathematical models can usually be translated in a straightforward manner into code; thus, the software for the central computation is relatively compact. However, since there is a great deal of uncertainty in selecting from among possible assumptions and models, the software must do extensive testing and adjustment to determine the best possible fit between the data and the assumptions. In a way, the special situations are the qualitative side of quantitative log interpretation.

The results of this study can be summarized in two observations.

1. *The complexity of writing log interpretation software arises from the wealth of knowledge it draws upon, not the algorithms employed.* That is, algorithm design, the primary focus of most automatic programming research (e.g., Barstow 1982, Bibel 1980, Smith 1980, Manna & Waldinger 1980), is not the hard part of programming in this domain. This is probably true of many other domains.

2. *The state of knowledge about log interpretation is constantly changing. New experiments are performed, new data is gathered, new theories are developed, new techniques are tested.* That is, evolution is an inherent feature of quantitative log interpretation, and hence a major problem for software developers. As with size complexity, this is an area which has not received a great deal of attention in automatic programming research. Of course, it could be argued that with fully automatic programming, there is no need to worry about evolution. For each change, the program can simply be rewritten. A counterargument is that, if the automatic programming system knows what it is doing, it should be able to document the program enough that it can make many changes easily.

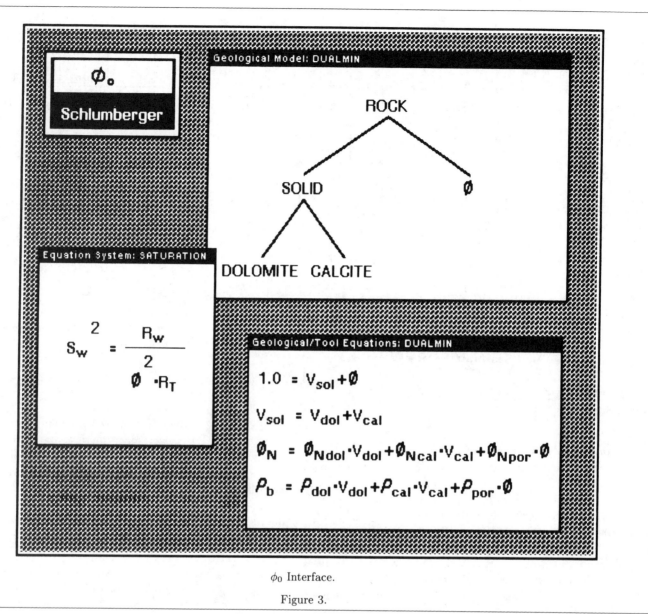

ϕ_0 Interface.

Figure 3.

An Experimental System. The second study involved the development of an experimental automatic programming system for a restricted class of quantitative log interpretation software, namely those programs written to test hypothesized models against real data during the trial-and-error process of developing new models. Such models are generally expressed in purely equational terms, and correspond roughly to the central computations of the software studied initially. This class was chosen for several reasons. First, it offered a chance to experiment with some simple kinds of interpretation knowledge (equations) without the need to consider more complex kinds such as heuristics. Second, in-house colleagues might be interested in using it, providing opportunities for testing with "real" users. Third, since the intended users typically spend from hours to days developing test programs, a system which produces programs in seconds or minutes would have immediate benefit. The system, called ϕ_0 ("phi-naught"), was implemented in INTERLISP-D which runs the XEROX 1100 series workstations. ϕ_0 is described in more detail elsewhere (Barstow *et al* 1982a, 1982b), so the major features will be discussed only briefly here.

The target user of ϕ_0 is a log analyst concerned with developing a new equational model for use in log interpretation. Such a user may be neither experienced in nor comfortable with traditional computer interfaces. An explicit goal was that ϕ_0 be easy for such people to use. Toward this end, ϕ_0 includes an icon- and menu-oriented interface incorporating the standard notations and concepts of the domain. Figure 3 shows the ϕ_0 interface during the process of developing a simple model. In this case, the model describes the responses of the neutron (denoted by ϕ_N) and density (ρ_b) tools in a formation consisting of calcite, dolomite, and porosity. (The fractional volumes of the three materials are denoted by V_{cal}, V_{dol} and ϕ, respectively. V_{sol} denotes the fractional volume of solid. ϕ_{Ncal}, ϕ_{Ndol} and ϕ_{Npor} denote the characteristic responses of the ϕ_N tool in the three materials; similarly, ρ_{cal}, ρ_{dol}, ρ_{por} denote the ρ_b responses.) Since the characteristic responses of the tools in the materials are known geophysical constants, this model is a system of four equations in six unknowns. Hence, it can be used to compute any four of the unknowns given values for the other two. Typically, the tool measurements at some depth in the well are known, and the equation system would be used to compute the fractional volumes of the different materials. Such equation systems consistitute the specifications given to ϕ_0's synthesizer.

At various times in its development ϕ_0 has written programs in several different target languages. For LISP and FORTRAN, the basic technique was to use an algebraic manipulation system to turn the implicit system into an explicit one. At each step, the size of the system is reduced by solving one equation for one term and substituting the result into the remaining equations. Figure 4 shows both the initial system and the solved system.[1] If the equations are considered in order, the terms on the right of each equation are either inputs or appear on the left of an earlier equation. In other words, they may be considered to be a sequence of assignment statements.[2]

Not all systems of equations can be solved explicitly. ϕ_0 used PROSE (1979), a mathematical package which uses numeric techniques to solve implicit systems of equations, as

---

[1] Appropriate values have been substituted for the geophysical constants, except that the responses of the tools in porosity (ϕ_{Npor} and ρ_{por}) have been left as run-time parameters which the user may adjust to reflect the nature of the fluid in the pore spaces.

[2] MACSYMA [Bogen et al 1975] has a similar facility for producing FORTRAN statements.

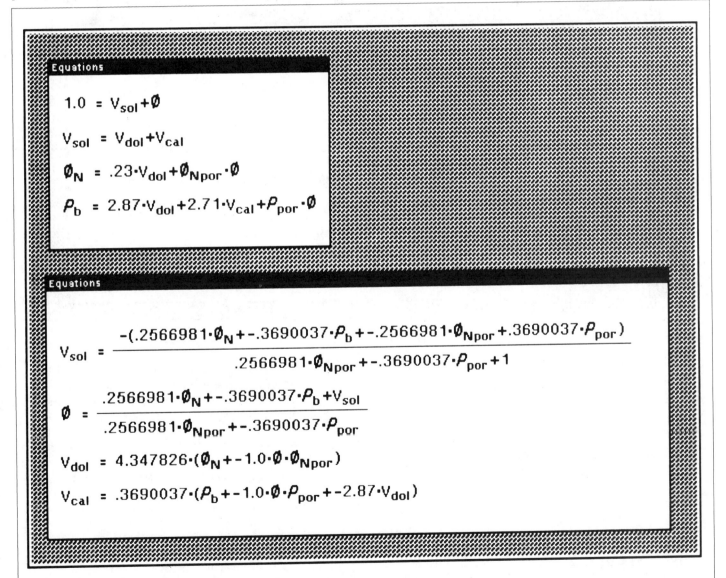

Algebraic Solution of an Equation System.

Figure 4.

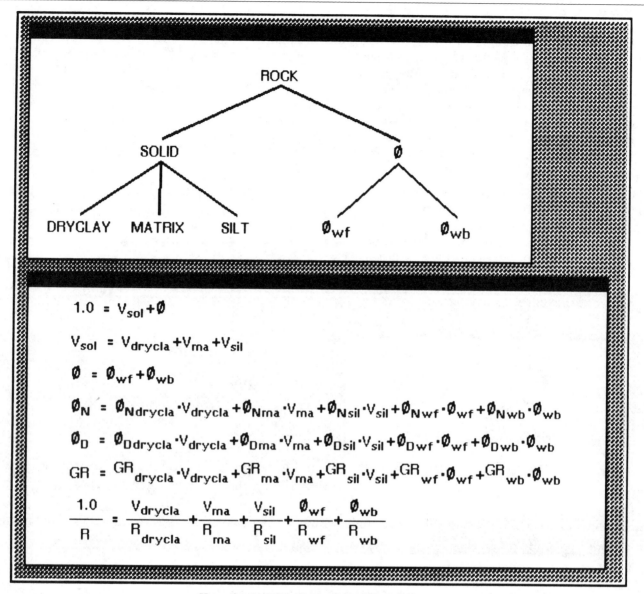

$$1.0 = V_{sol} + \emptyset$$

$$V_{sol} = V_{drycla} + V_{ma} + V_{sil}$$

$$\emptyset = \emptyset_{wf} + \emptyset_{wb}$$

$$\emptyset_N = \emptyset_{Ndrycla} \cdot V_{drycla} + \emptyset_{Nma} \cdot V_{ma} + \emptyset_{Nsil} \cdot V_{sil} + \emptyset_{Nwf} \cdot \emptyset_{wf} + \emptyset_{Nwb} \cdot \emptyset_{wb}$$

$$\emptyset_D = \emptyset_{Ddrycla} \cdot V_{drycla} + \emptyset_{Dma} \cdot V_{ma} + \emptyset_{Dsil} \cdot V_{sil} + \emptyset_{Dwf} \cdot \emptyset_{wf} + \emptyset_{Dwb} \cdot \emptyset_{wb}$$

$$GR = GR_{drycla} \cdot V_{drycla} + GR_{ma} \cdot V_{ma} + GR_{sil} \cdot V_{sil} + GR_{wf} \cdot \emptyset_{wf} + GR_{wb} \cdot \emptyset_{wb}$$

$$\frac{1.0}{R} = \frac{V_{drycla}}{R_{drycla}} + \frac{V_{ma}}{R_{ma}} + \frac{V_{sil}}{R_{sil}} + \frac{\emptyset_{wf}}{R_{wf}} + \frac{\emptyset_{wb}}{R_{wb}}$$

Hypothetical Synthesis: Initial Statement.

Figure 5.

a target language for those cases which could not be handled algebraically.

Several observations can be made as a result of the ϕ_0 experience:

- *Good user interfaces are crucial to automatic programming systems. They must provide both an appropriate set of concepts and convenient ways to describe problems using those concepts.* This statement may be obvious, but is worth making quite explicit.

- *Special-purpose automatic programming systems often have tight boundaries and are almost useless outside of these boundaries. If a system is going to be useful, it must either have wide boundaries or convenient ways to mix machine- and hand-written code.* ϕ_0 never came into widespread use, primarily because its boundaries were too narrow. The tar-

get class, equational interpretation models, was too restricted. In particular, certain procedural concepts (such as sequencing and conditionality) seem to be natural for some aspects of quantitative log interpretation; these concepts were outside the bounds of ϕ_0's capabilities.

- *Algebraic manipulation is quite powerful, but has obvious limitation.* Not all systems can be solved explicitly, and there are some questions about the numeric precision and stability of the computations resulting from the explicit solution of large systems. Domain knowledge may enable some of these limitations to be overcome. As a simple example, knowing the plausible range of values for terms in a quadratic equation may enable the selection of one of the two possible roots. This is an area ripe for further research.

Hypothetical Syntheses. The third (and on-going) study involves the construction of detailed, step-by-step descriptions of the process of writing particular programs. This methodology has provided useful insights in the past (*e.g.*, the classical work by Floyd (1971), Manna and Waldinger (1975), and the preliminary work on PSI (Green & Barstow 1977) and the Programmer's Apprentice (Rich & Shrobe 1978).) The key to the methodology is to pick good examples to work on. In our case, we are working on complete log interpretation programs, not just the central computations which ϕ_0 could deal with. For each such synthesis, the primary goal is to characterize the types of knowledge involved. In this section, a few steps from one hypothetical synthesis will be discussed.[3]

The problem under consideration is to perform a volumetric analysis assuming that the rock is composed of three materials (dry clay, silt, and matrix consisting of quartz) and that the fluid consists of two types of water (ϕ_{wf}) which flows freely in the pore spaces; and bound water (ϕ_{wb}) which is chemically attracted to clay). Measurements from four tools are available: neutron (ϕ_N), density porosity (ϕ_D), gamma ray (GR), The problem and the associated set of seven equations in seven unknowns are shown in Figure 5.

From a mathematical point of view, the system could be solved algebraically and translated directly into code. However, log analysts know that the GR and R_t equations are only rough approximations — they're not very reliable. A better way to write this program is to use a traditional interpretation heuristic — separate out the solid analysis from

Results for other syntheses are available elsewhere (Duffey & Smoliar 1983).

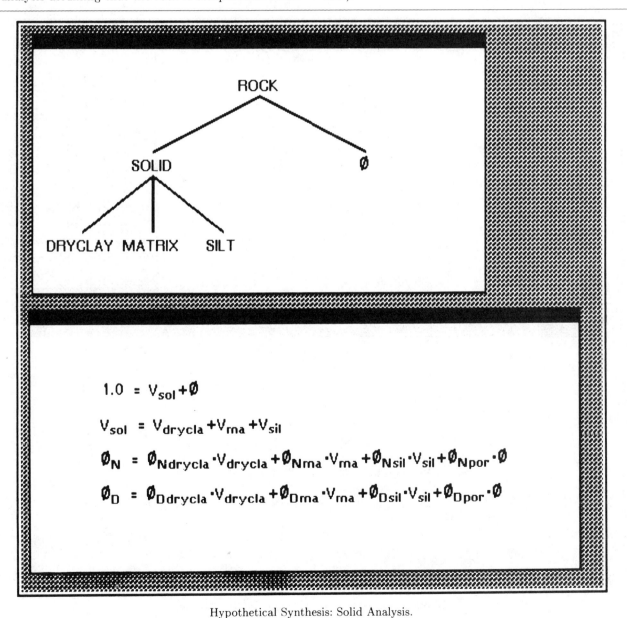

Hypothetical Synthesis: Solid Analysis.

Figure 6.

the fluid analysis, using whichever measurements are most appropriate for each. The resulting solid analysis part involves three materials but only two measurements, as shown in Figure 6.

We now have a system of reliable equations but it is underdetermined (four equations in five unknowns). Once again, knowledge of log interpretation resolves the problem. Since the matrix is made up of quartz, and silt is essentially ground up quartz, the responses of the two tools in matrix and silt are identical. Given only these two measurements, it would be impossible to distinguish between matrix and silt. Thus, the solution is to break the problem into two parts: one is concerned with porosity, quartz, and dry clay; the other is concerned with somehow distinguishing between matrix and silt. The first of these is a system with four equations and four unknowns, as shown in Figure 7.

At this point, the problem might seem to be one of straightforward algebraic manipulation. Recall, however, that explicitly solving a system of equations involves several choices: each step involves selecting a term and equation to solve. Such choices can be influenced by a variety of factors. For example, if the target architecture has several processors, it may be possible to take advantage of natural parallelism in the computation. Figure 8 shows a flow chart of the major data paths in the problem. Note that porosity (ϕ) is computed in one block and used in another. The second block could be computed on a second processor as soon as porosity is available. Thus, the equation system should be solved in such a way that porosity is computed first.

As these few steps suggest, many different types of knowledge play important roles in the development of log interpretation software. These include extensive knowledge of

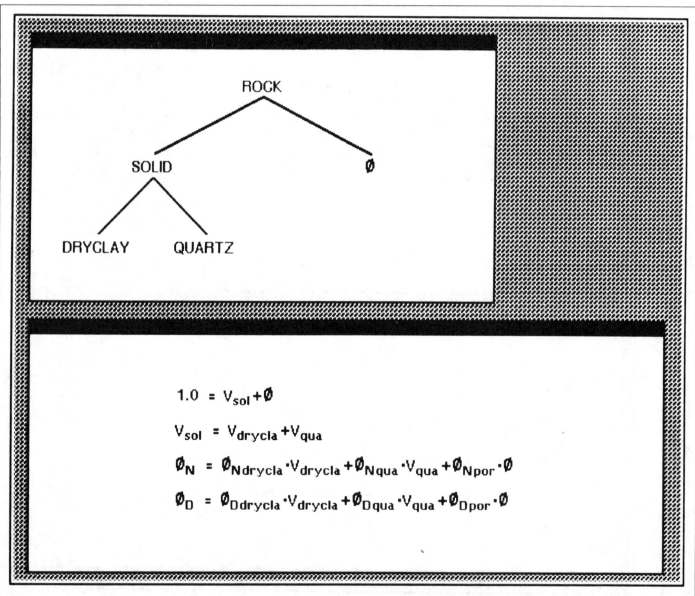

Hypothetical Synthesis: Simplified Solid Analysis.

Figure 7.

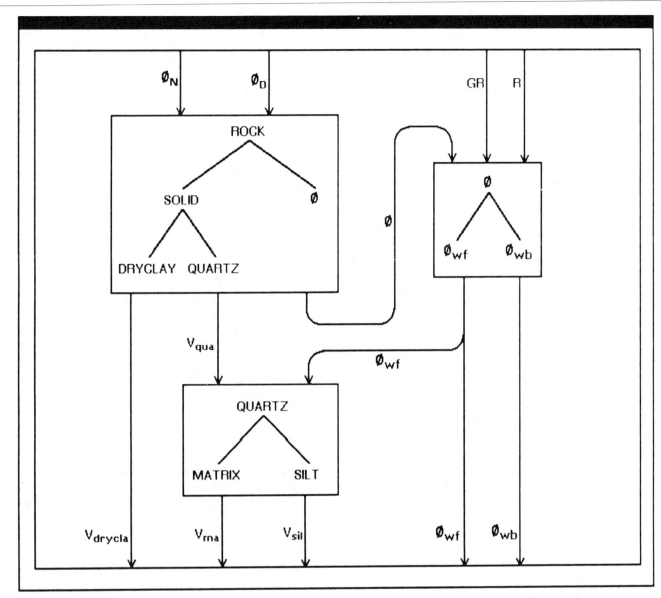

Hypothetical Synthesis: Data Flow Diagram.

Figure 8.

the domain, knowledge of various mathematical formalisms, knowledge of a variety of programming concepts, knowledge of the target language, and even knowledge of the target machine. In fact, this is what makes programming such a fascinating process to study — a wide variety of knowledge is used in a wide variety of ways.

The Role of Domain Knowledge

Perhaps the most consistent and important result of these studies has been the realization that knowledge of the domain plays several roles in the activities of an automatic programming system, during both interaction with the user and synthesis of the program.

User Interaction. Since a user may not be knowledgeable about, or comfortable with, the intricacies of programming systems, he or she must be able to describe problems in a natural way. The system must be able to deal effectively with the terms and notations of the domain. In the case of quantitative log interpretation, the user should be able to use concepts like "porosity," "water," and "shale," and notations like "ϕ_{wb}". The system should be able to deal with subtle nuances of the domain, for example, that most "shale indicators" are somewhat unreliable. In other words, the user must be able to interact with an automatic programming system in the same way that he or she would interact with another log interpreter.

One crucial part of the interaction between log interpreters is that they share more than just terminology and notations. They also share a great deal of detailed knowledge about log interpretation. They know the responses of the various tools in different materials, they know many mathematical relationships, they are intimately familiar with the interpretation charts which describe relationships diagrammatically, and they have had experience in using common interpretation techniques. When one interpreter describes a technique to another, there is no need to fill in all the details; because of their shared knowledge, the listener will be able to do that. The lesson for automatic programming systems is that they must also be able to fill in the missing pieces.[4]

In summary, the usability of an automatic programming system will depend largely on the nature of the specification process; the process must be both somewhat informal and highly interactive. These attributes can only be achieved if the system has access to a large and evolving base of knowledge about the domain. This role for domain knowledge might be considered a nice extra that could be ignored — simply provide a sufficiently high-level language for the user. The problem is that "No matter how high the level, it's still programming" (Smoliar & Barstow 1983). Unless that fundamental fact is changed, a wide class of users would still have to learn programming in order to benefit from such systems. Access to a body of domain knowledge is one way to bring about such a change.

Program Synthesis. One role for domain knowledge during synthesis is to reduce the complexity of the overall task. In the case of log interpretation, a typical FORTRAN program is over fifty pages long; the space of possible programs is enormous. Domain-specific problem-solving heuristics seem to be valuable aids in reducing the space to a more manageable size. As an example, consider the problem of determining the amount of hydrocarbon in a formation. Since hydrocarbons are not uniform (the density of gas varies considerably depending on such factors as temperature and depth), the effect of hydrocarbons on tool measurements is difficult to model precisely, and the models are difficult to deal with mathematically. Log interpreters doing hand calculations have developed a simple heuristic:

"Since light hydrocarbons are relatively uncommon, do all of the calculations assuming there are no light hydrocarbons; if the results are implausible, consider the possibility that light hydrocarbons may be present."

This heuristic is reflected in code in the form of "porosity analysis" and "hydrocarbon correction" routines. During program synthesis, this domain-specific heuristic enables a complex problem to be reduced to two simpler problems.

Domain knowledge is also needed during synthesis to assist in selecting among alternative implementation techniques. This is perhaps best explained by example. Consider first the problem of representing real numbers: a variety of techniques are possible and selecting an appropriate alternative depends on knowing the range of values and the needed accuracy. As another example, consider the problem of solv-

ing a complex system of non-linear polynomial equations. From a mathematical viewpoint, this may not be tractable, since an equation may have multiple solutions for the same unknown. However, there may be only one solution with a physically plausible range of values. Finally, consider an equation system which is still too complex to be solved algebraically, even given knowledge of ranges for the terms. In such cases some numeric technique must be employed, usually some form of successive approximation. It is sometimes possible to predict in advance the number of iterations necessary to achieve the accuracy desired. In such cases the loop can be coded with a counter or even open-coded as a sequence rather than a loop. This latter choice was taken in a case in which it was known that the tool readings were only reliable in the first two digits and that two applications of the loop body would achieve four-digit accuracy.

In summary, just as domain knowledge is crucial for the usability of an automatic programming system, it is crucial for the ability of a system to deal with realistic problems. It is needed both for writing large programs and for making appropriate choices among implementation alternatives.

Implications. In one sense, these observations are simply restatements of generally accepted maxims for building artificial intelligence systems: knowledge is crucial for natural interaction; knowledge can be used to reduce search. The important point is that the observations are concerned with domain knowledge rather than programming knowledge. Automatic programming systems will require large amounts of both kinds of knowledge — it isn't sufficient to build systems which only know about programming.

Of course, if this is true for automatic programming systems, it is probably also true for human programming systems. Among the implications for software engineering, two seem especially important:

1. Compilers for general purpose very high level languages may not be able to produce efficient code unless they have some sort of access to knowledge of the domain.
2. The traditional separation of software development into specification and implementation may not be feasible unless both specifiers and implementors are knowledgeable about the domain.[5]

The Perspective

These investigations have led to a particular perspective on automatic programming systems, especially those intended for use in real-world situations. This perspective may be summarized by a definition, an assertion, and a conclusion about research goals.

- Definition: An automatic programming system allows a computationally naive user to describe problems using the natural terms and concepts of a

---

[4]This argument is not new; Balzer *et al* (1977) made a similar argument several years ago.

[5]In a recent paper, Swartout and Balzer discuss this issue at length (Swartout and Balzer 1982).

domain, with informality, and imprecision and omission of details. An automatic programming system produces programs which run on real data to effect useful computations.

- Assertion: Such an automatic programming system is clearly specific to a particular domain. Knowledge of the domain is crucial to both the usability and the feasibility of such a system.

- Research goals: Therefore, a primary goal of automatic programming research should be the development of models of domain-specific programming and techniques for building domain-specific automatic programming systems.

Based on this perspective, several issues seem open for investigation. Some have been addressed, at least in part, in previous research efforts; however, no solid answers have been determined:

- *How can domain knowledge be structured for use by an automatic programming system?* A great deal of work on representing domain knowledge has been done in the context of expert systems. It would be a satisfying result if the same knowledge structured in the same way could be used by an automatic programming system. The idea is reminiscent of Green's early work (1969), in which the same axioms were used both to solve problems and to write programs, but it has yet to be tested in a complex domain.

- *How can programming knowledge be structured for use by an automatic programming system?* Work on this issue has been proceeding on two fronts. One is the relationship between abstract and concrete programming concepts. Notable work here includes the PSI project (Barstow 1979, Green 1977) and the Programmer's Apprentice project (Rich 1981). The other front involves techniques for constructing complex data structures. The work of Low (1978) and Katz and Zimmerman (1981) fit into this category. Overall, the groundwork for this issue has been laid. What is now required is rather methodical codification of many specific programming techniques.

- *What knowledge is required to choose an appropriate implementation from a variety of alternatives?* Here the question is essentially one of efficiency in the target program. It is interesting to note that Simon, in his description of the Heuristic Compiler in the early 1960's, explicitly recognized that the efficiency of the target code was an issue and also explicitly chose to ignore it (1963). There was her reference to the issue in the automatic programming literature for over a decade. Finally, Low (1978) considered it in his work on data structure selection. More recently, Katz and Zimmerman (1981) looked at it in the context of a data structure advisor and Kant (1981) considered the question in the context of the PSI project. This work is a good start, but the issue deserves much more attention than it has gotten. Our studies suggest that the use of domain knowledge will prove crucial to addressing it well.

In fact, Kant's work actually characterized one kind of domain knowledge that's needed for selecting the right alternative — knowledge of the plausible values and typical set sizes.

- *How can the interaction between an automatic programming system and the user be modeled?* In one sense, this is just a special case of human-computer interfaces, a topic which has been receiving a considerable amount of attention lately. With respect to the interface, there's probably nothing special about automatic programming systems. In another sense, however, this gets right to one of the core questions of artificial intelligence — how can two knowledgable agents communicate? Automatic programming systems provide a fruitful context in which to explore this question.

Unfortunately, the central issue suggested by the perspective, and the key to significant progress in automatic programming, has not been addressed in any substantial way:

How can the interaction between domain and programming knowledge during program synthesis be modeled?

An Experimental Approach

Given the importance of domain knowledge, the best way to address these issues is through experimentation in the context of specific domains. That is, we must develop models of programming for these domains and implement automatic programming systems which test these models. Based on such experiments, we can develop broader models and characterize the utility of different system-building techniques. The validity of this approach as a research methodology clearly depends on characteristics of the individual experiments. It is not sufficient simply to build a variety of application program generators. Unless the domains are suitable and the underlying models of programming are formulated well, it will not be possible to generalize to broader models or to characterize the techniques in a useful way.

While selecting domains and developing models is an art, it is possible to state some guidelines that may be helpful. By considering ϕ_0 in light of these guidelines, we may see why it is not particularly useful as a basis for more general models:

- *The domain must be non-trivial. There must be considerable room for variability in the class of target problems, the possibility of multiple target languages, or the types of programming techniques which may be employed.* ϕ_0's domain, purely equational interpretation models, was too simple. Some extensions which would have increased the complexity are: non-equational concepts; computations over zones in a well, rather than single levels; and some notion of the reliability of the stated relationships. ϕ_0 could write programs in several target languages, although the technique was essentially a "big switch." ϕ_0's repertoire of programming techniques was rather limited.

- *The model of programming for the domain must clearly characterize the roles played by domain and programming knowledge.* ϕ_0 provides a clear characterization of the roles played by domain and programming knowledge: all of the domain knowledge is embodied in the initial specification phase, with essentially no role for domain knowledge during the synthesis process itself. Unfortunately, it now seems that this strict separation is the wrong characterization.

- *The model must address the issue of choosing from among several alternative implementations.* For a given target language, there was essentially only one style of implementation.

- *The model must be supported by an implemented system intended for real users who need real programs to perform real computations.* As noted earlier, although ϕ_0 was intended for real users and real programs, it never came into widespread use, primarily because of limitations on its target class.

ϕ_{NIX}

As an illustration of an experiment which seems to fit the guidelines, we will consider some of the details of ϕ_{NIX}, another project currently underway at Schlumberger-Doll Research, the scope of which includes full-fledged quantitative log interpretation programs.[6] This class has considerably more variability than ϕ_0's for three reasons. First, it includes non-equational relationships such as charts, tables, and simple procedural concepts. Second, it includes computations over entire wells, not just the single level computations which ϕ_0 dealt with. Third, the target language and machine include simple kinds of parallelism.

To date, we have outlined a model of programming for this target class. The model addresses the two issues noted earlier: the interaction of domain knowledge and programming knowledge; and the selection of an appropriate program from a set of valid alternatives. However, the model is only speculative — it is neither tested nor supported by an implementation. Rather, it must be considered to be a proposal. Nonetheless, the model provides a good example — it suggests the kind of domain-specific model of programming which may generalize to other domains. For example, we hope that this model will generalize to other types of scientific software.

Overview of the Model of Programming. According to this model, programming for quantitative log interpretation involves four activities:

- *Informal problem solving:* This activity is concerned with informal problems involving inputs, outputs, assumptions, and relations stated primarily in domain-specific terms. The problems are informal in that they may be incomplete (not enough information is available to compute the outputs from the inputs) and the input set may not be quite correct (some inputs may be missing, others extraneous). Such problems might be paraphrased in English as "Try to find a way to compute X from Y using relationship Z." The result of the informal problem solving activity is a set of formal problems stated in terms of any of several different formalisms.

- *Formal manipulation:* This activity is concerned with problems stated in terms of mathematical formalisms: statistics, analytic geometry, and algebra. The results of these activities are algorithmic statements connected by data flow links.

- *Implementation selection:* This activity is concerned with selecting from among a variety of implementation techniques for each entity in the algorithmic descriptions produced by formal manipulation. The result of this activity is a complete description of the program in terms of concepts available in the target language.

- *Target language translation:* The major concern of this activity is the expression of the program in terms of the syntax of the target language. This is a fairly direct translation from the results of the implementation selection activity.

Each of these activities involves applying transformations based on knowledge of quantitative log interpretation and of programming. We will now consider each of the activities and the kinds of transformations involved in them.

Informal Problem Solving. An informal problem consists of a set of inputs, a set of outputs, a set of assumptions, and a set of relationships, all expressed in domain terms. For example, an English rendering of one such informal problem is:

Assume the only fluids in the pore spaces in the rock around the borehole are water which flows freely and water which is bound to clay. Try to find a way to compute bound water saturation (S_{wb}) from the resistivity (R) and gamma ray (GR) measurements.

The primary goal of the informal problem solving activity is to determine a set of formal problems which can be put together to solve the overall problem.

This activity has been named "informal" because the problems and subproblems considered during the activity are often incomplete. When inputs and outputs are stated, the intention is that some way of computing the outputs from the inputs is desired. In trying to find an appropriate computation some inputs may be ignored and additional inputs may be considered. Similarly, when relationships or assumptions are given, the intention is that the relationships be used, but there is no requirement that all or only these relationships be used. In other words, the parts of a problem statement provide a focus for, but not a restriction on, the informal problem solving activity.

---

[6] An early report on ϕ_{NIX} provides additional background (Barstow et al 1982b).

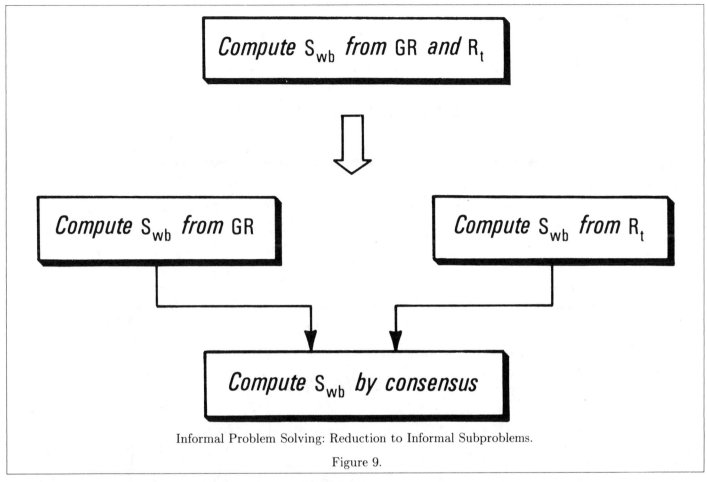

Informal Problem Solving: Reduction to Informal Subproblems.

Figure 9.

There are five types of transformations used during informal problem solving:

1. *Reduction to informal subproblems.* These transformations are often suggested by domain-specific heuristics. For example, the transformation shown in Figure 9 is based on the following heuristic: "If you have only unreliable indicators for a quantity, consider each indicator as a separate subproblem, and use some kind of consensus technique to determine a more reliable value." The result is three simpler informal problems.

2. *Translation into formal problems.* These transformations often involve definitions of domain concepts in terms of domain-independent mathematical formalisms. For example, the transformation shown in Figure 10 is based on the following rule (and the fact that GR is a linear indicator for S_{wb}): "If you have a linear indicator for the desired output, the problem may be expressed as a two-point linear relationship between indicator values for the minimum and maximum values of the output." The result is a problem stated in terms of formal concepts.

3. *Addition of information.* The formal problem, as stated, is underdetermined: it has one input (GR), one output (S_{wb}), and two other terms ($GR_{S_{wb}=0}$, $GR_{S_{wb}=1}$); since only the value of the input term is known, it is a system with one equation and

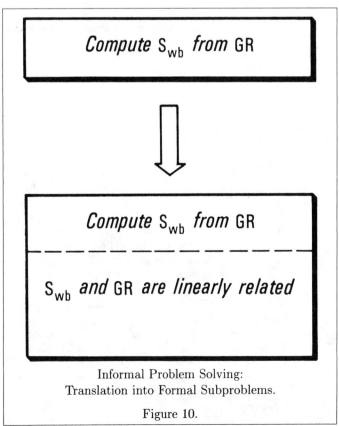

Informal Problem Solving:
Translation into Formal Subproblems.

Figure 10.

Compute S_{wb} from GR

- -

S_{wb} and GR *are linearly related*

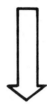

Compute S_{wb} from GR

- -

S_{wb} and GR *are linearly related*

$S_{wb}=0$ *when* GR *is minimum over the zone*

$S_{wb}=1$ *when* GR *is maximum over the zone*

Informal Problem Solving: Addition of Information.

Figure 11.

three unknowns, hence underdetermined. To resolve the difficulty, either additional relationships must be found or more inputs provided. In this case, a reasonable solution is to add two relationships, as shown in Figure 11. Additional information such as this may come from known facts and relationships of the domain or from assumptions the user is willing to make.

4. *Elaboration of general concepts.* Informal problems are often stated in terms of general concepts which do not have precise formal definitions. Before a formal problem can be stated, it is necessary to be more explicit about the desired relationship. For example, the concept of "consensus" covers a broad range of techniques for computing a single value from a set of values, no one of which is especially reliable. Since GR and R_t are equally unreliable as bound water indicators, and no information about the direction of their unreliability is available, the mean of their values is a good choice. This transformation is illustrated in Figure 12.

5. *Introduction of conditionals.* Computed results must often satisfy certain constraints. For example, volumetric results are computed as fractional volumes and must therefore be in the range $[0, 1]$. Such volumetric problems are often described in geometric terms by identifying the points, in a coordinate system whose axes are tool readings, representing 100% concentrations of the materials. Figure 13 shows the points for quartz, dry clay, and porosity in a coordinate system determined by the neutron (ϕ_N) and density-porosity (ϕ_D) logs. Geometrically, the $[0, 1]$ constraint corresponds to the condition that the data point (*i.e.,* specific values for ϕ_N and ϕ_D) fall within the triangle determined by the 100% points. Data points falling outside the triangle represent anomolous situations; identification of such anomalies leads to the introduction of a conditional on the inputs, several new informal problems, and perhaps a request to the user about how the anomolous situtation should be handled.

Compute S_{wb} from S_{wb}(GR) and S_{wb}(R_t) by consensus

Compute S_{wb} from S_{wb}(GR) and S_{wb}(R_t)

S_{wb} is the mean of S_{wb}(GR) and S_{wb}(R_t)

Figure 12. Informal Problem Solving: Elaboration of General Concepts.

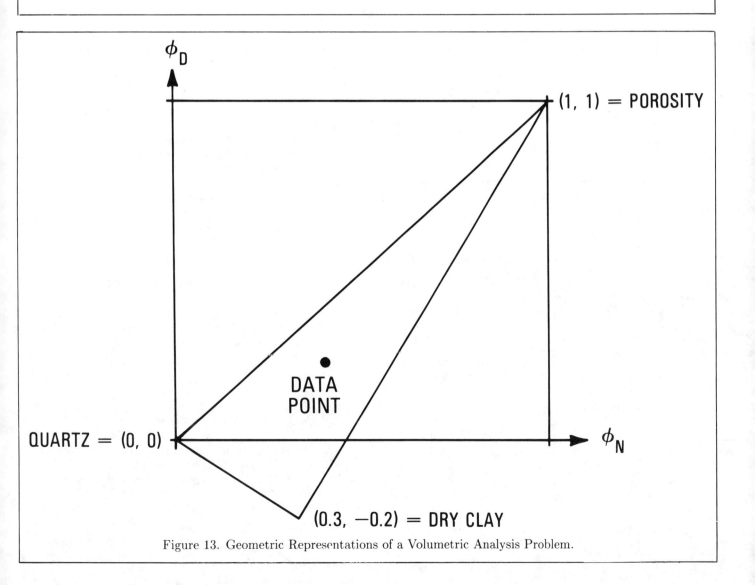

Figure 13. Geometric Representations of a Volumetric Analysis Problem.

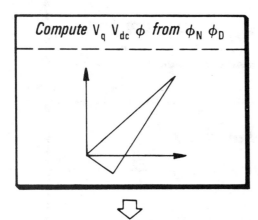

$$\textit{Compute } V_q\ V_{dc}\ \phi \textit{ from } \phi_N\ \phi_D$$

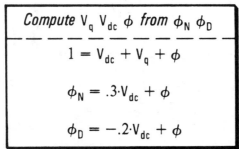

$$\textit{Compute } V_q\ V_{dc}\ \phi \textit{ from } \phi_N\ \phi_D$$

$$1 = V_{dc} + V_q + \phi$$

$$\phi_N = .3{\cdot}V_{dc} + \phi$$

$$\phi_D = -.2{\cdot}V_{dc} + \phi$$

Figure 14. Formal Manipulation:
Reformulation into a Different Formalism.

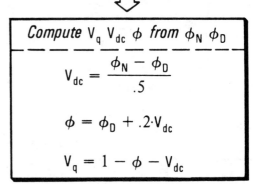

$$\textit{Compute } V_q\ V_{dc}\ \phi \textit{ from } \phi_N\ \phi_D$$

$$1 = V_{dc} + V_q + \phi$$

$$\phi_N = .3{\cdot}V_{dc} + \phi$$

$$\phi_D = -.2{\cdot}V_{dc} + \phi$$

$$\textit{Compute } V_q\ V_{dc}\ \phi \textit{ from } \phi_N\ \phi_D$$

$$V_{dc} = \frac{\phi_N - \phi_D}{.5}$$

$$\phi = \phi_D + .2{\cdot}V_{dc}$$

$$V_q = 1 - \phi - V_{dc}$$

Figure 15. Formal Manipulation:
Reformulation within a Formalism.

The key ideas behind this formulation of the informal problem solving activity are:

- The heuristics used by expert quantitative log interpreters can provide valuable guidance by suggesting subproblems for consideration.

- There is a large body of quantitative log interpretation facts and relationships which are best expressed in terms of simple statistics, analytic geometry, and algebra.

- Inability to define formal problems suggests incompleteness in the specification which can be resolved by using additional information found in the repository or suggested by the user.

- Analysis in terms of the mathematical formalisms can help identify anomolous conditions as special cases which a target program might encounter when it is run on real data.

Formal Manipulation. A formal problem consists of a set of inputs, a set of outputs, and a set of relationships stated in terms of mathematical formalisms: statistics, analytic geometry, and algebra. The primary goal of the formal manipulation activity is to transform each of the formal problems into an algorithmic form.

Three types of transformations are used during this activity:

1. *Reformulation into a different formalism.* The different mathematical formalisms are used by the informal problem solving activity primarily as a matter of convenience. For example, many experimentally determined relationships are represented as charts much more easily than as algebraic relationships. However, unless the target language has mechanisms for dealing directly with such concepts, they must be translated into other formalisms for which the appropriate concepts are available. In the case of quantitative log interpretation, these translations are usually from statistics and analytic geometry into algebra. For example, the transformation shown in Figure 14 involves the reformulation of the geometric problem posed earlier into an algebraic one.

2. *Reformulation within a formalism.* Often a problem may be formulated in several equivalent ways within a single formalism. For example, there are many equivalent systems of equations for representing numeric relationships among several terms. Some of these systems may be easier to deal with than others. As illustrated in Figure 15, the problem involving three equations in three unknowns may be reformulated as an equivalent upper-triangular system of equations.

3. *Translation into an algorithmic formalism.* The ultimate goal of the formal manipulation activity is to transform the formal problems into an algorithmic

representation. Once the appropriate formal manipulations have been done, this is a relatively straightforward process. For example, the transformation shown in Figure 16 yields a sequence of assignment statements.

Implementation Selection. The result of the formal manipulation activities is a set of simple algorithms described in terms of general computational concepts dealing with data flow and operations on three data types: real numbers, sequences, and mappings. For each of these general concepts, several implementation techniques are possible. The goal of this activity is to select techniques for each general concept.[7] These selections are guided by two considerations: whether or not the technique is appropriate for the target language, and the relative merit of alternative techniques given some preference criteria (*e.g.*, an efficiency measure).

Three types of transformations are applied during this activity:

1. *Data type refinement.* Since most programming languages cannot implement all three abstract data types directly, techniques for representing instances of the data types must be selected. For example, the porosity log measured by the neutron tool is abstractly viewed as a mapping of depths to porosity values. Logs are typically implemented by establishing a correspondence between depths and integers (in effect, a kind of discretization) and then indexing the log by the integers. This transformation is illustrated in Figure 17. With several more steps, this representation can be refined into two arrays, one for depths and one for log values.

---

[7]More precisely, a technique must be chosen for each instance of each general concept. For example, there is no reason for all numbers to be represented in the same way.

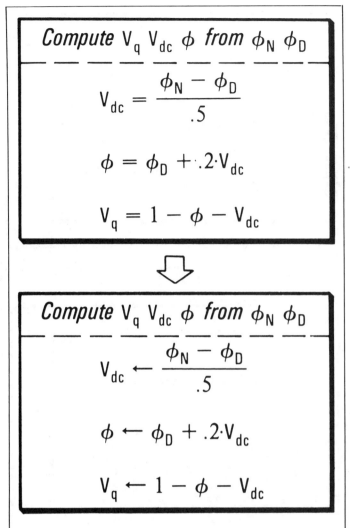

Figure 16. Translation into an Algorithmic Formalism.

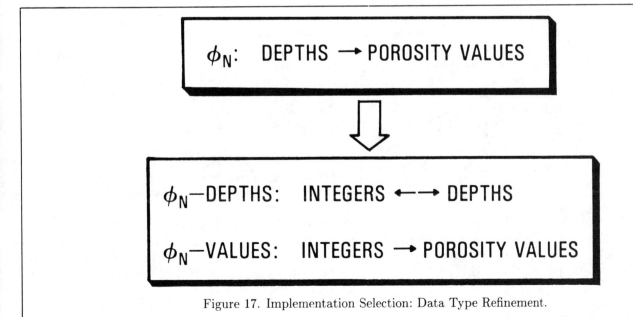

Figure 17. Implementation Selection: Data Type Refinement.

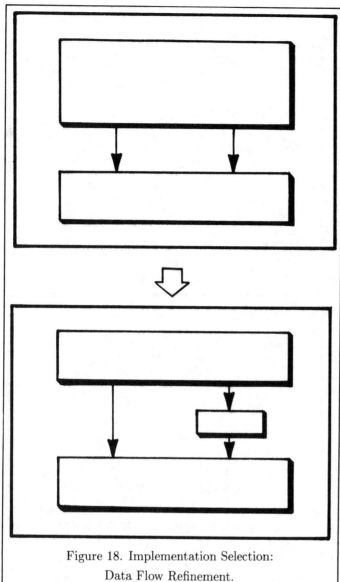

Figure 18. Implementation Selection:
Data Flow Refinement.

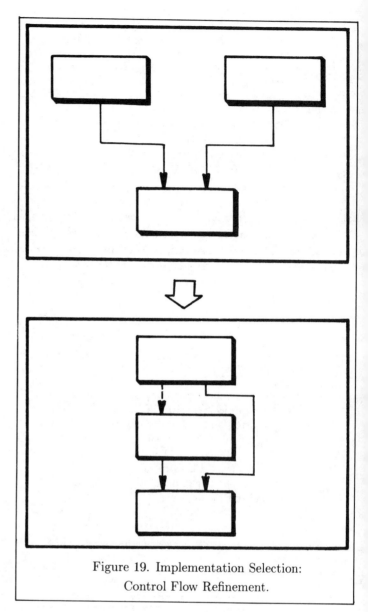

Figure 19. Implementation Selection:
Control Flow Refinement.

2. *Data flow refinement.* Most languages have a variety of ways to pass data from one computation to another, and a selection of particular techniques for each of the data flow links must be made. This is an area where different languages may vary significantly. For example, FORTRAN can deal with multiple return values more conveniently than most LISP dialects. Although many of the data flow decisions seem relatively mundane (*e.g.,* whether or not to use a variable) there are also some rather exotic possibilities, such as the conversion of one representation to another in the middle of a computation, as suggested in Figure 18. For example, a set may be represented as a mapping of potential elements to Boolean values while it is being built, and then changed to a sequence to make enumerations easier. This is a rather powerful technique — one which both humans and machines could profitably use.

3. *Control flow refinement.* Control flow techniques also differ among target languages. Among the relevant concepts are sequencing, iteration, recursion, conditionality, and function invocation. The dashed arrow in Figure 19 illustrates a simple sequencing of computations which are only partially ordered by data flow constraints.

Of course, these types of refinement may be closely linked. For example, deciding to use an array processor to perform similar computations on all elements of a vector has implications for all three types of refinements.

Target Language Translation. The last activity is a translation from the final algorithmic form into the syntax of the target language. Since the final algorithmic form involves only concepts available in the target language, this is a fairly simple activity. The greatest complexities involve the selection of variable names and producing the program in a readable format.

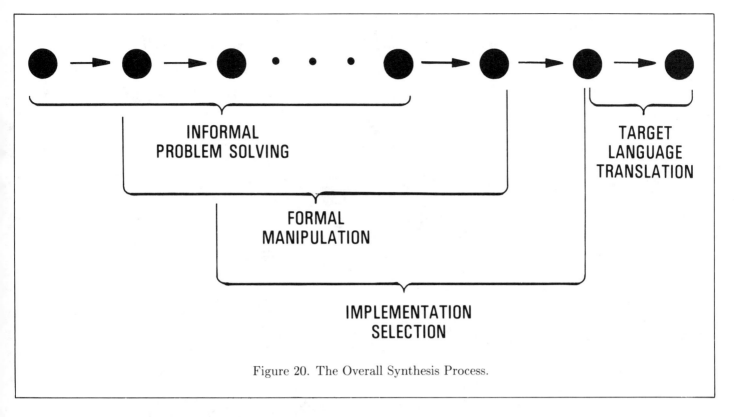

Figure 20. The Overall Synthesis Process.

The Synthesis Process. Since each activity involves the application of transformations, the overall process can be modeled as a sequence of transformations. In other words, the overall process is an instance of the transformational paradigm which has received considerable attention lately (*e.g.,* Balzer 1981, Cheatham 1979, and Kant & Barstow 1981).

Although the activities of the ϕ_{NIX} model were described separately, the overall process cannot be broken into four distinct stages corresponding. As suggested by Figure 20, there is a gradual shift in emphasis from informal problem solving through formal manipulation to implementation selection. To illustrate this mixing of activities, consider the use of an optimization strategy to deal with a complex system of equations. The decision to use the strategy is made during formal manipulation, but the initial point determination involves a new informal problem (which may, for example, have less stringent accuracy requirements).

At each stage in a sequence there may be many transformations which could plausibly be applied. Thus, the transformations of the different activities define a space of partially implemented programs; the overall synthesis process is one of exploring this space. (See Figure 21.) At the current time, it is only possible to characterize this space in general terms. Any complete sequence leads to a implementation of the initial problem. Given the informality of the specification, different implementations may have different input/output behavior, although any such differences would be within the accepted bounds of uncertainty in the domain. In addition, there may be considerable variability in terms of efficiency. There is also no guarantee that every sequence of transformations can be completed; there may be dead-end paths.

Characterizing the Activities. We may use this space to characterize the different activities:

- *Informal problem solving.* Due to the informal nature of informal problem solving, the transformations may not preserve equivalence. As a simple example, different elaborations of the consensus concept would lead to programs which are not equivalent, but which might all be plausible from the point of view of a log interpreter. Another aspect of informal problem solving is that there are likely to be many alternatives, of which only a small number don't lead to dead-ends. Thus, the primary concern will be to avoid dead-ends — almost any completable path is acceptable. This suggests a highly exploratory and opportunistic strategy.

- *Formal manipulation.* Formal manipulation seems to be much more cleanly structured. There are probably only a few transformations which produce algorithms directly; the other transformations are used to satisfy preconditions on these. For example, of the three transformations given earlier, the first satisfies preconditions of the second, which satisfies preconditions of the third, which produces an algorithm. Thus, simple backward-chaining is probably the right strategy.

- *Implementation selection.* During implementation selection, most paths will complete successfully and more traditional search strategies are probably appropriate, including quantitative evaluation functions and explicit construction of much of the space.

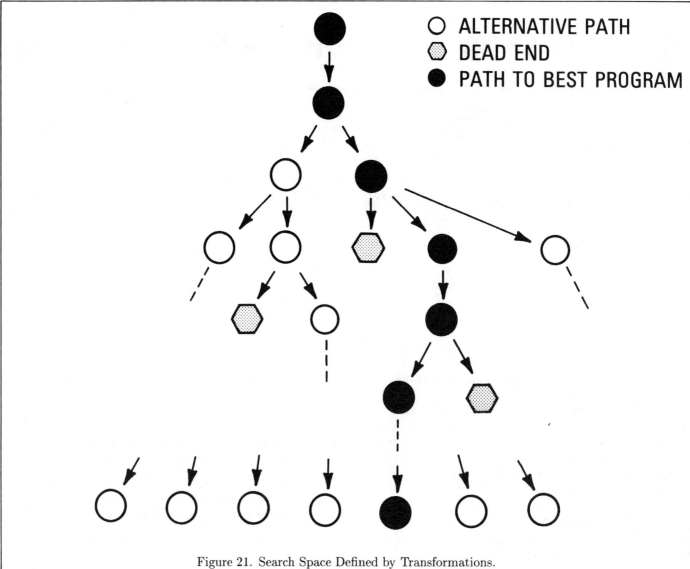

Figure 21. Search Space Defined by Transformations.

The refinement paradigm as developed in PSI's synthesis phase (Kant & Barstow 1981), seems to fit well here.

- *Target language translation.* This activity is quite straightforward, involvng little or no search.

Characterizing the Knowledge. Given this description of the overall process, it can be seen that knowledge plays two kinds of roles, as the transformations themselves and as selectors of appropriate transformations.[8] Figure 22 shows the roles played by various types of knowledge during the different activities.

- Log interpretation

  —*Facts and relationships derived from theoretical or empirical considerations:* These play a transfor-

mational role during informal problem solving by providing information which may be added to informal problems (*e.g.,* the end points of the linear $GR\text{-}S_{wb}$ relationship). They also play a selective role during formal manipulation and implementation selection by providing the basic information needed to make certain decisions (*e.g.,* the plausible range of a physical value).

—*Mechanisms for expressing log interpretation concepts in terms of mathematical formalisms:* These play a transformational role during informal problem solving by producing problems which can be handled by formal manipulation (*e.g.,* the expression of the linear $GR\text{-}S_{wb}$ relationship).

—*Problem-solving heuristics:* These are used during informal problem solving to help reduce problems to simpler problems; in effect, they play both a tranformational and a selective role (*e.g.,* the reduction of the original bound water problem into three simpler ones).

---

[8]In terms of traditional search theory, knowledge is embodied both in operators and in heuristics.

	I.P.S.	F.M.	I.S.	T.L.T.
LOG INTERPRETATION				
Facts and Relationships	T	S	S	
Formulation Mechanisms	T→			
P.S. Heuristics	T/S			
MATHEMATICAL FORMALISMS				
Taxonomy of Concepts	T			
Analytic Mechanisms	S			
Reformulation Mechanisms		T		
Algorithmic Transformations		T→		
PROGRAMMING TECHNIQUES				
Taxonomy of Techniques	S	S	T→	
Efficiency Analysis	S	S	S	
TARGET LANGUAGE				
Taxonomy of concepts	S	S	S	
Surface Syntax				T→

T — TRANSFORMED ROLE   → — INTRODUCES CONCEPTS
S — SELECTIVE ROLE   FOR NEXT ACTIVITY

Figure 22. Characterizing the Knowledge.

- Mathematical formalisms (simple statistics, analytic geometry, algebra)

  — *Taxonomy of concepts:* This plays a tranformational role during informal problem solving by indicating specializations for general concepts (*e.g.*, the use of the arithmetic mean as a consensus technique).

  — *Analytic mechanisms:* These play a selective role during informal problem solving (*e.g.*, the identification of the implausible regions of the ϕ_N-ϕ_D crossplot).

  — *Mechanisms for reformulation within a formalism or into a different formalism:* These play a tranformational role during formal manipulation by transforming problems into more convenient forms (*e.g.*, the reformulation of the geometric problem into an

algebraic one, and the solution of the system of equations).

  — *Mechanisms for translating a formal problem statement into an algorithmic form:* These play a transformational role during formal manipulation by producing algorithmic modules (*e.g.*, the translation of the solved system of equations into a sequence of assignment statements).

- Programming techniques

  — *Taxonomy of programming techniques (data flow, control flow, data types):* This plays a tranformational role during implementation selection, since it embodies certain refinement relationships (*e.g.*, knowledge of alternative representations for mappings). This also plays a selective role during formal manipulation, since it provides the target set of concepts for the activity.

— *Mechanisms for analyzing the efficiency of specific techniques:* These play a selective role during implementation selection. (*E.g.,* knowledge of the efficiency characteristics of alternative mapping representations). It also plays a selective role during informal problem solving in that certain transformations might be rejected on efficiency grounds.

- Target language

— *Taxonomy of computational concepts available in the language:* This is essentially a sub-taxonomy of the mathematical and programming techniques. It plays a selective role by acting as a filter during formal manipulation and implementation selection. For example, FORTRAN does not establish a new context for each subroutine call, so the use of recursive subroutines would be filtered out.

— *Mechanism for translating into the syntax of the language:* As the essence of the target language translation activity, this plays a transformational role.

In looking at the overall picture, note that domain knowledge is used during each of the activities, but in different ways. During informal problem solving, it is the source of many of the transformations. During later activities, it is used primarily to select from among alternative transformations. Note also that the domain knowledge is not specifically related to the programming task, it is simply used by it.

Summary

Let us now review the basic theme of this paper, overstating slightly for the sake of clarity:

The primary conclusion of our initial studies is that domain knowledge plays a critical role in the programming process. This role is so important that automatic programming systems without considerable domain knowledge will be neither usable by non-computer scientists nor feasible for non-trivial domains. Therefore, a primary goal of automatic programming research should be to develop models of programming which characterize the interaction of domain knowledge and programming knowledge. The best way to achieve this goal is to develop models of programming for specific non-trivial domains, and to test these models by building systems for real users who want real programs that can be run on real data. If these models clearly separate and characterize the roles played by domain and programming knowledge, then we will have the foundation for developing broader models of programming.

References

Archie, G. (1942) The electrical resistivity log as an aid in determining some reservoir characteristics. *Petroleum Technology,* 5:1, January.

Balzer, R. Transformational implementation: An example. (1981) *IEEE Transactions on Software Engineering,* 7:1, January.

Balzer, R., Goldman, N., & Wile, D. (1977) Informality in program specification. *IJCAI 5,* Cambridge, Massachusetts. August.

Barstow, D. (1979) *Knowledge-based Program Construction.* Elsev North Holland, New York.

Barstow, D. (1982) The roles of knowledge and deduction in algorithm design. In J. E. Hayes, D. Michie, Y.-H. Pao (Eds.) *Machine Intelligence 10,* Ellis Horwood Limited, Chichester.

Barstow, D., Duffey, R., Smoliar, S., & Vestal, S. (1982) An automatic programming system to support an experimental science. *Sixth International Conference on Software Engineering* Tokyo, Japan, September.

Barstow, D., Duffey, R., Smoliar, S., & Vestal, S. (1982) An overview of ϕ_{NIX}. *AAAI-82,* Pittsburgh, Pennsylvania, August. 367-369.

Bibel, W. (1980) Syntax-directed, semantics-supported program synthesis. *Artificial Intelligence,* 12:3, October.

Bogen, R. *et al,* (1975) MACSYMA *Reference Manual.* Massachusetts Institute of Technology, Laboratory for Computer Science.

Cheatham, T., Townley, J., & Holloway, G. (1979) A system for program refinement. *Fourth International Conference on Software Engineering,* Munich, Germany, September. Reprinted in D. Barstow, H. Shrobe, E. Sandewall (Eds.), *Interactiv Programming Environments,* McGraw-Hill, New York, 1984.

Duffey, R., & Smoliar, S. (1983) From geological knowledge to computational relationships: A case study of the expertise o programming. *Workshop on Program Transformation and Pro gramming Environments,* September.

Floyd, R. (1971) *Toward interactive design of correct programs* Stanford University, Computer Science Department, CS-235.

Green, C. (1969) Application of theorem proving to problem solving. *IJCAI-X,* Washington, D.C., May.

Green, C. (1977) A summary of the PSI program synthesis system. *Fifth International Conference on Artificial Intelligence* Cambridge, Massachusetts, August.

Green, C., & Barstow, D. (1977) A hypothetical dialogue exhibiting a knowledge base for a program understanding system. In E. Elcock & D. Michie (Eds.), *Machine Intelligence 8,* Ellis Horwood Limited, Chichester.

Kant, E. (1981) *Efficiency in Program Synthesis,* UMI Research Press, Ann Arbor.

Kant, E. & Barstow, D. (1981) The refinement paradigm: The interaction of coding and efficiency knowledge in program synthesis. *IEEE Transactions on Software Engineering,* 7:5, September. Reprinted in D. Barstow, H. Shrobe, & E. Sandewall (Eds.), *Interactive Programming Environments,* McGraw-Hill New York, 1984.

Katz, S., & Zimmerman, R. (1981) An advisory system for developing data representations. *Seventh International Conference on Artificial Intelligence,* Vancouver, British Columbia, August, 1030-1032.

Low, J. (1978) Automatic data structure selection: an example and overview. *Communications of the ACM,* 21:5, May.

Manna, Z., & Waldinger, R. (1980) A deductive approach to program synthesis. *ACM Transactions on Programming Languages and Systems,* 2:1, January.

Manna, Z., & Waldinger, R. (1975) Knowledge and reasoning in program synthesis. *Artificial Intelligence*, 6:2, Summer.

PROSE General Information Manual, (1979) PROSE, Inc., Palos Verdes Estates, California.

Rich, C. (1981) Inspection methods in programming. *Massachusetts Institute of Technology:* AI-TR-604, June.

Rich, C., Shrobe, H. (1978) Initial Report on the Programmer's Apprentice. *IEEE Transactions on Software Engineering*, 4:6, November. Reprinted in D. Barstow, H. Shrobe, & E. Sandewall (Eds.), *Interactive Programming Environments*, McGraw-Hill, New York, 1984.

Simon, H. (1963) Experiments with a heuristic compiler. *Journal of the Association for Computing Machinery*, 10:4, October. Reprinted in H. Simon, & L. Siklossy (Eds.), *Representation and Meaning*, Prentice-Hall, Englewood Cliffs, 1972.

Smith, D. (1983) A problem reduction approach to program synthesis. *Eighth International Joint Conference on Artificial Intelligence*, Karlsruhe, Germany, August, 32-36.

Smith, D. (1980) A survey of the synthesis of LISP programs from examples. *International Workshop on Program Construction*, Bonas, France, September.

Swartout, S. & Barstow, D. (1983) Who needs languages and why do they need them? or no matter how high the level it's still programming. *Symposium on Programming Language Issues in Software Systems*, San Francisco, California, June.

Swartout, W. & Balzer, R. (1982) An inevitable intertwining of specification and implementation, *Communications of the ACM*, 25:7, July.

Waldinger, R. & Lee, R. (1969) PROW: a step toward automatic programming. *IJCAI* Washington, D.C.

Waters, R. (1982) The Programmer's Apprentice: Knowledge-base program editing. *IEEE Transactions on Software Engineering*, 8:1, January. Reprinted in D. Barstow, H. Shrobe & E. Sandewall (Eds.), *Interactive Programming Environments*, McGraw-Hill, New York, 1984.

Knowledge Representation as the Basis for Requirements Specifications

Alexander Borgida, Rutgers University
Sol Greenspan, Schlumberger-Doll Research
John Mylopoulos, University of Toronto

Specification of many kinds of knowledge about the world is essential to requirements engineering. Research on knowledge representation in artificial intelligence provides a wealth of relevant techniques that can be incorporated into specification languages.

What facts must be recorded during the requirements phase of a software project? What does a language that is designed to express such facts look like? We provide some answers to these questions in this article.

For purposes of discussion, we define the "requirements phase" of the software life cycle as the stage that precedes the design of software system architecture. This phase includes analysis of customer needs, as well as specification of both the functional behavior of the proposed system and the nonfunctional requirements that must be met. It is clear that, to carry out these activities, the analyst must gain an understanding of the environment in which the software will be used and the use to which the software will be put. We contend that this understanding should be expressed and recorded as a model of the environment, and that the various requirements should be expressed in relation to this model. Once we have made a case for this contention, we present some features that we believe are desirable in any language intended to support requirements engineering. In the remainder of the article, we illustrate some features of the language RML and point out how it arose from the confluence of two streams of thought: the representation of knowledge in artificial intelligence and the traditional concern for abstraction found in software engineering. The article concentrates on language-design issues and pays little attention to such problems as the "implementation" of requirements specification languages and their use as prototyping tools, or the semiautomatic transformation of a specification into an effective program—problems frequently associated with the application of artificial intelligence to software engineering.[1]

The need for representing knowledge

The requirements for a software product often describe no more than its *functional specification,* that is, the product's behavior at an early point in its development. However, to understand or use such a specification requires a great deal more information than is usually given in the specification alone. It is assumed that users of the specification possess wide-ranging knowledge about the environment from which the specification is drawn, and they use it to interpret the meaning of the specification. This includes knowledge of terms, technical and scientific rules, everyday procedures and conventions, and the way various devices work—as well as commonsense knowledge.

Consider an environment, such as a hospital, in which there may be several computer-based systems. There may be interactive information systems (such as those used for patient registration), real-time systems (like those used for patient monitoring), and expert systems (such as those used to aid in medical diagnosis).* Writing a requirements specification for each of these systems is largely a matter of gathering and understanding information about patient's needs, diseases, medical procedures, administration policies, and so on.

In current practice, the requirements specification is restricted to describing only certain aspects of computer systems: the storage, retrieval and manipulation of data; the computation of desired results; the functional behavior of system tasks; and the types of information used by the system. Features of traditional languages, such as PSL and RSL, that are used for stating requirements reflect these limitations. This leads to problems because system developers are not usually experts in the application domain; therefore, the requirements specification must go beyond the limits of a strict functional specification to capture the broader context in which the system will be placed. For example, the rules for converting from Fahrenheit to Celsius are not usually directly retrievable from a medical information system, yet this knowledge could be quite important in writing the programs that make up the information system. To illustrate: The knowledge that a sensor reads temperatures to within an accuracy of, say, ±0.5°F would have a direct bearing on how the program that converts degrees Fahrenheit to degrees Celsius is written (the degree of precision required in the conver-

sion factor would be affected, for instance).

We feel that even in the functional specification, the requirements statements should be written with an eye to the real world entities and activities about which information is being kept. For example, the specification statement that "the system must maintain up-to-date information about all admitted patients, including their names, ages, attending physicians, next of kin,..." is preferable to "keep a file with patient's name, age, doctor's name, next-of-kin's phone number," which makes a number of implementation decisions. We base our preference on the view that requirements specifications should talk about the "what" rather than the "how" of a software system. As we shall see, requirements specifi-

cations dealing with the world must be more powerful and expressive than requirements specifications dealing with target systems only.

While it may seem obvious that to describe a system's requirements, functional and otherwise, it is first necessary to understand the real-world concepts involved, techniques for explicitly capturing this information have yet to be adopted in software engineering. Our feeling, which is shared by several other researchers,[1-5] is that a new kind of specification is needed—one that is more world-oriented than current functional specification methods allow. We wish to view this proposed specification as forming a model of the world. In such a model, the symbols and their definitions correspond to concepts/entities in the world, and the structure of the model mirrors the structure one perceives in the world. The task of requirements specification thus has at its core the

building of a *requirements model* for some portion of the world.

Perhaps the best way to understand our view of the role of this world model is to understand the relationship between the requirements model and the world, on the one hand, and the relationship between the requirements model and the software system, on the other.

The model and the world. The symbols in the requirements model are related to the world in that each represents some real-world entity or activity, such as a person, prescribing medication, or participating in a clinical trial. When constructing the requirements model, one is concerned with such issues as which real-world objects should be represented, which of their properties are relevant, and

> Requirements specifications should talk about the "what" rather than the "how" of a software system; specifications dealing with the world must be more powerful and extensive than those dealing with target systems.

how accurately and completely the model represents the world.

The value of explicitly expressing a world model is that it facilitates communication between users, can be subjected to automated aids, and can be otherwise manipulated in ways not possible with the unexpressed knowledge of a human. For example, the model can be queried to check if the represented information is correct and to derive facts not explicitly represented. The model can also be analyzed for various kinds of consistency. Furthermore, when a "context" of specific facts is provided, the model can be run as a simulation of the world being represented, and this can be used to check whether complex dynamic processes have been adequately captured. Once the requirements model has been constructed, it should, ideally, become the sole body of knowledge about the world being modeled that is used by system designers.

*Since our work has been primarily in the area of information systems, we draw our examples in this article from various information systems; however, we believe that what we have to say is applicable to any software system that is intimately related to the world outside the computer—avionics software and office systems software, for example.

The model and the software system. The software system is determined by establishing "boundaries" that define what portions of the world model will be realized in a computer-based system and what portions will be considered as the environment of that system. Therefore, only some portions of the model of reality will be realized by the implemented system. While the requirements model is as true as possible to reality, the software system may be more limited. For example, the requirements model may say that a person always has a birth date, but the system may not have this on record, as in the case of patients brought unconscious into the emergency room.

and those of Balzer[1] are among the first to meld concepts from AI knowledge representation with software engineering concerns so as to achieve better techniques and languages for software requirements specifications.

Some principles for requirements modeling languages

We feel that the central goal of a requirements specification language is to provide facilities for gathering and representing world knowledge in a natural and convenient fashion, and at the same time to organize and structure this knowledge so that it

We believe that most information systems being developed reflect the designer's perceptions of the world. We label such perceptions *concepts,* whether they are about ideas, entities or activities. Most concepts are like patients and surgery, in that they arise in everyday human experience (philosophers call these "natural kinds"), as opposed to the artificially defined concepts of, say, mathematics. When we describe natural kinds, we are faced with the problem that they do not have precise definitions: Patients are sick persons, but shouldn't the class of patients also include people coming back for a checkup after they are healed? The symptoms of pneumonia include fever, but some people get pneumonia and don't have fever. And so on. It appears that descriptions of natural kinds run the risk of being either hopelessly vague or subject to contradiction. Contrast this with specifying such mathematical concepts as sets or sequences, which always satisfy their constraints "by definition." Developers of languages for requirements modeling will have to take the problem of describing natural kinds into account.

It is necessary to combine several kinds of modeling facilities into one language; a good modeling language should allow the designer to describe discourse entities and events in the real world.

Of course, the implementation of the software system will represent the knowledge about the relevant portion of the world by making use of standard techniques, such as files of records.

The use of AI knowledge representation. We have argued that capturing knowledge about the world is a significant part of requirements engineering. At the same time, one of the key conclusions of the past two decades of artificial intelligence research is that machines can exhibit intelligent behavior (that is, communicate in English, understand pictures, and so on) only when they are equipped with a great deal of knowledge about the real world. For this reason, there has been much AI research on representing and organizing knowledge with computers.* It is therefore natural to apply what has been learned in AI to requirements modeling. Our studies

*The reader may find the October 1983 issue of *Computer* a useful survey of this area.

can be easily understood by system developers and by the end user. We identify the following criteria as basic to achieving these goals, though the list is clearly not exhaustive.

To begin with, a good modeling language should allow the designer to describe entities in the domain of discourse and changes (events) in the world, and to state constraints and assumptions. Some modeling languages and methods are good for describing the properties of entities (for example, languages that take entity-relationship approaches), but are weak with respect to describing change and constraints. Specification methods designed especially for processes, procedures, or events are more appropriate for describing change. Logics are the most convenient languages for stating constraints. Since a requirements modeling language must be able to describe all of these things, it is necessary to combine several kinds of modeling facilities into one language.

Also, we recognize that the passing of time is a cornerstone of our human experience and is intimately tied to the description of dynamic aspects of the world. Therefore, a requirements modeling language must be able to talk explicitly about time and the evolution of the world through time. A language that lacks such capabilities forces the designer either to consider only static aspects of the world, or to specify dynamics not by describing them, but by writing procedures.

The above concerns the kinds of knowledge that a requirements modeling language must be able to represent. Another important concern is a language's usefulness in organizing knowledge.

Abstraction is the foremost organizational issue. The requirements specification for a realistic software system is likely to be very large and detailed. Past experience in software engineering and elsewhere suggests that the proper way to deal with many details is to abstract out the most important ones and then introduce the others in successive passes of a refinement process. A requirements modeling language should support the process of abstraction both by providing guidelines as to what are currently relevant details and by providing language features that support the refinement process.

Languages can also help the specifier achieve more complete and accurate descriptions. One tool for this is redundancy: If the specifier views the same situation from multiple points of view, he is less likely to omit a significant fact. Furthermore, if multiple descriptions of the same situation do not agree, then at least one of them is incorrect—a fact that may not be uncovered if only one description is presented. In general, of course, we would like the language to have an associated notion of consistency/inconsistency so that we can recognize obviously incorrect software specifications—that is, those for which there cannot be an implementation.

Finally, like all language designers, we would like to make the language easy to learn and read and convenient to use.

A language for requirements modeling

We have developed a language called RML that meets the above criteria.[6,7] We do not provide an indepth description of this language here. Instead, we highlight some of the notable features of RML and point out their relationship to AI work on knowledge representation and to traditional software engineering concerns.

We remark that the RML language is used to state requirements and does not have an implementation per se. (Incidentally, we have used RML

to specify at least one sizable example[7]—a conference organization system.) RML is part of larger information systems development project that includes the database programming language Taxis[8] and associated tools for editing, interpreting, and compiling programs. We plan to acquire computer tools that will enable us to make deductions from our requirements model and to check its consistency by translating RML into one of the AI languages for knowledge representation.

An object-oriented framework. A requirements model specified in RML consists of interrelated objects. Each object in the model stands for some

---

Object-oriented frameworks make possible a direct, natural correspondence between a model and the world.

---

entity, or activity, or, more generally, some concept in the world being modeled. For example, in a hospital information system model there are objects corresponding to each patient, room, and doctor as well as to diseases, lab tests, and so on. Objects are related to each other by properties. For example, bob *hasPhysician* mm, mm *hasName* "Dr. Mickey Mouse," mm *hasSpecialty* cardiology.

Objects are organized into classes for the purpose of capturing common characteristics. (Thus, "bob" belongs to the class of PATIENTS and mm is in DOCTORS.) Once this is done, we can specify relationships between generic concepts, for example, PATIENT *hasPhysician* DOCTOR, or DOCTOR *hasSpecialty* MEDICAL_ SPECIALTIES. Generic information about a class restricts the relationships in which the members of the class can participate. For example, a particular patient cannot have as physician any object which is not in the class DOCTORs.

In our framework, building a requirements model consists mostly of identifying the appropriate classes and describing them in terms of applicable properties and constraints on their values. For example, a partial description of the class PATIENT is

```
PATIENT
   parts
      name: PERSON_NAMES
      address: ADDRESSES
      hasPhysician: DOCTOR
      hasDiagnosis: DISEASE
```

The chief advantage of object-oriented frameworks is that they make possible a direct and natural correspondence between the world and its model: When constructing the model, we select concepts mentioned in descriptions of the application domain and define corresponding classes of objects in the model. Each of these acts as a center around which we place information related to that concept.

Our object-oriented approach has its origins in AI knowledge representation techniques, especially semantic networks, and in programming languages such as Simula and Smalltalk.

Activities and assertions are also objects. We manipulate the objects in a requirements model to simulate the behavior of their counterparts in the world. In a conscious bid for uniformity, we also model as objects activities in the world, which results in the generation of activity objects, as opposed to entity objects. For example, the activity of admitting patients is modeled by the activity class ADMIT, some of whose properties are

```
ADMIT
   participants
      newPatient: PERSON
      toWard: WARD
      admitter: DOCTOR

   parts
      document: GET_INFO
         (from ←→ newPatient)
      checkIn: ASSIGN_BED
         (toWhom ←→ newPatient,
          onWard ←→ toWard)

   precondition
      canAdmit?: HAS_AUTHORITY
         (who ←→ admitter,
          where ←→ toWard)
```

ADMIT intends to convey the idea that admitting a new patient involves obtaining information from the new patient and assigning him a bed. The definition shows six properties (*new-Patient, toWard, admitter, document, checkIn, and canAdmit?*) that fall into three property categories (*participants, parts, and precondition*). The first three properties specify that each instance of ADMIT involves a patient, a ward, and a doctor. These three objects are participants in the activity. There are two parts: These relate each instance of ADMIT to the two named activity objects, which serve as

Generalization hierarchies. In designing RML, we followed yet another lead from semantic networks in AI: Classes in RML can be related to each other by the *subclass* or *IS-A* relationship (PATIENT IS-A PERSON, DOCTOR IS-A PERSON, and SURGEON IS-A DOCTOR, for example). One class is said to be a subclass of another only if it describes a more specialized concept and if every instance of the first class is an instance of the second class. The subclass relationship organizes the classes and their descriptions into a hierarchy, called the *generalization* or *IS-A* hierarchy. One

hierarchy. The IS-A relationship forms the basis for an abstraction mechanism called *generalization,* which is founded on the idea that it is often useful to ignore at first the detailed differences between several related classes and to present their common aspects as the description of some superclass instead. The differences between the classes can be introduced when the modeler describes how each differs as a subclass from the common superclass.

Generalization also suggests a particular methodology for developing a requirements specification. This methodology, called *stepwise refinement by specialization,*[9] prescribes that one describe first the most general classes of pertinent entities, activities and assertions occurring in the physical world. In the hospital world, these might include patients, doctors, admissions, treatments, and so on. In the next phase, important subclasses of each class are selected and described. For example, the modeler might differentiate between child and adult patients, internists and surgeons, chemotherapy and radiation therapy. Successive phases of the refinement process then introduce and describe smaller and smaller subclasses that model more and more specialized concepts. Inheritance is useful here because it allows the modeler to limit his specifications to the ways in which the subclass differs from the superclass—at each step, he need consider only information appropriate to that level.

Successive RML refinements introduce and describe smaller and smaller subclasses that model more and more specialized concepts: here inheritance allows the modeler to limit specifications to how the subclass differs from the superclass at each step.

---

components of the overall admit activity. The sixth property, *canAdmit,* relates each instance of ADMIT to an instance of the assertion class HAS AUTHORITY TO ADMIT. This assertion serves as a precondition, which means that at the time the activity instance starts, the related assertion instance is true.

As we have just seen, assertions, like activities, are objects that belong to classes. An assertion has properties that relate it to other objects and belong to categories such as *arguments, parts,* and *constraints.* Arguments are the objects that the assertion is about; parts are component formulas, and constraints are conditions that must be met for an instance of an assertion class to be true. Instances of an assertion class are true formulae in the form dictated by the containing class.

One of the distinguishing features of RML is that it combines the specification of entities, activities, and assertions into a framework in which all units of description (activities, assertions, and so on) are objects that belong to classes and have properties. It is a powerful language based on a small set of primitive concepts.

of the important consequences of this organization is that properties of a class can be inherited by its subclasses.

For example, if we write the definition

PERSON
    name: HUMAN_NAMES
    age: HUMAN_AGES
    address: ADDRESS
    tel#: TELEPHONE_NUMBER

and then specify that PATIENT IS-A PERSON to indicate that all patients are also persons, we need not restate the fact that patients have names, ages, and so on. These facts will be inherited from the description of PERSONs. Furthermore, the same saving of effort would occur if DOCTORs, ADMINISTRATORs, or other subclasses of PERSONs were specified.

A subclass can constrain inherited properties. For example, the *admittingPhysician* property can be restricted to SURGEONs where surgical patients are involved.

The IS-A relationship organizes classes of objects into a natural taxonomy of concepts that helps to make descriptions manageable: It highlights the similarities between classes by placing them close to each other in the

Generalization is the appropriate abstraction principle to exploit when the difficulty of modeling is caused by a large number of details and objects that need to be captured, rather than by algorithmic complexity. After all, taxonomic hierarchies have long been used in other disciplines, such as botany and zoology, to organize numerous observations. For example, the problems of specifying the ADMIT activity are related for the most part to the many variations introduced by the persons being admitted: Children don't have their own health insurance numbers, patients undergoing surgery must be put on special diets, and so on. We claim that many software development projects, especially information systems projects, deal with precisely this kind of situation. Note that this methodology is orthogonal and complementary to the well-known *stepwise refinement by decomposition*: Variants of a class of solutions can be introduced through specialization at any level of decomposition, including the final, programming-language level.

Refinement by specialization, which we describe more fully in another work,[9] is an interesting example of the advantages to be gained from the marriage of AI concepts (in this case, various kinds of inheritance schemes) with those of software engineering (here, abstraction).

Representing time. Time is a very important subject in a world-oriented modeling scheme. Time is inextricably involved in every fact we state: an object exists at a particular time, an activity starts and ends at particular points in time; an assertion is true at some particular time, and so on. RML captures the rich variety of references to time that occur in everyday discourse. Designers of specification languages typically do not include explicit references to time because they make some grossly simplifying assumptions, such as the assumption that events are totally ordered. Some requirements languages do supply a handful of time-related statement types; for example, those that say an event "happens so many times per month." However, a rich facility for talking about time and for talking about behaviors with reference to time is needed.

In designing RML, we adopted a relatively simple notion of time as an infinite and dense sequence of time points. Assertions are true at a given time point, and the value of an object's properties as well as its membership in a class is always evaluated with respect to a specified time. Furthermore, every event has associated start and end points.

Starting from this simple foundation, we can build surprisingly complex temporal descriptions within the object-oriented framework of RML, including the description of *time entities* that correspond to ordinary time concepts, such as dates of the year, times of the day, and so on. The passing of a period of time can be viewed as a *time activity* whose start and end points coincide with the start and end times of a given time interval. If we apply to activities the predicates for reasoning about time intervals that were developed by Allen,[10] we can express quite complex temporal relationships. Note that temporal predicates, such as DURING, BEFORE, and OVER-

> Time is inextricably involved in every fact we state: RML captures the rich variety of time references in everday discourse and builds complex temporal descriptions within its object-oriented framework.

LAPS, as well as classes of concepts such as ONE_HOUR_INTERVAL, can all be defined as classes in RML itself—they are like procedure definitions rather than extra language features. This attests to the power of the basic ideas on which RML is built.

RML also makes it easy to state commonly occurring expressions that concern time. A good example of this is the use of *property categories* to abbreviate time constraints. For instance, the statement that "a new patient's location after he has been admitted is the ward to which he is being admitted" would normally have to be written

```
ADMIT
    right_place:
        toWard of ADMIT at end(ADMIT) =
        location of (newPatient of ADMIT
        at end(ADMIT)) at end(ADMIT)*
```

because it is important to know when every property (such as *toWard, newPatient, or location*) is to be evaluated. Property categories can be used to

*This statement should be read as: "at the end of an ADMIT event, the value of the *toWard* property of the ADMIT event equals the value of the *location* property of the patient being admitted." The patient being admitted is the *newPatient* property of the ADMIT event.

specify default times when properties will be evaluated. For example, *final-condition* evaluates all properties that lack a temporal specification at the time point corresponding to the end of the activity. Thus, the above example can be abbreviated to

```
ADMIT
    final-condition
        right-place: (toWard of ADMIT =
        location of newPatient of ADMIT)
```

Property categories are also useful for abbreviating other time constraints. They are most often used to specify property values at those times when an object is inserted into a class or removed from a class, as well as throughout the interval when an object is in a class.

We wish to point out that there are many complexities surrounding the notion of time—complexities that we believe have been successfully dealt with by RML. These include the need to represent absolute and relative time (for example, "at eight o'clock" and "one hour from now," respectively), repetitive behavior ("the motion of the earth involves one rotation around its axis every 24 hours"), and vagueness ("on Thursday"), as well as the need to give extremely detailed descriptions of events.

The representation of time and time-related information is another area where there has been almost no relevant research in software engineering and where we have benefited from work in AI.[10]

Multiple levels of description

We do not wish to leave the impression that artificial intelligence research has covered all the relevant problems of requirements engineering. One area of key concern for software engineering but not for AI is building up detailed descriptions incrementally and introducing implementation details to arrive at a final software product. We have addressed this issue in our work[7] by considering the two language levels between which an RML description is sandwiched: We use SADT as a model language for initial descriptions,[11] and the Taxis[8] programming language for implementation.

In the initial stages of requirements engineering, the chief difficulty lies in deciding what concepts and phenomena are relevant. We propose that designers will find it easier to make such decisions if they use a language created for structured analysis, such as SADT, to build a "structured lexicon" of relevant terms. SADT diagrams accomplish this by making use of boxes and connecting arrows that are labelled by English terms. However, the interpretation of SADT diagrams is dependent on the meaning of the words and phrases of the embedded language and the accompanying natural language narrative.

At this stage, RML is used to introduce classes and properties that correspond to terms in the SADT diagrams: This makes the diagrammed information precise. Thus, for each feature of a diagram (box, node, arrow, split, join, and so on), an RML concept is specified in the requirements (RML) model. For example, each activity box has a class description with the various inputs and outputs as properties belonging to appropriate property categories like input, output, etc. Essentially, the designer decides on the precise meaning of the words in the SADT model and writes them down in RML. The semantic relationships expressed in the RML model are constrained, though, by the connectivity of the SADT diagram, which the designer uses as a "road map." He then uses the RML model to specify details that are not specifiable in the SADT diagrammatic notation because of their

precision (for example, whether some input is a stream of values or a single value). This scheme allows the designer to follow the SADT technique of systematically gathering terms needed for requirements so that he can build an imprecise but suggestive skeleton—another stepwise refinement process—that is fleshed out in RML.

The chief difficulty of the initial stages of requirements engineering is deciding what concepts and phenomena are relevant.

Our melding of SADT and RML is not accidental: It was suggested by SADT's uniform treatment of data and activity diagrams, which corresponds to our uniform treatment of entities and activities as objects with properties. The narrative text accompanying SADT diagrams can be encoded in the form of properties that fall into various categories. These properties give such information as activation conditions, initial and final conditions, and constraints (for example, mutual exclusion) affecting subparts. Also, RML assertions make it possible to capture arrow connections as general constraints (not data flow), as suggested by Ross.[11]

Given a statement of requirements, the usual next step for the designer is to proceed toward an implementation (possibly a prototype). It is natural to use the programming language Taxis[8] for information systems specified in RML, since Taxis was designed on many of the same principles as RML. Objects are described by properties and grouped into classes, and classes are organized along IS-A hierarchies. Taxis, however, is a procedural language with standard control constructs (loops, conditionals, assignment) and primitive operations for data manipulation. This means, for example, that descriptions of some

activities in RML can be mapped to procedures that manipulate data objects and are supposed to obey the constraints stated in the RML model. We are currently developing ways to add "design decisions" features at various points in the system so that designers can derive a Taxis program from an RML specification.

Current research directions

Our current research in adapting ideas from AI knowledge representation to requirements modeling is proceeding in a number of directions. We mention two of them here to give the reader further insight into the usefulness of viewing knowledge representation as a basis for requirements specification.

Dealing with over-abstraction. Consistency—the absence of contradictions—is one of the most important features of a specification. Unfortunately, in describing the natural world it is often very difficult to avoid making contradictory statements. For example, according to medical textbooks, all patients suffering from anemia have low red-blood-cell counts; however, a special kind of anemia—acute posthemorrhagic anemia—is not associated with low RBC, at least not at the beginning. A person's heart normally beats between 70 and 90 times a minute, but this is not so in the case of hyperthyroid patients. Situations such as these have been studied extensively in AI. The problem of "birds fly," "penguins are birds," but "penguins don't fly" is a classic case.

These examples appear to be cases of over-abstraction, that is, detailed differences are ignored at the beginning in a way that doesn't allow them to be introduced later on without destroying consistency. This is because most concepts lack precise definitions, and almost any rule will have exceptions.

When faced with contradictions, we can go back to the original description and make it more general—for example, we can say nothing about birds flying—so that we avoid contradictions. This has a number of disadvantages. Owing to inheritance, such a change may propagate to many other subclasses for which the original assertion was correct and useful (starlings, sparrows, storks, and so on all fly). The alternative of introducing new subclasses—for instance FLYING-BIRDS and NON-FLYING-BIRDS—can result in a combinatorial explosion of mostly uninteresting classes. A final problem is that in attempting to be as general as possible, we have no principle for deciding how far to go. Suppose we want to make an assertion about chairs. How should we characterize them? Chairs usually have four legs, but some have three, and surely carpenters have made chairs with five, six, and more legs.

From a methodological point of view, exceptions are definitely a fly in the ointment, since one can expect almost anything said at one level of refinement to be contradicted eventually at some lower level. We propose to deal with this by allowing the designer to specify exceptional classes or objects for which contradictions are explicitly acknowledged and resolved through *excuses.* (For instance, the assertion that hyperthyroid patients have high blood pressure excuses the assertion that patients in general have normal blood pressure.) Of course, we need to provide appropriate semantics for excuses so the final specification will be logically consistent. Research in AI on non-monotonic logics is one area that may provide insight on how to accomplish this.

Note that the excuse mechanism also has the advantage of supporting yet another abstraction principle, namely that of describing first the usual or normal case and then later refining this description by indicating special or exceptional cases later.[12]

Relationship of world, model, and system. One of the important problems confronting cognitive science is explicating the relationship, in humans and machines, between knowledge of the world and the actual state of the world. In particular, it is important to discover how one can proceed when these relationships are incomplete or even inaccurate. This is relevant to several significant distinctions that arise in requirements modeling, namely those between the world and the

---

AI research on non-monotonic logics may provide insight on how to make final specification logically consistent.

---

model of the world being built, and those between the model of the world and the model of the proposed information system, which will be part of the world. As an example, consider the distinctions between the blood pressure of a patient at a specific time, the pressure that we can read on the sphygmomanometer or that is read by a machine, and the value recorded in a database. Our goal is to provide easy ways for designers to talk about the concepts underlying these different but related readings so that they can include in their specifications such hospital requirements as "the recorded blood pressure at any time must be within 10 of the actual blood pressure." Drawing up such nonfunctional requirements is an important part of requirements engineering. One reason for this is that they can be extremely useful during the development phase. To use the example of blood pressure readings again, nonfunctional requirements can influence how frequently blood pressure is sampled by a device that is part of a software/hardware patient-monitoring environment.

We have argued that the requirements specification of a software system should consist of a detailed model of the world, or, more accurately, of our knowledge of the world.

We have presented several features of the language RML, which was crafted to help designers build requirements models. We used these features to support the claim that requirements modeling can draw significant inspiration from work on knowledge representation in AI, but noted that this transfer must be tempered by keeping in mind the traditional concerns of software engineering.

Also, we have touched on some of the principal problems of requirements engineering: creating high-level, world-oriented descriptions that deal with the application domain of discourse rather than with system design or implementation concepts; coping with large descriptions whose details must be effectively organized; designing coherent requirements languages that are based on a small number of concepts; providing methodological guidance for incrementally constructing requirements specifications; producing provably consistent descriptions; and proceeding from requirements modeling to the design of an information system.

By basing our work on results from knowledge representation, we have reached at least partial answers to questions that have barely been addressed in software engineering. We have given several examples of how our research on requirements has been influenced by knowledge representation. This area offers ideas and techniques for both the representation of many kinds of knowledge (such as concepts from the natural world, default knowledge, exceptions, information about time, uncertainty, and incompleteness of knowledge) and the organization of such knowledge for convenient processing by humans and computers.

As a final point, we wish to note that important groundwork has been done in AI on the formal semantics of representation schemes as well as on such topics as deduction and logical consistency within knowledge bases. We have given a formal account of RML[7] that shows that an RML specification translates into a relatively standard predicate logic. An RML specification can thus be usefully viewed as a logical theory.* Consistency in an RML model is shown in this account to be the standard notion of logical consistency, and since this is so, deductions and inferences can be made from the model. This opens up the possibility of using computer-based theorem provers as tools in an environment for developing requirements specifications; such theorem provers could be used to decide whether a requirements model is consistent, whether a certain situation can arise or not in the world, and so on.

In conclusion, we hope we have convinced the reader that

- the requirements specification for software must be much more than a statement of the external behavior of the final system;

- it is appropriate to view the requirements specification as a model of our knowledge of the application domain and to phrase various requirements in terms of this model;

- AI research on knowledge representation provides a wealth of ideas for world modeling; and

- RML has incorporated many such ideas into a novel, powerful, yet uniform framework based on a few concepts that nevertheless supports such traditional software engineering concepts as abstraction. □

Acknowledgment

The research for this article was supported in part by the National Science and Engineering Research Council of Canada and the US National Science Foundation under Grant MCS-82-1193.

*However, RML also provides facilities for structuring descriptions, which languages based on logics alone do not.

References

1. R. Balzer, N. Goldman and D. Wile, "Operational Specification as the Basis for Rapid Prototyping," *Proc. ACM Sigsoft Software Eng. Symp. Rapid Prototyping,* Columbia, Md., in *ACM Software Eng. Notes,* Vol. 7, No. 5, Dec. 1982, pp. 3-16.

2. M. L. Wilson, "A Requirements and Design Aid for Relational Data Bases," *Proc. Fifth Int'l Conf. Software Eng.,* IEEE-CS Press, Los Alamitos, Calif., 1981, pp. 283-293.

3. R. T. Yeh and R. T. Mittermeir, "Conceptual Modeling as a Basis for Deriving Software Requirements," *Int'l Computer Symp.,* Taipei, Taiwan, Dec. 1980.

4. J. A. Bubenko, Jr., "On Concepts and Strategies for Requirements and Information Analysis," SYSLAB Rept. No. 4, Dept. of Computer Science, Chalmers University of Technology, 1981.

5. N. Roussopoulos, "CSDL: A Conceptual Schema Definition Language for the Design of Data Base Applications," *IEEE Trans. Software Eng.,* Vol. SE-5, No. 5, Sept. 1979, pp. 481-496.

6. S. J. Greenspan, J. Mylopoulos, and A. Borgida, "Capturing More World Knowledge in the Requirements Specification," *Proc. Sixth Int'l Conf. Software Eng.,* IEEE-CS Press, Los Alamitos, Calif., 1982, pp. 225-234.

7. S. J. Greenspan, "Requirements Modeling: A Knowledge Representation Approach to Software Requirements Definition," PhD thesis, Dept. of Computer Science, University of Toronto, 1984.

8. J. Mylopoulos, P. A. Bernstein, and H. K. T. Wong, "A Language Facility for Designing Interactive Database-Intensive Application," *ACM Trans. Database Systems,* Vol. 5, No. 2, June 1980, pp. 185-207.

9. A. Borgida, J. Mylopoulos, and H. K. T. Wong, "Generalization as a Basis for Software Specification," *On Conceptual Modeling: Perspectives from Artificial Intelligence, Databases, and Programming Languages,* M. Brodie, J. Mylopoulos, and J. Schmidt, eds., Springer-Verlag, New York, 1984, pp. 87-114.

10. J. Allen, "Maintaining Knowledge about Temporal Intervals," *Comm. ACM,* Vol. 26, No. 11, Nov. 1983, pp. 832-843.

11. D. T. Ross, "Structured Analysis (SA): A Language for Communicating Ideas," *IEEE Trans. Software Eng.,* special issue on requirements analysis, Vol. SE-3, No. 1, Jan. 1977, pp. 16-34.

12. A. Borgida, "Intelligent Handling of Exceptions in Information Systems—An Overview," *Proc. First Int'l Workshop on Expert Database Systems,* L. Kerscheberg, ed., Institute for Information Management, Technology and Policy, University of South Carolina, Columbia, South Carolina, Oct. 1984, pp. 643-651.

Alexander Borgida has been an assistant professor in the Department of Computer Science at Rutgers University since 1981. His current research interests involve the application of ideas from artificial intelligence to the problems of software development, especially the development languages and methodologies for the specification and implementation of information systems. He is a member of ACM.

Borgida received his PhD in computer science from the University of Toronto, where he studied computational linguistics.

Questions about this article can be directed to Borgida at the Dept. of Computer Science, Rutgers University, New Brunswick, NJ 08903.

Sol J. Greenspan is a member of the research staff in the Systems Science Department at Schlumberger-Doll Research in Ridgefield, Connecticut. His main interests involve applying artificial intelligence findings to software engineering. His current work focuses on process control specifications and their use in an automatic programming system.

Before joining Schlumberger this year, Greenspan was on the Computer Science Faculty of the University of Toronto's Artificial Intelligence Group. From 1972 to 1975 he was member of the Technical Staff at Bell Laboratories. He has also held positions at IBM Research, San Jose, and Softech, Inc., Waltham, Massachusetts.

Greenspan received his PhD in computer science from the University of Toronto in 1984. His thesis investigated the use of knowledge representation in software requirements specification.

John Mylopoulos is currently a professor of computer science at the University of Toronto. His research interests include knowledge representation and its applications in the design of interactive information systems. He served as principal investigator for the Torus project, which involved the design of a natural-language front end for a relational database management system, and for the PSN project, which was concerned with the construction of a knowledge representation system. He is currently serving as principal investigator for the Taxis project, which is concentrating on the development of linguistic tools for the design of information systems. He was recently appointed senior research fellow for a national project on artificial intelligence, robotics and society, by the Canadian Institute for Advanced Research.

Mylopoulos holds a PhD in computer science from Princeton University.

XI / Artificial Intelligence Programming

Essentially all of the intelligent programming tools described in this volume are at most experimental prototypes. Given that these tools are still quite far from being commercial realities, it is worthwhile to note that there is a completely different way in which artificial intelligence research has (and will undoubtedly continue) to help programmers: Artificial intelligence researchers are themselves programmers. Since the earliest days of computers, artificial intelligence researchers have developed programming tools for their own use that have turned out to be very useful for programmers in general.

An area where this spinoff is of particular importance today is rapid prototyping and other forms of exploratory programming. The construction of large, complex, first-of-a-kind programs is an area of programming that is receiving greater and greater emphasis these days. As discussed in [Sheil, Chapter 33], creating such programs is more a problem of exploration than implementation and does not conform to conventional software lifecycle models. The artificial intelligence programming community has always been faced with this kind of exploratory programming and has therefore had a head start on developing appropriate language, environment, and hardware features.

[Bobrow and Stefik, Chapter 34] gives an overview of the key features of current artificial intelligence programming and discusses why these features are useful. In particular, Bobrow and Stefik discuss object-oriented programming, logic programming, constraint-oriented programming, and the interactive nature of artificial intelligence programming environments.

DATAMATION®

POWER TOOLS FOR PROGRAMMERS

by Beau Sheil

Emerging from AI labs, exploratory programming
environments can handle complex,
interactive applications that structured methods
box into a corner.

POWER TOOLS FOR PROGRAMMERS

by Beau Sheil

ILLUSTRATION BY DORIS ETTINGER

An oil company needs a system to monitor
and control the increasingly complex and frequently changing equipment used to operate
an oil well. An electronic circuit designer
plans to augment a circuit layout program to
incorporate a variety of vaguely stated design
rules. A newspaper wants a page layout system to assist editors in balancing the inter-
locking constraints that govern the placement
of stories and advertisements. A government
agency envisions a personal workstation that
would provide a single integrated interface to
a variety of large, evolving database systems.

Applications like these are forcing the
commercial deployment of a radically new
kind of programming system. First developed to support research in artificial intelligence and interactive graphics, these new
tools and techniques are based on the notion
of exploratory programming, the conscious
intertwining of system design and implementation. Fueled by dramatic changes in the cost
of computing, such exploratory programming environments have become a commercial reality virtually overnight. No fewer than
four such systems were displayed at NCC '82
and their numbers are likely to increase rapidly as their power and range of application
become more widely appreciated.

Despite the diversity of subject matter, a common thread runs through our example applications. They are, of course, all
large, complex programs whose implementations will require significant resources. Their
more interesting similarity, however, is that
it is extremely difficult to give complete
specifications for any of them. The reasons
range from sheer complexity (the circuit designer can't anticipate all the ways in which
his design rules will interact), through continually changing requirements (the equipment
in the oil rig changes, as do the information
bases that the government department is required to consult), to the subtle human factors issues that determine the effectiveness of
an interactive graphics interface.

Whatever the cause, a large programming project with uncertain or changing
specifications is a particularly deadly combi-

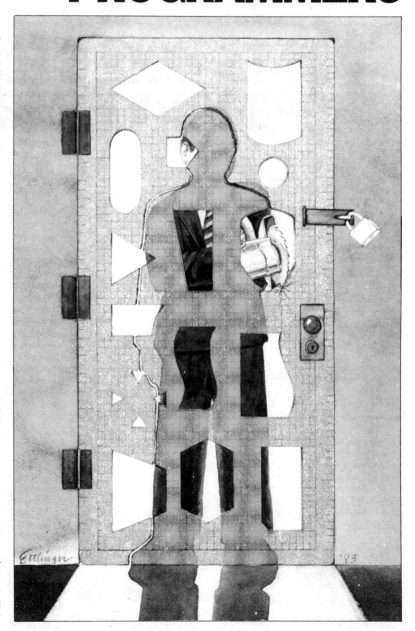

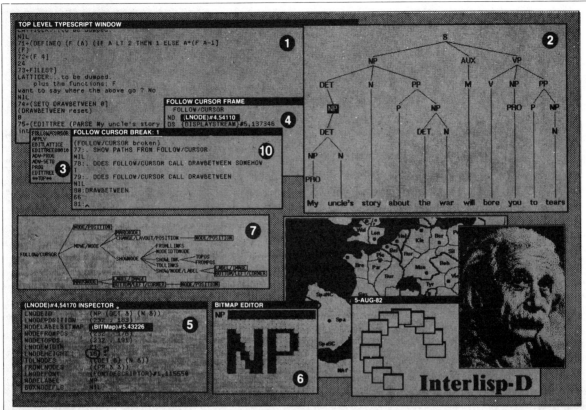

These two screen images show some of the exploratory programming tools provided in the Xerox Interlisp-D programming environment. The screen is divided into a series of rectangular areas or windows, each of which provides a view onto some data or process, and which can be reshaped and repositioned at will by the user. When they overlap, the occluded portion of the lower window is automatically saved, so that it can be restored when the overlapping window is removed. Since the display is bit-mapped, each window can contain an arbitrary mixture of text, lines, curves, and pictures composed of half-tones or solids. The image of Einstein, for instance, was produced by scanning a photograph and storing it digitally.

In the typescript window (labeled 1), the user has defined a program F (facto-rial) and has then immediately run it, giving an input of 4 and getting a result of 24. Next, in the same window, he queries the state of his files, finding that one file (LAT-TICER) has already been changed and one function (F) has been defined but not associated with any file yet. The user sets the value of DRAWBETWEEN to 0 in command 74, and the system notes that this is a change and adds DRAWBETWEEN to the set of "changed objects" that might need to be saved.

Then, the user runs the program EDITTREE, giving it a parse tree for the sentence "My uncle's story about the war will bore you to tears." This opens up the big window (2) on the right in which the sentence diagram is drawn. Using the mouse, the user starts to move the NP node on the left (which is inverted to show that it is being moved).

While the move is taking place, the user interrupts the tree editor, which suspends the computation and causes three "break" windows to appear on top of the lower edge of the typescript. The smallest window (3) shows the dynamic state of the computation, which has been broken inside a subprogram called FOLLOW/CURSOR. The "FOLLOW/CURSOR Frame" window (4) to the right shows the value of the local variables bound by FOLLOW/CURSOR. One of them has been selected (and so appears inverted) and in response, its value has been shown in more detail in the window (5) at the lower left of the screen. The user has marked one of the component values as suspicious by circling it using the mouse. In addition, he has asked to examine the contents of the BITMAP component, which has

nation for conventional programming techniques. Virtually all modern programming methodology is predicated on the assumption that a programming project is fundamentally a problem of implementation, rather than design. The design is supposed to be decided on first, based on specifications provided by the client; the implementation follows. This dichotomy is so important that it is standard practice to recognize that a client may have only a partial understanding of his needs, so that extensive consultations may be required to ensure a complete specification with which the client will remain happy. This dialog guarantees a fixed specification that will form a stable base for an implementation.

The vast bulk of existing programming practice and technology, such as structured design methodology, is designed to ensure that the implementation does, in fact, follow the specification in a controlled fashion, rathern than wander off in some unpredictable direction. And for good reason. Modern programming methodology is a significant achievement that has played a major role in preventing the kind of implementation disasters that often befell large programming projects in the 1960s.

The implementation disasters of the 1960s, however, are slowly being succeeded by the design disasters of the 1980s. The projects described above simply will not yield to conventional methods. Any attempt to obtain an exact specification from the client is bound to fail because, as we have seen, the client does not know and cannot anticipate exactly what is required. Indeed, the most striking thing about these examples is that the clients' statements of their problems are really aspirations, rather than specifications. And since the client has no experience on which to ground these aspirations, it is only by exploring the properties of some putative solutions that the client will find out what is really needed. No amount of interrogation of the client or paper exercises will answer these questions; one just has to try some designs to see what works.

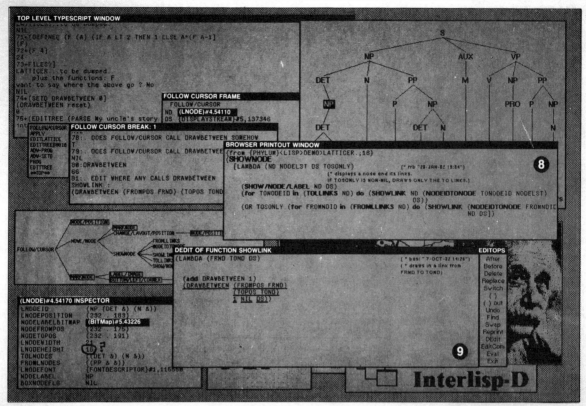

opened up a bitmap edit window (6) to the right. This shows an enlarged copy of the actual NP image that is being moved by the tree editor. Then, inside the largest of the three break windows (10) the user has asked some questions about the FOLLOW/CURSOR subprogram that was running when he interrupted, and queried the value of DRAW-BETWEEN (now 66). The SHOW PATHS command brought up the horizontal tree diagram on the left (7), which shows which subprograms call each other, starting at FOLLOW/CURSOR.

Each node in the call tree produced by the SHOW PATHS command is an active element that will respond to the user's selecting it with the mouse. In the second image, the user has selected the SHOWNODE subprogram, which has caused its source code to be retrieved from the file (‹LISP›DE-

MO›LATTICER) on the remote file server (PHYLUM) where it was stored, and displayed in the "Browser printout window" (8) which has been opened at middle right. User functions and extended Lisp forms (like *for* and *do*) are highlighted by system-generated font changes.

By selecting nodes in the SHOW PATHS window, the user could also have edited the code or obtained a summary description of any of its subprograms.

Instead, the user has asked (in the break typescript window (10)) to edit wherever anybody calls the DRAWBETWEEN system primitive (which draws lines between two specified points). This request causes the system to consult its dynamically maintained database of information about user programs, wherein it finds that the subprogram SHOWLINK calls DRAWBETWEEN. It

therefore loads the code for SHOWLINK into an edit window (9) that appears under the "Browser printout window." The system then automatically finds and underlines the first (and only) call on DRAWBETWEEN. Note that on the previous line DRAW-BETWEEN is used as a variable (the same variable the user set and interrogated earlier). The system, however, knows that this is not a subprogram call, so it has been skipped over. If the user were to make any change to this subprogram in the editor, not only would the change take effect immediately, but SHOWLINK would be marked as needing to be updated in its file and the information about it in the subprogram database would be updated. This, in turn, would cause the SHOW PATHS window to be repainted, as its display might no longer be valid.

The consequences of approaching problems like these as routine implementation exercises are dramatic. First, the implementation team begins by pushing for an exact specification. How long the client resists this coercion depends on how well he really understands the limits of his own grasp of the problem. Sooner or later, however, with more or less ill-feeling, the client accepts a specification and the implementation team goes to work.

The implementors take the specification, partition it, define a module structure that reflects this partitioning, freeze the interfaces between them, and repeat this process until the problem has been divided into a

large number of small, easily understandable, and easily implementable pieces. Control over the implementation process is achieved by the imposition of structure, which is then enforced by a variety of management practices and programming tools.

USE OF INTERNAL RIGIDITY

Since the specification, and therefore the module structuring, is considered fixed, one of the most effective methods for enforcing it is the use of redundant descriptions and consistency checking. Hence the importance of techniques such as interface descriptions and static type checking, which require that multiple

statements of various aspects of the design be included in the program text. These statements allow mechanical checks that ensure that each piece of the system remains consistent with the rest. In a well-executed conventional implementation project, a great deal of internal rigidity is built into the system, ensuring its orderly development.

The problems usually emerge at system acceptance time, when the client requests not just superficial, but radical changes, either as a result of examining the system or for some completely exogenous reason. From the point of view of conventional programming practice, this indicates a failure at specification time. The software engineer

The implementation disasters of the 1960s are slowly being succeeded by the design disasters of the 1980s.

should have been more persistent in obtaining a fuller description of the problem, in involving all the affected parties, etc. This is often true. Many ordinary implementation exercises are brought to ruin because the consequences of the specification were never fully agreed upon. But that's not the problem here. The oil company couldn't anticipate the addition of a piece of equipment quite different from the device on which the specification was based. No one knew that the layout editors would complain that it doesn't "feel right" now that they can no longer physically handle the copy (even in retrospect, it's unclear why they feel that way and what to do about it), etc., etc., etc. Nor would any amount of speculation by either client or software engineer have helped. Rather, it would have just prompted an already nervous client to demand whole dimensions of flexibility that would not in fact be needed, leaving the system just as unprepared for the ones that eventually turned out to matter.

Whatever the cause, the implementation team has to rework the system to satisfy a new, and significantly different, specification. That puts them in a situation that conventional programming methodology simply refuses to acknowledge—except as something to avoid. As a result, their programming tools and methods are suddenly of limited effectiveness. The redundant descriptions and imposed structure that were so effective in constraining the program to follow the old specification have lost none of their efficacy—they still constrain the program to follow the old specification. And they're difficult to change. The whole point of redundancy is to protect the design from a single unintentional change. But it's equally well protected against a single intentional change. Thus, all the changes have to be made everywhere. (Since this should never happen, there's no methodology to guide or programming tools to assist this process.) Of course, if the change is small (as it "should" be), there is no particular problem. But if it is large enough to cut across the module structure, the implementation team finds that it has to fight its way out of its previous design.

Still no major problem, if that's the end of the matter. But it rarely is. The new system will suggest yet another change. And so on. After a few iterations of this, not only are the client and the implementation team not on speaking terms, but the repeated assaults on the module structure have likely left it looking like spaghetti. It still gets in the way (fire walls are just as impenetrable if laid out at random as they are when laid out straight), but has long ceased to be of any use to anyone except to remind them of the project's sorry history. Increasingly, it is actively subverted (enter LOOPHOLES, UNSPECS, etc.) by programmers whose patience is running thin. Even if the design were suddenly to stabilize (unlikely in the present atmosphere), all the seeds have now been sown for an implementation disaster as well.

EXPLORE DESIGN PROBLEMS

The alternative to this kind of predictable disaster is not to abandon structured design for programming projects that are, or can be made to be, well defined. That would be a tremendous step backwards. Instead, we should recognize that some applications are best thought of as design problems, rather than implementation projects. These problems require programming systems that allow the design to emerge from experimentation with the program, so that design and program develop together. Environments in which this is possible were first developed in artificial intelligence and computer graphics, two research areas that are particularly prone to specification instability.

At first sight, artificial intelligence might seem an unlikely source of programming methodology. But constructing programs, in particular programs that carry out some intelligent activity, is central to artificial intelligence. Since almost any intelligent activity is likely to be poorly understood (once a program becomes well understood we usually cease to consider it "intelligent"), the artificial intelligence programmer invariably has to restructure his program many, many times before it becomes reasonably proficient. In addition, since intelligent activities are complex, the programs tend to be very large, yet they are invariably built by very small teams, often a single researcher. Consequently, they are usually at or beyond the manageable limits of complexity for their implementors. In response, a variety of programming environments based on the Lisp programming language have evolved to aid in the development of these large, rapidly changing systems.

The rapidly developing area of interactive graphics has encountered similar problems. Fueled by the swift drop in the cost of computers capable of supporting interactive graphics, there has been an equally swift development of applications that make heavy use of interactive graphics in their user interfaces. Not only was the design of such interfaces almost completely virgin territory as recently as 10 years ago, but even now, when there are a variety of known techniques (menus, windows, etc.) for exploiting this power, it is still very difficult to determine how easy it will be to use a proposed user interface and how well it will match the user's needs and expectations in particular situations. Consequently, complex interactive interfaces usually require extensive empirical testing to determine whether they are really effective and considerable redesign to make them so.

While interface design has always required some amount of tuning, the vastly increased range of possibilities available in a full graphics system has made the design space unmanageably large to explore without extensive experimentation. In response, a variety of systems, of which Smalltalk is the best known, have been developed to facilitate this experimentation by providing a wide range of built-in graphical abstractions and methods of modifying and combining them together into new forms.

In contrast to conventional programming technology, which restrains the programmer in the interests of orderly development, exploratory programming systems must amplify the programmer in the interests of maximizing his effectiveness. Exploration in the realm of programming can require small numbers of programmers to make essentially arbitrary transformations to very large amounts of code. Such programmers need programming power tools of considerable capacity or they will simply be buried in detail. So, like an amplifier, their programming system must magnify their necessarily limited energy and minimize extraneous activities that would otherwise compete for their attention.

SOURCES OF DESIGN POWER

One source of such power is the use of interactive graphics. Exploratory programming systems have capitalized on recent developments in personal computing with extraordinary speed. The Xerox 1108 Interlisp-D system, for example, uses a large format display and a "mouse" pointing device to allow very high bandwidth communication with the user. Designers of exploratory programming environments have been quick to seize on the power of this combination to provide novel programming tools, as we shall see.

In addition to programming tools, these personal machine environments allow the standard features of a professional workstation, such as text editing, file management, and electronic mail, to be provided within the programming environment itself. Not only are these facilities just as effective in enhancing the productivity of programmers as they are for other professionals, but their integration into the programming environment allows them to be used at any time during programming. Thus, a programmer who has encountered a bug can send a message reporting it while remaining within the debugger, perhaps including in the message some information, like a back-trace, obtained from the dynamic context.

Another source of power is to build the important abstract operations and objects

Redundancy protects the design from unintentional change—but it's equally well protected against intentional change.

of some given application area directly into the exploratory environment. All programming systems do this to a certain extent; some have remarkably rich structures for certain domains, (e.g., the graphics abstractions embedded within Smalltalk). If the abstractions are well chosen, this approach can yield a powerful environment for exploration within the chosen area, because the programmer can operate entirely in substantively meaningful abstractions, taking advantage of the considerable amount of implementation and design effort that they represent.

The limitations of this approach, however, are clear. Substantive abstractions are necessarily effective only within a particular topic area. Even for a given area, there is generally more than one productive way to partition it. Embedding one set of abstractions into the programming system encourages developments that fit within that view of the world at the expense of others. Further, if one enlarges one's area of activity even slightly, a set of abstractions that was once very effective may become much less so. In that situation, unless there are effective mechanisms for reshaping the built-in abstractions to suit the changed domain, users are apt to persist with them, at the cost of distorting their programs. Embedded abstractions, useful though they are, by themselves enable only exploration in the small, confined within the safe borders where the abstractions are known to be effective. For exploration in the large, a more general source of programming power is needed.

Of course, the exact mechanisms that different exploratory systems propose as essential sources of programming power vary widely, and these differences are hotly debated within their respective communities. Nevertheless, despite strong surface differences, these systems share some unusual characteristics at both the language and environment level.

THE LANGUAGE LEVEL

The key property of the programming languages used in exploratory programming systems is their emphasis on minimizing and deferring the constraints placed on the programmer, in the interests of minimizing and deferring the cost of making large-scale program changes. Thus, not only are the conventional structuring mechanisms based on redundancy not used, but the languages make extensive use of late binding, i.e., allowing the programmer to defer commitments for as long as possible.

The clearest example is that exploratory environments invariably provide dynamic storage allocation with automatic reclamation (garbage collection). To do otherwise imposes an intolerable burden on the programmer to keep track of all the paths through his program that might access a particular piece of storage to ensure that none of them access or release it prematurely (and that someone does release it eventually!). This can only be done by careful isolation of storage management or with considerable administrative effort. Both are incompatible with rapid, unplanned development, so neither is acceptable. Storage management must be provided by the environment itself.

Other examples of late binding include the dynamic typing of variables (associating data type information with a variable at run-time, rather than in the program text) and the dynamic binding of procedures. The freedom to defer deciding the type of a value until run-time is important because it allows the programmer to experiment with the type structure itself. Usually, the first few drafts of an exploratory program implement most data structures using general, inefficient structures such as linked lists discriminated (when necessary) on the basis of their contents. As experience with the application evolves, the critical distinctions that determine the type structure are themselves determined by experimentation, and may be among the last, rather than the first, decisions to evolve. Dynamic typing makes it easy for the programmer to write code that keeps these decisions as tacit as possible.

The dynamic binding of procedures entails more than simply linking them at load-time. It allows the programmer to change dynamically the subprocedures invoked by a given piece of code, simply by changing the run-time context. The simplest form of this is to allow procedures to be used as arguments or as the value of variables. More sophisticated mechanisms allow procedure values to be computed or even encapsulated inside the data values on which they are to operate. This packaging of data and procedures into a single object, known as object-oriented programming, is a very powerful technique. For example, it provides an elegant, modular solution to the problem of generic procedures (i.e., every data object can be thought of as providing its own definition for common actions, such as printing, which can be invoked in a standard way by other procedures). For these reasons, object-oriented programming is a widely used exploratory programming technique and actually forms the basic programming construct of the Smalltalk language.

The dynamic binding of procedures can be taken one step further when procedures are represented as data structures that can be effectively manipulated by other programs. While this is of course possible to a limited extent by reading and writing the text of program source files, it is of much greater significance in systems that define an explicit representation for programs as syntax trees or their equivalent. This, coupled with the interpreter or incremental compiler provided by most exploratory programming systems, is an extraordinarily powerful tool. Its most dramatic application is in programs that construct other programs, which they later invoke. This technique is often used in artificial intelligence in situations where the range of possible behaviors is too large to encode efficiently as data structures but can easily be expressed as combinations of procedure fragments. An example might be a system that "understands" instructions given in natural language by analyzing each input as it is received, building a program that captures its meaning, and then evaluating that program to achieve the requested effect.

A BASIC TECHNIQUE EXPANDED

Aside from such specialized applications, effective methods for mechanically manipulating procedures enable two other significant developments. The first is the technique of program development by writing interpreters for special purpose languages. Once again, this is a basic technique of artificial intelligence that has much wider applicability. The key idea is that one develops an application by designing a special language in which the application is relatively easy to state. Like any notation, such a language provides a concise representation that suppresses common or uninteresting features in favor of whatever the designer decides is more important.

A simple example is the use of notations like context-free grammars (BNF) to "metaprogram" the parsers for programming languages. Similar techniques can be used to describe, among other things, user interfaces, transaction sequences, and data transformations. Application development in this framework is a dialectic process of designing the application language and developing an interpreter for it, since both the language and the interpreter will evolve during development. The simplest way of doing this is to evolve the application language out of the base provided by the development language. Simply by allowing the application language interpreter to call the development language interpreter, expressions from the development language can be used wherever the application language currently has insufficient power. As one's understanding of the problem develops, the application language becomes increasingly powerful and the need to escape into the development language becomes less important.

The other result of having procedures that are easily manipulated by other procedures is that it becomes easy to write program manipulation subsystems. This in turn has two key consequences. First, the exploratory

Conventional programming technology restrains the programmer; exploratory systems amplify him.

programming language itself can grow. The remarkable longevity of Lisp in the artificial intelligence community is in large part due to the language having been repeatedly extended to include modern programming language syntax and constructions. The vast majority of these extensions were accomplished by defining source-to-source transformations that converted new constructions into more conventional Lisp. The ease with which this can be done allows each user, and even each project, to extend the language to capture the idioms that are found to be locally useful.

Second, the accessibility of procedures to mechanical manipulation facilitates the development of programming support tools. All exploratory programming environments boast a dazzling profusion of programming tools. To some extent, this is a virtue of necessity, as the flexibility necessary for exploration has been gained at considerable sacrifice in the ability to impose structure. That loss of structure could easily result in a commensurate loss of control by the programmer. The programming tools of the exploratory environment enable the programmer to reimpose the control that would be provided by structure in conventional practice.

Programming tools achieve their effectiveness in two quite different ways. Some tools are simply effective viewers into the user's program and its state. Such tools permit one to find information quickly, display it effectively, and modify it easily. A wide variety of tools of this form can be seen in the two Interlisp-D screen images (see box, p. 132), including data value inspectors (which allow a user to look at and modify the internal structure of an object), editors for code and data objects, and a variety of break and tracing packages. Especially when coupled with a high bandwidth display, such viewers are very effective programming tools.

A WIDE VARIETY OF TOOLS The other type of programming tool is knowledge based. Viewer-based tools, such as a program text editor, can operate effectively with a very limited understanding of the material with which they deal. By contrast, knowledge-based tools must know a significant amount about the content of a user's program and the context in which it operates. Even a very shallow analysis of a set of programs (e.g., which programs call which other ones) can support a variety of effective programming tools. A program browser allows a programmer to track the various dependencies between different parts of a program by presenting easy to read summaries that can be further expanded interactively.

Deeper analysis allows more sophisticated facilities. The Interlisp program analyzer (Masterscope) has a sufficiently detailed knowledge of Lisp programs that it can provide a complete static analysis of an arbitrary Lisp program. A wide variety of tools have been constructed that use the database provided by this analysis to answer complex queries (which may require significant reasoning, such as computing the transitive closure of some property), to make systematic changes under program control (such as making some transformation wherever a specified set of properties hold), or to check for a variety of inconsistent usage errors.

Finally, integrated tools provide yet another level of power. The Interlisp system notices whenever a program fragment is changed (by the editor or by redefinition). The program analyzer is then informed that any existing analysis is invalid, so that incorrect answers are not given on the basis of old information. The same mechanism is used to notify the program management subsystem (and eventually the user, at session end) that the corresponding file needs to be updated. In addition, the system will remember the previous state of the program, so that at any subsequent time the programmer can undo the change and retreat (in which case, of course, all the dependent changes and notifications will also be undone). This level of cooperation between tools not only provides immense power to the programmer, but relieves him of detail that he would otherwise have to manage himself. The result is that more attention can be paid to exploring the design.

A key, but often neglected, component of an exploratory programming system is a set of facilities for program contraction. The development of a true exploratory program is design limited, so that is where the effort has to go. Consequently, the program is often both inefficient and inelegant when it first achieves functional acceptability. If the exploration were an end in itself, this might be of limited concern. However, it is more often the case that a program developed in an exploratory fashion must eventually be used in some real situation. Sometimes, the time required to reimplement (using the prototype program as a specification) is prohibitive. Other times, the choice of an exploratory system was made to allow for expected future upheaval, so it is essential to preserve design flexibility. In either event, it is necessary to be able to take the functionally adequate program and transform it into one whose efficiency is comparable to the best program one could have written, in any language, had only one known what one was doing at the outset.

The importance of being able to make this post hoc optimization cannot be overemphasized. Without it, one's exploratory programs will always be considered toys; the pressure to abandon the exploratory environment and start implementing in a real one will

be overwhelming; and, once that move is made (and it is always made too soon), exploration will come to an end. The requirement for efficient implementation places two burdens on an exploratory programming system. First, the architecture must allow an efficient implementation. For example, the obligatory automatic storage allocation mechanism must either be so efficient that its overhead is negligible, or it must permit the user to circumvent it (e.g., to allocate storage statically) when and where the design has stabilized enough to make this optimization possible.

Second, as the performance engineering of a large system is almost as difficult as its initial construction, the environment must provide performance engineering tools, just as it provides design tools. These include good instrumentation, a first-class optimizing compiler, program manipulation tools (including, at the very least, full functionality compiler macros), and the ability to add declarative information where necessary to guide the program transformation. Note that, usually, performance engineering takes place not as a single "post-functionality optimization phase," but as a continuous activity throughout the development, as different parts of the system reach design stability and are observed to be performance critical. This is the method of progressive constraint, the incremental addition of constraints as and when they are discovered and found important, and is a key methodology for exploratory development.

Both of these concerns can be most clearly seen in the various Lisp-based systems. While, like all exploratory environments, they are often used to write code very quickly without any concern for efficiency, they are also used to write artificial intelligence programs whose applications to real problems are very large computations. Thus, the ability to make these programs efficient has long been of concern, because without it they would never be run on any interesting problems.

More recently, the architectures of the new, personal Lisp machines like the 1108 have enabled fast techniques for many of the operations that are relatively slow in a traditional implementation. Systems like Interlisp-D, which is implemented entirely in Lisp, including all of the performance-critical system code such as the operating system, display software, device handlers, etc., show the level of efficiency that is now possible within an exploratory language.

The increasing importance of applications that are very poorly understood, both by their clients and by their would-be implementors, will make exploratory development a key technique for the 1980s. Radical changes in the cost of computing power have already made such systems cost-effective vehicles for

The programming languages used in exploratory systems minimize and defer constraints on the programmer.

the delivery of application systems in many areas. As recently as five years ago, the tools and language features we have discussed required the computational power of a large mainframe costing about $500,000. Two years ago, equivalent facilities became available on a personal machine for about $100,000, and a year later, about $50,000. Now, a full-scale exploratory development system can be had for about $25,000. For many applications, the incremental cost has become so small over that required to support conventional technology that the benefits of exploratory development (and redevelopment!) are now decisive.

One consequence of this revolutionary change in the cost-effectiveness of exploratory systems is that our idea of exploratory problems is going to change. Exploratory programming was developed originally in contexts where change was the dominant factor.

There is, however, clearly a spectrum of specification instability. Traditionally, the cost of exploratory programming systems, both in terms of the computing power required and the run-time inefficiencies incurred, confined their use to only the most volatile applications. Thus, the spectrum was arbitrarily dichotomized into exploratory (very few) and standard (the vast majority). Unfortunately, the reality is that unexpected change is far more common in standard applications than we have been willing to admit. Conventional programming techniques strive to preserve a stability that is only too often a fiction. Since exploratory programming systems provide tools that are better adapted to this uncertainty, many applications that are now being treated as standard but which in fact seem to require moderate levels of ongoing experimentation may turn out to be more effectively developed in an exploratory environment.

We can also expect to see a slow infusion of exploratory development techniques into conventional practice. Many of the programming tools of an exploratory programming system (in particular, the information gathering and viewing tools) do not depend on the more exploratory attributes of either language or environment and could thus be adapted to support programming in conventional languages like FORTRAN and COBOL. Along with these tools will come the seeds of the exploratory perspective on language and system design, which will gradually be incorporated into existing programming languages

and systems, loosening some of the bonds with which these systems so needlessly restrict the programmer.

To those accustomed to the precise, structured methods of conventional system development, exploratory development techniques may seem messy, inelegant, and unsatisfying. But it's a question of congruence: precision and inflexibility may be just as dysfunctional in novel, uncertain situations as sloppiness and vacillation are in familiar, well-defined ones. Those who admire the massive, rigid bone structures of dinosaurs should remember that jellyfish still enjoy their very secure ecological niche.   ✳

Beau Sheil is on the research staff at the Palo Alto Research Center of the Xerox Corp., where he has been since receiving his PhD in computer science from Harvard University in 1976. His research interests include programming systems and the psychology of programming. Many of these ideas were first developed, and later polished, in discussions with John Seely Brown and other colleagues in cognitive and instructional sciences at Xerox PARC.

Perspectives on Artificial Intelligence Programming

Daniel G. Bobrow and Mark J. Stefik

Programs are judged not only by whether they faithfully carry out the intended processing but also by whether they are understandable and easily changed. Programming systems for artificial intelligence applications use specialized languages, environments, and knowledge-based tools to reduce the complexity of the programming task. Language styles based on procedures, objects, logic, rules, and constraints reflect different models for organizing programs and facilitate program evolution and understandability. To make programming easier, multiple styles can be integrated as sublanguages in a programming environment. Programming environments provide tools that analyze programs and create informative displays of their structure. Programs can be modified by direct interaction with these displays. These tools and languages are helping computer scientists to regain a sense of control over systems that have become increasingly complex.

PEOPLE WHO DEVELOP PROGRAMMING SYSTEMS NEED TO organize them in ways that make them comprehensible to other people and easy to modify. We will be concerned mainly with the practice of artificial intelligence (AI) programming and about the arguments and tensions that have shaped the current state of the art. An intelligent system should embody and apply information about itself so that it can assist in its own continuing development.

The programming culture of the AI community has a somewhat different emphasis than most "production" programming. The AI programming process is not a sequential progression from specification to implementation, testing, and release. Instead, an exploratory approach is used in which specification and implementation evolve together as the problem is understood and tested. Another difference is the frequent design of experimental specialized sublanguages that make it easier to express solutions to the problems being attacked.

List processing (1) is fundamental to AI programming (2). As an example, the list

(IBM (A-Kind-Of ComputerCompany)(Headquarters NYC))

can be used to represent relations between the thing represented by the symbol IBM and other things represented by the symbols ComputerCompany or NYC. Manipulations of these list structures can deduce implicit relations (3), for example, that IBM produces computers (because it is A-Kind-Of ComputerCompany). Programs can use lists to build structures of unpredictable sizes and shapes during execution without predetermined or artificial limits.

List structures are also used to represent programs in AI systems, and hence they are often used to build tools to infer implicit features

about programs themselves. This contrasts with typical programming systems that deal with programs as a sequence of characters; program changes are made by adding and deleting characters. Higher level organizations of programs, such as the module boundaries and the calls between packages and so on, are parsed from these characters but made available in very limited ways to the users. AI systems provide users with interactive displays that describe systems in these terms. A user can understand a system and change it directly through these displays rather than indirectly by manipulation of text.

A programming style is a way of organizing programs on the basis of some conceptual model of programming and an appropriate language to make programs written in the style clear. We will describe styles organized around procedures, objects, logic, rules, and constraints. Each style is a specialized language or sublanguage that shapes the organization of programs written in that style.

Different styles differ substantially in what can be stated concisely. Significant appeal arises from what does not have to be stated. By eliminating redundancy, the intent of the code can be more easily understood. This is an important virtue of, for example, automatic storage management facilities that allow omission of code for freeing storage. Different styles facilitate different kinds of program change that ensure appropriate properties of the program remain invariant. Experiments have led to systems in which a number of styles are integrated and to others in which one style dominates.

Programming Styles

Procedure-oriented programming. In this style, subroutines and data structures are the two (separate) primitive elements. Subroutine calls are the primary mechanism for program composition. Subroutines have the property that they carry out the same algorithm when called from different places. Adding a line to a calling program, and thus changing the position of the call to a subroutine, does not change the algorithm executed by the subroutine.

Data structure declarations allow programs to reference parts of a complex data structure by name rather than, for example, by index position in an array. In the declaration, a programmer can specify once the method for looking up the named substructure rather than specifying it in every place that the structure is referenced in the procedures. To change the lookup process, a programmer need only change the specification. AI systems provide automatic storage management facilities that ensure that any data structure no longer referenced directly or indirectly by the program is reclaimed. This avoids problems that occur in systems where a programmer must

Daniel G. Bobrow is a research fellow and Mark J. Stefik is a principal scientist in the Intelligent Systems Laboratory of the Xerox Palo Alto Research Center, Palo Alto, CA 94304.

take responsibility for storage management, such as failure to return unused storage or inappropriate deallocation of referenced storage.

Although programmers do not usually think about the invariants associated with subroutine call, data access, or storage management, they are essential for the composition of large programs. They confine and control the effects of change. To the extent that common changes are local, a language provides insulation from change-induced bugs.

Some languages augment the notion of subroutine with features intended to support better the sharing of code by several people. Modula-2 (4) and Ada (5), for example, provide mechanisms for defining modules—collections of related procedures and structure definitions—and interfaces—descriptions of elements of a module that may be used from outside that module. The interfaces are intended to minimize interference as people change different parts of a system.

The interface definition provides information about module data types and procedure requirements that can be used for module optimization. An implementation of a module is free to change any features not "advertised" in the interface. With these restrictions, independently developed, debugged, and compiled modules can be loaded together. The interface definition is the defined narrow pathway of interaction.

Object-oriented programming. This style (6, 7) has often been advocated for simulation programs, systems programming, graphics, and AI programming. Although there are variations in exactly what is meant by object-oriented programming (8), in all these languages there are objects that combine state and behavior.

There are three major ideas in object-oriented programming: (i) objects are defined in terms of classes that determine their structure and behavior; (ii) behavior is invoked by sending a message to an object; and (iii) descriptions of objects may be inherited from more general classes. Uniform use of objects contrasts with the distribution of information into separate procedures and data in procedural programming.

A message to an object contains a name for a behavior (often called its selector) and some other parameters. For example, in a traffic simulation we could have classes of vehicles such as Car and Truck. To cause Car-1, an instance of the class Car, to move in the simulation, a Loops (9) program would send a "Move" message to Car-1:

(send Car-1 Move 400 50)

Associated with the class Car is a particular method for Move that is run for this invocation. The class Truck has a different method, since trucks must obey different traffic rules and consume different fuel. The "message passing" style allows each class to implement its response to a message in its own way. These methods can be changed independently. In contrast, procedure-oriented programming would require that all the variations of Move be incorporated into the single procedure that implements Move.

Classes can inherit description from other classes. PoliceCar can be defined as a specialization of the class Car. Then PoliceCar has all of the structure and behavior of Car except that which is explicitly overridden or added in PoliceCar. For example, PoliceCar can add a two-way radio and a method for Move that can exceed the speed limit or interact with traffic light control. Such inheritance of a specialized class from its "superclass" reduces the need to specify redundant information and simplifies updating and modification, since information can be entered and changed in one place.

Specialization and message sending synergize to support program extensions that preserve important invariants. For example, splitting a class, renaming a class, or adding a new class does not affect simple

message sending unless a new method is introduced. Instances of a specialized class follow exactly the same protocols as a superclass until local specialized methods are defined. Similarly, deleting a class does not affect message sending if the deleted class does not have a local method involved in the protocol.

Changes to the inheritance network are common in program reorganization. Programmers often create new classes and reorganize their classes as they understand the opportunities for factoring parts of their programs. Together, message sending and specialization provide a robust framework for extending and modifying programs.

Access-oriented programming. In object-oriented programming, when an object is sent a message it may change the values of some variables that make up its internal state. In access-oriented programming (10), when an object changes the value of a variable a message may be sent to another object as a side effect if the value associated with that variable is an "annotated value." In terms of actions and side effects this is dual to object-oriented programming. The annotated value is a specialized object and can contain state other than the value.

Access-oriented programs are factored into parts that compute and parts that monitor the computations. For example, suppose one were to build a traffic simulation program with an interactive display showing the state of the simulation. By dividing it into a simulator and a display-controller, one can separate programming concerns.

The simulator represents the dynamics of traffic. It has objects for such things as automobiles, trucks, roads, and traffic lights. These objects exchange messages to simulate traffic interactions. For example, when a traffic light object turns green, it sends messages to start traffic moving.

The display-controller has objects representing images of the traffic and provides an interactive user interface for scaling and shifting the views. It has methods for presenting graphics information. The simulator and the display-controller can be developed separately, provided that there is agreement on the structure of the simulation objects.

Access-oriented programming provides the "glue" for connecting the simulator and display-controller. The process of connection is dynamic and reversible. When a user tells the display-controller to change the views, it can make and break connections to the simulator as needed for its monitoring. Thus at one time a user can monitor the simulation as if looking at a map of the town and at another time as if looking at the instrument panel of a particular car. For the former, active values attached to the positions of each vehicle are used to update the display; for the latter, probes on the speed of the auto and level of the gas tank can update pictorial gauges. Attaching such gauges does not change the behavior of the program being monitored.

Property annotations in annotated values can be used to store useful but subsidiary quantities. Some systems store a measure of the certainty of that value being correct. A reasoning system can store this annotation without having to change the structure of the represented object. Other values and rules used in computing this value could be stored as annotations, as in truth maintenance systems (11). Annotations also provide a place for documentation for human readability of data structures.

Access-oriented programming supports several invariants under program change. Annotations can be added to programs without causing them to stop working. Annotated values are invisible to programs that are not looking for them. They can be added to data that are already annotated. The same invariants hold for recursive annotated values, that is, for descriptions of descriptions. Nested active values enable multiple independent side effects on variable access.

Logic programming. There are both declarative and procedural interpretations of logic statements (*12*). The simplest statements in Prolog, the most popular logic-based language, is a statement of a relation; for example:

Brother(*Danny, Rusty*)

As a declarative statement, it has a truth value; procedurally it is a request to check the truth of the statement. Prolog uses a database of facts entered by statements of the form

Assert(Brother(*Danny, Rusty*))

to store this relation in a database. A query Brother(*Danny, X*) searches the database and returns *X = Rusty*. The same elementary fact could also be used to answer the query Brother(*X, Rusty*).

In addition to simple statements and queries, Prolog programs consist of sets of statements stored in the database. Each statement has the form

consequent :- antecedent-1, . . . , antecedent-*n*

This is read declaratively as, consequent is true if (:-) each of antecedent-1 to antecedent-*n* is true. In a procedural reading, the consequent is taken as a goal to be achieved, and the antecedents are subgoals to be tried in order. The declarative interpretation of the statement,

Uncle(*X, Y*) :- Brother(*X, Z*), Father(*Z, Y*)

is "*X* is an Uncle of *Y* if there is some *Z*, such that *X* is a Brother of *Z*, and *Z* is the Father of *Y*."

This statement can be read as directions for achieving a goal Uncle(*X, Y*): first find a *Z* such that Brother (*X, Z*), and then prove that *Z* is a Father of *Y*. To verify the truth of Uncle(*Danny, Johanna*), the system could find Brother(*Danny, Rusty*) and Father(*Rusty, Johanna*).

Unlike ordinary procedures, any number of the inputs to a program can be left unspecified. The system searches for one (or upon request, more) bindings of the input parameters that make the consequent true. By repeated application of the Uncle rule, starting with Uncle(*Danny, X*), the system will find all the nephews and nieces of *Danny*; Uncle(*X, Johanna*) can be used to find all the uncles of *Johanna*.

Since the given Uncle rule does not completely specify the Uncle relation, a second rule can be added after the first:

Uncle(*X, Y*) :- Brother(*X, Z*), Mother(*Z, Y*)

After searching the database (or using other rules) with the first rule, Prolog would then "backtrack" to use the second rule. In general, any number of ordered rules can be used to specify a relation. An advantage of using Prolog is that new rules can be easily added to modify the system behavior. The system will perform exhaustive search with all the rules, and with all clauses from the database, to find appropriate bindings for input parameters that are unspecified.

One of the important features of logic programming is that is separates the idea of goals from the statements of how to satisfy them. This reification of goals, rather than explicit calls to particular methods for achieving them (subroutines), allows new methods to be added without the need to change the goal statements. This is an advantage in the incremental development of a system, but it may make program behavior hard to understand.

Automatic search through the database of rules rather than explicit control has another disadvantage. Some obvious and inno-cent-looking rules, such as that expressing the commutativity of the Brother relation,

Brother(*X, Y*) :- Brother(*Y, X*)

can cause the system to go into an infinite loop. The problem of search control is an area of active research in the logic programming community.

Because Prolog provides simple rules with clear declarative se-mantics and a convenient interpretation for database search, it was chosen as the starting point for the fifth-generation computer project in Japan (*13*).

Rule-based programming. The widespread use of the term rule-based programming belies the considerable diversity in what it is used to mean (*14, 15*). Rule languages are used to support the building of knowledge bases. Rule environments include tools for generating explanations of program behavior, tools for answering questions, and tools for acquiring and integrating new rules into a program.

Rule languages use if-then statements as shown in this rule from Mycin (*16*):

If   the Gram stain of the organism is Gram-negative,
        the morphology of the organism is rod, and
        the aerobicity of the organism is anaerobic,
then   there is suggestive evidence (0.7) that the identity of the
        organism is bacteriodes.

This rule can be used by reasoning forward from laboratory tests to accumulate evidence about the identity of a disease organism. It is also used to reason backward from a goal of finding the identity of the invading organism to determine what tests should be run. The (0.7) in the above rule is a weighting for the evidence mentioned in the preconditions of the rule. Extensive work has been done in the context of rule-based systems on techniques for combining multiple pieces of evidence (*17*). Uncertain information is not usually handled in logic-based systems.

Rule-based systems provide explanations of results to users by keeping track of which rules were invoked in a consultation. After a consultation they can explain the reasoning the system used. A fundamental assumption in these systems is that the display of rules applied is a reasonable explanation of system behavior. Explanations do not reflect assumptions underlying rules, causal mechanisms, or the current knowledge of the user.

For small tasks, rules are viewed as independent, and getting them right is easy because rules are small and manageable. For large tasks, the interactions of rules must be considered. Some rule languages organize rules into hierarchical rule sets that describe how the rules are to be applied. Some provide problem-solving frameworks in which rules can be organized. For example, each subtask in a network can carry its own relevant rules, as in Pride, an expert system for aiding in a mechanical design (*18*). In Blackboards (*19*), rules are attached to nodes of a general problem-solving model. In structured systems, the programming task of adding new rules also requires deciding where to put them.

In summary, the available rule languages are important in narrow, carefully chosen applications, often for expert systems. Their funda-mental strength—the construction in terms of independent individ-ual rules—is also their limiting factor.

Constraint-oriented programming. The idea of developing pro-gramming languages around the concept of constraint satisfaction has appealed to computer scientists for years (*20*). The idea is that a programmer need only declare certain relations among program variables without saying precisely how they should be achieved. The details of the computation can then be figured out by the system by means of implicit, automatic constraint satisfaction techniques.

For example, the equation $x + y = 5$ can be viewed as a constraint on possible values for the variables x and y. If numeric values for x and y are given, we can substitute those values into the equation and determine whether the constraint is satisfied. In this example, a

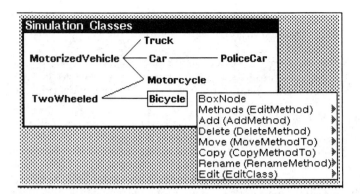

Fig. 1. A browser, showing the inheritance of classes for the simulation. On the right is an interactive menu for some of the operations that can be done by pointing to elements of this browser. The Add item on the menu allows addition of structure, methods, or classes. As indicated, the default operation is to add a method. Such browsers provide a simple way of specifying common changes and maintain an up-to-date display of the program structure throughout the process.

numeric value for either variable together with the constraint is enough to determine the value of the other variable.

The most widely used and practical systems based on constraints are the spread-sheet programs that have been popular on personal computers. Spread-sheet programs provide a matrix of rows and columns for organizing values and constraints among them. For example, in a rental income application, columns of the matrix could correspond to months of a year and rows could correspond to income and categories of expense. Constraints connect dependent elements, so that total monthly expense is maintained as the sum of the individual expenses in the same column. When monthly rental rate, taxes, and utilities variables are filled in' for the first month, constraints in a spread-sheet fill in as much of the table as possible, including various subtotals.

The constraints in a spread-sheet program differentiate between dependent and independent variables. When the independent variables are filled in, values for dependent variables are updated immediately. Reasoning in both directions is provided in some applications, for example, in graphics and simulation (21).

Constraint satisfaction systems have always been specialized to exploit the nature of the particular kinds of constraints and hence have not been considered general purpose. Nonetheless, there are several research efforts aimed at increasing the breadth of applicability of constraint languages for specifying the behavior of computers (22).

Use of Multiple Paradigms

Programming language development has often consisted of the honing of a particular paradigm for organizing programs (23). Advocates of multiple styles in a single system (24, 25) argue that, just as there are many tools in a carpenter's toolbox, each specialized to its purpose, there should be many tools in the programmer's kit. One should not be forced to pry up nails with a screwdriver. However, use of multiple paradigms does involve an additional cost of learning more than one style, and programs may be required to transform between different representations of the same information chosen to optimize processing within a style.

When a problem does not fit well in a style, resulting programs may be both awkward and long. For large applications, the various costs for using a particular style can vary across parts of the program. In addition to the cost of the initial writing of the program and the

cost of running the program, the costs of debugging and change as the program and its specifications evolve must be considered. The total cost of a system can be lower when more than one style is used. For example, many expert systems are developed in which object-oriented programming is used for representing the basic concepts, rules are used to specify the inferences, access-oriented programming is used to drive the graphics display, and procedures are used for the overall control structure.

Sometimes the search for integration can lead to a language that gracefully subsumes the different styles. This is illustrated in the deep integration of procedure-oriented programming and object-oriented programming in CommonLoops (26). In ordinary procedure calls, the code to carry out an operation is looked up by using only the name of the procedure. In object-oriented programming, the code lookup process for message sending uses both an operation name (the selector) and also the class of the first argument.

Procedure call and message sending are generalized in Common-Loops, so that code lookup uses the selector and the types of as many arguments as desired (multimethods). Thus, CommonLoops does more than just provide both message sending and procedure call. The integration yields a continuum of method definitions from simple procedures to methods with many arguments whose types are specified. The familiar methods of object-oriented programming fall out as a special case where the type (class) of only the first argument is used. A programmer using code developed by others need not be aware of whether there are multiple implementations that depend on the types of multiple arguments.

Computer scientists are just beginning to develop examples of the integration of styles in hybrid or integrated languages and criteria for judging them (25). Different programming languages are no longer just focusing on a particular style; styles now coexist and are beginning to evolve together (27).

Programming Environments

Programming languages reduce the complexity of programming by simplifying the expression of instructions. Programming environments are the set of tools used to build, change, and debug programs. Operating systems have played this role, but now specialized environments (28) that know about the language and program structure reduce complexity by taking some responsibility for managing changes to programs.

AI programming environments provide tools that analyze program structure and create informative displays that help programmers to develop mental models of the systems. They also provide simplified means for specifying changes to a program that free a programmer from specifying many of the details. Tools may also be used to compensate for a particular distribution of information imposed by one or more styles of programming. These tools are particularly important in the exploratory programming style (29) used in AI, where the specifications for a task are developed as parts of it are implemented.

Understanding and changing the static structure of a program. Traditionally, the main descriptions of programs available to programmers have been the text of program instructions. This is useful when a program fits on a few pages, but stacks of program listings are inadequate for visualizing large programs. Nor is the situation much improved by computerizing the same view with text editors and window systems. Text editors do not provide a flexible overview and are of limited use in making many important kinds of systematic changes.

The primary struggle is often to simplify the organization of a system. Simplification may require exploring and changing the boundaries between and within subsystems. It is now possible to create automatically more informative views of programs that reflect the kinds of questions that programmers ask when they are modifying or trying to understand a large system.

For procedure-oriented programming, tools can display interactive graphs that show where procedures and variables are defined and used (30). In object-oriented programming, changes to the inheritance network are common in program reorganization. An interactive class browser such as that shown in Fig. 1 can make it easy to add, delete, and rename classes and methods, examine documentation, trace the inheritance of particular methods or variables, and move definitions of methods and variables in the inheritance lattice.

Understanding and changing the dynamic structure of a program. Testing, debugging, and performance tuning are all important parts of the task of programming. In the current state of the art, these tasks cannot be done practically by an analysis of static program structure, and so programming environments provide interactive tools for them.

Conventional programming practice has long included means for tracing the execution of programs to aid in debugging. In the simplest case, tracing is achieved by inserting statements into a program to cause printing when various parts of a program are activated and to print out indications of the internal state. Other capabilities allow interruption of program execution when certain conditions arise, such as when a particular procedure is called, a variable is accessed, or a value is set that is outside a specified range.

An improvement on tracing is the use of gauges, as shown in Fig. 2. Several systems that support access-oriented programming provide a suite of gauges that can be attached to the variables of running programs to display the monitored values. Attaching a gauge to a program variable is analogous to attaching a voltmeter to a circuit. The gauge does not interfere with the operation of the program, and it is not necessary to search through a long listing to find values for variables. A programmer can create an array of gauges on the display and watch them while the program runs.

Modern environments let a programmer examine the state of a computation when a program is interrupted, either by an error or by a user request. If a bug is found and a fix made, the user can back up from a nested computation to a call that invoked it and try the computation again from that point. Some systems can also run a program at slow speed or one step at a time. The ability to interrupt a program's execution to make changes can make a dramatic difference in the overall productivity of programming because this enables a programmer to identify and correct several errors in a single short session.

Many of these interactive capabilities for controlling execution are not new ideas. Some of them have been available in Basic and Lisp systems for several years. They are mentioned because they are less common in production programming environments for large systems, they are important for incremental debugging, and they are usefully combined with tools for analyzing and modifying program structure.

AI programming environments tend to do late-binding by default. This means that they usually provide the flexibility for programmers to change a running program without losing the state of the computation. Programmers are concerned about the time it takes to complete a cycle of revision: discover a problem, find a bug, make a revision, and test again. Late-binding systems tend to speed up this cycle.

Late-binding can slow program execution. Optimization facilities in AI systems allow compilation of efficient programs before release for wide use. Exploratory programming encourages a style of programming in which exploration is followed by analysis, which is

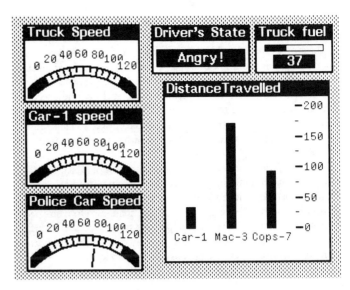

Fig. 2. Gauges, which can be attached to any object variable at any time to view the changing value of a variable. A set of attached gauges allows a simultaneous view of the dynamic state of a program.

then followed by optimization. In this approach, optimization is focused where it is needed. This leads to effective optimization guided by real measurements rather than being based on preconceptions (often misconceptions) of system designers. A program's performance can be largely determined by the performance profile of underlying system facilities, whose performance on particular cases may not be known ahead of time.

A graphical view of timing analysis, as shown in Fig. 3, can be useful for understanding the incremental and integrated time spent in any part of the system during a particular computation.

Narrow Knowledge-Based Systems

Work on programming environments can be understood as an application of computer technology to the task of writing and maintaining programs. The same theme can be seen in the work on compilers. Compilers convert high-level language descriptions into specific instructions. They use their knowledge of machine architecture to yield efficient implementations. Compilers, like programming environments, are intended to be used for all kinds of programming tasks.

An important strategy for making tools that can give more comprehensive kinds of assistance is to incorporate specific knowledge into them. In the 1960's work on compilers was sometimes called automatic programming. Current research on automatic programming (31, 32) follows this direction of incorporating increasing amounts of knowledge about programming. The most successful uses of automatic programming are even more narrowly focused; these are the application generators now used commercially for creating specially tailored systems for business applications, such as accounting and inventory.

The same trend toward knowledge-intensive systems can be seen in the creation of so-called shells for expert systems. An expert system shell is a specialized sublanguage and environment designed to support a set of closely related applications. Shells are an intermediate point between specific applications and general-purpose "knowledge-engineering" environments. Shells can be built for such applications as planning, scheduling, and a variety of specialized office tasks.

Shells have four things that general programming tools do not:

prepackaged representations for important concepts, inference and representation tools tuned for efficient and perspicuous use in the applications, specialized user interfaces, and generic knowledge about the application. For example, a shell for a planning application could have representations for modeling goals and agents. Its specialized knowledge could include rules, such as one specifying that an agent can be only at one place at a time. It would have generic categories for things such as time, tasks, serially reusable resources (such as a room), and interfaces for interacting with alternative plans.

These knowledge-intensive systems blur the boundaries between environments and languages, since they combine features of both. Domain-specific knowledge enables a system to take on more of the responsibility for checking and installing changes. Domain-specific knowledge also enables systems to provide specialized user interfaces that are intended to be closer to the concepts of the application. General-purpose environments have broad applicability; specialized systems can do more in a narrower domain.

Directions and Themes Revisited

The developments we have discussed in programming languages, environments, and knowledge systems provide different perspectives on what a program is. Conventionally, a program is a set of instructions for a machine that specifies how information is to be processed. Programming is the process of translating user intentions and requirements into a formal language understandable by a computer.

Variations in programming languages determine what can be stated concisely, what must be stated in multiple places, and what need not be stated in a program. Objects, rules, procedures, constraints, and other programming concepts make different trade-offs in the way that they organize information. If a programming language allows one to write procedures but not constraints, then expressing desired relations among variables requires having statements in all those parts of the program that can potentially change the values of the variables. Inheritance allows structural description

and methods to be shared by classes without redundant specification.

When a system makes directly manipulatable the concepts of an application, programs become more understandable. For example, some bookkeeping and accounting concepts are represented and manipulated directly in spread-sheet programs. While the state of the art has no dependable cognitive metric for how much this helps, the issue is a recurring theme in the design of languages and knowledge-based systems. It has to do with reducing the levels of abstraction that must be penetrated to understand system behavior.

In contrast, many of the programs for modern physics experiments have become large and perhaps unmanageable. There are so many levels of mathematical technique and abstraction between the terminology of physics and the text of the programs that they have become unwieldy and hard to understand. Indeed, one important role for AI systems is as an impedance matcher, or natural bridge, between mental concepts and program symbols. The Sophie system (33) is an example of a program that, among other things, provides an interface between descriptions of circuits and Spice, the underlying simulation program for modeling circuit behavior. Hybrids like this suggest ways of using programs in different contexts, thus "preserving programming capital."

Programming environments provide us with another answer to what a program is. Environments determine what a programmer sees when writing or modifying a program. They include different kinds of interactive browsers, as seen in Figs. 1 to 3, that provide different views of a program based on automatic analysis. These visualizations are designed to help programmers gain perspective on their programs, and in doing this they blur the boundary between language and environment.

As browsers are increasingly used for understanding and changing systems, they displace program listings. Ultimately they are more powerful (because they are active), can employ specialized knowledge, and can provide alternative views. Today's programs are parts of larger complex systems, and the main activity of programming has moved from the origination of new programs to the modification of existing ones (34). Programs are increasingly judged not only by whether they faithfully carry out the intended processing but also

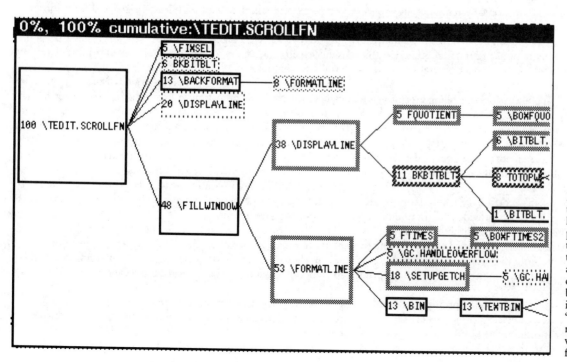

Fig. 3. Spy timing-analysis tree in Interlisp-D (35). The height of each box is proportional to the fraction of the time spent in the routine. Large boxes are associated with potential candidates for optimization. The border of each box is used to indicate modes, such as "time includes called subroutines," "appears elsewhere on display," and so forth.

by whether they are understandable and easily changed. Thus computer tools that bring computational leverage to programming are helping computer scientists to regain a sense of control over systems that have become increasingly complex.

REFERENCES AND NOTES

1. J. McCarthy, *Commun. ACM* **3**, 185 (1960).
2. E. Charniak, C. Riesbeck, D. McDermott, *Artificial Intelligence Programming* (Erlbaum, Hillsdale, NJ, 1980).
3. R. Davis, *Science* **231**, 957 (1986).
4. N. Wirth, *Programming in Modula-2* (Springer-Verlag, New York, 1985).
5. B. Wichman, *Commun. ACM* **27**, 98 (1984).
6. G. Birtwistle, O. Dahl, B. Myhrhaug, K. Nygaard, *Simula Begin* (Auerbach, Philadelphia, 1973).
7. A. Goldberg and D. Robson, *Smalltalk-80, The Language and Its Implementation* (Addison-Wesley, Reading, MA, 1983).
8. M. Stefik and D. G. Bobrow, *AI Magazine* **6**, 40 (1985).
9. D. G. Bobrow and M. J. Stefik, *The Loops Manual* (Xerox Corporation, Palo Alto, CA, 1983).
10. M. Stefik, D. G. Bobrow, K. Kahn, *IEEE Software* **3**, 10 (1986).
11. J. Doyle, *Artif. Intell.* **12**, 231 (1979).
12. R. A. Kowalski, *Commun. ACM* **22**, 424 (1979).
13. T. Moto-oka, Ed., *Fifth Generation Computer Systems* (Elsevier/North-Holland, Amsterdam, 1982).
14. R. Davis and J. King, in *Machine Intelligence*, E. Elcock and D. Michie, Eds. (Wiley, New York, 1976), vol. 8, pp. 300–332.
15. D. Waterman and F. Hayes-Roth, Eds., *Pattern-Directed Inference Systems* (Academic Press, New York, 1978).
16. B. G. Buchanan and E. H. Shortliffe, *Rule-Based Expert Programs: The MYCIN Experiments of the Stanford Heuristic Programming Project* (Addison-Wesley, Reading, MA, 1984).
17. J. Gordon and E. H. Shortliffe, *Artificial Intelligence* **26**, 323 (1985).
18. S. Mittal, C. L. Dym, M. Morjaria, in *Applications of Knowledge-Based Systems to Engineering Analysis and Design*, C. L. Dym, Ed. (American Society of Mechanical Engineers, New York, 1985), p. 99.
19. B. Hayes-Roth, *Artif. Intell.* **26**, 251 (1985).
20. I. E. Sutherland, thesis, Massachusetts Institute of Technology, Cambridge (1963).
21. A. Borning, *ACM TOPLAS* **3**, 353 (1981).
22. G. Steele, thesis, Massachusetts Institute of Technology, Cambridge (1980).
23. H. Abelson and G. Sussman, *Structure and Interpretation of Computer Programs* (Massachusetts Institute of Technology Press, Cambridge, 1985).
24. R. Fikes and T. Kehler, *Commun. ACM* **28**, 904 (1985).
25. D. G. Bobrow, *IEEE Trans. Software Eng.* **SE:11**, 10 (1985).
26. D. Bobrow, K. Kahn, G. Kiczales, L. Masinter, M. Stefik, *CommonLoops, A Graceful Merger of Common Lisp and Object-Oriented Programming* (Xerox Corporation, Palo Alto, CA, 1985).
27. B. Hailpern, *IEEE Software* **3**, 6 (1986).
28. A. Goldberg, in *Interactive Programming Environments*, D. Barstow, H. Shrobe, E. Sandewall, Eds. (McGraw-Hill, New York, 1984), p. 141.
29. B. Sheil, *ibid.*, p. 19.
30. W. Teitelman and L. Masinter, *ibid.*, p. 83.
31. D. Barstow, *AAAI Magazine* **5**, 5 (1984).
32. C. Rich and H. Shrobe, in *Interactive Programming Environments*, D. Barstow, H. Shrobe, E. Sandewall, Eds. (McGraw-Hill, New York, 1984), p. 443.
33. J. S. Brown, R. Burton, J. de Kleer, in *Intelligent Tutoring Systems*, D. Sleeman and J. S. Brown, Eds. (Academic Press, New York, 1983), p. 227.
34. T. Winograd, *Commun. ACM* **22**, 391 (1979).
35. M. Sanella, *Interlisp-D Reference Manual* (Xerox Corporation, Palo Alto, CA, 1983).
36. We thank J. S. Brown, J. de Kleer, K. Kahn, G. Kiczales, M. Miller, and J. Shrager for comments on earlier versions of this paper.

BIBLIOGRAPHY

Abbott, R. "Program Design by Informal English Descriptions", *Comm. of the ACM* V26 #11, Nov. 1983:882–894.

Adam, A. and J. Laurent. "LAURA, a System to Debug Student Programs", *Artificial Intelligence* V15, 1980:75–122.

Aho, A., J. Hopcroft, and J. Ullman. *The Design and Analysis of Computer Algorithms*, Addison-Wesley, 1974.

Allen, F. and J. Cocke. "A Catalogue of Optimizing Transformations", in *Design and Optimization of Compilers*, R. Rustin *ed.*, Prentice-Hall, 1972:1–30.

Amey, W. "Computer Assisted Software Engineering (CASE) System", *4th Int. Conf. on Software Engineering*, 1979.

Andreae, P. "Justified Generalization: Acquiring Procedures from Examples", MIT PhD Thesis, MIT/AI/TR-834, Jan. 1985.

Asirelli, P., *et al.*, "A Flexible Environment for Program Development Based on a Symbolic Interpreter", *4th Int. Conf. on Software Engineering*, 1979.

Balzer, R. "A Global View of Automatic Programming", *3rd Int. Joint Conf. on Artificial Intelligence*, 1973:494–499.

——— . "Transformational Implementation: An Example", *IEEE Trans. on Software Engineering* V7 #1, Jan. 1981:3–13.

——— . "A 15 Year Perspective on Automatic Programming", *IEEE Trans. on Software Engineering*, V11 #11, Nov. 1985:1257–1267.

Balzer, R., *et al.*, "Domain-Independent Automatic Programming", *Information Processing* V74, 1974:326.

Balzer, R. and N. Goldman. "Principles of Good Software Specification and Their Implications for Specification Languages", *Specification of Reliable Software Conf.*, 1979:58–67.

Balzer, R., N. Goldman, and D. Wile. "Meta-Evaluation as a Tool for Program Understanding", *5th Int. Joint Conf. on Artificial Intelligence*, 1977:398–403.

——— . "Informality in Program Specifications", *IEEE Trans. on Software Engineering* V4 #2, March 1978:94–103.

——— . "Operational Specification as the Basis for Rapid Prototyping", *ACM Sigsoft Software Engineering Symp. on Rapid Prototyping*, Columbia MD, *ACM SIGSOFT Software Engineering Notes* V7 #5, Dec. 1982:3–16.

Balzer, R., C. Green, and T. Cheatham. "Software Technology in the 1990s: Using a New Paradigm", *IEEE Computer Magazine*, Nov. 1983.

Barr, A. and E. Feigenbaum *eds.*, *The Handbook of Artificial Intelligence*, Kaufmann, 1982.

Barstow, D. *Knowledge-Based Program Construction*, Elsevier North-Holland, 1979.

——— . "An Experiment in Knowledge-Based Automatic Programming", *Artificial Intelligence* V12 #1–2, 1979:73–119.

——— . "The Roles of Knowledge and Deduction in Algorithm Design", *Machine Intelligence 10*, J. Hayes, D. Michie and Y. Pao *eds.*, Wiley, 1982.

——— . "A Perspective on Automatic Programming", *AI Magazine* V5 #1, Spring 1984:5–27.

——— . "On Convergence Toward a Database of Program Transformations", *ACM Trans. on Programming Languages and Systems* V7 #1, Jan. 1985:1–9.

——— . "Domain-Specific Automatic Programming", *IEEE Trans. on Software Engineering* V11 #11, Nov. 1985:1321–1336.

Barstow, D., R. Duffy, S. Smoliar, and S. Vestal. "An Automatic Programming System to Support an Experimental Science", *6th Int. Conf. on Software Engineering*, 1982.

——— . "An Overview of ΦNIX", *2nd Nat. Conf. on Artificial Intelligence,* 1982:367–369.

Barstow, D., E. Sandewall, and H. Shrobe eds., *Interactive Programming Environments,* McGraw-Hill, 1983.

Basili, V. and H. Mills. "Understanding and Documenting Programs", *IEEE Trans. on Software Engineering* V8 #3, May 1982:270–283.

Basu, S. "A Note on Synthesis of Inductive Assertions", *IEEE Trans. on Software Engineering* V6 #1, Jan. 1980:32–39.

Basu, S. and J. Misra. "Proving Loop Programs", *IEEE Trans. on Software Engineering* V1 #1, March 1975:76–86.

——— . "Some Classes of Naturally Provable Programs", *2nd Int. Conf. on Software Engineering,* 1976.

Bates, J. "A Logic for Correct Program Development", Cornell PhD Thesis, report 79–388, Aug. 1979.

Bates, J. and R. Constable. "Proofs as Programs", *ACM Trans. on Programming Languages and Systems* V7 #1, Jan. 1985:113–136.

Bauer, F. "Programming as an Evolutionary Process", in *Language Hierarchies and Interfaces,* F. Bauer and K. Samelson eds., *Lecture Notes in Computer Science* V46, Springer-Verlag, 1976:153–182.

Bauer, F., *et al.,* "Towards a Wide Spectrum Language to Support Program Specification and Program Development", *ACM SIGPLAN Notices* V13 #12, 1978:15–24.

Bauer, M. "Programming by Examples", *Artificial Intelligence* V12, 1979:1–21.

Bayman, P. and R. Mayer. "A Diagnosis of Beginning Programmers' Misconceptions of BASIC Programming Statements", *Comm. of the ACM,* V26 #9, Sept. 1983:677–679.

Beck, L. and T. Perkins. "A Survey of Software Engineering Practice: Tools, Methods and Results", *IEEE Trans. on Software Engineering* V9 #9, Sept. 1983:541–561.

Beichter, F., O. Herzog, and H. Petzsch. "SLAN-4: A Language for the Specification and Design of Large Software Systems", *IBM J. of Research and Development* V27 #6, Nov. 1983.

Bentley, J. and M. Shaw. "An Alphard Specification of a Correct and Efficient Transformation on Data Structures", *Specification of Reliable Software Conf.,* 1979:222–233.

Bianchi, M. and J. Wood. "A User's Viewpoint on the Programmer's Workbench", *2nd Int. Conf. on Software Engineering* 1976:193–199.

Bibel, W. "Syntax-Directed, Semantics-Supported Program Synthesis", *Artificial Intelligence* V14 #3, 1980:243–261.

Bidoit, M., B. Biebow, M. Gaudel, C. Gresse, and G. Guiho. "Exception Handling: Formal Specification and Systematic Program Construction", *IEEE Trans. on Software Engineering* V11 #3, March 1985:242–251.

Bidoit, M., C. Gresse, and G. Guiho. "A System Synthesizes Array-Manipulating Programs From Specifications", *6th Int. Joint Conf. on Artificial Intelligence,* 1979:63–65.

Biermann, A. "On the Inference of Turing Machines From Sample Computations", *Artificial Intelligence* V3 #3, 1972.

——— . "The Inference of Regular LISP Programs from Examples", *IEEE Trans. on Systems, Man, and Cybernetics* V8 #8, Aug. 1978:585–600.

Biermann, A., R. Baum, and F. Petry. "Speeding up the Synthesis of Programs from Traces", *IEEE Trans. on Computers* V24 #2, Feb. 1975:122–136.

Biermann, A., G. Guiho, and Y. Kodratoff eds., *Automatic Program Construction Techniques,* Macmillan, 1984.

Biermann, A. and R. Krishnaswamy. "Constructing Programs from Example Computations", *IEEE Trans. on Software Engineering* V2 #3, Sept. 1976.

Bledsoe, W. and D. Loveland eds., *Automated Theorem Proving: After 25 Years,* American Mathematical Society Contemporary Mathematical Series, 1984.

Bobrow, D. and M. Stefik. "Perspectives On Artificial Intelligence Programming", *Science* V231, Feb. 1986:951–957.

Boehm, H. "Side Effects and Aliasing Can Have Simple Axiomatic Descriptions", *ACM Trans. on Programming Languages and Systems* V7 #4, Oct. 1985:637–655.

Bonar, J. and E. Soloway. "Uncovering Principles of Novice Programming", *10th ACM Symp. on the Principles of Programming Languages,* 1983:10–13.

Borgida, A., S. Greenspan, and J. Mylopoulos. "Knowledge Representation as the Basis for Requirements Specifications", *IEEE Computer Magazine,* April 1985:82–90.

Borning, A. "The Programming Language Aspects of Thinglab, A Constraint-Oriented Simulation Laboratory", *ACM Trans. on Programming Languages and Systems* V3 #4, Oct. 1981.

Boyer, R. and J. Moore. "Proving Theorems About LISP Functions", *J of the ACM* V22 #1, Jan. 1975:129–144.

——— . *A Computational Logic,* Academic Press, 1979.

——— . "Metafunctions: Proving Them Correct and Using Them Efficiently as New Proof Procedures", in *The Correctness Problem in Computer Science,* R. Boyer and J. Moore eds., Academic Press, 1981.

———. "Proof Checking the RSA Public Key Encryption Algorithm", *The American Mathematical Monthly* V91 #3, March 1984:181–189.

———. "A Mechanical Proof of the Unsolvability of the Halting Problem", *J of the ACM* V31 #3, July 1984:441–458.

———. "Program Verification", *Journal of Automated Reasoning* V1 #1, 1985:17–22.

Boyle, J. and M. Muralidharan. "Program Reusability Through Program Transformation", *IEEE Trans. on Software Engineering* V10 #5, Sept. 1984:574–588.

Brachman, R. and H. Levelsque *eds.*, *Readings in Knowledge Representation*, Morgan Kaufmann, 1985.

Brode, B. "Precompiliation of FORTRAN Programs to Facilitate Array Processing", *IEEE Computer Magazine*, Sept. 1981:46–51.

Brown, J. and K. VanLehn. "Repair Theory: A Generative Theory of Bugs in Procedural Skills", Xerox Palo Alto Research Center report CIS-4, Aug. 1980.

Broy, M. and P. Pepper. "Program Development as a Formal Activity", *IEEE Trans. on Software Engineering* V7 #1, Jan. 1981:14–22.

Burstall, R. "Some Techniques for Proving Correctness of Programs Which Alter Data Structures", *Machine Intelligence 7*, D. Michie and B. Meltzer *eds.*, Edinburgh Univ. Press, 1972:23–50.

Burstall, R. and J. Darlington. "A Transformation System for Developing Recursive Programs", *J of the ACM* V24 #1, Jan. 1977.

Burstall, R. and J. Goguen. "Putting Theories Together to Make Specifications", *5th Int. Joint Conf. on Artificial Intelligence*, 1977:1045–1058.

———. "The Semantics of CLEAR, A Specification Language", Edinburgh Univ. report CSR-65-80, Feb. 1980.

Caio, F., G. Cuida, and M. Somalvico. "Problem Solving as a Basis for Program Synthesis: Design and Experimentation of the BIS System", *Int. J of Man-Machine Studies* V17, 1982:173–188.

Cartwright, R. and J. McCarthy. "First Order Programming Logic", *6th ACM Symp. on the Principles of Programming Languages*, 1979:68–80.

Chapman, D. "A Program Testing Assistant", *Comm. of the ACM* V25 #9, Sept. 1982:625–634.

Cheatham, T. "An Overview of the Harvard Program Development System", in *Software Engineering Environments* H. Hunke *ed.*, North-Holland, 1981:253–266.

———. "Reusability Through Program Transformations", *IEEE Trans. on Software Engineering* V10 #5, Sept. 1984:589–595.

Cheatham, T., G. Holloway, and J. Townley. "Symbolic Evaluation and the Analysis of Programs", *IEEE Trans. on Software Engineering* V5 #4, July 1979:402–417.

———. "Program Refinement by Transformation", *5th Int. Conf. on Software Engineering*, 1981.

———. "A System for Program Refinement", *4th Int. Conf. on Software Engineering*, 1979.

Cheng, T., E. Lock, and N. Prywes. "Use of Very High Level Languages and Program Generation by Management Professionals", *IEEE Trans. on Software Engineering* V10 #5, Sept. 1984:552–563.

Claybrook, B. "A Specification Method for Specifying Data and Procedural Abstractions", *IEEE Trans. on Software Engineering* V8 #5, Sept. 1982:449–459.

Cohen, J. "Computer-Assisted Microanalysis of Programs", *Comm. of the ACM* V25 #10, Oct. 1982:724–733.

———. "Describing Prolog by Its Interpretation and Compilation", *Comm. of the ACM* V28 #12, Dec. 1985:1311–1324.

Constable, R. "Constructive Mathematics and Automatic Program Writers", *IFIP*, Ljubljana Yugoslavia, Aug. 1971:229–233.

Cristian, F. "Robust Data Types", *Acta Informatica* V17, 1982:365–397.

Curry G. and R. Ayers. "Experience with Traits in the Xerox Star Workstation", *ITT Workshop on Reusability in Programming*, Newport RI, Sept. 1983:83–96.

Darlington, J. "Automatic Theorem Proving With Equality Substitutions and Mathematical Induction", *Machine Intelligence 3*, D. Michie and B. Meltzer *eds.*, Edinburgh Univ. Press, 1986:113–127.

———. "A Synthesis of Several Sort Programs", *Acta Informatica* V11 #1, 1978:1–30.

———. "An Experimental Program Transformation and Synthesis System", *Artificial Intelligence* V16, 1981:1–46.

Darlington, J. and R. Burstall. "A System Which Automatically Improves Programs", *Acta Informatica* V6, 1976:41–60.

De Millo, R., R. Lipton, and A. Perlis. "Social Processes and Proofs of Theorems and Programs", *Comm. of the ACM* V22 #5, May 1979:271–280.

Dennis, J. "First Version of a Data Flow Procedure Language", *Symp. on Programming*, Univ. of Paris, April 1974:241–271.

Dershowitz, N. "Program Abstraction and Instantiation", *ACM Trans. on Programming Languages and Systems* V7 #3, July 1985:446–477.

———. "Synthetic Programming", *Artificial Intelligence* V25, 1985:323–373.

Dershowitz, N. and Z. Manna. "The Evolution of Programs: Automatic Program Modification",

IEEE Trans. on Software Engineering V3 #6, Nov. 1977:377–385.

——— . "Inference Rules for Program Annotation", *IEEE Trans. on Software Engineering* V7 #2, March 1981:207–222.

Dewar, R., A. Grand, S. Liu, and J. Schwartz. "Programming by Refinement, as Exemplified by the SETL Representation Sublanguage", *ACM Trans. on Programming Languages and Systems* V1 #1, July 1979:27–49.

Dewar, R., M. Sharir, and E. Weixelbaum. "Transformational Derivation of a Garbage Collection Algorithm", *ACM Trans. on Programming Languages and Systems* V4 #1, Oct. 1982:650–667.

Dolotta, T., R. Haight, and J. Mashey. "The Programmer's Workbench", in *Interactive Programming Environments*, D. Barstow, E. Sandewall and H. Shrobe *eds.*, McGraw-Hill, 1983.

Dolotta, T. and J. Mashey. "An Introduction to the Programmer's Workbench", *2nd Int. Conf. on Software Engineering*, 1976:164–168.

Donzeau-Gouge, V., *et al.*, "A Structure-Oriented Program Editor; A First Step Towards Computer Assisted Programming", *Int. Computing Symp.*, Antibes, 1975.

Eares, R., C. Hitchon, R. Thall, and J. Brackett. "An Environment for Producing Well-Engineered Microcomputer Software", *4th Int. Conf. on Software Engineering*, 1979.

Earley, J. "Toward an Understanding of Data Structures", *Comm. of the ACM* V14 #10, Oct. 1971:617–627.

——— . "High Level Iterators and a Method for Automatically Designing Data Structure Representation", *Computer Languages* V1 #4, 1975:321–342.

Ellozy, H. "The Determination of Loop Invariants for Programs with Arrays", *IEEE Trans. on Software Engineering* V7 #2, March 1981:197–206.

Elshoff, J. and M. Marcotty. "Improving Computer Program Readability to Aid Modification", *Comm. of the ACM* V25 #8, Aug. 1982:512–521.

Emery, J. "Small-Scale Software Components", *ACM SIGSOFT Software Engineering Notes* V4 #4, Oct. 1979:18–21.

Faust, G. "Semiautomatic Translation of COBOL into HIBOL", MIT MS Thesis, MIT/LCS/TR-256, March 1981.

Feather, M. "A System for Assisting Program Transformation", *ACM Trans. on Programming Languages and Systems* V4 #1, Jan. 1982:1–20.

——— . "Program Specification Applied to a Text Formatter", *IEEE Trans. on Software Engineering* V8 #5, Sept. 1982:490–498.

——— . "A Survey and Classification of Some Program Transformation Approaches and Techniques", *IFIP Working Conf. on Program Specification and Transformation*, Bad Tolv Germany, April 1986.

Feather, M. and P. London. "Implementing Specification Freedoms", *Science of Computer Programming 2*, 1982:91–131.

Feiler, P. and R. Medina-Mora. "An Incremental Programming Environment", *5th Int. Conf. on Software Engineering*, 1981.

Fickas, S. "Automating the Transformational Development of Software", *IEEE Trans. on Software Engineering* V11 #11, Nov. 1985:1268–1277.

Fickas, S. and R. Brooks. "Recognition in a Program Understanding System", *6th Int. Joint Conf. on Artificial Intelligence*, 1979:266–268.

Fischer, G. and H. Boecker. "The Nature of Design Processes and How Computer Systems Can Support Them", in *Integrated Interactive Computing Systems*, P. Degano and E. Sandewall *eds.*, North-Holland, 1983.

Fischer, G. and M. Schneider. "Knowledge-Based Communication Processes in Software Engineering", *7th Int. Conf. on Software Engineering*, 1984.

Flon, L. and J. Misra. "A Unified Approach to the Specification and Verification of Abstract Data Types", *Specification of Reliable Software Conf.*, 1979:162–169.

Floyd, R. "Assigning Meaning to Programs", in *Mathematical Aspects of Computer Science* V19, J. Schwartz *ed.*, American Mathematical Society, 1967:19–32.

——— . "Toward Interactive Design of Correct Programs", *IFIP*, Ljubljana Yugoslavia, Aug. 1971:7–11.

——— . "1978 ACM Turing Award Lecture: The Paradigms of Programming", *Comm. of the ACM* V22 #8, Aug. 1979.

Follett, R. "Synthesising Recursive Functions with Side Effects", *Artificial Intelligence* V13, 1980:175–200.

Freeman, P. "Reusable Software Engineering: Concepts and Research Directions", *ITT Workshop on Reusability in Programming*, Newport RI, Sept. 1983:2–16.

Freeman, P. and A. Newell. "A Model for Functional Reasoning in Design", *2nd Int. Joint Conf. on Artificial Intelligence*, 1971:621–640.

Freudenberger, S., J. Schwartz, and M. Sharir. "Experience with the SETL Optimizer", *ACM Trans. on Programming Languages and Systems* V1 #1, Jan. 1983:26–45.

Geller, M. "Test Data as an Aid in Proving Program Correctness", *Comm. of the ACM* V21 #5, May 1978:368–375.

Genesereth, M. "Automated Consultation for Complex Computer Systems", Harvard PhD Thesis, Sept. 1978.

Gerhart, S. "Knowledge About Programs: A Model and Case Study", in *Int. Conf. on Reliable Software,* June 1975:88–95.

Gerhart, S., *et al.*, "An Overview of Affirm: A Specification and Verification System", *Information Processing 80,* S. Lavington *ed.*, North Holland, 1980.

German, S. and B. Wegbreit. "A Synthesizer of Inductive Assertions", *IEEE Trans. on Software Engineering* V1 #1, March 1975:68–75.

Ginsparg, J. "Natural Language Processing in an Automatic Programming Domain", Stanford PhD Thesis, Stanford report AIM-316, June 1978.

Glass, R. "Persistent Software Errors", *IEEE Trans. on Software Engineering* V7 #2, March 1981:162–168.

Goad, C. "Computational Uses of the Manipulation of Formal Proofs", Stanford report STAN-CS-80-819, Aug. 1980.

Goguen, J. "Parameterized Programming", *ITT Workshop on Reusability in Programming,* Newport RI, Sept. 1983:138–150.

——— . "Parameterized Programming", *IEEE Trans. on Software Engineering* V10 #5, Sept. 1984:528–543.

Goguen, J., J. Thatcher, and E. Wagner. "An Initial Algebra Approach to the Specification, Correctness and Implementation of Abstract Data Types", *Current Trends in Programming Methodology V4,* R. Yeh *ed.*, Prentice-Hall, 1978.

Goldman, N. "Three Dimensions of Design Development", USC Information Sciences Institute report ISI/RS-83-2, July 1983.

Goldstein, I. "Summary of MYCROFT: A System for Understanding Simple Picture Programs", *Artificial Intelligence* V6 #3, 1975.

Goldstein, I. and D. Bobrow. "A Layered Approach to Software Design", Xerox Palo Alto Research Center report CSL-80-5, 1980.

Gonnet, G. and F. Tompa. "A Constructive Approach to the Design of Algorithms and Their Data Structures", *Comm. of the ACM* V26 #11, Nov. 1983:912–920.

Good, D. "Mechanical Proofs About Computer Programs", *Philosophical Transactions of the Royal Society of London* V312 #1522, *Mathematical logic and programming languages,* M. Atiyah, C. Hoare and J. Shepherdson *eds.*, Oct. 1984:389–409.

Good, D., R. London, and W. Bledsoe. "An Interactive Program Verification System", *IEEE Trans. on Software Engineering* V1 #1, March 1975:59–67.

Goto, S. "Program Synthesis from Natural Deduction Proofs", *6th Int. Joint Conf. on Artificial Intelligence,* 1979:339–341.

Green, C. "Theorem Proving by Resolution as a Basis for Question-Answering Systems", *Machine Intelligence 4,* D. Michie and B. Meltzer *eds.*, Edinburgh Univ. Press, 1969.

——— . "Application of Theorem Proving To Problem Solving", *1st Int. Joint Conf. on Artificial Intelligence,* 1969.

——— . "A Summary of the PSI Program Synthesis System", *5th Int. Joint Conf. on Artificial Intelligence,* 1977:380–381.

——— . "The Design of the PSI Program Synthesis System", *3rd Int. Conf. on Software Engineering,* 1978:4–18.

——— . "What is Program Synthesis?", *Journal of Automated Reasoning* V1 #1, 1985:37–40.

Green, C., *et al.*, "Results in Knowledge Based Program Synthesis", *6th Int. Joint Conf. on Artificial Intelligence,* 1979:342–344.

Green, C. and D. Barstow. "Some Rules For the Automatic Synthesis of Programs", *4th Int. Joint Conf. on Artificial Intelligence,* 1975:232–239.

——— . "A Hypothetical Dialogue Exhibiting a Knowledge Base For a Program Understanding System", *Machine Intelligence 8,* D. Michie and B. Meltzer *eds.*, Edinburgh Univ. Press, 1976.

——— . "On Program Synthesis Knowledge", *Artificial Intelligence* V10 #3, Nov. 1978:241–279.

Green, C., D. Luckham, R. Balzer, T. Cheatham, and C. Rich. "Report on a Knowledge-Based Software Assistant", Rome Air Development Center report RADC-TR-83-195, Aug. 1983.

Green, C. and S. Westfold. "Knowledge-Based Programming Self-Applied", *Machine Intelligence 10,* J. Hayes, D. Mitchie and Y. Pao *eds.*, Wiley, 1982:339–359.

Greenspan, S., A. Borgida, and J. Mylopoulos. "A Requirements Modeling Language and its Logic", *Information Systems* V11 #1, Pergammon Press, 1986:9–23.

Greenspan, S., J. Mylopoulos, and A. Borgida. "Capturing More World Knowledge in the Requirements Specification", *6th Int. Conf. on Software Engineering,* 1982:225–234.

Grosz, B., B. Webber, and K. Sparck Jones *eds.*, *Readings in Natural Language Processing,* Morgan Kaufmann, 1986.

Guttag, J. "Abstract Data Types and the Development of Data Structures", *Comm. of the ACM* V20 #6, June 1977:396–404.

——— . "Notes on Abstraction (Version2)", *IEEE Trans. on Software Engineering* V6 #1, Jan. 1980:13–23.

Guttag, J. and J. Horning. "Formal Specification As a Design Tool", *7th ACM Symp. on the Principles of Programming Languages*, 1980:251–261.

Guttag, J., E. Horowitz, and R. Musser. "Abstract Data Types and Software Validation", *Comm. of the ACM* V21 #12, Dec. 1978:1048–1064.

Haase, V. and G. Koch. "Application-Oriented Specifications", *IEEE Computer Magazine*, May 1982:10–60.

Hansson, A. and S. Tarnlund. "A Natural Programming Calculus", *6th Int. Joint Conf. on Artificial Intelligence*, 1979:348–355.

Harandi, M. "A Knowledge-Based Programming Support Tool", *IEEE Trends & Applications conf.*, Gaithersburg MD, May 1983:233–239.

——— . "Knowledge-Based Program Debugging: A Heuristic Model", *Softfair Conf.*, Arlington VA, July 1983:282–288.

Harandi, M. and M. Lubars. "A Knowledge-Based Dataflow Design Aid", Univ. of IL report, 1983.

Hardy, S. "Synthesis of LISP Functions from Examples", *4th Int. Joint Conf. on Artificial Intelligence*, 1975:240–245.

Hayward, V. and A. Osorio. "A System to Automatically Analyze Assembled Programs", *IEEE Trans. on Software Engineering* V9 #2, 1983:210–213.

Hedrick, C. "Learning Production Systems from Examples", *Artificial Intelligence* V7, 1976:21–49.

Heidorn, G. "Automatic Programming Through Natural Language Dialogue: A Survey", *IBM J. of Research and Development* V20 #4, July 1976:302–313.

Heitmeyer, C. and J. McLean. "Abstract Requirements Specification: A New Approach and Its Application", *IEEE Trans. on Software Engineering* V9 #9, Sept. 1983:580–589.

Hewitt, C. and B. Smith. "Towards a Programming Apprentice", *IEEE Trans. on Software Engineering* V1 #1, March 1975:26–46.

Hoare, C. "Proof of Correctness of Data Representations", *Acta Informatica* V1 #4, 1972:271–281.

Horowitz, E., A. Kemper, and B. Narasimhan. "A Survey of Application Generators", *IEEE Software*, Jan. 1985:40–54.

Howden, W. "Contemporary Software Development Environments", *Comm. of the ACM* V25 #5, May 1982:318–329.

Ianov, Y. "The Logical Schemes of Algorithms", English translation in *Problems of Cybernetics V1*, Pergammon Press, 1960:82–140.

Ishida, T., S. Isoda, and Y. Kobayashi. "Global Compaction of Horizontal Microprograms Based on the Generalized Data Dependency Graph", *IEEE Trans. on Computers* V32 #10, Oct. 1983:922–933.

Ivie, E. "The Programmer's Workbench—A Machine for Software Development", *Comm. of the ACM* V20 #10, Oct. 1977:746–753.

Johnson, M. "A Software Debugging Glossary", *ACM SIGPLAN Notices* V17 #2, Feb. 1982:53–70.

Johnson, W. and E. Soloway, "PROUST: Knowledge-Based Program Understanding", *IEEE Trans. on Software Engineering* V11 #3, March 1985:267–275.

Jones, C. "A Survey of Programming Design and Specification Techniques", *Specification of Reliable Software Conf.*, 1978:91–103.

Kahney, H. "An In-Depth Study of the Cognitive Behaviour of Novice Programmers", Human Cognition Research Laboratory (England) PhD Thesis, report TR #5, Dec. 1982.

Kant, E. "A Knowledge-Based Approach to Using Efficiency Estimation in Program Synthesis", *6th Int. Joint Conf. on Artificial Intelligence*, 1979:457–462.

——— . "On the Efficient Synthesis of Efficient Programs", *Artificial Intelligence* V20 #3, May 1983:253–306.

——— . "Understanding and Automating Algorithm Design", *IEEE Trans. on Software Engineering* V11 # 11, Nov. 1985:1361–1374.

Kant, E. and D. Barstow. "The Refinement Paradigm: The Interaction of Coding and Efficiency Knowledge in Program Synthesis", *IEEE Trans. on Software Engineering* V7 #5, Sept. 1981:458–471.

Katz, S. and R. Zimmerman. "An Advisory System for Developing Data Representations", *7th Int. Joint Conf. on Artificial Intelligence*, 1981:1030–1036.

Kedzierski, B. "Communication and Management Support in System Development Environments", *Conf. on Human Factors in Computer Systems*, March 1982.

Knuth, D. *The Art of Computer Programming* V1, V2 & V3, Addison-Wesley, 1968, 1969 & 1973.

Kodratoff, Y. and J. Jouannaud. "Synthesizing LISP Programs: Working on the LISP Level of Embedding", in *Automatic Program Construction Techniques*, A. Biermann, G. Guiho and Y. Kodratoff eds., Macmillan, 1984:325–374.

Koffman, E. and S. Blount. "Artificial Intelligence and Automatic Programming in CAI", *Artificial Intelligence* V6, 1975:215–234.

Komoda, N., K. Haruna, H. Kaji, and H. Shinozawa. "An Innovative Approach to System Requirements Analysis By Using Structural Modeling Method", *5th Int. Conf. on Software Engineering*, 1981:305–313.

Kowalski, R. "Algorithm = Logic + Control", *Comm. of the ACM* V22 #7, July 1979:424–436.

——— . *Logic for Programming*, North-Holland, 1979.

Lanski, J. "An Approach to Loop Program Debugging", *ACM SIGPLAN Notices* V14 #11, Nov. 1979:64–72.

——— . "On Readability of Programs with Loops", *ACM SIGPLAN Notices* V14 #11, Nov. 1979:73–83.

Laski, J. and B. Korel. "A Data Flow Oriented Program Testing Strategy", *IEEE Trans. on Software Engineering* V9 #3, May 1983:347–354.

Laubsch, J. and M. Eisenstadt. "Domain Specific Debugging Aids for Novice Programmers", *7th Int. Joint Conf. on Artificial Intelligence*, 1981:964–969.

——— . "Using Temporal Abstraction To Understand Recursive Programs Involving Side Effects", *2nd Nat. Conf. on Artificial Intelligence*, 1982:400–403.

Leclerc, Y., S. Zucker, and D. Leclerc. "A Browsing Approach to Documentation", *IEEE Computer Magazine*, June 1982:46–49.

Ledgard, H. and R. Taylor. "Two Views of Data Abstraction", *Comm. of the ACM* V20 #6, June 1977:382–384.

Lesser, V., N. Carver, and D. McCue. "Focusing in Plan Recognition", *4th Nat. Conf. on Artificial Intelligence*, 1984.

Lewis, J. "Beyond ALBE/P: Language Neutral Form", *5th Int. Conf. on Software Engineering*, 1981:422–429.

Lieberman, H. and C. Hewitt. "A Session with TINKER: Interleaving Program Testing with Program Design", *LISP Conference*, Stanford Univ., Aug. 1980.

Lientz, B. and E. Swanson. "Problems in Application Software Maintenance", *Comm. of the ACM* V24 #11, Nov. 1981:763–769.

Liskov, B. and S. Zilles. "Specification Techniques for Data Abstractions", *IEEE Trans. on Software Engineering* V1 #1, March 1975:7–19.

London, B. and W. Clancy. "Plan Recognition Strategies in Student Modeling: Prediction and Description", Stanford report STAN-CS-82-909, May 1982.

Loveman, D. "Program Improvement By Source to Source Transformation", *J of the ACM* V24 #1, Jan. 1977:121–145.

Low, J. "Automatic Data Structure Selection: An Example and Overview", *Comm. of the ACM* V21 #5, May 1978:376–384.

Low, J. and P. Rovner. "Techniques For the Automatic Selection of Data Structures", *3rd ACM Symp. on the Principles of Programming Languages*, 1976:58–67.

Lukey, F. "Understanding and Debugging Programs", *Int. J of Man-Machine Studies* V12, 1980:189–202.

Manna, Z. *Mathematic Theory of Computation*, McGraw-Hill, 1974.

Manna, Z. and R. Waldinger. "Toward Automatic Program Synthesis", *Comm. of the ACM* V14 #3, 1971.

——— . "Knowledge and Reasoning in Program Synthesis", *Artificial Intelligence* V6, 1975:175–208.

——— . "The Logic of Computer Programming", *IEEE Trans. on Software Engineering* V4 #3, May 1978:199–229.

——— . "The Synthesis of Structure Changing Programs", *3rd Int. Conf. on Software Engineering*, 1978:175–187.

——— . "Synthesis: Dreams ⇒ Programs", *IEEE Trans. on Software Engineering* V5 #4, July 1979:294–327.

——— . "A Deductive Approach to Program Synthesis", *ACM Trans. on Programming Languages and Systems* V2 #1, Jan. 1980:90–121.

Mayer, R. "A Psychology of Learning BASIC", *Comm. of the ACM* V22 #11, Nov. 1979:589–593.

McCune, B. "The PSI Program Model Builder: Synthesis of Very High-Level Programs", *Symp. on Artificial Intelligence and Programming Languages*, Rochester NY, Aug. 1977:130–139.

——— . "Building Program Models Incrementally from Informal Descriptions", Stanford PhD Thesis, Stanford report AIM-333, Oct. 1979.

——— . "Incremental, Informal Program Acquisition", *1st Nat. Conf. on Artificial Intelligence*, 1980:71–73.

McCune, B. and J. Dean. "Advanced Tools for Software Maintenance", Rome Air Development Center report RADC-TR-82-313, Dec. 1982.

McMullin, P. and J. Gannon. "Combining Testing with Formal Specifications: A Case Study", *IEEE Trans. on Software Engineering* V9 #3, May 1983:328–334.

Medina-Mora, R. and P. Feiler. "An Incremental Programming Environment", *IEEE Trans. on Software Engineering* V7 #5, Sept. 1981.

Michalski, R., J. Carbonell, and T. Mitchell *eds.*, *Machine Learning*, Morgan Kaufmann, 1983.

Miller, L. "Behavioral Studies of the Programming Process", IBM Watson Research Center report 31711, Oct. 1978.

Miller, M. "Planning and Debugging in Elementary Programming", MIT PhD Thesis, Feb. 1979.

——— . "A Structured Planning and Debugging Environment for Elementary Programming", in *Intelligent Tutoring Systems*, D. Sleeman and J. Brown *eds.*, Academic Press, 1982.

Misra, J. "A Technique of Algorithm Construction on Sequences", *IEEE Trans. on Software Engineering* V4 #1, Jan. 1978: 65–69.

——— . "An Approach to Formal Definitions and Proofs of Programming Principles", *IEEE Trans. on Software Engineering* V4 #5, Sept. 1978:410–413.

——— . "Some Aspects of the Verification of Loop Computations", *IEEE Trans. on Software Engineering* V4 #6, Nov. 1978:478–485.

Mitchell, J. and B. Wegbreit. "Schemes: A High Level Data Structuring Concept", Xerox Palo Alto Research Center report, Jan. 1977.

Moll, R. and J. Ulrich. "The Synthesis of Programs by Analogy", *6th Int. Joint Conf. on Artificial Intelligence*, 1979:592–594.

Moriconi, M. "A Designer/Verifier's Assistant", *IEEE Trans. on Software Engineering* V5 #4, July 1979:387–401.

Mostow, J. "Automating Program Speedup by Deciding What to Cache", *9th Int. Joint Conf. on Artificial Intelligence*, 1985:165–172.

Mostow, J., *ed.*, "Special Issue on Artificial Intelligence and Software Engineering", *IEEE Trans. on Software Engineering* V11 #11, Nov. 1985.

Musser, D. "Abstract Data Type Specification in the AFFIRM System", *IEEE Trans. on Software Engineering* V6 #1, Jan. 1980:24–32.

Negrini, R. and M. Sami. "Some Properties Derived from Structural Analysis of Program Graph Models", *IEEE Trans. on Software Engineering* V9 # 2, March 1983:172–178.

Neighbors, J. "The Draco Approach to Constructing Software from Reusable Components", *IEEE Trans. on Software Engineering* V10 #5, Sept. 1984.

Nelson, G. "Verifying Reachability Invariants of Linked Structures", *10th ACM Symp. on the Principles of Programming Languages*, 1983:186–195.

O'Dunlaing, C. and C. Yap. "Generic Transformation of Data Structures", *23rd Annual Symp. on Foundations of Computer Science*, New York Univ., Nov. 1982:38–47.

Oldehoeft, R. "Program Graphs and Execution Behavior", *IEEE Trans. on Software Engineering* V9 #1, Jan. 1983:103–108.

Oppen, D. "Reasoning about Recursively Defined Data Structures", *5th ACM Symp. on the Principles of Programming Languages*, 1978.

Partsch, H. and R. Steinbruggen. "Program Transformation Systems", *ACM Computing Surveys* V15 #3, 1983:199–236.

Perlis, A. and S. Rugaber. "Programming With Idioms in APL", *APL79 Conf.*, Rochester NY, June 1979.

Phillips, J. "A Framework For the Synthesis of Programs From Traces Using Multiple Knowledge Sources", *5th Int. Joint Conf. on Artificial Intelligence*, 1977.

Plotkin, G. "A Note On Inductive Generalization", *Machine Intelligence 5,* D. Michie and B. Meltzer *eds.*, Edinburgh Univ. Press, 1969.

Polak, W. "An Exercise in Automatic Program Verification", *IEEE Trans. on Software Engineering* V5 #5, Sept. 1979:453–458.

Prywes, N. and A. Pnueli. "Compilation of Nonprocedural Specifications into Computer Programs", *IEEE Trans. on Software Engineering* V9 #3, May 1983:267–279.

Ramsey, H., M. Atwood, and J. VanDoren. "Flowcharts vs. Program Design Languages: An Experimental Comparison", *Comm. of the ACM* V26 #6, June 1983:445–449.

Redwine, S., Jr. "An Engineering Approach to Software Test Data Design", *IEEE Trans. on Software Engineering* V9 #2, March 1983:191–200.

Reilly, G. "SEA—A LISP Programmer's Apprentice", Univ. of PA report, 1982.

Reiss, S. "Generation of Compiler Symbol Processing Mechanisms from Specifications", *ACM Trans. on Programming Languages and Systems, V5 #2,* April 1983:127–163.

Renner, S. "Diagnosis of Logical Errors in PASCAL Programs", Univ. of IL MS Thesis, 1984.

Reynolds, J. "Reasoning About Arrays", *Comm. of the ACM* V22 #5, May 1979:290–298.

Rich, C. "Multiple Points of View in Modeling Programs", *Workshop on Data Abstraction, Data Bases and Conceptual Modeling, ACM SIGPLAN Notices, V16 #1,* Jan. 1981:177–179.

——— . "Inspection Methods in Programming", MIT PhD Thesis, MIT/AI/TR-604, June 1981.

——— . "A Formal Representation for Plans in the Programmer's Apprentice", *7th Int. Joint Conf. on Artificial Intelligence,* 1981, 1044–1052. (Reprinted in *On Conceptual Modelling,* M. Brodie, J. Mylopoulos and J. Schmidt *eds.,* Springer-Verlag, 1984:243–269)

——— . "Knowledge Representation Languages and Predicate Calculus: How to Have Your Cake and Eat It Too", *2nd Nat. Conf. on Artificial Intelligence,* 1982.

——— . "The Layered Architecture of a System for Reasoning about Programs", *9th Int. Joint Conf. on Artificial Intelligence,* 1985.

Rich, C. and H. Shrobe. "Initial Report on a LISP Programmer's Apprentice", *IEEE Trans. on Software Engineering* V4 #6, Nov. 1978.

Rich, C. and R. Waters. "The Disciplined Use of Simplifying Assumptions", *ACM SIGSOFT Second Software Engineering Symp.: Workshop on Rapid Prototyping, ACM Software Engineering Notes* V7 #5, Dec. 1982.

———— . "Formalizing Reusable Software Components", *ITT Workshop on Reusability in Programming,* Newport RI, Sept. 1983.

Robinson, L. and K. Levitt. "Proof Techniques for Hierarchically Structured Programs", *Comm. of the ACM* V20, April 1977:271–283.

Rosenschein, S., and S. Katz. "Selection of Representations for Data Structures", *Artificial Intelligence and Programming Languages,* Rochester NY, Aug. 1977:147–154.

Rovner, P. "Automatic Representation Selection for Associative Data Structures", Univ. of Rochester report TR10, 1976.

Rowe L. and F. Tonge. "Automating the Selection of Implementation Structures", *IEEE Trans. on Software Engineering* V4 #6, Nov. 1978:494–506.

Ruth, G. "Intelligent Program Analysis", *Artificial Intelligence* V7, 1976:65–85.

———— . "Protosystem I: An Automatic Programming System Prototype", *AFIPS Conf.,* Anaheim CA, 1978:675–681.

Schonberg, E., J. Schwartz, and M. Sharir. "Automatic Data Structure Selection in SETL", *6th ACM Symp. on the Principles of Programming Languages,* 1979:197–210.

———— . "An Automatic Technique for Selection of Data Representations in SETL Programs", *ACM Trans. on Programming Languages and Systems* V3 #2, April 1981:126–143.

Schwartz, J. "Automatic Data Structure Choice in a Language of Very High Level", *Comm. of the ACM* V18, Dec. 1975:722–728.

Sedlmeyer, R., W. Thompson, and P. Johnson. "Diagnostic Reasoning in Software Fault Localization", *8th Int. Joint Conf. on Artificial Intelligence,* 1983:29–31.

Shapiro, D. "Sniffer: a System that Understands Bugs", MIT MS Thesis, MIT/AIM-638, June 1981.

Shapiro, D. and B. McCune. "The Intelligent Program Editor", *IEEE Trends & Applications conf.,* Gaithersburg MD, May 1983:226–232.

Shapiro, E. *Algorithmic Program Debugging,* MIT Press, 1983.

Shaw, D., W. Swartout, and C. Green. "Inferring LISP Programs from Examples", *4th Int. Joint Conf. on Artificial Intelligence,* 1975:260–267.

Shaw, M. "Abstraction and Verification in Alphard: Design and Verification of a Tree Handler", *5th Texas Conf. on Computing Systems,* 1976:86–94.

Shaw, M., W. Wulf, and R. London. "Abstraction and Verification in Alphard: Defining and Specifying Iteration and Generators", *Comm. of the ACM* V20 #8, Aug. 1977:553–563.

Sheil, B. "The Psychological Study of Programming", *ACM Computing Surveys* V13 #1, March 1981:101–120.

———— . "Power Tools for Programmers", *Datamation,* Feb. 1983:131–143.

Shrobe, H. "Explicit Control of Reasoning in the Programmer's Apprentice", *4th Int. Conf. on Automated Dedication,* Feb. 1979.

———— . "Dependency Directed Reasoning for Complex Program Understanding", MIT PhD Thesis, MIT/AI/TR-503, April 1979.

———— . "Common-Sense Reasoning About Side Effects to Complex Data Structures", *6th Int. Joint Conf. on Artificial Intelligence,* 1979.

Siekmann, J. and Wrightson *eds., Automation of Reasoning: Classical Papers on Computational Logic 1957–70,* Springer-Verlag, 1983.

Siklossy, L. and D. Sykes. "Automatic Program Synthesis from Example Problems", *4th Int. Joint Conf. on Artificial Intelligence,* 1975:268–273.

Sleeman, D. and J. Brown *eds., Intelligent Tutoring Systems,* Academic Press, 1982.

Smith, C. "The Power of Pluralism for Automatic Program Synthesis", *ACM Trans. on Programming Languages and Systems* V29 #4, Oct. 1982:1144–1165.

Smith, D. "The Synthesis of LISP Programs from Examples: A Survey", in *Automatic Program Construction Techniques,* A. Biermann *et al. eds.,* Macmillan, 1984:307–324.

———— . "Top-Down Synthesis of Divide-and-Conquer Algorithms", *Artificial Intelligence* V27, 1985:43–96.

Smith, D., G. Kotik, and S. Westfold. "Research on Knowledge-Based Software Engineering Environments at Kestrel Institute", *IEEE Trans. on Software Engineering,* V11 #11, Nov. 1985:1278–1295.

Smith, J. and D. Smith. "Database Abstractions: Aggregation and Generalization", *ACM Transactions on Database Systems* V2 #2, 1977:105–133.

Soloway, E., *et al.,* "MENO-II: An Intelligent Programming Tutor", *J of Computer-Based Instruction* V10 #1–2, Summer 1983.

———— . "Bug Catalogue: I", Yale, Oct. 1983.

Soloway, E., J. Bonar, and K. Ehrlich. "Cognitive Strategies and Looping Constructs: An Empirical Study", *Comm. of the ACM* V26 #11, Nov. 1983:853–860.

Soloway, E. and K. Ehrlich. "Tacit Programming Knowledge", *4th Cognitive Science Conf.,* Ann Arbor MI, 1982.

———— . "Empirical Studies of Programming Knowledge", *IEEE Trans. on Software Engineering* V10 #5, Sept. 1984:595–609.

Spitzen, J., K. Leavitt, and L. Robinson. "An Example of Hierarchical Design and Proof" *Comm. of the ACM* V21 #12, Dec. 1978:1064–1075.

Squires, S., ed., *2nd ACM SIGSOFT Software Engineering Symp.: Workshop on Rapid Prototyping, ACM Software Engineering Notes* V7 #5, Dec. 1982.

Srivas, M. "Automatic Synthesis of Implementations for Abstract Data Types from Algebraic Specifications", MIT/LCS/TR-276, June 1982.

Standish, T., D. Harriman, D. Kibler, and J. Neighbors. *The Irvine Program Transformation Catalogue,* UC Irvine, 1976.

Steele, G. "The Definition and Implementation of a Computer Programming Language Based on Constraints", MIT PhD Thesis, MIT/AI/TR-595, Aug. 1980.

Stefik, M. and D. Bobrow. "Object-Oriented Programming: Themes and Variations", *AI Magazine* V6 #4, Winter 1986, 40–62.

Stefik, M., D. Bobrow, and K. Kahn. "Integrating Access-Oriented Programming into a Multiparadigm Environment", *IEEE Software Magazine,* Jan. 1986:10–18.

Steier, D. and E. Kant. "The Roles of Execution and Analysis in Algorithm Design", *IEEE Trans. on Software Engineering* V11 #11, Nov. 1985:1375–1385.

Summers, P. "A Methodology for LISP Program Construction from Examples", *J of the ACM* V24 #1, Jan. 1977:161–175.

Sunshine, C., *et al.,* "Specification and Verification of Communication Protocols in AFFIRM Using State Transition Models", *IEEE Trans. on Software Engineering* V8 #5, Sept. 1982:460–489.

Swartout, W. "The GIST Behavior Explainer", *3rd Nat. Conf. on Artificial Intelligence,* 1983:402–407.

Swartout, W. and R. Balzer. "On the Inevitable Intertwining of Specification and Implementation", *Comm. of the ACM* V25 #7, July 1982:438–440.

Swartout, W. and D. Barstow. "Who Needs Languages and Why Do They Need Them? Or No Matter How High The Level It's Still Programming", *Symp. on Programming Language Issues in Software Systems,* San Francisco CA, June 1983.

Tamir, M. "ADI: Automatic Derivation of Invariants", *IEEE Trans. on Software Engineering* V6 #1, Jan. 1980:40–48.

Teitelbaum, T. and T. Reps. "The Cornell Program Synthesizer: A Syntax-Directed Programming Environment", *Comm. of the ACM* V24 #9, Sept. 1981:563–573.

Teitelman, W. "A Display Oriented Programmer's Assistant", *5th Int. Joint Conf. on Artificial Intelligence,* 1977.

Thatcher, J., E. Wagner, and J. Wright. "Data Type Specification: Parameterization and the Power of Specification Techniques", *ACM Trans. on Programming Languages and Systems* V4 #1, Oct. 1982:711–732.

Verkshop III—A Formal Verification Workshop, ACM Software Engineering Notes V10 #4, Aug. 1985.

Warren, M. "Program Generation by Questionnaire", *Information Processing 68,* North-Holland, 1969.

Waters, R. "A Method for Analyzing Loop Programs", *IEEE Trans. on Software Engineering* V5 #3, May 1979:237–247.

———. "The Programmer's Apprentice: Knowledge Based Program Editing", *IEEE Trans. on Software Engineering* V8 #1, Jan. 1982.

———. "KBEmacs: A Step Toward the Programmer's Apprentice", MIT/AI/TR-753, May 1985.

———. "The Programmer's Apprentice: A Session with KBEmacs", *IEEE Trans. on Software Engineering* V11 #11, Nov. 1985:1296–1320.

———. "KBEmacs: Where's the AI?", *AI Magazine* V7 #1, Spring 1986.

———. "Program Translation via Abstraction and Reimplementation", *IEEE Trans. on Software Engineering,* 1986.

Wegbreit, B. "Constructive Methods in Program Verification", *IEEE Trans. on Software Engineering* V3 #3, May 1977:193–209.

Weiser, M. "Programmers Use Slicers When Debugging", *Comm. of the ACM* V25 #7, July 1982:446–452.

———. "Program Slicing", *IEEE Trans. on Software Engineering* V10 #4, July 1984.

Weiss, D. and V. Basili. "Evaluating Software Development by Analysis of Changes: Some Data from the Software Engineering Laboratory", *IEEE Trans. on Software Engineering* V11 #2, Feb. 1985:157–169.

Wertheimer, J. "A Library of Programming Knowledge for Implementing Rule Systems", MIT MS Thesis, 1986.

Weyhrauch, R. "Prolegomena to a Theory of Mechanized Formal Reasoning", *Artificial Intelligence* V13 #1–2, 1980:133–170.

White, J. "On the Multiple Implementation of Abstract Data Types Within a Computation", *IEEE Trans. on Software Engineering* V9 #4, July 1983:395–410.

Wile, D. "Type Transformations", *IEEE Trans. on Software Engineering* V7 #1, Jan. 1981:32–39.

———. "Program Developments: Formal Explanations of Implementations", *Comm. of the ACM* V26 #11, Nov. 1983:902–911.

Wile, D., R. Balzer, and N. Goldman. "Automated Derivation of Program Control Structure from Natural Language Program Descriptions", *Symp.*

on *Artificial Intelligence and Programming Languages,* Rochester NY, Aug. 1977.

Willis, R. and E. Jensen. "Computer Aided Design of Software Systems", *4th Int. Conf. on Software Engineering,* 1979.

Winograd, T. "Breaking the Complexity Barrier (Again)", *SIGIR-SIGPLAN Interface Meeting,* Nov. 1973. (Reprinted in *Interactive Programming Environments,* D. Barstow, E. Sandewall and H. Shrobe eds., McGraw-Hill, 1984.)

———. "Beyond Programming Languages", *Comm. of the ACM* V22 #7, July 1979.

Wirth, N. *Systematic Programming, An Introduction,* Prentice-Hall, 1973.

Wos, L., *et al., Automated Reasoning: Introduction and Applications,* Prentice-Hall, 1984.

Wulf, W., R. London, and M. Shaw. "An Introduction to the Construction and Verification of Alphard Programs", *IEEE Trans. on Software Engineering,* V2 #4, Dec. 1976:253–265.

Yau, S. and P. Grabow. "A Model for Representing Programs Using Hierarchical Graphs", *IEEE Trans. on Software Engineering* V7 #6, Nov. 1981:556–574.

Yeh, R. and R. Mittermeir. "Conceptual Modeling as a Basis for Deriving Software Requirements", *Int. Computer Symp.,* Taipei Taiwan, Dec. 1980.

Zave, P. "Executable Requirements for Embedded Systems", *5th Int. Conf. on Software Engineering,* 1981.

———. "An Operational Approach to Requirements Specification for Embedded Systems", *IEEE Trans. on Software Engineering* V8 #3, May 1982:250–269.

Zelinka, L. "Automated Program Recognition", MIT MS Thesis, 1986.

INDEX